iGAAP 2009

Financial instruments: IAS 32, IAS 39 and IFRS 7 explained

Fifth edition

iGAAP 2009

Financial instruments: IAS 32, IAS 39 and IFRS 7 explained

Fifth edition

Veronica Poole
Andrew Spooner

Deloitte LLP

LexisNexis®

International Accounting Standards Board Material:

Extracts from International Financial Reporting Standards, International Accounting Standards, Exposure Drafts, Discussion Papers and Educational Guidance are reproduced with the permission of the International Accounting Standards Committee Foundation.

Published by LexisNexis, a Division of Reed Elsevier (UK) Ltd, Halsbury House, 35 Chancery Lane, London, WC2A 1EL, and London House, 20–22 East London Street, Edinburgh EH7 4BQ

ISBN 978 0 7545 3769 4

British Library Cataloguing-in-Publication Data

A catalogue record of this book is available from the British Library.

Typeset by Letterpart Ltd, Reigate, Surrey

Printed in the UK by CPI William Clowes Beccles NR34 7TL

Standards covered

This book covers the following standards that are effective for reporting periods beginning on or after 1 January 2009:

- International Accounting Standard 32 – *Financial Instruments: Presentation* (IAS 32)
- International Accounting Standard 39 – *Financial Instruments: Recognition and Measurement* (IAS 39)
- International Financial Reporting Standard 7 – *Financial Instruments: Disclosures* (IFRS 7)
- International Financial Reporting Standard 1 – *First-time Adoption of International Financial Reporting Standards* (IFRS 1)

This book also includes the amendments to:

- IAS 32 – *Puttable Financial Instruments and Obligations Arising on Liquidation* effective for annual periods beginning on or after 1 January 2009
- IFRS 7 – *Improving Disclosures about Financial Instruments* effective for annual periods beginning on or after 1 January 2009
- IAS 1, IAS 39 and IFRS 7 included in *Improvements to IFRSs* effective for annual periods beginning on or after 1 January 2009
- IAS 39 – *Eligible Hedged Items* effective for annual periods beginning on or after 1 July 2009
- IFRS 3 – *Business Combinations* effective for annual periods beginning on or after 1 July 2009

This book incorporates relevant discussions from meetings of the International Accounting Standards Board and International Financial Reporting Interpretations Committee that took place up to the end of March 2009.

This book also highlights differences in financial instrument accounting between IFRS and US GAAP. The US GAAP comparisons are intended to be high-level summaries of certain aspects of comparable US GAAP. They do not describe all guidance that may apply under US GAAP to a specific fact pattern. Additionally, the absence of a US GAAP comparison for a particular section or sub-section is not intended to imply that the requirements of US GAAP and the equivalent IFRS are the same. Similarly, the existence of a US GAAP comparison in a particular section or sub-section does not necessarily mean that all potential differences in that area have been addressed. Consult with a professional where appropriate.

Foreword

This book has been written at a time of unprecedented stress in the financial markets and the wider economy. Increasing column inches in the press have focused on not only the financial results of companies, but the part that the accounting standards played in determining those results and the impact of accounting on the economic system. This spotlight is inevitable and reflects the importance of financial reporting as a key tool in communicating with investors and other stakeholders.

If ever there was an accounting standard that generates strong, and opposing, emotions, IAS 39 is it. The IASB recognises this and the importance of getting financial instruments accounting right. Accordingly, the Board issued proposals to replace the derecognition requirements of IAS 39 in March of this year. The Board has also set itself a bold target to issue an exposure draft to replace other parts of IAS 39 this year. The depth of this book illustrates the complexity that has evolved in the financial instruments standards and their application since IAS 39 was originally issued ten years ago. The replacement to IAS 39 will attempt to call time on this complexity and in doing so will make the accounting standard more accessible, its application more understandable and the financial information presented more usable to investors.

In the meantime, we must work with the tools we have. There is no doubt that preparers and users find financial instruments accounting tough to navigate. Hence, I welcome the fifth edition of this book in bringing together so comprehensively the IASB's guidance with the practical insight experienced by its authors and other Deloitte professionals.

Stephen Cooper
International Accounting Standards Board member

May 2009

Acknowledgements

We would like to express our thanks to the following who contributed to this edition:

Angela Bacarella	USA
Jens Berger	UK
Joseph Berry	USA
Kirk Crews	USA
Christine Colleu	France
Mario Enxuto	USA
Ryan Jankowski	USA
Madhu Gopinath	USA
Mateusz Lasik	UK
Magnus Orrell	USA
Kushal Patel	UK
Sarah Sandford	USA
Kallol Sen	UK

Summary of contents

Table of contents

1 Scope

1 Introduction

There are three Standards that deal with the accounting for financial instruments.

- IAS 32 *Financial Instruments: Presentation* deals with the presentation and classification of financial instruments as financial liabilities or equity.
- IAS 39 *Financial Instruments: Recognition and Measurement* contains all the key guidance for recognition and measurement of financial instruments other than equity.
- IFRS 7 *Financial Instruments: Disclosures* prescribes the disclosure of financial instruments.

All three Standards have detailed scoping paragraphs that exclude from their scope certain financial instruments. In addition, the scoping paragraphs of the Standards differ slightly:

- all financial instruments that are scoped out of IAS 32 are also scoped out of IAS 39;
- financial instruments that an entity issues with a discretionary participation feature are accounted for under IFRS 4 *Insurance Contracts* and are scoped out of IAS 39. They are within the scope of IFRS 7 and IAS 32 except that, for such contracts, the requirements of IAS 32 regarding the distinction between financial liabilities and equity instruments are not applicable;
- IAS 39 has some additional scope exclusions that go beyond the scope exclusions in IAS 32 (see **section 3** below); and
- IAS 39 excludes all instruments classified as equity from its scope, whereas IFRS 7 appears to only exclude derivatives over own equity classified as equity, making no reference to non-derivative instruments, such as ordinary shares. It appears that this difference does not have any practical effect (see **3.1** below).

The definition of a financial instrument is broad: a financial instrument is defined as any contract that gives rise to a financial asset of one entity and a financial liability or equity instrument of another entity. Trade receivables and payables, bank loans and overdrafts, issued debt, ordinary and preference shares, investments in securities like shares and bonds, and various derivatives are just some of the examples of financial instruments. In addition, certain contracts to buy or sell non-financial items are specifically scoped in on the basis that they behave and are used in a similar way to financial instruments (see **2.5** below). The chapters that follow explain the concepts of financial assets, financial liabilities, equity, derivatives, embedded derivatives and hedge accounting and demonstrate that many items that entities have not previously considered to be financial instruments may well be within the scope of IAS 32 and/or IAS 39 and IFRS 7.

This chapter explains which items that meet the definition of a financial instrument are scoped out of IAS 32 and/or IAS 39 and IFRS 7. In general, items are scoped out of IAS 32, IAS 39 and IFRS 7 if another Standard is more prescriptive. As an example, interests in subsidiaries will be scoped out of all three Standards as they are within the scope of IAS 27 *Consolidated and Separate Financial Statements*. The detailed scope exclusions of IFRS 7 are included in **section 2** of **chapter 11**.

This chapter deals with the scope of all three Standards in the following sections:

Section 2	Financial instruments scoped out of IAS 32, IAS 39 and IFRS 7
Section 3	Additional scope exclusions of IAS 39

2 Financial instruments scoped out of IAS 32, IAS 39 and IFRS 7

A summary of the scope of IAS 32, IAS 39 and IFRS 7 with respect to financial instruments only is included below.

Financial instrument	**Within scope of IAS 32?**	**Within scope of IFRS 7?**	**Within scope of IAS 39?**
Interest in subsidiaries, associates and joint ventures accounted for in accordance with IAS 27, IAS 28 or IAS 31 respectively	No	No	No

Financial instrument	**Within scope of IAS 32?**	**Within scope of IFRS 7?**	**Within scope of IAS 39?**
Interest in subsidiaries, associates and joint ventures accounted for in accordance with IAS 39 as permitted by IAS 27(2008).38(b) (previously IAS 27(2003).37(b))	Yes	Yes	Yes
Investment in equity securities (available-for-sale investments and fair value through profit or loss)	Yes	Yes	Yes
Investment in debt securities (available-for-sale investments, fair value through profit or loss, loans and receivables, held to maturity investments)	Yes	Yes	Yes
Trade receivables and payables	Yes	Yes	Yes
Finance lease receivables of the lessor	Yes	Yes	No *
Construction contract receivables accounted for under IAS 11 *Construction Contracts* (see **2.7** below)	No	No	No
Cash and cash equivalents	Yes	Yes	Yes
Borrowings and other financial liabilities such as some preference shares	Yes	Yes	Yes

Financial instrument	Within scope of IAS 32?	Within scope of IFRS 7?	Within scope of IAS 39?
Derivatives (and non-closely related embedded derivatives)	Yes	Yes	Yes
Derivatives over interests in subsidiaries, associates and joint ventures in the individual financial statements	Yes	Yes	Yes
Derivatives over interests in associates and joint ventures in the consolidated financial statements	Yes	Yes	Yes
Contracts over non-financial items that do not meet the purchase, sale or usage exemption in IAS 39.5	Yes	Yes	Yes
Contingent consideration in a business combination (acquirer or seller)**	Yes	Yes	Yes
Deferred consideration in a business combination (acquirer or seller)	Yes	Yes	Yes
Warranty obligations and other provisions under IAS 37 that will be settled by the delivery of cash or other financial assets	Yes	Yes	Yes
Financial guarantee contracts for the writer that are not treated as insurance contracts	Yes	Yes	Yes
Finance lease obligations of the lessee	Yes	Yes	No ***

Financial instrument	Within scope of IAS 32?	Within scope of IFRS 7?	Within scope of IAS 39?
Own equity shares	Yes	No ****	No
Derivatives over own equity shares that are classified as equity (including derivatives over shares in non-controlling interest in the consolidated financial statements)	Yes	No	No
Contracts between an acquirer and a vendor in a business combination to buy or sell an acquiree at a future date	Yes	Yes	No
Loan commitments that cannot be settled net in cash or another financial instrument, and are not designated as at financial liabilities at fair value through profit or loss	Yes	Yes	No
Employer's rights and obligations under employee benefit plans covered by IAS 19	No	No	No
Share based payment arrangements covered by IFRS 2	No	No	No
Insurance contracts for the writer or holder of insurance (settled in cash or other financial assets)	No	No	No

* Except for the requirements on derecognition, impairment and embedded derivatives.

** If the version of IFRS 3 *Business Combinations* issued in 2008 is not applied contingent consideration in a business combination for the acquirer is not in the scope of all three standards. Contingent consideration for the seller is always in the scope of all three standards.

*** Except for the requirements on derecognition and embedded derivatives.

**** Scope exclusion refers only to derivatives over own equity but can be applied broadly to all equity instruments of the issuer – see **3.1** below

IAS 32 applies to all financial instruments except for the following items:

- interests in subsidiaries, associates and joint ventures (see **2.1** below);
- employers' rights and obligations under employee benefit plans (see **2.2** below);
- rights and obligations arising under insurance contracts as well as financial instruments that are within the scope of IFRS 4 because they contain a discretionary participation feature (see **2.3** below);
- for entities that have not yet adopted IFRS 3(2008), contracts for contingent consideration in a business combination (see **2.4** below); and
- financial instruments, contracts and obligations under share-based payment transactions (see **2.6** below).

IAS 39 also scopes out these instruments, but has some additional scope exemptions (see **section 3** below).

Additionally, IAS 32, IAS 39 and IFRS 7 include within their scopes certain contracts to buy or sell non-financial assets (see **2.5** below) even though they do not meet the definition of a financial instrument.

Each of the above is considered in turn.

2.1 Interests in subsidiaries, associates and joint ventures

Interests in subsidiaries, associates and joint ventures that are accounted for under IAS 27 *Consolidated and Separate Financial Statements*, IAS 28 *Investments in Associates* or IAS 31 *Interests in Joint Ventures* are not within the scope of IAS 32. However, if in certain circumstances specified by IAS 27, IAS 28 or IAS 31 an entity accounts for an interest in a subsidiary, associate or joint venture under IAS 39, then that interest in a subsidiary, associate or joint venture also falls into the scope of IAS 32 and IFRS 7 (see **2.1.1** below). In such a case, the applicable disclosure requirements of IAS 27, IAS 28 and IAS 31 are given in addition to those of IFRS 7. For example, in the parent's separate financial statements, if the parent chooses to record its investment in its subsidiary in accordance with IAS 39 as an available-for-sale financial asset (see **chapter 2**), then that investment having been clearly scoped into IAS 39 also falls into the scope of IFRS 7.

Improvements to IFRSs issued in May 2008 has confirmed the interaction of IFRS 7, IAS 28 and IAS 31 as described above. The amendments made by *Improvements to IFRSs* are effective for periods beginning on or after 1 January 2009 and earlier application is permitted, but an entity choosing to apply the amendments early must disclose that fact. The amendments may be applied prospectively.

Derivatives that are linked to interests in subsidiaries, associates and joint ventures are always within the scope of IAS 32. Where a derivative on an interest in a subsidiary meets the definition of equity in the consolidated financial statements in accordance with IAS 32 (see **chapter 3**) that derivative is scoped out of IAS 39 and IFRS 7 and is accounted for as equity under IAS 32. This is the case for a derivative over shares in a subsidiary where the derivative will be settled by delivery of a fixed amount of shares for a fixed amount of cash or other financial asset. The derivative meets the definition of equity in the consolidated financial statements as shares in a subsidiary in the consolidated financial statements are presented as non-controlling interest which is part of consolidated equity. In contrast, shares in an associate or joint venture are never considered part of equity in the consolidated financial statements and therefore in consolidated financial statements a derivative over an interest in an associate or joint venture will never meet the definition of equity and as a result will always be within the scope of IAS 39 and IFRS 7.

Where derivatives over interests in subsidiaries, associates and joint ventures are within the scope of IAS 39 they are covered by the normal measurement requirements for derivatives as detailed in **chapter 4**.

Example 2.1A

Written call over equity of subsidiary (1)

Parent X and Subsidiary Y are part of Group Z.

Subsidiary Y writes a call option to an entity outside the group over a fixed number of its own equity shares that is exclusively physically settled in all cases and the strike price of the option is a fixed amount of cash. For Subsidiary Y, the written call option meets the definition of equity in accordance with IAS 32 and therefore in the financial statements of Subsidiary Y it is treated as an equity item.

In the financial statements of Group Z, the instrument is within the scope of IAS 32 as it is a derivative over an interest in a subsidiary. It is outside the scope of IAS 39 and IFRS 7 because the instrument meets the definition of equity in the financial statements of Subsidiary Y in accordance with IAS 32, and therefore it is non-controlling interest in the consolidated financial statements of Group Z.

Example 2.1B

Written call over equity of subsidiary (2)

As **example 2.1A** above except Parent X writes the call option over a fixed number of shares in Subsidiary Y for a fixed amount of cash.

In the separate financial statements of Parent X the instrument is a derivative that is in the scope of IAS 39 and IFRS 7 as the derivative does not meet the definition of equity in Parent X's financial statements as the derivative is not over Parent X's equity.

In the consolidated financial statements of Group Z, the instrument is within the scope of IAS 32 as it is a derivative over an interest in a subsidiary which is presented as non-controlling interest. The instrument is outside the scope of IAS 39 and IFRS 7 because the instrument meets the definition of equity.

2.1.1 *Investments in subsidiaries, associates and joint ventures*

Where an entity prepares separate financial statements (as defined in IAS 27), an investment in a subsidiary, associate or joint venture should be accounted for either:
[IAS 27(2008).38, previously IAS 27(2003).37]

(a) at cost; or

(b) in accordance with IAS 39.

If the investment is accounted for in accordance with IAS 39, then it will be classified as either at fair value through profit or loss or available-for-sale (see **section 3.1** and **3.5** of **chapter 2**).

Investments that cease to be subsidiaries, but that do not become associates or joint ventures, are accounted for in accordance with IAS 39 from the date they cease to be subsidiaries. Their carrying amount on that date is their initial cost.

Similarly, investments that cease to be associates, but that do not become subsidiaries or joint ventures, are accounted for in accordance with IAS 39 from the date the entity ceases to have significant influence. Investments that cease to be joint ventures, that do not become subsidiaries or associates, are accounted for in accordance with IAS 39 from the date the entity ceases to have joint control. The carrying amount on the date that the investment ceases to be an associate or joint venture is regarded as its initial cost.

Venture capital organisations, mutual funds, unit trusts, investment-linked insurance funds and similar entities that upon initial recognition choose to designate their interests in associates and joint ventures as at fair value through profit or loss or classify them as held for trading in the entity's individual or consolidated financial statements must account for such interests under IAS 39, i.e. measure them at fair value with changes in fair value recognised in profit or loss. [IAS 28.1, IAS 31.1] A venture capital organisation or similar entity is not permitted to apply IAS 39 to their investments in subsidiaries in the consolidated financial statements.

A group may consist of a venture capital entity or similar entity and other operations. This is common in large financial institutions where the organisation consists of a venture capital business as well as other banking operations, such as retail and investment banking. It would seem acceptable for the venture capital operation within the larger organisation to choose to apply IAS 39 for its interests in associates and joint ventures. It is not permitted to apply IAS 39 to interests in associates and joint ventures outside of the venture capital operation.

US GAAP comparison: Unlike IAS 39, the fair value option for financial instruments under US GAAP, in principle, is available also for investments in associates (Statement 159). Similar to IFRS, the fair value option under US GAAP cannot be elected for investments in subsidiaries that the entity is required to consolidate. Under US GAAP, special accounting requirements apply to mutual funds and other investment companies. Investment companies are precluded from consolidating or applying the equity method of accounting to investments in non-investment company investees. Instead those investments are accounted for at fair value.

2.2 Employers' rights and obligations under employee benefit plans

Employers' rights and obligations under employee benefit plans are outside the scope of IAS 32, IAS 39 and IFRS 7. They are within the scope of IAS 19 *Employee Benefits*.

2.3 Rights and obligations arising under insurance contracts

Contracts that meet the definition of an insurance contract in IFRS 4 *Insurance Contracts* are outside the scope of IAS 32, IAS 39 and IFRS 7. In addition, financial instruments that are within the scope of IFRS 4 because they contain a discretionary participation feature are outside the scope of IAS 32 and IAS 39. A discretionary participation feature is the right to receive, in addition to guaranteed benefits, significant further benefits that are at the discretion of the issuer and are based on the performance of a specified pool of contracts, investment returns or profit or loss of a company, fund or other entity that issues the contract. [IFRS 4.2 and Appendix A] The issuer of such instruments is exempt from applying the paragraphs in IAS 32 with respect to the distinction between financial liabilities and equity instruments. However, these instruments are subject to all the other requirements of IAS 32. Furthermore, IAS 32 applies to derivatives that are embedded in these instruments that are required to be separately accounted for in accordance with IAS 39 (see **2.3.1** below).

An insurance contract is defined in IFRS 4 as a contract under which one party (the insurer) accepts significant insurance risk from another party (policyholder) by agreeing to compensate the policyholder if a specified uncertain future event (the insured event) adversely affects the policyholder. [IFRS 4, Appendix A] An insurance risk is a pre-existing risk that the policyholder transfers to the insurer and is a risk other than financial risk, i.e. other than a risk of a possible future change in either a financial variable (e.g. interest rate, commodity price, credit rating, etc) or a non-financial variable that is not specific to a party to the contract. The insurance risk has to be significant: it has to have a discernible effect on the economics of the transaction, i.e. significant additional benefits including claims handling and assessment costs could become payable. An adverse effect on a policyholder as a result of an insured event is a precondition for payment, however the payment itself does not have to be limited to the financial loss suffered by the policyholder.

IFRS 4 contains numerous examples of insurance contracts, and also examples of those contracts that do not meet the definition of an insurance contract and may fall within the scope of IAS 32, IAS 39 and IFRS 7.

Example 2.3

Insurance risk

A life insurance contract in which the insurer bears no significant mortality risk will be in the scope of IAS 39 if it creates financial assets or liabilities. [IFRS 4.B19]

2.3.1 *Derivatives embedded in insurance contracts*

Derivatives embedded within insurance contracts are within the scope of IAS 32, IAS 39 and IFRS 7 if they require separation in accordance with IAS 39. The only exception is if a derivative embedded in an insurance contract is itself an insurance contract. [IFRS 4.7]

Example 2.3.1

Embedded derivatives in insurance contracts

[IFRS 4.IG4, Example 2.16]

A contractual feature within an insurance contract provides a return that is contractually linked (with no discretion) to the return on specified assets. The embedded derivative is not an insurance contract and is not closely related to the contract (IAS 39.AG30(h)). Fair value measurement is required [*i.e. the embedded derivative will be separated from the insurance contract and fair valued*].

2.3.2 *Financial guarantee contracts*

If an entity has issued a financial guarantee to a third party, the entity will need to consider whether that instrument meets the definition of a financial guarantee contract as laid out in IAS 39. The Standard defines such contracts as those that require the issuer to make specified payments to reimburse the holder for a loss it incurs because a specified debtor fails to make payment when due in accordance with the original or modified terms of a debt instrument. The issuer of such a contract shall in accordance with the requirements of IAS 39 initially recognise the financial guarantee contract at fair value and subsequently measure it at the higher of:
[IAS 39.47(c)]

- the amount determined in accordance with IAS 37 *Provisions, Contingent Liabilities and Contingent Assets*; and
- the amount initially recognised less when appropriate cumulative amortisation in accordance with IAS 18 *Revenue*.

This treatment in respect of initial recognition and subsequent measurement applies with the following three exceptions:

- if the financial guarantee contract was entered into or retained on a transfer of a financial asset and prevented derecognition of the financial asset or resulted in continuing involvement (see **3.3** and **3.4** in **chapter 7** for further details); [IAS 39.47(b)]

- if the financial guarantee contract was designated at fair value through profit or loss at inception (see **7.1** in **chapter 3** for further details); [IAS 39.47(a)] and

- if the issuer has previously asserted explicitly that it regards such contracts as insurance contracts and has used accounting applicable to insurance contracts; in such cases the issuer may elect to apply either IAS 39 or IFRS 4 *Insurance Contracts*; it should be noted that this election may be made on a contract by contract basis but the election for each contract is irrevocable. [IAS 39.2(e)]

An entity may have written financial guarantee contracts but not as a core business activity. It has historically considered these contracts as insurance and asserted that they were insurance contracts, or alternatively it may have made such an assertion at the time of transition to IFRSs.

It should be noted that financial guarantee contracts held, as opposed to those issued, are specifically outside the scope of IAS 39. [IAS 39.IN6]

The following decision tree summarises the treatment of issued financial guarantees.

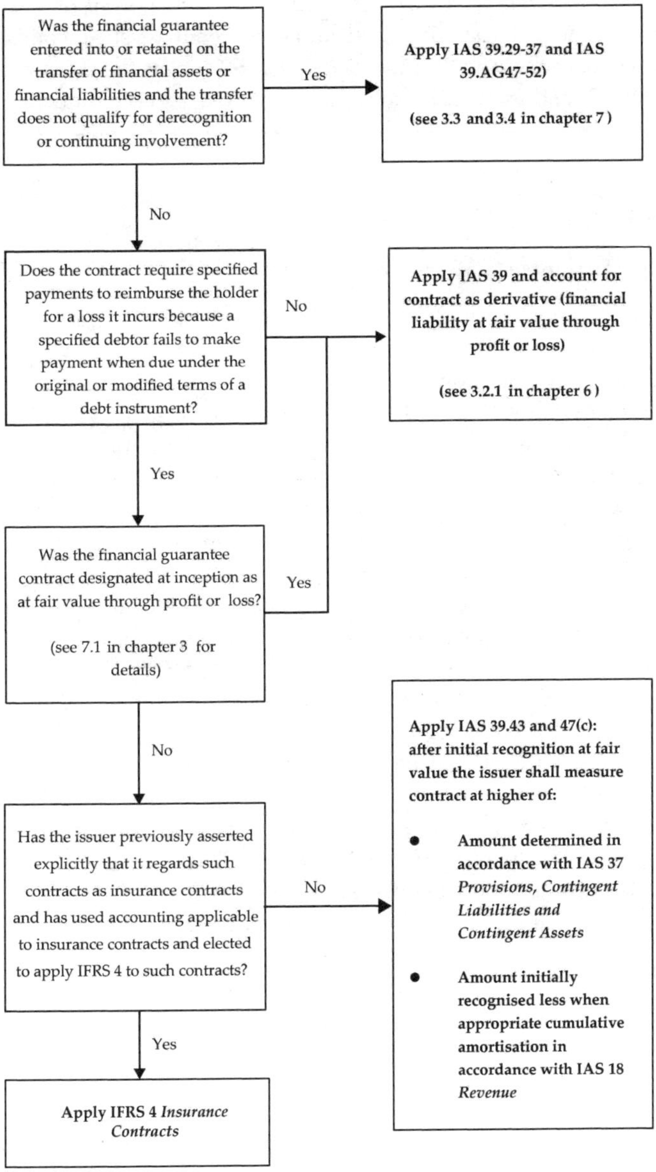

Example 2.3.2A

Financial guarantee contracts (1)

Entity A owns CU100 million of Entity X bonds that mature in twenty years. Entity X is rated BBB by the rating agencies. Entity A is concerned that Entity X may be downgraded and the value of bonds would decline. To protect against such a decline, Entity A enters into a contract with a bank that will pay Entity A for any decline in the fair value of the Entity X bonds related to a credit downgrade to BB or below. The contract is for a five-year period, and Entity A pays CU2 million to enter into the contract. As the contract pays Entity A in the event of a downgrade, and not in the event of a failure by Entity X to meet its payment obligations under the issued bonds, it is a derivative instrument within the scope of IAS 39 from the point of view of both Entity X and the bank who is the counterparty to the contract.

Example 2.3.2B

Financial guarantee contracts (2)

Entity X owns CU100 million of single family residential mortgage loans. Entity X is concerned that defaults may increase as a result of a recession, so purchases a guarantee contract from Entity B, a mortgage insurance entity. The contract requires Entity B to pay Entity X the loss it suffers in the case where mortgages default and there is foreclosure by Entity X. The contract has a CU5 million cap. Entity X pays Entity B a CU2 million fee for the contract. Because the contract provides for specified payments to be made to reimburse Entity X for a loss it incurs in the event of a failure of a specified debtor to pay when due, the contract meets the definition of a financial guarantee contract. Accounting by the holder of the financial guarantee contract is not specifically addressed in IAS 39. In the books of the writer of the financial guarantee contract, i.e. in the books of Entity B, the instrument is within the scope of IAS 39 and should follow the guidance set out above. Unless the contract is designated at fair value through profit or loss at inception, the contract will be recognised initially at fair value and then measured at the higher of the amount determined in accordance with IAS 37 and the amount initially recognised less cumulative amortisation in accordance with IAS 18. However, if Entity B had previously asserted explicitly that it regards such contracts as insurance contracts and has used accounting applicable to insurance contracts it could elect to apply either IAS 39 or IFRS 4 to the specific contract. Although the election in respect of this contract would not affect the availability of the election in respect of other similar contracts, it is irrevocable in respect of this individual contract.

IAS 39 does not provide clear guidance for the accounting for financial guarantee contracts for the holder. IAS 39.IN6 states: "financial guarantee contracts held are not within the scope of the Standard", yet in the body of IAS 39 there is no reference to the scoping out of financial guarantee contracts held. The IASB decided to clarify the reason why financial guarantee contracts held are outside the scope of IAS 39. The clarification was issued in January 2008 as part of editorial changes to standards. The editorial change was made to IAS 39.IN6 only, which now states that financial guarantee contracts for the holder are not in the scope of IAS 39 because they are insurance contracts. The scope exclusion does not state which standard does apply in accounting for these arrangements.

As financial guarantee contracts held are not in the scope of IAS 39 they will generally be recognised as an asset equal to the premium paid with amortisation of the asset to income over the period in which the benefit of the guarantee is obtained. Only if the entity considers it virtually certain that its claim under the financial guarantee contract will be successful will the asset be remeasured upwards to reflect the claim in accordance with IAS 37. The contract is not accounted for in accordance with IFRS 4 as this standard only applies to the accounting for the issuer of insurance contracts, not the holder.

Example 2.3.2C

Financial guarantee contracts (3)

Entity A has a wholly-owned subsidiary, Entity B. Entity B entered into a third party bank loan. Entity A wrote a financial guarantee contract to the bank over the loan. In the separate financial statements of Entity A, the financial guarantee contract will be accounted for as set out above. In the consolidated financial statements of Group A, the financial guarantee contract is not separately recognised as the group as a single entity has simply borrowed money from a third party.

If Entity A had provided a guarantee directly to Entity B in respect of its bank loan, in the separate financial statements of Entity A, the guarantee is not recognised separately as Entity A has agreed to contribute more money to its subsidiary which will generally be accounted for as a capital contribution as and when it is contributed. The promise by the parent to inject money at a future date is not recognised upfront.

In some jurisdictions, regulatory or statutory requirements state that an ultimate parent company or subsidiary (the guarantor) must, or can elect to, make representations that it will make payments to unspecified parties outside the group should a subsidiary (obligor) fail to make payments under its obligations to those parties. The guarantor will make a payment to the debtor equal to the amount that the obligor has failed to pay. The representation is open-ended (i.e. it relates to all currently recognised obligations as well as to all obligations that the subsidiary may enter into in the future) and does not have a specified counterparty. Care needs to be taken in determining whether such representations by the guarantor are financial guarantee contracts in the guarantor's financial statements.

Before considering whether the representation meets the definition of a financial guarantee contract in accordance with IAS 39.9, the entity must consider whether the instrument meets the definition of a financial instrument. If it does not, the instrument is not within the scope of IAS 39 and cannot be a financial guarantee contract.

Representations to unspecified parties do not meet the definition of a financial instrument because they are not a contractual arrangement between the guarantor and a specified third party or parties. IAS 32.13 states that a contract is "an agreement between two or more parties that has clear economic consequences that the parties have little, if any, discretion to avoid, usually because the agreement is enforceable by law". A representation to meet the subsidiary's obligations should the subsidiary fail to meet its obligations is a representation of unspecified amounts held by unspecified parties. As such, the representation is not a contractual arrangement and is outside the scope of IAS 32 and IAS 39. In addition, IAS 32.AG12 clarifies that "liabilities or assets that are not contractual (such as income taxes that are created as a result of statutory requirements imposed by governments) are not financial liabilities or financial assets". Therefore, the guarantor would apply IAS 37 and provide for the amount it could be required to pay under the arrangement if the criteria in IAS 37.14 are met.

If the representation is a contractual arrangement between the guarantor and a specified third party over a specified amount and, therefore, does meet the definition of a financial instrument and is within the scope of IAS 39, the entity must consider whether the instrument meets the definition of a financial guarantee contract in IAS 39.9. A financial guarantee contract only exists when the guarantor agrees to make specified payments to reimburse the holder for a loss it incurs because a specified debtor fails to make payment when due in accordance with the original or modified terms of a debt instrument. If the guarantor has not explicitly stated that it regards financial guarantee contracts as insurance under IFRS 4 it must measure the contract as described in this section above.

A contractual arrangement that does meet the definition of a financial instrument but does not meet the definition of a financial guarantee contract is measured at fair value through profit or loss because the contractual arrangement meets the definition of a derivative in IAS 39.9. Such a contractual arrangement meets the definition of a derivative because: (1) the initial investment received by the guarantor is small compared with the amount that could be required to be paid if a claim is made under the contractual arrangement, (2) the fair value of the arrangement is driven by the credit risk of the obligor, and (3) the arrangement will be settled either at a future date, should the holder make a claim against the guarantor, or at its maturity since expiration at maturity is a form of settlement. [IAS 39.IG.B.7]

An arrangement whereby a parent agrees to make future contributions or to lend to a subsidiary is not a financial guarantee contract for the parent in its separate financial statements. The arrangement is not a financial guarantee contract as the parent is not making payments in the instance when the subsidiary has suffered loss on a specified debt instrument. Even if the subsidiary only makes a claim from the parent when it is in financial difficulty, the exercise of the claim is more akin to either a claim under a loan commitment (and written and purchased loan commitments are outside the scope of IAS 39 – see **3.5** below) or a commitment for a capital contribution which by analogy to loan commitment accounting would also be considered outside the scope of IAS 39.

A contract that requires an entity to make payments when the counterparty to a derivative contract (for example a foreign currency forward contract or an interest rate swap) fails to make payment is not a financial guarantee contract. A financial guarantee contract is a contract 'that requires the issuer to make specified payments to reimburse the holder for a loss it incurs because a specified debtor fails to make payment when due in accordance with the original or modified terms of a debt instrument'. [IAS 39.9] As a derivative is not a debt instrument, the contract does not meet the definition of a financial guarantee contract.

2.3.3 *Weather derivatives*

Contracts requiring payments based on climatic, geological or other physical variables are inside the scope of IFRS 4 if they meet the definition of an insurance contract. Those based on climatic variables are sometimes referred to as 'weather derivatives'. Examples of climatic, geological and other physical variables include:

- the number of inches of rainfall or snow in a particular area;
- temperature in a particular area or for a specified period of time; and
- the severity of earthquakes.

If these contracts are not within the scope of IFRS 4, and they meet the definition of a derivative in **chapter 4**, they are within the scope of IAS 32, IAS 39 and IFRS 7.

US GAAP comparison: Exchange traded weather derivatives are accounted for as derivative instruments (FAS 133). Non-exchange traded weather derivatives that are entered into for trading purposes or for the purpose of speculation would initially be valued at fair value, with subsequent changes in fair value recorded currently in profit or loss (EITF 99–2). Written non-exchange traded weather derivative options should be accounted for in a similar manner as a freestanding written option which is not in the scope of any specific US GAAP literature (e.g. FAS 133, FAS 150, etc), i.e. at fair value with changes in fair value reported in earnings. Non-exchange traded forward-based and purchased option based weather derivatives not entered into for speculation or trading should be accounted for using an intrinsic value method.

2.4 Contracts for contingent consideration in a business combination

For entities that have not yet adopted IFRS 3(2008), contracts for contingent consideration in a business combination are excluded from IAS 32, IAS 39 and IFRS 7. They are subject to the provisions of IFRS 3(2004).) This exemption applies only to the acquirer, not to the seller.

The revised version of IFRS 3 *Business Combinations* issued in January 2008 amended IAS 32, IAS 39 and IFRS 7. Under IFRS 3(2008), contracts for contingent consideration are no longer outside the scope of these standards for the acquirer. Thus, if a contract for contingent consideration meets the definition of a financial instrument it will be in the scope of these standards for both the acquirer and the seller. Paragraph BC349 in the Basis for Conclusions accompanying IFRS 3(2008) states that 'the boards noted that most contingent consideration obligations are financial instruments, and many are derivative instruments'. IFRS 3(2008) applies prospectively to business combinations for which the acquisition date is on or after the beginning of the first annual reporting period beginning on or after 1 July 2009.

Irrespective of whether IFRS 3(2008) has been adopted, a seller's contract for contingent consideration is not scoped out of IAS 32, IAS 39 and IFRS 7. The seller will recognise a financial asset arising from the contract for contingent consideration. The measurement of this financial asset will depend on the facts and circumstances of the contractual arrangement. As the cash flows under the contract for contingent consideration are often derived from an underlying such as the future performance of the entity that has been sold the asset will often meet the definition of a derivative in its entirety (see **chapter 4**) and will therefore be measured at fair value through profit or loss. Alternatively, the contingent consideration asset may be partly a loan and receivable measured at amortised cost to the extent part of the consideration is not contingent with a non-closely related embedded derivative measured at fair value through profit or loss (see **chapter 5**) if the whole contingent consideration is not designated as at fair value through profit or loss at initial recognition.

2.5 Contracts to buy or sell non-financial items

IAS 32, IAS 39 and IFRS 7 primarily deal with contracts that are financial items, however, they also capture some contracts to buy or sell non-financial items. Contracts to buy or sell non-financial items that can be settled net (either in cash or by exchanging financial instruments) are within the scope of IAS 32, IAS 39 and IFRS 7 unless they were entered into, and continue to be held for the purpose of the receipt of the non-financial item in accordance with the entity's expected purchase, sale or usage requirements. [IAS 39.5]

2.5.1 *Net settlement*

Net settlement can be in cash, another financial instrument, or by exchanging financial instruments. It can be achieved in many ways:
[IAS 39.6]

(a) the contractual terms may permit either party to settle it net in cash or by exchanging financial instruments;

(b) settlement may not be explicit under the terms of the contract, but the entity has a past practice of net settling similar contracts (see **2.5.3** below);

(c) for similar contracts, the entity has a past practice of taking delivery of the underlying and selling it within a short period after delivery for the purpose of generating a profit from short-term price fluctuations or from dealer's margin; or

(d) the non-financial item that is the subject of the contract is readily convertible to cash.

2.5.2 *Non-performance penalties*

The terms of a contract need to be evaluated in detail since net settlement provisions may be implicit rather than explicit.

A non-performance penalty in a purchase order, where the amount of the penalty is calculated by reference to the changes in the price of the item that is the subject of the contract, is an example of an implicit net settlement provision.

> **Example 2.5.2A**
>
> **Non-performance penalty equivalent to net settlement**
>
> Entity A enters into a forward purchase agreement with Entity B to buy 100 units of a commodity at CU1.00 per unit. Entity A defaults on the forward when the prevailing market price of the commodity is CU0.75 per unit. Under the non-performance penalty provisions incorporated into the contract, Entity A has to pay Entity B a penalty of CU25, i.e. 100 x (CU1.00 – CU0.75). The non-performance penalty represents an implicit net settlement provision.

Conversely, fixed penalties or normal handling fees do not amount to net settlement.

> **Example 2.5.2B**
>
> **Non-performance penalty not equivalent to net settlement**
>
> Entity A enters into a contract to purchase wheat, which will be used in its manufacturing operations. The delivery contract requires a non-performance penalty of CU1 million if Entity A fails to take delivery of the wheat. This is a fixed penalty and does not provide for net settlement because the CU1 million payment amount is not based on changes in the price of wheat (the reference asset).

2.5.3 *Past practice*

Contracts where there is a past practice of either net settling or purchasing and selling the underlying within a short period after delivery with a view to making a short-term profit (i.e. (b) or (c) in the above list in **2.5.1**) are always within the scope of the financial instruments Standards. Such contracts cannot be argued to be entered into and continue to be held for the purpose of the receipt or delivery of the non-financial item in accordance with the entity's expected purchase, sale or usage requirements, since the entity's activities clearly indicate that this is not the case.

Example 2.5.3A

Rolling contracts until physical delivery

Entity C is in the business of milling maize and using it as input into its production process. Entity C's procurement strategy for maize includes purchasing futures on a futures exchange. Due to the significant quantity of maize needed, Entity C enters into forward purchases of maize to secure the level required for the running of its business. The intention at the outset is to take physical delivery of the maize under these contracts.

In January 20X6, Entity C procures maize for its 20X6 requirements. The longest available maturity of maize futures contracts is to July 20X6. C's purchasing policy requires it to secure maize at least for 9 months, i.e. as far out as September 20X6. Hence, Entity C enters into a larger number of July 20X6 contracts with a view to rolling some of them to September 20X6.

In April 20X6, Entity C will close out some of its July 20X6 futures at market value at the time, and take out September 20X6 futures. As a result, Entity C will take physical delivery of the maize under the September contracts only.

Entity C's practice of net settling some of its July futures contracts (i.e. its practice of net settling similar contracts) prevents it from arguing that it enters into futures contracts for the receipt of maize in accordance with its expected purchase, sale or usage requirements. Accordingly, both the July and September contracts are within the scope of IAS 39.

Example 2.5.3B

Choice of cash or physical settlement (1)

[Extract from IAS 39.IG.A.1]

Entity XYZ enters into a fixed price forward contract to purchase one million kilograms of copper in accordance with its expected usage requirements. The contract permits XYZ to take physical delivery of the copper at the end of twelve months or to pay or receive a net settlement in cash, based on the change in fair value of copper.

If XYZ intends to settle the contract by taking delivery and has no history for similar contracts of settling net in cash or of taking delivery of the copper and selling it within a short period after delivery for the purpose of generating a profit from short-term fluctuations in price or dealer's margin, the contract is not accounted for as a derivative under IAS 39. Instead, it is accounted for as an executory contract [*i.e. outside the scope of IAS 39*].

Example 2.5.3C

Choice of cash or physical settlement (2)

Entity A is a copper manufacturer. Entity A enters into forward contracts to sell its copper cathode to its customers. The forward contracts are homogenous and permit the entity to:

- provide physical delivery of copper at the end of the contract; or
- pay or receive a net settlement in cash based on the change in fair value of copper.

Based on its inventory levels and its production capacity, Entity A is able to meet the obligation to deliver copper should it decide to provide physical delivery of copper relating to all of its outstanding forward sales contracts.

The stated intention in entering into the forward sales contracts is for the purpose of delivery of copper in accordance with its sales requirements. Historically, Entity A has a practice of net settling a portion of similar forward contracts, provided the contracts are in the money. For contracts that are out of the money, historically Entity A has opted to physically deliver.

These contracts are all homogenous and the fact that Entity A has a past practice of net settling a portion of similar forward contracts means that it cannot assert that the contracts are held for the purpose of the delivery of copper in accordance with Entity A's expected sale requirements. Hence, the forward contracts are in the scope of IAS 39 and will be accounted for as derivatives.

There are instances where an entity will net settle as part of its normal operating cycle, as opposed to net settling in order to generate profits from short-term movements in prices. This is particularly common for utility entities that need to balance the demand from their customers with the supply contracts. For example, a retail gas supplier purchases gas under long-term take-or-pay contracts. The buyer's intent is to use the contracted volumes to serve its customers. However, the demand in certain periods (usually in the summer months) falls below the minimum required contractual take. The buyer is forced to settle net since the relative scarcity of natural gas storage capacity makes it difficult to store it for later use (storage of electricity is effectively impossible, so a similar situation is likely under a power contract). This 'balancing' activity is common for gas and power entities serving retail customers since customer demand forecasts cannot be precise. The practice of net settling similar contracts makes it difficult to claim that the long-term contracts meet the definition of own use requirements contracts, and therefore they are likely to be scoped into IAS 39.

It is a matter of judgement what is past practice of net settlement. An entity will need to consider its historical behaviour, reasons for past net settlement, and relative frequency. In some cases it may be argued that an occurrence of a net settlement in the past is a result of an isolated non-recurring event that could not have been reasonably anticipated.

2.5.4 *Written options*

In addition to the restriction on contracts where there is a past practice of settling net or a practice of taking delivery of the underlying and selling it within a short period after delivery, a written option to buy or sell a non-financial item that can be settled net contractually or where the non-financial item that is the subject of the option is readily convertible to cash is always within the scope of IAS 39.

Example 2.5.4A

Written call with no net settlement

Entity XYZ owns an office block. It writes Entity ABC an option, allowing ABC to purchase the office block for a fixed price on a future date. The terms of the contract do not allow for it to be net settled, and the office block is not readily convertible to cash. Therefore, although Entity XYZ has written an option, the option does not fall within the scope of IAS 39.

Example 2.5.4B

Written put with possible net settlement

[Extract from IAS 39.IG.A.2]

Entity XYZ owns an office building. Entity XYZ enters into a put option with an investor that permits XYZ to put the building to the investor for CU150 million. The current value of the building is CU175 million. The option expires in five years. The option, if exercised, may be settled through physical delivery or net cash, at XYZ's option.

XYZ's accounting depends on XYZ's intention and past practice for settlement. Although the contract meets the definition of a derivative, XYZ does not account for it as a derivative [*i.e. the contract would not be in the scope of IAS 39*] if XYZ intends to settle the contract by delivering the building if Entity XYZ exercises its option and there is no past practice of settling net (IAS 39.5 and IAS 39.AG10).

The investor, however, cannot conclude that the option was entered into to meet the investor's expected purchase, sale or usage requirements because the investor does not have the ability to require delivery (IAS 39.7). In addition, the option may be settled net in cash. Therefore, the investor has to account for the contract as a derivative [*i.e. within the scope of IAS 39*]. Regardless of past practices, the investor's intention does not affect whether settlement is by delivery or in cash. The investor has written an option, and a written option in which the holder has a choice of physical settlement or net cash settlement can never satisfy the normal delivery requirement for the exemption from IAS 39 because the option writer does not have the ability to require delivery.

IAS 39 does not define a written option, with only limited discussion of written options provided in the context of hedge accounting. IAS 39.AG94 states that the potential loss on an option an entity writes could be significantly greater than the potential gain in value of a related hedged item.

Different schools of thought exist as to what is considered to be a written option in the context of contracts over non-financial items. Some focus on the existence of a premium received. This treatment is analogous to the approach described in the hedge accounting guidance, as receiving a premium, whether upfront or over the life, indicates that the party to the option is taking on a greater risk of loss and therefore is being compensated by a premium. However, in the context of contracts over a non-financial item this approach has its difficulties, largely because it can be extremely difficult to ascertain whether a premium is received over the life when this 'premium' may be included in the pricing of the non-financial item that will be delivered under the contract.

An alternative approach is to consider whether the holder of the option has the ability to exercise the option in order to make a profit. This approach assesses the pay-off characteristics of the contract. In instances where the behaviour of the holder in exercising the option is independent of price, i.e. the holder exercises the option for reasons other than the value of the underlying being greater than the strike price under the option, it could be argued that the holder exercises the option not in order to profit, but to take delivery of the non-financial item so as to meet the expected purchase, sale or usage requirements. Examples of this are electricity supply contracts to retail customers since generally electricity is considered to be readily convertible to cash in the hands of the writer of the option. As the holder of the option, the retail customer has no ability to take delivery of the electricity, store it, and sell the electricity on at a profit, i.e. the holder is unable to realise a profit from the contract. The holder's behaviour is driven simply from the need for electricity to meet the usage requirements. From the perspective of the writer of the option, i.e. the electricity seller, it can then be argued that it has not written an option.

In March 2007 the IFRIC finalised a rejection notice titled *Written Options in Retail Energy Contracts*. The IFRIC discussed what is meant by 'written option' within the context of IAS 39.7. The discussion was primarily concerned with the accounting for energy supply contracts to retail customers. The rejection notice states that following an analysis of such contracts the IFRIC believes that in many situations these contracts do not meet the net settlement criteria laid out in IAS 39.5 & 6 and if this is the case, such contracts would not be considered to be within the scope of IAS 39. It is not entirely clear from the IFRIC's rejection notice whether they considered these contracts as written options over an underlying that is not readily convertible into cash and therefore not net settled per IAS 39.6(d), or whether they did not consider them written options at all and therefore viewed an analysis of ready convertibility of the underlying into cash as irrelevant.

Often an entity enters into an agreement to buy a fixed quantity of a non-financial item, but has an option to buy further quantities at the contracted price. For example, an entity enters into an agreement to buy 100 units of a non-financial item that is readily convertible into cash, which includes the ability for it to purchase a further 15 units at the same contracted price. These contracts are often referred to as having 'volumetric flexibility'. If the seller concludes that the option on the 15 units is a written option, then the whole contract for 115 units is a written option. This is because IAS 39 looks at the arrangements based on their contractual terms. The contract is a single contract over 115 units and thus it is not possible to split it into (1) a forward over 100 units classified as a normal usage requirements contract outside the scope of IAS 39, and (2) a written option over 15 units in the scope of IAS 39.

US GAAP comparison: US GAAP contains extensive and in some respects very detailed guidance about the requirements that must be met in order for different types of contract to purchase or sell non-financial items to be exempt from derivative accounting. Under US GAAP, this exception is referred to as the 'normal purchases and normal sales' exception (FAS 133). Under US GAAP contracts with optionality features that modify the quantity of the asset to be delivered usually cannot qualify for the 'own use' ('normal purchases and normal sales) exemption. However, in some circumstances such contracts are scoped out of derivative accounting for other reasons (for example, so-called 'requirements contacts' that lack a determinable notional amount). Special rules apply to power purchase and sales agreements that qualify as capacity contracts (as defined in FAS 133).

The SEC has a longstanding position related to the accounting for written options which was reiterated in EITF 08–8, *Accounting for an Instrument (or an Embedded Feature) with a Settlement Amount That Is*

Based on the Stock of an Entity's Consolidated Subsidiary. If the contract is considered a freestanding written option and is not in the scope of FAS 133, it cannot qualify, for example, for the normal purchases and sales exemption and should be accounted for at fair value.

IAS 39 does not permit a written option over a non-financial item that is 'readily convertible to cash' to be scoped out of IAS 39. IAS 39 does not provide guidance on what is considered readily convertible to cash and therefore similar guidance in US GAAP is worthy of consideration. FASB Concepts Statement No. 5 *Recognition and Measurement in Financial Statements of Business Enterprises*, paragraph 83(a), states that assets that are readily convertible to cash 'have (i) interchangeable (fungible) units and (ii) quoted prices available in an active market that can rapidly absorb the quantity held by the entity without significantly affecting the price'. US literature provides further guidance in the Derivative Interpretations Group (DIG) Implementation Issues which considers amongst other issues, the extent to which the cost of converting the item to cash impacts whether the instrument is a derivative or not.

2.5.5 *Expected purchase, sale and usage requirements*

Non-optional contracts or purchased options over non-financial items where either the terms of the contract permit net settlement, or where the non-financial item that is subject to the contract is readily convertible to cash (for example, many commodity contracts) must be assessed to see if they were entered into for the receipt or purchase of the item in accordance with the entity's expected purchase, sale or usage requirements.

Example 2.5.5

Purchase contract with possible net settlement

Entity X enters into a fixed-price forward contract to purchase one million tonnes of copper. Copper is traded on the London Metals Exchange and is readily convertible to cash. The contract permits X to take physical delivery of the copper at the end of 12 months or to pay or receive a net settlement in cash, based on the change in fair value of copper. Entity X does not have a practice of settling similar contracts net or taking physical delivery of copper and selling it within a short period after delivery for the purposes of generating a profit from short-term fluctuations in price.

Entity X needs to demonstrate that the contract was entered into and continues to be held for the purpose of the receipt of copper in accordance with its expected purchase or usage requirements in order for the contract to be scoped out of IAS 39. In addition to past practice, factors like the quantities involved, quality and grades of the commodity, and delivery locations would need to be considered.

Where the reporting entity, opposed to the counterparty, has the choice of net cash settlement the reporting entity may be able to demonstrate that it does not intend to exercise its right to net cash settlement and therefore the existence of the net cash settlement feature does not result in arrangement being scoped into IAS 39. Where the choice of net cash settlement is with the counterparty it will generally not be possible for the reporting entity to demonstrate that the non-financial item will be delivered under the contract as the reporting entity does not control the cash settlement decision. If the reporting entity cannot insist that the counterparty delivers the non-financial item the reporting entity cannot demonstrate that it intends to receive the non-financial item in accordance with its expected purchase, sale or usage requirements.

Each contract must be evaluated in its entirety. For example, an entity may have a contract for 100 units, yet its expected usage requirement is for 80 units only. The entity intends to net settle the part of the contract it does not need in its normal course of business. Such partial net settlement can be achieved in different ways, for example, by entering into an offsetting contract for 20 units, or by taking delivery of all 100 units and selling 20 straight away. The entire contract falls within the scope of IAS 39 since the entire contract cannot be argued to be in accordance with the entity's expected usage requirements.

US GAAP comparison: FAS 133 requires an entity to document its designation of a purchase or sale contract as 'normal'. DIG Issue C12 clarifies failing to document this designation prohibits the entity from using this scope exemption even if an entity is eligible for using it. Hence, 'own use' is a de facto accounting choice for the entity. However, an entity that has once documented a contract as 'normal' is not later permitted to change its election and treat the contract as a derivative. IAS 39 has no requirement to designate a contract as 'own use'. Once a contract is established as own use it is accounted for as such for as long as its meets the conditions for own use in IAS 39.

The following decision tree illustrates how to evaluate whether contracts to buy or sell non-financial items are within the scope of IAS 32, IAS 39 and IFRS 7.

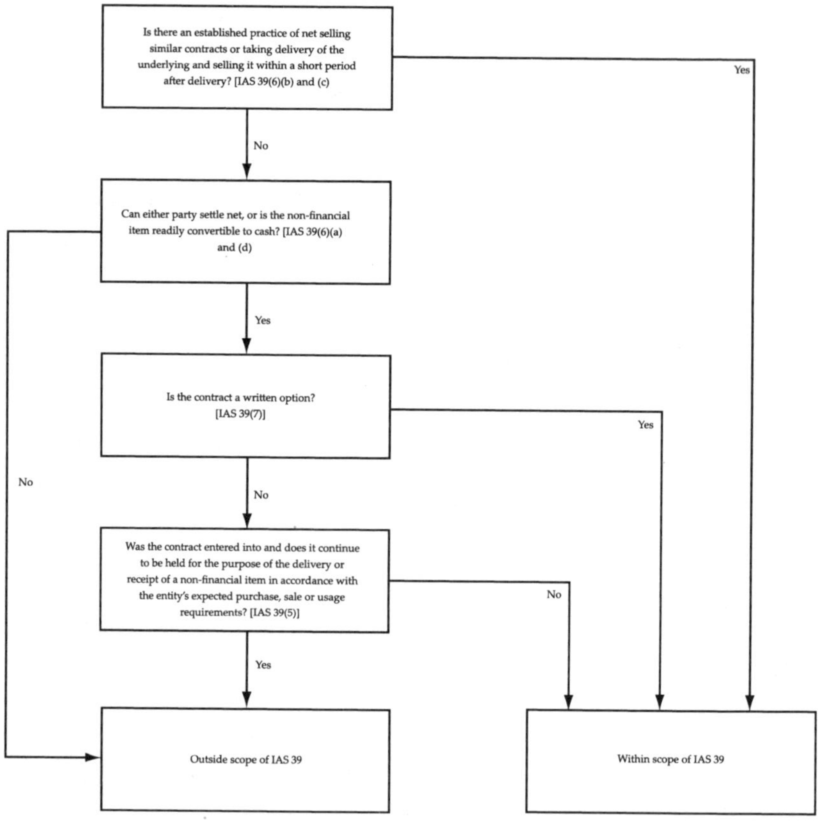

Entities may enter into multiple contracts with the same contractual terms for different reasons. Care needs to be taken in determining whether the contracts themselves should have the same accounting treatment or not. A conglomerate may enter into contracts to buy non-financial items that are used in the conglomerate's production processes for the provision of finished goods. These contracts are always physically delivered. A separate part of the business may enter into contractual arrangements with the same contractual terms but does not always physically receive the non-financial item, rather it cash settles the contract or enters into offsetting contracts as part of a trading strategy. From a group perspective it may be possible to differentiate the two portfolios of contracts in the two separate businesses within the conglomerate and therefore account for them differently only if the contracts are entered into separately and not in contemplation of each other; there are no transfers between the businesses within the group; the businesses are managed independently of each other; and the strategy of each business is sufficiently different that the different settlement behaviour of each business is reasonable. In practice, it is unlikely that such a distinction is possible as different parts of a group often choose to transact with each other as opposed to separately entering into offsetting transactions outside the group and incurring additional transaction costs.

2.5.6 *Change of settlement terms*

The terms of a contract, or the intentions of an entity, may change over time. A contract outside the scope of IAS 39 will continue to be treated as such only if it continues to be held for the purpose of the receipt or delivery of a non-financial item in accordance with the entity's expected purchase, sale or usage requirements.

Example 2.5.6

Change of terms to include net settlement

Two parties enter into a contract for the delivery of a non-financial asset. There is no net settlement provision in the contract, no established market mechanism or side agreement, and no history of net settlement.

Subsequently, the parties agree to settle the contract net. From the time the decision to settle net is made, the contract will be recognised and measured under IAS 39 since from that point the contract no longer continues to be for the purpose of the receipt of the non-financial asset in accordance with the expected purchase, sale or usage requirements.

2.6 Share-based payments

IAS 32, IAS 39 and IFRS 7 exclude from their scope financial instruments, contracts and obligations under share-based payment arrangements to which IFRS 2 *Share-based Payment* applies, except for contracts over non-financial items that are within the scope of IAS 39 (see **2.5** above). However, the scope of IAS 32 makes it clear that treasury shares that are purchased, sold, issued or cancelled in connection with employee share option plans, employee share purchase plans, and all other share-based payment arrangements, are in the scope of IAS 32 (see **section 5** of **chapter 3**).

US GAAP comparison: Similar to IAS 39, the US derivative accounting standard (Statement 133) excludes from its scope contracts issued by the entity under share-based payment transactions subject to

FASB Statement No. 123(R), *Share-Based Payment*. However, if a contract is no longer subject to Statement 123(R), then it must be evaluated to determine the applicable accounting literature (Statement 133, Statement 150, or other guidance).

2.7 Construction contract receivables

Construction contract receivables are measured and presented in accordance with IAS 11 *Construction Contracts*. The financial instruments standards do not specifically scope out these contracts and therefore consideration must be given as to whether such receivables are financial instruments. A right to cash or another financial asset is critical in the definition of a financial asset. In construction contract arrangements the amount of work incurred by the constructor may be in excess of the amount that is billed. IAS 11.42 requires 'the gross amount due from customers for contract work' to be recognised in the statement of financial position. This amount is determined in accordance with IAS 11.43 as the net amount of costs incurred plus recognised profits less the sum of recognised losses and progress billings, for all contracts in progress for which costs incurred plus recognised profits (less recognised losses) exceeds progress billings. An entity must consider whether the amount recognised in accordance with IAS 11 can be contractually billed or recovered.

Example 2.7

Gross amount due from customer for contract work

Entity A has entered into a contract with Entity B for the construction of a single asset, such as a building. The contract is within the scope of IAS 11, but is specifically not within the scope of IFRIC 12 *Service Concession Arrangements*. Because the outcome of the contract can be estimated reliably, contract revenue and contract costs associated with the construction contract are recognised as revenue and expenses, respectively, by reference to the stage of completion of the contract activity at the end of the reporting period in accordance with IAS 11.22. At the end of the reporting period, costs incurred plus recognised profits (less recognised losses) exceed progress billings and Entity A presents an amount in its statement of financial position as 'the gross amount due from customers for contract work'.

Entity A bills Entity B in accordance with the construction contract only when specific work performed by Entity A has been certified as completed. These billings are recognised in the statement of financial position as a separate financial asset because they represent a contractual right to receive cash and thus meet the definition of a financial asset in IAS 32.11.

The gross amount due from customer for contract work is not a financial asset in accordance with IAS 32.11. Such amounts cannot contractually be billed and recovered from Entity B because Entity A's work has not been certified as completed. The asset is not a financial asset because, in accordance with IAS 32.11, it is not 'a contractual right to receive cash or another financial asset from another entity' at the end of the reporting period. It is only when Entity A's work is certified as completed that (i) Entity A becomes party to a contractual right to receive cash or other financial asset and (ii) the gross amount due from customers for contract work becomes a separate financial asset.

If a construction contract receivable is not a financial instrument then IAS 39 and IFRS 7 do not apply to that balance.

3 Additional scope exclusions of IAS 39

In addition to the above scope exemptions, IAS 39 has some further exemptions as follows:

- financial instruments issued by the entity that meet the definition of equity instruments in accordance with IAS 32 (see **3.1** below);
- contracts to buy or sell an acquiree in a business combination (see **3.2** below);
- certain reimbursement rights (see **3.3** below);
- rights and obligations under leases, although in certain circumstances the derecognition, impairment and embedded derivative provisions of IAS 39 apply (see **3.4** below); and
- certain loan commitments (see **3.5** below).

Each of the above is considered in turn.

3.1 Equity instruments of the entity

Financial instruments issued by an entity that meet the definition of equity instruments in IAS 32 (see **section 2** of **chapter 3**) are outside the scope of IAS 39. This exemption includes standalone equity instruments, such as ordinary shares, as well as derivatives over own equity that exchange a fixed amount of cash or other financial asset for a fixed number of equity instruments. The exemption applies only to the issuer of the equity instrument. The holder of the instrument should apply the recognition and measurement criteria of IAS 39.

Following the amendment to IAS 32, *Puttable Financial Instruments and Obligations Arising on Liquidation*, issued in February 2008, some instruments previously classified as financial liabilities are classified as equity (see **2.1.2.1 and 2.3** in **chapter 3**. The IAS 32 amendment also amended IFRS 7 to exclude these instruments classified as equity from the scope of IFRS 7. [IFRS 7.3(f)]

IFRS 7 scopes out derivatives over own equity that meet the definition of equity. IFRS 7 does not appear to have a scope exception for non-derivative instruments classified as equity, such as ordinary shares. This appears to be an oversight in the drafting of the Standard as IFRS 7.BC8 states that the scope exception of IFRS 7 is intended to be the same as IAS 32 (prior to IFRS 7 being issued) with one exception, namely 'derivatives based on interests in subsidiaries, associates or joint ventures if the derivatives meet the definition of an equity instrument in IAS 32'. The basis of conclusions justifies this position by stating that these instruments are not remeasured and hence 'do not expose the issuer to balance sheet and income statement risk' and the disclosures about the significance of financial instruments for financial position and performance are not relevant to equity instruments. In addition, it states that these instruments are excluded from the scope of IFRS 7, but they are within the scope of IAS 32 for the purpose of determining whether they meet the definition of equity instruments. It appears reasonable to conclude that the scope exclusions for derivatives over own equity that meet the definition of equity would also apply to non-derivatives that meet the definition of equity as the justification in the basis of conclusions of IFRS 7 would be equally relevant.

3.2 Contracts to buy or sell an acquiree in a business combination

Contracts between an acquirer and a vendor in a business combination to buy or sell an acquiree at a future date are outside the scope of IAS 39. The application of IAS 39.2(g) is assessed at the time the holder enters into the derivative contract. If the contract is a forward contract, whether partly prepaid or not, which will lead to a certain business combination, the exemption applies and the forward contract is outside the scope of IAS 39. The same analysis would be applied to a combination of a put and a call option where the strike prices, exercise dates and notionals are equal, such that the combination of the put and the call is economically equivalent to a forward contract that will result in a business combination that is certain to occur. Equally, an option that is very deeply in-the-money at inception because the strike price is very low compared with the value of the shares to be delivered under it, which is analogous to a forward contract, is also outside the scope of IAS 39. Contracts that have settlement alternatives that may not result in all cases in the delivery of shares to the acquirer will be within the scope of IAS 39 as the exemption within IAS 39.2(g) will not apply.

The above scenarios should be distinguished from contracts between an acquirer and vendor that are options which are not economically equivalent to a forward contract. IAS 27 provides guidance as to whether an option represents a 'potential voting right that is currently exercisable or convertible'. If the option is currently exercisable but is not an in-substance present ownership interest, the appropriate accounting will depend on whether control currently exists. If control does exist, the parent's proportion of the acquiree in the consolidated financial statements is determined taking into account the present ownership interests which do not reflect the possible exercise or conversion of potential voting rights. In such circumstances the ownership interest that excludes the exercise of the currently exercisable option is a subsidiary as there is control and therefore thought will need to be given as to whether the currently exercisable option (to acquire a non-controlling interest) meets the definition of equity in the consolidated financial statements (see **section 6** in **chapter 3**). If the option meets the definition of equity it is outside the scope of IAS 39. Otherwise, it will be within the scope of IAS 39 and the exemption in IAS 39.2(g) does not apply.

If the option (that is not economically equivalent to a forward) is currently exercisable and it gives the holder the ability to control the target entity, and is an in-substance present ownership interest, then control exists and the parent's proportion of the acquiree in the consolidated financial statements is determined reflecting the in substance present ownership interest in accordance with IAS 27. The option is not subject to the requirements of IAS 39 in such a case as it is treated as giving rise to a present ownership interest rather than being a derivative to acquire such an interest in the future.

If the option (that is not economically equivalent to a forward) is not currently exercisable and would give the holder the ability to control the target entity only when it becomes exercisable the scope exemption within IAS 39.2(g) also does not apply. The option will not always result in a business combination to buy or sell an acquiree at a future date and therefore is in the scope of IAS 39.

The IAS 39.2(g) exemption applies equally to the acquirer and the vendor. Therefore, if the acquirer applies the exemption on the basis that the contract will result in a future business combination, the vendor equally applies the exemption and scopes out its contract to sell its subsidiary to the acquirer in its consolidated financial statements. Irrespective of IAS 39.2(g), the contract may also be outside the scope of IAS 39 for the vendor as the contract may meet the definition of equity in the case where the contract is a forward sale of shares in a subsidiary for a fixed amount of functional currency cash.

In 2007 the IFRIC was asked to interpret whether the IAS 39.2(g) scope exemption applies only to binding contracts to acquire shares that constitute a controlling interest in another entity within the period necessary to complete a business combination, or if it applies more widely, and also whether it applies to similar transactions, such as those to acquire an interest in an associate. In January 2008 the IFRIC acknowledged that the wording in IAS 39.2(g) was ambiguous and could lead to diversity in practice. For this reason, the IFRIC referred the issue to the IASB where the Board agreed to amend IAS 39.2(g) as proposed in the exposure draft, *Improvements to IFRSs*, issued in August 2008. The proposed amendment to IAS 39.2(g) states that the scope exception applies only to forward contracts entered into before the acquisition date (i.e. before the date the acquirer obtains control of the acquiree) between an acquirer and a vendor in a business combination, to buy or sell an acquiree at a future date and at a specified price (or on a specified price basis). In the basis of conclusions of the exposure draft the Board makes it clear that the exception in IAS 39.2(g) should not be applied by analogy to investments in associates and similar transactions because an investment in an associate does not represent an acquisition of the constituent assets of the investee.

3.3 Certain reimbursement rights

Rights to payments to reimburse the entity for expenditure it is required to make to settle a liability that it recognises as a provision in accordance with IAS 37 *Provisions, Contingent Liabilities and Contingent Assets*, or for which, in an earlier period, it recognised a provision in accordance with IAS 37, are outside the scope of IAS 39. [IAS 39.2(j)] Such rights are within the scope of IAS 37 and are recognised as a separate asset when, and only when, it is virtually certain that the reimbursement will be received if and when the entity settles the liability. [IAS 37.53]

3.4 Rights and obligations under lease contracts

Rights and obligations under lease contracts may meet the definition of a financial instrument. In a finance lease, a lease receivable recognised by the lessor represents the lessor's right to receive a stream of cash flows. This receivable is substantially the same as blended payments of principal and interest under a loan agreement. Hence, a finance lease is a contract that gives rise to a financial asset in the hands of the lessor and also gives rise to a financial liability in the hands of the lessee. Operating leases, on the other hand, are generally regarded as uncompleted contracts whereby lessors provide the use of assets in exchange for a fee for their service. Accordingly an operating lease is not regarded as a financial instrument (except as regards individual payments currently due and payable). This continues to be the case even if the operating lease is regarded as an onerous contract and a provision has been recognised in accordance with IAS 37 *Provisions, Contingent Liabilities and Contingent Assets.* IAS 17 *Leases* sets out the accounting framework for leases and hence leases are, for the most part, outside of the scope of all three Standards. However:

- lease receivables recognised by a lessor are subject to the derecognition (see **section 3** of **chapter 7**) and impairment (see **section 6** of **chapter 6**) requirements of IAS 39;
- finance lease payables recognised by a lessee are subject to the derecognition requirements of IAS 39 (see **section 3** of **chapter 7**);
- derivatives embedded in lease contracts are within the scope of IAS 39 (see **section 9** of **chapter 5**); and
- finance leases are within the scope of IFRS 7.

US GAAP comparison: The US derivative accounting standard (Statement 133) does not specifically scope out leases, however EITF Issue No. 01–8, "Determining Whether an Arrangement Contains a Lease" explicitly states that leases within the scope of the US lease accounting literature (Statement 13) are not derivative instruments subject to Statement 133."

3.5 Loan commitments

Loan commitments that cannot be settled net in cash or another financial instrument are outside the scope of IAS 39, unless the entity designates them as financial liabilities at fair value through profit or loss. If an entity has a past practice of selling the asset resulting from a loan commitment shortly after its origination, it should apply IAS 39 to all loan commitments in the same class.

Loan commitments that can be settled net in cash or another financial instrument are derivatives within the scope of IAS 39. Instalment payments do not constitute net settlement. Thus, for example, a mortgage construction loan that is paid out in instalments in line with the progress of the construction is not within the scope of IAS 39. [IAS 39.2(h)]

A financial institution may write a loan commitment to a large corporate borrower as a lead lender with the expressed intention to sell part of the loan immediately to other financial institutions when lent. The intention to sell part of the loan is part of its predetermined credit risk management. At inception of the loan commitment the financial institution cannot assert that it does not have a past practice of selling the asset resulting from a loan commitment shortly after its origination and therefore cannot consider the loan commitment wholly outside the scope of IAS 39. The financial institution may be able to demonstrate that, consistent with its predetermined credit risk management, only part of the loan that may be originated from the loan commitment is intended to be sold, and if so, only that proportion of the loan commitment is in the scope of IAS 39 and is fair valued through profit or loss. If the loan is originated the part of the loan commitment that is fair valued through profit or loss will be derecognised and will be incorporated into the initial carrying value of the resulting loan.

If an entity commits to providing a loan at a below-market interest rate it should initially recognise the commitment at fair value. Subsequently, the commitment is measured at the higher of:
[IAS 39.47(d)]

(i) the amount determined under IAS 37 *Provisions, Contingent Liabilities and Contingent Assets*; and

(ii) the amount initially recognised less, where appropriate, cumulative amortisation recognised in accordance with IAS 18 *Revenue*.

Loan commitments can either be optional, i.e. provide a borrower with the right to borrow in the future from a specified lender, or be non-optional, i.e. the borrower must borrow from the specified lender. In all cases the lender will lend funds to the borrower either when the borrower exercises its right to borrow or, in the case of non-optional loan commitments, per the specified conditions in the contract. If a contract requires or gives the option for an entity to *acquire* a debt instrument, as opposed to lending funds to the borrower under the commitment, this arrangement is not a loan commitment as a lending will not take place. The arrangement is a derivative financial instrument which will be measured at fair value through profit or loss except if it meets the regular way exemption as described in **section 2** in **chapter 7**.

The scoping out of loan commitments as described above applies equally to the holder (the borrower) as it does to the writer (the lender) of the loan commitment. If a loan commitment is not within the scope of IAS 39, the writer accounts for in accordance with IAS 37 and IAS 18; however, all loan commitments are subject to the derecognition provisions of IAS 39.

IFRS does not provide specific guidance on the measurement of a loan commitment that is outside the scope of IAS 39 from the perspective of the holder. Where the holder of the loan commitment pays the writer of the loan commitment compensation for entering into the loan commitment the fair value of the compensation should be recognised as an asset. From the holder's perspective the asset represents the right for the entity to borrow in the future at pre-specified terms which may be favourable. For the holder, the asset should be released to profit or loss on a systematic basis reflecting the periods over which the holder has the right to exercise the loan commitment.

If the loan commitment is fully drawn down by the holder and no further amounts can be drawn down it would be appropriate to recognise the remaining unamortised loan commitment asset as part of the carrying value on initial recognition of the borrowing as a transaction cost (see **2.2** in **chapter 6**). If the loan is not measured at fair value through profit or loss this will form part of the instrument's effective interest rate (see **4.1** in **chapter 6**).

Where the fee paid by the holder is more akin to a facility fee where the amounts and timing of the draw down, and repayment of the borrowing, can vary at the discretion of the borrower, for example, an overdraft fee, it would not be appropriate to capitalise the fee as a transaction cost when amounts are drawn down. The fee is not specific to an amount borrowed and therefore a systematic release of the fee over the period of the facility is more appropriate.

Where the loan to be originated under a loan commitment will include a non-closely related embedded derivative (see **section 3** in **chapter 5**) the question arises as to whether it is still permissible for the loan commitment to be scoped out of IAS 39. Once the loan is originated under the commitment, the non-closely related embedded derivative will be separated from the host loan contract and separately accounted for at fair value through profit or loss (unless the whole loan is designated at fair value through profit or loss at initial recognition – see **3.1** in **chapter 2** and **7.1.2** in **chapter 3**). It could be argued that applying the scope exemption in such a situation creates a measurement inconsistency between the measurement of the loan commitment (outside the scope of IAS 39 and not measured at fair value) and the subsequent measurement of the loan (within the scope of IAS 39 and either wholly at fair value through profit or loss if so designated or in part measured at fair value in the case of a separately recognised embedded derivative). However, it should be noted that the Standard already allows such a measurement inconsistency where a loan commitment that will result in a loan not containing any embedded derivatives is outside the scope of IAS 39 (and not measured at fair value) and the loan subsequently originated under the commitment is designated at fair value through profit or loss under certain conditions. It seems, therefore, appropriate that the scope exemption for loan commitments that will result in loans with separately accounted embedded derivatives should still apply if the relevant conditions are met, i.e. the loan commitment cannot be settled net in cash, the entity has not designated it as at fair value through profit or loss, and the entity does not have a past practice of selling the assets resulting from loan commitments shortly after origination.

To illustrate, Entity X may enter into a firm commitment to lend to Entity Y. The loan to be originated under the commitment will be a loan which the lender can convert into a fixed number of equity shares of the borrower. Once originated, the lender will have a loan asset with a non-closely related embedded derivative and the analysis in the paragraph above would apply. For Entity X the loan commitment would be outside the scope of IAS 39.

From Entity Y's perspective, the loan commitment is a right to jointly borrow cash and issue a derivative over its own equity. The loan commitment is partly a derivative over debt and partly a derivative over a derivative over own equity. The definition of a financial liability (see **section 2** in **chapter 3**) makes it clear that a derivative over a derivative over own equity would itself not meet the definition of equity and therefore it could be argued that the loan commitment cannot be considered to be outside the scope of IAS 39. However, IAS 39.BC15 recognises that all loan commitments are in fact derivatives that are excluded from the scope of IAS 39. Consequently, it is reasonable to consider such a loan commitment for Entity Y as also being outside the scope of IAS 39.

US GAAP comparison: The US derivative accounting literature (Statement 133) excludes from its scope holders of loan commitments (i.e. potential borrowers). In addition, issuers of loan commitments to originate mortgage loans that will be held for investment purposes or any other types of loans are not subject to Statement 133.

2 Financial assets

1 Introduction

IAS 39 prescribes how a financial asset should be classified. The classification of an asset will then drive how the asset is subsequently measured.

All financial assets are required to be classified into one of the four primary classification categories. Two of these categories, 'held-to-maturity' and 'loans and receivables' result in amortised cost measurement and the other two categories 'fair value through profit or loss' and 'available-for-sale' result in fair value measurement.

This chapter discusses financial assets in the following sections:

Section 2	Definition of a financial asset
Section 3	Classification of financial assets
Section 4	Reclassifications
Section 5	Classification of financial assets acquired in a business combination

2 Definition of a financial asset

IAS 32.11 defines a financial asset as any asset that is:

(a) cash;

(b) an equity instrument of another entity;

(c) a contractual right:

   (i) to receive cash or another financial asset from another entity; or

   (ii) to exchange financial assets or financial liabilities with another entity under conditions that are potentially favourable to the entity; or

(d) a contract that will or may be settled in the entity's own equity instruments and is:

(i) a non-derivative for which the entity is or may be obliged to receive a variable number of the entity's own equity instruments; or

(ii) a derivative that will or may be settled other than by the exchange of a fixed amount of cash or another financial asset for a fixed number of the entity's own equity instruments. For this purpose the entity's own equity instruments do not include puttable financial instruments classified as equity instruments in accordance with IAS 39.16A and 16B, instruments that impose on the entity an obligation to deliver to another party a pro rata share of the net assets of the entity only on liquidation and are classified as equity instruments in accordance with IAS 39.16C and 16D, or instruments that are contracts for the future receipt or delivery of the entity's own equity instruments.

A deposit of cash with a bank or similar institution is a financial asset because it represents the contractual right of the depositor to obtain cash from the institution or to draw a cheque or similar instrument against the balance in favour of a creditor in payment of a financial liability.

Common examples of financial assets representing a contractual right to receive cash in the future are trade accounts receivable, notes and loans receivable, and debt securities. Another type of financial asset is one for which the economic benefit to be received is a financial asset other than cash, for example, a note payable in treasury bonds which gives the holder the contractual right to receive treasury bonds, not cash.

Gold bullion is not a financial instrument, it is a commodity. Although bullion is highly liquid, there is no contractual right to receive cash or another financial asset inherent in the bullion. [IAS 39.IG.B.1] Where the future economic benefit is the receipt of goods or services, such as prepaid expenses, the asset is not a financial asset. Also, assets that represent rights to receive cash but are not contractual such as tax receivables are not financial assets as they arise from statutory requirements. [IAS 32.AG12]

The definition of a financial asset also includes certain derivative and non-derivative contracts indexed to, or settled in, an issuer's equity instruments.

Example 2

Derivative financial asset

On 1 February 20X0 Entity E enters into a contract with Entity F to receive the fair value of 1,000 of Entity E's own ordinary shares in exchange for a payment of CU104,000 in cash (i.e. CU104 per share) on 31 January 20X1.

> Under the terms of the contract, settlement will be net in cash. The market price per share on 1 February 20X0 is CU100.
>
> The initial value of the forward contract on 1 February 20X0 is zero. On 31 December 20X0, the share price has increased and, as a result, the fair value of the forward contract has increased to CU6,300. Entity E recognises a derivative asset of CU6,300.

For further detail on the classification of contracts indexed to or settled in an entity's own equity instruments as derivative assets or liabilities, gross liabilities or equity, by the issuer, see **section 6** in **chapter 3**.

3 Classification of financial assets

Every financial asset that falls within the scope of IAS 39 must be classified into one of the following four primary categories:

- at fair value through profit or loss (FVTPL);
- available-for-sale (AFS);
- loans and receivables (LR); or
- held-to-maturity (HTM).

This classification is important as it drives the subsequent measurement of the asset (i.e. whether the asset is held at fair value or amortised cost). In the above list, assets in the first two categories are measured at fair value, whilst those in the last two categories are measured at amortised cost. The only exception to this rule is equity instruments that do not have a quoted market price in an active market and whose fair value cannot be reliably measured, and derivatives that are linked to and must be settled by delivery of such an unquoted equity instrument, which are instead held at cost, see **3.1.6** in **chapter 6**.

Different classification categories that are possible for different financial assets are illustrated below.

	Type of instrument		
Classification	**Investment in a debt security**	**Investment in an equity security for which fair value can be reliably measured**	**Derivatives and embedded derivatives**
FVTPL			
• held for trading	■	■	■
• designated as at FVTPL	■	■	
Loans and receivables	■		
Held-to-maturity	■		
Available-for-sale	■	■	

3.1 Financial assets at fair value through profit or loss (FVTPL)

FVTPL has two sub-categories. The first includes any financial asset that is designated on initial recognition as one to be measured at fair value with fair value changes in profit or loss (except for investments in equity instruments and derivatives that are linked to and must be settled by delivery of equity instruments, where the equity instrument does not have a quoted market price in an active market for which fair value is reliably determinable – see **3.1.6** in **chapter 6**). This designation is irrevocable. The second category includes financial assets classified as held for trading. All derivative assets are held for trading financial assets measured at FVTPL, except for derivatives that are designated and effective hedging instruments. If a derivative asset is a hedging instrument in a cash flow hedge or a hedge of a net investment in a foreign operation, part of the fair value gains/losses will be recognised in other comprehensive income. Fair value gains/losses for a derivative asset that is a hedging instrument in a fair value hedge will always be recognised in profit or loss, i.e. the same treatment applies as if the instrument was not in a hedge relationship at all. See **2.2** in **chapter 8** on cash flow hedge accounting and **2.3** in **chapter 8** on hedges of a net investment in a foreign operation.

3.1.1 Designation as at FVTPL

There are many reasons why an entity may wish to designate a financial instrument as at FVTPL:

- it eliminates an accounting mismatch;
- it allows an entity to avoid the burden of hedge accounting requirements (see **chapter 8**), for example designating, assessing, and measuring effectiveness where classification of both items as at fair value through profit or loss achieves a similar result as if fair value hedge accounting had been applied;
- it de-emphasises interpretative issues of when an item is appropriately considered to be 'held for trading'; or
- when applied to hybrid instruments (see **chapter 5**), it eliminates the burden of separating embedded derivatives that are not considered to be closely related to the host contract as the fair value of the whole contractual arrangement is then recognised in profit or loss.

A financial asset or a financial liability may upon initial recognition be designated as at FVTPL only if it meets one of the following conditions:

(a) it eliminates or significantly reduces a measurement or recognition inconsistency that would otherwise arise from measuring assets or liabilities or recognising the gains and losses on them on different bases (commonly referred to as an 'accounting mismatch');

(b) a group of financial assets, financial liabilities or both is managed and its performance is evaluated on a fair value basis, in accordance with a documented risk management or investment strategy, and information about the group is provided internally on that basis to the entity's key management personnel (as defined in IAS 24 *Related Party Disclosures*), for example the entity's board of directors and chief executive officer; or

(c) in the case of a hybrid contract containing one or more embedded derivatives, an entity may designate the entire hybrid (combined) contract as a financial asset or financial liability as at FVTPL unless:

  - the embedded derivative does not significantly modify the cash flows that otherwise would be required by the contract; or
  - it is clear with little or no analysis when a similar hybrid instrument is first considered that separation of the embedded derivative is prohibited, for example a prepayment option embedded in a loan that permits the holder to prepay the loan for approximately its amortised cost, (see **7.1** in **chapter 5**).

The election to FVTPL has to be made at initial recognition of the financial instrument. Once an entity has elected to use the fair value option for a financial asset or a financial liability it is cannot revoke this election. This is the case even if the instrument giving rise to an accounting mismatch is derecognised. This is different from the approach taken when employing hedge accounting (see **chapter 8**) where an entity is free to revoke such a designation at any time.

The fair value option is unavailable for investments in equity instruments that do not have a quoted market price in an active market, and whose fair value cannot be reliably measured (see **3.1.6** in **chapter 6**).

It should be noted that the requirements for determining a reliable measure of the fair value of a financial asset or a financial liability apply equally to items that are measured at fair value and to those that are only disclosed at fair value.

The decision by an entity to designate a financial asset or a financial liability as at FVTPL is similar to an accounting policy choice in that the result of applying the fair value option should provide reliable and more relevant information about the effects of transactions, other events and conditions on the entity's financial position, financial performance or cash flows. [IAS 39.AG4C] However, an important difference between an accounting policy choice and the fair value option is that the latter can be applied on an instrument-by-instrument basis. The fair value option cannot be applied to a part of a financial instrument, it must be applied to the financial instrument in its entirety.

US GAAP comparison: As discussed in **3.1.1.3** below, FAS 155 *Accounting For Certain Hybrid Financial Instruments* provides a fair value option for hybrid financial instruments that contain an embedded derivative that otherwise would have been required to be separated from the host contract.

Subsequent to the issuance of FAS 155, the US FASB issued FAS 159, *The Fair Value Option for Financial Assets and Financial Liabilities* which provides a fair value option for all financial assets and liabilities. The fair value option in FAS 159 is broader than the equivalent option in IAS 39 as it does not have the qualifying criteria in IAS 39.9 & 11A. The items that the fair value option can be applied to and the documentation requirements under FAS 159 and IAS 39 are broadly similar. However, there are some differences in scope and therefore the two standards do not always permit the fair value option for the same items. For example, FAS 159 permits election of the fair value option for certain contracts that are outside the scope of IAS 39, such as certain insurance contracts and certain warranties that are not financial instruments.

Furthermore, FAS 159 permits application of the fair value option to most equity method investments. With limited exceptions described in **2.1** of **chapter 1**, IAS 39 excludes equity method investments, 'associates', from being fair valued, and therefore if the interest in the associate is outside the scope of IAS 39 the fair value option cannot be applied. Unlike IAS 39, FAS 159 permits the fair value option to be elected not only upon initial recognition of an eligible item but also on certain subsequent election dates such as when (1) an "investment becomes subject to the equity method of accounting"; (2) an investment is deconsolidated and (3) "an event that requires an eligible item to be measured at fair value at the time of the event" (such as a business combination, consolidation or deconsolidation, or a significant debt modification).

3.1.1.1 Eliminates or significantly reduces an accounting mismatch

The following are examples of where applying the fair value option can significantly reduce a measurement or recognition inconsistency.

- In the absence of designation as at FVTPL, a financial asset would often be classified as available-for-sale (with most changes in fair value recognised in other comprehensive income) while a related liability would often be measured at amortised cost (with changes in fair value not recognised). In such circumstances, an entity may conclude that its financial statements would provide more relevant information if both instruments were classified as at FVTPL. [IAS 39.AG4D]

- An entity's liabilities may have cash flows that are contractually linked to the performance of assets that would often be classified as available-for-sale. For example, an insurer may have liabilities that pay benefits based on realised / unrealised investment returns on a specified pool of the insurer's assets. If the measurement of those liabilities reflects current market prices, classifying the assets as at FVTPL means that changes in the fair value of the financial assets are recognised in profit or loss in the same period as related changes in the value of the liabilities. [IAS 39.AG4E(a)]

- An entity may have liabilities under insurance contracts whose measurement incorporates current information (as permitted by IFRS 4 *Insurance Contracts*), and related financial assets would often be classified as available-for-sale or measured at amortised cost. Classifying the assets as at FVTPL means that changes in the fair value of the financial assets are recognised in profit or loss in the same period as related changes in the value of the liabilities. [IAS 39.AG4E(b)]

- An entity may have financial assets, financial liabilities or both that share a risk, such as interest rate risk, that gives rise to opposite changes in fair value that tend to offset each other. Yet, often only some of the instruments are measured at FVTPL (for example, derivatives). Furthermore, the requirements for hedge accounting may not be met, for example because the requirements for effectiveness are not met. Classifying the assets and liabilities as at FVTPL will achieve an accounting offset that reflects the existing natural economic offset. [IAS 39.AG4E(c)]

- An entity may have financial assets, financial liabilities or both that share a risk, such as interest rate risk, that gives rise to opposite changes in fair value of those assets and liabilities that tend to offset each other. The assets and liabilities may be measured on a different basis and hedge accounting cannot be applied because none of the instruments is a derivative. Classifying the assets and liabilities as at FVTPL will achieve an accounting offset that reflects the existing natural economic offset. [IAS 39.AG4E(d)]

Example 3.1.1.1A

Fair value option: issued fixed rate debt

Entity A issues fixed rate debt. In order to economically hedge the fair value risk associated with interest payments on fixed rate debt, Entity A concurrently enters into an interest rate swap with a bank (receive fixed, pay floating), which has the same terms and payment dates as the debt. The interest rate swap is a derivative that must be fair valued through profit or loss. The entity does not wish to apply fair value hedge accounting as it does not wish to prepare any hedge documentation and does not have the processes in place to monitor hedge effectiveness. By designating the fixed rate debt as at FVTPL on initial recognition, the entity will achieve a natural substantial offset in profit or loss with the held for trading derivative. As the instruments both share a common risk (interest rate risk) the entity will seek to demonstrate that applying the fair value option results in more relevant information because it significantly reduces a measurement inconsistency that would otherwise arise from measuring the derivative at fair value with gains and losses in profit or loss, and carrying the debt at amortised cost. [IAS 39.9]

Example 3.1.1.1B

Fair value option: intragroup derivative

Subsidiary S issues a five-year fixed rate bond. To hedge against the interest rate risk it enters into a pay-variable-receive-fixed interest rate swap with its Parent P. In the subsidiary's financial statements, the bond is designated as at FVTPL. The designation cannot be applied in the consolidated financial statements as the derivative is eliminated on consolidation. If the parent or another group entity had a derivative instrument with a third party that shares a common risk with the bond, a different designation could be made for the bond in the consolidated financial statements provided the designation is made upon initial recognition.

In the examples above, the entity need not have entered into all of the assets and liabilities giving rise to the measurement or recognition inconsistency at exactly the same time. The fair value option is available provided that each transaction is designated as at fair value through profit or loss at its initial recognition, the delay between entering into the separate transactions is reasonably short, and any remaining transactions are expected to occur. [IAS 39.AG4F]

It would not be acceptable to designate only some of the financial assets and financial liabilities giving rise to the inconsistency as at FVTPL if to do so would not eliminate or significantly reduce the inconsistency and would therefore not result in more relevant information. However, it would be acceptable to designate only some of a number of similar financial assets or financial liabilities if doing so achieves a significant reduction (and possibly a greater reduction than other allowable designations) in the inconsistency. [IAS 39.AG4G]

Example 3.1.1.1C

Fair value option: lack of accounting mismatch (1)

Entity A has borrowed (through a single instrument) €1,000,000 with a third party bank and at the same time has used some of the borrowing to acquire 10 similar financial assets each of a value of €50,000 that add up to €500,000 which are all classified as held for trading. Entity A wants to reduce the measurement inconsistency by designating the liability as at FVTPL. However, if the financial liability was fair valued, Entity A would create an accounting mismatch in profit or loss related to the €500,000 of liabilities that are not matched by financial assets that are held for trading. This accounting mismatch is comparable to the mismatch it would have had had it not contemplated applying the fair value option in the first place. Therefore, Entity A cannot apply the fair value option as it does not significantly reduce the accounting mismatch between the assets and the liability.

Example 3.1.1.1D

Fair value option: lack of accounting mismatch (2)

Entity B buys an equity share for CU100 which does not meet the definition of held for trading. At the same time the entity buys a put option for CU20 over the same share with a strike price of CU100. Entity B is contemplating whether it could designate the equity share as a financial asset at fair value through profit or loss at initial recognition by claiming that doing so eliminates or significantly reduces an accounting mismatch that arises as a result of entering into the put option. If the fair value option is not applied the share will be measured at fair value with gains and losses immediately recognised in other comprehensive income unless there is an impairment in which case the cumulative losses are reclassified from equity to profit or loss prior to derecognition of the share. The put option will be accounted for at fair value through profit or loss in the absence of hedge accounting.

In considering whether an accounting mismatch is eliminated or significantly reduced Entity B considers various share price scenarios.

If the share price increases above CU100 the gain in fair value of the share will be recognised in other comprehensive income, while the fall in fair value of the option will be recorded in profit or loss. However, it should be noted that while the share price could rise well beyond CU120 (i.e. the fair value gain could be in excess of CU20) the corresponding possible fall in the value of the option is limited to CU20 as the value of the purchased put option cannot decline below zero). Gains from the share that arise from increases in the share price above CU120 will not have a corresponding loss from the put option. Thus, the degree of offset between the share and the option if the fair value option was applied is limited to certain share price scenarios only. In addition, when the share increases between CU100 and CU120 the decline in fair value of the option will not be linear compared with the increase in the fair value of the share as the option's fair value includes time value but the share's does not.

If the share price falls and the fall is not considered significant or prolonged then the fair value loss will be recognised in other comprehensive income while the increase in the fair value of the option would be recorded in profit or loss. As noted above the increase in fair value of the option will not be fully offset by the decrease in the fair value of the share as the option's fair value will also include changes in time value.

If there is an impairment the cumulative loss recognised in other comprehensive income will be reclassified from equity to profit or loss as a reclassification adjustment (see **section 6** in **chapter 6**). Once the impairment has occurred, future falls in fair value of the shares and further increases in intrinsic value of the option will be recognised in profit or loss and will achieve the same accounting result had the fair value option not been applied. In the period when the impairment occurs not applying the fair value option would result in a greater one-off loss in profit or loss as a result of reclassification from equity compared to the net loss when applying the fair value option.

Considering all the various scenarios it is not possible for the entity to claim that applying the fair value option does provide an elimination or significant reduction in an accounting mismatch.

3.1.1.2 Managed and performance evaluated on a fair value basis

Examples of where an entity can apply the fair value option on the basis that financial assets, financial liabilities or both are managed and their performance evaluated on a fair value basis, in accordance with a documented risk management or investment strategy include the following.

- An entity that is a venture capital organisation, mutual fund, unit trust or similar entity whose business is investing in financial assets with a view to profiting from their total return in the form of interest or dividends and changes in fair value. An entity may designate such investments as at FVTPL, provided it does not hold a controlling interest in them. [IAS 39.AG4I(a)]

- An entity may have financial assets and financial liabilities that share one or more risks and those risks are managed and evaluated on a fair value basis in accordance with a documented policy of asset and liability management. An example could be an entity that has issued 'structured products' containing multiple embedded derivatives and manages the resulting risks on a fair value basis using a mix of derivative and non-derivative financial instruments. [IAS 39.AG4I(b)] This is particularly evident for investment banks that issue structured medium-term note programmes linked to a basket of equities or corporate bonds, where the bank economically hedges its liability by purchasing equity and corporate bonds in the cash market, and/or enters into derivative contracts where the underlying is the referenced equities or corporate bonds. It is common for investment banks to manage the portfolio of assets and liabilities on a fair value basis.

- An insurer holds a portfolio of financial assets, manages it so as to maximise its total return (i.e. interest / dividends and changes in fair value), and evaluates its performance on that basis. For example, a portfolio may be held to back specific liabilities in which case the investment policy and evaluation on a fair value basis may apply to either the assets and liabilities, or to the assets alone. [IAS 39.AG4I(c)]

- An entity that designates financial instruments as at FVTPL on the basis that it manages and evaluates their performance on that basis must designate all eligible financial instruments that are managed and evaluated together, i.e. it cannot cherry-pick. [IAS 39.AG4J]

The risk management or investment strategy must be documented, though documentation need not be extensive. For example, if the performance management system as approved by the entity's key management personnel clearly demonstrates that the performance is evaluated on a total return basis, no additional documentation is required. The documentation does not need to be on an item-by-item basis (it may be on a portfolio basis), or at the level of detail required for hedge accounting.

3.1.1.3 Contracts containing one or more embedded derivative

IAS 39.11A allows a hybrid contract containing one or more embedded derivatives to be designated in its entirety at FVTPL unless:

- the embedded derivative does not significantly modify the cash flows that otherwise would be required by the contract; or
- it is clear with little or no analysis when a similar hybrid instrument is first considered that separation of the embedded derivative is prohibited, for example a prepayment option embedded in a loan that permits the holder to prepay the loan for approximately its amortised cost (see **7.1** in **chapter 5**).

Example 3.1.1.3

Fair value option: Commodity-linked debt

Entity Q issues a debt instrument that has interest payments linked to a basket of commodity prices. The linking to commodity prices is considered to be a non-closely related embedded derivative that would require separation and measurement as at FVTPL. Entity Q may choose at initial recognition to designate the whole debt instrument as at FVTPL to avoid separating out the embedded derivative.

IAS 39 applies to financial instruments within its scope. However, certain requirements like embedded derivatives apply to a wider range of contracts. For example, an operating lease that is not a financial instrument may have an embedded derivative that is separately recognised in the statement of financial position. A question arises whether the fair value option provisions can be extended to hybrid contracts where the host contract is a non-financial item or a financial item outside the scope of IAS 39. At its meeting in March 2007, the IFRIC was asked to consider this question. In November 2007 the IFRIC recommended that the Board should clarify IAS 39.11A by specifying whether it applies only to contracts with embedded derivatives that have financial hosts, or whether the fair value option can be applied to all contracts with embedded derivatives. In August 2008 the IASB issued an exposure draft, *Improvements to IFRSs*, which proposed amending IAS 39.11A to make it clear that the fair value option could only apply to financial instruments within the scope of IAS 39. In the basis of conclusions to the exposure draft the Board acknowledged that the wording in paragraph 11A was not clear. The Board noted that prior to the restricted fair value option that was issued in June 2005 that continues to apply in IAS 39, the standard had an unrestricted fair value option which could only be applied to financial instruments within the scope of

IAS 39. The objective of fair value option that was introduced in 2005 was to restrict, not broaden, an entity's ability to designate financial instruments as at FVTPL. At its January 2009 meeting, the IASB decided to defer its redeliberations on the fair value option for a future period and therefore would not be included in the finalised amendments expected to be issued in April 2009.

It would be surprising to conclude otherwise since it would mean that any host contract that is outside the scope of IAS 39, and in many cases has been specifically excluded from IAS 39 in paragraph 2, could be fair valued through profit or loss as this would override the recognition and measurement guidance of more specific Standards, like IAS 17 *Leases*, IFRS 4 *Insurance Contracts* or IAS 11 *Construction Contracts*. It would also mean that executory host contracts, like sale and purchase contracts, would be 'grossed up' in the statement of financial position.

The rules on embedded derivatives contained in non-financial host contracts were introduced as an anti-abuse measure to stop entities from stapling financial instruments on to non-financial contracts. Once the embedded derivative is separated, that part of the hybrid instrument is in the scope of IAS 39, but the host contract always remains outside the scope of IAS 39. The fair value option provisions are contained in IAS 39, the Standard that deals with financial instruments and contracts that behave like financial instruments, and therefore it seems logical for embedded derivative to conclude that the fair value option is restricted only to contracts that are in the scope of IAS 39.

IFRIC 9 *Reassessment of Embedded Derivatives* allows an entity to reconsider whether an embedded derivative is closely related only if there is a change in the terms of the contract that significantly modifies the cash flows that otherwise would be required under the contract (or if the instrument is a hybrid (combined) financial asset that is reclassified out of fair value through profit or loss and an assessment of embedded derivatives is performed for the first time). As the fair value option can only be applied at initial recognition if the cash flows are modified sufficiently for the original instrument to be derecognised would an entity be able to designate the modified instrument as at fair value through profit or loss (see **section 3** in **chapter 5**).

The revised version of IFRS 3 *Business Combinations*, issued in January 2008, clarified that if a contractual arrangement is acquired as part of a business combination the acquirer must determine what is the classification of the contractual arrangement at the date of acquisition as this is the date of initial recognition (see **section 5** below). At the date of acquisition the acquirer will need to consider whether the contractual arrangement has any embedded derivatives that require separation. The acquirer is not *reassessing* an embedded derivative at this point as the acquirer is recognising the contractual arrangement for the first time and will be able to apply the fair value option election as appropriate.

US GAAP comparison: FAS 155, *Accounting For Certain Hybrid Financial Instruments* amended FAS 133 in a number of respects, one of which was the introduction of a 'fair value option' to hybrid financial instruments. If an entity would be required to separate out a non-closely related embedded derivative, an entity can instead choose to elect irrevocably to fair value the whole instrument for initial and subsequent measurement with fair value gains and losses recognised in profit or loss. The fair value election must be supported by concurrent documentation or a pre-existing documented policy for automatic election. The election may be made on an instrument-by-instrument basis. The introduction of a fair value option to hybrid financial instruments in FAS 155 is comparable to the fair value option permitted under IAS 39.11A. In addition, with the issuance of FAS 159, US GAAP allows an entity to designate financial assets or liabilities at fair value through earnings as described in **3.1.1** above.

3.1.1.4 Fair valuing through alternative designations

In some cases an entity could achieve fair value accounting through profit or loss by using alternative designation strategies. The choice of that designation strategy must be made at initial recognition of the instruments concerned.

Example 3.1.1.4A

Fair value option: alternative designations (1)

Bank A issues structured notes that contain non-closely related embedded derivatives linked to specific securities. Bank A manages the risk of these embedded derivatives by immediately investing in the underlying securities that do not meet the definition of held for trading. Bank A also manages the performance of the portfolio of underlying securities and issued structured notes on a fair value basis.

Bank A has a number of choices:

(a) designate the portfolio of financial assets (underlying securities) and financial liabilities (structured notes) as at FVTPL as it is managed on a fair value basis; or

(b) designate the hybrid financial liabilities (structured notes) as at FVTPL as they contain non-closely related embedded derivatives; or

(c) designate the financial assets (underlying securities) as at FVTPL as there is an accounting mismatch with the embedded derivative that is separately accounted for as at FVTPL; or

(d) designate the financial assets (underlying securities) as at FVTPL as there is an accounting mismatch with the financial liabilities if they are designated as at FVTPL under (b) above.

In some scenarios a particular choice of designation will produce more meaningful information about the effects of transactions, other events and conditions on the entity's financial position, financial performance or cash flows. As the decision to designate an instrument is similar to an accounting policy choice the entity should choose the designation strategy that results in reliable and the *most* relevant information.

Example 3.1.1.4B

Fair value option: alternative designations (2)

Entity B issues a mandatory convertible instrument that at maturity converts into the shares of Entity D. The instrument consists of a debt host contract and a non-closely related embedded derivative, i.e. a forward to deliver Entity D's shares. Entity B economically hedges its exposure to Entity D by acquiring shares in Entity D. The shares in Entity D are not held for trading as Entity B does not intend to sell them in the short term, but intends to deliver the shares to the holder of the mandatory convertible instrument. Absent the fair value option, Entity B therefore would need to classify the investment in Entity D's shares as available-for-sale.

Entity B has a non-closely embedded derivative in its issued mandatory convertible instrument that relates to Entity D's share price. This embedded derivative will be fair valued through profit or loss. Entity B may choose to designate Entity D's shares as at FVTPL as this will significantly reduce the recognition inconsistency that would have existed from gains or losses in Entity D's shares being recognised through equity.

Arguably, Entity B could choose to designate the mandatory convertible instrument as at FVTPL on initial recognition as it has an embedded derivative that is not closely related. If Entity B fair valued through profit or loss the entire hybrid instrument there would still be a recognition inconsistency as the investment in the shares is an available-for-sale investment with fair value gains or losses recognised in other comprehensive income. A further election to designate Entity D's shares as at FVTPL would significantly reduce this inconsistency, but the reduction in the inconsistency is less than would be achieved had the entity applied the fair value option designation as described in the paragraph above. Designating the entire hybrid instrument would result in the fair value of the entity's credit risk being recognised in profit or loss which would not be the case had the entity not applied the fair value option.

3.1.2 Held for trading financial assets

A financial asset is held for trading if it is acquired principally for the purpose of sale in the near term, on initial recognition it is part of a portfolio of identified financial instruments that are managed together and for which there is evidence of a recent actual pattern of short-term profit-taking or if it is a derivative (except for a derivative that is a designated and effective hedging instrument).

Held for trading financial assets are measured at fair value through profit or loss.

Examples of held for trading financial assets are:

- equity securities bought and sold by defined benefit pension plans and investment companies that are actively traded by the entity;
- a portfolio of debt and/or equity securities managed by a trading desk;
- reverse repurchase agreements that form part of a trading book; or
- derivative financial instruments that are not effective hedging instruments.

In March 2009 the IFRIC issued a tentative agenda decision titled, *Classification of failed loan syndications*. The IFRIC was asked whether a loan amount resulting from a loan syndication that the originator intends to sell in the near term must always be classified as held for trading. The question arises when loans are originated with an intention of syndication but the arranger fails to find sufficient commitments from other participants (failed syndications). The arranger then tries to sell the surplus loan amount to other parties in the near term rather than holding it for the foreseeable future. The IFRIC noted that the definitions of loans and receivables and financial asset or financial liability at fair value through profit or loss in IAS 39.9 determine the classification of a loan in such circumstances. The definition of loans and receivables explicitly requires a loan (or portion of a loan) that is intended to be sold immediately or in the near term to be classified as held for trading on initial recognition. IAS

39.AG14 describes characteristics that *generally* apply to financial instruments classified as held for trading. The IFRIC noted, however, that these general characteristics are not a prerequisite for all instruments the standard requires to be classified as held for trading.

The IFRIC also noted that, in accordance with IAS 39.50D, an entity would be permitted to consider reclassifying the surplus loan amount that it no longer intended to sell.

The IFRIC did not expect significant diversity in practice because of the specific requirements in IAS 39 and therefore tentatively agreed not to issue an interpretation. At the date of writing the agenda decision was not finalised.

US GAAP comparison: US guidance has less stringent criteria for the classification of debt and equity securities as "trading." FAS 115 provides for securities to be classified as trading that are bought and held principally for near term selling, generally with the objective of receiving profits on short term differences in market prices. However, FAS 115 does not preclude classification of a security as trading simply because the entity does not intend to sell the security in the near term. Similar to IFRS, trading securities are measured at fair value with unrealised holding gains and losses included in earnings.

Financial assets that are not in security form (such as loan receivables) cannot be classified as "trading" under FAS 115 because they are not within the scope of that guidance. However, they may be eligible for election under the fair value option in FAS 159.

3.1.2.1 A portfolio with a recent actual pattern of short-term profit taking

Although the term 'portfolio' is not explicitly defined in IAS 39, the context in which it is used suggests that a portfolio is a group of financial assets that are managed together as part of a group. [IAS 39.IG.B.11 & 12] If there is evidence of a recent actual pattern of short-term profit taking on financial instruments included in such a portfolio, those financial instruments qualify as held for trading even though an individual financial instrument in the portfolio may in fact be held for a longer period of time. [IAS 39.IG.B.11]

In May 2008 the IASB issued *Improvements to IFRSs*. The improvements amended the definition of held for trading to clarify that a non-derivative financial instrument that is traded as part of a portfolio of identified financial instruments that are managed together and for which there is evidence of a recent actual pattern of short-term profit-taking can qualify for the trading classification only if it is included in such a portfolio on initial recognition. The amendments made to IAS 39 by *Improvements to IFRSs* apply for annual periods beginning on or after 1 January 2009, but earlier application is permitted. An entity choosing to apply the amendments early must disclose that fact.

3.1.2.2 Indicators of trading activities

The term 'trading' generally reflects active and frequent buying and selling. Determining whether or when an entity is involved in trading activities is a matter of judgement that depends on the relevant facts and circumstances. The facts and circumstances can be assessed based on an evaluation of various activities of the entity rather than solely on the terms of the individual transactions. Inherent in that assessment is an evaluation of the entity's intent in entering into financial instrument contracts and using particular types of financial instruments. Indications that financial instruments are entered into for trading purposes are set out below. The absence of any or all of the indicators in any category, by itself, would not necessarily avoid the classification of financial assets or liabilities as held for trading. All available evidence should be considered to determine whether, based on the weight of that evidence, an operation is involved in trading activities.

Organisational characteristics (nature of operations):

- the primary assets/liabilities of the operation are financial instrument contracts;

- the operation does not use its own capital as the primary source of funding its activities and instead makes extensive use of other techniques such as leveraging and credit enhancement as sources of risk capital;

- the operation develops and utilises its own proprietary models to price financial instrument contracts it offers or trades; and

- the operation offers financial instruments as a dealer, not as a 'user'.

Customers, counterparties and competitors:

- the majority of the counterparties to the financial instrument contracts and competitors are banks, brokers/traders or fund managers;
- the volume and prevalent direction (buying/selling) of transactions are indicative of trading;
- the change in the value of financial instrument contracts is expected to move in a direction that does not mitigate or offset the risk of other exposures;
- the volume of transactions differs significantly from the operation's historical requirements for such contracts;
- there has been a change in the volume of transactions that is significant relative to the change in demand arising from the entity's primary operating environment and financial structure;
- contracted quantities far exceed normal needs and exposure levels or result in opposite exposures;
- the operation does not consume the financial instruments to meet its normal needs (or make use of physical delivery to settle the contracts); and
- there is a high turnover rate in the portfolio of financial instrument contracts.

Management and controls:

- compensation and/or performance measures are tied to the short-term results generated from financial instrument transactions (that is, the operation is measured based on trading profits or changes in the market values of its positions);
- the operation communicates internally in terms of 'trading strategy' (that is, management reports identify contractual positions, fair values, hedging activities, risk exposure etc.);
- the operation sets limits on market positions and related strategies, sets policies governing what types of contracts it will transact in, and sets the controls it will follow; in addition,

management is involved in reviewing compliance with those limits, strategies, policies, and controls on a daily or frequent basis;

- the word 'trading' appears in the name of or documentation of the operation for internal or external purposes;
- employees of the operation are referred to as 'traders' or 'dealers' or have prior experience in banking, broking, derivatives trading or risk management activities;
- assessment of net market positions of the operation is done on a regular and frequent basis (for example hourly or overnight);
- infrastructure of the operation is similar to that of a trading operation of a bank or investment bank's front office, middle office, and back office (that is, there is a segregation of back office processing and front office trading functions);
- an infrastructure exists that enables the operation to capture price and other risks on a real-time basis;
- the activities are managed on a portfolio or 'book' basis; and
- management searches for opportunities to take advantage of favourable price spreads, arbitrage opportunities, or outright positions in the marketplace.

Transactions/contracts

- the operation has a history of pairing off (entering into offsetting contracts) or otherwise settling the transactions without physically receiving or delivering the underlying item. In other words, past practices of the operation have resulted in net cash settlement, offsetting, as well as netting out, and the type of settlement has changed quickly from one type to another to maximise profits/mitigate losses;
- the contracts do not permit physical delivery and must be settled net in the market or in cash; and
- the financial instrument contracts are not customarily used for general commercial (operational) business purposes or by the industry in general.

3.1.3 Reclassification into the financial assets at FVTPL category

Reclassification into the 'fair value through profit or loss' financial category while an asset is held is prohibited in accordance with IAS 39.50. Reclassifications out of the FVTPL category are permitted for non-derivative financial assets subject to meeting specified criteria. See **4.2** below.

The following changes in circumstances are not reclassifications: [IAS 39.50A]

- a derivative that was previously a designated and effective hedging instrument in a cash flow hedge or net investment hedge no longer qualifies as such;
- a derivative becomes a designated and effective hedging instrument in a cash flow hedge or net investment hedge; and
- financial assets are reclassified when an insurance company changes its accounting policies in accordance with IFRS 4.45.

IAS 39.50A was introduced by *Improvements to IFRSs* issued in May 2008. The amendments made to IAS 39 by *Improvements to IFRSs* apply for annual periods beginning on or after 1 January 2009, but earlier application is permitted. An entity choosing to apply the amendments early must disclose that fact.

It should be noted that a change in a fair value valuation technique, say from using quoted market prices to using a valuation technique in the instance when there is no longer a quoted market price, is not a reclassification. This applies if the item is classified as at fair value through profit or loss or as an available-for-sale financial asset.

3.2 Held-to-maturity investments (HTM)

HTM investments are financial instruments with fixed or determinable payments and fixed maturity that an entity has the positive intention and ability to hold to maturity, other than those that the entity, upon initial recognition, elects to designate as at FVTPL or available-for-sale or that meet the definition of loans and receivables. [IAS 39.9]

HTM investments are measured at amortised cost using the effective interest rate method.

An asset cannot be classified as HTM if it can be contractually prepaid or otherwise extinguished by the issuer in such a way that the holder would not recover substantially all of its recorded investment, i.e. those contracts where the issuer has a right to settle at an amount significantly below amortised cost. In addition, a debt security with the right of the issuer to redeem early should be evaluated to determine whether it contains an embedded derivative that must be accounted for separately. See **chapter 5** on embedded derivatives.

Some host debt instruments from which an embedded derivative has been separated can be classified as HTM.

US GAAP comparison: Under US GAAP, only financial assets that are in the form of debt securities can be classified as HTM. In addition, the classification of an investment in a debt security as HTM does not consider whether the debt security trades in an active market. Under US GAAP, therefore, an investment in a debt security potentially could be classified as HTM even if it is not traded in an active market. Under IAS 39, however, because the definition of loans and receivables includes investments that are not quoted in active markets and the definition of an HTM investment excludes loans and receivables, an investment that is not traded in an active market cannot be classified as HTM under IAS 39.

3.2.1 *Fixed or determinable payments and fixed maturity*

HTM investments are financial instruments with fixed or determinable payments and fixed maturity, which means that the contractual arrangement defines the amounts and dates of payments to the holder, such as interest and principal payments.

Equity instruments cannot be HTM investments either because they have an indefinite life (such as ordinary shares) or because the amounts the holder may receive can vary in a manner that is not predetermined (such as for share options, warrants and similar rights). [IAS 39.AG17]

Preference shares with fixed or determinable payments and a fixed maturity, determined to be financial liabilities in accordance with IAS 32 for the issuer, can be classified in the HTM category for the holder, for example, mandatorily redeemable preference shares.

A debt instrument with a variable interest rate can satisfy the criteria for a HTM investment. [IAS 39.AG17] The terms of the contract determine the amounts and dates of payments to the holder. An example is a five-year debt instrument which pays a variable rate of interest specified as LIBOR plus 150 basis points, with interest payments receivable semi-annually in arrears.

Example 3.2.1A

HTM: debt host contract (1)

Entity G has a bond asset with interest payments indexed to the price of gold. The bond has a fixed payment at maturity and a fixed maturity date.

Interest payments contain an embedded derivative (indexation to gold) that is separated and accounted for as a derivative at fair value (unless Entity G elects on initial recognition to designate the bond as a financial asset at FVTPL or it cannot separate and measure the embedded derivative in which case the whole instrument is designated as at FVTPL). Once the embedded derivative is separated, the host debt instrument can be classified as HTM provided Entity G has the positive intention and ability to hold the bond to maturity.

Example 3.2.1B

HTM: debt host contract (2)

Entity A purchases a five-year equity indexed-linked note with an original issue price of CU10 at a market price of CU12 at the time of purchase. At maturity, the note requires payment of the original issue price of CU10 plus a supplemental redemption amount that depends on whether a specified share price index exceeds a predetermined level at the maturity date. The supplemental amount paid at redemption is a formula that incorporates the change in the share index. If the share price index does not exceed or is equal to the predetermined level, no supplemental redemption amount is paid. Entity A has the positive intention and ability to hold the note to its maturity.

Entity A can classify the note as HTM because it has a fixed payment of CU10 and fixed maturity and Entity A has the positive intention and ability to hold it to maturity. However, the equity index feature is an embedded derivative that is not closely related to the debt host, and must be separated. The purchase price of CU12 is allocated between the host debt instrument and the embedded derivative. For example, if the fair value of the embedded option at acquisition is CU4, the host debt instrument is measured at CU8 on initial recognition. In this case, the discount of CU2 that is implicit in the host bond (principal of CU10 minus the original carrying amount of CU8) is amortised to profit or loss over the term to maturity of the note using the effective interest method. [IAS 39.IG.B.13]

It is important to note in this example that the instrument has a floor on the redemption equal to CU10. Absent that floor, Entity A would not be able to assert an intention to hold to maturity, because an issuer's right to settle a financial asset at an amount significantly below its amortised cost precludes an entity from asserting a positive intention to hold to maturity. [IAS 39.AG16]

If the terms of a 'perpetual' debt instrument (such as 'perpetual' bonds, debentures and capital notes) provide the holder with the contractual right to receive payments of interest at fixed dates into perpetuity, the instrument cannot be classified as HTM because the instrument does not have a fixed maturity date.

It can be argued that a perpetual debt instrument with fixed or determinable payments for which the only cash payments under the terms of the instrument are interest payments during a limited period, for instance, 10 years, can be classified as HTM provided the amount invested is recovered through fixed or determinable payments, and the rights to zero interest after year 10 have no present value at inception. In that case one would need to argue that the final date on which interest is paid is in effect the maturity date of such a financial instrument. Despite the legal form being a perpetual, the substance is that of a finite life instrument.

3.2.2 *Positive intention and ability to hold to maturity*

An entity cannot classify a financial asset as HTM if the entity intends to hold the financial asset for only an undefined period. A debt security, for example, should not be classified as HTM if the entity anticipates that the security would be available to be sold in response to:
[IAS 39.AG16(b)]

- changes in market interest rates and related changes in the investment's prepayment risk;
- liquidity needs (for example, due to the withdrawal of deposits, increased demand for loans, surrender of insurance policies, or payment of insurance claims);
- changes in the availability of and the yield on alternative investments;
- changes in funding sources and terms; or
- changes in foreign currency risk.

In summary, classification of an investment as HTM means that the entity is indifferent to future opportunities to profit from changes in the asset's fair value.

For this reason IAS 39 prohibits the hedging of a HTM investment for interest rate risk or prepayment risk as the entity, in classifying the investment as HTM, has expressed its commitment to retaining the financial asset and collecting all of its contractual cash flows, irrespective of the impact of changes in market interest rates on the asset's fair value and any option the issuer may have to redeem the asset prior to its contractual maturity.

IAS 39 states that an asset is not classified as HTM if it can contractually be repaid or otherwise extinguished by the issuer in such a way that the holder of the asset would not recover substantially all of its recorded investment. Any premium paid and capitalised transaction costs are considered in determining whether the carrying amount would be substantially recovered. In the circumstances where the holder will recover substantially all of its investment, for example, in the case of a debt instrument where the issuer exercises its call option on the asset and the option's exercise price is approximately equal to the instrument's amortised cost, the debt instrument's maturity date is viewed as being accelerated. The issuer's exercise of a call feature in such circumstances does not invalidate the holder's treatment of the investment as held-to-maturity, provided the holder intends to hold it until it is called.

Convertible debt instruments generally bear a lower interest rate than debt instruments without a conversion feature because the investor pays for the right to benefit from the appreciation in value of the option embedded in the debt instrument. The conversion feature would normally be separated out from the debt host contract and accounted for as an embedded derivative. If the conversion feature can be exercised only at maturity of the instrument, then it may be reasonable for the holder to argue that it has the positive intent and ability to hold the debt host contract to maturity. However, generally, it would be contradictory to assert the positive intention to hold the debt host contract to its maturity if the conversion right that has been purchased by the holder allows the holder to convert the instrument into equity at any point. In the latter case, the holder does not have the positive ability to hold the debt host contract to maturity as exercising the option prior to maturity of the instrument will extinguish the debt host contract early.

For a debt instrument held that is subject to a purchased put option, the existence of the option will prima facie undermine any statement of intention to hold the instrument to maturity. Paying for a put feature is inconsistent with expressing an intention to hold the financial asset until maturity. An entity should not classify a financial asset as HTM if it has the intention to hold the instrument for only an undetermined period or if it stands ready to sell the asset in response to general market conditions.

Therefore, unless the terms of the put option are such that it can be exercised only in one of the permitted, isolated, non-recurring circumstances (see **3.3.2** below), it will not be acceptable to classify a puttable security as HTM. [IAS 39.AG19]

US GAAP comparison: IAS 39 does not permit the classification of puttable debt instruments as held to maturity whereas US GAAP permits such classification if the entity has the positive intent and ability to hold to maturity (FAS 115). However, the exercise of a put option will call into question an investor's stated intent to hold other debt securities to maturity in the future.

Example 3.2.2A

HTM: sale due to credit rating triggers

An investment fund holds high-yield debt securities (bonds, etc) as specified in the portfolio guidelines. The fund only sells assets if the credit rating of the assets deteriorates below a certain specified level (rather than only when significant deterioration has occurred). The fund's assets cannot be classified as HTM because the fund cannot claim at initial recognition that there is a positive intention to hold the assets to maturity – the intention is to hold assets only while their credit rating is within the prescribed parameters.

Example 3.2.2B

HTM: managing debt duration

Entity X has a portfolio of debt securities and wishes to classify the investments as HTM. The investment policy allows management to transfer every HTM security to a more liquid portfolio at a specific predetermined date (e.g. 24 months prior to each security's stated maturity). The policy is designed to permit Entity X the flexibility to sell debt securities and thereby manage the duration of the portfolio.

Entity X's policy would preclude classifying its debt securities as HTM because it does not have the positive intention to hold those securities to maturity – the intention is to hold until the date 24 months prior to stated maturity and that date is not sufficiently close to maturity to meet the exception of tainting certain transfers out of HTM (see **3.3.2** below).

Example 3.2.2C

HTM: regulatory constraint (1)

Entity P would like to designate as HTM its portfolio of high quality assets held for the purpose of complying with regulatory requirements on liquidity.

> Entity P cannot designate the portfolio as HTM because Entity P cannot claim that there is a positive intention to hold the assets to maturity – the intention is to hold whilst the assets continue to be of the appropriate quality and Entity P is not required to realise them for regulatory purposes.

A significant risk of default by the issuer does not preclude classification of a financial asset as HTM provided its contractual payments are fixed or determinable and the other criteria for classification as HTM are met. [IAS 39.AG17]

Even if there is a significant risk of default on interest and principal on a bond, for example, due to significant business, financial, or economic uncertainties and, as evidenced, for instance, by a low-grade rating of the bond issue, the contractual payments on the bond may be fixed or determinable. The likelihood of default is not a consideration in qualifying for the HTM category as long as there is an intent and ability, considering the credit condition existing at the acquisition date, to hold the instrument to maturity.

Where an entity classifies a high-risk debt security as HTM knowing that if at some future date there is a further credit deterioration it will sell in response to such a downgrade, it may be difficult, absent a bankruptcy, to substantiate that a significant credit deterioration occurred and that the sale, if significant, does not 'taint' the HTM portfolio.

Securities that have been pledged as collateral for borrowings or are subject to a repurchase agreement or securities lending agreement (i.e. have been transferred to another party under a repo or securities lending transaction but continue to be recognised), can be classified as HTM provided that the entity intends and expects to be able to repay the borrowings without being required to dispose of the asset. [IAS 39.IG.B.18]

For financial assets classified as HTM, management should consider whether the entity has both the financial ability as well as the regulatory ability to obviate the need to dispose of HTM investments prior to maturity. The assessment of an entity's financial ability takes into account such factors as its funding position and its ability to maintain any over-collateralisation requirements. The assessment of an entity's financial ability also takes into account such factors as its regulatory capital requirements, its liquidity position (including specified holdings of liquid assets), its loans-to-one-borrower ratio, growth prospects and related financing requirements and its investment authority (including permitted asset-mix).

Example 3.2.2D

HTM: regulatory constraint (2)

Entity Q, a regulated entity, would like to classify securities as HTM. Its regulators may require Entity Q to dispose of these securities in the normal course of business.

Entity Q cannot classify the securities as HTM. Even though the entity may have the positive intention to hold the securities to maturity, it does not have the ability. Certain financial institution regulators have designated specific financial instruments – such as certain collateralised mortgage obligations (CMOs) or other, similar stripped securities (for example, interest-only and principal-only securities) – as high-risk securities, and may require a regulated entity to sell such securities as a result of changes in interest rates. If a financial instrument is subject to such regulatory requirements, classification as HTM is not appropriate since management would not be able to demonstrate the ability to hold securities to maturity as a result of the regulator being able to require the sale of the security.

3.2.3 *Frequency of assessment of positive intention and ability to hold to maturity*

Both the positive intention and ability to hold are assessed at the end of each reporting period. [IAS 39.AG25]

Example 3.2.3

HTM: sale after the reporting period

Entity X, with a 31 December year end, has a portfolio of financial assets classified as HTM. Early in January 20X2, prior to the issuance of the 20X1 financial statements, Entity X sells a portion of the financial assets held, and the factors motivating the sale do not qualify under the exceptions provided in **3.3.2** below.

The entire HTM securities portfolio is required to be reclassified as available-for-sale in the statement of financial position as at 31 December 20X1, since the actions in January call into question the entity's assertion of intent at year end.

3.3 Tainting of the HTM portfolio

'Tainting' is the term used to describe the effect of disposing of or reclassifying a HTM investment before its maturity date in situations where such disposal or reclassification disqualifies the entity from using the HTM classification for the remaining portfolio of securities held.

Except for certain limited circumstances described in **3.3.2** below, a sale or reclassification of a HTM investment casts doubt on the entity's stated intention or ability to hold the rest of its HTM portfolio to maturity. As a consequence, where an entity has, during the current year, sold or reclassified more than an insignificant amount of HTM investments before maturity, i.e. tainting of the HTM portfolio occurs, all of the entity's HTM investments generally must be reclassified into the available-for-sale category. Furthermore, the entity is prohibited from classifying any investments as HTM for the next two financial years.

Example 3.3

HTM: sale of single asset

Entity X has a portfolio of HTM financial assets comprising both municipal and corporate bonds. A sale or transfer of a single corporate bond which comprises more than an insignificant amount of the portfolio does not meet the specific exceptions in **3.3.2** below and therefore would result in tainting of all remaining bonds, municipal and corporate.

US GAAP comparison: Under US GAAP sales or transfers from the held-to-maturity category prior to maturity are expected to be rare (FAS 115). Similar to IAS 39, such transactions would call into question the classification of other held-to-maturity securities and could require the transfer of such other securities to the available for sale category. While FAS 115 does not specify the specific time period that must pass before investments can again be classified as held to maturity following a tainting event, for public entities US regulators (SEC) suggest a two-year period, and for non-public entities practice is to apply a similar period.

3.3.1 *Sub-categorisation for the purposes of applying the 'tainting' rule*

An entity cannot create two different categories of HTM financial assets, for example, debt securities denominated in US dollars and debt securities denominated in Euros. The 'tainting rule' applies to the portfolio of HTM investments in its entirety. If an entity has sold or reclassified more than an insignificant amount of HTM investments, it cannot classify any financial assets as HTM financial assets. [IAS 39.IG.B.20]

3.3.2 *Sales or reclassification of HTM financial assets which do not taint the HTM portfolio*

Sales or reclassifications in strictly defined and limited circumstances specified in IAS 39 do not taint the remaining HTM portfolio. These are sales or transfers that:
[IAS 39.9]

- are so close to maturity or the financial asset's call date (for example, less than three months before maturity) that changes in the market rate of interest would not have a significant effect on the financial asset's fair value;
- occur after the entity has collected substantially all of the financial asset's original principal through scheduled payments or prepayments;
- are attributable to an isolated event that is beyond the entity's control, is non-recurring and could not have been reasonably anticipated by the entity; or
- do not involve 'more than insignificant' amount of the entity's HTM portfolio (more than insignificant in relation to the total amount of HTM investments).

Selling an asset close enough to its maturity does not taint the remaining HTM portfolio if the effect of movements in interest rates between the repurchase date and the maturity is expected to have an insignificant impact on the fair value of the asset. For instance, if an entity sells a financial asset less than three months prior to maturity, the present value of the amount received from the sale usually will not be significantly different from the amount received at maturity. This is unlikely to be the case if the instrument's maturity is several months away.

IAS 39 does not provide guidance as to what is considered to be 'substantially all' of the financial asset's original principal. Prior to the 2004 revisions to IAS 39, Implementation Guidance contained an example that illustrated that collecting 90 per cent or more of the original principal was considered to be substantially all. In the amended Implementation Guidance this interpretation has been removed, and therefore judgement must be applied on a case-by-case basis in determining what is considered to be substantially all.

US GAAP comparison: US guidance is more specific as to what it considers to be the collection of a substantial portion of an asset. It considers that the entity must have collected at least 85 per cent of the principal outstanding due either to prepayments on the debt security or to scheduled payments on a debt security payable in equal instalments (both principal and interest) over its term (FAS 115).

For an event to be isolated, non-recurring, beyond the entity's control and could not have been reasonably anticipated, the event would need to be extremely remote and unlikely to occur in practice. Not many events are likely to meet this criterion.

A sale, or a transfer of a HTM investment due to one of the following isolated, non-recurring events is not considered to be inconsistent with its original classification as HTM and does not raise a question about the entity's intention to hold other investments to maturity:
[IAS 39.AG22]

(a) a significant deterioration in the issuer's credit-worthiness;

(b) a change in tax law that eliminates or significantly reduces the tax-exempt status of interest on the HTM investment (but not a change in tax law that revises the marginal tax rates applicable to interest income);

(c) a major business combination or major disposal (such as sale of a segment) that necessitates the sale or transfer of HTM investments to maintain the entity's existing interest rate risk position or credit risk policy (although the business combination is an event within the entity's control, the changes to its investment portfolio to maintain an interest rate risk position or credit risk policy may be consequential rather than anticipated);

(d) a change in statutory or regulatory requirements significantly modifying either what constitutes a permissible investment or the maximum level of particular types of investments, thereby causing an entity to dispose of a HTM investment;

(e) a significant increase in the industry's regulatory capital requirements that causes the entity to downsize by selling HTM investments; and

(f) a significant increase in the risk weights of HTM investments used for regulatory risk-based capital purposes.

Note that a disaster scenario that is only remotely possible, such as a run on a bank or a similar situation affecting an insurance company, is not something that is assessed by an entity in deciding whether it has the positive intention and ability to hold an investment to maturity. [IAS 39.AG21]

Catastrophic losses or high levels of policy surrenders are 'reasonably probable' of occurring in the insurance industry. They cannot be considered to be non-recurring or isolated and would not meet the exception under IAS 39.9. As a result, the sale of investments classified as HTM in order to meet excessive levels of claim obligations or because of policyholder withdrawals would taint the entity's held-to-maturity category.

The following factors, amongst others, would be relevant in determining whether there has been a significant deterioration in the issuer's creditworthiness. [IAS 39.AG22(a)]

The deterioration in the issuer's creditworthiness should have occurred after the security was acquired. Low credit ratings or creditworthiness concerns existing at acquisition would generally lead to a conclusion that a subsequent not insignificant sale from the HTM category taints the rest of the HTM portfolio.

There should be evidence of actual deterioration of the issuer's creditworthiness. A downgrading by a rating agency may provide objective evidence of a significant credit deterioration. An expectation of deterioration should be supported by objective evidence. Some of the financial measures that may provide objective evidence are:

- cash flows from operations (i.e. decline in cash flows, available cash flows, liquidity);
- broker/analyst reports on the issuer;
- adverse performance compared to projections;
- sustained decline in earnings or other key measures; and
- violation of covenants or other evidence that the issuer is in peril of violating covenants.

An increase in yield relative to a risk-free rate may be indicative of a change in the market's evaluation of the risk associated with holding the issuer's debt. In many situations, an effective measure of a significant deterioration is a significant increase in the yield on the debt of an entity when compared to the change in the yield of a risk-free security of a similar maturity.

Guidance used in determining impairment may also be useful in assessing a significant decline in the issuer's creditworthiness (see

section 6 of **chapter 6**). Information, such as the current and near-term projected financial condition and performance of the issuer, the issuer's dividend payment and earnings performance, the general market conditions and prospects of the region and industry in which the issuer operates, and specific adverse news or events affecting the issuer may provide objective evidence of impairment that may be indicative of a significant decline in the issuer's creditworthiness.

To provide evidence of a significant deterioration in the issuer's creditworthiness, general market or industry factors should have a direct or demonstrable effect on a specific issuer. For example, widespread difficulties experienced by others in the industry (e.g. due to over-leveraging or weak assets) that are not expected to affect the issuer are not relevant.

In contrast, the development of severe competition, adverse tax or regulatory developments, or declining markets may have a direct bearing on the creditworthiness of specific issuers.

A sale of a HTM investment following a downgrade of the issuer's credit rating by a rating agency would not necessarily raise a question about the entity's intention to hold other investments to maturity. A downgrade indicates a decline in the issuer's creditworthiness. IAS 39 specifies that a sale due to a significant deterioration in the issuer's creditworthiness could satisfy the condition in IAS 39 and therefore not raise a question about the entity's intention to hold other investments to maturity. However, the deterioration in creditworthiness must be significant judged by reference to the credit rating at initial recognition. A credit downgrade of a notch within a class or from a rating class to the immediately lower rating class could often be regarded as reasonably anticipated. If the rating downgrade in combination with other information provides evidence of impairment, the deterioration in creditworthiness often would be regarded as significant. [IAS 39.IG.B.15]

A permitted, i.e. non-tainting, sale in accordance with IAS 39.AG22(a) should be in response to an actual deterioration rather than in advance of a deterioration in creditworthiness and should not be based on mere speculation or in response to industry statistics.

The deterioration should be supported by evidence about the issuer's creditworthiness though the entity need not await the formal notification of an actual downgrading in the issuer's published credit rating or inclusion on a 'credit watch' list.

Where an entity uses internal ratings for assessing exposures, changes in those internal ratings may help to identify issuers for which there has been a significant deterioration in creditworthiness, provided the entity's approach to assigning internal ratings and changes in those ratings give a consistent, reliable and objective measure of the credit quality of the issuers.

If an entity does not sell a debt instrument immediately in response to a significant credit deterioration, but continues to classify the instrument in the HTM portfolio, a sale of that instrument at a future date would not satisfy the conditions for permitted sales. As an entity is required to make an ongoing assessment of its ability and intent to hold an instrument to its maturity, by not reclassifying the instrument out of HTM when the credit deterioration occurred, the entity effectively reconfirmed its intent to hold the instrument to its maturity.

An exchange of debt securities classified as HTM pursuant to a bankruptcy generally qualifies as a permitted sale out of HTM since bankruptcy is the ultimate form of credit deterioration. However, if the investor had anticipated the bankruptcy at the acquisition date and was able to control the outcome, then such a sale would not satisfy the conditions for permitted sales due to a significant deterioration in the issuer's creditworthiness.

Example 3.3.2A

HTM: sale due to cash need

Entity P, an insurance entity, sells financial assets that have been classified as HTM due to cash needs arising from the failure of one of its principal reinsurers.

A sale from the HTM portfolio for this reason would be inconsistent with the positive intent and ability to hold the security to maturity. This situation is not analogous to significant deterioration in an issuer's creditworthiness, because the deterioration does not relate specifically to the issuer of the security sold but to the entity's reinsurer.

Example 3.3.2B

HTM: counterparty restructuring

Entity N, a life insurance entity, purchased a debt security in a private placement offering. At acquisition, Entity N classified the debt as HTM. The issuer, a private entity, is currently in bankruptcy proceedings and is restructuring its debt. The issuer is contemplating swapping its debt security to Entity N in exchange for new debt and shares. Entity N has no control over the outcome of the issuer's restructuring arrangements.

Prior to the issuer's determination of the final restructuring arrangements, Entity N can continue to classify the debt security as HTM. The HTM classification is acceptable because the issuer's termination of the original debt is not under Entity N's control. The restructuring is analogous to an issuer's call option. In some circumstances it may not be possible to hold a security to its original stated maturity, such as when the security is called by the issuer prior to maturity. The issuer's exercise of the call option effectively accelerates the security's maturity and is not viewed as being inconsistent with the HTM classification. Under these circumstances, the maturity date is accelerated to the date of early redemption or when the debt security is exchanged. Accordingly, Entity N's classification as HTM is appropriate. Entity N should determine whether impairment has occurred, and if so, write down the financial instrument (see **section 6** of **chapter 6**).

Prior to the issuer's determination of the final restructuring arrangements, Entity N could have transferred the debt security from the HTM to the available-for-sale category if the intention and ability to hold to maturity is no longer appropriate, without tainting its HTM portfolio, since a transfer resulting from evidence of a significant deterioration in the issuer's credit-worthiness will not call into question an entity's intent to hold other financial assets.

Sales out of HTM in anticipation of future tax law changes that have not become law will taint the HTM portfolio if sales are significant in comparison to the HTM portfolio. To reduce the risk of tainting the tax change must already have become law prior to the disposal of the assets.

Example 3.3.2C

HTM: change in tax treaty

Entity X, an entity operating in Canada, has a portfolio of financial assets classified as held-to-maturity, which contains a Malaysian bond issue. At the date that Entity X purchased the security, a tax treaty existed between the Canadian tax jurisdiction and Malaysia which the entity anticipated would continue for the foreseeable future and at least as long as the bonds were outstanding. This treaty allowed the use of Canadian foreign tax credits to reduce the onerous tax consequences that would otherwise result from inclusion of interest on the Malaysian security in taxable income in both tax jurisdictions (assuming Entity X, also, is taxed on the income in Malaysia).

Entity X cannot reclassify the security from its HTM category in anticipation of the treaty's expiration without calling into question the intent to hold other financial assets to maturity. If the treaty does expire, however, reclassification may be permitted which will not taint any remaining HTM securities.

A disposal out of HTM is permitted if it is consequential to a major business combination or disposal of a business and affects existing interest rate risk or credit risk positions which must be maintained in accordance with risk management policies. Hence, an entity may reassess the classification of HTM securities concurrently with or shortly after a major business combination and not necessarily call into question its intent to hold other securities to maturity in the future. As time passes, it becomes increasingly difficult to demonstrate that the business combination, and not other events or circumstances, necessitated the transfer or sale of HTM securities.

Sales in anticipation of a business combination, e.g. for the purpose of financing it, will taint the HTM category.

Sales out of the HTM category as a result of a change in senior management in connection with a restructuring of the entity will result in tainting. A change in management is not identified as an instance of sales or transfers from HTM that does not compromise the classification as HTM as change in management or restructuring cannot be argued to be an isolated, non-recurring event that could not have been reasonably anticipated. [IAS 39.IG.B.16]

In some countries, regulators of banks or other industries may set capital requirements on an *entity-specific* basis based on an assessment of the risk in that particular entity.

Sales of HTM investments in response to an unanticipated significant increase by the regulator in the *industry*'s capital requirements do not taint the entity's intent to hold remaining investments to maturity. However, sales of HTM investments imposed by regulators, due to a significant increase in *entity-specific* capital requirements applicable to a particular entity, but not to the industry, 'taint' the entity's intent to hold other financial assets as HTM. Entity-specific capital requirements could only be disregarded in exceptional cases if it can be demonstrated that the sales result from an increase in capital requirements which is an isolated event that is beyond the entity's control and that is non-recurring and could not have been reasonably anticipated by the entity. [IAS 39.IG.B.17]

In consolidated financial statements, intragroup sales of HTM investments between group entities generally would not taint the HTM portfolio from a group perspective, as long as the business purpose of the transfer and the investment policies of the 'buyer' are consistent with a continued positive intention and ability to hold to maturity.

The impact on each entity's stand-alone financial statements should be assessed separately; in the financial statements of the selling entity, the stated intention of holding securities to maturity will have been undermined, even though the sale was made to another entity within the consolidated group.

Note that an entity cannot apply the conditions separately to HTM financial assets held by different entities in a consolidated group, even if those group entities are in different countries with different legal or economic environments. If the consolidated entity in total across the group has sold or reclassified more than an insignificant amount of investments classified as HTM, it cannot classify any financial assets as HTM investments in its consolidated financial statements unless such sales and transfers do not taint the HTM portfolio.

As a remedy to protect the investor from the issuer's violation of a debt covenant, a contractual right of foreclosure that was negotiated at arm's length at the issuance date would not preclude an investor classifying an investment as HTM. Similarly, the exercise of such a right or foreclosure on the violation of a substantial covenant would not taint an investor's remaining HTM portfolio.

Example 3.3.2D

HTM: sale following acceptance of tender offers

Entity A, an insurance company, initially classified 100 per cent of its property liability fixed income portfolio as available-for-sale, 50 per cent of its life fixed income securities portfolio as HTM, and 50 per cent as available-for-sale. Entity A considered various factors in making these classifications, including its investment policy, security characteristics, liquidity needs, and asset-liability management strategy.

In a subsequent year, Entity A began receiving unsolicited tender offers from issuers with respect to its fixed income portfolio (including its HTM portfolio) which was prompted by a very volatile interest rate environment. Entity A accepted certain tender offers involving the exchange of debt securities classified as HTM as these exchanges were on economically favourable terms.

As a consequence, Entity A is required to transfer 100 per cent of previously classified HTM securities to available-for-sale because it can no longer assert it has the positive intent to hold all of these securities to maturity. The sale of a security in response to a tender offer typically is motivated not by a need for cash, but instead by the investor's desire for additional possible profit – a motive inconsistent with the HTM classification. Further, none of the exceptions for sales that do not taint HTM portfolio applies.

In the context of open-ended funds, for example a mutual fund, where investors do not have an investment in equity shares in the fund, but own 'units' in the fund, and can require redemption of their share of the net assets of the fund in cash, it is difficult to argue that the possibility of unit-holders asking for redemption of their units is a non-recurring situation that could not have been reasonably anticipated.

In fact, it could reasonably be argued that the entity, e.g. the mutual fund is *'subject to an existing legal or other constraint that could frustrate its intention to hold the financial asset to maturity'* and therefore that HTM classification of the fund's portfolio of investments would be inappropriate.

Where a large number of unit-holders require redemption of their share in the net assets of the fund, the fund could be obliged to sell assets in order to fulfil its obligation to deliver cash to the unit-holders exiting the fund. Although IAS 39.AG21 states that a *'disaster scenario that is only remotely possible, such as a run on a bank or a similar situation affecting an insurer, is not something that is assessed by an entity in deciding whether it has the positive intention and ability to hold an investment to maturity,'* the possibility of unit-holders asking for their redemption in cash (and in large numbers) and thereby forcing the sale of fund assets does not constitute a disaster scenario but is readily possible in the course of operation of a mutual fund, and consequential liquidity needs have to be considered by the fund manager at any time.

A sale or transfer of a security classified as HTM for reasons other than those that are specifically permitted does not indicate that the previous financial statements were issued in error. As the accounting for financial assets as HTM is based primarily on a representation of intent by management, the sale or transfer of a security classified as HTM does not represent an error of previously issued financial statements, provided there was no evidence that existed at the time the financial statements were issued demonstrating that the entity did not have the positive intent and ability to hold the security to maturity. However, such a sale or transfer may call into question the entity's intent to hold other debt securities to maturity in the future.

If 'tainting' of the HTM portfolio occurs in a period, resulting in reclassification of the portfolio as available-for-sale (see **4.6** below), comparative figures for the period are not restated for the reclassification, since this would disguise the consequences of 'tainting.'

If an entity plans to sell a security from the HTM category in response to one of the permitted conditions that do not taint the HTM portfolio, the instrument can continue to be classified in the HTM category. There is no requirement in IAS 39 for the security to be reclassified as available-for-sale if an entity intends to sell in response to one of the permitted conditions.

3.4 Loans and receivables

Loans and receivables are non-derivative financial assets with fixed or determinable payments that are not quoted in an active market, other than those the entity intends to sell immediately or in the short-term (which must be classified as held for trading), and those that the entity on initial recognition designates as either at FVTPL or available-for-sale. [IAS 39.9]

Note that financial assets that do not meet the definition of loans and receivables may still satisfy the criteria for classification in the HTM category as the HTM definition is different from the loans and receivables definition. See **3.2** above on HTM assets.

Loans and receivables are measured at amortised cost using the effective interest method (see **4.1** of **chapter 6** on measurement).

A financial asset cannot be classified as a loan and receivable if it can be contractually prepaid or otherwise extinguished by the issuer in such a way that the holder would not recover substantially all of its recorded investment, other than because of credit deterioration. [IAS 39.9] Such assets are accounted for as available-for-sale or at FVTPL.

For example, a fixed rate interest-only strip created in a securitisation and subject to prepayment risk cannot be classified as a loan and receivable because there is a risk that the purchaser may not recover substantially all of its investment due to prepayment.

Loans and receivables are created by providing money, goods or services to a debtor. Examples are deposits held in banks, trade receivables, loan assets, including loans originated by the entity, loans acquired in a syndication, and other loans purchased in a secondary market provided that the market is not active and the loans are not quoted. Investments in debt securities that are not quoted in an active market can also be classified as loans and receivables.

When banks make term deposits with a central bank or other banks and the proof of deposit is negotiable, the deposit does meet the definition of a loan and receivable unless the depositor bank intends to sell the deposit immediately or in the near term, in which instance the deposit must be classified as held for trading.

Financial assets purchased after origination do qualify for classification as loans and receivables provided they meet all of the criteria for loans and receivables. However, the purchase of an interest in a pool of assets that are not themselves loans and receivables such as an interest in a mutual fund or a similar fund for example, is not a loan or receivable.

The principal difference between loans and receivables and HTM investments is that loans and receivables are not subject to the tainting provisions that apply to HTM investments. Loans and receivables not held for trading can be classified as such even if an entity does not have the positive intention and ability to hold them until maturity. As a consequence, the ability to measure a financial asset at amortised cost without consideration of the entity's intention and ability to hold the asset until maturity is only appropriate when there is no active market for that asset. [IAS 39.BC27]

Example 3.4

Loan in security form

An entity acquires a debt security issued by a government at original issuance. The debt security will be quoted in an active market.

The debt security does not qualify for classification as a loan and receivable because the debt security is quoted in an active market. The definition of loans and receivables in IAS 39 does not distinguish between loans that take the form of securities and those that do not. However, only debt securities that are not quoted in an active market can be classified in the 'loans and receivables' financial asset category.

As with any financial asset, the characteristics of a loan and receivable should be evaluated to determine whether the contractual arrangement contains an embedded derivative that must be accounted for separately (see **chapter 5**).

Following the separation of an embedded derivative from a debt host contract, the debt host contract may be accounted for as a loan and receivable provided the classification criteria for loans and receivables are met.

US GAAP comparison: The classification of loans and receivables under US GAAP differs significantly from IFRS. IAS 39 determines the classification and measurement of all financial assets (including debt securities, loans and trade receivables). FAS 115 establishes accounting for equity securities with readily determinable fair values and all debt securities, and specifies that they should be classified as held for trading, available for sale, or held to maturity. However, FAS 115.137 provides that trade accounts receivable and loans receivable do not meet the definition of a security and unless they have been securitised would not meet the definition of a debt security. SOP 01–6 establishes recognition and measurement principles for various aspects of loan and trade receivables for banks, savings institutions, credit unions, finance companies, and certain other entities that lend to or finance the activities of others. SOP 01–6 specifies that loans not held for sale (held for investment) that management has the ability and intent to hold for the foreseeable future or until maturity should be reported at outstanding principal balance less charge-offs and allowance for loan losses, while non-mortgage loans held for sale should be reported at the lower of cost or fair value. Similarly, FAS 65 specifies that mortgage loans held for sale should be reported at the lower of cost or fair value. US GAAP permits an entity to apply a fair value option for a hybrid financial instrument or loans and receivables under FAS 155 and FAS 157 respectively.

IFRS permits the classification of debt securities that are not traded in an active market and not held for trading as loans and receivables, while no such provision exists within US GAAP. Instead all debt securities are classified as held for trading, available for sale, or held to maturity under FAS 115.

3.4.1 *Definition of loans and receivables: equity security*

Equity instruments cannot be loans and receivables because the amounts the holder may receive can vary in a manner that is not predetermined (such as for ordinary shares, share options, warrants and similar rights). A preference share that is a non-derivative equity instrument of the issuer with fixed or determinable payments can be classified in the loans and receivables category for the holder provided it is not quoted in an active market [IAS 39.IG.B.22]. An example of such a preference share is a privately issued mandatorily redeemable preference share.

3.4.2 *Securitised loans*

The purchase of an interest in a pool of assets that are themselves loans and receivables can be classified as loans and receivables if it meets the definition of a loan and receivable. If an entity acquires a beneficial interest in a securitised pool of loans and receivables this would not meet the definition of loan and receivable if the beneficial interest is quoted in an active market.

3.5 Available-for-sale financial assets (AFS)

AFS financial assets are those non-derivative financial assets that are designated as AFS, or are not classified as loans and receivables or HTM investments, are not held for trading and are not designated as at FVTPL on initial recognition.

AFS financial assets are measured at fair value with fair value gains or losses recognised in other comprehensive income. On sale or impairment of the asset, the cumulative gain or loss previously recognised in other comprehensive income is reclassified to profit or loss as a reclassification adjustment.

However, interest calculated using the effective interest method on interest-bearing AFS financial assets, impairment losses and foreign exchange gains and losses on monetary AFS financial assets are recognised in profit or loss (see **chapter 6** on measurement).

Dividends on an AFS equity instrument are recognised in profit or loss when the entity's right to receive payment is established.

Examples of AFS financial assets are equity investments that are not designated on initial recognition as at FVTPL, debt securities that are quoted in an active market, which may or may not have put features that would also prohibit them being HTM assets, and other financial assets held for liquidity purposes.

Example 3.5

Held for trading versus available-for-sale
[IAS 39.IG.B.12]

Entity A has an investment portfolio of debt and equity securities. The documented portfolio management guidelines specify that the equity exposure of the portfolio should be limited to between 30 and 50 per cent of total portfolio value. The investment manager of the portfolio is authorised to balance the portfolio within the designated guidelines by buying and selling equity and debt instruments. Is Entity A permitted to classify the instruments as available for sale?

It depends on Entity A's intentions and past practice. If the portfolio manager is authorised to buy and sell instruments to balance the risks in a portfolio, but there is no intention to trade and there is no past practice of trading for short-term profit, the instruments can be classified as available for sale. If the portfolio manager actively buys and sells instruments to generate short-term profits, the financial instruments in the portfolio are classified as held for trading.

US GAAP comparison: Under US GAAP, financial assets that are not in security form (such as loan receivables) cannot be classified as "available for sale" under FAS 115 because they are not within the scope of that guidance. However, mortgage loans and other loan receivables may be eligible for classification as "held for sale" under FAS 65 or SOP 01–6.

4 Reclassifications

An amendment to IAS 39, *Reclassification of Financial Assets*, was issued in October 2008. The amendment was issued to address differences between the reclassification requirements of IAS 39 and US GAAP. Prior to this amendment the ability to reclassify financial assets from one category to another under IFRS was limited to reclassifying certain debt instruments out of HTM to AFS and vice versa. The amendment to IAS 39 introduced new guidance that permitted reclassification of certain financial assets out of FVTPL and AFS. The amendment does not permit reclassification of financial liabilities, derivatives or financial assets for which the fair value option was elected.

4.1 Into FVTPL

IAS 39.50 does not permit an entity to reclassify any financial instrument into the fair value through profit or loss category after initial recognition.

Although IAS 39.50 is categorical that reclassifications into FVTPL are prohibited, there does appear to be one exception to this prohibition, which is described in IAS 39.12. If an entity is not able to measure an embedded derivative separately at a financial reporting date subsequent to acquisition the entity is required to designate the entire hybrid (combined) contract as at FVTPL. As embedded derivatives are only required to be separated from contracts that are not measured as at FVTPL the situation described in IAS 39.12 would appear to be a reclassification from a measurement category other than FVTPL to FVTPL.

US GAAP comparison: Under US GAAP, paragraph 15 of Statement 115 states, "Given the nature of a trading security, transfers into or from the trading category . . . should be rare." However, while such a transfer should be rare, it is not prohibited.

4.2 Out of FVTPL

As described in **3.1** above financial assets may be classified at initial recognition as at FVTPL if certain conditions are met. In some cases this classification is mandatory, for example, in the case of derivatives that are not designated as effective hedging instruments or non-derivative financial assets that are deemed held for trading. In other cases the classification is by election, for example, in the case where an entity applies the fair value option. IAS 39 as amended in October 2008 only permits reclassification out of FVTPL, subject to specified criteria, for financial assets that were originally classified as at FVTPL because they met the definition of held for trading. Therefore, financial assets that are classified as at FVTPL because they are derivatives or are designated as at FVTPL under the fair value option cannot be reclassified under any circumstances.

Loan commitments that are within the scope of IAS 39 and recognised and measured as at FVTPL cannot be reclassified as they meet the definition of derivatives and derivatives cannot be reclassified. In addition, a financial asset cannot be reclassified if it is designated as at FVTPL under the fair value option which would also prohibit loan commitments designated as at FVTPL in accordance with IAS 39.4(a). Also, in the case of written loan commitments they are financial liabilities and financial liabilities cannot be reclassified.

The first condition to be met in order to reclassify a financial asset from FVTPL is that the financial asset is no longer held for the purpose of selling or repurchasing it in the near term [IAS 39.50(c)]. This criterion applies irrespective of whether the asset was initially classified as held for trading because (i) it was acquired principally for the purpose of selling in the near term or (ii) because it is part of a portfolio of identified financial instruments that are managed together and for which there is evidence of a recent actual pattern of short-term profit-taking.

If an entity wishes to reclassify a financial asset that was classified as held for trading because it was part of a portfolio of identified financial instruments that are managed together and for which there was evidence of a recent actual pattern of short-term profit-taking the entity must demonstrate that the specific asset subject to reclassification is not intended to be sold in the near term. For an asset that forms part of a portfolio of assets this may be difficult to demonstrate unless the asset has been isolated from the portfolio or the mandate of the portfolio has changed such that there is no longer evidence of short-term profit taking.

IAS 39.50(c) refers to "selling or repurchasing it in the near term" which is the same terminology that is used in the held for trading definition. Both selling *and* repurchasing is relevant in the held for trading definition as the held for trading definition applies to both financial assets and financial liabilities. The reference to "repurchasing" in IAS 39.50(c) appears to be superfluous as this relates to financial liabilities and financial liabilities cannot be reclassified.

The second condition to be met in order to reclassify a financial asset from FVTPL is whether the financial asset meets the definition of a loan and receivable. If it does, the financial asset may be reclassified out of FVTPL if the entity has the intention and ability to hold the financial asset for the foreseeable future or until maturity [IAS 39.50D]. If it does not meet the definition of a loan and receivable it may be reclassified out of FVTPL only in rare circumstances [IAS 39.50B].

A summary of the criteria for reclassifying out of FVTPL is below:

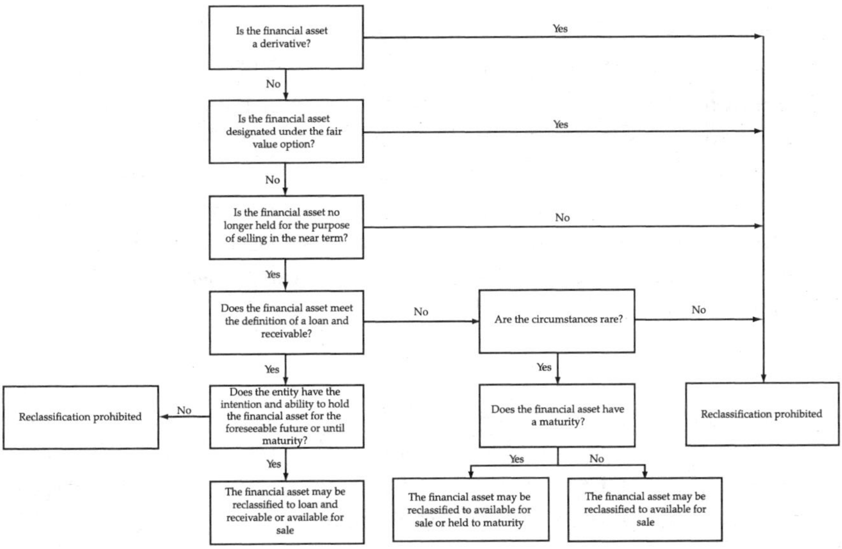

IAS 39 does not state explicitly at what date an entity shall determine whether the financial asset met the definition of a loan and receivable when assessing whether it can reclassify a financial asset. Two interpretations are acceptable: (i) assess the definition of a loan and receivable at the date of initial recognition of the financial asset, or (ii) assess the definition of a loan and receivable at the date of reclassification of the financial asset. This is particularly relevant for financial assets that would not have met the definition of loans and receivables at initial recognition (e.g. because the instrument was traded in an active market), but meets the definition at the date of reclassification.

An entity should decide on the appropriate interpretation and apply it as an accounting policy choice consistently to all reclassification assessments that require the entity to apply the loan and receivable definition. If the accounting policy is considered relevant for the understanding of the financial statements it has to be disclosed in accordance with IAS 1.117.

The financial asset reclassified from FVTPL should be reclassified at its fair value on the date of reclassification. Any gain or loss recognised in profit or loss up until the date of reclassification shall not be reversed. The fair value of the financial asset on the date of reclassification becomes its new cost (in the case of equity instruments) or amortised cost (in the case of debt instruments). [IAS 39.50C]

For financial assets reclassified out of FVTPL the entity will start to apply the impairment guidance described in IAS 39.58–70 for that asset. Prior to the date of reclassification an assessment of impairment was not required as the asset was measured at FVTPL. As the instrument's fair value at the date of reclassification becomes its new deemed cost or deemed amortised cost the recognition of impairment losses after the reclassification date may differ compared to the impairment losses that would have been recognised had the instrument never been previously measured at FVTPL. See **6.4.3** in **chapter 6** for more detail.

US GAAP comparison: Under US GAAP, paragraph 15 of Statement 115 states, "Given the nature of a trading security, transfers into or from the trading category . . . should be rare." However, while such a transfer should be rare, it is not prohibited.

A financial asset reclassified out of FVTPL is subject to extensive disclosures (see **4.1.4** in **chapter 11**)

4.2.1 *Rare circumstances*

IAS 39 does not provide specific guidance on how an entity should determine what are rare circumstances. However, the Board expressed in IAS 39.BC104D that rare circumstances arise from a single event that is unusual and highly unlikely to recur in the near term. In a press release that accompanied issuance of the amendment to IAS 39, *Reclassification of Financial Assets*, in October 2008 the IASB stated that "the deterioration of the world's financial markets that has occurred during the third quarter of this year is a possible example of rare circumstances cited in these IFRS amendments".

In order for circumstances to be considered rare there should be cause and effect between those circumstances and the financial assets held that are subject to reclassification. In the second half of 2008 some markets for asset-backed securities became in effect closed as there was a stark reduction in new instruments being issued and very low trading volumes for existing instruments, partly due to a lack of price transparency and lack of investor appetite. An entity with investments in asset-backed securities in those markets, which had originally been classified as held for trading, may have ceased to have intent to hold the investments for trading purposes, and, due to rare circumstances in those markets, was unable to sell the assets. The mere reduction in the price of assets is generally not evidence of rare circumstances as falling prices, even in a stock market crash, are not in themselves rare. In addition, the reduction in the value of an asset, for example an investment in an equity security, does not necessarily have an effect on the intentions or investment strategy of the holder of the instrument. Often the only effect is the fair value loss that would be realised should the entity dispose of the asset, and the realisation of a fair value loss is not in itself rare.

4.2.2 *Foreseeable future*

IAS 39 does not provide guidance on how an entity should assess whether it intends to hold the financial asset for the foreseeable future.

'Foreseeable future' is not a new term introduced in the IAS 39 amendment as it is a term used in other IFRSs. IAS 21.15 permits the foreign exchange gains/losses on a monetary item that is a receivable from or a payable to a foreign operation to be deferred in consolidated other comprehensive income if settlement is neither planned nor likely to occur in the foreseeable future. IAS 12 requires recognition of deferred tax liabilities in circumstances when it is probable that temporary differences will not reverse in the foreseeable future.

What is deemed foreseeable future will depend on the facts and circumstances and intentions of the entity and the specific asset that is being assessed for reclassification. If an entity is actively marketing the asset in an attempt to sell the asset this activity would be inconsistent with the assertion that the entity does not intend to sell the asset in the foreseeable future. An entity may at the date of reclassification have the intention to retain the asset for the foreseeable future yet later it may receive an unsolicited offer and choose to sell the asset. An entity determines foreseeable future at the date of reclassification and it does not need to revisit this assessment. However, to the extent an entity sells reclassified assets shortly after the reclassification date this would call into question the entity's ability to assert that it has the intention to hold other assets that it wishes to reclassify until the foreseeable future.

US GAAP comparison: Under US GAAP, mortgage loans held for sale may be reclassified to a "long-term investment" classification if the entity has both the ability and intent to hold the loan for the foreseeable future or until maturity (FAS 65).

4.2.3 Assessing embedded derivatives

Following the amendments to IAS 39 certain financial assets classified as at FVTPL could be reclassified to other categories. These assets may be hybrid contracts that contain embedded derivatives which were not separately accounted for as these hybrid contracts were measured at fair value through profit or loss (see **section 3** in **chapter 5**). A question arises, therefore, as to whether IFRS requires or prohibits an entity from assessing for embedded derivatives at the date the financial asset is reclassified.

In March 2009 the IASB issued amendments to IAS 39 and IFRIC 9 titled, *Embedded Derivatives*. The amendments state that upon reclassification of a financial asset out of FVTPL an entity is required to assess whether embedded derivatives should be separated from the host financial contract. In addition, if an entity is unable to measure separately the embedded derivative that would have to be separated on reclassification of a hybrid (combined) contract out of the FVTPL category, that reclassification is prohibited. In such circumstances the hybrid (combined) contract remains classified as at FVTPL in its entirety. The Board noted that when IFRIC 9 was issued, reclassifications out of the FVTPL category were prohibited and hence IFRIC 9 did not consider the possibility of such reclassifications. The Board believed it was appropriate that embedded derivatives should be assessed at the date of reclassification. Not to require this would allow an entity to circumvent the need to assess embedded derivatives by classifying a financial asset initially as at FVTPL and subsequently reclassifying the asset.

The amendments also state that when assessing for embedded derivatives at the date of reclassification the assessment shall be made on the basis of the circumstances that existed at the later of when the entity first became a party to the contract and the date of change in the terms of the contract that significantly modifies the cash flows that otherwise would have been required under the contract. The Board considered that looking to circumstances when the entity became party to the contract was consistent with one of the stated purposes of embedded derivative accounting which is to prevent circumvention of the recognition and measurement requirements for derivatives and provide some degree of comparability. Furthermore, because the terms of the embedded features in the hybrid (combined) financial instrument have not changed, the Board did not see a reason for arriving at an answer on separation different from what would have been the case at initial recognition of the hybrid (combined) contract.

The amendments to IAS 39 and IFRIC 9 shall be applied for annual periods ending on or after 30 June 2009.

> The Board's decision to look to circumstances when the party became party to the contract when determining whether an embedded derivative is closely related to the host financial contract will be most relevant when determining whether puts, calls, or other prepayment options in debt instruments are closely related. IAS 39.AG30(g) requires such options to be separated from the host contract if the option's exercise price is not approximately equal to the amortised cost of host debt instrument. At the date of reclassification an entity will be required to make the embedded derivative assessment it would have made had the debt instrument not been initially classified as at FVTPL, i.e. the entity will need to determine the instrument's amortised cost for all dates when the instrument may be put, called, or prepaid and compare the amortised cost with the exercise price of the option on those dates.

4.3 Into AFS investments

A debt or equity instrument may be reclassified out of held for trading, part of the FVTPL category, into AFS, in accordance with IAS 39.50 (see **4.2** above). As the instrument is fair valued both before and after reclassification there is no gain/loss on reclassification and all amounts previously recognised in profit or loss prior to the date of reclassification are retained in profit or loss.

An entity must reclassify a debt instrument from HTM to AFS if there is no longer the intention and ability to hold the debt instrument to maturity. Also, all debt instruments must be reclassified out of HTM into AFS in the instance when there are sales or reclassifications of more than an insignificant amount of HTM investments that do not meet any of the conditions in IAS 39.9 (see **4.6** below). At the date of reclassification, the difference between their carrying amount and fair value shall be recognised in other comprehensive income. [IAS 39.52]

If the fair value of an investment in an unquoted equity instrument becomes sufficiently reliable following a period where the investment was measured at cost in accordance with IAS 39.53, resulting in the measurement of that investment at fair value this is not a reclassification from one of the four financial asset classification categories to another. Investments in equity instruments can only ever be classified in either FVTPL or AFS (of which both are required to be measured at fair value) and IAS 39 does not have a fifth classification category. Therefore, although IAS 39.53 refers to financial assets that become reliably measurable where the measure was not previously available and this paragraph is included in the section titled, 'Reclassifications', it is not apparent what category such assets could be reclassified to. It is reasonable to consider such assets as continuing to belong to the same classification category to which they were originally classified, but change their basis of measurement to fair value. The difference between cost and fair value at the date the fair value becomes reliably measureable shall be recognised in other comprehensive income if the asset is classified as an available-for-sale asset. See **4.10** and **4.11** below.

4.4 Out of AFS investments

Investments in debt instruments may be reclassified out of AFS. Investments in equity instruments classified as AFS cannot be reclassified.

If the fair value of an investment in an unquoted equity instrument classified as an available-for-sale asset becomes unreliable and therefore an entity ceases to measure this investment at fair value and starts measuring it at cost in accordance with IAS 39.54, this is not a reclassification from one of the four financial asset classification categories to another. Investments in equity instruments can only ever be classified in either FVTPL or AFS (both of which require measurement at fair value) and IAS 39 does not have a fifth classification category. Therefore, although IAS 39.54 refers to examples where the fair value of an investment in an unquoted equity instrument becomes unreliable, and this paragraph is included in the section of the Standard titled, 'Reclassifications', it is not apparent what category such assets could be reclassified to. It is reasonable to consider such assets as continuing to belong to the same classification category to which they were originally classified, but change their basis of measurement to cost. See **4.10** and **4.11** below.

A financial asset classified as available-for-sale may be reclassified to held-to-maturity if the entity has the intent and ability to hold the asset to maturity. The asset may be reclassified during the instrument's life except during the 2-year tainting period (see **3.3** above) if the entity has disposed of more than an insignificant amount of held-to-maturity assets.

A financial asset classified as available-for-sale may be reclassified out of the available-for-sale category to the loans and receivables category if it meets the definition of a loan and receivable and the entity has the intention and ability to hold the financial asset for the foreseeable future or until maturity.

As described in **4.2** above an entity should determine an accounting policy with respect to the date it determines whether a reclassified AFS debt instrument meets the definition of a loan and receivable. Two interpretations are acceptable: (i) assess the definition of a loan and receivable at the date of initial recognition of the financial asset, or (ii) assess the definition of a loan and receivable at the date of reclassification of the financial asset. An entity should decide on an appropriate interpretation and apply it as an accounting policy choice consistently to all reclassification assessments that require the entity to apply the loan and receivable definition. If the accounting policy is considered relevant for the understanding of the financial statements it has to be disclosed in accordance with IAS 1.117.

If an entity's accounting policy is to assess the definition of a loan and receivable at the date of initial recognition then the entity will not be able to reclassify an AFS debt instrument where that AFS debt instrument was classified as such because it did not meet the definition of a loan and receivable at initial recognition due to the fact that it was traded in an active market.

If an entity's accounting policy is to assess the definition of a loan and receivable at the date of reclassification then the debt instrument may no longer be traded in an active market and thereby be able to reclassify the AFS debt instrument even though it did not meet the definition of a loan and receivable at initial recognition.

A summary of the criteria for reclassifying out of AFS is below:

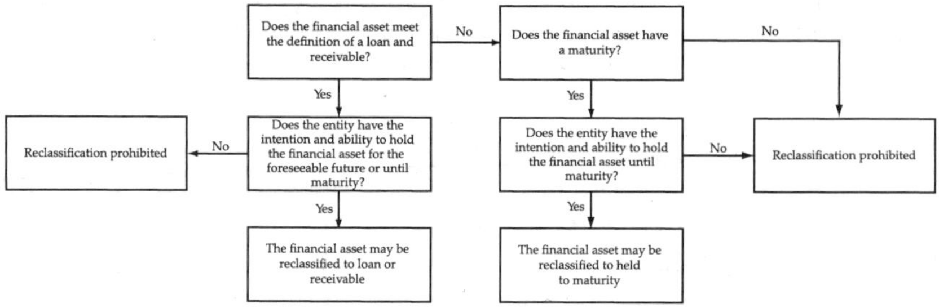

The financial asset reclassified from AFS should be reclassified at its fair value on the date of reclassification. Any gain or loss already recognised in profit or loss shall not be reversed. The fair value of the financial asset on the date of reclassification becomes its new amortised cost.

Any previous gain or loss on an AFS asset that has been recognised in other comprehensive income shall be amortised to profit or loss over the remaining life of the investment using the effective interest method in the case of an instrument with a fixed maturity. Any difference between the new amortised cost (being the asset's fair value at the date of reclassification) and its maturity amount shall also be amortised over the remaining life of the financial asset using the effective interest method, similar to the amortisation of a premium or a discount. In the case of a financial asset that does not have a fixed maturity, e.g. a perpetual debt instrument reclassified from available-for-sale to loans and receivables, the gain or loss shall be recognised in profit or loss when the financial asset is sold or otherwise disposed of or impaired. If the reclassified financial asset is subsequently impaired any previous gain or loss that has been recognised in other comprehensive income is reclassified from equity to profit or loss irrespective of whether or not the asset has a fixed maturity. [IAS 39.54]

A financial asset reclassified out of AFS to loans and receivables is subject to extensive disclosures (see **4.1.4** in **chapter 11**)

4.5 Into HTM investments

A financial asset classified as at fair value through profit or loss may be reclassified to held to maturity if the financial asset is no longer held for the purpose of selling or repurchasing it in the near term [IAS 39.50(c)] and it meets the definition of a held to maturity investment. The criteria for reclassification are described in **4.2** above.

A financial asset classified as AFS may be reclassified to HTM if the entity has the intent and ability to hold the asset to maturity. The asset may be reclassified during the instrument's life except during the 2-year tainting period if the entity has disposed of more than an insignificant amount of held to maturity assets. When the two-year period subsequent to the period in which tainting occurred has passed, the entity is allowed to reclassify the assets back into HTM provided it intends and is able to hold these assets to maturity. On the date of reclassifications the assets' carrying amount, i.e. their fair value at the date of reclassification, becomes the assets' new amortised cost. [IAS 39.54] Any previous fair value gain or loss on the assets that has been recognised directly in equity is amortised to profit or loss over the remaining life of the financial asset using the effective interest method.

4.6 Out of HTM investments

Where, as a result of a change in intention or ability, it is no longer appropriate to classify an investment as HTM, it is reclassified to AFS and re-measured at fair value [IAS 39.51]. The 'tainting' provisions of IAS 39 (see **3.3** above) apply not only to sales but also to reclassifications of HTM investments. Hence, reclassifications of more than an insignificant amount of HTM investments, which do not meet any of the conditions for permitted sales, taint the HTM portfolio and all remaining HTM investments must be reclassified into AFS.

On reclassification out of HTM into the AFS category, as a consequence of tainting, the difference between the assets' carrying amount and their fair value is recognised in equity. [IAS 39.51 and IAS 39.55(b)] This difference must be disclosed in addition to the reason for reclassification. [IFRS 7.12]

When an entity taints its HTM portfolio in the current reporting period, and is required to reclassify all of its HTM investments into the AFS category, it does not restate its comparatives for the reporting period to reflect this change of classification, since this would conceal the impact of 'tainting' the portfolio.

4.7 Into loans and receivables

Reclassifications of financial assets classified as at either FVTPL or AFS to loans and receivables category are permitted in certain circumstances. The criteria for reclassifying out of these classification categories is described in **4.2** and **4.4** above.

4.8 Out of loans and receivables

IAS 39 does not state explicitly whether an entity is permitted (or is potentially required) to reclassify a loan and receivable to a different classification category. As an asset cannot be reclassified to fair value through profit or loss and the held to maturity definition specifically excludes assets that meet the definition of a loan and receivable it would appear the only category available to reclassify to would be to available-for-sale. However, IAS 39 assumes the classification made at initial recognition is retained for the instrument's life except where the Standard specifically permits an entity to reclassify to an alternative classification category. As IAS 39 does not specifically permit reclassification out of loans and receivables, once an asset is classified as a loan and receivable it cannot be reclassified.

4.9 Summary of reclassifications

The summary of reclassifications below excludes investments in equity instruments (or derivatives linked to them and settled by delivery of an unquoted equity instrument) for which fair value is unreliable, see **4.10** and **4.11** below.

Out of	Into	Criteria	Example
FVTPL	L&R	*Debt instrument meets the definition of a L&R* The asset is no longer held for the purpose of selling in the near term and the entity has the intention and ability to hold the financial asset for the foreseeable future.	A trade receivable that at initial recognition was intended to be sold where the intent no longer applies.

Out of	Into	Criteria	Example
FVTPL	HTM	*Debt instrument does not meet the definition of a loan & receivable (if the instrument met the definition of a L&R it could not be reclassified to HTM as the HTM definition specifically excludes L&Rs)* The asset is no longer held for the purpose of selling in the near term and the entity has the intention and ability to hold the financial asset until maturity (this requirement applies for all HTM assets) and the circumstances are rare.	A debt security that at initial recognition was intended to be sold and is a security that is traded in an active market (e.g. corporate debt, government bond) and where the entity now considers it has the intent and ability to hold to maturity.
FVTPL	AFS	*Debt instrument meets the definition of a L&R* The asset is no longer held for the purpose of selling in the near term and the entity has the intention and ability to hold the financial asset for the foreseeable future.	A trade receivable that at initial recognition was intended to be sold where the intent no longer applies.
FVTPL	AFS	*Equity instrument or debt instrument does not meet the definition of either a L&R* The asset is no longer held for the purpose of selling in the near term and the circumstances are rare.	A debt security that at initial recognition was intended to be sold and is a security that is traded in an active market (e.g. corporate debt, government bond).
AFS	L&R	*Debt instrument meets the definition of a L&R* The entity has the intention and ability to hold the financial asset for the foreseeable future.	A trade receivable that at initial recognition was designated as AFS.

Out of	Into	Criteria	Example
AFS	HTM	*Debt instrument does not meet the definition of a L&R* The asset is held with the intention and ability to hold to maturity.	A debt security that at initial recognition was intended to be sold prior to maturity and is a security that is traded in an active market (e.g. corporate debt, government bond) and where the entity now considers it has the intent and ability to hold to maturity.
AFS	FVTPL	Not permitted	Not permitted
HTM	AFS	Debt instrument is no longer held with the intent and ability to hold to maturity. If there are more than an insignificant amount of sales or reclassifications of HTM assets the HTM portfolio is 'tainted' and the whole portfolio must be reclassified to AFS.	A debt security that at initial recognition was considered traded in an active market (e.g. corporate debt, government bond) and the entity had the intent and ability to hold to maturity but the intent or ability no longer applies.
HTM	L&R	Not permitted	Not permitted
HTM	FVTPL	Not permitted	Not permitted
L&R	HTM	Not permitted	Not permitted
L&R	AFS	Not permitted	Not permitted
L&R	FVTPL	Not permitted	Not permitted

4.10 Investments in equity instruments for which fair value becomes insufficiently reliable

Where fair value becomes insufficiently reliable to warrant an unquoted equity instrument (or derivative linked to it and settled by delivery of an unquoted equity instrument) to be measured at fair value, then the instrument must be measured at cost. The carrying amount of the asset on this date becomes its cost. [IAS 39.54] Any fair value gains and losses recorded in profit or loss to that date will not be reversed; equally any fair value gains and losses that were included in equity will remain in equity until the financial asset is sold, at which point these movements will be recognised in profit or loss. However, even where the asset is carried at cost it is still subject to an impairment assessment (see **section 6** in **chapter 6**).

4.11 Investments in equity instruments for which fair value becomes reliably determinable

When subsequently a reliable measure becomes available for an equity instrument (or derivative that is linked to and must be settled by delivery of an unquoted equity instrument) that was previously held at cost, the asset is measured at fair value. [IAS 39.53]

The difference between the financial asset's carrying amount and its fair value is recognised in profit or loss for assets classified as at FVTPL or directly in equity for assets classified as AFS.

US GAAP comparison: Under US GAAP, only investments in equity securities with readily determinable fair values (FAS 115) are recorded at fair value. Investments in equity securities without readily determinable fair values are recorded at cost (unless the investor exercises significant influence over the investor) unless the holder elects to apply the fair value option under FAS 159.

5 Classification of financial assets acquired in a business combination

When financial assets are acquired in a business combination those assets must be classified in the consolidated financial statements of the acquirer into one of the permitted categories described in **section 3** above. It is entirely possible that the classification of a financial asset for these purposes may differ from its classification in the financial statements of the acquiree. For example, the acquirer in its consolidated financial statements may choose to designate a financial asset as at fair value through profit or loss or as an available-for-sale asset on initial recognition that the acquiree did not when the acquiree initially recognised the asset. Also, the acquirer may choose to classify an asset as held-to-maturity that the acquiree did not. There are many other variations where the classification in the acquirer could be different to the existing accounting in the acquiree for the same financial asset. These differences arise as the acquirer is recognising the financial assets acquired in a business combination for the first time and therefore makes its classification decisions on that initial recognition.

The revised version of IFRS 3 *Business Combinations* issued in January 2008 provides clear guidance stating that at the acquisition date the acquirer shall make any classifications or designations concerning financial assets acquired or financial liabilities assumed in a business combination in accordance with the contractual terms, economic conditions, the acquirer's operating or accounting policies, and other factors as of that date that are pertinent in subsequently applying other IFRSs. IFRS 3(2008) applies prospectively to business combinations for which the acquisition date is on or after the beginning of the first annual reporting period beginning on or after 1 July 2009.

3 Financial liabilities and equity

1 Introduction

IAS 32 *Financial Instruments: Presentation* requires an issuer of a financial instrument to classify the financial instrument, or its component parts, as a financial liability or as equity in accordance with the substance of the contractual arrangement and the definitions of a financial liability and an equity instrument. The overriding principles are that where the issuer does not have an unconditional right to avoid the obligation to deliver cash, and where the contract does not, in substance, evidence a residual interest in the net assets of the issuer after deducting all of its liabilities, the instrument is not an equity instrument (see **section 2** below).

A more complex area, where the Standard provides additional guidance, is the treatment of derivative and non-derivative contracts indexed to, or settled in, an entity's own equity instruments. The definitions of a financial asset and a financial liability also include certain contracts on own equity and are applied to evaluate whether such contracts are, in substance, equity, financial liabilities or derivatives (derivatives could be either financial assets or financial liabilities). For example, a written put on own shares that will be settled, if the option is exercised by the holder, by delivering cash in exchange for the entity's own shares, is a financial liability as the entity will have an obligation to deliver cash (see **6.3** below).

This chapter addresses the application of the financial liability and equity definitions to various types of financial instruments issued in practice and contracts indexed to and settled in an entity's own equity. It also indicates the implications of classification as either debt, equity or a derivative for the measurement of that contract or its component parts.

This chapter discusses financial liabilities and equity in the following sections:

Section 2	Principles of liability/equity classification
Section 3	Compound instruments
Section 4	Treatment of interest, dividends, gains and losses, and other items
Section 5	Treasury shares

Section 6	Derivatives over own equity
Section 7	Classification of financial liabilities
Section 8	Reassessing classification
Section 9	Future developments

2 Principles of liability/equity classification

A financial instrument or its component parts should be classified upon initial recognition as a financial liability or equity instrument according to the substance of the contractual arrangement, not its legal form, and the definitions of a financial liability and an equity instrument. [IAS 32.15 & 18] Whilst some instruments may have the legal form of equity, their substance is one of a liability. A preference share, for instance, may display either equity or liability characteristics depending on the substance of the rights that attach to it. The appropriate classification is determined by the entity at the point of initial recognition and is not changed subsequently unless the terms of the instrument change, except as discussed in **section 8** below, or when the specific requirements for puttable instruments and instruments that contain an obligation to deliver a pro rata share of net assets at liquidation described in **2.1.2.1** and **2.3** respectively no longer apply or start to apply. When classifying a financial instrument in consolidated financial statements, an entity considers all terms and conditions agreed upon between members of the group and the holders of the instrument. A financial instrument issued by a subsidiary could be classified as equity in the individual financial statements and as a liability in the consolidated financial statements if another group entity has provided a guarantee to make payments to the holder of the instrument.

IAS 32 defines a financial liability as any liability that is:
[IAS 32.11]

(a) a contractual obligation:

  (i) to deliver cash or another financial asset to another entity (e.g. a payable);

  (ii) to exchange financial assets or financial liabilities with another entity under conditions that are potentially unfavourable to the entity (e.g. a financial option written by the entity); or

(b) a contract that will or may be settled in the entity's own equity instruments and is:

(i) a non-derivative contract for which the entity is or may be obliged to deliver a variable number of its own equity instruments (e.g. an instrument that is redeemable in own shares to the value of the carrying amount of the instrument); or

(ii) a derivative contract over own equity that will or may be settled other than by the exchange of a fixed amount of cash (or another financial asset) for a fixed number of the entity's own equity instruments (e.g. a net-share settled written call over own shares). For this purpose the entity's own equity instruments do not include puttable financial instruments that are classified as equity instruments in accordance with paragraphs 16A and 16B, instruments that impose on the entity an obligation to deliver to another party a pro rata share of the net assets of the entity only on liquidation and are classified as equity instruments in accordance with paragraphs 16C and 16D, or instruments that are contracts for the future receipt or delivery of the entity's own equity instruments.

As an exception, an instrument that meets the definition of a financial liability is classified as an equity instrument if it has all the features and meets the conditions in paragraphs 16A and 16B or paragraphs 16C and 16D.

The Standard defines an equity instrument as any contract that represents a residual interest in the assets of an entity after deducting all of its liabilities.

US GAAP comparison: US GAAP incorporates a more limited definition of financial liabilities resulting in a different assessment of certain instruments. Similar to IAS 32, under FAS 150 the following types of freestanding financial instruments are classified as financial liabilities in their entirety by the issuer:

(1) a mandatorily redeemable financial instrument (e.g. an outstanding share that is mandatorily redeemable);

(2) a financial instrument, other than an outstanding share, that at inception embodies an obligation to repurchase the issuer's equity shares by transferring assets (e.g. a forward purchase of own equity shares or a written put option on own equity shares); and

(3) a financial instrument that embodies an unconditional obligation, or a financial instrument other than an outstanding share that embodies a conditional obligation, that the issuer must or

may settle by issuing a variable number of its equity shares provided that, at inception, the monetary value is based solely or predominantly on any one of the following: (a) a fixed monetary amount (e.g. a share-settled note payable), (b) variations in something other than the issuer's equity shares (e.g. an indexed obligation that will be settled in the issuer's own equity shares), or (c) variations inversely related to the fair value of the issuer's equity shares (e.g. a written put option that can be net share settled).

Unlike IAS 32, under US GAAP outstanding shares that are redeemable at the option of the holder or upon the occurrence of an event that is not solely within the control of the issuer are not classified as financial liabilities in their entirety. However, issuers must also consider:

(a) whether the holder's redemption option is an embedded derivative instrument that is required to be recognised separately from the outstanding shares, including whether that option, on an as-if-freestanding basis, would qualify for a scope exception afforded instruments indexed to the issuer's own equity shares and classified in equity (FAS 133) and

(b) whether the outstanding shares are required to be classified outside of the 'permanent equity' section of the balance sheet in a separate section entitled 'temporary equity' or 'mezzanine equity' between permanent equity and liabilities either because the issuer is an SEC registrant or a non-SEC registrant electing to follow SEC guidance (EITF D-98).

2.1 Contractual obligation to deliver cash or another financial asset

The key feature in determining whether a financial instrument is a liability is the existence of a contractual obligation of one party (the issuer) to deliver cash or another financial asset to another party (the holder), or to exchange financial assets or liabilities under conditions that are potentially unfavourable. In contrast, in the case of an equity instrument (e.g. ordinary shares) the right to receive cash in the form of dividends or other distributions is at the issuer's discretion and as such no obligation to deliver cash or another financial asset to the holder of the instrument exists. The exception to this rule is permitted for certain puttable instrument and instruments with an obligation to deliver a pro rata share of net assets only at liquidation (see **2.1.2.1** and **2.3** below).

Items such as deferred revenue or warranty obligations require delivery of goods or services rather than an obligation to deliver cash or another financial asset and therefore are not financial liabilities. [IAS 32.AG11] Obligations to pay tax, company registration fees and other similar charges are obligations to pay cash. However these are statutory rather than contractual requirements and hence are not financial liabilities. Accounting for income taxes is dealt with in IAS 12 *Income Taxes*. Similarly, constructive obligations, as defined in IAS 37 *Provisions, Contingent Liabilities and Contingent Assets*, do not arise from contracts and are not financial liabilities. [IAS 32.AG12]

Liability characteristics are established in practice in a number of ways as demonstrated below.

2.1.1 *Mandatory redemption and/or mandatory interest payments*

Where the instrument requires mandatory redemption by the issuer for a fixed or determinable amount, a contractual obligation to deliver cash at redemption exists and therefore the instrument includes, and is presented as a liability. The exception to this principle applies for certain puttable instruments and certain instruments that contain an obligation to deliver a pro rata share of net assets at liquidation as described in **2.1.2.1** and **2.3**.

Example 2.1.1A

Mandatory redeemable preference shares

Entity A issues preference shares that are mandatorily redeemable at par in 10 years. A contractual obligation to deliver cash exists for the repayment of principal – the issuer cannot avoid the outflow of cash in year 10.

Perpetual instruments provide the holder with no right to require redemption. However, the terms of such instruments often require the issuer to make coupon payments into perpetuity. A perpetual instrument with a mandatory coupon is a liability in its entirety since the whole of its value is derived from the stream of future coupon payments.

Example 2.1.1B

Perpetual coupon-bearing preference shares

A perpetual instrument is issued at a par amount of CU100 million requiring coupon payments of 6 per cent to be made annually. Provided 6 per cent is the market rate of interest for this type of instrument when issued, the issuer has assumed a contractual obligation to make a future stream of 6 per cent interest payments. The net present value of the interest payments is CU100 million and represents the fair value of the liability.

Many traditional debt instruments such as bonds and bank loans involve both mandatory redemption and mandatory interest payments.

Other instruments may require a mandatory payment of a percentage of the profits of an entity (to the extent that such profits are generated) instead of a traditional interest payment. Such an instrument meets the definition of a liability as it is a contractual obligation of the issuer to deliver cash or another financial asset to the holder. The issuer has no discretion over paying out a percentage of its profits.

Care is needed in distinguishing between those cases where the issuer genuinely contractually has no discretion over the making of interest payments (or payments representing a percentage of profits) and those where, if a payment is not made, there are other consequences (even if significant) to such a decision. For example, in some jurisdictions an entity may issue instruments under which it contractually has the discretion to make payments representing a percentage of profits, though if a payment is not made the entity ceases to benefit from a favourable tax treatment. In such cases, while the entity may in fact always plan to make the payments in light of the significant tax benefits, there is no contractual obligation to deliver cash (or other financial asset) to the holder of the instrument and the instrument is not a financial liability.

2.1.2 *Puttable instruments*

A puttable instrument is defined as a financial instrument that gives the holder the right to put the instrument back to the issuer for cash or another financial asset or is automatically put back to the issuer on the occurrence of an uncertain future event or the death or retirement of the instrument holder. [IAS 32.11]

2.1.2.1 *Puttable instruments presented as equity*

As a puttable instrument contains a contractual obligation for the issuer to deliver cash or another financial asset to the holder such instruments are generally classified as financial liabilities. However, certain puttable instruments that meet specified criteria must be presented as equity. The criteria for equity classification is extensive and restrictive.

The criteria for equity classification for certain instruments originated from an amendment to IAS 32 issued in February 2008, *Puttable Financial Instruments and Obligations Arising on Liquidation*. The purpose of the amendment was to provide a limited scope exception to the definition of a financial liability that would apply to certain financial instruments that contain obligations, but, in the IASB's view, also represent a residual interest in the net assets of the issuing entity. As the title of the amendment suggests the exception applies to puttable instruments (described in this section) as well as instruments containing an obligation to deliver a pro rata share of the net assets of the entity only on liquidation (see **2.1.3** below). As the requirements of the amendment are designed as an exception, the application of the requirements should be applied strictly, and should not be used by analogy (IAS 39.96B). Failure to meet one of the requirements results in failure to meet the exception, and the instrument will not meet the criteria to be classified as equity.

A puttable instrument is classified as equity if it meets all of the following criteria:
[IAS 32.16A]

(a) the holder is entitled to a pro rata share of the entity's net assets in the event of the entity's liquidation.

The entity's net assets are those assets that remain after deducting all other claims on its assets. A pro rata share is determined by: (i) dividing the entity's net assets on liquidation into units of equal amount; and (ii) multiplying that amount by the number of the units held by the financial instrument holder. The IASB decided that the instrument must entitle the holder to a pro rata share of the net assets on liquidation because the net assets on liquidation represent the ultimate residual interest of the entity. [IAS 32.BC57]

An instrument that has a preferential right on liquidation of the entity is not an instrument with an entitlement to a pro rata share of the net assets of the entity. For example, an instrument has a preferential right on liquidation if it entitles the holder to a fixed dividend on liquidation, in addition to a share of the entity's net assets, when other instruments in the subordinate class with a right to a pro rata share of the net assets of the entity do not have the same right on liquidation. [IAS 32.AG14C]

(b) the instrument is in the class of instruments that is subordinate to all other classes of instruments.

For an instrument to be in the most subordinate class, the financial instrument must have no priority over other claims to the assets of the entity on liquidation and does not need to be converted into another instrument before it is in the class of instruments that is subordinate to all other classes of instruments. [IAS 32.BC58] The instrument must be in the class of instruments that is subordinate to all other classes of instruments on liquidation in order to represent the residual interest in the entity.

When determining whether an instrument is in the subordinate class, an entity evaluates the instrument's claim on liquidation as if it were to liquidate on the date when it classifies the instrument. An entity shall reassess the classification if there is a change in relevant circumstances. For example, if the entity issues or redeems another financial instrument, this may affect whether the instrument in question is in the class of instruments that is subordinate to all other classes. [IAS 32.AG14B]

If an entity has only one class of financial instruments, that class shall be treated as if it were subordinate to all other classes. [IAS 32.AG14D]

In some circumstances the most subordinate class of instruments are immaterial compared to the overall capital structure of the entity. This is particularly the case where the most subordinate instrument is 'founder shares', i.e. shares issued when the entity was formed, yet the entity is capitalised by other issued instruments, for example, puttable instruments issued after the founder shares were issued. The founder shares in this case, although immaterial, cannot be ignored in determining whether the puttable instruments should be classified as equity. As the puttable instruments are not the most subordinate instruments issued by the entity they are not classified as equity.

(c) all financial instruments in the class of instruments that is subordinate to all other classes of instruments have identical features. For example, they must all be puttable, and the formula or other method used to calculate the repurchase or redemption price is the same for all instruments in that class.

In January 2009 the IFRIC issued a rejection notice, *Classification of puttable and perpetual instruments*. The IFRIC considered whether a puttable instrument is most subordinate to all other classes of instruments when an entity also has perpetual instruments that meet the definition of equity instruments.

The IFRIC noted that a financial instrument is first classified as a liability or equity instrument in accordance with the general requirements of IAS 32. That classification is not affected by the existence of puttable instruments. As a second step, if a financial instrument would meet the general definition of a liability because it is puttable to the issuer, the entity considers the conditions in IAS 32.16A & 16B to determine whether it should be classified as equity. Consequently, the IFRIC noted that IAS 32 does not preclude the existence of several classes of equity.

The IFRIC also noted that IAS 32.16A(c) applies only to 'instruments in the class of instruments that is subordinate to all other classes of instruments'. IAS 32.16A(b) specifies that the level of an instrument's subordination is determined by its priority in liquidation. Accordingly, the existence of the put does not of itself imply that the puttable instruments are less subordinate than the perpetual instruments.

Given the requirements in IAS 32, the IFRIC did not expect significant diversity in practice to develop and therefore the IFRIC did not add this issue to its agenda.

(d) apart from the contractual obligation for the issuer to repurchase or redeem the instrument for cash or another financial asset, the instrument does not include any contractual obligation to deliver cash or another financial asset to another entity, or to exchange financial assets or financial liabilities with another entity under conditions that are potentially unfavourable to the entity, and it is not a contract that will or may be settled in the entity's own equity instruments as set out in subparagraph (b) of the definition of a financial liability.

Limiting equity classification to instruments where the only obligation in the instrument is the put right held by the holder ensures that the limited scope exception does not apply to instruments with other obligations. To include puttable instruments with obligations other than the put right within the limited scope exception would include instruments that may not represent a residual interest of the entity because the holder may have a claim to some of the net assets in preference to other instrument holders. [IAS 32.BC60]

(e) The total expected cash flows attributable to the instrument over the life of the instrument are based substantially on the profit or loss, the change in the recognised net assets or the change in the fair value of the recognised and unrecognised net assets of the entity over the life of the instrument (excluding any effects of the instrument).

Profit or loss and the change in the recognised net assets shall be measured in accordance with relevant IFRSs. [IAS 32.AG14E]

IAS 32 provides guidance on how to distinguish whether transactions and arrangements between the instrument holder and the issuing entity should be considered to have bee entered into in a capacity as an owner or a non-owner. This is relevant when applying the criteria in IAS 32.16A described above. The general principle is that cash flows and contractual terms and conditions of a transaction or arrangement between the instrument holder (in the role as a non-owner) and the issuing entity must be similar to an equivalent transaction that might occur between a non-instrument holder and the issuing entity. In other words, the arrangement with the owner must be similar to an arrangement that could exist with a non-owner.

If an instrument holder is also an employee of the issuing entity, the cash flows payable to the instrument holder in their capacity as an employee of the entity are ignored as those cash flows do not arise in their capacity as an owner. Similarly, a profit or loss sharing arrangement that allocates profit or loss to the instrument holders on the basis of services rendered or business generated during the current and previous years are arrangements with instrument holders in their role as non-owners and should not be considered when assessing the features listed in IAS 32.16A. However, if the profit or loss sharing arrangement allocates profit or loss based on the nominal amount of the instrument holder's interest relative to others in the class, this would represent an arrangement with the holders in their capacity as owners and should be considered when applying IAS 32.16A. [IAS 32.AG14H]

IAS 32.AG14G provides a further example of a partnership structure where some partners provide a guarantee to the entity and are remunerated for that guarantee. In determining whether the partners' interests in the partnership are identical, the guarantee is ignored as the guarantee is not provided by the partners in their capacity as owners.

For a puttable instrument to be classified as equity, in addition to meeting the above criteria in IAS 32.16A, the issuer must have no other financial instrument or contract that has:
[IAS 32.16B]

(a) total cash flows based substantially on the profit or loss, the change in the recognised net assets or the change in the fair value of the recognised and unrecognised net assets of the entity (excluding any effects of such instrument or contract), and

(b) the effect of substantially restricting or fixing the residual return to the puttable instrument holders.

When applying (a) and (b) above, the issuer shall not consider non-financial contracts with a holder of an instrument described in IAS 32.16A that have contractual terms and conditions that are similar to the contractual terms and conditions of an equivalent contract that might occur between a non-instrument holder and the issuing entity. If the entity cannot determine that this condition is met, it shall not classify the puttable instrument as an equity instrument.

IAS 32.AG14J provides examples of some instruments and arrangements that when entered into on normal commercial terms with unrelated parties, are unlikely to prevent instruments that otherwise meet the criteria in IAS 32.16A from being classified as equity:

(a) instruments with total cash flows substantially based on specific assets of the entity.

(b) instruments with total cash flows based on a percentage of revenue.

(c) contracts designed to reward individual employees for services rendered to the entity.

(d) contracts requiring the payment of an insignificant percentage of profit for services rendered or goods provided.

If a puttable instrument is presented as equity IAS 1 *Presentation of financial statements* requires the following disclosure:
[IAS 1.136A]

- summary quantitative data about the amount classified as equity;
- the entity's objectives, policies and processes for managing its obligation to repurchase or redeem the instruments when required to do so by the instrument holders, including any changes from the previous period;
- the expected cash outflow on redemption or repurchase of that class of financial instruments; and
- information about how the expected cash outflow on redemption or repurchase was determined.

Where a puttable instrument is presented as equity, but subsequently fails to meet any of the criteria detailed in IAS 32.16A & 16B, the entity shall reclassify it from the date when the instrument ceases to have all the features or meet all the conditions set out in those paragraphs. The financial liability shall be measured at the instrument's fair value at the date of reclassification with any difference between the carrying value of the equity instrument and the fair value of the financial liability at the date of reclassification recognised in equity. Similarly, if an entity redeems all its issued non-puttable instruments and any puttable instruments that remain outstanding have all of the features and meet all the conditions in IAS 32 16A & 16B, the entity shall reclassify the puttable instruments as equity instruments from the date when it redeems the non-puttable instruments. The reclassification to equity shall be at the carrying value of the financial liability at the date of reclassification. [IAS 32.16E & 16F]

IAS 1 requires that where an entity reclassifies a puttable financial instrument between financial liabilities and equity, it shall disclose the amount reclassified into and out of each category, and the timing and reason for that reclassification. [IAS 1.80A(a)]

As the treatment of some puttable instruments as equity, rather than a financial liability, is an exception to the principles in IAS 32, the Standard does not permit the extension of this amendment to the classification of non-controlling interests in the consolidated financial statements. Therefore, puttable instruments presented as equity in the separate or individual financial statements that represent non-controlling interests in the consolidated financial statements are classified as financial liabilities in the consolidated financial statements.

Example 2.1.2.1A

Puttable instruments held by non-controlling interests

Entity P controls Entity Q and therefore forms part of Entity P's consolidated financial statements. Entity Q's capital structure consist partly of puttable instruments, partly held by Entity P and other external investors, which meet the requirements of equity classification in its separate financial statements. Entity P's interest in the puttable instruments is eliminated on consolidation. Even though the puttable instruments held by the non-controlling interest meet the definition of equity in Entity Q's separate financial statements they are presented as a financial liability in the consolidated financial statements of Entity P.

The prohibition of equity classification in the consolidated financial statements for an equity instrument issued by a subsidiary appears at odds with the principles in IAS 27 *Consolidated Financial Statements* where equity instruments issued by subsidiaries not held by the parent are presented as non-controlling interests. This is further evidence that the requirement to present certain puttable instruments as equity is a limited scope exception that not only overrides the general principle of a financial liability, but also overrides other principles within IFRSs.

2.1.2.2 *Puttable instruments presented as a financial liability*

Puttable instruments that do not meet the definition of equity as described in **2.1.2.1** above will be classified either wholly as a financial liability, or partly as a financial liability in the case of an instrument that is a compound instrument (i.e. the instrument consists partly of a financial liability and partly an equity component). In considering whether an instrument is a financial liability or equity an entity must first apply the criterion in section **2.1.2.1** to determine whether the instrument is equity. If it is not, this section is relevant.

The fact that the contractual put right in a puttable instrument is conditional upon the holder exercising its right to require redemption does not negate the existence of a financial liability, as the issuer does not have the unconditional right to avoid delivering cash or another financial asset. [IAS 32.19(b)] An obligation is not negated where the instrument gives the holder the right to a residual interest in the assets of the issuer, as is the case for example, for a unit in a mutual fund [IAS 32.18(b)]

Example 2.1.2.2A

Preference shares puttable at par

An entity issues preference shares that are puttable at par at the option of the holder at a particular date. The issuer recognises a financial liability for the present value of the obligation to redeem the preference shares at par in exchange for cash on that date.

Example 2.1.2.2B

Instrument puttable at net asset value

Entity A issues Class B shares that allow the holder of the instrument to put the instrument back to Entity A at a price equal to the number of Class B shares owned, divided by the total number of Class B shares outstanding, multiplied by the net assets of Entity A (excluding the Class B shares from the net asset calculation). The Class B shares are not the most subordinate class of shares. Although Class B shareholders are in a similar position to owners, in that they participate in the performance of the net assets of Entity A, the fact that Entity A has a contractual obligation to pay the holder of the

Class B shares cash if the holder chooses to put the instrument back to the Entity, and the terms of that Class B shares do not meet the criteria to be classified as equity in IAS 32.16A, means Entity A must treat Class B shares as a financial liability. The participation feature is an embedded derivative that is not closely related to the host liability and, therefore, needs to be separated out from the host contract and accounted for separately. The accounting treatment for embedded derivatives is dealt with in **chapter 5**.

Example 2.1.2.2C

Discretion to refuse redemption

Entity A has instruments in issue that allow the holders to exercise their right to request redemption of their instrument at specified dates and amounts. All other characteristics of the instrument are equity. Entity A's governing charter states that the entity has a choice whether to accept the holder's request. There are no other conditions on the level of redemptions or any limitations on the entity's discretion to redeem or make payments to holders. In its history, Entity A has never refused to redeem holders' shares, although the governing board has the right to do so. As Entity A does not have an obligation to transfer cash or another financial asset, the instrument is equity. A history of, or intention to make, discretionary payments does not trigger liability classification. [IAS 32.AG26]

Under IAS 32 the interests in many open-ended mutual funds, unit trusts, partnerships and some co-operative entities, which embody the right of the holder to require the issuer to redeem the interests for a cash amount equivalent to their share of net assets, but do not meet the narrow criteria for equity classification described in **2.1.2.1** above, require classification as financial liabilities. This may lead to a situation where some entities have no equity capital in their financial statements. IAS 32 permits the use of an appropriate description of the line item relating to puttable instruments and provides an illustrative example of such presentation, which is reproduced below:

Example 2.1.2.2D

Presentation of an entity without equity

[Extracts from IAS 32 Illustrative Examples (Example 7)]

Statement of financial position as at 31 December 20X1

		20X1		20X0
	CU	CU	CU	CU
ASSETS				
Non-current assets (classified in accordance with IAS 1)	91,374		78,484	
Total non-current assets		91,374		78,484

		20X1		20X0
	CU	CU	CU	CU
Current assets (classified in accordance with IAS 1)	1,422		1,769	
Total current assets		1,422		1,769
Total assets		92,796		80,253
LIABILITIES				
Current liabilities (classified in accordance with IAS 1)	647		66	
Total current liabilities		(647)		(66)
Non-current liabilities excluding net assets attributable to unitholders (classified in accordance with IAS 1)	280		136	
		(280)		(136)
Net assets attributable to unitholders		91,869		80,051
Statement of comprehensive income for the year ended 31 December 20X1				
		20X1		**20X0**
		CU		CU
Revenue		2,956		1,718
Expenses (classified by nature or function)		(644)		(614)
Profit from operating activities		2,312		1,104
Finance costs:				
– other finance costs		(47)		(47)
– distributions to unitholders		(50)		(50)
Change in net assets attributable to unitholders		2,215		1,007

Where an entity has no instruments classified as equity, the normal requirements for presenting certain gains and losses in other comprehensive income continue to apply. For example, hedging gains and losses on cash flow hedging (see **2.2** in **chapter 8**) and net investment hedging (see **2.3** in **chapter 8**), as well as gains and losses on available-for-sale investments (see **3.5** in **chapter 2**) ,are recognised in other comprehensive income following the normal recognition and measurement rules.

In the case of some co-operatives, the entity has an unconditional right to refuse a member's request to redeem their shares, as prescribed in the entity's governing charter. In certain jurisdictions, local law, or regulation imposes prohibitions on redemption. Such a prohibition may be absolute in that all redemptions are prohibited; it may also be proportional, in that it prohibits redemption of members' shares if, by redeeming, the number of members' shares or amount of paid-in capital from members' shares would fall below a specified level.

IFRIC Interpretation 2 *Members' Shares in Co-operative Entities and Similar Instruments*, provides guidance on the application of IAS 32's principles to classification of members' shares in a co-operative entity as liabilities, or part equity and part liability, in accordance with the entity's charter or local legal and regulatory requirements. The Interpretation clarifies the following.

- The contractual right of a member to request redemption of contracts identified as members' shares does not, in itself, give rise to a liability. Rather, the entity must consider all of the terms of the contract in determining classification as a liability or equity (including relevant local laws, regulations and the entity's governing charter in effect at the date of the classification). Expected future amendments to those laws, regulations or charter, however, should not be considered. [IFRIC 2.5]
- Members' shares that give the member a right to request redemption are equity of the entity if the entity has an unconditional right to refuse redemption. [IFRIC 2.7]
- Local law, regulation or the entity's governing charter can impose prohibitions on the redemption of members' shares that are unconditional or dependent on certain conditions being met (or not met), e.g. prohibitions based on liquidity criteria. If redemption is unconditionally prohibited, members' shares are equity. However, provisions in local law, regulation or the entity's governing charter that prohibit redemption only if conditions (e.g. liquidity constraints) are met (or not met) do not result in members' shares being equity. [IFRIC 2.8]
- An unconditional prohibition may be absolute (i.e. all redemptions are prohibited) or partial in prohibiting redemption of members' shares if redemption would cause the number of shares or paid-in capital from members' shares to fall below a specified level. In the latter case, members' shares in excess of the prohibition against redemption are liabilities, unless the entity has an unconditional right to refuse redemption, or the member's shares meet the criteria allowing certain puttable instruments (see **2.1.2.1** above) and obligations arising on liquidation (see **2.1.3** below) to be classified as equity. [IFRIC 2.9]

Example 2.1.2.2E

Limited discretion to refuse redemption

Local law governing the operations of co-operatives, or the terms of the entity's governing charter, prohibit an entity from redeeming members' shares if, by redeeming them, it would reduce paid-in capital from members' shares below 90 per cent of the highest amount of paid-in capital from members' shares. The highest amount for a particular co-operative is CU1,000,000. With the exception of the 90 per cent restriction, the paid in capital for this co-operative is redeemable at the option of the member. The instruments in each class of paid in capital are not identical. At 31 December 20X0 the balance of paid-in capital is CU750,000. At this date, the entire balance of paid-in capital CU750,000 is classified as equity. At 31 December 20X1 the balance of paid-in capital is CU950,000. At this date, CU900,000 is classified as equity and CU50,000 is classified as a financial liability.

In certain cases, the number of shares or amount of paid-in capital subject to a redemption prohibition may change over time. If this is the case, such a change may lead to a transfer between financial liabilities and equity. [IFRIC 2.9] Consistent with the requirements of IAS 39, demand deposits, including current accounts, deposit accounts and similar contracts that arise when members act as customers, are financial liabilities of the entity. [IFRIC 2.6]

Example 2.1.2.2F

Reclassification due to change in local law

Continuing the example in **2.1.2.2E** above, at 31 December 20X2, local law governing the operations of co-operatives, or the terms of the entity's governing charter, change so that redemption of members' share is up to 20 per cent of the highest amount of members' shares, as opposed to 10 per cent. The entity would reclassify CU100,000 from equity to financial liabilities, with no gain or loss resulting, at the date the local law or governing charter is amended. The entity must disclose separately the amount, timing and reason for the transfer.

US GAAP comparison: Under US GAAP, puttable shares are not classified as financial liabilities. FAS 150 limits the meaning of mandatorily redeemable financial instruments, which are required to be classified as financial liabilities, to unconditional obligations to redeem the instrument by transferring assets at a specified or determinable date or upon an event certain to occur. Therefore, outstanding shares that *could* be redeemed at the option of the holder or upon some contingent event that is outside the control of the issuer and the holder generally are not classified as financial liabilities. However, due to the fact that a puttable instrument has a redemption feature that is not solely within the control of the issuer, SEC registrants are required to present these instruments in the balance sheet between permanent equity and liabilities in a section entitled 'temporary equity' or 'mezzanine equity' (EITF D-98).

2.1.3 *Instruments containing an obligation to deliver a pro rata share of the net assets of the entity only on liquidation*

Where liquidation of an entity is certain to occur and outside the control of the entity (for example an entity with a limited life) or is uncertain to occur but is at the option of the holder of an instrument issued by the entity (for example, in some partnership interests), the entity has a contractual obligation to pay cash or another financial asset that the entity cannot avoid. Therefore, such entities will generally recognise a financial liability with respect to the amounts payable by the entity on liquidation. However, IAS 32 has an exception for certain instruments, or components of instruments, where the issuer has an obligation to deliver to another party a pro rata share of the net assets of the entity only on liquidation. This limited scope exception was introduced at the same time as the equivalent limited scope exception for puttable instruments described in **2.1.2.1** above.

The criteria for equity classification is similar, but not the same, to the criteria described in IAS 32.16A & 16B for puttable instruments. The instrument must meet all of the following criteria to be presented as equity:
[IAS 32.16B]

(a) it entitles the holder to a pro rata share of the entity's net assets in the event of the entity's liquidation.

(b) it is in the class of instruments that is subordinate to all other classes of instruments.

(c) all financial instruments in the class of instruments that is subordinate to all other classes of instruments must have an identical contractual obligation for the issuing entity to deliver a pro rata share of its net assets on liquidation.

> The three criteria above are equivalent to the criteria in IAS 32.16A(a – c) for puttable instruments. The shaded boxes that accompany the criteria described in **2.1.2.1** above equally apply to the criteria in IAS 32.16B reproduced immediately above.

For an instrument, or component of a financial instrument, containing an obligation to deliver a pro rata share of the net assets of the entity only on

liquidation, to be classified as equity, in addition to meeting the above criteria in IAS 32.16C, the issuer must have no other financial instrument or contract that has:
[IAS 32.16D]

(a) total cash flows based substantially on the profit or loss, the change in the recognised net assets or the change in the fair value of the recognised and unrecognised net assets of the entity (excluding any effects of such instrument or contract), and

(b) the effect of substantially restricting or fixing the residual return to the puttable instrument holders.

When applying (a) and (b) above, the issuer shall not consider non-financial contracts with a holder of an instrument described in IAS 32.16C that have contractual terms and conditions that are similar to the contractual terms and conditions of an equivalent contract that might occur between a non-instrument holder and the issuing entity. If the entity cannot determine that this condition is met, it shall not classify the puttable instrument as an equity instrument.

IAS 32.16D reproduced immediately above is equivalent to the IAS 32.16B for puttable instruments. The guidance and shaded boxes that accompany IAS 32.16B for puttable instruments, and the inability to classify puttable instruments held by non-controlling interests as equity in the consolidated financial statements (as described in **2.1.2.1** above) equally apply to instruments containing an obligation to deliver a pro rata share of the net assets of the entity only on liquidation.

The Board acknowledged in their basis for conclusions that many of those requirements, and the reasons for them, are similar for puttable financial instruments and instruments that contain an obligation to deliver a pro rata share of the net assets only at liquidation. As highlighted in IAS 32.BC67 the criteria for the latter instruments differ from the former as:

(a) there is no requirement that there be no other contractual obligations;

(b) there is no requirement to consider the expected total cash flows throughout the life of the instrument;

(c) the only feature that must be identical among the instruments in the class is the obligation for the issuing entity to deliver to the holder a pro rata share of its net assets on liquidation.

The Standard explains that the reason for the differences is the timing of settlement of the obligation. In the case of obligations settled only on liquidation the life of the financial instrument is the same as the life of the issuing entity, as the extinguishment of the obligation can occur only on liquidation. Therefore, the IASB concluded that it was appropriate to focus only on the obligations that exist on liquidation. The instrument must be subordinate to all other classes of instruments and represent the residual interests only at that point in time. However, if the instrument contains other contractual obligations, those obligations may need to be accounted for separately in accordance with the requirements of IAS 32 (i.e. the instrument may be a compound instrument containing a financial liability and equity component).

IAS 1 *Presentation of financial statements* requires that where an entity reclassifies an instrument between financial liabilities and equity that imposes on the entity an obligation to deliver to another party a pro rata share of the net assets of the entity only on liquidation, it shall disclose the amount reclassified into and out of each category (financial liabilities or equity), and the timing and reason for that reclassification. [IAS 1.80B(b)]

In the case of a limited life entity disclosure is required of information regarding the length of the entity's life. [IAS 1.138(d)]

2.1.4 *Restrictions on ability to satisfy contractual obligation*

A restriction on the contractual obligation of the entity to deliver cash or another financial instrument, such as the need to obtain regulatory approval for payment, does not in itself negate that obligation. The entity does not in such cases have an unconditional right to avoid delivering cash or another financial asset. [IAS 32.19(a)]

Example 2.1.4

Inability to satisfy put feature

Entity A issued preference shares that are puttable for CU1 million by the holders to Entity A at any time after a specified date. Under the terms of the shares, Entity A will have to satisfy this obligation under the put out of its distributable reserves.

The put creates an obligation for Entity A. The potential inability of Entity A to satisfy the obligation under the put if it were to find that it has insufficient distributable reserves does not negate the obligation.

2.1.5 *Contractual obligation that is not explicit*

An obligation may be established indirectly through the instrument's terms and conditions. IAS 32 gives two examples of how such an obligation can be created.

- A financial instrument may contain a non-financial obligation that must be settled if, and only if, the entity fails to make distributions or to redeem the instrument. If the entity can avoid a transfer of cash or another financial asset only by settling the non-financial obligation the financial instrument is a financial liability. [IAS 32.20(a)]

- A financial instrument is a financial liability if it provides that on settlement the entity will deliver either cash or another financial asset, or its own shares whose value is determined to exceed substantially the value of the cash or other financial asset. Although the entity does not have an explicit obligation to deliver cash or another financial asset, the holder of the asset has in substance been guaranteed a minimum amount equal to at least the cash/other financial asset settlement option amount. [IAS 32.20(b)]

In March 2006, the IFRIC, in response to a submission for a possible agenda item, discussed the role of contractual and economic obligations in the classification of two different financial instruments under IAS 32. The first instrument was an irredeemable, callable financial instrument with dividends payable only if dividends are paid on the ordinary shares of the issuer which included a 'step-up' dividend clause that would increase the dividend at a pre-determined date in the future unless the instrument had previously been called by the issuer. The second instrument was an irredeemable, callable financial instrument with dividends that must be paid if interest was paid on another, linked, instrument.

The IFRIC agreed that IAS 32 is clear that a contractual financial obligation was necessary in order that a financial instrument be classified as a liability (ignoring the classification of financial instruments that may or will be settled in the issuer's own equity instruments). Such a contractual obligation could be established explicitly or indirectly. However, the obligation must be established through the *terms and conditions* of the financial instrument. IFRIC also noted that IAS 32 is clear that economic obligations, commonly known as *economic compulsion*, by itself, would not result in a financial instrument being classified as a liability. The IFRIC also discussed the role of 'substance' in the classification of financial instruments. It noted that IAS 32 restricted the role of 'substance' to consideration of the contractual terms of an instrument, and that anything outside the contractual terms was not considered for the purpose of assessing whether an instrument should be classified as a liability under IAS 32. These points were subsequently confirmed by the IASB through their discussions in June 2006.

In November 2006 the IFRIC agreed not to add the issue to its agenda as the Board's and IFRIC's discussions demonstrated that the Standard was sufficiently clear.

Example 2.1.5

Perpetual instrument with coupon step-up and dividend pusher

Bank A issues a perpetual instrument with the following terms.

- €100m notional with 8 per cent interest payments for 8 years. Bank A has a call option embedded in the instrument that allows the instruments to be repurchased at the end of year 8, and every year after, for €100m.
- If the instrument is not called by the issuer at the end of year 8 the interest on the instrument increases to 14 per cent per annum (commonly referred to as a 'step-up' feature).
- The interest payments before and after the call date are only payable if Bank A pays a dividend on its ordinary shares which are classified wholly as equity (commonly referred to as a 'dividend pusher').
- Bank A has consistently chosen to pay dividends on its ordinary shares. The cost of borrowing for Bank A for 8 years when the instrument is issued is approximately 8 per cent.

Bank A does not have an indirect or direct obligation to pay cash or other financial asset in respect of the perpetual instrument. The instrument is therefore classified wholly as equity.

Bank A has no obligation to pay interest as it can always avoid paying interest by exercising its discretion and not paying dividends on its ordinary shares. The bank has no obligation to exercise its right to call the instrument at year 8 as the call right is an option and it could always choose not to exercise that right. As the instrument is perpetual, there is no redemption date, and therefore the instrument does not contain any contractual obligation to pay cash or other financial asset.

In determining the substance of the contractual arrangement an entity must assess whether the terms of the instrument provide the issuer with a genuine choice whether to deliver cash or another financial asset. In this case the entity has a genuine choice as to whether or not it wishes to pay an ordinary dividend. Even though it is highly likely that the entity will choose to pay ordinary dividends and thereby will be forced to pay interest under the perpetual instrument, the high likelihood is of itself not sufficient for the instrument to be classified as a financial liability. Although it is very likely that the Bank will pay interest on the perpetual instrument and will exercise its call at year 8, thus making the instrument economically equivalent to an 8-year loan, this of itself is not sufficient for the instrument to be classified as a financial liability.

When considering the instrument's terms and conditions only genuine terms should be taken into account. If an instrument contains an option that gives an entity a choice between paying cash or ceasing to be a going concern, such an option is not a genuine term of the instrument as the directors cannot choose to stop being a going concern as they have to act in their fiduciary capacity. Equally, a link to an intragroup instrument that has a mandatory dividend is not a genuine term as intragroup transactions are generally not enforceable.

US GAAP comparison: When the FASB exposed FAS 150, they concluded that increasing-rate preferred shares would be classified in equity to the extent the shares are not mandatorily redeemable and no enforceable obligation to pay dividends exists. In the redeliberations of the exposure draft, this issue was postponed to Phase 2 of FASB's liabilities and equity project. [FAS 150.B24] Although the FASB had stated that its next step would be to redeliberate the remaining issues discussed in the exposure draft and not resolved by FAS 150, the FASB subsequently changed its plan. The new plan was to start over and attempt to develop a convergent set of classification principles that would avoid the issues raised by FAS 150, as well as resolve the remaining issues. This project, renamed the financial instruments with characteristics of equity project, is now a joint project of the FASB and IASB and has not yet been completed. Under the guidance in SEC SAB Topic 5-Q, these instruments are classified in permanent equity (unless an investor put causes them to be in temporary equity), however, the issuer is required to accrue dividends on an expected yield basis rather than on a cash basis.

2.1.6 Shares to the value of, or issuer settlement option

Some instruments may contain an obligation for the issuer to deliver a variable number of its own equity instruments such that the fair value of the entity's own equity that is delivered under the arrangement equals the amount of the contractual obligation. The amount of the contractual obligation may be fixed or may fluctuate in part or in full in response to a variable other than the market price of the issuer's own equity.

Such instruments do not meet the definition of equity as the issuer is merely using its own shares as currency to extinguish its obligation. The contract therefore does not evidence a residual interest in the entity's assets after deducting all of its liabilities. [IAS 32.21]

Example 2.1.6A

Variable number of shares to the value of a fixed obligation

Entity A issues CU0.01 nominal preference shares that will pay out CU1 over three years. Entity A will pay the CU1 in its own ordinary shares so that the number of shares issued will vary to equate to CU1 in value.

The instrument is a financial liability as Entity A issues shares such that the fair value of the shares delivered always equals the amount of the contractual obligation.

Example 2.1.6B

Variable number of shares to the value of a variable obligation

Entity B issues an instrument for CU100 that pays no interest payments before maturity. At maturity Entity B is required to deliver as many of its own equity instruments as are equivalent in value to the original issue price of CU100 plus a supplemental redemption amount depending on whether a designated share price index has exceeded a predetermined level at the maturity date. The supplemental amount is determined as a multiple of the percentage increase in the share price index from the date of issue of the instrument to maturity and the original issue price. If the share price index has fallen over the life of the instrument, there is no supplemental redemption amount.

The instrument is a financial liability as the amount of the contractual obligation varies in response to a variable other than the market price of the issuer's own equity.

2.1.7 Contingent settlement provisions

Financial instruments may be structured such that the obligation to deliver cash or another financial instrument arises only on the occurrence or non-occurrence of uncertain future events (or on the outcome of uncertain circumstances) that are beyond the control of both the issuer and the holder of the instrument. The issuer does not have an unconditional right to avoid the obligation to deliver cash or another financial instrument and hence such instruments are financial liabilities of the issuer unless: [IAS 32.25]

- the contingent settlement provision that could require payment in cash or another financial asset is not genuine; or

- settlement in cash or another financial asset can only be required in the event of liquidation of the issuer.
- the instrument meets the specified criteria for a puttable instrument or an obligation arising on liquidation to be classified as equity (see sections **2.1.2.1** and **2.3** respectively).

'Genuine' is generally understood to be not spurious or counterfeit, i.e. a genuine provision is one that is authentic and has commercial substance. A provision that is extremely rare, highly abnormal and very unlikely to occur is not considered genuine. [IAS 32.AG28]

Future events that are beyond the control of both the issuer and the holder of the instrument include:

(a) a change in macroeconomic, industry and other indices such as the stock market index, consumer price index, growth in Gross Domestic Product or total sector production;

(b) changes in law, government regulations, and other regulatory requirements (such as changes in taxation, pricing controls or accounting requirements); and

(c) changes in the key performance indicators of the issuer that are beyond the control of both the issuer and the holder such as revenues, net income or debt to equity ratio.

Example 2.1.7A

Contingent settlement provisions: change in accounting or tax law

Entity A issues preference shares bearing 5 per cent non-cumulative dividends that are at the discretion of the issuer. The shares will be redeemed if the applicable taxation or accounting requirements were to change.

Given that the contingent event is outside the control of both the issuer and the holder, is genuine, and can result in the issuer having to deliver cash or another financial asset at a time other than the issuer's liquidation, the instrument is classified as a financial liability. However, the 5 per cent dividend is at the discretion of the issuer and is therefore equity of the issuer. Hence, the preference share contains both debt and equity features, i.e. it is a compound instrument (see **section 3** below).

Example 2.1.7B

Contingent settlement provisions: initial public offering (1)

Entity B issues shares for CU1 million. Dividends are discretionary. The issuer must redeem the shares for par in the event of a flotation / Initial Public Offering (IPO) of the entity. The issuer cannot guarantee a successful floatation / IPO, but it does have the discretion whether or not to instigate proceedings to try and float or IPO. Given that the issuer can avoid redeeming the shares by avoiding the floatation/IPO the instrument is classified as equity.

Example 2.1.7C

Contingent settlement provisions: initial public offering (2)

Entity B issues shares for CU1 million. Dividends are discretionary. The issuer must redeem the shares for par in the event that the entity is *not* subject to a successful flotation / Initial Public Offering ('IPO') of the entity within 5 years from the date of issue of the shares. Given that the contingent event, being a successful floatation/IPO, is not in the control of the issuer, it is a contingent settlement provision. As the issuer cannot avoid redeeming the shares, the instrument is classified as a financial liability.

Example 2.1.7D

Contingent settlement provisions: change of control

Entity B issues shares for CU1 million. Dividends are discretionary. The issuer must redeem the shares for par in the event that the control of the entity changes. A change of control is defined as a change in ownership of at least 51% of the ordinary shares of the entity. Given that the contingent event, being the sale of the entity from one set of shareholders to another, is not in the control of the issuer, it is a contingent settlement provision. As the issuer cannot avoid redeeming the shares, the instrument is classified as a financial liability.

US GAAP comparison: If a share is mandatorily redeemable only upon the occurrence of specified conditions that are not certain to occur, the instrument in its entirety only becomes classified as a liability once the condition occurs, the condition is resolved, or the event becomes certain to occur. Prior to the condition occurring, being resolved or becoming certain to occur, entities must also consider: (a) whether the instrument contracts an embedded derivative and whether it qualifies for a scope exception for instruments indexed to the entity's own equity shares and classified in equity and (b) whether EITF Topic D-98 would apply. Topic D-98 requires classification outside permanent equity, if the specified conditions are outside the control of the issuer. This analysis may result in liability, temporary (mezzanine) equity or permanent equity treatment depending on the terms of the instrument and other relevant facts.

If a share is only optionally redeemable (at the holder's choice) upon occurrence of specified events (not solely within the issuer's control), US GAAP would regard the share as a mezzanine equity item from the inception of the instrument (for SEC registrants or non-SEC registrants electing to follow guidance in EITF D-98) or permanent equity item (for issuers that are not SEC registrants). In this context, mezzanine equity is a temporary equity item presented between liabilities and permanent equity. Note that this assumes that the entity has appropriately concluded that the instrument either does not contain an embedded derivative or that the embedded derivative qualifies for a scope exception for instruments indexed to the entity's own equity shares and classified in equity (i.e. that the instrument is not required to be classified as a liability under US GAAP).

2.2 Equity instruments

In classifying a financial instrument as liability or equity, equity classification is appropriate only if the instrument fails the definition of a financial liability as detailed in **section 2** above.

The key requirement in determining whether an instrument is equity is the issuer's unconditional ability to avoid delivery of cash or another financial asset. That ability is not affected by:

- the history of making distributions;
- an intention to make distributions in the future;
- a possible negative impact on the price of ordinary shares of the issuer if the distributions are not made on the instrument concerned;
- the amount of the issuer's reserves;
- an issuer's expectations of a profit or loss for the period; or
- an ability or inability of the issuer to influence the amount of its profit or loss for the period.

Provided the dividends are at the discretion of the issuer, it is irrelevant whether dividends are cumulative or non-cumulative. [IAS 32.AG26]

Once a dividend is properly declared and the issuer is legally required to pay it, a contractual obligation to deliver cash comes into existence and a financial liability for the amount of the declared dividend needs to be recognised. Similarly, on a winding up a liability arises to distribute to the shareholders the residual assets in the issuer, i.e. any remaining assets after satisfying all of its liabilities.

The existence of an option whereby the issuer can redeem equity shares for cash does not trigger liability classification as the issuer retains the unconditional right to avoid delivering cash or another financial asset. A contractual obligation would only arise at the point where the issuer exercised its right to redeem. This principle applies to all instruments that are not derivatives over own equity.

Specific rules apply to derivatives over own equity. For example, a purchased call option over a fixed number of shares will allow the issuer to buy back shares at a fixed price in the future. The issuer always has a choice whether it wishes to pay cash, as it always has a choice as to whether it wishes to exercise its option. However, this instrument is only treated as equity if it is gross physically settled in all cases when the issuer chooses to exercise, i.e. the option cannot ever be net settled.

Often instruments are issued with various links to dividend payments on other types of instruments, most commonly ordinary shares. A 'dividend stopper' is a contractual term that requires no dividend to be paid on the ordinary shares if the payment is not made on the instrument concerned. A 'dividend pusher' is a term that requires a dividend to be paid on the instrument concerned if a payment of dividend is made on ordinary shares.

Provided the link is to the dividends on an instrument like an ordinary share where the issuer has the discretion over the decision whether or not to pay a dividend, a 'dividend pusher' or a 'dividend stopper' does not of itself result in the instrument concerned being classified as a liability. This is because the issuer continues to have the discretion over the decision whether or not to pay on the instrument, though that decision will need to be made in conjunction with the decision on whether to pay on ordinary shares. The fact remains that the issuer has an unconditional right to avoid outflow of cash (or other financial assets).

Example 2.2A

Dividend stopper

Entity Y issues 6 per cent cumulative preference shares with discretionary dividends which are subject to availability of distributable reserves. The directors of Y can decide at each period end whether and the extent to which a dividend on the preference shares will be paid. The terms of the instrument include a dividend stopper, i.e. if no dividend is paid on the preference shares, then no dividend is paid on Entity Y's ordinary shares. Entity Y has an unconditional right to avoid the obligation to deliver cash, as dividends on the preference shares are entirely at Entity Y's discretion.

Example 2.2B

Dividend pusher

Entity M issues preference shares bearing 6 per cent discretionary non-cumulative dividends which are subject to availability of distributable reserves. The directors of M can decide at each period end whether and the extent to which a dividend on the preference shares will be paid. However, the terms of the instrument include a dividend pusher, i.e. if a dividend is paid on Entity M's ordinary shares, then a dividend must be paid on the preference shares. Dividends on its ordinary shares are at the discretion of Entity M and therefore Entity M has an unconditional right to avoid the obligation to pay cash on the preference shares. The preference shares are equity.

2.3 Entities with annual reporting periods beginning before 1 January 2009

In February 2008 the IASB published an amendment to IAS 32 and IAS 1 titled *Puttable Financial Instruments and Obligations Arising on Liquidation*. The amendment is reflected in **2.1.2.1** and **2.1.3** above. For those entities with annual reporting periods beginning before 1 January 2009 that do not early adopt, these amendments are not applicable.

The pre-amended version of IAS 32 required all financial instruments that met the definition of a financial liability to be classified as a liability. Therefore, all instruments puttable for cash or another financial asset to the issuer by the holder, and obligations arising on liquidation, where liquidation is either certain and outside of the control of the issuer or uncertain and at the option of the holder, are classified as financial liabilities.

A comparison of the difference in presentation of certain financial instruments prior to the amendment to IAS 32 and post the amendment is illustrated below.

Issued financial instrument	**Classification under IAS 32 prior to the amendment**	**Classifica-tion under amended IAS 32**
Share puttable throughout its life at fair value, that is also the most subordinate, does not contain any other obligation, with discretionary dividends based on profits of the issuer	Liability	Equity
Share puttable at fair value, that is not the most subordinate	Liability	Liability
Share puttable at fair value only on liquidation, that is also the most subordinate, but contains a fixed non-discretionary dividend	Liability	Compound (part equity, part liability)
Share puttable at fair value only on liquidation, that is also the most subordinate, but contains a fixed discretionary dividend and does not contain any other obligation	Liability	Equity
Any of the instruments described above issued by a subsidiary held by non-controlling parties, in the consolidated financial statements	Liability	Liability

If entities adopt the amendments to IAS 32 for a period beginning before 1 January 2009, consequential amendments to IFRS 7 *Financial Instruments: Disclosures*, IAS 39 and IFRIC 2 should be adopted from the same earlier date. The fact that the amendments have been adopted in advance of their effective date should be disclosed.

If an entity applies the amendments and as a result would have recognised a financial instrument in the past that would have been a compound instrument, but the financial liability is no longer outstanding at the date of applying the amendments, it does not need to restate retained earnings for the profit or loss impact that would have arisen from that financial liability. This is the same exemption that applies to the accounting for compound instruments in IFRS 1 *First-time Adoption of International Financial Reporting Standards*.

3 Compound instruments

The terms of a financial instrument may be structured such that it contains both equity and liability components (i.e. the instrument is neither entirely a liability, nor entirely an equity instrument). Such instruments are defined in IAS 32 as compound instruments. An example of a compound instrument is a bond that is convertible, either mandatorily or at the option of the holder, into a fixed number of equity shares of the issuer. Compound instruments come in many forms and are not restricted solely to convertible instruments. The liability and equity components of a compound instrument are required to be accounted for separately. [IAS 32.28]

The requirement to separate out the equity and financial liability components of a compound instrument is consistent with the principle that a financial instrument must be classified in accordance with its substance, rather than its legal form. A compound instrument has a legal form of a single instrument, while the substance is that both a liability and an equity instrument exist.

For example, a convertible bond that pays fixed coupons and is convertible by the holder into a fixed number of ordinary shares of the issuer has the legal form of a debt contract. Yet, its substance is that of two instruments.

1. A financial liability to deliver cash (by making scheduled payments of coupon and principal) which exists as long as the bond is not converted.

2. A written call option granting the holder the right to convert the bond into a fixed number of ordinary shares of the entity.

The economic effect of the instrument is substantially the same as issuing simultaneously a debt instrument with an early settlement provision, and separately issuing warrants to issue ordinary shares.

US GAAP comparison: Separating a convertible debt instrument into different liability and equity components is generally precluded with certain exceptions, including:

(a) debt instruments that are issued with detachable share purchase warrants (including warrants with an exercise price that may be settled by surrendering the debt instrument) that meet the requirements for equity classification (FAS 150, FAS 133, EITF 00–19 and EITF 01–6 or EITF 07–5) (APB 14);

(b) convertible debt that is issued at a substantial premium (APB 14);

(c) convertible debt with a conversion option that upon issuance is required to be separated as a derivative liability component because it meets the criteria to be separated from the debt host contract as an embedded derivative instrument (FAS 133), but subsequently fails to meet those criteria (EITF 06–7);

(d) convertible debt instruments that, by their stated terms, may be settled in cash (or other assets) upon conversion, including partial cash settlement, and for which the embedded conversion option is not required to be separated as a derivative liability component under FAS 133 (FSP APB 14–1);

(e) convertible debt instruments with a conversion option that is in the money for the holder at the commitment date (generally this is the date a firm commitment to issue convertible debt is reached) and that is not required to be separated either as a derivative liability component under FAS 133 or as an equity component under FSP APB 14–1 (EITF 98–5, EITF 00–27 and EITF 08–4).

Additionally, separation of a convertible debt instrument into debt host and derivative liability components may be required if the conversion option meets the definition of a derivative instrument (including not qualifying for the scope exception afforded instruments indexed to the entity's own equity shares and classified in equity) under FAS 133. Separation of the conversion option under FAS 133 precludes the separation into different liability and equity components for the instruments described in (d) and (e) above. Further, recognition of the detachable warrants noted in (a) above as a liability component separate from the debt instrument may be required if the warrants fail to meet equity classification requirements under FAS 150, FAS 133, EITF 01–6 or EITF 07–5 and EITF 00–19.

3.1 Separating the liability and equity components

Separation of the instrument into its liability and equity components is made upon initial recognition of the instrument and is not subsequently revised. The method used is as follows:

- firstly, the fair value of the liability component is calculated, and this fair value establishes the initial carrying amount of the liability component; and

- secondly the fair value of the liability component is deducted from the fair value of the instrument as a whole, with the resulting residual amount being the equity component.

This method of allocating the liability and equity components is consistent with the definition of equity being a residual interest in the assets of an entity after deducting all of its liabilities. It ensures that no gain or loss arises on initial recognition of the two components.

The fair value of the liability component on initial recognition is the present value of the contractual stream of future cash flows (including both coupon payments and redemption amount) discounted at the market rate of interest that would have been applied to an instrument of comparable credit quality with substantially the same cash flows, on the same terms, but without the conversion option.

Example 3.1A

Convertible debt

Entity A, a CU functional currency entity, issues 2,000 convertible bonds on 1 January 20X5. The bonds have a three-year term, and are issued at par with a face value of CU1,000 per bond, giving total proceeds of CU2 million. Interest is payable annually in arrears at an annual interest rate of 6 per cent. Each bond is convertible, at the holder's discretion, at any time up to maturity into 250 ordinary shares. When the bonds are issued, the market interest rate for similar debt without the conversion option is 9 per cent.

On initial recognition the liability component is valued first, and the difference between the proceeds of the bond issue (being the fair value of the instrument in its entirety) and the fair value of the liability is assigned to the equity component. The present value (i.e. fair value) of the liability component is calculated using a discount rate of 9 per cent, the market interest rate for similar bonds with the same credit standing having no conversion rights. The calculation, which excludes the income tax entries, is illustrated below:

	CU
Present value of principal at the end of 3 years*	1,544,367
Present value of interest (CU120,000 payable annually in arrears for 3 years **)	303,755
Total liability component (B)	1,848,122
Residual equity component (A-B)	151,878
Proceeds of bond issue (A)	2,000,000
*present value of principal amount at 9%: 2,000,000/(1.09)^3 =	1,544,367
**present value of interest (CU120,000) payable at the end of each of 3 years:	
interest at end of year 1: 120,000/1.09 =	110,092
interest at end of year 2: $120{,}000/(1.09)^2$ =	101,002
interest at end of year 3: $120{,}000/(1.09)^3$ =	92,661
Total net present value of interest payments	**303,755**

Upon initial recognition of the convertible instrument in the financial statements of the issuer the following entries are appropriate:

Dr	Cash	CU2,000,000
Cr	Financial liability	CU1,848,122
Cr	Equity	CU151,878

Any transaction costs are allocated between the debt component and the equity component, using their relative fair values.

The financial liability component will be subsequently measured in accordance with the measurement requirements in IAS 39 depending on its classification (either as a financial liability at fair value through profit or loss, or as an 'other' liability, measured at amortised cost using the effective interest rate method).

The equity component will not be re-measured.

Example 3.1B

Perpetual interest-bearing preference shares

Entity A, a Euro functional entity, issues non-redeemable preference shares. The preference shares have a cumulative, mandatory dividend fixed at €424 per share per year. If earnings are not sufficient to cover the dividend in any given year, such dividends will be paid in future years. Additional dividends may be declared but must be distributed evenly throughout the different classes of shares.

The preference share is a compound financial instrument that contains both liability and equity components. The liability is the contractual obligation by the issuer to deliver cash (€424 per year), while the equity component is represented by the holder's right to receive an equity return in the form of additional dividends, if declared.

The fair value of the liability will be calculated as the present value of the mandatory dividend of €424 per share per year in perpetuity discounted at the market interest rate for a similar instrument that does not contain a residual benefit to discretionary dividends. The equity component is calculated as the residual amount after deducting from the fair value of the instrument as a whole the amount separately determined for the liability component.

US GAAP comparison: As noted in **section 3** above, separating a convertible debt instrument into different liability and equity components is generally precluded with certain exceptions. When such a separation is required, the method used to allocate proceeds between the components is determined by the exception requiring the separation:

(a) debt instruments that are issued with detachable share purchase warrants that are classified in equity: the initial carrying amounts are determined by allocating the proceeds based on the relative fair values of the debt and the warrants (APB 14);

(b) convertible debt that is issued at a substantial premium: the premium is treated as additional paid-in capital (APB 14);

(c) convertible debt with a conversion option that upon issuance is required to be separated as a derivative liability component because it meets the criteria to be separated from the debt host contract as an embedded derivative instrument, but subsequently fails to meet those criteria: the carrying amount (i.e. its fair value) of the derivative liability for the conversion option is reclassified as an equity component and the carrying amount of the debt liability component is not impacted (i.e. any debt discount recognised based on the initial allocation of the proceeds to the debt liability component should continue to be amortised) (EITF 06–7);

(d) convertible debt instruments that may be settled in cash upon conversion (including partial cash settlement) and for which the conversion option does not require separation under FAS 133: the initial carrying amounts are determined by first allocating proceeds equal to the fair value of a similar debt instrument without an associated equity component to the liability component and then allocating the residual proceeds to the equity component (FSP APB 14–1);

(e) convertible debt instruments with a conversion option that is in the money for the holder at the commitment date and does not require separation under either FAS 133 or FSP APB 14–1: the initial carrying amounts are determined by first allocating proceeds equal to the intrinsic value of the conversion option to the equity component and then allocating the residual proceeds to the liability component (EITF 98–5, EITF 00–27 and EITF 08–4).

Additionally, the initial carrying amounts for a convertible debt instrument that requires separation of the conversion option as a derivative liability are determined by first allocating proceeds equal to the fair value of the conversion option to the derivative liability component and then allocating the residual proceeds to the debt host liability component (FAS 133, DIG B6). Further, if the detachable warrants noted in (a) above fail to meet equity classification requirements, the initial carrying amounts are determined by first allocating proceeds equal to the fair value of the warrants to the separate warrant liability component and then allocating the residual proceeds to the debt instrument (FAS 133, DIG B6).

3.2 Separating the liability and equity components where the instrument has embedded derivatives

In addition to the financial liability and equity components, a compound instrument may also have embedded derivatives (see **chapter 5**). For example, the instrument may contain a call option exercisable by the issuer. The value of any such embedded derivative features must be allocated to the liability component. [IAS 32.31] Thus, the carrying amount of the liability component is established by measuring the fair value of a similar liability (with similar terms, credit status and embedded non-equity derivative features) but without an associated equity component. The carrying amount of the equity component is then determined by deducting the fair value of the liability component from the fair value of the compound instrument as a whole.

A further assessment is required to establish whether the embedded derivative is closely related to the liability component (see **chapter 5**). This assessment is made before separating the equity component. No gain or loss arises from initially recognising the components of the instrument separately.

Example 3.2A

Convertible debt with issuer call

A CU functional currency entity issues a bond with a principal amount of CU60 million carrying a coupon of 5 per cent payable annually in arrears.

The instrument is issued for proceeds of CU60 million. The instrument is convertible into a fixed number of equity shares of the issuer after a specified date. The instrument has no fixed maturity. However, it contains an issuer call option that allows the issuer to redeem the bond at par at any point in time.

It is established that the value of a similar bond, of similar credit status with similar features except one not containing a call or equity conversion option at current market rates would be CU57 million. Based on an option pricing model it is further determined that the value of the issuer purchased call option on a similar bond without a conversion option is CU2 million. In this case the value allocated to the liability and equity components should be as follows:

Liability component: CU55 million (CU57 million less CU2 million)

This represents the inclusion of the value of the additional embedded derivative feature in the liability component.

Equity component: CU5 million (CU60 million – CU55 million)

This represents the equity residual arrived at by subtracting from the fair value of the whole instrument the fair value of the liability component (which includes the value of the embedded derivative feature in the form of the purchased call feature).

The issuer call option will not be separately accounted for since its exercise price is set at par (CU60 million), which is equal to the amortised cost of the instrument on each exercise date on the basis that the assessment is made prior to separating out the written equity call option, i.e. the embedded derivative is closely related to the host debt instrument.

In the example described above, the initial amortised cost of the financial liability is established as the fair value of issued callable debt. Assuming the call feature over the debt instrument is not separated, the effective interest rate applied at inception and throughout the life of the instrument is the same rate of interest that would apply to plain callable debt. To the extent that interest rates change subsequent to issue, this will impact the likelihood that callable debt will be called by the issuer, and therefore the carrying amount will be updated (see **4.1.1** in **chapter 6**).

Example 3.2B

Convertible debt with issuer call and holder put

Entity X has issued a convertible debt instrument in May 2008 with a contractual maturity of 16 years. One bond allows the holder to obtain, at any time, one share of the issuer (the conversion option). Coupon is 2 per cent payable annually. Issue price is 100 per cent and redemption price is 140 per cent.

> The instrument is puttable by the holders on three different dates, during the life of the instrument (May 2012, May 2016 and May 2020).
>
> The instrument is also callable by the issuer, starting 2012, if the price of the issuer's shares increases beyond 125 per cent of the redemption price.
>
> In the case of exercise of the put/call option, the redemption price is equivalent to the amortised cost of the issued instrument (prior to the equity conversion option being separated). The embedded call/put options, therefore, are closely related to the instrument and are not accounted for as derivatives with changes in fair value recognised in profit or loss. On initial recognition, Entity X considers that there is a very high probability that the instrument will be redeemed by the holders on the first exercise date of the put (i.e. 2012), given the low price of its shares.
>
> Entity X will account for the issued bond as a compound instrument. On initial recognition X needs to consider the contractual cash flows in order to measure the value of the debt component of the compound instrument.
>
> The fair value of the straight debt instrument without a call/put or equity conversion option, is equivalent to the present value of the contractually determined stream of future cash flows until maturity (in this case 2024) discounted at the rate of interest that applies to instruments of comparable credit quality and providing substantially the same cash flows on the same terms but without the call, put or conversion option (i.e. debt instruments with a 2024 maturity date).
>
> Entity X then determines the value of the call and put options embedded in the debt instrument using an option pricing model. The call and put options are valued as if they were a call and a put embedded in a debt instrument that did not have any equity conversion feature. Both the purchased call and the written put are deducted and added to the debt in order to obtain the fair value of the total liability component.
>
> Finally, Entity X determines the value of the embedded conversion option (equity component) by subtracting the total liability component from the total net proceeds received on issuance.

If the financial liability is not designated as at fair value through profit or loss, the effective interest rate must be applied in determining amortised cost. If an entity designates financial instruments as at fair value through profit or loss it should have a policy as to whether it recognises the effective interest rate in profit or loss separately for such items (see **4.3.1** in **chapter 11**). An issuer must apply the effective interest rate to the financial liability ignoring the likelihood that the financial liability may be forgiven if the equity conversion is exercised. This treatment is consistent with the principle that the likelihood of conversion is reflected in the value of conversion option and is recognised as a separate financial instrument in equity.

US GAAP comparison: As noted in **section 3** above, separating a convertible debt instrument into different liability and equity components is generally precluded with certain exceptions. Whether the convertible debt instrument is separated into different liability and equity components or not, whenever an embedded derivative instrument is required to be separated as a derivative liability pursuant to FAS 133, the initial carrying amounts are generally determined by first allocating proceeds equal to the fair value of the embedded derivative instrument to the derivative liability component and then allocating the residual proceeds between the remaining components to be recognised using the same model that would have been used absent the derivative liability component (FAS 133, DIG B6). However, for convertible debt instruments that may be settled in cash upon conversion (including partial cash settlement) and for which the conversion option does not require separation under FAS 133, the initial carrying amounts are determined by first allocating proceeds equal to the fair value of a similar debt instrument including the embedded derivative instrument without an associated equity component to the liability component then allocating the residual proceeds to the equity component (FSP APB 14–1). The proceeds allocated to the liability component would then be further allocated first to the derivative liability component based on its fair value with the residual proceeds then allocated to the debt host liability component. Further, if both the conversion option and another embedded derivative feature are required to be separated under FAS 133, they should be accounted for as a single, compound derivative instrument (FAS 133, DIG B15) with the initial carrying amounts determined by first allocating proceeds equal to the fair value of the compound derivative to the derivative liability component and then allocating the residual proceeds to debt host liability component.

3.3 Conversion of a compound instrument

Upon conversion of a compound instrument equity is issued and the liability component is derecognised. The original equity component recognised at inception remains in equity (although it may be reclassified from one line item of equity to another). No gain or loss is recognised on conversion. [IAS 32.AG32]

Example 3.3A

Convertible debt: issue of new shares

Assume the facts are as in **example 3.1A** but the date now is 31 December 20X6 (i.e. the end of year 2 of the instrument's life). Assume that due to a rapidly rising share price all holders of the bond exercise their right to convert it into a fixed number of equity instruments of the entity at this point in time.

The liability has been accounted for at amortised cost using the effective interest rate method (see **4.1** in **chapter 6**).

At 31 December 20X6 the following applies:

- the amortised cost carrying amount of the liability (determined using the effective interest rate method) just before conversion is CU1,944,954;
- the original equity component just before conversion still stands at the original CU151,878; and
- upon conversion 500,000 equity shares will be issued (250 equity shares per bond x 2,000 bonds issued) where each equity share has a nominal value of CU1.

The accounting entries on conversion are as follows:

Dr	Bond	1,944,954	to remove the liability from the statement of financial position on conversion
Cr	Equity	1,944,954	to recognise the issue of shares as a result of conversion

The original component of equity, CU151,878, may be reclassified to another line item within equity.

Example 3.3B

Convertible debt: issue of treasury shares

Assume the facts as in **example 3.1A** above except that instead of issuing new shares upon conversion the entity satisfies the requirement for equity shares to be delivered to the bondholders through the use of treasury shares. Rather than issuing 500,000 new equity shares the entity will deliver to bondholders upon conversion 500,000 of its own shares that it had previously repurchased and held as treasury shares.

The accounting entries in this case would be:

Dr	Bond	1,944,954	to remove liability from statement of financial position as a result of conversion
Cr	Equity	1,944,954	to remove the treasury shares from equity

The original component of equity, CU151,878, may be reclassified to another line item within equity.

US GAAP comparison: US GAAP indicates that upon **extinguishment** of convertible debt the difference between the cash acquisition price of the debt and its net carrying amount should be recognised currently in income in the period of extinguishment as losses or gains (APB 26). However, APB 26 does not apply to a **conversion** of debt nor does it specify the accounting for conversion of debt. In practice, the carrying amounts of the debt, including any unamortised premium or discount, and any separately recognised derivative liability are credited to the capital accounts upon conversion to reflect the shares issued and no gain or loss is recognised (AIN-APB 26, EITF 85–17, EITF 08–4). US GAAP further clarifies that the conversion of debt to common or preferred shares is not an extinguishment if the conversion represents the exercise of a conversion right contained in the terms of the debt at issuance (FTB 80–1). Exceptions to this general practice include:

(1) At conversion of convertible debt that has been either (a) separated into a debt host and a derivative liability and the derivative liability has been subsequently reclassified to equity (EITF 06–7), or (b) separated into a liability and an equity component because the conversion option is in the money for the holder at the commitment date (EITF 98–5, EITF 00–27, and EITF 08–4), any unamortised discount associated with the debt is immediately recognised as interest expense.

(2) At conversion of convertible debt that has been bifurcated into a liability and an equity component because the convertible debt may be settled in cash upon conversion (including partial cash settlement) (FSP APB 14–1), a portion of the fair value of the shares transferred is allocated to the extinguishment of the liability component equal to the fair value of that component immediately prior to conversion and a gain or loss is recognised and the remaining portion is allocated to reacquisition of the equity component as a reduction of equity.

US GAAP indicates that upon **extinguishment** of convertible debt the difference between the cash acquisition price of the debt and its net carrying amount should be recognised currently in income in the period of extinguishment as losses or gains (APB 26). However, APB 26 does not apply to a **conversion** of debt nor does the Opinion specify the accounting for conversion of debt. In practice, the carrying amount of the debt, including any unamortised premium or discount, is credited to the capital accounts upon conversion to reflect the stock issued and no gain or loss is recognised (AIN-APB 26). US GAAP further clarifies that the conversion of debt to common or preferred stock is not an extinguishment if the conversion represents the exercise of a conversion right contained in the terms of the debt at issuance (FTB 80–1).

3.4 Early redemption of compound instrument

Where an entity redeems or repurchases a convertible instrument before its maturity (without altering the conversion feature) through a tender offer the consideration paid to do so (including any transaction costs) is allocated to the liability and equity components at the date of the early redemption/early repurchase. The method used to make this allocation is the same as that used to make the original allocation of the proceeds of the issue of the instrument between the liability and equity components upon initial recognition. [IAS 32.AG33]

To the extent that the amount of the consideration allocated to the liability component exceeds the carrying amount of the liability component at that point in time, a loss is recognised in profit or loss. Conversely, to the extent that the consideration allocated is smaller than the carrying amount of the liability a gain is recognised in profit or loss.

The amount of consideration allocated to equity is recognised in equity with no gain or loss being recognised (the equity component that is not eliminated may be reclassified to another line item within equity).

Example 3.4

Convertible debt: repurchase

Using the same scenario as in **example 3.1A** assume that one year has elapsed and it is now 31 December 20X5 (i.e. the convertible bonds have been outstanding for one year).

In respect of the first year (year ended 31 December 20X5) the following accounting entries will have been made:

Dr	Interest Expense	166,331
Cr	Bond Liability	166,331

To recognise the interest expense and amortised cost of the bond using an effective interest rate of 9 per cent.

Dr	Bond Liability	120,000
Cr	Cash	120,000

To recognise the cash payment of interest.

This gives a carrying amount of the liability at the end of the first year equal to CU1,894,453.

	CU
Initial carrying amount at inception	1,848,122
Accretion in year 1 using the effective interest method	166,331
Cash coupon payment at end of year 1	(120,000)
Carrying amount at end of year 1	1,894,453

At the end of the first year Entity A repurchases the convertible bonds for a cash amount of CU2,100,000. It is established that at the date of repurchase the entity could have issued a non convertible instrument with a term of 2 years bearing a coupon rate of 7 per cent.

The consideration paid is allocated to the liability and equity components using the same method as used on initial recognition of the convertible bonds. Namely, the fair value of consideration paid is first allocated to the liability component with the residual being assigned to the repurchase of the equity component:

	Fair value of repurchase consideration	**Carrying amount prior to repurchase**	**Differ-ence**
	CU	CU	CU
Liability component:			
Present value of 2 remaining interest payments of CU120,000 discounted at 7 per cent and 9 per cent respectively	216,963	211,093	
Present value of principal amount due in 2 years time of CU2 million discounted at 7 per cent and 9 per cent respectively	1,746,877	1,683,360	
	1,963,840	1,894,453	69,387
Equity component	136,160*	151,878	(15,718)
Total	2,100,000	2,046,331	53,669

* The amount of CU136,160 represents the difference between the repurchase price of CU2,100,000 and the amount of the consideration paid allocated to the liability component.

Having completed the allocation of the repurchase price, the following entries are made by Entity A in respect of the repurchase of the bonds:

Dr	Bond liability	CU1,894,453
Dr	Debt extinguishment loss	CU69,387
Cr	Cash	CU1,963,840

To recognise the repurchase of the liability and the loss on doing so

Dr	Equity	CU136,160
Cr	Cash	CU136,160

To recognise the portion of the cash paid in respect of the repurchase of the equity component.

The remaining balance of CU15,718 can be transferred into a different line item in equity.

3.4.1 Early redemption of convertible bond by the issuer exercising an embedded call option

Repurchase through a tender offer of convertible debt is explicitly addressed in the application guidance to IAS 32 as described above but early redemption via the issuer exercising an embedded call option is not. Consider the following scenario. Entity B (whose functional currency is Euro) issues a convertible bond for €10m on 1 January 20X0. The bond is redeemable at the par amount of €10m at 31 December 20X9. The bond pays interest of 4% on the par amount on 31 December throughout its life. The holder can convert the bond into a fixed number of equity shares at any point from 1 January 20X5 to 31 December 20X9. In addition under the terms of the call option embedded in the convertible bond the issuer may redeem the instrument early by paying the par amount of €10m at any point between 1 January 20X5 and 31 December 20X9.

The convertible bond is classified as a compound instrument with a financial liability and equity component by Entity B. As discussed in **section 7.1** in **chapter 5** the call option is deemed to be closely related and is therefore not separately accounted for on the basis of a comparison of the exercise price of the option (amount repayable if called) to the amortised cost of the instrument before separating the equity component under IAS 32. Assume the issuer does make use of the call option on 1 January 20X5 and redeems the instrument under the terms of the option at this date. The question then arises as to how to account for the redemption of the convertible bond by Entity B.

One way of accounting for the use of the call option would be to account for it as part of the debt instrument to which it is closely related. This would necessitate remeasuring the amortised cost of the financial liability component of the convertible debt under IAS 39.AG8 as discussed in **section 4.1.2** in **chapter 6.** This would involve discounting the revised estimate of cash flows payable under the instrument (to include the €10m that will be payable immediately under the terms of the option) at the original effective interest rate established at initial recognition of the financial liability component of the convertible debt. The difference between the previous amortised cost carrying amount and the newly remeasured amount would be recognised in profit or loss. This would have the effect of recognising a loss equal to par less the carrying amount from the prior reporting period.

Alternatively, it may be argued that the guidance under IAS 32.AG33 discussed earlier in this section should be applied as this refers to redemption. Under this approach the consideration paid to redeem the convertible debt would be allocated to the financial liability and equity components at the date of the early redemption using the same method as that used to make the allocation between the financial liability and equity component on initial recognition of the compound instrument. However, as the fair value of the financial liability component once the option has been exercised is likely to be equal to the redemption price this method would allocate all of the consideration (i.e. the redemption price) to the financial liability component. Therefore the effect would be likely to be substantially the same as the remeasurement under IAS 39.AG8 as discussed above.

US GAAP comparison: As noted in **section 3** above, US GAAP does not generally require separation of an equity component, with certain exceptions. Accordingly, upon early redemption, entities do not generally allocate proceeds between the debt and equity components. Instead, entities generally derecognise the instrument and recognise a gain or loss in earnings for any difference between the current carrying amount and the redemption proceeds (see **3.3** above). When separation is required due to an exception, there are exceptions to the general practice of derecognition as well, including:

1) At early redemption of convertible debt that has been separated into a debt host and a derivative liability and the derivative liability has been subsequently reclassified to equity (EITF 06–7), the portion of the reacquisition price equal to the fair value of the conversion option at the date of the extinguishment should be allocated to equity and the remaining reacquisition price should be allocated to the extinguishment of the debt to determine the amount of gain or loss.

2) At early redemption of convertible debt that has been separated into a liability and an equity component because the conversion option is in the money for the holder at the commitment date

(EITF 98–5, EITF 00–27, and EITF 08–4), the portion of the reacquisition price equal to the intrinsic value of the conversion option at the date of extinguishment should be allocated to equity and the remaining reacquisition price should be allocated to the extinguishment of the debt to determine the amount of gain or loss.

3) At early redemption of convertible debt that has been separated into a liability and an equity component because the convertible debt may be settled in cash upon conversion (including partial cash settlement) (FSP APB 14–1), a portion of the fair value of the shares transferred is allocated to the extinguishment of the liability component equal to the fair value of that component immediately prior to conversion and a gain or loss is recognised and the remaining portion is allocated to reacquisition of the equity component as a reduction of equity.

US GAAP further clarifies that the issuance of equity securities to settle a debt instrument (pursuant to the instrument's original conversion terms) that became convertible upon the issuer's exercise of a call option should be accounted for as a conversion if the debt instrument contained a substantive conversion feature as of its issuance date. That is, no gain or loss should be recognised related to the equity securities issued to settle the instrument. The issuance of equity securities to settle a debt instrument that became convertible upon the issuer's exercise of a call option should be accounted for as a debt extinguishment if the debt instrument did not contain a substantive conversion feature as of its issuance date. That is, the fair value of the equity securities issued should be considered a component of the reacquisition price of the debt (EITF 05–1).

3.5 Amendment of the terms of a compound instrument to induce early conversion

An entity may amend the terms of the convertible instrument during its life so as to make conversion more attractive through either offering a more favourable conversion ratio, paying additional consideration in the event of conversion before a specified date, or a combination of both. In such instances the difference between the fair value of the consideration that the holder receives upon conversion under the revised terms and the fair value of the consideration that the holder would have received upon conversion under the original terms, measured at the date when the terms are amended, should be recognised in profit or loss as a loss. [IAS 32.AG35]

Example 3.5

Convertible debt: inducement to convert

Assume the same scenario as in **example 3.1A**, but at 31 December 20X5 (i.e. the end of year 1 of the instrument's life) to induce holders to convert promptly Entity A amends the terms in one of two ways in respect of conversions that take place prior to 1 March 20X6:

Scenario 1: Entity A alters the terms such that each of the 2,000 bonds converts into 300 equity shares of the entity, instead of 250 equity shares as under the original conversion terms (assume the market value of the equity shares at the date of the amendment is CU5).

Scenario 2: Entity A states that it will pay an additional CU1 in cash in relation to each share converted.

The liability and equity components have the following carrying amounts in the statement of financial position at 31 December 20X5:

	CU
Liability component:	
- present value of 2 remaining interest payments of CU120,000 discounted at 9 per cent	211,093
- present value of principal amount of CU2m due in 2 years time discounted at 9 per cent	1,683,360
	1,894,453
Equity component	151,878*
Total	**2,046,331**

* The equity component remains unchanged since the allocation on initial recognition.

The following entries will be necessary to recognise the amendment of the terms of the convertible:

Scenario 1

Number of equity shares to be issued to bondholders under the *amended* conversion terms:

- number of bonds issued	2,000
- number of shares to be issued per bond on conversion	300
Total number of equity shares to be issued on conversion	600,000

Number of equity shares to be issued to bondholders under *original* conversion terms:

- number of bonds issued	2,000
- number of shares to be issued per bond on conversion	250
Total number of equity shares to be issued on conversion	500,000

Number of incremental equity shares to be issued to bondholders upon conversion: 100,000

Value of incremental equity shares to be issued to bondholders upon conversion:

100,000 * CU5 = CU500,000

Therefore the entry needed to recognise the amendment of the terms is:

Dr	Expense on amendment of terms of convertible (profit or loss)	CU500,000
Cr	Equity	CU500,000

Upon conversion the accounting would follow the approach laid out in **example 3.3A.**

Scenario 2

The additional consideration to be paid in the event of conversion would amount to:

500,000 * CU1 = CU500,000

This would again be recognised through the following double entries:

Dr	Expense on amendment of terms of convertible (profit or loss)	CU500,000
Cr	Financial liability	CU500,000

Upon conversion the accounting would follow the approach laid out in **example 3.3A** except in so far as an extra entry would be necessary to recognise the payment of the additional cash inducement as follows:

Dr	Financial liability	CU500,000
Cr	Cash	CU500,000

Upon non-conversion an entry would be necessary to derecognise the inducement that the holder has not taken up:

Dr	Financial liability	CU500,000
Cr	Gain upon non-exercise of inducement (profit or loss)	CU500,000

As described in **3.3** above, upon conversion of a compound instrument equity is issued and the liability component is derecognised. The original equity component recognised at inception remains in equity (although it may be reclassified from one line item of equity to another) and no gain or loss is recognised on conversion. This treatment equally applies for conversion of a compound instrument where previously there was an inducement and an expense in profit or loss and increase in equity was recognised. Upon conversion of the compound instrument the financial liability is derecognised and reclassified to equity. Equity will therefore consist of the original equity component recognised on issue of the compound instrument, the amount recognised in equity as a result of inducement, plus the reclassification of the liability upon conversion. Amounts may be transferred within equity from one line item to another upon conversion of the compound instrument.

US GAAP comparison: US GAAP indicates that when convertible debt is converted to equity securities of the debtor pursuant to an inducement offer the debtor enterprise should recognise an expense equal to the fair value of all securities and other consideration transferred in the transaction in excess of the fair value of securities issuable pursuant to the original conversion terms (FAS 84, FSP APB 14–1). The conversion accounting discussed in **3.3** above would then be applied using the fair value of the consideration that was issuable in accordance with the original conversion terms.

3.6 Treatment of mandatorily convertible instruments

An entity may issue an instrument that at the end of its life is mandatorily convertible into a fixed number of its equity shares (rather than conversion being at the option of the holder). This instrument is, in substance, a prepaid forward purchase of the entity's equity shares. As the instrument carries an obligation for the issuer to make fixed interest payments during the life of the mandatorily convertible, the instrument includes a financial liability component. The following example illustrates the entries for a mandatorily convertible debt instrument.

Example 3.6

Mandatorily convertible instrument

A CU functional currency entity issues a mandatorily convertible instrument for CU100,000 on 1 January 20X5. The instrument obligates the entity to make cash coupon payments of CU5,000 on both 31 December 20X5 and 31 December 20X6. In addition, at the end of the instrument's life on 31 December 20X6, after the last coupon payment is made, the instrument will mandatorily convert into 5,000 CU1 ordinary shares of the entity.

At inception of the instrument the following two elements will be separated.

- A liability component arising from the coupon payments of CU5,000 to be made on 31 December 20X5 and 31 December 20X6. This will be determined as the present value of the payments discounted at the rate that would have been applicable if the entity had issued a debt instrument with similar features and of similar credit standing but without the mandatory conversion feature.

- An equity component representing the delivery of equity in the future. This amount will be determined as the residual amount after the liability component is deducted from the fair value of the whole compound instrument at inception (CU100,000).

If on the basis of the above method the liability component is determined to constitute, for example, CU9,000 at inception (based on a discount rate of 7.32 per cent) the following entries will be necessary on initial recognition of the instrument:

Dr	Cash	CU100,000
Cr	Financial liability	CU9,000
Cr	Equity	CU91,000

Over the life of the instrument the following entries will be made with respect to the liability such that by the end of the instrument's life the liability component will no longer be present:

Year end 31 December 20X5

Dr	Interest expense	CU659
Cr	Financial liability	CU659

To account for the liability at amortised cost using the effective interest rate of 7.32 per cent.

Dr	Financial liability	CU5,000
Cr	Cash	CU5,000

To account for the cash coupon payment of CU5,000

Year end 31 December 20X6

Dr	Interest expense	CU341
Cr	Financial liability	CU341

To account for the liability at amortised cost using the effective interest rate of 7.32 per cent.

Dr	Financial liability	CU5,000
Cr	Cash	CU5,000

To account for the cash coupon payment of CU5,000

When the instrument is mandatorily converted into 5,000 ordinary shares of the entity via the issue of new ordinary shares (with nominal value of CU1 each) the following entries will be necessary to reclassify the amount originally recognised as equity:

Dr	Equity	CU91,000
Cr	Equity – share capital	CU5,000
Cr	Equity – share premium	CU86,000

3.7 Convertible debt with multiple settlement options

Throughout **section 3** so far, it was assumed that the equity conversion option can only be gross physically settled, i.e. a fixed number of shares is delivered on conversion of the bond. However, this may not always be the case. As explained in **section 6** below, if the settlement of the call option can be achieved in ways other than by delivery of a fixed number of shares for a fixed amount of cash, the call option is treated as a derivative and is carried at fair value with gains and losses recognised in profit or loss.

Some convertible debt instruments include cash settlement options. The contractual terms of such an instrument allow that in the event of the holder of the instrument demanding conversion the issuer has a choice over the manner in which the call option is settled: the issuer may deliver either a fixed number of shares to the holder, or an amount of cash equal to the market value of the fixed number of shares on the date of conversion or an average price in a period before conversion. As the issuer will not always deliver a fixed amount of equity for receipt of a fixed amount of cash upon conversion, the conversion feature does not meet the definition of equity. The written call option is accounted for as a derivative liability. The convertible debt is a hybrid instrument containing a host debt contract and an embedded derivative liability (written call option over own shares). The embedded derivative is measured at fair value with changes in fair value recognised in profit or loss. The treatment of hybrid instruments is explained in **chapter 5**.

Example 3.7

Convertible debt: cash settlement choice at conversion

On 1 January 20X1 Entity X issues a convertible bond with a face value of CU10 million at par. The instrument has a maturity of 10 years and pays an annual coupon of 5 per cent on 31 December. The bond is convertible at maturity at the discretion of the holder. However, if the holder does exercise the right to convert Entity X can either:

- deliver a fixed number of Entity X's ordinary shares; or
- pay an amount of cash equal to the fixed number of shares under the conversion option multiplied by the average share price of Entity X's ordinary shares in the 10 days immediately preceding maturity.

As the written call option within the convertible instrument may be settled in cash rather than through the delivery of a fixed number of shares it does not meet the definition of equity and must be accounted for as an embedded derivative. Entity X will need to recognise a derivative liability at fair value on 1 January 20X1. The difference between the fair value of the total hybrid instrument and the fair value of the embedded derivative is assigned to the host contract, with the host accounted for at amortised cost. This accounting treatment applies if the entire financial instrument is not designated as at fair value through profit or loss at initial recognition (see **3.1.1** in **chapter 2**).

Assume that at 1 January 20X1 the fair value of the written call option is equal to CU1.5 million. The entries on 1 January 20X1 would be as follows:

Dr	Cash	CU10,000,000
Cr	Financial liability (host contract)	CU8,500,000
Cr	Derivative financial liability	CU1,500,000

Entity X will account for the host contract at amortised cost by applying the effective interest rate of 7.15 per cent, and the derivative will be re-measured to its fair value. On 31 December 20X1 the amortised cost of the host debt contract is equal to CU9,107,750 and the fair value of the embedded derivative is equal to CU2,450,000. Therefore, the entries are as follows:

Dr	Interest expense	CU607,750
Cr	Financial liability (host contract)	CU607,750
Dr	Financial liability (host contract)	CU500,000
Cr	Cash	CU500,000

To recognise the host debt contract at amortised cost and payment of contractual coupon

Dr	Derivative loss	CU950,000
Cr	Derivative financial liability	CU950,000

To recognise fair value movement of embedded derivative in profit or loss

US GAAP comparison: As noted in **section 3** and **3.1** above, convertible debt instruments that, by their stated terms, may be settled in cash (or other assets) upon conversion, including partial cash settlement, and for which the embedded conversion option is not required to be separated as a derivative liability component under FAS 133 (FSP APB 14–1) are required to be separated into different liability and equity components with the initial carrying amounts determined by first allocating proceeds equal to the fair value of a similar debt instrument without an associated equity component to the liability component and then allocating the residual proceeds to the equity component.

3.8 Foreign currency denominated convertible debt

An entity may issue an instrument denominated in a foreign currency (currency other than functional currency of the entity) that is convertible into a fixed number of ordinary shares of the entity. Such an instrument contains a written option to exchange a fixed number of equity instruments for a fixed amount of cash that is denominated in a foreign currency.

As explained in **section 6** of this chapter a derivative contract over an entity's own equity is accounted for as equity only where it will be settled exclusively by the entity delivering (or receiving) a fixed number of its own equity instruments in exchange for a fixed amount of cash or another financial asset.

For foreign currency denominated convertible debt the question arises whether the equity conversion option meets the definition of equity when the consideration the issuer receives for issuing a fixed number of shares is forgiveness of a debt instrument that is variable in functional currency terms. The same question also applies to freestanding instruments, for example, a stand alone physically settled written call over own shares that will be settled at exercise through an exchange of a fixed number of own shares for a fixed amount of foreign currency cash.

A gross physically settled derivative over a fixed number of own equity shares meets the definition of equity only if the amount of cash or financial assets paid or received is fixed in the *functional currency* of the issuer. The following guidance is relevant.

- A derivative over a fixed number of equity shares that is exchanged for a variable amount of cash is a derivative, and not equity. For example, an instrument that requires an exchange of a fixed number of equity shares for a variable amount of cash calculated to equal the value of 100 ounces of gold is a derivative since the fair value of the derivative is driven from movements in the gold price as well as the equity price. [IAS 32.24]

- IAS 39 considers that although foreign denominated monetary items and foreign currency forecast transactions are fixed in foreign currency terms, they are variable in functional currency terms and, therefore, are eligible to be designated in a cash flow hedge. [IAS 39.IG.F.3.3 & F.3.4]

Applying this guidance to foreign currency denominated convertible debt, it is clear that (1) the foreign currency convertible whilst fixed in foreign currency terms, is variable in functional currency terms and therefore a fixed number of shares will be delivered in exchange for a variable amount of cash; and (2) conversion will occur based on the interaction of not only the equity price but the foreign currency value of the bond that is forgiven.

The IFRIC referred the issue to the IASB where, in September 2005, the Board explored whether to amend IAS 32 to permit contracts to be classified as equity if they are to be settled by an entity delivering a fixed number of its own equity instruments for a fixed amount of cash or another financial asset denominated in a foreign currency. The Board noted the amendment would result in equity and foreign exchange features whose values are interdependent being recognised in equity, and that excluding from equity the value attributable to the foreign exchange features would require arbitrary rules. The Board also noted that allowing dual indexed contracts (to share price and foreign exchange rates) to be classified as equity would require additional and detailed guidance to avoid structuring opportunities aimed at obtaining a desired accounting result. The Board therefore decided not to proceed with an amendment to IAS 32.

Example 3.8

Foreign currency denominated convertible debt

Entity A has a functional currency of Sterling. Entity A issues a convertible bond denominated in US dollars that, if converted, will result in the gross physical delivery of a fixed number of Entity A's Sterling-denominated shares.

The convertible bond will be classified in it entirety as a financial liability as upon conversion a fixed amount of shares will be delivered in exchange for a variable amount of functional currency cash, being the forgiveness of the bond obligation.

If a parent and subsidiary have the same functional currency and either the parent issues a foreign currency denominated convertible bond that is convertible into a fixed number of subsidiary's shares, or the subsidiary issues a foreign currency convertible bond that is convertible into a fixed number of parent's shares, the instrument in both cases would be classified wholly as a liability in the consolidated financial statements as a fixed number of shares is exchanged for a variable amount of functional currency cash.

The accounting for convertible debt issued by an entity in the group that is convertible into a fixed number of equity instruments of another entity in the group is more complex when the bond is denominated in the functional currency of one of the entities. The IFRIC discussed this scenario but did not take the issue onto their agenda as they considered the issue was too narrow. In the absence of specific guidance it is not clear whether a group should look to the functional currency of the issuer of the fixed number of shares or the functional currency of the issuer of the convertible bond. A group should establish a policy as to how it determines what is a fixed amount of functional currency cash in the instance when different entities in the group issue the convertible instrument and issue the shares, should the instrument be converted. This policy should be applied consistently to all similar instruments.

US GAAP comparison: A conversion option embedded in a convertible debt instrument that is denominated in a currency other than the issuer's functional currency is not considered to be indexed to the issuer's own equity shares (EITF 07–5). Such an option would not qualify for the scope exception afforded instruments indexed to the issuer's own equity shares (and classified in equity) and if it otherwise met the definition of a derivative, it would be required to be separated from the debt host as a derivative liability under FAS 133.

3.9 Anti-dilutive provisions in convertible debt

Convertible debt will normally include anti-dilutive provisions within the contractual terms of the instrument to ensure that the holder of the convertible bond's potential interest in the equity of the issuer is not diluted in certain events. For an equity conversion feature to be considered equity it must result in the exchange of a fixed amount of cash or other financial asset for a fixed number of equity instruments (the 'fixed-for-fixed criterion'). As anti-dilutive provisions result in the number of shares that will be delivered to the holder of the convertible bond upon conversion changing subject to specified events, care needs to be taken in determining whether such provisions result in the equity conversion feature failing equity treatment because it fails the fixed-for-fixed criterion.

IAS 32 does not provide any guidance on whether anti-dilutive provisions in convertible debt result in the equity conversion feature failing equity treatment. Most anti-dilutive provisions are structured so as to 'make-whole' the holder of the convertible bond if certain events occur. For example, if the issuer decides to issue more ordinary shares while the convertible debt is outstanding, e.g. through a bonus issue, the conversion feature will be adjusted to reflect the increased number of shares in issue. This adjustment attempts to put the convertible debt holder in the same economic position relative to existing ordinary share holders as they were immediately prior to the issue of the new shares. An adjustment to the number of shares to be delivered under the conversion option that makes whole the holder of the convertible debt relative to existing ordinary shareholders is not deemed to breach the 'fixed-for-fixed' criterion. A different conclusion would be reached if the adjustment to the conversion ratio benefited the convertible bondholder at the expense of the expense of the non-convertible bondholders. The same principle can be applied in the instance when the number of shares is adjusted due to the issuer entering into a buy back of its own shares in the market while the convertible debt is outstanding. In this instance, the number of shares under the conversion feature will decrease reflecting that there are less ordinary shares outstanding. If the adjustment to the conversion ratio only reflects the reduction in the number of outstanding shares and does not advantage the convertible bondholder the existence of the anti-dilution feature would not breach the 'fixed-for-fixed' criterion.

Convertible debt may permit the holder to convert into a fixed percentage of the outstanding shares of the entity, say 5% of the entity. In this instance the number of shares does potentially vary, as the number of shares that may be delivered under conversion of the debt is not known until the date of conversion. Even though the number of shares is not fixed in this instance, the conversion feature does not breach the 'fixed-for-fixed' criterion as the feature ensures that the holder of the convertible debt has the same relative potential equity interest in the issuer relative to the existing ordinary shareholders. This feature is economically the same as fixing the conversion ratio at date of issue of the convertible debt but then including anti-dilutive provisions for bonus issues, share buy backs etc as described above to preserve the potential equity interest of the convertible debt holder.

Anti-dilutive provisions linked to dividend payments are also common. Should the issuer pay dividends on its existing ordinary shares an adjustment to the conversion ratio may occur which attempts to compensate the holder of the convertible debt in the instance when dividends paid are in excess of a specified level. This provision attempts to compensate the holder of the convertible bond in the instance when a 'special dividend' is paid which is akin to a return of capital to the existing ordinary shareholders. In this instance the conversion ratio that was determined when the convertible bond was issued assumes a certain level of dividend payments between the date when the instrument was issued and the date when conversion can occur. The adjustment to the conversion features makes-whole the difference between the amount of the special dividend and the amount of the dividends expected to be paid. An alternative provision is where the number of shares under the conversion feature is adjusted for the actual dividend paid in a period while the convertible bond is outstanding. In this instance, the conversion ratio that was determined when the convertible bond was issued assumed no dividend payments between the date when the instrument was issued and the date when conversion can occur. The number of shares to be delivered under the conversion feature is adjusted so the conversion price is equal to that which would have been determined had the issuer known at inception exactly what dividends it was going to be paying in the future. Both anti-dilutive provisions in this case are not deemed to breach the 'fixed-for-fixed' criterion as they both compensate the holder of the convertible debt relative to existing ordinary shareholders.

Many convertible debt instruments contain change of control protection clauses in the terms and conditions of the instruments. The clauses vary considerably so it is not possible to generalise whether such clauses prevent compound instrument accounting for convertible debt. A common clause attempts to provide the convertible bond holders with an enhanced conversion ratio following a change of control of the issuer in order to compensate the convertible bond holders for the loss of time value in the option if the bond holder converts early. The instrument will often contain a right for the issuer to redeem early the convertible bond for par for a period immediately following a change of control. It is this issuer call that may incentivise the convertible bond holders to convert and in doing so entitle them to an additional number of shares to reflect that, absent conversion, the newly acquired entity will buy back the convertible bond at par and the convertible bond holder will lose the remaining value of the conversion option.

The terms and conditions of the instrument will generally either stipulate a predetermined adjusted conversion ratio which varies depending on when the change of control occurs during the life of the instrument (with the conversion ratio adjusted less the closer the change of control occurs to maturity of the instrument) or be include a formula which attempts to determine the value of the remaining time value in the conversion option at the date of change of control and adjusts the conversion ratio to reflect this value.

If the objective of the change in the conversion ratio is to preserve the rights and value of the bond holders following a change of control by providing additional shares on conversion equal to the value of the remaining time value of the conversion option on the date of change of control, this feature would not breach the fixed-for-fixed criterion.

US GAAP comparison: A conversion option embedded in a convertible debt instrument that meets the definition of a derivative on an as-if-freestanding basis is not separated from the debt host as a derivative liability if it qualifies for the scope exception afforded instruments indexed to the entity's own equity shares and classified in equity. To be considered indexed to the entity's own equity shares (i.e., the first part of the scope exception), the conversion option must pass a two-step evaluation (EITF 07–5):

(1) any exercise contingency is not based on (a) an observable market, other than the market for the entity's equity shares (if applicable), or (b) an observable index, other than an index calculated or measured solely by reference to the entity's own operations and

(2) either the settlement amount of the conversion option would need to equal the difference between the fair value of a fixed number of the entity's equity shares and a fixed monetary amount ('fixed-for-fixed') or, if the conversion option's strike price or the number of shares used to calculate the settlement amount are not fixed (e.g. because of anti-dilution provisions), the only variables that could affect the settlement amount would need to be inputs to the fair value of a "fixed-for-fixed" option on equity shares.

The fair value inputs of a fixed-for-fixed option on equity shares may include the entity's share price and additional variables, including the strike price of the instrument, term of the instrument, expected dividends or other dilutive activities, share borrow cost, interest rates, share price volatility, the entity's credit spread, and the ability to maintain a standard hedge position in the underlying shares.

If a conversion option's strike price or the number of shares used to calculate the settlement amount would be adjusted upon the occurrence of an exercise contingency, the exercise contingency would be evaluated under Step 1 and the potential adjustment to the conversion option's settlement amount would be evaluated under Step 2.

3.10 Other variations in convertible debt

It is not possible to provide an exhaustive list of different variations in conversion features in convertible debt. However, some further examples and discussion of the accounting analysis are included below.

3.10.1 Discounted convertible debt

Convertible debt may be issued such that the investor receives some of the interest on the instrument in the form of fixed cash coupons and some in the form of accretion up to the par amount. For instance an entity may issue convertible debt for CU90 that is convertible into a fixed number of equity shares at any time and pays an annual coupon of 1% based on the par amount of CU100. If the holder does not choose to convert the instrument into the fixed number of equity shares the bond will be redeemed at maturity for the par amount of CU100. When considering whether "fixed cash" is being received as consideration for issuing shares under the conversion option the amount of the liability forgiven needs to be considered. The amount of the liability forgiven could be argued to change with the passage of time, i.e. is variable, because the instrument has been issued at a discount and therefore the investor is giving up a bond piece that is changing over the life as the discount is unwound. However, it would seem inappropriate to consider this a breach of the 'fixed cash' criteria for two reasons. Firstly, the par amount remains constant and therefore the nominal of the bond remains unchanged. Secondly, the unwinding of the discount to par is part of the interest on the bond component. When compared to a conventional fixed rate convertible debt issued at par (i.e. without a discount) the conversion option always results in the holder giving up a variable amount of future interest receipts. As the instrument's life shortens the amount of interest forgiven by the holder reduces. Such variability in the amount forgiven by the holder is not considered variability in cash in determining whether the conversion option meets the definition of equity.

3.10.2 *LIBOR-linked convertible debt*

Convertible debt usually carries a fixed rate of interest, or as described above may be partly issued at a discount and therefore economically pays a fixed amount of interest at maturity. If the interest on convertible debt is linked to LIBOR (or an equivalent benchmark interest rate) and the instrument is not issued at a discount then all interest flows are variable. It could be argued that the conversion feature breaches the 'fixed cash' criteria as the interest forgiveness is always changing. Similar to the analysis above for discounted convertible bond it would be inappropriate to consider variable interest to be a breach of the 'fixed cash' criteria. Firstly, the par amount remains constant and therefore the nominal of the bond remains unchanged Secondly, IAS 32.22 specifically states that *"changes in the fair value of a contract arising from variations in market interest rates that do not affect the amount of cash or other financial assets to be paid or received on settlement of the contract"* do not preclude equity classification. If the fixed cash is considered the par amount and the LIBOR interest is considered to be merely servicing the 'fixed cash' criterion is not breached. Such an instrument would therefore be treated as a compound instrument that contains a financial liability and an equity component.

If instead the interest payments were driven not by LIBOR, but say by another variable that was not a market rate of interest, for example changes in inflation, the same conclusion would not be appropriate and therefore the instrument would not be a compound instrument, rather it would be treated as a financial liability in its entirety. The issuer would need to consider whether the inflation linkage was a closely related embedded derivative in the case where the instrument was not classified as at fair value through profit or loss. Guidance on embedded derivatives is detailed in **chapter 5**.

3.10.3 *Convertible debt where conversion is into a differing number of shares that depends on the share price at the date of conversion*

Convertible debt that permits the holder to convert the instrument into a number of shares that is not always a fixed number as it changes with share price at the date of conversion is not a compound instrument. For example, the conversion feature may be forgiveness of a fixed amount of functional currency debt (i.e. principal and any future interest) for a fixed number of shares, say 10.0 shares, if the share price is above CU100 but below CU110, but 9.5 shares if the share price is above CU110 but below CU120, and 9.0 shares if the share price is above CU120. The number of shares to be delivered is based on a sliding scale that reduces as the share price increases. In this case, the conversion feature does not meet the definition of equity as the conversion does not result in the delivery of a fixed number of shares.

It is not possible to consider the conversion feature as three separate conversion features that each have a right to convert the same fixed amount of cash (being principal and interest) for a fixed amount of shares as the conversion features are mutually exclusive. There can only ever be one conversion feature that can be exercised (equally there can only ever be one fixed amount of cash that is forgiven as consideration for the issue of shares) as following conversion the instrument is extinguished.

3.10.4 *Convertible debt where conversion is into a fixed number of shares or variable number of shares to the value of the debt component*

Consider an example where convertible debt permits the holder to convert into a fixed number of shares when the share price is above a specified level, but also allows the holder to forgive the debt component (being principal and interest) by electing for a variable number of shares equal to the par value of the debt component when the share price is below that specified level. On the face of it, and consistent with the example described above, as the instrument does not always result in the delivery of a fixed number of shares it could be argued that the instrument does not have any equity element, i.e. the entire instrument is a financial liability. However, the right for the holder to require repayment of debt in a variable number of shares is not itself a conversion feature, rather it is a settlement alternative inherent in the debt component. The payment of interest and principal, regardless of how it is settled is a financial liability. The inclusion of a feature that permits the holder to early redeem the instrument by requiring the issuer to deliver a variable number of shares equal to the par amount of the debt when the share price is below a specified level is merely an early redemption option. Put another way, when the share price is below a specified level the holder can require the convertible debt to be early redeemed and the issuer is required to use its own shares as currency for this early redemption. The right to convert into a fixed number of shares when the share price is above the specified level is an equity instrument as it permits the holder to require the issuer to deliver a fixed amount of shares in exchange for a fixed amount of cash (being the principal and interest, and the 'shares to the value of' settlement alternative on that principal and interest).

3.10.5 *Convertible debt that is convertible only on a contingent event*

The issuer of convertible debt that is convertible only upon the occurrence of a contingent event that is outside the control of the holder and the issuer must first determine whether, if the event occurs, the conversion would result in the delivery of a fixed number of equity instruments for a fixed amount of functional currency cash. Put another way, ignoring the contingent element, would the instrument be a compound instrument with an equity and debt component? If the answer to this question is yes, then the fact that the holder can only convert if a contingent event has occurred does not prevent the conversion feature being presented as equity. The inclusion of the contingency merely reduces the likelihood of the conversion occurring and therefore for a stated amount of proceeds would result in the value of the equity instrument being lower (because of a corresponding higher contractual interest rate) compared to an equity component on convertible debt without the contingency included in the conversion feature.

3.11 Treatment of reverse convertible instruments

A conventional convertible bond generally entitles the holder to convert the bond into shares of the issuer. If the conversion option meets the definition of equity, the conversion option is recognised in equity and the bond component is recognised as a financial liability. The accounting treatment for this is clear in IAS 32 and reflects the fact that, until conversion, the issuer always has an obligation to pay the bond component, which will either be settled by paying cash or by another financial asset or be forgiven by the holder should the holder choose to exercise their conversion option.

The accounting treatment in IAS 32 is less clear for reverse convertible instruments where the issuer, as opposed to the holder, has the choice whether to settle a bond with cash or another financial asset or deliver a fixed number of shares. In this case, the holder does not have the choice whether to convert. This raises the question whether the issuer ever has an obligation to pay cash as the issuer can always choose to deliver shares.

Example 3.11

Reverse convertible bond

Entity X is a CU functional currency entity and issues a reverse convertible instrument for CU100m. The instrument has a maturity of 5 years. The instrument has non-discretionary annual interest payments over its life of CU10 million. At maturity, the issuer has a choice of either (i) paying cash equal to the principal amount (CU100 million); or (ii) issuing a fixed number of 15 of its own equity shares. The value of 15 shares at issue of the instrument does not substantially exceed the value of the cash settlement alternative under (i).

Given the lack of clear guidance in IAS 32, two interpretations are possible. Whichever interpretation Entity X chooses to adopt, it should apply it consistently in accordance with IAS 8.13, *Accounting Policies, Changes in Accounting Estimates and Errors.*

Interpretation 1

From Entity X's perspective, the instrument is a compound instrument analysed as an obligation to pay cash as interest during the life and principal at maturity, which is a financial liability, and a purchased put over own shares (i.e. an option to exchange the obligation to pay CU100 million for a fixed number of shares), which is equity. Economically, the high interest payments represent the interest rate on a plain vanilla bond (without the conversion feature) plus the option premium in respect of the purchased put spread over the life. This approach is consistent with the approach taken for conventional convertible debt where the holder has the choice of conversion. The equity component of the reverse convertible bond will be determined as the difference between the fair value of the instrument as a whole and the fair value of the financial liability (comprising the obligation to pay cash in relation to interest and principal).

Interpretation 2

From Entity X's perspective the instrument is a compound instrument analysed as an obligation to pay cash in respect of interest over the life and an option to either pay CU100 million or issue 15 shares at maturity in settlement of the principal. As Entity X can avoid paying cash in relation to the principal amount through delivery of a fixed number of own equity shares, this feature does not give rise to a financial liability.

This is different from a conventional convertible bond where the holder has the choice of conversion and the issuer always has an obligation to pay the principal in cash as it cannot control whether the conversion option is exercised. In the case of the reverse convertible bond, the issuer can avoid the outflow of cash by exercising its right to convert and delivering the fixed number of equity shares.

Proponents of this approach view it as being consistent with IAS 32.20(b) that states that an entity has a financial liability if the terms of the instrument provide that on settlement the entity will deliver either: (i) cash or another financial asset or (ii) its own shares whose value is determined to exceed substantially the value of the cash or other financial asset. As IAS 32.20(b) only requires financial liability treatment if the value of the shares is determined to substantially exceed the value of the cash alternative, the settlement choice at maturity for this reverse convertible bond is not a financial liability.

The equity component of the reverse convertible bond will be determined as the difference between the fair value of the instrument as a whole and the fair value of the financial liability (comprising only the obligation to pay cash in relation to interest).

US GAAP comparison: A reverse convertible instrument would generally be analysed as a debt host with a potential embedded derivative feature that enables the issuer to sell a fixed number of its own shares to the holder in settlement of the fixed amount of the issuer's debt obligation (i.e. a purchased put option). Separation of a reverse convertible instrument into different liability and equity components would be precluded as it is not one of the exceptions noted in **section 3** above.

Further, separation of a reverse convertible instrument into debt host and derivative liability components would not be required if the embedded put option does not meet the definition of a derivative instrument on an as-if-freestanding basis or qualifies for the scope exception afforded instruments indexed to the entity's own equity shares and classified in equity.

4 Treatment of interest, dividends, gains and losses and other items

The classification of a financial instrument or a component of a financial instrument as either a financial liability or an equity instrument determines the treatment of interest, dividends, and other gains and losses relating to that instrument or component of that instrument. Interest, dividends, losses and gains relating to a financial liability, or a component of a compound instrument that is a financial liability, are recognised as income or expense in profit or loss. Distributions to holders of equity instruments are recognised directly in equity net of any related income tax benefit. Similarly, transaction costs of an equity transaction are accounted for as a deduction from equity. [IAS 32.35]

The following items are treated as income or expense in profit or loss: [IAS 32.37]

- interest payments on a bond issued by an entity;
- dividend payments on preference shares that are classified as a financial liability;
- gains and losses associated with redemption or refinancing of an instrument classified as a financial liability (notwithstanding the fact that the instrument may take the legal form of a share);
- gains and losses related to the carrying amount of an instrument that is a financial liability notwithstanding the fact that the instrument gives the holder a right to participate in the residual interest of an entity (e.g. certain puttable instruments such as units in a mutual fund that fail equity classification); and
- costs of an equity transaction that is abandoned.

Dividends classified as an expense in profit or loss may be presented either with interest on other liabilities or as a separate item.

The following items are accounted for within equity:
[IAS 32.37]

- dividend payments on shares classified wholly as equity; and

- incremental directly attributable costs incurred in successfully issuing or acquiring an entity's own equity instruments (including transaction costs, regulatory fees, amounts paid to regulatory, legal, accounting and other professional advisers, printing costs, stamp duties).

The amount of transaction costs that are accounted for as a deduction from equity in the period is disclosed in line with the requirements of IAS 1 *Presentation of Financial Statements*. Also, the related amount of income taxes recognised directly in equity is included in the aggregate amount of current and deferred tax credited or charged to equity and is disclosed under IAS 12 *Income Taxes*. [IAS 32.39]

Example 4A

Effective interest rate and dividends for a compound instrument

Entity A issues a non-cumulative preference share that is mandatorily redeemable for cash of CU10 million in 10 years' time. During the life of the instrument dividends are payable at the discretion of Entity A. The non-cumulative preference share is issued for CU8 million.

The non-cumulative redeemable preference share is a compound instrument. The liability component is determined as the present value of the eventual redemption amount of CU10m discounted at the rate at which the entity could issue a similar instrument with a similar credit standing but without the feature of discretionary dividends during its life.

Assuming the liability component is equal to CU7.8 million, the residual amount of CU0.2 million will be treated as the equity component. The unwinding of the discount (between the redemption of CU10 million and its present value of CU7.8 million) on the liability component is accounted for using the effective interest rate method as an interest expense and reported in profit or loss. Any dividends actually paid are treated as relating to the equity component and thus are classified as an equity distribution.

Transaction costs that are incremental and directly attributable to the issue of a compound financial instrument (i.e. would have been avoided if not for the issue of the compound instrument) are allocated to the liability and equity components in proportion to the allocation of the proceeds (see **3.1** above). In cases where costs represent the joint cost relating to more than one transaction (for instance a joint and concurrent offering of some equity instruments and an issue of instruments classified as liabilities) these are allocated using a basis that is rational and consistent with similar transactions. [IAS 32.38]

Example 4B

Transaction costs: placing and new issue of shares

Entity B places its privately held ordinary shares that are classified as equity with a stock exchange and simultaneously enters into a new capital raising by issuing new ordinary shares on the stock exchange. Transaction costs are incurred in respect of both transactions. As the issue of new shares is the issue of an equity instrument, but the placing of the existing equity instruments with the exchange is not, the transaction costs will need to be allocated between the two transactions. Transaction costs in respect of the capital raising will be recognised in equity whereas the transaction costs incurred in placing the existing shares with the stock exchange will be recognised in profit or loss.

In July 2008, the IFRIC issued a rejection notice titled *Transaction costs to be deducted from equity*. The IFRIC received a request for guidance on the extent of transaction costs to be accounted for as a deduction from equity in accordance with IAS 32.37 and on how the requirements of IAS 32.38 to allocate transaction costs that relate jointly to more than one transaction should be applied. This issue relates specifically to the meaning of the terms 'incremental' and 'directly attributable'.

The IFRIC noted that only incremental costs directly attributable to issuing new equity instruments or acquiring previously outstanding equity instruments are related to an equity transaction in accordance with IAS 32. The IFRIC also noted that judgement will be required to determine which costs are related solely to other activities undertaken at the same time as issuing equity, such as becoming a public company or acquiring an exchange listing, and which costs are related jointly to both activities and must be allocated in accordance with IAS 32.38. In view of the existing guidance, the IFRIC decided not to add this issue to its agenda.

However, the IFRIC also noted that the terms 'incremental' and 'directly attributable' are used with similar but not identical meanings in many Standards and Interpretations. The IFRIC recommended that common definitions should be developed for both terms and added to the Glossary as part of the Board's annual improvements project.

US GAAP comparison: As noted in **section 3** above, separating a convertible debt instrument into different liability and equity components is generally precluded with certain exceptions. When such a separation is required because the convertible debt instrument may be settled in cash upon conversion (including partial cash settlement) and the conversion option does not require separation under FAS 133

(FSP APB 14–1), transaction costs incurred with third parties other than the investor(s) that directly relate to the issuance shall be allocated to the liability and equity components in proportion to the allocation of proceeds and accounted for as debt issuance costs and equity issuance costs, respectively. When such separation is required because the convertible debt instrument has a conversion option that is in the money for the holder at the commitment date and does not require separation under either FAS 133 or FSP APB 14–1, transaction costs are allocated entirely to the liability component and accounted for as debt issuance costs.

5 Treasury shares

Where an entity reacquires its own shares, these shares (known as treasury shares) are deducted from equity. No gain or loss is recognised in profit or loss on the purchase, sale, issue or cancellation of an entity's own equity instruments. The acquisition and subsequent resale by an entity of its own equity instruments represents a transfer between owners (specifically between those who have given up their equity interest and those who continue to hold an equity instrument) rather than a gain or loss to the entity. Accordingly, any consideration paid or received is recognised in equity. [IAS 32.33]

Example 5A

Acquisition of equity

Entity A buys back 100,000 of its own equity shares in the market for CU5 a share. The shares will be held as treasury shares to enable Entity A to satisfy its obligations under its employee share option scheme. The following entries will be made to recognise the purchase of the treasury shares as a deduction from equity:

Dr	Equity	CU500,000
Cr	Cash	CU500,000

Example 5B

Treasury shares held as a economic hedge

Entity F is a large financial institution. The entity's shares are included in the FTSE 100 index. Entity F issues a bond whose principal amount varies with the movement in the FTSE 100 share index (an 'index tracker bond'). In order to hedge economically the equity derivative that is embedded in the bond, F purchases a portfolio of the shares contained in the FTSE 100 index and classifies them as held for trading.

Entity F cannot classify its own purchased shares as held for trading in order to hedge economically the index tracker bond. IAS 39 excludes from its scope instruments issued by an entity that meet the definition of equity in IAS 32. Furthermore, IAS 32 requires that treasury shares are presented in the statement of financial position as a deduction from equity and not as assets, and that no gain or loss should be recognised in profit or loss on such shares.

The amount of treasury shares held is disclosed separately either in the statement of financial position or in the notes in accordance with IAS 1 *Presentation of Financial Statements.* An entity provides disclosure in accordance with the requirements of IAS 24 *Related Party Disclosures* in instances where the entity reacquires its own equity instruments from related parties. [IAS 32.34]

Where an entity holds its own shares on behalf of others (as is the case when a financial institution holds its own shares on behalf of a client as a custodian), this represents an agency relationship and as a result the shares are not included in the statement of financial position of the entity. [IAS 32.AG36]

US GAAP comparison: US GAAP establishes the general principle that an entity should not recognise gains and losses on repurchases of its own equity shares within earnings. Instead such amounts should be reflected within retained earnings or paid in capital as appropriate (ARB 43 Chapter 1B). However, facts and circumstances associated with a share repurchase may suggest that the total payment relates to other than the shares repurchased. An entity offering to repurchase shares only from a specific shareholder (or group of shareholders) suggests that the repurchase may involve more than the purchase of treasury shares. Also, if an entity repurchases shares at a price that is different from the price obtainable in transactions in the open market or transactions in which the identity of the selling shareholder is not important, some portion of the amount being paid is likely to represent a payment for stated or unstated rights or privileges that shall be given separate accounting recognition. For example, the selling shareholder may agree to abandon certain acquisition plans, forego other planned transactions, settle litigation, settle employment contracts, or restrict voluntarily the ability to purchase shares of the entity or its affiliates within a stated time period. (FTB 85–6)

Transactions do arise, however, in which a reacquisition of an entity's equity shares may take place at prices different from routine transactions in the open market. For example, to obtain the desired number of shares in a tender offer to all or most shareholders, the offer may need to be at a price in excess of the current market price. In addition, a block of shares representing a controlling interest will generally trade at a price in excess of market, and a large block of shares may trade at a price above or below the current market price depending on whether the buyer or seller initiates the transaction. An entity's reacquisition of its shares in those circumstances is solely a treasury share transaction properly accounted for at the purchase price of the treasury shares. Therefore, in the absence of the receipt of stated or unstated consideration in addition to the shares, the entire purchase price shall be accounted for as the cost of treasury shares. (FTB 85–6)

Payments by an entity to a shareholder or former shareholder attributed, for example, to a standstill agreement, or any agreement in which a shareholder or former shareholder agrees not to purchase additional shares, shall be expensed as incurred. (FTB 85–6)

Although IFRS does not have the equivalent specific guidance detailed in US GAAP in FTB 85–6 the guidance described above may be appropriate.

6 Derivatives over own equity

A derivative contract over an entity's own equity is accounted for as equity *only* where it will be settled by the entity delivering (or receiving) a fixed number of its own equity instruments and receiving (or delivering) a fixed amount of cash or another financial asset. Any consideration received (such as the premium received in relation to written options over own shares or warrants on the entity's own shares that satisfy the above condition) is added directly to equity. Similarly, any consideration paid for such an instrument (such as premium paid for a purchased option that satisfies the above condition) is deducted from equity. Changes in fair value of the equity instrument are not recognised in the financial statements. [IAS 32.22] At a group level, derivatives over own equity include derivatives over shares of subsidiaries.

Example 6A

Purchased call

On 1 February 20X5 Entity MNO, a CU functional currency entity, purchases for CU5,000 a call option over 1,000 of its own ordinary shares. The option is a European type option with exercise at a strike price of CU102 per share exercisable only on 31 January 20X6. The option is gross physically settled, i.e. Entity MNO takes delivery of 1,000 of its own shares in exchange for an amount of cash paid to the counterparty equal to the option exercise price of CU102,000 (CU102 per share × 1,000 shares).

The entries are as follows:

1 February 20X5

On inception of the contract the following entry will be needed in order to recognise the cash paid in exchange for the right to receive a fixed number of own shares in exchange for a fixed amount of cash:

Dr	Equity	CU5,000
Cr	Cash	CU5,000

The premium is recognised in equity because the instrument meets the definition of an equity instrument.

31 December 20X5

No entry is made on 31 December 20X5 because no cash is paid or received and a contract that gives a right to receive a fixed number of the entity's own shares in exchange for a fixed amount of cash meets the definition of an equity instrument of the entity. Hence, the fair value of the option is irrelevant as the equity instrument is not remeasured.

31 January 20X6

The entity exercises the call option and the contract is gross physically settled through the entity taking delivery of 1,000 of its own shares in exchange for a payment of CU102,000 to the counterparty. This is recognised as follows:

Dr	Equity	CU102,000
Cr	Cash	CU102,000

Any contract with a single or multiple settlement option that contains an obligation for the entity to purchase its own equity for cash or another financial asset gives rise to a financial liability for the present value of the repurchase price, even if the obligation to purchase is conditional on the holder exercising its right to sell the shares to the entity. Examples of instruments that give rise to a liability include forward contracts to buy own equity and written put options that allow the holder to put the shares back to the entity at a fixed or variable amount (for example a fixed amount plus inflation). At inception such contracts are recognised at an amount equal to the present value of the obligation inherent in the contract. This is the case notwithstanding the fact that the contract itself may be an equity instrument (as it can be settled only through the entity delivering a fixed amount of cash in exchange for a fixed number of its own shares). [IAS 32.23] The presentation is equivalent to buying back own shares today but with an obligation to still pay the cash under the buy-back to the seller.

The liability is subsequently remeasured through profit or loss, i.e. interest is accrued in accordance with the effective interest method up to the share redemption amount. In the case of a gross liability based on a variable amount of cash, the re-measurement of the amount of the eventual liability (for example, for changes in inflation) would also be recognised through profit or loss.

Example 6B

Forward purchase contract

Assume that, instead of purchasing a call option over own shares that will be gross physically settled, on 1 February 20X5 Entity MNO enters into a forward contract to buy 1,000 of its own ordinary shares on 31 January 20X6 for CU104 per share.

This contract will be gross physically settled, i.e. Entity MNO will take delivery of 1,000 of its own shares in exchange for paying to the counterparty an amount of CU104,000 (CU104 per share × 1,000 shares).

The entries are as follows:

1 February 20X5

The entity has an unconditional obligation to deliver CU104,000 in cash in one year's time to the counterparty in exchange for a fixed amount of own equity shares. The following entry is made to recognise this obligation to deliver CU104,000 in one year at its present value of CU100,000 discounted using an appropriate interest rate:

Dr	Equity	CU100,000
Cr	Liability	CU100,000

31 December 20X5

The following entry is necessary to accrue interest in accordance with the effective interest method on the liability for the share redemption amount.

Dr	Interest expense	CU3,660
Cr	Liability	CU3,660

31 January 20X6

The following entry accrues further interest for the remaining month of January 20X6 in accordance with the effective interest method on the liability for the share redemption amount.

Dr	Interest expense	CU340
Cr	Liability	CU340

On the same date the following entry will be needed to recognise the settlement of the liability for the share redemption amount:

Dr	Liability	CU104,000
Cr	Cash	CU104,000

Example 6C

Written put

On 1 February 20X5 Entity PQR writes a put option over 1,000 of its own ordinary shares and receives a premium of CU5,000 for doing so. The option is a European type option with exercise at a strike price of CU98 per share exercisable only on 31 January 20X6. The option will be gross physically settled, i.e. if the option is exercised the entity will receive 1,000 of its own shares in exchange for paying to the counterparty an amount equal to the option exercise price of CU98,000 (CU98 per share × 1,000 shares).

The accounting entries are as follows:

1 February 20X5

At inception of the contract the following entry will be needed in order to recognise the cash received in exchange for writing the put option giving the counterparty the right to receive a fixed amount of cash in exchange for delivering a fixed number of the entity's own shares:

Dr	Cash	CU5,000
Cr	Equity	CU5,000

The premium is recognised in equity because the instrument meets the definition of an equity instrument.

The following additional entry is needed in order to recognise the present value of the CU98,000 obligation on 31 January 20X6:

Dr	Equity	CU95,000
Cr	Liability	CU95,000

31 December 20X5

The following entry is necessary to accrue interest in accordance with the effective interest method on the liability for the share redemption amount.

Dr	Interest expense	CU2,745
Cr	Liability	CU2,745

31 January 20X6

The following journal accrues further interest for the remaining month of January 20X6 in accordance with the effective interest method on the liability for the share redemption amount.

Dr	Interest expense	CU255
Cr	Liability	CU255

On the same date the following entry will be needed to recognise the settlement of the liability for the share redemption amount:

Dr	Liability	CU98,000
Cr	Cash	CU98,000

If the written put was not exercised by the counterparty, the following entry would be required instead:

Dr	Liability	CU98,000
Cr	Equity	CU98,000

It is common for a group to acquire an interest in an entity which upon acquisition will be a subsidiary (but not wholly owned) and as part of the acquisition also to enter into a written put option with the seller that permits the seller to put their remaining interest in the acquired entity to the group at a specified price. These puts are written by the acquiring entity to allow the existing owners an exit mechanism for their remaining shares. The acquisition of shares that results in the interest being recognised as a subsidiary will be accounted for in accordance with IFRS 3 *Business Combinations.* If the written put can be physically settled, i.e. subsidiary's shares are physically delivered and paid for by cash or other financial asset, irrespective of whether the strike price of the put is a fixed or variable price, a gross obligation must be recognised at an amount equal to the present value of the amount that could be required to be paid to the counterparty in accordance with IAS 32. Changes in the measurement of the gross obligation due to the unwinding of the discount or changes in the amount that the group could be required to pay are always recognised in profit or loss. It is not permissible to recognise these gains/losses against the goodwill that arose on acquiring the interest in the subsidiary as changes in the value of the gross obligation relate to the potential *future* acquisition of the remaining shares in the subsidiary.

In November 2006 the IFRIC considered the classification and presentation of written puts and forward purchase arrangements entered into by a parent over shares of a subsidiary, otherwise known as puts and forwards over non-controlling interests (previously known as 'minority interests'). The IFRIC confirmed that in the consolidated financial statements a financial liability must be recognised in accordance with IAS 32.23 for the obligation to pay cash in the future to purchase the shares held by non-controlling interests, even if the payment of that cash is conditional on the option being exercised by the holder. After initial recognition any liability to which IFRS 3 *Business Combinations* is not being applied will be accounted for in accordance with IAS 39. The parent will reclassify the liability to equity if a put expires unexercised.

The IFRIC recognised that there is likely to be divergence in practice in how the related debit to equity is presented. However, the IFRIC did not believe that it could reach a consensus on this matter on a timely basis and therefore it decided not to add this item to its agenda.

The debit that is recognised in equity on initial recognition of a written put or forward purchase over a non-controlling interest may be presented in equity in one of two ways. The debit may be recognised as a deduction from non-controlling interests or may be presented in other reserves, alongside non-controlling interests, illustrating that the transaction represents a future transaction involving the non-controlling interests. The latter seems preferable, i.e. the non-controlling interests balance is unaffected by the transaction, as this preserves the net assets of the subsidiary that are attributed to those non-controlling interest holders.

Example 6D

Written put over equity of subsidiary

On 1 January 20X8 Entity Q, the ultimate parent of Group Q, acquires a 60% interest in Entity P from Entity O. As part of the acquisition agreement Entity Q also writes a put option over 40% of shares in Entity P to Entity O. Entity Q pays CU1,000m under the purchase agreement. The written put option allows Entity O to put the 40% interest in Entity P to Entity Q at CU275m plus 20% of Entity P's post acquisition cumulative profits. The put can be exercised by Entity O at 1 July 20Y0 and at every anniversary thereafter until 1 July 20Y2. Cumulative profits are determined based on audited financial statements of Entity P up to the year ended immediately prior to exercise of the put option. Group Q's reporting period end is 31 December.

At 1 January 20X8 the fair value of 60% of the shares in Entity P was CU1,100m and the fair value of the written put option was CU100m. Entity Q's estimation of profits of Entity P for the two year period ending 31 December 20X9 is CU50m. Entity Q's cost of debt funding is 10%.

At 31 December 20X8 the fair value of the written put option was CU90m. Entity Q revises its estimate of Entity P's profits for the two year period ending 31 December 20X9 to CU80m.

Entity Q separate financial statements

The written put is over a third party's equity and therefore does not meet the definition of equity for Entity Q. The put option will be classified as at fair value through profit or loss.

1 January 20X8

Dr	Cost of investment	1,100m
Cr	Cash	1,000m
Cr	Written put option – FVTPL	100m

To recognise the cost of investment of the subsidiary and the written put option at fair value at initial recognition.

31 December 20X8

Dr	Written put option – FVTPL	10m
Cr	Profit or loss	10m

To recognise the re-measurement of the put option as at fair value through profit or loss.

Group Q consolidated financial statements

The written put permits a third party, Entity O, to put up to 40% of the shares in a subsidiary of Group Q to Group Q. As Group Q could be required to pay cash or other financial asset as settlement for the acquisition of shares in a subsidiary, in this case non-controlling interest of the group, Group Q must recognise a gross obligation for the potential future acquisition of these equity shares.

1 January 20X8

At the date of acquisition Group Q consolidates Entity P and recognises a 40% non-controlling interest. The fair value of consideration used to acquire 60% of the shares in Entity P for the purposes of determining any goodwill arising on acquisition is CU1,100m. The difference between this amount and the total consideration paid to Entity O is the premium that Entity Q received for writing the put option.

The estimated present value of the amount Group Q could be required to pay Entity O should Entity O exercise its put option at the earliest opportunity, being 1 July 20Y0, is CU225m. This is determined as follows: [CU275m + (CU50m x 20%)] x $1/(1.1^{2.5})$.

Dr	Net assets acquired / goodwill *	1,100m
Dr	Equity	125m
Cr	Cash	1,000m
Cr	Gross obligation under put option	225m

To recognise the acquisition of the subsidiary and the recognition of the present value of the gross obligation under the written put over the non-controlling interest.

31 December 20X8

The estimated present value of the amount Group Q could be required to pay Entity O, should Entity O exercise its put option at the earliest opportunity, being 1 July 20Y0, is CU252m. This is determined as follows: [CU275m + (CU80m x 20%)] x $1/(1.1^{1.5})$.

Dr	Profit or loss – finance cost	27m
Cr	Gross obligation under put option	27m

To recognise the re-measurement of the present value of the gross obligation under the written put over the non-controlling interest.

* for simplicity the non-controlling interests' share of net assets has not been split out and is not recognised

All derivatives over own equity (other than forward purchases and written puts) where settlement is not exclusively by the exchange of a fixed number of equity shares for a fixed amount of cash (or another financial asset) are treated as derivatives (derivative financial assets or liabilities) and are accounted for in accordance with the requirements of IAS 39, namely the fair value of the instrument is recognised on the balance sheet with changes in fair value recorded in profit or loss. A forward purchase or written put that may result in the receipt of equity shares for delivery of cash (or another financial asset) is recognised as a financial liability that represents the entity's gross obligation to deliver cash or another financial asset to the counterparty. All other forward purchase and written put contracts over own shares are fair valued through profit or loss.

Hence, the following derivatives over own equity are accounted for as held for trading derivatives that are fair valued through profit or loss:

- those that are exclusively net settled in cash (or other financial assets);
- those that are exclusively net settled in own equity shares; and
- any derivative over own equity which gives either party a choice over how it is settled unless all the settlement alternatives result in the exchange of a fixed number of own shares for a fixed amount of cash or another financial asset (or in the case of a forward purchases or written put over own shares where one of the settlement alternatives is gross physical settlement).

Example 6E

Forward sale contract: net share settlement

On 1 February 20X5 Entity XYZ, a CU functional currency entity, enters into a forward sale contract over 1,000 of its own ordinary shares on 31 January 20X6 at a fixed price of CU104 per share. The terms of the contract are that it will be net settled in shares, i.e. settlement will take the form of receipt/ delivery by Entity XYZ of a variable number of shares such that the market value of the shares at the date of settlement is equal to the market value of the forward contract.

The accounting entries are as follows:

1 February 20X5

The price per share when the contract is entered into on 1 February 20X5 is CU104. The initial fair value of the forward contract on 1 February 20X5 is zero. Thus, no entry is required because the fair value of the derivative is zero and no cash is paid or received.

31 December 20X5

On 31 December 20X5, the market price per share has increased to CU110 and, as a result, the fair value of the forward contract has decreased to CU6,000.

The following entry is necessary to recognise the decrease in the fair value of the forward contract:

Dr	Loss	CU6,000
Cr	Forward liability	CU6,000

31 January 20X6

On 31 January 20X6, the market price per share has decreased to CU106. The fair value of the forward contract is CU2,000 ([CU106 x 1,000] – CU104,000). Thus, the following entry is needed to recognise the increase in the fair value of the contract:

Dr	Forward liability	CU4,000
Cr	Gain	CU4,000

On the same day, the contract is settled net in shares (with Entity XYZ delivering an amount of its own shares to the counterparty equivalent to the fair value of the contract). The following entry is therefore necessary to recognise the settlement of the contract net in own equity shares:

Dr	Forward Liability	CU2,000
Cr	Equity	CU2,000

For illustrative purposes only the fair value of the forward contract is not discounted.

Example 6F

Total return swap

An entity enters into a total return swap ('TRS') over 1,000 of its own equity shares on 1 February 20X5. The contract matures on 31 January 20X6. Due to the nature of the total return swap (whose fair value is driven by changes in the entity's share price), gross settlement is not possible and it will be settled net (either in cash or in a variable number of shares). Thus, the instrument does not qualify as an equity instrument and therefore will be accounted for as a derivative as follows:

1 February 20X5

The initial fair value of the swap on 1 February 20X5 is zero. No entry is required because the fair value of the derivative is zero and no cash is paid or received.

31 December 20X5

The fair value of the swap at 31 December 20X5 is CU4,500, hence the following entry is required to recognise the increase in fair value:

Dr	Swap asset	CU4,500
Cr	Profit or loss	CU4,500

31 January 20X6

The fair value of the swap at 31 January 20X6 is CU3,750, hence the following entry is required to recognise the decrease in fair value:

Dr	Profit or loss	CU750
Cr	Swap asset	CU750

The entries necessary upon settlement will depend on which of the two methods of net settlement is chosen. If net share settlement is chosen the following entry will be made:

Dr	Equity	CU3,750
Cr	Swap asset	CU3,750

In this scenario settlement will take place through the entity taking receipt of 150 of its own shares (CU3,750 / CU25) (the market value of the entity's share on this date is CU25)

If net cash settlement is chosen the following entry will be made at settlement of the contract:

Dr	Cash	CU3,750
Cr	Swap asset	CU3,750

The following table illustrates application of the above rules to different derivatives over own equity, with different settlement mechanisms:

	Settlement options available			
	A	B	C	D
	Net cash settlement(1)	**Net share settlement**(2)	**Gross physical settlement**(3)	**Settlement options**(4)
Forward to buy equity shares (the forward may be over a fixed or variable number of equity shares for a fixed or variable amount of functional or foreign currency cash)	Derivative financial asset/ liability	Derivative financial asset/ liability	Gross liability	If C exists as an alternative, treat as a Gross liability If C does not exist as an alternative, treat as a Derivative financial asset/ liability
Forward to sell a fixed number of equity shares for a fixed amount of functional currency cash	Derivative financial asset/ liability	Derivative financial asset/ liability	Equity	Derivative financial asset/ liability
Forward to sell a fixed number of equity shares for a fixed amount of foreign currency cash or variable amount of functional currency cash	Derivative financial asset/ liability	Derivative financial asset/ liability	Derivative financial asset/ liability	Derivative financial asset/ liability
Forward to sell a variable number of equity shares for a fixed or variable amount of functional or foreign currency cash	Derivative financial asset/ liability	Derivative financial asset/ liability	Derivative financial asset/ liability	Derivative financial asset/ liability

	Settlement options available			
	A	B	C	D
	Net cash settlement[1]	Net share settlement[2]	Gross physical settlement[3]	Settlement options[4]
Purchased call option on a fixed number of equity shares for a fixed amount of functional currency cash	Derivative financial asset	Derivative financial asset	Equity	Derivative financial asset
Purchased call option on a fixed number of equity shares for a fixed amount of foreign currency cash or variable amount of functional currency cash	Derivative financial asset	Derivative financial asset	Derivative financial asset	Derivative financial asset
Purchased call option on a variable number of equity shares for a fixed or variable amount of functional or foreign currency cash	Derivative financial asset	Derivative financial asset	Derivative financial asset	Derivative financial asset
Written call option on a fixed number of equity shares for a fixed amount of functional currency cash	Derivative financial liability	Derivative financial liability	Equity	Derivative financial liability
Written call option on a fixed number of equity shares for a fixed or variable amount of foreign currency cash or variable amount of functional currency cash	Derivative financial liability	Derivative financial liability	Derivative financial liability	Derivative financial liability
Written call option on a variable number of equity shares for a fixed or variable amount of functional or foreign currency cash	Derivative financial liability	Derivative financial liability	Derivative financial liability	Derivative financial liability
Purchased put option on a fixed number of equity shares for a fixed amount of functional currency cash	Derivative financial asset	Derivative financial asset	Equity	Derivative financial asset

	Settlement options available			
	A	B	C	D
	Net cash settlement[(1)]	**Net share settlement**[(2)]	**Gross physical settlement**[(3)]	**Settlement options**[(4)]
Purchased put option on a fixed number of equity shares for a fixed or variable amount of foreign currency cash or variable amount of functional currency cash	Derivative financial asset	Derivative financial asset	Derivative financial asset	Derivative financial asset
Purchased put option on a variable number of equity shares for a fixed or variable amount of functional or foreign currency cash	Derivative financial asset	Derivative financial asset	Derivative financial asset	Derivative financial asset
Written put option on equity shares (the option may be over a fixed or variable number of equity shares for a fixed or variable amount of functional or foreign currency cash)	Derivative financial liability	Derivative financial liability	Gross liability	If C exists as an alternative, treat as a Gross liability If C does not exist as an alternative, treat as a Derivative financial asset/ liability

(1) **Net cash settlement**. Where the one party's net gain/loss is settled in cash and no shares are exchanged.

(2) **Net share settlement (shares for shares)**. A variable number of shares is delivered/received having an aggregate current fair value equal to the amount of the gain/loss to the relevant party.

(3) **Gross physical settlement**. The buyer/seller delivers/receives cash in return for shares from the seller/buyer.

(4) **Settlement options**. Where either the issuer or the holder has a right to choose among two or more of the above ways of settlement.

US GAAP comparison: Forward contracts to buy an entity's own shares that require physical settlement are accounted for as liabilities and measured initially at the fair value of the shares to be repurchased and subsequently at the present value of the amount to be paid at settlement provided the settlement date and amount is fixed or else at the amount that would be paid if settlement occurred at the reporting date (FAS 150). Furthermore, forward and option contracts that could require the issuer to net cash settle are treated as derivative contracts (FAS 133 and EITF 00–19). These contracts are initially recognised as an asset or liability at fair value, with subsequent changes in fair value being recognised in profit or loss.

Under FAS 150, written puts over own shares are measured at fair value with gains/losses recognised in income regardless of the settlement alternatives rather than at the present value of the redemption amount.

Unlike IAS 32, forward sale contracts, purchased call options, written call options and purchased put options on own equity, which are subject to net share settlement (or are readily convertible to cash), may be classified as equity instruments under US GAAP, provided specified conditions are met (EITF 00–19 and EITF 07–5 or EITF 01–6).

6.1 Other variations of terms of derivatives over own equity

As described immediately above, the guidance on multiple settlement alternatives for standalone derivatives over own equity is consistent with the multiple settlement alternatives guidance for convertible debt described in **3.7** above. The guidance is consistent as in order to determine whether an equity conversion option in convertible debt is considered to be equity for the issuer, the derivatives over own equity guidance is applied. As a result, the guidance on foreign currency convertible debt described in **3.8** above equally applies to standalone derivatives over own equity, i.e. for a derivative over own equity to meet the definition of equity it must be an exchange of a fixed number of shares for a fixed amount of functional currency cash. Also, the guidance on anti-dilutive provisions in **3.9** above also applies to standalone derivatives over own equity.

It is not possible to provide an exhaustive list of different variations in the terms of derivatives over own equity. However, some examples and the accounting analysis are included below.

6.1.1 Contracts where the number of own equity shares or amount of cash is predetermined but still subject to variability

Derivatives over own equity may be structured so that they can be exercised at various points in time and the number of shares or the amount of cash is predetermined upfront but varies with time. One must consider whether such derivatives involve exchange of a fixed amount of cash or other financial asset for a fixed amount of equity. Consider the following example:

Entity A, a US$ functional currency, enters into two standalone contracts to deliver own equity to a third party:

- Contract 1: a written call option that gives the counterparty the right to buy equity of Entity A for US$100 over a three year period. The number of shares that will be delivered to the counterparty on exercise will depend on when the counterparty exercises the option. If the counterparty exercises the option at the first anniversary 10 shares are delivered, at the second anniversary 11 shares are delivered, or at the third anniversary 12 shares are delivered. If the option is not exercised by the end of year 3 the call option expires. If the option is exercised at any time in the 3 year period there is no further right to buy shares under the arrangement.

- Contract 2: a written call option that gives the counterparty the right to buy equity of Entity A for US$100 over a three year period. The number of shares that will be delivered to the counterparty on exercise will depend on when the counterparty exercises the option and the rate of LIBOR at that date. If the counterparty exercises the option at the first anniversary the number of shares delivered is 10 x (1+LIBOR), at the second anniversary 10 x $(1+LIBOR)^2$, and at the third anniversary 10 x $(1+LIBOR)^3$. If the option is not exercised by the end of year 3 the call option expires. If the option is exercised at any time in the 3 year period there is no further right to buy shares under the arrangement.

In the case of Contract 1 the contract meets the definition of equity as, if exercised, the issuer will receive a fixed amount of cash for delivering a fixed amount of own equity. Even though the number of shares that the instrument may be converted into does vary, it only varies with the passage of time and not with other variables, i.e. the number of shares is fixed at inception of the contract. The arrangement is considered to be an exchange of a fixed number of shares for a fixed amount of cash. Therefore, the premium received for writing the call option is credited to equity and changes in the fair value of the instrument are not recognised in the financial statements in accordance with IAS 32.

In the case of Contract 2 the contract meets the definition of a financial liability as, if exercised, the issuer will deliver a variable number of shares for a fixed amount of cash. Even though the number of shares is determinable, i.e. it is determined by a specified index, in this case LIBOR, the number of shares is not fixed in advance and does vary due to factors other than the passage of time, in this case, interest rates. The contract is therefore not an exchange of a fixed number of shares for a fixed amount of cash. The written option must be initially recognised at fair value, and subsequently measured as at fair value through profit or loss in accordance with IAS 39.

6.1.2 *Contract to exchange a fixed number of shares of a parent for a fixed number of shares in a subsidiary*

In the consolidated financial statements such a contract is an exchange of a fixed number of shares of the issuer, being the parent, which are equity instruments, for a fixed number of shares of a subsidiary, being non-controlling interest, which are also equity of the group. IAS 32 does not consider this fact pattern as the standard assumes that for a derivative over equity to be classified as equity the exchange will always involve receipt or delivery of a fixed amount of cash (or other financial asset) for a fixed amount of equity. As the arrangement is an exchange of a fixed number of two equity instruments, at the consolidated level, it is reasonable that the instrument be presented as equity as the holder is exchanging one fixed amount of residual interest in one group entity for another.

6.1.3 *Contract to exchange a fixed or variable number of shares of a parent for a fixed number of shares in a subsidiary*

Consider an example of such a contract. Entity R (the parent of Group R) writes a call option over 10% of its subsidiary, Entity S, to Entity T. The call option allows Entity T to buy the 10% stake in Entity S by delivering shares in Entity R as consideration at a fixed date in the future. The call option can only be physically settled by the delivery of shares in Entity S to Entity T and the delivery of shares in Entity R from Entity T to Entity R. However, the strike price of the call option, being the consideration that Entity T will pay Entity R if the option is exercised depends on the value of Entity S at the exercise date as follows:

(a) if the value of Entity S is equal to CU100m or more Entity R will receive from Entity T a fixed number of its own shares, i.e. Entity R shares; and

(b) if the value of Entity S is less than CU100m Entity T will deliver a variable number of share in Entity R equal to the value of the 10% interest in Entity S.

Assume that both the shares of Entity R and Entity S are equity instruments in accordance with IAS 32.

In the consolidated financial statements the contract is an exchange of a fixed number of shares in a subsidiary (being non-controlling interest that is presented as equity) for a fixed, or under certain scenarios variable, number of equity shares in the parent. IAS 32.21 makes itclear that a contract is not an equity instrument solely because it may result in the receipt or delivery of the entity's own equity instruments. IAS 32.21 draws a distinction between two types of arrangements:

(a) obligations to be settled in own equity shares where the fair value of the obligation may be for a fixed amount or an amount that fluctuates in part or in full in response to changes in a variable *other* than the market price of the entity's own equity instruments; and

(b) obligations to be settled in own shares where the fair value fluctuates in response to changes in the market price of an entity's own equity instruments.

The paragraph appears to suggest that contracts to deliver a variable number of own shares may display characteristics of equity, i.e. characteristics of a residual interest in the entity's assets after deducting all of its liabilities. In the above example, Entity R receives its own shares for delivering a fixed number of shares in its subsidiary. The only variable that determines the number of shares to be received is the value of Entity S's shares. Therefore, the principles of IAS 32 would suggest that the contract does evidence a residual interest and therefore Entity R should account for it as equity in its consolidated financial statements.

If the variability in the number of shares was driven by a factor other than the market price of Entity S's shares such as for example the fair value of a certain quantity of gold, as mentioned in IAS 32.21, then it would be inappropriate to classify the contract as an equity instrument. In this case the variable number of equity shares is derived from a variable other than the market price of the shares and the contract does not evidence a residual interest in the entity's assets after deducting all of its liabilities.

US GAAP comparison: US GAAP differs from IFRS when evaluating whether contracts that settle in shares of a subsidiary are derivatives. US GAAP indicates that, stock of a subsidiary is not considered equity of the parent (reporting entity). As a result, derivatives indexed to, and potentially settled in, the stock of a consolidated subsidiary do not meet the scope exclusion for contracts indexed to, and classified in own equity in FAS 133.11(a). If those derivatives meet the definition of a derivative instrument in FAS 133.6, they should be accounted for as derivatives at fair value under Statement 133. For example, derivatives indexed to, and potentially settled in, the stock of a consolidated subsidiary that may be net-cash or net-share settled meet the definition of a derivative instrument in FAS 133.6 and, therefore, should be accounted for under Statement 133. [EITF Issue 00–6]

In some cases careful judgement is needed in order to determine whether a contractual arrangement is a derivative over own equity. Consider the following example. Entity A enters into an arrangement with a potential investor whereby it receives CU100 on day one. Under the terms of the arrangement Entity A has a choice of delivering either a fixed number of equity shares of Entity A to the potential investor or returning CU100 back to the potential investor. One way of analysing the transaction would be to regard it as an option purchased by Entity A that would allow it to put a fixed number of its own equity shares to the potential investor under which the strike price of CU100 has already been prepaid by the investor and therefore is potentially returnable to the potential investor (should Entity A choose not to exercise the put option). However, viewing this transaction as a derivative over own equity does not seem to be the most faithful representation of the contractual arrangement. Under a conventional purchased put option over own equity the purchaser of the option (Entity A in this case) would suffer the cost of the option (in the form of premium) that would not be returnable if the option were not exercised. In this fact pattern Entity A does not suffer any premium. Another possible view might be to liken the arrangement to a prepaid forward to sell own shares with a predetermined requirement for the return of the prepaid cash leg in the case of non-performance by Entity A (i.e. if it chooses not to deliver its own shares). However, this also is not the most faithful representation as a conventional forward to sell own shares would not allow for the potential investor to claim damages for economic losses due to non-performance under the contract. Indeed, the whole nature of the contractual arrangement is that if Entity A chooses not to deliver shares it is entitled to do so and this is not non-performance.

Consistent with the two different interpretations applied to reverse convertible bonds in **Example 3.11** above the instrument could be interpreted in one of two ways. The first interpretation is to view the arrangement as an instrument which will be settled by Entity A either delivering cash or issuing a fixed number of own shares and not to apply the rules regarding derivatives over own equity. Viewed in this way the arrangement should, on initial receipt of CU100, be accounted for as equity since Entity A has the unconditional right to avoid delivering cash by choosing to deliver own shares. This is the case only if the value of the alternative to deliver shares instead of cash is not determined to exceed substantially the value of the cash alternative. [IAS 32.21] A financial liability would only be recognised at the point where Entity A has chosen not to deliver own shares and has therefore incurred an obligation to deliver cash. If the value of the share settlement was determined to exceed substantially the value of the cash then the instrument would be considered a financial liability as in substance the holder has been guaranteed receipt of an amount that is at least equal to the cash alternative.

The second interpretation is to view the instrument as a debt host contract, being the obligation to deliver CU100, and an embedded purchased put which permits the issuer to deliver its own equity shares as extinguishment for the debt host contract. As the number of shares delivered by the issuer and the debt host contract forgiven is fixed the purchased put would meet the definition of equity.

6.2 Share buy-back arrangements

An entity may enter into arrangements with a third party, usually with a financial institution, for that third party to buy back the entity's equity shares in the market for delivery to the entity. It is important to determine in these instances whether the third party is acting as principal or as agent for the entity. If the third party is acting as agent then the contractual arrangement between the entity and third party is not a financial instrument. In such cases, only when shares are acquired by the third party will the entity recognise a financial liability to pay the third party and a debit in equity for the shares to be delivered, and when the shares are delivered to the entity will the entity settle the financial liability with cash or other financial asset and re-present within equity that treasury shares have been acquired or shares cancelled.

In some jurisdictions an entity will enter into an arrangement immediately prior to its period end which allows a financial institution to acquire shares in the entity at the financial institution's discretion with delivery of those shares to the entity. These arrangements are normally subject to a cap and/or floor on the amount of shares the financial institution can acquire and a maximum amount of shares that can be acquired in a trading day. The financial institution acquires the shares in the market and then transfers them to the entity at a market price subject to some adjustments and a fee. These arrangements are entered into to ensure the entity's buy back programme continues during the 'quiet period' (the period between the entity's period end and the release of the financial results) without the entity breaching regulatory rules. The financial institution has the unfettered discretion to buy back shares, is not under instruction from the entity and is therefore considered as a principal.

The entity will need to recognise at the period end that it has a financial obligation to acquire its own equity, i.e. a 'gross obligation'. This financial liability will be initially recognised at the present value of the maximum amount the entity could be required to pay to the financial institution with a corresponding debit in equity. Changes in the present value of this liability, say, due to the unwind of the discount rate, or changes in the market price of the entity's shares, will be recognised in profit or loss. If the arrangement limits the maximum amount the entity can pay to the financial institution, the financial liability will be initially measured at the present value of this amount. In this case, the entity may not have variability in the amount it will pay due to changes in the entity's share price as the entity could always be required to pay the maximum amount to the financial institution.

When the financial institution buys back the entity's shares and delivers them to the entity and the entity settles the obligation with cash or other financial asset, the entity derecognises the part of the financial liability equal to the amount that the entity has paid. If at the end of the buy-back period the financial institution has not acquired the maximum amount of shares or utilised the maximum amount that the entity can spend on buying back shares, a financial liability will remain. This amount should be reversed with a corresponding credit in equity to show that the financial liability has been extinguished.

7 Classification of financial liabilities

IAS 39 *Financial Instruments: Recognition and Measurement* requires that financial liabilities are classified into one of two categories:

- financial liabilities at fair value through profit or loss; and
- other financial liabilities (measured at amortised cost).

7.1 Financial liabilities at fair value through profit or loss

This class of financial liabilities can further be divided into the following two sub-categories:

- financial liabilities classified as held for trading; and
- financial liabilities designated by the entity as at fair value through profit or loss.

7.1.1 Financial liabilities classified as held for trading

A financial liability is held for trading if it falls into one of the following categories:
[IAS 39.9]

- financial liabilities incurred with the intention of repurchasing them in the near term;
- financial liabilities that on initial recognition form part of a portfolio of identified financial instruments that are managed together and for which there is evidence of a recent actual pattern of short-term profit-taking; and
- derivative liabilities, unless the derivative forms part of a designated and effective hedging relationship (see **chapter 8**).

In May 2008 the IASB issued *Improvements to IFRSs*. The improvements amended the definition of held for trading to clarify that a non-derivative financial instrument that is traded as part of a portfolio of identified financial instruments that are managed together and for which there is evidence of a recent actual pattern of short-term profit-taking can qualify for the trading classification only if it is included in such a portfolio on initial recognition. The amendments made to IAS 39 by *Improvements to IFRSs* apply for annual periods beginning on or after 1 January 2009, but earlier application is permitted. An entity choosing to apply the amendments early must disclose that fact.

The fact that a liability is used to provide funding for trading activities does not of itself mean that liability is to be classified as held for trading. [IAS 39.AG15] Thus, a borrowing that a bank uses to fund its trading portfolio of debt and equity securities would not automatically be classified as held for trading.

Example 7.1.1

Held for trading liabilities

The following are examples of liabilities that would be classified as held for trading and thus included in the fair value through profit or loss category:

(a) an interest rate swap that has negative fair value that is not accounted for as a hedging instrument;

(b) a derivative liability incurred upon writing a foreign exchange option that is not accounted for as a hedging instrument;

(c) an obligation to deliver financial assets borrowed by a short seller (i.e. an entity that sells financial assets it has borrowed and does not yet own); and

(d) a quoted debt instrument that the issuer plans to buy back in the near term depending on movements in the debt instrument's fair value, i.e. a financial liability that is incurred with an intention to repurchase it in the near term.

IAS 39.47 states that derivatives (including derivatives embedded in other non-derivative arrangements) are not measured at fair value if they are linked to and must be settled by the delivery of an unquoted equity instrument whose fair value cannot be reliably measured. Such instruments are measured at cost. In the case of non-optional derivatives, for example, forward contracts, the cost may be nil. In the case of written options there will normally be a cost which reflects the option's time value.

As IAS 39 states that subsequent measurement must be at cost it does not appear to allow an entity to amortise the carrying value of the liability measured at cost to profit or loss over the period of the derivative. Therefore, to the extent the derivative liability has a cost it will be recognised in profit or loss only on derecognition of the derivative liability, i.e. when the instrument is extinguished. This will typically be when the obligation is discharged by transferring the obligation to a third party, settlement by delivering or receiving the unquoted equity instrument, or expiration in the case of an option that matures unexercised.

7.1.2 *Financial liabilities designated as at fair value through profit or loss*

Designation as at fair value through profit or loss is available notwithstanding the fact that in the absence of such a choice the liability would have been classified within the category of 'other financial liabilities' and measured at amortised cost. The ability to fair value through profit or loss a financial liability that is not held for trading is restricted to those instances where specified criteria are met. The criterion for financial liabilities is the same as for financial assets, and is detailed in **3.1.1** in **chapter 2**. The designation is, however, irrevocable so the liability cannot subsequently be reclassified into another category during its life (see **3.1.1** in **chapter 2**).

If an entity has designated a financial liability as at fair value through profit or loss, it must disclose the amount of change in its fair value that is due to credit risk which can be determined as the amount of change that is not attributable to changes in market conditions that give rise to market risk (i.e. benchmark interest rate). [IFRS 7.10] (See **4.1.3** in **chapter 11**.)

Where an entity transfers an asset but neither retains nor transfers substantially all of the risks and rewards of ownership of a financial asset, and retains control of that asset, the entity continues to recognise the asset to the extent of its continuing involvement (see **3.4** in **chapter 7**). A corresponding liability is also recognised in accordance with IAS 39.31 and measured in such a way that the net carrying amount of the asset and the liability is:

- the amortised cost of the rights and obligations retained, if the asset is measured at amortised cost; or
- the fair value of the rights and obligations retained, if the asset is measured at fair value.

The specific measurement guidance as described above means that a continuing involvement liability cannot be classified as at fair value through profit or loss. This is reinforced in IAS 39.35 where it states that if the transferred asset is measured at amortised cost an entity is prohibited from designating the associated financial liability as at fair value through profit or loss.

When an entity transfers an asset but retains substantially all the risks and rewards of ownership of the asset a financial liability is recognised equal to the consideration received. IAS 39 is not clear whether this 'failed sale' financial liability can be designated as at fair value through profit or loss. The recognition of such financial liabilities is common in the case of repurchase obligations ('repos') or in structured transactions where an asset is legally transferred but the risks and rewards related to the transferred asset are passed back to the transferor via guarantees and/or derivatives. IAS 39.47 requires all financial liabilities to be measured at amortised cost with some exceptions that include liabilities fair valued through profit or loss (whether held for trading or designated as at fair value through profit or loss) and financial liabilities that arise when a transfer of a financial asset does not qualify for derecognition. In the case of a financial liability initially recognised at the fair value of the consideration received on a failed derecognition transaction the terms of the liability are imputed from the transfer arrangement and the liability is regarded as an in substance collateralised borrowing. IAS 39.29 states that the transferor shall recognise any income on the transferred asset that continues to be recognised in the transferor's statement of financial position "and any expense incurred on the financial liability". As the Standard is not clear whether 'expense' is limited to interest expense only on the deemed collateralised borrowing or could include fair value gains/losses, it is reasonable that an entity can designate the financial liability as at fair value through profit or loss if all the criteria for designation is met.

US GAAP comparison: Under US GAAP, non-derivative liabilities are generally measured at amortised cost. However, FAS 159 permits entities to elect to measure most financial liabilities at fair value through earnings.

7.2 Other financial liabilities

Financial liabilities not classified as at fair value through profit or loss (and which, therefore, are classified in the 'other financial liabilities' category) are measured at amortised cost.

7.3 Reclassification

7.3.1 Into and out of fair value through profit or loss

Reclassifications in and out of this category are prohibited. The following changes in circumstances are not reclassifications:
[IAS 39.50A]

- a derivative that was previously a designated and effective hedging instrument in a cash flow hedge or net investment hedge no longer qualifies as such; and

- a derivative becomes a designated and effective hedging instrument in a cash flow hedge or net investment hedge.

IAS 39.50A was introduced by *Improvements to IFRSs* issued in May 2008. The amendments made to IAS 39 by *Improvements to IFRSs* apply for annual periods beginning on or after 1 January 2009, but earlier application is permitted. An entity choosing to apply the amendments early must disclose that fact.

7.4 Classification of financial liabilities acquired in a business combination

When financial liabilities are assumed in a business combination those liabilities must be classified in the consolidated financial statements of the acquirer into one of the permitted categories described in **section 7** above. It is entirely possible that the classification of a financial liability for these purposes may differ from its classification in the financial statements of the acquiree. For example, the acquirer in its consolidated financial statements may choose to designate a financial liability as at fair value through profit or loss at initial recognition that the acquiree did not classify in that category when it initially recognised the liability. The difference in classification arises as the acquirer at the time of acquisition recognises the financial liabilities of the acquiree for the first time and has to make its own classification decision.

The revised version of IFRS 3 *Business Combinations*, issued in January 2008, provides clear guidance stating that at the acquisition date the acquirer shall make any classifications, designations concerning financial assets acquired or financial liabilities assumed in a business combination in accordance with the contractual terms, economic conditions, the acquirer's operating or accounting policies, and other factors as of that date that are pertinent in subsequently applying other IFRSs. IFRS 3(2008) is effective for accounting periods beginning on or after 1 July 2009.

8 Reassessing classification

The liability-equity classification made at initial recognition is reconsidered if there are changes to the contractual terms of the instrument. In November 2006 the IFRIC issued a rejection notice that included a reassessment of liability-equity classification in the case of a change in terms of the instrument that resulted in a financial liability being reclassified to equity. IFRIC 2.5 also states that in determining liability-equity classification the entity considers all terms and conditions at the date of classification, "but not expected future amendments to those laws, regulations or charter". The IFRIC that Example 3 in IFRIC 2 provides an example of reclassification from equity to financial liability following a change in the entity's governing charter.

IAS 32 is less clear in what circumstances it is appropriate to reconsider the liability-equity classification in the case where the terms of the instrument do not change. Generally, an entity would not reconsider the classification of the arrangement though it may be necessary to do so if due to changed circumstances as demonstrated in the examples below.

Example 8A

Convertible debt with change in functional currency

Entity B, a US$ functional currency entity, issues a Euro denominated convertible bond that is convertible at the holder's choice into a fixed number of equity shares of Entity B. As the conversion feature will not be settled by the exchange of a fixed amount of functional currency cash and a fixed number of shares the convertible bond is recognised entirely as a financial liability.

One year after the date of issue Entity B's functional currency changes to the Euro. The terms of the conversion feature meet the definition of equity at the date Entity B's functional currency changes as the conversion option will now be settled by the exchange of a fixed amount of functional currency cash and a fixed number of shares. At the date the functional currency changes it would be reasonable to reclassify the conversion feature to equity as its then carrying value, being its fair value. No gain or loss is recognised as the conversion feature is recognised at fair value. It would be inappropriate to recognise the conversion feature at its fair value at the date of issue of the convertible bond as this would result in a gain or loss on derecognition of the conversion feature financial liability which would effectively be reversing the gains or losses recognised since initial recognition. The financial liability component that remains is the debt component, being the interest payable over the life and the principal payable at maturity if the instrument is not converted which will continue to be recognised as a financial liability.

If the fact pattern were to be reversed so that Entity B's functional currency was Euro and the convertible bond was recognised as a compound instrument, had Entity B's functional currency then changed to US$, at that date the conversion option would fail to meet the definition of equity and would be reclassified to profit or loss at its fair value. Any difference between the fair value at the date of reclassification and the original amount recognised in equity would be recognised in equity consistent with the reclassification described in IFRIC rejection notice in November 2006. The reclassification from equity to financial liability must not result in a gain or loss in profit or loss consistent with IAS 32.33.

Example 8B

Derivative over interest in a subsidiary with subsequent disposal of the subsidiary

Entity C is a Euro functional currency entity. It has a 60% owned subsidiary, Entity D. Entity C acquires a call option enabling it to purchase a further 10% of Entity D. The option is over 100,000 shares and Entity D and is not exercisable until the end of year 2. The option can only be exercised through gross physical settlement, i.e. through receipt of a fixed number of shares for a fixed amount of Euro cash).

Upon entering into the call option Entity C determines that the call option meets the definition of equity in the consolidated financial statements as it will be settled exclusively through the exchange of a fixed amount of functional currency cash for a fixed number of equity shares.

Subsequent to entering into the call option but before the option is exercisable at the end of year 2 Entity C disposes of half of its 60% interest in Entity D such that following the disposal it has a 30% shareholding and the pre-existing purchased call option over an additional 10%. Control is lost at the date of disposal, but Entity C acquires significant influence over Entity D.

At the date of disposal the purchased call option no longer meets the definition of equity in the consolidated financial statements as the shares delivered under the option are not longer group equity, rather they are shares in an associate. At the date of disposal the purchased call option must be reclassified from equity to a derivative measured at fair value through profit or loss. Any difference between the fair value at the date of reclassification and the original amount recognised in equity is recognised as a gain or loss in equity.

If the fact pattern were to be reversed so that Entity C's interest in Entity D was originally an investment in a an associate the purchased call option would have not met the definition of equity at initial recognition and would have been fair valued through profit or loss. If Entity C subsequently acquired a further 30% interest in Entity D (independent of the call option) and thus acquired control of Entity D, then the purchased call option would be reclassified at its fair value to equity at the date of acquisition.

An example of a written put financial liability expiring and the simultaneous recognition of an equity instrument is illustrated in **example 4B** in **chapter 7**.

9 Future developments

In February 2008 the IASB issued a discussion paper entitled *Financial Instruments with Characteristics of Equity*. The discussion paper follows the issue in November 2007 of a preliminary views document with the same title issued by the US Financial Accounting Standards Board (FASB). The discussion paper was issued by the IASB as part of its memorandum of understanding with the FASB to issue due process documents relating to a proposed standard on the distinction between liabilities and equity. The discussion paper comprised an invitation to comment on the FASB's preliminary views document. At the time of writing the project was on IASB's active agenda and is being undertaken jointly with the FASB.

The FASB document describes three approaches for distinguishing equity instruments from non-equity instruments: (i) basic ownership, (ii) ownership-settlement and (iii) reassessed expected outcomes. Subsequently, the FASB has discussed a fourth approach – the so-called perpetual approach.

The IASB decided that future deliberations would use the principles underlying the perpetual and basic ownership approaches. Under the perpetual approach, an instrument would be classified as equity if it lacks a settlement requirement and entitles the holder to a share of the entity's net assets on liquidation. Under the basic ownership approach, an instrument would be classified as equity if it is the most subordinated claim and entitles the holder to a share of the entity's net assets. The IASB acknowledged that there may be exceptions to the basic principles as it continues to develop an approach to identify equity instruments. The Board tentatively decided that all perpetual instruments (including perpetual basic ownership instruments) should be classified as equity and that derivatives on an issuer's own equity instruments should be classified as non-equity (although whether derivative instruments within the scope of IFRS 2 *Share-based Payment* would be subject to that classification principle has not been determined) and at the time of writing the Board directed the staff to analyse further an approach that would identify different types of instruments and consider whether those types should be classified differently. For example, the Board discussed the following types of instruments: (i) instruments that are puttable or mandatorily redeemable on a specified date or dates and (ii) instruments that are puttable or mandatorily redeemable upon the occurrence of an event that is certain to occur (such as death or retirement).

At the date of writing, the IASB expects to issue an exposure draft on distinguishing equity from non-equity instruments in the second half of 2009 and a final standard on this subject in 2011.

4 Derivatives

1 Introduction

IAS 39 requires that all derivatives are accounted for in the statement of financial position at fair value, irrespective of whether they are used as part of a hedging relationship. Changes in fair value are recognised in profit or loss unless the contract is part of an effective cash flow or net investment hedging relationship (see **chapter 8** and **9** on hedge accounting). If a derivative is part of an effective cash flow or net investment hedge, the change in fair value of the effective portion of the hedge is recognised in other comprehensive income. As the definition of a derivative is so broad, many contracts are likely to be caught, and therefore will have to be accounted for at fair value. For example, certain contracts to buy or sell non-financial items fall within the scope of IAS 39 and meet the definition of a derivative (see **2.5** in **chapter 1**).

A fixed price commitment to buy or sell a financial instrument at a future date meets the definition of a derivative financial instrument. However, as a practical expedient these are not accounted for as derivatives if the commitment has a short duration accepted by market convention. These are referred to as regular way purchases or sales. Regular way contracts are subject to special accounting rules. This is dealt with in **2.2** in **chapter 7**.

This chapter discusses derivatives in the following sections:

Section 2	Definition of a derivative
Section 3	Scoped-in contracts
Section 4	Examples of contracts that meet the definition of a derivative
Section 5	Presentation of derivatives

2 Definition of a derivative

IAS 39 defines a derivative as a financial instrument or other contract within the scope of the Standard with all three of the following characteristics:
[IAS 39.9]

- its value changes in response to the change in a specified interest rate, financial instrument price, commodity price, foreign exchange rate, index of prices or rates, credit rating or credit index, or other variable, provided in the case of a non-financial variable that the variable is not specific to a party to the contract (sometimes called the 'underlying');

- it requires no initial net investment or an initial net investment that is smaller than would be required for other types of contracts that would be expected to have a similar response to changes in market factors; and
- it is settled at a future date.

2.1 Underlying

An underlying is a variable that, along with either a notional amount or a payment provision, determines the settlement amount of a derivative.

Examples of underlyings include:

- a security price or security price index;
- a commodity price or commodity price index;
- an interest rate or interest rate index;
- a credit rating or credit index;
- a foreign exchange rate or foreign exchange rate index;
- an insurance index or catastrophe loss index;
- a climatic or geological condition (e.g. temperature, earthquake severity, or rainfall), another physical variable, or a related index; or
- another variable (e.g. volume of sales).

The value or cash flows of all assets, liabilities, and purchase and sale commitments change in response to changes in the market factors in which they are founded. There is nothing unique in this regard about derivatives, except that the market factor is referred to as an index, a variable or an underlying and, in many instances, the referenced underlying is not delivered at settlement but is used as a basis for computing a settlement amount, usually in cash.

Prior to the issue of IFRS 4 *Insurance Contracts*, IAS 39 scoped out derivatives where the variable is based on climatic, geological and other physical variables. However, since IFRS 4 was issued, IAS 39 has been amended to scope these contracts into IAS 39 unless they meet the definition of an insurance contract (see **2.3** of **chapter 1**). If an insurance contract contains an embedded derivative that needs to be separately accounted for, then it is only the embedded derivative part of the insurance contract that will be accounted for as a derivative in accordance with IAS 39. Embedded derivatives are considered in **chapter 5**.

Additionally, a derivative where the underlying is a specific commodity, for example oil, may be scoped out of IAS 39 if the contract is considered a normal purchase, sale or usage requirement contract (see **2.5** of **chapter 1**). Whether the instrument is scoped in or out of IAS 39 is dependent on the entity's normal business requirements as well as the settlement terms of the instrument, the entity's past practice, and whether the instrument is a written option and the underlying is readily convertible to cash.

The definition of a derivative was amended by the IASB when it issued IFRS 4 *Insurance Contracts* to scope out contracts over non-financial variables that are specific to a party to the contract. This amendment was required to ensure that insurance risk was scoped out of IAS 39 and instead accounted for in accordance with IFRS 4. Some argue that the term 'non-financial variable specific to a party to the contract' was intended to scope out contracts beyond just insurance contracts. For example, if the amount of interest payable on issued debt is linked to the sales volume of the issuer or based on a proportion of profits of the issuer, then this could be argued to be 'a non-financial variable specific to a party to the contract.' If this literal interpretation applied then the sales or profit linking feature would never meet the definition of a derivative, and therefore could never be an embedded derivative. However, this would not seem to be a valid interpretation considering that both IAS 39.IG.B.8 and IAS 39.AG33(f)(ii) clearly indicate that derivatives and embedded derivatives can be based on sales volumes and revenue. In addition, IAS 39.IG.A.2 states that an option to put a non-financial asset, such as an office building, is a derivative if it is not scoped out of IAS 39 as a purchase, sale or usage requirements contract (see **2.5** of **chapter 1**). If the literal interpretation described above was appropriate then the implementation guidance Q&A would be incorrect as the put option in that case is over an office building that is a non-financial variable that is specific to a party to the contract. It follows, therefore, from IAS 39.11 that a debt instrument with interest linked to sales volume of the issuer or other non-financial variables contains an embedded derivative that is not closely related to the host debt contract. The embedded derivative is therefore separated from the host contract and accounted for as a derivative under IAS 39. See **chapter 5** on embedded derivatives.

In February 2007 the IFRIC recommended that the Board should make an amendment to IAS 39 to make it clear that the term 'non-financial variable specific to a party to the contract' included in the definition of a derivative is restricted to scoping out insurance contracts from IAS 39. The Board unanimously agreed to this recommendation. In October 2007 the IASB issued an Exposure Draft titled *Improvements to International Financial Reporting Standards* that proposed to amend the definition of a derivative in IAS 39 by deleting the reference to 'non-financial variables specific to a party to the contract' and as a result contracts linked to those variables will be within the scope of IAS 39 and classified as derivatives. The Board recognised that it introduced the exclusion for some non-financial variables when it issued IFRS 4 to exclude from the scope of IAS 39 contracts within the scope of IFRS 4. The Board observed that the proposed amendment would not affect the scope of IAS 39, because contracts within the scope of IFRS 4 are excluded from IAS 39.2(e) anyway.

In October 2008 the IASB redeliberated the definition of a derivative following comments received from constituents on its proposals that were issued in October 2007. The Board tentatively decided not to proceed with the proposed amendment in the annual improvements project but will consider addressing this issue in a future project.

US GAAP comparison: Under US GAAP contracts that are not exchange traded in which the underlying is a specified volume of sales or service revenues of one of the parties to the contract are exempted from derivative accounting (FAS 133.10(e)(3)). Non-derivative treatment is intended to apply to contracts with settlements based on the volume of items sold or services rendered (such as royalty agreements). It is not intended to apply to contracts based on changes in sales or revenues due to changes in market prices.

2.2 Notionals and payment provisions

A derivative usually has a notional amount, which is an amount of currency, a number of shares, a number of units of weight or volume or other units specified in the contract. However, instead of having a notional amount, a derivative contract could instead require a fixed payment or payment of an amount that can change (but not proportionally to a change in the underlying) as a result of some future event that is unrelated to a notional. This is referred to as a payment provision.

Example 2.2A

Payment provision based on interest rates

Entity ABC receives CU200 to enter into a contract that requires it to pay CU500 if six-month LIBOR increases by 75 basis points over the next six months. Even though this contract does not have a notional, it contains a payment provision that does not move proportionally with the underlying.

Example 2.2B

Payment provision based on share price

Entity XYZ enters into a contract that requires it to pay CU10 million if Entity ABC's share price increases by CU5 per share during a six-month period; conversely XYZ will receive CU10 million if ABC's share price decreases by CU5 per share during the same six-month period.

In this example, the underlying is the price of ABC shares. There is no notional amount to determine the settlement amount. Instead, there is a payment provision that does not move proportionally with the underlying. The absence of a notional amount does not preclude the instrument from meeting the definition of a derivative because there is a payment provision.

It is sometimes the case that a contract has neither a notional, nor a fixed payment provision. In addition, a contract may have multiple underlyings.

Example 2.2C

Foreign currency forward contract linked to sales

Entity X, a Euro functional currency entity, sells products in Switzerland. The sales are denominated in Swiss francs. Entity X enters into a contract with an investment bank to convert Swiss francs to Euros at a fixed exchange rate. The contract requires Entity X to remit Swiss francs based on its sales volume in Switzerland in exchange for Euros at a fixed exchange rate of 1.60.

The contract with the bank has two underlyings (sales volume and the Euro/Swiss franc exchange rate). The contract does not have a specified notional amount or a fixed payment provision, but still meets the definition of a derivative.

US GAAP comparison: The first part of the definition of a derivative in IFRS focuses on the existence of an underlying. The equivalent guidance under US GAAP focuses on the existence of an underlying and a notional amount or a payment provision, or both. [FAS 133.6(a)]. The US definition is therefore narrower in that if a contract does not have either a notional or a payment provision it can never be a derivative. This is especially significant given the fact that US GAAP requires that in cases where a contract does not specify a fixed number of units the conclusion that a notional exists can only be reached if there is a reliable way of determining the notional amount

(DIG A6). Because the IFRS definition focuses simply on the existence of an underlying, a contract could meet the definition of a derivative in IFRS but not US GAAP where the contract does not have a notional or payment provision.

2.3 Interaction of notional amounts with the underlying

The settlement amount of a derivative instrument with a notional amount is determined by the interaction of that notional amount with the underlying. The interaction may be simple multiplication, or it may involve a formula with leverage factors or other constants.

Example 2.3

Interest rate swap

XYZ enters into an interest rate swap that requires XYZ to pay a fixed rate of interest and receive a variable rate of interest. The fixed interest rate amount is 7.5 per cent, while the variable interest rate amount is three-month LIBOR, reset on a quarterly basis. The notional amount of the swap is CU100 million.

The underlying is an interest rate index, three-month LIBOR. Net regular settlements are calculated by applying the difference between 7.5 per cent and three-month LIBOR to the notional of CU100 million.

2.4 Initial net investment

The second part of the definition of a derivative is that there is either no initial net investment, or that any initial investment is smaller than would be required for other contracts that are expected to have a similar response to changes in market factors. This is a comparative measure, and excludes any margin accounts (which are instead treated as collateral). Consider the following examples.

2.4.1 Interest rate swaps

Example 2.4.1

Interest rate swap

Entity B enters into a contract with a counterparty that requires it to pay a LIBOR-based variable rate of interest, and receive a fixed rate of 8 per cent. The contract is an interest rate swap with a notional amount of ¥10 billion. Entity B did not pay or receive cash at inception, i.e. the contract is at market at inception, and therefore does not require an initial net investment by either party.

In some instances, the terms of the interest rate swap may be favourable or unfavourable and may require one of the parties to make an up-front initial investment in the contract. If the initial investment represents a premium or discount for market conditions, the initial net investment would normally still be smaller than the notional on the debt instrument from which the interest rate cash flows are derived, and so would satisfy the initial net investment criterion of a derivative.

2.4.1.1 Interest rate swap with fixed leg prepaid

Example 2.4.1.1

Prepaid fixed leg

Entity X enters into an eight-year pay-fixed at 7 per cent, receive LIBOR interest rate swap on CU100 million. It prepays the fixed leg at inception. The amount it pays is calculated as CU7 million (CU100 million x 7 per cent) for 8 years, discounted at market rates.

This initial payment is significantly less than the amount Entity X would have to pay to acquire an instrument that would have a similar response to changes in market factors. Entity X would need to acquire CU100 million debt with a LIBOR return in order to replicate the return on the floating rate leg of the swap. Therefore, the swap with a prepaid fixed leg will still meet the definition of a derivative.

If the fixed rate payment obligation on the interest rate swap is prepaid after initial recognition the payment would be considered termination of the old swap and an origination of a new instrument that would need to be classified for the first time. [IAS 39.IG.B.4]

US GAAP comparison: While the IAS 39.IG.B.4 is clear on the treatment of a prepaid interest swap as a derivative, US GAAP considers those instruments as hybrid contracts with a non-derivative host. According to DIG Issue A23 the entity is required to bifurcate interest rate swaps with a prepaid fixed leg into a debt host contract (i.e. the present value of the prepaid fixed rate payments) and an interest rate swap with a fair value of zero at inception. The latter is consistent with the guidance in DIG Issue B20.

2.4.1.2 Interest rate swap with floating leg prepaid

Example 2.4.1.2

Prepaid floating leg

Entity A enters into a six-year pay LIBOR, receive-fixed 5 per cent interest rate swap on CU100 million. It prepays the variable leg at inception. The cash inflows that the entity continues to receive are akin to those of a financial instrument with a fixed annuity of 5 per cent per year for the next six years.

As the amount prepaid will be about the same as what would have been paid to purchase a fixed annuity instrument paying 5 per cent over the next six years, the initial net investment test is failed. The contract would not be accounted for as a derivative, but instead as a loan made by Entity A. [IAS 39.IG.B.5]

2.4.2 Options

For an option the premium paid could be significant. However, it is likely to be smaller than the amount that would be required to buy an instrument with a similar response to changes in market factors, i.e. the underlying instrument to which the option relates.

Example 2.4.2A

Deep in-the-money option (1)

Entity A purchases, for CU1.1 million, an option to buy 80,000 shares in Entity B at CU75 per share in three months' time. When it purchased the option, Entity B's shares were trading at CU70 per share. The cost of the option, CU1.1 million, is less than what it would cost to buy 80,000 shares in Entity B, so it meets this part of the definition. This will even be the case for many deep-in-the-money options, as demonstrated below.

Example 2.4.2B

Deep in-the-money option (2)

Entity XYZ purchases a deep-in-the-money call option on Entity ABC shares. ABC's share price is €100 per share. The option is an American option with a 180-day maturity. The option has a strike price of €10 per share and XYZ pays a premium of €91. The initial investment in the option of €91 is less than the notional amount applied to the underlying, i.e. €100 (the notional amount is one share and the underlying is €100 per share).

Although the option has a significant initial net investment, it is smaller than the investment that would be required for other types of contracts that would be expected to have a similar response to changes in market factors. The invested amount of €91 does not approximate the notional amount applied to the underlying (€100) and, therefore, the option meets the initial net investment criterion for a derivative instrument.

2.4.3 *Currency swap*

Currency swaps typically require an initial exchange of currencies. These swaps will still satisfy the initial net investment criterion as the exchange is of amounts with an equal fair value, so that on a net basis the fair value at inception is zero.

> **Example 2.4.3**
>
> **Currency swap**
>
> Entity X enters into a three-year currency swap with Bank Z. At inception, when the Sterling/Euro exchange rate is 1.5, the swap results in Entity X paying Bank Z £100 million and Bank Z paying Entity X €150 million. Although there has been an exchange of cash, the amounts exchanged are of equal fair value.

2.4.4 *Prepaid forward contract*

> **Example 2.4.4**
>
> **Prepaid forward contract**
>
> Entity X enters into a forward contract to purchase one million ordinary shares in Entity T in one year. The current market price of Entity T's shares is €50 per share, and the one-year forward price is €55 per share. Entity X prepays the forward contract at inception with a €50 million payment.
>
> The initial net investment approximates the investment that would be required for other types of contracts that would be expected to have a similar response to changes in market factors because one million of Entity T's shares could be purchased at inception for the same price of €50 million. Accordingly, the prepaid forward contract does not meet the initial net investment criterion of a derivative instrument. [IAS 39.IG.B.9]

2.4.5 *Offsetting loans*

Two or more non-derivative contracts should be considered together when the substance of the aggregate position is that of a derivative. IAS 39.IG.B.6 states that indicators of such a situation are when the contracts are:

- entered into at the same time, and in contemplation of each other;
- have the same counterparty;
- relate to the same risk; and

- there is no apparent economic need or substantive business purpose for structuring the transactions separately that could not also have been accomplished in a single transaction.

Example 2.4.5

Offsetting loans

Entity A makes a five-year fixed rate loan to Entity B on market terms. Simultaneously, Entity B makes a five-year variable rate loan to Entity A on market terms over the same notional. The combination of these two loans is akin to an interest rate swap. Even if amounts are exchanged at inception of the two loans, the net fair value of the amounts exchanged is zero. Therefore, the loans must be considered together, and the entire arrangement accounted for as a derivative.

2.5 Future settlement

The third part of the definition of a derivative is that it is settled at a future date. Settlement can occur in different ways, either gross or net [IAS 39.IG.B.3], and does not just mean exchange of cash. For example, it may be expected that an out-of-the-money option will not be exercised. However, expiry of the contract is a form of settlement, even if at maturity of the instrument no cash or underlying changes hands. [IAS 39.IG.B.7]

US GAAP comparison: The US GAAP definition of a derivative requires the presence of a net settlement characteristic in the financial instrument or other contract (FAS 133.6(c)). Under US GAAP, the net settlement criterion can be met if a financial instrument or other contract can readily be settled net by a means outside the contract or if the terms of the instrument provide for delivery of an asset that puts the recipient in a position not substantially different from net settlement (e.g. where the asset to be delivered is readily convertible to cash because it is exchange traded). Stated differently, net settlement exists when a market mechanism facilitates net settlement or when the asset to be delivered under the contract is readily convertible to cash or is itself a derivative instrument. Because the IAS 39 definition of a derivative permits gross or net settlement but does not require net settlement, some financial instruments could meet the definition of a derivative under IAS 39 but not under US GAAP. For example, a purchased option on an unquoted security may not meet the definition of a derivative under US GAAP because the underlying security is not readily convertible to cash (i.e., does not meet the net settlement criterion).

3 Scoped-in contracts

Certain contracts to buy or sell non-financial items are within the scope of IAS 39 (see **2.5** of **chapter 1**). If a contract to buy or sell a non-financial item is within the scope of IAS 39 and meets the definition of a derivative it will be recognised at fair value.

Example 3

Contract over a non-financial item

Entity A enters into a futures contract to purchase 1,000 bushels of corn for CU1 per bushel in three months. No cash is paid at inception. Assuming the contract is within the scope of IAS 39 (i.e. because it is not entered into for the purpose of the receipt of the corn bushels), the contract meets the definition of a derivative.

It has an underlying (the price of corn bushels), there is no initial investment, and the contract will be settled in the future. The contract must be recognised in Entity A's statement of financial position at fair value, with changes in fair value recognised in profit or loss unless the contract qualifies as a hedging instrument in an effective hedge relationship.

4 Examples of contracts that meet the definition of a derivative

Some common examples of derivatives are included below:

Contract	Notional/ payment provision	Underlying	Initial invest-ment	Future settlement
A futures contract to buy 1,000 barrels of crude oil at $60 a barrel in 1 month and the contract is not entered into for the physical delivery of oil for the entity's normal business usage requirements	1,000 barrels of crude oil	Price of oil barrels	$0	Yes – 1 month
A forward to buy $500 for £300 in 1 year	$500 (or £300)	£/$ exchange rate	£0	Yes – 1 year
An option to buy 80,000 shares in Entity B at CU75 per share in 1 month. The option costs CU1.1 million	80,000 shares	Entity B's share price	CU1.1 million	Yes – 1 month
A pay LIBOR + 25 basis points, receive fixed 5% interest rate swap over CU100 million, settled quarterly	CU100 million	LIBOR	CU0	Yes – quarterly

Contract	Notional/ payment provision	Underlying	Initial invest-ment	Future settlement
A pay-floating £ on £100 million, receive-floating US$ on $170 million currency swap, settled annually	£100 million or $170 million	£/$ exchange rate	£0	Yes – annually
A contract to receive CU10 million if Entity A's share price increases by CU5 per share at the end of six-months. The contract costs CU1.0 million to enter into	Payment provision	Entity A's share price	CU1.0 million	Yes – 6 months
A pay-variable Euro amount based on the entity's sales, receive £ at a fixed exchange rate of €1.5:£1 based on the entity's sales, settled monthly	Variable notional	€/£ exchange rate and sales volume	£0	Yes – monthly
A 5-year interest rate cap over CU100 million. The cap will pay if LIBOR increases beyond 8%. The premium paid to enter into the cap is CU1.0 million	CU100 million	LIBOR	CU1.0 million	Yes – if in Year 5 LIBOR exceeds 8%.

The definition of a derivative is very broad and therefore can capture many contractual arrangements that traditionally would not be considered derivatives. One example is bets in the gaming industry. A bookmaker will take a bet from a customer on the outcome of a specified event (for example a horse race, general election, or football match) in cash for stated or variable odds. When the event occurs, depending on the outcome, the bookmaker will pay any winnings to the customer. The contract for the bet is no different to a derivative contract without a notional and with a payment provision. The bookmaker has written an option to the customer, where the bookmaker will receive an up-front premium in return for bearing potential downside risk should the uncertain event occur.

Where the customer does not 'fix' the odds, i.e. has variable odds, the derivative will be far less sensitive to changes in the probability of the uncertain event occurring, and therefore the derivative will be far less sensitive to changes in market prices. However, where the holder of the bet 'fixes' the odds, the fair value of the bet will change with changes in the probability of the uncertain event occurring.

The bookmaker will take bets on many different outcomes for one event and expects to make a profit irrespective of that event's outcome. If a bookmaker has taken too many bets from customers on one outcome, it may 'lay off' bets with another bookmaker, i.e. it enters into an offsetting bet to lay off the risk. This is a form of economic hedging. The entity cannot apply hedge accounting as a derivative is not a qualifying hedged item (see **3.6** in **chapter 8**). As such, in accordance with IAS 39, bookmakers should recognise all bets, whether written or purchased, as derivative assets and liabilities measured at fair value through profit or loss.

In May 2007 the IFRIC issued a rejection notice on gaming transactions stating that an unsettled wager is likely to meet the definition of a derivative and will therefore be accounted for under IAS 39. The IFRIC recognised that, in other situations, a gaming institution does not take a position against a customer but instead provides services to manage the organisation of games between two or more gaming parties. In these instances, the gaming institution earns a commission regardless of the outcome of the wager and therefore it is likely that the commission would meet the definition of revenue and would be recognised when the conditions in *IAS 18 Revenue* were met.

5 Presentation of derivatives

5.1 Current versus non-current

A derivative that has a maturity of less than twelve months from the end of the reporting period or has a maturity greater than twelve months but is expected to be settled within twelve months should be presented as a current asset or liability in the statement of financial position. A derivative that has a maturity of more than twelve months from the end of the reporting period and is not intended to be settled within twelve months will be presented as a non-current asset or liability.

Prior to the issue of *Improvements to IFRSs* in May 2008, there was ambiguity as to whether derivatives with a maturity greater than twelve months that are not intended to be settled within twelve months and were not part of a designated and effective hedge accounting relationship could be presented as non-current as these instruments also met the definition of held for trading in IAS 39.9. An amendment to IAS 1 included as part of *Improvements to IFRSs* clarified that in such instances the derivatives should be presented as non-current as the derivative is not held primarily for trading purposes. The amendments made to IAS 1 by *Improvements to IFRSs* apply for annual periods beginning on or after 1 January 2009, but earlier application is permitted. An entity choosing to apply the amendments early must disclose that fact.

For guidance on the presentation of embedded derivatives see **section 13** in **chapter 5**.

5.2 Income statement presentation

5.2.1 *Fair value gains and losses on derivatives in hedge accounting relationships*

IAS 39 provides limited guidance where gains and losses on derivatives in highly effective hedge accounting relationships should be presented in the income statement. However, an analogy can be drawn with the principle in IAS 39.IG.G.2 that describes where cash flows arising from hedging instruments should be classified in statements of cash flows. The implementation guidance states that cash flows arising from hedging instruments are classified as operating, investing or financing activities, on the basis of the classification of the cash flows arising from the hedged item. Therefore, it appropriate that gains and losses in highly effective hedge accounting relationships are presented in the same line in the income statement as the hedged item impacts profit or loss. Where gains and losses are material separate presentation of those gains and losses in the income statement would be required. An item that is not sufficiently material to warrant separate presentation on the face of the income statement may nevertheless be sufficiently material for it to be presented separately in the notes. [IAS 1.30]

5.2.2 *Fair value gains and losses on derivatives that are economic hedges*

IAS 39 requires gains and losses on derivatives to be reported in profit or loss when hedge accounting is not applied. However, the Standard does not specify where such gains and losses would be presented within profit or loss.

Example 5.2.2

Presentation of non-hedge accounting derivative

Entity A enters into a derivative contract (forward contract) to hedge a foreign currency cash flow under a highly probable forecast revenue stream. The entity does not apply hedge accounting.

Presentation of the gains and losses on the derivative within revenue or elsewhere in operating profit is not precluded, provided the chosen presentation is applied consistently from period to period to all similar items and follows the nature of the transaction to which it is linked. The policy adopted should be disclosed in the financial statements.

5 Embedded derivatives

1 Introduction

IAS 39 introduces a new accounting concept, that of an embedded derivative. The definition of an embedded derivative and the principle of separation is relatively simple, but the application is complicated as most of the guidance in the Standard is provided by means of examples. Furthermore, the scope is wide as an entity will need to consider whether embedded derivatives may reside in contracts other than financial instruments. They may be found in any contract, such as a lease, an insurance contract, or a sale or a purchase contract.

The challenge extends beyond searching for all embedded derivatives. Once one has been found, it must then be determined whether the embedded derivative needs to be separately accounted for under IAS 39. Not all embedded derivatives should be separated out from the host contract in which they reside.

Embedded derivatives that have to be separated are accounted for in the same way as stand-alone derivatives, i.e. at fair value with gains and losses recognised in profit or loss at each measurement date, unless the embedded derivative qualifies as an effective hedging instrument in a cash flow or a net investment hedge in a foreign operation.

This chapter discusses embedded derivatives in the following sections:

Section 2	Definitions
Section 3	Separation conditions
Section 4	Terms of the embedded derivative and the debt host contract
Section 5	Determination of host contract: debt vs. equity
Section 6	Multiple embedded derivatives
Section 7	Embedded derivatives in debt host contracts
Section 8	Embedded derivatives in equity host contracts
Section 9	Embedded derivatives in lease contracts

2 Definitions

IAS 39 defines an embedded derivative as a component of a hybrid (combined) instrument that also includes a non-derivative host contract – with the effect that some of the cash flows of the combined instrument vary in a way similar to a stand-alone derivative. An embedded derivative causes some or all of the cash flows that otherwise would be required by the contract to be modified according to a specified interest rate, financial instrument price, commodity price, foreign exchange rate, index of prices or rates or other variable (provided in the case of a non-financial variable that the variable is not specific to a party to the contract, see **2.1** of **chapter 4**). [IAS 39.10]

The hybrid contract is the entire contract, within which there may be an embedded derivative. The host contract is the main body of the contract, excluding the embedded derivative. The diagram and examples below demonstrate the application of these terms.

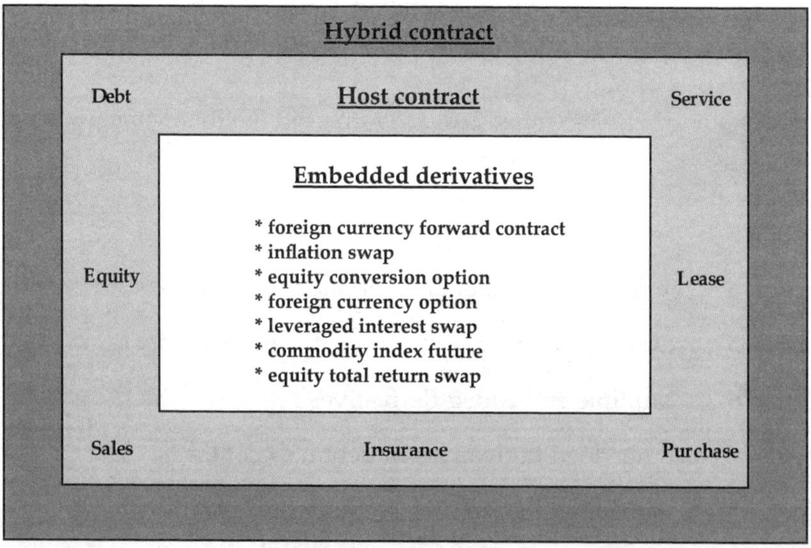

Example 2A

Debt host contract

Entity X holds a bond which is convertible into the ordinary shares of Entity Y. The hybrid contract is the convertible bond; the host contract is the bond asset, and the embedded derivative is the conversion option.

Example 2B

Lease host contract

Entity A enters into a lease with an inflation factor, such that each year rentals are adjusted for changes in a retail price index. The hybrid contract is the entire lease; the host is the lease contract, and the embedded derivative is the adjustment to the retail price index.

Example 2C

Executory host contract

Entity T, a UK entity whose functional currency is Sterling, enters into a contract to sell a non-financial item in US dollars. The hybrid contract is the entire sale contract which will be settled in US dollars; the host contract is the Sterling sale contract; the embedded derivative is the foreign exchange Sterling/US dollar forward.

A derivative that is attached to a financial instrument but is contractually transferable independently of that instrument, or has a different counterparty from that instrument, is not an embedded derivative, but a separate financial instrument. [IAS 39.10]

Example 2D

Contractually separate derivative

Entity A issues floating rate debt. To protect itself against rising interest rates, it purchases an interest rate cap, capping interest payable at 8 per cent. The cap is contractually separate from the debt, so it is not an embedded derivative, but a free-standing derivative.

Entity A could have instead issued floating rate debt, where the debt instrument itself is capped, such that once interest rates go beyond 8 per cent, it only pays out 8 per cent until rates fall below this level. In this case, there is an embedded derivative within the debt, i.e. the interest rate cap, and this cap will need to be assessed to see if it must be separately accounted for.

3 Separation conditions

Not all embedded derivatives should be separated from their host contracts. An embedded derivative is separated from its host contract and accounted for separately as a stand-alone derivative when:
[IAS 39.11]

(a) the economic characteristics and risks of the embedded derivative are not closely related to the economic risks and characteristics of the host contract;

(b) a separate instrument with the same terms as the embedded derivative would meet the definition of a derivative; and

(c) the hybrid instrument is not measured at fair value with changes in fair value recognised in profit or loss.

Condition (b) above means that an embedded feature should only be separated from its host contract if it itself meets the definition of a derivative, i.e. it has an underlying, no initial net investment (or an initial net investment that is smaller than would be required for other types of contracts that would be expected to have a similar response to changes in market factors) and it is settled at a future date (see **chapter 4** for more details on the definition of a derivative).

Example 3A

No underlying

A lease contract contains a provision that rentals increase by CU100 each year. The price adjustment feature does not meet the definition of a derivative on a stand-alone basis since its value does not change in response to changes of some 'underlying' – there is no underlying.

US GAAP comparison: As described in **section 2** in **chapter 4**, the definition of a derivative in US GAAP differs from IFRS. This difference in definition equally applies to the definition of embedded derivatives. In addition, US guidance is more detailed in providing more examples of which embedded derivatives are considered to be closely related. These additional examples may be of use in determining whether embedded derivatives under IFRS are closely related.

Condition (c) means that any financial asset or financial liability that is held at fair value with changes in fair value recognised through profit or loss should not be assessed to see if it contains any embedded derivatives. Any embedded derivative that is not closely related to its host will be accounted for as if it were a stand-alone derivative – i.e. measured at fair value, with changes in fair value recognised in profit or loss. If the entire contract is already being accounted for in this way the embedded derivative is automatically accounted for at fair value and therefore it is not required to be separated.

An entity can elect to classify a hybrid instrument at fair value through profit or loss at initial recognition, even though the instrument would not meet the definition of held for trading (see **3.1** in **chapter 2**).

Such an election cannot be made if:

(a) the embedded derivative does not significantly modify the cash flows that otherwise would be required by the contract; or

(b) it is clear with little or no analysis when a similar hybrid instrument is first considered that separation of the embedded derivative is prohibited, as in the case of a prepayment option embedded in a loan that permits the holder to prepay the loan for approximately its amortised cost (see **7.1** in this chapter).

Designating a hybrid instrument as at fair value through profit or loss may provide benefit to entities with more complex instruments where the search for and analysis of embedded derivatives significantly increases the cost of complying with IAS 39. This will also benefit entities that issue or acquire structured products, for example equity-linked notes or callable range-accrual notes, which may contain more than one embedded derivative that is not closely related to the host contract. For issuers of these instruments, who normally invest in derivatives as an economic hedge of the issued notes, fair valuing the hybrid instrument reduces the accounting mismatch which would have resulted had the host contract been measured at amortised cost. For the acquirer of the notes, assuming the product has been transacted with a financial institution, the fair value of the combined instrument may be more readily available for the hybrid instrument as a whole than for the host contract and the individual embedded derivative separately. [IAS 39.BC77A – 78]

Example 3B

Pricing adjustment to a contract over a non-financial item

An entity enters into a forward contract to purchase wheat. The contract meets the definition of a derivative, but does not meet the 'expected purchase, sale or usage requirements' scope exemption as the entity has a history of net cash settling similar contracts (see **2.5** of **chapter 1**). Embedded in the forward contract is the following price adjustment: if the retail price index were to increase by 3 per cent during the term of the contract, the contracted price is doubled.

As the contract is within the scope of IAS 39 and meets the definition of a derivative, it will be accounted for at fair value with changes in fair value recognised in profit or loss. The embedded derivative will automatically be accounted for at fair value through profit or loss, hence no further consideration of embedded derivatives is necessary.

Condition (a) is the most difficult of the three to assess, as there is no definition of 'closely related'. In the appendix to IAS 39 there are two lists: one list gives examples of embedded derivatives that are closely related to their hosts, and the other gives examples of embedded derivatives that are not closely related to their hosts.

When an embedded derivative is not included in one of these lists, a significant degree of judgement will be required and conclusions may need to be drawn by analogy to the specific examples given. Ultimately, the conclusion reached should be consistent with the underlying principle that an embedded derivative should be separated from its host contract when its economic characteristics and risks differ from those of the host contract.

In summary, the following decision tree can be used to determine whether an embedded derivative needs to be separated from its host contract.

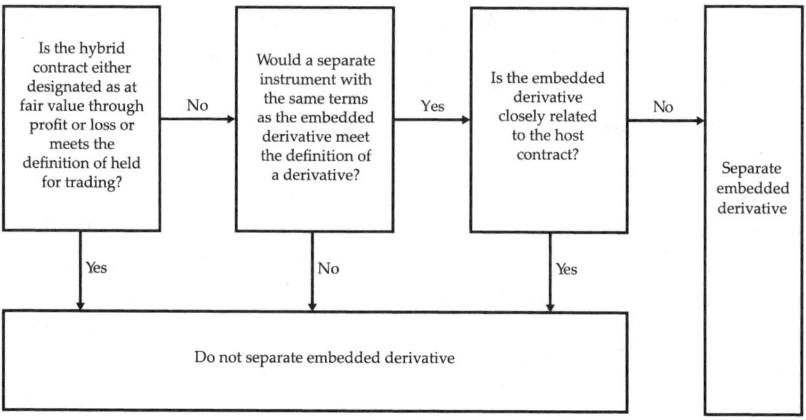

Once it is determined that an embedded derivative is closely related to the host contract, it cannot be separated as the entire hybrid contract is accounted for in accordance with the relevant Standard that deals with the host contract. For example, if an embedded derivative is identified in a lease contract, but it is deemed to be closely related, then the entire contract is accounted for in accordance with IAS 17 *Leases*.

If an identified embedded derivative is not closely related to the host contract, then it must be separately accounted for as if it were a free-standing derivative. This is considered further in **section 12** below.

US GAAP comparison: US GAAP uses the phrase "clearly and closely related" rather than the phrase "closely related". While the phrases "clearly and closely related" and "closely related" convey a similar principle, there are application differences. For instance, FAS 133 has more detailed application guidance on some topics than IAS 39. Thus, an entity may not necessarily reach the same conclusion under IAS 39 as under US GAAP. IAS 39 and US GAAP also differ in their guidance on how to apply the principle.

IFRIC Interpretation 9 *Reassessment of Embedded Derivatives*, published in March 2006, provides guidance on whether an entity should assess embedded derivatives as closely related at the time the entity first becomes a party to the contract or on an ongoing basis. The Interpretation clarifies the following.

- An entity is generally prohibited from reassessing its conclusion as to whether an embedded derivative needs to be separated from the hybrid contract after it is initially recognised.
- An entity is required to revisit its assessment if there is a change in the terms of the contract that significantly modifies the cash flows that would otherwise be required under the (original) contract. The significance of the change in cash flows is evaluated by considering the extent of the change in the cash flows of the embedded derivative, the host contract or both and whether these changes are significant relative to the previously expected cash flows of the contract.

A first-time adopter of IFRSs should make its assessment on the basis of conditions existing at the later of the date it first became a party to the contract and the date a reassessment is required. In all cases, the Interpretation should be applied retrospectively.

Example 3C

Reassessment of embedded derivatives: common currency

Entity G operates in Country Y and had entered into long-dated supply contracts denominated in US$. When Entity G entered into the contracts an assessment was made as to whether the US$ was considered to be a 'common currency' per IAS 39.AG33(d)(iii) with a view to establishing whether an embedded derivative would need to be separated out. At the time Entity G entered into the contracts the US$ was considered a common currency for Country Y. The functional currency of Entity G and the counterparty to the contracts is not US$.

At the end of the current reporting period the US$ is no longer considered a common currency in Country Y. Entities within that country now use the domestic currency instead as this is now traded cross-border and is considered a 'hard' currency by other countries.

Entity G should not reconsider the embedded derivative assessment it made when it originally entered into the contracts as the terms of the arrangement have not changed. The accounting treatment is unchanged even though, had Entity G entered into the same contract today, the US$ would not be considered a common currency and an embedded derivative would need to be recognised.

It should be noted that as part of the IASB's Annual Improvements project it has proposed amending the requirements of IAS 39.33(d)(iii). See **10.5** below.

Example 3D

Reassessment of embedded derivatives: change in correlation of energy prices

Entity T, a coal fired power station, entered into contracts to supply electricity prior to the deregulation of the energy market. The price paid for the supply of electricity was partly linked to the gas price. Entity T always intended to physically deliver electricity to the counterparty so the supply contract was always considered to be an executory contract that was outside the scope of IAS 39. At the date the contract was entered into, the prices for gas and electricity were highly correlated and therefore Entity T considered the linkage to gas prices was a closely related embedded derivative.

Following deregulation of the market the two prices were no longer highly correlated and, had Entity T entered into the contract today, it would have concluded that the linkage to gas prices was an embedded derivative that was not closely related to the electricity supply contract. Entity T does not reconsider its embedded derivative assessment made when it entered into the electricity supply contract as the terms of the arrangement are unchanged. This is the case even though, had Entity T entered into the same contract today, it would have concluded that the embedded derivative would require separation.

Example 3E

Reassessment of embedded derivatives: equity conversion terms

On 1 January 20X1, Entity Y, a US$ functional currency entity, issued US$ denominated convertible bonds with a par of US$30 million. The convertible bonds will mature on the third anniversary of the date of issue at par unless they are converted into ordinary shares prior to maturity. The conversion price is the lower of US$1.50 and 90 percent of Y's average closing price, determined based on the last 10 trading days immediately before 1 January 20X3.

The equity conversion option does not deliver a fixed amount of cash for a fixed number of equity shares and therefore does not meet the definition of equity (see **example 3.8** in **chapter 3**). The instrument is therefore not a compound instrument, it is a hybrid financial instrument wholly in the scope of IAS 39. The instrument will be separated into a debt host contract and a non-closely related embedded derivative with respect to the equity conversion option that must be measured at fair value through profit or loss.

IFRIC 9 does not permit an entity to reconsider its closely related decision made at initial recognition of the hybrid instrument unless there is a significant change to the cash flows under the contract. At 1 January 20X3 Entity Y will know how many shares it will deliver to the holder if the convertible bond is converted but this is not known at the time when the instrument was issued. As the terms of the instrument have not changed, Entity Y must continue to account for the equity conversion option as a non-closely related embedded derivative.

Example 3F

Reassessment of embedded derivatives: novation within group

Group A has a US$ functional currency subsidiary, Subsidiary B, which enters into contracts to sell non-financial items at a fixed future date with a Euro functional counterparty, outside of Group A, called Entity D. The contract is denominated in US dollars.

The foreign currency embedded derivative is not separately recognised as Subsidiary B has a US$ functional currency and is a substantial party to the contract. In Group A's consolidated financial statements the same treatment is applied.

Sometime later, Subsidiary B novates the contract to a fellow subsidiary, Subsidiary C, which has a Sterling functional currency. At the date of novation there are no changes to the terms of the contract other than Subsidiary C has stepped into Subsidiary B's place as the seller. Subsidiary C is a principal to the transaction following the novation.

In the individual financial statements of Subsidiary C, at the novation date it becomes a party to the contract for the first time and therefore must consider whether the contract has any embedded derivatives. The contract is not denominated in either Subsidiary C's or Entity D's functional currency and therefore a non-closely related embedded derivative must be recognised by Subsidiary C, being a currency forward contract between Sterling and US$.

In Group A's consolidated financial statements, as the group is presented as a single economic entity, there has been no change in the contractual terms of the contract and therefore the group would not reassess the embedded derivative assessment it made when Subsidiary B entered into the arrangement.

In March 2009 the IASB issued amendments to IFRIC 9 and IAS 39 titled, *Embedded Derivatives*. The amendments clarify that upon reclassification of a financial asset out of FVTPL (see **section 4** in **chapter 2**) an entity is required to assess whether embedded derivatives should be separated from the host financial contract. In addition, if an entity is unable to measure separately the embedded derivative that would have to be separated on reclassification of a hybrid (combined) contract out of the FVTPL category, that reclassification is prohibited. In such circumstances the hybrid (combined) contract remains classified as at FVTPL in its entirety. The Board noted that when IFRIC 9 was issued, reclassifications out of the FVTPL category were prohibited and hence IFRIC 9 did not consider the possibility of such reclassifications. The Board believed it was appropriate that embedded derivatives should be assessed at the date of reclassification. Not to require this would allow an entity to circumvent the need to assess embedded derivatives by classifying a hybrid contract initially as at FVTPL and subsequently reclassifying it. The Board noted that the inability to reclassify if the embedded derivative that would have to be separated cannot be measured separately would prevent reclassification of a hybrid (combined) financial asset out of that category between financial reporting dates, and hence avoid a requirement to reclassify the hybrid (combined) financial asset back into the fair value through profit or loss category at the end of the financial reporting period.

The amendments also state that when assessing for embedded derivatives at the date of reclassification the assessment shall be made on the basis of the circumstances that existed at the later of when the entity first became a party to the contract and a change in the terms of the contract that significantly modifies the cash flows that otherwise would have been required under the contract. The Board considered that looking to circumstances when the entity became party to the contract was consistent with one of the stated purposes of embedded derivative accounting which is to prevent circumvention of the recognition and measurement requirements for derivatives and provide some degree of comparability. Furthermore, because the terms of the embedded features in the hybrid (combined) financial instrument have not changed, the Board did not see a reason for arriving at an answer on separation different from what would have been the case at initial recognition of the hybrid (combined) contract.

The amendments to IAS 39 and IFRIC 9 shall be applied for annual periods ending on or after 30 June 2009.

US GAAP comparison: Except for certain types of embedded features (e.g. certain interest rate features), practice under US GAAP is to reassess at least at the end of each period the appropriateness of an entity's assertions regarding hybrid contracts. An entity therefore monitors and evaluates continuously whether embedded derivatives are closely related.

IFRIC 9 does not address remeasurement issues arising from a reassessment of embedded derivatives. [IFRIC 9.4] This will require careful consideration depending on particular facts and circumstances.

Example 3G

Reassessment of embedded derivatives: modification to terms

Entity B, a Euro functional currency entity is party to a contract to purchase a set quantity of electricity at a future date for £10m. The electricity will always be physically delivered under the contract and will be used for Entity B's production processes. The contract is a hybrid contractual arrangement containing a host contract that is an executory contract to purchase electricity in Euros and a non-closely related embedded foreign currency derivative based on the guidance in **10.5** below. The two elements are:

(i) non-closely related embedded €/£ forward with an initial fair value of zero to buy €12m, sell £10m; and

(ii) host purchase contract to buy a set quantity of electricity with a purchase price of €12m (that matches the Euro leg of the foreign currency forward in (i) above).

Upon entering into the contract Entity B separates out the non-closely related foreign currency embedded derivative and measures it at fair value through profit or loss.

At a later date there is a contractual modification to the terms such that the currency in which the contract is denominated changes to the functional currency of Entity B, i.e. Euro. The embedded derivative had a negative fair value at the date of modification of €1m. Due to the redenomination of the currency of the contract Entity B pays the counterparty €1m which is equal to the value of the change in contractual terms of the arrangement. Entity B derecognises the embedded derivative.

The change in denomination of the contract in this case is a significant modification that triggers reassessment under IFRIC 9. As the denomination of the contract after modification is in the functional currency of Entity B the contract no longer has a non-closely related embedded derivative and the entire arrangement will be accounted for prospectively as an executory contract outside the scope of IAS 39.

Care is needed in determining how the carrying amount of an embedded derivative is treated when the embedded derivative is no longer closely related. This is particularly relevant when the modification occurs without cash consideration or when the cash consideration differs with the value of the embedded derivative derecognised. The carrying amount of the embedded derivative, being its fair value, at the date of modification of the contract, will be recognised in profit or loss, remain in the statement of financial position or be recognised in other comprehensive income in the period or future periods depending on the substance of the modified terms of the contract. Consideration will need to be given as to whether the pricing of the remaining contract is modified to reflect the value of the change in terms of the arrangement; whether any other goods or services are provided or received as part of the modification; or an equity transaction occurs between the entity and the counterparty.

Consideration will also need to be given to the substance of the modification when a non-closely related embedded derivative is recognised for the first time following the modification of a contract where previously the embedded derivative was closely related. The substance of the arrangement will determine whether, having recognised the derivative at fair value, the counter entry impacts profit or loss, the statement of financial position or other comprehensive income.

A further issue arises when an instrument is acquired in a business combination, since the determination of whether an embedded derivative should be separated, performed at the time of the business combination, may produce a different result compared to the conclusion reached when the assessment was first performed at the time the contract was first entered into by the acquiree. IFRIC 9.5 does not address the reassessment of embedded derivatives in a business combination. However, as the group becomes a party to the contract at the time of acquisition, reassessment at the time of acquisition is appropriate for the acquirer and therefore the accounting treatment in the consolidated financial statements may differ to that in the individual financial statements of the acquiree.

In January 2008, a revised version of IFRS 3 *Business Combinations* was issued. The revised Standard confirms that the assessment as to whether an embedded derivative is closely related to its host contract is to be made on the basis of pertinent factors at the acquisition date. IFRS 3(2008) applies prospectively to business combinations for which the acquisition date is on or after the beginning of the first annual reporting period beginning on or after 1 July 2009.

In January 2009 the IASB issued ED/2009/1, *Post-implementation Revisions to IFRIC Interpretations*, that included proposed amendments to IFRIC 9. IFRIC 9.5 states that the interpretation does not address the acquisition of contracts with embedded derivatives in a business combination nor their possible reassessment at the date of acquisition. ED/2009/1 proposes to amend IFRIC 9.5 by extending the scope exemption to embedded derivatives in contracts acquired in a combination of entities or businesses under common control as described in IFRS 3(2008).B1–B4 or through the formation of a joint venture as defined in IAS 31.

4 Terms of the embedded derivative and the debt host contract

The term 'debt host contract' that is applied below includes debt instruments that are issued by an entity, and therefore are financial liabilities, as well as debt instruments that an entity may invest in that are recognised as financial assets.

The terms of the host contract must reflect the stated or implied terms of the hybrid contract; i.e. the embedded feature must be clearly present in the hybrid contract. In the absence of implied or stated terms a judgement may have to be made, but an entity cannot create cash flows that do not contractually exist.

Example 4A

Fixed versus floating debt host contract (1)

Entity A issues floating-rate debt. The contract cannot be seen as fixed-rate debt with an embedded interest rate swap that swaps fixed-rate cash flows into floating-rate cash flows. The terms of the contract do not contain any fixed cash flows, so there can be no embedded feature with fixed rate cash flows.

Example 4B

Fixed versus floating debt host contract (2)

A five-year debt instrument has fixed annual payments, and a principal repayment at the end of the contract which is conditional on changes in the FTSE 100 index. This instrument must be treated as a host fixed-rate debt contract with an embedded equity feature. It cannot be classified as floating-rate debt with an embedded equity swap that has an offsetting floating-rate leg. The host is a fixed-rate contract because there are no variable interest rate payments in it.

Embedded non-optional derivatives must be determined so that they have a fair value of zero at inception of the contract. If this were not stipulated, it would be possible to split one instrument into an infinite number and variety of hosts with embedded derivatives. This could be done by separating embedded derivatives with terms that create leverage, asymmetry or another risk exposure that does not exist in the hybrid contract. [IAS 39.AG28 & IG.C.1]

Embedded optional derivatives will not necessarily have a fair value (or intrinsic value) of zero at inception. The fair value of such an embedded derivative will depend on its strike price or rate. Therefore, the separation of an option from a hybrid contract should be based on the stated terms of the option feature. [IAS 39.AG28 and IG.C.2)]

US GAAP comparison: Guidance in US GAAP on separation of embedded derivatives is broadly similar to IFRS. US GAAP provides further guidance on the separation of option-based embedded derivatives in DIG Issue No. B22. When separating an option-based embedded derivative from the host contract the terms of the option-based embedded derivative should not be adjusted to result in the derivative being at-the-money at inception of the hybrid. In separating an option-based embedded derivative from the host contract, the strike price of the embedded derivative should be based on the stated terms documented in the hybrid contract. As a result, the option based embedded derivative at inception may have a strike that does not equal the market price of the asset associated with the underlying.

5 Determination of host contract: debt vs. equity

If a hybrid contract has both debt and equity features, a determination must be made as to whether the host contract is debt or equity. Often, this will be a relatively straightforward task, as the 'majority' of the contract will behave like debt or equity (more usually debt). However, this will not always be the case.

From the perspective of the holder of a contract, if the host contract has no stated or predetermined maturity and represents a residual interest in the net assets of the issuer, then its economic characteristics and risks are those of an equity instrument. Any embedded derivative would need to possess equity characteristics of the issuer to be regarded as closely related. If the host contract is not an equity instrument and meets the definition of a financial asset or liability, then its economic characteristics and risks are those of a debt instrument. [IAS 39.AG27]

Most commonly, the host contract will not represent a residual interest in an entity and, thus, the economic characteristics and risks of a financial host contract will be considered that of a debt instrument. For example, even though an overall hybrid instrument may provide for repayment of principal linked to the market price of the issuer's ordinary shares, the host contract may not involve any existing or potential residual rights in the net assets of the issuer (i.e. rights of ownership) so would not be an equity instrument. The host contract is a debt instrument, and the embedded derivative, the indexation to the market price of the issuer, is not closely related to the host contract.

Example 5A

Debt host contract (1)
[IAS 39.IG.C.5]

Entity A purchases a five-year 'debt' instrument issued by Entity B with a principal amount of CU1 million that is indexed to the share price of Entity C. At maturity, Entity A will receive from Entity B the principal amount plus or minus the change in the fair value of 10,000 shares of Entity C. The current share price is CU110. No separate interest payments are made by Entity B. The purchase price is CU1 million. Entity A classifies the debt instrument as available for sale. Entity A concludes that the instrument is a hybrid instrument with an embedded derivative because of the equity-indexed principal. For the purposes of separating an embedded derivative, is the host contract an equity instrument or a debt instrument?

The host contract is a debt instrument because the hybrid instrument has a stated maturity, i.e. it does not meet the definition of an equity instrument (IAS 32.11 and IAS 32.16). It is accounted for as a zero coupon debt instrument. Thus, in accounting for the host instrument, Entity A imputes interest on CU1 million over five years using the applicable market interest rate at initial recognition. The embedded non-option derivative is separated so as to have an initial fair value of zero (see IAS 39.IG.C.1).

Example 5B

Debt host contract (2)

Entity A invests in instruments that are classified as available-for-sale that are issued by Entity B. The instruments have the legal form of shares, and embedded within them is a put option allowing Entity A to put the 'shares' back to Entity B for the higher of (i) the fair market value of the shares and (ii) an amount based on the initial investment with compounded interest based on LIBOR. The option is exercisable five years after the initial investment is made.

Whilst the instruments have the legal form of shares, they do not evidence a residual interest in Entity B. Entity A will receive a rate of return that is at least equal to the return on a debt instrument. Entity A should account for the instruments as a debt host contract with an embedded derivative.

In January 2007 the IFRIC issued a rejection notice on the classification by the holder of financial instruments that are puttable by the holder at an amount other than fair value. The issuer accounts for the instrument as a financial liability in accordance with IAS 32. The IFRIC was asked whether the holder's accounting should be symmetrical with that of the financial statements of the issuer. The IFRIC noted that IAS 32 and IAS 39 do not directly address whether the accounting for financial instruments in the financial statements of the holder should be symmetrical with that of the issuer. However, the IFRIC noted that the issuer of a financial instrument is required to classify it in accordance with IAS 32, whereas the holder is required to classify and account for it in accordance with IAS 39. The IFRIC also noted that IAS 39 requires the holder to identify embedded derivatives in hybrid financial instruments and requires separate accounting for the embedded derivatives if all the conditions in IAS 39.11 are met. These requirements apply to the holder regardless of whether any embedded derivatives are accounted for separately in the financial statements of the issuer. In light of the existing guidance in IAS 39, the IFRIC decided that the issue should not be taken onto its agenda.

Judgement is required in determining whether the put feature in puttable shares is closely related to the equity host contract where the host is classified as an available-for-sale asset. If the hybrid instrument is classified as at fair value through profit or loss the embedded derivative guidance is not applicable as the whole instrument is fair valued through earnings.

If the shares are puttable at fair value it may be argued that the amount received by the holder upon exercise of the put (being the fair value of the shares) represents the fair value of the equity host, because the amount payable to the holder is the fair value of the residual interest in the assets of the entity after deducting all of its liabilities, and therefore by definition has characteristics of equity. The put would be closely related as its risk characteristics are similar to the equity host. The whole hybrid instrument would be classified as available-for-sale with gains and losses recognised in other comprehensive income and no embedded derivative would be recognised. This treatment could also apply where the issuer is an unquoted entity and the put strike price is derived from a formula which is aimed at being a surrogate for the fair value of the shares of the issuing entity. Greater care would need to be taken in determining whether the put strike is equivalent to the fair value of the underlying shares and therefore the put could be considered closely related.

If the shares are puttable at a fixed amount or an amount determined on the basis of an index that is unrelated to the fair value of the equity host (e.g. the price of gold) then the put would not have equity characteristics and therefore would not be closely related. As the investor can force the issuer to pay an amount not equal to the proportionate share of the net assets of the entity, the holder has downside protection and therefore is not exposed to the residual net assets of the entity. The put would be accounted for separately at fair value through profit or loss and the host contract would be classified as an available-for-sale asset.

US GAAP comparison: US GAAP has a notion similar to "closely related" and therefore it also requires that entities determine whether a host contract is more "debt-like" or more "equity- like". Paragraphs FAS 133.60 & 61 and DIG Issues B1, B8, B12, B19, and B36 contain relevant guidance.

In EITF Topic No. D-109, Determining the Nature of a Host Contract Related to a Hybrid Financial Instrument Issued in the Form of a Share under FASB Statement No. 133 (Topic D-109), the SEC staff expressed its position that all stated and implied substantive terms and features of a hybrid instrument issued in the form of a share must be considered when determining the nature of the economic characteristics and risks of the host contract. Based on the SEC staff's position in Topic D-109, two acceptable methods for determining the nature of the host contract for a hybrid financial instrument issued in the form of a share are available to SEC registrants. In practice, these methods are sometimes identified as (1) the "chameleon" approach and (2) the "whole instrument" approach.

Chameleon Approach – The chameleon approach determines the nature of host contract by considering all stated and implied substantive terms and features of the hybrid instrument *excluding* the particular embedded feature being analysed for separation. When using the chameleon approach to analyse a hybrid instrument with multiple embedded features, the nature of the host contract may change as each embedded feature is analysed separately. For example, assume an entity acquires a preferred share puttable by the holder for a fixed amount of cash equal to par and convertible by the holder into common shares at a fixed conversion price. Under the chameleon approach, the entity typically would conclude that the host contract is an equity host when analysing the put feature, because absent the put feature the holder's payoff profile is that of an equity security. When analysing the conversion option, however, the entity typically would conclude that the host contract is a debt host, because the put feature provides the holder with downside protection similar to a debt security.

Whole-Instrument Approach – In contrast, the whole instrument approach determines the nature of the host contract by considering all stated and implied substantive terms and features of the hybrid instrument *including* the embedded feature being analysed for bifurcation. When using the whole instrument approach to analyse a hybrid instrument with multiple embedded features, the nature of the host contract should not change as each embedded feature is analysed separately. For example, assume an entity issues a preferred share puttable by the holder for a fixed amount of cash equal to par and convertible by the holder into common shares at a fixed conversion price. Under the whole-instrument approach, the entity typically would conclude that the host contract is a debt host when analysing both the put and conversion features, because the put feature provides the holder with downside protection similar to a debt security.

Under either approach, if the put or conversion option are considered not clearly and closely related to the host contract they will be separated and recognised at fair value through profit or loss if the embedded derivative is in scope of FAS 133. If both the put and conversion option are considered not clearly and closely related and are both within the scope of FAS 133 they will be recognised as a single compound embedded derivative that is fair valued through profit or loss.

6 Multiple embedded derivatives

It is possible for a contract to contain more than one embedded derivative. In such a case, each embedded derivative needs to be individually assessed to see if it is closely related to the host contract.

Example 6

Conversion feature and put option

Entity A holds convertible bonds. In addition to the conversion feature, Entity A can choose to put the bonds back to the issuer. When searching for embedded derivatives, it will be necessary to consider both the conversion option and the put option, and assess each separately.

When contracts contain multiple embedded derivatives they are generally treated as a single compound embedded derivative. Only if the embedded derivatives relate to different risk exposures and are readily separable and independent of each other are they accounted for separately from each other. [IAS 39.AG29]

US GAAP comparison: US GAAP requires that entities treat multiple embedded features as if they were a single compound embedded (DIG B15), regardless of inter-dependencies. See the discussion in **5** above regarding host contract determination.

If an embedded derivative must be separated from its host contract, but it cannot be valued, the entity must first determine both the fair value of the whole contract and the fair value of the host contract, and the balance represents the fair value of the derivative instrument. If an entity is unable to do this, the entity must designate it as at fair value through profit or loss.

7 Embedded derivatives in debt host contracts

Financial liabilities are discussed at some length in **chapter 3.** These include traditional debt contracts like bonds and bank borrowings, and also certain other securities that are in substance liabilities, like mandatory redeemable preference shares.

7.1 Puts, calls and prepayment options

Contractual terms that allow either party to terminate the contract early and accelerate the repayment of the outstanding principal, either in whole or in part, are often embedded derivatives. Examples of such terms include call options of the issuer, put options of the holder, or prepayment features.

These embedded derivatives are not closely related to the host debt contract unless the exercise price is approximately equal to the debt's amortised cost on each exercise date. [IAS 39.AG30(g)]

From the perspective of the issuer of a convertible debt instrument with an embedded call or put option feature, the assessment of whether the call or put option is closely related to the host debt contract is made before separating the equity element under IAS 32 as discussed in **section 3** of **chapter 3**. [IAS 39.AG30(g)]

Example 7.1A

Issuer call option

Entity A issues a five-year zero-coupon bond for CU75 million, with a face value of CU100 million. Embedded in the debt is a call option allowing Entity A to repay the debt after three years for CU90 million, when its amortised cost will be CU89 million. As the repayment amount is approximately equal to its amortised cost on that date, the call option is closely related to the host contract and so is not separated from it. This is the case for both the issuer and holder of the bond.

If the terms were instead such that Entity A could call the debt at any time, but would have to redeem it at a fixed amount, for example at par of CU100 million, then the call option would not be closely related, as the repayment amount would not approximately equal the debt's amortised cost on each date that the call can be exercised. For example, the week after issuing the bond (when the bond's amortised cost is approximately CU75 million), Entity A could call it back but would have to pay CU100 million to do so. This situation arises because the bond was issued at a substantial discount, and hence its amortised cost will not approximate to its par value, except in the years close to its maturity.

Example 7.1B

Investor put option

Entity X issues 10-year bonds with a par value of CU1 million for proceeds of CU1 million. The bonds have a coupon of 10 per cent. Embedded in the bonds is a clause that allows the investors to put the bonds back to the issuer for CU1 million in the event the FTSE declines by 5 per cent. It is reasonably possible that the FTSE will decline by 5 per cent in the near future. The issue costs are insignificant.

The embedded put option would not be accounted for separately, even though the put is contingent on an event that is not related to the host instrument (i.e. a trigger other than interest rates or credit). The tests in IAS 39 relate to the exercise price (settlement amount), not the trigger. The likelihood of the put being exercised is also irrelevant in determining whether the embedded derivative is closely related, although this will affect valuation. In this case, the bonds will be put back at an amount that approximates amortised cost. It is not relevant that the put only becomes exercisable if an equity index performs in a particular manner.

Example 7.1C

Investor contingent put option

Entity A issues CU100 million cumulative preference shares to investors with a dividend of 7 per cent. Dividends are payable quarterly subject to the availability of distributable profits. Issue costs are insignificant. The preference shares are puttable at par to Entity A for cash if interest rates move by 150 basis points. Any dividend that remains accumulated and not paid becomes payable when the shares are put to Entity A.

The embedded put option would not be separated from the host contract under the embedded derivative requirements. The preference shares are classified as a liability under IAS 32 (see **chapter 3**). The put feature is an option that is considered to be closely related to the host since the exercise price of the put is the amortised cost of the preference shares.

Sometimes derivatives may be 'embedded' subsequent to the issuance of the instrument.

Example 7.1D

Remarketable put bonds

Entity X issues 10-year bonds with a 6 per cent coupon to a bank and receives proceeds of €103 million. The debt is puttable by the holder at the end of three years. The three-year debt rate for vanilla debt instruments (i.e. those without put or call features) is 6 per cent. The bank staples a call option and sells the two instruments to an investor. This call option enables the bank to reacquire the bonds in the event that it wishes to exercise its put option inherent in the bond issued by Entity X.

A party other than the issuer (i.e. the bank) has stapled the call option into the debt instrument. Thus, the investor would not be able to consider the call option to be closely related to the host debt instrument. The holder of the call option would have a free-standing derivative that would be recognised at fair value.

Note that Entity X does not have to consider the accounting for the call option because Entity X is not a party to the call option.

A debt instrument that may be called by the issuer or put or prepaid by the holder must be assessed in order to determine whether these features are considered to be closely related. The outcome of this assessment is dependent on comparing the strike price under the option, i.e. the amount the issuer would pay the holder on exercise of the option, with the amortised cost of the instrument. What is less clear is whether calls, puts and prepayment options that are likely to be exercised should be taken into account in determining amortised cost.

Consider the following example. A fixed rate debt instrument is issued at par with a 10 year term. The debt can be put by the holder anytime after year 5 for an amount equal to 110 per cent of par. If the issuer at initial recognition considers it likely that the holder will put at year 5, the host contract could be considered a 10 year host redeeming at 100 per cent or a 5 year host that early redeems at 110 per cent. If the former view is applied the put option is not closely related as 110 per cent is not approximately equal to 100 per cent, whereas if the latter view is applied the put would be closely related as 110 per cent would equal to 110 per cent.

The above example illustrates that where a significant penalty is payable on early redemption the accounting would differ depending on which view is applied. Ironically, if an entity did take into account a put option that is likely to be exercised in determining the host contract it would result in that put option not being recognised. If the put option was less likely to be exercised, it would result in the put option being recognised.

Extending the example above, assume the holder can put at any time in the ten years for an amount equal to 110 per cent of par. The issuer still believes it is most likely the holder will put at year 5. If the issuer was to consider the 5 year put as part of the amortised cost of the host contract, and thereby not recognise an embedded derivative for that put, it would still need to consider whether the puts from years 2 to 4 were considered closely related. If the host contract is considered a discounted instrument, issued for 100 per cent and redeemable at 110 per cent at year 5, then some of the puts between years 2 to 4 would be non-closely related embedded derivatives as their exercise price of 110 per cent would not be approximately equal to amortised cost.

If early redemption features in debt instruments were reflected in the host contract's amortised cost when determining whether those features are closely related, it is not clear how an entity should account for the instrument should there be changes in the likelihood of the early redemption feature being exercised. Applying the example above, if the issuer subsequently estimated the put was now likely to be exercised after year 5, two views exist. The first view is that the change in timing of cash flows is simply a re-measurement of estimated cash flows and the revised changes in cash flows should be discounted by the original effective interest rate in accordance with IAS 39.AG8. An alternative view is that the host contract is deemed a 5 year instrument; therefore, the right for the holder to put the instrument after year 5 is equivalent to a term extension option, which, if the extension is not at market interest rates, would be considered a non-closely related embedded derivative.

In October 2007 the IASB issued an Exposure Draft titled *Annual Improvements to International Financial Reporting Standards*. Included within the exposure draft was a proposed amendment to IAS 39.AG30(g) for specific prepayment options embedded in a debt host contract that are designed to ensure the lender is compensated for loss of interest when the borrower prepays by reducing the economic loss from reinvestment risk. Such prepayment options are not equal to the amortised cost of the debt host contract because the amount prepaid will include an adjustment to reflect the then market interest rate. At the IASB's Board meeting in December 2008 the Board agreed to amend IAS 39 so that such prepayment options are closely related to the host debt contract. The Board intends to issue the amendment as part of its annual improvements in April 2009 with an effective date of 1 January 2010.

US GAAP comparison: US GAAP has more guidance on whether calls and puts that can accelerate the settlement of debt instruments should be considered to be clearly and closely related to the debt host. Usually, call or put options that can accelerate the repayment of principal on a debt instrument are considered to be clearly and closely related to a debt instrument that requires principal repayments unless both (1) the debt involves a substantial premium or discount (which is common with zero-coupon bonds) **and** (2) the put or call option is only contingently exercisable, provided the put or call are also considered clearly and closely related to the debt host.

DIG B16 further clarifies that calls and puts are **not** clearly and closely related if the payoff amount is indexed to an underlying other than interest rates or credit risk. In addition, FAS 133.13 indicates that a put or call is **not** clearly and closely related to the debt host if (1) the hybrid can be settled in a way that the investor would not recover substantially all of its initial recorded investment **or** (2) there is a possible interest rate scenario that would double the investor's initial rate of return on the host contract **and** would result in a rate of return that is at least twice what otherwise would be the then-current market return for a contract having the same terms as the host.

A further consideration is whether the option is a prepayment option over an interest-only or principal-only strip. The embedded derivative will be closely related provided the host contract:

(a) initially resulted from separating the right to receive contractual cash flows of a financial instrument that itself did not contain an embedded derivative; and

(b) does not contain any terms not present in the original host debt.

Example 7.1E

Interest-only strip: no additional terms

A pool of floating rate mortgages is split into an interest-only and principal-only strip, with different entities acquiring each part. The terms of the mortgages allow the borrower to prepay the mortgage at amortised cost prior to the contractual maturity of the mortgage. Because this prepayment option is at amortised cost it does not require separation.

Entity K purchases an interest-only strip from the pool of floating rate mortgages. The floating rate interest-only strip has the same terms as the floating rate on the original instrument. Entity K must consider whether the interest only strip has embedded derivatives that require separation.

As the interest-only strip does not contain any terms not present in the original host debt contract and the prepayment option was not separated in the accounting for the original mortgage, the prepayment option is considered closely related to the interest-only strip and therefore is not separated. [IAS 39.AG33(e)]

Example 7.1F

Interest-only and principal-only strip: additional terms

Transferor X securitises CU100 million of mortgage loans with an 8 per cent coupon in a securitisation structure that meets the requirements for derecognition (derecognition is discussed further in **chapter 7**). The issued beneficial interests consist of a principal-only strip of CU100 million and an interest-only strip that pays 8 per cent based on the principal amount.

Transferor X received proceeds of CU60 million for the principal-only strip. If market 30-year mortgage rates exceed 10 per cent, the coupon on the interest-only strip increases to 10 per cent. The additional 2 per cent will be paid from the principal-only cash receipts. The conditional 2 per cent payment is an option, sometimes referred to as a caplet.

The embedded caplet is required to be separated because it was not present in the original financial instrument.

7.2 Term extending features

Where the term of the debt is extendable, and there is no concurrent adjustment to the approximate current market rate of interest at the time of the extension, the embedded term extension option is not closely related to the host debt contract. To be closely related the reset to market rates must result in a reset of both current interest rates and current credit spread for the issuer.

If an entity issues a debt instrument and the holder of that debt instrument writes a call option on the debt instrument to a third party, the issuer regards the call option as extending the term to maturity of the debt instrument provided the issuer can be required to participate in or facilitate the remarketing of the debt instrument as a result of the call option being exercised. [IAS 39.AG30(c)]

Example 7.2A

Term extension feature (1)

Entity X issues CU10 million fixed rate debt with an 8 per cent coupon and maturity of five years. At the end of five years, Entity X has an option to extend the term for an additional three years. If extended, the coupon will remain at 8 per cent. If the option is exercised it will significantly extend the term of the debt and the coupon will not reset to current market rates. Therefore, this term extending option is an embedded derivative that is not closely related to the host contract.

Example 7.2B

Term extension feature (2)

Entity X issues debt of CU10 million with an 8 per cent coupon and a maturity of five years. If LIBOR increases by 200 basis points within any one year, the maturity of the bonds will be extended for another three years at the same 8 per cent coupon rate. The embedded derivative would be accounted for separately from the host contract because the coupon following extension does not reset to the current market rate.

The likelihood of LIBOR increasing by 200 basis points in a year is not a consideration when determining whether the embedded derivative is closely related. It will, however, impact the valuation of the embedded derivative. If the possibility of LIBOR increasing by 200 basis points is considered low, the value of the embedded derivative will be relatively small.

Five-year fixed rate debt with an option to extend for three years (as detailed in **example 7.2A** above) is economically no different from eight-year fixed rate debt that is puttable at the end of five years.

However, the criteria for determining whether there is an embedded derivative in these instruments are different.

The form of the instrument is relevant when determining whether an embedded derivative must be accounted for separately. Thus, two instruments that are economically the same may be treated differently under IAS 39. An entity cannot separate a prepayment option if the debt is prepayable at its amortised cost, but would be required to separate out a term extending option if that option did not result in the interest being reset to market rates.

7.3 Indexed interest and principal payments

Where interest or principal payments in a debt contract are indexed to changes in a specified security price, commodity price, foreign exchange rate, or index of prices or rates, the host debt contract contains an embedded derivative.

Such an embedded derivative will not be closely related to the host debt contract if the amounts of interest or principal are indexed to the price of a commodity or to the change in value of an equity instrument. [IAS 39.AG30(d) & (e)]

Example 7.3A

Commodity price adjustment

Entity X issues 10-year notes with no stated coupon. Embedded in the notes is a clause that adjusts the interest paid by reference to changes in the price of corn.

The embedded derivative would be accounted for separately because the adjustment to interest payments based on changes in corn prices is not closely related to the host debt instrument.

Example 7.3B

Equity price adjustment

Entity X issues 10-year notes to a bank. Embedded in the notes is a provision that requires interest paid to be adjusted based on changes in the share price of Entity Y.

The embedded derivative will be separated because the interest payments are indexed to changes in the share price of Entity Y, and therefore the adjustment is not closely related to the host debt instrument.

Generally, an embedded derivative that adjusts interest and/or principal amounts paid on the debt contract will not be closely related to the host debt where the underlying that drives the value of the derivative is different from the economic factors that drive the value of the host debt contract. The guidance would equally apply to indexation to a basket of commodities, share indices like the FTSE 100, or net asset value changes of a fund.

Example 7.3C

Equity index adjustment

A bank issues 10-year notes with a coupon of 5 per cent to an entity. At maturity, the entity receives cash equal to the higher of the initial proceeds and an amount based on the Standard and Poor's 500 ('S&P 500').

The embedded cash-settled S&P 500 call option is an embedded derivative that is not closely related to the host debt contract.

Even if the interest or principal payments are determined by changes in underlyings that are typically associated with debt (e.g. interest rates, inflation or creditworthiness of the issuer) there may still be an embedded derivative that is not closely related to the host debt contract, for example, when interest or principal repayments are determined based on leveraged, complex or formulaic features.

These features must be such that **either** the holder would not recover substantially all of its recognised investment **or** the issuer would pay more than twice the market rate of the host contract at inception (of issuing the instrument) **and** could result in a rate of return that is at least twice what the market return would be for a similar host contract (sometimes referred to as the 'double double test'). [IAS 39.AG33(a)]

The test is based on the contractual terms, so the determination is made for both parties to the contract based on the return or loss to the investor. Thus, if the holder separately accounts for an embedded derivative because it could lose substantially all of its initial investment, the issuer would generally do the same.

Example 7.3D

Recovery of recognised investment (1)

Entity X issues CU10 million in debt with an 8 per cent coupon. However, if LIBOR increases by 500 basis points within any one year, the bonds mature and the holder receives CU8 million in total.

An embedded derivative exists and should be separately accounted for because there is a payment provision that may cause the holder not to recover substantially all of its recognised investment if LIBOR increases by 500 basis points.

The likelihood of LIBOR increasing by 500 basis points in the above example is not relevant when making this determination. The test in IAS 39 is based around the possibility of the holder not recovering its recognised investment or obtaining double its initial rate of return. Even if it is unlikely that LIBOR will increase by 500 basis points, the contingent embedded derivative must be separated from the host contract. However, if the probability of this event occurring is low then the fair value of the embedded derivative at inception will be relatively small compared to the fair value of the host contract.

The condition that the holder will not recover substantially all of its recognised investment is only met if the holder can be forced to accept a settlement amount that is substantially below its recognised investment. If the terms of the contract permit, but do not require the holder to settle the instrument in such a manner, then the feature is closely related to the host contract.

US GAAP comparison: DIG Issue B39 allows for an exception to the US GAAP equivalent of the double-double test in FAS 133.13(b) for an embedded call option in a hybrid instrument containing a debt host if the right to accelerate the settlement of the debt can be exercised only by the debtor (issuer/borrower). This is because in the case of an issuer call, the investor does not have the unilateral ability to obtain the right to receive the high rate of return. IFRS does not have specific guidance to this effect.

The 'double-double test' is performed at the date that the hybrid instrument is initially recognised. The first step is it to determine whether there is a possible future interest rate scenario, no matter how remote, in which the embedded derivative would at least double the investor's initial return on the host contract. In making this assessment, it is important to differentiate the return on the host contract from the return on the hybrid contract. The host contract has terms identical to the hybrid contract being tested, except that it does not contain the embedded derivative. IAS 39.AG33(a) describes this step as requiring that the embedded derivative could at least double the holder's initial rate of return on the host contract. An embedded derivative that does not breach this threshold would be considered closely related to its host. If the embedded derivative does breach the threshold, a second step must be performed to determine whether it is closely related to the host contract. The second step is to review each interest rate scenario identified in the first step for which the investor's initial rate of return on the host contract would be doubled, and determine whether, for any of the scenarios, the embedded derivative would at the same time result in a rate of return that is at least twice what otherwise would be the then-current market return for a contract that has the same terms as the host contract and that involves a debtor with a credit quality similar to the issuer's credit quality at inception. If the embedded derivative does not breach the threshold it would not be considered closely related to its host contract. If the threshold is breached in any one of the scenarios then the embedded derivative would be considered not closely related to the host contract and it must be separated.

A vanilla variable rate debt instrument does not contain an embedded derivative even though the investor could pay a rate more than twice the rate at inception. A rate that is always equal to the current market rate is not an embedded derivative.

Example 7.3E

Double-double interest rate test (1)

On 1 January 20X1, an investor purchases a bond where interest payments are linked to LIBOR. The bond also incorporates an interest rate cap whereby if LIBOR equals or exceeds 8 percent at any interest rate reset date, the investor will receive a return of 10 percent. On the date the investor purchases the bond, it also could purchase at par a variable-rate bond not containing a cap that pays LIBOR minus 1 percent from a debtor that has the same credit quality as the issuer of the investor's bond. As of 1 January 20X1, LIBOR is 5 percent. The bond cannot be contractually settled such that the investor would not recover substantially all of its initial recorded investment in the bond.

To perform the first test in paragraph IAS 39.AG33(a), the investor must determine whether there is any interest rate scenario, no matter how remote, under which the embedded derivative (the cap) would at least double the investor's initial rate of return on the host contract. This analysis is summarised in the following table:

A	B	C	D	
Interest rate change	**Return reflecting the effect of the cap**	**Initial rate of return on the host (LIBOR – 1%)**	**Initial rate of return on the host doubled**	**Is the first test met, i.e. is A > D?**
0 – 7.99%	0 – 7.99%	4%	8%	No
8% and up	10%	4%	8%	Yes

Since the first test is met, the investor must perform the second test described in paragraph IAS 39.AG33(a) to determine whether the embedded cap is closely related to its bond host. For this test, the investor must determine, for each interest rate scenario identified above for which the investor's initial rate of return on the host contract would be doubled, whether the embedded cap would simultaneously result in a rate of return that is at least twice what otherwise would be the then-current market return for a contract that has the same terms as the host contract and that involves a debtor with a credit quality similar to the issuer's credit quality at inception. The investor's analysis for this test can be summarised as follows:

A	B	C	
Interest rate scenario identified in the first test above for which the cap would at least double the investor's initial rate of return on the host contract	Return reflecting the effect of the cap under the interest rate scenario in A	Current market rate of return for the host contract under the interest rate scenario in A (LIBOR – 1%)	Is the second test met, i.e. is B at least twice C for any scenario?
8% and up	10%	7%	No

As the first test in IAS 39.AG33(a) is met, but the second test is not, the embedded cap is considered closely related to the bond host.

Example 7.3F

Double-double interest rate test (2)

Entity A invests in 30-year variable-rate debt issued by Entity B. The debt is indexed to the three-month LIBOR (3m LIBOR) rate plus 4 percent. As of the date of issuance, the 3m LIBOR rate was 2 percent. The debt's terms also specify that if the 3m LIBOR rate increases to 5 percent, the debt issuer is required to pay 23 percent for the remaining term of the bonds. The bond cannot be contractually settled such that the investor would not recover substantially all of its initial recorded investment in the bond.

If Entity B were to issue 30-year variable-rate debt without any embedded derivatives (i.e. the interest rate reset feature), it would pay a coupon of 3m LIBOR plus 6 percent. Consequently, the initial rate of return on the host contract is 8 percent (3m LIBOR of 2 percent plus 6 percent). It is necessary to determine whether the embedded derivative could at least double the investor's initial rate of return on the host contract, which was 8 percent at the date of issuance, in any of the possible interest rate environments. Therefore, when 3m LIBOR increases to 5 percent, the 23 percent interest rate feature more than doubles the initial rate of return of 8 percent on the host contract.

It is then necessary to perform an analysis to determine whether the embedded derivative results in a rate of return that is at least twice what otherwise would be the then-current market rate of return for a host contract when 3m LIBOR is at 5 percent. When 3m LIBOR increases to 5 percent the rate of return on the host contract would be 11 percent (3m LIBOR of 5 percent plus 6 percent) for a bond of similar credit quality that does not contain any embedded derivatives. Therefore, when 3m LIBOR increases to 5 percent, the 23 percent interest rate feature is more than twice the then-current market rate of return of the host contract of 11 percent (3m LIBOR of 5 percent plus 6 percent.)

Entity A and Entity B each would be required to treat the feature as a non-closely related embedded derivative.

Example 7.3G

Double-double interest rate test (3)

Entity A issues CU10 million debt with a coupon of 8 per cent and a term of 10 years. Entity A's market rate for 10-year debt is 8.25 per cent. Embedded in the debt is an interest rate adjustment that resets the interest rate to 16.40 per cent if three-month LIBOR increases to 7 per cent or greater during the first three years of the debt.

The adjustment feature is an embedded derivative, but it would not be accounted for separately. The derivative could not cause the rate of return on the host contract to double.

Example 7.3H

Recovery of recognised investment (2)

Entity X issues CU10 million in debt with a coupon of 8.25 per cent and a term of 10 years. Entity X's market rate for 10-year debt is 8 per cent. Embedded in the debt is a clause that states if interest rates increase beyond a specified level, the holder of the debt must give the issuer an additional CU1 million in borrowings maturing in 10 years on which the holder will receive no interest.

The adjustment feature is a written option issued by the holder. The issuer pays for this option through a higher interest cost when compared to debt without the option. The embedded derivative would not be accounted for separately because the holder will recover all of its recognised investment, being CU10 million advanced at inception and CU1 million if it is advanced at a later date. In all cases the investor will recover all its recognised investment. There is no circumstance that can result in the issuer paying a rate that is more than double the market rate of the host contract at inception.

Note the 'recognised investment' is based on the amount advanced by the holder. The likelihood of the option being exercised or the present value of the loan are not considered when determining whether the holder will recover its recognised investment.

7.4 Inflation features

IAS 39 does not specifically address whether an inflation feature within a debt contract is closely related to the host contract. Where an embedded derivative is not specifically addressed by the Standard, significant judgement will need to be used. In these situations, drawing analogies to specific examples given will often prove helpful.

IAS 39 does address inflation features within lease contracts. Finance lease contracts are similar to debt contracts, and therefore the guidance below is based on the examples given for contracts with lease hosts.

Example 7.4

Inflation-linked bond

Entity X purchases an inflation-linked bond. The bond pays a coupon of 4 per cent annually, with a repayment of principal on maturity of the bond. The principal payment is indexed to the domestic retail price index but cannot decrease below par.

As the bond is denominated in the local currency, the indexation of the principal payment to domestic inflation rates is closely related to the host contract.

An inflation feature in a host debt contract is closely related to the host provided that the inflation index is not leveraged, cannot cause the investor not to recover substantially all of its initial investment and is the inflation rate of the economic environment for the currency in which the debt is denominated.

Inflation features that are leveraged will not be closely related to a host debt contract. This is discussed further in the context of a lease host contract in **9.1** below.

7.5 Credit derivatives and liquidity features

IAS 39 does not explicitly address adjustments to the terms of a debt instrument as a result of issuer default, changes in the issuer's credit rating or creditworthiness. It does, however, provide guidance on embedded credit derivatives that relate to other reference entities. Further, certain credit sensitive contracts embedded in other instruments may meet the definition of a financial guarantee contract (see **2.3.2** of **chapter 1**).

7.5.1 *Adjustment for issuer's credit risk*

IAS 39 does not provide specific guidance when the cash flows on debt instruments are adjusted for changes in the issuer's creditworthiness.

It is reasonable to conclude that credit features that relate to the credit quality of the issuer (for example the issuer's credit rating, default or ratios indicative of its credit status) should be viewed as closely related to the host debt contract. In economic terms such features directly affect the value of the host debt contract.

US GAAP comparison: US GAAP indicates that the creditworthiness of the debtor and the interest rate on a debt instrument are considered clearly and closely related (FAS 133.61(c)).

Example 7.5.1A

Interest adjustment: debt covenants

Entity X issues bonds with a BBB rating. The terms of the bond are such that if Entity X violates a specified debt-to-equity ratio covenant, or Entity X's credit rating is downgraded, the interest rate will reset to the then current market rate for Entity X.

The interest rate reset is considered to be closely related to the host contract since it relates to default in a credit risk-related covenant and Entity X's own credit rating, and hence the embedded derivative would not be accounted for separately.

Example 7.5.1B

Interest adjustment: credit risk and share price

Entity Y issues bonds with a BBB rating. The terms of the bond are such that if both of the following conditions are met the coupon on the bond will be reduced by 50 basis points:

(a) the rating of the bonds by a specific rating agency is upgraded to at least BBB+; and

(b) the average share price of the ordinary shares of Entity Y exceeds a certain level over a certain 20 day period

As the adjustment to the interest payments only occurs if both conditions are met it is appropriate to consider the provision as a single embedded derivative in line with IAS 32.AG29 as discussed in **section 6** above, rather than two embedded derivatives. Although one of the underlyings of the derivative is related to credit quality of the issuer (i.e. Entity Y's credit rating) and the other underlying relates to Entity Y's equity price the whole derivative would be considered not to be closely related to the host debt contract. This is because one of the underlyings (i.e. equity price) is considered not to be closely related to the economic characteristics and risks of debt (see **7.3** above).

By contrast if the feature operated such that there were two independent adjustments to the interest paid on the bond (of 25 basis points each) one of which were triggered by changes to Entity Y's credit rating and the other by movements in Entity Y's equity price it would be appropriate to treat the two features as separate embedded derivatives. The credit rating triggered feature would be closely related but the equity triggered feature would not be closely related to the debt host contract and as a consequence would be accounted for separately as at fair value through profit or loss.

7.5.2 *Adjustment for liquidity of issuer's debt*

IAS 39 does not provide specific guidance when the cash flows of a debt instrument are adjusted for changes in the relative liquidity of that debt instrument. Provided the adjustments are not geared, the adjustment is likely to be closely related to the debt host contract as the liquidity of the instrument is inherent in the debt host contract.

Example 7.5.2

Interest adjustment: liquidity

Entity X issues a debt instrument that is repayable at par at maturity that pays a fixed rate of interest. On issue of the debt the instrument is not listed. The debt instrument contains a contractual provision specifying that if the debt instrument ever becomes listed then the rate of interest payable on the instrument will decrease by 0.5%. The interest rate will be reset to its initial level should the debt instrument subsequently be delisted.

The listing of the debt instrument is likely to increase the liquidity of the debt instrument. The lower liquidity of an unlisted instrument is a cost borne by the holders as it limits their ability to sell their holding of the debt instrument in the instance when the borrower's ability to meet its obligations as they fall due may be in question. The listing of the debt instrument is likely to improve its liquidity and to provide the holders with an exit mechanism before maturity. The holder's willingness willing to accept a reduction in the interest rate in exchange for increased liquidity would be considered closely related to the host debt contract.

7.5.3 *Adjustment for third party credit*

IAS 39 views a credit derivative that transfers credit risk of a particular reference asset (which the entity, the 'beneficiary', may not own) to another party, the 'guarantor', as not closely related to the host debt contract. [IAS 39.AG30(h)]

Example 7.5.3A

Credit-linked note

Entity X issues credit-linked bonds. The bonds are linked to the performance of a portfolio of third party corporate bonds held by a third party bank. The bonds pay a rate of interest in excess of Entity X's normal cost of funds as, in the event that one of the referenced corporate bonds defaults, Entity X will pay a reduced principal to the holders.

The embedded credit-related provision would be accounted for separately because the credit of a third party entity is not considered to be closely related to the debt host contract issued by Entity X.

Example 7.5.3B

Cash versus synthetic credit default obligations

Collateralised debt obligation (CDO) special purpose entities (SPEs) are set up to issue notes to investors which pay based on the performance of specified named corporate debt. The interest and principal on the assets is used to service and repay the CDO liability. If there is default under the named corporate debt, then the investors of the CDO notes will suffer loss. The losses are shared by investors in a pre-agreed manner, often with the most junior notes suffering most of the expected loss.

There are two types of structure:

- the assets in the SPE are actual corporate debt (e.g. GM & Ford corporate bonds), referred to as 'cash CDOs' as the SPE has to own the actual cash instruments; or
- the assets in the SPE are derivatives over the corporate debt (e.g. credit default swaps (CDS) over GM & Ford), referred to as 'synthetic CDOs' as the SPE will or may hold synthetic instruments, as opposed to holding cash instruments.

A CDO is illustrated below:

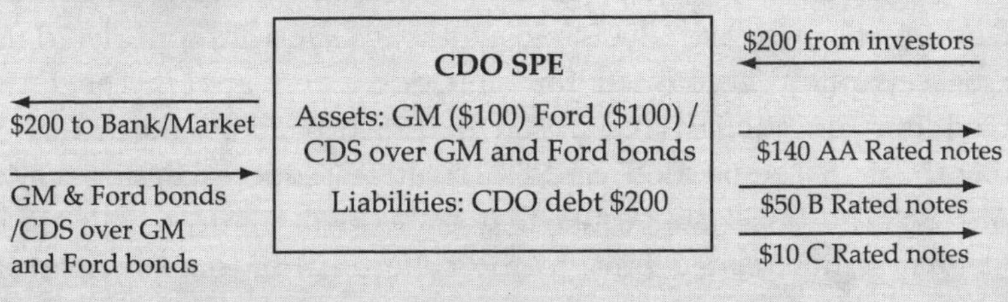

Whether the CDO structure is cash or synthetic will impact the accounting for the notes:

Cash CDO

If an issued CDO liability is not fair valued through profit or loss the SPE will need to assess whether the CDO liability has embedded credit derivatives that require separation. As the entity must own the underlying cash instruments the issued CDO liability does not have a credit derivative that requires separation. The beneficiary (the SPE) is transferring the credit risk of its referenced assets to a guarantor (the investor in the CDO notes).

Synthetic CDO

As the SPE is required to pay returns on the CDO liability that is linked to the performance of corporate bonds, but without actually needing to own these cash instruments (e.g. it can purchase credit derivatives over the reference corporate bonds), the notes issued by the SPE have credit embedded derivatives that require separation. The beneficiary (the SPE) is transferring the credit risk of referenced assets to a guarantor (the investor of the CDO notes) but does not own the underlying referenced assets.

The guidance on whether to separate out an embedded derivative in CDOs equally applies to the issuer and the holder of the CDO notes.

US GAAP comparison: FAS 155, *Accounting For Certain Hybrid Financial Instruments.* amended FAS 133 in a number of respects, one of which was the accounting for beneficial interests in securitisations. FAS 155 states that changes in cash flows attributable to changes in the creditworthiness of an interest resulting from securitised financial assets and liabilities (including derivative contracts) that represent the assets or liabilities that are held by the issuing entity shall not be considered an embedded derivative. Therefore, synthetic or cash CDOs as illustrated above would not have separately recognised embedded derivatives with respect to the linkage to third party credit. FAS 155 therefore creates a difference with IFRS with respect to synthetic CDOs because under IFRS an embedded derivative is separately recognised if the instrument is not classified as at fair value through profit or loss.

In January 2009, the FASB issued proposed DIG Issue C22 to clarify how to determine which embedded credit derivative features, including those in cash CDOs and synthetic CDOs are considered not to be separately accounted for embedded derivatives. The FASB noted that questions have arisen in practice about the intended breadth of the embedded credit derivative scope exception under FAS 133. The FASB suggested that embedded features with credit risk that is not related only to the subordination of one financial instrument to another must be evaluated for potential embedded derivatives. At the date of writing, the proposed amendment had not been finalised.

7.6 Foreign currency features

Debt contracts may require the issuer to make payments of interest or principal in a foreign currency. An example of such a contract is a dual currency bond where principal is paid in a foreign currency, whereas interest is paid in the entity's functional currency. The foreign currency feature in a dual currency bond is an embedded derivative (foreign currency swap or foreign currency forward) but it is not separated from the host debt instrument because foreign currency gains and losses on a dual currency bond are already recognised in profit and loss following the requirements of IAS 21 *The Effects of Changes in Foreign Exchange Rates*.

Certain currency features may need to be separated. A debt contract may, for example, contain a provision that would allow the holder to choose to receive interest payments in an alternative currency. This provision is a foreign currency option, written by the issuer.

Foreign currency option features are generally viewed by IAS 39 as taking on an additional foreign currency risk that is not normally present in transactions and will not be fully reflected by the requirements of IAS 21. Such an option in a debt host is not closely related and needs to be accounted for separately.

7.7 Caps, floors and collars on interest rates

Floating rate debt contracts often include features that 'cap', 'floor' or 'collar' the amount of interest payable on the debt.

7.7.1 Definitions

A 'cap' is an option contract that puts an upper limit on a floating interest rate. The purchaser of the cap is paid the difference between the current floating interest rate and the strike rate of the cap whenever the current floating rate exceeds the strike rate.

Example 7.7.1

Interest rate cap

Entity A purchases an interest rate cap, paying a premium of CU1 million. The cap has a notional of CU100 million and a strike rate of 6 per cent. Currently, LIBOR is 4.5 per cent.

The cap will pay Entity A the difference between LIBOR and 6 per cent whenever LIBOR exceeds 6 per cent. Thus, if LIBOR moves to 6.5 per cent, the cap will pay Entity A CU500,000, i.e. 0.5 per cent (the difference between LIBOR and 6 per cent) applied to the notional of the cap (CU100 million).

A 'floor' is an option contract that puts a lower limit on a floating interest rate. The writer of the floor will pay the difference between the current floating interest rate and the strike rate of the floor whenever the current floating rate drops below the strike rate. A floor is effectively the opposite of a cap. The writer of a floor will receive a premium which compensates it for the risk it has taken on (i.e. the risk that rates drop below a certain level).

Entities often want to protect themselves against rises in interest rates, so they purchase caps. However, these can be expensive. To reduce or limit the cost, entities will often simultaneously write a floor. Thus, they have achieved an interest rate collar. A 'collar' is an instrument that combines a cap and a floor. The holder of an interest rate collar will be exposed to interest rate movements only within a specified range. It protects the holder against a significant rise in interest rates, but limits the benefits of a drop in interest rates.

7.7.2 *In-the-money and out-of-the-money caps, floors and collars*

A cap is 'in-the-money' if its strike rate is lower than the market rate of interest. It is 'out-of-the-money' if its strike rate is higher than the market rate of interest. If a cap has a strike rate of 6 per cent, it will be in-the-money whenever interest rates are above 6 per cent and out-of-the-money whenever interest rates are below 6 per cent.

A floor is in-the-money if its strike rate is higher than the market rate of interest. It is out-of-the-money if its strike rate is lower than the market rate of interest. If a floor has a strike rate of 4 per cent, it will be in-the-money whenever interest rates are below 4 per cent and out-of-the-money whenever interest rates are above 4 per cent.

A collar has two strike prices, the upper and lower limits. A collar is out-of-the-money if interest rates are between these two strike rates; it is in-the-money otherwise.

7.7.3 *Embedded caps, floors and collars*

An embedded cap or floor on the interest rate of a debt instrument, where the cap or floor is not leveraged, is closely related to the host debt contract provided the cap is at or above the market interest rate and the floor is at or below the market interest rate when the instrument is issued. The assessment as to whether an embedded cap or floor is closely related to a host debt contract is made at issuance and is not subsequently revised. [IAS 39.AG33(b)]

Example 7.7.3

Embedded interest rate cap

Entity X issues CU100 million debt with a five-year maturity. The interest is payable at LIBOR plus a credit spread of 150 basis points. LIBOR at issuance is 4.5 per cent, and therefore the rate at inception of the debt is 6 per cent. There is a provision in the debt contract that if LIBOR were to rise, the rate payable on the debt would not rise above 7 per cent.

The cap is an embedded derivative that is closely related to the host debt contract, since at the time of the issuance of the debt the cap is out-of-the-money.

While the Standard does not specifically address a collar embedded in a debt contract, a simple analogy to caps and floors can be made. If a debt contract has an embedded collar which caps interest rates at 7 per cent and has a floor of 4 per cent, the collar will be closely related to the host debt contract provided both the cap and the floor are out-of-the-money when the debt is issued and are not leveraged.

US GAAP comparison: FAS 133.61(f) specifies that an embedded floor or cap on interest rates on a debt instrument is clearly and closely related to the host contract unless the contract could be contractually settled such that the investor would not recover substantially all its initially recorded investment or the embedded derivative could double the investor's initial rate of return and simultaneously result in a rate of return that is twice what otherwise would be the then-current market return.

7.8 Conversion and equity features

A conversion feature that allows the holder of the debt contract to convert the outstanding amount into equity of the issuer is an embedded derivative that is not closely related to the host debt contract.

Accounting for convertible debt is different for the holder and issuer of the instrument if from the issuer's perspective, the conversion feature is an equity instrument which is outside the scope of IAS 39. Issuer accounting is addressed in **chapter 3**.

Example 7.8

Equity conversion feature

Entity X issues debt that is convertible into a fixed number of its ordinary shares in five years. The conversion feature represents an embedded written call option on the shares of Entity X, settled in a fixed number of shares.

For Entity X, the convertible debt is a compound instrument that should be split into its liability and equity components. Entity X will not account for the written call option as an embedded derivative because the option is an equity instrument of Entity X (see **chapter 3**).

The investor will account for the embedded purchased option separately as, under IAS 39, the equity conversion feature is not closely related to the host debt contract.

Another form of equity embedded derivative is an 'equity kicker'. These are debt instruments which provide for the lender to receive shares of the borrower for nothing, or a very low amount if the borrower lists its shares on a stock exchange. The debt remains outstanding following the delivery of the shares. Typically, the lender is a venture capitalist. Similar to convertible debt, debt with an equity kicker carries a coupon that is lower than the rate on a comparable debt without the equity kicker.

The equity kicker meets the definition of a derivative as its value will change in response to changes in the borrower's share price. It has little initial net investment, and is settled at a future date. This is true even though the right to receive the shares is contingent on an unrelated event. [IAS 39.IG.C.4] By analogy to convertible debt, the embedded derivative is not closely related to the host debt contract.

US GAAP comparison: For holders of instruments, US GAAP indicates that the changes in fair value of an equity interest and the interest rates on a debt instrument are not clearly and closely related. Accordingly, a conversion option in a debt host must be separated from the debt host contract and accounted for as a derivative instrument if the conversion option would, as a freestanding instrument, be a derivative instrument subject to FAS 133.

For issuers of instruments, under US GAAP, the issuer may be eligible for a scope exception from the bifurcation requirements of FAS 133. Also, as discussed in **chapter 3**, IFRS requires the issuer to separate a hybrid instrument into the debt component and the equity component. US GAAP does not have this requirement. Separate accounting by the issuer for a hybrid with a debt and equity component is typically only permitted if the conversion feature is an embedded derivative that is required to be bifurcated under FAS 133 or the issuer is permitted to settle the instrument in whole or in part in cash upon conversion.

7.9 Non-cash settlement of interest or principal

Debt contracts that allow for the payment of interest or principal in non-cash consideration may contain embedded derivatives that are not closely related to the host debt contract.

For example, Entity A lends Entity B CU10 million for 10 years. Each year instead of paying interest, Entity B agrees to give Entity A a predetermined amount of free advertising space in a newspaper. A will not use the advertising space in its own business, so it pre-sells all the advertising space in advance. The feature embedded in the loan meets the definition of a derivative as it has an underlying, which is the price of the advertising space, no initial net investment, and will be settled at future dates. The economic characteristics and risks of the embedded derivative and debt are not closely related. The derivative is net settled and therefore does not get the purchase, sale or usage requirements exemption (see **2.5** of **chapter 1**).

Where Entity A intends to utilise the advertising space in its normal course of business, and therefore does not intend to net settle the advertising space, the provision of advertising space will meet the purchase, sale or usage requirements exemptions and therefore will not be in the scope of IAS 39.

7.10 Unit linking features embedded in host debt instrument

A unit linking feature embedded in a host debt instrument is closely related to the host debt instrument if the unit-denominated payments are measured at current unit values that reflect the fair values of the assets of the fund. A unit linking feature is a contractual term that requires payments denominated in a unit of an internal or external investment fund. [IAS 39.AG33(g)]

IFRS 4.IG Example 2: 2.15 provides the example of a policyholder option to surrender a contract for account value equal to the fair value of a pool of equity investments, possibly after deducting a surrender charge. The example makes reference to IAS 39.AG33(g) and states that if such a feature is embedded in a host investment contract then, if the insurer regards the account value as the amortised cost or the fair value of that portion of its obligation, no further adjustment is needed for the option (unless the surrender value differs significantly from the account value). Otherwise the embedded derivative feature would be required to be classified separately as at fair value through profit or loss. A host investment contract is described in IFRS 4.IG 4 as a financial instrument that does not meet the definition of an insurance contract.

The above guidance suggests that unit linking features would only be considered closely related where the unit denominated payments are measured in such a way that they reflect the fair value of the assets of the fund to which they are linked. In any case, even if the unit linking feature is determined to be closely related to a debt host contract IAS 39.AG8 would be applicable for subsequent measurement of the hybrid instrument if it was measured at amortised cost (see **4.1.2** in **chapter 6**). Applying IAS 39.AG8 would result in the carrying value of the hybrid instrument reflecting the amount expected to be paid or received which would incorporate the unit linking feature.

7.11 Further examples of embedded derivatives in host debt contracts

The table below provides further examples of derivative instruments embedded in debt host contracts.

Type of instrument	**Economic characteristics**	**Embedded derivative**	**Closely related**
Inverse floater	Bond accrues interest at 5.25% for three months to July 20X4; thereafter at 10.75% less six-month LIBOR to January 20X5.	Fixed-to-floating interest rate swap	No. Para AG 33(a)
Leveraged inverse floater	Bond accrues interest at 6% to June 20X5; thereafter, at 14.55% – (2.5 x 3 month LIBOR).	Leveraged interest rate swap	No. Para AG 33(a)
Ratchet floater	Bond accrues interest at three-month LIBOR + 50 basis points. In addition to having a lifetime cap of 7.25%, the coupon will be collared each period between the previous coupon and the previous coupon plus 25 basis points.	Combinations of purchased and written options that create changing caps and floors	Yes. Para AG 33(b)

Type of instrument	Economic characteristics	Embedded derivative	Closely related
Fixed-to-floating note	A bond that pays a varying coupon (first-year coupon is fixed; second- and third-year coupons are based on LIBOR).	Forward-starting interest rate swap	Yes. Para AG 33(a)
Indexed amortising note	A bond that repays principal based on a predetermined amortisation schedule or target value. The amortisation is linked to changes in the relevant interest rate index. The maturity of the bond changes as the related index changes.	Conditional exchange option that requires partial or early payment of the note	Yes. Para AG 33(a)
Equity-indexed note	A bond for which the return of interest, principal, or both is tied to a specified equity security or index (for example, the Standard and Poor's 500 (S&P 500) index). This instrument may contain a fixed or varying coupon rate and may place all or a portion of principal at risk.	Forward exchange contracts or option contracts	No. Para AG 30(d)
Variable principal redemption bond	A supplemental principal payment will be paid to the investor, at maturity, if the final S&P 500 closing value (determined at a specified date) is less than its initial value at date of issuance and the 10-year constant maturity treasuries (CMT) is greater than 2% as of a specified date. In all cases, the minimum principal redemption will be 100% of face amount.	Purchased option	No. Para AG 30(d)
Crude-oil knock-in note	A bond that has a 1% coupon and guarantees repayment of principal with upside potential based on the strength of the oil market.	Option contract	No. Para AG 30(e)
Gold-linked bull note	A bond that has a fixed 3% coupon and guarantees repayment of principal with upside potential if the price of gold increases.	Option contracts	No. Para AG 30(e)
Step-up bond	A bond that provides an introductory above-market yield that is less than twice the market rate at inception and steps up to a new coupon, which will be below then-current market rates or, alternatively, the bond may be called in lieu of the step-up in the coupon rate.	Call option	Yes. Para AG 33(a)
Credit-sensitive bond	A bond that has a coupon rate of interest that resets based on changes in the issuer's credit rating.	Conditional exchange contract or option	Yes. Para AG 33(a)
Inflation bond	A bond with a contractual principal amount that is indexed to the non-leveraged inflation rate of the economic environment of the issuer, but cannot decrease below par; the coupon rate is below that of traditional bonds of a similar maturity.	Conditional exchange contract or option	Yes. Para AG 33(a) and (f)(i)

Type of instrument	Economic characteristics	Embedded derivative	Closely related
Specific equity-linked bond	A bond that pays a coupon slightly below that of traditional bonds of similar maturity; however, the principal amount is linked to the stock market performance of an equity investee of the issuer.	Series of forward contracts or option contracts	No. Para AG 30(d)
Dual currency bond	A bond providing for repayment of principal in one currency (e.g. Euro) and periodic interest payments denominated in a different currency (e.g. Yen).	Foreign currency forward	Yes. Para AG 33(c)
Short-term loan with foreign currency option	A US lender issues a loan at an above-market interest rate. The loan is made in US dollars, the borrower's functional currency, and the borrower has the option to repay the loan in US dollars or in a fixed amount of a specified foreign currency.	Foreign currency option	No. Para AG 33(d)
Participating mortgage	A mortgage in which the investor receives a below-market interest rate and is entitled to participate in the appreciation in the market value of the project that is financed by the mortgage upon sale of the project, at a deemed sale date, or at the maturity or refinancing of the loan. The mortgagor must continue to own the project over the term of the mortgage.	Call option	No. Para AG 30(e)

8 Embedded derivatives in equity host contracts

It is not common to find derivatives embedded in equity host contracts. **Chapter 3** provides guidance on when instruments are classified as debt or equity. Sometimes it may be difficult to determine whether the host contract is debt or equity. Further examples are considered in **section 5** above.

8.1 Equity option triggered by an unrelated factor

Example 8.1

Contingent share conversion based on interest rates

Entity A issues €100 million of perpetual, irredeemable preference shares that pay a fixed dividend rate of 10 per cent. The shares meet the definition of equity per IAS 32 as the entity has true discretion as to whether or not, and the extent to which, dividends will be paid.

The shares include a provision stating that if interest rates increase by 200 basis points, the holders will additionally receive 100,000 ordinary shares in Entity A.

The embedded option is not separated by the issuer because it and the host instrument are both equity instruments of the issuer. Although the option is triggered by a change in interest rates, the value of the option is indexed to the change in fair value of, and is settled in, the issuer's shares. Equally, from the holder's perspective, the embedded option is closely related to the host.

8.2 Conditional cash return on perpetual preference shares

Example 8.2

Contingent cash payment based on interest rates

Entity A issues $100 million of perpetual, irredeemable preference shares that pay a discretionary, fixed dividend rate of 8 per cent. The shares meet the definition of equity per IAS 32 as the entity has true discretion as to whether or not, and the extent to which, dividends are paid. Embedded in the shares is a provision that states if LIBOR increases to 12 per cent or more, the holders will become entitled to receive a one-off payment of cash calculated by a predetermined formula.

The issuer cannot avoid an outflow of cash in respect of the amount prescribed by the formula if LIBOR reaches 12 per cent, i.e. the embedded feature is an embedded derivative liability. Both the holder and the issuer account for this derivative separately from the host instrument. Accounting for the host instrument by the issuer is different from that by the holder as for the issuer equity is outside the scope of IAS 39.

8.3 Convertible preference shares

Example 8.3

Convertible preference shares

Entity X issues perpetual preference shares where any dividends are entirely at the discretion of the issuer. The preference shares are convertible into a fixed number of ordinary shares at any time after a specified date. The preference shares meet the definition of equity under IAS 32.

The preference shares are equity of X. The conversion feature represents an embedded call option on Entity X's ordinary shares that also meets the definition of equity. Entity X does not account for the embedded option separately because both the option and the host are equity instruments of Entity X.

The same considerations apply to the investor; however the accounting in the investor's books will be different from that of the issuer since for the issuer equity is outside the scope of IAS 39. For the holder, the perpetual preference share is a financial asset which consists of an equity host contract with a closely related equity embedded derivative.

US GAAP comparison: US GAAP indicates that because the changes in fair value of an equity interest and interest rates on a debt instrument are not clearly and closely related, the terms of the preferred stock (other than the conversion option) must be analysed to determine whether the preferred stock (and thus the potential host contract) is more akin to an equity instrument or a debt instrument. FAS 133.61(l) further clarifies that a typical cumulative fixed-rate preferred stock that has a mandatory redemption feature is more akin to debt, whereas cumulative participating perpetual preferred stock is more akin to an equity instrument. If it is more like equity, then the conversion option is clearly and closely related and no further analysis is required (i.e., bifurcation is not permitted). If it is more like debt, then the conversion feature is not clearly and closely related (see the US GAAP comparison in **5** and **7.8** above).

8.4 Puttable equity instruments

If an instrument has an equity host and is puttable at a fixed amount or an amount determined on the basis of an index that is unrelated to the fair value of the equity host (e.g. the price of gold) then the put would not have equity characteristics and therefore would not be closely related. In the case of fixed strike price the investor has downside protection and therefore does not share in a residual interest in the net assets of the issuer, and in the case of a strike price linked to a variable other than the net assets of the issuer, the investor is not exposed to the residual net assets of the entity. The put would not be considered closely related to the equity host contract and therefore would be separated and classified as at fair value through profit or loss.

9 Embedded derivatives in lease contracts

Embedded derivatives can exist in lease contracts, whether an entity is acting as a lessee or a lessor in either a finance or an operating lease.

9.1 Inflation factors

An embedded derivative in a host lease contract is closely related to the host contract if the embedded derivative is an inflation-related index, for example, where lease payments are indexed to a retail price index, provided that the index is not leveraged, and the index relates to inflation in the entity's own economic environment. [IAS 39.AG33(f)(i)]

9.1.1 Entity's economic environment

IAS 39 does not give any guidance on what constitutes the entity's own economic environment. It is reasonable to assume that where an entity operates in a certain country and enters into a lease agreement on, say, a property located in that country, the inflation of the country concerned will be the relevant inflation index, since that index is related to the value of the lease and is present in the environment in which the entity operates.

Example 9.1.1

Inflation-adjusting lease payments

Entity X, a UK entity, has extensive operations in Europe and the US. Entity Y, Entity X's subsidiary, leases property in Paris with a lease term of 10 years. The functional currency of Entity Y is the Euro. Lease payments are to be made in Euros. Embedded in the lease is a provision that requires the lease payments to be adjusted every two years for the change in the UK consumer price index, which is not the index of the economic environment of Entity Y.

The embedded inflation indexed payment would be accounted for separately because, although the rate of inflation is not leveraged, the inflation index is in a different economic environment from the entity entering into the lease.

9.1.2 Leverage factors

The second consideration when assessing whether an inflation adjustment in a lease contract is an embedded derivative that requires separate accounting is leverage. IAS 39 does not define leverage in the context of inflation. However, the concept of leverage is used in the assessment of the features present in debt contracts. For debt contracts it is assumed that a leverage feature that can double the holder's initial rate of return and could result in a rate of return that is at least twice what the market return would be for a contract with the same terms as the host contract is not closely related to the host debt contract.

By analogy, it can be argued that an inflation adjustment for two times or more of the inflation index will be seen as leveraged. Careful consideration of the terms of the lease is required for a decision on whether any inflation adjustment included in it is indeed leveraged.

Example 9.1.2

Leveraged inflation-adjusting lease payments

Entity X, a UK entity, leases property in London with a lease term of 10 years. Lease payments are to be made in Sterling. Embedded in the lease is a provision that requires the lease payment to be adjusted annually for three times the changes in UK's retail price index.

The embedded inflation adjustment will be accounted for separately because it is leveraged.

In the above example, it is quite clear that there is a leveraged inflation feature that needs to be separated. However, what is less clear is whether the derivative that needs separation is the total inflation adjustment, i.e. three times the retail price index, or just the leveraged portion, i.e. two times the retail price index.

The argument for the latter is that adjustment by the retail price index is seen as closely related. However, there are two counter-arguments to that: firstly, separation of only a portion of the embedded derivative amounts to splitting the derivative into two parts which is not generally permitted under IAS 39; secondly, separation could be argued to create cash flows that are not evident in the contract, which once again is not the general practice under IAS 39. On balance, the total inflation adjustment should be split out.

9.2 Foreign currency features

There are no specific rules addressing currency features in lease contracts. There are two pieces of guidance included in IAS 39 which analyse foreign currency features embedded in contracts: foreign currency derivatives embedded in host debt instruments; and foreign currency derivatives embedded in a host contract that is not a financial instrument.

For the former, the foreign currency feature is not separately accounted for because the instrument is a monetary item and, under IAS 21, foreign currency gains and losses are already recognised in profit or loss. For the latter, the assessment is more complicated. A foreign currency derivative embedded in a host contract that is not a financial instrument is closely related to the host provided it is not leveraged, does not contain an option, and requires payments denominated in:

- the functional currency of any substantial party to the contract;
- the currency in which the price of the related good or service that is acquired or delivered is routinely denominated in commercial transactions around the world; or
- a currency that is commonly used in contracts to purchase or sell non-financial items in the economic environment in which the transaction takes place.

It can be argued that trade receivables and payables recognised under finance leases are akin to a debt host, and therefore are covered by the same requirements in IAS 21 to recognise foreign currency gains and losses in profit or loss on monetary items. Hence, it would be reasonable to analogise from the foreign currency guidance on debt contracts when considering foreign currency features in finance lease payables and receivables.

Operating leases are non-financial instruments. Hence, the considerations that apply to non-financial items detailed in **10.5** below will equally apply to operating leases. These considerations include foreign currency options, leverage factors, the functional currency of substantial parties to the contract, and the currency that is commonly used in contracts in the economic environment in which the transaction takes place.

9.2.1 Examples of embedded foreign currency features

The following examples apply the analysis that is described in **9.2** above.

Example 9.2.1A

Operating lease denominated in functional currency of a party

Entity X, a Dutch entity, leases property from Entity Y, a UK entity, under an operating lease. The lease payments are denominated in Sterling. The functional currency of Entity X is the Euro and the functional currency of Entity Y is Sterling.

The provision to pay in Sterling would not require separate accounting, because Sterling is the functional currency of a substantial party to the contract, Entity Y.

Example 9.2.1B

Operating lease not denominated in functional currency of a party

Entity X, a New Zealand entity, leases property under an operating lease from Entity Y, an Australian entity. The lease payments are denominated in US dollars. The functional currency of Entity X is the New Zealand dollar and the functional currency of Entity Y is the Australian dollar.

The provision to pay in US dollars would require separate accounting because it is not the currency of the primary economic environment of either counterparty to the contract, and the price of this asset is not denominated routinely in that currency in international commerce.

If the property was leased under a finance lease (which is a financial instrument), the lease payments would represent monetary items, and therefore be within the scope of IAS 21. The embedded derivative would not be separated.

Example 9.2.1C

Choice of settlement in foreign currencies

A lease contract between a Sterling functional currency entity and a US dollar one, whereby the lessee can choose to make payments in either Sterling or US dollars, contains an embedded option which is not closely related to the host lease contract. This is true even though both of the settlement currencies are functional currencies of one of the counterparties to the lease. This answer would apply regardless of whether the lease was an operating or finance lease.

9.2.2 *Substantial party*

A 'substantial party' to the contract in the examples above is a party acting as a principal to the contract. The criterion for a 'substantial party' would not be satisfied if the party is an agent that is being engaged by the entity solely to comply with the requirement that payments be denominated in the functional currency of any substantial party to the contract.

Example 9.2.2

Substantial party

Entity X would like to lease property from Entity Y under an operating lease and have the payments denominated in US dollars. The functional currency of both entities is Sterling. To accomplish a US dollar-denominated lease, Entity Y leases the property to an investment bank whose functional currency is US dollars. The investment bank then subleases the property to Entity X. The sublease agreement requires Entity X to pay US dollars.

The investment bank is acting solely as an agent for Entity X and, accordingly, is not at risk (i.e. the investment bank would be indemnified by Entity Y for any losses incurred due to a default by Entity X). The bank cannot be viewed as a substantial party to the lease. Hence, the embedded foreign currency derivative requires separate accounting.

US GAAP comparison: US GAAP does not separate an embedded foreign currency derivative from a non-financial host contract in the case where the contract is denominated in the local currency of any substantial party to the contract, or the currency used by a substantial party to the contract as if it were the functional currency because the primary economic environment in which the party operates is highly inflationary.

9.3 Referenced underlyings

A lease with contingent rentals that are based on related sales or on variable interest rates contain an embedded derivative (linkage to sale or interest) which is deemed to be closely related to the host lease contract.

9.3.1 *Contingent rentals based on variable interest rates*

Example 9.3.1

Lease linked to interest rates

Entity A, a UK entity, enters into a lease whose payments are indexed to six-month LIBOR. The embedded derivative does not need to be separated as the indexation is to interest rates inherent in its local economy.

IAS 39 does not give any guidance on what constitutes a variable interest rate. It is reasonable to assume that where an entity operates in a certain country and enters into a lease agreement in that country, a variable interest rate would be similar to the benchmark interest rate achieved on a debt instrument where the proceeds are used to invest in an asset where the debt is secured on that asset.

9.3.2 *Contingent rentals based on related sales*

Example 9.3.2A

Lease linked to sales

Entity X leases a property, which it uses as a retail outlet, selling custom made umbrellas. Embedded in the lease is a clause requiring lease payments to increase for each 1,000 sales after the first 100,000 umbrellas are sold.

Contingent rentals based on related sales are considered to be closely related to the host lease contract, so the sales related derivative should not be separated from the lease.

Example 9.3.2B

Lease linked to throughput

Entity Y leases shop premises in an airport terminal on an operating lease. The lease payments are contingent on the number of passengers who pass through the terminal.

While the contingent rentals are not based directly on related sales, it is clear that sales are directly affected by the number of passengers passing through the terminal. Thus, the embedded derivative is closely related to the host lease contract and does not need to be separately accounted for.

9.3.3 *Contingent rentals based on other balances*

IAS 39 states that contingent rentals based on related sales are closely related to the host lease contract. However, no guidance is given on contingent rentals based on other balances, such as profit or net assets or based on ratios.

It is not reasonable to extend the guidance given to cover other balances, such as profit. Sales within a retail unit may directly affect how much rent can be charged on the unit, as it will be an indicator of how many customers frequent the premises. However, the sales figure is a gross figure, whereas any profit figure will be a net figure, comprising several balances. To argue that profit is closely related to rentals, it would be necessary to argue that each balance that comprises the profit figure is individually closely related to rentals. It is not clear how figures such as cost of sales can be argued to be closely related to rentals. They are not analogous to sales.

Similarly, a net asset position comprises several asset and liability positions all added together. To argue that net assets are closely related to lease payments, it would be necessary to show that each asset and liability position that makes up the net asset position is individually closely related to the lease payments; i.e. that they have economic characteristics and risks that are similar to those in a lease contract, or that they are analogous to sales. It is not clear how, for example, an overdraft or an investment in securities is closely related to rentals, or analogous to sales.

Example 9.3.3

Lease linked to profits

Entity Z, a UK entity, leases a retail unit in a large shopping mall located in the UK. Embedded in the lease is a provision requiring lease payments to increase for each £1,000 profit after tax made over £1,000,000.

While contingent rentals based on related sales are closely related to a host lease contract, the same is not true of contingent rentals based on profit after tax. Several of the balances that are added together to reach profit after tax (such as cost of sales and tax) do not have economic characteristics and risks similar to those of the lease contract.

9.3.4 Other referenced underlyings

Lease contracts in which payments are determined by changes in a referenced underlying that is not generally connected with the normal pricing of a traditional lease contain embedded derivatives that need to be separated. Examples of underlyings include security prices, commodity prices, an unrelated index of prices or rates, credit ratings or a credit index.

Example 9.3.4

Lease linked to share price index

Entity A has several investments in FTSE 100 shares. It enters into a lease contract and negotiates a clause whereby lease payments are indexed to changes in the FTSE 100.

Contingent rentals based on changes in FTSE 100 are not closely related to the host lease contract, so the embedded derivative would need to be separated from the host lease.

10 Embedded derivatives in purchase, sale and service contracts

There is very little guidance on assessing embedded derivatives in purchase, sale and service contracts, particularly service contracts. Conclusions will need to be reached by analogising from the guidance and principles applicable to other host contracts.

10.1 Adjustments for ingredients

Pricing of sales, purchase and service contracts is often structured so as to pass on to customers the cost of an ingredient used in the production or delivery of an asset or service.

There is no guidance from which to draw an analogy. Hence, the assessment should be based on the consideration of the economic characteristics and risks of the contract. This should include a combination of qualitative and quantitative factors.

For example, a physically delivered contract to purchase electricity is assessed and found to be a 'normal' purchase, sale and usage requirement contract. However, there is a pricing adjustment with respect to a different commodity, gas. Gas is used as an ingredient in the production of the electricity that will be physically delivered. The pricing adjustment is achieved through a formula that incorporates many other pricing inputs and variables. The prices of gas and electricity in this case are not highly correlated.

Commodity-based contracts that are entered into and continue to meet the entity's expected purchase, sale, or usage requirements are outside the scope of IAS 39 and are therefore not financial instruments. (This is discussed further in **2.5** of **chapter 1**.) However, even if a contract is not a financial instrument in its entirety, it may include an embedded derivative that is potentially required to be accounted for separately.

The guidance in IAS 39 focuses on economic characteristics and risks in determining whether the embedded derivative is closely related. The guidance does not specifically refer to a purely quantitative assessment, nor does it refer to a purely qualitative assessment of the relationship. Therefore an entity would need to determine whether both quantitative and qualitative factors are relevant in determining whether the pricing adjustment is closely related to the host contract or not.

In this instance a quantitative assessment would establish that the economic characteristics are different, due to a lack of correlation between the pricing adjustment and the price of the commodity that is delivered under the contract. However, this quantitative assessment should not be applied exclusively in determining whether the embedded derivative is closely related, as qualitative factors may also be relevant to the decision. If the supplier of the electricity (who is the counterparty to the arrangement) is a gas powered power station, then this qualitative characteristic is relevant in determining whether the pricing adjustment should be separately accounted for. As the pricing adjustment is specifically relevant to the production of the commodity to be delivered under the contract then the pricing adjustment is considered to be closely related to the host contract. However, if it cannot be demonstrated that the pricing adjustment is directly relevant to the counterparty, for example, the counterparty is an electricity exchange/broker and did not use the indexed commodity (gas) in the production of the commodity (electricity) that was to be physically delivered, or the counterparty is a nuclear powered electricity supplier and does not use gas in the production of the electricity, then this pricing adjustment does not have qualitative merit, and therefore a quantitative assessment should take precedence.

10.2 Inflation factors

There is no specific guidance on inflation factors within purchase, sale or service contracts, but an analogy can be established with lease contracts. An embedded inflation-related index in a host lease contract is closely related to the host contract provided that the index is not leveraged and the index relates to inflation in the entity's own economic environment.

Example 10.2

Executory contract linked to inflation

Entity A, a UK entity, enters into a long-term service contract under which it agrees to clean and maintain specified buildings owned by Entity B for the next 10 years. All the buildings are located within the UK. A receives a fixed annual fee. Embedded in the contract is a clause providing for a one-off adjustment half-way through the contract such that the fee receivable is adjusted for changes in the UK's retail price index from the beginning of the contract. Thereafter, the fee remains fixed at the new amount.

The embedded inflation indexed payment is closely related to the host service contract because the rate of inflation is not leveraged, and the inflation index is that of the local economic environment.

In determining whether the inflation feature within a sale, purchase or service contract is leveraged or is that of the entity's local environment, similar considerations to those used when assessing host lease contracts should be applied (see **9.1** above).

10.3 Adjustments for unrelated factors

Purchase and sale contracts in which payments are determined by changes in a referenced underlying that is not generally connected with the normal pricing of such a contract contain embedded derivatives that need to be separated. Examples of pricing adjustments of this type include adjustments by reference to interest rates, security prices, unrelated commodity prices, and various indices of prices or rates.

Example 10.3

Executory contract linked to share price index

Entity A contracts to buy goods from Entity B for a fixed amount plus or minus an indexation feature linked to movements in the FTSE 250. The embedded derivative based on the FTSE 250 would need to be separated from the host purchase contract.

US GAAP comparison: Pricing terms unrelated to the good to be purchased or delivered must be separated under IFRS. The remaining contractual terms have to be evaluated again if the 'own use' exemption applies. Under US GAAP such unrelated pricing terms taint the whole contract and hence this exemption is not available for such contracts (FAS 133).

10.4 Caps, floors and collars

In some purchase, sales and service contracts, the price is set as a market price at the time of the payment, but is 'capped', 'floored', or 'collared' within a range. The concepts of caps, floors and collars are explained in the context of interest rates in **7.7** above.

Similar consideration can be applied here, i.e. provisions included in a contract to purchase or sell an asset that establish a cap and a floor on the price to be paid or received for the asset are closely related to the host contract if both the cap and floor are out-of-the-money at inception and are not leveraged. [IAS 39.AG33(b)] This can be extended to collars included in purchase and sales contracts, i.e. collars are closely related to the host contract if they are out-of-the-money at inception.

The assessment is made at inception of the contract, and is not subsequently revised.

Whilst IAS 39 does not specifically mention caps, floors and collars embedded in service contracts, it is reasonable to analogise to the guidance given on purchase and sale contracts.

Example 10.4

Executory contract with embedded cap

Entity A enters into a contract to purchase tin in 12 months at the market price of tin at the point of purchase. Embedded in the contract is a cap that puts an upper limit on the price A will pay. The cap is out-of-the-money at inception of the contract, i.e. the cap is set above the current price for tin.

The cap is closely related to the host purchase contract, so it will not be separated. The cap is closely related to the host contract for the life of the contract, irrespective of whether tin prices rise so that the cap becomes in-the-money.

US GAAP comparison: US GAAP has guidance that applies to a purchase contract with a selling price subject to a cap and a floor. That guidance indicates that if the embedded options (due to the presence of the cap and floor) are indexed to the purchase price of the asset that is the subject of the purchase contract, the embedded options are considered clearly and closely related (DIG B14).

10.5 Foreign currency features

An embedded foreign currency derivative in a host contract that is not a financial instrument is closely related to the host contract provided it is not leveraged, does not contain an option feature and requires payments denominated in one of the following currencies:
[IAS 39.AG33(d)]

(i) the functional currency of any substantial party to the contract;

(ii) the currency in which the price of the related good or service that is acquired or delivered is routinely denominated in commercial transactions around the world (such as the US dollar for crude oil transactions), or

(iii) a currency that is commonly used in contracts to purchase or sell non-financial items in the economic environment in which the transaction takes place (for example, a relatively stable and liquid currency that is commonly used in local business transactions or external trade).

The three criteria in IAS 39.AG33(d) are not mutually exclusive. For example, an entity in country Y may export oil in US$. One, two or all three of the following may apply: the exporting entity may have US$ as its functional currency; oil is considered a non-financial item that is routinely denominated in US$ throughout the world; or US$ may be a common currency for either internal or external transactions for country Y.

The term 'substantial party' is discussed further in **9.2.2** above.

The assessment of the functional currency of a substantial party to the contract in (i) above requires care. For example, a substantial party to a contract may be a subsidiary of a larger group. The presentation currency of the group (see IAS 21 *The Effects of Changes in Foreign Exchange Rates*) is not relevant to this assessment, as it is the functional currency of the subsidiary that is relevant. In many cases judgement will be required when the subsidiary is in a jurisdiction which does not produce individual entity financial statements under IFRSs and therefore its functional currency is not evident. Too much reliance should not be placed on the country of incorporation or geographical location of a substantial party to the contract as the evaluation of the functional currency in IAS 21 includes many other factors.

The currency in which the price of the related goods or services is routinely denominated in commercial transactions around the world is only a currency that is used for similar transactions all around the world, not just in one local area. For example, if cross-border transactions in natural gas in North America are routinely denominated in US dollars and such transactions are routinely denominated in Euros in Europe, neither the US dollar nor the Euro is the currency in which the goods or services are routinely denominated in commercial transactions around the world. [IAS 39.IG.C.9]

By definition, a currency in which a good or service is routinely denominated around the world has to be one currency. However, the existence of a relatively small proportion of transactions in one or two markets, or a particular jurisdiction, that are denominated in a local currency does not preclude a non-financial item from being considered to be routinely denominated in a particular currency in commercial transactions around the world.

The number of non-financial items that would qualify under IAS 39.AG33(d)(ii) is likely to be limited. In practice, such items will primarily be commodities that are traded in US dollars in commercial transactions throughout the world.

For certain types of commodity transactions, contracts may be based on a dominant currency (such as the US dollar) but may be denominated in local currencies in certain markets for regulatory or other reasons, i.e. the price is translated at the spot rate into local currencies (a "convenience translation" mechanism). For example, although the dominant currency for crude oil transactions as noted in IAS 39.AG33(d)(ii) is the US dollar, some contracts for crude oil may be denominated in Canadian dollars in Canada, where the Canadian dollar price is a convenience translation of the US dollar crude oil price. A simple convenience translation into local currencies of a commodity that is routinely denominated in a dominant currency would not negate the view that the commodity is routinely denominated in a single currency in commercial transactions around the world. On the other hand, if a commodity transaction is regularly denominated in various currencies in commercial transactions around the world where such foreign currency prices are not convenience translations of a dominant currency price, that commodity would not be considered to be routinely denominated in a particular currency.

The existence of an organised commodity exchange where a commodity is traded in a single currency provides a useful starting point in determining the dominant currency in which transactions in that commodity are denominated and, accordingly, whether such a commodity can be considered to be "routinely denominated" in that particular currency. The organised commodity exchanges may establish liquid markets for commodities quoted in a particular currency, and transactions between counterparties that are not conducted through the exchange are also denominated in that particular currency because to do otherwise would present arbitrage opportunities. For example, copper and gold are traded in US dollars on organised commodity exchanges and transactions between various counterparts that are not conducted through the exchange are also denominated in US dollars given the liquid markets established by the exchanges.

Certain commodities are not traded on organised exchanges, but global pricing forums exist that publish "spot prices" denominated in a dominant currency for that particular commodity. Transactions between market participants are based on those published spot prices. For example certain organisations independently may monitor market activities and publish US dollar prices that have become generally accepted as spot prices for the given commodity. Contracts between market participants are denominated in US dollars based on these published spot prices. In Japan and Europe, transactions may be conducted in Japanese Yen or Euros, respectively, but such Yen and Euro price equivalents are convenience translations of the US dollar spot price. Accordingly, the given commodity would in such a scenario be considered to be routinely denominated in US dollars in commercial transactions around the world.

In January 2008 the Emerging Issues Committee of the Canadian Institute of Chartered Accountants issued Abstract EIC 169 *"Determining Whether a Contract is Routinely Denominated in a Single Currency"*. The Abstract provides an interpretation regarding paragraph 3855.A34(d) of Canadian GAAP which is equivalent to IAS 39.AG33(d)(ii). The Abstract is therefore **not an interpretation of IFRS** and it is not issued by the IASB or the IFRIC. Although not issued by the IASB or the IFRIC the Abstract may be a useful starting point when considering what non-financial items are denominated in a common currency. The Appendix to the Abstract (which is an integral part of the Abstract) provides examples of commodities and certain other items that are considered to be routinely denominated in US dollars based on consideration of the factors discussed in the Abstract. The list of examples in the Abstract is as follows:

- aluminium
- coal (coking and thermal)
- copper
- crude oil
- diamonds [rough/raw and polish (wholesale market)]

- gold
- iron ore
- jet fuel
- lead
- nickel
- NBSK pulp
- palladium
- platinum
- silver
- tin
- titanium
- uranium
- wide-bodied aircraft
- zinc

The Abstract notes that the list is not intended to be exhaustive. Rather, it is a listing of commodities and certain other items that are routinely denominated in US dollars that have been identified at the date of the Abstract which may be used to support an assertion under paragraph 3855.A34(d) that these goods are routinely denominated in US dollars in commercial transactions around the world. The Abstract notes further that preparers should consider any circumstances arising subsequent to the date of its issue that might impact whether an item should remain on the list.

The concept of a 'currency that is commonly used in contracts to purchase or sell non-financial items in the economic environment in which the transaction takes place' as described in IAS 39.AG33(d)(iii) was introduced to address situations where entities operate in economies in which it is common for business contracts to be denominated in a foreign currency. [IAS 39.BC39]

'Economic environment' should be considered for the country concerned as a whole. It may be the case that more than one currency is commonly used. The Standard provides an example of a common currency as a 'relatively stable and liquid currency that is commonly used in local business transactions **or** external trade' (emphasis added). Therefore, a currency that is common for *either* external or internal transactions will be considered common for that country.

Looking at external trade, it may be possible that a country has multiple currencies that are commonly used to purchase or sell non-financial items. For instance, import and export transactions in and out of a small country (with counterparties in other small countries) may be commonly denominated in a range of internationally liquid, stable currencies (such as the Euro and the US dollar) rather than just one internationally liquid, stable currency. In such a case, if there is a significant level of transactions in each of the currencies, it may be possible that more than one currency is commonly used in the economic environment of external trade for that country.

Similarly, it may be possible that in certain hyperinflationary economies more than one foreign currency is used in local business transactions (because large sections of the general population view amounts in terms of one foreign currency and significant other sections of the population view amounts in another foreign currency). Also, this may be the case where a particular industry dominates the economy and commonly uses a foreign currency in local business transactions whilst the entirety of the remaining part of the economy uses the local currency. The judgement as to whether there is more than one common currency will depend on how significant the use of a particular currency is with respect to the local or external trade transactions of the country as a whole.

In determining whether a currency is common in a particular jurisdiction the analysis should focus on *all* transactions in that jurisdiction. For example, in determining whether external trade is commonly denominated in Euros, transactions with the Euro zone should not be excluded from the analysis. Equally, if an entity is determining whether a country with large oil exports is considered to have US$ as a common currency, the analysis of that country should not exclude exports of oil which would be expected to be denominated in US$ as oil is routinely denominated in US$ throughout the world.

In May 2007 the IFRIC published a tentative rejection notice in response to a submission on the application of IAS 39.AG33(d)(iii), in particular, what is the economic environment when determining whether a currency is commonly used in contracts to buy or sell non-financial items. In the draft rejection notice the IFRIC noted that the paragraph requires an entity to identify where the transaction takes place and to identify currencies that are commonly used in the economic environment in which the transaction takes place. The IFRIC was proposing not to take the issue on to its agenda because any guidance developed would be more in the nature of application guidance than an interpretation.

Following responses by constituents and further debate at IFRIC the IFRIC agreed to refer the matter to the Board for amendment to clarify the standard and eliminate any diversity in practice. At its December 2007 meeting the IASB noted that IAS 39.AG33(d) is intended to prohibit the separation of embedded foreign currency derivatives if the embedded derivatives are integral to the contractual arrangement. The IASB noted that embedded foreign currency derivatives are likely to be integral to the contractual arrangement if the foreign currency has one or more of the characteristics of a functional currency as set out in IAS 21.9. Accordingly, the Board decided to amend IAS 39.AG33(d)(iii) to refer to a currency that has one or more of the characteristics of a functional currency as set out in IAS 21.9.

At its January 2009 meeting, the Board decided to defer its redeliberations of the proposal relating to the bifurcation of an embedded foreign currency derivatives to a future period and therefore would not be included in the finalised amendments expected to be issued in April 2009.

The following examples demonstrate the application of the guidance in IAS 39.AG33.

Example 10.5A

Routinely denominated currency (1)

Two entities, both of whose functional currency is the Japanese yen, enter into a three-year supply contract. If payments were either denominated in or linked to the US dollar, and the US dollar is not the currency in which the service is routinely denominated in commercial transactions around the world, the embedded foreign currency forward would need to be separated from the host supply contract.

Where a transaction is denominated in a currency that is a common currency in the economic environment of one or both of the substantial parties to the contract it is reasonable to consider the currency denomination of the contract is closely related for both parties.

Contracts where a party has the option over which currency the contract may be settled in contain foreign currency features that are not closely related to the host purchase or sale contract.

Example 10.5B

Choice of settlement in foreign currencies

Entity A, a car dealership, contracts to purchase cars from Entity B, a car manufacturer. Companies A and B have functional currencies of Sterling and Euro respectively. The purchase agreement allows A to choose whether to settle the contract in a fixed amount of either Sterling or Euros.

The embedded foreign currency option must be separated from the host purchase contract. This treatment applies even though both settlement currencies are functional currencies of counterparties to the sales agreement.

Example 10.5C

Leveraged foreign currency adjustment

Entity X, a UK entity, enters into a sales contract with Entity Z, a US entity. Payments are in US dollars, but embedded in the contract is a clause such that payments are adjusted for twice the change in the US dollar exchange rate for the period that the payment is outstanding.

The sales contract contains an embedded derivative that is not closely related to the host sales contract, as leveraged foreign currency features are not closely related to host sales contracts.

Example 10.5D

Routinely denominated currency (2)

Entity A, a UK entity, contracts to buy oil from Entity B, also a UK entity. The functional currency of both entities is Sterling, however, the contract is to be settled in a fixed number of US dollars.

The embedded foreign currency feature is closely related to the host purchase contract, even though it is not in the functional currency of either counterparty to the contract. This is because oil is routinely denominated in US dollars in commercial transactions around the world. Therefore two

Sterling functional currency entities can transact in oil in US dollars and the foreign currency embedded derivative is deemed to be closely related to the host purchase or sale contract.

Example 10.5E

Common currency in local economic environment

Entity A operates in a South American country that is assessed as having a high inflation economy. Like all other local businesses, it chooses to conduct its business in US dollars, a relatively stable currency. Thus, all purchase and sale contracts are denominated in US dollars.

The embedded foreign currency derivative does not need to be separated from a host purchase or sales contract, as these contracts are denominated in a currency that is commonly used in the local economic environment.

If A chose to use the Euro where all other local businesses used the US dollar, this exemption would not be available. To avoid separation of the embedded derivative, A would have to demonstrate that it met one of the other exemptions noted above.

Determination of contractual terms of the separated embedded derivative should be done by reference to the contractual terms of the non-financial host contract. For example, if a foreign currency derivative that needs separation is embedded in a purchase contract of a non-financial item which specifies delivery in two months' time, the maturity of the foreign currency derivative is two months.

The purchase contract stops being an executory (non-financial) contract once the delivery of the non-financial item takes place and a financial instrument, a foreign currency payable, comes into existence. The foreign currency translation of the payable is recognised in profit or loss in accordance with IAS 21 as it is a foreign currency denominated monetary item. When the non-financial item is recognised the embedded derivative is derecognised and its carrying value is included in the cost of the non-financial item (see **section 12** below).

US GAAP comparison: Although US GAAP is similar to IFRS in this area, there are differences. The most notable of these is that in IFRS, a foreign currency derivative embedded in a non-financial (or insurance) host contract may be considered closely related to that host if it requires payments denominated in a currency that is commonly used in contracts to purchase or sell non-financial items in the economic environment in which the transaction takes place (e.g., a relatively stable and liquid currency that is commonly used in local business transactions or external trade). This exception is worded more broadly than in US GAAP, which requires such payments to either be denominated in the local currency of any substantial party to the contract (the same as IFRS), or the currency used by a substantial party to the contract as if it were the functional currency because the primary economic environment in which the party operates is highly inflationary.

If a purchase or sales contract that would otherwise qualify for the 'normal purchase or sales' exemption contains an embedded foreign currency derivative that is not clearly and closely related, this would disqualify the entity from applying the normal purchase or sales exemption. If the purchase/sale contract met the definition of a derivative in FAS 133 the contract would be fair valued through profit or loss in its entirety. IFRS does not contain this provision and, therefore, an embedded derivative is separated and fair valued through profit or loss while the host contract meets the normal purchase or sale exemption and is treated as an executory contract. See **example 12A** below.

11 Embedded derivatives in insurance contracts

As discussed in **2.3** of **chapter 1**, derivatives embedded in insurance contracts are within the scope of IAS 39 if they require separation in accordance with IAS 39, except if a derivative embedded in an insurance contract is itself an insurance contract. [IFRS 4.7] An insurance contract is a contract under which one party (the policyholder) accepts significant insurance risk from another party by agreeing to compensate the policyholder if a specified uncertain future event adversely affects the policyholder.

As an exception to IAS 39, an insurer need not separate and measure at fair value a policyholder's option to surrender an insurance contract for a fixed amount (or for an amount based on a fixed amount and an interest rate), even if the exercise price differs from the carrying amount of the host insurance liability. However, the requirement in IAS 39 does apply to a put option or cash surrender option embedded in an insurance contract if the surrender value varies in response to the change in a financial variable (such as an equity or commodity price or index), or a non-financial variable that is not specific to a party to the contract. Furthermore, this requirement also applies if the holder's ability to exercise a put option or cash surrender option is triggered by a change in such a variable (e.g. a put option that can be exercised if a stock market index reaches a specified level). This applies equally to options to surrender a financial instrument containing a discretionary participation feature. [IFRS 4.8 & 9]

IFRS 4.IG Example 2: 2.15 provides the example of a policyholder option to surrender a contract for account value equal to the fair value of a pool of equity investments, possibly after deducting a surrender charge. The example makes reference to IAS 39.AG33(g) and states that if such a feature is embedded in a host insurance contract then if the insurer measures that portion of its obligation at account value, no further adjustment is needed for the option (unless the surrender value differs significantly from account value). Otherwise the embedded derivative is to be measured separately as at fair value through profit or loss.

A unit linking feature embedded in a host insurance contract is closely related to the host contract if the unit-denominated payments are measured at current unit values that reflect the fair values of the assets of the fund. A unit linking feature is a contractual term that requires payments denominated in a units of an internal or external investment fund. [IAS 39.AG33(g)] For equivalent guidance on debt host contracts see **7.10** above.

This is a complex area, and must be considered in conjunction with IFRS 4 *Insurance Contracts*. Below are a few examples of applying the above guidance.

Example 11A

Surrender value indexed to share price index

A policyholder has an option to surrender an insurance contract for a surrender value based on the FTSE 100. The option is not closely related to the host contract (unless the option is life-contingent to a significant extent), so should be separated from the host contract and accounted for as a derivative.

Example 11B

Death benefit linked to share price index

A host insurance contract contains a death benefit linked to equity prices or equity index, payable only on death or annuitisation and not on surrender or maturity. The equity-index feature is an insurance contract (unless the life-contingent payments are insignificant), because the policyholder benefits from it only when the insured event occurs. Thus, the contract is outside the scope of IAS 39.

Example 11C

Interest rate linked surrender value

A host insurance contract contains an embedded guarantee of minimum interest rates to be used in determining its surrender or maturity values.

If the guarantee is in-the-money on issue, or is leveraged, then the embedded guarantee is not an insurance contract (unless the embedded guarantee is life-contingent to a significant extent), so will need to be separated from the host contract.

Example 11D

Dual-indexed payout feature

Entity A purchases an insurance contract that contains a dual trigger such that payment is contingent on a breakdown in power supply that adversely affects the holder (first trigger) and a specified level of electricity prices (second trigger). The contingent payment is made only if both triggering events occur.

The embedded derivative is an insurance contract (unless the first trigger lacks commercial substance). A contract that qualifies as an insurance contract, whether at inception or later, remains an insurance contract until all rights and obligations are extinguished or expire. Therefore, although the remaining exposure is similar to a financial derivative after the insured event has occurred, the embedded derivative is still an insurance contract.

A derivative embedded in an insurance contract is closely related to the host insurance contract if the embedded derivative and host insurance contract are so interdependent that an entity cannot measure the embedded derivative separately (i.e. without considering the host contract). [IAS 39.AG33(h)]

US GAAP comparison: Because FAS 133 does not contain guidance similar to IAS 39.AG33(h), the conclusions reached under US GAAP may be different from those reached under IFRSs. In addition, the application guidance in US GAAP and IFRS on assessing embedded derivatives in insurance contracts sometimes differs. Under US GAAP, entities should consider, for example, DIG Issues B7 to B10, B25 to B31, and B36.

12 Measuring embedded derivatives at initial recognition

If an embedded derivative is separated from its host contract (because it is not closely related to the host), then it must be accounted for as if it were a free standing derivative. The embedded derivative should be recognised in the statement of financial position at fair value, with changes in fair value recognised in profit or loss as they arise, unless it is designated as an effective hedging instrument in a cash flow or a net investment hedge (see **chapter 8**).

The host contract is accounted for under IAS 39 if it is a financial instrument within the scope of the Standard, otherwise it is accounted for under the appropriate Standard (e.g. under IAS 17 *Leases*, if it is a lease contract).

Example 12A

Accounting for foreign currency derivative embedded in executory contract

Entity A, a UK-based entity with Sterling as its functional currency, enters into a contract to purchase cocoa from a local supplier, Entity B, in six months for a fixed amount of US dollars. US dollars is not the functional currency of either party to the transaction. The cocoa will be delivered and used over a reasonable period in the normal course of business.

As the cocoa will be physically delivered and is for use in the normal course of business, the contract qualifies for the normal purchase requirements scope exception. This means that the entire contract is not a derivative recognised in the statement of financial position at fair value with changes in fair value recognised in profit or loss.

The contract still needs to be assessed for embedded derivatives. The contract contains an embedded foreign currency forward that is not closely related as the contract will be settled in US dollars and US dollars is neither the functional currency of either counterparty to the contract, nor the currency in which the price of cocoa is routinely denominated in commercial transactions throughout the world. It is also not the currency commonly used in contracts to purchase or sell non-financial items in the UK. This embedded derivative must be separated from the host purchase contract and accounted for in the statement of financial position at fair value. Changes in fair value (arising from changes in the Sterling/US dollar exchange rate) will be recognised in profit or loss.

Assume the contract is entered into on 1 January 20X5. The contract is over a specified amount of cocoa for US$150,000. The six-month forward exchange rate is US$1.5:£1. The three-month forward exchange rate on 31 March 20X5 (Entity A's year end) is US$1.2:£1, and the spot exchange rate on 30 June 20X5 (when the cocoa is delivered) is US$1.25:£1. From the point of view of Entity A, the contract will be accounted for as a foreign currency forward to sell US dollars and buy Sterling, and an unrecognised executory contract to sell Sterling and buy inventory.

There are no entries on 1 January as the embedded derivative is a non-optional derivative with a fair value of zero at inception. At 31 March, the forward exchange rate has moved and so Entity A now expects $150,000 to be equivalent to £125,000, rather than £100,000. There is a fair value loss on the forward, so the entry is:

Dr	Profit or loss	£25,000
Cr	Forward liability	£25,000

On 30 June, the forward liability has decreased in value, as $150,000 will cost £120,000. The entry is:

Dr	Forward liability	£5,000
Cr	Profit or loss	£5,000

A now pays $150,000 to buy the cocoa under the purchase contract:

Dr	Inventories	£120,000
Cr	Cash	£120,000

It must also remove the embedded derivative from its statement of financial position:

Dr	Forward liability	£20,000
Cr	Inventories	£20,000

The inventory is recognised in the statement of financial position at £100,000. This is $150,000 translated at the forward rate contracted on 1 January. When the inventory is sold, the cost of sales will be £20,000 lower than expected (based on cash paid on 30 June). This is because a £20,000 loss has already been recognised in profit or loss as a result of fair valuing the embedded derivative.

Note: for illustrative purposes only, this example ignores the time value of money for the purpose of valuing the forward contract.

At inception, an entity must determine the fair value of the embedded derivative first. The difference between the consideration paid or received to acquire the entire contract and the fair value of the embedded derivative is assigned to the host contract.

Example 12B

Allocating the proceeds to the embedded derivative

Entity A invests CU1 million in a convertible bond. The bond has a coupon of 6 per cent, a maturity of five years, and is convertible into a fixed number of equity shares at maturity of the bond. Using a Black-Scholes model, it is determined that the fair value of the conversion option is CU100,000. Assuming that the entire bond is not carried at fair value through profit or loss, separation of the embedded derivative is necessary. The amount assigned to the bond is determined by subtracting the fair value of the option from the consideration paid to purchase the bond. The entry on purchasing the asset is:

Dr	Bond	CU900,000
Dr	Equity conversion option	CU100,000
Cr	Cash	CU1,000,000

It will not always be easy to establish the fair value of embedded derivatives, but there is little room for manoeuvre. If an embedded derivative needs to be separately accounted for, but the entity is unable to determine reliably the fair value of the embedded derivative on the basis of its terms and conditions (e.g. because the embedded derivative results in the delivery of an unquoted equity investment), the entity must determine the fair value of the whole contract and the fair value of the host contract, and the balance represents the derivative instrument. [IAS 39.13] If an entity is unable to do this, the entity must designate the whole contract as at fair value through profit or loss. [IAS 39.12] The entity might conclude, however, in the above example of an equity embedded derivative that results in the delivery of unquoted equity investment, that the equity component of the combined instrument may be sufficiently significant to preclude it from obtaining a reliable estimate of the fair value of the entire instrument. In that case the combined instrument is measured at cost less impairment. [IAS 39.IG.C.11]

13 Presentation of embedded derivatives

IFRSs do not provide specific guidance on the presentation of embedded derivatives in the statement of financial position or in profit or loss. IAS 39.11 has an explicit statement that it does not address whether an embedded derivative shall be presented separately in the statement of financial position.

It seems appropriate for an entity to choose as an accounting policy whether it presents non-closely related embedded derivatives as separate financial assets or liabilities. This policy should be applied consistently to all hybrid contracts.

In instances where the host contract is a debt instrument held at amortised cost an entity may have a preference for presenting embedded derivatives as separate instruments rather than presenting the hybrid instrument as a single instrument, part measured at fair value and part measured at amortised cost. Conversely, if an entity has available-for-sale investments with separate embedded derivatives, i.e. the hybrid instrument is fair valued in its entirety, an entity may prefer to present the embedded derivative along with the host contract as a single financial instrument. If an entity chooses to present an embedded derivative together with the host contract as a single financial instrument, the entity must be aware of the need to comply with IFRS 7.8 to present either in the statement of financial position or in the notes the carrying amounts of financial instruments classified into appropriate financial instrument categories. Hence, if the contract is presented as a single financial instrument in the statement of financial position, the measurement by category of financial instrument will need to be included in the notes to the financial statements.

IAS 1 *Presentation of Financial Statements* requires an entity to determine whether assets and liabilities are presented as current or non-current. IAS 1 does not provide guidance as to whether in determining current or non-current presentation of embedded derivatives an entity should look to the settlement of the embedded derivative as if it is a standalone derivative (consistent with the way it is measured) or whether the settlement should be considered based on the settlement of the whole hybrid contract (consistent with the fact that the embedded derivative, even if measured separately, is nonetheless part of a hybrid contract).

If an embedded derivative is recognised in the statement of financial position separately from its host contract an entity should choose one of the two following policies in determining whether the embedded derivative is current or non-current:

- consider the timing of the cash flows of the embedded derivative as if it is a standalone contract; or

- consider the timing of the cash flows of the whole hybrid arrangement.

If the first policy is being applied, consideration should be given to *Improvements to IFRSs* issued in May 2008. This amended IAS 1 to clarify that, even though derivatives meet the held for trading definition in IAS 39.9, they are not presented as current unless they are due for settlement or expected to be settled in less than twelve months after the end of the reporting period. The amendments made to IAS 1 by *Improvements to IFRSs* apply for annual periods beginning on or after 1 January 2009, but earlier application is permitted. An entity choosing to apply the amendments early must disclose that fact.

If an embedded derivative is not recognised in the statement of financial position separately from its host contract the entity should determine the presentation as current or non-current based on the timing of the cash flows of the whole hybrid arrangement.

Example 13

Presentation of embedded derivative in the statement of financial position

Entity D issues 5 year callable debt in the period where Entity D has the choice to redeem the instrument prior to maturity at an amount not approximately equal to the amortised cost. Entity D measures the host contract at amortised cost and measures the non-closely embedded derivative, the call option, at fair value through profit or loss. At the period end Entity D can choose within the next twelve months to call the debt but does not expect to exercise its right to call. As the call option is a right for Entity D to buy the debt back, the embedded derivative will always have a positive fair value for Entity D.

Entity D has an accounting policy choice as to whether it presents the embedded derivative separately, in this case as a derivative financial asset, or together with the host contract as a single financial instrument. If the latter policy is applied, the hybrid financial instrument is presented as a single financial liability (as the embedded derivative will have a fair value less than the amortised cost of the host contract debt liability). If the former policy is applied, Entity D has a further choice as to whether it determines the embedded derivative as current or non-current based on the timing of the cash flows of the embedded derivative as if it were a standalone derivative or based on the timing of cash flows of the whole hybrid arrangement.

Policy based on timing of the cash flows of the embedded derivative as if it were a standalone derivative

Entity D does not have the intention to settle the embedded derivative within twelve months following the end of the reporting period as it does not expect to exercise the call option. The embedded derivative asset that is separately recognised in its statement of financial position will therefore be classified as non-current. The debt host contract liability will be presented as non-current as Entity D cannot be forced to settle the liability within twelve months of the end of the reporting period.

If in a future period Entity D believes it will choose to call the debt within twelve months of the end of the reporting period the embedded derivative will be presented as current at the end of the reporting period. The debt host contract liability will continue to be presented as non-current as Entity D cannot be forced to settle the liability within twelve months of the end of the reporting period.

Should the debt mature within twelve months of the end of the reporting period both the embedded derivative and debt host contract will be presented as current.

Policy based on timing of the cash flows of the whole hybrid instrument

If at the end of a reporting period the contractual maturity of the debt is more than twelve months and Entity D does not intend to call the debt within twelve months the whole instrument will be presented as non-current.

If at the end of a reporting period the contractual maturity of the debt is less than twelve months the whole hybrid contract will be presented as current.

US GAAP comparison: While US GAAP does not explicitly address presentation of embedded derivatives, in *Current Accounting and Disclosure Issues in the Division of Corporation Finance* (as updated November 30, 2006), the staff of the SEC's Division of Corporation Finance indicated that "although bifurcated for measurement purposes, embedded derivatives should be presented on a combined basis with the host contract, except in circumstances where the embedded derivative is a liability and the host contract is equity." Thus, under US GAAP, SEC registrants would present the embedded derivative on a combined basis with its related host, except when the embedded derivative is a liability and the host contract is equity.

6 Measurement

1 Introduction

IAS 39 requires the use of a mixed measurement model, with certain assets and liabilities measured at fair value and others on a cost basis. The model is based on the classification of financial assets and liabilities discussed in **chapters 2** and **3**. The Standard provides requirements for certain financial assets to be measured at fair value, and an option to measure other financial assets at fair value under specific circumstances. For example, the use of fair value is not required where an asset is to be held to its maturity. Financial liabilities are typically measured at amortised cost, though fair values should be used for derivative liabilities and separate rules apply to liabilities forming part of a hedge.

The rationale for using fair values is that, from a measurement point of view, the most relevant information that can be provided for financial assets is normally the amount that will be realised from their disposal, commonly referred to as 'exit price'. The relevance of fair value information for financial liabilities is less clear. Unless held for speculative or hedging purposes, liabilities generally form part of an entity's financing arrangements. It is often argued that it would be unhelpful for the carrying amount (and associated interest expense) of such liabilities to be remeasured to take account of changes in fair values, particularly those caused by changes in own credit risk. Such concerns are reflected in IAS 39's requirements for financial liabilities and the additional disclosure requirements when the fair value option is applied to financial liabilities. A fair value approach is particularly important for derivative instruments, where cost is typically negligible.

Since IAS 39 was originally issued in 1998 it has continued to have a mixed measurement model. The Joint Working Group of Standard Setters explored the possibility of moving towards a full fair value regime, but progress has been slow and it is expected that the mixed measurement model retained in IAS 39 will be here for some time to come. As part of the memorandum of understanding with the US Financial Accounting Standards Board, the IASB issued a discussion paper, *Reducing Complexity in Reporting Financial Instruments*, in March 2008 that will provide a basis for future discussions of issues related to the measurement of financial instruments (including hedge accounting issues). The ultimate goal of this project is to publish an IFRS that would significantly improve and simplify financial instrument reporting, i.e. would replace IAS 39.

The Financial Stability Forum issued a report in April 2008, *Enhancing Market and Institutional Resilience,* which had two recommendations for the IASB. Firstly, the IASB should enhance its guidance on valuing financial instruments when markets are no longer active, and secondly, strengthen its standards to achieve better disclosures about valuations, methodologies and the uncertainty associated with valuations. In response to the report the IASB's Expert Advisory Panel was set up and in October 2008 issued a report, *Measuring and disclosing the fair value of financial instruments in markets that are no longer active.* This report provides useful information and educational guidance for measuring and disclosing fair values. The report has not been approved by the IASB and does not establish new requirements. The measurement aspects of the report are referred to in this chapter but, as they do not represent official positions of the IASB, are identified in a shaded box.

This chapter addresses the approach to measurement that is adopted in the Standard, covering not only the basic rules, but also issues relating to the measurement of fair value and amortised cost, and the Standard's impairment model.

This chapter discusses measurement in the following sections:

2 Initial measurement

2.1 Fair value

IAS 39 requires that financial assets and liabilities are measured initially at 'fair value'. The concept of fair value is central to the approach of the Standard – it is defined as the amount for which an asset could be exchanged, or a liability settled, between knowledgeable, willing parties in an arm's length transaction. [IAS 39.9] (Note that transaction costs will often be added to/deducted from fair value on initial recognition – see **2.2** below.)

Section 5 below contains guidance on the appropriate determination of fair value for financial assets and liabilities.

Assuming transactions are conducted on arm's length terms, the fair value of a financial instrument acquired should normally be equal to the fair value of the consideration given or received (the 'transaction price'). Consequently, IAS 39 states that for initial recognition purposes, the transaction price is normally the best evidence of the fair value of a financial instrument. [IAS 39.AG64]

An exception to this general rule exists where the fair value of an instrument is evidenced by comparison with other observable current market transactions in the same instrument (i.e. without modification or repackaging) or based on a valuation technique whose variables include only data from observable markets. [IAS 39.AG76] This point is of particular significance for some entities, including those operating in the investment banking and insurance industry. An immediate gain may arise on the recognition of a financial instrument only where there is strong, market-based evidence of the fair value of the said instrument (see **5.3.5** below).

In certain situations, it may be difficult to identify and measure the fair value of consideration paid or received for a financial instrument. For example, where part of the amount involved in a transaction represents consideration for something other than the instrument itself. It would then be necessary to value the instrument directly using a valuation technique (see **5.3** below). This issue may arise when a credit card balance is acquired (particularly where there is a discounted rate being offered on the balance transferred and/or on purchases over an introductory period):

Example 2.1A

Separating financial instruments from total consideration (1)

An entity acquires a credit card balance (from the original lender), offering discounted rates on purchases in an introductory 12-month period. The credit card expires in three years.

The purchase consideration consists of four elements.

(i) The financial asset (i.e. the amount outstanding).

(ii) The borrower's option to borrow at preferential rates over the next 12 months.

(iii) The borrower's option to borrow at market rates over the following two years.

(iv) An intangible asset, being the expected future cash flows associated with generating a relationship with the borrower.

Item (i) should be calculated by discounting the expected repayments of the amount outstanding at an interest rate appropriate for the risk profile of the borrower. The commitment to lend at preferential rates should initially be recognised at fair value, and subsequently measured at the higher of (i) the amount recognised under IAS 37 *Provisions, Contingent Liabilities and Contingent Assets*, and (ii) the amount initially recognised less, where appropriate, cumulative amortisation recognised in accordance with IAS 18 *Revenue*. The commitment to lend at future market rates does not have any value for the buyer. However, it might be argued that certain behavioural aspects of credit card relationships (i.e. borrowers will often make purchases even when it would be more rational to obtain finance from another source) would often result in such commitments being viewed as assets (in effect part of the intangible item (iv)). The entity would need to determine whether the relationship met the definition of an intangible asset in IAS 38 *Intangible Assets*.

A similar issue might arise where an entity makes a low-interest, or interest-free, loan to an employee.

Example 2.1B

Separating financial instruments from total consideration (2)

On 1 January 20X0, an entity grants an interest-free loan of CU100 to an employee. It is repayable on 31 December 20X0. The market rate of interest for a loan to this individual would be 8 per cent. Consideration paid is made up as follows:

(i) CU92.59 is the fair value of the acquired financial asset (i.e. CU100/1.08).

(ii) CU7.41 is employee remuneration. This amount represents the fair value of the entity providing its employee with interest-free finance and is accounted for under IAS 19 *Employee Benefits*.

Another potential complication may arise if an initial fee is paid or received in compensation for subsequent cash flows that are above or below market rates. A simple example is given below:

Example 2.1C

Fair value of consideration

An entity originates a loan of CU100. The entity receives an up-front fee of CU10 from the borrower. Interest of CU5 is receivable annually over the next five years and the principal amount is repaid at the end of year five.

The entity should recognise its financial asset at its fair value, being the fair value of the net consideration paid, i.e. CU90 (principal less the fee) and apply the effective interest method (see **4.1** below):

Year	Carrying amount b/f	Interest income at 7.47%	Cash flow	Carrying amount c/f
1	90.00	6.72	(5.00)	91.72
2	91.72	6.85	(5.00)	93.57
3	93.57	6.99	(5.00)	95.56
4	95.56	7.14	(5.00)	97.70
5	97.70	7.30	(105.00)	0.00

The effective interest rate, of 7.47 per cent, will also be the prevailing market rate for this instrument, on the assumption that the arrangement is at arm's length terms.

In some instances the difference between the consideration paid or received and the fair value of the financial instrument may represent a distribution or a capital contribution.

Example 2.1D

Interest free loan

A subsidiary, Entity S, granted an interest free fixed-term loan to its parent, Entity P. As the loan Entity S has provided to Entity P is not on market terms, there will be a difference between the cash advanced to Entity P and the initial recognition amount of the loan at fair value.

This fair value adjustment is, in substance, a distribution from the subsidiary to its parent because it does not meet the definition of an expense under paragraph 70 of the *Framework for the Preparation and Presentation of Financial Statements*. Hence, the adjustment to recognise the loan at its fair value should be taken directly to equity as a deemed distribution.

The deemed distribution would be recognised in equity irrespective of whether the subsidiary had distributable profits. The legal framework in Entity S's jurisdiction will govern whether the transfer of funds from a subsidiary with no legally distributable profits to its parent, by way of a deemed distribution, would render management of the subsidiary in breach of either their fiduciary duties and/or the corporate governance rules in that jurisdiction. Therefore, the level of distributable profits may be a factor affecting Entity S's decision to provide an interest-free loan to its parent but will not impact the accounting if a loan is made.

In May 2008 the IASB issued *Improvements to IFRSs*. The improvements amended IAS 20 *Accounting for Government Grants and Disclosure of Government Assistance* to rectify an apparent inconsistency between IAS 20 and IAS 39. When a loan is received from a government with a below-market rate of interest IAS 20 before the amendment stated that no interest should be imputed for such a loan, whereas IAS 39 requires all loans to be recognised at fair value, thus imputing interest on loans with a below-market rate of interest. The improvements removed this inconsistency by amending IAS 20 so that loans received from a government that have a below-market rate of interest are recognised and measured in accordance with IAS 39. The benefit of the government loan is quantified by the imputation of interest in accordance with IAS 39. This benefit is accounted for in accordance with IAS 20. The amendment to IAS 20 applies prospectively to government loans received in periods beginning on or after 1 January 2009. If the amendments are applied to an earlier period the entity shall disclose this fact.

2.2 Transaction costs

For a financial asset or liability that is not classified as 'at fair value through profit or loss' (FVTPL), transaction costs that are directly attributable to the acquisition or issue of the asset or liability should be added to or deducted from the fair value on initial recognition.

The consequences of this are summarised below.

(a) For financial instruments that are carried at amortised cost (see **section 4** below), transaction costs are included in the calculation of the effective interest rate – in effect, they will be amortised through profit or loss over the term of the instrument.

(b) For available-for-sale financial assets where the effective interest method is applied, transaction costs will initially be recognised as part of the carrying amount of the financial asset. The transaction costs will be amortised through profit or loss over the term of the instrument under the effective interest method as with assets and liabilities measured at amortised cost. If the available-for-sale asset does not have fixed or determinable payments or has an indefinite life, and therefore the effective interest rate is not applied (e.g. the asset is an investment in an equity security), transaction costs are recognised in profit or loss only upon impairment or derecognition.

(c) For financial instruments classified as at FVTPL, transaction costs are immediately recognised in profit or loss on initial recognition.

Transaction costs are defined as incremental costs that are directly attributable to the acquisition, issue or disposal of a financial asset or a financial liability. An incremental cost is one that would not have been incurred if the entity had not acquired, issued or disposed of the financial instrument. [IAS 39.9]

Transaction costs are interpreted as including fees and commissions paid to agents, advisers, etc., as well as levies, taxes and duties. However, debt premiums/discounts, financing costs, internal administrative costs and holding costs should not be included. [IAS 39.AG13] In practice, the interpretation of this definition may require significant judgement. A particular issue arises in relation to the treatment of origination fees (see **4.1.3** below).

US GAAP comparison: Under US GAAP, all costs paid directly to the seller of an investment in a debt security that is classified as HTM or AFS and fees paid less fees received are included as part of the initial investment in the debt security and recognised as an adjustment to the yield of the debt security over its remaining life. All other costs incurred as part of the acquisition are expensed immediately as incurred.

Under both IFRS and US GAAP, certain loan origination costs are recognised over the life of the loan as an adjustment to its effective interest rate. Under US GAAP, however, such costs include not only incremental costs that would not have been incurred if the entity had not entered into the loan, but also certain other costs directly related to specified activities performed by the lender for that loan (such as compensation or payroll-related costs related to evaluating the prospective borrower's financial condition; evaluating and recording guarantees, collateral, and other security arrangements; negotiating loan terms; preparing and processing loan documents; and closing the transaction).

2.3 Settlement date accounting

The accounting for regular way trades is considered at **2.2** in **chapter 7**. When an entity uses settlement date accounting for an asset that is subsequently measured at cost or amortised cost, the asset is recognised initially at the settlement date, but at the fair value that existed at the trade date (discussed further in **3.5** below). Movements in fair value between trade and settlement date are not recognised (other than impairment losses). For assets carried at fair value, the change in fair value between trade and settlement date is recognised in profit or loss if the asset is measured at fair value through profit or loss, or in other comprehensive income if the asset is available-for-sale. [IAS 39.57]

3 Subsequent measurement

3.1 Financial assets

As discussed in **section 3** of **chapter 2**, financial assets (including derivatives that are assets) are classified into one of four categories. This classification largely determines their subsequent measurement:

3.1.1 Financial assets at fair value through profit or loss (FVTPL)

Assets falling within this category, which includes those classified as held for trading, are measured at fair value. Gains and losses that arise on changes in fair value are recognised in profit or loss, except for derivatives that are designated in effective cash flow hedges or hedge of a net investment in a foreign operation. **Section 5** below contains guidance on the appropriate determination of fair value.

Gains and losses that arise between the end of the last annual reporting period and the date an instrument is derecognised do not constitute a separate 'profit/loss on disposal'. Such gains and losses will have arisen prior to disposal, while the item is still being held at FVTPL, and should be recognised in profit or loss as they occur.

Transaction costs that might be incurred upon future disposal are **not** deducted from fair value in determining the carrying amount. Some argue that this is inconsistent with the use of exit prices (i.e. fair value) for measurement purposes, but the Standard is clear that such costs are viewed as being related to the act of disposal and, therefore, are recognised only in the period of disposal itself.

3.1.2 Held-to-maturity investments

Held-to-maturity investments are measured at amortised cost using the 'effective interest method'. This method is discussed in detail in **section 4** below.

3.1.3 Loans and receivables

Loans and receivables are also measured at amortised cost using the effective interest method, as discussed in **section 4** below.

3.1.4 *Available-for-sale financial assets*

Assets classified as available-for-sale are measured at fair value. As with financial assets at FVTPL, no deduction is made for transaction costs that might be incurred upon future disposal. **Section 5** below contains guidance on the appropriate determination of fair value.

Gains and losses that arise on changes in fair value are recognised in other comprehensive income, with three exceptions:

(i) interest, calculated using the effective interest method, is recognised in profit or loss (see **section 4** below);

(ii) impairment losses are recognised in profit or loss (see **section 6** below); and

(iii) foreign exchange gains and losses on monetary financial assets (the approach adopted in relation to foreign currency gains and losses is discussed in **3.3** below).

When an available-for-sale asset is derecognised, the cumulative gain or loss previously recognised in other comprehensive income is reclassified from equity to profit or loss. This reclassification of previous fair value gains and losses is frequently referred to as 'recycling'.

The following example illustrates the concept of 'recycling'.

Example 3.1.4A

Available-for-sale debt instrument

A zero coupon bond is acquired for its fair value of CU95 on 1 January 20X0 and classified as available-for-sale. Transaction costs arising on acquisition are CU5. The bond redeems for CU130 on 31 December 20X4. On 31 December 20X0, the bond's fair value is CU103. On 31 December 20X1, the entity sells the bond for its fair value of CU108.

In its 20X0 accounts, the entity records the following entries:

(1) Initial recognition (at fair value, including transaction costs)

Dr	Asset	CU100
Cr	Cash	CU100

(2) Interest income (calculated under the effective interest method – the rate of 5.39 per cent is calculated so as to include transaction costs as explained in **4.1** below)

Dr	Asset	CU5.39
Cr	Interest income	CU5.39

(3) Fair value adjustment (such that the asset is stated at its fair value of CU103)

Dr	Equity	CU2.39
Cr	Asset	CU2.39

In its 20X1 the following entries are recognised:

(1) Interest income (calculated under the effective interest method)

Dr	Asset	CU5.68
Cr	Interest income	CU5.68

(2) Fair value adjustment (such that the asset is stated at its fair value of CU108)

Dr	Equity	CU0.68
Cr	Asset	CU0.68

(3) Sale of asset

Dr	Cash	CU108
Cr	Asset	CU108

(4) Reclassification to profit or loss of fair value losses previously recognised in other comprehensive income

Dr	Profit or loss	CU3.07
Cr	Equity	CU3.07

If an available-for-sale asset is derecognised, with the consideration received being another available-for-sale asset, the fair value gain or loss previously recognised in other comprehensive income should nonetheless be reclassified to profit or loss. As the original asset has been derecognised the deferred gain or loss is not attributable to the new asset and does not remain in other comprehensive income. [IAS 39.IG.E.3.1]

Example 3.1.4B

Available-for-sale equity instrument – group restructuring (1)

Entity A has a directly-held wholly-owned subsidiary, Entity B. Entity A accounts for its investments in subsidiaries in accordance with IAS 39 in its separate financial statements as permitted by IAS 27(2008).38(b) (previously IAS 27(2003).37(b)). Entity A designates its investment in Entity B as an available-for-sale investment in its separate financial statements and therefore measures its investment at fair value with fair value gains/losses recognised in other comprehensive income.

As part of a group reorganisation a new holding entity is created, Entity C, whose shares are issued to Entity A in return for Entity A's investment in Entity B. Entity C has no other assets or liabilities or transactions other than the issue of shares to Entity A and the acquisition of shares in Entity B. At the date of the group reorganisation Entity A has a gain in other comprehensive income attributable to the increase in value of Entity B. The group structure is illustrated below:

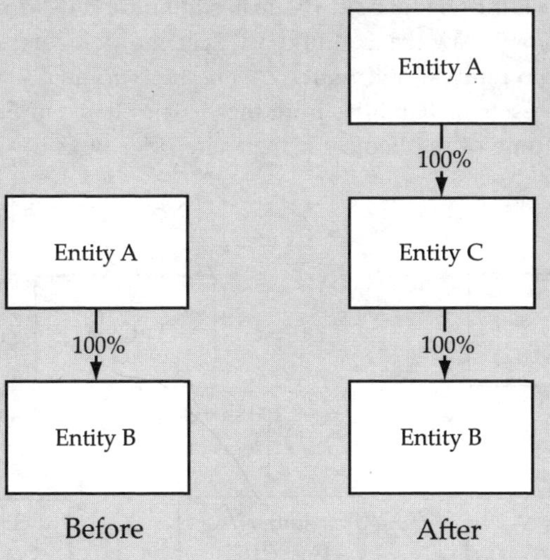

In the separate financial statements of Entity A it will not derecognise its investment in Entity B. Although Entity A has transferred its contractual rights to receive cash flows under the Entity B shares in accordance with IAS 39.18(a), Entity A has not transferred substantially all the risks and rewards of ownership of the Entity B shares in accordance with IAS 39.20(b) as the consideration received for transferring the shares in Entity B are shares in Entity C, the entity whose only asset is the investment in Entity B. Entity A's exposure to the risks and rewards of Entity B are equivalent to its new investment in Entity C. As Entity A has not derecognised the shares in Entity B the fair value gain recognised in other comprehensive income and accumulated in the available-for-sale reserve in equity will not be reclassified to profit or loss at the date of the group reorganisation.

Example 3.1.4C

Available-for-sale equity instrument – group restructuring (2)

Entity X purchases 100 equity shares of Entity Y, a listed entity, for CU1,000 (i.e. at a price of CU10 per each share). The investment is classified as an available-for-sale investment. At Entity X's period end, 31 December 20X1, the price of the shares has increased to CU20 per share. As a result the fair value of Entity X's holding has increased to CU2,000 with Entity X recognising a fair value gain on its available-for-sale financial asset of CU1,000 in other comprehensive income.

On 1 January 20X2 Entity Y undergoes a corporate restructuring such that certain assets, liabilities and activities of Entity Y are transferred into a newly created Entity Z whose shares will be distributed to the shareholders of Entity Y. The restructuring means Entity Y will continue with certain core activities while Entity Z will undertake certain other activities that were previously undertaken by Entity Y. As part of the demerger shareholders in Entity Y will receive 1 new share in Entity Z (in addition to retaining their existing shares in Entity Y) for each share owned in Entity Y. After the reorganisation Entity X will hold 100 shares in Entity Z in addition to the 100 shares it originally owned in Entity Y. Post the demerger all assets and liabilities within Entity Y and Entity Z were those originally within Entity Y with no new assets or liabilities introduced. The shares in Entity Z are not listed. At the time of the demerger the share price of Entity Y decreases to CU5 per share.

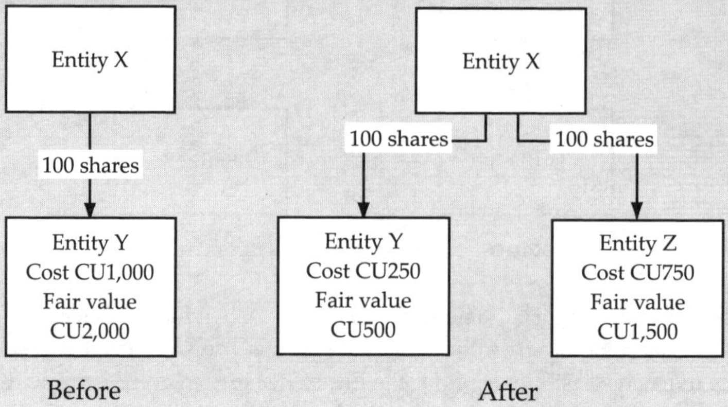

On receipt of the additional shares in Entity Z the available-for-sale reserve should not be reclassified to profit or loss as the original financial asset, Entity Y shares, does not meet the requirements for derecognition. Entity X has not transferred the contractual rights to receive cash flows from the Entity Y shares nor has it retained the contractual rights to receive the cash flows of the financial asset, but assumed a contractual obligation to pay the cash flows to one or more recipients in an arrangement that meets the pass through conditions (IAS 39.18). At the point of the demerger, from the point of view of Entity X, some of the value of the Entity Y shares has been distributed to the newly set up Entity Z. In addition, Entity X's investment in Entity Y is not considered to be impaired as the reduction in fair value of Entity Y shares is only the result of a redistribution of assets to existing shareholders for nil consideration.

Although the gain of CU1,000 previously recognised in other comprehensive income should not be reclassified to profit or loss at the point of the demerger, Entity X will need to perform the following:

(i) recognise the shares in Entities Y and Z at their fair values upon the demerger. The fair value of the Entity Y shares upon demerger will be equal to CU500 (fair value of CU5 multiplied by 100 shares). The fair value of the shares in Entity Z should be estimated using a valuation technique in the absence of a quoted market price. In the event that the fair value of Entity Z shares cannot be estimated reliably the shares will be held at cost less impairment. In such case the cost will be deemed to equal CU1,500 (the value of Entity Y shares prior to the demerger, CU2,000, less the value of those shares upon demerger, CU500); and

(ii) allocate the gain of CU1,000 in other comprehensive income in relation to the investment in Entity Y shares across the shares in Entity Y and Z. This allocation should be performed in line with the proportions of fair value/estimated cost of the shares upon the demerger as established in (i) above.

If available-for-sale assets are distributed to owners as dividends-in-kind (also known as 'dividends in specie'), the cumulative gains or losses recognised in other comprehensive income should still be reclassified to profit or loss on derecognition of the available-for-sale assets even though the dividend is accounted for in equity. This treatment is equivalent to the entity selling the available-for-sale assets for cash and distributing that cash to owners as a dividend.

Dividends on an available-for-sale equity instrument are recognised in profit or loss when the entity's right to receive payment is established. [IAS 39.55(b) and IAS 18.30(c)]]

Example 3.1.4D

Dividends on available-for-sale equity instruments

On 1 January 20X0, Entity X acquires an equity instrument of Entity Y for its fair value of CU100. It is classified as available-for-sale. Entity Y immediately declares a dividend of CU10 and, consequently, the fair value of the equity instrument in Entity Y decreases to CU90. Entity X records the following entries:

(1) Initial recognition

Dr	Asset	CU100
Cr	Cash	CU100

(2) Dividend income

Dr	Cash	CU10
Cr	Dividend income	CU10

(3) Fair value adjustment (such that the asset is stated at its fair value of CU90)

Dr	Other comprehensive income	CU10
Cr	Asset	CU10

The accounting treatment in the example above appears unfortunate, since the realisation of part of the value of an asset will lead to the recognition of two offsetting amounts – one in profit or loss and the other in other comprehensive income. (Historically, there was also an apparent conflict here with IAS 18.32, which, until it was amended in May 2008, required dividends out of pre-acquisition profits to be treated as a reduction of the cost of investment, rather than being taken to profit or loss.) Nevertheless, IAS 39 explicitly requires that dividends received are included in profit or loss. In addition, an entity would need to consider in all cases whether a reduction in fair value recognised in other comprehensive income needs to be reclassified to profit or loss in the instance when the asset is impaired (see **6.1.2** below).

3.1.5 Hedged items

IAS 39 includes specific requirements to be applied when accounting for a financial asset that is a hedged item. These requirements are discussed in detail in **chapters 8** and **9**.

3.1.6 Unquoted equity instruments

Investments in equity instruments that do not have a quoted market price in an active market, and whose fair value cannot be reliably measured, are measured at cost. The term 'active market' is discussed further in **5.2** below. Cost is also applied for derivatives (whether assets or liabilities) that are linked to and must be settled by delivery of such unquoted equity. [IAS 39.46(c)] Examples of such derivatives would include purchased call options over a third party's equity shares requiring physical settlement, or a forward purchase of such shares.

The application guidance to the Standard (IAS 39.AG80 & AG81) makes it clear that it will normally be possible to estimate the fair value of an asset that has been acquired from an outside party. Cost should be used **only** if there is a significant range of possible fair value estimates and the probabilities of the various estimates cannot be reasonably assessed.

US GAAP comparison: Equity investments that do not have readily determinable fair values are generally measured at cost, as opposed to fair value. This is different from IFRS where unquoted equity investment should be fair valued unless the entity can demonstrate that the valuation is not sufficiently reliable.

Restricted shares (i.e. shares for which sale is restricted due to governmental or contractual requirements) where the restriction is for more than one year are measured at cost less impairment (including temporary impairment) as this type of share is scoped out of FAS 115.

Derivatives over unquoted equity investments should be fair valued under US GAAP if the definition of a derivative is met, though as noted in **section 2** of **chapter 4**, the definition of a derivative in US GAAP is narrower than that in IFRS and includes a requirement for net settlement. Derivatives on unquoted equity instruments which do not contain a net settlement provision do not meet the definition of a derivative in FAS 133 as unquoted equity is not readily convertible to cash. However, the SEC requires written options to be accounted for at fair value irrespective of whether they are within the scope of FAS 133.

3.1.7 *Instruments whose fair value is 'unreliable'*

If IAS 39 requires a financial instrument to be measured at fair value, there is no exception from measuring on that basis except for equity instruments described in **3.1.6** above. In all other cases, fair value is deemed to be reliable and any measurement assumptions are disclosed. See **chapter 11**.

In November 2006 the IFRIC finalised a rejection notice on the valuation of electricity derivatives where the contract fails to meet the normal purchase, sale or usage exemption in IAS 39.5 and therefore is wholly within the scope of IAS 39. The question asked was whether such contracts fell under the exception from fair valuation that applies to derivatives linked to unquoted equity instruments. Valuation issues arise as the derivative in this case has a variable notional amount and the term of the derivative might extend well beyond the period for which there is any observable market data. The IFRIC noted that the only exception in IAS 39 from the requirement to fair value derivatives after initial recognition is given in IAS 39.46(c), amplified by paragraphs AG80 and AG81, which is in respect of unquoted equity investments, and that it was not appropriate to extend this exemption to other derivatives. The IFRIC noted further that IAS 39 contains general principles on how to measure fair value. The IFRIC decided that it should not seek to develop more detailed guidance on this topic, since the subject was too specific.

3.1.8 *Negative fair value*

If the fair value of a financial instrument, previously recognised as a financial asset, falls below zero, then it is a financial liability and measured as discussed in **3.2** below.

3.2 Financial liabilities

Financial liabilities are measured at amortised cost using the effective interest method (see **section 4** below), with the following exceptions.

3.2.1 *Financial liabilities at fair value through profit or loss (FVTPL)*

Such liabilities, which include those classified as held for trading and derivative liabilities that are not designated as effective hedging instruments, and those designated as at FVTPL, are measured at their fair value with gains and losses recognised in profit or loss. However, a derivative liability that is linked to, and must be settled by delivery of, an unquoted equity instrument whose fair value cannot be reliably measured is measured at cost (discussed further in **3.1.6** above).

A consequence of including a financial liability in this category is that the effect of an entity's own credit risk will be reflected in its statement of comprehensive income. For example, if an entity that has elected to fair value its issued debt experiences financial difficulties, it is likely to recognise a gain in profit or loss reflecting the instrument's worsening creditworthiness.

> **US GAAP comparison**: US GAAP does not include a classification of liabilities as held for trading. Nevertheless, derivative liabilities are accounted for at fair value in accordance with FAS 133. Additionally, FAS 159 provides an option under US GAAP to carry financial liabilities (e.g., accounts payable or issued debt) at fair value with changes in fair value recognised in earnings.

3.2.2 *Financial liabilities arising on the transfer of a financial asset*

A liability may arise when a transfer of a financial asset does not qualify for derecognition or is accounted for using the 'continuing involvement' approach. The approach used when measuring such liabilities is discussed in **chapter 7**.

3.2.3 *Hedged items*

IAS 39 includes specific requirements to be applied when accounting for a financial liability that is a hedged item. These requirements are discussed in detail in **chapters 8** and **9**.

3.3 Foreign currency

Where a financial asset or liability is a monetary item under IAS 21 *The Effects of Changes in Foreign Exchange Rates*, foreign exchange gains and losses should be recognised in profit or loss in accordance with that Standard. Monetary items are defined as units of currency held and assets and liabilities to be received or paid in a fixed or determinable number of units of currency. [IAS 21.8]

For financial assets and liabilities that are classified as at FVTPL, this requirement is easy to apply since all gains and losses are recognised in profit or loss in any case. However, the situation is not so straightforward for assets measured at amortised cost and, in particular, for available-for-sale financial assets.

IAS 39 requires that 'for the purpose of recognising foreign exchange gains and losses under IAS 21, a monetary available-for-sale financial asset is treated as if it were carried at amortised cost in the foreign currency.' [IAS 39.AG83] Hence, exchange differences resulting from changes in amortised cost are recognised in profit or loss, with other changes in carrying amount recognised in other comprehensive income under IAS 39.55(b). The result of this is that the cumulative gain or loss recognised in other comprehensive income is the difference between the amortised cost (adjusted for impairment, if any) and the fair value of the instrument in the functional currency of the reporting entity.

IAS 39.IG.E.3.2 illustrates the approach and is reproduced below.

Example 3.3

IAS 39 and IAS 21 – Available-for-sale financial assets: separation of currency component
[IAS 39.IG.E.3.2]

For an available-for-sale monetary financial asset, the entity recognises changes in the carrying amount relating to changes in foreign exchange rates in profit or loss in accordance with IAS 21.23(a) and IAS 21.28 and other changes in the carrying amount in other comprehensive income in accordance with IAS 39. How is the cumulative gain or loss that is recognised in other comprehensive income determined?

It is the difference between the amortised cost (adjusted for impairment, if any) and fair value of the available-for-sale monetary financial asset in the functional currency of the reporting entity. For the purpose of applying IAS 21.28 the asset is treated as an asset measured at amortised cost in the foreign currency.

To illustrate: on 31 December 20X1 Entity A acquires a bond denominated in a foreign currency (FC) for its fair value of FC1,000. The bond has five years remaining to maturity and a principal amount of FC1,250, carries fixed interest of 4.7 per cent that is paid annually (FC1,250 × 4.7 per cent = FC59 per year), and has an effective interest rate of 10 per cent. Entity A classifies the bond as available for sale, and thus recognises gains and losses in other comprehensive income. The entity's functional currency is its local currency (LC). The exchange rate is FC1 to LC1.5 and the carrying amount of the bond is LC1,500 (= FC1,000 × 1.5).

Dr	Bond	LC1,500
Cr	Cash	LC1,500

On 31 December 20X2, the foreign currency has appreciated and the exchange rate is FC1 to LC2. The fair value of the bond is FC1,060 and thus the carrying amount is LC2,120 (= FC1,060 × 2). The amortised cost is FC1,041 (= LC2,082). In this case, the cumulative gain or loss to be recognised in other comprehensive income and accumulated in equity is the difference between the fair value and the amortised cost on 31 December 20X2, i.e. LC38 (= LC2,120 – LC2,082).

Interest received on the bond on 31 December 20X2 is FC59 (= LC118). Interest income determined in accordance with the effective interest method is FC100 (=1,000 × 10 per cent). The average exchange rate during the year is FC1 to LC1.75. For the purpose of this question, it is assumed that the use of the average exchange rate provides a reliable approximation of the spot rates applicable to the accrual of interest income during the year (IAS 21.22). Thus, reported interest income is LC175 (= FC100 × 1.75) including accretion of the initial discount of LC72 (= [FC100 – FC59] × 1.75). Accordingly, the exchange difference on the bond that is recognised in profit or loss is LC510 (= LC2,082 – LC1,500 – LC72). Also, there is an exchange gain on the interest receivable for the year of LC15 (= FC59 × [2.00 – 1.75]).

Dr	Bond	LC620
Dr	Cash	LC118
Cr	Interest income	LC175
Cr	Exchange gain	LC525
Cr	Fair value change in other comprehensive income	LC38

On 31 December 20X3, the foreign currency has appreciated further and the exchange rate is FC1 to LC2.50. The fair value of the bond is FC1,070 and thus the carrying amount is LC2,675 (= FC1,070 × 2.50). The amortised cost is FC1,086 (= LC2,715). The cumulative gain or loss to be accumulated in equity is the difference between the fair value and the amortised cost on 31 December 20X3, i.e. negative LC40 (= LC2,675 – LC2,715). Thus, the amount recognised in other comprehensive income equals the change in the difference during 20X3 of LC78 (= LC40 + LC38).

Interest received on the bond on 31 December 20X3 is FC59 (= LC148). Interest income determined in accordance with the effective interest method is FC104 (= FC1,041 × 10 per cent). The average exchange rate during the year is FC1 to LC2.25. For the purpose of this question, it is assumed that the use of the average exchange rate provides a reliable approximation of the spot rates applicable to the accrual of interest income during the year (IAS 21.22). Thus, recognised interest income is LC234 (= FC104 × 2.25) including accretion of the initial discount of LC101 (= [FC104 – FC59] × 2.25). Accordingly, the exchange difference on the bond that is recognised in profit or loss is LC532 (= LC2,715 – LC2,082 – LC101). Also, there is an exchange gain on the interest receivable for the year of LC15 (= FC59 × [2.50 – 2.25]).

Dr	Bond	LC555
Dr	Cash	LC148
Dr	Fair value change in other comprehensive income	LC78
Cr	Interest income	LC234
Cr	Exchange gain	LC547

When some portion of the change in carrying amount is recognised in other comprehensive income and some portion is recognised in profit or loss, for example, if the amortised cost of a foreign currency bond classified as available-for-sale has increased in foreign currency (resulting in a gain in profit or loss) but its fair value has decreased in the functional currency (resulting in a loss in other comprehensive income), an entity cannot offset those two components for the purposes of determining gains or losses that should be recognised in profit or loss or in other comprehensive income. [IAS 39.IG.E.3.4]

IAS 21 specifically scopes out the measurement of foreign currency items that are subject to hedge accounting. These items are discussed in **chapters 8** and **9** on hedge accounting.

For available-for-sale financial assets that are not monetary items under IAS 21 (for example, equity investments), the gain or loss that is recognised in other comprehensive income includes any related foreign currency component.

IAS 39.IG.E.3.4 includes a further discussion of the interaction between IAS 39 and IAS 21. It states that the measurement of a financial asset or financial liability at fair value, cost or amortised cost is first determined in the foreign currency in which the item is denominated in accordance with IAS 39. Then, the foreign currency amount is translated into the functional currency using the closing rate or a historical rate in accordance with IAS 21. [IAS 39.AG83]

For example, if a monetary financial asset (such as a debt instrument) is carried at amortised cost under IAS 39, amortised cost is calculated in the currency of denomination of that financial asset. Then, the foreign currency amount is recognised using the closing rate in the entity's financial statements. [IAS 21.23] That applies regardless of whether a monetary item is measured at cost, amortised cost or fair value in the foreign currency.

[IAS 21.24] A non-monetary financial asset (such as an investment in an equity instrument) is translated using the closing rate if it is carried at fair value in the foreign currency [IAS 21.23(c)] and at a historical rate if it is not carried at fair value under IAS 39 because its fair value cannot be reliably measured. [IAS 21.23(b) & IAS 39.46(c)]

As an exception, if the financial asset or financial liability is designated as a hedged item in a fair value hedge of the exposure to changes in foreign currency rates under IAS 39, the hedged item is remeasured for changes in foreign currency rates even if it would otherwise have been recognised using a historical rate under IAS 21 [IAS 39.89]. This exception applies to non-monetary items that are carried in terms of historical cost in the foreign currency and are hedged against exposure to foreign currency rates. [IAS 21.23(b)]

A summary of how foreign currency is treated for the various financial asset and liability classifications is included below.

Classification	**Monetary or non-monetary item**	**Foreign currency gains and losses from re-measurement (prior to its disposal) ***
Available-for-sale	Monetary item (e.g. debt security)	Profit or loss
Available-for-sale	Non-monetary item (e.g. equity security)	Equity
Loan and receivable	Always a monetary item	Profit or loss
Held-to-maturity	Always a monetary item	Profit or loss
Fair value through profit or loss	Not applicable	Profit or loss
Liability carried at amortised cost	Always a monetary item	Profit or loss

* Assumes the item is not being hedged for foreign currency, or is not a hedging instrument in a foreign currency hedge

US GAAP comparison: If an instrument is fair valued through other comprehensive income, the amount will include all gains and losses in respect of that instrument, including any foreign exchange gains/losses (EITF 96–15). This approach is different from that under IFRS whereby for investments in monetary available-for-sale assets, like investments in foreign currency denominated debt securities, the foreign exchange gain or loss is recorded in profit or loss with the remaining changes in fair value recognised in other comprehensive income.

3.3.1 *Dual currency bonds*

IAS 39.AG33(c) states that a foreign currency derivative that provides a stream of principal or interest payments that are denominated in a foreign currency and is embedded in a host debt instrument (e.g. a dual currency bond) is closely related to the host debt instrument. Such a derivative is not separated from the host instrument because IAS 21 requires foreign currency gains and losses on monetary items to be recognised in profit or loss.

IAS 39 and IAS 21 do not provide specific guidance on how to measure dual currency bonds. As IAS 39 states that the foreign currency gains and losses are accounted for under IAS 21 it is reasonable to assume that the accounting treatment is equivalent to isolating the foreign currency cash flows and measuring them as if they were a separate instrument. For example, if interest is denominated in a foreign currency, but the principal is not, an entity could measure the interest flows as if it was a foreign currency denominated interest rate strip and treat the principal cash flow as a functional currency denominated zero coupon bond. Conversely, if the principal is denominated in a foreign currency, but the interest is not, an entity could measure the principal as if it was a foreign currency denominated zero coupon bond and treat the interest flows as a functional currency denominated interest rate strip.

Example 3.3.1

Accounting for a dual-currency bond

Entity A, a Sterling functional currency entity, issues a dual currency bond on 1 January 20X4 where the interest is denominated in its functional currency, but the principal is denominated in US dollars. The bond has a notional of US$200m, has a maturity of three years and is issued at par.

Entity A determines the carrying amount of a US$-denominated three year zero coupon bond at inception by discounting US$200m by the 3-year US$ zero coupon rate reflecting Entity A's credit quality which is 10% (US$200m / 1.1^3 = US$150.26m). Entity A then converts this amount into its functional currency at the US$:£ spot rate at inception (US$150.26m / US$2:£1 = £75.13m). The difference between this amount and the functional currency equivalent net proceeds received from issuing the dual-currency bond is allocated to the functional currency interest only strip [(US$200m / US$2:£1) – £75.13m = £24.87m]. Each period the US$ effective interest rate of 10% is applied to the US$-denominated zero coupon bond in US$ and this US$ carrying amount is converted into £ in accordance with IAS 21.

Entity A determines the £ effective interest rate for the interest only strip which is the 3-year interest rate for an equivalent 3-year amortising loan. For illustration purposes this interest rate is also 10% though in practice the interest rates for the respective currencies will differ.

The foreign exchange rates for the three period were as follows:

	Period end rate (US$:£)	**Average rate (US$:£)**
20X3	2.00	–
20X4	1.80	1.90
20X5	2.10	1.95
20X6	1.90	2.00

The carrying value of the foreign currency zero coupon bond in US$ is determined by applying the US$ effective interest rate in US$.

	20X4	**20X5**	**20X6**
Opening carrying value (US$)	150.26	165.29	181.82
Interest at 10% (US$)	15.03	16.53	18.18
Closing carrying value (US$)	165.29	181.82	200.00

The carrying amount of the foreign currency zero coupon bond in £ is determined by converting the opening carrying value in US$ at the opening rate, adding interest at the average rate, adding/subtracting foreign exchange gains or losses so that the closing value in £ is equal to the US$ closing value at the period end rate.

	20X4	**20X5**	**20X6**
Opening carrying amount (£)	75.13	91.83	86.58
Interest at average rates (£)	7.91	8.48	9.09
Foreign currency (gains) losses (£)	8.79	(13.72)	9.59
Closing carrying amount (£)	91.83	86.58	105.26

The carrying value of the interest only strip in £ is determined by adding the effective interest rate and deducting the cash payments for each period.

	20X4	20X5	20X6
Opening carrying amount	24.87	17.36	9.10
Interest at 10%	2.49	1.74	0.90
Less cash paid	(10.00)	(10.00)	(10.00)
Closing carrying amount	17.36	9.10	–

The entries are summarised below.

£	Description	Cash	Debt	Interest expense	Foreign currency gain/(loss)
1/1/X4	Issue debt	100.00	(100.00)		
20X4	Interest on US$ zero coupon bond		(7.91)	7.91	
	Foreign currency movement		(8.79)		(8.79)
	Interest on interest only strip	(10.00)	7.51	2.49	
20X5	Interest on US$ zero coupon bond		(8.48)	8.48	
	Foreign currency movement		13.72		13.72
	Interest on interest only strip	(10.00)	8.26	1.74	
20X6	Interest on US$ zero coupon bond		(9.09)	9.09	
	Foreign currency movement		(9.59)		(9.59)
	Interest on interest only strip	(10.00)	9.10	0.90	
31/12/X6	Repayment of dual currency bond	(105.26)	105.26		

3.4 Reclassifications

The measurement consequences of reclassifying financial assets at the date of reclassifications are discussed in **section 4** of **chapter 2**. The measurement guidance after the date of reclassification is generally consistent with the measurement guidance that would have applied had the financial asset been initially measured in accordance with the classification category that it has been reclassified to. The only exceptions are:

- measurement of the effective interest rate for debt instruments reclassified out of FVTPL, and those reclassified out of AFS to loans and receivables, in the case where there is an increase in the recoverability of cash flows following the date of reclassification, see **4.1.2.1** below.
- determining impairment for equity and debt instruments reclassified out of FVTPL, see **6.4.1** and **6.4.3** respectively below.

3.5 Settlement date accounting

When an entity uses settlement date accounting for an asset that is subsequently measured at cost or amortised cost, the asset is recognised initially at its fair value on the trade date. Any change in fair value between the trade date and settlement date is not recognised (other than impairment losses). Changes in value between the trade date and settlement date for assets that are subsequently measured at fair value are recognised (i) in profit or loss for financial assets classified as at FVTPL; and (ii) in other comprehensive income for available-for-sale financial assets. This subject is discussed in greater detail at **2.2** in **chapter 7**.

4 Amortised cost

On acquisition, the carrying amount of a financial instrument, being its fair value (normally the transaction price), represents the discounted amount of the expected future cash flows that will arise under that instrument. For financial assets and liabilities that are measured at amortised cost, the unwinding of that discount is included in profit or loss as interest income or interest expense.

Short-term receivables and payables with no stated interest rate may be measured at the original invoice amount if the effect of discounting is immaterial. [IAS 39.AG79]

Amortised cost is defined as the amount at which the financial asset or financial liability is measured at initial recognition minus principal repayments, plus or minus the cumulative amortisation using the effective interest method of any difference between that initial amount and the maturity amount, and minus any reduction (directly or through the use of an allowance account) for impairment or uncollectibility. [IAS 39.9]

The effective interest method is discussed in **4.1** below.

Amortised cost measurement is required for financial assets that are classified as either 'loans and receivables' or 'held-to-maturity investments', and for financial liabilities that are not at FVTPL. In addition, while interest-bearing available-for-sale financial assets are measured at fair value, with changes in fair value recognised in other comprehensive income, the Standard nonetheless requires interest income or expense (calculated on an amortised cost basis) to be included in profit or loss. This approach is illustrated in **example 3.1.4A** above. For financial assets or liabilities at FVTPL, interest is effectively wrapped up in the fair value adjustment that is included in profit or loss in each accounting period and is not required to be separately disclosed although an entity may choose to do so as an accounting policy choice.

4.1 The effective interest method

IAS 39 requires that the amortised cost of a financial asset or liability is calculated using the 'effective interest method'. This method allocates interest income/expense over the relevant period by applying the 'effective interest rate' to the carrying amount of the asset or liability.

The effective interest rate is defined as the rate that exactly discounts estimated future cash payments or receipts through the expected life of the financial instrument or, when appropriate, a shorter period to the net carrying amount of the financial asset or financial liability. When calculating the effective interest rate, an entity shall estimate cash flows considering all contractual terms of the financial instrument (for example, prepayment, call and similar options) but shall not consider future credit losses. The calculation includes all fees and points paid or received between parties to the contract that are an integral part of the effective interest rate (see IAS 18 *Revenue*), transaction costs, and all other premiums or discounts. There is a presumption that the cash flows and the expected life of a group of similar financial instruments can be estimated reliably. However, in those rare cases when it is not possible to estimate reliably the cash flows or the expected life of a financial instrument (or group of financial instruments), the entity shall use the contractual cash flows over the full contractual term of the financial instrument (or group of financial instruments). [IAS 39.9]

Since transaction costs are taken into account when determining the initial net carrying amount, their recognition in profit or loss is effectively spread over the life of the instrument.

Example 4.1

Effective interest rate

On 1 January 20X0, an entity acquires a bond for consideration of CU90, incurring transaction costs of CU5. Interest of CU4 is receivable annually over the next 5 years (31 December 20X0 to 31 December 20X4). The bond has a mandatory redemption of CU110 on 31 December 20X4.

Year	Carrying amount b/f	Interest income at 6.96%	Cash flow	Carrying amount c/f
20X0	95.00	6.61	(4.00)	97.61
20X1	97.61	6.79	(4.00)	100.40
20X2	100.40	6.99	(4.00)	103.39

Year	Carrying amount b/f	Interest income at 6.96%	Cash flow	Carrying amount c/f
20X3	103.39	7.19	(4.00)	106.58
20X4	106.58	7.42	(114.00)	0.00

The effective interest rate of 6.96 per cent is the rate that discounts the expected cash flows on the bond to the initial carrying amount, i.e.:

$4/1.0696 + 4/1.0696^2 + 4/1.0696^3 + 4/1.0696^4 + 114/1.0696^5 = 95$

The effective interest rate is determined based on the initial carrying amount of the financial asset or liability. Therefore, the effective interest rate applied to any financial instrument, including interest bearing available-for-sale assets is not recalculated to reflect fair value changes in the carrying amount of the asset.

4.1.1 *Cash flows*

When calculating the effective interest rate, the **estimated** cash flows arising from the asset or liability (or, where relevant, the group of assets or liabilities) should be used. The Standard explicitly states that all contractual terms of the instrument (for example prepayment, call and similar options) should be considered, but that future credit losses should **not** be taken into account. This last point is consistent with the fact that the impairment model adopted in the Standard requires impairment losses to be recognised as they are incurred, rather than when they are expected (see **section 6** below).

In contrast, credit losses that have already been incurred on an instrument by the time it is acquired by the reporting entity should be taken into account when calculating the effective interest rate. This might be the case where a financial asset is acquired at a deep discount because credit losses that have occurred are reflected in the transaction price. As mentioned above, IAS 39 requires impairment losses to be recognised as incurred. If previously incurred losses are not factored into the calculation, an overstated interest income amount would be offset by the recognition of impairment losses that have already been incurred.

If a debt instrument has a prepayment, put, or call feature embedded in the terms of the instrument, the entity must firstly determine whether that feature is an embedded derivative that needs to be separately accounted for. See **7.1** in **chapter 5** for further guidance on embedded derivatives. Briefly, such embedded derivatives will be separately accounted for unless the option's exercise price is approximately equal to the instrument's amortised cost on each exercise date. [IAS 39.AG30(g)]

If the embedded derivative is separately accounted, the impact of this feature must not be used in determining the estimated cash flows of the debt host contract when determining the effective interest rate. If the feature was taken into account, it would result in double counting of the prepayment, put or call feature in profit or loss as it would be included in the effective interest rate on the debt host contract as well as in the fair value movements of the embedded derivative.

US GAAP comparison: Under US GAAP, interest typically is recognised by applying the effective interest method on the basis of the contractual cash flows over the contractual life (FAS 91). Prepayments of principal are not anticipated. However, there are several exceptions to this method of recognising interest, including the following:

- If an investment in a loan or debt security is part of a pool of prepayable financial assets and the timing and amount of prepayments are reasonably estimable, an entity is allowed to anticipate future principal prepayments when determining the appropriate effective interest rate (FAS 91).
- If an investment in a loan or debt security is purchased with evidence of credit deterioration, an interest method based on expected rather than contractual cash flows, must be applied (SOP 03–3).
- For investments in beneficial interests in securitised financial assets that (1) are not of high credit quality or (2) can be contractually prepaid or otherwise be settled such that the holder would not recover substantially all of its investment, the interest method articulated in EITF 99–20, which is based on estimated rather than contractual cash flows, must be applied.
- If an investment in a debt security is considered other-than-temporarily impaired after acquisition, an interest method based on estimated rather than contractual cash flows, must be applied (FSP FAS 115/124–1).

- If an investment in a debt security is considered a structured note but does not contain an embedded derivative that is required to be separated under FAS 133, the interest method articulated in EITF 96–12, which is based on estimated rather than contractual cash flows, must be applied.

- If the loan's stated interest rate increases during the term of the loan (so that interest accrued under the interest method in early periods would exceed interest at the stated rate), interest income shall not be recognised to the extent that the net investment in the loan would increase to an amount greater than the amount at which the borrower could settle the obligation. Prepayment penalties shall be considered in determining the amount at which the borrower could settle the obligation only to the extent that such penalties are imposed throughout the entire loan term.

- The issuer of a convertible debt instrument that may be settled in cash upon conversion (including partial cash settlement) and that does not contain a separately recognised embedded derivative uses the interest method described in FSP APB 14–1. Under this method, debt discounts and debt issuance costs are amortized over the expected life of a similar liability that does not have a conversion option.

4.1.2 *Changes in cash flows*

For floating rate instruments, when cash flows are re-estimated to reflect movements in market rates of interest, the effective interest rate is updated. If the instrument is initially recognised at an amount equal to the amount receivable or payable on maturity, re-estimating future cash flows for this reason will not normally have a significant effect on its carrying amount. [IAS 39.AG7]

The re-estimation of future cash flows for any other reason (except in the case of certain reclassified debt instruments) or in the case of an instrument that is not a floating rate instrument will normally result in a change in carrying amount since the revised estimated cash flows are discounted at the instrument's original effective interest rate. The required adjustment is recognised in profit or loss. [IAS 39.AG8] The one exception to recognising an immediate gain or loss in profit or loss for changes in cash flows when applying IAS 39.AG8 is for certain financial assets that are reclassified out of the fair value through profit or loss category or reclassified from available-for-sale to loans and receivables. See **4.1.2.1** below. With the exception of such reclassified debt instruments the changes in estimated cash flows will immediately impact profit or loss. For example, this will be the case for an instrument where the timing or amount of interest or principal payments varies due to the presence of an embedded derivative but the embedded derivative but the feature is not accounted for separately as an embedded derivative and the instrument is also not considered a floating rate instrument.

The difference in approach in IAS 39.AG7 and AG8 reflects the fact that varying interest receipts/payments are a contractual term of a floating rate instrument. In this situation, it would be inappropriate to determine at inception a single rate to discount estimated future cash flows. Instead, the Standard requires an entity to reflect changes in the interest rate in profit or loss as such changes occur.

Judgement is required in determining what constitutes a floating rate debt instrument. A debt instrument may have variable cash flows linked to market interest rates which differ from standard floating rate debt instruments. If the instrument is considered a floating rate debt instrument then IAS 39.AG7 is applied, if it is not, then IAS 39.AG8 applies.

In 2008 the IFRIC received a request for guidance on the application of the effective interest rate method to a financial instrument with future cash flows linked to changes in an inflation index. The IFRIC did not add the issue to its agenda but recommended that the Board should consider clarifying or expanding the relevant guidance in IAS 39. As part of its annual improvements project in October 2008 the IASB decided tentatively that a floating rate financial instrument is an instrument with contractual variable cash flows arising from changes in market variables. The Board decided not to define the term market variable but may instead provide examples.

Before the IASB clarifies its guidance the choice between applying IAS 39.AG7 or AG8 continues to be available. It is an accounting policy choice and must be applied consistently to similar instruments.

Consider an example of a Sterling functional currency entity that has issued a Sterling denominated bond where principal and interest payments are indexed to unleveraged UK inflation. The inflation-linking feature is considered a closely related embedded derivative (see **7.4** in **chapter 5**). If the entity chooses to apply IAS 39.AG8 the effective interest rate will be calculated at initial recognition of the bond, as the rate that exactly discounts the expectations of inflation at initial recognition to the initial carrying amount (being fair value less transaction costs). This effective interest is never updated. At the end of each subsequent reporting period the cash flows are re-estimated, reflecting the then current expectations of future inflation, and are discounted using the original effective interest rate. Any difference between the carrying amount of the instrument before and after such re-estimation is recognised in profit or loss.

If the entity chooses to apply IAS 39.AG7 it may follow one of two possible approaches. One approach is to update the expected cash flows at each period end in line with changes in expectations of inflation in the same way as applying IAS 39.AG8, but unlike IAS 39.AG8 the changes in expectations do not to result in an immediate gain/loss in profit or loss. Instead, the effective interest rate is revised each period, i.e. the gain/loss is spread forward. At initial recognition, the effective interest rate is calculated at a rate that discounts the estimated cash flows of principal and interest (which includes the estimation of future inflation) to the initial carrying amount. That initial effective interest rate is used to account for the instrument at amortised cost until the end of the next reporting period. The carrying amount at the end of the first reporting period will be equal to the initial fair value, plus the effective interest on the carrying amount, less any cash payments/receipts in the period. The entity then determines a new effective interest rate as the rate that discounts the new estimated cash flows of the instrument (taking into account the revised estimation of future inflation) back to the period end carrying amount. This new effective interest rate is applied for the new reporting period. This approach is repeated at each subsequent reporting period until the instrument is derecognised.

An alternative approach in applying IAS 39.AG7 is for profit or loss to reflect only the accrued inflation for the period up to the reporting date, i.e. the effective interest rate is not determined by looking forward to expectations of future inflation. This approach is consistent with the tentative conclusion of the IASB at its Board meeting in October 2008 where the Board tentatively agreed that expectations (and changes in expectations) of future cash flows are not considered when calculating the effective interest rate for floating rate instruments.

The proposed amendment is expected to be included in the exposure draft of proposed annual improvements, which is due to be issued in the second half of 2009. At the date of writing the exposure draft has not yet been issued.

Applying one of the IAS 39.AG7 approaches described above will result in a less volatile profit or loss when compared to applying IAS 39.AG8. The application of the latter approach results in changes in expectations of future inflation impacting profit or loss immediately at each re-estimation date.

In March 2009 the IFRIC issued a tentative agenda decision titled, *Participation rights and calculation of the effective interest rate*. The IFRIC was asked for guidance on how an issuer should account for a financial liability that contains participation rights by which the instrument holder shares in the net income and losses of the issuer. The holder receives a percentage of the issuer's net income and is allocated a proportional share of the issuer's losses. Losses are applied to the nominal value of the instrument to be repaid on maturity. Losses allocated to the holder in one period can be offset by profits in subsequent periods. The IFRIC considered the issue without reconsidering the assumptions described in the request that the financial liability:

- does not contain any embedded derivatives
- is measured at amortised cost using the effective interest rate method, and
- does not meet the definition of a floating rate instrument.

The IFRIC noted that IAS 39.AG6–8 provide the relevant application guidance for measuring financial liabilities at amortised cost using the effective interest rate method. The IFRIC also noted that it is inappropriate to analogise to the derecognition guidance in IAS 39 because the liability has not been extinguished. Because specific application guidance already exists, the IFRIC tentatively agreed not to issue an interpretation. At the date of writing the agenda decision was not finalised.

Guidance on the accounting treatment of financial instruments where interest is determined as a proportion of profit of the issuer is referred to in **2.1** in **chapter 4** with respect to the definition of a derivative.

Changes in any expected cash flows that relate to an embedded prepayment, put or call option will not normally have an effect on carrying amount. This is because one of the following two circumstances will apply.

(i) The embedded derivative is separately accounted for. As discussed in **4.1.1** above, this means that the derivative is ignored when determining the effective interest rate of the host contract.

(ii) The embedded derivative is not separately accounted for because the option's exercise price is approximately equal to the instrument's amortised cost on each exercise date. In this situation, since prepayment/put/call can only occur at an amount (approximately) equal to amortised cost, the discounted amount of future cash flows will be (approximately) unaffected by any change in expectations with respect to the exercise of said options.

This statement is not applicable for embedded prepayment, put or call options embedded in compound instruments because of the unique way in which the embedded prepayment, put or call options are assessed as being closely related and the way the liability component is separated from the instrument as a whole.

Where a prepayment, put or call option is embedded in an issued compound instrument the assessment of whether the prepayment, put or call option is considered closely related to the debt host contract is made *prior* to the instrument being split into liability and equity parts. See **3.2** in **chapter 3**. If the exercise price of the prepayment, put or call option is approximately equal to the amortised cost (prior to splitting the instrument into its liability and equity parts) it is closely related and therefore it is not separately recognised. If the embedded derivative is not separately recognised the embedded prepayment, put or call option is taken into account in determining the timing and amount of the expected cash flows for the liability component when determining its amortised cost in future periods. As the liability is initially recognised at a discount to the proceeds of the instrument as a whole, yet in most cases it can be early redeemed at an amount equal to the proceeds of the instrument as a whole, changes in the likelihood that the prepayment, put or call option will be exercised will impact the liability's carrying amount.

Example 4.1.2A

Issuer call and holder put in convertible debt

Entity X issued a convertible debt instrument in May 20X2 with a contractual maturity of 16 years. Each bond allows the holder to convert, at any time, into one share of the issuer. The issue price is 100 per cent and redemption price is 140 per cent.

The instrument is puttable by the holders on three different dates, during the life of the instrument (May 20X6, May 20Y0 and May 20Y4). At initial recognition, Entity X considers that there is a very high probability that the instrument will be redeemed by the holders at the first put date (i.e. May 20X6), given the low price of its shares. The instrument is also callable by the issuer, starting May 20X6, if the price of the issuer's shares increases beyond 125 per cent of the redemption price. The issuer does not expect to call the instrument.

All the embedded call and put options over the instrument (excluding the conversion option that is treated as equity) are considered closely related to the debt component as the exercise prices are equal to the amortised cost of the instrument prior to the equity conversion option being separated. The embedded call and put options are therefore not separated and form part of the debt component recognised as a financial liability. The financial liability is not designated as at FVTPL, rather it is subsequently measured at amortised cost.

The fair value of the debt component at initial recognition is the contractual cash flows of the instrument, being interest and principal at maturity, discounted by the entity's normal borrowing rate, plus the fair value of the written put less the fair value of the purchased call. The effective interest rate is the rate that exactly discounts this carrying amount with the estimated early redemption payment, in this case at May 20X6. This is the instrument's *original* effective interest rate. The difference between the total liability that includes the written put and the purchased call and the net proceeds at issue is assigned to the equity component.

Assuming that the expectation of repayment in May 20X6 does not change, the carrying amount of the debt component will change only for the application of the effective interest rate, i.e. it will increase by the difference between the effective interest rate and interest paid in the period. At May 20X6, the carrying amount of the liability will therefore equal par. If the put is exercised as expected, the early redemption will result in nil gain or loss.

If, however, expectations of repayment were to change (e.g. a change in market conditions were to cause the issuer to consider that the bond will be put back to the issuer on May 20Y0 instead of May 20X6), a recalculation of the carrying amount of the liability component would be required. The new carrying amount of the liability would be the re-estimated cash flows, being interest up to, and principal payable in, May 20Y0, discounted by the *original* effective interest rate. Any difference between the new carrying amount and the old carrying amount will be recognised in profit or loss.

Example 4.1.2B

Example of calculating amortised cost using IAS 39.AG8: financial asset

[Extract from IAS 39.IG.B.26]

Entity A purchases a debt instrument with five years remaining to maturity for its fair value of CU1,000 (including transaction costs). The instrument has a principal amount of CU1,250 and carries fixed interest of 4.7 per cent that is paid annually (CU1,250 × 4.7 per cent = CU59 per year). The contract also specifies that the borrower has an option to prepay the instrument and that no penalty will be charged for prepayment. At inception, the entity expects the borrower not to prepay.

It can be shown that in order to allocate interest receipts and the initial discount over the term of the debt instrument at a constant rate on the carrying amount, they must be accrued at the rate of 10 per cent annually. The table below provides information about the amortised cost, interest income and cash flows of the debt instrument in each reporting period.

Year	**(a) Amortised cost at the beginning of the year**	**(b = a x 10%) Interest income**	**(c) Cash flows**	**(d = a + b – c) Amortised cost at the end of the year**
20X0	1,000	100	59	1,041
20X1	1,041	104	59	1,086
20X2	1,086	109	59	1,136
20X3	1,136	113	59	1,190
20X4	1,190	119	1,250 + 59	–

On the first day of 20X2 the entity revises its estimate of cash flows. It now expects that 50 per cent of the principal will be prepaid at the end of 20X2 and the remaining 50 per cent at the end of 20X4. In accordance with IAS 39.AG8, the opening balance of the debt instrument in 20X2 is adjusted. The adjusted amount is calculated by discounting the amount the entity expects to receive in 20X2 and subsequent years using the original effective interest rate (10 per cent). This results in the new opening balance in 20X2 of CU1,138. The adjustment of CU52 (CU1,138 – CU1,086) is recorded in profit or loss in 20X2. The table below provides information about the amortised cost, interest income and cash flows as they would be adjusted taking into account the change in estimate.

Year	**(a) Amortised cost at the beginning of the year**	**(b = a x 10%) Interest income**	**(c) Cash flows**	**(d = a + b – c) Amortised cost at the end of the year**
20X0	1,000	100	59	1,041
20X1	1,041	104	59	1,086
20X2	1,086 + 52	114	625 + 59	568
20X3	568	57	30	595
20X4	595	60	625 + 30	–

If the debt instrument becomes impaired, say, at the end of 20X3, the impairment loss is calculated as the difference between the carrying amount (CU595) and the present value of estimated future cash flows discounted at the original effective interest rate (10 per cent).

US GAAP comparison: Under US GAAP, interest typically is recognised on the basis of the contractual cash flows of the security as discussed above. For investments in loans or debt securities for which recognition of interest income is based on estimated rather than contractual cash flows, several methods exist for recognising changes in estimated cash flows depending on the type of the financial asset:

- If an entity anticipates estimated prepayments when measuring interest income of an investment in a loan or debt security that is part of a pool of prepayable financial, that entity must continually recalculate the appropriate effective yield as prepayment assumptions change. That is, if the estimated future cash flows of a debt security change, the effective yield of a debt security must be recalculated to take into account the new prepayment assumptions. The adjustment must be applied on a retrospective basis. That is, the carrying value is adjusted to reflect what the carrying value should have been had the new effective yield been used since the acquisition with a corresponding charge or credit to current period earnings.

- If an investment in a loan or debt security is within the scope of SOP 03–3 because there is evidence of credit deterioration, an entity must prospectively recalculate the amount of accretable yield if it is probable that there is a significant increase in cash flows previously expected to be collected or if actual cash flows are significantly greater than cash flows previously expected.

- For a beneficial interest in securitised financial assets within the scope of EITF 99–20, an entity must prospectively recalculate the amount of accretable yield of the debt security whenever it is probable that there is a favourable or adverse change in estimated cash flows from the cash flows previously projected.

- If an investment in a debt security is within the scope of FSP FAS 115/124–1 because it is other-than-temporarily impaired, an entity must prospectively recalculate the amount of accretable yield as if the debt security had been purchased on the measurement date of the other-than-temporary impairment in a manner consistent with the method described in SOP 03–3.

- If an investment in a debt security is a structured note within the scope of EITF 96–12, an entity must retrospectively recalculate the amount of accretable yield for the debt security on the basis of the current estimated future cash flow as of the reporting date. However, if the recalculated effective yield is negative, a zero percent effective yield is used instead.

4.1.2.1 Changes in cash flows following reclassification

The amendment to IAS 39 that was issued in October 2008, *Reclassification of Financial Assets*, amended IAS 39.AG8 for debt instrument assets reclassified out of the fair value through profit or loss, or available-for-sale to loans and receivable (see **4.2** and **4.4** respectively in **chapter 2**). The amendment requires that any increases in estimates of future cash receipts as a result of increased recoverability of those cash receipts after the date of reclassification shall be recognised as an adjustment to the effective interest rate from the date of the change in estimate rather than as an adjustment to the carrying amount of the asset at the date of the change in estimate. The impact of this amendment is to 'spread' the impact of increased recoverability of cash flows forward through a higher effective interest rate as opposed to recognising a gain in profit or loss at the time the re-estimation of cash flows is made. The aim of the IASB in amending IAS 39.AG8 was to attempt to align the post-reclassification gains/losses on reclassified debt instruments with US GAAP as best it could but acknowledging that there remain broader GAAP differences in this area that could not be eliminated as part of the amendment.

Example 4.1.2.1

Reclassification from FVTPL to L&R with subsequent increase in recoverability of cash flows

In June 20X0, Bank A purchases asset-backed securities that are linked to an underlying portfolio of corporate bonds held by the issuer of the asset-backed securities. The investment is known as a "cash CDO". The investment matures in 20Y0 at its par value of CU100 million although, depending on the performance of the underlying corporate bond portfolio, the asset-backed securities may redeem earlier. The investment is classified by Bank A as at FVTPL at initial recognition because it has the intent to trade the instrument.

At 30 June 20X3, the investment has declined in value to CU70 million and the asset-backed securities and the underlying portfolio of corporate bonds are no longer traded in an active market.

On 1 July 20X3, Bank A reclassifies the investment to the loans and receivables category as the entity has the intention and ability to hold the investment until the foreseeable future. Bank A has an accounting policy of applying the loans and receivables definition at the date of reclassification, as opposed to the date of initial recognition (see 4.2 in chapter 2). At the date of reclassification its opening amortised cost equals its fair value, being CU70 million. Bank A estimates that it will recover the following contractual cash flows on the investment with an expected redemption in June 20X8:

Date	**Coupon – CU million**	**Principal – CU million**
30 June 20X4	6	
30 June 20X5	6	

Date	Coupon – CU million	Principal – CU million
30 June 20X6	6	
30 June 20X7	6	
30 June 20X8	6	80

The EIR that exactly discounts the estimated future cash flows to the fair value of the investment at the date of reclassification is 10.9%. This new EIR is then used to amortise the difference between the amortised cost of the cash CDO at the date of reclassification and the redemption value until the expected maturity date. Accordingly, the amortised cost will accrete as follows:

Date	Amortised cost b/f – CU million	Interest income at 10.9% – CU million	Coupons – CU million	Amortised cost c/f – CU million
30 June 20X4	70.0	7.6	(6.0)	71.6
30 June 20X5	71.6	7.8	(6.0)	73.4
30 June 20X6	73.4	8.0	(6.0)	75.4
30 June 20X7	75.4	8.2	(6.0)	77.6
30 June 20X8	77.6	8.4	(6.0)	80.0

On 30 June 20X6, Bank A estimates there is an increase in the recoverability of cash flows. Bank A expects that it will receive 90% of principal, instead of 80% as previously expected.

Date	Coupon – CU	Principal – CU
30 June 20X7	6	
30 June 20X8	6	90

As the increase in recoverability of cash flows occurred after a reclassification of a debt instrument Bank A must determine a new effective interest in accordance with IAS 39.AG8. The EIR that exactly discounts these future cash flows to the amortised cost carrying value of the investment at 30 June 20X6 is 16.9%. Accordingly, the amortised cost will accrete as follows:

Coupon Date	Amortised cost b/f – CU million	Interest income at 16.9% – CU million	Coupons – CU million	Amortised cost c/f – CU million
30 June 20X7	75.4	12.7	(6.0)	82.1
30 June 20X8	82.1	13.9	(6.0)	90.0

If the asset was subject to an impairment event in a future period the effective interest rate that would be used to discount the expected recoverable cash flows to determine the impairment loss would be the revised effective interest rate, i.e. 16.9%.

If the asset was instead subject to further increases in the recoverability of cash flows in a future period the effective interest rate would once again be revised in accordance with IAS 39.AG8.

4.1.3 Fees

The definition of the effective interest rate states that 'the calculation includes all fees and points paid or received between parties to the contract that are an integral part of the effective interest rate (see IAS 18).' [IAS 39.9] The appendix to IAS 18 includes material relevant to the determination of whether or not fees should be viewed as an integral part of the effective interest rate (and, therefore, taken into account in the calculation). The interpretation of this material will be far from straightforward in many instances. A number of examples are discussed below.

Origination fees. The appendix to IAS 18 specifically addresses origination fees received by the entity, which may include compensation for activities such as evaluating the borrower's condition, evaluating and recording security arrangements, negotiating terms, preparing and processing documents and closing the transaction. Such fees (relating to the creation or acquisition of a financial asset) are an integral part of generating an ongoing involvement with the resulting financial instrument. As such, they are deferred and recognised as an adjustment to the effective interest rate.

Commitment fees. Where a commitment fee is received by an entity to originate a loan when the loan commitment is outside of the scope of IAS 39, the Standard draws a distinction based on whether it is probable that the entity will enter into the related specific lending arrangement. If it is probable, the fee should be viewed as compensation for an ongoing involvement with the acquisition of a financial instrument (i.e. defer and recognise as an adjustment to the effective interest rate). If it is unlikely that the arrangement will be entered into, the fee is viewed as being compensation for a service provided (i.e. making the borrowing facility available for a period of time) and should be recognised on a time proportion basis over the commitment period. This will be an area in which judgement will be required in many instances.

The choice of the terms 'probable' and 'unlikely' to cover the two possible alternatives is slightly unusual. It is suggested that 'unlikely' should be interpreted as meaning anything less than probable.

Loan servicing fees. Such fees are received for the provision of a service and should be recognised as revenue as those services are provided.

Fees earned on the execution of a significant act. IAS 18 identifies the following examples of such fees: commission on the allotment of shares to a client; placement fees for arranging a loan between two third parties; and loan syndication fees. Such amounts should be recognised as revenue when the significant act has been completed.

Prepayment penalties. A borrower may be required to make a penalty payment to the lender upon early repayment. The definition of the effective interest rate explicitly states that prepayment options, along with all other contractual terms, should be taken into account. This would imply that related penalty payments, along with the effect on cash flows of the early repayment itself, should be included in the calculation. Typically, such penalties represent some form of compensation to the borrower for not receiving interest over the full term of the instrument. However, where such penalties represent only the reimbursement of administrative costs associated with an early repayment, they would not be taken into account in determining the effective interest rate on the instrument. It is also noted that such prepayment options may meet the definition of an embedded derivative that requires separate accounting – the requirements for such instruments are explained in **chapter 5**.

Unless a fee can be clearly demonstrated to relate to a particular service or the execution of a significant act (to use IAS 18 terminology), it will normally be appropriate to view the amount as an adjustment to the effective interest rate. However, it will be necessary to consider such fees carefully, on a case-by-case basis.

The appendix to IAS 18 indicates that, where fees are viewed as an integral part of generating an involvement with a financial instrument (e.g. origination or commitment fees) and are therefore treated as an adjustment to the effective interest rate, 'related transaction costs' should also be deferred. Related transaction costs should include only 'incremental costs that are directly attributable to the acquisition, issue or disposal of a financial asset or financial liability'.

US GAAP comparison: FAS 91 provides guidance about the types of costs that should be deferred and used to adjust the effective interest rate of an originated loan. For instance, for a completed loan the types of origination costs that should be deferred include incremental direct costs of loan origination incurred in transactions with independent third parties and certain costs directly related to specified activities performed by the lender for that loan (e.g. evaluating the prospective borrower's financial condition, evaluating and recording guarantees, collateral, and other security arrangements, negotiating loan terms, preparing and processing loan documents, and closing the transaction). The costs directly related to those activities include that portion of the employees' total compensation directly related to time spent performing those activities for that loan and other costs related to those activities that would not have been incurred but for that loan. All other lending-related costs, including costs related to activities performed by the lender for advertising, soliciting potential borrowers, servicing existing loans, and other ancillary activities related to establishing and monitoring credit policies, supervision and administration should be charged to expense as incurred, as well as compensation cost related to unsuccessful loan origination efforts and idle time. Administrative costs, rent, depreciation, and all other occupancy and equipment costs are considered indirect costs and charged to expense as incurred.

4.1.4 Amortisation period

The definition of the effective interest rate (see **4.1** above) requires the amortisation of premiums/discounts, fees, points paid or received and transaction costs (those that are taken into account in calculating the effective rate) over 'the expected life of the financial instrument or, when appropriate, a shorter period.' A shorter period will be appropriate if it is the period to which the relevant premiums/discounts, fees, points paid or received or transaction costs relate. [IAS 39.AG6] For example, if a fee is received as compensation for a discounted interest rate over an initial period (which ends with a repricing to market interest rates), then that fee should be amortised over that initial period, rather than the expected life of the instrument. In general, where the variable to which the fee, transaction costs, discount or premium relates is repriced to market rates before the expected maturity of the instrument, a shorter period will be used. However, if it is another variable that is repriced, the expected life of the instrument will be used. This would be the case where the premium/discount on an instrument results from changes in the credit spread over the specified floating rate, but it is the interest rate that is repriced.

4.1.5 Measurement

There is a presumption that it will be possible to estimate reliably the cash flows and expected life of an instrument or group of similar instruments, such that the effective interest rate can be determined. However, in those 'rare cases' where that is not so, the rate should be calculated based on the contractual cash flows over the full contractual term of the instrument. [IAS 39.9]

The application of the effective interest method is illustrated in the examples below.

Example 4.1.5A

Example of calculating amortised cost: debt instruments with stepped interest payments

[Extract from IAS 39.IG.B.27]

On 1 January 20X0, Entity A issues a debt instrument for a price of CU1,250. The principal amount is CU1,250 and the debt instrument is repayable on 31 December 20X4. The rate of interest is specified in the debt agreement as a percentage of the principal amount as follows: 6.0 per cent in 20X0 (CU75), 8.0 per cent in 20X1 (CU100), 10.0 per cent in 20X2 (CU125), 12.0 per cent in 20X3 (CU150), and 16.4 per cent in 20X4 (CU205). In this case, the interest rate that exactly discounts the stream of future cash payments through maturity is 10 per cent. Therefore, cash interest payments are reallocated over the term of the debt instrument for the purposes of determining amortised cost in each period. In each period, the amortised cost at the beginning of the period is multiplied by the effective interest rate of 10 per cent and added to the amortised cost. Any cash payments in the period are deducted from the resulting number. Accordingly, the amortised cost in each period is as follows:

Year	(a) Amortised cost at the beginning of the year	(b = a x 10%) Interest income	(c) Cash flows	(d = a + b – c) Amortised cost at the end of the year
20X0	1,250	125	75	1,300
20X1	1,300	130	100	1,330
20X2	1,330	133	125	1,338
20X3	1,338	134	150	1,322
20X4	1,322	133	1,250 + 205	–

Example 4.1.5B

Accounting for a loan with a separated embedded derivative

On 1 January 20X0, an entity originates a loan of CU100. Interest of CU4 is receivable annually over the next 5 years (on 31 December 20X0 to 31 December 20X4). The loan is repayable at an amount of CU110 on 31 December 20X4. However, the borrower can prepay (at CU111 plus accrued interest for the year) at any time. As the prepayment option will result in the loan potentially being prepaid by the borrower at an amount that is not approximately equal to the amortised cost, the prepayment option is separately accounted for as an embedded derivative. The prepayment option is effectively an option written by the originator allowing the borrower to repay the borrowing at any time. Economically, the borrower will prepay the liability if the fair value of the instrument rises above CU111 (plus accrued interest).

On 1 January 20X0, the fair value of the prepayment option for the originator is a CU3 liability. Therefore, the remaining balance of CU103 is the host contract asset.

(1) Initial recognition at 1 January 20X0

Dr	Asset	CU103.00
Cr	Cash	CU100.00
Cr	Prepayment option	CU3.00

The effective interest rate on the host contract is 5.11 per cent (calculated as the rate that exactly discounts interest of CU5 and principal of CU100 to the carrying value of CU103).

At the end of 20X0 interest rates have fallen slightly, and the fair value of the option has risen from CU3 to CU5. The following entries are recorded in the entity's 20X0 financial statements:

(2) Interest income

Dr	Asset	CU5.26
Cr	Interest income	CU5.26

Interest income is determined at the effective interest rate of 5.11 per cent (5.11% x CU103.00)

(3) Interest receipt

Dr	Cash	CU4.00
Cr	Asset	CU4.00

The carrying amount of the loan as at 31 December 20X0 is therefore CU104.26.

(4) Embedded derivative

Dr	Profit or loss	CU2.00
Cr	Embedded derivative liability	CU2.00

By the end of 20X1 interest rates have fallen further, so on 31 December 20X1 the borrower repays the borrowing early. At the year end the fair value of the prepayment option is CU6

(5) Interest income

Dr	Asset	CU5.33
Cr	Interest income	CU5.33

Interest income is determined at the effective interest rate of 5.11 per cent (5.11% x CU104.26)

(6) Interest receipt

Dr	Cash	CU4.00
Cr	Asset	CU4.00

The carrying amount of the loan prior to early repayment is therefore CU105.59.

(7) Embedded derivative

Dr	Profit or loss	CU1.00
Cr	Embedded derivative liability	CU1.00

(8) Early repayment of loan

Dr	Cash	CU111.00
Dr	Embedded derivative liability	CU6.00
Cr	Asset	CU105.59
Cr	Profit or loss	CU11.41

The credit in profit or loss on early repayment of the loan represents the cumulative catch-up of the fair value of the host contract. As the host contract is not measured at fair value during its life, when the instrument is terminated, this results in a gain in profit or loss due to the impact of movements in interest rates that have not previously been recognised in the financial statements. As interest rates have fallen considerably, the fair value of the host contract has risen.

The above example assumes that at inception the holder of the loan considers that the put option is not likely to be exercised. If the put option was considered likely to be exercised there is an argument that the likely exercise of the put option would form part of the instrument's amortised cost and therefore would result in a different host contract being identified (see **7.1** in **chapter 5**).

Example 4.1.5C

Effective interest rate for fixed-rate perpetual debt

An entity issues a perpetual debt instrument for consideration of CU100. Interest of CU6 is payable annually in perpetuity. The instrument is not redeemable. The effective rate (i.e. the rate that discounts CU6 annually in perpetuity to CU100) is 6 per cent. Interest of CU6 is recognised in profit or loss and there is no amortisation of the principal amount. This would also be the case for a floating rate instrument since, as discussed in **4.1.2** above, the effective rate is adjusted for changes in market rates for floating rate instruments.

Example 4.1.5D

Effective interest rate for stepped fixed-rate perpetual debt

An entity issues a perpetual debt instrument where the interest rate is fixed at 10% for the first 10 years and 8% for each year thereafter.

The 10% interest payments in the first ten years represent a part payment of redemption. Consequently when these payments are made the difference between 10% and 8% is treated as a reduction in the carrying amount of the liability. In the period from year ten the effective interest will be recognised at 8% as all payments relate to interest and not repayment of principal.

An alternative way of considering the higher payments in the first ten years is the sum of the differential between the 10% and 8% represents repayments on an amortising loan. The value of the amortising loan at inception less the proceeds from the instrument as a whole represents the carrying value of the perpetual debt instrument.

IAS 39.IG.B.25 has a similar fact pattern as **example 4.1.5D** above except that after year ten the interest rate reduces to zero. The implementation guidance states that the amortised cost is zero after year ten because the present value of the stream of future cash payments in subsequent periods is zero.

An alternative argument to one used in the implementation guidance is that after the final payment is made at year ten the financial liability is derecognised as the entity has fully discharged any obligation to pay cash or other financial asset.

4.1.6 *Interaction of effective interest rate and fair value hedge accounting*

When an entity applies fair value hedge accounting to a hedge of a debt instrument the carrying value of the debt is adjusted for movements in the hedged risk to the extent the hedge is highly effective. Fair value hedge accounting is explained in detail at **2.1** in **chapter 8**. IAS 39.92 requires the fair value adjustment to be amortised to profit or loss as early as the adjustment is made and no later than when the hedged item ceases to be fair value adjusted. This amortisation is included as part of the revised effective interest rate. Therefore, if an entity chooses to amortise the fair value adjustment as soon as the adjustment is made, then assuming the fair value adjustment changes for each subsequent reporting period as there is a change in the fair value of the hedged risk and the hedge is highly effective, a revised effective interest rate will need to be determined at the start of each reporting period. Alternatively, if an entity chooses to start to amortise the adjustment when hedge accounting ceases the entity will only need to recalculate the effective interest rate at that point.

In May 2008 the IASB issued *Improvements to IFRSs*. The improvements amended IAS 39 to make it clear that the effective interest rate that is used when applying IAS 39.AG8 when revisions in estimates of cash flows occur is the original effective interest rate, except when IAS 39.92 as described above applies in which case it is the revised effective interest rate that includes the effects of the fair value hedge adjustment is used. The amendment to IAS 39.AG8 applies for annual periods beginning on or after 1 January 2009. If the amendment is applied to an earlier period the entity shall disclose this fact.

5 Fair value

The concept of fair value is central to the approach of IAS 39. The Standard is based on the premise that the most relevant information, in relation to a financial instrument will normally be its fair value. In this context, fair value is viewed as an 'exit' rather than an 'entry' price for subsequent measurement, i.e.:

- for an asset, the amount which would be realised from the disposal of the asset, rather than the amount it would cost to acquire it; and
- for a liability, the amount it would cost to discharge the liability, rather than the amount that would be received in return for taking it on.

In determining fair value, the Standard requires the maximum possible use of observable market data and the minimum use of entity-specific factors. [IAS 39.48A] If available, a quoted market price will give the best evidence of fair value, given that fair value is defined as 'the amount for which an asset could be exchanged, or a liability settled, between knowledgeable, willing parties in an arm's length transaction.' [IAS 39.9] The use of such amounts, as opposed to entity-specific information, is intended to promote consistent measurement across entities.

Nonetheless, the use of fair values gives rise to numerous issues of measurement. IAS 39.AG69 – AG82 provide assistance in the determination of fair value as defined in the Standard. The publication of the IASB's Expert Advisory Panel report, *Measuring and disclosing the fair value of financial instruments in markets that are no longer active,* provides further, non-authoritative, guidance to assist in determining fair value, particularly when using valuation techniques. This section outlines and amplifies this material, identifying additional issues that may arise.

It should be noted that IAS 39.AG69 explicitly states that underlying the definition of fair value is a presumption that an entity is 'a going concern without any intention or need to liquidate, to curtail materially the scale of its operations or to undertake a transaction on adverse terms.' In addition, a forced transaction does not establish fair value (see **5.1** below).

In November 2006 the IASB issued a discussion paper entitled *Fair Value Measurement*. This discussion paper is equivalent to FAS 157, which was issued by the US FASB some months earlier. The issue of the discussion paper is part of the IASB and FASB's convergence agenda. At the time of writing the IASB is formulating its exposure draft on fair value measurement with the expectation of issuing it in the second quarter of 2009. The proposals included in the discussion paper and the Board's tentative conclusions in formulating their exposure draft are detailed in the future developments in **section 8** below.

US GAAP comparison: Under US GAAP, one defining characteristic of fair value is that it is assumed to be the exit price. FAS 157 defines exit price as the price that would be received or paid by the reporting entity "in an orderly transaction between market participants to sell the asset or transfer the liability at the measurement date". Unlike IAS 39, FAS 157 assumes that fair value of a liability is the amount that a market participant would pay to transfer the liability as of the measurement date to another market participant.

5.1 Forced transactions

IAS 39.AG69 states that the amount an entity would receive or pay in a forced transaction, involuntary liquidation or distress sale (collectively, a 'forced transaction') is not fair value. IAS 39 does not provide guidance as to how to distinguish between a transaction that is forced, and therefore is not at fair value, and the one that is not forced.

The IASB's Expert Advisory Panel report provides further clarity in determining what a forced transaction is. The report notes that an imbalance between supply and demand (for example, fewer buyers than sellers) is not always a determinant of a forced transaction. The report also notes that although a seller might be under financial pressure to sell, the seller can still sell at a market price that is fair value if there is more than one potential buyer in the market and a reasonable time is available to market the instrument. Paragraph 24 of the report lists some indicators that might evidence a forced transaction:

- a legal requirement to transact, for example a regulatory mandate;
- a necessity to dispose of an asset immediately and no sufficient time to market the asset to be sold; or
- the existence of a single potential buyer as a result of the legal or time restrictions imposed.

The report further states that if an entity sells assets to market participants to meet regulatory requirements, the regulator does not establish the transaction price and the entity has a reasonable amount of time to market the assets, the transaction price provides evidence of fair value. Similarly, transactions initiated during bankruptcy should not automatically be assumed to be forced. The determination of whether a transaction is forced requires a thorough understanding of the facts and circumstances of the transaction.

If a transaction is identified as being forced then it does not form part of a fair value measurement. This applies equally when determining fair values for financial instruments quoted in active markets and those that are not. Therefore, an entity should not use the price of forced transaction when determining the price of an instrument that is quoted in an active market or use a forced transaction as an input in determining the valuation of an instrument using a valuation technique.

Example 5.1

Forced transactions

Entity A is acting as an administrator on behalf of the creditors of Entity B who is subject to bankruptcy proceedings. The administrator's role is to seek to maximise the return to Entity B's creditors. As part of the administrator's responsibilities it auctions a portfolio of Entity B's financial assets. The administrator promotes the auction to interested parties with the expectation of receiving bids for the financial assets over a specified period. Although Entity B's assets are being sold as part of its bankruptcy proceedings, the sale of the financial assets by auction is not a forced transaction as the sale is not immediate and there is sufficient time to market the assets to other market participants.

If transactions are occurring between willing buyers and sellers in a manner that is usual and customary for transactions involving such instruments, then these are not forced transactions. Persuasive evidence is required to establish that an observable transaction is a forced transaction.

In March 2009 the IASB issued a request for views on a proposed FSP No. FAS 157-e *Determining Whether a Market is Not Active and a Transaction is Not Distressed* issued by the US FASB. The FSP provides guidance on how to determine whether a market is active or inactive. In addition, it states that if a market is inactive it is presumed that a transaction in that market is distressed unless the reporting entity has evidence that (a) there was sufficient time before the measurement date to allow for usual and customary marketing activities for the asset and (b) there were multiple bidders for the asset. The IASB did not participate in the development of the FSP and therefore represents the views of the FASB only. At the date of writing the comment periods for the FSP and the IASB's request for views remained open.

5.2 Quoted in an active market

It will normally be relatively straightforward to determine the fair value of a financial instrument that is quoted in an active market. IAS 39 defines such a market as one in which quoted prices are readily and regularly available from an exchange, dealer, broker, industry group, pricing service or regulatory agency, and those prices represent actual and regularly occurring market transactions on an arm's length basis. [IAS 39.AG71]

'Regularly occurring market transactions' does not mean that there must be a consistent number of market transactions from one period to another. A significantly lower than normal volume of transactions does not automatically mean that either there is not an active market, transactions are forced (see **5.1** above), or that the transactions that are occurring are motivated other than by normal business considerations. It would not be appropriate to disregard observable prices in an active market even if the market is relatively thinner or illiquid as compared to previous periods.

The absence of transactions for a short period does not automatically mean that a market has ceased to be active. If transactions are occurring frequently enough to obtain reliable pricing information on an ongoing basis, then that market would be considered active. However, if observed transactions are no longer regularly occurring even if prices might be available, or the only observed transactions are forced transaction, then the market would no longer be considered active. What is 'regularly occurring' is a matter of judgement and depends upon the facts and circumstances of the market for the instrument being measured at fair value. The fact that there is no active market in one financial instrument should not be taken to imply that there are no active markets in other similar financial instruments.

The IASB's Expert Advisory Panel report notes that there is no bright line between active and inactive markets. The biggest distinction between prices observed in active markets and prices observed in inactive markets is typically that, for inactive markets, an entity needs to put more work into the valuation process to gain assurance that the transaction price provides evidence of fair value or to determine the adjustments to transaction prices that are necessary to measure the fair value of the instrument. The focus therefore is not about the market activity per se, but whether the transaction price observed represents fair value.

Characteristics of an inactive market include a significant decline in the volume and level of trading activity, significant variance of available prices over time or among market participants and the prices are not current. However, these factors alone do not necessarily mean that a market is no longer active.

Irrespective of whether the market is active or not, the objective in establishing fair value is to determine the price at which a transaction would occur in the relevant instrument, in the instrument as it is without modification or repackaging.

5.2.1 *Which market?*

Market quotations may vary widely from dealer to dealer and from broker to broker. It may be necessary to obtain more than one quotation from these markets to ensure that the fair value estimate is appropriate. If there is more than one quote, there may be effectively more than one market and the fair value should be based on the most advantageous market to which the entity has immediate access. [IAS 39.AG71]

It is sometimes possible for an entity to have access to more than one exit market for a financial instrument, and prices in those markets may be different – for example, where the same instrument is traded in different geographical markets, or where dealers and brokers give different quotes for the same instrument and effectively create more than one market.

The following considerations are relevant.

- An entity should consider alternative prices only if it has access to the exit markets involved. An entity has access to a market if there is no legal impediment to its participation in that market.
- Where only portfolios of instruments can be traded in a particular market, an entity has access to that market only if it holds a portfolio that could be traded in that market.
- The entity should adjust the price in the more advantageous market to reflect differences in counterparty credit risk.

The term 'most advantageous' should be interpreted in view of the generic objective of maximising profits or net assets. The 'most advantageous' price for an asset is a higher market exit price; for a liability, a lower market exit price is the 'most advantageous'. When estimating the exit value for an instrument, any specific objective of an entity, or management intent, should be disregarded.

It is important that when deciding what is the 'most advantageous' price a comparison is made on a 'like-with-like' basis. Any dissimilarities need to be adjusted for as there could be some differences in transaction costs or value enhancements. Ignoring transaction costs for comparison purposes will not show what is most advantageous to the entity. However, once the comparison is made, the price actually used as an estimate of fair value should not be adjusted to include transaction costs (see **3.1** above and **example 5.2.1A** below).

The following examples are relevant.

Example 5.2.1A

Transactions costs in different markets

An entity can sell a financial asset in two different markets:

Market	Quoted market price	Transaction costs
A	CU80	CU2
B	CU85	CU10

Transaction costs should be taken into account when determining the most advantageous market. This will be Market A since the net cash inflow from disposal of CU78 exceeds that available from Market B (CU75). Therefore, the estimate of fair value that is appropriate is CU80 (i.e. disregarding transaction costs that will be incurred on disposal).

Example 5.2.1B

Most advantageous price

If an entity needs to sell an asset quickly and therefore will not be able to realise the optimum price, it should not adjust the market price and report the asset at a value lower than the 'most advantageous' price. Any subsequent loss is the result of the sub-optimal disposal (and should be recorded only when that disposal occurs).

US GAAP comparison: Under US GAAP, FAS 157 states, in part, "A fair value measurement assumes that the transaction to sell the asset or transfer the liability occurs in the principal market for the asset or liability or, in the absence of a principal market, the most advantageous market for the asset or liability." This concept is considered from the reporting entity's perspective and can result in different fair value measurements by different reporting entities for the same asset or liability. For example, assume a retail counterparty enters into an interest rate swap with a securities dealer in a retail market. The retail counterparty will use its exit price in the retail market (its principal market) to measure the fair value of the swap, while the securities dealer will use its exit price in the interdealer market (its principal market) to measure the fair value of the swap.

5.2.2 *Which price?*

Exchange markets provide the most reliable estimate of fair value since closing prices and volumes are readily and regularly available. The fair value is simply the closing price at the end of the last trading day of the reporting period for an instrument identical to the one being measured. Listed shares, some options, some futures and many fixed income securities are traded on public exchanges like the London Stock Exchange, the New York Stock Exchange and Euronext. IAS 39.AG71 states that where such published price quotations exist, they should be used provided quoted prices represent actual and regularly occurring market transactions.

In dealer markets, such as the US NASDAQ and UK Alternative Investment Market (AIM), dealers stand ready to trade for their own account. Quotations are in the form of bid and ask amounts and are typically more readily available than information about closing prices and volume levels. Dealer markets are the principal exchanges for more narrowly traded securities, corporate bonds, commercial and industrial loans, asset-backed and mortgage-backed securities.

A bid quote normally represents an exit price for an asset, already adjusted for some exit costs (dealer's profit); whilst an ask quote normally represents an exit price for a liability, already adjusted for some exit costs (dealer's profit). The Standard clarifies that when these terms are used, the 'bid-ask spread' (i.e. the difference between the bid and ask for a particular instrument) should be interpreted as including only transaction costs. The quote that will normally be appropriate will differ, depending on whether the relevant instrument is an asset/liability that is held/to be acquired.

	Asset	**Liability**
Held	Bid	Ask *
To be acquired	Ask *	Bid

* Sometimes referred to as the 'current offer' price

The appropriate quoted market price for an asset held or liability to be issued is usually the current bid price and, for an asset to be acquired or liability held, the asking price. When an entity has assets and liabilities with offsetting market risks, it may use mid-market prices as a basis for establishing fair values for the offsetting risk positions and apply the bid or asking price to the net open position as appropriate. [IAS 39.AG72]

Example 5.2.2A

Mid-market prices (1)

Entity X has the following financial instruments:

Asset:
Investment in 100 shares of Entity Y (an unrelated third party). The assets are classified as available-for-sale.

Liability:
Obligation to deliver 80 shares of Entity Y. The liability is held for trading. The liability was created following the entity selling shares in Entity Y that, at the time of the arrangement, Entity X did not own. This is commonly referred to as 'shorting' the shares.

The bid price for shares in Entity Y is CU100, the ask price is CU102. Therefore, the mid-price is CU101 per share.

	Asset	**Liability**
Held	Bid (CU100)	Ask (CU102)
To be acquired	Ask (CU102)	Bid (CU100)

Entity X will value its financial instruments as follows:

Asset:	
Investment in 80 shares of Entity Y at mid price	CU8,080
Investment in 20 shares of Entity Y at bid price	CU2,000
Sum	CU10,080
Liability:	
Obligation to deliver 80 shares of Entity Y at mid price	CU8,080

The net of the asset and the liability is equal to CU2,000, being the bid price applied to the open net asset position.

Example 5.2.2B

Mid-market prices (2)

An investment fund holds financial assets and puttable financial liabilities linked to the performance of the assets. The entity elects to designate both the assets and liabilities as at fair value through profit or loss. As the assets and liabilities have offsetting market risks, i.e. the market risk of the assets is offset by the market risk of the liabilities, it is permitted to apply mid-market prices for both. As the liability is linked to the performance of all invested assets there will be no open net position in this case.

US GAAP comparison: Under US GAAP, FAS 157 permits mid-market pricing as a practical expedient. Moreover, FAS 157 indicates that a reporting entity should measure fair value by using the price within the bid-ask spread that is most representative of fair value. If the practical expedient is not used, a reporting entity would most likely use the bid price to measure the fair value of its assets and the ask price to measure the fair value of its liabilities.

The existence of regulations that require a different measurement for specific purposes is not justification for overriding the general requirements of IAS 39.AG72. For example, a regulator may require investment funds to report net asset values based on mid-market prices. If measuring at mid-prices was not compliant with IAS 39, then the entity could not apply such a technique in measuring its financial instruments. In reporting its net asset values to investors, an investment fund may wish to provide a reconciliation between fair values recognised in its statement of financial position and the prices used for the net asset value calculation. [IAS 39.IG.E.2.1]

In certain types of market, published price quotations will often not be available. Brokered markets, in which brokers attempt to match buyers and sellers but do not trade for their own account, can sometimes provide quotations for comparable completed transactions. Such information, provided it can reasonably be obtained from brokers, may represent 'actual and regularly occurring market transactions', but that will not always be the case. Similarly, prices obtained from industry groups, pricing services, regulatory agencies and other sources will need to be considered on their own merits.

5.2.3 *Other issues*

Components. If a published price quotation does not exist for a financial instrument in its entirety, but active markets exist for its component parts, fair value is determined on the basis of the market prices of those components. [IAS 39.AG72]

Large holdings. The fair value of a large holding of financial instruments is the product of the number of instruments in the holding and the fair value of an individual instrument. [IAS 39.AG72] No adjustment should be made for any premium or discount that might result from selling the portfolio as a whole. For example, an entity with a significant shareholding in another entity would often realise an amount per share in excess of, or perhaps less than, that share's market price if it were to dispose of its entire shareholding in a single transaction. The carrying amount of such a shareholding should not be adjusted to reflect this fact. The IASB's concept of fair value is based on estimating the price that would be achieved in a routine arm's length transaction under the market conditions at the measurement date. The definition is drawn within a going concern context, hence it does not assume that the entity needs to liquidate the whole position or enter into a transaction on adverse terms by accepting a discount to the market price.

Current prices unavailable. Where current prices are not available, the price of the most recent transaction in that instrument will often provide evidence of its current value. This is essentially the use of a valuation technique and is discussed in **5.3** below.

Restrictions. An entity may enter into restrictions which limit its ability to sell an underlying financial instrument. These contractual arrangements must be considered carefully to determine whether the restriction forms part of the underlying financial instrument or is a separate contractual arrangement that has been entered into by the holder of the instrument. Restrictions that form part of the contractual terms of the instrument would be incorporated into the fair value of that instrument. However, restrictions that are not part of the contractual terms of the instrument do not form part of that instrument and should not impact its fair value. For example, if the fair value of an investment in an equity security is traded in an active market but the entity separately agrees not to sell that security within a specified period, the fair value is equal to the price quoted in that active market. The opportunity loss from not being able to sell the security arises because of the separate agreement the holder has entered into (which would not normally be recognised in the statement of financial position) and does not arise from the equity security itself.

The IFRIC received a request for guidance on whether a discount must be applied to the quoted market price when establishing the fair value of a security quoted in an active market when there is a contractual, governmental or other legally enforceable restriction that prevents the sale of the security for a specified period. Guidance was requested only in situations in which the restriction applied to the current holder of the security and would not transfer to another entity. In November 2008 the IFRIC noted that any guidance it could provide would be in the nature of implementation guidance rather than an Interpretation. In its view, any additional guidance that is necessary should be provided by the Board in its project on fair value measurement (see **8.1** below). The IFRIC therefore decided not to add the issue to its agenda.

US GAAP comparison: If an equity security has a restriction that is governmental or contractual by nature and that restriction lasts more than twelve months from the end of the reporting period, it is scoped out of FAS 115 and is measured at cost. A pledge is not considered a restriction for that purposes. FAS 157 provides guidance for securities with restrictions on its sale or use. A fair value measurement for a restricted security under FAS 157 should consider the effect of the restriction if other market participants would consider the effect of the restriction in pricing the security (i.e. the restriction would pass along to the market participant acquiring the security).

5.3 Valuation techniques

If the market for a financial instrument is not active, it will be necessary to use a valuation technique to ascertain fair value. Depending on the type and complexity of the instrument involved, and the availability of reliable input data, the nature of the appropriate technique may differ markedly. The main types are considered in the remainder of this section. Valuation techniques should incorporate all factors that market participants would consider in setting a price. [IAS 39.AG76]

Choosing a valuation technique is a highly judgemental exercise involving the selection of a method, formulae and assumptions. The risk that a technique is incorrectly specified, is based on questionable assumptions, or does not accurately reflect the true behaviour of the market is known as model risk. Model risk will be present whenever a valuation technique is used, since no technique is a perfect substitute for values evidenced by market transactions. Regardless of the level of sophistication, valuation techniques produce only a theoretical representation of market value.

Most valuation techniques are founded on arbitrage arguments, i.e. that there is no such thing as a risk-free profit in the marketplace. If there is no risk-free profit, the theoretical value of a financial instrument will be equal to the value of an equivalent alternative investment. Most techniques therefore involve evaluation of the cash flows of equivalent alternative investments.

In general, if there is a technique that is frequently used and well accepted by market participants, the entity should use that technique. However, care should be taken to ensure that the techniques used have historically provided reliable estimates of the prices obtained in actual transactions. [IAS 39.AG74] In order to assess the validity of the technique used, an entity should periodically calibrate its valuation techniques using prices from a current market transaction or based on any available observable market data. [IAS 39.AG76]

The IASB's Expert Advisory Panel report notes that where a valuation technique uses unobservable inputs an entity may use multiple valuation techniques to corroborate the results of each model. An entity should consider (and weigh) the different valuation techniques in arriving at the fair value of the instrument, placing more weight on the approaches that use observable inputs.

For any valuation technique that is used an entity includes appropriate risk adjustments that market participants would make. These will include adjustments for liquidity and credit risk. A valuation technique that does not include all the factors that a market participant would make in pricing the instrument does not represent an estimate of a current transaction price on the measurement date. Model risk adjustments that reflect deficiencies in models highlighted through calibration of the model may also be needed. As market conditions change it may be necessary to either change the models used or to make additional adjustments to model valuations. Adjustments are not appropriate if they adjust the measurement away from fair value, for example for conservatism or prudence.

The report acknowledges that different entities can come to different conclusions as to what is the fair value of an instrument in an inactive market. The fact that different estimates of fair value exist reflects the different judgements and assumptions applied and the inherent uncertainty of estimating the fair value of instruments that do not have prices quoted in an active market. The report notes, however, that a single entity should apply judgement consistently, across time and by type of instrument, when measuring fair value.

5.3.1 Inputs to valuation techniques

IAS 39.AG75 states explicitly that the valuation techniques used to estimate fair value should make the maximum use of market inputs and rely as little as possible on entity-specific inputs. This approach is consistent with the Standard's overall notion of fair value and promotes comparability between entities. The estimates and assumptions used in a valuation technique should be consistent with those that market participants would use in setting a price for a financial instrument and therefore will include adjustments, for example for liquidity and credit risk, that a market participant would make in determining fair value.

The technique used should not just attempt to replicate the market's valuation technique, it should also ensure that the inputs to the technique reflect market conditions on the measurement date and represent the market's assessment of the return required for an instrument of similar risk to that which is being measured (i.e. instrument specific factors).

If a rate, rather than a price, is quoted in an active market, that market-quoted rate should be used as an input into a valuation technique. [IAS 39.AG73]

IAS 39.AG82 identifies a number of factors that may influence the fair value of a financial instrument:

- time value of money (i.e. interest at the risk-free rate);
- credit risk (both counterparty credit risk for a financial asset and own credit risk for a financial liability);
- foreign currency exchange rates;
- commodity prices;
- equity prices;
- volatility;
- prepayment or surrender risk; and
- servicing costs.

The list is not intended to be exhaustive and will apply in the valuation of non-derivative and derivative financial instruments.

Although liquidity risk is not included in the list in IAS 39.AG82 reproduced above the IASB's Expert Advisory Panel report refers to the inclusion of a market participant's view of liquidity risk as a factor that should be incorporated in valuation techniques.

The IASB's Expert Advisory Panel report notes that there are various potential sources for reflecting own credit risk in a valuation of a financial liability. For example, the senior debt issue credit curve of the entity, credit default swap spreads, structured loan note issue curves and asset swap spreads. The curve, as well as any adjustments from that curve, that are used as an input in fair valuing a financial liability will depend on the instrument being valued as well as quality of the data available. The credit data that is incorporated into the valuation technique must be the most relevant and representationally faithful information that market participants would use to reflect the entity's credit risk in measuring the fair value of the instrument.

Credit risk adjustments should reflect any collateral that is 'ring fenced' (i.e. legally separated from the obligor). Collateral may include charges on specific assets, or assets that have the same counterparty as the counterparty to the financial liability. In the case of default by the obligor under a master netting arrangement the credit exposure of the obligor is limited to the net liability position it has with the counterparty and therefore the credit risk adjustment applied to the financial liabilities will reflect this. This is common in netting arrangements between financial institutions.

The seniority of the rights the counterparty has to claim against the obligor in case of default will impact the obligor's credit risk adjustment. All other things being equal, the credit risk is greater for more junior liabilities compared to senior liabilities. Also, the extent to which some financial liabilities are secured with collateral will impact the credit risk of other, less secured, financial liabilities.

In March 2009 the IFRIC issued an agenda notice titled, *Fair value measurements of financial instruments in inactive markets: determining the discount rate.* The agenda notice was responding to a proposal on how a discount rate should be determined when fair value is established using a valuation technique. The IFRIC were not supportive of the proposal as they considered it may suggest that a valuation technique should consider factors differently from the way a market participant would be expected to consider them so as to arrive at a price that is different from the price a market participant would determine. This approach would not be consistent with IAS 39. The IFRIC noted that IAS 39 states that the objective of using a valuation technique is to establish what the transaction price would have been on the measurement date in an arms length exchange motivated by normal business considerations. Therefore, that measurement incorporates all factors that market participants would consider in setting a price and is consistent with accepted economic methodologies for pricing financial instruments. The IFRIC also noted that the Expert Advisory Panel report explains how experts measure and disclose the fair values of financial instruments in inactive markets. The IFRIC believed that any new or amended guidance that is necessary should be provided as a result of the Board's joint activities with the FASB and its fair value measurement project. Therefore the IFRIC decided not to add this issue to its agenda.

The IASB's Expert Advisory Panel report notes that there are various potential sources for reflecting own credit risk in a valuation of a financial liability. For example, the senior debt issue credit curve of the entity, credit default swap spreads, structured loan note issue curves and asset swap spreads. The curve, as well as any adjustments from that curve, that are used as an input in fair valuing a financial liability will depend on the instrument being valued as well as quality of the data available. The credit data that is incorporated into the valuation technique must be the most relevant and representationally faithful information that market participants would use to reflect the entity's credit risk in measuring the fair value of the instrument.

Credit risk adjustments should reflect any collateral that is 'ring fenced' (i.e. legally separated from the obligor). Collateral may include charges on specific assets, or assets that have the same counterparty as the counterparty to the financial liability. In the case of default by the obligor under a master netting arrangement the credit exposure of the obligor is limited to the net liability position it has with the counterparty and therefore the credit risk adjustment applied to the financial liabilities will reflect this. This is common in netting arrangements between financial institutions.

The seniority of the rights the counterparty has to claim against the obligor in case of default will impact the obligor's credit risk adjustment. All other things being equal, the credit risk is greater for more junior liabilities compared to senior liabilities. Also, the extent to which some financial liabilities are secured with collateral will impact the credit risk of other, less secured, financial liabilities.

The extent to which an entity may place reliance on a value or input provided by a third party (for example, a broker quote or pricing service) for an instrument that is not quoted in an active market, will depend on how the third party has derived that valuation and whether it is in accordance with the requirements of IAS 39. The greater the transparency as to how a third party has derived the price, the greater the ability to validate the price and place reliance on it. Factors to consider include:

- whether it reflects a price at which the entity could be expected to transact (for example, a market to which the entity has access);
- whether and how the valuation incorporates recent market events (for example, does it include 'stale' prices);
- how frequently the valuation is updated to reflect changing market conditions;
- the number of sources from which the valuation is derived (a valuation derived from many quotes or data sources is generally preferable to one based on a small number of observations);
- whether it reflects actual transactions or binding offers (for example, a market maker) or merely indicative prices or indicative spreads; and

- whether it is consistent with available market information, including any current market transactions in the same or similar instruments.

The IASB's Expert Advisory Panel report provides a significant amount of guidance on using prices obtained from brokers and/or pricing services. The report notes that a price from a broker or pricing service is not necessarily determinative of fair value if an active market does not exist for the instrument. In an inactive market brokers and price services will likely rely on valuation techniques using inputs that are not necessarily based on actual transactions. An entity cannot rely on third party brokers and pricing services without understanding the basis on which the price is determined and whether it is consistent with the definition of fair value in IAS 39.

Sourcing prices from multiple sources, as opposed to a single source, will typically provide a better indication of fair value. If multiple sources are used an understanding is needed of the pricing differences between sources and whether these differences fall within an acceptable range without an need for further investigation. A narrow range is likely to be more indicative of fair value. If prices are widely dispersed, an entity will consider the price in the range that best represents the price at which an orderly transaction would take place between market participants on the measurement date. This is preferable to simply averaging the various prices as an average price will not represent a price at which a transaction would take place.

The Panel noted that if an entity is measuring fair values that are material to the financial statements it is normally not appropriate to rely on a single broker quote. More reliance can be placed on prices from a broker that has a larger presence in the market compared to other brokers, has experience and expertise to provide a representationally faithful quote, and on brokers who originally brokered the instrument and therefore benefit from information asymmetry. In validating a third party's ability to provide prices that represent fair value it may be possible to compare previous prices obtained from brokers and pricing services with subsequent actual transactions to determine how well they compared. Care will be required if the timing between the quote and the actual transaction is significant or market conditions had changed.

Broker quotes or pricing services may be used to validate an entity's own valuation models. To the extent the entity's own model produces prices within an acceptable range of prices derived from third party brokers or pricing services it may rely on its own model. If the model prices fall outside the range of prices from third parties the entity will use judgement in weighting the third party prices as an input to a fair value measurement.

Pricing services may provide prices based on a consensus of prices provided to them from their subscribers. Subscribers may be large financial institutions with a good track record of valuations and depth in the market for the underlying instruments being valued. The pricing service is independent of the prices being submitted and attempts to 'cleanse' submitted prices in order to provide its subscribers information about how closely their prices compare with the generated consensus price. The reliance that can be placed on a consensus price used to calibrate an entity's valuation technique will depend on the degree to which subscriber's prices are derived from actual transactions, knowledge and market presence of the subscriber, and the quality of the cleansing process that eliminates outlying prices. An entity will need to consider all these factors before relying on a consensus price as representative of fair value, or as an input into a valuation technique.

5.3.2 *Recent transaction price*

The most straightforward 'valuation technique' is to base the estimate of fair value on a recent transaction price in an identical instrument. The initial acquisition or origination of a financial asset, or incurrence of a financial liability, is a market transaction for this purpose.

A recent transaction price will provide evidence of current fair value, as long as there has been no significant change in economic conditions since the relevant transaction occurred. If conditions have changed, fair value should be adjusted to reflect that change by reference to current prices or rates for similar instruments. [IAS 39.AG72] For example, a significant announcement made after the date of the most recent transaction might indicate that, if a trade were to take place at the period end, it would not establish the same price as that observed at the time of that transaction.

Example 5.3.2

Valuation including changes in market interest rates

An entity holds an investment in a corporate bond of Entity X. Nominal value is CU100. The most recent transaction price, observed on the day before the measurement date, is CU117. The bond pays interest annually at a rate of 10 per cent. The next interest payment is due on the measurement date itself. On the measurement date, interest rates rose by 0.5 per cent. What is the fair value of the investment at the measurement date?

> There is a payment of interest on the measurement date and, all other factors staying equal, the fair value will be reduced to CU107 by the payment of the coupon. The fair value will also need to be adjusted for the change in market conditions: an increase in general interest rates would mean that there will be an upward adjustment to the market rate expected for an instrument of the same terms and credit risk as the bond of Entity X. Hence, the future cash flows of that bond will be discounted at a rate higher than that implied by the most recent transaction price and will produce a valuation lower than CU107.

It will not always be so straightforward to make the appropriate adjustments to a recent transaction price, since the necessary information will not always be readily available. For example, an entity holding a debt instrument that is not actively traded may not be able to determine the level of credit and other risk that market participants would attribute to the relevant counterparty when pricing the instrument. IAS 39.AG78 indicates that, in the absence of evidence to the contrary (e.g. information from other recent transactions that might indicate the appropriate credit spread), it would be reasonable to assume that no adjustment is necessary to the credit spread that existed when the instrument was acquired/originated. However, the entity would be expected to take reasonable steps to determine whether there is evidence that there has been a change in such factors.

Any events post period-end which would affect fair value would not normally be adjusted for since they would be expected to reflect circumstances arising in the following period rather than provide further evidence of the conditions existing at the end of the reporting period. IAS 10 *Events after the Reporting Period* treats a decline in market value of investments between the end of the reporting period and the date when the financial statements are authorised for issue as a non-adjusting event. IAS 10.11 states that 'the decline in market value does not normally relate to the condition of the investments at the end of the reporting period, but reflects circumstances that have arisen subsequently. Therefore, an entity does not adjust the amounts recognised in its financial statements for the investments. Similarly, the entity does not update the amounts disclosed for the investments as at the end of the reporting period, although it may need to give additional disclosure.'

A further complication will arise if it can be demonstrated that the last transaction price was not representative of fair value. This might be the case if, for example:

- the recent transaction occurred between two entities, one or both of which were experiencing severe financial difficulties such as bankruptcy, court orders, orders from regulators, or other extreme legal or financial pressures;

- the price established in a recent transaction would have been different if not for other transactions, contracts, or agreements between the transacting parties;
- the recent transaction is between related parties;
- the recent transaction was the sale of a large holding; or
- some publicly acknowledged errors or irregularities were affecting the observed price at the time of the recent transaction.

An entity will need to consider whether the valuation of a financial instrument should incorporate additional information that adjusts the last transaction price in order for the valuation technique to generate a fair value.

5.3.3 *Comparison to a similar instrument*

Another method of establishing fair value is to draw a comparison with a similar instrument to that being valued. Such an approach will be appropriate, provided the estimation of the effects of differences between the instruments on fair value is practicable.

The process of estimating fair value of an instrument by reference to a market exit price for a similar instrument is a three step process.

(i) Understand the instrument that needs to be measured.

(ii) Identify a similar instrument with a quoted market price (or a recent transaction that can be used to establish its fair value).

(iii) Quantify the effect of any differences and adjust the market price of the similar instrument for this effect.

In order for an instrument to be 'similar' for this purpose, it will be necessary for the two instruments to have contractually specified cash flows which are similar in amounts and timings, and have similar risk attributes. Risk attributes will be similar if both instruments have similar prepayment expectations, credit risk (including collateral) and marketability, and are issued by entities with similar industry and geographical bases.

Similarity can be affected by the absolute size of the investment: CU1 million placed on deposit often earns interest at a higher rate than CU1,000 placed on deposit. Therefore, the contractual cash flows of a CU1 million term deposit will be greater than those one would calculate using 1000 times the return on CU1,000, hence an adjustment would be required to achieve similarity.

It is important to note that the effect of any differences must be reasonably determinable. For example, with individual equity investments the differences are so significant that no two equity investments are ever likely to be similar – the value is affected by intangibles and other 'soft' assets like reputation and quality of management which, under the current reporting framework, are not recorded in the statement of financial position or measured in any consistent fashion, but which do affect the market price.

5.3.4 *Other valuation techniques*

It is not always possible to establish the fair value of an instrument by reference to market prices, as outlined above. In such situations it will be necessary to use an alternative technique. Appropriate techniques might range from simple discounted cash flow calculations to complex option pricing models (such as Black-Scholes-Merton and binomial models).

In applying a discounted cash flow analysis, an entity uses discount rates equal to the prevailing rates of return for financial instruments having substantially the same terms and characteristics, including the credit quality of the instrument, the remaining term over which the contractual interest rate is fixed, the remaining term to repayment of the principal and the currency in which payments are to be made. The discount rate is used to discount the contractual (or expected) cash flows. An alternative to discounting contractual cash flows by a market rate of return is to use probability-weighted cash flows and a risk-free rate of return to arrive at fair value. Irrespective of the technique used the objective in establishing fair value remains the same, being the price of an orderly transaction between market participants, remains the same.

The IASB's Expert Advisory Panel report provides some factors that might affect the market rate of return or probability-weighted cash flows to be used in a discounted cash flow technique:

- the timing of cash flows for the instrument;
- any uncertainty about the amount and timing of the cash flows;
- the risk that payments will not be made when due (credit risk);
- the liquidity of the instrument, and
- the currency in which payments are to be made.

As market prices reflect the market's best estimate of the present value of the future cash flows arising from an instrument, in one way or another, an alternative valuation technique will attempt to estimate this present value. The technique/model selected will need to be consistent with the objectives and criteria previously discussed in this section.

The IASB's Expert Advisory Panel report notes that over time valuation models evolve as techniques are refined to better reflect the price market participants would transact at. For example, as markets become more or less liquid, the model may be less capable of representing fair value. As models and/or assumptions used in models change it does not mean that models previously used to measure fair value were inappropriate. Changes to the model and assumptions are appropriate when it can be demonstrated that the new model and assumptions provide a better estimate of fair value.

5.3.5 *Day 1 P&L*

IAS 39 provides guidance on the initial and subsequent measurement of financial instruments where a valuation technique does not solely use observable market data (this is commonly referred to as 'day 1 p&l'). In such cases no gain or loss should be recognised on initial recognition of a financial instrument. Furthermore, a gain or loss shall be recognised subsequently only to the extent that it arises from a change in a factor (including time) that market participants would consider in setting a price. [IAS 39.AG76A]

Example 5.3.5A

Day 1 P&L (1)

Bank A sells a 30 year cash settled forward sale contract over a commodity to Entity B.

Forward prices for the specific commodity are freely quoted in the market for 10, 15, and 20 year periods. Bank A uses an extrapolation technique and its proprietary pricing system to estimate the 30 year forward rate and incorporates an additional premium on top of this internal price. Some of the premium may be received in cash at inception and some may be included in the contracted price of the forward contract.

The valuation technique uses both the available forward prices and Bank A's estimates of the commodity prices between years 20 and 30. As some of the inputs are entity specific and not observable, a day 1 profit cannot be recognised.

Example 5.3.5B

Day 1 P&L (2)

Investment Bank X issues credit-linked notes to institutional investors.

The credit-linked notes are debt instruments with an interest rate higher than normal bonds issued by the Bank because the performance of the notes is linked to the performance of a basket of underlying corporate bonds. The terms require that if a corporate bond in the basket defaults, then the notional principal will be reset on the next payment date to reflect the outstanding value of the remaining bonds in the basket. This term is commonly referred to as 'first-to-default', as it is the first bond in the basket that defaults which results in the early repayment of the notes at an amount less than was originally invested by the holder.

Bank X does not actually hold the corporate bonds that the credit-linked notes are linked to. Instead Bank X purchases a large number of credit default options over the individual corporate bonds. These purchased options serve as an economic hedge in case any of the referenced credits default. The remaining proceeds from issuing the credit-linked notes are invested in high quality government debt.

If the credit-linked notes are not traded in an active market, then Bank X must use a valuation technique to measure the financial liability. At inception it is assumed that the proceeds received from the issuance of the notes are equal to their fair value.

It would not be possible to recognise an upfront profit on initial recognition of the credit-linked notes, even if the sum paid to purchase the government bonds and the credit options is less than the proceeds from the notes if:

- there are no other observable current market transactions in the same credit-linked notes with the same terms over the same portfolio of corporate credits; or
- if the valuation of the credit-linked notes includes non-observable market data, e.g. default correlation data between the different corporate credits where this data is not sourced from observable markets.

Using unobservable inputs to calculate a fair value different to the transaction price on day 1 involves a high degree of subjectivity and therefore the day 1 profit should not be recognised immediately. There is little clarity as to when this gain or loss can be recognised. The deferred gain or loss should be released to profit or loss such that it reaches a value of zero at the time when the entire contract can be valued using active market quotes or verifiable objective market information. IAS 39BC222(u)(v)(ii) notes that straight-line amortisation may be an appropriate method in some cases, it will not be appropriate in others. If the instance where the item acts in a non-linear fashion, for example option based contracts, non-linear amortisation may be appropriate. An entity should determine a policy for amortisation. The following policies may be appropriate (i) calibrate your unobservable inputs to your transaction price and recognise the deferred gain or loss as your best estimate of those unobservable inputs change based on observable information, (ii) release the day 1 gain or loss in a reasonable fashion based on the facts and circumstances.

Example 5.3.5C

Day 1 P&L (3)

Entity A writes a call option over a specified financial asset to Entity B and receives a premium from Entity B. The option can be exercised by Entity B any time during the instrument's life. The written call option meets the definition of a derivative and is classified by Entity A as at fair value through profit or loss. Entity A uses its proprietary valuation model to fair value the written option as the instrument is not traded in an active market. The model uses observable inputs to the extent possible but also includes significant unobservable inputs. Entity A is not permitted to recognise an upfront gain or loss at initial recognition and measures the derivative at the transaction price. Per IAS 39.AG76A, Entity A should recognise in profit or loss changes in the fair value of the derivative that have occurred subsequent to initial recognition.

To illustrate, Entity A received CU500 for the written call option and the entity's proprietary model valued the instrument at CU300. Entity A initially recognises a derivative liability at CU500 equivalent to the consideration received. At the next measurement date, using the same proprietary model, the fair value of the instrument has fallen by CU100 and this fair value gain is recognised in profit or loss.

Entity A must determine an accounting policy for recognition of the initial difference of CU200 (CU500 – CU300) in profit or loss. Any amounts not recognised in profit or loss at the date of exercise or maturity will be recognised in profit or loss on that date.

US GAAP comparison: FAS 157 nullifies the previous guidance in EITF 02–3 that prohibited recognition of day 1 gains and losses, which was broadly similar to the guidance in IAS 39. Although FAS 157 notes that "in many cases, the transaction price will equal the exit price and, therefore, represent the fair value of the asset or liability at initial recognition," in certain instances such as the ones, listed below, the transaction price may not be equal to initial fair value:

- The transaction is between related parties.

- The transaction occurs under duress or the seller is forced to accept the price in the transaction. For example, that might be the case if the seller is experiencing financial difficulty.

- The unit of account represented by the transaction price is different from the unit of account for the asset or liability measured at fair value. For example, that might be the case if the asset or liability measured at fair value is only one of the elements in the transaction, the transaction includes unstated rights and privileges that should be separately measured, or the transaction price includes transaction costs.

- The market in which the transaction occurs is different from the market in which the reporting entity would sell the asset or transfer the liability, that is, the principal or most advantageous market. For example, those markets might be different if the reporting entity is a securities dealer that transacts in different markets, depending on whether the counterparty is a retail customer (retail market) or another securities dealer (inter-dealer market).

5.3.6 *Applying the fair value hierarchy*

The following table sets out how the fair value hierarchy is applied for instruments commonly used in the energy markets, starting from those quoted in an active market down to those which require other valuation techniques where a greater degree of subjectivity exists and greater use of judgement is required.

Price derivation process	**Example instruments**
Quoted price in an active (liquid) market.	Standard short dated wholesale trades such as NYMEX.
Comparable/proxy instrument with quoted price in an active market if there is a high degree of correlation with the instrument being valued. For example, quoted NBP gas prices may be used to value a contract for gas delivery at delivery point if there is a high level of correlation between NBP and delivery point market prices.	Standard short dated wholesale trades such as NBP '97, IPE, GTMA and oil swaps.

Price derivation process	Example instruments
Conventional model based on direct 'market' inputs.	Bilateral deals such as capacity, storage; non-market delivery periods such as overnights and short-dated vanilla options.
Conventional model based on indirect market inputs, such as interpolations of price curves or proxy market inputs. Interpolations can be used for unpriced periods using quoted market prices for points before and after that are not significantly spread apart in price and time, or for implied traded option volatility. Example proxy inputs would be using observable gas prices and heat rates to determine electricity prices if historical evidence and observable market information indicates there is a high degree of correlation with the proxy.	Bilateral deals such as capacity, storage; non-market delivery periods such as overnights and short-dated vanilla options.
Model based on more subjective inputs or proprietary models. Some subjective inputs may include: • estimates of option volatility (e.g. based on historical prices of the underlying); • forward curves constructed using econometric data such as expected supply and demand of commodities; and • extrapolation of price curves for terms beyond the periods in which there are active market quotes.	Complex bilateral contracts which: • are relatively long-term in comparison with similar contracts; • involve underlyings that are not supported by deep and active markets such as with developing contract types; and • involve complex or long-dated optionality.

US GAAP Comparison: The illustration above is an example of the application of valuation techniques using the guidance in IAS 39. FAS 157 in US GAAP has a specific hierarchy that must be applied in determining fair value of an instrument FAS 157 classifies valuation technique inputs into the following three broad levels:

- Level 1 — Inputs based on quoted prices (unadjusted) in active markets for identical assets or liabilities.
- Level 2 — Inputs based on observable market information.
- Level 3 — Inputs based on unobservable information.

This hierarchy was established to develop increased consistency and comparability within and between reporting entities. FAS 157 requires entities to use valuation techniques that maximise the use of observable inputs and minimise the use of unobservable inputs. FSP FAS 157–3, issued by the FASB in October of 2008, provides further clarification in applying the US GAAP hierarchy in specific instances of inactive markets or unobservable inputs. The concept of a fair value hierarchy underpins the IASB's discussion paper that is intended to be a base for future IFRS fair value guidance as discussed in **section 8** below.

5.4 Demand features

IAS 39 clarifies the approach that should be adopted in relation to financial liabilities with a demand feature (e.g. demand deposits). It states that the fair value of such liabilities is not less than the amount payable on demand, discounted from the first date that the amount could be required to be paid. [IAS 39.49] Put another way, it is not appropriate to apply a further discount to such liabilities to reflect an expectation that repayment will not be required on the first date possible (even if this expectation is supported by empirical evidence).

6 Impairment

IAS 39 requires all financial assets, with the exception of those measured at FVTPL, to be reviewed for impairment. The approach specified in the Standard is explained in this section.

The two most notable characteristics of the IAS 39 impairment model are:

(i) impairment losses should be recognised when they are incurred, rather than as expected;

(ii) an impairment loss should be regarded as incurred if, and only if, there is objective evidence of impairment as a result of one or more events that occurred after initial recognition (a 'loss event').

6.1 Evidence of impairment

The Standard requires an assessment, at the end of each reporting period, of whether there is any objective evidence that a financial asset or group of financial assets is impaired. An asset is impaired, and an impairment loss recognised, if and only if, such evidence exists. [IAS 39.58]

6.1.1 *Loss events*

Impairment losses are incurred on a financial asset or a group of financial assets if, and only if, there is objective evidence of an impairment that results from one or more events that occurred after the initial recognition of the asset (a 'loss event'). [IAS 39.59]

The following points are important to note.

- Such loss events must have an impact on the estimated future cash flows of the asset, or group of assets, that can be reliably measured.
- An impairment may occur as the result of the combined effect of several events – it is not always possible to identify a single, discrete event that caused the impairment.
- Losses expected as a result of future events are not recognised (no matter how likely those events might be).

The Standard gives a number of examples of possible loss events: [IAS 39.59]

(a) significant financial difficulty of the issuer or obligor;

(b) a breach of contract, such as a default or delinquency in interest or principal payments;

(c) the lender, for economic or legal reasons relating to the borrower's financial difficulty, granting to the borrower a concession that the lender would not otherwise consider;

(d) it becoming probable that the borrower will enter bankruptcy or other financial reorganisation;

(e) the disappearance of an active market for that financial asset because of financial difficulties; or

(f) observable data indicating that there is a measurable decrease in the estimated future cash flows from a group of financial assets since the initial recognition of those assets, although the decrease cannot yet be identified with the individual financial assets in the group, including:

(i) adverse changes in the payment status of borrowers in the group (e.g. an increased number of delayed payments or an increased number of credit card borrowers who have reached their credit limit and are paying the minimum monthly amount); or

(ii) national or local economic conditions that correlate with defaults on the assets in the group (e.g. an increase in the unemployment rate in the geographical area of the borrowers, a decrease in property prices for mortgages in the relevant area, a decrease in oil prices for loan assets to oil producers, or adverse changes in industry conditions that affect the borrowers in the group).

The following are not, in themselves, evidence of an impairment.

- In contrast to (e) above, the disappearance of an active market because an entity's financial instruments are no longer publicly traded.
- A downgrading of an entity's credit rating, in the absence of other information suggesting the occurrence of a loss event.
- A decline in the fair value of a financial asset below its cost or amortised cost (the Standard gives the example of a decline in the fair value of a debt instrument resulting from an increase in the risk-free interest rate).

A change in the fair value of a fixed rate debt investment due to movements in the *risk-free interest rate* would never by itself be objective evidence of impairment. Also, changes in the fair value of a fixed rate debt investment due to movements in market interest rates will generally not be indicative of impairment as movements in market interest rates are never specific to the credit quality of the investment that is held. [IAS 39.IG.E.4.10]

However, it is possible that a fall in fair value due to an increase in the borrower's specific interest rate (i.e. due to an increase in the credit spread of the borrower) could be indicative of impairment when considered with other evidence supporting that a loss event has been incurred. [IAS 39.AG22(a)]

In the case of available-for-sale debt investments that have already been subject to recognition of impairment losses and there continues to be evidence of impairment, further declines in the fair value of the investment due to a change in the risk-free interest rate is evidence of impairment. See **6.4.3.2** below.

US GAAP Comparison: Under US GAAP, an entity recognises an impairment loss on an AFS or HTM security if a decline in fair value below amortised cost is other than temporary. An other-than-temporary impairment loss must be recognised if it is probable that the investor will not (1) collect all amounts contractually due (including principal and interest) on a debt security (FAS 115) or (2) recover an amount equal to or greater than the carrying value of the security (SAB Topic 5.M). Impairment of a loan is recognised when, based on current information and events, it is probable that a creditor will be unable to collect all amounts due according to the contractual terms of the loan agreement.

In March 2009 the FASB issued a proposed FSP, *Recognition and Presentation of Other-Than-Temporary Impairments*. The proposal would require entities to separate out an other-than-temporary impairment of a debt security into two components when there are credit losses associated with an impaired debt security for which management asserts that it does not have the intent to sell the security and it is more likely than not that it will not have to sell the security before recovery of its cost basis. The two components would be (a) the credit component and (b) the non-credit component (residual related to other factors). The IASB also issued a request for views on the proposed FSP in March 2009. As the IASB did not participate in the development of the FSP the proposals represents views of the FASB only. At the date of writing the comment periods for the FSP and the IASB's request for views remained open.

Losses that are expected to arise as a result of future events are not recognised. This holds true no matter how likely such events might be. The most obvious example of an expected future event in this context is the future default of a counterparty if a default was expected already at origination. Often an entity will have reliable empirical evidence of the rate of default for a particular class of borrower. However, the existence of such evidence does not imply that an impairment loss should be recorded. Otherwise, a 'day-one' loss would be recorded upon the origination or acquisition of many financial assets (future cash flows used to calculate the effective interest rate do not reflect future credit losses – see **4.1.1** above). At origination, the effective interest rate assumes the borrower will meet all their contractual obligations and will not default even though the probability of default is factored into the interest rate the lender will charge the borrower. This 'incurred loss', as opposed to 'expected loss', approach is a key characteristic of the impairment model of IAS 39.

For example, if a financial asset is purchased at a discount to its initial issue price because there has been a worsening of the credit quality of the counterparty (but there is no loss event) between the issue date and the acquisition date, the effective interest rate will reflect the rate that exactly discounts the cash flows until maturity without taking into account expected credit losses. The effective interest rate therefore will be higher than the rate that would have been achieved had the asset been purchased originally at the issue date. Even though the credit spread inherent in the effective interest rate is higher than it is at inception, this is not evidence of impairment itself. When a loss event occurs, only then will an impairment loss be recognised.

In some cases, financial assets are acquired at a deep discount that reflects incurred credit losses. Entities include such incurred credit losses in the estimated cash flows when computing the effective interest rate. [IAS 39.AG5]

It is not necessary to be able to identify a single, discrete event in order to conclude that an impairment loss has occurred. In addition to point (e) of the list above, the following factors should be considered in determining whether there is objective evidence that an impairment loss has been incurred:
[IAS 39.IG.E.4.1]

- information about the counterparty's liquidity, solvency and business and financial risk exposures;
- levels of and trends in delinquencies for similar financial assets;
- national and local economic trends and conditions; and
- the fair value of collateral and guarantees.

In assessing financial assets or groups of financial assets for impairment an entity considers financial guarantees and any existing collateral. IAS 39.AG84 states that when considering impairment an entity should take into account the cash flows from the foreclosure of collateral. IAS 39.IG.E.4.1 states that in determining whether there is objective evidence that an impairment loss has been incurred the entity must consider the existence of guarantees over the financial asset. The accounting for financial guarantee contract is detailed at **2.3.2** in **chapter 1**. As the effect of guarantees are incorporated into the impairment assessment an entity will not recognise both a contingent asset for the claim under a financial guarantee contract in the case of loss under a specified asset and an equal impairment loss on that recognised specified asset. Instead the existence of the guarantee will limit the impairment loss recognised.

6.1.2 *Equity investments*

In addition to the potential loss events discussed above, further factors will apply when considering the impairment of equity investments. Information about significant changes with an adverse effect that have taken place in the technological, market, economic or legal environment in which the issuer operates may constitute objective evidence of an impairment. A significant or prolonged decline in fair value (below cost) is objective evidence of impairment and therefore will result in the fair value loss being reclassified from other comprehensive income to profit or loss. [IAS 39.61] Also see **6.4.1** below.

When considering what is a 'significant or prolonged decline in fair value' of an equity security below cost, the investor must compare the original cost in the investor's functional currency at the date of acquisition compared with the fair value of the equity security, also in the investor's functional currency, on the re-measurement date. If an entity purchased a listed foreign currency denominated equity security whose fair value in local currency terms has remained relatively stable since acquisition, but the currency depreciated significantly or has been depreciating for a prolonged period, this would constitute impairment, as losses that are attributable to foreign currency losses are a portion of the overall net fair value loss of an equity security.

US GAAP comparison: Under US GAAP, a decline in the fair value of an investment in an equity security below cost is recognised as an impairment loss if the decline is considered other than temporary (FAS 115). To determine whether a decline is other than temporary requires significant judgement, and management should consider various factors including the intent and ability of the investor to hold the investment until its forecasted recovery and the severity and duration of the impairment. This could lead to timing differences in the recognition of impairment under US GAAP and IFRS.

The Standard contains separate rules for the measurement of impairment losses to be applied to financial assets that are (i) carried at amortised cost; (ii) carried at cost; and, (iii) classified as available-for-sale.

6.2 Assets carried at amortised cost

The requirements outlined in this section are relevant for financial assets classified as either loans and receivables or held-to-maturity.

Once an impairment loss has been identified, its amount is measured as the difference between the asset's carrying amount and the present value of estimated future cash flows, discounted at the original effective interest rate. This amount is then recognised in profit or loss. The carrying amount of the asset is reduced, either directly or through use of an allowance account. [IAS 39.63] However, as a practical expedient, the impairment loss can be measured on the basis of an asset's fair value using an observable market price. [IAS 39.AG84]

In circumstances in which there is a range of possible amounts, a loss equal to the best estimate within that range should be recognised. Where there is a continuous range of possible amounts, and each point in that range is as likely as any other, the mid-point of the range is used.

For collateralised assets, the estimated cash flows that should be used to calculate any impairment reflect the cash flows that might result from foreclosure, less the costs of obtaining and selling the collateral. [IAS 39.AG84] Collateral should not be recognised as a separate asset before foreclosure. [IAS 39.IG.E.4.8]

6.2.1 Discount rate

In calculating an impairment loss, expected future cash flows are discounted at the original effective interest rate. As a result, **only** the effect of the reduction in cash flows is recognised as a loss – that amount is not affected by other factors (for example, changes in the market interest rate, or the credit rating of the borrower) that might impact on the fair value of the asset.

Where the terms of a loan are renegotiated due to the financial difficulties of the borrower/issuer, any impairment is still measured by reference to the original effective interest rate before the modification of terms. [IAS 39.AG84]

Two particular instances in which a different rate should be used are as follows.

(i) For a variable rate asset, impairment should be measured using the current effective interest rate determined under the contract (see **4.1.2** above).

(ii) The carrying amount of an asset designated as a hedging item in a fair value hedge of interest rate risk will be adjusted for fair value changes attributable to interest rate movements. The original effective interest rate then becomes irrelevant and the rate is recalculated using the adjusted carrying amount of the loan. [IAS 39.IG.E.4.4]

The IAS 39 impairment model is illustrated in the simple example below.

Example 6.2.1A

Determining the amount of impairment for a loan

On 1 January 20X0, an entity originates a loan of CU100. The loan attracts five annual repayments of CU25 on 31 December 20X0 to 31 December 20X4. Ignoring future credit losses, it is expected that all contractual cash flows will be received, hence the effective interest rate is 7.93 per cent and the following entries are recorded in the entity's 20X0 accounts:

(1) Initial recognition

Dr	Asset	CU100.00
Cr	Cash	CU100.00

(2) Interest income

Dr	Asset	CU7.93
Cr	Interest income	CU7.93

(3) Repayment

Dr	Cash	CU25.00
Cr	Asset	CU25.00

The carrying amount of the loan as at 31 December 20X0 is therefore CU82.93. On 1 January 20X1, the entity receives information regarding the future prospects of the sector in which the borrower operates. This information coincides with a downgrading of the borrower's credit rating. Together, these two occurrences are deemed to constitute a loss event and it is now expected that the 20X3 and 20X4 repayments will not be received.

The revised carrying amount of the loan is calculated by discounting the expected future cash flows (i.e. the 20X1 and 20X2 repayments) at the original effective interest rate:

CU25/1.0793 + CU25/1.0793^2 = CU44.62

Therefore an impairment loss of CU38.31 (i.e. CU82.93 – CU44.62) is recorded:

Dr	Profit or loss	CU38.31
Cr	Asset	CU38.31

If an investment in a debt instrument is reclassified out of FVTPL or AFS the entity must determine an effective interest rate at the date of reclassification because the fair value of the date of reclassification becomes its new deemed amortised cost. In the case of a debt instrument reclassified out of AFS any amounts recognised in other comprehensive income must be amortised to profit or loss as part of the revised effective interest rate if the debt instrument has a maturity. If the reclassified debt instrument is subsequently impaired any unamortised amounts in other comprehensive income must be reclassified from other comprehensive income to profit or loss along with the impairment loss. (IAS 39.54(a) & 50F)

Example 6.2.1B

Reclassification from AFS to L&R and subsequent impairment

In June 20X0, Bank A purchases asset-backed securities that are linked to an underlying portfolio of corporate bonds held by the issuer of the asset-backed securities. The investment is known as a "cash CDO". The investment matures in 20Y0 at its par value of CU100 million although, depending on prepayments and restructuring of the underlying corporate bond portfolio, the asset-backed securities may redeem earlier. The investment is classified by Bank A as AFS.

At 30 June 20X3, the investment has declined in fair value to CU70 million and the asset-backed securities and the underlying portfolio of corporate bonds are no longer traded in an active market. The AFS reserve in other comprehensive income is CU30 million as the investment has not been subject to impairment.

On 1 July 20X3, Bank A reclassifies the investment to the loans and receivables category as the entity has the intention and ability to hold the investment for the foreseeable future. Bank A has an accounting policy of applying the loans and receivables definition at the date of reclassification, as opposed to the date of initial recognition (see **4.2** in **chapter 2**). At the date of reclassification its opening amortised cost equals its fair value, being $70 million. Bank A estimates that it will recover all the contractual cash flows on the investment with an expected redemption in June 20X8. The contractual cash flows are as follows:

Date	**Coupon – CU**	**Principal – CU**
30 June 20X4	6	
30 June 20X5	6	
30 June 20X6	6	
30 June 20X7	6	
30 June 20X8	6	100

The EIR that exactly discounts these future cash flows to the fair value of the investment at the date of reclassification is 14.9%. This new EIR is then used to amortise the difference between the amortised cost of the CDO at the date of reclassification and the redemption value until the expected maturity date. Accordingly, the amortised cost will accrete as follows:

Date	**Amortised cost b/f – CU**	**Interest income at 14.9% – CU**	**Coupons – CU**	**Amortised cost c/f – CU**
30 June 20X4	70.0	10.5	(6.0)	74.5
30 June 20X5	74.5	11.1	(6.0)	79.6
30 June 20X6	79.6	11.9	(6.0)	85.5
30 June 20X7	85.5	12.7	(6.0)	92.2
30 June 20X8	92.2	13.8	(6.0)	100.0

The debit in the available-for-sale reserve in OCI of CU30 million is frozen at the date of reclassification and will be amortised to profit or loss over the remaining life of the CDO by applying an effective interest rate. As a result, profit or loss impact will be as follows:

Date	AFS reserve b/f – CU	Amortisation of AFS reserve in profit or loss – CU	AFS reserve c/f	Interest income at 14.9% – CU	Net interest income – CU
30 June 20X4	(30.0)	(4.5)	(25.5)	10.5	6.0
30 June 20X5	(25.5)	(5.1)	(20.4)	11.1	6.0
30 June 20X6	(20.4)	(5.9)	(14.5)	11.9	6.0
30 June 20X7	(14.5)	(6.7)	(7.8)	12.7	6.0
30 June 20X8	(7.8)	(7.8)	0	13.8	6.0

On 30 June 20X6, Bank A estimates there is a reduction in the recoverability of cash flows due to objective evidence of impairment. Bank A expects that it will no longer receive any coupon and that only 70% of principal amount will be recovered (i.e., CU70 million).

Applying IAS 39.54(a) & 67, Bank A reclassifies all of the residual AFS reserve in OCI (CU14.5) to profit or loss. Additionally, it records an impairment loss measured as the difference between the investment's carrying amount (CU85.5) and the present value of estimated future cash flows discounted at the investment's revised EIR (i.e., the EIR determined at the date of reclassification).

The present value of the expected future cash flows discounted using the EIR determined at the date of reclassification (14.9%) is CU53.0 million. The total impact on profit or loss is as follows:

Coupon Date	Net interest income – CU	Reclassification of AFS reserve to profit or loss – CU	Impairment loss on the investment – CU	Total impact on profit or loss – CU
30 June 20X6	6.0	(14.5)	(32.5)	(41.0)

The amortised cost of the investment will then accrete as follows:

Coupon Date	Amortised cost b/f	Interest income at 14.9% – CU	Coupons – CU	Amortised cost c/f
30 June 20X7	53.0	7.9	0	60.9
30 June 20X8	60.9	9.1	0	70.0

Following the impairment, the net amount recorded in profit or loss is only the interest income recorded using the EIR of 14.9% since the entire AFS revaluation has already been reclassified to profit or loss.

6.2.2 *Reversals*

If the amount of a past impairment loss decreases and the decrease can be related objectively to an event occurring after the impairment was recognised, then the impairment is reversed through profit or loss. However, the carrying amount should not be increased to an amount that exceeds what the amortised cost would have been (at the date of the reversal) had the impairment not been recognised. [IAS 39.65] It should be noted that, to qualify for recognition, a reversal does **not** need to have resulted from the same factor that caused the original impairment.

US GAAP comparison: An investor in debt security classified as held-to-maturity shall consider whether a decline in fair value below the amortised cost basis is other than temporary (FAS 115). If it is probable that the investor will be unable to collect all amounts due according to the contractual terms of a debt security not impaired at acquisition, an other-than-temporary impairment shall be considered to have occurred. If the decline in fair value is judged to be other than temporary, the cost basis of the individual security shall be written down to fair value as a new cost basis and the amount of the write-down shall be included in profit or loss. The new cost basis shall not be changed for subsequent recoveries in fair value. This is different from IFRS, where a loss event must occur in order to recognise an impairment loss on a held-to-maturity investment, and if an asset is impaired, reversals of impairment losses are permissible in certain circumstances.

6.2.3 *Subsequent interest*

Once an impairment loss has been recognised, subsequent interest income is recognised using the rate of interest used to discount the future cash flows in measuring that impairment. [IAS 39.AG93] IAS 39 does not allow for non-accrual of interest following impairment.

In the case of a floating rate financial asset the rate used to discount future cash flows in measuring impairment will be the current effective interest rate since the effective interest rate is updated through the asset's life as the market rates change (see **6.2.1** above). This is consistent with the requirements of IAS 39.AG93 which states that once a financial asset has been written down as a result of an impairment loss, interest income is thereafter recognised using the rate of interest used to discount the future cash flows for the purpose of measuring the impairment loss. In this case, the 'rate' of interest, is a 'floating rate'. Entities may have a preference for 'freezing' the effective interest rate at the date of impairment, as opposed to updating the effective interest rate after the impairment date, but this is contrary to the principle in the Standard that interest income on floating rate loans is recognised at the current floating rate.

6.2.4 *Groups of assets*

IAS 39 contains specific requirements to be employed when considering the impairment of a group of financial assets. It is first necessary to consider whether there is objective evidence of an impairment for financial assets that are 'individually significant'. Assets that are not individually significant may be assessed either individually or collectively. [IAS 39.64] There is no guidance on the appropriate interpretation of the term 'individually significant' and it is, undoubtedly, an area of considerable judgement for management.

Measurement of impairment on a portfolio basis may be applied to groups of small balance items and to financial assets that are individually assessed and found not to be impaired when there is indication of impairment in a group of similar assets and impairment cannot be identified with an individual asset in that group. [IAS 39.IG.E.4.7]

If a collective assessment is to be undertaken, it should include financial assets that have been considered individually, whether or not they are individually significant, for which no impairment has been recorded. Assets that have been considered individually, and for which an impairment is (or continues to be) recognised, are not included in the collective assessment.

Where an asset is assessed for impairment individually and an impairment loss would have been recognised but for the existence of collateral, the asset is not impaired and is not included in the collective assessment of impairment. Had the same asset not been collateralised, an impairment loss would have been recognised on an individual basis, and the asset would also not be included in the collective assessment.

The asset groups used for collective assessment of impairment should be defined to include financial assets with similar credit risk characteristics. IAS 39.AG87 gives the example of using 'a credit risk evaluation or grading process that considers asset type, industry, geographical location, collateral type, past-due status and other relevant factors.' If groups sharing similar risk characteristics cannot be identified, the collective assessment cannot be performed.

In determining the impact of external factors on whether an impairment loss should be recognised on an individual or collective basis, each external factor needs to be considered carefully to determine whether that factor relates only to the specific counterparty to the referenced asset, or more widely to the industry in which that counterparty operates in.

For example, the fact that an external factor affects the counterparty to a much greater degree than its competitors within the same industry may suggest that this factor is more relevant in an individual impairment analysis. The factor may need to be reapplied, along with other factors, on a collective impairment assessment if it also affects the rest of the industry.

It should be noted that the characteristics of assets that have been assessed individually, and found not to be impaired, will differ from those assets assessed only on a collective basis. This should be taken into account in performing the collective assessment and, as a result, a different amount of impairment may be required.

As soon as information is available that specifically identifies losses on individual assets, those assets are removed from the collective assessment. [IAS 39.AG88]

The application guidance to IAS 39 provides further guidance on how to perform a collective impairment assessment. [IAS 39.AG89-AG92] The main elements of this guidance are as follows.

- Future cash flows for an asset group are estimated on the basis of historical loss experience for assets with similar credit risk characteristics to the group.
- Information about historical loss rates should be applied to groups that are defined in a manner consistent with the groups for which that information was observed.
- Peer-group experience is used if there is no, or insufficient, entity-specific loss experience.
- Historical loss experience is adjusted on the basis of current observable data so that it is consistent with current conditions.
- The methodology and assumptions used to estimate future cash flows are reviewed regularly.

Most importantly, collective assessments of impairment will still reflect the incurred loss model and will not result in the recognition of expected future losses. The aim is to reflect, on a portfolio basis, the effect of loss events that have occurred with respect to individual assets in the group (but have not yet been identified on an individual asset basis). IAS 39 provides an example of an entity that determines on the basis of historical experience that one of the main causes of default on credit card loans is the death of the borrower. The entity may observe that the death rate is unchanged from one year to the next. Nevertheless, some of the borrowers in the entity's group of credit card loans may have died in that year, indicating that an impairment loss has occurred on those loans, even if, at the year-end, the entity is not yet aware which specific borrowers have died. It would be appropriate for an impairment loss to be recognised for these 'incurred but not reported' losses. However, it would not be appropriate to recognise an impairment loss for deaths that are expected to occur in a future period, because the necessary loss event (the death of the borrower) has not yet occurred. [IAS 39.AG90]

Consistent with the principle of only recognising incurred but not reported losses, if a formulae-based approach or statistical method is employed, the method must not give rise to an impairment loss on initial recognition. Such methods may be used only if they are consistent with the guidance above and:

- incorporate the effects of the time value of money;
- consider the cash flows for the whole of the remaining life of an asset; and
- consider the age of loans within the portfolio.

It is not permissible to set aside additional provisions or reserves in excess of the amount of impairment or bad debt losses that are recognised under IAS 39. [IAS 39.IG.E.4.6]

US GAAP comparison: Similar to IAS 39, US GAAP employs different accounting models depending on whether impairment is evaluated on a single item or at a group level. An entity assesses larger loans regularly for evidence of impairment on an item by item basis (FAS 114). If the entity concludes that an individual loan is impaired, it generally measures the amount of impairment in a similar way to IAS 39. Additionally, an entity is required to assess homogeneous groups of loans collectively for impairment in accordance with FAS 5. Unlike IAS 39, FAS 5 does not require expected cash flows to be discounted in measuring impairment for groups of loans. Compared with IAS 39, US GAAP contains less prescriptive guidance about how to measure impairment in groups of loans. SEC and US bank regulators have emphasised that arriving at an appropriate allowance involves a high degree of judgement and results in a range of estimated losses (EITF D-80). Banks should maintain prudent, conservative, but not excessive, loan loss allowances that fall within an acceptable range of estimated losses. The overall allowance should appropriately reflect a margin for imprecision inherent in most estimates of expected credit losses.

6.3 Assets carried at cost

Unquoted equity instruments (and derivatives that result in physical delivery of unquoted equity investments) whose fair value cannot be reliably measured are shown at cost (see **3.1.6** above). For such instruments, if there is objective evidence of an impairment (as discussed in **6.1** above), the amount of the impairment loss is measured as the difference between carrying amount and the present value of estimated future cash flows discounted at the current rate of return for a similar financial asset. [IAS 39.66]

Once an impairment loss has been recognised on a financial asset recognised at cost a reversal of that impairment is not permitted.

6.4 Available-for-sale financial assets

If a decline in the fair value of an available-for-sale financial asset has been recognised in other comprehensive income under the requirements discussed in **3.1.4** above, and there is objective evidence of an impairment (as discussed in **6.1.1** for debt instruments and **6.1.1** and **6.1.2** for equity instruments), the cumulative loss that had been recognised in other comprehensive income is reclassified from equity to profit or loss. The amount of cumulative loss is the difference between the acquisition cost (net of principal repayments and amortisation for debt instruments) and the current fair value, less any impairment loss previously recognised in profit or loss. [IAS 39.67 & 68] Any portion of the cumulative net loss that is attributable to foreign currency movements that had been recognised in other comprehensive income in the case of a non-monetary item, e.g. for equity instruments, is also reclassified from equity to profit or loss. [IAS 39.IG.E.4.9]

6.4.1 Impairment measurement – equity instruments

An impairment of an available-for-sale equity investment does not establish a new deemed cost for that investment. The test of whether there has been a 'significant or prolonged decline in the fair value of an investment in an equity instrument below its cost' is with reference to the original cost on initial recognition (not the carrying amount after the previous impairment) and 'prolonged' should be evaluated against that period in which the fair value of the investment has been below original cost at initial recognition. [IAS 39.61] IAS 39 does not allow entities to consider only the period since the last impairment loss was recognised in profit or loss nor does it allow entities to segregate different loss events in order to evaluate the significance and duration of each event separately. Therefore, once an impairment loss is recognised in profit or loss, any further decline in value must be recognised immediately in profit or loss. [IAS 39.IG.E.4.9] This was confirmed by the IFRIC in April 2005.

If an investment in an equity instrument is reclassified from FVTPL to AFS consideration should be given as to whether "cost" is the original acquisition cost at initial recognition or the fair value at the date of reclassification. Prior to the IAS 39 amendment on reclassifications of financial assets cost always meant 'acquisition cost' because it was not possible to reclassify an equity investment from one fair value measurement category to another and therefore, the amount recognised in equity always represented the difference between the acquisition cost of the equity investment and its fair value. For an investment in an equity instrument reclassified from FVTPL to AFS the amounts in equity will be the difference between the fair value at the date of the reclassification and the fair value at the balance sheet date. The IAS 39 amendment on reclassifications introduced IAS 39.50C which states that the fair value at the date of reclassification "becomes its new cost". The requirements to assess impairment were not applicable prior to reclassification as any impairment is automatically included in profit or loss for assets carried at fair value through profit or loss (IAS 39.58) Therefore, subsequent to reclassification, in assessing whether the fair value of an equity investment is significantly below its cost it is appropriate to compare the fair value at the balance sheet date with the fair value at the date of reclassification. Similarly, in assessing whether there has been a prolonged decline in fair value below cost it is appropriate to look at how long the equity investment's fair value has been below the 'new cost' established at the date of reclassification.

It is unlikely that an entity could apply a portfolio approach for assessing impairment of available-for-sale equity securities. As equity securities are issued by different entities they are unlikely to have similar risk characteristics as their exposure to equity price risk will differ.

If an entity holds an investment in a fund that invests in equity securities, and the investment is classified as an available-for-sale investment, the investor should assess impairment based on a comparison of cost and fair value of the investment in the fund, not by looking through the fund to the individual equity securities held by the fund.

6.4.2 *Impairment reversals – equity instruments*

Once an impairment loss has been recognised on an available-for-sale equity investment, it is not permitted to recognise a reversal through profit or loss. [IAS 39.69] This approach differs from the approach for debt instruments where reversal is permitted (see **6.4.4** below).

IAS 39.BC127 – BC130 explain the rationale for this difference in approach. Primarily, the IASB took the view that reversals of impairments in debt instruments are more objectively determinable than those in equity instruments. In particular, for equity instruments the IASB 'could not find an acceptable way to distinguish reversals of impairment losses from other increases in fair value.' This is consistent with the approach taken for unquoted equity instruments measured at cost (see **6.3** above).

A puttable instrument issued by an entity (e.g. a fund), under which the holder can put it back to the issuer at any time for cash equal to a proportionate share of the net asset value of the entity, should be considered an equity instrument when establishing whether a reversal of impairment is appropriate. As the instrument does not have specified payments and a fixed maturity it is an equity investment and, therefore, any reversal of a previously recognised impairment through profit or loss account is not permitted if it is classified as an available-for-sale financial asset.

6.4.2.1 *Interim financial reporting and impairment*

IFRIC Interpretation 10 *Interim Financial Reporting and Impairment*, published in July 2006, provides guidance on the interaction between the requirements of IAS 34 *Interim Financial Reporting* and the recognition of impairment losses for certain financial assets under IAS 39. In respect of investments in equity instruments or a financial asset carried at cost, the Interpretation clarifies that an entity should not reverse an impairment loss recognised in a previous interim period.

Example 6.4.2.1

Interaction of impairment and interim financial reporting

On 1 January 20X1 Entity A and Entity B each buy small shareholdings of equity instruments of Entity X for CU100. Both entities classify their investments in the quoted equity instruments as available-for-sale. Accordingly, IAS 39.55(b) requires gains and losses to be recognised initially in other comprehensive income except for impairment losses which are recognised in profit or loss.

Entity A is listed on its national stock exchange which requires interim reports in accordance with IFRSs on a semi-annual basis. Entity B is required to prepare IFRS financial statements on an annual basis for statutory purposes. On 30 June 20X1 Entity X shows signs of severe financial difficulties with the share price declined to CU80. While preparing its interim report Entity A concludes that its investment in Entity X is impaired and recognises an impairment loss of CU20 in profit or loss. As Entity B is not required to prepare a semi-annual report it does not review its equity instruments for evidence of impairment at that point in time.

On 31 December 20X1 the financial condition of Entity X has fully recovered due to a successful debt restructuring with the share price having risen to CU120. Both Entity A and Entity B conclude that the original cost of the investment is recoverable. However, while Entity B does not recognise an impairment loss in its annual IFRS financial statements, Entity A is prohibited from reversing the impairment loss recognised in its interim report. The result is that Entity A and Entity B have different results for exactly the same equity instrument.

6.4.3 *Impairment measurement – debt instruments*

Impairment losses to be recognised on an available-for-sale debt instrument is the cumulative fair value loss that is recognised in equity that is reclassified to profit or loss. As the impairment loss is recognised on a fair value basis this differs from a loss on a debt instrument measured at amortised sot where the loss is determined as the difference between the asset's carrying value and its recoverable amount calculated as the sum of the estimated future recoverable cash flows discounted at the asset's original effective interest rate. The reason for this difference is that the impairment loss on an available-for-sale debt instruments includes a market participant's view of recoverable cash flows discounts by a rate that reflects current market interest rates, adjusted for liquidity and other factors a market participant would include in determining fair value.

If a debt instrument is reclassified from FVTPL to AFS the impairment requirements in IAS 39.58–70 apply for the first time. As the asset was previously measured at FVTPL an assessment of impairment was not required. If there is objective evidence of impairment following reclassification an impairment loss is recognised and this is treated as the first impairment event irrespective of the history of the asset prior to the reclassification. Only gains/losses since the date of reclassification are reclassified to profit or loss.

6.4.3.1 *Subsequent interest*

IAS 39.AG93 requires that the interest recognition following impairment for all debt instruments is recognised using the rate of interest used to discount the future cash flows for the purpose of measuring the impairment loss. In the case of fixed rate debt instruments measured at amortised cost the discount rate will be the original effective interest rate. For floating rate debt instruments measured at amortised cost the discount rate will be the effective interest rate at the date of impairment. As the impairment loss on AFS debt instruments is equal to the fair value loss recognised in equity that is reclassified to profit or loss, the interest rate subsequent to the impairment loss is based on a market interest at the date of impairment. The market interest rate reflects the rate that was used in determining the asset's fair value. A further reason for applying a market interest rate for interest recognition subsequent to the date of impairment, as opposed to the original effective interest rate, is that, assuming there are no further impairment losses, or reversals of impairment losses, the amount in equity at maturity will be zero.

Examples 6.4.3.1 and **6.4.3.2** deal with investments in zero coupon bonds as opposed to interest-bearing debt instruments. This is for illustrative purposes only. An entity is required to revise the effective interest rate at the date of impairment for all available-for-sale debt instruments.

Example 6.4.3.1

Interest recognition subsequent to impairment losses on AFS debt instruments

Entity B acquires a zero coupon bond debt security and classifies it as available for sale at initial recognition at 1/1/X6. The instrument is acquired for CU82.6 and has a maturity in 2 years with a redemption of CU100. The effective interest rate is 10%. Entity B has a calendar year reporting period end.

At 31/12/X6 Entity B determines there is objective evidence of impairment. Entity B estimates the expected recoverable cash flows to be CU80 at maturity, instead of CU100. The fair value of the debt security is CU70. The difference between CU82.6 plus interest at the instrument's original effective interest rate of 10% less its fair value of CU70 is a fair value of CU20.86 and is recognised in the available for sale reserve in equity. In accordance with IAS 39.67 the fair value loss in equity is reclassified to profit or loss.

Dr	Available-for-sale asset	CU8.26
Cr	Interest income – profit or loss	CU8.26

To recognise interest income at the original effective interest rate of 10%

Dr	Other comprehensive income	CU20.86
Cr	Available-for-sale asset	CU20.86

To recognise the fair value loss directly in other comprehensive income

Dr	Impairment loss – profit or loss	CU20.86
Cr	Equity	CU20.86

To reclassify the impairment loss recognised in equity to profit or loss.

Entity B must revise the instrument's effective interest rate at 1/1/X7. The effective interest rate is the rate that discounts the estimated recoverable cash flows, being CU80 in one year, to the instrument's carrying value, being CU70. The revised effective interest rate is 14.3%.

At the instrument's maturity at 31/12/X7 the cash flows received equal Entity B's estimated recoverable cash flows at 31/12/X6, i.e. there was no further impairment losses or reversal of impairment losses.

Dr	Available-for-sale asset	CU10.00
Cr	Interest income – profit or loss	CU10.00

To recognise interest income at the revised effective interest rate of 14.3%

The amount in equity is zero as the instrument's carrying value following recognition of the revised effective interest rate equals to CU80, being its fair value at maturity.

For illustrative purposes only, had Entity B not revised the effective interest rate to 14.3% from 10% at the date of impairment loss then the interest income of CU7 (being CU70 x 10%) would be understated and the amount in equity would have been overstated being a credit of CU3 (being CU77 – CU80).

If following an impairment loss there are further impairment losses and fair value losses are reclassified from equity to profit or loss, then the effective interest rate for interest recognition subsequent to the further impairment will need to be revised. The basis for revising the effective interest rate is the same as with the first revision, being the rate that exactly discounts the estimated recoverable cash flows to the instrument's carrying value.

If following an impairment loss there is a reversal of an impairment loss that requires fair value gains previously recognised in other comprehensive income to be reclassified from equity to profit or loss then the effective interest rate will also need to be revised at that date. The revised effective interest rate will be used for subsequent interest recognition after the impairment reversal. The basis for revising the effective interest rate immediately following a reversal of an impairment loss is the same as for the first revision, being the rate that exactly discounts the estimated recoverable cash flows to the instrument's carrying value. For reversals, see **6.4.4** below.

US GAAP comparison: If it is probable that an investor in a debt security classified as available-for-sale will be unable to collect all amounts due, the investor shall recognise an other-than-temporary impairment so that the cost basis of the security is written down to fair value as a new cost basis with the amount of the write-down included in profit or loss (FAS 115). The new cost basis shall not be changed for subsequent recoveries in fair value. Subsequent increases in the fair value of available-for-sale securities shall be included in the separate component of equity; subsequent decreases in fair value, if not an other-than-temporary impairment, also shall be included in the separate component of equity. This is different from IFRS, where reversals of impairment of available-for-sale debt securities are recognised in profit or loss, as opposed to equity as in US GAAP.

6.4.3.2 *Fair value losses subsequent to impairment*

If an available-for-sale debt instrument has been impaired and amounts are reclassified from equity to profit or loss, and the asset continues to have an impaired status, i.e. the expected recoverable contractual cash flows to be received are lower than at initial recognition, further fair value losses recognised in other comprehensive income should also be reclassified equity to profit or loss. Effectively, if an asset is impaired, IAS 39 does not distinguish between fair value losses that arise due to further declines in recoverability of cash flows, and those fair value losses that arise due to other factors, e.g. changes in risk-free interest rates, liquidity risk etc.

Example 6.4.3.2

Fair value losses subsequent to impairment – debt instruments

Entity Q acquires an investment in an available-for-sale debt instrument at 1/1/X1. Entity D has a calendar year reporting period end.

At 31/12/X3 there was objective evidence of impairment and the fair value loss recognised in other comprehensive income is reclassified to from equity profit or loss in accordance with IAS 39.67.

At 31/12/X4 a further fair value loss is recognised in other comprehensive income and Entity Q estimates the recoverable cash flows remaining due are lower than at 1/1/X1, i.e. the asset continues to be impaired. The fair value loss recognised in initially in other comprehensive income in the period must be reclassified from equity to profit or loss.

6.4.4 *Impairment reversals – debt instruments*

If the fair value of an available-for-sale debt instrument increases and the increase can be related objectively to an event occurring after the impairment was recognised, then the impairment is reversed through profit or loss. [IAS 39.70] It should be noted that, to qualify for recognition, a reversal does **not** need to have resulted from the same factor that caused the original impairment. The amount of the gain recognised in profit or loss on reversal of an impairment loss is unlikely to be equal to the amount of the original impairment loss recognised in profit or loss. This is because the amount of the original impairment loss and the reversal are based on the *fair value* loss and gain respectively that are recognised in other comprehensive income at the reporting date.

IAS 39.70 allows reversal of impairment losses on an available-for-sale debt instrument if there is objective evidence of "an event occurring after the impairment was recognised". IAS 39.70 does not state what event is sufficient to warrant an impairment reversal. It is assumed the event must be a credit event as opposed to a non-credit event like a change in the risk-free interest rate. This is consistent with the approach described in IAS 39.65 for amortised cost financial assets which loos specifically to an event like an improvement in the debtor's credit rating.

Example 6.4.4A

Impairment reversals – debt instruments (1)

Entity D acquires an investment in an available-for-sale debt instrument at 1/1/X1. Entity D has a calendar year reporting period end.

At 31/12/X3 there was objective evidence of impairment and the fair value loss recognised in other comprehensive income is reclassified from equity to profit or loss in accordance with IAS 39.67.

At 31/12/X4 there is objective evidence that the impairment loss has reversed and therefore the gain recognised in other comprehensive income is reclassified from equity to profit or loss. The amount of the gain recognised in profit or loss will not necessarily equal the amount of loss recognised in profit or loss at 31/12/X3.

Example 6.4.4B

Impairment reversals – debt instruments (2)

Entity E acquires a zero coupon bond debt security and classifies it as an available-for-sale investment at initial recognition at 1/1/X1. The instrument is acquired for CU68 and has a maturity of five years with a redemption amount of CU100. The effective interest rate is 8.0%. Entity E has a calendar year reporting period end.

At 31/12/X1 Entity E determines there is objective evidence of impairment. Entity B estimates the expected recoverable cash flows to be CU90 at maturity, instead of CU100. The fair value of the debt security is CU65. The difference between CU68 plus interest at the instrument's original effective interest rate of 8.0% less its fair value CU65 is a fair value loss of CU8.5

recognised in other comprehensive income in the AFS reserve in equity. In accordance with IAS 39.67 the fair value loss initially recognised in other comprehensive income is reclassified from equity to profit or loss as an impairment loss.

Dr	Available-for-sale asset	CU5.5
Cr	Interest income – profit or loss	CU5.5

To recognise interest income at the original effective interest rate of 8.0%. The effective interest rate is applied to the instrument's opening fair value which also equals its opening amortised cost for the purposes of calculating the instrument's interest income.

Dr	Other comprehensive income	CU8.5
Cr	Available-for-sale asset	CU8.5

To recognise the fair value loss directly in other comprehensive income.

Dr	Impairment loss – profit or loss	CU8.5
Cr	Other comprehensive income	CU8.5

To reclassify the fair value loss initially recognised in other comprehensive income to profit or loss as an impairment loss.

Entity E must revise the instrument's effective interest rate at 1/1/X2. The effective interest rate is the rate that discounts the estimated recoverable cash flows, CU90 in four years, to the instrument's carrying value, CU65. The revised effective interest rate is 8.5%.

At 31/12/X2 Entity E determines there is further impairment due to a further decline in recoverable cash flows. Entity E estimates the expected recoverable cash flows to be CU85 at maturity, instead of CU90 as was previously estimated. The fair value of the debt security is CU66. The difference between CU65 plus interest at the instrument's revised effective interest rate of 8.5% less its fair value of CU66 is a fair value loss of CU4.5 and is recognised initially in other comprehensive income in the available-for-sale reserve. In accordance with IAS 39.67 the amount initially recognised in other comprehensive income is reclassified from equity to profit or loss.

Dr	Available-for-sale asset	CU5.5
Cr	Interest income – profit or loss	CU5.5

To recognise interest income at the revised effective interest rate of 8.5%. The effective interest rate is applied to the instrument's opening fair value, not the prior period's amortised cost because the effective interest rate was reset following the reclassification of the impairment loss from equity to profit or loss.

Dr	Other comprehensive income	CU4.5
Cr	Available-for-sale asset	CU4.5

To recognise the fair value loss directly in other comprehensive income.

Dr	Impairment loss – profit or loss	CU4.5
Cr	Other comprehensive income	CU4.5

To reclassify the fair value loss initially recognised in other comprehensive income from equity to profit or loss as an impairment loss.

Entity E must revise the instrument's effective interest rate at 1/1/X3. The effective interest rate is the rate that discounts the estimated recoverable cash flows, CU85 in three years, to the instrument's carrying value, CU66. The revised effective interest rate is 8.8%.

At 31/12/X3 there is objective evidence of a reversal of a credit event that has led to an increase in recoverability in cash flows. Entity E estimates the expected recoverable cash flows to be CU98 at maturity, instead of CU85 as was previously estimated. The fair value of the debt security is CU84. The difference between CU66 plus interest at the instrument's revised effective interest rate of 8.8% less its fair value of CU84 is a fair value gain of CU12.2 and is recognised in other comprehensive income in the available-for-sale reserve. In accordance with IAS 39.70 the fair value gain initially recognised in other comprehensive income is reclassified from equity to profit or loss as a reversal of an impairment loss.

Dr	Available-for-sale asset	CU5.8
Cr	Interest income – profit or loss	CU5.8

To recognise interest income at the revised effective interest rate of 8.8%. The effective interest rate is applied to the instrument's opening fair value, not the prior period's amortised cost because the effective interest rate was reset following the reclassification of the impairment loss from equity to profit or loss.

Dr	Available-for-sale asset	CU12.2
Cr	Other comprehensive income	CU12.2

To recognise the fair value gain directly in other comprehensive income

Dr	Other comprehensive income	CU12.2
Cr	Impairment reversal – profit or loss	CU12.2

To reclassify the fair value gain initially recognised in other comprehensive income from equity to profit or loss as a reversal of an impairment loss.

Entity E must revise the instrument's effective interest rate at 1/1/X4. The effective interest rate is the rate that discounts the estimated recoverable cash flows, being CU98 in two years, to the instrument's carrying value, being CU84. The revised effective interest rate is 8.0%.

At 31/12/X4 the estimated recoverable cash flows remain unchanged since the last reporting period end. The fair value of the debt security is CU95. The difference between CU84 plus interest at the instrument's revised effective interest rate of 8.0% less its fair value CU95 is a fair value gain of CU4.3 and is recognised in other comprehensive income in the available-for-sale reserve.

Dr	Available-for-sale asset	CU6.7
Cr	Interest income – profit or loss	CU6.7

To recognise interest income at the revised effective interest rate of 8.0%. The effective interest rate is applied to the instrument's opening fair value, not the prior period's amortised cost because the effective interest rate was reset following the reclassification of the fair value gain from equity to profit or loss upon reversal of the impairment loss.

Dr	Available-for-sale asset	CU4.3

Cr	Other comprehensive income	CU4.3

To recognise the fair value gain directly in other comprehensive income.

At 31/12/X5 the cash flows at maturity are equal to the estimated recoverable cash flows at the end of the prior reporting period. The fair value of the debt security is equal to its settlement amount of CU98. The difference between CU95 (being the prior period's closing fair value) plus interest at the instrument's revised effective interest rate of 8.0% on the instrument's opening amortised cost less its fair value of CU98 is a CU4.3 loss that is recognised in the AFS reserve in other comprehensive income.

Dr	Available-for-sale asset	CU7.3
Cr	Interest income – profit or loss	CU7.3

To recognise interest income at the revised effective interest rate of 8.0%. The effective interest rate is applied to the instrument's opening amortised cost (CU90.7, being CU84.0 + CU6.7), not the opening fair value, as the effective interest rate was not reset because there were no impairment losses or reversals of impairment losses in the previous period.

Dr	Other comprehensive income	CU4.3
Cr	Available-for-sale asset	CU4.3

To recognise the fair value loss directly in other comprehensive income.

At maturity the AFS reserve in equity equals zero. A summary of the entries is illustrated below.

Date	**Available-for-sale asset**	**Cash**	**Profit or loss Dr/(Cr)**	**Other comprehensive income Dr/(Cr)**
Opening – 1/1/X1	68.0	(68.0)		
Interest	5.5		(5.5)	
Fair value loss	(8.5)			8.5
Impairment loss	—		8.5	(8.5)
Closing – 31/12/X1	65.0			
Interest	5.5		(5.5)	
Fair value loss	(4.5)			4.5
Impairment loss	—		4.5	(4.5)
Closing – 31/12/X2	66.0			
Interest	5.8		(5.8)	
Fair value gain	12.2			(12.2)
Reversal of impairment loss	—		(12.2)	12.2
Closing – 31/12/X3	84.0			
Interest	6.7		(6.7)	
Fair value gain	4.3			(4.3)
Closing – 31/12/X4	95.0			

Date	Available-for-sale asset	Cash	Profit or loss Dr/(Cr)	Other comprehensive income Dr/(Cr)
Interest	7.3		(7.3)	
Fair value loss	(4.3)			4.3
Closing – 31/12/X5	98.0	98.0		
	___	___	___	___
	___	30.0	(30.0)	0

IAS 39.70 states that if following an impairment of an available-for-sale debt instrument the fair value increases and the increase can be objectively related to an event occurring after the impairment loss was recognised in profit or loss the impairment loss shall be reversed and the amount of the reversal recognised in profit or loss. Although IAS 39.70 refers to increases in fair value, this paragraph should be applied to instances where there are fair value gains recognised in other comprehensive income following impairment. For example, a debt instrument may increase in fair value over the reporting period but will not necessarily result in a gain being recognised in other comprehensive income. If the increase in fair value over the reporting period is lower than the interest recognised by applying the effective interest rate less cash received in the period, the amount in other comprehensive income will be a fair value loss.

If there has been a decline in the recoverability of cash flows on an available-for-sale debt instrument that has previously been impaired the amount recognised directly in other comprehensive income may not necessarily be a fair value loss. Similar to above, if the decrease in fair value over the reporting period is smaller than the interest recognised calculated by applying the effective interest rate less cash received in the period, the amount in other comprehensive income will be a fair value gain. It would be inappropriate to reclassify this fair value gain in profit or loss as there has not been a reversal of a credit event as described in IAS 39.70. Equally, even though there has been a decline in the recoverability in cash flows there has not been an impairment loss that should be recognised in profit or loss as the amount in other comprehensive income is a fair value gain, not a fair value loss.

6.5 Measurement difficulties

The IASB acknowledges that in some cases, the observable data required to estimate the amount of an impairment loss on a financial asset may not be available or relevant to current circumstances. [IAS 39.62] In such cases, the use of 'experienced judgement' is required. In a collective impairment assessment, **6.2.4** above gives guidance on the approach to be adopted if measurement is less than straightforward.

6.6 Distressed debt

An entity must determine the effective interest rate of acquired distressed debt on the date the debt is acquired, ignoring future credit losses that may be expected to occur. The impact of previous impairment will have already been reflected in the purchase of the debt.

Example 6.6

Effective interest rate on distressed debt

Entity B acquires distressed debt. The fair value of the consideration paid to acquire the debt is CU60. The debt is contracted to redeem at par (CU100) at its maturity. The low consideration paid reflects the fact that prior to Entity B's acquisition of the debt, the debt was subject to impairment.

In order to determine the interest to be received on the debt Entity B must determine the effective interest rate at acquisition. The effective interest rate will incorporate the cash flows expected to be received on the debt (i.e. it will incorporate the impact of the impairment event) because incurred credit losses are considered in computing the effective interest rate for financial assets acquired at a deep discount. [IAS 39.AG5] This treatment is consistent with the prohibition on recognising expected future losses in the effective interest rate [IAS 39.59] as upon acquisition of the distressed debt, the impairment event had already occurred. [IAS 39.BC32]

To the extent the recoverability of the asset improves as a result of a reversal of factors that led to the original impairment, this shall not be recorded as a reversal of impairment as the original impairment charge was not included in Entity B's financial statements. Instead, Entity B would revise its estimate of expected cash flows and recognise a cumulative catch-up in profit or loss to adjust the carrying amount of the asset by discounting the revised expected cash flows at the original effective interest rate (the effective interest rate computed at initial recognition when Entity B acquired the asset). [IAS 39.AG8]

7 Implications for business combinations

The revised version of IFRS 3 *Business Combinations* issued in January 2008 requires the acquirer to recognise all identifiable assets and liabilities at fair value at the date of the business combination and to reassess classifications and designations of all contractual arrangements, with the exception of classification of leases as finance or operating leases and the classification of insurance contracts. The acquirer, in the group financial statements, will make all the classification decisions it would have made had the entity acquired the acquiree's financial instruments separately, i.e. not as part of a business combination.

It is worth noting that subsequent measurement of financial instruments by the acquirer in the group financial statements may differ to the acquiree's financial statements. The acquirer may make different classification decisions than those that were originally made by the acquiree. For example, the acquirer may designate a financial instrument carried by the acquiree at amortised cost as at fair value through profit or loss or available-for-sale. Even if classification and the measurement basis are the same, for example, an asset is classified as a loan and receivable held at amortised cost in both the acquiree's financial statements and the acquirer's group financial statements, the amounts recognised in the group's statement of financial position and statement of comprehensive income in respect of that asset may be different from the amounts recognised by the acquiree. The acquirer recognises the asset at fair value at the time of acquisition and that amount may be different from the carrying value of the asset in the financial statements of the acquiree both at initial recognition and at the date of acquisition. Thus, going forward, the acquirer will record a different effective interest rate to that recorded by the acquiree. This effective interest rate will impact interest recognition and measurement of any future impairment. Also, the acquiree may reverse an impairment loss in its own financial statements but the acquirer will not if the reversal is an impairment that occurred in the acquiree prior to the acquisition date.

The above illustrations are not exhaustive as there are many other differences that can arise when comparing the subsequent measurement of financial instruments by the acquiree and acquirer.

8 Future developments

8.1 Fair value measurement

In November 2006 the IASB issued a discussion paper titled Fair Value Measurement. This discussion paper is equivalent to FAS 157 in US GAAP that is effective for financial statements issued for financial years beginning after 15 November 2007. As the IASB has issued the US standard only as a discussion paper, it will be some time before the IASB issues a standard on fair value measurement and in the meantime GAAP differences will remain between the US standard and the current fair value literature in IFRSs. At the time of writing the IASB were finalising the exposure draft that is intended to be issued in the second quarter of 2009. The IASB expects a final Standard to be issued in 2010.

Most accounting standards that include fair value focus on what to measure at fair value, whereas the discussion paper instead focuses on how to measure fair value. Dispersed throughout accounting standards are inconsistent definitions of fair value and only limited guidance on application. The discussion paper remedies this by providing a 'one-stop shop' for the definition of fair value and related measurement guidance. In other words, the discussion paper does not propose to introduce any new requirements mandating the use of fair value; instead, it would unify the meaning of fair value and add important disclosures.

Highlights of the discussion paper include the following:

- a new definition of fair value;
- a fair value hierarchy used to classify the source of information used in fair value measurements (i.e. market based or non-market based);
- new disclosures of assets and liabilities measured at fair value based on their level in the hierarchy;
- a modification of the long-standing accounting presumption that the transaction price of an asset or liability equals its initial fair value;
- questions and answers on the application of the discussion paper.

The proposals are intended to apply to any asset or liability that is measured at fair value, not just financial instruments. The discussion paper defines 'fair value' as 'the price that would be received to sell an asset or paid to transfer a liability in an orderly transaction between market participants at the measurement date.' While the words may have a similar ring to past definitions, there are some key differences. First, the definition is based on an exit price (for an asset, the price at which it would be sold) rather than an entry price (for an asset, the price at which it would be bought), regardless of whether the entity plans to hold or sell the asset. This is the same approach that is currently applied in IAS 39 for subsequent measurement, but is not applied to initial recognition of some other assets where an entry price is applied instead. A second key point of the definition is that it, like IAS 39, emphasises that fair value is market based rather than entity specific, i.e. fair values must be based on assumptions that market participants would use in pricing the asset or liability.

A fair value hierarchy underpins the discussion paper. The hierarchy ranks the quality and reliability of information used to determine fair values — quoted prices are the most reliable valuation inputs, whereas model values that include inputs based on unobservable data are the least reliable. The table below provides a description of the levels in the hierarchy and examples.

Level and 'Inputs' (Information Used in Determining Fair Value)	Examples
Level 1 — Quoted market prices for *identical* assets or liabilities in *active* markets	• Entity A common stock traded and quoted on the New York Stock Exchange.
Level 2 — Observable market-based inputs, other than Level 1 quoted prices (or unobservable inputs that are corroborated by market data)	• Entity Z common stock traded and quoted only on an inactive market in an emerging country. • A privately placed bond of Entity Z whose value is derived from a similar Entity Z bond that is publicly traded. • An over-the-counter interest rate swap, valued based on a model whose inputs are observable LIBOR forward interest rate curves.
Level 3 — Unobservable inputs (that are not corroborated by observable market data)	• A long-dated commodity swap whose forward price curve, used in a valuation model, is not directly observable or correlated with observable market data. • Shares of a privately held entity whose value is based on projected cash flows.

The discussion paper proposed extensive disclosures based on the three-level hierarchy described above.

In March 2009 the IASB issued an amendment to IFRS 7, *Improving Disclosures about Financial Instruments*. The amendments includes a requirement to classify fair value measurements using a fair value hierarchy that reflects the significance of the inputs used in making the measurements. The fair value hierarchy had three levels similar to that described in the table above. For fair value measurements recognised in the statement of financial position an entity would be required to disclose for each class of financial instruments (i) the level in the fair value hierarchy into which the fair value measurements are categorised in their entirety, and (ii) for financial instruments included in the Level 3 category a reconciliation from the beginning balances to the ending balances, showing where movement in fair value are recognised, purchases, sales, issues and settlements (net), and transfers into and/or out of Level 3. For more detail on the amendments to IFRS 7 see **chapter 11**.

A fair value measurement assumes that the transaction to sell the asset or transfer the liability occurs in the principal market for the asset or liability or, in the absence of a principal market, the most advantageous market for the asset or liability. The principal market is the market in which the reporting entity would sell the asset or transfer the liability with the greatest volume and level of activity for the asset or liability. The most advantageous market is the market in which the reporting entity would sell the asset or transfer the liability with the price that maximises the amount that would be received for the asset or minimises the amount that would be paid to transfer the liability, considering transaction costs in the respective market(s). IAS 39 does not distinguish between the principal and the most advantageous market, rather it refers solely to the market that is most advantageous.

The discussion paper proposes to allow an entity to record an upfront profit, 'day 1 p&l', if its valuation technique suggests that fair value is different from the transaction price. This would be a change from IAS 39 which, like US guidance prior to FAS 157 being issued, does not allow an entity to recognise an upfront profit absent observable market data.

Fair value should not be adjusted for transaction costs. Transaction costs that represent the incremental direct costs to sell the asset or transfer are also not an attribute of the asset or liability, instead, they are specific to a transaction and will differ depending on how the reporting entity transacts. However, transaction costs should be taken into account in determining the most advantageous market that the entity has access to. The discussion paper provides guidance on transportation costs and states that these are an element of fair value in the instance when location is an attribute of the asset or liability (as might be the case for a commodity), but not otherwise. Thus, the price in the principal market used to measure the fair value of the asset or liability should be adjusted for the costs, if any, that would be incurred to transport the asset or liability to (or from) its principal (or most advantageous) market.

When a quoted price in an active market exists, the fair value is the product of the quoted price and the number of units. The fair value of the instrument is not affected by the size of the investment the entity has. The unit of account for Level 1 items is therefore a single instrument. This is the same as IAS 39. The discussion paper does not state what the unit of account would be for items that are not Level 1.

When measuring instruments in active markets the discussion paper is less specific than IAS 39 as to using bid, ask, or mid-market prices. The discussion paper would preserve the ability of securities brokers (and other types of entities) to use a price within the bid-ask spread that is most representative of fair value, as long as this is consistently applied. The discussion paper does not preclude the use of mid-market pricing or other pricing conventions as a practical expedient for fair value measurements within a bid-ask spread.

As part of the IASB's deliberations in formulating an exposure draft on fair value measurement the IASB tentatively agreed not to preclude the use of mid-market pricing or another pricing convention as a practical expedient for a fair value measurement within the bid-ask spread across all levels of the hierarchy.

The discussion paper clarifies that a fair value measurement for a restricted asset should consider the effect of the restriction if market participants would consider the effect of the restriction in pricing the asset. This would usually be the case when the restriction is specific to (an attribute of) the asset and would transfer to market participants.

As part of the IASB's deliberations in formulating an exposure draft on fair value measurement the IASB tentatively agreed that if a restriction on the sale or use of an asset would transfer to market participants it is an attribute of the asset and will affect the fair value. If the restriction would not transfer to a market participant it will not affect the asset's fair value. Restrictions on liabilities differ as the fair value of a liability is not a function of marketability, but of performance.

8.2 Reducing complexity

In March 2008 the IASB issued a discussion paper *Reducing Complexity in Reporting Financial Instruments*. Although the discussion paper was drafted by the IASB, the US Financial Accounting Standards Board also issued the discussion paper as part of the memorandum of understanding between the two standard setters. The aim of the discussion paper is to provide a basis for future discussions of issues related to the measurement of financial instruments (including hedge accounting issues). The ultimate goal of this project is to publish an IFRS that would significantly improve and simplify financial instrument reporting, i.e. it would replace IAS 39.

The discussion paper sets out the IASB's long-term objective of full fair value accounting for all financial instruments, i.e. elimination of the existing mixed measurement approach in IAS 39. The discussion paper acknowledges that instead of immediately moving to its long-term goal the Board may instead consider alternative intermediate approaches, all of which retain a mixed measurement model.

7 Recognition and derecognition

1 Introduction

Recognition addresses the question of whether or not a financial instrument is included in the statement of financial position. Derecognition, not surprisingly, is the reverse of recognition and is the removal of a previously recognised financial instrument from the statement of financial position.

A financial instrument is recognised when, and only when, the entity becomes a party to the contractual provisions of the instrument. A previously recognised financial asset is derecognised when, and only when, either the contractual rights to the cash flows from that asset expire, or the entity transfers the asset such that the transfer qualifies for derecognition. A financial liability is derecognised when, and only when, it is extinguished.

The criteria that are applied to transfers of financial assets are a mix of risks and rewards and control tests. IAS 39 establishes a hierarchy of the tests and provides many examples to clarify the meaning of the concepts used and application of the tests to various transfer transactions.

Although the broad principles of derecognition may appear to be simple, a significant degree of judgment will be required when applying these principles in practice. This is particularly so in more mature financial markets where the complexity of transactions is ever increasing.

This chapter discusses recognition and derecognition in the following sections:

Section 2 Initial recognition

Section 3 Derecognition of financial assets

Section 4 Derecognition of a financial liability

Section 5 Future developments

2 Initial recognition

2.1 General principle

An entity should only recognise a financial asset or a financial liability in its statement of financial position when it becomes a party to the contractual provisions of the instrument. [IAS 39.14]

Example 2.1

Recognised and unrecognised financial instruments

Arrangements that are recognised as financial assets and liabilities are as follows.

- Unconditional receivables are recognised as an asset when the entity becomes a party to the contract and, as a consequence, has a legal right to receive cash. [IAS 39.AG35(a)]
- Issued debt is recognised as a liability when the entity that issues it becomes a party to the contractual terms of the debt, and therefore has a legal obligation to pay cash to the debt holder.
- A derivative is recognised as an asset or a liability on the commitment date, rather than on the date on which settlement takes place. At inception the fair values of the right and obligation created by the derivative may be equal, in which case the fair value of the derivative will be zero. [IAS 39.AG35(c)]

Arrangements that are not recognised as financial assets and liabilities are as follows.

- Planned future transactions, no matter how likely, are not assets and liabilities because the entity has not become a party to a contract. [IAS 39.AG35(e)]
- Derivative contracts to buy or sell non-financial items that are scoped out of IAS 39 are not recognised as financial assets and liabilities as they are executory contracts.
- Assets to be acquired and liabilities to be incurred as a result of a firm commitment are generally not recognised until at least one of the parties has performed under the agreement. [IAS 39.AG35(b)]

A firm commitment to acquire a non-financial item is not recognised until the asset is acquired if the commitment itself is deemed to be outside the scope of IAS 39 (see **2.5** of **chapter 1**). A firm commitment to buy a financial asset, or a commitment to buy a non-financial item where the commitment is in the scope of IAS 39, is generally recognised as a derivative on the date the commitment is entered into (see **chapter 4**) unless the 'regular way' exemption is applied (see **2.2** below). If a previously unrecognised firm commitment is subject to a highly effective fair value hedge, changes in the fair value of the hedged risk of the firm commitment are recognised in the statement of financial position. This appears to run counter to non-recognition of certain firm commitments. The argument for permitting such an approach is that all firm commitments are recognised, but generally at a historic cost of nil, and the fair value hedge requirements merely remeasure part of that commitment to fair value. [IAS 39.BC152]

If an entity transfers or receives cash as collateral for an arrangement careful consideration is needed to determine whether the cash should be recognised as a financial asset in the hands of the recipient. If the cash received by the recipient is not legally segregated from the recipient's other assets and the recipient can use the cash unfettered, then the cash meets the definition of an asset. This is because the ultimate realisation of a financial asset is its conversion into cash and, therefore, no further transformation is required before the economic benefits of the cash transferred by the provider of the collateral are realised by the recipient. In this case, the recipient would recognise the cash as a financial asset and recognise a concurrent financial liability to return the cash to the provider of the collateral. The provider of the collateral would derecognise the cash and recognise a receivable from the collateral holder. [IAS 39.IG.D.1]

Derivatives that prevent a transfer of financial assets from achieving derecognition are not recognised if recognising both the derivative and the asset that failed derecognition would amount to accounting for the same rights and obligations twice. [IAS 39.AG49]

2.1.1 Linked transactions

IAS 39 does not contain guidance when two separate financial instruments entered into concurrently should be recognised as a single combined instrument. IAS 39 does, however, provide specific implementation guidance in IAS 39.IG.B.6 where a loan receivable and a payable are considered as a single transaction, an interest rate swap. It seems reasonable that the guidance in this example can be applied to other transactions. Two financial instruments should therefore be recognised and measured as a single combined instrument if:

- they are entered into at the same time and in contemplation of each other;
- they have the same counterparty;

- they relate to the same risk; and
- there is no economic need or substantive business purpose for structuring the transactions separately that could not also have been accomplished in a single transaction.

One of the most common benefits of structuring transactions separately, even if their substance is that of a single arrangement, is tax benefits that accrue. It is difficult to see how it can be argued that structuring for tax benefits is a substantive business purpose, particularly when those tax benefits derive from the accounting treatment adopted (in this example, from treating the transactions separately for accounting purposes).

2.1.2 *Modification that leads to initial recognition of a new instrument*

An entity may become a party to the contractual provisions of a financial instrument as a result of a substantial modification of an instrument that it already recognised in the statement of financial position. The entity will need to consider whether the modification results in derecognition of the existing instrument and recognition of a new instrument. Derecognition of financial assets is detailed in **section 3** below and derecognition of financial liabilities is detailed in **section 4** below.

Example 2.1.2

Initial recognition following modification

An entity had previously issued a perpetual instrument with an issuer option to redeem after 15 years. Under the terms of the instrument the entity had the option to defer interest payments indefinitely, except upon liquidation of the entity. Consequently, the instrument met the definition of an equity instrument and was presented as equity at its net proceeds.

During the year the entity and the holder of the instrument make a modification to the terms of the instrument which creates a contingent settlement provision that is considered to be 'genuine' in accordance with IAS 32.25. If a prescribed contingent event occurs, the entity is required to pay all deferred interest and lose the right to defer future interest. In accordance with IAS 32.25, after this modification the instrument is classified as a financial liability. The modification involves no compensation payment to the holders of the instrument or a change in the expected cash flows, and no fees in respect of the modification are paid.

All financial instruments are measured at their fair value at initial recognition. The initial recognition date of the financial liability in this example is the date of the modification as at this date the old equity instrument is derecognised and a new financial liability is recognised. Therefore, the entity must recognise the financial liability at its fair value, which will incorporate expectations of cash flows and market interest rates at the date of the modification. Any difference between the previous carrying amount recognised in equity and the fair value of the financial liability is recognised as an adjustment within equity.

If the entity does not designate the financial liability as at fair value through profit or loss, the liability is measured at amortised cost which will include any directly attributable transaction costs.

In November 2006 the IFRIC issued a rejection notice on changes in the contractual terms of an existing equity instrument that results in the instrument being reclassified to a financial liability for the issuer. Two issues were discussed: (i) on what basis the financial liability should be measured at the date when the terms were changed and (ii) how any difference between the carrying amount of the previously recognised equity instrument and the amount of the financial liability recognised at the date when the terms were changed should be accounted for. The IFRIC noted that at the time when the contractual terms were changed, a financial liability was initially recognised, and, furthermore, that a financial liability on initial recognition is measured at its fair value in accordance with IAS 39.43. The IFRIC observed that Example 3 of IFRIC 2 *Members' Shares in Co-operative Entities and Similar Instruments* deals with a similar situation. In that example, at the time when the financial liabilities are recognised, as a result of a change in terms, they are recognised at their fair value.

The IFRIC observed that the change in the terms of the instrument gave rise to derecognition of the original equity instrument. The IFRIC noted that IAS 32.33 states that no gain or loss shall be recognised in profit or loss on the purchase, sale, issue or cancellation of an entity's own equity instruments. The IFRIC, therefore, believed that, at the time when the terms were changed, the difference between the carrying amount of the equity instrument and the fair value of the newly recognised financial liability should be recognised in equity.

2.2 Trade date and settlement date accounting

'Regular way' purchases and sales of financial assets are recognised by applying either trade or settlement date accounting. A 'regular way' purchase or sale is defined as a transaction whose contractual terms 'require delivery of the asset within a time frame established generally by regulation or convention in the marketplace concerned'. [IAS 39.9] A marketplace is not limited to a formal stock exchange or organised over-the-counter market. Rather, it means the environment in which the financial asset is customarily exchanged. An acceptable time frame would be the period reasonably and customarily required for the parties to complete the transaction and prepare and execute closing documents. [IAS 39.IG.B.28] The trade date is the date of the commitment to buy or sell the financial asset. The settlement date is the date of the delivery of the asset. If a transaction is considered 'regular way' a derivative is not recognised for the time period between trade and settlement date.

Where trade date accounting is applied, the entity recognises the financial asset to be received and the corresponding liability to pay for it at the trade date; on disposal, the financial asset is removed from the statement of financial position on the trade date. [IAS 39.AG55]

Under the settlement date accounting approach, the asset is recognised on the day on which it is received by the entity; on disposal, the asset continues to be recognised until such time as the asset is delivered to the buyer. Between the trade date and settlement date, although the asset itself is not yet recognised, the entity is required to account for changes in its fair value, applying the same measurement basis that will be used to account for the acquired asset once it is recognised (i.e. changes in fair value are recorded in profit or loss for assets to be classified as at fair value through profit or loss, in other comprehensive income for assets to be classified as available-for-sale, and not recognised for assets to be carried at amortised cost). [IAS 39.AG56] An entity must choose between trade date and settlement date accounting for each category of financial asset as defined by IAS 39. [IAS 39.AG53]

Example 2.2A

Trade and settlement date accounting for a purchase of an asset

The following example illustrates the amounts to be recorded for a purchase of a financial asset.

The dates that are relevant to the example are:

- trade date: 29 December 20X1
- period end date: 31 December 20X1; and
- settlement date: 4 January 20X2

TRADE DATE ACCOUNTING

Journal entries	Held to maturity	Available-for-sale	Fair value through profit or loss
29 December 20X1			
	Dr Asset 1,000 Cr Liability 1,000	Dr Asset 1,000 Cr Liability 1,000	Dr Asset 1,000 Cr Liability 1,000

TRADE DATE ACCOUNTING

Journal entries	Held to maturity	Available-for-sale	Fair value through profit or loss
Description	*To recognise asset and to record payable*	*To recognise asset and to record payable*	*To recognise asset and to record payable*
31 December 20X1			
	–	Dr Asset 2	Dr Asset 2
	–	Cr Equity 2	Cr Profit or loss 2
Description		*With the increase in fair value to date*	*With the increase in fair value to date*
4 January 20X2			
	–	Dr Asset 1	Dr Asset 1
	–	Cr Equity 1	Cr Profit or loss 1
Description		*With the increase in fair value to date*	*With the increase in fair value to date*
	Dr Liability 1,000	Dr Liability 1,000	Dr Liability 1,000
	Cr Cash 1,000	Cr Cash 1,000	Cr Cash 1,000
Description	*With the amount contracted to pay for the asset*	*With the amount contracted to pay for the asset*	*With the amount contracted to pay for the asset*

SETTLEMENT DATE ACCOUNTING

Journal entries	Held to maturity	Available-for-sale	Fair value through profit or loss
29 December 20X1			
	–	–	–
	–	–	–
31 December 20X1			
	–	Dr Receivable 2	Dr Receivable 2
	–	Cr Equity 2	Cr Profit or loss 2
Description		*With the increase in fair value to date*	*With the increase in fair value to date*
4 January 20X2			
	–	Dr Receivable 1	Dr Receivable 1
	–	Cr Equity 1	Cr Profit or loss 1
Description		*With the increase in fair value to date*	*With the increase in fair value to date*
	Dr Asset 1,000	Dr Asset 1,003	Dr Asset 1,003
	Cr Cash 1,000	Cr Cash 1,000	Cr Cash 1,000
	–	Cr Receivable 3	Cr Receivable 3
Description	*With the amount contracted to pay for the asset*	*With the amount contracted to pay for the asset and its change in fair value since trade date*	*With the amount contracted to pay for the asset and its change in fair value since trade date*

When the settlement provisions of a financial instrument differ between various active markets the entity must apply the provisions that apply in the market in which the purchase or sale under the financial instrument actually takes place.

Example 2.2B

Regular way contracts: which customary settlement provisions apply?

[Extract from IAS 39.IG.B.30]

Entity XYZ purchases one million shares of Entity ABC on a US stock exchange, for example, through a broker. The settlement date of the contract is six business days later. Trades for equity shares on US exchanges customarily settle in three business days. Because the trade settles in six business days, it does not meet the exemption as a regular way trade.

However, if XYZ did the same transaction on a foreign exchange that has a customary settlement period of six business days, the contract would meet the exemption for a regular way trade.

Where the regulation or convention for settlement differs between a derivative over the underlying, say a call option over a share, and the underlying itself, say the share, the regulation or convention that is used to determine whether the financial instrument is regular way would be the regulation or convention specific to that instrument. For example, if the call option over the share is regularly settled within 14 days of exercise of the option in the option markets, but a direct acquisition of a share requires 3 day settlement, the entity will look to the options market in determining whether an option is regular way or not. [IAS 39.IG.B.31]

Example 2.2C

Application of trade and settlement date accounting for different categories of financial asset

Entity P has an accounting policy of settlement date accounting for loans and receivables and trade date accounting for available-for-sale financial assets. Entity P enters into a regular way transaction whereby it will sell a loan in exchange for an available-for-sale equity instrument. At the date of entering into the arrangement, 30 March 20X8, both assets had the same fair value. The settlement date is 2 April 20X8. Entity P's reporting period is 31 March 20X8.

	Amortised cost US$	**Fair value US$**
30 March 20X8		
Loan and receivable	10,000	
Available-for-sale asset		10,400
31 March 20X8		
Loan and receivable	10,005	
Available-for-sale asset		10,350
2 April 20X8		
Loan and receivable	10,015	
Available-for-sale asset		10,325

30 March 20X8

Dr	Available-for-sale asset	10,400
Cr	Financial liability	10,400

To recognise the acquisition of the available-for-sale asset at trade date

31 March 20X8

Dr	Available-for-sale reserve (equity)	50
Cr	Available for sale asset	50

To recognise the change in fair value of the available-for-sale equity security

Dr	Loan and receivable	5
Cr	Interest income	5

To recognise interest earned on an effective interest rate basis

2 April 20X8

Dr	Loan and receivable	10
Cr	Interest income	10

To recognise interest earned on an effective interest rate basis

Dr	Available for sale reserve (equity)	25
Cr	Available for sale asset	25

To recognise the change in fair value of the available-for-sale equity security

Dr	Financial liability	10,400
Cr	Loan and receivable	10,015
Cr	Profit or loss	385

To recognise the gain on disposal of the loan and receivable at the date of derecognition. The gain represents the difference between the proceeds received, being the fair value of the available-for-sale asset at the date the contract is entered into, and amortised cost of the loan and receivable at the settlement date.

Trade or settlement date accounting for regular way transactions is not limited to exchanges of securities for cash as exchanges of large amounts of foreign currency are also subject to market convention. For example, an entity may agree to exchange an amount of foreign currency cash recognised in its statement of financial position for an amount of functional currency cash at a predetermined foreign currency exchange rate but with deferred delivery in, say, 2 days after the agreement was entered into subject to normal market settlement convention.

If the market settlement convention is not deemed normal, i.e. this is not a regular way transaction, the entity would continue to recognise the foreign currency cash balance and recognise a foreign currency forward contract to sell foreign currency and buy functional currency in 2 days time at fair value through profit or loss. At maturity of the foreign currency forward contract the foreign currency cash and the foreign currency forward contract would both be derecognised and the functional currency recognised.

If the market settlement convention is deemed normal, i.e. the transaction is a regular way one, the accounting would depend on the entity's accounting policy of applying either trade or settlement date accounting.

Example 2.2D

Trade and settlement date accounting for an exchange of foreign currency cash

Entity A agrees to sell US$200m that are recognised in its statement of financial position for £100m with settlement 2 days after trade date ('t+2'). Entity A has a Sterling functional currency. T+2 is considered to be the normal market settlement convention in the market Entity A is transacting in for the size and type of asset being exchanged. Entity A, therefore, consider the transaction regular way.

The dates and currency rates that are relevant are as follows:

- trade date: 30 December 20X1; US$2:£1 spot rate
- period end date: 31 December 20X1; and
- settlement date: 1 January 20X2

If Entity A's policy is trade date accounting the following entries would apply.

30 December 20X1

Dr	Receivable – £	£100m	(the balance should be discounted unless the effect is immaterial)
Cr	Cash – US$	£100m	

to derecognise the US$ cash at the trade date and recognise a receivable for the Sterling amount to be received at 1 January 20X2

31 December 20X1

As the US$ asset has been recognised there is no foreign currency monetary item that requires translation (had the receipt been in a foreign currency the receivable would be retranslated to Entity A's functional currency at the period end).

1 January 20X1

Dr	Cash – £	£100m
Cr	Receivable – £	£100m

to derecognise the Sterling receivable and recognise the Sterling cash at the settlement date.

If Entity A's policy is settlement date accounting the following entries would apply.

30 December 20X1

No entries are required because the US$ cash remains recognised until settlement date.

31 December 20X1

As Entity A has agreed to sell the US$ at 1 January 20X1 at a fixed amount of Sterling it does not have exposure to foreign currency risk. Entity A does not retranslate the US$ to Sterling after the trade date. This is consistent with IAS 39.IG.D.2.2 that states 'A change in the fair value of a financial asset that is sold on a regular way basis is not recorded in the financial statements between trade date and settlement date even if the entity applies settlement date accounting because the seller's right to changes in the fair value ceases on the trade date'. Therefore, no entries are required.

1 January 20X1

Dr	Cash – £	£100m
Cr	Cash – US$	£100m

to derecognise the US$ cash and recognise the Sterling cash at the settlement date

If an entity derecognises a financial asset using settlement date accounting but receives non-cash consideration for selling the asset which, when classified under IAS 39, will be recognised using trade date accounting the entity must apply trade date accounting to the non-cash financial asset to be received.

Example 2.2E

Settlement date accounting: exchange of non-cash financial assets

[Extract from IAS 39.IG.D.2.3]

On 29 December 20X2 (trade date) Entity A enters into a contract to sell Note Receivable A, which is carried at amortised cost, in exchange for Bond B, which will be classified as held for trading and measured at fair value. Both assets have a fair value of CU1,010 on 29 December, while the amortised cost of Note Receivable A is CU1,000. Entity A uses settlement date accounting for loans and receivables and trade date accounting for assets held for trading. On 31 December 20X2 (financial year-end), the fair value of Note Receivable A is CU1,012 and the fair value of Bond B is CU1,009. On 4 January 20X3, the fair value of Note Receivable A is CU1,013 and the fair value of Bond B is CU1,007. The following entries are made:

29 December 20X2

Dr	Bond B	CU1,010
Cr	Payable	CU1,010

31 December 20X2

Dr	Trading loss	CU1
Cr	Bond B	CU1

4 January 20X3

Dr	Payable	CU1,010
Dr	Trading loss	CU2
Cr	Note Receivable A	CU1,000
Cr	Bond B	CU2
Cr	Realisation gain	CU10

In January 2007 the IFRIC issued a rejection notice on accounting for short sales of securities when the terms of the short sales require delivery of the securities within the time frame established generally by regulation or convention in the marketplace concerned. A fixed price commitment between trade date and settlement date of a short sale contract meets the definition of a derivative. As IAS 39.AG55 and AG56 only permit a choice of trade or settlement date accounting for recognition and derecognition of financial assets traded under regular way purchases and regular way sales of long positions, the Standard would require a short sale to be recognised as a derivative until delivery of the security. The IFRIC acknowledged that an interpretation that is applied in practice is that entities choose trade date or settlement date accounting for short sales. Specifically, practice recognises the short sales as financial liabilities at fair value with changes in fair value recognised in profit or loss. Under the industry practice, the same profit or loss amount is recognised as would have been recognised if short sales of securities were accounted for as derivatives but the securities are presented differently in the statement of financial position. The IFRIC acknowledged that requiring entities to account for the short positions as derivatives may create considerable practical problems for entities' accounting systems and controls with little, if any, improvement to the quality of the financial information presented. For these reasons and because there is little diversity in practice, the IFRIC decided not to take the issue onto its agenda.

IAS 39 does not provide guidance on whether the trade date exemption can be applied if an entity delivers a financial instrument under a regular way contract but the delivery date is delayed, and the asset is delivered outside the normal convention for that type of contract. For example, a contract has a delivery date of t+3 days, but there is a delay in delivery and the instrument is delivered at t+5. A delay should not preclude use of the regular way exemption if the delay is outside the control of the entity.

US GAAP comparison: Whether a particular entity applies trade date or settlement date accounting is often dependent on the industry in which an entity operates. US GAAP accounting guidance indicates that trade-date accounting is required for regular-way security trades for certain types of entities, including broker-dealers, banks and saving institutions, credit unions, finance companies, mortgage companies, investment companies, and employee benefit plans.

FAS 133 specifically excludes from its scope contracts that are considered regular way security trades unless a contract permits or requires net settlement or a market mechanism exists to facilitate net settlement. However, if recognition of a contract on its trade date is required, regardless of the contract permitting net settlement, trade date accounting is followed.

3 Derecognition of financial assets

A financial asset is derecognised, i.e. removed from the statement of financial position, when, and only when, either the contractual rights to the asset's cash flows expire, or the asset is transferred and the transfer qualifies for derecognition.

The decision whether a transfer qualifies for derecognition is made by applying a combination of risks and rewards and control tests. The risks and rewards tests seek to establish whether, having transferred a financial asset, the entity continues to be exposed to the risks of ownership of that asset and/or continues to enjoy the benefits that it generates. The control tests are designed with a view to understand which entity controls the asset, i.e. which entity can direct how the benefits of that asset are realised.

This approach of using two types of tests is often criticised for being a mix of two accounting models that can create confusion in application. IAS 39 addresses this criticism by providing a clear hierarchy of application of the two sets of tests: risks and rewards tests are applied first, with the control tests used only when the entity has neither transferred substantially all risks and rewards of the asset nor retained them.

Inherent in the IAS 39 derecognition model is the notion of 'stickiness', i.e. it is more difficult to remove an asset from an entity's statement of financial position than it is to recognise that asset in the first place. Derecognition cannot be achieved by merely transferring the legal title to a financial asset to another party. The substance of the arrangement must be assessed in order to determine whether an entity has transferred the economic exposure associated with the rights inherent in the asset, i.e. its risks and rewards, and in some cases control of those rights.

US GAAP comparison: The differences in financial instrument accounting between US GAAP and IFRS are greatest in the area of derecognition as different derecognition models apply. Broadly, US GAAP applies a financial-components approach that focuses on control. Under this model, after there has been a transfer of financial assets, an entity recognises the financial assets it controls and the liabilities it has incurred, derecognises financial assets when control has been surrendered, and derecognises liabilities when extinguished.

FAS 140 *Accounting for Transfers and Servicing of Financial Assets and Extinguishments of Liabilities* states that a transfer of financial assets in which the transferor surrenders control over those assets is accounted for as a sale to the extent that consideration other than beneficial interests in the transferred assets is received in exchange. The transferor has surrendered control over transferred assets if, and only if, all of the following conditions are met.

(a) The transferred assets have been isolated from the transferor – put presumptively beyond the reach of the transferor and its creditors, even in bankruptcy or other receivership.

(b) Each transferee (or, if the transferee is a qualifying special-purpose entity (SPE), each holder of the beneficial interests in the SPE) has the right to pledge or exchange the assets (or their beneficial interests), and no condition constrains the transferee (or holder) from taking advantage of its right to pledge or exchange and no condition provides more than a trivial benefit to the transferor.

(c) The transferor does not maintain effective control over the transferred assets through either (1) an agreement that both entitles and obligates the transferor to repurchase or redeem them before their maturity or (2) the ability to cause unilaterally the holder to return specific assets, other than through a clean-up call.

The control based model in US GAAP will result in significantly different accounting assessments when compared to IFRS in many instances. For example, if a transferor sells a portfolio of short-term receivables to a transferee and at the same time issues a guarantee of credit risk in respect of those receivables equal to several times expected credit losses (but not necessarily the full amount), and there is no other significant risk of the assets, the application of the US

GAAP criteria may lead to derecognition, provided the transferor is able to obtain a legal opinion that indicates that the receivables have been legally isolated from the transferor and its creditors, including in bankruptcy. If the transferor is not able to obtain such a legal opinion, the transferred receivables are not derecognised. In contrast, under IFRS the arrangement would fail derecognition simply because substantially all the risks and rewards of ownership of the assets have been retained by the transferor (see **3.1.5** below).

In summary, because IAS 39 is primarily a risk-and-rewards model, a transferor can transfer substantially all the risks and rewards of ownership of a particular asset while still retaining control over the transferred asset and achieve derecognition. However, under US GAAP, if a transferor continues to control a transferred financial asset regardless of whether substantially all risks and rewards of that asset are transferred to a third party, it must continue to recognise the asset until control is surrendered. Additionally, IAS 39 does not include a notion of legal isolation. Under IFRSs, control of a financial asset may be surrendered regardless of whether the transferor's creditors have the ability to reclaim the transferred asset in the event of bankruptcy.

In December 2008, the FASB issued FASB Staff Position (FSP) and FIN 46(R)-8-*Disclosures by Public Entities (Enterprises) about Transfers of Financial Assets and Interests in Variable Interest Entities*. The disclosures required by this FSP are intended to provide greater transparency to financial statement users about a transferor's continuing involvement with transferred financial assets and an enterprise's involvement with variable interest entities and qualifying SPEs.

3.1 The IAS 39 derecognition decision tree

IAS 39 provides a decision tree, reproduced below, that clarifies the hierarchy of application of the derecognition tests.

[IAS 39.AG36]

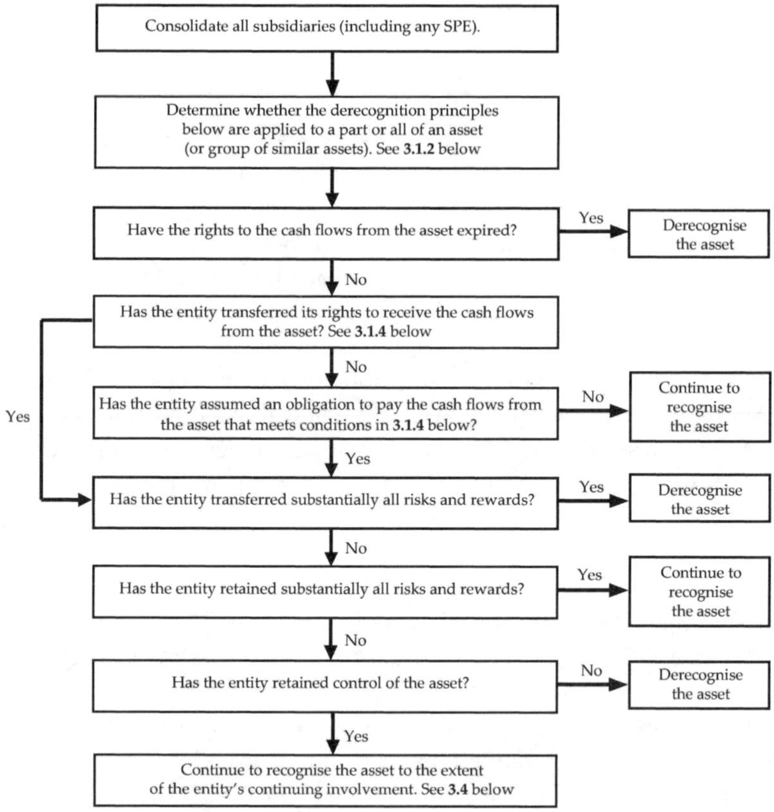

The steps of this decision tree are explained below.

3.1.1 *Consolidate all subsidiaries including any Special Purpose Entity (SPE)*

The first step is to define at which level the derecognition decision is to be applied: in the parent's separate financial statements or in the consolidated financial statements. Where derecognition of financial assets is to be applied in the consolidated financial statements, the reporting group must first consolidate all subsidiaries in accordance with IAS 27 *Consolidated and Separate Financial Statements* and SIC-12 *Consolidation – Special Purpose Entities*. [IAS 39.15]

This first step ensures that the derecognition decision is consistent regardless of whether the transfer of assets is direct to investors or through a consolidated SPE that obtains the financial assets, and transfers these financial assets, or their portion, to third party investors. [IAS 39.BC64]

IAS 27 requires consolidation of all entities that are controlled by the reporting entity. SIC-12 requires consolidation of an SPE when the substance of the relationship between an entity and the SPE indicates that the SPE is controlled by the entity.

Special purpose entities may take the form of a corporation, trust, partnership or unincorporated entity and are often created with legal arrangements that impose strict and sometimes permanent limits on the decision-making powers of their governing board, trustees or management over the operations of the SPE. Frequently, these provisions specify that the policy guiding the ongoing activities of the SPE cannot be modified, other than perhaps by its creator or sponsor (i.e. they operate on so-called 'autopilot').

Structured transactions, such as securitisations and certain other asset-based financing arrangements, typically seek, as their primary economic objective, to isolate legally the assets from the party providing them (and from that party's creditors) to avoid the investor having a credit exposure to the transferor. This isolation is often achieved through a SPE. For many sellers of financial assets, structured arrangements that isolate the assets permit access to capital markets at more favourable prices than might otherwise be available since credit agencies and investors require a lower return from structures that avoid the consequences arising from bankruptcies. This ability is particularly important for those entities whose credit ratings may reflect the adverse effects of financial, operational or environmental risks not directly attributable to the assets being transferred. However, this bankruptcy isolation does not automatically lead to the conclusion that the sponsor is not required to consolidate the SPE. Other factors set out in SIC-12 have to be considered. Consolidation may, through its impact on the sponsor's financial ratios, negate certain of the benefits of isolating the SPE.

A SPE may issue different types of beneficial interests, multiple classes of interests and classes of interests with different maturities. Several forms of SPE are common, depending on the asset being securitised, the securities issued by the entity and the legal framework governing the entity's operations. These include grantor trusts, owner trusts, revolving trusts, master trusts, special purpose corporations and REMICS (Real Estate Mortgage Investment Conduits).

Typically, the SPE is prevented from selling, assigning or pledging its direct interest in any financial asset it holds; however, the owners of the beneficial interests generally have the right to pledge or exchange their beneficial interests.

In November 2006 the IFRIC issued a rejection notice on the application of SIC-12. The IFRIC was asked for the relative weight to be given to the various indicators in SIC-12.10 in determining who should consolidate a SPE. The issue focused on a situation in which all the decisions necessary for the ongoing activities of the SPE had been predetermined by its creator and in which the majority of the 'equity interest tranche' had been transferred to a third party. The question was whether in such a situation the benefits and risks factors specified in SIC-12.10(c) and (d) took precedence over the activities and decision-making factors in SIC-12.10(a) and (b). The IFRIC noted that, under IAS 27 *Consolidated and Separate Financial Statements*, control, which is the basis for consolidation, has two components: power to govern and rights to obtain benefits. The IFRIC noted that the factors set out in SIC-12.10 are indicators only and not necessarily conclusive. The IFRIC believed that this approach was deliberate, in acknowledgement of the fact that circumstances vary case by case. In the IFRIC's view, SIC-12 requires that the party having control over an SPE should be determined through the exercise of judgement and skill in each case, after taking into account *all* relevant factors.

In December 2008, the IASB published its new consolidation standard for exposure, ED10. The exposure draft is proposed to replace IAS 27, *Consolidated and Separate Financial Statements*, and SIC-12, *Consolidation – Special Purpose Entities*. The main objectives of ED10 are to (1) provide a single consolidation model for all entities, (2) improve the definition of control and (3) improve disclosure requirements about consolidated and unconsolidated entities. A reporting entity controls another entity when the reporting entity has the power to direct the activities of that other entity to generate returns for the reporting entity. The exposure draft would require *continuous* consideration of *both power and returns* together when assessing control.

US GAAP comparison: Under US GAAP, there are two different models for determining whether consolidation is appropriate. If a reporting enterprise has an interest in an entity that meets the definition of a variable interest entity (VIE) in FIN 46(R), the risk and rewards model under FIN 46(R) should be applied. Under this model, consolidation is based on which interest holder absorbs a majority of the risks and rewards of a VIE. However, if a reporting entity has an interest in an entity that is not considered a VIE or that is not within the scope of FIN 46(R), the consolidation model in ARB 51 must be applied. Under this model, consolidation is based on whether the reporting entity has a controlling financial interest in the entity.

Under US GAAP, a transferor that transfers assets to an SPE that does not have the ability to freely pledge or exchange the transferred asset can still derecognise the transferred asset if the transferee SPE meets the definition of a Qualifying SPE (QSPE) provided the underlying beneficial interest holders in the QSPE have the ability to freely pledge or exchange their beneficial interest and the other conditions for derecognition are met. In other words, the transferor can 'look through' a QSPE and consider whether the underlying beneficial interest holders in the QSPE have the ability to pledge or exchange their beneficial interests. Under US GAAP, a transferor of assets to an entity that meets the definition of a QSPE is not permitted to consolidate that entity. Note that the FASB has tentatively decided that it will remove the concept of QSPE from FAS 140.

3.1.2 *Determine whether the derecognition principles are applied to a part or all of an asset (or group of similar assets)*

An entity needs to determine what is being subjected to an evaluation for derecognition: a whole financial asset; a group of financial assets; a part of a financial asset; or a part of a group of similar financial assets.

An entity may apply the derecognition principles to a part of a financial asset (or a group of similar financial assets) if the part comprises one of the following:

- specifically identified cash flows, e.g. an interest or principal strip from a debt instrument;
- a fully proportionate share of the cash flows, e.g. the rights to the cash flows on 90 per cent of all cash flows arising from a debt instrument; or
- a fully proportionate share of specifically identified cash flows, e.g. 90 per cent of the cash flows that arise on the interest strip from a debt instrument.

In all other cases the financial asset (or the group of financial assets) is considered in its entirety. [IAS 39.16(b)]

Example 3.1.2

Determining the part of a financial asset subject to transfer

Entity X, the transferor, transfers the right to the first CU90 of cash flows that are derived from a debt instrument; the fair value of the asset is CU100 on the date of transfer.

The transferor cannot apply the derecognition model to part of the asset because the transferor has neither transferred specifically identifiable cash flows, nor a fully proportionate share of all or part of the cash flows. The transferor effectively agrees to absorb the first CU10 of losses from the asset that has been subject to the transfer.

It should be noted, however, that if the transferor had transferred a 90 per cent pro rata share of all cash flows from the asset, then the derecognition model could be applied to the part of the asset that has been transferred, i.e. 90 per cent. In that case, the transferor and the transferee would have agreed to participate in a fully proportionate share of losses.

The Standard does not provide guidance on what makes assets 'similar'. 'Similar' generally means that the two instruments have contractually specified cash flows which are similar in amounts and timings, and have similar risk attributes. An entity shall consider the similarity of terms, e.g. prepayment features, interest rates, currency denomination. By definition, there will always be some differences between similar instruments, otherwise such instruments would be identical. A portfolio of mortgages transferred by a bank is often deemed to contain similar financial assets. Also, a portfolio of corporate bonds transferred by a bank is often deemed to contain similar financial assets. However, no two portfolios are ever precisely alike. A transfer of a portfolio of mortgages would need to be assessed separately from a transfer of a portfolio of corporate bonds even if the two transfers happen at the same time. With individual equity investments, the differences are so significant that no two equity investments are ever likely to be similar – the value is affected by intangibles and other 'soft' assets, like reputation, which are not recorded on the statement of financial position or measured in any consistent way, but which do affect perceptions and hence market price.

In September 2006 the Board was asked by the IFRIC for input and advice on what is the meaning of 'similar' for group of financial assets (in IAS 39.16). The Board responded with its view, which the IFRIC used as a basis for a tentative rejection wording, along with other derecognition issues, in November 2006. The Board believed that derivative assets (which are often transferred together with non-derivative financial assets) are not 'similar' to non-derivative financial assets. Therefore, an entity would apply the derecognition tests in IAS 39 to non-derivative financial assets (or groups of similar non-derivative financial assets) and derivative financial assets (or groups of similar derivative financial assets) separately, even if they are transferred at the same time. The Board also indicated that transferred derivatives that could be either assets or liabilities (such as interest rate swaps) would have to meet both the financial asset and the financial liability derecognition tests.

Following comments from constituents, at the IFRIC meeting in January 2007, the IFRIC decided to withdraw its tentative agenda decision and decided to add a project on derecognition to its agenda. However, in March 2009 the IFRIC decided to remove this issue from its agenda as the IASB accelerated its project to develop a replacement for the sections of IAS 39 on derecognition which was issues as an exposure draft in March 2009 with an expectation of a new derecognition standard to be issued no later than 2010.

US GAAP comparison: Under US GAAP, FAS 140 does not provide specific requirements that must be met for a portion (an undivided interest) of a financial asset to be derecognised. Rather, FAS 140 provides that a portion of a financial asset may be derecognised if control over that specified portion is surrendered and the conditions for sale accounting in FAS 140 are met. For example, if the transferor has surrendered control over 90 percent of the cash flows of a transferred asset, derecognition of that portion of the financial asset is appropriate regardless of a credit guarantee that compensates the transferee for credit losses up to a specified percentage.

3.1.3 *Have the rights to the cash flows from the asset expired?*

An entity derecognises a financial asset when the rights to the cash flows from that financial asset expire. [IAS 39.17]

The rights to the cash flows expire when, for example, a financial asset reaches its maturity and there are clearly no further cash flows arising from that asset, or a purchased option reaches its maturity unexercised. An entity may have a right to receive certain or all cash flows from a financial asset over a specified period of time which may be shorter than the contractual maturity of that financial asset. In that case, the entity's right to the cash flows expires once the specified period expires.

3.1.4 *Has the entity transferred its rights to receive the cash flows from the asset?*

An entity may transfer the contractual rights to the cash flows that comprise a financial asset, or it may retain the contractual rights to the cash flows, but assume a contractual obligation to pass on those cash flows to one or more recipients, in what is often referred to as a 'pass-through' arrangement.

In some pass-through arrangements an entity acts as an agent of the eventual recipients of the cash flows that derive from the asset. The entity agrees to receive cash flows and has a concurrent obligation to pay those cash flows to the eventual recipient. For this to be the case, the following conditions on the transfer have to be satisfied:
[IAS 39.19]

- the entity has no obligation to pay amounts to the eventual recipients unless it collects equivalent amounts from the original asset, i.e. the entity does not benefit or suffer from performance or non-performance of the asset;
- the entity is prohibited by the terms of the transfer arrangement from selling or pledging the original asset other than as security to the eventual recipients for the obligation to pay them cash flows, i.e. the entity does not have control of the future economic benefits associated with the transferred asset; and
- the entity has an obligation to pass on or remit the cash flows that it has collected on behalf of the eventual recipients *without material delay*, is prohibited from re-investing the cash flows received in the short settlement period between receiving them and remitting them to the eventual recipient in anything other than cash or cash equivalents and any interest earned on such investments must be passed on to the eventual recipients, i.e. the entity has no access to the benefits of the asset.

Even if the entity passes on the interest earned, the delay in passing on the cash flows alters the credit risk characteristics of the original asset such that the eventual recipient of the cash flows is exposed to, not only the original asset subject to the arrangement, but to additional credit risk on the investment cash flows from the asset.

> *Without material delay* does not mean instantaneously, nor does it imply an extended length of time. The contractual arrangement will need to be considered in full in order to make an assessment as to whether the timeframe between the collection of cash flows on the

underlying assets and the point at which they are passed on to the eventual recipients is material in the context of the contractual arrangements of the transfer.

In some arrangements, the cash collected on the underlying assets occurs sporadically throughout a period of time. For example, if an entity retains the rights to the cash flows arising on a group of credit card receivables, the payments arising on those credit cards are likely to occur on any given day throughout the month. The contractual arrangement of the transfer may require that those cash flows are remitted to the eventual recipients, weekly, monthly, quarterly or even annually. There is a trade-off between passing on the cash flows almost as soon as they arise and the administrative burden that goes along with passing on those cash flows. Half-yearly, and certainly annual payments, to the eventual recipients would be considered a material delay as the conditions specified above fail and therefore derecognition would be inappropriate in these circumstances. It appears reasonable that the entity can invest the cash flows from the assets for up to three months without breaching the condition that all cash flows must be passed to the eventual recipient without material delay.

When the contractual arrangement that passes the cash flows on the transferred asset to the eventual recipient is legally structured as a share, as opposed to a conventional obligation to a creditor, the form of the share may prevent the pass-through tests being met. For example, if a dividend under the share, being the cash received under the transferred asset, is only required to be paid if there are sufficient distributable profits in the entity, then a lack of distributable profits will limit the transferor's ability to make payments to the eventual receipts without material delay. The potential for a dividend block in this case will prohibit the transferor meeting the pass-through criteria. Consideration should be given to other restrictions, either inherent in the terms of the instrument, or in the articles of the entity that would limit the entity's ability to pay amounts to the eventual recipients when due without material delay.

The likelihood that the transferor will default under the pass-through arrangements as a result of a default on other creditor obligations is not considered an impediment to meeting the pass-through criteria as the transferor is assumed to be a going concern. In many cases the transferee may limit this risk by ensuring that the transferred assets reside in a bankruptcy remote special purpose entity so that the wider credit risk of the transferor is not borne by the transferee.

An entity may provide credit enhancement in a transfer arrangement so that it suffers the first loss on the asset up to a specified amount. This credit enhancement may be in the form of over-collateralisation or may be in the form of purchasing a subordinated interest in a consolidated SPE (in the latter case the entity is applying the pass-through tests at a consolidated level). Providing credit enhancement will not in itself result in failure of the pass-through tests if all cash received on transferred assets, if received by the transferor, is paid by the transferor to the eventual recipient, though it may result in failure of derecognition due to the entity retaining substantially all the risks and rewards of ownership of the assets. The pass-through tests must be considered prior to considering the entity's exposure to risk and rewards.

An entity may pass all three of the pass-through tests even when it provides credit enhancement. In such cases the entity will pay cash it receives on the asset without material delay to the eventual recipients should the debtor pay. If the debtor fails to pay, the entity will absorb the first loss fully, with the eventual recipient only suffering a loss after the first loss has been fully absorbed.

If a greater amount of cash is realised on the assets than is needed to pay the eventual recipient, i.e. the eventual recipient's initial investment is fully paid, then the entity will retain the remainder of the cash and will not pass it on. In all cases the entity passes 'any cash it collects on behalf of the eventual recipients'.

Example 3.1.4

Pass-through arrangements

Entity B enters into an arrangement with Entity C where Entity C pays Entity B CU0.9m in return for receiving cash flows on CU1.0m of assets when expected losses on the assets are 10 per cent of all cash flows (interest and principal). Entity B retains the contractual rights to receive the cash flows from the assets but assumes an obligation to pay cash flows from the asset to Entity C. The maximum cash flows that Entity C can receive under the arrangement are interest and principal on a notional of CU0.9m. If actual credit losses are lower than expected, say only 5 per cent, Entity B will pay Entity C CU0.9m and retain CU0.05m.

Entity B will pass the pass-through tests, assuming all other conditions are met, as Entity B will pass interest and principal on a notional up to CU0.9m of the cash flows to Entity C.

However, if the form of the transaction was different, in that Entity C pays Entity B CU1.0m for the assets and purchases a financial guarantee contract from Entity B for CU0.1m then the pass-through tests would not be met as

Entity B will pay the eventual recipient, Entity C, even when it does not collect the equivalent amount from the original assets.

In a revolving structure cash received on the assets is reinvested in buying new receivables assets. In other words, cash 'revolves' into new assets instead of being returned immediately to the investors. Upon maturity the reinvested assets are used to repay the beneficial interest holders. Such 'revolving' structures do not meet the pass-through tests as they involve a material delay before the original cash is passed onto the eventual recipients and the reinvestment would typically be not in cash or cash equivalents. The treatment of revolving structures described above was confirmed by the IFRIC in September 2005.

US GAAP comparison: Under US GAAP, FAS 140 does not allow for derecognition of a financial asset if the rights to the contractual cash flows of that financial asset are retained by the transferor. While FAS 140 does not allow an entity to derecognise assets in which the contractual right to the cash flows are retained, a transferor may be able to achieve a result similar to the pass-through concept in IAS 39 by transferring assets to a trust that meets the definition of a qualifying special purpose entity (QSPE).

Under US GAAP, if a revolving structure meets the definition of a qualifying special purpose entity (QSPE), the transferor of assets into the revolving structure typically meets the criteria for derecognition. In this case, derecognition of the transferred asset may be appropriate even if cash from maturing receivables is continually reinvested rather than being passed onto the eventual recipients. In November 2008, the FASB issued a proposed amendment to FAS 140, which would remove the concept of a QSPE from FAS 140.

An entity enters into an arrangement with a third party to transfer the contractual rights to receive the cash flows of a financial asset, but may agree to continue to act as an agent to administer collection and distribution of cash flows to the recipient (i.e. it retains servicing rights on the cash flows).

IAS 39.18(a) focuses on whether an entity transfers the contractual rights to receive the cash flows from a financial asset. The determination of whether the contractual rights to cash flows have been transferred is not affected by the transferor retaining the role of an agent to administer collection and distribution of cash flows. Retention of servicing rights by the entity transferring the financial asset does not, in itself, cause the transfer to fail the requirements in IAS

39.18(a). However, careful judgement must be applied to determine whether the entity providing servicing is acting solely as an agent for the owner of the financial asset, i.e. whether it has transferred all risks and rewards.

The IFRIC confirmed in September 2005 that the existence of servicing does not prevent an entity from transferring the contractual rights to the cash flows of the asset.

When the Board considered a number of derecognition issues in September 2006 at the request of the IFRIC it discussed whether the pass-through test is applicable to all transfers in which legal ownership of the financial asset is not transferred. In other words, they considered whether a transfer of legal ownership of the transferred asset is a pre-requisite to be considered a transfer of contractual rights under IAS 39.18(a). The Board indicated that a transaction in which an entity transfers *all* the contractual rights *to receive the cash flows* [emphasis added in the IASB Update] (without necessarily transferring legal ownership of the financial asset), would not be treated as a pass-through. An example might be a situation in which an entity transfers all the legal rights to specifically identified cash flows of a financial asset (e.g. a transfer of the interest or principal of a debt instrument). Conversely, the pass-through test would be applicable to situations when the entity does not transfer all the contractual rights to cash flows of the financial asset, such as disproportionate transfers (see IAS 39.16(b)).

The Board's view in this case would mean that if an arrangement transferred all the legal rights to cash flows for a full proportionate interest in an asset (say 50 per cent of all cash flows), even though legal title of the asset was not transferred to the transferee, the transferor would apply paragraph 18(a) to the transfer, and therefore would avoid the pass-through tests in paragraph 18(b).

The Board also discussed whether conditional transfers should be treated as pass-through transactions. Conditions attached to a transfer could include provisions ensuring the existence and value of transferred cash flows at the date of transfer or conditions relating to the future performance of the asset. The Board indicated that such conditions would not affect whether the entity has transferred the contractual rights to receive cash flows (under IAS 39.18(a)). However, the existence of conditions relating to the future performance of the asset might affect the conclusion related to the transfer of risks and rewards as well as the extent of any continuing involvement by the transferor in the transferred asset.

The Board's view on conditional transfers would allow the pass-through criteria to be met for a transfer of trade receivables even when there is a promise to compensate the transferee should the transferor issue a credit note to the customer if the goods are returned. In this case the transferor is obligated to pay cash to the transferee when the transferee did not collect cash from the asset.

The Board's views were included in a draft rejection notice issued by the IFRIC in November 2006. Following comments from constituents, at the IFRIC meeting in January 2007, the IFRIC decided to withdraw the rejection notice and add a project on derecognition to its agenda. However, in March 2009 the IFRIC decided to remove all the outstanding derecognition issues from its agenda as the IASB accelerated its project to develop a replacement for the sections of IAS 39 on derecognition which was issued as an exposure draft in March 2009. The expectation is a new standard on derecognition will be issued no later than 2010.

3.1.5 *Has the entity transferred substantially all of the risks and rewards of ownership of the asset?*

Determining the extent to which the risks and rewards of the transferred asset have been transferred and retained is critical in determining the accounting outcome for a transfer. The greater the risks and rewards retained the greater is the likelihood of continued recognition. The degree to which risks and rewards have been transferred and its effect on the accounting outcome can be illustrated as follows.

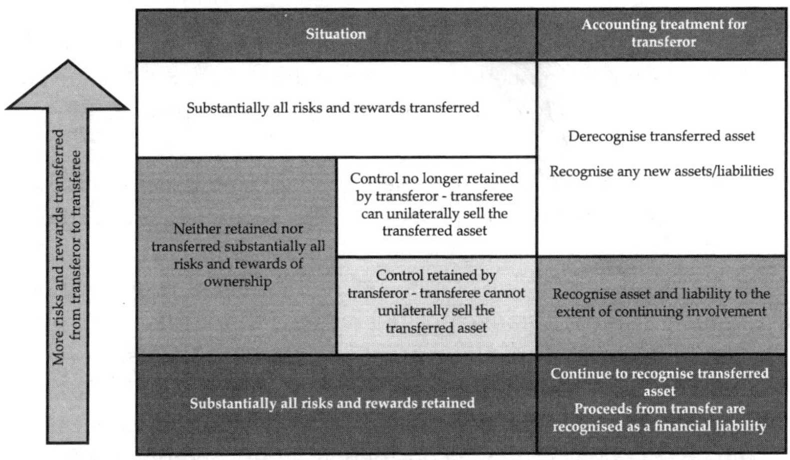

Where the entity transfers substantially all of the risks and rewards of ownership of the financial asset, the asset should be derecognised. The entity may have to recognise separately any rights and obligations created or retained in the transfer. [IAS 39.20(a)]

There is no 'bright line' provided in IAS 39 as to what is meant by 'substantially all' and a significant degree of judgement is required when applying the risks and rewards test.

There are other references in the Standard to various yardsticks that need to be met when applying certain paragraphs. For example, when comparing the old and new terms of a financial liability, the terms are considered to be 'substantially different' if the present value of the cash flows under the new terms is at least 10 per cent different from the discounted present value of the remaining cash flows of the original financial liability (see **4.1** below).

While IAS 39 does not apply the 90 per cent test to derecognition of financial assets, it would seem imprudent to conclude that substantially all risks and rewards of ownership have been transferred where the computations show that the entity still retains more than 10 per cent of the exposure to the variability in present value of the expected future cash flows post transfer.

IAS 39 provides three examples of when an entity has transferred substantially all of the risks and rewards of ownership:
[IAS 39.AG39]

- an unconditional sale of a financial asset;
- a sale of a financial asset together with an option to repurchase the financial asset at its fair value at the time of repurchase; and
- a sale of a financial asset together with a put or call option that is deeply out of the money (i.e. an option that is so far out of the money, it is highly unlikely to be in the money before expiry).

In the first example, it is clear that there has been a transfer of all the risks and rewards of ownership of the asset. In the second example, the entity has sold the asset and, although it can call the asset back, this can only be done at the fair market value of the asset at the time of re-acquisition. The entity is in the same economic position as having sold the asset outright, with the ability to go into the market to reacquire the asset, i.e. it has transferred the full price risk of the asset. In the third example the option is highly unlikely ever to be exercised and has very little value, which is substantially the same economic position as an unconditional sale.

US GAAP comparison: Under US GAAP, an analysis of whether the transferred assets are readily obtainable in the market is required to determine if derecognition is appropriate. In contrast to the second example above, if a transferor sells an asset with an option to repurchase the asset at its fair value, derecognition is allowed only if the transferred assets are readily obtainable in the market place. In this case, control of the transferred asset is not relinquished if the transferee does not have the ability to freely pledge or exchange the asset for fear that the transferor will exercise its option and it will not be able to obtain that asset in the market place.

Pass-through arrangements that meet the criteria in **3.1.4** above may not satisfy the transfer of substantially all risks and rewards test.

Example 3.1.5A

Interaction of pass-through tests and risk and reward tests

Entity A originates a portfolio of five-year interest-bearing loans of CU10,000. Entity A enters into an agreement with Entity C whereby in exchange for a cash payment of CU9,000, Entity A agrees to pay to Entity C the first CU9,000 (plus interest) of cash collected from the loan portfolio. Entity A retains rights to the last CU1,000 (plus interest), i.e. it retains a subordinated residual interest. If Entity A collects, say, only CU8,000 of its loans of CU10,000 because some debtors default, Entity A would pass on to Entity C all of the CU8,000 collected and Entity A keeps nothing of the CU8,000 collected. If Entity A collects CU9,500, it passes CU9,000 to Entity C and retains CU500. Expected losses are CU500.

Even though all cash flows that derive from the portfolio of assets are passed onto Entity C up to a maximum of CU9,000, Entity A has not transferred substantially all the risks and rewards of ownership because of the subordinated retained interest. The residual interest absorbs the likely variability in net cash flows, i.e. the expected losses.

IAS 39 acknowledges that in many cases it will be clear whether or not the entity has transferred substantially all of the risks and rewards of ownership following a transfer of an asset. Where it is unclear whether or not there has been a transfer of substantially all of the risks and rewards of ownership of the financial asset, then the entity will have to evaluate its exposure before and after the transfer by comparing the variability in the amounts and timing of the net cash flows of the transferred asset. [IAS 39.21] If the exposure to the present value of the future net cash flows from the financial asset does not change significantly as a result of the transfer, then the entity has not transferred substantially all of the risks and rewards of ownership.

The computational comparison is made using an appropriate current market interest rate as the discount rate. All reasonably possible outcomes should be considered and a greater weight given to those outcomes that are more likely to occur. This is an expected cash flow model and should include all risks inherent in the cash flows.

There is no example in the Standard that describes the methodology that should be used in performing the risks and rewards assessment. A methodology that is used should be consistently applied to all transfers that are similar in nature. It would be inappropriate to use multiple methodologies for similar transactions and to 'cherry pick' the methodology that produced the desired degree of transfer of risks and rewards.

A common approach is to use a standard deviation statistic as the basis for determining how much variability has been transferred and retained by the transferor. To apply this approach the transferor will need to consider various future scenarios that will impact the amount and timing of cash flows of the transferred assets and calculate the present value of these amounts both before and after the transfer. In the case of a transfer of loans and receivables, scenarios will incorporate among other factors, changes in the amount of cash flows due to changes in the rate of default by the borrower and recovery of any collateral in the case of default; changes in the timing of when cash flows are received due to changes in prepayments rates. The expected cash flows on the transferred assets will be allocated to the transferor and the transferee based on the rights and obligations following the transfer. For example, if the transferor guarantees part of the transferred assets or invests in a subordinated loan, a subordinated interest only strip or excess spread issued by the transferee, this will result in some of the exposure to the assets coming back to the transferor.

The transferor will need to assess the probability of the various scenarios occurring so it can take the various present values described above and multiply them by those probabilities in order to determine probability weighted present values. These values are used for calculating the standard deviation, which can be thought of as the exposure, or volatility, that the transferor has to the transferred asset both before and after the transfer. This will form the basis for judging whether the transferor has retained or transferred substantially all the risks and rewards of ownership of the transferred assets.

The example below is aligned with the fact pattern included in the illustration in IAS 39.AG52, reproduced in **example 3.4.2** below, where prepayable loans are transferred to a transferee in return for cash proceeds and an investment in a subordinated interest only strip, subordinated principal only strip, and an excess spread. The illustration in the Standard concludes that the transferor has neither retained nor transferred substantially all the risks and rewards of ownership.

Example 3.1.5B

Determining the extent of risk and reward transferred

Entity A has a portfolio of similar prepayable fixed rate loans with a remaining maturity of two years, a coupon and effective interest rate of 10%. The principal and amortised cost is CU10,000. On 1/1/X0 Entity A transfers the loans for cash consideration of CU9,115 to Entity B, an entity not consolidated in Entity A's consolidated financial statements. In order to acquire the loans Entity B issues a senior note, linked to the performance of the transferred assets, to third parties where the holders of the notes obtain the right to CU9,000 of any collections of principal plus interest thereon at 9.5 per cent. Entity A agrees to retain rights to CU1,000 of any collections of principal plus interest thereon at 10 per cent, plus the excess spread of 0.5 per cent on the remaining CU9,000 of principal. Collections from prepayments are allocated between the transferor and the transferee proportionately in the ratio of 1:9, but any defaults are deducted from the entity's interest of CU1,000 until that interest is exhausted. Entity A's retained interest is therefore more subordinate to the senior notes as it suffers the loss of any defaults on the transferred assets prior to the holders of the senior notes.

Interest is due on the transferred assets annually on the anniversary of the date of transfer.

In order to determine the extent to which Entity A has retained the risks and rewards of the transferred assets Entity A, considers a number of scenarios where amounts and timings of cash flows on the transferred assets vary and assigns a probability for each scenario occurring in the future. For illustration purposes only four scenarios are included below, though in practice a greater number of scenarios is likely to be required. A risk-free rate of 8.5% is used to determine net present values. All amounts are denominated in CU.

Scenario		Total	Senior note holders	Retained by Entity A
1. All loans prepay immediately with no defaults. Probability is 20%	1/1/X0 – undiscounted	10,000	9,000	1,000
	Total net present value	*10,000*	*9,000*	*1,000*
2. All loans prepay in one year with no defaults. Probability is 30%	1/1/X0 – undiscounted	-	-	-
	1/1/X1 – undiscounted	11,000	9,855 (9.5% x 9,000) + 9,000	1,145 (0.5% x 9,000) + (10% x 1,000) + 1,000
	Total net present value	*10,138*	*9,083*	*1,055*

Scenario		Total	Senior note holders	Retained by Entity A
3. All loans run to their contractual maturity of 1/1/X2 with no defaults. Probability is 30%	1/1/X0 – undiscounted	-	-	-
	1/1/X1 – undiscounted	1,000	855 (9.5% x 9,000)	145 (0.5% x 9,000) + (10% x 1,000)
	1/1/X2 – undiscounted	11,000	9,855	1,145
	Total net present value	*10,265*	*9,159*	*1,106*
4. All loans default at 1/1/X1 and due to immediate foreclosure and sale of the collateral, a total of CU10,741 is recovered. Probability is 20%	1/1/X0 – undiscounted	-	-	-
	1/1/X1 – undiscounted	10,741	9,855	886 Proceeds from sale of collateral less amount paid to senior note holders
	Total net present value	*9,900*	*9,083*	*817*

The net present values for each scenario are multiplied by the probability of each scenario to determine a probability weighted present value. The variance before and after the transfer is determined using the profitability weighted present values as illustrated below:

Entity A's variability before the transfer

Scenario	PV of cash flows	Probability	Probability weighted PV	Variability in PV	Probability weighted variability
	a	b	c = a x b	e = a – d	f = e² x b
1	10,000	20%	2,000	(101)	2040
2	10,138	30%	3,041	37	411
3	10,265	30%	3,080	164	8,069
4	9,900	20%	1,980	(201)	8,080
Total			10,101 [d]		18,600
Square root of f					**136**

Entity A's variability after the transfer

Scenario	PV of cash flows	Probability	Probability weighted PV	Variability in PV	Probability weighted variability
	a	b	c = a x b	e = a – d	f = e² x b
1	1,000	20%	200	(12)	29
2	1,055	30%	317	43	555
3	1,106	30%	332	94	2,651

Scenario	PV of cash flows	Probability	Probability weighted PV	Variability in PV	Probability weighted variability
4	817	20%	163	(195)	7,605
Total			1,012 [d]		10,840
Square root of f					**104**

Senior note holders' variability after the transfer

Scenario	PV of cash flows	Probability	Probability weighted PV	Variability in PV	Probability weighted variability
	a	b	c = a x b	e = a – d	f = e^2 x b
1	9,000	20%	1,800	(90)	1,620
2	9,083	30%	2,725	(7)	15
3	9,159	30%	2,748	69	1,428
4	9,083	20%	1,817	(7)	10
Total			9,090 [d]		3,073
Square root of f					**55**

Entity A determines whether substantially all of the risks and rewards of ownership of the transferred assets are retained by dividing the variability retained after the transfer by the variability of the portfolio as a whole [$^{104}/_{136}$ = 76%]. Consequently, Entity A concludes that substantially all the risks and rewards of ownership are neither transferred nor retained. Entity A would then need to address whether it has control of the transferred asset as described in detail in **3.1.7** below to determine whether Entity A can derecognise the asset in full or continue to recognise its continuing involvement in the transferred assets.

It is worth noting that the sum of variability of Entity A after the transfer (CU104) plus variability of the senior note holders (55) is greater than the variability of the portfolio as a whole (CU136). This arises because the portfolio of loans as a whole has less risk due to the diversification of the loans within the portfolio. Some of this diversification is reversed when the portfolio is split into pieces. More complex mathematical techniques can be applied to show Entity B's variability to the loans after transfer that include the diversification effect that exists in the portfolio prior to the transfer. Such techniques are not covered in this publication.

3.1.6 Has the entity retained substantially all of the risks and rewards of ownership of the asset?

If the entity has retained substantially all of the risks and rewards of ownership of a financial asset, the entity shall continue to recognise that financial asset. [IAS 39.20(b)]

Once again, where it is unclear whether the entity has retained substantially all of the risks and rewards of ownership of the asset it should look at its exposure before and after the transfer by comparing the variability in the amounts and timing of the net cash flows of the transferred asset. [IAS 39.21]

IAS 39 provides examples of transfers where substantially all of the risks and rewards of ownership have been retained and therefore derecognition is not permitted:
[IAS 39.AG40]

- a sale and repurchase transaction where the repurchase price is a fixed price or the sale price plus a lender's return;
- a securities lending transaction;
- a sale of a financial asset together with a total return swap that transfers the market risk back to the entity;
- a sale of a financial asset together with a deep in-the-money written put or purchased call option (i.e. an option that is so far in the money that it is highly unlikely to go out of the money before expiry); and
- a sale of short-term receivables in which the entity guarantees to compensate the transferee for credit losses that are likely to occur.

In a typical repurchase agreement, the entity might, for example, own government securities that it sells to a third party with an agreement to repurchase the securities at a specified price, generally within a short period of time. At inception, the lender transfers the securities to the borrower and receives cash or other consideration as collateral; if the consideration is cash, it is then invested in other assets that earn a return. At a defined date, the transferor repurchases the securities. Dollar repurchase agreements (dollar rolls) are similar transactions in which the transferor repurchases similar but not identical assets to those originally sold. Economically, the lender is motivated in these transactions by the liquidity afforded by the agreement and/or the excess returns it expects to earn on the collateral.

Repurchase agreements are commonly referred to as repos. In many countries, these are actively traded on listed exchanges or in the over-the-counter market and often are used as a source of funding or yield enhancement mechanism. The terminology, however, varies from country to country and the form taken, also, can be different. In some countries, a distinction is made between a repurchase agreement where legal title passes (also known as 'sell/ buy-backs') and a carry (typically, a short term repo that is sometimes known as a classic repo) where title does not pass. Terminology also differs depending on which party is 'buying' or 'selling' the security (hence the use of terms such as reverse repos, inward and outward carries).

In a securities lending transaction the transferor (lender of the security) transfers a security to the transferee (borrower of the security) for a period of time. The transferee generally is required to provide collateral, which may be cash, other securities, or a standby letter of credit with a value that can be slightly higher than the value of the security borrowed (sometimes referred to as a 'haircut'). These transactions are typical when an entity needs a specific security to cover a short sale or a customer's failure to deliver securities sold. The transferor is compensated for lending the security by earning a fee or a return on the collateral invested if the collateral is cash.

US GAAP Comparison: FAS 140 provides specific conditions that must be considered in addition to the general derecognition criteria to determine whether derecognition of a financial asset subject to a repurchase agreement is appropriate. The additional conditions focus on whether the asset to be returned to the transferor is substantially the same as the originally transferred asset and whether the transferor has certain rights to the transferred asset if the transferee defaults.

In February 2008, the FASB issued FSP 140–3 which provides guidance on accounting for a transfer of a financial asset and a repurchase financing. When a transferor initially transfers a financial asset and also enters into a repurchasing agreement with the transferee, there are typically three transfers of the financial asset: (1) an initial transfer of the financial asset to the transferee, (2) the transferee transfer of the financial asset back to the transferor as collateral for financing, and (3) the transferor transfer of the financial asset back to the transferee upon settlement of the financing. The FSP clarified that the initial transfer and the repurchase financing transaction would be considered separately only when there is a valid business purpose and the repurchase financing does not return control of the financial asset back to the initial transferor. If there is no valid business purposes or the repurchase financing transfers control back to the transferor, then the two transactions shall be considered linked and evaluated together to determine if the combined transaction meets the requirements of sale or derecognition accounting under FAS 140.

A sale and repurchase transaction with a fixed price establishes a lending arrangement whereby the transferor is always going to reacquire the asset in the future. The fixed price is usually set to reflect the cost of borrowing over the period of the transaction. As the transferor is required to reacquire the asset for a fixed price, the transferor is exposed to the market risk of the asset. The same analysis applies to a securities lending transaction. [IAS 39.AG51(a)]

A sale of a financial asset together with a total return swap that transfers the market risk back to the entity also establishes the economic equivalent of a lending arrangement. Under the terms of the total return swap, the transferor will usually pay an amount equivalent to a borrowing rate to the transferee over time and the transferee will reimburse the transferor for the performance of the asset. For example, the transferred asset may be an equity security: if the equity price goes up, the transferor receives the benefits of the rise in value of the transferred equity security from the transferee and pays an amount equivalent to a borrowing rate to the transferee; if the equity security price falls, the transferor pays an amount equivalent to a borrowing rate and, in addition, pays an amount equivalent to the fall in value of the equity security. The transferor continues to be exposed to the rise and fall in the equity security price after the transfer and hence, has retained substantially all of the risks and rewards of ownership of the asset. [IAS 39.AG51(o)]

Where an entity sells an asset, but retains the right to buy the asset back at a price that is sufficiently low (option is deep in the money) that the option is highly likely to be exercised, the entity retains substantially all the risks and rewards of ownership. Similarly, where an entity sells an asset and gives the transferee the right to put the asset back at a sufficiently advantageous price (option is deep in the money) so that the option is likely to be exercised, the entity retains substantially all the risks and rewards of ownership. [IAS 39.AG51(f)]

Example 3.1.6A

Transfer of receivables with a deep in-the-money written put option (1)

Transferor X transfers receivables that are carried at amortised cost with a carrying amount of $90 and a put option which expires in 10 days to Transferee Y. Transferee Y pays $150 for the receivables, which have a fair value of $100. Under the terms of the put option, Transferee Y may put the receivables to Transferor X for $151. The possibility of the fair value of the receivables increasing to $151 in 10 days is considered remote and, therefore, exercise of the option appears virtually assured at inception.

Since at inception it is virtually certain that the put option will be exercised, Transferor X has retained substantially all of the risks and rewards of ownership over the receivables, and this transaction should be accounted for as a secured borrowing of $150 with the difference between the consideration received and the put strike price, being $1, amortised to profit or loss using the effective interest rate method.

However, the same analysis is not appropriate where the option is not deep in the money and further derecognition tests should be applied.

In a sale of short-term receivables where the main risk of ownership is credit risk (i.e. the risk that the debtor will fail to pay), and the entity guarantees to compensate the transferee for credit losses that are likely to occur, the transferor has retained substantially all of the risks of ownership. [IAS 39.AG40(e)]

All the terms of a transfer need to be carefully evaluated. For example, penalty provisions attached to the agreement may affect the analysis of whether the risks and rewards have been transferred.

Example 3.1.6B

Transfer of receivables with a deep in-the-money written put option (2)

Transferor X transfers receivables with a carrying amount of $90 and a put option that expires in 10 days' time to Transferee Y. In the exchange, Transferee Y pays Transferor X $100, the fair value of the receivables. Under the terms of the put option, Transferee Y may put the receivables back to Transferor X for $101. However, if Transferee Y does not put the receivables back to Transferor X, Transferee Y must pay Transferor X an additional $50. The possibility of the fair value of the receivables increasing to $151 in 10 days is remote and, therefore, exercise of the option appears virtually assured at inception.

Since at inception it is virtually certain that the put option will be exercised, Transferor X has effectively retained substantially all the risks and rewards of ownership, and therefore the transaction should be accounted for as a secured borrowing of $100 with the difference between the consideration received of $100 and the put strike price, of $101, amortised to profit or loss using the effective interest rate method.

Typical risks included in a risk and reward analysis are interest rate risk, credit risk (i.e. risk of default), late payment risk, and currency risk. In many securitisation transactions an entity, typically a special purpose entity ('SPE'), acquires assets and issues notes that are backed by those assets. The overall securitisation has liquidity risk associated with the fact that there is a mismatch in the timing of cash inflows and outflows. It is important to recognise that liquidity risk arising in the SPE from differences in the contractual timing of cash flows of the assets and the notes issued to acquire the assets is not part of the transferred asset. This compares to late payment risk and credit default risk which is inherent in the asset. However, if an asset pays late, the transferee may not be able to meet its obligations under the notes. This liquidity risk is not part of the transferred asset as it only results when the assets are placed inside the securitisation structure. The liquidity risk associated with late payment risk is therefore not included in the transferor's risk and rewards assessment in determining derecognition for the transferor. However, the impact of liquidity risk will be included as part of the risks and rewards analysis of the SPE in determining whether an entity should consolidate that SPE.

Derivatives are often included in the contractual arrangements that transfer financial assets and may affect the analysis of whether the risks and rewards of those assets have been transferred. Their presence and contractual terms may not be obvious and careful review of all the terms of the transfer agreement is required.

In some instances, derivatives are included in a transfer or a securitisation structure and are not explicitly defined as derivatives. For example, the terms of a securitisation may call for the allocation of all principal cash flows to outside investors, with any remainder going to the retained interest of the seller. This provision may be in the form of a call option, put option, or forward contract. Identifying the implicit derivative in this example requires a thorough understanding of the transfer structure, terms, and conditions. A further assessment is required in these circumstances to determine the applicability of the embedded derivative provisions (see **chapter 5**).

Derivatives commonly found in transfers of financial assets include put options, call options, forward or repurchase contracts, forward sales contracts and swap agreements. Put options provide the transferee with the right to require the transferor to repurchase some or all of the financial assets that were sold, for example, to repurchase delinquent receivables. Call options provide the transferor with the right to repurchase some or all of the financial assets sold to the transferee. Forward or repurchase agreements require the transferee to sell and the transferor to buy some or all of the financial assets that were sold before their scheduled maturity. Forward sales contracts require the transferor to sell and the transferee to buy additional financial assets in the future. Swap agreements effectively change one or more cash flows of the underlying transferred assets (or debt issued by a special purpose entity). For example, an interest rate swap may convert a variable rate asset to a fixed rate.

Derivatives can operate automatically or require exercise by one of the parties; they can be exercised freely or only after the occurrence of a future event. Such a future event may be certain of occurring, such as the passage of time, or may be conditional upon another event, such as a loan becoming delinquent. The certainty of occurrence varies with conditional events. Some conditional events may be probable of occurring, possible of occurring, or their occurrence may be considered remote. The exercise price of a derivative can be fixed above, below or equal to the market value of the financial assets at inception or it can be variable, equal to the market value at exercise date, or the result of a formula that is a function of market conditions or other future events. Derivatives can be combined to form different types of derivatives. Each of these factors impacts the extent to which risks and rewards have been retained by the transferor.

US GAAP comparison: Under US GAAP, there is an exception to the derecognition provisions for a call option that meets the definition of a clean-up call in FAS 140. In many cases, a call option held by the transferor over the transferred financial assets causes the transferor to maintain effective control over the transferred assets, resulting in a failed sale. However, if a transferor is the servicer of transferred financial assets and holds a call option on the transferred financial assets that meets the definition of a clean-up call, FAS 140 exempts that call option from the derecognition provisions (i.e. FAS 140 does not preclude derecognition of the transferred financial assets).

Where a transferor transfers a fixed rate debt instrument for cash or other consideration and at the same time enters into an interest rate swap with the transferee so that the transferor receives a fixed rate and pays floating rate based on a notional equal to the par amount of the transferred debt instrument the interest rate swap does not preclude derecognition of the debt instrument as long as payments under the swap are not conditional on payments being made on the transferred debt. [IAS 39.AG51(p)] Even though the interest rate swap results in the transferor receiving cash flows similar to the underlying cash flows it would have received under the debt instrument, this does not prevent derecognition as the transferor's exposure before and after the transfer is different. Prior to the transfer the transferor is exposed to fixed interest only and the credit risk of the issuer of the debt instrument. After the transfer the transferor is exposed to the net of fixed and floating interest rates and the credit risk of the transferee to the extent that the transferee owes the transferor any amounts under the interest rate swap. If the cash flows under the swap were contingent on the cash flows received under the debt instrument then credit risk of the interest flows under the debt instrument would be retained by the transferor and a different derecognition conclusion is likely to result.

Where a transferor transfers a prepayable fixed rate debt instrument for cash or other consideration and at the same time enters into an amortising interest rate swap with the transferee so that the transferor receives fixed rate and pays floating rate, the transferor will have retained prepayment risk if the repayment profile on the debt instrument matches the amortising profile of the interest rate risk. In this case, the transferor will either continue to recognise fully the fixed rate debt instrument or will recognise the transferred asset to the extent of its continuing involvement. If the amortisation of the notional of the swap is not linked to the principal amount outstanding of the transferred asset, the swap will not result in the transferor retaining prepayment risk on the asset. [IAS 39.AG51(q)] For the same reasons as described above for non-amortising swaps, as long as the interest flows on the swap are not conditional on the cash flows under the debt instrument and the swap does not result in the transferor retaining any other significant risks and rewards of ownership, then derecognition of the asset would apply.

3.1.7 *Has the entity retained control of the asset?*

Where an entity determines that it has neither transferred nor retained substantially all of the risks and rewards of ownership of the transferred assets it has to make an assessment as to whether or not it has retained control of the asset.

- If the entity has not retained control of the financial asset, the entity shall derecognise the financial asset and recognise separately as assets or liabilities any rights and obligations created or retained in the transfer.

- If the entity has retained control of the financial asset, the entity shall continue to recognise the financial asset to the extent of its continuing involvement in the financial asset. [IAS 39.20(c)]

An entity controls a financial asset when it is able to sell that asset. Where the transferee has the *practical ability* to sell the asset in its entirety to an *unrelated* third party and is able to exercise that ability *unilaterally* and *without* the imposition of additional *restrictions* on the transfer, the transferee controls the asset, and hence the transferor must have relinquished control. [IAS 39.23]

Where the transferred asset is traded in an active market the transferee generally has the practical ability to sell the asset. This is because there is a ready market and the transferee can repurchase the asset if and when it is required to return the asset back to the transferor. [IAS 39.AG42]

However, the fact that the transferred asset is traded in an active market is not in itself sufficient to conclude that the transferee has the 'practical ability' to sell the asset. For example, the settlement terms of repurchase, which are driven by the market conventions, may differ significantly from the settlement terms in the transfer agreement such that the transferee will not be able to get hold of the asset quickly enough to deliver the asset to the transferor so as to comply with the contractual provisions of the transfer agreement. In this case the transferee is forced to hold the asset in order to ensure that it can deliver the asset back to the transferor when required.

Other factors may affect the entity's practical ability to sell the asset:

- a financial asset that would satisfy the call option or forward contract may have to be purchased from a third party at a price significantly above its estimated fair value, thus indicating that the assets are not liquid;

- financial assets available to satisfy the call option or forward contract may be held by one or a small number of investors, thus indicating that the assets are not liquid; or

- the quantity of financial assets necessary to satisfy the call option or forward contract may be too large compared to that traded in the market and the terms of the transfer do not allow delivery of the assets over a period of time.

Intuitively, the wider the range of assets that may be used to satisfy the call option, the more likely it is that the entity has practical ability to sell the asset. For instance, assets identical to those originally transferred may not be readily obtainable, but, if the call option permits delivery of assets that are similar to the transferred assets, they may be readily obtainable. Where a call option permits settlement in cash as an alternative to delivering the financial asset, and the cash settlement alternative does not contain an economic penalty rendering it unfeasible, the transferee has the practical ability to sell the asset as cash is a readily obtainable asset.

Unilateral and unrestricted ability to sell means that there can be no 'strings' attached to the sale. If the transferee has to attach a call option over the asset when it sells it, or introduce conditions over how the asset is serviced, in order to satisfy the terms of the original transfer, then 'strings' exist and the test of 'practical ability' is failed.

The 'strings' can be created by other instruments that form a contractual part of the transfer arrangement and are sufficiently valuable to the transferee, so that if the transferee were to sell the asset it would rationally include similar features within that sale. For example, a guarantee may be included in the initial transfer and may have such potential value to the transferee that the transferee would be reluctant to sell the asset and forgo any payments that may fall due under the guarantee.

The transfer agreement may have an explicit restriction that prohibits the transferee from selling the asset. When that restriction is removed or lapses, and as a result the transferee has the practical ability to sell the asset, derecognition would then be appropriate.

The fact that the transferee may or may not choose to sell the asset should not form part of the decision making process, it is the transferee's practical ability to do so that is important.

Example 3.1.7A

Transfer of readily obtainable bonds with written put option

Transferor X sells South African government bonds that are readily obtainable in the market with a book value of 100 Rand to Transferee Y for 103 Rand. The transfer includes an option for Transferee Y to put the assets back to Transferor X up to one year after the transfer date at 103.50 Rand. Transferee Y exercises its option 30 days after the initial sale. The option had a fair value of 2 Rand at the exchange date consisting of time value of 1.50 Rand and intrinsic value of 0.50 Rand.

In this example, the transferor has neither transferred nor retained substantially all the risks and rewards of ownership because the option is neither deeply in, or deeply out of the money. The transferor has not retained control because the assets are readily obtainable. This put option does not therefore preclude derecognition.

Example 3.1.7B

Transfer of mortgage loans with right to call

Transferor X transfers a portfolio of mortgage loans to a third party, Transferee Y. The transferred loans can be repurchased by Transferor X at any time prior to their maturity. The agreement contains no explicit conditions restraining Transferee Y from selling, exchanging or pledging the assets to a third party.

Transferee Y does not have the practical ability to sell the portfolio of mortgage loans since it must have access to the original mortgage loans that were transferred in the event Transferor X exercises its right under the call option, and the mortgage loans cannot be readily obtained from another source.

IAS 39 envisages instances where the transferee does not have the unilateral and unrestricted ability to sell the asset due to arrangements such as a call option held by the transferor. The Standard is less clear on the accounting treatment that should apply when a call option is held by a party other than the transferor. Consider the following example.

Example 3.1.7C

Transfer of asset with purchased call not held by transferor

Bank A transfers loans to a non-consolidated SPE. The funds that the SPE used to purchase the loans were generated through a securitisation involving notes being issued by the SPE to third parties. Bank A invests in a note that comprises an interest-only strip on the transferred loans and also provides a subordinated loan to the SPE. The SPE is consolidated by Bank B (independent third party relative to Bank A) due to it providing a larger subordinated loan and investing in the most junior notes of the SPE such that it is exposed to the majority of the risks and rewards of the vehicle. Bank B has a call on the assets of the SPE that is exercisable at a fixed price.

As Bank A has invested in the interest-only strip and provided the subordinated loan it is considered to neither have transferred nor retained substantially all of the risks and rewards of the transferred loans. Bank A must assess whether it has retained control of the asset, i.e. whether the *transferee* has the practical ability to sell the asset in its entirety to an unrelated third party and is able to exercise that ability unilaterally and without imposition of additional restrictions.

In this example, if the SPE is considered to be the transferee, it does not have such practical ability to sell the loans without restrictions. If it were to sell the loans it would need to attach restrictions such that it could honour its obligations under the call option which allows Bank B to call the remaining loans. The call option written by the SPE limits the SPE's ability to sell the asset. However, if the transferee in this case is viewed as the consolidated group of Bank B (which therefore includes the SPE) then the transferee does have the unrestricted ability to sell the assets as the call option is eliminated on consolidation. Also, it can be argued that Bank A has not retained control of the asset, given that it has no mechanism within the arrangements for buying back the loans or being forced to acquire the loans. It is appropriate, therefore, for Bank A to derecognise the loans, and therefore not to apply continuing involvement accounting (see **3.4** below), and instead initially recognise the interest only strip and subordinated loan at fair value.

US GAAP comparison: Under US GAAP, if the transferor does not relinquish control of a transferred asset, it continues to recognise the transferred asset in its statement of financial position and separately recognise a secured borrowing equal to the proceeds received. This differs from IAS 39 which requires the transferor to recognise the financial asset only to the extent of its continuing involvement in the financial asset in the case where substantially all the risks and rewards of ownership are neither retained nor transferred.

In addition, the control tests under IAS 39 and US GAAP are slightly different. As discussed above, IAS 39 requires that the transferee have the practical ability to sell the asset in its entirety to an unrelated party and is able to exercise that ability unilaterally and without imposition of additional restrictions on the transfer. Under US GAAP, control is relinquished if, among other things, the transferee has the right to freely pledge or exchange the transferred asset and no condition both constrains the transferee and provides more than a trivial benefit to the transferor. In this case, control may be relinquished if the transferee can pledge the transferred asset in such a way that it obtains all or most of the cash inflows that are the primary economic benefits of financial assets. Further, under US GAAP, control may be relinquished even if a constraint on the transferee exists as long as that constraint does not provide the transferor with more than a trivial benefit. This is different from IAS 39 which requires that the transferee is able to readily obtain the transferred asset in the market.

3.2 Transfers that qualify for derecognition

Where an entity concludes that derecognition of a financial asset is appropriate (the rights to the cash flows from the asset expired, or the entity has transferred substantially all of its risks and rewards, or the entity no longer retains control of the asset), the asset is removed from the statement of financial position and any new financial assets obtained, financial liabilities assumed and any servicing obligation are recognised at fair value. [IAS 39.25]

Often the transferor continues to service the transferred assets for a fee, which may take the form of part of the interest receipts on the transferred assets that an entity retains as compensation for servicing those assets.

Servicing refers to activities associated with the collection of cash flows from receivables or other financial assets after origination and the distribution of that cash to investors if the receivables are owned by other entities. Servicing may include the temporary investment and distribution to the financial asset owners of all or a portion of the cash collected. Servicing activities, also, may include monitoring delinquencies, advancing delinquent payments, restructuring receivables, and foreclosing on the collateral underlying the receivables when necessary. If the receivables are mortgage loans, servicing activities often include collecting and disbursing escrow payments for taxes and insurance. Servicing activities are inherent in all receivables; however, they do not need to be performed by the owner of the receivables. If the receivables are being serviced for another entity, the servicer generally receives a fee for performing these activities. This fee is usually a contractual amount received based on a fixed percentage of the outstanding receivables for the period. Servicers may also receive additional compensation by retaining late charges, other ancillary fees, and the float, which is the net interest earned on funds held by the servicer before disbursement. The compensation received by the servicer is referred to as the benefits of servicing.

Where the benefits of servicing are not expected to cover the costs of servicing the assets, then the entity should recognise a liability for the fair value of the service obligation that it has entered into as a result of the transfer. [IAS 39.24] The servicing in this instance represents an obligation, because the servicer would have to pay another entity to assume the servicing contract or use its assets in the future to perform under the servicing contract.

When the benefits of servicing exactly compensate the servicer for performing the servicing but provide no additional benefits, the servicer has neither an asset nor a liability and the fair value of this servicing contract is zero. A servicing contract with a positive fair value is considered to be one that would be favourable for a substitute servicer should one be required, and includes the profit that would be demanded in the marketplace. The amount allocated to a servicing right is treated as a retained interest and the amount allocated to it is determined by allocating the carrying amount of the larger financial asset. [IAS 39.24]

US GAAP comparison: Under US GAAP, FAS 156, *Accounting for Servicing of Financial Assets*, requires all separately recognised servicing assets and liabilities to be initially recognised at fair value. In the case of a sale in which the transferor retains a servicing right, the servicing asset is not treated as retained interest that is recognised at its allocated carrying value.

FAS 156 permits an entity to subsequently measure a recognised servicing asset or liability ether at fair value or amortised cost. If subsequent measurement at fair value is elected, that election is irrevocable and the period change in fair value of the servicing asset or liability is recognised in current period earnings. If subsequent measurement at amortised cost is elected, the servicing asset or liability is amortised to earnings in proportion to and over the period of estimated net servicing income (or loss).

Example 3.2

Allocating consideration received between sold and retained interests

Entity A owns CU1,000,000 face amount of loans that contractually yield 10 per cent interest over their life. The carrying amount of these loans after recognising impairment of CU20,000 is CU980,000. Entity A sells 90 per cent of the principal, plus the right to receive interest income of 8 per cent without recourse to an investor for CU900,000 in cash. The part of the asset that has been transferred meets all the criteria for derecognition.

Entity A retains the right to service these loans, and the servicing contract stipulates a 1 per cent fee as compensation for performing the servicing. Entity A also retains an interest-only strip for the portion of the interest coupon not sold (1 per cent). At the date of transfer, the fair value of the retained 10 per cent of the loan is CU100,000; the fair value of the servicing asset is CU15,000; and the fair value of the interest-only strip is CU35,000.

The following table demonstrates the allocation of this loan between the sold and retained interests assuming the entity has already determined that it has transferred substantially all risks and rewards of ownership of the transferred asset (for example substantially all the credit losses and the majority of interest rate risk on the loans transferred):

Interest	**Fair value**	**Percentage of total fair value**	**Allocated carrying amount (1)**	**Sold interests**	**Retained interests**
Loans sold	CU900,000	85.71	CU840,000	CU840,000	–
Loans retained	CU100,000	9.53	CU93,333		CU93,333
IO strip	CU35,000	3.33	CU32,667		CU32,667
Servicing asset	CU15,000	1.43	CU14,000		CU14,000
Total	CU1,050,000	100.00	CU980,000	CU840,000	CU140,000

(1)The allocated carrying amount is calculated as the percentage of total fair value multiplied by the aggregate carrying amount prior to the transfer (CU980,000).

The difference between:

- the carrying amount allocated to the part derecognised and
- the sum of (i) the consideration received for the part derecognised (including any new asset obtained less any new liability assumed)

and, for available-for-sale assets, (ii) any cumulative gain or loss allocated to it that had been recognised in other comprehensive income

is recognised in profit or loss. A cumulative gain or loss, for available-for-sale assets, that had been recognised in other comprehensive income is allocated between the part that is derecognised and the part that continues to be recognised on the basis of their relative fair values. [IAS 39.27]

In the above example the assets were carried at amortised cost and the amount recognised in the profit or loss is calculated as the difference between the consideration of CU900,000 and the allocated carrying amount of the derecognised asset of CU840,000.

There are likely to be instances in which applying basis allocation based on the 'relative fair value method' is difficult to apply because it is difficult to obtain the fair value of the parts of the asset that are subject to derecognition and continued recognition. The Standard acknowledges that where an entity has a historical practice of selling parts similar to the part that is continued to be recognised, or other market transactions for such parts exist, recent prices for actual transactions would best reflect the fair value of the parts. Where there are no price quotes available, the best estimate of the fair value is the difference between the fair value of the larger financial asset as a whole and the consideration received from the transferee for the part of the asset that is derecognised. [IAS 39.28]

3.3 Transfers that do not qualify for derecognition

Where a financial asset is precluded from being derecognised in its entirety, i.e. the transferor retains substantially all of the risks and rewards of ownership, the entity continues to recognise the asset in its entirety and recognises a financial liability for the consideration received. [IAS 39.29] The asset and liability cannot be offset and, similarly, any income arising from the asset cannot be offset against any expense incurred on the liability. [IAS 39.36] The asset's classification, measurement basis and income recognition does not change as a result of the transfer. This accounting treatment is often referred to as 'gross presentation' or 'secured borrowing' presentation.

Example 3.3

Transfer of receivables with credit guarantee

Entity X transfers short term receivables to Entity Y and provides a credit guarantee to Entity Y over the expected losses of those receivables.

Entity X continues to recognise the receivables in its statement of financial position because it has retained substantially all the risks and rewards of ownership of the receivables. Entity X will recognise a financial liability for the proceeds received. The substance of the arrangement is that of a secured borrowing, i.e. short term receivables provide security for the cash advanced by Entity Y.

Where a derivative financial instrument forms part of the transfer arrangement and precludes the asset from being derecognised, the derivative is not accounted for separately as this would result in the derivative being effectively counted twice. [IAS 39.AG49]

IAS 39 does not provide specific guidance on the accounting for the transferee in the case where the transferor continues to recognise the asset in its entirety. It is reasonable to assume that the accounting for the transferee is the inverse of the accounting for the transferor in this case. For example, if the transferor continues to recognise the asset and therefore recognises a collateralised borrowing for the consideration received, then the transferee will not recognise the asset but will instead recognise a collateral lending to the transferor. If a derivative is entered into between the transferor and transferee as part of the arrangement but is not recognised by the transferor because it is an impediment to derecognition, then similarly the derivative will not be recognised by the transferee. The terms of the collateralised lending will include the cash consideration paid at the date of transfer, the contractual cash flows of the derivative, as well as the imputed repayment of principal.

US GAAP comparison: US GAAP does provide for symmetry in accounting between a transferor and a transferee. Specifically, the basis of financial components approach used under US GAAP provides that "transferors and transferees should account symmetrically for transfers of financial assets".

3.4 Continuing involvement in the transferred assets

Where an entity neither transfers, nor retains substantially all of the risks and rewards of ownership of a financial asset, and retains control of that asset, the entity continues to recognise the asset to the extent of its continuing involvement. Continuing involvement represents the extent to which the transferor continues to be exposed to the changes in the value of the transferred asset. A corresponding liability is also recognised and measured in such a way that the *net* carrying amount of the asset and the liability is:

- the amortised cost of the rights and obligations retained, if the asset is measured at amortised cost; or
- the fair value of the rights and obligations retained, if the asset is measured at fair value. [IAS 39.31]

The liability that is recognised at the date of transfer will not necessarily equate to the proceeds received in transferring the asset which would ordinarily be the case if the asset continued to be fully recognised and the proceeds received were recognised as a collateralised borrowing. In some cases, the liability appears to be the 'balancing figure' that is the result of applying the specific guidance for continuing involvement accounting. IAS 39 acknowledges that measuring the liability by reference to the interest in the transferred asset is not in compliance with the other measurement requirements of the standard. [IAS 39.31]

This requirement for consistent measurement of the asset and associated liability means that designation of the liability as at fair value through profit or loss is not available if the transferred asset is measured at amortised cost (see **7.1.2** in **chapter 3**).

The entity cannot offset the asset and the associated liability. Any subsequent changes in the fair value of that asset and that liability are measured consistently and are not offset. [IAS 39.33] Any income on the asset to the extent of the entity's continuing involvement and any expense incurred on the associated liability are not offset. [IAS 39.32]

Where an entity transfers assets, but retains a guarantee over the transferred assets that absorb future credit losses and that guarantee (as well as other continuing involvement) results in the transferor neither transferring nor retaining substantially all the risks and rewards of ownership, the transferor must recognise the guarantee as part of its continuing involvement. Assuming for illustration only, that the guarantee represents the transferor's only continuing involvement in the transferred asset, then:

- the transferred asset at the date of transfer will be measured at the lower of (i) the carrying amount of the asset; and (ii) the maximum amount of the consideration received in the transfer that the entity could be required to repay; and
- the associated liability is measured initially at the amount in (ii) above plus the fair value of the guarantee.

The initial fair value of the guarantee is recognised in profit or loss on a time proportion basis in accordance with IAS 18 *Revenue* and the carrying amount of the asset is reduced by any impairment losses. [IAS 39.AG48(a)]

Example 3.4A

Continuing involvement: guarantee over first default losses

Transferor X transfers an asset that is carried at, and is worth, CU100 on the date of transfer to Transferee Y. Transferee Y pays CU105. Transferor X provides a guarantee to Transferee Y to pay for the first default losses up to a value of CU8. The fair value of the guarantee at the date of transfer is CU5. Expected future losses on the portfolio are CU12. Transferor X considers that substantially all the risks and rewards of ownership have neither been transferred, nor retained. Transferee Y does not have the practical ability to sell the assets, i.e. Transferor X controls the asset.

Transferor X determines its continuing involvement as the extent to which it continues to be exposed to the changes in the value of the transferred asset, i.e. the lower of:

(i) the carrying amount of the asset (CU100); and

(ii) the maximum amount of the consideration received in the transfer that Transferor X could be required to repay ('the guarantee amount') (CU8).

Transferor X records its continuing involvement in the asset at CU8, and derecognises the part of the asset transferred, i.e. CU92. The associated liability is initially measured at CU13, being the guarantee amount (CU8) plus the fair value of the guarantee (CU5). Subsequently, the initial fair value of the guarantee is recognised in profit or loss on a time proportion basis.

The following entries would be made at the date of transfer:

Dr	Cash	CU105
Cr	Financial asset	CU92
Cr	Financial liability	CU13

If at the end of the guarantee period, no amounts have been paid under the guarantee then the following entries will be required:

Dr	Financial liability	CU8	(the fair value of the guarantee of CU5 will have been fully amortised by the end of the guarantee period)
Cr	Financial asset	CU8	

If at the end of the guarantee period, the full amount of the guarantee is claimed by Transferee Y then the following entries will be required:

Dr	Financial liability	CU8	
Cr	Cash	CU8	
Dr	Profit or loss	CU8	(the fair value of the guarantee of CU5 will have been fully amortised by the end of the guarantee period)
Cr	Financial asset	CU8	

Example 3.4B

Continuing involvement: guarantee over slow payment risk

Entity A transfers short term receivables to Bank B under a factoring arrangement. Entity A transfers the credit risk of the receivables but retains the slow payment risk up to a maximum of 120 days. If the receivable is outstanding after 120 days the risk is absorbed by Bank B as the receivable is deemed to be in default. Entity A is charged a market interest rate of 10% for the slow payment risk on the outstanding balance for the period if it is deemed to be a slow paying receivable. At the date of transfer receivables with a nominal value and amortised cost carrying value of CU300m are transferred and the fair value of the late payment guarantee is CU1m. The total consideration received by Entity A is CU288m.

Entity A considers it has neither retained nor transferred substantially of all the risks and rewards of ownership and is deemed to control the receivables as Bank B does not have the practical ability to sell the transferred assets.

Entity A determines its continuing involvement as the extent to which it continues to be exposed to the late payment risk of the transferred asset, i.e. the lower of:

(i) the carrying amount of the asset (CU300m); and

(ii) the maximum amount of the consideration received in the transfer that Entity A could be required to repay ('the guarantee amount') (CU3m, being CU300m x 120/360 x 10%).

Entity A records its continuing involvement in the asset at CU3m, and derecognises the part of the asset transferred, i.e. CU297m. The associated liability is initially measured at CU4m, being the guarantee amount (CU3m) plus the fair value of the guarantee (CU1m). Subsequently, the initial fair value of the guarantee is recognised in profit or loss on a time proportion basis.

Dr	Cash	288
Dr	Continuing involvement in the transferred asset	3
Dr	Loss on disposal	13
Cr	Receivables	300
Cr	Continuing involvement liability	4

To record the derecognition of the receivables and the recognition of the continuing involvement.

The interest in the continuing involvement asset of CU3m less the continuing involvement liability CU4m is equal to the fair value of the guarantee at the date of transfer, being CU1m.

3.4.1 Continuing involvement through options

Transfer arrangements often contain written or purchased options, or combinations thereof, so that the transferor neither retains, nor transfers substantially all the risks and rewards of ownership, and controls the transferred asset. This is the case when the option is neither deeply-in, nor deeply-out of the money at the date of transfer. In such transfer arrangements, with the exception of arrangements that contain a put option written by the transferor where the transferor measures the asset at its fair value, the entity's continuing involvement in the asset is the amount of the transferred asset that the entity may repurchase. In the case of the arrangement that contains a put option written by the transferor where the transferor measures the asset at its fair value, the continuing involvement is the lower of the asset's fair value and the option exercise price. [IAS 39.30(b)] This is because in such a transfer arrangement the entity has no right to increases in fair value of the transferred asset above the exercise price of the option.

The table below sets out the measurement bases for the asset and associated liability for transfers that contain written or purchased options, or combinations thereof, where the transferor continues to recognise its continuing involvement in the asset. The manner of settlement of the options, gross or net cash settled, does not affect the accounting analysis below. However, a cash settled option in of itself is less likely to restrict the transferee's practical ability to sell the transferred asset, so may result in derecognition rather than continuing involvement accounting.

Derivative involved	**Measurement basis of transferred asset prior to the transfer**	**Measurement basis of transferred asset after the transfer**	**Measurement basis of the associated financial liability**
Purchased call option	Amortised cost	Amortised cost	Amortised cost: cost on initial recognition (being consideration received) is adjusted for amortisation of the difference between that cost and amortised cost of the asset on the expiration date of the option.
Written put option	Amortised cost	Amortised cost	Amortised cost: cost on initial recognition (being consideration received) is adjusted for amortisation of the difference between that cost and amortised cost of the asset on the expiration date of the option.

Derivative involved	Measurement basis of transferred asset prior to the transfer	Measurement basis of transferred asset after the transfer	Measurement basis of the associated financial liability
Purchased call option	Fair value	Fair value	Where the *option is in or at the money* - the call option exercise price less the time value of the option. Where the *option is out of the money* - the fair value of the transferred asset less the time value of the option. This ensures that the net carrying amount of the asset and associated liability is the fair value of the call option right.
Written put option	Fair value	Fair value (limited to the lower of the fair value of the asset and the option exercise price)	Option exercise price plus the time value of the option. This ensures that the net carrying amount of the asset and associated liability is the fair value of the put option obligation.
Collar (combination of purchased call and a written put)	Amortised cost	Amortised cost	Amortised cost: cost on initial recognition (being consideration received) is adjusted for amortisation of the difference between that cost and amortised cost of the asset on the expiration date of the options.
Collar (combination of purchased call and a written put)	Fair value	Fair value	Where the *call option is in or at the money* - the sum of the call exercise price and fair value of the put option less the time value of the call option. Where the *call option is out of the money* - the sum of the fair value of the asset and the fair value of the put option less the time value of the call option. This ensures that the net carrying amount of the asset and associated liability is the fair value of the options held and written.

The examples below apply the requirements set out in the table above:

Example 3.4.1

Continuing involvement: options

(a) Out of the money purchased call

Entity A transfers an asset to Bank X and receives $92. The amortised cost of the asset on the date of transfer is $98. The amortised cost of the asset on the expiration of the option will be $100. The fair value of the asset on the date of transfer is $95. The exercise price of the purchased call option is $99 (being out of the money at the date of transfer) and therefore the premium paid to purchase the option consists entirely of the time value, being $3, at the date of transfer.

The asset is held at amortised cost. On the date of transfer the asset will continue to be recognised at $98. The associated liability will be recognised at the fair value of the consideration received, $92, with the difference between $92 and $100 being recognised in profit or loss using the effective interest rate method.

The asset is held at fair value. On the date of transfer the asset will continue to be recognised at $95. The associated liability will be recognised at $92, being the fair value of the transferred asset, $95, less the time value of the option, $3.

(b) In or at the money purchased call

Entity A transfers an asset to Bank X and receives $87. The amortised cost of the asset on the date of transfer is $98. The amortised cost of the asset on the expiration of the option will be $100. The fair value of the asset on the date of transfer is $95. The exercise price of the purchased call option is $90 (being in the money at the date of transfer) and therefore the premium paid to purchase the option consists of intrinsic value, being $5, and time value, being $3, at the date of transfer.

The asset is held at amortised cost. On the date of transfer the asset will continue to be recognised at $98. The associated liability will be recognised at the fair value of the consideration received, $87, with the difference between $87 and $100 being recognised in profit or loss using the effective interest rate method.

The asset is held at fair value. On the date of transfer the asset will continue to be recognised at $95. The associated liability will be recognised at $87, being the option exercise price, $90, less the time value of the option, $3.

(c) Written put

Entity A transfers an asset to Bank X and receives $95. The amortised cost of the asset on the date of transfer is $98. The amortised cost of the asset on the expiration of the option will be $100. The fair value of the asset on the date of transfer is $92. The exercise price of the written put is $90 (out of the money at the date of transfer) and therefore the premium received for writing the option consists entirely of time value, being $3.

The asset is held at amortised cost. On the date of transfer the asset will continue to be recognised at $98. The associated liability will be recognised at the fair value of the consideration received, $95, with the difference between $95 and $100 being recognised in profit or loss using the effective interest rate method.

The asset is held at fair value. The asset will be recorded at the lower of its fair value and the option exercise price, i.e. at $90. The associated liability will be recognised at $93, being the option exercise price, $90, plus the time value of the option, $3.

(d) Collar

Entity A transfers an asset to Bank X and receives $98. The amortised cost of the asset on the date of transfer is $98. The amortised cost of the asset on the expiration of the option will be $100. The fair value of the asset on the date of transfer is $92. The cost of the collar at the date of transfer is zero. The exercise price of the written put is $80 (out of the money at the date of transfer) and the exercise price of the purchased call is $120 (out of the money at the date of transfer).

The asset is held at amortised cost. On the date of transfer the asset will continue to be recognised at $98. The associated liability will be recognised at the fair value of the consideration received, $98, with the difference between $98 and $100 being recognised in profit or loss using the effective interest rate method.

The asset is held at fair value. On the date of transfer the asset will continue to be recognised at $92. The associated liability will be recognised at $92, which is calculated as the sum of the fair value of the asset, $92, and the fair value of the put, less the time value of the call. The fair value of the put will be equal to the time value of the call, as the put's fair value represents only time value, and the sum of the two premiums on the options (both representing time value only) is zero.

Where an option expires unexercised, the transferor derecognises financial assets that were subject to the option and also derecognises the associated liability. The transferee recognises the financial assets and eliminates the receivable due from the transferor.

3.4.2 *Continuing involvement in a part of a financial asset*

In a situation where an entity has a continuing involvement in only a part of a financial asset, the entity allocates the previous carrying amount of the financial asset between the part it continues to recognise under continuing involvement, and the part it no longer recognises based on the relative fair values of those parts at the date of transfer. [IAS 39.34]

The allocation exercise and the calculation of the gain or loss on the disposal of the part of the asset are done in the same way as in **3.2** above. In addition to the part retained, the transferor also recognises its continuing involvement in the asset and the associated liability. IAS 39.AG52 contains a numerical illustrative example of continuing involvement in a part of an asset which is reproduced below.

Example 3.4.2

Continuing involvement: part of a financial asset

[Extract from IAS 39.AG52]

Assume an entity has a portfolio of prepayable loans whose coupon and effective interest rate is 10 per cent and whose principal amount and amortised cost is CU10,000. It enters into a transaction in which, in return for a payment of CU9,115, the transferee obtains the right to CU9,000 of any collections of principal plus interest thereon at 9.5 per cent. The entity retains rights to CU1,000 of any collections of principal plus interest thereon at 10 per cent, plus the excess spread of 0.5 per cent on the remaining CU9,000 of principal. Collections from prepayments are allocated between the entity and the transferee proportionately in the ratio of 1:9, but any defaults are deducted from the entity's interest of CU1,000 until that interest is exhausted. The fair value of the loans at the date of the transaction is CU10,100 and the estimated fair value of the excess spread of 0.5 per cent is CU40.

The entity determines that it has transferred some significant risks and rewards of ownership (for example, significant prepayment risk) but has also retained some significant risks and rewards of ownership (because of its subordinated retained interest) and has retained control. It therefore applies the continuing involvement approach.

To apply [IAS 39], the entity analyses the transaction as (a) a retention of a fully proportionate retained interest of CU1,000, plus (b) the subordination of that retained interest to provide credit enhancement to the transferee for credit losses.

The entity calculates that CU9,090 (90 per cent × CU10,100) of the consideration received of CU9,115 represents the consideration for a fully proportionate 90 per cent share. The remainder of the consideration received (CU25) represents consideration received for subordinating its retained interest to provide credit enhancement to the transferee for credit losses. In addition, the excess spread of 0.5 per cent represents consideration received for the credit enhancement. Accordingly, the total consideration received for the credit enhancement is CU65 (CU25 + CU40).

The entity calculates the gain or loss on the sale of the 90 per cent share of cash flows. Assuming that separate fair values of the 90 per cent part transferred and the 10 per cent part retained are not available at the date of the transfer, the entity allocates the carrying amount of the asset in accordance with paragraph 28 as follows:

	Estimated fair value	**Percentage**	**Allocated carrying amount**
Portion transferred	9,090	90%	9,000
Portion retained	1,010	10%	1,000
Total	10,100		10,000

The entity computes its gain or loss on the sale of the 90 per cent share of the cash flows by deducting the allocated carrying amount of the portion transferred from the consideration received, i.e. CU90 (CU9,090 – CU9,000). The carrying amount of the portion retained by the entity is CU1,000.

In addition, the entity recognises the continuing involvement that results from the subordination of its retained interest for credit losses. Accordingly, it recognises an asset of CU1,000 (the maximum amount of the cash flows it would not receive under the subordination), and an associated liability of CU1,065 (which is the maximum amount of the cash flows it would not receive under the subordination, i.e. CU1,000 plus the fair value of the subordination of CU65).

The entity uses all of the above information to account for the transaction as follows:

	Debit	Credit
Original asset	–	9,000
Asset recognised for subordination or the residual interest	1,000	–
Asset for the consideration received in the form of excess spread	40	–
Profit or loss (gain on transfer)	–	90
Liability	–	1,065
Cash received	9,115	–
Total	**10,155**	**10,155**

Immediately following the transaction, the carrying amount of the asset is CU2,040 comprising CU1,000, representing the allocated cost of the portion retained, and CU1,040, representing the entity's additional continuing involvement from the subordination of its retained interest for credit losses (which includes the excess spread of CU40).

In subsequent periods, the entity recognises the consideration received for the credit enhancement (CU65) on a time proportion basis, accrues interest on the recognised asset using the effective interest method and recognises any credit impairment on the recognised assets. As an example of the latter, assume that in the following year there is a credit impairment loss on the underlying loans of CU300. The entity reduces its recognised asset by CU600 (CU300 relating to its retained interest and CU300 relating to the additional continuing involvement that arises from the subordination of its retained interest for credit losses), and reduces its recognised liability by CU300. The net result is a charge to profit or loss for credit impairment of CU300.

A number of observations can be drawn from the example in IAS 39.AG52 reproduced above. A concern that is often cited is that the example advocates 'double-counting', i.e. the continuing involvement in the asset is accounted for twice. This is best illustrated using the numbers in the example above. The transferor continues to recognise a fully proportionate interest in 10% of all cash flows which equals an amortised cost of CU1,000 (being 10% x CU10,000 carrying amount) and also recognises an additional CU1,000 being the 'asset recognised for subordination or the residual interest'. This may appear odd as the interest in the assets is limited to a disproportionate interest in the transferred asset up to CU1,000. However, the reason for presenting the transferor's interest in the transferred asset 'grossed up' is to reflect that the transferor's interest in 10% of the asset is in fact subordinated (and therefore is not a fully proportionate interest) as any losses borne by the transferred assets continue to be borne by the transferor until their remaining interest is exhausted. In order to recognise the transferor's continuing involvement liability the entity needs to 'gross-up' its statement of financial position by recognising a further asset.

As the transferor's interest in the transferred asset is deemed to be a fully proportionate share of the asset (plus that interest being subordinated) the calculation of the gain/loss on partial disposal of the asset is also based on a fully proportionate basis. On the face of it this calculation may also appear odd as the entity has not economically sold a fully proportionate share in the asset to the transferee, rather it has retained a disproportionate share of the cash flows of the asset.

The example also recognises another new asset that it refers to as the 'asset for the consideration received in the form of excess spread'. It is worth noting that the amount recognised for the excess spread is equal to the fair value of the excess spread at the date of transfer, being CU40, even though it appears the loans themselves were not originally measured at fair value, i.e. they were originally measured at amortised cost. As the objective of accounting for continuing involvement is to ensure that the measurement of the net involvement (being the net of the continuing involvement asset and continuing involvement liability) is consistent with the measurement of the transferred assets, it is surprising that the excess spread in the example is initially recognised at fair value, as opposed to amortised cost. We suspect this was an oversight when the example was developed.

3.4.3 *Accounting by the transferee in the case of continuing involvement*

Example 3.4.3

Bank S owns a 16 per cent equity stake in a thinly traded entity. The investment is classified by Bank S as an available-for-sale financial asset. Bank S enters into an agreement with Entity K whereby Entity K pays CU102 to Bank S in return for:

- the 16 per cent equity interest in the thinly traded entity; and
- a put option that allows Entity K to put the shares back to Bank S for a price of CU96 at a pre-specified date.

On the date of the transfer, the fair value of the shares is CU97 and the time value of the put option is CU5 (CU102 minus CU97), i.e. the option is out of the money at inception.

Transferor accounting

Bank S, the transferor, will apply continuing involvement accounting as it has neither transferred nor retained substantially all the risks and rewards of the shares and Entity K does not have the practical ability to sell the shares since it is a significant holding in an entity that is thinly traded and therefore Bank S is deemed to control the shares.

As the arrangement involves the transferor writing a put option on an asset that is measured at fair value, the extent of the continuing involvement for Bank S is limited to the lower of the fair value of the shares and the option exercise price. [IAS 39.30(b) & AG48]

At the transaction date, the following entries will be required:

Dr	Cash	102
Cr	Available-for-sale financial asset	1
Cr	Financial liability	101

This entry recognises a liability of CU101, consisting of a strike price of CU96 and time value of the put option of CU5.

The shares continue to be recognised by Bank S and measured as an available-for-sale financial asset, though changes in their value above the strike price of CU96 are not recognised.

If the put is exercised by Entity K because the share price is below CU96 the following entry will be required:

Dr	Financial liability	96
Cr	Cash	96

The difference in the opening and closing carrying value of the liability of CU5 (CU101 less CU96) will be recognised in profit or loss over the life of the arrangement. Fair value loss on the available-for-sale investment below CU96 will be recognised in other comprehensive income. Fair value losses recognised in equity will only be reclassified from equity to profit or loss when the asset is impaired or is subsequently derecognised.

If the put is not exercised by Entity K because the share price is above CU96 the following entry will be required:

Dr	Financial liability	96
Cr	Available-for-sale investment	96

The difference in the opening and closing carrying value of the liability of CU5 (CU101 less CU96) will be recognised in profit or loss over the life of the arrangement. Any amounts retained in the available-for-sale reserve in equity will be reclassified to profit or loss as the available-for-sale investment has been derecognised.

Transferee accounting

Entity K has paid cash of CU102 in return for a right to receive cash of CU96 (through exercise of its purchased put option) and rights to all the upside on the shares above CU96 (i.e. by not exercising its put and physically retaining the transferred shares). Entity K economically has an investment in shares with no downside risk below CU96.

Entity K should recognise its interest in the arrangement as an available-for-sale financial asset, but not recognise any changes in fair value below the strike price of CU96, as Entity K has no exposure to fair value movements below this amount. This is the inverse of the accounting by the transferor, Bank S. Both parties recognise an available-for-sale investment with Entity K recognising fair value gains above CU96, and Bank S recognising fair value gains below CU96.

At the date of transfer the following entry will be required:

Dr	Available-for-sale financial asset	102
Cr	Cash	102

This entry will recognise the financial asset consisting of the fair value of the shares of CU97 plus the value of the purchased put option of CU5. Increases in the fair value of the available-for-sale investment above CU96 will be recognised in other comprehensive income. The available-for-sale asset and the purchased put will be re-measured in other comprehensive income. As the purchased put provides a 'floor' of CU96, changes in fair value of the security below this amount will not be recognised. At maturity of the option the time value of the option will have been fully eroded resulting in the security either being put at CU96 and thereby being derecognised, or continuing to be fair valued in other comprehensive income as the transferee has not exercised the put. The put option is not fair valued through profit or loss since for the transferor it is not recognised as it is an impediment to derecognition, and for the transferee it forms part of its involvement in the asset.

If the put is exercised by Entity K because the share price is below CU96 the following entry will be required:

Dr	Cash	96
Cr	Available-for-sale financial asset	96

An amount of CU1 would have already been recognised in other comprehensive income when the fair value of asset had decreased to CU96. Fair value movements below CU96 are not recognised. The

CU1 in other comprehensive income is reclassified from equity to profit or loss when the put is exercised by Entity K and the available-for-sale asset is derecognised.

If the put is not exercised by Entity K because the share price is above CU96 no further entry will be required to recognise the shares as they are already recognised in Entity K's statement of financial position. After the expiration of the option all gains or losses on the available-for-sale investment will be recognised in other comprehensive income (except impairment losses recognised in profit or loss) as Entity K will be exposed to movements in the share price in both directions.

3.5 Collateral

A transfer arrangement may require a transferor to provide non-cash collateral (e.g. a debt or an equity instrument) to the transferee. The transferee's entitlement to the collateral is conditional upon the transferor's default and while the transferor continues to perform under the contract, the transferor continues to benefit from substantially all of the collateral's risks and rewards. Normal recognition and derecognition principles apply to the collateral: the transferee is not entitled to recognise the collateral until it becomes contractually entitled to it, which will not be the case until the transferor defaults under the terms of the contract; the transferor retains all of the risks and rewards of ownership of the asset pledged as collateral and therefore cannot derecognise it.

If the transferee has the right by contract or custom to sell or repledge the collateral, then the asset that has been pledged by the transferor should be reclassified in its statement of financial position separately from its other assets and described as a loaned asset, pledged equity instrument or repurchase receivable. If the transferee uses that right and sells the collateral, it shall recognise the proceeds from the sale and a liability measured at fair value for its obligation to return the collateral. [IAS 39.37]

In the event of a default by the transferor the risks and rewards of the collateral, within the confines of the collateral agreement, are transferred to the transferee. Hence, the transferor derecognises the collateral and the transferee, who after the default becomes contractually entitled to it, recognises the collateral at its fair value, unless the transferee has already sold the collateral, in which case, it derecognises its obligation to return the collateral to the transferor.

3.6 Sale and repurchase agreements and stock lending

A sale and repurchase agreement usually takes the form of an agreement to sell a security (i.e. transfer all the rights attaching to a security) with a simultaneous agreement to repurchase it at a specified price at a fixed future date. The consideration involved is either in the form of cash or security. The repurchase price is normally structured higher than the sale price; alternatively, the two prices can be the same, but with an explicit interest rate charged instead. The transferee will require that it is assured of a lender's return on its investment and the transferor will require that the transferee earns no more than this return. In the event that the transferee is entitled to retain any coupons or dividends that are paid on the asset during the term of the repurchase agreement, the transaction price is adjusted to reflect the fact (see **3.1.6** above).

The table below considers some common terms of sale and repurchase transactions and applies IAS 39 derecognition principles to those transactions.

Features	Applying derecognition in IAS 39
The repurchase price is an agreed price higher than the market value at the date of sale.	If the repurchase price results in a lender's return for the transferee, then the transferor has not transferred, but has retained substantially all of the risks and rewards of ownership of the asset. The lender's return earned by the transferee is consistent with the arrangement being a collateralised borrowing for the transferor, and a collateralised lending for the transferee.
The repurchase provision is an option for the transferor to repurchase the asset at a fixed price (where the call option is neither deeply in nor out of the money), and the asset is readily obtainable in the market.	The asset is derecognised since the transferor neither transferred nor retained substantially all of the risks and rewards of ownership, and has lost control over the asset. The transferor will recognise a standalone call option in the statement of financial position at fair value with gains or losses recognised in profit or loss.

Features	Applying derecognition in IAS 39
The repurchase provision is an option for the transferor to repurchase the asset at a fixed price (where the call option is neither deeply in nor out of the money), and the asset is *not* readily obtainable in the market.	The transferor has neither transferred nor retained substantially all of the risks and rewards of ownership but has retained control of the asset. Hence, the transferor continues to recognise the asset to the extent of its continuing involvement: where the asset is measured at fair value and the option is out of the money the transferor records a liability for the fair value of the transferred asset less the time value of the option; where the asset is measured at fair value and the option is at or in the money the transferor records a liability for the option exercise price less the time value of the option; where the asset is measured at amortised cost the transferor records a liability for the consideration received and adjusts it for the amortisation between the consideration received and amortised cost of the asset on the expiration date of the option.
The repurchase provision is a put option at a fixed price (where the put option is neither deeply in nor out of the money) and the asset is readily obtainable in the market.	The asset is derecognised since the transferor has neither retained nor transferred substantially all of the risks and rewards of ownership, and has lost control over the asset. The transferor recognises a standalone put option in the statement of financial position at fair value with gains or losses recognised in profit or loss.
The repurchase provision is a put option at a fixed price (where the put option is neither deeply in nor out of the money) and the asset is *not* readily obtainable in the market.	The transferor has neither transferred nor retained substantially all of the risks and rewards of the asset and has retained control of the asset; hence, it continues to recognise the asset to the extent of its continuing involvement. Hence, the transferor continues to recognise the asset to the extent of its continuing involvement: where the asset is measured at fair value the transferor records a liability equal to the option exercise price plus the time value of the option; where the asset is measured at amortised cost the transferor records a liability for the consideration received and adjusts it for the amortisation between the consideration received and amortised cost of the asset on the expiration date of the option.
The asset sold is subject to the transferor receiving a deferred consideration receipt/payment based on the increases/decreases in the fair value of the asset respectively for a specified period of time.	The deferred consideration passes the changes in the fair value of the asset back to the transferor, thus the transferor has retained substantially all of the risks and rewards of ownership of the asset; hence, the transferor continues to recognise the asset and recognises a liability for the initial cash consideration received.

Features	Applying derecognition in IAS 39
The asset is subject to a varying repurchase price such that original purchase price is adjusted retrospectively to pass variations in the value of the asset to the transferor.	The variation in the repurchase price so as to pass the changes in the value of the asset back to the transferor means that the transferor retains substantially all the risks and rewards of ownership; hence, the transferor continues to recognise the asset and recognises a liability for the cash consideration received.
The transferor provides a residual value guarantee to the transferee or subordinated debt to protect the transferee from falls in the value of the asset.	Provided the asset has upside potential, the transferor neither retained nor transferred substantially all the risks and rewards of ownership (transferred the upside, but retained the downside). The transferor continues to control the asset where the guarantee is sufficiently valuable to the transferee and limits its ability to transfer the asset, and therefore the transferor continues to recognise the asset to the extent of its continuing involvement, i.e. at the date of the transfer the asset is measured at the lower of its carrying amount and the guarantee amount. The transferor records an associated liability equal to the guarantee amount plus the fair value of the guarantee. Where the guarantee does not restrict the transferee's ability to sell the asset, the transferor derecognises the asset.
The repurchase price, whether put/call or forward, is the market price at the time of repurchase.	The transferor has transferred substantially all of the risks and rewards of ownership of the asset since the transferor can only repurchase it at its fair value. Hence, the asset is derecognised.
Asset repurchased is substantially the same as the asset that is transferred or the transferee can substitute the asset with one that is similar or is of equal fair value.	The transferor retains substantially all the risks and rewards of ownership of the asset and therefore derecognition is precluded.

3.7 Debt factoring

Debt factoring is used extensively as a method for obtaining one or more of the following benefits: obtaining financing, bad debt protection or sales ledger administration. A factoring transaction normally takes the form of an entity receiving cash consideration in exchange for the rights to cash collected from its receivables. In many situations the rights to the cash flows on the receivables are subject to certain restrictions or guarantees. Sometimes the transferee may have recourse to the transferor over the performance of the receivables either up to a certain limit or to the extent to which there is a shortfall of the cash collected on the receivables. In a non-recourse transaction, there is no obligation of the transferor to make good the transferee for any shortfall on the assets. In order to receive a market return from the receivables (the receivables are collected over time) the transferee charges interest.

The table below sets out some of the common features of debt factoring transactions and application of derecognition principles to a 'vanilla' debt factoring transaction (an entity receives cash consideration in exchange for the rights to cash collected from its receivables) with each of those features. It is assumed that the transferee cannot sell receivables, i.e. the transferor continues to control them.

Features	Applying derecognition in IAS 39
For all receivables not recovered after a certain period, e.g. 120 days, whether due to late payment or default, the transferor provides a guarantee.	The guarantee may represent substantially all the risks of ownership of receivables (e.g. where most receivables are long term due to the credit terms offered). If so, derecognition is precluded. Where the transferor has neither transferred nor retained substantially all the risks and rewards of ownership, the transferor continues to recognise receivables to the extent of its continuing involvement, i.e. to the extent that amounts may be repaid under the guarantee.
In the event of a receivable going bad beyond but not prior to a certain period (e.g. the period commencing after 120 days), the transferor provides credit protection on that receivable.	The credit protection may represent substantially all the risks of ownership (e.g. where credit terms are 120 days or more and thus the risk of a receivable going bad stays with the transferor). If it does, derecognition is precluded. Depending on the likelihood of default prior to 120 days and other risks transferred to the transferee, the transferor may determine that substantially all the risks and rewards of ownership are neither transferred nor retained and thus the transferor continues to recognise receivables to the extent of its continuing involvement, i.e. to the extent that amounts may be repaid under the credit protection.
The transferor receives an element of non-returnable consideration for the receivables, but either the transferor or the transferee has rights to some further sums from the other party to the transaction. This further sum depends on whether or when cash is collected from the receivables, e.g. through deferred consideration, a retrospective adjustment to the sale price or rebates of certain charges.	Where the further sums from the other party are not considered to be substantially all of the risks and rewards of ownership, the transferor has neither transferred nor retained substantially all the risks and rewards of ownership and continues to recognise the receivables to the extent of its continuing involvement. The transferor derecognises receivables to the extent of the non-returnable consideration.

Features	Applying derecognition in IAS 39
The transferor provides a warranty over the quality/condition of the receivables at the moment of transfer, e.g. at the point of delivery of the goods, the customer had not breached their credit limit.	The warranty provision may result in the transferor retaining some risks and rewards, for example, if the transferor has to reimburse the transferee should the transferor's representations as to the quality/condition of the asset prove to be wrong. If the warranty results in the transferor neither transferring nor retaining substantially all the risks and rewards of ownership it continues to recognise the receivables to the extent of its continuing involvement, i.e. to the extent that amounts may be repaid under the warranty. If the warranty as to quality/condition of the assets at the date of transfer results in the entity transferring substantially all the risks and rewards of ownership then the transferor will derecognise the assets. (The IFRIC considered conditional transfers in November 2006 – see **3.1.4** above.)
The transferor continues to service the receivables by administering the sales ledger for a fee that is based upon the total amount of receivables factored at each month end. The charge is at market price. The transferor is not subject to any recourse and the transferor has not retained any residual interest in the receivables.	A servicing arrangement at a market price with no further continuing involvement in the receivables is considered to be a transfer of substantially all of the risks and rewards of ownership of the assets, and therefore derecognition by the transferor is appropriate. If the charge for the servicing arrangement is not at market price such that the benefits of servicing the assets are not commensurate with the administration charges, but did not otherwise involve further transfer of exposure to risk back to the transferor, a servicing asset or servicing liability will arise and be recorded separately.
The transferor has a call option to purchase outstanding receivables from the transferee at a predetermined price when the amount of outstanding assets falls to a specified level at which the cost of servicing those assets is too high as compared to the benefits of servicing. This is sometimes known as a clean-up call.	Provided that the clean-up call results in the entity neither retaining nor transferring substantially all the risks and rewards of ownership, it precludes derecognition only to the extent of the amount of the assets subject to the call option.

3.8 Securitisations

Securitisation is a means of making use of a portfolio of assets, usually receivables held by an entity (such as loans, mortgages, credit cards, etc.), to obtain cost effective funding. These assets are usually purchased by a transferee who then re-packages the receivables as asset-backed securities and sells them on in the market to investors for cash consideration. The normal process is to re-package these securities in a vehicle specifically set up for that purpose, a Special Purpose Entity ('SPE', see **3.1.1** above). The notes issued to the investors are secured on the underlying assets that have been transferred to the SPE. It is usual for investors to require a form of credit enhancement which can take many forms:

- subordination: typically the transferor acquires a junior (often the most junior) note issued by the SPE that absorbs the first losses incurred by the transferred assets;
- over-collateralisation: the face amount of the transferred assets is larger than the funding used to buy the assets;
- excess spread: after all interest has been received and paid and expenses of the SPE settled, an amount is retained in the arrangement which will absorb first losses should they occur;
- reserve fund: similar to excess spread except a separate fund is created;
- guarantees: the SPE may obtain guarantees either from the transferor or from third parties, for example from well rated insurance companies;
- letters of credit: the SPE may obtain letters of credit from well rated banks where the bank will stand ready to reimburse the SPE for losses incurred up to a specified amount;
- cash collateral account: similar to a letter of credit except the bank lends cash upfront which is invested in highly rated short-term commercial paper. The SPE has some credit risk on its investments but this is less than would be the case for a letter of credit where the borrower runs the risk that the lender will fail to meet its lending commitment when demanded by the borrower. Alternatively, the transferor may deposit a percentage of its proceeds from the securitisation in a cash collateral or maintenance account.

Some forms of credit enhancement, like subordination and over-collateralisation, some cash collateral accounts deposited by the transferor, transfer risks and rewards of the transferred asset back to the transferor. Others, like letters of credit and some cash collateral accounts, transfer risks and rewards to third parties. The types of risk transfer determine whether the transferor is able to achieve derecognition for the transferred assets.

As explained in **3.1.1** above, it is important to determine whether or not the entity needs to consolidate the SPE. If the SPE is consolidated, the extent of derecognition achieved is the same irrespective of whether the transfer is direct to investors or through a consolidated SPE that obtains the financial assets and, in turn, transfers them to third party investors.

In many securitisations the SPE is consolidated and the assets are not transferred to a third party, i.e. the right to receive the cash flows from the assets remains with the group. The group may assume a contractual obligation to pass on those cash flows to ultimate investors in a 'pass-through' arrangement that meets all three conditions detailed in **3.1.4** above. Nevertheless, the group may still have retained all the risks and rewards of ownership of the assets (e.g. where credit risk is the main risk and credit enhancement provided by the group covers all expected losses) and may still need to continue to recognise the assets. The IASB recognises that many securitisations will not qualify for derecognition either because one of the three conditions in the pass-through test will not be met or because the credit enhancement required by the ultimate investors will mean that the group retains substantially all the risks and rewards of ownership of the assets. [IAS 39.BC63] Where credit enhancement provided by the group is such that the group neither retains nor transfers all the risks and rewards of ownership, the group will continue to recognise the assets only to the extent of its continuing involvement, i.e. the credit enhancement provided.

The table below sets out some of the common features of securitisations where the SPE that purchases the assets is *not consolidated* by the transferor and application of derecognition principles to securitisations with each of those features. It is assumed that the SPE cannot sell receivables, i.e. the transferor continues to control them and the transferor has no exposure to the assets other than stated.

Features	Applying derecognition in IAS 39
Credit enhancement is provided for the transferred receivables by an independent third party, e.g. third party credit insurance or guarantee.	The transferor has transferred the rights to receive cash flows on the assets to the SPE and also transferred substantially all the risks and rewards of ownership of those assets, hence full derecognition is appropriate.
As above, but the transferor acts as the servicing agent on the portfolio of the assets.	The retention of a servicing right at market price does not preclude derecognition, since substantially all of the risks and rewards of the assets have been transferred and accordingly derecognition is appropriate. If the charge for the servicing asset is not at market price such that the benefits of servicing the assets are not commensurate with the administration charges, but do not otherwise involve further retention of exposure to risk, a servicing asset or liability arises and is recorded separately.

Features	Applying derecognition in IAS 39
A call option is held by the transferor that allows it to call back some of the assets from the portfolio. The transferor has the choice of which balances can be recalled but the total amount of balances that can be recalled is restricted.	Assuming the transferor is economically rational, the transferor will repurchase those assets that will yield the highest return, thereby avoiding assets that are expected to default. This interest in the assets indicates that the transferor has neither transferred nor retained substantially all the risks and rewards of ownership, and hence is required to continue to recognise the assets to the extent of its continuing involvement, i.e. the extent to which the transferred assets are subject to the call option.
The transferor has a call option enabling it to insist on the return of some specific assets from the portfolio; the amount of balances that can be recalled is restricted and the transferor cannot choose the balances to be recalled.	Assuming the call option is not deeply in nor out of the money, the transferor has neither retained nor transferred all the risks and rewards of ownership and will continue to recognise the assets to the extent of its continuing involvement, i.e. the extent to which the transferred assets are subject to the call option. If the call option is deeply out of the money, e.g. the assets that can be recalled are in default, derecognition is appropriate.
The transferor services the assets and has a clean-up call to purchase outstanding receivables from the SPE when the amount of outstanding assets falls to a specified level at which the cost of servicing those assets is too high as compared to benefits of servicing.	Provided the clean-up call results in the transferor neither retaining nor transferring substantially all the risks and rewards of ownership, the clean-up call precludes derecognition only to the extent of the amount of the assets subject to the call option.

US GAAP comparison: Under US GAAP, a call option that is considered a clean-up call does not preclude derecognition for any of the assets transferred. If a transferor (that is also the servicer) retains a clean-up call that allows the transferor to purchase the remaining financial asset at the point in time when the costs of servicing the remaining assets outweigh the benefits, the transferor is allowed to derecognise all assets transferred including those subject to the clean up call.

The table below sets out some of the common features of securitisations where the SPE that purchases the assets *is consolidated* by the transferor and application of derecognition principles to securitisations with each of those features. It is assumed that the SPE has not transferred the assets to a third party, but instead assumed a contractual obligation to pass the cash flows to external investors. Other than indicated, the pass-through tests (see **3.1.4** above) are met and the group has not retained substantially all the risks and rewards of ownership.

Features	Applying derecognition in IAS 39
The SPE has provisions for a revolving investment facility (i.e. securitisation of revolving assets such as credit card receivables) in which for a given time period the SPE reinvests cash receipts in similar assets. This is common where the receivables have a much shorter life than the securitisation programme.	The pass-through conditions are not met as the reinvestment is in assets other than cash and cash equivalents and the cash flows are not passed on without material delay. Derecognition by the group is precluded.
A rebalancing swap is taken on by the SPE to ensure that the cash flows due on the notes are met at their predetermined payment dates as the timing of cash flows on the underlying assets is often unpredictable.	Short term advances to the investors from the group do not violate the pass through tests as long as the investors still bear the risk of recovery of the assets. Hence, provided the amounts paid to investors are recovered by the group if the group suffers loss on the assets and any advances are only short term, derecognition is appropriate.
The group is granted rights to cash collected from the portfolio of assets and any remaining cash after the payments due on the securities issued to the investor, e.g. deferred sale consideration, dividend payments or other fees.	This right to collect the excess cash flows is often designed to create a similar payoff profile for the group as if the group had retained a subordinated interest in a non-consolidated SPE. The extent of subordination as compared to expected credit losses on the assets determines whether the group has retained substantially all the risks and rewards of ownership and thus continues to recognise the assets or whether the group has neither retained nor transferred substantially all of the risks and rewards of ownership and thus continues to recognise the assets only to the extent of its continuing involvement, i.e. to the extent of its subordinated interest.

Example 3.8

Securitisation – sponsor consolidates SPE

A Bank creates a special purpose entity (SPE) in order to facilitate the acquisition of specified assets (long-term loans) from third parties. The consideration received by the third party transferors from the SPE is less than the fair value of the assets transferred, i.e. the SPE is overcollateralised (10%), and as such the transferors suffer expected losses. The SPE raises external debt through the issue of a rolling short-term commercial paper programme (i.e. the commercial paper is repaid and new paper is issued over the life of the arrangement). All the proceeds of the initial issue are used to finance the acquisition of the assets from the third parties which are co-mingled in the SPE. When all the underlying assets have been repaid the proceeds from the assets will be used to repay the final round of commercial paper. In order to support the whole programme the sponsoring bank will provide the SPE with a short-term liquidity facility should it require any short-term funds. In addition, the sponsoring bank will agree to be the lender to the SPE should the SPE fail to issue short-term commercial paper to investors (this facility is generally known as programme wide credit enhancement).

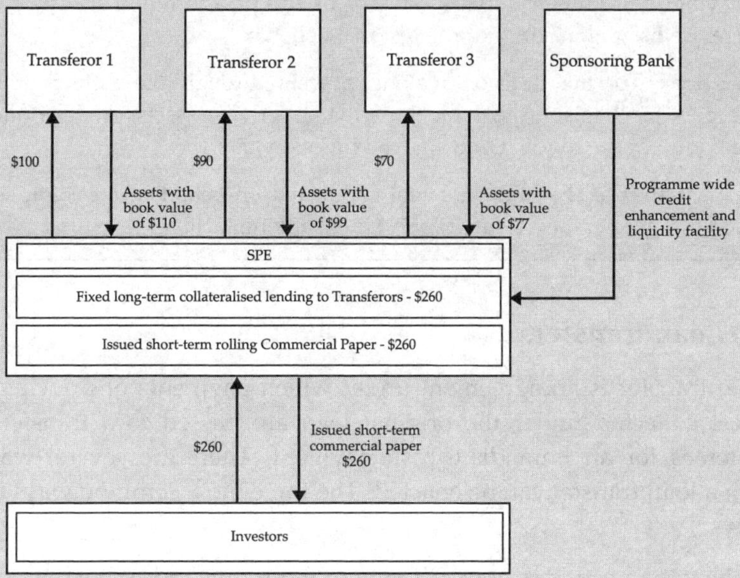

Transferor accounting

The transferors must first consider whether they consolidate the SPE. Applying the tests in SIC-12 to each transferor, the SPE is not controlled by any of the transferors as the SPE's activities are not being conducted on behalf of any one particular transferor; the transferors do not have the decision making powers to obtain the majority of benefits of the SPE; they do not have the right to the majority of the benefits and majority of residual risks of the SPE.

Each transferor must therefore apply the derecognition model to the transfer of the assets to the SPE. As each transferor retains substantially all the risks and rewards of ownership of the transferred assets due to the over-collateralisation, each transferor fails derecognition, and recognises a collateralised borrowing equal to the proceeds received from the SPE.

Sponsoring bank accounting

The Sponsoring Bank needs to consider whether it consolidates the SPE. The assets of the SPE are collateralised loans to the third party transferors (not the underlying transferred long-term loans as these continue to be recognised by the transferors) and liabilities under the short-term commercial paper. The Sponsoring Bank consolidates the SPE for the following reasons.

The Bank has agreed to provide support to the SPE through the programme wide credit enhancement and liquidity facility. If the assets of the SPE under-perform, which is driven by the performance of the assets transferred by the transferors, the Bank has to step in and finance the programme. If the assets under-perform in excess of the expected loss, the bank's lending is not going to be fully repaid, i.e. it bears the residual risk of the SPE.

If the assets perform better than expected the cash retained in the SPE after repaying the commercial paper lenders all will pass to the Bank. The Bank therefore has the majority of the residual benefits.

The Bank has the decision making powers through the setting of the autopilot mechanism (the Bank chose the underlying assets, predetermined the nature of the funding and sourced investors).

The activities of the SPE are being conducted on behalf of the Bank as it receives remuneration through providing banking facilities.

3.9 Loan transfers

A loan transfer is an agreement under which payments of principal and interest collected under the original loan are passed to a transferee or transferees for an immediate cash payment. There are several ways in which a loan transfer can be enacted. The three most common ways are as follows.

(a) Novation – this is normally where the rights and obligations of the loan are cancelled or amended and renegotiated such that the identity of the lender has been changed. In this case, the borrower is released from its obligation to the transferor and instead has an obligation to the transferee.

(b) Assignment – this is a similar process to novation but the original borrower may or may not be made aware of the change in assignment depending on whether or not the assignment is statutory or equitable respectively. Any cash flows paid to the transferor are passed on to the transferee.

(c) Sub-participation – the borrower still has an obligation to the transferor but at the same time the transferor enters into a non-recourse back-to-back agreement with the transferee to pass on the cash flows collected on the original loan.

Under novation the transferor's rights to the cash flows expire and hence derecognition is appropriate. In an assignment or sub-participation where the cash flows paid to the transferee reflect in full the collections from the original loan and there is no recourse to the transferor it is likely that the pass-through tests in **3.1.4** above are met and the transferor does not retain the risks and rewards of ownership of the assets i.e. derecognition is appropriate.

The table below sets out common features of loan sub-participations and application of derecognition principles to sub-participations with each of those features. Other than indicated, the pass-through tests are met and there is no recourse to the transferor (i.e. risks and rewards are transferred).

Features	**Applying derecognition in IAS 39**
The terms of the transfer provide that additional funds that are not part of the terms of the original loan will be made available to the borrower in the event of restructuring of the debt; this facility is not provided to the transferee under the terms of the sub-participation.	In the event of restructuring, the entity will not pass all the restructured cash flows to the transferee, i.e. pass-through tests are not met and derecognition is precluded.
A proportionate share of all future cash flows on the original loan is transferred, e.g. 40 per cent.	A fully proportionate share of the cash flows from the original loan (40 per cent) constitutes part of the loan. It is assumed that the pass-through tests applied to that part of the loan are met and the transferor has transferred all the risks and rewards of ownership of that part of the loan. Hence, derecognition of the part of the loan is appropriate.
The transferor continues to administer the original loan for a fee.	The servicing right at market price does not preclude derecognition since substantially all of the risks and rewards of the asset have been transferred. If the charge for the servicing asset is not at market price such that the benefits of servicing the asset are not commensurate with the administration charges, but does not otherwise involve further transfer of exposure to risk, a servicing asset or liability arises and is recorded separately.
The assigned loan or sub-participation is floating rate, whilst the original loan carries a fixed rate coupon.	The pass-through tests are not met since the transferor may be required to pay amounts that are not collected on the original loan to the transferee and equally not all cash flows collected on the original loan are passed to the transferee. Hence, derecognition is precluded.
Both the original loan and the assigned loan or sub-participation are floating rates instruments but they are priced off different floating rate indices, e.g. 6 month LIBOR and 6 month EURIBOR.	The pass-through tests are not met since the transferor may be required to pay amounts that are not collected on the original loan to the transferee and equally not all cash flows collected on the original loan are passed to the transferee. Hence, derecognition is precluded.
The original loan and the assigned loan or sub-participation are in different currencies.	The pass-through tests are not met since the transferor may be required to pay amounts that are not collected on the original loan to the transferee and equally not all cash flows collected on the original loan are passed to the transferee. Hence, derecognition is precluded.

Features	Applying derecognition in IAS 39
The sub-participation is in the same currency, but concurrently the transferor and transferee enter into a cross currency swap over the same notional as the original loan which converts the payments made to the transferee into a different currency. If the original loan defaults the swap can be terminated at its fair value at the time; the amounts and timing of the payments on the swap are not adjusted to reflect any changes that may occur in the amounts and timing of the cash flows of the original loan.	The sub-participation qualifies for derecognition since all of the risks and rewards of ownership of the original loan are transferred to the transferee. The cross currency swap is recognised separately as a derivative at fair value through profit or loss and may qualify for hedge accounting in the books of the transferee.

3.9.1 *Loan syndication*

Loan syndication is an agreement between several lenders to fund jointly a large loan. Each lender will advance a loan of a specific amount to the borrower and has the right to repayment from the borrower. Such a syndication agreement does not involve a loan transfer and should be accounted for as recognition of a financial asset by each of the lenders involved.

In some loan syndications, a lead lender may advance cash to the borrower and transfer the loan to a number of other lenders so that repayments by the borrower are made to the lead lender who then distributes the collections to the other lenders in the syndicate. Such loan syndications are just another form of a loan sub-participation and the lead lender would need to consider whether the pass-through tests are met. In other syndications, the pass-through tests are not relevant as the lead lender transfers the contractual rights to a proportion of the loan to third parties.

3.10 Transfers with total return swaps

A total return swap is a derivative that transfers the exposure of a referenced asset between two parties. Typically, one entity would pay amounts equal to increases in the fair value of the referenced asset to the counterparty, and at the same time receive amounts equal to decreases in the fair value of the asset plus a floating rate interest return calculated on a fixed notional amount. This floating funding interest compensates the entity for the theoretical cost of borrowing cash in order to buy the referenced asset, or put another way, is equal to a cost that would have been borne by the entity if the entity had instead chosen to expose itself to the referenced asset by acquiring the referenced asset as opposed to entering into the total return swap. These types of instruments are common in transfers of financial assets as they allow the transferor some or all of the participation in the underlying asset. As discussed in **3.1.6** above a transfer of an asset for cash consideration and a total return swap would not result in the transferor derecognising the transferred asset as the transferor continues to be exposed to substantially all the risks and rewards of ownership as a result of the total return swap. However, total return swaps can be used in transfer arrangements in other ways. Below are some illustrations which explain the consideration that would need to be given in assessing whether derecognition is appropriate.

Example 3.10

Transfers of financial assets with a total return swap

(i) Transfer of a financial asset with deferred consideration and a TRS

Transferor A transfers a debt instrument where the transfer agreement requires Transferee B to pay the transferor a fixed sum in 6 months time. The transferor and transferee also enter into a total return swap whereby the transferor receives cash equal to increases in fair value of the asset from the transferee and pays cash equal to decreases in the fair value of the asset plus LIBOR plus a fixed spread every quarter based on a notional equal to the fair value of the debt instrument at the date of transfer. The transferee also pays the transferor any interest that it receives on the transferred asset.

Transferor A must first determine whether the contractual rights to cash flows have been transferred to Transferor B in accordance with IAS 39.18(a). As Transferee B has all rights to cash flows under the asset the answer is yes. Transferor A must then consider whether it has transferred substantially all the risks and rewards of ownership to Transferor B. The existence of the total return swap results in the transferor continuing to be exposed to the risks and rewards of ownership of the transferred asset, being both fair value risk and the interest earned. The risks and rewards are retained by the transferor and therefore derecognition is not appropriate even though the transferor has taken on an additional risk that it did not have prior to the transfer, being the credit risk of the transferee who has yet to pay the transferor cash consideration for the transferred asset.

As the total return swap is an impediment to derecognition it will not be recognised by the transferor in accordance with IAS 39.AG49. Transferor A will continue to recognise the assets until maturity of the total return swap. At that date, the total return swap will not be an impediment to derecognition as it will have matured and therefore the transferor will not have retained substantially all the risks and rewards of ownership, cash consideration for the asset will be received from the transferee and a gain/loss will be recognised by the transferor on disposal.

(ii) Transfer of a financial asset with deferred delivery of the asset at maturity of a TRS

Entity C enters into a 6 month TRS with Entity D over Entity C's debt instrument whereby Entity C will pay Entity D cash equal to increases in fair value of the asset and receive from Entity D cash equal to decreases in the fair value of the asset plus LIBOR plus a fixed spread every quarter based on a notional equal to the fair value of the debt instrument at the date of entering into the arrangement. Entity C will also pay Entity D any interest that it receives on the transferred asset immediately after Entity C receives the interest from the issuer of the debt instrument. If Entity C does not receive interest on the debt instrument it has no obligation to pay Entity D. Equally, Entity C does not provide Entity D with any guarantee to pay further amounts. At maturity of the TRS Entity C will physically deliver the referenced asset to Entity D for a fixed amount of cash determined upon entering into the arrangement.

Entity C must first determine whether the contractual rights to cash flows have been transferred to Entity D in accordance with IAS 39.18(a). As the transferor retains all the rights to cash flows under the asset then the answer is no. Entity C must then consider whether the pass-through requirements in IAS 39.18(b) are met. It is clear that *all* the contractual cash flows under the asset are not passed to Entity D as the only cash flows that are passed to Entity D are interest flows on the asset for 6 months. As these interest flows are specifically identified cash flows from a financial asset, i.e. they constitute a portion of the asset, under IAS 39.16(a)(i) and the cash flows are immediately paid by Entity C to Entity D when Entity C receives the cash, then Entity C could apply the pass-through requirements to the portion of the asset that represents the interest flows for 6 months only. Assuming that both the pass through and risks and rewards tests lead to the conclusion that the portion of the asset representing the interest flows for 6 months should be derecognised, Entity C would need to recognise a debtor from Entity D as no upfront consideration is received by Entity C. The debtor recognised would be equal to the fair value of the interest flows for the next 6 months and may differ in amount to the portion of the asset derecognised in the case where the asset is not measured at fair value, i.e. it is measured at amortised cost, with the difference recognised in profit or loss as a gain/loss on disposal.

The remaining portion of the financial asset is not subject to a transfer and therefore will continue to be recognised and measured consistently with the period prior to the transaction occurring. The TRS will be recognised as at fair value through profit or loss. When the referenced asset is physically delivered to Entity D at maturity of the TRS, Entity C transfers the contractual right to cash flows under the asset and derecognises it. This scenario is illustrated below.

- Entity C's fixed-rate debt instrument has an amortised cost of €100, and fair value of €110 at 1 January 20X8. The amortised cost of the remaining interest flows, being the present value discounted at the original effective interest rate, is €3, and the fair value, being the present value discounted at current market rates, is €4.

- Entity C enters into a TRS with Entity D for 6 months over the fixed-rate debt instrument. Entity C will pay Entity D increases in fair value of the debt instrument and Entity D will pay Entity C decreases in fair value as well as a funding rate of 6m LIBOR + 50 basis points set in advance. At the maturity of the TRS Entity C will transfer the debt instrument to Entity D for €110. LIBOR at 1 January 20X8 was 5.5%.

- At 30 June 20X8 the fair value of the debt instrument is €106.

1 January 20X8

Dr	Loan and receivable	€4
Cr	Debt instrument	€3
Cr	Profit or loss	€1

To recognise the profit on derecognition of the portion of the debt instrument representing the 6m interest flows that were subject to the pass-through tests.

No further entries are required at 1 January 20X8 as the contractual rights to the cash flows of the remaining portion of the asset have not been transferred and the pass-through requirements for the remaining portion of the asset do not apply.

30 June 20X8

Dr	Total return swap asset	€7
Cr	Profit or loss	€7

To recognise the TRS at FVTPL. For illustration purposes, the fair value of the TRS is equal to the decrease in fair value of the debt instrument (€4) plus 6m LIBOR accrued for 6 months (6% x 6/12).

Dr	Cash	€117
Cr	Total return swap asset	€7
Cr	Debt instrument	€97
Cr	Loans and receivables	€4
Cr	Profit or loss	€9

To recognise the consideration received on transfer of the debt instrument with the corresponding derecognition of the TRS, the debt instrument, and the receivable that was recognised on entering into the pass-through arrangement.

The gain on disposal represents the unrealised gain on the debt instrument immediately prior to entering into the arrangement, being €10, less the gain of €1 recognised on 1 January 20X8 upon entering into the pass-through arrangement.

4 Derecognition of a financial liability

A financial liability is derecognised when, and only when, it is extinguished, i.e. when the obligation in the contract is *discharged, cancelled* or *expired*. [IAS 39.39]

An entity discharges its obligation by paying amounts of cash, other financial assets, or by delivering other goods or services to the counterparty. An obligation may expire due to the passage of time (e.g. an unexercised written option). An obligation is cancelled when through the process of law, or via negotiation with a creditor, an entity is released from its primary obligation to pay the creditor.

Example 4A

Extinguishment of financial liabilities

Situations may arise where a liability is considered unlikely to result in an outflow of economic resources. The following examples illustrate three scenarios in which a liability might never be extinguished absent a statute of limitation in the applicable jurisdiction:

Unredeemed travellers cheques

Entity A is in the business of issuing travellers cheques to customers. Historical statistical analysis indicates that five per cent of travellers cheques will never be redeemed. Travellers cheques do not have an expiry date.

As travellers cheques do not have an expiry date, the entity is obliged to honour the redemption of travellers cheques on demand. The financial liability will be measured at the amount the Entity A can be required to pay on demand. This obligation may carry on indefinitely into the future unless the jurisdiction allows for legal release from that obligation when a specified period of time has passed.

Goods received but not invoiced

Entity B is a media buying entity that purchases advertising space in newspapers, television and radio on behalf of its customers, thereby incurring a liability to pay for that advertising space. Historical analysis shows that invoices have never been received by Entity B in respect of five per cent of the advertising space purchased. The jurisdiction of Entity B contains a 'statute of limitations' under which the counterparty is no longer able legally to enforce payment if it does not claim payment from Entity B within a period of six years from the date the goods or services are provided.

Until six years have expired since the transaction, Entity B is legally obligated to pay the counterparty should they make a claim. The financial liability will be measured at the amount the Entity B can be required to pay on demand. At six years, Entity B should derecognise the financial liability.

Dormant bank accounts

Bank C cannot locate all its customers that deposit cash with the bank. The depositor may have moved from their home without notifying the bank and there have been no transactions on the account for a considerable period of time (the account is dormant). However, the depositor or its legal representatives, including the depositor's executor of the estate, have the right to claim the deposited amounts indefinitely. Historically, five per cent of dormant accounts held with the bank are never reclaimed.

In the absence of a statute of limitation in Bank C's jurisdiction Bank C will continue to recognise the financial liability to return the cash to the depositor at the amount repayable on demand. In other jurisdictions the law may allow the bank, or the bank may be forced, to transfer the deposit to a third party, for example, a government body, after a specified period of time. The legal release on transfer to the government body is a legal release for the bank if the depositor has no recourse to the bank.

Where an entity pays another party to assume its obligation under a contract, sometimes referred to as 'in substance defeasance', the liability is not extinguished until a legal release from the obligation is obtained. [IAS 39.AG59]

Legal release from an obligation extinguishes the liability, but if concurrently an entity assumes another obligation to a third party or indeed to the original creditor, the new obligation is recognised. For example, an entity may be released from its primary obligation to the creditor, but assumes a guarantee if the party assuming the primary obligation defaults, in which case it derecognises the original liability and recognises the new liability for the guarantee. [IAS 39.AG60]

When a liability is extinguished, the difference between its carrying amount and consideration paid including any non-cash assets transferred and any new liabilities assumed is recognised in profit or loss. [IAS 39.41] In the above example, the difference between the carrying amount of the liability and consideration paid to the creditor including the fair value of the guarantee provided to the creditor is recognised in profit or loss. Where only part of a liability is extinguished (e.g. repurchased by an entity), the allocation of the previous carrying amount between the amount that continues to be recognised and the part that is derecognised is performed by reference to the relative fair values of those parts on the date of repurchase (see **3.2** above).

Example 4B

Expiry of embedded written put option

Entity F issues an instrument that contains a written put option embedded in the instrument that allows the holder to redeem the instrument for par in cash three years after the instrument is issued. The instrument also contains an entitlement to a fixed coupon payable at the discretion of the entity to the extent the instrument remains outstanding. If the put is not exercised by the holder the instrument will remain outstanding in perpetuity. The instrument contains no other financial liability component other than the written put element. In accordance with IAS 32, at initial recognition the difference between the net proceeds and the fair value of the financial liability in respect of the written put measured at the present value of the strike price of the written put at year 3, is recognised in equity.

If the put is exercised by the holder at the end of year 3 the whole instrument is extinguished as therefore is derecognised. Due to the unwinding of the discount on the financial liability recognised in profit or loss the carrying amount of the financial liability will equal the exercise price of put option, and thus the put will be settled with no gain or loss.

If the put is not exercised by the holder at the end of year 3 the instrument remains outstanding and the written put is extinguished as it has not been exercised by the holder as is therefore derecognised. The financial liability is derecognised at its closing carrying amount and reclassified to equity. In this instance the terms of the instrument have not changed but the written put ceases to be a financial liability and starts to be recognised as equity. No gain or loss is recognised on derecognition of the financial liability in this case as the holder has chosen not to exercise its put right to redeem the instrument but rather chose to retain the instrument and have an entitlement to a fixed coupon payable at the discretion of the issuer which is classified as equity.

US GAAP comparison: Similar to IAS 39, under US GAAP a liability is derecognised only if it has been extinguished. A liability is extinguished by paying the debtor or obtaining legal release from being the primary obligor (FAS 140).

4.1 Renegotiation of a financial liability

Often entities will seek to renegotiate debt instruments for a variety of reasons. Sometimes the entity will be seeking more favourable terms from the lender. Sometimes the borrower may be in financial difficulty and need to alter the contractual terms of the liability such as the maturity of the instrument or the coupon on the instrument.

Where the existing borrower and lender exchange instruments with terms that are substantially different, the exchange is accounted for as an extinguishment of the original liability and recognition of a new liability. Similarly, modification of the terms of a liability is accounted for as an extinguishment of the original liability and recognition of a new liability where the modification is substantial. [IAS 39.40]

The terms are deemed to be substantially different if the net present value of the cash flows under the new liability, including any fees paid and received, is at least 10 per cent different from the net present value of the remaining cash flows of the existing liability, both discounted at the original effective interest rate of the original liability. Similarly, modification is deemed to be substantial if the net present value of the cash flows under the modified terms, including any fees paid or received, is at least 10 per cent different from the net present value of the remaining cash flows of the liability prior to the modification, in both discounted at the original effective interest rate of the liability prior to the modification. [IAS 39.AG62]

When performing the 10 per cent test described above the entity must exclude from the original effective interest rate the effects of hedge accounting (whether fair value hedging or cash flow hedging). For example, if the issuer is fair value hedge accounting the interest rate risk portion of its issued fixed rate debt, the effective interest rate on this debt will reflect current floating rates at the date of exchange. As the terms of the original debt are fixed, not floating, the original effective interest determined at initial recognition of the debt prior to any hedge accounting, should be the rate that is used in applying the 10 per cent test.

The above treatment for fair value hedge accounting is consistent with applying the original effective interest rate at initial recognition had the issuer designated the debt as at fair value through profit or loss. Designating the debt as at fair value through profit or loss for subsequent measurement does not negate the issuer determining the original effective interest rate at the date the instrument was initially recognised for the purposes of applying the 10 per cent test.

Example 4.1A

Debt modification: change in interest and term

Entity A borrowed CU1 million on 1 January 20X0, at a fixed rate of 9 per cent per annum for 10 years. Entity A incurred issue cost of CU50,000. Interest on the loan is payable annually in arrears. The original effective interest rate ('EIR') is 9.807 per cent. During 20X5, Entity A approached the lender for a modification of the terms of the debt (this modification could have been as a result of a deteriorating financial condition of the borrower or because of a fall in interest rates). The following modified terms were agreed with effect from 1 January 20X6:

- Interest rate will be reduced to 7.5 per cent payable yearly in arrears.
- The original amount, payable on maturity, remains unchanged but the maturity of the loan is extended by two years to 31 December 20Y1.

No fees for renegotiating the finance are payable.

	Opening	Interest	Payments	Closing
		EIR of 9.807%	-950,000	
31 Dec 20X0	950,000	93,166	90,000	953,166
31 Dec 20X1	953,166	93,477	90,000	956,643
31 Dec 20X2	956,643	93,818	90,000	960,461
31 Dec 20X3	960,461	94,192	90,000	964,654
31 Dec 20X4	964,654	94,604	90,000	969,257
31 Dec 20X5	969,257	95,055	90,000	**974,312**
31 Dec 20X6	974,312	95,551	90,000	979,863
31 Dec 20X7	979,863	96,095	90,000	985,958
31 Dec 20X8	985,958	96,693	90,000	992,651
31 Dec 20X9	992,651	97,349	1,090,000	0

The present value of the modified debt at the original effective interest rate is calculated as follows:

	Payments
31 Dec 20X6	75,000
31 Dec 20X7	75,000
31 Dec 20X8	75,000
31 Dec 20X9	75,000
31 Dec 20Y0	75,000
31 Dec 20Y1	1,075,000
Present value at 1 January 20X6 discounting at original EIR of 9.807%	**898,954**

The entity must determine whether the modification is considered to be an extinguishment of the original debt. [IAS 39.AG62] As the difference between the amortised cost of the debt instrument at the date of modification and the present value of the new debt instrument, discounted by the original effective interest rate, is less than 10 per cent, the modification is not considered an extinguishment of the original debt. The difference, CU75,359, will be recognised in profit or loss in future periods through the revised effective interest rate.

For the avoidance of doubt, at the date of modification only, the issuer should not apply IAS 39.AG8, as this will result in an immediate gain/loss in profit or loss on modification which is contrary to the issuer not achieving derecognition. The issuer will apply IAS 39.AG8 following the date of modification if the estimates of future cash flows change. The revised cash flows must be discounted at the revised effective interest rate that was determined at the date of modification.

A modification of debt terms may include changes to any one or a combination of the following:

- stated interest rate for the remaining original life of the debt;
- maturity date or dates;
- face amount of the debt;

- accrued interest;
- recourse or non-recourse features;
- priority of the obligation;
- collateral (requirement for or changes in the type of the collateral);
- covenants and/or waivers;
- currency denomination;
- the guarantor (or elimination of the guarantor); or
- option features.

Example 4.1B

Debt modification: change in notional, interest, term

Entity P borrowed CU100 million on 1 January 20X0 at a fixed interest rate of 10 per cent per annum for 10 years. Entity A incurred no issue costs. Interest on the loan is payable annually in arrears. The original effective interest rate is 10 per cent. At the end 20X4, Entity P is offered a number of alternatives to refinance its issued debt with effect from 1 January 20X0. The current market interest rate including a credit premium for Entity P's credit risk (which has remained unchanged) is 5 per cent for the remaining time to maturity of its existing debt, i.e. half the contractual cash flows on the original debt issued at the start of 20X0.

All proposed new borrowings are with the same counterparty and are used to buy back existing debt with the issue and buy back being in contemplation of one another. Assume for illustrative purposes only, the yield curve is flat at 1 January 20X5. All amounts are in CU million.

The fair value of the outstanding debt at 31 December 20X4 is determined as follows:

Period	Cash flows 10% x CU100	Discount factor at 5%	Present value
20X5	10	0.952	9.52
20X6	10	0.907	9.07
20X7	10	0.864	8.64
20X8	10	0.823	8.23
20X9	110	0.784	86.19
		Fair value	121.65

Scenario 1 – new borrowing at current market interest rate of 5% with notional equal to the amount needed to buy back the outstanding debt at market price

Entity P determines the present value of remaining cash flows on its existing debt at the original effective interest rate and compares this with the cash flows on the new debt also discounted at the same original effective interest rate.

The new debt has a notional of CU121.65m and an interest rate of 5% and matures in 20X9.

Period	Cash flows Existing debt	Cash flows New debt 5% x CU121.65	Discount factor at 10%	Present value Existing debt	Present value New debt
20X5	10	6.08	0.909	9.09	5.53
20X6	10	6.08	0.826	8.26	5.03
20X7	10	6.08	0.751	7.51	4.57
20X8	10	6.08	0.683	6.83	4.15
20X9	110	127.73	0.621	68.31	79.31
				100.00	98.59

The difference between the present value of the existing and new debt discounted at the original effective interest rate is CU1.41 (1.41%). As the difference is within the '10% test' the existing debt will not be derecognised.

Scenario 2 – same as Scenario 1 but term of new debt is extended by one year (assuming yield curve is flat)

The new debt has a notional of CU121.65m and an interest rate of 5% and matures in 20Y0.

Period	Cash flows New debt 5% x CU121.65	Discount factor at 10%	Present value New debt
20X5	6.08	0.909	5.53
20X6	6.08	0.826	5.03
20X7	6.08	0.751	4.57
20X8	6.08	0.683	4.15
20X9	6.08	0.621	3.78
20Y0	127.73	0.564	72.10
			95.16

The difference between the present value of the existing and new debt discounted at the original effective interest rate is CU4.84 (4.84%). As the difference is within the '10% test' the existing debt will not be derecognised.

The difference in the present value calculations of the new debt in scenario 1 and new debt in scenario 2 arises because scenario 2 has an additional interest flow at current market rates and deferral of the principal by a year.

Scenario 3 – same as Scenario 2 but the yield curve is not flat in 20Y0

The yield curve remains flat until 20X9 as in scenario 2 but then falls in 20Y0 and beyond. The 6-year yield curve at 1/1/X5 (i.e. until 20Y0) is 4.85% compared to 5% in scenario 2.

Period	Cash flows New debt 4.85% x CU121.65m	Discount factor at 10%	Present value New debt
20X5	5.90	0.909	5.37
20X6	5.90	0.826	4.88
20X7	5.90	0.751	4.43
20X8	5.90	0.683	4.03
20X9	5.90	0.621	3.67
20Y0	127.55	0.564	71.99
			94.37

The difference between the present value of the existing and new debt discounted at the original effective interest rate is CU5.63 (5.63%). As the difference is within the '10% test' the existing debt will not be derecognised.

The difference in the present value calculations of the new debt in scenario 2 and the new debt in scenario 3 has increased because, even though both scenarios 2 and 3 have the same maturity and notional, the effective interest rate on the new debt differs. As the additional contractual interest flows on the new debt extending beyond the term of the existing debt are locking in a lower interest rate environment this exaggerates the difference in present value calculations between the existing and new debt. If the term was to extend further, and/or interest rates were even lower, then the present value of the new debt may be greater than 10% of the existing debt which would result in derecognition of the existing date and recognition of the new debt at fair value in accordance with IAS 39.43.

It is possible in a scenario of higher interest rates that when the term of the debt is extended beyond the term of the existing date that the '10% test' is breached and derecognition of the existing debt is required.

Example 4.1C

Debt modification: change in basis of interest

Entity C issued 5 year debt at a fixed rate of interest of 7 per cent on 1/1/X3 at par for €100m. The debt is measured at amortised cost. On 1/1/X5 the debt is exchanged with the original lender for a new debt instrument that has floating rate, LIBOR, for the remaining 3 year term that is set annually in advance. The current LIBOR rate is 4 per cent and the yield curve is flat for the next 3 years. As interest rates have fallen from 7 per cent to 4 per cent, and credit spreads have remained unchanged, the fair value of the debt has risen above par. In order to put the current debt holders in the same economic position following the debt exchange the issuer agrees to increase the notional of the new debt to €108.70m.

Entity C applies the 10 per cent per cent test to the debt exchange. Entity C sums the cash flows on the new debt discounted by the original effective interest rate of 7 per cent:

- €4.3m for 3 years (4 per cent x €108.70m, as the LIBOR curve is flat at the date of exchange); and
- the principal of €108.70m payable at the end of year 3.

The net present value of the new debt discounted using the original effective interest rate is €100m.

Entity C then sums the remaining cash flows on the old debt of €7m for 3 years and a principal of €100m discounted by the original effective interest rate of 7 per cent, which is also €100m.

The net present value of the old debt and modified debt discounted by the original effective interest rate are the same, i.e. €100m. Entity C therefore does not derecognise the old debt.

For the remaining three years Entity C applies a modified effective interest rate that consists of current LIBOR for the period plus the amortisation from €100m to €108.70m based on a constant yield. The internal rate of return for the amortisation is 2.82 per cent per year and represents the current discount to par on the modified debt. This is the same accounting as for a discounted floating rate bond. The amortisation for the remaining three years is:

Period ending 31/12/05: 2.82% x €100m = €2.82m
Period ending 31/12/06: 2.82% x €102.82m = €2.90m
Period ending 31/12/07: 2.82% x €105.72m = €2.98m

At 31/12/X5 Entity C accrues both LIBOR for the period plus the amortisation less the LIBOR interest paid in the period. As LIBOR is set in advance, the interest payment is €4.3m, being 4 per cent on the modified notional of the debt of €108.70m. The period end carrying amount is therefore €102.82m (being €100m + €4.3m + €2.82m – €4.3m).

For illustrative purposes, assuming LIBOR remains the same for the remaining term of the instrument the period end carrying amounts for 31/12/X6 and 31/12/X7 are as follows:

1/1/X6	€102.82m
LIBOR	€4.3m
Amortisation of discount	€2.90m
Less cash paid	(€4.3m)
31/12/X6	€105.72m
LIBOR	€4.3m
Amortisation of discount	€2.98m
Less cash paid	(€4.3m)
31/12/X7	€108.70m

At 31/12/X7 Entity C settles the modified debt instrument for €108.70m, being its par amount.

In most instances 'substantially different' will be determined by using the 10 per cent test. However, in limited cases a simple qualitative assessment will be sufficient to establish that the terms of the modified liability are substantially different from those of the original one. One example of modification where a qualitative assessment is relevant is where the denomination of the original liability is changed to a different currency such that the entity is left in a different economic position due to the new currency exposure taken on.

In some instances entities renegotiate debt in such a way that under the new terms the lender is granted equity instruments in full settlement of the obligation under the original contract (i.e. a debt for equity swap). Such a restructuring is treated as an extinguishment of debt and a simultaneous issuance of new shares. The shares are recognised at the fair value of the consideration received, with any difference to the carrying amount of the debt being recognised in profit or loss.

This approach is consistent with the rationale that the restructuring could be seen as a 'shortcut' for issuing shares to the lender and using the consideration received to repay the debt. The alternative school of thought is that the consideration for the shares is the carrying amount of the debt then the debt will be reclassified at its carrying amount with no gain or loss recognised. As the transaction is with a third party it seems appropriate to assume that shares are issued at fair value and therefore if this amount differs to the carrying amount of the debt a gain or loss will be recognised in profit or loss.

US GAAP comparison: Under US GAAP special rules apply for contractual modifications for troubled debt restructurings (FAS 15). IAS 39 does not distinguish between a normal renegotiation and a troubled debt restructuring. The rules of FAS 15 have to be applied if debt is restructured for economic or legal reasons that a creditor would not consider otherwise. In case of a modification of the contractual terms the accounting treatment depends on a comparison of carrying amount with the undiscounted future cash flows. If the carrying amount does not exceed the total future cash payments, no change in the carrying amount shall be made, and hence, to reflect the new cash flow profile, the effective interest rate has to be adjusted. If the future undiscounted cash flows under the modified terms are below the carrying amount, than the entity reduces the carrying amount to this new amount and recognises a gain on restructuring of debt. All future cash payments on this debt shall be accounted for as a reduction of the carrying amount and, hence, no interest expense is to be recognised.

IAS 39 provides less guidance on renegotiations and exchanges of debt instruments. IFRS is broadly based on the equivalent guidance in US GAAP. However, US GAAP has a greater amount of guidance in certain areas. An entity may find the guidance in EITF 96–19 *Debtor's Accounting for a Modification or Exchange of Debt Instruments* useful in applying IFRSs.

The following guidance included in the EITF 96–19 may be relevant in applying the '10 per cent' test under IFRSs:

- the cash flows have to include all cash flows specified by the terms of the new debt instrument (plus any amounts paid by the debtor to the creditor and less any amounts received by the debtor from the creditor as part of the exchange or modification);

- if either the old or the new debt instrument or both have a variable interest rate, an entity has to use the rate effective as at the date of exchange or modification to calculate the cash flows;

- if either the old or the new debt instrument has a call or a put option then separate cash flow analyses for exercise and non-exercise has to be performed and the scenario that generates the smaller change would be used to decide whether the 10 per cent hurdle is breached;

- judgement is to be used when determining the cash flows if the instrument contains contingent payment terms or unusual interest rate terms;

- if the exchanged or modified debt instrument is exchanged or modified again within one year, the terms of the original debt should be used as starting point to perform the '10 per cent' test;

- in the case of an intermediary acting as an agent for the debtor, the assessment of the transaction should "look through" that intermediary; and

- if the intermediary is identified as acting as a principal it is treated like any other creditor.

In EITF 06–6 in US GAAP, unlike IAS 39, specific guidance is given for modifications (or exchanges) of convertible debt instruments. Among its guidance it states that a modification or an exchange of debt instruments that adds a substantive conversion option or eliminates a conversion option that was substantive at the date of the modification or exchange would always be considered substantial, and debt extinguishment accounting would be required in those circumstances.

Where an investment bank is used to facilitate a debt exchange it is important to establish all the terms of the arrangement in order to establish whether the investment bank is acting as agent or principal to the transaction. An investment bank can undertake a number of roles in debt exchanges. For example, if an entity wishes to exchange its issued debt it may request an investment bank to seek out the holders of the debt in order for those holders to be offered the new debt instrument. If the investment bank is remunerated by way of a predetermined fee for this service, it is likely the bank is acting as an agent to enable the issuer to exchange its existing debt instruments.

If the existing debt holders acquire the new debt in exchange for returning the old debt to the issuer, and the investment bank simply facilitates this exchange as an agent of the issuer, then this is considered a debt exchange between the issuer and existing debt holders and therefore the 10 per cent test would need to be applied by the issuer. On the other hand, if debt is transferred from one debt holder to another, the issuer's accounting is not impacted as long as funds do not pass through the issuer or its agent.

In some instances the investment bank buys the existing debt from the debt holders by using its own funds and bears market risk of the debt, and therefore is considered principal to the original debt. If the investment bank subsequently exchanges or modifies the debt with the issuer, the investment bank is considered the original debt holder and the issuer must determine whether the debt exchange between the investment bank and the issuer breaches the 10 per cent test. The investment bank would not be acting as principal, i.e. would be acting as an agent, if it merely places the new notes in the market and only buys the new debt that it has contractually agreed to sell to others.

If an exchange of debt instruments or modification of terms is accounted for as an extinguishment, any costs or fees incurred are recognised as part of the gain or loss on the extinguishment. Where the terms of the new/modified instrument are not substantially different, then any fees or costs paid in the exchange/modification are treated as an adjustment to the carrying amount of the original liability and are amortised over the remaining life of the new/modified liability. [IAS 39.AG62]

US GAAP comparison: EITF 96–19 draws a distinction between fees paid or received between the counterparties and directly related cost incurred with third parties. While counterparty fees are recognised in profit or loss when the exchange/modification is treated as an extinguishment they are amortised over the remaining life of the new instrument if this is not the case. Costs incurred with third parties are treated the other way around. If the exchange/modification leads to an extinguishment of debt, the costs are amortised over the remaining life of the new instrument, and in the absence of extinguishment accounting they are expensed as incurred. IAS 39 does not distinguish between fees paid to third parties and those paid to counterparties.

5 Future developments

In response to the global financial crisis and the recommendations made by the Financial Stability Forum, in March 2009, the IASB issued an exposure draft, ED/2009/3, of proposed amendments to IAS 39 and IFRS 7, *Derecognition*. The exposure draft forms part of the IASB and FASB's Memorandum of Understanding which sets out a Roadmap of Convergence between IFRSs and US GAAP. As illustrated in the US GAAP comparisons included in this chapter the two accounting regimes differ in many ways and the exposure draft represents the first step in aligning them. The final IFRS on derecognition is expected in the first half of 2010.

The exposure draft proposes a control-based model. The model requires derecognition of an asset when:

- the contractual rights to the cash flows expire;
- there is a transfer and the transferor has no continuing involvement in the asset, or
- there is a transfer and there is retention of continuing involvement, but the transferee has the practical ability to transfer the asset for its own benefit.

Compared to the existing Standard, the new model does not include either a risk and reward assessment or the pass-through tests; also, a transferred asset is not subject to the specific measurement requirements on continuing involvement measurement. The model is applied to the whole asset, part of an asset if the cash flows are specifically identifiable (e.g. an interest only strip of a loan), or a fully proportionate share of an asset (e.g. 60% of all cash flows). The right to receive the first 90% of cash flows on an asset is not deemed specifically identifiable and therefore the model would be applied to the whole asset. To the extent an entity derecognises an asset and retains some continuing involvement, proposed amendments to IFRS 7 would require extensive disclosures on the nature of and risks associated with the transferor's continuing involvement.

In practice, compared to the existing requirements, many more repurchase arrangements over assets that are highly liquid would get derecognition under the proposed model. The transferor will derecognise the asset and recognise a forward contract to buy the transferred asset back from the transferee; the transferee will recognise the asset and a forward contract to sell the transferred asset back to the transferor. In contrast, many securitisations and factoring arrangements would likely fail derecognition as it is common for the transferor to retain a disproportionate interest in the cash flows of the asset, usually credit risk, and the transferee does not usually have the right to transfer the asset for its own benefit.

The exposure draft contains an alternative approach proposed by a significant minority of Board members. Like the model described above, it is based on control. However, the model would require that if a transferor does not have access to *all* the cash flows the transferor recognised prior to the transfer, then the asset is derecognised and a new asset is recognised for any interest in part of the asset transferred. This is sometimes referred to as a 'components approach'. This model does not distinguish between a disproportionate or fully proportionate interest in cash flows and therefore would result in a many more transfers achieving derecognition.

8 Hedge accounting – basics

1 Introduction

Entities enter into many transactions that aim to reduce risk, and ultimately reduce the variability in cash flows that arise from these risks. Entities enter into hedging transactions to hedge risks that are evident in items that are already recognised in the statement of financial position, as well as hedge risks for future transactions that have yet to occur.

Hedge accounting is a method of presentation that may be voluntarily applied to hedging transactions. The objective of hedge accounting is to ensure that the gain or loss on the hedging instrument is recognised in profit or loss in the same period when the item that is being hedged affects profit or loss. In other words, applying hedge accounting results in the 'matched' timing of recognition of gains and losses in profit or loss. Where an entity is perfectly hedged, the gains and losses on the hedging instrument and the hedged item perfectly offset in profit or loss in the same period.

IAS 39 allows an entity to apply hedge accounting if an entity specifically designates the hedging instrument and the hedged item at inception of the hedge accounting relationship. Generally, there are two ways in which hedge accounting achieves the matching of gains and losses on the hedging instrument and the hedged item:

- changes in the fair value of the hedging instrument are recognised in profit or loss at the same time that a recognised asset or liability that is being hedged is adjusted for movements in the hedged risk with that adjustment also recognised in profit or loss in the same period. This is referred to as a fair value hedge because it is the exposure to changes in the fair value of the hedged item due to the designated risk that is being hedged; or
- changes in the fair value of the hedging instrument are recognised initially in other comprehensive income and reclassified from equity to profit or loss when the hedged item affects profit or loss. This is known as a cash flow hedge because it is the exposure to the variability in future cash flows that is being hedged.

A third and final category of hedge accounting is hedging a net investment in a foreign operation. This is accounted for similarly to cash flow hedges.

There are specific rules in the Standard that limit which financial instruments can be considered hedging instruments, and which items can be considered hedged items. In summary, a hedging instrument can be a derivative financial instrument or a non-derivative financial instrument (for hedges of foreign exchange risk only). The hedged item must be an identified hedged item or a group of items that could affect profit or loss.

When an entity wishes to apply hedge accounting, it must formally document in writing its intention to apply hedge accounting prospectively. Hedge accounting cannot be applied retrospectively. Additionally, hedge accounting must be consistent with the entity's established risk management strategy for that hedge relationship. The hedge documentation must identify the hedging instrument, the hedged item or transaction, the nature of the risk being hedged and specify how the 'effectiveness' of the hedge relationship will be assessed and ineffectiveness measured.

Hedge accounting is only permitted if the hedge relationship is expected to be highly effective and it is actually effective within a quantitative range. To the extent that the hedging instrument and hedged item are not perfectly effective at offsetting each other, this ineffectiveness is immediately recognised in profit or loss.

IAS 39 does not mandate the use of hedge accounting. Hedge accounting is voluntary. If an entity does not wish to use hedge accounting it does not need to designate and document its hedging relationships. Where an entity applies the normal recognition and measurement requirements of IAS 39 it may find in some cases that the effect on profit or loss of applying hedge accounting could be substantially the same as where hedge accounting is not applied. In such cases, an entity may well choose not to apply hedge accounting because there is very little benefit in doing so.

In some instances the fair value option (see **3.1.1** in **chapter 2**) can be used as an alternative to hedge accounting. If an accounting mismatch exists, which will result in profit or loss volatility, an entity may apply the fair value option to reduce this volatility instead of complying with the onerous conditions of hedge accounting. For example, where a derivative provides an economic hedge of a financial instrument that is not measured at fair value through profit or loss, an accounting measurement mismatch exists. In that situation, the fair value option applied to the hedged item would reduce the measurement mismatch. The simplicity of applying the fair value option does, however, come at a cost:

- hedge accounting can be discontinued at any time but fair value through profit or loss designation is irrevocable; and
- if fair value option is used, the entire change in fair value of the designated item must be recognised in profit or loss. This amount

will not be an exact offset to the change in fair value of the hedging instrument where the hedging instrument is not hedging all the risks of the item that is designated under the fair value option. Hedge accounting allows the specific hedged risk to be designated, and therefore can achieve a greater reduction in profit or loss volatility.

This chapter discusses hedge accounting in the following sections:

Section 2	Definitions and mechanics of hedge accounting
Section 3	Hedged items
Section 4	Hedging instruments
Section 5	Hedge effectiveness
Section 6	Documentation

US GAAP comparison: The hedge accounting rules under US GAAP, detailed in FAS 133, are similar in many respects to IAS 39. However, there are differences which are highlighted throughout this chapter. In addition, US GAAP has a greater number of interpretations in the form of questions and answers issued by the Derivative Implementation Group (DIG), the interpretive body for FAS 133 issues.

The FASB issued an exposure draft to amend FAS 133 in June 2008 to, among other things, simplify accounting for hedging activities, improve the financial reporting of hedging activities to make the accounting model and associated disclosures easier to understand for users of financial statements, resolve major practice issues related to hedge accounting that have arisen under FAS 133, and address differences resulting from recognition and measurement anomalies between the accounting for derivative instruments and the accounting for hedged items or transactions. Currently, the exposure draft and related matters are under redeliberation by the FASB.

The more complex aspects of hedge accounting and detailed examples are included in **chapters 9** and **10** respectively.

2 Definitions and mechanics of hedge accounting

IAS 39 recognises three types of hedge accounting depending on the nature of the risk exposure:

- a fair value hedge;

- a cash flow hedge; and
- a hedge of a net investment in a foreign operation ('net investment hedge').

2.1 Definition of a fair value hedge

A fair value hedge is a hedge of the exposure to changes in fair value of a recognised asset or a liability or an unrecognised firm commitment or an identified portion of such an asset, a liability or a firm commitment that is attributable to a particular risk and could affect profit or loss. [IAS 39.86(a)]

2.1.1 Examples of fair value exposure

Fair value exposures arise from existing assets or liabilities, including firm commitments. Fixed-rate financial assets and liabilities, for example, have a fair value exposure to changes in market rates of interest and changes in credit quality. Non-financial assets have a fair value exposure to changes in their market price, e.g. a commodity price. Some assets and liabilities have fair value exposures arising from more than one type of risk, e.g. interest rate, credit, foreign currency risk.

The following assets and liabilities are commonly fair value hedged:

- fixed rate liabilities like loans;
- fixed rate assets like investments in bonds;
- investments in equity securities; and
- firm commitments to buy/sell non-financial items at a fixed price.

Examples of fair value hedges include:

- a hedge of exposure to changes in the fair value of fixed rate debt as a result of changes in market interest rates (such a hedge could be entered into either by the issuer or by the holder);
- a hedge of the foreign currency risk of an unrecognised contractual commitment by an airline to purchase an aircraft for a fixed amount of a foreign currency at a future date; and
- a hedge of the change in fuel price relating to an unrecognised contractual commitment by an electricity utility to purchase fuel at a fixed price at a specified date, with payment in its functional currency.

Further examples

A detailed illustration of the mechanics of a fair value hedge of interest rate risk of fixed rate debt is included in **2.1** of **chapter 10**.

2.1.2 *Fair value hedge accounting*

A fair value hedge that meets all the hedge accounting criteria is accounted for as follows:
[IAS 39.89]

(a) the gain or loss from re-measuring the hedging instrument at fair value (for a derivative hedging instrument) or the foreign currency component of its carrying amount (for a non-derivative hedging instrument) is recognised immediately in profit or loss; and

(b) the carrying amount of the hedged item is adjusted through profit or loss for the gain or loss on the hedged item attributable to the hedged risk. This applies even if the hedged item is an available-for-sale asset measured at fair value with changes in fair value recognised in other comprehensive income. This also applies if the hedged item is otherwise measured at cost.

2.1.3 *Firm commitment*

A firm commitment is a binding agreement for the exchange of a specified quantity of resources at a specified price on a specified future date or dates. [IAS 39.9]

A commitment is binding if it is enforceable either legally or otherwise. If the commitment is with a related party, consideration should be given as to whether in practice the right can be enforced. To be enforceable, the agreement should provide for remedies that are available to the parties to the contract in the event of non-performance. For example, a penalty could be specified at a fixed amount or equal to the change in market price of the item under the contract. Alternatively, the penalty may not be specifically stipulated in the agreement but may otherwise be applicable (for example remedies under law). When an entity is preparing its individual entity only financial statements the entity needs to consider carefully whether transactions between group entities meet the definition of a firm commitment as they may not be subject to remedies for non-performance either as part of the contract or under law. In many instances, particularly, in the absence of non-controlling interests that may require protection from the controlling interest, an agreement between group entities would not be binding.

Hedges of firm commitments are generally treated as fair value hedges under IAS 39. However, there is one exception: if an entity is hedging the foreign currency risk in a firm commitment this may be accounted for either as a fair value hedge or a cash flow hedge. [IAS 39.87]

Example 2.1.3A

Hedging foreign currency risk of a firm commitment

Entity B sells machinery at fixed prices in many jurisdictions. Entity B's functional currency is Sterling. Entity B enters into a contract with Entity D, whose functional currency is Euro, to sell machinery for delivery in six months' time at a fixed price in Euro that is determined today. In other words, Entity B has entered into a firm commitment with Entity D.

Entity B simultaneously enters into a foreign currency forward contract to hedge its future exposure to Euro arising from its firm commitment. This foreign currency forward contract can either be designated as a hedging instrument in a fair value hedge or a cash flow hedge as it is hedging the foreign currency risk of a firm commitment.

Example 2.1.3B

Fair value hedging a firm commitment

Entity E is a discount grocery chain with over 400 stores in the US, which enters into forward contracts to purchase various inventory items for its stores. On 1 June 20X0, Entity E enters into a forward contract to purchase 300,000 bushels of wheat from a wheat producer for a fixed price of US$1.40 per bushel on 1 August 20X0. Entity E will use the wheat in its bakery operations. Entity E intends taking physical delivery of the wheat in accordance with its expected purchase requirements. If Entity E failed to take delivery of the wheat, it would be required to pay for any decrease in the value of the wheat and legal remedies will be available to the wheat producer.

The transaction is a firm commitment because it is a binding agreement for the exchange of a specified quantity of wheat at a specified price on a specified future date. The forward contract is not accounted for as a derivative because Entity E intends to take physical delivery of wheat and has no past practice of settling similar contracts net. Entity E could enter into a contract to hedge the fair value exposure of the firm commitment due to the change in the price of wheat between 1 June 20X0 and 1 August 20X0, e.g. a net cash settled forward contract to sell wheat for a fixed price on 1 August. Such a contract would qualify as a hedging instrument in a fair value hedge of a firm commitment.

2.1.4 *Fair value hedges of unrecognised firm commitments*

When an unrecognised firm commitment is designated as a hedged item, the subsequent cumulative change in the fair value of the firm commitment attributable to the hedged risk is recognised as an asset or a liability with a corresponding gain or loss recognised in profit or loss. [IAS 39.93]

The changes in the fair value of the hedging instrument will also be recognised in profit or loss.

The initial carrying amount of the asset or the liability that results from the entity fulfilling the firm commitment is adjusted to include the cumulative change in the fair value of the firm commitment attributable to the hedged risk that was recognised in the statement of financial position. **Example 2.2** in **chapter 10** demonstrates the entries required when an entity hedges foreign currency risk of a firm commitment.

2.1.5 *Discontinuance of fair value hedge accounting*

An entity must discontinue prospectively fair value hedge accounting if: [IAS 39.91]

- the hedging instrument expires or is sold, terminated or exercised (the replacement or rollover of a hedging instrument into another hedging instrument is not an expiration or termination if it formed part of the entity's documented hedging strategy from inception) (for rollover hedging strategies see **3.8** in **chapter 9**);
- the hedge no longer meets the hedge accounting criteria (for example, it is no longer highly effective or its effectiveness is no longer measurable); or
- the entity de-designates the hedge relationship.

Any adjustment to the carrying amount of the hedged item for the designated risk for interest-bearing financial instruments is amortised to profit or loss, with amortisation commencing no later than when the hedged item ceases to be adjusted. [IAS 39.92] The amortisation is based on a recalculated effective interest rate at the date amortisation commences such that the adjustment is fully amortised by maturity.

Where amortisation begins as soon as a fair value adjustment exists, the adjustment to the carrying amount affects the effective interest rate calculation for the hedged item. In practice, to ease the administrative burden of amortising the adjustment while the hedged item continues to be adjusted for changes in fair value attributable to the hedged risk, it may be easier to defer amortising the adjustment until the hedged item ceases to be adjusted for the designated hedged risk. This is particularly true when the life of the hedge is the same as that of the hedged item. For example, if a fixed rate loan is issued at par and redeems at par, its fair value will move away from par over its life in response to changes in interest rates but will be pulled back to par on maturity. Therefore, any fair value adjustments to the carrying amount of the bond under a fair value hedge for interest rate risk will be reversed by the end of the hedge and will not require amortisation.

However, if an interest-bearing instrument is hedged for only a portion of its term to maturity (see **2.2** in **chapter 9** for partial term hedging), deferring amortisation until cessation of the hedge relationship will result in a skewed effective interest rate in the remaining years to the maturity of the hedged item.

An entity must apply the same amortisation policy for all of its debt instruments, i.e. it cannot defer amortising fair value adjustments on some items and not on others.

Example 2.1.5

Amortising fair value hedge adjustments

Bank J has a ¥10 million fixed-rate loan asset that is classified as an available-for-sale asset. Bank J hedged the fair value exposure of the asset using a forward contract. As a result of the hedge, the loan asset has been adjusted for changes in the fair value of the risk being hedged and that adjustment is recognised in profit or loss. If Bank J does not elect to start amortising the hedging gain or loss while the hedge is outstanding, the adjustment will remain as part of the available-for-sale asset, until the loan is sold or until the loan is no longer hedged. If hedge accounting ceases prior to the loan being sold, the fair value adjustment of the loan will be amortised through the revised effective interest over the expected remaining life of the loan.

If an entity discontinues hedge accounting by de-designating the hedging relationship, an entity may elect to designate prospectively a new hedging relationship with the same derivative hedging instrument provided the new hedging relationship meets the requirements for hedge accounting.

2.2 Definition of a cash flow hedge

A cash flow hedge is a hedge of the exposure to variability in cash flows that:
[IAS 39.86(b)]

- is attributable to a particular risk associated with a recognised asset or liability (such as all or some future interest payments on variable rate debt) or a highly probable forecast transaction; and

- could affect profit or loss.

Common assets and liabilities and forecast transactions that are cash flow hedged include:

- variable rate liabilities like loans;
- variable rate assets like investments in bonds;
- highly probable future issuance of fixed rate debt;
- forecast reinvestment of interest and principal received on fixed rate assets; and
- highly probable forecast sales and purchases.

An example of a cash flow hedge is a hedge of variable rate debt with a floating to fixed interest rate swap. The variability in cash flow arises due to the reset of interest rates. The cash flow hedge reduces future variability of interest cash flows on the debt. Another example of a cash flow hedge is a hedge of anticipated reinvestment of cash inflows and the anticipated refinancing or rollover of a financial liability. A hedging instrument that swaps one variable rate for another, e.g. LIBOR for EURIBOR, would not qualify in a cash flow hedge relationship as it does not reduce cash flow variability, it merely swaps the existing cash flow variability of the debt for cash flow variability determined on a different basis.

2.2.1 *Forecast transactions*

A forecast transaction is an uncommitted but anticipated future transaction. [IAS 39.9]

It is important to distinguish between forecast transactions and firm commitments as forecast transactions are always cash flow hedged, whereas firm commitments are generally fair value hedged. The following table illustrates some examples of forecast transactions and, also illustrates the difference between a forecast transaction and a firm commitment:

Example 2.2.1

Examples of forecast transactions and firm commitments

Forecast transaction	*Firm commitment*
In May 20X1 an entity forecasts the purchase of 100,000 bushels of corn to be used in its manufacturing process in October 20X1.	An entity has signed a legally binding purchase agreement to take delivery of 100,000 bushels of corn on 30 September 20X1 for US$2 per bushel.
Corporate Treasury forecasts the sale of an available-for-sale debt instrument at the end of the fourth quarter.	Corporate Treasury signs a legally binding agreement with a third party to sell a specific available-for-sale debt instrument for par on 30 December 20X1.
Corporate Treasury forecasts the purchase of a £25 million bond on 23 March 20X1 from an investment bank.	Corporate Treasury enters into a legally binding purchase agreement with a bank to take delivery of a £25 million bond for par on 23 March 20X1.

Cash flow hedge accounting can be applied to a forecast transaction only if the transaction is highly probable. [IAS 39.88(c)].

Highly probable is not defined in IAS 39. The probability of occurrence must be significantly in excess of a 50 per cent likelihood, but not necessarily as high as 100 per cent as the entity can never claim a transaction that is not yet committed can be guaranteed to occur. IFRS 5.BC81 also refers to 'highly probable' although in a different context. It states that in IFRS 'probable' is defined as "more likely than not" and that the 'highly probable' is regarded as implying a significantly higher probability than 'more likely than not' and as being equivalent to the phrase "likely to occur".

Probability is assessed based on observable facts and the relevant circumstances. In assessing the likelihood that a transaction will occur, consideration should be given to the following:

- the frequency of similar past transactions;
- the financial and operational ability of the entity to carry out the transaction;

- substantial commitments of resources to a particular activity (for example, a manufacturing facility that can be used in the short run only to process a particular type of commodity);
- the extent of loss or disruption of operations that could result if the transaction does not occur;
- the likelihood that transactions with substantially different characteristics might be used to achieve the same business purpose (for example, an entity that intends to raise cash may have several ways of doing so, ranging from a short-term bank loan to a common stock offering); and
- the entity's business plan.

In addition, both the length of time until a forecast transaction is projected to occur and the quantity of the forecast transaction should be considered in determining probability. Other factors being equal, the more distant a forecast transaction is, the less likely it is that the transaction would be considered probable and the stronger the evidence that would be needed to support an assertion that it is probable. For example, a transaction forecast to occur in five years may be less likely than a transaction forecast to occur in one year.

Other factors being equal, the greater the physical quantity or future value of a forecast transaction, the less likely it is that the transaction would be considered probable and the stronger the evidence that would be required to support an assertion that it is highly probable. For example, it is easier to support forecast sales of 100,000 units in a particular month than support forecast sales of 300,000 units in that month by an entity, where recent sales have averaged 300,000 units per month for the past three months. [IAS 39.IG.F.3.7]

IAS 39.IG.F.2.4 provides an example of an airline operator that could use sophisticated models based on experience and economic data to project its revenues in various currencies. If it can demonstrate that forecast revenues for a period of time into the future in a particular currency are 'highly probable' it may designate a currency borrowing as a cash flow hedge of the future revenue stream.

To meet the 'highly probable' requirement an entity is not required to predict and document the exact date a forecast transaction is expected to occur. However, it is required to identify and document the time period during which the forecast transaction is expected to occur within a reasonably specific and generally narrow range of time from a most probable date, as a basis for assessing hedge effectiveness. To determine that the hedge will be highly effective it is necessary to ensure that changes in the fair value of the expected cash flows are offset by changes in the fair value of the hedging instrument and this test may be met only if the cash flows occur within close proximity to each other. [IAS 39.IG.F.3.11]

A pattern of discovering that hedged forecast transactions are no longer expected to occur would call into question both an entity's ability to predict accurately forecast transactions and the propriety of using hedge accounting in the future for similar transactions. [IAS 39.IG.F.3.7]

A hedged forecast transaction must be identified and documented with sufficient specificity so that when the transaction occurs, it is clear whether the transaction is the designated hedged transaction. Hence, a forecast transaction may be identified as the sale of the first 15,000 units of a specific product during a specified three-month period, but it could not be identified as the last 15,000 units of that product sold during a three-month period because the last 15,000 units cannot be identified with sufficient specificity: it could be units 20,001 to 35,000 or units 120,001 to 135,000. [IAS 39.IG.F.3.10]

For the same reason, a forecast transaction cannot be specified solely as a percentage of sales or purchases during a period.

While sufficient specificity is required when identifying forecast transactions, a description of the transaction that is *too* specific increases the risk of failure of hedge accounting in its entirety. For example, an entity may have a forecast fixed rate debt issuance of CU100m in six months' time. The movement in interest rates between the date of designation and the date the debt is to be issued is hedged using a forward starting interest rate swap which will be closed out on the date the debt is issued. The changes in interest rates prior to the date of issuing the debt influences the determination of the fixed rate on that future debt.

If the entity designated the forecast debt issuance as being a fixed rate debt issuance then, should the forecast debt issuance not occur, the hedge will be entirely ineffective and hedge accounting will not be permitted. This will be the case even where the entity decides at the issuance date to issue floating rate debt instead of fixed rate debt. All gains/losses recognised in other comprehensive income on the forward starting interest rate swap would need to be reclassified from equity to profit or loss. The reclassification of amounts from equity to profit or loss is required because the specific forecast fixed rate debt issuance did not occur, even though, economically, at the date of issuance the entity would be indifferent as to whether it chooses to issue fixed or floating rate debt.

As an alternative, the entity could make its designation a bit less specific as to the ultimate basis of interest that will be issued. Instead, it could designate the hedged risk more broadly, for example, as changes in interest rates between the date of designation and the date when CU100m of debt is issued. As long as the debt, when issued, is referenced to the same interest rate as is evident in the forward starting interest rate swap, the hedge will, all other things being equal, be highly effective, and therefore the entity will continue to recognise the effective gains and losses in the cash flow hedge reserve in equity irrespective of whether the entity chooses to issue fixed or floating rate debt. The amounts recognised in other comprehensive income will be reclassified from equity to profit or loss when the interest impacts profit or loss.

US GAAP comparison: In order to qualify as a hedged item in a cash flow hedge, FAS 133 specifies that a forecast transaction must be 'probable' (rather than 'highly probable', which is the requirement in IAS 39). US GAAP generally defines 'probable' as 'likely to occur' and suggests that it is a higher level of likelihood than 'more likely than not' (FAS 5 and related guidance). As explained above 'highly probable' in IFRS is generally understood to be equivalent to 'likely to occur' and thus the difference in terminology should not lead to a difference in practice.

2.2.2 *Cash flow hedge accounting*

A cash flow hedge (assuming it meets all other hedge accounting requirements) is accounted for as follows:
[IAS 39.95]

(a) the portion of the gain or loss on the hedging instrument that is determined to be an effective hedge is recognised in other comprehensive income; and

(b) the ineffective portion of the gain or loss on the hedging instrument is recognised immediately in profit or loss.

In particular:

(a) the separate component of equity associated with the hedged item is adjusted to the lesser of the following (in absolute amounts):

- the cumulative gain or loss on the hedging instrument from inception of the hedge; and
- the cumulative change in fair value (present value) of the expected future cash flows on the hedged item from inception of the hedge; and

(b) any remaining gain or loss on the hedging instrument (which is not an effective hedge) is included in profit or loss.

An entity may exclude the time value of an option or interest element of a forward from the hedge designation, in which case the component of the fair value gain or loss related to that component is recognised in profit or loss. Alternatively, an entity may exclude a proportion of a derivative (or a non-derivative instrument for hedges of foreign currency risk), for example 50 per cent of a derivative, or a proportion of hedged item, for example, 50 per cent of a debt instrument, from the hedge relationship, in which case the gain or loss on the proportion excluded from the designation is recognised by applying the instrument's normal classification guidance (see **chapter 2** for financial assets and **chapter 3** for financial liabilities). [IAS 39.96]

The effective portion of the gain or loss on the hedging instrument recognised in other comprehensive income is subsequently reclassified from equity to profit or loss in the same period or periods during which the hedged item affects profit or loss, so as to offset the changes in the cash flows of the hedged item for the designated risk (e.g. if sales are hedged, the reclassification from equity to profit or loss will occur when the sales occur).

In August 2008 the IASB issued an exposure draft, *Annual Improvements to IFRSs*. The exposure draft proposed amending IAS 39.97 that describes when an amount in equity shall be reclassified to profit or loss. IAS 39.97 currently states that the associated gains or loss that are recognised directly in equity shall be reclassified into profit or loss in the period during which the asset acquired or liability assumed affects profit or loss (such as in the periods that interest income and interest expense is recognised). The IASB understood there was some uncertainty about how this paragraph applied when the designated cash flow exposure being hedged differs from the financial instrument arising from the hedged forecast cash flows. The IASB proposed making the paragraph clearer by removing the references to an 'asset acquired or liability assumed' and instead refer to the 'hedged forecast cash flows' that affect profit or loss.

US GAAP comparison: Under FAS 133, a hedge of a foreign currency denominated variable-rate asset or variable-rate liability only qualifies for cash flow hedge accounting if the variability in the cash flows from the asset or liability is eliminated *in full* by the cash flows from the hedging instrument. Hence, when hedging a variable rate foreign currency asset or liability with a float for float cross currency swap this would not qualify for cash flow hedge accounting under US GAAP as not all variability in cash flows is eliminated (the cash flow risk from changing interest rates remains). Such a designation would be permissible under IFRS if the swap is highly effective at hedging the designated foreign currency risk.

Further examples

Detailed illustrations of cash flow hedges are included in **chapter 10** in the following sections.

- 3.1 Cash flow hedging a forecast sale of a non-financial item
- 3.2 Cash flow hedging a forecast sale for foreign currency risk
- 3.3 Basis adjusting the acquisition of a non-financial item
- 3.4 Cash flow hedging a forecast sale and subsequent receivable
- 3.5 Cash flow hedging variable rate interest with an interest rate swap
- 3.7 Cash flow hedging foreign currency risk of floating rate debt
- 3.8 Cash flow hedging foreign currency risk of fixed rate debt
- 3.9 Cash flow hedging foreign currency risk of zero coupon debt
- 3.10 Cash flow hedging foreign currency risk of the principal only on interest-bearing debt
- 3.14 Cash flow hedging share appreciation rights

In a cash flow hedge of a forecast transaction where the spot foreign exchange rate is being hedged, the effective amount recognised in other comprehensive income is calculated on a discounted basis, i.e. it is based on the present value of the spot element of the derivative. [IAS 39.IG.F.5.6]

Where an entity hedges the spot foreign exchange rate in a forecast transaction using a non-derivative hedging instrument, such as foreign currency denominated debt, the amount recognised in other comprehensive income should be the undiscounted spot rate as this is the rate that the foreign currency denominated debt is translated at in accordance with IAS 21.

A foreign currency monetary item, for example a loan, can be cash flow hedged for foreign currency risk for both interest and principal, interest only, or principal only, or any proportion thereof.

If an entity hedges both interest and principal with a derivative, in order for the hedging instrument to be highly effective, it will need to have contractual cash flows that match the foreign currency interest and principal flows but swap them into the functional currency equivalent cash flows. An example would be a cross-currency interest rate swap with gross physical exchange of principal at inception and at maturity. Example **3.7** and **3.8** in **chapter 10** illustrate this approach for hedging floating rate and fixed rate loans respectively.

If an entity hedges only the interest cash flows with a derivative, in order for the hedging instrument to be highly effective, it will need to have contractual cash flows that match the foreign currency interest flows but swap them into the functional currency equivalent interest flows. An example would be a cross-currency interest rate swap without gross physical exchange of principal at inception and at maturity.

If an entity hedges only the principal cash flow with a derivative, in order for the hedging instrument to be highly effective, it will need to have contractual cash flows that match the foreign currency principal cash flows but swap it into the functional currency equivalent principal cash flows. An example would be a foreign currency forward contract. Example **3.10** in **chapter 10** illustrates a cash flow hedge of foreign currency risk of the principal only on an interest-bearing debt instrument.

For hedges of forecast transactions, it is permitted, but not required, to adjust the carrying amount of an acquired non-financial asset or a non-financial liability by the effective gain or loss on the hedging instrument as explained below.

2.2.3 *Basis adjustments*

An entity has a choice of accounting policy regarding the presentation of gains and losses recognised in other comprehensive income if a cash flow hedge of a forecast transaction subsequently results in the recognition of a *non-financial* asset (or a *non-financial* liability), or if a forecast transaction for a non-financial asset or a non-financial liability becomes a firm commitment for which fair value hedge accounting is applied. The accounting policy chosen must be applied consistently to all such hedges. [IAS 39.99]

The accounting policy choices are as follows. The entity can either: [IAS 39.98]

(a) reclassify the associated gains and losses from equity to profit or loss in the same period or periods during which the asset acquired or liability assumed affects profit or loss (such as in the periods that depreciation expense or cost of sales is recognised); or

(b) remove the associated gains and losses that were recognised in other comprehensive income and include them in the initial cost or other carrying amount of the asset or liability (in which case they will automatically impact profit or loss when the item is depreciated or sold).

However, if an entity expects that all or a portion of a loss recognised in other comprehensive income will not be recovered in one or more future periods, it must reclassify the amount that is not expected to be recovered into profit or loss immediately.

IAS 39 only allows a basis adjustment for non-financial items. This exception simplifies the accounting and tracking of gains and losses that would have otherwise been retained in equity. This exception does not apply for financial items as allowing basis adjustments would be contrary to recognising all financial instruments at fair value on initial recognition.

US GAAP comparison: FAS 133 does not permit accumulated gains or losses in a cash flow hedge to be reflected as a basis adjustment to the initial cost or other carrying amount of the acquired asset or liability.

Further examples

A detailed illustration of a cash flow hedge of a non-financial item where an entity has a policy of basis adjusting is included in **3.3** of **chapter 10**.

2.2.4 *Discontinuance of cash flow hedge accounting*

An entity must discontinue prospectively hedge accounting if: [IAS 39.101]

- the hedging instrument expires or is sold, terminated or exercised (the replacement or rollover of a hedging instrument into another hedging instrument is not an expiration or termination if it formed part of the entity's documented hedging strategy from inception);

- the hedge no longer meets the hedge accounting criteria (for example, it is no longer highly effective or its effectiveness is no longer measurable);
- the forecast transaction is no longer expected to occur; or
- the entity de-designates the hedge relationship.

The cumulative gain or loss on the hedging instrument recognised in other comprehensive income continues to be separately classified in equity until the forecast transaction occurs, at which point it is reclassified from equity to profit or loss.

When a forecast transaction is no longer highly probable but is still expected to occur, it no longer qualifies for cash flow hedge accounting as it does not satisfy the 'highly probable' criterion. Further recognition of fair value gains and losses on the hedging instrument in other comprehensive income is prohibited, i.e. subsequent changes in the fair value of the hedging instrument are recognised in profit or loss.

The cumulative gain or loss on the hedging instrument recognised in other comprehensive income prior to the transaction ceasing to be highly probable remains in equity until the transaction occurs, or until it is determined that the forecast transaction is no longer expected to occur. In the former case, the gain or loss is reclassified from equity to profit or loss when the hedged item impacts profit or loss or is used to adjust the initial cost of the carrying amount of a non-financial item. In the latter case, the gain or loss is reclassified from equity to profit or loss as soon as it is discovered that the transaction is no longer expected to occur.

Example 2.2.4A

Change in term of forecast debt issuance

Entity D, a Euro functional entity intends to issue Euro denominated debt in six months' time with a maturity of five years that will pay fixed interest on a six monthly basis. The transaction is highly probable and therefore there is a stream of ten highly probable six monthly interest payments. In order to hedge its future profit or loss exposure as a result of the fixed interest payments on the debt due to changes in the six-month LIBOR rate between now and the issuance of the debt (in six months' time), Entity D enters into a forward starting receive six-month LIBOR pay fixed interest rate swap with terms matching the critical terms of the forecast debt issuance such as start date, maturity, notional and payment dates. The entity designates the swap as a cash flow hedge of the profit or loss exposure arising from the series of six monthly interest payments on the forecast issuance of debt. Assuming all conditions necessary for hedge accounting under IAS 39 are satisfied, the effective portion of the gain and loss on the swap will be recognised in other comprehensive income.

On the forecast issue date Entity D issues seven-year Euro denominated fixed rate debt, rather than debt with a five-year term as previously anticipated. The entity closes out the swap at the date of issuance. Ten forecast highly probable interest payments are still likely to occur, even though they will now be interest payments on debt with a seven-year maturity. The gain or loss recognised in other comprehensive income will be reclassified from equity to profit or loss when the individual interest payments for the first five years of the debt impact profit or loss. An allocation of the amount deferred in equity when the debt is issued will be required to determine the amount of the swap that relates to the individual interest payments that were forecast and are still expected to occur. As the fair value of the swap recognised in other comprehensive income consists of the present value of 10 future fixed cash flows, this present value amount is allocated specifically to those 10 future interest periods, and accordingly is released to profit or loss in those future periods.

US GAAP comparison: US GAAP states that if a forecast transaction is no longer probable of occurring at the originally documented specified time period, or within an additional two-month period thereafter, the amount associated with the derivative that has been recognised in 'accumulated other comprehensive income' (the equivalent of amounts deferred in equity under IFRS) should be reclassified into profit or loss. However, in rare cases, the existence of extenuating circumstances that are related to the nature of the forecasted transaction and are outside the control or influence of the reporting entity may cause the forecasted transaction to be probable of occurring on a date that is beyond the additional two-month period of time, in which case the net derivative gain or loss related to the discontinued cash flow hedge shall continue to be reported in other comprehensive income. DIG Issues G3 and G16 provide additional guidance when hedging forecast transactions in long-term contracts where there are changes in expectations in the timing of forecast cash flows.

IFRS does not have equivalent guidance in this area.

Where the timing of a transaction moves forward, i.e. the transaction is expected to occur sooner, the forecast transaction continues to be highly probable and hence continues to qualify as a hedged item. [IAS 39.IG.F.5.4]

Example 2.2.4B

Change in timing of forecast sale of a non-financial item

Entity S designates a derivative as a hedging instrument in a cash flow hedge of a forecast sale of silver. The hedging relationship meets all the hedge accounting conditions, including the requirement to identify and document the period in which the transaction is expected to occur within a reasonably specific and generally narrow range of time.

In a subsequent period, the forecast transaction is expected to occur in an earlier period than originally anticipated.

The change in timing of the forecast transaction does not affect the validity of the designation. Entity S can conclude that the transaction is the same as the one that was designated as being hedged. However, the change in timing of the hedged transaction may affect the assessment of hedge effectiveness going forward since the hedging instrument must continue to be designated for the whole of its remaining period to maturity. Also, the amount recognised in other comprehensive income up to this point will need to be adjusted to be the lower of the cumulative gain or loss on the derivative from inception of the hedge and the cumulative change in fair value of the future cash flows of the forecast transaction.

If the hedged transaction is no longer expected to occur, then the cumulative amounts in other comprehensive income are reclassified from equity to profit or loss. [IAS 39.101(c)]

Example 2.2.4C

Change in timing of forecast debt issuance

Entity D is hedging the forecast issuance of £100 million of 10-year, fixed-rate debt using a rate lock agreement (a derivative). The entity designates the rate lock agreement as a hedge of the variability in the total cash flows arising on the forecast debt issuance. Entity D expects to issue the debt in the second quarter of 20X0. Entity D's credit rating is BB. In the first quarter of 20X0, the spreads between government and corporate bond rates widen significantly. As a result, Entity D does not expect to issue its bonds in the second quarter. Entity D's advisors believe that the markets may stabilise in the first quarter of 20X1. Entity D will now make a decision on the type of funding in the first quarter of 20X1 and therefore closes out its rate lock agreement. At the time of closure the fair value of the lock agreement was negative.

Entity D should recognise the entire loss in profit or loss because the forecast debt issuance is not expected to occur.

An entity can de-designate a hedge relationship at any point in time. Any gains or losses recognised in other comprehensive income up to the point of de-designation will remain in equity until the forecast transaction occurs. [IAS 39.101(d)] Gains or losses on the hedging instrument after de-designation will be recognised in profit or loss if the hedging instrument continues to be held.

2.2.5 *Reclassification from equity to profit or loss after a business combination*

Following a business combination, where the acquiree has applied cash flow hedging and recognised gains or losses in other comprehensive income prior to the acquisition, the acquirer will not be able to reclassify those gains and losses to consolidated profit or loss. Because the pre-acquisition reserves of the subsidiary do not exist in the consolidated financial statements of its new parent, any amounts recognised in other comprehensive income by the subsidiary prior to the business combination cannot be reclassified. Thus, the group can only hedge account for the specific relationship that the acquiree has prospectively from the date of acquisition with only post acquisition amounts in other comprehensive income being reclassified from equity to consolidated profit or loss in accordance with IAS 39.95.

2.3 Net investment hedge

A hedge of a net investment in a foreign operation is a hedge of the foreign currency exposure to changes in the reporting entity's share in the net assets of that foreign operation. IAS 21 *The Effects of Changes in Foreign Exchange Rates* requires that the reporting entity's share in the net assets of a foreign operation is translated into the functional currency of the ultimate parent with the retranslation gain or loss recognised in other comprehensive income. It does not matter what denomination the monetary assets and liabilities are in the foreign operation, as all those monetary items are firstly retranslated into the foreign operation's functional currency. It is the translation of those net assets of the foreign operation into the parent's functional currency that is the designated hedged risk.

IFRIC 16 *Hedges of a Net Investment in a Foreign Operation* was issued in July 2008 and is effective for annual periods beginning on or after 1 October 2008. One of the questions it addressed was whether the hedged risk in a net investment hedge was the difference between the functional currency of the foreign operation and the presentation currency of the group, or the functional currency of the foreign operation and the functional currency of the parent. The IFRIC consensus was that the latter interpretation is correct. The IFRIC acknowledged that this question will only be relevant to the extent that the presentation currency of the group differs from the functional currency of the parent. The IFRIC recognised that there were arguments for either view but on balance considered that the arguments in favour of looking to the functional currency of the parent were more compelling. The IFRIC concluded that the presentation currency does not create an exposure to which an entity may apply hedge accounting. The functional currency is determined on the basis of the primary economic environment in which the entity operates. Accordingly, functional currencies create an economic exposure to changes in cash flows or fair values; a presentation currency does not. [IFRIC 16.BC14]

A hedge of a net investment in a foreign operation, including a hedge of a monetary item that is accounted for as part of the net investment as defined in IAS 21, assuming it meets all other requirements for hedge accounting, is accounted for similarly to a cash flow hedge:
[IAS 39.102]

(a) the portion of the gain or loss on the hedging instrument that is determined to be an effective hedge is recognised in other comprehensive income; and

(b) the ineffective portion of the gain or loss on the hedging instrument is recognised immediately in profit or loss.

The descriptions of fair value and cash flow hedges in **2.1** and **2.2** above respectively make specific reference to the presence of an exposure attributable to a particular risk that could affect profit or loss. The equivalent statement is not made with respect to a hedge of a net investment in a foreign operation. However, this can be seen as simply an omission rather than a substantive difference. The hedged risk in a net investment hedge, being the foreign currency exposure on the retranslation of the reporting entity's share of the net assets of the foreign operation under IAS 21, does affect profit or loss because IAS 21.48 & 48C require the cumulative exchange differences of the foreign operation to be reclassified from equity to profit or loss on the disposal (or, in some cases, the partial disposal) of that foreign operation.

Goodwill and any fair value adjustments arising on acquisition of a foreign operation are treated as assets and liabilities of the foreign operation, expressed in the foreign currency and translated at the closing rate, and thus are considered net assets of the foreign operation. [IAS 21.47] Equally, a monetary item that is receivable from or payable to a foreign operation for which settlement is neither planned nor likely to occur in the foreseeable future is, in substance, part of the entity's net investment in that foreign operation, and therefore forms part of the net assets of that foreign operation. [IAS 21.15]

Example 2.3

Identifying net assets available to be hedged

Parent A, £ functional currency, has an investment in a foreign operation, its wholly-owned Subsidiary B that has a US$ functional currency. Parent A heads Group A. The investment in Subsidiary B was made on 1 January 20X0 when Parent A acquired 100 per cent of the share capital for US$100m. At the date of acquisition the fair value of the identifiable net assets of Subsidiary B was US$70m. In applying purchase accounting under IFRS 3 *Business Combinations* US$30m of goodwill was recognised in the consolidated financial statements of Parent A. At the acquisition date, Parent A extended a loan of £10m to Subsidiary B when the US$/£spot exchange rate was US$2:£1. Settlement of this loan is neither planned nor likely to occur in the foreseeable future.

At the acquisition date, Group A wishes to designate as a hedged item its net investment in its foreign operation, Subsidiary B, in the consolidated financial statements. The maximum amount of the net investment in the foreign operation that can be designated as a hedged item is US$120m. This comprises three elements:

- US$70m of the identifiable net assets of the foreign operation acquired upon acquisition;
- US$30m of goodwill that forms part of the net assets of the foreign operation; and
- US$20m of additional net assets as a result of the loan extended by Parent A to Subsidiary B, being a monetary item for which settlement is neither planned nor likely to occur in the foreseeable future, i.e. the loan forms part of the net investment in Subsidiary B.

It should be noted that if the loan extended to Subsidiary B was expected to be settled in the foreseeable future, the maximum amount of the net investment in the foreign operation that could be designated would be US$100m as the loan would not form part of the net investment in Subsidiary B.

The gain or loss on the hedging instrument relating to the effective portion of the hedge that has been recognised in other comprehensive income is reclassified from equity to profit or loss when the net investment affects profit or loss, i.e. on the disposal of the net investment in the foreign operation. [IAS 39.102] This makes it necessary to track the amount of gains and losses on hedging instruments recognised in other comprehensive income in relation to the hedge of each individual foreign operation separately, so as to be able to identify how much of the total amount recognised in other comprehensive income should be reclassified from equity to profit or loss on the sale of a particular foreign operation. This may be complex in large groups with many foreign operations and with many hedging instruments used over different periods of time.

A more detailed discussion of complex issues that can arise with net investment hedging is included in **section 5** in **chapter 9**.

IAS 21 *The Effects of Changes in Foreign Exchange Rates* defines what a net investment in a foreign operation is. IAS 21 defines a net investment in a foreign operation as the amount of the reporting entity's interest in the net assets of that operation. [IAS 21.8]

Net investment hedging is only permitted in consolidated financial statements, as it is only in consolidated financial statements that the net assets of the foreign operation are recognised. The only exception to this is where a foreign operation is not a separate legal entity but is a branch of the reporting entity and the branch has a functional currency different to the functional currency of the reporting entity. In this instance the reporting entity may apply net investment hedging in the individual financial statements of the investor in the branch by designating the translation risk of the net assets of the foreign operation branch. This view is acknowledged in IFRIC 16.2.

In the individual financial statements of the investor, an investment in a subsidiary is recognised either at cost or in accordance with IAS 39, i.e. as an available-for-sale asset or at fair value through profit or loss. [IAS 27(2008).38, previously IAS 27(2003).37] Similarly, an investment in an associate or a jointly controlled entity is recognised either at cost or in accordance with IAS 39. [IAS 28.35 & IAS 31.46] The carrying amount under either of these methods will not be equivalent to the net assets of that operation and therefore net investment hedging cannot be applied.

However, as an alternative, the investor may wish to apply fair value hedge accounting for the foreign exchange risk of its investment in its foreign operation. For example, if an investor makes an investment in a foreign operation that meets the definition of a subsidiary, the investor will hold its investment either at cost or in accordance with IAS 39. [IAS 27(2008).38, previously IAS 27(2003).37] The investing entity will be exposed to a risk that will impact profit or loss, i.e. the foreign currency risk that arises upon disposal of the foreign subsidiary. If the investing entity has a foreign currency derivative, or a foreign denominated liability that was used to fund the investment in the foreign operation, it could designate it as a hedging instrument in respect of a portion of the foreign currency risk of the investment in the subsidiary equivalent to the notional on the hedging instrument. In order to do so the entity must be able to determine that foreign currency risk with respect to the investment in the subsidiary exists on an amount equal to at least the notional of the hedging instrument. For the entity to make this claim it must either be able to fair value the investment in local currency terms, or at a minimum be able to determine that the fair value in local currency terms is not below the notional of the hedging instrument. Applying fair value hedge accounting would result in the gain or loss on the hedging instrument being recognised in profit or loss along with the associated foreign currency risk on the designated portion of the investment in the subsidiary.

It is worth noting that this approach is very different to applying net investment in a foreign operation hedge accounting at a consolidated level where both the hedging instrument and the foreign exchange translation on the net assets of the foreign operation are recognised in other comprehensive income. Additionally, it should be noted that fair value hedge accounting cannot be applied in the consolidated financial statements to an equity method investment or an investment in a consolidated subsidiary. [IAS 39.AG99] Fair value hedge accounting for such items can only be applied in the separate financial statements of the investor.

2.3.1 *Hedging net investments with loans*

In the absence of hedge accounting, foreign exchange gains and losses on re-translating the net assets of a foreign operation are recognised in other comprehensive income and taken to a separate component of equity (in accordance with IAS 21), whilst those on the loan are recognised in profit or loss. This creates a mismatch in foreign currency translation. When net investment hedge accounting is applied, this mismatch is eliminated as the gains and losses on the loan, to the extent effective, are recognised in other comprehensive income.

When the hedging instrument in a net investment hedge is a foreign denominated non-derivative financial liability, for example, a foreign denominated loan, it is always the spot re-translation risk that is the hedged risk (as opposed to the forward rate) as it is only the spot rate that is recognised from retranslating the foreign currency non-derivative liability.

2.3.1.1 *Loan is less than or equal to the net assets of subsidiary*

Example 2.3.1.1

Loan is less than or equal to the net assets of subsidiary

Entity A, a UK entity with a Sterling functional currency, has a US subsidiary with a US dollar functional currency, Entity B. To finance this subsidiary, Entity A has a US$50 million US dollar loan with a third party bank. Entities A and B have the same 31 December year end and the net assets of Entity B at 31 December 20X1 and 31 December 20X2 were US$70 million.

The loan is designated as a hedging instrument of the first US$50 million of net assets of Entity B. The designation is spot retranslation risk only. The hedge is determined to be highly effective. The US$/£ spot rate on 31/12/X1 is 1.6 and on 31/12/X2 it is 1.7.

On 31/12/X2 the entries are as follows:

Dr	Loan	£1.84m
Cr	Other comprehensive income	£1.84m

To recognise the foreign exchange gain on the loan. This is the difference between US$50m translated at 1.6 and 1.7.

Dr	Other comprehensive income	£2.57m
Cr	Net assets	£2.57m

To retranslate the net assets. This is the difference between US$70m translated at 1.6 and 1.7.

The entire exchange difference on retranslating the net assets of the foreign operation is taken to other comprehensive income in accordance with IAS 21. The application of hedge accounting results in the remeasurement of the loan being recognised in other comprehensive income as opposed to profit or loss. No hedge ineffectiveness has been recognised. Hedge ineffectiveness would have arisen if the net assets of the foreign operation fell below US$50m at the period end.

2.3.1.2 *Loan exceeds net assets of subsidiary*

Hedge accounting is still possible when the amount of the loan exceeds the net assets of the foreign operation.

Example 2.3.1.2

Loan exceeds net assets of subsidiary

The same scenario applies as in **example 2.3.1.1** except the loan is US$100m.

The entity designates US$70 million of the loan as a hedging instrument of the first US$70 million net assets of Entity B. The designation is spot retranslation risk only. The hedge is determined to be highly effective. The US$/£ spot rate on 31/12/X1 is 1.6 and on 31/12/X2 it is 1.7.

On 31/12/X2 the entries are as follows:

Dr	Loan	£3.68m
Cr	Other comprehensive income	£2.57m
Cr	Profit or loss	£1.11m

To recognise the foreign exchange gain on the loan.

The entire loan must be reported at the closing rate, giving rise to an exchange gain. The exchange gain that relates to the designated and effective hedging instrument (i.e. US$70 million of the loan) is reported in other comprehensive income. The remainder is reported in profit or loss.

Dr	Other comprehensive income	£2.57m
Cr	Net assets	£2.57m

To retranslate the net assets.

2.3.1.3 Net assets of the foreign operation change

Both of the above examples were simplified as the net assets of the subsidiary remained the same at the start and at the end of the reporting period. In practice this will rarely be the case. As documentation and designation must be in place at inception of the hedge, the hedged item will be based on the opening net asset position. Hedge ineffectiveness arises to the extent to which the net asset position falls below the designated amount of net assets at the date that hedge effectiveness is assessed, which is, at a minimum, at the end of each reporting period.

Example 2.3.1.3

Net assets of foreign operation change

Entity A, a UK entity with a Sterling functional currency, has a US subsidiary with a US dollar functional currency, Entity B. To finance this subsidiary, Entity A has a US$80 million US dollar loan with a third party bank. The year end of both entities is 31 December. On 31 December 20X1 the net assets of Entity B were US$90m, and are expected to remain at approximately this level, so the entire loan was designated as hedging the spot retranslation risk associated with the first US$80 million net assets of Entity B.

On 31 December 20X2, the net assets of B were US$75m. The US$/£ spot rate on 31/12/X1 is 1.6 and on 31/12/X2 is 1.7.

Hedge ineffectiveness arises as there are no longer US$80 million of net assets that are being hedged. The hedge, nonetheless, is assessed as highly effective and hedge accounting is required for the period. Hedge ineffectiveness must be reported immediately in profit or loss.

Dr	Loan	£2.94m
Cr	Other comprehensive income	£2.76m
Cr	Profit or loss	£0.18m

To recognise the foreign exchange gain on the loan.

The foreign exchange gain that relates to the designated and effective hedging instrument is recognised in other comprehensive income (i.e. the exchange gain on US$75 million), whilst the ineffective portion is recognised in profit or loss.

On 31 December 20X2 the group may choose to redesignate prospectively the hedging instrument to be only US$75 million of the loan.

In the above example, ineffectiveness was caused by the net assets of the foreign operation falling below the level of the loan hedging it. This ineffectiveness can be minimised by monitoring the net assets of the foreign operation and redesignating as appropriate.

2.3.2 *Hedging net investments with forward contracts*

If no hedge accounting was applied, then the foreign exchange gains and losses on re-translating the net assets of the foreign operation would be taken to other comprehensive income (in accordance with IAS 21.39) and the change in fair value of the forward contract would be recognised in profit or loss.

When hedging net investments with forward contracts, it is important to specify what risk is being hedged: i.e. the forward or the spot foreign currency exchange rate. If the forward rate is hedged, the full change in fair value of the forward is recognised in other comprehensive income if it is fully effective, whereas if the spot rate is hedged, the spot element of the forward is recognised in other comprehensive income and the remainder (being the forward points) is recognised in profit or loss. Any element recognised in other comprehensive income as an effective gain or loss is reclassified from equity to profit or loss when the underlying net investment is sold.

For the purpose of both assessing effectiveness and measuring ineffectiveness in net investment hedging it is possible to identify the spot element of a forward contract as the undiscounted spot. This is because the risk being hedged is the risk of the retranslation of the net assets of the net investment in accordance with IAS 21 *The Effects of Changes in Foreign Exchange Rates*, which is calculated on an undiscounted basis. This is equally true when an entity designates foreign currency denominated debt as a hedge of a net investment in a foreign operation. In this case, both the hedged item and hedging instrument are retranslated to undiscounted spot in accordance with IAS 21 and therefore the hedged risk is the undiscounted spot.

Whether the spot rate or the forward rate is the designated hedged risk, the overall effect on profit or loss is the same, but the timing of the recognition of the fair value of the forward points is different.

It is not permitted in any hedge relationship to amortise any premium or discount on a forward contract. Derivatives must always be measured at fair value in the statement of financial position. Changes in fair value are either recognised in profit or loss, or in other comprehensive income, if the derivative is designated as an effective hedge in a cash flow or net investment hedge. [IAS 39.IG.F.6.4]

US GAAP comparison: US GAAP states that hedge ineffectiveness will be nil when hedging a net investment in a foreign operation when ineffectiveness is assessed on changes in forward exchange rates, the notional amount of the derivative equals the portion of the net investment designated as being hedged, the derivative's underlying exchange rate is the rate between the functional currency of the foreign operation and the investor's functional currency, and the derivative hedging instrument is not a cross-currency interest rate swap in which both legs are not based on comparable interest rate curves. [DIG H8]

Further examples

A detailed illustration of a net investment hedge using a forward contract is included in the following sections of **chapter 10**.

- 4.1 Net investment hedging the spot foreign currency risk.
- 4.2 Net investment hedging the forward foreign currency risk.

Hedging with cross currency swaps is very similar to hedging with forward contracts, see **4.3** and **4.4** in **chapter 10** for further guidance.

2.4 Exposures and types of hedges: summary

The following table provides examples of assets, liabilities, forecast transactions, firm commitments that may be hedged, and the type of hedge accounting that could apply.

Exposures and types of hedges

Fixed-rate assets and liabilities	*Variable-rate assets and liabilities*
Examples:	Examples:
Fixed-rate loans and receivables	Variable-rate loans and receivables
Fixed-rate debt securities	Variable-rate debt securities
Fixed-rate issued debt of the entity	Variable-rate debt of the entity

Exposures and types of hedges

Fixed-rate assets and liabilities
Examples:

Fixed-rate deposit liabilities

Exposure	*Hedge accounting*
Overall fair value	FV (Fair Value)
Interest rates	FV
Credit of the issuer	FV or CF**
Foreign currency	FV or CF
Termination options	FV

Variable-rate assets and liabilities
Examples:

Variable-rate deposit liabilities

Exposure	*Hedge accounting*
Overall fair value	FV
Interest rates	FV* or CF (Cash flow)
Credit of the issuer	FV or CF**
Foreign currency	FV or CF
Termination options	FV

Firm commitments to purchase or sell financial instruments
Examples:

Commitment to purchase fixed-rate debt
Fixed-rate loan commitments

Exposure	*Hedge accounting*
Overall fair value	FV
Interest rates	FV
Credit	FV
Foreign currency	FV or CF***

Forecast purchases and sales of financial instruments
Examples:

Forecast purchase of fixed-rate debt
Forecast loan originations

Exposure	*Hedge accounting*
Overall fair value	CF
Interest rates	CF
Credit	CF

Firm commitment to purchase or sell non-financial assets
Examples:

Committed sale of inventory
Committed purchase of inventory

Exposure	*Hedge accounting*
Overall fair value	FV
Foreign currency	FV or CF

Forecast purchases and sales of non-financial instruments
Examples:

Forecast sale of inventory
Forecast purchase of inventory

Exposure	*Hedge accounting*
Overall fair value	CF
Foreign currency	CF

Other Assets
Examples:
Equity investments

Exposure	*Hedge accounting*
Overall fair value	FV
Foreign currency	FV or CF

* FV hedging is generally permitted for hedging the fair value risk associated with the fixing of interest between floating reset dates.

** CF hedging would only be appropriate if the credit spread on the instrument was variable.

*** IAS 39 recognises that firm commitments create fair value exposure. However, it does allow hedges of the foreign currency risk of a firm commitment to be accounted for as either a fair value hedge or a cash flow hedge. [IAS 39.87]

3 Hedged items

IAS 39 defines a hedged item as follows:

A hedged item is a recognised asset, liability, unrecognised firm commitment, highly probable forecast transaction or net investment in a foreign operation that:
[IAS 39.9]

(a) exposes the entity to risk of changes in fair value or future cash flows; and

(b) is designated as being hedged.

A hedged item can be:

(a) a single asset, liability, firm commitment, highly probable forecast transaction or net investment in a foreign operation;

(b) group of assets, liabilities, firm commitments, highly probable forecast transactions or net investments in foreign operations with similar risk characteristics; or

(c) in a portfolio hedge of interest rate risk only a portion of the portfolio of financial assets/liabilities that share the risk being hedged.

The basic application of the rules on qualifying hedged items is covered in the remainder of this section, with more complex issues dealt with in **section 2** in **chapter 9**.

3.1 Unrecognised assets

Unrecognised assets (other than unrecognised firm commitments) cannot be designated as hedged items. For example, it is not possible to hedge account for an unrecognised intangible asset such as a core deposit intangible that is not recognised in the statement of financial position. [IAS 39.IG.F.2.3]

3.2 Intragroup items

As a general rule only assets, liabilities, firm commitments or highly probable forecast transactions that are with a party or parties external to the reporting entity can be a designated hedged items. Transactions between entities within the same group can only be designated as hedged items in the entity only financial statements and not in the consolidated financial statements of the group. This is because intragroup transactions do not generally expose the group to a risk that affects consolidated profit or loss. [IAS 39.80]

There are two exceptions to this general rule. The first is where the foreign currency exposure of an intragroup monetary item does not fully eliminate on consolidation under IAS 21 *The Effects of Changes in Foreign Exchange Rates* (discussed further in **3.2.1 below**). The second is for the foreign currency risk of forecast intragroup transactions (discussed further **3.2.2 below**).

Within a group, an entity exposed to a hedged risk is not required to be party to the hedging instrument if hedge accounting is applied at the group level. An entity may decide not to apply hedge accounting in its individual financial statements, but hedge accounting can be applied in the consolidated financial statements which include that entity. For example, it is common in many groups that trading subsidiaries do not enter into derivative transactions; instead corporate treasury does so on their behalf. Unless there are internal derivatives transactions between the trading subsidiary and corporate treasury, the subsidiary would not be able to apply hedge accounting in its entity only financial statements because it has not entered into any hedging instruments. Hedge accounting may, though, be applied at the consolidated group level if the external hedging instrument entered into by corporate treasury is an effective instrument at the consolidated group level.

US GAAP comparison: For foreign currency cash flow hedging, FAS 133 requires that either the operating unit that has the foreign currency exposure is a party to the hedging instrument, or another member of the consolidated group that has the same functional currency as the operating unit is a party to the hedging instrument. If another member of the consolidated group is a party to the hedging instrument then there can be no intervening subsidiary with a different functional currency. IFRS does not have equivalent guidance; in fact in IAS 39.IG.F.2.14 it explicitly states that IAS 39 does not require that the operating unit that is exposed to the risk being hedged is a party to the hedging instrument.

3.2.1 Intragroup monetary items and interest

In accordance with IAS 21, foreign currency gains and losses on intragroup monetary assets and liabilities do not fully eliminate on consolidation when the intragroup monetary item is transacted between two group entities that have different functional currencies. As these gains and losses impact consolidated profit or loss, foreign currency risk on such intragroup monetary assets and liabilities is eligible to be hedged. [IAS 39.80]

Example 3.2.1

Foreign currency risk on intragroup loans

A Sterling functional currency ultimate parent entity makes a 5-year US$ denominated fixed rate interest bearing loan to its US dollar functional currency subsidiary. The loan does not form part of the parent's investment in the US subsidiary. In the parent's separate financial statements, this loan will need to be remeasured at the end of each reporting period in accordance with IAS 21, and will give rise to an exchange gain or loss. However, there will be no corresponding foreign currency gain or loss in the subsidiary's financial statements as its functional currency is the US dollar and the loan is denominated in US dollars.

The parent hedges the foreign currency risk of both interest and principal by entering into a cross-currency swap with a counterparty outside of the group where the parent receives Sterling-fixed and pays US$ fixed on the interest payment dates of the intercompany loan with a gross exchange of US$ for Sterling at inception and Sterling for US$ in 5 years time equivalent to the US$ notional of the loan.

In the consolidated financial statements, an exchange gain or loss on the intragroup balance will not be eliminated, but will be reported in the profit or loss as an exchange gain or loss on a monetary item.

The loan may be designated as a hedged item in both the parent only financial statements and in the consolidated financial statements. In the parent's entity only financial statements the cross-currency swap is expected to be fully effective as a cash flow hedge of the US$ foreign currency risk arising on the interest and principal of the loan.

However, in the consolidated financial statements the cross-currency swap will be less effective as the impact on profit or loss in the parent only and consolidated financial statements differs, and therefore the hedged risk differs. In the parent only financial statements the impact on profit or loss will be the foreign currency risk associated with both interest and principal cash flows denominated in a foreign currency. In the consolidated financial statements the hedged risk differs as part of the risk that resides in the parent only financial statements does not survive consolidation. The parent's interest income (measured at spot or an average rate) in the parent's financial statements and the subsidiary's interest expense (measured at spot or an average rate) in the subsidiary financial statements should eliminate in the consolidated financial statements. As the hedged risk differs, the hypothetical derivative will differ, and its fair value will differ to the actual derivative entered into by the parent (for detail on the hypothetical derivative method see **4.4.1** in **chapter 9**). The difference in the actual and hypothetical derivative will need to be determined as part of the prospective hedge effectiveness assessment to establish whether the hedge is expected to be highly effective.

3.2.2 *Foreign currency risk of a highly probable forecast intragroup transaction*

Foreign currency risk of a highly probable intragroup transaction qualifies as a hedged item in the consolidated financial statements provided the following two conditions are met:
[IAS 39.80]

- the transaction is denominated in a currency other than the functional currency of the entity entering into that transaction; and
- the foreign currency risk will affect consolidated profit or loss.

The entity can be a parent, subsidiary, associate, joint venture or branch. [IAS 39.AG99A]

In many cases the forecast intragroup transaction does not affect consolidated profit or loss, as is the case for royalty payments, interest payments or management charges, unless there is a related external transaction. Such transactions for which there are no related external transactions do not qualify as hedged items. By contrast, in the case of forecast sales or purchases of inventories between members of the same group where there is an onward sale of the inventory to a party external to the group there will be an effect on consolidated profit or loss (see **example 3.2.2B** below). Similarly, a forecast intragroup sale of plant and equipment from the group entity that manufactured it to a group entity that will use the plant and equipment in its operation will affect consolidated profit or loss. This is because the amount initially recognised by the purchasing entity for the plant and equipment, and thus depreciated through its profit or loss, will vary with movements in foreign currency prior to the plant and equipment being recognised when the forecast intragroup transaction is denominated in a currency other than the functional currency of the purchasing entity (see **example 3.2.2A** below). [IAS 39.AG99A]

If a hedge of a forecast intragroup transaction qualifies for hedge accounting, any gain or loss recognised in other comprehensive income is reclassified from equity to profit or loss in the same period or periods during which the foreign currency risk of the external hedged transaction affects consolidated profit or loss. [IAS 39.AG99B]

Example 3.2.2A

Hedging foreign currency risk of intragroup transactions (1)

Entity A (a Sterling functional currency entity) is expecting, with a high degree of probability, to purchase a machine from Entity B (a Euro functional currency entity) for €10m in 1 year's time. Entity A and Entity B are part of the same group and Entity A will use the machine in its production process to make goods for external sale. The cost of the machine will be capitalised and depreciated over its useful economic life in both the individual financial statements of Entity A and the consolidated financial statements (including both Entity A and Entity B). Entity A enters into a buy Euro sell Sterling forward contract with a third party to hedge the expected foreign currency risk on the forecast purchase.

The forecast intragroup purchase will qualify as a hedged item in the consolidated financial statements in a cash flow hedge of the currency risk because:

- the purchase is highly probable;
- the purchase is denominated in a currency (Euro) other than Entity A's functional currency (Sterling); and
- the depreciation of the machine will result in the foreign currency risk of the forecast transaction affecting consolidated profit or loss. The Euro/Sterling exchange rate at the date of purchase will affect the amount initially recognised in respect of the machinery, and thus will impact the associated depreciation charge.

Example 3.2.2B

Hedging foreign currency risk of intragroup transactions (2)

In all scenarios below, the group has two subsidiaries (Entity C – Euro (€) functional currency and Entity D – US dollar (US$) functional currency).

Scenario 1

Entity C incurs external production costs in € towards goods it manufactures and sells on in € to a fellow subsidiary Entity D. This creates a foreign currency risk in Entity D to the €/US$ exchange rate with regard to its forecast purchase from Entity C (purchase of goods in €). Entity D also intends to sell the goods externally outside of the group in US$. In order to hedge the exposure associated with the forecast purchase from Entity C, Entity D enters into a forward contract with a third party (buy €/ sell US$). The group wishes to designate the forward contract as hedging the foreign currency risk of the forecast intragroup purchase by Entity D from Entity C in a cash flow hedging relationship in the consolidated financial statements.

Scenario 2

Same as Scenario 1 above except that the sale of goods from Entity C to Entity D is denominated in US$, and therefore there is foreign currency risk for Entity C on the sale of goods to Entity D. Entity C enters into a forward contract with a third party to mitigate its foreign currency risk of the forecast sale to Entity D in US$ (buy €/ sell US$). The group wishes to designate the forward contract as hedging the foreign currency risk of the forecast intragroup sale by Entity C to Entity D in a cash flow hedging relationship in the consolidated financial statements.

Scenario 3

Same as Scenario 1 above except that the sale of goods from Entity C to Entity D is denominated in Sterling, and therefore there is foreign currency risk for Entity C on the sale of goods to Entity D and there is also foreign currency risk for Entity D on the purchase of goods from Entity C. Entity C enters into a buy €/ sell £ forward contract with a third party to mitigate its foreign currency risk of the forecast sale to Entity D, and Entity D enters into a buy £/sell US$ forward contract with a third party to mitigate its foreign currency risk of the forecast purchase from Entity C.

In both scenarios 1 and 2 the internal transaction being designated is denominated in a currency other than the functional currency of the entity entering into it: in Scenario 1 the forecast intragroup purchase by Entity D (functional currency of US$) is denominated in €; in Scenario 2 the forecast intragroup sale by Entity C (functional currency €) is denominated in US$. Also, in both cases the onward sale of the goods by Entity D will affect consolidated profit or loss. Thus, in both cases the forecast intragroup transaction could be designated as the hedged item in a cash flow hedge of foreign currency risk in the consolidated financial statements, assuming all other conditions of hedge accounting are met.

In Scenario 3, in the individual financial statements of both entities, cash flow hedge accounting can be applied. The provision to hedge intragroup forecast transactions was included in IAS 39 for situations where one of the parties to the internal transaction passes their foreign currency risk to the other, as in Scenarios 1 and 2 above. This is the currency risk that exists and cannot be avoided because the two parties have different functional currencies. In Scenario 3 the parties to the internal transaction are taking on a new foreign currency risk and therefore the amendment cannot be applied. Furthermore, although the sum of the two derivatives result in a net buy €/ sell US$ position, these two derivatives cannot be designated in combination in the consolidated financial statements as a hedge of the external € purchases or a hedge of the external US$ sales, as Entity C does not have a US$ exposure, and Entity D does not have a € exposure.

Example 3.2.2C

Hedging foreign currency risk of intragroup transactions (3)

Entity E (Sterling functional currency entity) has a wholly-owned subsidiary, Entity F (Yen functional currency entity). Entity F generates substantial profits and regularly pays Yen dividends on its ordinary shares to its sole shareholder and parent, Entity E. In order to hedge the Yen exposure associated with the dividend income Entity E enters into a series of sell Yen buy Sterling forward contracts. Entity E also expects to pay dividends on its own ordinary shares (classified as equity in accordance with IAS 32 *Financial Instruments: Presentation*) using the proceeds from dividends received from its shareholding in Entity F.

The forecast intragroup transaction (the dividend income in the hands of Entity E) will not qualify as a hedged item in the consolidated financial statements of the group in a cash flow hedge of the currency risk as the foreign currency risk will not affect consolidated profit or loss. Even though Entity E may expect to make an onward declaration and payment of dividends on its own shares, IAS 32 requires that distributions to holders of an equity instrument shall be debited by the entity directly to equity and thus, this will not give rise to a gain or loss in consolidated profit or loss.

Example 3.2.2D

Hedging foreign currency risk of intragroup transactions (4)

Entity A is a Euro functional currency entity that has a fellow subsidiary Entity B, a US$ functional currency entity. Entity A borrows a specified amount of Euro from a party external to the group at fixed interest rates. Entity A lends the proceeds of the borrowing to Entity B on the same terms as the external borrowing. As Entity B has borrowed in Euro at fixed rates and has a US$ functional currency, it enters into a Receive Euro fixed Pay US$ fixed cross currency swap with a party external to the group to hedge the foreign currency risk of the interest and principal payments on its borrowing from Entity A.

In the separate financial statements of Entity B it can designate the foreign currency risk arising from the Euro denominated interest payments and principal of its borrowing from Entity A in a hedging relationship with the hedging instrument being the external cross currency swap.

In the consolidated financial statements the cross currency swap cannot be designated as a hedge of the foreign currency risk of the forecast intragroup interest payments by Entity B as the interest payments in Entity B are eliminated against the interest receipts in Entity A. Entity B's interest payments do not impact consolidated profit or loss and therefore cannot be designated as a hedged item in the consolidated financial statements.

The foreign currency exposure generated on the intragroup loan will not be fully eliminated on consolidation in accordance with IAS 21 as the loan is measured in Entity B in US$ but measured in Entity A in Euro. It is unlikely that this foreign currency risk could be designated as a hedged item in an effective hedge relationship with the external cross currency swap as a hedging instrument in the consolidated financial statements as the swap's fair value is derived from both interest and principal payments and receipts whereas the foreign currency risk that survives consolidation is limited to Entity B's translation of the opening and closing carrying amounts of the intragroup loan.

3.3 Overall business risks

Overall business risk cannot be hedged because it cannot be specifically identified and measured. [IAS 39.AG98] For example, an entity could not apply hedge accounting to a hedge of a risk of a transaction not occurring which will result in less revenue. This is an overall business risk. [IAS 39.IG.F.2.8]

A firm commitment to acquire a business in a business combination cannot be a hedged item, except for foreign exchange risk, because the other risks being hedged cannot be specifically identified and measured. These other risks are general business risks. [IAS 39.AG98]

Example 3.3

Hedging foreign currency risk of a firm commitment to acquire a business

Entity D, a € functional currency entity, is the parent company of Group D. Entity D enters into an agreement to acquire Entity E in two months' time for US$50m. Entity D will produce consolidated financial statements. To hedge the US$ foreign currency risk of the purchase consideration, Entity D enters into a foreign currency forward contract to buy US$50m and sell € at a specified foreign currency rate that matures in two months.

As Entity D is hedging the foreign currency risk of a firm commitment, it may designate the foreign currency forward contract as a fair value or as a cash flow hedge.

If Entity D designates the derivative in a fair value hedge, the gains or losses will be recognised in profit or loss, and the movements in the fair value of the firm commitment due to foreign currency risk will also be recognised in profit or loss with the other side of the entry recognised in the statement of financial position. At acquisition, this balance will be derecognised and will adjust the amount of goodwill.

If Entity D designates the derivative in a cash flow hedge, the gain or loss will be recognised in other comprehensive income. As discussed in **2.2.3** above, the entity has a choice as to whether to apply a basis adjustment when cash flow hedging the acquisition of a non-financial item (the acquisition of a business). If Group D applies a basis adjustment, it will remove the gain or loss on the derivative from equity and basis adjust the goodwill that is recognised on acquisition. The amount of the basis adjustment will impact profit or loss, for example, if any resulting goodwill is impaired. If Group D does not apply a basis adjustment, it will continue to recognise the gain or loss on the derivative in other comprehensive income until it would have affected profit or loss had goodwill been basis adjusted.

US GAAP comparison: US guidance permits neither fair value hedge accounting for a firm commitment to enter into a business combination nor cash flow hedge accounting for a forecast business combination (FAS 133). Unlike US GAAP, IFRS specifies that a firm commitment to acquire a business in a business combination can be hedged for foreign currency risk.

3.4 Held-to-maturity assets

A held-to-maturity (HTM) investment cannot be a hedged item with respect to interest rate risk or prepayment risk. This is irrespective of whether the interest is fixed or variable. To be able to designate an asset as HTM, an entity must be indifferent to future profit opportunities for that asset, i.e. it must have the positive intent to hold the asset to maturity irrespective of changes in its market value (see **3.2** in **chapter 2**). However, an HTM asset can be a hedged item with respect to foreign currency risk and credit risk. [IAS 39.79]

A forecast purchase of a financial asset that an entity intends to classify as HTM can be a hedged item. The prohibition for hedges of interest rate risk and prepayment risk is only for HTM assets already held, hence until the asset is acquired, it may be a hedged item. [IAS 39.IG.F.2.10]

Example 3.4A

Hedging interest risk for forecast acquisition of a held-to-maturity asset

Entity A forecasts the purchase of a fixed rate financial asset that it intends to classify as HTM. To protect itself against movements in interest rates between now and when the asset is purchased, Entity A enters into a derivative contract that will mature when the forecast transaction occurs with the intent of locking in the current forward rate for the day when the asset is expected to be purchased. The derivative is designated as a hedge of the forecast purchase of the financial asset, and qualifies for hedge accounting.

IAS 39 does not prohibit an entity from hedging its forecast interest receipts on debt instruments resulting from the reinvestment of interest receipts from an HTM asset. [IAS 39.IG.F.2.11]

Example 3.4B

Hedging interest risk of forecast reinvestment of cash flows from a held-to-maturity asset

Entity XYZ owns a variable rate asset that it has classified as HTM. The variable interest rate receipts are reinvested in debt instruments. Entity XYZ enters into a derivative to lock in the current interest rate on the reinvestment of the variable cash flows, and designates the derivative as a cash flow hedge of the forecast future interest receipts on debt instruments.

Entity XYZ qualifies for hedge accounting, even though the interest payments that are being reinvested derive from an HTM asset. Whilst an HTM asset itself cannot be hedged with respect to interest rate risk, it is possible to designate the derivative as hedging cash flow risk from debt instruments that were purchased using the interest receipts from the HTM asset. The source of the funds used to purchase the debt instruments in the future is not relevant.

The same would be true if Entity XYZ's HTM assets had been fixed rather than variable rate assets.

US GAAP comparison: US guidance allows an investor to hedge the overall fair value of a written prepayment option in a held-to-maturity asset. This is different from IFRS that explicitly prohibits an entity from hedging the prepayment risk of a held to maturity asset.

3.5 Loans and receivables

Assets classified as loans and receivables are measured at amortised cost. Even though a loan or receivable is not measured at fair value, it can still be a hedged item in a fair value hedge or cash flow hedge. For example, if a loan earns fixed rate interest, it could be hedged for changes in fair value due to movements in interest rates. Further, as there is no presumption of holding loans and receivables until their maturity it is possible to hedge the cash flows that arise from their future disposal where their disposal is considered to be highly probable.

3.6 Derivatives

Derivatives cannot be designated as hedged items. [IAS 39.IG.F.2.1] As an exception, IAS 39 permits a written option to qualify as a hedging instrument if it is designated as an offset to a purchased option, including one that is embedded in another financial instrument (for example, a written call option used to hedge a callable liability). [IAS 39.AG94]

The inability to designate a derivative as a hedged item will be relevant if an entity attempts to apply hedge accounting to a net risk position that includes a derivative. For example, an entity may enter into a derivative to hedge a debt instrument and then layer on a second derivative to hedge part of the net exposure of the debt and the first derivative. The inclusion of the first derivative as part of the hedged item is prohibited because it would result in the first derivative being a hedged item, rather than it being a hedging instrument.

Example 3.6

Entity K has a US$ functional currency. Entity K issues fixed rate Euro denominated 10-year debt. It chooses to issue the debt in the Euro market because it perceives the net interest cost after hedging to be cheaper than issuing directly in the US market. At the date of issue it immediately swaps all the foreign currency cash flows on the debt into its functional currency by entering into a 10-year receive € fixed pay US$ floating cross-currency interest rate swap as Entity K does not wish to be exposed to foreign currency risk. As Entity K has an interest rate policy of fixing interest rates for 5 years it also enters into a 5-year receive US$ floating pay US$ fixed interest rate swap to fix its interest cost for the 5 years after issue of the debt.

Entity K is prohibited from designated the interest rate swap as a cash flow hedge of changes in US$ interest rates of the issued debt and the cross-currency interest rate swap (i.e. the net synthetic US$ fixed rate debt achieved by swapping all fixed Euro cash flows into US$ fixed cash flows). The cross-currency interest rate swap is a derivative and therefore is not a qualifying hedged item.

However, Entity K could designate the cross-currency swap and the interest rate swap in combination as a partial-term hedge of foreign currency hedge of the debt for the first 5 years and a hedge of foreign currency risk and interest rate risk for the latter 5 years. IAS 39 permits a combination of derivatives to be designated jointly as a hedging instrument and permits partial-term hedging, see **3.2** and **2.2** in **chapter 9** respectively.

3.7 Designation of financial items

Provided that effectiveness can be measured, it is possible to designate only a portion of either the cash flows or fair value of a financial instrument as the hedged item.

It is possible to designate:
[IAS 39.81]

- one or more contractual cash flows of an instrument;
- one or more portions of one or more contractual cash flows of an instrument; or
- a proportion (i.e. percentage) of the cash flows or fair value of the instrument.

The example below illustrates different permissible hedge designations for a fixed rate bond. For more detailed guidance on hedging portions and partial term hedging see **2.1** and **2.2** in **chapter 9** respectively.

Example 3.7A

Permitted hedge designations of financial items

Entity B has a 5-year fixed rate bond asset. Entity B wishes to hedge part, or all, of the bond. The instrument is not classified as held-to-maturity. There are many options available to Entity B in applying hedge accounting:

- hedge the full fair value of the cash flows on the debt (all contractual cash flows);
- hedge the fair value on a proportion of debt, e.g. fair value of 50 per cent of the debt (proportion of all the contractual cash flows);
- hedge the fair value on all cash flows due to the impact of a specific risk only such as the impact of changes in risk-free interest rates (rather than all risks);
- hedge part of the cash flows due to a specific risk, e.g. designate the impact of movements in interest rates on 50 per cent of the cash flows (hedging a specific risk on a proportion of all cash flows);
- hedge an isolated set of cash flows due to all risks, e.g. hedging the fair value movement on the principal only (hedging a portion of cash flows);
- hedge an isolated set of cash flows due to a specific risk, e.g. hedging the fair value movement due to interest rate risk on the principal only (hedging a specific risk only on a portion of cash flows); or
- hedging the full fair value above or below a specified amount, e.g. hedging fair value decreases below a specified amount (hedging a part of the fair value).

US GAAP comparison: US guidance is more restrictive about what can be the designated risk in a hedge relationship. In a hedge of a financial asset or a financial liability, the designated risk can be risk of changes in overall fair value of the entire hedged item or changes in the fair value associated with changes in the designated benchmark interest rate, foreign currency rates, and/or creditworthiness of the issuer.

In calculating the change in the hedged item's fair value attributable to changes in the benchmark interest rate, the estimated cash flows used in calculating fair value must be based on all of the contractual cash flows of the entire hedged item. An entity cannot exclude a disproportionate (i.e. non pro rata) portion of the hedged item's contractual cash flows (for example, the portion of the interest coupon in excess of the benchmark interest rate) like under IFRS.

IAS 39 does not require risk reduction on an entity-wide basis as a condition for hedge accounting. Exposure is assessed on a transaction basis. [IAS 39.IG.F.2.6]

Example 3.7B

Risk reduction

An entity has a fixed rate asset and a fixed rate liability, each having the same principal amount. The entity receives interest on the asset of 10 per cent, and pays interest of 8 per cent on the liability, with payments and receipts occurring in the same period, so the entity always has a net cash inflow of 2 per cent.

The entity enters into a receive-floating, pay-fixed interest rate swap on a notional amount equal to the principal of the asset and designates the interest rate swap as a fair value hedge of the fixed rate asset. The entity qualifies for hedge accounting, even though the effect of the swap on an entity-wide basis is to create an exposure to interest rate changes that did not previously exist. The specific asset being hedged has a fair value exposure to interest rate movements that is offset by the interest rate swap.

3.7.1 *Hedge of portions*

As illustrated in **example 3.7A** above, an entity has many options available to it on how to dissect the cash flows of a hedged financial item. An entity may hedge part or all of the cash flows due to all risks inherent in the hedged item, or it may choose to hedge part or all of the cash flows due to specific risks only. This approach is known as hedging portions and is only allowed if the risk can be identified and hedge effectiveness can be assessed and measured reliably.

Hedging portions of cash flows and risks can be helpful in ensuring that the designated terms of the hedged item are similar to the terms of the hedging instrument, which reduces hedge ineffectiveness.

Example 3.7.1A

Hedging interest rate risk portion (1)

Entity A wishes to issue 5-year fixed rate debt. Based on market rates of interest and A's credit rating, it is able to issue debt at 6.5 per cent. This comprises a 5-year interest rate risk of 4.5 per cent, and a credit spread of 2 per cent. Entity A may designate the hedged risk as changes in fair value of the debt associated with changes in interest rate risk only, i.e. it may exclude from the designation its own credit spread.

Excluding the credit spread from the designation will increase the effectiveness of the hedge relationship as the equivalent credit risk inherent in the debt is not reflected in the terms of the interest rate swap.

An individual leg on an interest rate swap (or other derivative) that is not exactly the same as the cash flows on the hedged item does not necessarily preclude hedge accounting. The fair value of a hedging instrument is determined by the valuation of its net cash flows, and therefore when determining whether a hedging relationship is effective, an entity would not consider the terms of a single leg of the swap, without also considering the impact of the other leg of the swap.

Instead of entering into swaps that receive or pay a LIBOR flat equivalent amount (i.e. LIBOR without a credit spread), entities often enter into swaps where one of the legs exactly matches the cash flows on their debt.

Example 3.7.1B

Hedging interest rate risk portion (2)

Entity Z has a credit rating of B. It issues fixed-rate debt at 6 per cent, which includes a credit spread of 100 basis points, i.e. the rate comprises a LIBOR rate of 5 per cent and a credit spread of 1 per cent. To hedge its exposure to changes in interest rate movements, it enters into a receive-fixed, pay-floating interest rate swap.

Instead of entering into a swap where the pay leg exactly matches the equivalent of LIBOR (i.e. receive 5 per cent, pay LIBOR), Entity Z enters into a swap where the fixed leg exactly matches its debt. As the receive leg is 6 per cent, the pay leg is increased correspondingly, to LIBOR + 100 basis points. As the fair value of the swap is derived from its net settlements, the receive 5 per cent, pay LIBOR swap and the receive 6 per cent, pay LIBOR + 100 basis points will have the same fair value for a given movement in interest rates. Therefore, Entity Z may still designate the LIBOR portion of its debt as the hedged item.

3.8 Designation of non-financial items

If the hedged item is a non-financial asset or liability, it may only be designated as a hedged item:

(a) for foreign currency risk; or

(b) in its entirety for all risks. [IAS 39.82]

It is often difficult to isolate and directly measure the change in cash flows or fair value associated with a specific risk for a non-financial item, other than foreign currency risk, when compared to measuring separately specific risks of financial items, for example, interest rate risk. For this reason, the Standard only permits hedging of a non-financial item for foreign currency risk or in its entirety for all risks, even though it may be argued that in some cases it is possible to, at least indirectly, isolate the changes in cash flows or fair value attributable to a particular risk. This position was confirmed by the IFRIC in October 2004 where the IFRIC also noted that to allow separation of a non-financial asset into price risk components with the separate components being designated as the hedged item would require an amendment to IAS 39 rather than an Interpretation.

Example 3.8A

Hedging a forecast acquisition of a non-financial item: foreign currency risk

Entity D, a € functional currency entity, has a highly probable forecast transaction to purchase tyres from an external US$ functional currency entity. Because the tyres are a non-financial item, Entity D can either hedge the purchase of tyres for all risks or for just the foreign currency risk.

Entity D is able to hedge the foreign currency risk that will arise from buying the tyres as the foreign currency risk between the Euro and the US$ is identifiable and measurable. However, it is not possible to hedge just the cost of rubber in the purchase of tyres as this is not the entirety of all risks in the forecast transaction.

Example 3.8B

Hedging a forecast acquisition of a non-financial item: all risks

Entity B purchases bronze for its inventory of raw materials used in manufacturing its products. Entity B enters into a forward contract indexed to copper and wishes to designate it as a hedge of the copper component in forecasted purchases of bronze.

The price of copper is only a portion of the exposure to changes in the price of bronze. Entity B cannot designate as the hedged item changes in the value of the future purchase of bronze due to changes in the price of copper. However, if Entity B is able to demonstrate that the hedging instrument will be highly effective in hedging the price of bronze, it may be able to designate the forward contract as a hedging instrument in hedging the price of bronze. Any hedge ineffectiveness that arises from the hedge relationship must be reported in profit or loss.

The term 'entirety of all risks' in IAS 39.82 includes variability in cash flows that will be incurred in getting the non-financial item to the condition and location in which it must be delivered where these costs are included by the seller as a single unit price. For example, if an entity has forecast purchases of non-financial items where the buyer is billed for the cost of the non-financial item (which includes some conversion of a commodity into a finished good) plus the delivery of that finished good to the buyer, the entirety of all risks is the entire variability in cash flows, which includes the cost of conversion and delivery.

Where transportation is undertaken by a third party provider, not the counterparty, the variability in the cost of transportation does not form part of the non-financial item, as it a separate service undertaken by an unrelated party.

The restriction to hedge the item in its entirety for all risks or just foreign currency risk can give rise to practical problems for entities that hedge the purchase or sale of commodities where the grade of the hedging instrument is not equivalent to the grade of the commodity in the purchase. This is often referred to as a basis risk.

Example 3.8C

Hedging a forecast acquisition of a non-financial item: basis risk

Entity E hedges the forecast purchase of cocoa using cocoa futures. The cocoa futures contracts specify a grade of quality of cocoa that differs from the grade of quality of the forecast purchase of the non-financial item. The difference in the grade of the quality of cocoa between the hedged item and the hedging instrument is referred to as basis risk. The basis risk will cause hedge ineffectiveness.

Example 3.8D

Hedging a forecast acquisition of a non-financial item: transportation

Entity C acquires commodities for use in its business. Entity C acquires the commodities at spot prices on the date Entity C requires the commodity for use in its business. The amount Entity C pays for the commodity from the supplier is an amount referenced to the London Metal Exchange (LME), plus an amount for transportation of the commodity from the supplier to the entity.

If an entity designates a non-financial item as a hedged item it must be designated as a hedged item for (a) foreign currency risk only, or (b) in its entirety.

If Entity C is hedging the cash flow price variability of its future commodity purchases in its entirety, the entity must include the costs, whether fixed or variable, it will pay the supplier in bringing the non-financial item to its current location. Should the transportation paid to the supplier be variable, this would result in greater cash flow variability that will potentially result in greater hedge ineffectiveness.

If Entity C enters into the hedging instrument to hedge the variability in the LME price only, yet the transportation costs also are paid to the supplier and are variable, Entity C may choose to adjust the hedge ratio (i.e. so it is not 1-to-1) to reduce the amount of hedge ineffectiveness that may result from changes in the cash flow variability of transportation costs.

Example 3.8E

Hedging a non-financial item: operating leases

Entity A is a leasing entity which rents out machinery on both operating and finance lease arrangements. Entity A may wish to hedge future lease receipts. The ability to hedge these future receipts depends on whether the lease arrangement is a finance lease or an operating lease. An operating lease is an executory contract committing the lessor to provide the use of an asset in future periods in exchange for cash receipts. As the lease is a non-financial item, Entity A would need to either hedge account all the risks of the future lease receipts or foreign currency risk only. This is different from a finance lease, since a finance lease is a financial instrument which gives Entity A greater flexibility in designating the hedged item in a qualifying hedge relationship.

Example 3.8F

Hedging a non-financial item: inventory

[Extract from IAS 39.IG.F.3.6]

Can an entity designate inventories, such as copper inventory, as the hedged item in a fair value hedge of the exposure to changes in the price of the inventories, such as the copper price, although inventories are measured at the lower of cost and net realisable value under IAS 2 Inventories?

Yes. The inventories may be hedged for changes in fair value due to changes in the copper price because the change in fair value of inventories will affect profit or loss when the inventories are sold or their carrying amount is written down. The adjusted carrying amount becomes the cost basis for the purpose of applying the lower of cost and net realisable value test under IAS 2.

As described in **2.2.3** above IAS 39 permits an accounting policy choice as to whether to basis adjust non-financial items that are subject to a cash flow hedge. As described above, IAS 39.IG.F.3.6 states that a basis adjustment is included in the cost when applying the lower of cost or net realisable value test in IAS 2. If an entity has an accounting policy of not basis adjusting non-financial items subject to a cash flow hedge, IAS 39 does not state amounts reclassified from the cash flow hedge reserve to profit or loss should be the same as when an entity adopts a policy of basis adjusting.

It is reasonable to assume that this should be the case. Therefore, if an entity does not basis adjust inventory the reclassification from equity to profit or loss should result in the same net profit or loss amount that would have been achieved had the entity basis adjusted that inventory.

For guidance on other aspects of hedging non-financial items, such as hedging assets held at cost, or hedging for all risks except foreign currency risk see 3.10 in chapter 9.

3.9 Hedging net positions

A hedge of an overall net position, does not qualify for hedge accounting since hedge effectiveness is required to be measured by comparing the change in fair value or cash flows of a hedging instrument and a specific hedged item (or group of similar items). However, almost the same effect on profit or loss can be achieved by designating part of the underlying items, assets or liabilities, equal to the net position as the hedged item. [IAS 39.AG101]

Example 3.9A

Hedging a net payable

Entity A, a Sterling functional currency entity, has payables of US$100, and receivables of US$80. Instead of entering into two separate derivatives, it wishes to hedge the net US$20 position for foreign currency risk. The Standard does not allow it to designate the net position as the hedged item. Instead Entity A can designate US$20 of payables as the hedged item.

Similarly, if an entity had £500 fixed rate assets and £350 fixed rate liabilities and entered into a hedge of the net position, it could designate £150 of assets as being a hedged item in a fair value hedge of interest rate risk.

The net exposure from a forecast purchase and a forecast sale cannot be designated as a hedged item. Once again, almost the same effect on profit or loss can be achieved by designating part of the forecast purchases or forecast sales equal to the net position as the hedged item.

Example 3.9B

Hedging a net sale

Entity A, a UK entity, has highly probable forecast sales of US$100, and highly probable forecast purchases of US$80. Entity A enters into a single foreign currency forward contract to hedge the net exposure of US$20. Entity A can designate that derivative as hedging the first US$20 of sales.

An entity cannot hedge net profit as this is also a net number of many items. If an entity has sufficiently stable net profit margins it may be able to hedge the net number by designating as the hedged item a portion of sales equal to that amount.

Example 3.9C

Hedging a net profit

Entity A's functional currency is Sterling. A fifth of Entity A's profits is generated in US$ and thereby this exposes the entity's net profit to foreign currency risk. The US$ sales are expected to be $100m per month and have a relatively stable net profit margin of 15 per cent (i.e. US$ purchases are expected to be $85m per month).

Entity A wishes to hedge the exposure of net profit to changes in US$ / Sterling currency rate. As Entity A cannot hedge a net amount, and therefore cannot hedge the net profit, Entity A chooses instead to designate the hedging instrument as a cash flow hedge of the first $15m of US$ sales per month.

As long as Entity A makes at least $15m of US$ sales per month, the hedge relationship will be effective.

3.10 Hedging own equity

Transactions in own equity cannot be designated as hedged items. An entity's own equity transactions cannot be hedged because they do not expose the entity to a risk that can affect reported profit or loss. For example, a forecast dividend payment could not be designated as a hedged item, as IAS 32 requires that distributions to owners are debited directly to equity and therefore do not impact profit or loss. However, a properly declared dividend that has not yet been paid and is recognised as a financial liability by the payer or financial asset by the recipient may qualify as a hedged item for foreign currency risk if it is denominated in a foreign currency as changes in the foreign currency will impact profit or loss. [IAS 39.IG.F.2.7]

An entity may be able to designate share based payment transactions that are exclusively cash settled in an effective hedge accounting relationship. Even though the amount of cash payable varies by reference to the entity's share price, there is a cash flow variability that will impact profit or loss.

Example

An illustration of the accounting entries recorded for a cash flow hedge of equity price risk arising from a company's IFRS 2 *Share-based Payment* charge, using an equity call option, is shown at **3.14** in **chapter 10**.

3.11 Hedging issued convertible debt

As explained at **3.1** in **chapter 3**, convertible debt is separated at issue into a financial liability and equity conversion option which is included in equity. The financial liability is recognised at the present value of the contractual interest flows and principal, discounted at an interest rate for a debt without the equity conversion option. As the financial liability is measured as if the entity had issued a partly discounted bond, the hedging of the interest rate risk on this financial liability must also take into account this discount. In addition, because the financial liability will be extinguished when the convertible bond is converted, the hedging instrument should mirror this termination feature in order to increase hedge effectiveness.

3.12 Equity method investments and investments in consolidated subsidiaries

An equity method investment cannot be a hedged item in a fair value hedge in consolidated financial statements because the equity method recognises the investor's share of the associate's profit or loss, rather than changes in the investment's fair value.

For a similar reason, an investment in a consolidated subsidiary cannot be a hedged item in consolidated financial statements in a fair value hedge because consolidation recognises the subsidiary's profit or loss, rather than changes in the investment's fair value. [IAS 39.AG99]

Although in the consolidated financial statements it is not possible to apply fair value hedge accounting for an equity method investment or investment in a consolidated subsidiary, it may be possible to apply fair value hedge accounting to such a hedge in the investor's separate financial statements.

Whether fair value hedge accounting is permitted is dependent on whether the investment in the equity security can actually be fair valued for the hedged risk. It is inconsistent to claim fair value hedge accounting when the fair value of the investment cannot be reliably measured, e.g. where the investment is in an unquoted equity and the variability in the range of reasonable fair value estimates is too high and the entity is attempting to fair value hedge the investment for equity price risk.

A more complex scenario may arise when in its individual financial statements the investor attempts to apply fair value hedging with respect to foreign currency risk in relation to an equity investment in a foreign subsidiary. This scenario is discussed in more detail in **section 2.3** above.

A hedge of a net investment in a foreign operation is different because it is a hedge of the foreign currency exposure, not a fair value hedge of the change in the value of the investment. Hedges of net investments in foreign operations are dealt with in **2.3** above.

4 Hedging instruments

A hedging instrument is a designated derivative, or for a hedge of the risk of changes in foreign currency exchange rates a designated non-derivative financial asset or non-derivative financial liability, whose fair value or cash flows are expected to offset changes in the fair value or cash flows of a designated hedged item. [IAS 39.9]

Unless it is a written option (see **4.5** below), a derivative carried at fair value may always be designated as a hedging instrument, provided that:

(a) it meets the effectiveness requirements (see **section 5** below); and

(b) the necessary documentation is in place that supports the hedging relationship (see **section 6** below).

Investments in unquoted equity that are carried at cost (because their fair value cannot be reliably measured) and derivatives that are linked to and must be settled by delivery of such an unquoted equity instrument, cannot be designated as hedging instruments. [IAS 39.AG96] This is because a hedging instrument is defined as a designated financial instrument whose fair value or cash flows are expected to offset changes in the fair value or cash flows of a designated hedged item. However, if the instrument is carried at cost because it is not possible to reliably measure it, then there can be no expectation that its change in fair value or cash flows will offset those of the hedged item.

Any derivative, other than one that is linked to and will result in the delivery of an unquoted equity investment, is considered to be measurable with sufficient reliability. Therefore, an entity may designate any derivative as a hedging instrument, assuming all other qualifying criteria are met, even though the derivative's valuation may use a significant amount of unobservable data. However, significant judgement will need to be exercised in these circumstances when assessing hedge effectiveness, determining the gain/loss attributed to the hedged risk for the hedged item in a fair value hedge (pursuant to IAS 39.89(b)), and for cash flow hedges determining the cumulative change in fair value of the expected future cash flows on the hedged item from inception of the hedge.

A derivative may only be designated as an effective hedging instrument if it is a derivative in the scope of IAS 39. The term 'derivative' does not extend to other types of derivatives that are scoped out of IAS 39. For example, a derivative over own equity that meets the definition of equity in accordance with IAS 32 also meets the definition of a derivative in IAS 39 as it has an underlying, requires a small initial net investment, and is settled at a future date. However, such a derivative is an equity instrument recognised and measured in accordance with IAS 32 and cannot therefore be designated as a hedging instrument.

The basic application of the rules surrounding qualifying hedging instruments is covered in the remainder of this section, with more complex issues dealt with in **section 3** of **chapter 9**.

4.1 Hedging with non-derivatives

A non-derivative financial instrument may only be designated as a hedging instrument when hedging foreign currency risk. [IAS 39.72] An entity can use foreign currency denominated loans, deposits and other non-derivative financial instruments as hedging instruments. A common example of a non-derivative financial instrument used as a hedging instrument is a foreign denominated debt liability used in a hedge of a net investment in a foreign operation (see **2.3.1** above).

Example 4.1A

Hedging a financial asset with a non-derivative (1)

Entity J, whose functional currency is Sterling, has issued 5 million five-year US$ fixed rate debt. It also acquired a 5 million five-year fixed rate US$ bond which it has classified as available-for-sale.

Entity J cannot designate its US$ liability as a hedging instrument in a fair value hedge of the entire fair value exposure of its US$ bond, as a non-derivative may only be used as a hedging instrument of foreign currency risk.

Entity J could consider the use of the fair value option (see **3.1.1** in **chapter 2**) at initial recognition of the loan and liability. By designating both items as at fair value through profit or loss this designation would result in substantial offset of gains and losses in profit or loss, and unlike treating the asset as available-for-sale and the liability at amortised cost, it will result in no or little volatility in equity.

If Entity J did not apply the fair value option it could designate the US$ liability as a hedge of the foreign currency component of the bond (as either a fair value or cash flow hedge), but hedge accounting will not provide any advantage over not applying hedge accounting at all: the foreign currency gains and losses on both the monetary asset and monetary liability are already recognised in profit or loss in the period, in accordance with IAS 21, i.e. there is already a natural offset of foreign currency risk in profit or loss.

It should be noted that this natural offset would not apply if the hedged item was a non-monetary financial instrument, such as an equity security held as available-for-sale. This is because the foreign exchange gains and losses on an equity security that is recognised at fair value would be recognised in other comprehensive income, and foreign exchange gains and losses from reporting the monetary financial liability would be recognised in profit or loss under IAS 21. An entity could therefore attempt to apply either fair value or cash flow hedge accounting to achieve offset in profit or loss or other comprehensive income respectively, but variations in the US$ fair value of the equity security could result in significant ineffectiveness as the foreign currency component of the shares is derived from the fair value of the shares in local currency, being US$.

Example 4.1B

Hedging a firm commitment with a non-derivative (2)

Entity XYZ's functional currency is Euro. It has issued a US$5m fixed rate debt instrument with semi-annual interest payments that matures in two years. Entity XYZ has also entered into a US$5m fixed price sale commitment of a non-financial item that matures in two years and is not accounted for as a derivative because it meets the exemption as a contract that is entered into and continues to be held for the purpose of the delivery of a non-financial item in accordance with the entity's expected sale requirements.

Entity XYZ cannot designate its US$ liability in a fair value hedge of the entire fair value exposure of its fixed price sale commitment as a non-derivative liability can only be used in a hedge of a foreign currency risk.

However, Entity XYZ can designate its US$ liability in a fair value or a cash flow hedge of the foreign currency risk of its fixed price sale commitment.

Note that Entity XYZ cannot designate the fixed price sale commitment as the hedging instrument instead of the hedged item, as only a derivative or non-derivative financial instrument can be designated as a hedging instrument in a hedge of a foreign currency risk. The fixed price sale commitment in this case is neither, as it is scoped out of IAS 39.

If the foreign currency component of the sale commitment was separated as an embedded derivative that was not considered to be closely related to the sale contract, the embedded derivative could be designated as a hedging instrument of the foreign currency risk of the fixed rate debt instrument. However, applying hedge accounting would not provide the entity with any presentation benefit as both the foreign currency risk on the debt and the embedded derivative hedging instrument would be recognised in profit or loss.

Further examples

A detailed illustration of a fair value hedge of foreign currency risk on a firm commitment, using a foreign denominated deposit is included in **2.2** of **chapter 10**.

A financial asset that is classified as held-to-maturity may be designated as a hedging instrument in a hedge of foreign currency risk.

US GAAP comparison: US GAAP is more restrictive than IFRS in designating a non-derivative item as a hedging instrument in hedging foreign currency risk. US guidance only allows foreign denominated debt to be a designated hedging instrument of unrecognised firm commitments and a hedge of a net investment in a foreign operation. IFRS allows these two items to be hedged, but also allows debt to be a hedging instrument for foreign currency risk in hedging both forecast transactions and recognised assets and liabilities.

4.2 Splitting a derivative

A hedging relationship must be designated for a hedging instrument in its entirety. This is because there is usually only one fair value for a hedging instrument, and the factors contributing to that fair value are interdependent. Two exceptions to designating a hedging instrument in its entirety are: [IAS 39.74]

(i) the intrinsic and time value of an option may be separated, with only the intrinsic element designated as the hedging instrument; and

(ii) the interest and spot elements of a forward may be separated, with only the spot element designated as the hedging instrument.

In both of these situations, the element of the derivative that is not designated as a hedging instrument (i.e. the time value of an option, or the interest element of a forward) will be fair valued through profit or loss.

The above exceptions are permitted because the intrinsic value of an option and the spot element of a forward can usually be measured separately. However, the principle of reliable separate measurement cannot be extended. Even if it can be demonstrated that a reliable measure of an element of a derivative can be determined, it cannot be excluded from the hedge designation except if it is one of the two exceptions described above.

US GAAP comparison: US GAAP is less restrictive than IFRS on what elements of a hedging instrument may be excluded from an entity's assessment of hedge effectiveness. Excluded elements must be recognised in profit or loss. Both IFRS and US GAAP allow an entity to exclude the time value of an option or interest element of a forward, but US guidance is more flexible in that it allows an entity to exclude components of the change in an option's time value from the assessment of hedge effectiveness (DIG Issue E19). The components that can be excluded from the designation are the portion of the change in time value attributable to: the passage of time (theta); changes due to volatility (vega); and changes due to interest rates (rho).

As part of a hedge relationship an entity can choose to designate only a proportion of the derivative as the hedging instrument (e.g. 50 per cent of the notional), and then apply one of the exceptions as described above should it wish to. Designation of proportions of hedging instruments is discussed in **4.3** below.

Example 4.2

Fair value hedging with a purchased put

Entity A has an investment in shares of Entity XYZ, which it has classified as available-for-sale ('AFS'). To protect itself against a decrease in the share price, it purchases a put option over those shares. A designates the intrinsic value of the put as a hedging instrument in a fair value hedge of the XYZ shares.

The put has a strike price of CU50 per share – i.e. it allows A to sell the shares at CU50. When Entity A purchased the put, Entity XYZ shares were trading at CU55 per share. The put option will be fully effective in offsetting any price decrease below CU50, as Entity A designated only the intrinsic value as a hedging instrument. Any change in price above CU50 is not hedged.

Changes in the fair value of Entity XYZ shares are recognised in other comprehensive income. To the extent that the shares are hedged, changes in the fair value attributable to the hedged risk are recognised in profit or loss and offset with the gains and losses on the hedging instrument (i.e. the gains or losses on the hedged item below CU50 will be recognised in profit or loss and offset with the gains or losses on hedging instrument). Changes in the fair value of the option that relate to time value will be recognised in profit or loss.

4.3 Designation of portions and proportions of hedging instruments

A proportion of the entire hedging instrument may be designated as the hedging instrument in a hedge relationship. [IAS 39.75]

Example 4.3A

Designating part of a derivative: proportion

Entity A has a pay-fixed, receive-variable interest rate swap that it wishes to designate as hedging its issued variable rate debt. The notional on the swap is CU100 million and the notional on the debt is CU60 million. Entity A may designate CU60 million of the swap (i.e. 60 per cent) as the hedging instrument of the variable rate debt. The remaining CU40 million (i.e. 40 per cent) of the notional of the swap will be treated as a held for trading item, unless it is designated as a hedging instrument in another hedge relationship.

A hedging relationship may not be designated for only a portion of the time period that the hedging instrument is outstanding. [IAS 39.75] This restriction is clarified in IAS 39.IG.F.2.17 which indicates that a portion of cash flows of a hedging instrument that are not a fully proportionate part of all cash flows of a financial instrument cannot be designated as a hedging instrument. For example, the cash flows during the first three years of a ten-year borrowing denominated in a foreign currency cannot qualify as a hedging instrument in a cash flow hedge of the first three years of revenue in the same foreign currency.

Example 4.3B

Designating part of a derivative: portion

Entity A has a pay-fixed, receive-variable interest rate swap that it wishes to designate as hedging its issued variable rate debt. The swap has a 10-year term and the debt has a 7-year term. Entity A cannot designate seven of the ten years of the swap as the hedging instrument.

Note that the converse can be applied as IAS 39 permits partial term hedging. If in the above example the terms of the debt and swap were reversed, it would be possible to hedge the debt for the first seven years that it remains outstanding. Partial term hedges are discussed further in **2.2** in **chapter 9**.

The inability to designate a hedging instrument for only a portion of the time period that the hedging instrument remains outstanding is an extension of the rule that does not allow derivatives to be split up. It is not permitted to designate part of a derivative that is not a proportion of the derivative as a whole, unless the part of the derivative excluded from the hedge relationship is the time value of an option or forward points of a forward contract as discussed in **4.2** above.

This should not be confused with designating a hedging instrument for only part of its life, if for that part of its life it is expected to be a highly effective hedge. For example, it is possible to hedge a 10-year debt instrument using a 10-year interest rate swap, but apply hedge accounting for only one year. Hedge accounting is permitted, assuming the relationship is highly effective, for as long as the designation is applied.

4.4 Hedging more than one risk

A hedging instrument is often designated as hedging one risk only.

However, a hedging instrument can be designated as hedging more than one risk provided that:
[IAS 39.76]

(i) the risks being hedged can be clearly identified;

(ii) the effectiveness of the hedge can be demonstrated; and

(iii) it is possible to ensure that there is specific designation of the hedging instrument and different risk positions.

If a single hedging instrument is hedging more than one risk, and each risk is being hedged using a different form of hedge accounting (for example one as a fair value hedge and one as a cash flow hedge), separate disclosures will be needed for each.

Hedging risks in multiple hedged items using a single hedging instrument and hedging with more than one derivative is dealt with in **3.1** and **3.2** in **chapter 9** respectively

4.4.1 Hedging more than one risk in a single hedged item

IAS 39 allows the use of one instrument to hedge more than one risk. Cross currency interest rate swaps are commonly used to swap foreign currency floating rate debt into functional currency fixed rate debt, or to swap foreign currency fixed rate debt into functional currency floating rate debt.

If a single derivative hedging instrument is used to hedge multiple risks in a single hedged item or in multiple hedged items and the risks are hedged using different types of hedge accounting (e.g. cash flow hedging, fair value hedging or net investment hedging), the entity will need to isolate the derivative's fair value relating to each type of hedge. In such cases the guidance on hedging multiple hedged items detailed in **3.1.1** in **chapter 9** should be applied.

Example 4.4.1

Hedging both interest rate and foreign currency risk

Entity A, a Sterling functional currency entity, issues floating US dollar debt. To hedge its exposure to foreign currency exchange rates and to interest rate risk it enters into a cross currency interest rate swap. The terms of the swap match those of the debt. Under the swap, Entity A receives floating US dollars and pays fixed Sterling. IAS 39 allows the swap to be designated as a cash flow hedge of both US$ interest rate risk and US$:£ foreign currency risk designated in a single hedge relationship, or a cash flow hedge of US$ interest rate risk and a fair value hedge of the US$:£ foreign currency risk as two separate hedge relationships. The former designation is preferable to the latter as the entity incorporates two risks in a single cash flow hedge and therefore does not need to separate notionally the derivative instrument across multiple hedge relationships. The latter designation requires notional separation of the derivative across two hedge relationships: (i) hedge of cash flow variability due to US$ interest rates in foreign currency terms (being receive US$ floating, pay US$ fixed) and (ii) a hedge of the foreign currency risk into the entity's functional currency (being receive US$ fixed, pay £ fixed). The foreign currency hedge may prove more complex because the hedged item does not have fixed US$ cash flows.

Similarly, Entity A could have issued fixed US dollar debt, and used a cross currency interest rate swap to convert the position into floating Sterling debt. IAS 39 would permit the entity to designate the swap as a fair value hedge of both the interest rate and foreign currency risk designated as a single hedge relationship, or a fair value hedge of US$ interest rate risk and a cash flow hedge of the US$:£ foreign currency risk as two separate hedge relationships. The former designation is preferable to the latter as the entity incorporates two risks in a single fair value hedge and therefore does not need to separate notionally the derivative instrument across multiple hedge relationships. The latter designation would require notional separation of the derivative across two hedge relationships: (i) a fair value hedge of US$ interest rate risk and (ii) a hedge of the foreign currency risk into the entity's functional currency (being receive US$ fixed, pay US$ floating). The foreign currency hedge may prove more complex because the hedged item is fair value adjusted for fair value movements in US$ interest rates and therefore the carrying amount, and the foreign currency translation risk thereon, will change from period to period.

Assuming all other hedge accounting criteria are met it is possible to use a single derivative to hedge both foreign currency and interest rate risks if both risks are evident in the hedged item.

4.5 Written options

The Standard does not allow a written option to be designated as a hedging instrument unless it is designated as an offset to a purchased option (including one that is embedded in another financial instrument). The written option is not effective in reducing the profit or loss exposure of a hedged item since the potential loss on an option that an entity writes could be significantly greater than the potential gain in value of a related hedged item. [IAS 39.AG94] An instrument containing multiple options (written and purchased) may qualify as a hedging instrument provided it is not a net written option. See **3.3** in **chapter 9** for further detail.

4.6 Purchased options

Unlike written options, a purchased option may be designated as a hedging instrument, provided all the other criteria for hedge accounting are met. This is because a purchased option has a potential gain equal to or greater than the loss on a hedged item and therefore has the potential to reduce profit or loss exposure from changes in fair values or cash flows. [IAS 39.AG94]

Example 4.6A

Hedging an available-for-sale asset with a purchased put

Entity XYZ owns 1,000 shares of Entity ABC which are publicly traded, and has classified the shares as an available-for-sale asset. At 1 January 20X0, these shares are trading at CU50 per share and Entity XYZ has an unrealised gain of CU25,000 recognised in other comprehensive income. XYZ would like to lock in the unrealised gain and purchases a put option on Entity ABC's shares from Entity A for CU9,000. The purchased put option allows Entity XYZ to put the 1,000 shares to Entity A at CU50 per share on 31 December 20X2. Subject to the other hedge accounting criteria being met, the purchased put option may be designated as a hedge of the exposure to the decline in the fair value of the investment in ABC shares below CU50 per share.

In order to demonstrate that the hedge will be highly effective, Entity XYZ designates just the intrinsic value of the purchased put as a hedging instrument so when the fair value of the shares falls below CU50 the option will be fully effective. When the share price rises above CU50 per share the put option is out of the money and has no intrinsic value. Accordingly, gains and losses on the 1,000 shares in Entity ABC above CU50 are not attributable to the hedged risk for the purposes of assessing hedge effectiveness and recognising gains and losses on the hedged item.

Entity XYZ reports a change in the fair value of the shares in other comprehensive income if it is associated with the price increases above CU50. [IAS 39.55 & 90] Changes in the fair value of the shares associated with price decreases below CU50 form part of the designated fair value hedge and are recognised in profit or loss under IAS 39.89(b). Assuming the hedge is effective, those changes are offset by changes in the intrinsic value of the put, which are also recognised in profit or loss. [IAS 39.89(a)] Changes in the time value of the put are excluded from the designated hedge relationship and recognised in profit or loss under IAS 39.55(a). Changes in the intrinsic value of the put provide protection against the changes in the fair value of the investment in ABC shares below CU50 per share. [IAS 39.IG.F.1.10]

Further examples

A detailed illustration of a cash flow hedge of interest rate risk on variable rate debt, using a purchased interest rate cap, is included in **3.6** of **chapter 10**.

5 Hedge effectiveness

IAS 39 requires a hedge to be 'highly effective', prospectively and retrospectively, for it to qualify for hedge accounting. [IAS 39.88] Highly effective refers to the degree to which the hedge relationship is assessed as having a high level of hedge effectiveness. If hedge accounting is applied in the period any ineffectiveness is required to be measured and recorded immediately in profit or loss.

Hedge effectiveness assessment is different to hedge effectiveness measurement. An entity is required to *assess prospectively* whether it believes that a hedge relationship will be highly effective. This assessment forms part of the hedge documentation that an entity needs to complete in order to earn the right to apply hedge accounting. The prospective assessment is forward looking. An entity is required to *assess retrospectively* whether in any particular period the hedge relationship was highly effective. This retrospective assessment determines whether an entity can apply hedge accounting in the period, i.e. it looks back to establish how well the hedge has performed. If an entity has passed the retrospective assessment it will reflect hedge accounting in its financial statements and recognise any hedge ineffectiveness. Determining the amount of hedge ineffectiveness involves measurement and recognition of hedge ineffectiveness in profit or loss.

5.1 Hedge effectiveness assessment

The Standard does not prescribe a specific method for assessing hedge effectiveness. [IAS 39.AG107] However, it requires an entity to specify at inception of the hedge relationship the method it will apply to assess hedge effectiveness, and to apply that method consistently for the duration of the hedging relationship. The method specified must be consistent with management's risk management strategy and objective. A method of assessing hedge effectiveness must be applied consistently to all similar hedges unless different methods are explicitly justified. [IAS 39.IG.F.4.4]

Several mathematical techniques can be used to assess hedge effectiveness, including ratio analysis and various statistical methods like regression analysis. The appropriateness of a given method will depend on the nature of the risk being hedged and the type of hedging instrument used.

US GAAP comparison: FAS 133 requires that an entity define at the time it designates a hedging relationship the method it will use to assess the hedge's effectiveness in achieving offsetting changes in fair value or offsetting cash flows attributable to the risk being hedged. Similar to IAS 39, it also requires that an entity use that defined method consistently throughout the hedge period (a) to assess at inception of the hedge and on an ongoing basis whether it expects the hedging relationship to be highly effective in achieving offset and (b) to measure the ineffective part of the hedge.

5.1.1 The 'highly effective' criterion

IAS 39.AG105 specifies that a hedge is regarded as highly effective only if both of the following conditions are met:

(a) at the inception of the hedge and in subsequent periods, the hedge is expected to be ***highly effective*** in achieving offsetting changes in fair value or cash flows attributable to the hedged risk during the period for which the hedge is designated. Such an expectation can be demonstrated in various ways, including a comparison of past changes in the fair value or cash flows of the hedged item that are attributable to the hedged risk with past changes in the fair value or cash flows of the hedging instrument ('ratio analysis' or the 'dollar offset method' – see **5.1.8.1** below), or by demonstrating a high statistical correlation between the fair value or cash flows of the hedged item and those of the hedging instrument (for example 'regression analysis' – see **5.1.8.2** below). The entity may choose a hedge ratio of other than one to one in order to improve the effectiveness of the hedge (see **4.3.2** in **chapter 9**).

(b) The actual results of the hedge are within a range of 80–125 per cent.

When actual results are within a range of 80–125 per cent, but not 100 per cent exactly, any deviation from 100 per cent means that the hedge relationship is partly ineffective and ineffectiveness must be recognised in profit or loss.

Hedge ineffectiveness arises in a fair value hedge when the change in the fair value of the hedging instrument differs from that of the hedged risk of the hedged item. Since changes in fair value of the hedging instrument are recognised in profit or loss so as to offset changes in the fair value due to the hedged risk on the hedged item, all hedge ineffectiveness is automatically recognised in profit or loss in the period. Hedge ineffectiveness is recognised in profit or loss for both under and over hedges, i.e. ineffectiveness is recognised when the fair value of the hedging instrument changes, either to a lesser or greater extent respectively when compared to the changes in the fair value of the hedged item.

In a cash flow hedge, the portion of the hedging instrument that is considered to be effective, and therefore is recognised in other comprehensive income, is the lesser of (i) and (ii):
[IAS 39.96]

(i) the cumulative gain or loss on the hedging instrument from inception of the hedge; and

(ii) the cumulative change in fair value (present value) of the expected future cash flows on the hedged item from inception of the hedge.

In an over-hedge, where the change in fair value of the hedging instrument is greater than the change in fair value of the expected future cash flows on the hedged item, the difference is recognised in profit or loss as hedge ineffectiveness. However, where the change in fair value of the hedging instrument is less than the change in the fair value of expected future cash flows on the hedged item, the entire change in fair value of the hedging instrument is recognised in other comprehensive income, i.e. no ineffectiveness arises in an under-hedge, unless the hedge is determined no longer to be highly effective.

5.1.1.1 *Assessment on cumulative basis*

IAS 39 permits the assessment of hedge effectiveness either on a period-by-period basis or cumulatively over the life of the hedging relationship, provided the approach to be taken is documented formally at inception of the hedge relationship. [IAS 39.IG.F.4.2]

If hedge effectiveness is assessed on a cumulative basis and the hedge is not expected to be highly effective in a particular period, hedge accounting is not precluded if effectiveness is expected to remain sufficiently high over the life of the hedging relationship. The entity is still required to recognise any ineffectiveness in profit or loss as it occurs.

Example 5.1.1.1

Assessment on cumulative basis

Entity S designates a LIBOR-based interest rate swap that resets every 3 months as a hedge of its LIBOR based borrowing which carries interest at LIBOR plus a credit spread, where LIBOR resets every 6 months. Entity S documents that it will assess hedge effectiveness on a cumulative basis. Over the life of the hedge relationship, the hedge is expected to be almost perfect. However, there will be periods when the variability in cash flows on the borrowing is not perfectly offset by the variability in the interest rate swap.

Entity S is required to recognise any ineffectiveness in profit or loss as it arises. Because it assesses hedge effectiveness on a cumulative basis, Entity S will be able to hedge account for this relationship provided hedge effectiveness is expected to remain sufficiently high over the remainder of the life of the hedge.

5.1.1.2 *Effectiveness outside the 80 to 125 per cent range*

Effectiveness outside the range of 80 to 125 per cent at any measurement period may preclude hedge accounting not only in the period but also for future periods if it is an indication of further expected ineffectiveness.

A hedge relationship must be discontinued for the period in which the hedge fails to meet the effectiveness criteria. [IAS 39.88] IAS 39.IG.F.6.2 issue (i) states that "if there is a hedge effectiveness failure, the ineffective portion of the gain or loss on the derivative instrument is recognised immediately in profit or loss and hedge accounting based on the previous designation of the hedge relationship cannot be continued. In this case, the derivative instrument may be redesignated prospectively as a hedging instrument in a new hedging relationship provided this hedging relationship satisfies the necessary conditions". Generally, hedge accounting will be discontinued from the previous effectiveness testing date, though where it is possible to identify the event that caused the hedging relationship to fail the effectiveness test and to demonstrate that the hedge was effective before the event occurred, hedge accounting will be discontinued from the date the event occurred. [IAS 39.AG 113]

Where hedge effectiveness is outside the 80–125 per cent range, hedge accounting in subsequent periods would only be appropriate if a strong historical relationship exists and there is an expectation that the hedge will be highly effective in future periods. The same hedge relationship can be re-designated for hedge accounting prospectively provided the entity can demonstrate that the new hedge relationship is expected to be highly effective in the future. An entity may wish to change the hedge ratio of the existing hedged item and hedging instrument, designate a new hedging instrument, or utilise the hedging instrument in hedging a different hedged item in order to improve effectiveness.

Where a hedge is re-designated after an effectiveness failure, the previous hedge relationship is considered to be extinguished and a new hedge relationship created. Accordingly, subsequent retrospective effectiveness testing will only assess hedge effectiveness since the date of the new hedge designation and will not be tainted by the poor historical performance. Prospective tests will, nevertheless, be affected where the entity's chosen method of prospective effectiveness testing incorporates historical performance data.

5.1.2 Principal terms of the hedged item and hedging instrument match

If the principal terms of the hedged item and the hedging instrument match, then there is likely to be a high degree of offset between the hedged item and the hedging instrument. The principal terms of a hedged item and a hedging instrument will include: the notional and principal, the maturity, and the underlying. Different hedge relationships will have different principal terms.

For fair value hedges of investments in equity securities, if the underlying of the derivative equals that of the equity security and the derivative has a fair value of zero, then there will be an expectation of a high degree of offset in their fair values.

For hedges of interest rate risk there is a greater number of principal terms to consider, in particular depending on whether:

- the notional amount of the derivative matches the principal amount of the interest-bearing asset or liability;

- for cash flow hedges, repricing dates and interest rate indices match;
- the derivative is on-market at inception and therefore has a fair value of zero;
- the formula for computing net settlements under the interest rate swap is the same for each net settlement (i.e. the fixed rate is the same throughout the term, and the variable rate is based on the same index and includes either the same constant adjustment or no adjustment, say, for credit spread); and
- if the hedged item has prepayment features, these features are also reflected in the derivative.

For hedges of firm commitments, the principal terms will depend on which risk is being hedged. If the foreign currency risk of a firm commitment is being hedged then the principal terms will include the maturities of the commitment and the derivative, the underlying (i.e. the foreign currency), and the notional of each. Where an entity is hedging all the fair value of a firm commitment, the underlying will reflect the exact quality, grade, type, if the underlying is a non-financial item, or exact index, timing of cash flows, if the underlying is a financial item.

Similarly, for cash flow hedges of forecast transactions, the maturity of the hedging instrument is compared to the period when the designated forecast transactions are expected to impact profit or loss. Other principal terms that need to be considered are similar to those described above for hedges of firm commitments. In addition, where a forward contract is designated as a hedging instrument, for the terms to match, either the change in the discount or premium on the forward contract needs to be excluded from the assessment of effectiveness and recognised in profit or loss, or the change in expected cash flows on the highly probable forecast transaction needs to be based on the forward price for the non-financial item.

Even where the principal terms of the hedging instrument and of the entire hedged asset or liability or hedged forecast transaction are the same, an entity cannot assume hedge effectiveness without subsequent effectiveness testing as significant hedge ineffectiveness may arise from other sources, for example, as a result of changes in the liquidity of the hedging instruments or their credit risk. [IAS 39.IG.F.4.7]

Example 5.1.2A

Matched terms: hedge effectiveness not assumed

Entity X enters into a firm commitment to buy 10,000 ounces of gold at the current six-month forward rate of US$310. This contract is not recognised as a financial instrument as it is a purchase or usage requirements contract in accordance with IAS 39.5. On the same day, Entity X enters into a cash settled forward contract to sell 10,000 ounces of gold at the current six-month forward rate of US$310 which is designated as a fair value hedge of all risks with respect to the firm commitment to purchase gold. Hedge effectiveness will be measured based on changes in the six-month forward price of gold.

Because the principal terms of the firm commitment and the forward contract match (quantity of gold, contract maturity, forward rate) Entity X may conclude that the changes in the fair value of the firm commitment are expected to offset the change in the fair value of the derivative. However, ineffectiveness must still be assessed, at a minimum, at the end of each reporting period.

Example 5.1.2B

Matched terms: fair value derived from net settlements

If the form of an interest rate swap is such that the variable leg is adjusted for a fixed spread, for example LIBOR + 150 basis points, the adjustment can be considered as an adjustment of the fixed leg of the swap.

For example, for a fair value hedge of a 7 per cent fixed rate issued debt where the credit spread at issue was 1 per cent, the hedged risk, being the LIBOR portion, would be equivalent to 6 per cent. If the terms of the derivative were receive 7.5 per cent, pay LIBOR + 150 basis points, the terms of the swap would not invalidate a conclusion of minimal ineffectiveness as the swap's fair value is derived from its net settlements, and the net receive leg is equivalent to 6 per cent, being the hedged risk.

If the principal terms of the hedging instrument and the hedged item do not match, an entity will be subject to a larger degree of hedge ineffectiveness. For example, if, at inception of a cash flow hedge, the fair value of the swap is not zero, i.e. it is off-market, there will be ineffectiveness due to the interest rate risk on an up-front payment or receipt. For example, where an entity enters into an interest rate swap that has been structured to be significantly in-the-money at inception, the price paid to purchase the interest rate swap will be reimbursed to the buyer via a higher receive leg, or a lower pay leg. The upfront payment of cash by the buyer of the swap is like financing, and therefore any costs or income with respect to the financing will result in hedge ineffectiveness.

US GAAP comparison: FAS 133 allows an entity to assume no ineffectiveness (i.e. it allows an entity not to assess or measure ineffectiveness during the life of a hedge relationship) in certain hedges of interest rate risk. Cash flow and fair value hedges have slightly different conditions that need to be met in order for an entity to apply this technique. This technique is commonly referred to as the 'shortcut method'. IFRS does not permit such a technique.

In January 2008, the FASB issued FAS 133 DIG E23 which addresses certain implementation issues when applying the shortcut method in both fair value and cash flow hedges.

5.1.3 Minimising ineffectiveness

To improve hedge effectiveness, an entity can elect to designate only certain risks inherent in a hedged item as being hedged. The ability to hedge portions of cash flows or fair value generally applies to hedges of financial items only. The ability to designate only certain risks in non-financial items is limited and is discussed in **3.7** above. 'Hedging portions', i.e. designating an identifiable and separable portion of the risk on the financial asset or liability as the hedged item [IAS 39.81], can result in a higher degree of effectiveness as the designated risk is a specifically identifiable risk inherent in the hedged item. Designating portions is discussed in greater detail in **3.6** above and in **2.1** in **chapter 9**.

Example 5.1.3

Hedging the LIBOR swap rate

Entity A enters into a receive-fixed, pay-variable LIBOR interest rate swap and designates the swap as a fair value hedge of its issued fixed rate debt. As the interest rate index in the hedging instrument is LIBOR, and the LIBOR rate reflects the credit quality of AA financial institutions, even though Entity A is not a AA rated entity, it may designate the portion of risk inherent in its issued debt equivalent to this rate, i.e. hedge the LIBOR swap rate only. Entity A designates the risk of fair value movements in respect of the LIBOR swap rate on its issued fixed rate debt. By hedging just this portion of risk, Entity A has excluded from the designation fair value movements of the debt due to movements in its own credit quality.

It should be noted that if Entity A is charged an additional spread on the interest rate swap by the counterparty because Entity A's credit quality relative to the counterparty is worse, this may impact hedge effectiveness. The spread on the derivative will be relatively small when compared to the credit spread charged on the cash instrument, i.e. the debt. The entity will need to monitor the impact of the credit spread of the interest rate swap as part of its assessment of hedge effectiveness.

There is a number of ways to minimise hedge ineffectiveness. The following sections in **chapter 9** provide further guidance.

- 4.3.1 designating a cash flow hedge in layers;

- 4.3.2 hedging with a ratio other than one to one;
- 4.3.3 hedging on an after tax basis;
- 4.3.4 excluding forward points from forward contracts, and
- 4.3.5 excluding time value from options.

5.1.4 *Embedded call, prepayment or termination features*

Any derivative feature embedded in the hedged item or features embedded in the hedging instrument will have some impact on the changes in the fair value of these instruments. Differences in terms between the hedged item and hedging instrument will lead to differences in changes in fair value of the respective instruments. A termination, cancellation, call or prepayment feature embedded in the hedged item which is not replicated in the hedging instrument may result in a hedge relationship failing to qualify for hedge accounting.

Example 5.1.4A

Hedging callable issued debt

Entity X issues 10-year fixed-rate debt that is callable at the end of the sixth year. It decides to convert the interest payments on the bond from fixed-rate to floating-rate by entering into a 10-year receive-fixed, pay-floating interest rate swap. The interest rate swap is not cancellable at the end of year six. Entity X would like to designate the swap as the hedging instrument in a fair value hedge of the interest rate risk only on the fixed-rate debt.

The call feature may impede designation of the hedging relationship, particularly if it is probable that during the first six years of the debt it will be in-the-money. The assessment of whether it will be in the money can be based on a probability-weighted analysis of possible future changes in interest rates. Even if the option is unlikely to be exercised, the fact that there is a possibility of exercise, i.e. time value, will impact the debt's sensitivity to changes in interest rates.

If, during the first six years, interest rates decrease, the gain on the swap will be greater than the loss on the debt because the fair value of the debt will take into consideration the call feature, which will be in-the-money when interest rates fall below the rate on the debt. Economically, the debt will behave more like 6-year term debt, rather than 10-year term debt. Consequently, the changes in fair value of the debt due to movements in interest rates and the interest rate swap are unlikely to fully offset, potentially resulting in the prospective or retrospective hedge effectiveness tests being failed.

Example 5.1.4B

Hedging puttable issued debt

Bank C has a fixed-rate commercial loan maturing in five years. The borrower can prepay the loan without penalty after year two.

If Bank C wants to hedge the fair value of the loan due to changes in interest rate risk, it must consider the effect on fair value of the embedded option (a prepayment option forms a sub-component of the overall interest rate risk). A five-year receive-variable, pay-fixed swap might or might not be sufficiently effective to qualify as a hedging instrument. A swap, cancellable at Bank C's option after year two with the same terms as the prepayment feature in the loan, would be a more effective hedging instrument because it hedges all of the interest rate risk, including the embedded prepayment option.

5.1.5 *Credit risk*

Changes in credit risk impact the fair value of financial instruments. As derivative financial instruments are always fair valued, credit risk will directly impact the fair valuation of the instrument and therefore will impact hedge effectiveness assessments.

5.1.5.1 Counterparty credit risk

The effect of counterparty credit risk on hedge effectiveness cannot be disregarded. An entity must consider the counterparty's creditworthiness (and changes therein) in assessing hedge effectiveness. [IAS 39.IG.F.4.3] In addition, IAS 39.AG109 states that a hedge of interest rate risk using a derivative would not be fully effective if part of the change in the fair value of the derivative is attributable to the counterparty's credit risk. IAS 39.IG.F.4.7 goes further and states that an entity "cannot assume hedge effectiveness even if the principal terms of the hedging instrument and the hedged item are the same, since hedge ineffectiveness may arise because of other attributes such as the liquidity of the instruments or their credit risk".

Example 5.1.5

Cash flow hedge ineffectiveness

[Extract from IAS 39.IG.F.5.2]

Entity A has a floating rate liability of CU1,000 with five years remaining to maturity. It enters into a five-year pay-fixed, receive-floating interest rate swap in the same currency and with the same principal terms as the liability to hedge the exposure to variable cash flow payments on the floating rate liability attributable to interest rate risk. At inception, the fair value of the swap is zero. Subsequently, there is an increase of CU49 in the fair value of the swap. This increase consists of a change of CU50 resulting from an increase in market interest rates and a change of minus CU1 resulting from an increase in the credit risk of the swap counterparty. There is no change in the fair value of the floating rate liability, but the fair value (present value) of the future cash flows needed to offset the exposure to variable interest cash flows on the liability increases by CU50. Assuming that Entity A determines that the hedge is still highly effective, is there ineffectiveness that should be recognised in profit or loss?

No. A hedge of interest rate risk is not fully effective if part of the change in the fair value of the derivative is attributable to the counterparty's credit risk (IAS 39.AG109). However, because Entity A determines that the hedge relationship is still highly effective, it recognises the effective portion of the change in fair value of the swap, i.e. the net change in fair value of CU49, in other comprehensive income. There is no debit to profit or loss for the change in fair value of the swap attributable to the deterioration in the credit quality of the swap counterparty, because the cumulative change in the present value of the future cash flows needed to offset the exposure to variable interest cash flows on the hedged item, i.e. CU50, exceeds the cumulative change in value of the hedging instrument, i.e. CU49.

Dr	Swap	CU49	
Cr	Other comprehensive income		CU49

If Entity A concludes that the hedge is no longer highly effective, it discontinues hedge accounting prospectively as from the date the hedge ceased to be highly effective in accordance with IAS 39.101.

Would the answer change if the fair value of the swap instead increases to CU51 of which CU50 results from the increase in market interest rates and CU1 from a decrease in the credit risk of the swap counterparty?

Yes. In this case, there is a credit to profit or loss of CU1 for the change in fair value of the swap attributable to the improvement in the credit quality of the swap counterparty. This is because the cumulative change in the value of the hedging instrument, i.e. CU51, exceeds the cumulative change in the present value of the future cash flows needed to offset the exposure to variable interest cash flows on the hedged item, i.e. CU50. The difference of CU1 represents the excess ineffectiveness attributable to the derivative hedging instrument, the swap, and is recognised in profit or loss.

Dr	Swap	CU51	
Cr	Other comprehensive income		CU50
Cr	Profit or loss		CU1

For a cash flow hedge, if it becomes probable that a counterparty will default, an entity will be unable to conclude that the hedge is expected to be highly effective in achieving offsetting cash flows. As a consequence, hedge accounting would be discontinued.

A change in the creditworthiness of the counterparty of the derivative in a fair value hedge would have an immediate impact on the assessment of whether the hedge relationship is effective and qualifies for hedge accounting because the fair value of the hedging derivative will change and will result in immediate recognition of ineffectiveness in profit or loss.

The impact of changes in credit risk on the fair value of a derivative hedging instrument and the resulting impact on hedge effectiveness are easier to understand for fair value hedges than for cash flows hedges. For fair value hedges the derivative hedging instrument will always be measured at fair value through profit or loss and, to the extent the hedge relationship is highly effective, there will be either a full or partial offset in profit or loss with the change in fair value of the hedged risk of the hedged item. The fair value hedge adjustment to the hedged item that is reflected in profit or loss is independent of the change in fair value of the hedging instrument and therefore does not reflect the changes in credit risk reflected in the derivative's fair value. The existence of changes in the derivative's fair value due to changes in credit risk, whether counterparty or own credit risk, will directly impact the hedge effectiveness of the hedge relationship.

Cash flow hedges are often a hedge of forecast transactions, for example, the foreign currency risk of forecast sales or purchases, or the interest rate risk of variable interest cash flows on floating-rate debt. Similar to fair value hedges described above the hedged item does not incorporate movements in the credit risk of the derivative hedging instrument. The credit risk of the derivative hedging instrument is entirely independent of the change in cash flows of the hedged item. Therefore, when determining hedge ineffectiveness it is not possible to infer the changes in the credit risk and its impact on the fair value of the hedging instrument onto the hedged item and assume perfect hedge effectiveness. If the fair value of the derivative changes due to changes in counterparty or own credit risk, this change will not be offset by a change in the hedged item, and therefore hedge ineffectiveness will arise. An entity should monitor the impact of changes in credit risk for both prospective and retrospective hedge effectiveness assessment.

If an entity wished to fair value hedge the counterparty credit risk of a non-derivative asset, for example, a loan and receivable, hedge ineffectiveness will still arise from changes in the fair value of the derivative hedging instrument. The hedged risk is the credit risk of the counterparty to the loan, but the hedging instrument includes the credit risk of the counterparty and the entity's own credit risk. The counterparty credit risk of the loan differs to the counterparty or own credit risk of the derivative hedging instrument and therefore ineffectiveness will arise.

US GAAP comparison: Certain issues have been raised regarding the determination of the fair value of derivatives under FAS 157 and the effect on assessing hedge effectiveness of fair value hedges under FAS 133. FAS 157 indicates that credit risk (both the counterparty's and the entity's own) affects the determination of the fair value of derivatives. Some reporting entities pool derivatives by counterparty to estimate the appropriate credit valuation adjustment in determining the fair value of that pool. Preparers of financial statements have asked (1) whether credit risk must be considered in hedge effectiveness assessments and, if so, (2) whether credit risk can be assessed separately through qualitative analysis.

The SEC staff has confirmed that reporting entities must consider the impact of credit risk on the fair value of the designated derivative, as discussed in DIG G10. However, reporting entities may separately demonstrate the credit-risk effect of the designated derivative on the effectiveness of the hedge relationship by performing a qualitative analysis in which the entities determine that the changes in fair value that are attributable to credit risk would not affect the highly effective nature of the fair value hedge. Effectively, reporting entities can exclude credit risk from their periodic quantitative fair value hedge effectiveness assessments if they determine qualitatively that credit risk would not cause the hedging relationship to fail its periodic effectiveness assessment. This qualitative determination should take into account (1) the magnitude of the credit valuation adjustment in relation to the portfolio size and (2) the level of effectiveness of each individual hedging relationship before credit risk is considered.

When a reporting entity cannot or does not determine qualitatively that credit risk would not cause the hedging relationship to fail its periodic effectiveness assessment, it must include credit risk in its periodic quantitative assessments of fair value hedging relationships. FAS 133 requires reporting entities to perform this assessment at the individual hedge relationship level.

5.1.5.2 Own credit risk

The impact of change in own credit risk will impact hedge effectiveness assessment in the same way as counterparty credit risk described in **5.1.5.1** above.

5.1.6 Clean versus dirty prices

Clean prices are prices that exclude any interest accruals. Dirty prices include interest accruals.

Clean prices can be used when assessing whether a hedge is expected to be highly effective.

Where a retrospective test of hedge effectiveness is performed using dirty prices for a hedge of a debt instrument with an interest rate swap, ineffectiveness will be observed if the test is performed between interest payment dates. The swap's value will include a net interest accrual being the net of the interest receivable on the receive leg and the interest payable on the pay leg. The loan's value will include a gross interest accrual. The accrued interest component of the swap's value will therefore be far smaller than that of the debt causing hedge ineffectiveness.

It is important to note that excluding accrued interest in an effectiveness test does not eliminate the ineffectiveness that can be caused by the first fixing of the swap. When an interest rate swap fixes in advance, the interest rate on the floating leg of the swap is fixed until the next reset date. Therefore, between reset dates, as market interest rates change, this fixed portion of the floating leg builds up value. The build up of value between reset dates is not mirrored in the fair value movements of the hedged debt. This ineffectiveness is not eliminated by excluding accrued interest from the hedge effectiveness testing.

When measuring the actual results of the hedge (see **5.7 below**) the dirty value of the instruments must be used.

5.1.7 Frequency of hedge effectiveness assessment

Effectiveness must be assessed, at a minimum, at inception and at the end of each reporting period, including interim financial statements. [IAS 39.AG106]

US GAAP comparison: US guidance requires that hedge effectiveness assessments be undertaken at inception of the hedging relationship, whenever an entity prepares financial statements, and no less than every quarter. IFRS only requires hedge effectiveness assessments to be undertaken at a minimum at the end of each reporting period.

5.1.8 Ratio analysis and regression analysis

Hedge effectiveness is the degree to which changes in the fair value or cash flows of the hedged item that are attributable to a hedged risk are offset by changes in the fair value or cash flows of the hedging instrument.

A perfect hedge relationship might be illustrated as follows:

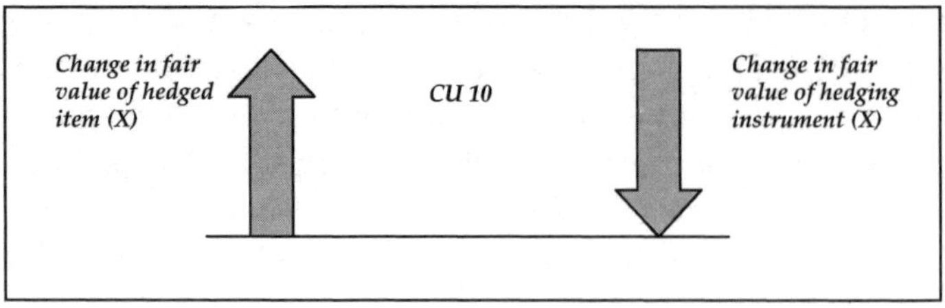

For each CU10 change in value of the hedged item, there is an equal and opposite (CU10) change in value of the hedging instrument, i.e. the hedging instrument is perfectly negatively correlated in this example with the risk it hedges. The negative sign results from the offsetting effect between the derivative and the hedged item.

Correlation is a term that originates from probability theory and relies on statistical analysis, but it is often estimated from historical data. It is a measure of the extent to which two variables move in relation to one another. The correlation can range from perfectly negative through totally uncorrelated to perfectly positive. Quantitatively, it is expressed as a value ranging from -1 (perfectly negatively correlated) to 1 (perfectly positively correlated).

5.1.8.1 Ratio analysis

Ratio analysis establishes, as a percentage, the extent of effectiveness of the hedging instrument in offsetting the hedged item for the designated risk over a defined period of time, i.e. the degree to which the changes in fair value of the hedging instrument and the hedged item are negatively correlated. It is relatively simple to compute and is well suited for measuring the effectiveness of short-term hedges (where there may be insufficient data to perform a statistical test, such as regression) and is also used to measure the level of actual offset.

5.1.8.2 Regression analysis

Regression analysis is a statistical measurement technique for determining the validity and extent of a relationship between an independent and dependent variable. It is more complex than ratio analysis and is explained in more detail in **4.6** in **chapter 9**.

5.2 Measuring hedge ineffectiveness

Section 5.1 above looked at the various ways in which hedge effectiveness can be assessed. These techniques are used to support the entity's claim that a hedge relationship has been highly effective in the period, and will continue to be so for future periods. Consistent application of these techniques in assessing hedge effectiveness is used to support the continued application of hedge accounting.

Measurement of hedge effectiveness relates to the actual amount of ineffectiveness that needs to be reported in the period's profit or loss.

In many instances, the techniques used for assessing hedge effectiveness, i.e. whether the hedge relationship is effective for this period and future periods, will be different to the technique used in measuring ineffectiveness for the period. The difference arises because recognition of ineffectiveness is based on actual offset. The degree of offset is more consistent with ratio analysis techniques (otherwise known as 'the dollar offset test') as opposed to statistical techniques such as regression. Equally, where clean prices are used for assessing hedge effectiveness the measurement of the actual results of the hedge must be based on the actual performance of the derivative, i.e. it is not possible to exclude from its measurement a portion of fair value that is due to the interest accrual. This means that measurement of hedge effectiveness is always based on dirty prices.

The extent to which hedge ineffectiveness will be recognised will depend on whether the hedge is a fair value hedge, or a cash flow hedge.

5.2.1 *Fair value hedge effectiveness measurement*

Once a fair value hedge has been assessed as being highly effective for the period, and there is an expectation of high effectiveness for future periods, the entity has earned the right to measure the hedged item in a manner consistent with fair value hedging, i.e. adjusting the hedged item for fair value movements in the hedged risk.

Actual measurement of hedge ineffectiveness will be recognised in profit or loss of the period because both the adjustment to the hedged item with respect to fair value movements in the hedged risk, and the fair value movements on the hedging instrument are both recognised in profit or loss. To the extent that these two amounts do not fully offset, this difference, being hedge ineffectiveness, will be recognised in profit or loss.

If an entity was applying a retrospective assessment of hedge effectiveness using ratio analysis (i.e. dollar offset test) using period-to-period data, then the percentage of hedge ineffectiveness derived from using this technique would be consistent with the measurement of ineffectiveness in the period.

5.2.2 *Cash flow hedge effectiveness measurement*

As described in **5.1.1** above, effectiveness measurement in a cash flow hedge effectiveness is different from effectiveness measurement in a fair value hedge. With cash flow hedges, no hedge ineffectiveness is recognised in profit or loss if the cumulative gain or loss on the hedging instrument from inception of the hedge is less than the cumulative change in fair value of the expected future cash flows on the hedged item from inception of the hedge. As described in **5.1** this results in hedge ineffectiveness being recognised in profit or loss only when the change in the hedging instrument's fair value exceeds the change in the present value of future cash flows on the hedged item.

If an entity was applying a retrospective assessment of hedge effectiveness using ratio analysis (i.e. dollar offset test) using cumulative data, then in the case of over-hedging, the percentage of hedge ineffectiveness derived from using this technique would be consistent with the measurement of the cumulative ineffectiveness over the life.

6 Documentation

There are several conditions to achieving hedge accounting under IAS 39. In the previous sections of this chapter the conditions have focused on what is considered to be an eligible hedged item and hedging instrument. Even if the hedge relationship is considered to be eligible for hedge accounting, documentation of the hedge relationship must be in place at inception of the hedge relationship. Until the necessary documentation is in place, an entity cannot apply hedge accounting. There can be no retrospective designation of a hedge relationship. [IAS 39.IG.F.3.8]

Example 6

Timing of hedge documentation

Entity A issues fixed rate debt on 1 January. On the same date it enters into a receive-fixed, pay-floating interest rate swap, with all the terms of the debt and swap matching. Entity A does not complete the required documentation until 1 February.

A may adopt hedge accounting from 1 February. From 1 January to 1 February, it will account for the debt and the derivative on the normal measurement basis, i.e. amortised cost for the debt, and fair value for the derivative, with changes in fair value recognised in profit or loss.

IAS 39 states that at the inception of the hedge there must be formal designation and documentation of:
[IAS 39.88]

- the hedging relationship; and
- the entity's risk management objective and strategy for undertaking the hedge.

That documentation shall include identification of:

- the hedging instrument;
- the hedged item or transaction;
- the nature of the risk being hedged; and
- how the entity will assess the hedging instrument's effectiveness in offsetting the exposure to changes in the hedged item's fair value or cash flows attributable to the hedged risk.

Broadly, the documentation requirements fall into two categories:

- specific documentation for every hedge entered into. This will give details of the hedged item, hedged risk, hedging instrument, how effectiveness will be assessed prospectively and retrospectively, and how effectiveness will be measured retrospectively; and
- overall risk management objectives and strategies.

6.1 Risk management objectives and strategies

There are no rules governing this area, except that to achieve hedge accounting, an entity must have documented its objectives and strategies. The hedge relationships that the entity wishes to apply hedge accounting to, must be consistent with these stated policies. Therefore the policies and objectives should as a minimum include a list of the risks that the entity is exposed to, and how the entity intends to manage those risks.

6.2 Specific hedge documentation

Below is one example of how the specific documentation requirements for each hedge relationship could be met. It is based on the minimum that could reasonably be provided.

Example 6.2

Entity XYZ

Accounting hedge designation and assessment summary

Policy declaration

This relationship is in accordance with our Risk Management and Accounting Policies for IAS 39 [insert specific reference to policy within the policy manual]. The risk management objective and strategy for undertaking the hedge is as follows [to be inserted].

Risk identification

Nature of risk hedged

e.g. overall fair value, interest, credit, foreign currency, equity risk.

Specific hedged risk

e.g. for overall fair value, commodity price risk, for foreign currency, forward or spot rate; for interest rate risk, specific portion such as the benchmark interest rate.

Hedge type

	Yes	No
Cash Flow Hedge		
Fair Value Hedge		
Net Investment Hedge		

Date of designation of hedging relationship

Indicate date of designation of the hedging relationship.

Process required for the de-designation of the hedging relationship, including date on which the hedging relationship was de-designated

Indicate process required to formally de-designate the hedging relationship and date of de-designation.

Details of Hedging Instrument

Nature of hedging instrument	
Deal reference number	
Contractual parties of thc hedging instrument	
Start date	
Maturity date	
Currency	
Principal/Notional	
Cash flows to be received and paid – amount, basis (e.g. LIBOR) and timing	
Amount of Principal/Notional designated as a hedging instrument	
If non-optional derivative is used, will movements in forward points be excluded?	
If optional derivative is used, will the movement in time value be excluded?	
Attachments (include any other information to explain the nature and profile of the instrument, e.g. the swap has an amortising notional)	

Details of hedged item

Nature of hedged item	
Deal reference number (if applicable)	
Contractual parties of the hedged item	
Start date	
Maturity date	
Currency, amount (and basis e.g. LIBOR) and timing	
Principal/Notional	
Amount designated as hedged item	
Attachments (e.g. if cash flow hedging forecasts sales then sales forecasts will be attached which show the level of designated sales compared with the total forecast	

Effectiveness testing

Prospective effectiveness testing

Can hedge effectiveness be reliably measured?	
Expectation of hedge effectiveness	
Type of test	
Period by period or cumulative assessment	
Frequency of hedge effectiveness test	

Results of prospective effectiveness testing

Date of test					
Results of Test					
Attachments (include any details of the results of the assessment)					

Retrospective effectiveness testing

Can hedge effectiveness be reliably measured?	
Expectation of hedge effectiveness	
Type of test	
Period by period or cumulative assessment	
Frequency of hedge effectiveness test	

Result of retrospective effectiveness testing

Date of test					
Results of Test					
Attachments (include any details of the results of the assessment)					

Result of retrospective effectiveness testing

Date of test					
Results of Test					
Attachments (include any details of the results of the assessment)					

Accounting

Basis Adjustment

If the hedge is a cash flow hedge and results in the recognition of a non-financial asset or non-financial liability, whether the gains and losses are reclassified directly out of equity into profit or loss or whether the gains and losses are removed from equity on initial recognition of the non-financial asset or liability and included in the initial carrying value of the asset or liability.

Reconciliation of gain or loss deferred in equity for cash flow and net investment hedges

	Cash flow hedging	Net investment hedging
Balance brought forward in equity as effective gains/losses		
Effective gains and losses recognised in equity in period		
Gains and losses reclassified out of equity in period		
Balance carried forward in equity as effective		

Hedge documentation prepared by: ________________

Hedge documentation reviewed by: ________________

Date: ________________

9 Hedge accounting – complex

1 Introduction

Hedge relationships and hedge accounting strategies can range from the basic to the very complex. The purpose of this chapter is to discuss the more complex aspects of hedge accounting. The basic rules of hedge accounting are discussed in detail in **chapter 8** and equally apply to this chapter.

This chapter is presented in the following sections:

Section 2	Hedged items
Section 3	Hedging instruments
Section 4	Hedge effectiveness
Section 5	Net investment hedges – advanced
Section 6	Cash flow hedge – portfolio hedge of interest rate risk
Section 7	Fair value hedge – portfolio hedge of interest rate risk

2 Hedged items

The basic requirements governing the qualification of hedged items are discussed in detail in section 3 in chapter 8. This section provides additional application guidance on the basic requirements and also covers less common, more complex scenarios.

Section 2.1	Hedges of portions of a financial instrument
Section 2.2	Partial term hedging
Section 2.3	Financial instruments subject to prepayment
Section 2.4	Hedging foreign currency exposure in equity securities
Section 2.5	Foreign currency risk of a forecast foreign currency debt issuance
Section 2.6	Hedging capitalised borrowing costs
Section 2.7	Hedging non-financial items

Section 2.8 Designation of groups of items

2.1 Hedges of portions of a financial instrument

As it is a requirement for all hedge relationships that effectiveness can be assessed and measured [IAS 39.88(d)], it is essential that the hedged portion is identifiable and separately measurable. For instance, the risk free rate or benchmark interest rate risk component of either a fixed or floating interest-bearing asset or liability is an identifiable and separately measurable portion (as illustrated in **example 3.7.1A** in **chapter 8**). However, in other cases it may not be possible to establish that a given variable is an identifiable and separately measurable portion if that portion is not identifiable when the instrument was originally issued and priced. This is illustrated in the following example:

Example 2.1A

Ineligible portion of interest rate risk

Entity C has issued Euro denominated debt with a floating interest rate based on the European Central Bank (ECB) rate. It has also entered into a receive EURIBOR pay fixed Euro interest rate swap with a notional equal to the principal of the debt.

The receive EURIBOR pay fixed interest rate swap cannot be designated as a hedge of the portion of the ECB cash flows that are due to changes in EURIBOR. There is no EURIBOR component in the ECB variable cash flows. The interest rate risk that can be designated as the hedged risk is variability in the ECB rate.

Alternatively, Entity C could hedge the variability of the ECB floating interest rate with a EURIBOR swap, however this is unlikely to be a perfectly effective hedging instrument even if the notional amounts of the two swaps are the same, because of the basis difference between ECB rate and EURIBOR. Changes in the cash flows of the floating interest rate on the debt will not necessarily be offset by variability in EURIBOR on the swap.

It may be possible to adjust continually the number of EURIBOR swaps to be equivalent to the variability in cash flows generated by variability in the ECB rate in order to achieve a highly effective hedge relationship. This is a dynamic hedging strategy. If a sufficiently high correlation can be demonstrated between EURIBOR and ECB rates then a statistical relationship could be used to adjust the hedge ratio in order to demonstrate prospectively a highly effective hedge in line with the principles described in **4.3.2** below.

In July 2008 the IASB issued an amendment to IAS 39 titled *Eligible Hedged Items*. The aim of the amendment was to clarify two issues in relation to hedge accounting: (i) identifying inflation as a hedged risk or portion; and

(ii) hedging with options. The amendments are to be applied retrospectively for annual periods beginning on or after 1 July 2009.

The amendments state that inflation may only be hedged in the instance where changes in inflation constitute a contractually-specified portion of cash flows of a recognised financial instrument. This may be the case where an entity acquires or issues inflation-linked debt. In such circumstances, the entity has a cash flow exposure to changes in future inflation that may be cash flow hedged. The amendments, therefore, do not permit an entity to designate an inflation component of issued or acquired fixed-rate debt in a fair value hedge such a component is not deemed separately identifiable and reliably measurable. The amendments also clarify that a risk-free or benchmark interest rate portion of the fair value of a fixed-rate financial instrument will normally be separately identifiable and reliably measurable, and therefore may be hedged. The amendments are effective retrospectively for annual periods beginning on or after 1 July 2009 with early adoption permitted

The clarification on hedging with options is detailed in **3.4** below.

Where an entity issues debt at a negative spread to LIBOR (i.e. the coupon is set at a rate below the LIBOR rate at inception), it cannot designate a 'LIBOR' portion as the hedged risk. This would entail splitting the fixed rate of the debt into a LIBOR portion and a discount to LIBOR (or negative credit spread component). IAS 39 specifies that if a portion of the cash flows of a financial asset or a financial liability is designated as the hedged item that designated portion must be less than the total cash flows of the asset or liability. [IAS 39.AG99C]

Example 2.1B

Fair value hedging sub-LIBOR fixed rate debt

Entity XYZ issues fixed rate debt at 3.75 per cent when LIBOR is 4 per cent. Entity XYZ would like to hedge its debt for interest rate risk arising from changes in the benchmark interest rate, i.e. LIBOR.

Entity XYZ cannot designate a LIBOR component (4 per cent) as the hedged risk as this amount is greater than the contractual cash flow on the hedged item. However, XYZ can designate all of the contractual cash flows of the debt instrument as the hedged item and specify that these cash flows are hedged for changes that are attributable to LIBOR. In order for XYZ to have a high expectation of hedge effectiveness, XYZ may need to choose a hedge ratio other than one to one in order to improve the effectiveness of the hedge as described in **4.3.2** below.

US GAAP comparison: FAS 133 specifically allows the benchmark interest rate to be the designated hedged risk in a hedge of interest rate risk regardless of the credit risk inherent in the hedged item. In order to qualify as a benchmark interest rate, that rate must be a widely recognised and quoted rate in an active financial market that is broadly indicative of the overall level of interest rates attributable to high-credit quality obligors in that market. In the United States, currently only the interest rates on direct Treasury obligations of the US government and the LIBOR swap rate are considered to be benchmark interest rates. For example, the LIBOR swap rate could be the designated hedged risk in an AAA-rated security even if the overall market interest rate of the instrument is less than the LIBOR swap rate.

If an entity enters into a fair value hedge of a fixed rate asset or a liability some time after its initial recognition, IAS 39 permits the entity to designate as the hedged item a portion of the cash flows equal to the benchmark rate (e.g. LIBOR) that is higher than the contractual fixed rate received or paid on the asset or liability, provided the benchmark rate is less than the recalculated effective interest rate on the asset or liability calculated as if the entity had purchased or issued the instrument on the date it first designates the hedged item. [IAS 39.AG99D]

Assume an entity issues a fixed rate bond at par that will redeem at par. Some time later it enters into an interest rate swap to hedge its exposure to changes in the fair value of the liability attributable to the benchmark interest rate. If the swap has a fair value of zero at inception and interest rates have fallen since the bond was issued, the coupons on the bond will be higher than the contracted fixed receipts on the interest rate swap. As the fixed receipts on the swap are lower than the contractual fixed rate coupons on the bond, the entity can designate as the hedged item a portion of each coupon cash flow equal to the fixed receipts of the swap. The fixed receipts of the swap and the cash flows on the designated portion of the bond will match and the hedge is likely to be highly effective.

If interest rates have risen since the bond was issued, the coupons on the bond may be lower than the contractual fixed receipts on the interest rate swap. The entity can designate the bond as hedged for the benchmark interest rate portion of its fair value interest rate risk, provided the benchmark rate is less than the effective interest rate of the hedged item, calculated based on the assumption that the entity had issued the bond on the date the hedge is designated. [IAS

39.AG99D] This is achieved by designating as the hedged risk both the contractual coupon payments and an amount of discount which is included in the difference between the current fair value of the bond and the amount repayable at maturity. A hedge designated in this way is likely to exhibit ineffectiveness because the fixed cash flows of the swap will have a different profile to the fixed cash flows of the hedged item: the fixed interest cash flows of the swap are composed of equal payments, while the hedged interest cash flows on the bond comprise lower contractual payments and a discount to par. The different cash flow profiles will result in different changes in fair value in response to changes in interest rates.

To minimise ineffectiveness an entity may need to enter into a swap with a fixed leg rate equal to or lower than the contractual coupons on the bond. Such a swap does not have a zero fair value at inception as it is not entered into at market interest rates. Where the upfront payment on the swap is structured to be equivalent to the discount on the bond, the swap will be more effective at hedging the bond.

Example 2.1C

Fair value hedging fixed rate debt when interest rates have moved since issue

Entity FGH originated a four-year 5 per cent fixed-rate loan of CU10,000 on 1 January 20X2, with a maturity date of 31 December 20X5. Of the 5 per cent coupon, 0.4 per cent represents credit spread, i.e. the market rate of interest was 4.6 per cent. Interest is receivable annually. The effective interest rate of FGH's loan at inception is 5 per cent.

Scenario 1: Interest rates fall between 1/1/20X2 and 31/12/20X2

One year later interest rates have fallen. At 31 December 20X2, the loan has a fair value of CU10,251. FGH wishes to protect its loan asset against an increase in interest rates by entering into a fair value hedge of interest rate risk. The current market rate of interest is now 3.5 per cent, rather than 4.6 per cent.

Entity FGH enters into a receive-variable rate, pay-fixed rate of 3.5 per cent interest rate swap on 31 December 20X2 with a maturity of 31 December 20X5 to hedge its fair value interest rate exposure. The swap is on-market, i.e. it has a fair value of zero at inception.

If FGH had originated the loan when the hedging swap was entered into, it would not have originated the loan at 5 per cent, but rather at 3.9 per cent, i.e. at the benchmark interest market rate plus the appropriate margin given the counterparty's credit rating (3.5 per cent + 0.4 per cent). In this case, the effective interest rate of the loan would have been 3.9 per cent and not 5 per cent. The benchmark interest rate of 3.5 per cent is lower than the effective interest rate of this 'hypothetical loan' and hence FGH is permitted to designate as the hedged item a portion equal to the benchmark rate (e.g. LIBOR).

Scenario 2: Interest rates increase between 1/1/20X2 and 31/12/20X2

One year later interest rates have increased. At 31 December 20X2, the loan has a fair value of CU9,081. FGH wishes to protect its loan asset against a further increase in interest rates by entering into a fair value hedge of the interest rate risk. The current market rate of interest is now 6 per cent, rather than 4.6 per cent.

Entity FGH enters into a receive-variable rate, pay-fixed rate of 6 per cent interest rate swap on 31 December 20X2 with a maturity of 31 December 20X5 to hedge its fair value interest rate exposure. The swap is on-market, i.e. it has a fair value of zero at inception.

If FGH had originated the loan when the hedging swap was entered into, it would not have originated the loan at 5 per cent, but at 6.4 per cent, i.e. at the benchmark interest market rate plus the appropriate margin given the counterparty's credit rating, i.e. the (6 per cent + 0.4 per cent). The benchmark interest rate of 6 per cent is lower than the effective interest rate of this 'hypothetical loan' and hence FGH is permitted to designate as the hedged item a portion equal to the benchmark rate (e.g. LIBOR) that is higher than the contractual fixed rate received on the asset.

2.2 Partial term hedging

Hedging only a part of a financial instrument's term is an extension of hedging portions of cash flows of the instrument.,It is possible to hedge for a shorter period than the term of the whole hedged item, by hedging only selected cash flows in that item. As with all hedge relationships, this is only permitted if hedge effectiveness can be demonstrated and measured (and the other hedge criteria are met). [IAS 39.IG.F.2.17]

Example 2.2A

Partial term hedging fixed rate debt (1)

XYZ plc issues 10-year fixed-rate debt. To hedge against changes in interest rates, it enters into a 6-year receive-fixed pay-floating interest rate swap. XYZ may designate the swap as hedging the fair value exposure of the interest rate payments relating to the first 6 years of the debt with respect to movements in interest rates only.

IAS 39.75 states a hedging relationship may not be designated for only a portion of the time period during which a hedging instrument remains outstanding. In practice, this prohibition is intended to preclude an entity splitting the fair value of a derivative (other than a fully proportionate share of the entire derivative) and only designating the fair value attributable to a portion of the time period during which is remains outstanding. For example, it would not be permissible to designate the portion of an interest rate swap relating to the next 5 years, when the instrument has a maturity in 7 years, as a cash flow hedge of variability in interest rate risk on a debt instrument for the next 5 years.

The concept of being able to hedge on a partial term basis is driven by the relationship between spot rates and forward rates for any given yield curve. The spot rate today, and the anticipated spot rates in the future periods are used to construct the yield curve today. The yield curve is a reflection of the anticipated rates in the future based on an assessment today.

By dissecting a longer dated current yield curve into 'mini-curves' it is possible to isolate the fair value movements of a longer dated instrument due to movements in the shorter part of the yield curve.

Example 2.2B

Partial term hedging fixed rate debt (2)

Facts as in **example 2.2A**.

At issuance of the bond the entity can obtain the yield curve for the stated maturity of the whole instrument, in this case, a ten year yield curve.

The ten year yield curve can be dissected into mini-yield curves.

- Spot interest rate today (t0) for interest due in a year (t1).
- Expected spot interest rate starting in a year's time (t1) due at the end of that year (t2) [one-year forward rate starting in a year].
- Expected spot interest rate starting at year 2 (t2) due at the end of that year (t3) [one-year forward rate starting in year 2].

If the entity wishes to fair value hedge for movements in the interest rate curve that matures in six years' time, it only has to consider movements in the first six years of the ten year yield curve in computing the change in the fair value of the hedged item. Because a six-year interest swap is priced of the six-year yield curve, in order to demonstrate hedge effectiveness, the entity discounts the six years of cash flows using the spot rates at the date hedge effectiveness is measured.

In one year's time, the entity will compare the change in the fair value of the derivative (with five years remaining) with the change in fair value of the hedged selected cash flows on the bond as well as the principal payment due at maturity to the extent affected by changes in the spot yield curve for the next five years, and so on.

US GAAP comparison: Although selected cash flows may be designated as the hedged item under US GAAP, the approach illustrated above to measuring hedge effectiveness for a partial term fair value hedge is not permitted under US GAAP (DIG Issue F2). Instead an appropriate derivative to hedge six years of interest cash flows of a ten-year bond would be a derivative that hedges the change in the fair value of a group of zero-coupon bonds that correspond in timing and amount to each individual interest payment being hedged.

An entity is permitted to partial term cash flow hedge a financial instrument as IAS 39 provides greater flexibility in designating portions when hedging financial instruments compared to hedging non-financial items. For hedges of non-financial items an entity is limited to hedging all foreign currency risk or all risks in their entirety (see **3.9** below). An entity that has a derivative with a maturity that is shorter than the timing of the cash flow exposure of the non-financial hedged item must designate all of the derivative (with the exception of the forward points in a forward contract or time value in an option) as hedging all foreign currency risk or all risks in their entirety up to the timing of the cash flow of the hedged item. As the hedged item is non-financial, the entity cannot designate a derivative for part of the time period until the forecast transaction occurs.

For example, a derivative that matures in 9 months' time could be perfectly effective as a hedge of a forecast sale or purchase of a non-financial item that is highly probable of occurring in 9 months' time. If the transaction is highly probable of occurring in 10 months' time, the same derivative could not be designated as a hedge of the 9 month portion of time until the transaction is expected to occur as a non-financial item cannot be partial-term hedged.

2.3 Financial instruments subject to prepayment

An instrument that contains an embedded prepayment option may still be designated as a hedged item. However, the effect of the prepayment option should be considered when designating the hedged item and assessing whether the hedge relationship will be highly effective.

If the entire asset or liability is designated as being hedged, for the hedging instrument to be highly effective it may have to include an equivalent option that coincides with the prepayment option in the hedged item. Inclusion of such an option in the hedging instrument ensures that fair value of the hedging instrument is as sensitive as the hedged item to the designated hedged risk.

Alternatively, the hedging relationship could be designated for just a portion of the term of the instrument prior to the prepayment option being capable of being exercised, provided the hedging instrument is designated for the entirety of its term. For example, if a debt instrument can be prepaid by the issuer after year five, the investor may wish to hedge the debt instrument for a period before the prepayment option can be exercised, i.e. for the first five years only.

An investor in a prepayable asset may decide to hedge cash flows in the period in which the prepayment option is exercisable (or in the period after the date on which the option can be exercised). In order to demonstrate that the hedging instrument is expected to be highly effective in the period, the cash flows must be highly probable. For example, cash flows in the period when the prepayment option is exercisable may qualify as highly probable if they result from a group or pool of similar assets (for example, mortgage loans) for which prepayments can be estimated with a high degree of accuracy or if the prepayment option is significantly out of the money. [IAS 39.IG.F.2.12]

Example 2.3A

Hedging prepayable loans for interest rate risk (1)

Entity A purchases a perpetual debt instrument which pays a market rate of interest of 5 per cent on par. The issuer of the debt instrument has an option to prepay the perpetual debt at an amount that is equal to the instrument's par amount after 5 years.

As the debt instrument is not quoted in an active market, Entity A classifies the instrument as a loan and receivable and determines that the embedded prepayment option is closely related to the host contract since the option's exercise price is approximately equal to the debt instrument's amortised cost on the exercise date of the option (i.e. par). Entity A enters into a non-prepayable swap with Bank B to pay fixed 5 per cent and to receive LIBOR for 20 years. The interest rate swap is designated as a partial term fair value hedge of the LIBOR portion of the perpetual debt instrument for 20 years. Apart from the issuer call prepayment option, all terms and conditions of the swap match those of the hedged item.

Entity A must compare the changes in fair value of the interest rate swap to the changes in the fair value of the perpetual debt instrument, where the latter includes both the change in fair value of the contractual cash flows and the change in fair value of the prepayment option. Hedge ineffectiveness will arise since the hedged item is prepayable, whilst the hedging instrument is not. Hedge ineffectiveness is likely to be so significant in that it will be difficult to demonstrate prospective hedge effectiveness. If 5 years after the issue, the perpetual debt has not been called by the issuer, Entity A may be able to designate the interest rate swap as a partial term hedge of the LIBOR portion of the perpetual debt for the next 15 years. It is not appropriate to exclude the prepayment risk out of the designation of the hedging relationship since prepayment risk and interest rate risk are closely interrelated.

Example 2.3B

Hedging prepayable loans for interest rate risk (2)

Facts as in **example 2.3A**, except that Entity A enters into a swap with Bank B whereby the swap can be terminated after 5 years at Entity A's option. The swap will be terminated at the swap's then fair value.

Entity A must compare the changes in fair value of the interest rate swap to the changes in the fair value of the perpetual debt instrument. In both cases the change in fair value includes both the change in fair value of the contractual cash flows as well as the change in fair value of the prepayment option which for the swap has negligible value as the swap terminates at fair value. Hedge ineffectiveness will still arise since the hedged item is prepayable at par whilst the hedging instrument can only be terminated at its then fair value, which will include the fair value of the expected future cash flows on the remaining 15 years of the swap. Thus, changes in the fair value of the hedged item will not be offset by changes in the fair value of the hedging instrument. The lack of offset may be significant enough to prevent hedge accounting.

Example 2.3C

Hedging prepayable loans for interest rate risk (3)

Facts as in **example 2.3A**, except that Entity A enters into a swap with Bank B whereby the swap can be terminated after 5 years at Entity A's option. The swap will be terminated at zero value.

Entity A must compare the changes in fair value of the interest rate swap to the changes in the fair value of the perpetual debt instrument. In both cases the change in fair value includes the change in fair value of the contractual cash flows as well as the change in fair value of the prepayment option. The hedging relationship is expected to be highly effective at hedging the interest rate risk of the debt for part of its term since both the hedging instrument and the hedged item are pre-payable at par.

2.4 Hedging foreign currency exposure in equity securities

Available-for-sale ('AFS') assets are held at fair value with changes in fair value recognised in other comprehensive income. A non-monetary AFS asset, such as a listed equity security in an unrelated party can be hedged, provided there is a clear and identifiable exposure to changes in foreign exchange rates. This would normally be the case where:

- the equity instrument is not traded on an exchange (or in another established marketplace) where trades are denominated in the same currency as the functional currency of the entity; and
- dividends received by the investor are not in the same currency as the functional currency of the investor.

If a share is traded in multiple currencies and one of those currencies is the functional currency of the reporting entity, hedge accounting for the foreign currency component of the share price is not permitted.

[IAS 39.IG.F.2.19]

Example 2.4A

Hedging foreign currency of a equity security: qualifying

Entity ABC is a UK-based manufacturing entity. Entity ABC owns shares in Entity X, which is listed on the New York Stock Exchange. The security is classified as available-for-sale. Dividends are paid in US dollars and the share price is quoted in US dollars.

As the shares in Entity X are not traded on a Sterling-denominated exchange and the dividends are not in the functional currency of Entity ABC, there is a clear and identifiable exposure to changes in foreign exchange rates, and the investment in shares can qualify as a hedged item.

Entity ABC could hedge its exposure to foreign currency risk by, for example, entering into a forward foreign currency contract to sell US dollars. Additionally, it could choose to designate only a portion of the shares, provided effectiveness can be measured. For example, if the fair value of the shares was US$1,000, it could designate the foreign currency risk associated with, say, US$800 of the fair value of the shares.

Entity ABC could designate the forward contract as a fair value hedge of the investment in Entity X, or as a cash flow hedge of the forecast sale of the shares if the timing of the sale is highly probable.

Example 2.4B

Hedging foreign currency of a equity security: non-qualifying

Group A is a group headed by a Japanese resident parent whose shares are publicly traded on the Tokyo Stock Exchange (TSE). Group A has a secondary listing on the New York Stock Exchange (NYSE) where the parent's shares are listed as American Deposit Receipts (ADRs). Trading on the NYSE is comparatively low compared to trading on the TSE as Group A has a small number of US investors. The prices on the NYSE closely approximate the prices of the shares on the TSE multiplied by the current foreign exchange rate between Japanese Yen and US dollars.

An investor is prohibited from hedging the foreign currency risk of an investment in a share denominated in multiple currencies where one of the currencies is the functional currency of the investor. Even where the trading volume is low compared to its primary listing as in the above scenario the Parent's shares remain dual listed. As the investor is a US dollar functional currency investor, and the shares are denominated in US dollars on a stock exchange, the investor cannot hedge their foreign currency risk in respect of the shares acquired from the TSE that are denominated in Japanese Yen. [IAS 39.IG.F.2.19]

2.5 Foreign currency risk of a forecast foreign currency debt issuance

An entity that has a highly probable forecast debt issuance may wish to cash flow hedge the interest rates and/or the foreign currency risk associated with the issuance. Hedging the interest rate risk is permitted and is described in **Example 2.2.4A** in **chapter 8** above and also in IAS 39.IG.F.5.5.

IAS 39 does not provide guidance on whether a hedge of the variability in functional currency equivalent proceeds attributable to foreign exchange risk that is to be received from a highly probable forecast issue of debt denominated in a currency other than the entity's functional currency can qualify for hedge accounting. It would not appear to be possible to designate the variability in the functional currency equivalent cash flows of a forecast debt issuance in a foreign currency as the foreign currency risk does not impact profit or loss. Foreign currency risk only arises from the date the debt is recognised in the statement of financial position as it is translated thereafter into the entity's functional currency under IAS 21. The quantum of this foreign currency risk that will impact profit or loss following the issue of the debt bears no relation to the quantum of foreign currency risk that arises prior to the date the debt is issued.

Example 2.5

Hedging foreign currency risk of forecast foreign currency debt issuance

On 1 January, Entity C, a US$ functional currency entity, has a highly probable forecast 10% fixed rate debt issuance of €100m in one month's time, and wishes to hedge the variability in the US$ equivalent proceeds that it will receive from the point in time when the hedging instrument is entered into and the point in time when the debt is issued. Entity C will enter into a foreign currency forward contract to sell €100m and to buy an equivalent amount of US$, based on the forward rate for delivery when the debt is expected to be issued. At the date Entity C enters into the foreign currency forward contract, it is expected that the combination of the net cash flows from the forward contract and the Euros to be received from issuing the debt should equal US$100m, all other things being equal.

Entity C cannot designate the changes in foreign currency risk between the date of entering into the derivative and the date the forecast debt is expected to be issued as a qualifying hedge exposure. This is because the foreign currency risk on the debt will only arise and impact profit or loss from the date it is recognised as a liability and is retranslated from Euro to Entity C's US$ functional currency during the period it remains outstanding. The gains/losses on the forward contract prior to the debt being issued bear no relationship to the foreign currency gains/losses that will be recognised after the debt is issued. Furthermore, the functional currency amount of interest in future periods is unaffected by movements in foreign currency prior to the debt being issued, as illustrated below.

Assume the foreign currency exchange rate at 1 January is US$1:€1 and at 1 February is US$1.5:€1. Using the 1 January exchange rate, the annual interest in US$ would be US$10m. At the rate of exchange prevailing on 1 February, the amount of Euro proceeds necessary to raise US$100m would be €67m. The related annual interest, assuming constant interest rates, would be €6.7m. However, translating € into US$, the annual interest is still US$10m (since €6.7m x 1.5 = US$10m). As demonstrated, the annual interest expense in functional currency terms is unaffected by a change in exchange rates between the date the foreign currency forward contract is entered into and the date the debt is issued.

Once the debt is issued it will be a recognised monetary item and will be retranslated from Euro to US$ on an ongoing basis in accordance with IAS 21 with any resulting foreign exchange gains or losses recognised in profit or loss. Once recognised, the debt could be designated in either a cash flow or fair value hedge of foreign currency risk.

2.6 Hedging capitalised borrowing costs

IAS 39 and IAS 23 *Borrowing Costs* do not provide guidance on whether an entity can cash flow or fair value hedge interest rate risk when the interest is partly or fully capitalised under IAS 23 as part of a qualifying asset. IAS 23 makes references in its basis of conclusions that US GAAP does provide specific guidance in this area for fair value hedges. IAS 23.BC21 states that 'EITF Issue No. 99–9 concludes that derivative gains and losses (arising from the effective portion of a derivative instrument that qualifies as a fair value hedge) are part of the capitalised interest cost. IAS 23 does not address such derivative gains and losses'.

The capitalisation of borrowing costs in and of itself should not prohibit any entity from applying hedge accounting for interest rate risk for debt that is used to fund a qualifying asset under IAS 23. IAS 39 requires that a hedge must result in the hedged risk impacting profit or loss, which will be the case when interest on debt is capitalised as the qualifying asset will impact profit or loss either through amortisation, impairment or sale. The example below sets out two scenarios where cash flow and fair value hedge accounting of interest rate risk is applied when the interest on the borrowing is capitalised under IAS 23.

Example 2.6

Hedging capitalised borrowing costs

Entity A borrows CU10m to finance the construction of a 'qualifying asset' in accordance with IAS 23. The related borrowing costs are eligible for capitalisation.

Scenario 1: Entity A borrows at fixed rates

Entity A enters into an interest rate swap (with the same notional and term as the debt) to receive fixed pay 3m LIBOR and designates this as a hedge of the fair value exposure to changes in interest rates (say 3m LIBOR) of its debt. Entity A will capitalise under IAS 23 the synthetic floating rate borrowing costs that have been achieved as a result of entering into the effective hedge accounting relationship.

(i) Entity A will determine the effectiveness of the fair value hedge and recognise any ineffectiveness in profit or loss. If the hedge is highly effective the debt will be fair value adjusted for changes in interest rates with the corresponding entry in profit or loss. The fair value adjustment will be amortised to profit or loss either immediately when the adjustment is made or no later than the debt ceases to fair value hedge adjusted.

(ii) The synthetic floating interest rate that is achieved as a result of the highly effective hedge is capitalised. This amount will include the actual fixed rate on the debt plus the effect of swapping this fixed rate into floating rates.

Scenario 2: Entity A borrows at floating rates

Entity A enters into an interest rate swap to receive 3m LIBOR pay fixed rates (same notional and term as debt) and designates the swap as hedging the variability in its debt due to changes in 3m LIBOR. Entity A intends to cash flow hedge the variability in interest rates on its borrowings even though the interest on the borrowings is capitalised under IAS 23.

Entity A can apply cash flow hedge accounting of the interest rate risk on its variable rate borrowings but the gain/loss on the derivative that is recognised in other comprehensive income is reclassified from equity to profit or loss when the interest component of the qualifying asset impacts profit or loss.

Entity A will apply the following steps in order:

(i) Capitalise the variable rate interest on the borrowing in accordance with IAS 23.

(ii) Determine the effectiveness of the cash flow hedge and recognise any ineffectiveness in profit or loss. Recognise the effective gain/loss on the derivative in other comprehensive income.

(iii) The amount recognised in other comprehensive income will be reclassified from equity to profit or loss when the hedged risk impacts profit or loss. The hedged interest that is capitalised as part of the qualifying asset will impact profit or loss when the qualifying asset is amortised, impaired, or is sold. The net effect in profit or loss from this reclassification is that the impact in profit or loss will be equivalent to the entity borrowing at fixed rates and capitalising fixed borrowing costs.

If an entity does not apply hedge accounting, and therefore the derivatives are classified as at fair value through profit or loss, it is not appropriate for the entity to capitalise part of the derivative as part of the borrowing costs under IAS 23. All gains/losses on non-hedging derivatives must be immediately recognised in profit or loss.

US GAAP comparison: EITF 99–9 provides specific guidance on the effect of qualifying hedging relationships on the capitalisation of interest on borrowings used to fund construction of a qualifying asset. When variable-rate interest on a specific borrowing is associated with an asset under construction and capitalised as a cost of that asset, the amounts in accumulated comprehensive income related to a cash flow hedge of the variability of that interest should be reclassified into earnings over the depreciable life of the constructed asset, since that depreciable life coincides with the amortisation period of the capitalised interest cost on the debt. FAS 133 prohibits the capitalisation of the gain or loss on the hedging instrument in a cash flow hedge.

2.7 Hedging non-financial items

As described in **3.7** in **chapter 8** a non-financial asset or liability may qualify as a hedged item in limited circumstances. More complex aspects of hedging non-financial items are described below.

2.7.1 Hedging foreign currency risk of non-financial asset held at cost

If an entity is hedging foreign currency risk, this risk must be separately measurable. A non-financial asset that was purchased in a foreign currency cannot be hedged for foreign currency risk because foreign currency risk is not evident in that non-financial item. However, the foreign currency risk associated with a forecasted sale of that non-financial item could qualify as a hedged item.

It is important to distinguish between hedging foreign currency risk of a non-financial item and hedging foreign currency risk in relation to the forecast sale or purchase of that non-financial item.

Example 2.7.1 below illustrates that it is not possible to hedge the foreign currency risk of a non-financial item as the foreign currency risk is not evident and not separately measurable. However, if an entity is purchasing or selling a non-financial item in a foreign currency, it is a fixed amount of foreign currency that will be needed to buy or will be received from selling that non-financial item, and a qualifying foreign currency exposure therefore exists.

Example 2.7.1

Hedging a non-financial item: held at cost

Entity A, a Sterling functional currency entity acquires some plant and machinery in US$ from Entity B, an unrelated third party US$ functional currency entity. In the financial statements of Entity A the plant and machinery will be translated at the US$:£ exchange rate at the date of the purchase (i.e. at historic rate).

If Entity A used US$ borrowing to finance the purchase of the plant and machinery, these US$ borrowings cannot be used as a hedging instrument in a fair value hedge of the foreign currency risk of the plant and machinery because the hedged item does not contain any separately measurable foreign currency risk.

If Entity A was to demonstrate that the disposal of the plant and machinery in US$ was highly probable, then the US$ denominated debt could be used as a hedging instrument against the forecast sale in US$ provided that the timing of the future cash flows on the debt coincided with the timing of the future cash flow on the disposal.

Non-derivatives can be used as hedging instruments only when hedging foreign currency risk. This is discussed further in **4.1** in **chapter 8**.

2.7.2 *Hedging all risks except foreign currency*

IAS 39 is clear that hedges of a non-financial instrument are possible for all risks or just foreign currency risk. Therefore, by deduction, it is possible to hedge all risks except foreign currency risk, assuming all other hedge accounting criteria are met. IAS 39.IG.E.3.4 on the interaction between IAS 39 and IAS 21 supports this assertion. For financial instruments fair value is firstly determined in the currency in which the contract is denominated, and translation of the contract into the functional currency of the entity is secondary. If it can be clearly demonstrated that the exposure to fair value of the non-financial instrument excluding foreign currency risk can be identified and measured, and hedged for all risks except foreign currency risk, such exposure is a permissible hedging designation.

Example 2.7.2

Hedging a non-financial item: all risks except foreign currency

Entity O has an anticipated purchase of 1,000 barrels of oil in 6 months that is highly probable of occurring. The purchase price will be the market price at the date of purchase and will be priced in US$. Entity O's functional currency is the Australian dollar.

Entity O purchases oil futures on 500 barrels of oil to fix the price at US$60 for those 500 barrels. The duration (and other terms) of the forecast transaction and the futures contracts match so that Entity O believes the hedge will be highly effective over its term.

Entity O has two risk exposures: foreign currency risk and fair value risk.

The oil futures hedge price risk only. Entity O does not co-terminously hedge its exposure to the US$ on the purchase contract.

The oil futures can be designated as a hedge of the forecast purchase of oil (provided the other hedge accounting criteria are satisfied). A forward purchase of oil (a non-financial asset) does not have inherent foreign exchange risk. The foreign exchange risk arises from the fact that the reporting entity's functional currency is not the US$, not from the market price risk inherent in a forward purchase of oil.

2.8 Designation of groups of items

It is possible to group together similar assets or similar liabilities and hedge them as a group, but only if the individual items within the group share the same risk exposure that is designated as being hedged. The change in fair value attributable to the hedged risk of each item in the group must be approximately proportional to the change in fair value attributable to the hedged risk of the entire group. [IAS 39.83]

IAS 39 does not provide specific guidance as to what is approximately proportional. It is reasonable to assume that while it is not expected that the items within a portfolio have exactly the same sensitivity to the hedged risk, the items must show a high degree of similarity for a given movement in the hedged risk.

US GAAP comparison: FAS 133.21(a) provides more guidance on what it considers to be 'generally proportionate' when comparing the change in fair value attributable to the hedged risk for each individual item in a hedged portfolio and the overall change in fair value of the aggregate portfolio attributable to the hedged risk. If the change in fair value of a hedged portfolio attributable to the hedged risk was 10 per cent during a reporting period, the change in the fair values attributable to the hedged risk for each item constituting the portfolio should be expected to be within a fairly narrow range, such as 9 per cent to 11 per cent. In contrast, an expectation that the change in fair value attributable to the hedged risk for individual items in the portfolio would range from 7 per cent to 13 per cent would be inconsistent with this provision.

Investments in debt instruments that have different credit ratings and different maturities can be combined and hedged as a portfolio. In order to comply with the requirement that all items in the portfolio share the same risk exposure for which they are designated and that changes in their fair values are expected to be approximately proportional to the overall change in the fair value attributable to the hedged risk of the group, only portions of risks related to these instruments can be designated as being hedged and only for a portion of their terms that is common to all instruments in the portfolio. For example, the risk-free interest rate component that is shared by these instruments can qualify as being hedged. Alternatively, if an entity wanted to designate the entire risk of each instrument in the portfolio as being hedged, it would have to segregate the loans into portfolios in which each item in the portfolio is similar. This can be done by classifying loans according to their predominant risk characteristics, including:

- date of origination;
- loan type;
- loan size;
- geographical location;

- nature and location of collateral;
- interest rate type (fixed or variable) and the coupon interest rate (if fixed) or the timing of reset dates (if variable);
- scheduled maturity, prepayment history of the loans; and
- expected prepayment performance in varying interest rate scenarios.

Example 2.8

Hedging a group of similar items

On 1 April 20X4, Bank S has a CU100 million portfolio of corporate bonds that have a range of coupons from 7.5 per cent to 9.0 per cent and a maturity range of 10–11 years. Bank S would like to hedge the interest rate exposure on the CU100 million bond portfolio. It performs a sensitivity analysis and determines that the fair value exposure with respect to movement in interest rate risk only of all of the items individually respond within a range of 95 to 105 per cent of the overall change in price of the portfolio as a whole.

Bank S can designate an interest rate swap as a hedge of interest rate risk of the portfolio as a whole since all items within the portfolio share the same risk exposure, and the change in value of the items within the portfolio is expected to be approximately proportional to the change in value of the portfolio as a whole.

It is unlikely that a pool of shares could be grouped together and hedged as a portfolio. For example, it would not be possible to hedge a portfolio of shares that equate to the FTSE-100 index with a FTSE-100 total return swap. Although on an aggregated basis the hedge may be highly effective, it is clear that the individual equity securities that make up the portfolio do not share the exposure to risk, in that the fair value of each individual equity share does not move proportionally to the changes in value of the overall FTSE-100 index. [IAS 39.IG.F.2.20]

3 Hedging instruments

The basic requirements governing the qualification of hedging instruments are discussed in detail in section 4 in chapter 8. This section provides additional guidance beyond the basic requirements incorporating less common, more complex scenarios.

Section 3.1 Hedging more than one risk

Section 3.2 Hedging with more than one derivative

Section 3.3 Written options and combinations of options

Section 3.4 Purchased options

3.1 Hedging more than one risk

A hedging instrument is often designated as hedging one risk only.

However, a hedging instrument can be designated as hedging more than one risk provided that:
[IAS 39.76]

(i) the risks being hedged can be clearly identified;

(ii) the effectiveness of the hedge can be demonstrated; and

(iii) it is possible to ensure that there is specific designation of the hedging instrument and different risk positions.

IAS 39 allows the use of one instrument to hedge more than one risk. Cross currency interest rate swaps are commonly used to swap foreign currency variable rate debt back into functional currency fixed rate debt, or to swap foreign currency fixed into functional currency variable. See **4.4.1** in **chapter 8** for further guidance.

3.1.1 Hedging multiple hedged items

IAS 39 provides limited guidance on how to assess hedge effectiveness when an entity uses a single hedging instrument to hedge multiple hedged items. There are many instances where an entity could use a single derivative financial instrument to hedge one risk (say foreign currency risk) or multiple risks (say foreign currency risk and interest rate risk) where those risks reside in more than one hedged item.

IAS 39.IG.F.1.13 provides an example of an entity hedging two hedged items for the same risk. The example describes a Japanese Yen functional currency entity that has a 5-year floating rate US$ liability and a 10-year fixed rate £-denominated note receivable and chooses to hedge both items with a single foreign currency forward contract where it will receive US$

and pay £ in 5 years. As the principal amounts of the asset and liability when converted into Japanese Yen are the same, the entity designates the dual foreign currency forward contract as hedging foreign currency risk for both items. Even though foreign currency risk is defined by reference to the entity's functional currency, and the foreign currency forward contract does not have a cash flow in the functional currency, i.e. Japanese Yen, the foreign currency forward contract may still be designated as hedging *both* foreign currencies as the exposure to both currencies has been eliminated by the forward. Put another way, if the entity entered into a receive US$ pay Japanese Yen forward, and a receive Japanese Yen pay £ forward, each forward could have been designated separately as hedging the foreign currency risk of the liability and asset respectively, even the fair value of the two Japanese Yen legs would offset each other perfectly. In a single forward to receive US$ pay £, the receive Japanese Yen leg and the pay Japanese Yen leg do not exist but this does not create hedge ineffectiveness as the fair value of both legs offsets to zero. However, in assessing and measuring hedge effectiveness with a single forward contract the entity will need to impute the two notional Japanese Yen legs into the hedge designation in order to determine the hedge effectiveness of the two hedges of foreign currency risk. Imputing the two notional cash flows for assessing hedge effectiveness is permitted as doing so does not create any additional cash flows as both notional cash flows offset each other perfectly.

In July 2007 the IFRIC issued a rejection notice on hedging multiple risks with a single derivative financial instrument. The IFRIC recognised that IAS 39's interpretative guidance does result in an entity needing to impute a notional leg as a means of splitting the fair value of the derivative into multiple components in order to assess hedge effectiveness. IFRIC considered that this was acceptable in assessing hedge effectiveness as this conclusion did not conflict with IAS 39.IG.C.1 which prohibits an entity from recognising embedded derivatives that result in the *recognition* [emphasis added in the July 2007 IFRIC Update] of cash flows that do not contractually exist. The IFRIC's rejection notice highlights that should any entity need to notionally split a derivative for assessing hedge effectiveness when that derivative is hedging multiple risks then the process of splitting should not result in any new cash flows and any new risks arising which were not evident in the contractual terms of the derivative.

Example 3.1.1A

Hedging a net investment in a foreign operation and interest rate risk of issued debt

Parent P, a € functional currency entity, has issued a €100m denominated fixed rate debt. Parent P consolidates Subsidiary S, a US$ functional currency foreign operation with opening net assets of US$300m. Parent P's objective is to hedge (i) the foreign currency risk of part of its foreign operation (being the € equivalent of US$150m net assets) and (ii) the fair value due to changes in interest rates on its issued debt (being interest rate risk on €100m). In order to minimise transaction costs the entity enters into a single derivative to Receive € fixed on €100m, Pay US$ 3m-US$ LIBOR on US$150m with the fair value of the cross-currency interest rate swap equal to zero at the transaction date, i.e. the derivative is on-market.

Parent P designates in the consolidated financial statements the cross-currency interest rate swap as a hedge of the foreign currency risk of Subsidiary S's net assets equal to US$150m and the fair value interest rate risk on €100m of its €-denominated debt. In order to assess hedge effectiveness for net investment hedge and fair value hedge Parent P notionally splits the derivative into the following: (i) Receive fixed €100m, Pay 3m-EURIBOR on €100m (notional derivative 1), and (ii) Receive 3m-EURIBOR on €100m, Pay 3m-US$ LIBOR US$150m (notional derivative 2). Parent P fair values the two notional derivatives at inception and both have a fair value of zero so the sum of the fair values equals the fair value of the actual contractual derivative. Each period the notional derivatives are fair valued in order to assess and measure hedge effectiveness and to ensure that the sum of these fair values equals the fair value of the actual contractual derivative entered into.

Example 3.1.1B

Hedging cash flow variability of both an asset and liability

Entity B, a Sterling functional currency entity, has issued 3m-LIBOR £200m denominated debt and has an investment in an inflation-linked bond that receives 3% + UK CPI on a notional of £200m (the inflation linkage is considered a closely related embedded derivative). The asset and liability have the same 5 year maturity.

Entity B's objective is to hedge the cash flow variability on both its asset and its liability. In order to minimise transaction costs the entity enters into 5-year Receive 3m-LIBOR £200m Pay 3% + UK CPI £200m and designates this basis swap as a hedge of the cash flow variability of both its assets and its liability. In order to assess hedge effectiveness Entity B notionally splits the derivative into the following: (i) 5-year Receive 3m LIBOR £200m, Pay 6% £200m (notional derivative 1), and (ii) Receive 6% £200m, Pay 3% + UK CPI £200m (notional derivative 2). Entity B fair values the two notional derivatives at inception and both have a fair value of zero so the sum of the fair values equals the fair value of the actual contractual derivative. Each period the notional derivatives are fair valued in order to assess and measure hedge effectiveness and to ensure that the sum of these fair values equals the fair value of the actual contractual derivative entered into.

Example 3.1.1C

Hedging cash flow variability of both a foreign currency sale and purchase

Entity C, a Euro functional currency entity, has forecast sales in US dollars and forecast purchases in Japanese Yen. Entity C enters into a series of foreign currency forward contracts under which it receives a fixed amount of Japanese Yen and pays a fixed amount of US dollars every month. The fair value of each forward contract is zero at inception as the terms are on-market at that date. Entity C's objective is to hedge the variability in functional currency cash flows of its US dollar sales and Japanese Yen purchases.

In order to assess hedge effectiveness Entity C notionally splits the derivative into the following: (i) receive fixed amount of Japanese Yen, pay fixed amount of Euro, and (ii) receive fixed amount of Euro, pay a fixed amount of US dollars. Entity C fair values the two notional derivatives at inception and both have a fair value of zero so the sum of the fair values equals the fair value of the actual contractual derivative. Each period the notional derivatives are fair valued in order to assess and measure hedge effectiveness and to ensure that the sum of these fair values equals the fair value of the actual contractual derivative entered into.

If the hedge is highly effective the effective gains/losses on the series of forward contracts will initially be recognised in other comprehensive income and will be reclassified to profit or loss when the sales and purchases impact profit or loss. It should be noted that the timing of the impact to profit or loss of the two hedged items may differ. This is because purchases would normally result in recognition of inventory and the sale of the inventory acquired in Japanese Yen could occur in a period after the sales in US dollars. The entity must allocate the fair value gains/losses recognised in equity to the two individual hedge relationships so it can determine the appropriate amount to be reclassified to profit or loss when the purchase or sale impacts profit or loss.

Judgement is required in determining what is an appropriate split when allocating the fair value of derivatives to multiple hedged items for assessing hedge effectiveness. It would not be appropriate to create multiple notional derivatives which introduce notional legs over risks which did not exist in the contractual derivative or are not specific to the entity entering into the transaction, for example the entity's functional currency. Taking **example 3.1.1A** above, the notional legs introduced are in the functional currency of the entity, being Euro, which is a reference point that is specific to the entity; the frequency of reset of EURIBOR on the notional leg is equal to the frequency of reset on the US$-LIBOR leg of the actual derivative. Taking **example 3.1.1B** above, the notional legs introduced are the Sterling fixed rate for a 5-year interest rate swap priced off the

Sterling 5-year LIBOR curve. In both examples it would be unacceptable to impute notional legs which although could offset each other would introduce an unrelated risk, say equity prices or an unrelated currency.

If a single hedging instrument is designated as a hedge of more than one risk the hedge accounting criteria must be satisfied in respect of all the designated hedged risks. If the criteria are not met in respect of one of the risks being hedged, no hedge accounting treatment is allowed for the period. If one designation fails to meet the effectiveness test or no longer exists, continuing hedge accounting would result in split accounting for the hedging instrument, treating one part as a hedge and the other as a trading instrument which is not permitted. (see **4.2** in **chapter 8**)

3.2 Hedging with more than one derivative

Two or more offsetting derivatives, or proportions thereof, can be jointly designated as a hedging instrument if none of them are a written or net written option. [IAS 39.77] Further, when hedging foreign currency risk, two or more non-derivatives (or proportions) or a combination of non-derivatives and derivatives can be viewed in combination. Common situations where two or more offsetting derivatives are designated in combination as a hedging instrument are:

- where an entity issues fixed-rate debt, swaps the entirety of the debt instrument to floating, and then re-fixes some of the instrument's cash flows;
- where an entity uses a combination of long and short foreign currency forwards to hedge its net investments in a foreign operation (e.g. when it manages foreign currency risk on the net assets of the foreign operation where the value of those net assets changes on a frequent basis); and
- where an entity uses a combination of a basis swap and a floating to fixed interest rate swap in the instance where there is not enough liquidity directly to enter into a floating to fixed interest rate swap that has a floating leg that matches the specific risk of the hedged item.

Example 3.2A

Hedging with multiple derivatives (1)

Entity A has a forecast purchase of copper. To hedge the price risk associated with the forecast purchase it enters into a futures contract to buy copper.

However, the grade of copper in the futures contract is lower than that required by the entity. It therefore also enters into a basis swap which swaps between the different grades of copper between the futures contracts and the forecast purchase. Subject to the other hedge accounting criteria being satisfied, Entity A may jointly designate the futures and the basis swap as hedging its forecast purchase of copper.

Where a combination of derivatives (or non-derivative instruments with respect to hedges of foreign currency risk only) is used as a hedging instrument, the hedge effectiveness of this relationship is based on the combination as a whole.

Example 3.2B

Hedging with multiple derivatives (2)

Entity X issues fixed-rate 10-year debt. At the same time, it enters into a receive-fixed, pay-floating interest rate swap whose terms exactly match those of the debt.

The swap was entered into as Entity X did not want to be exposed to changes in interest rates over the 10-year period of the debt. However, it would like to fix its cash flows for the next 12 months, so enters into a 1-year receive-floating, pay-fixed interest rate swap. Entity X has now re-fixed its cash flows for the first year of the debt.

Subject to the other hedge accounting criteria being satisfied, Entity X may designate both swaps as a partial term fair value hedge of interest rate risk for years 2 to 10 (even though the second swap partially offsets the effects of the first swap). Partial term hedging is discussed further in **2.2** above.

Example 3.2C

Hedging with derivatives and non-derivatives

Entity A, a UK entity, has a US subsidiary, Entity Z. Entity A hedges its net investment in Entity Z in its consolidated financial statements using forward foreign currency contracts and loans. It manages the net asset position quarterly, and as the net asset position changes, it enters into further forwards to sell US$ and buy £ that cover the increased exposure (if the US$ net asset position increases), or if the exposure decreases (if the US$ net asset position falls) the entity enters into forward contracts to sell £ and buy US$. In the latter case any sold US$ forwards will partially offset the purchased US$ forwards.

The loans and forwards may be viewed in combination and jointly designated as a hedge of the spot foreign currency risk of the net investment in Entity Z, even though some of the forward positions may offset each other. This is discussed further in **3.2.1** below.

Example 3.2D

Hedging with multiple derivatives (3)

Entity C is a Euro functional currency entity. Entity C issues Mexican Peso floating rate debt. Entity C has a policy of swapping all floating rate debt into fixed and into its functional currency. Because of limited liquidity for Peso/Euro swaps, Entity C does not enter into a Receive Mexico Peso floating, Pay Euro fixed cross currency interest rate swap. Instead, Entity C enters into a Receive Mexico Peso floating, Pay US Dollar floating cross currency swap, and a Receive US Dollar floating, Pay Euro fixed cross currency interest rate swap, and designates these two swaps in combination as a cash flow hedge of both interest rates and foreign currency of its Mexican Peso floating debt.

Where an entity enters into two derivative transactions at the same time and in contemplation of each other with the same counterparty, so that the terms of the second derivative fully offset the terms of the first one, the two derivatives are viewed as one unit and cannot be used in separate hedge designations. [IAS 39.IG.B.6] This is commonly referred to as 'round-tripping'. However, where there is a substantive business purpose for structuring transactions separately, then the two derivatives are not viewed as one unit. Judgement is applied to determine whether there is a substantive business purpose. Achieving hedge accounting treatment with respect to one of the two derivative transactions is not by itself considered a substantive business purpose. [IAS 39.IG.F.1.14]

Example 3.2E

Roundtripping

[Extract from IAS 39.IG.F.1.14]

Some entities have a policy that requires a centralised dealer or treasury subsidiary to enter into third-party derivative contracts on behalf of other subsidiaries within the organisation to hedge the subsidiaries' interest rate risk exposures. The dealer or treasury subsidiary also enters into internal derivative transactions with those subsidiaries in order to track those hedges operationally within the organisation. Because the dealer or treasury subsidiary also enters into derivative contracts as part of its trading operations, or because it may wish to rebalance the risk of its overall portfolio, it may enter into a derivative contract with the same third party during the same business day that has substantially the same terms as a contract entered into as a hedging instrument on behalf of another subsidiary. In this case, there is a valid business purpose for entering into each contract.

3.2.1 *Hedging with a combination of a derivative and a non-derivative*

If an entity is hedging foreign currency risk it may designate a non-derivative as a hedging instrument. An entity can also designate a combination of derivatives or a combination of a derivative and a non-derivative in a hedge of foreign currency risk. If a combination of a derivative and a non-derivative is jointly designated as a hedge of foreign currency risk the derivative cannot be a written or a net written option. [IAS 39.77]

Example 3.2.1

Hedging with derivatives and non-derivatives

Parent A, a Sterling functional currency entity, has an investment in a Yen functional currency foreign operation. Parent A has US$100 million floating issued debt. Parent A also has a cross-currency swap to receive US$ floating over a notional of US$100 million, pay Yen floating over a fixed notional of Yen (equivalent to US$100 million on the trade date of the swap). Both the US$ debt and the cross-currency swap have the same maturity. The Yen notional on the swap is less than the net assets of the Yen foreign operation.

Group A can designate the US$ denominated debt and US$/Yen cross-currency swap jointly as a hedging instrument in hedging the £/Yen foreign currency risk of its net investment in its Yen foreign operation.

Even though the US$ debt and the US$/Yen swap have a shared risk, being US$, that offsets when the two instruments are used in combination, the non-derivative and the derivative may be designated in combination as a hedging instrument of foreign currency risk, being £/Yen foreign currency risk, as the swap is not a written or net written option. It is assumed all other hedge accounting criteria are met.

3.3 Written options and combinations of options

3.3.1 *Written options*

The Standard does not allow a written option to be designated as a hedging instrument unless it is designated as an offset to a purchased option (including one that is embedded in another financial instrument). The written option is not effective in reducing the profit or loss exposure of a hedged item since the potential loss on an option that an entity writes could be significantly greater than the potential gain in value of a related hedged item. [IAS 39.AG94]

Example 3.3.1A

Hedging an available-for-sale asset with a written put

Entity A owns shares in Entity XYZ, an unrelated entity. It classifies these shares as available-for-sale. Entity A purchased the shares when the share price was CU10. The share price is currently CU15. Entity A writes an option over its shares in XYZ, allowing the purchaser of the option to acquire the shares for CU17, and for this Entity A receives a premium of CU0.50.

A may not designate the option as a hedge of its shares in XYZ because it is a written option.

All hedging instruments must be assessed to consider whether they contain a written option as this will often disqualify their designation as hedging instruments.

Example 3.3.1B

Embedded written options in interest rate swaps

Entity A issues twenty-year fixed rate debt. To hedge its fair value exposure to interest rate risk, it enters into a receive fixed, pay floating interest rate swap, such that all the terms of the swap match the debt. Owing to the long-term nature of the swap, the counterparty to the swap, the Bank, inserts a break clause into the swap giving the Bank the option to terminate the swap after ten years, so that on termination no cash will be exchanged. No cash is exchanged at the start of the transaction.

Entity A has effectively written an option to the bank allowing it to terminate the swap after ten years. While no cash was exchanged up-front, Entity A will have been recompensed for writing this option by receiving a favourable rate on one of the legs of the swap.

The swap cannot be designated as a hedge of the issued debt, as it contains a written option. The written option cannot be split out of the swap contract (leaving a vanilla twenty year interest swap) since a derivative must be designated as a hedging instrument in its entirety (with only two exceptions as described in **4.2** in **chapter 8**).

If the terms of the break-clause resulted in termination of the swap at fair value at the time of termination, and fair value excluded any additional compensation paid/receivable to either party in excess of the interest rate swap, the swap would still contain a written option, but the value of the option would be zero. The legs of the swap would be no different from a swap without a break clause. In this case the swap could be used as a hedging instrument.

IAS 39.AG94 states that a written option can only be used as a hedging instrument where it is designated as an offset to a purchased option. The purchased option can be either a stand-alone derivative, or one embedded in another contract. Thus, a written option could be designated as hedging a callable liability where the issuer has the right to call the debt back early.

3.3.2 *Net written options*

If two options, one written and one purchased, are structured as a single instrument (for example as a collar), this instrument must be assessed to see whether overall it is a net written option.

Even where the critical terms and conditions of the written option component and the purchased option component are largely the same (e.g. underlying variable(s), currency denomination and maturity date are the same) a combination of written and purchased options is deemed to be net written (and therefore not allowed to be designated as a hedging instrument) if:

(i) a net premium is received, either at inception or over the life of the combination of options; or

(ii) the notional on the written option exceeds that on the purchased option. [IAS 39.IG.F.1.3]

Example 3.3.2

Hedging with a collar

Entity A issues CU100 million variable rate debt. To hedge against interest rate increases, it purchases an interest rate collar at the date of issuance of the debt that hedges interest rates above 8 per cent and below 4 per cent. Current fixed interest rates for the same term as the debt are 6 per cent. The collar costs CU0.5 million as forward rates indicate that interest rates are expected to rise over the term of the debt and therefore there is a greater likelihood that the purchased cap will be in the money, when compared to the written floor. The purchased cap at 8 per cent and written floor at 4 per cent included in the collar have the same notional of CU100 million.

Entity A may designate the collar as a cash flow hedge of the variable rate debt, as there is no net premium received (there is a net premium payable of CU0.5 million) and the notional on the floor does not exceed that on the cap.

If there was a premium received on the collar, it could not have been designated as a hedging instrument. Equally, if the notional on the floor was greater than CU100 million, the collar could not have been designated as a hedging instrument.

It is not permissible to split a single instrument that consists of a number of options, for example an interest rate collar, and designate just the purchased option component as a hedging instrument. IAS 39.74 specifies that a derivative is designated as a hedging instrument in its entirety except when splitting the time value and intrinsic value of an option and splitting the interest element and spot price on a forward. [IAS 39.IG.F.1.8]

As is the case for all hedging instruments, in order for a combination of interest rate options structured as a single instrument to qualify as a hedging instrument, the combination of options must be expected to be highly effective in achieving offsetting changes in fair value or cash flows attributable to the hedged risk.

US GAAP comparison: US GAAP has further guidance on what tests are performed for the purposes of determining whether a written option, or a net written option may be designated as a hedging instrument. One of the tests detailed in US GAAP but not detailed in IFRS is a comparison of the potential gains and losses on the sum of the derivative and hedged item in various market scenarios. This test is performed to see whether the sum of the derivative and the hedged item provides at least as much potential for gains as a result of favourable change in the fair value of the combined instruments as exposure to losses from an unfavourable change in their combined fair value. If in all favourable market scenarios the gain is at least as much as the loss that would be incurred from unfavourable market scenarios of the same percentage then the derivative is not a written option that is precluded from designation as a hedging instrument.

3.3.3 *Combination of derivatives that includes a written option*

Only a combination of separate contractual derivatives that does not include a written or a net written option can be designated as a single qualifying hedging instrument. [IAS 39.77]

When an entity enters into purchased and sold options at the same time it is necessary to consider by analogy to the following indicators contained in IAS 39.IG.B.6, whether the two options are separate instruments or the combination of the two options is in substance a single arrangement. Factors that indicate that the instrument is a single arrangement are:

- they are entered into at the same time and in contemplation of one another;
- they have the same counterparty;
- they relate to the same risk; and

- there is no apparent economic need or substantive business purpose for structuring the transactions separately that could not also have been accomplished in a single transaction.

If the combination of options is not considered to be one arrangement, and one of the instruments is a written option or net written option, the combination of options cannot be designated as a hedging instrument.

However, a combination of options structured as a single instrument (that may economically be equivalent to options in a combination of contractually separate instruments) qualifies for designation as a hedging instrument as long as the single instrument is not a net written option as described in **3.3.1** above. This is the case for a zero cost collar that combines a purchased option and a written option and passes the test of not being a net written option overall.

3.4 Purchased options

When designating an option in a cash flow hedge accounting relationship it is common to designate just the intrinsic value of the option as permitted by IAS 39.74(a) and not designate the time value of the option. This approach ensures that when the option is 'in-the-money' the option is fully effective at hedging the variability in cash flows of the hedged item. As the time value of the option is not designated as part of the hedge relationship the gains/losses relating to time value are immediately recognised in profit or loss. These gains/losses are not considered hedge ineffectiveness as time value did not form part of the hedge accounting relationship. Had an entity chosen instead to designate the entirety of the option, the fair value gains/losses that result from changes in time value would cause hedge ineffectiveness, perhaps to such a great degree that the entity could not claim that the hedge is expected to be highly effective.

In July 2008 the IASB issued an amendment to IAS 39 titled *Eligible Hedged Items*. The amendment clarified that a purchased (or net purchased) option can be designated as a hedging instrument in a hedge of a financial or non-financial item. An entity may designate an option as a hedge of changes in the cash flows or fair value of a hedged item above or below a specified price or other variable (a one-sided risk). The amendments make it clear that the intrinsic value, not the time value, of an option reflects a one-sided risk and therefore an option designated in its entirety cannot be perfectly effective. The time value of a purchased option is not a component of the forecast transaction that impacts profit or loss. Therefore, if an entity designates an option in its entirety as a hedge of a one-sided risk arising from a forecast transaction hedge ineffectiveness will arise. Alternatively, an entity may choose to exclude time value as permitted by the Standard in order to improve hedge effectiveness. As a result of this designation, changes in the time value of the option will be recognised immediately in profit or loss. The amendments are effective retrospectively for annual periods beginning on or after 1 July 2009 with early adoption permitted.

US GAAP comparison: US GAAP has greater flexibility as to how hedge effectiveness is determined when using purchased options in a cash flow hedge relationship. This applies only to European-style options that can be exercised only on a single date. US guidance allows an entity to determine hedge effectiveness by focusing on the terminal value of the option, i.e. the amount of the option at maturity when all time value has been eroded (DIG Issue G20). If such an approach is used, the hedge relationship will be perfectly effective if the critical terms of the hedging instrument completely match the forecast transaction, the strike price of the option matches the exposure being hedged, and the cash flow from the option at its maturity date completely offsets the change in the hedged transaction's cash flows for the risk being hedged. The result of applying this technique is that because the relationship is deemed to be perfectly effective all derivative gains/losses will initially be recognised in other comprehensive income. Amounts recognised in other comprehensive income are reclassified into income as the hedged item affects profit or loss.

If a purchased option or a net purchased option is in-the-money at the date of designation and the entity excludes time value from the hedge relationship a question arises as to whether the intrinsic value that exists at the date of designation is itself effective at hedging future cash flows in a cash flow hedge. As the objective of a cash flow hedge is to hedge against future changes in cash flow variability and any intrinsic value that exists at the date of designation does not itself hedge this future variability then in determining hedge effectiveness in this case an entity should compare the actual in-the-money option with an at-the-money option in determining the future change in intrinsic value that should be recognised in other comprehensive income. Only future changes in intrinsic value that result in the at-the-money option being in the money in future periods are deemed effective and therefore can be recognised in other comprehensive income. This is illustrated in the example in **3.12** in **chapter 10**.

3.5 Dynamic hedging strategies

IAS 39.74 states that 'a dynamic hedging strategy that assesses both the intrinsic value and time value of an option contract can qualify for hedge accounting', i.e. the Standard permits an entity to apply hedge accounting for a 'delta-neutral' or other dynamic hedging strategy under which the quantity of the hedging instrument is constantly adjusted in order to maintain a desired hedge ratio. For example, an entity may wish to achieve a delta-neutral position insensitive to changes in the fair value of the hedged item.

Example 3.5

Delta-neutral hedging

An entity hedges the fair value of an equity security by using a combination of purchased options that aims to achieve a delta-neutral position. As the delta of the options changes, the number of options required will change to ensure the hedge is considered to be highly effective for movements in the fair value of the equity securities. This strategy can qualify for hedge accounting.

To qualify for hedge accounting, all the usual conditions must be met. These will include documenting how effectiveness will be assessed and measured, and demonstrating an ability to track properly all terminations and re-designations of the hedging instrument. Also, the entity must be able to demonstrate an expectation that the hedge will be highly effective for any specified short period of time during which the hedge is not expected to be adjusted. [IAS 39.IG.F.1.9]

3.6 'All-in-one' hedges

A derivative instrument within the scope of IAS 39 that will be settled by physical delivery of an underlying asset at a fixed price can be designated as the hedging instrument in a cash flow hedge of that gross settlement. Without the derivative there would be an exposure to variability in the purchase or sale price. The derivative eliminates this exposure, i.e. it acts as a hedging instrument. [IAS 39.IG.F.2.5] This hedge strategy is suitable when the underlying hedged item, when it is recognised, will not subsequently be measured at fair value.

The rationale for allowing hedge accounting for 'all-in-one' hedges is that an entity should not be disadvantaged from not achieving hedge accounting if a transaction is structured as a single instrument or as a combination of two transactions. Consider the following example:

Entity A normally sells products at variable prices. Entity A could concurrently enter into derivative transactions to fix the price of its forecast sales. Derivative instruments would be recognised at fair value with gains or losses recorded in profit or loss, unless hedge accounting is applied. Assuming the sales are highly probable and cash flow hedge accounting is applied, Entity A would recognise the gains and losses on its hedging instruments in other comprehensive income and reclassify them from equity to profit or loss when the sales occur.

Entity A now decides that it is no longer going to sell its products at variable prices and swap them back into fixed prices via derivatives, but instead is going to fix the sales price today directly with the customer. If the fixed price contract with the customer fell within the scope of IAS 39 it will be recognised at fair value with gains and losses recognised in profit or loss. By applying an all-in-one hedge accounting strategy, Entity A can obtain the same accounting treatment (i.e. recognise gains and losses on the derivative in other comprehensive income until the sale occurs under cash flow hedging), as had been the case in the former scenario where hedge accounting was applied to the derivative and the forecast sale separately.

Example 3.6A

All-in-one hedge of a non-financial item

An entity enters into a fixed price contract to sell a commodity and that contract is accounted for as a derivative under IAS 39. (This may be because the entity has a practice of settling similar contracts net in cash or taking delivery of the underlying and selling it within a short period after delivery for the purpose of generating a profit from short-term fluctuations in price or dealer's margin.) The entity may designate the fixed price contract as a cash flow hedge of the variability of the consideration to be received on the sale of the asset (a future transaction) even though the fixed price contract is the contract under which the asset will be sold.

Example 3.6B

All-in-one hedge of a debt instrument

An entity enters into a forward contract to purchase a debt instrument that will be settled by physical delivery of the debt instrument. The forward contract is a derivative in the scope of IAS 39 because its term exceeds the regular way delivery period in the marketplace. The entity may designate the forward as a cash flow hedge of the variability of the consideration to be paid to acquire the debt instrument (a forecast transaction), even though the derivative is the contract under which the debt instrument will be acquired.

US GAAP comparison: US guidance is more specific as to what hedged items can be designated in an all-in-one cash flow hedge. FAS 133.29(d) specifies that if the item that will be delivered will be subsequently measured at fair value through profit or loss then the forecasted transaction does not qualify for cash flow hedge accounting. IFRS does not have equivalent guidance. However, it is reasonable that an equivalent conclusion would be reached under IFRS in the case of a non-interest bearing instrument (e.g. an equity security) that when physically delivered under the derivative would be classified as at fair value through profit or loss. In this case, there is no systematic basis for reclassifying the amount recognised in other comprehensive income from equity to profit or loss in a cash flow hedge as all gains and losses after initial recognition on the equity security will immediately be recognised in profit or loss. See **example 3.6C** below.

Example 3.6C

All-in-one hedge of an equity instrument

Entity P, a US$ functional currency entity, enters into a forward contract to buy an equity share of Entity XYZ in 6 months' time at $10. The current share price of Entity XYZ is $10. At maturity of the forward contract the share price is $15 and therefore the forward contract has a positive fair value at maturity of $5.

Entity P cannot designate the forward as an all-in-one hedge of the future acquisition of a share in Entity XYZ in 6 months' time if Entity P intends to classify the share as at fair value through profit or loss, either because it is designated as such, or Entity P intends to sell the share in the short-term after initial recognition and therefore would meet the definition of held for trading. If the share is measured as at fair value through profit or loss there is no systematic basis in which the hedged risk impacts profit or loss and therefore Entity P cannot determine how the amount recognised in other comprehensive income can be reclassified from equity to profit or loss.

To illustrate why the forward cannot be designated in an all-in-one hedge consider the accounting entries that would result if cash flow hedging was applied: (i) at initial recognition of the equity security there would be a gain of $5 in other comprehensive income that would require reclassification from equity to profit or loss when the hedged risk of the hedged item impacts profit or loss, and (ii) the shares will be recognised at fair value, being $15 (Dr Shares $15, Cr Cash $10, Cr Derivative asset $5). If the share price rose or fell and thus affected profit or loss, there would be no basis for determining how much of the gain recognised in other comprehensive income should be reclassified. If the equity security was classified as an available-for-sale asset on initial recognition the amount recognised in other comprehensive income as a cash flow hedge would be reclassified from equity to profit or loss when the equity security was disposed of, or earlier if the security is impaired.

3.7 Splitting a derivative to exclude embedded financing

It is not possible to split the embedded financing from a non-optional derivative that has a fair value other than zero at the time of designation and account for it as a separate amortising loan whilst designating the zero fair value derivative as the hedging instrument.

If a non-optional derivative, such as a forward contract or swap, has a fair value other than zero at inception of the hedge, future changes in its fair value are impacted by that starting value. The derivative includes an embedded financing element which contributes to its fair value movements and causes them to differ from the changes in fair value of the hedged item when the hedged item does not have an equal and opposite financing element.

IAS 39 does not prohibit non-zero fair value non-optional derivatives being designated as hedging instruments as long as the hedging instrument is expected to be highly effective. In fact, IAS 39 allows hedging instruments to be designated part way through their lives, and therefore it is quite common for a derivative to have a starting value on designation other than zero. If the derivative can pass the prospective assessment of hedge effectiveness, the non-zero element of the derivative at initial designation will cause ineffectiveness that will be recognised in profit or loss over the term of the hedge. This is particularly the case for cash flow hedges as the 'hypothetical derivative' is deemed to be on-market at the date of designation, which for a non-optional derivative would have a fair value of zero (see **4.4.1** below).

The ineffectiveness arises because the embedded financing element is economically similar to a fixed rate amortising loan embedded in the derivative and this 'loan' will change in fair value as interest rates move. By the time the derivative matures, the loan will have been fully eliminated along with the derivative.

3.8 Rollover hedging strategies

A combination of more than one derivative or a derivative and a non-derivative may be used in 'rollover' hedging strategies when applying cash flow hedge accounting. IAS 39 envisages hedging strategies may include the replacement or rollover of one hedging instrument into another as they are referred to in IAS 39.101(a): an entity shall discontinue prospectively hedge accounting when "the hedging instrument expires or is sold, terminated or exercised (for this purpose, the replacement or rollover of a hedging instrument into another hedging instrument is not an expiration or termination if such replacement or rollover is part of the entity's documented hedging strategy)" (see **2.2.4** in **chapter 8**).

The benefit of a rollover strategy is that derivatives that have a maturity shorter than the timing of the underlying exposure of the hedged item can be designated as part of a rollover strategy as a hedge of that long-dated exposure. Where the hedged item is a financial instrument this technique offers no advantage as an entity could instead apply partial term hedging, i.e. hedge a risk of the hedged item for part of its life (see **2.2** above), but for hedges of non-financial items it is beneficial as for non-financial items an entity can only hedge foreign currency risk or all risk in its entirety, i.e. it is not possible to apply partial term hedging.

The following example illustrates how a rollover hedging strategy can be applied in a cash flow hedge relationship.

Example 3.8

Rollover strategies

On 1 January 20X1, Entity A, a £ functional currency, determines with high probability that it will have US$10m worth of sales on 30 September 20X1. Entity A enters into short dated forward contracts as part of a rollover strategy in order to hedge the US$:£ risk on its highly probable US$ sales.

On 1 January 20X1 Entity A enters into a 6-month forward contract (F1) to sell US$10m and buy £ which is intended to rollover into a new 3-month US$:£ forward contract (F2), also with a notional of US$10m, to coincide with the timing of the highly probable sales.

Entity A could designate the hedge relationship in one of two ways:

Designation 1

Designate the US$:£ foreign currency *spot* rate risk relating to the first US$10m of highly probable sales due to occur on 30 September 20X1 with the hedging instrument being the original forward contract (F1) recognised in the statement of financial position at the date of designation and rolled over into a new forward contract (F2) as part of the entity's hedging strategy.

In determining hedge effectiveness (see **section 4** below for detail), the hypothetical derivative will be the spot element of an on-market forward contract for US$:£ that is entered into on 1 January 20X1 and matures on 30 September 20X1. The forward points will be excluded from the fair value of the hypothetical derivative as it does not form part of the hedge relationship. The hypothetical derivative has a maturity date of 30 September 20X1 to coincide with the timing of the forecast transaction.

This designation will not be perfectly effective for a hedge of spot rates as there will be some ineffectiveness in the first six months as the fair value of the spot element of F1 will be discounted from 30 June 20X1, whereas the fair value of the hypothetical derivative will be discounted from 30 September 20X1. In the second period there will be no additional ineffectiveness due to discounting as both F2 and the hypothetical derivative terminate on the same date. Changes in the fair value of the forward points of the derivatives, F1 in the first period and F2 in the second period, will be immediately recorded in profit or loss as forward points do not form part of the hedge relationship.

Designation 2

Designate the US$:£ foreign currency *forward* rate risk relating to the first US$10m of highly probable sales due to occur on 30 September 20X1 with the hedging instrument being the original forward contract (F1) recognised in the statement of financial position at the date of designation and rolled over into a new forward contract (F2) as part of the entity's hedging strategy.

In determining hedge effectiveness, the hypothetical derivative will be a forward contract for US$:£ that is entered into on 1 January 20X1 and matures on 30 September 20X1 when the forecast transaction is expected to occur.

As the forward points form part of the hedge relationship the fair value of this hypothetical derivative will be compared with the fair value of the hedging instrument. Forward points in this case are not excluded from the hedge designation as Entity A is hedging the forward foreign currency exchange rate.

The effectiveness of the hedging relationship will be evaluated by comparing the cumulative change in the present value of the hedged item's cash flows due to the hedged risk (being the *forward* foreign currency exposure), which will equal the hypothetical derivative, with the fair value of the hedging instrument. This hedge will not be perfectly effective. Like in Designation 1, the differing maturities of F1 and the hypothetical derivative in the first period will be a source of ineffectiveness. In addition, the forward rate that is locked into in F1 will differ from the forward rate implicit in the hypothetical derivative which will be a further source of ineffectiveness.

If F1 is rolled over into a non-derivative financial instrument, a liability to deliver US$10m on 30 September 20X1, Entity A could apply the following designation:

Rollover of a derivative to a non-derivative

Assume the first derivative, F1, is gross cash settled (gross exchange of US$ and £) and Entity A borrows US$ at 30 June 20X1 in order to deliver under the gross cash settled derivative, F1, and the borrowing matures on 30 September 20X1. Entity A could intend to designate the anticipated rollover of derivative, F1, into a non-derivative, the US$ borrowing, as a hedging instrument of the US$:£ foreign currency *spot* rate relating to the first US10$m of highly probably sales due to occur on 30 September 20X1. Entity A can only designate the *spot* US$:£ rate, not the *forward* US$:£ rate, as the liability is only subject to spot retranslation under IAS 21. The same level of ineffectiveness would result as per Designation 1.

3.9 Forwards versus futures

Forward contracts and futures contracts share similar characteristics in that both contracts result in the exchange of a specified amount of cash or other financial asset for an underlying at a specific future date. The terms of a forward contract are negotiable as the two parties will agree the notional, forward price, maturity date, etc, subject to their specific needs. Futures are traded via a third party futures exchange which acts as an intermediary between two parties in a contract. The futures contract is normally standardised in size and over one of the pre-established underlyings (in the case of non-financial items, one of the pre-established grades and locations). A party to the futures contract will generally cash settle the market value of the futures contract on a regular basis, usually daily, with the futures exchange. Assuming the futures exchange has a buyer and a seller of equivalent futures contracts, the daily cash settlements will be paid to the futures exchange by one party and paid by the future exchange to the other party. These daily settlements are referred to as variation margin. In addition, the future exchange will also require the posting of collateral with the future exchange at inception, referred to as initial margin, to reduce the counterparty credit risk in the case where a party owes the futures exchange but fails to pay.

For the purposes of hedge accounting, the most significant difference between forwards and futures is the regular settlement of the fair value of futures contracts with the futures exchange which results in futures having a different fair value to a comparable forward contract with the same underlying, maturity and specified price for the underlying. To determine the fair value of the forward contract the cash flows will be discounted because the cash flows will occur at a future date, whereas the futures contract will not be discounted as the cash flows (being the settlements of the daily fair value movements) are occurring every day. The difference in fair value between a forward and a future will result in these instruments having different degrees of hedge effectiveness. Whether forwards or futures are more effective for hedge accounting depends on the individual circumstances and the hedge designation.

Example 3.9

Forwards versus futures

Entity P has an investment in Entity W which is classified as available-for-sale equity security. Entity P is considering entering into one of two contracts described below to hedge the available-for-sale equity security. Entity P believes it is highly probable that it will sell the investment in Entity W in six months' time, being the end of June 20X9. Assume that the forward price of the available-for-sale security is equal to the spot price at the start of January 20X9 when the hedging instrument will be entered into.

Entity P is considering the following two contracts:

- A forward contract to sell the available-for-sale equity security in six months' time for a fixed amount, equal to the spot price when the forward is entered into. The instrument is net cash settled with all cash flows settled at maturity of the contract.
- A futures contract to sell the available-for-sale equity security in six months' time for a fixed amount, equal to the spot price when the future is entered into. Entity P provides an initial margin to the futures exchange and pays/receives a daily variation margin equal to the fair value movements in the futures contract. The initial margin is deemed to be a collateral for the futures contract in accordance with IAS 39.IG.B.10 and therefore does not impact the fair value of the futures contracts as it is a separate financial asset. The daily settlement of daily variation margin is not a collateral and is deemed to be daily settlement of the futures contract.

Entity P considers designating one of these hedging instruments in a fair value hedge of the available-for-sale equity security.

If Entity P enters into the forward contract the hedge will not be perfectly effective as the change in fair value of the forward contract will not equal the change in fair value of the available-for-sale equity security. The difference is due to the discounting of the fair value of the forward as settlement is not due until six months' time, whereas the fair value movements of the available-for-sale equity security are not discounted as they are recognised as they arise.

If Entity P enters into the futures contract the hedge will be perfectly effective (all other things being equal) as the change in fair value of the futures contract will equal the change in fair value of the available-for-sale equity security. The futures contract is not discounted as there is daily settlement equal to the change in its fair value which is equal to the recognised gains/losses on the available-for-sale equity security.

For this designation the future is more effective than the forward for a given period.

If a forward contract is used Entity P could improve hedge effectiveness by designating a proportion, i.e. a percentage, of the equity security. The proportion of the equity security hedged would be equal to the fair value of the security at inception of the hedge discounted for 6 months. As the effect of discounting reduces over the life of the forward contract the hedge designation would need to be adjusted continuously by increasing the proportion of the equity security hedged.

Entity P considers designating one of these hedging instruments in a cash flow hedge of the forecast sale of the available-for-sale equity security in six months' time.

If Entity P enters into the forward contract the hedge will be perfectly effective (all other things being equal) as the cumulative change in fair value of the forward contract is expected to equal the cumulative change in fair value of the expected future cash flow on the hedged item. This is because the forward contract and the forecast transaction occur on the same date in the future and therefore are discounted by the same factor.

If Entity P enters into the futures contract the hedge will not be perfectly effective as the cumulative change in fair value of the futures contract is not expected to equal the cumulative change in fair value of the expected future cash flow on the hedged item. The futures contract is not discounted whereas the cash flow on the forecast transaction is when calculating the expected hedge effectiveness. The futures contract will 'over-hedge' the forecast transaction as it is expected to generate more gains/losses than the hedged item.

For this designation the forward is more effective than the future for a given period.

The technique described in the above example is often applied in practice when hedging forecast transactions with futures. It involves entering into futures contracts with a lower notional (or less futures contracts) compared with that of the hedged item. For a given notional the futures contract will have a larger fair value movement than the forecast transaction, so this technique attempts to ensure that the fair value movements of the futures contracts (which are undiscounted) match the fair value movements in the fair value of the forecast cash flows (which are discounted). The effect of discounting which is greater at the start of the hedge and all other things being equal reduces over time as the timing of the forecast transaction gets nearer. Adjusting the size of the notional of the futures to compensate for these differences is known as 'tailing' the futures hedge. This technique improves hedge effectiveness, and may also be applied for economic reasons as the benefit of a lower notional offsets the downside of financing the variation margin receipts and payments.

3.10 Deal contingent derivatives

An entity that expects to enter into transactions whose occurrence depends on a future event sometimes enter into derivatives that mirror the possibility of non-occurrence of the future event, i.e. the derivative has a knock-out option that is exercised if the future event does not occur. These are often referred to as deal contingent derivatives. If the future event occurs the derivative remains outstanding, if the event does not occur, the derivative ceases to exist and no settlements between the parties are made. It is unlikely that these instruments can be considered qualifying hedging instruments as illustrated in the example below.

Example 3.10

Hedging with deal contingent forwards

An entity believes it will enter into a highly likely business combination at a future date where the consideration for the acquiree is specified in a foreign currency. The prospective acquirer is awaiting approval by the acquiree's current shareholders, regulatory agencies, governments, or other parties etc. The prospective acquirer chooses to economically hedge their exposure by entering into a deal contingent foreign currency forward contract, such that if the business combination does not proceed the forward contract knocks-out and is terminated with no cash settlement between the parties. The value of this derivative contract is driven not only by the foreign currency component but also by the probability of the business combination occurring.

The business combination is unlikely to be seen as being highly probable, and therefore it would be inappropriate to designate the deal contingent forward contract as a hedge of the currency risk of the forecast business combination. The existence of a knock-out option adds strength to the argument that the business combination is not highly probable as the knock-out feature would not be needed if it was. IAS 39 presupposes that if an entity is hedging a transaction that it claims to be highly probable it expects the transaction to occur, while here the entity is economically entering into an additional hedge: the hedge of the non-occurrence of the transaction. The fair value of the deal contingent forward includes the probability that the business combination will not occur, which when compared to the fair value of a hypothetical derivative, a vanilla forward that assumes the transaction will occur, will be different. This difference may be so significant that the entity cannot claim on a prospective assessment of hedge effectiveness that the hedge is expected to be highly effective.

The ineffectiveness cannot be minimised by designating additionally the risk of non-occurrence of the transaction for two reasons: (i) the risk of non-occurrence is considered to be a general business risk and hence is not eligible to be a hedged item [IAS 39.IG.F.2.8] and, (ii) with the exceptions set out in IAS 39.74 an entity must designate a derivative instrument in its entirety.

3.11 Internal hedges

In a group that has a central treasury function a group entity or division that wishes to enter into hedging transactions uses their central treasury function rather than using an external group counterparty. The central treasury function then aggregates all its internal positions and enters into external transactions to offset the internal ones on a net basis thereby taking advantage of any natural offsets and hedging the exposures of the group in a cost efficient way.

At a group level, if the central treasury function enters into external derivatives these can be used as hedging instruments, but only as a hedge of a gross position. As discussed in **3.12** above, a net position cannot be a hedged item. Therefore, even though the external derivative was entered into to offset a net position, it can be used as a hedging instrument but only if it is designated as hedging (a portion of) a gross position.

Example 3.11A

Hedging an external gross position (1)

Entity A has a central treasury division. The central treasury division aggregates the internal derivative contracts with other group entities, and enters into external derivatives that offset the internal derivatives on a net basis.

Central treasury has three internal receive-fixed, pay-variable interest rate swaps and one internal receive-variable, pay-fixed interest rate swap. It enters into an interest rate swap with an external counterparty that exactly offsets the four internal swaps as follows:

Swap	Counterparty	Description	Notional
1	Internal	Receive-fixed, pay-variable	£100 million
2	Internal	Receive-fixed, pay-variable	£60 million
3	Internal	Receive-fixed, pay-variable	£30 million
4	Internal	Receive-variable, pay-fixed	£150 million
5	External	Receive-variable, pay-fixed	£40 million

Swap 5 cannot hedge an overall net position, i.e. it cannot be used to hedge all of the items that the internal derivatives 1–4 are hedging. IAS 39 states that an overall net position cannot qualify as a hedged item.

However, Swap 5 can qualify as a hedging instrument in a hedge of the underlying hedged items residing in the group companies on a gross basis, i.e. it could hedge £40 million of fixed rate assets or £40 million of variable rate liabilities.

IAS 39.IG.F.1.4 gives further guidance on the use of internal derivatives. The guidance derives from the principles of preparing consolidated financial statements in IAS 27 *Consolidated and Separate Financial Statements,* which require that 'intragroup balances, transactions, income and expenses shall be eliminated in full'. [IAS 27(2008).20, previously IAS 27(2003).24]

Only a derivative that is external to the reporting entity, i.e. external to the group or individual entity that is being reported, can be designated as a hedging instrument. In the consolidated financial statements intragroup derivatives cannot be hedging instruments as these are not external to the reporting entity and eliminate on consolidation. However, they may be used in the entity only financial statements since from that entity's perspective such derivatives are with a third party. [IAS 39.73]

Example 3.11B

Hedge accounting in the group versus entity only financial statements

Entity A has a 100 per cent subsidiary, Entity B. The group treasury policy requires that only Entity A enters into derivatives with external parties. If Entity B wishes to enter into a foreign currency forward it notifies Entity A. Entity A enters into a forward with a bank (forward 1), and then enters into an equal and opposite forward contract with Entity B (forward 2).

From a consolidated perspective, only the forward contract with the bank, forward 1, can be a designated hedging instrument. In Entity B's entity only financial statements, forward 2 may be designated as a hedging instrument. This would be true even if Entity A had not entered into forward 1 with the bank.

In Entity A's entity only financial statements there will be two equal and opposite derivatives. These must be presented separately in its statement of financial position. They cannot be offset as they do not meet the offset requirements of IAS 32 (see **section 7** in **chapter 11**).

Entities sometimes enter into netting agreements with a bank such that derivatives held with that bank are settled on a net basis. This does not in itself preclude those instruments being designated as hedging instruments. [IAS 39.IG.F.2.16]

Example 3.11C

Hedging an external gross position (2)

Entity A has several subsidiaries. Entity A acts as a central treasury function, so that if any subsidiary wants to lay off risk it must do so with Entity A. For each internal derivative, Entity A enters into an equal and opposite external contract with a bank. Thus, if it has a 3-year pay 6 per cent receive LIBOR interest rate swap with a subsidiary, it will enter into a 3-year receive 6 per cent pay LIBOR interest rate swap with a bank, such that all of the terms of the two contracts match. Each internal derivative is hedging a gross exposure.

The external derivatives can be designated as hedging instruments of the underlying gross exposures in the group's consolidated financial statements. This is true even if the external derivatives are settled on a net basis.

Provided the contracts are legally separate and serve a valid business purpose (such as laying off risk exposures on underlying gross positions) they qualify as hedging instruments.

Entities sometimes have external positions that offset each other. This can arise (as in the above example) because there is a policy of hedging every exposure separately (i.e. gross), or because an entity wishes to manage its external portfolio in a certain way.

Example 3.11D

Hedging an external gross position (3)

Continuing with **example 3.11C**, assume Entity A manages the portfolio of offsetting external derivatives separately from other exposures of the entity and enters into an additional, single derivative to offset the risk of the portfolio.

The individual external derivative contracts in the portfolio can still be designated as hedging instruments of the underlying gross exposures even though a single external derivative is used to offset fully the market exposure created by entering into these external contracts.

The purpose of structuring the external derivative contracts in this manner is consistent with the entity's risk management objectives and strategies. As noted in **3.2** above, external derivative contracts that are structured separately and serve a valid business purpose qualify as hedging instruments. [IAS 39.IG.F.2.16]

Detailed guidance on achieving hedge accounting in the group consolidated financial statements where a central treasury function exists is provided in the Implementation Guidance of IAS 39. Specifically, IAS 39.IG.F.1.5 provides guidance on offsetting internal derivative contracts used to manage interest rate risk, and IAS 39.IG.F.1.6 and IAS 39.IG.F.1.7 provide guidance on offsetting internal derivative contracts used to manage foreign exchange risk.

4 Hedge effectiveness assessment

IAS 39 requires a hedge to be 'highly effective', prospectively and retrospectively, for it to qualify for hedge accounting. [IAS 39.88] The highly effective criterion is used in the assessment of hedge effectiveness. If an entity passes the highly effective criterion and applies hedge accounting in a period, any ineffectiveness is required to be measured and recorded immediately in profit or loss.

The concept of hedge effectiveness and the basic methods for assessing hedge effectiveness are discussed in section **5** in **chapter 8**. This section discusses techniques to minimise hedge ineffectiveness and explores more advanced methods of assessing hedge effectiveness such as regression analysis.

4.1 Hedge effectiveness – gains/losses versus carrying amount

Assessing hedge effectiveness is based on comparing changes in the fair value of the hedging instrument and changes in the fair value of the hedged item attributable to the hedged risk. In determining the change in fair value of the hedging instrument an entity considers gains and losses, not the carrying amount of the hedging instrument in the statement of financial position. It is the gains/losses that are recognised in profit or loss, whereas changes in the carrying amount of the hedging instrument may result from receipts or payments of cash which do not impact profit or loss. Similarly for the hedged item, it is the impact of the hedged risk of the hedged item that impacts profit or loss and is therefore considered in assessing hedge effectiveness and not the carrying amount of the hedged item itself.

Example 4.1

Cash flow hedge ineffectiveness: off-market swaps

Entity B designates an off-market receive LIBOR, pay 7% interest rate swap in a cash flow hedge of variability in interest rates on its issued variable rate debt. The interest rate swap is off-market because at initial designation the swap has a negative fair value as expectations of interest rates have fallen since the swap was originally priced. The current yield curve for the remaining time to maturity is 5%.

Entity B assesses hedge effectiveness using the hypothetical derivative method and at the date of designation determines that a hypothetical derivative that would have a fair value of zero is the same as the actual derivative except that it would receive LIBOR, pay 5% (not receive LIBOR, pay 7%). In assessing hedge effectiveness Entity B models the actual and hypothetical derivative under various interest rate scenarios and compares the two in reaching its conclusion that the actual derivative, even though off-market, will still be effective at cash flow hedging its variable debt and therefore can qualify as a hedging instrument in a qualifying hedge relationship. The 2% extra that Entity B will pay on the actual derivative compared to the hypothetical derivative is not the amount of hedge ineffectiveness that will arise in the future periods. The 2% is part of the cash flows of the actual derivative. The amount of hedge ineffectiveness will depend on how future interest rates affect the cumulative fair value gains/losses on the actual derivative from inception of the hedge as compared to the effect they will have on the hypothetical derivative. Another way of viewing the 2% difference between the pay leg of the actual derivative and hypothetical derivative is viewing Entity B as paying loan instalments equal to 2% of the notional of the swap every period to the swap counterparty on an amortising loan. The cash payments on the 'loan' do not impact profit or loss, but changes in fair value of these future cash flows do.

4.2 Hedge ineffectiveness

4.2.1 Basis risk

It is not always possible for an entity to find a hedging instrument with exactly the same terms as the item it wishes to hedge. Basis differences result from using a hedging instrument that is based on a specific risk that is similar, but not identical to the risk being hedged in the hedged item. For example, there may not always be an active market for the grade or location of a commodity that an entity is seeking to hedge.

For interest sensitive items, basis differences result from differences in interest indices, e.g. LIBOR versus Treasury rates, in terms, e.g. three-month LIBOR versus six-month LIBOR, and in credit risk differences.

Example 4.2.1A

Basis risk: commodities

Entity Z has 20,000 therms of natural gas stored at its location in the United Kingdom. Entity Z ultimately intends on selling this gas to customers in continental Europe, and is concerned that prices may fall in the future. To hedge the exposure of its sales of natural gas, Entity Z sells the equivalent of 20,000 therms of natural gas under a forward contract (which the entity intends on net settling in cash by entering into an offsetting position in the spot market at delivery). The forward contract's price is based on delivery of natural gas at the Zeebrugge gas collection point in Belgium. Because prices in the UK (as based on the price quoted in the UK National Balancing Point, or NBP, market) and at Zeebrugge will differ as a result of regional factors (e.g. location, pipeline transmission costs, and supply and demand), Entity Z cannot assume that the hedge will be highly effective in achieving offsetting changes in fair value. Entity Z appropriately documents the hedging strategy and states that effectiveness will be measured based on the spot prices of natural gas in the UK NBP market and the spot prices at the Zeebrugge hub.

Entity Z is required to demonstrate effectiveness at inception and on an ongoing basis. This is achieved typically, through a correlation method such as regression analysis, or ratio analysis. If such analysis does not result in an expectation that correlation would be between 80 to 125 per cent, Entity Z is not permitted to apply hedge accounting. However, even if the effectiveness test is met, Entity Z may have ineffectiveness due to the difference in the basis of the hedged item and the hedging instrument and such ineffectiveness is recognised in profit or loss.

Example 4.2.1B

Basis risk: interest rate resets

Entity D designates an interest rate swap as hedging a debt instrument. The interest rate swap's rate settles every three months but is indexed to the six-month LIBOR rate and the debt settles every three months but is indexed to the three-month LIBOR rate, i.e. the three-month LIBOR index on the debt does not match the six-month LIBOR index on the swap. To the extent that there is high empirical correlation between these rate indices, Entity D may designate the swap as the hedge of the interest rate risk on the debt instrument, but the different rate indexation may result in ineffectiveness that needs to be measured and recognised.

Example 4.2.1C

Basis risk: foreign currency risk

Entity X's functional currency is the Euro. Entity X's forecast purchase of equipment from Brazil is expected to cost R$100,000. Entity X wishes to hedge its foreign currency risk. As the US$/ Euro currency market is more liquid than the R$/ Euro dollar currency market, Entity X enters into a forward contract to receive US$33,300 and pay €27,000. The US$ will then be converted into Brazilian Real in the liquid spot market for payment to the supplier.

Because the bases of foreign currency for the purchase of the equipment and the foreign exchange forward contract are different (R$ vs. US$), Entity X will have to demonstrate that US$/€ is highly effective in hedging R$/€ both at inception and on an ongoing basis. The entity could use a correlation method to demonstrate the effectiveness of this relationship.

To the extent that there is a basis difference between R$ and US$, hedge ineffectiveness will result and will be recognised in profit or loss.

Further examples

An illustration of the entries for a cash flow hedge of interest rate risk on a forecast debt issuance using an interest rate swap with a different basis to the hedged item is included in **3.13** in **chapter 10**.

4.2.2 *Hedge ineffectiveness – forecast transaction occurs earlier than expected*

Where the forecast transaction that an entity has designated as a hedged item in a cash flow hedge, for example a forecast sale of a commodity, is expected to occur in an earlier period than originally anticipated, the entity can conclude that this transaction is the same as the one that was designated as being hedged. The change in timing of the forecast transaction does not affect the validity of the designation. [IAS 39.IG.F.5.4]

However, it may affect the assessment of the effectiveness of the hedging relationship as the hedging instrument would need to be designated as a hedging instrument for the whole remaining period of its existence in order for it to continue to qualify as a hedging instrument. If the forecast transaction was expected to occur prior to the date documented in the hedge documentation, the relationship is likely to be ineffective because the hedging instrument matures after the transaction has occurred. The hedging instrument cannot be split into a part that is fully effective up to the date of the transaction, and a part that is excluded from the designation. However, if the forecast transaction was delayed, and was expected to occur after the date documented in the hedge documentation, the hedge could be re-designated as a hedge for the period up to the maturity of the hedging instrument. The effective part of this hedge will be recognised in other comprehensive income, and reclassified from equity to profit or loss when the transaction impacts profit or loss. In the latter case, the hedging instrument is being designated for its full life.

4.3 Minimising hedge ineffectiveness

4.3.1 *Designating a cash flow hedge in layers*

In order to improve effectiveness an entity may choose to hedge forecast transactions in layers. For example, instead of hedging a single layer of the first US$1m of forecast sales, an entity could designate the hedge relationship in layers: the first US$0.6m of forecast sales and a second layer of US$0.4m forecast sales. Designation in layers will only result in better hedge effectiveness where in future periods the amount of previously designated highly probable forecast transactions falls. In such a situation an entity may be able to recognise a greater amount in other comprehensive income if it designates in layers as hedge effectiveness will be assessed on each individual layer.

Further examples

An illustration of the entries for a cash flow hedge designated in layers for foreign currency risk of forecast revenue using forward exchange contracts is included in **3.11** in **chapter 10**.

4.3.2 *A hedge ratio of other than one to one*

For the purposes of designating a hedge relationship that satisfies the highly effective criterion, the amount of the hedging instrument designated may be greater or less than that of the hedged item if this improves the effectiveness of the hedging relationship.

For example, if an entity hedges an item with a hedging instrument with a different basis (IAS 39.100 uses the example of a transaction based on Brazilian coffee prices hedged with a transaction based on Columbian coffee prices), a regression analysis (see **4.6** below) could be performed to establish a statistical relationship between the two items. If a valid statistical relationship between the two variables (i.e. between the unit prices of Brazilian coffee and Columbian coffee) can be demonstrated, the slope of the regression line could be used to establish the hedge ratio that would maximise expected effectiveness.

If the slope of the regression line is, say, 1.02, a hedge ratio based on 0.98 quantities of hedged items to 1.00 quantities of the hedging instrument will maximise expected effectiveness.

Example 4.3.2

Hedge ratio other than one

Entity R periodically issues new bonds to refinance maturing bonds, provide working capital, and for various other purposes. Entity R hedges the risk of changes in the long-term interest rates from the date it decides to issue the bonds to the date the bonds are issued.

Entity R performed historical correlation studies and determined that a treasury bond of the same maturity adequately correlates to the bonds Entity R expects to issue, assuming a hedge ratio of 0.93 futures on treasury bonds to one debt unit. In order to achieve an effective hedge of the future issuance of the bond, Entity R enters into the futures on treasury bonds using this ratio.

Hedge ineffectiveness is measured on the basis of the actual amounts designated. It is not possible to designate an exposure based on a specified notional, but measure ineffectiveness on a different notional.

4.3.3 *Hedging on an after-tax basis*

IAS 39 permits assessment of hedge effectiveness on an after-tax basis, provided this approach is documented formally at inception. [IAS 39.IG.F.4.1]

It may be advantageous to assess hedge effectiveness on a post tax basis where the hedged item and hedging instrument are taxed differently. However, it must be borne in mind that any subsequent changes in the basis or rate of tax of either the hedged item or hedging instrument, will result in hedge ineffectiveness.

Further examples

An illustration of the entries for a net investment hedge of a foreign operation assessed for hedge effectiveness on an after tax basis is included in **4.5** in **chapter 10**.

4.3.4 *Forward points*

Where a forward contract is designated as a hedging instrument in a cash flow hedge of a forecast transaction the entity can choose to exclude the fair value movements of the forward points from the hedge relationship. In other words, an entity may include in its designation the whole fair value movements of the forward contract, or just the fair value movements of the forward contract that relate solely to movements in spot rates.

Example 4.3.4

Hedging the forward foreign currency rate

Entity X is a Euro functional entity. Entity X makes sales to US customers in US$. Entity X wishes to hedge its exposure to US$ by entering into a forward contract to sell US$ and buy € at a fixed rate at a specified delivery date that coincides with the timing of the sales.

Entity X can choose to designate the hedged risk as movements in either the spot US$/€ rate, or the forward US$/€ rate that terminates when the sales occur and the hedging instrument matures.

If the entity chooses to hedge the spot rate, then movements in the fair value of the forward contract due to movements in spot rate from period to period are recognised in other comprehensive income (to the extent this is effective).

The fair value movements in the forward contract due to the fair value of the forward points will be recognised immediately in profit or loss throughout the hedge relationship.

If the entity chooses to hedge the forward rate, then the full movement in the fair value of the forward contract is recognised in other comprehensive income (to the extent this is effective). Compared to designating the spot rate only, the fair value changes of the forward points are recognised in other comprehensive income (instead of profit or loss) throughout the hedge relationship. If the hedge was perfectly effective over the life, then the fair value of the forward points would never be recognised in profit or loss (at maturity of the hedging relationship and hedging instrument the fair value of the forward points will be zero as there will be no more forward points left). The fair value of the forward contract at maturity will be equivalent to the difference between the spot rate at maturity and the contracted rate.

4.3.5 *Time value of options*

By splitting the time and intrinsic value of an option that is a qualifying hedging instrument, and designating only the intrinsic value in the hedging relationship, a higher level of effectiveness may be achieved. Depending on the length of time to the maturity of the option, the relative volatility of the option, and other factors that affect the time value, this designation may make the difference as to whether the relationship qualifies for hedge accounting.

Generally, if options are being used to hedge financial instruments that have a linear response to changes in the hedged risk, such as cash instruments, it is beneficial to exclude the time value of the option from the hedge relationship as the time value evident in the option is not evident in the hedged item. Designating the gains and losses on the hedging instrument with respect to intrinsic value only as an offset of the gains and losses on the hedged item creates a greater likelihood that the hedge will be highly effective in achieving offsetting changes in fair value or cash flows attributable to the hedged risk.

The disadvantage of not including time value in the hedge designation is that changes in the value of the component that is not designated in the hedging relationship, i.e. change in time value, must be recognised immediately in profit or loss.

Example 4.3.5

Hedging intrinsic value only

Entity X owns 1,000 shares of Entity A worth CU50 each. Entity X classifies these securities as available-for-sale and recognises changes in the fair value of these securities in other comprehensive income. Entity X would like to hedge its downside equity price risk. Entity X purchases an at-the-money put option (i.e. the put option has a strike price of CU50) on 1,000 Entity A shares expiring in three years' time. The premium paid for the option is CU9,000.

Entity X designates the intrinsic value of the put option as a fair value hedge of its investment in Entity A. The hedge strategy is consistent with Entity X's established risk management strategies. Entity X measures effectiveness by comparing decreases in fair value of the investment below the CU50 strike price with changes in the intrinsic value of the option on a quarterly basis. The time value of the option is not included in the assessment of effectiveness.

Because the hedging instrument and the hedged item have the same basis and are based on the same number of shares, increases in the intrinsic value of the option are expected to be fully effective in offsetting decreases in the fair value of the investment.

In this example, the entire CU9,000 premium is time value because the option purchased was at-the-money. Changes in the fair value of the time value of the option are recognised directly in profit or loss. Effectiveness of the hedge is assessed based on the intrinsic value rather than the fair value of the option. To the extent that the fair value of the option changes due to other variables such as volatility and the risk free rate, Entity X calculates the fair value of the option and then deducts the intrinsic value to arrive at the 'time' value component. In other words, the time value component reflects the effect of all variables on the option's price other than the intrinsic value. Based on Entity X's designation of effectiveness, the time value component is not part of the hedge relationship and is therefore recognised directly in profit or loss.

When the fair value of the shares falls below the strike price of the option, i.e. CU50, the entity will recognise fair value movements on the hedged item below this amount in profit or loss (instead of other comprehensive income) which will offset the intrinsic value on the hedging instrument that will be recognised in profit or loss in the same period.

The Standard does not provide a definition of time value or intrinsic value for the purposes of identifying these two elements. This raises the question of what should be taken as intrinsic value, especially in the case of European options where the value of the option is driven from the expected price of the underlying in the future, and not its current price. For example, in the case of a cap on an interest rate index that is exercisable at the maturity of the option, there is a question whether intrinsic value at any point in time should be measured based on the current level of the given index (i.e. intrinsic value based on the spot rate) or by reference to the forward rate of the index that coincides with the actual exercise date (i.e. intrinsic value based on the forward rate)?

The latter view would seem to be more in line with the economic reality for a European option as the intrinsic value of the option is entirely a function of where the rate of interest is predicted to be at the exercise date as opposed to where it currently is, given that the option cannot be presently exercised. This view of intrinsic value is supported by the fact that there is a readily observable prediction of future interest rates, i.e. the forward rates derived from the yield curve. In this respect European options over interest rate indices are different from those over other underlyings such as equity shares. IFRS 2 *Share-based Payment* Appendix A defines the intrinsic value of a share option as the difference between the fair value of the shares and the exercise price of the option, pointing towards a spot based view of intrinsic value, which is consistent with the fact that for equity shares there is no readily observable prediction of future prices as there is for interest rates.

Consider the case of a purchased European interest rate cap in an environment of an inverted interest rate curve (i.e. a yield curve that predicts that future interest rates will be below current levels). An entity may purchase a European interest rate cap at 5 per cent with a maturity of 2 years when the current spot rate is 6 per cent and the current market prediction as illustrated by the yield curve is that the interest rate is expected to be 4.5 per cent at the exercise date of the option. If intrinsic value is based on the spot rate, the intrinsic value will effectively 'build in' an assumption of the interest rate remaining at 6 per cent, i.e. in excess of the cap even though the yield curve predicts that this will not be the case. This will lead to a value being attributed to intrinsic value that is in excess of the total fair value of the option. As a result 'negative' value will be attributed to the time value in order for the sum of the time and intrinsic values to equal the total fair value of the option. It would seem strange that IAS 39 would require an entity to attribute 'negative' time value to a purchased option and therefore it is reasonable for an entity to assess intrinsic value based on forward rather than spot interest rates, assuming it documents this as part of its risk management strategy and applies this consistently for similar hedging relationships.

US GAAP comparison: US GAAP provides more guidance than IAS 39 about how to compute the time value of options (DIG Issue E19). For both fair value and cash flow hedges, the following two methods for computing time value are permitted: (a) deducting from the total option value the intrinsic value of the option (defined as the difference between the strike price and the spot price of the underlying asset) or (b) deducting from the total option value the minimum value of the option (defined as the present value of the difference between the strike price and the forward price of the underlying asset). For cash flow hedges, time value can also be determined by deducting from the total option value the undiscounted difference between the strike price and the forward price of the underlying.

4.4 Methods for assessing effectiveness for cash flow hedges

IAS 39 does not provide specific guidance as to how an entity should measure hedge effectiveness. However, IAS 39.IG.F.5.5 provides an illustrative example of measuring hedge effectiveness in a cash flow hedge of forecast issuance of fixed rate debt. The implementation guidance recognises that there are at least two methods of accomplishing this measurement. The two methods: the hypothetical derivative method and changes in fair value method, are explained in the following section.

4.4.1 *The 'hypothetical derivative' method*

The hypothetical derivative method measures hedge ineffectiveness by comparing the change in fair value of the actual derivative designated as the hedging instrument and the change in fair value of a 'hypothetical derivative' that would result in perfect hedge effectiveness for the designated hedged item, i.e. the hypothetical derivative would have terms that exactly match the critical terms of the hedged item. For example, for a hedge of a variable rate financial asset or liability, the hypothetical derivative would be a swap with the same notional amount and same repricing dates as the hedged asset or liability. In addition, the index on which the hypothetical swap's variable rate is based would match the index on which the asset or liability's variable rate is based, including, where present, any caps and floors and any other embedded features in the hedged item. Further, it would be an on-market swap, i.e. have a zero fair value at inception.

Under the 'hypothetical derivative method' the change in the fair value of the 'perfect' hypothetical swap is regarded as a proxy for the change in the present value of the expected future cash flows on the hedged transaction.

The determination of the fair value of both the 'perfect' hypothetical swap and the actual swap will use discount rates based on the relevant swap curves.

The amount of ineffectiveness recognised in profit or loss for a cash flow hedge equals the excess of the cumulative change in the fair value of the actual swap over the cumulative change in the fair value of the 'perfect' hypothetical swap.

Example 4.4.1A

Identifying the hypothetical derivative

Entity PQR has a 4-year variable rate loan asset with a notional of €100 and a maturity of 31/12/X5. The benchmark rate on the loan (i.e. the coupon excluding credit spread) is 3-month EURIBOR. Interest is received quarterly. Entity PQR does not hedge its loan asset on origination, 1/01/X2.

However, at the end of 20X2, Entity PQR forecasts a fall in interest rates and designates a pay variable overnight indexed swap rate (OIS), receive 5 per cent fixed interest rate swap with a notional of €100 and annual interest payments as a cash flow hedge of the interest rate risk on the loan.

Entity PQR formally designates the hedging relationship and meets all of the hedge accounting criteria including the prospective effectiveness test.

To measure effectiveness of the hedging relationship Entity PQR compares the change in fair value of the hedging pay variable OIS, receive 5 per cent fixed interest rate swap to the changes in value of the 'hypothetical derivative,' i.e. the derivative that would result in perfect hedge effectiveness for a hedge of the loan. In this instance the hypothetical derivative is a pay 3-month EURIBOR, receive 4.9 per cent interest rate swap with quarterly payment dates. The 4.9 per cent fixed rate for the remaining 3 years is the market EURIBOR swap rate.

Note that the fixed rates on the actual hedging swap and the hypothetical swap differ as they are priced off different yield curves (i.e. OIS versus EURIBOR).

The hypothetical derivative method can be used universally for all cash flow hedge relationships where a derivative is used as a hedging instrument. This method would not be appropriate in the case of hedging foreign currency risk with a non-derivative instrument as clearly the hedging instrument is not a derivative.

The other method discussed below, the change in fair value method, will have greater applicability when determining hedge effectiveness on variable rate financial assets and liabilities and the forecast issuance of fixed rate debt.

The hypothetical derivative method is referred to as Method B in IAS 39.IG.F.5.5.

Hedge ineffectiveness will arise if the timing or amount of a forecast transaction changes as the fair value (present value) of the expected future cash flows on the hedged item from inception of the hedge will not equal the cumulative fair value on the hedging instrument from inception of the hedge.

Determining the degree of hedge ineffectiveness when the timing or amount of forecast transactions change can be a complex exercise. If an entity applies the hypothetical derivative method in assessing hedge effectiveness then this method will also be reapplied when the timing or amount of the hedged item changes. For example, if the timing of the cash flows on the derivative hedging instrument and the hedged item coincide at inception of the hedge and the derivative is deemed to be the hypothetical derivative, then only to the extent that the cash flows continue to coincide will the hedge be fully effective. If the timing of the forecast cash flows changes during the life of the hedge relationship then a new hypothetical derivative needs to be determined which will be equal to the hypothetical derivative that the entity would have determined when they entered into the hedge accounting relationship that reflects the revised timing of the forecast cash flows. Put another way, the revised hypothetical derivative is the one the entity would have determined had it been able to foresee the revised timing of the forecast cash flows. A comparison of the cumulative gain/loss on the actual hedging instrument and the revised hypothetical derivative will determine the degree of hedge effectiveness and the amount of hedge ineffectiveness to be measured under IAS 39.96(a).

Further examples

A detailed illustration of the application of the hypothetical derivative method for a cash flow hedge of interest rate risk on a forecast issuance of debt where the timing of the forecast cash flows change is included in **3.15** of **chapter 10**.

4.4.2 *The 'change in fair value' method*

The change in fair value method requires a computation of the change in fair value of the cash flows that would have been achieved had the variable cash flow exposure been a fixed cash exposure. For example, if an entity is hedging variable rate debt, the change in fair value method will compare the cumulative changes in the present value of the fixed cash flows that would have been achieved at inception, discounted at the new interest rate, with the fair value of the derivative that is designated as the hedging instrument.

In the instance that an entity is hedging the variable interest rate risk of a variable rate financial asset or liability, the fair value of the hedged item is generally equal to its par amount, as it is not sensitive to fair value movement when interest rates change. This method overcomes this problem by discounting the cash flows that would have been achieved had the instrument been fixed from inception.

Example 4.4.2

Change in fair value method

Facts as in **example 4.4.1A**.

Applying the change in fair value method, Entity PQR will determine the fixed rate that would have been achieved on 4-year fixed rate loan that is priced off EURIBOR.

The entity will discount the fixed cash flows that would have been achieved on a 4 year fixed rate loan at the new EURIBOR interest rate curve. The cumulative present value of these cash flows will be compared with the fair value of the interest rate swap that is priced off OIS. The change in fair value method will recognise ineffectiveness due to the different basis of interest rates between the hedging instrument and the hedged item.

The change in fair value method is referred to as Method A in IAS 39.IG.F.5.5.

4.4.3 *The 'change in variable cash flows' method*

The change in variable cash flows method compares the floating rate cash flows of the hedged item with the floating rates cash flows on the derivative. For example, if an entity was assessing hedge effectiveness for a variable rate financial asset or liability, the entity would compare the present value of the cumulative changes in the expected future cash flows on the variable leg of an interest rate swap with the present value of the cumulative change in expected future interest cash flows on the hedged item. The fixed rate leg of the interest rate swap is excluded from the analysis as it is assumed that the derivative's fair value that is attributable to the fixed rate leg is not relevant to the variability of the variable cash flows on the hedged item. Such an assumption is only valid when the derivative has a fair value of zero at inception, i.e. it is an on-market instrument, and there is no impact on the fair value of the hedging instrument of non-performance risk of the reporting entity and the derivative counterparty. If the derivative did not have a fair value of zero at inception, the derivative would have a higher or lower fixed rate leg to compensate the entity for the upfront payment or receipt at inception. Because the fixed rate leg is adjusted to reflect this upfront payment or receipt, the fixed rate leg includes a financing element that cannot be ignored. It is for the above reason that IAS 39.IG.F.5.5 purposely prohibits use of the variable cash flows method.

In March 2007, the IFRIC finalised a rejection notice titled *Assessing hedge effectiveness of an interest rate swap in a cash flow hedge*. The IFRIC stated that it was not permissible to consider only the undiscounted changes in cash flows of the hedging instrument and the hedged item in assessing hedge effectiveness in a cash flow hedge of interest rate risk when using an interest rate swap. The IFRIC noted that such a method for assessing hedge effectiveness would not be in accordance with IAS 39.74 that does not allow the designation of a portion of a derivative as the hedging instrument, and would ignore the fact that one of the reasons for ineffectiveness is the mismatch of the timing of interest payments or receipts of the swap and the hedged item.

US GAAP comparison: US guidance does allow the *change in variable cash flows method* to be used as a method of assessing cash flow hedge effectiveness. (An entity could only apply this technique if the derivative had a fair value of zero, or near zero, at inception of the hedge). IFRS does not allow an entity to exclude a leg of a swap in determining hedge effectiveness.

4.5 Hedge designations in Business Combinations

Phase 1 of the Business Combinations project that led to the publication of the original version of IFRS 3 *Business Combinations* in 2003 had no specific guidance about whether hedge relationships that exist in the acquiree need to be re-designated by the acquirer should the acquirer wish to continue hedge accounting in the group financial statements. IAS 39 also has no specific requirements with respect to business combinations. Phase 2 of the Business Combinations project that led to the issue of the revised version of IFRS 3 *Business Combinations* in January 2008 has specific guidance on reassessment of contractual arrangements, including financial instruments. IFRS 3(2008) applies prospectively to business combinations for which the acquisition date is on or after the beginning of the first annual reporting period beginning on or after 1 July 2009.

The revised standard requires reassessment of classification and designation of all contractual arrangements based on the pertinent conditions as they exist at the acquisition, with the exception of two cases which are classification of leases as finance or operating leases, and the classification of insurance contracts. IFRS 3(2008).16(b) and BC185 specifically refer to designation of a derivative instrument as a hedging instrument in accordance with IAS 39 and requires reassessment of classification and designation.

The implication of the requirement to reassess hedge relationships at the date of business combinations is that, without re-designation at the group level, the hedge accounting that may continue to be applied at the level of the acquiree will not be applied by the group. If the group wishes to apply hedge accounting at the group level immediately post-acquisition a new hedge relationship will need to be designated at the date of the business combination. When designating cash flow hedges the hypothetical derivative will reflect the conditions that exist at the date of re-designation and therefore may be substantially different to the hypothetical derivative that was originally designated in the acquiree's financial statements. Assuming the group attempts to designate the existing derivative of the acquiree in the same hedge relationship as the acquiree, any difference in the hypothetical derivative will result in a different amount of hedge effectiveness recognised at the group level. The hypothetical derivative may be so different to the actual derivative that the group is unable to pass the assessment of prospective hedge effectiveness and therefore is unable to apply hedge accounting post-acquisition. It is worth noting that any re-designation by the group does not affect the acquiree's financial statements assuming the acquiree retains its original hedge designation.

Consideration will need to be given to both hedge documentation and effectiveness where derivative financial instruments are transferred between entities within the same group. This transaction may or may not be part of a transaction that meets the definition of a common control transaction. In the separate financial statements of the entity acquiring the derivative, the instrument will be recognised as a financial instrument for the first time. Should that entity wish to designate that instrument in a hedge accounting relationship a new hedge relationship will need to determined and documented. In the case of a cash flow hedge, consideration will need to be given as to whether the actual derivative is equal to the hypothetical derivative at the date the hedge is designated (for detail on the hypothetical derivative method see **4.4.1** above). Hedge ineffectiveness will arise to the extent the actual and hypothetical derivative differ and may be significant enough to prevent the entity passing the prospective hedge effectiveness assessment. This will be the case even if the hedged item (as well as the derivative) is transferred to the acquirer.

Where a hedged item and hedging instrument are transferred from one group entity to another group entity and hedge accounting is applied immediately prior to the transfer, the original hedge accounting relationship may continue to apply in the consolidated financial statements if the relationship is highly effective. This will only be the case where there is no period where the hedge accounting relationship ceases and the hedge relationship, including the hedged risk, remain the same. In this limited case, the hypothetical derivative will not need to be to reset. Care should be taken in the case where the functional currency of the selling entity and the acquirer differ and foreign currency risk is being hedged as the difference in functional currencies will result in different hedged risks before and after the transfer and therefore a new hedge designation and a new hypothetical derivative will need to be determined in the consolidated financial statements. In some cases, the hedge relationship may no longer qualify for hedge accounting, e.g. if the functional currency of the acquirer is the same the denomination as the hedged item so no foreign currency exists, or the hedging instrument does not hedge the foreign currency risk of the hedged item into the acquirer's functional currency.

4.6 Regression analysis

Regression analysis is a statistical measurement technique for determining the validity and extent of a relationship between an independent and dependent variable. It is more complex than ratio analysis and requires appropriate interpretation and understanding of the statistical inferences. Where regression analysis is used, the entity's documented policies for assessing effectiveness must specify how the results of the regression will be assessed. A regression analysis can be used for either a cash flow or a fair value hedge.

Example 4.6A

Regression analysis (1)

Where the changes in value of a hedged item in Euros is X(t) and the change in value of the hedging instrument in Euros is Y(t), then if Y is a 'good hedge' for X then the observed points (X,Y) should be clustered close to a straight line with a slope equal to -1 and intercept equal to the value of the hedged position, C.

$Y(t) - X(t) = C$ or $Y = X + C$

C is the (constant) value of the hedged position.

For the purposes of illustration, assuming a constant of zero, the slope of the regression equation is equivalent to the ratio of effectiveness and, therefore, should lie within the range of -0.8 to -1.25 (corresponding to a ratio of 80 to 125 per cent) for a 1 to 1 hedge relationship. In the absence of further statistical evidence derived from the same data, a correlation coefficient, R^2, between the values of 0.8 to 1 typically is representative of a highly effective offsetting relationship between the hedged item and the hedging instrument. In other words, an R^2 of 0.8 indicate that 80 per cent of the movement in the dependent variable is 'explained' by variation in the independent variable. As the objective of hedge effectiveness is to assess the degree of offset between two variables, a simple linear regression is an acceptable technique for demonstrating the effectiveness of a hedge relationship.

The slope coefficient is the slope of the straight line of best fit of the regression. For a fully effective hedge relationship the slope coefficient will approximate to -1. A slope coefficient of -1 means that for a specified movement in the hedged item the hedging instrument will move by an equal but opposite extent. A slope coefficient of -0.85 means that for every €1 change in the hedged item it will generally result in an opposite change of €0.85 in the hedging instrument.

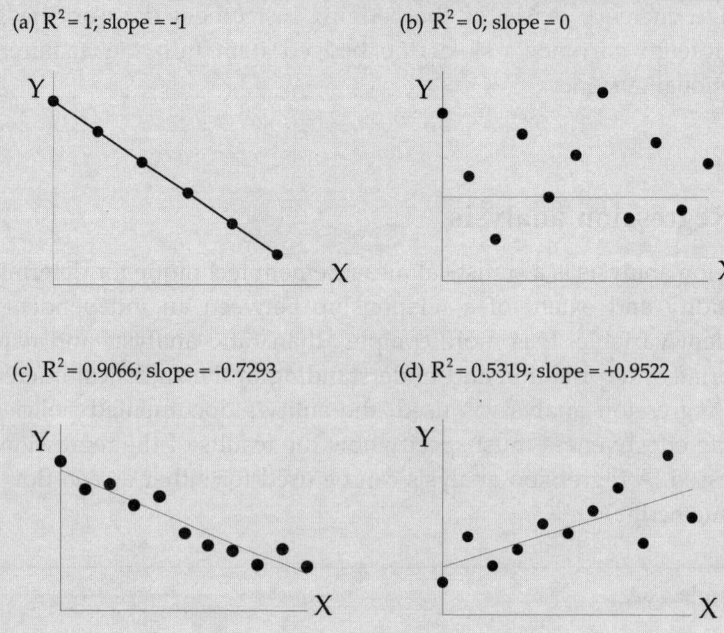

Regression analysis is best suited for measuring the strength of empirical relationships. This relationship can then be used to assess probability of offset, and establish hedge ratios. Such analysis is essential for indirect hedges, i.e. hedges with basis risk where the hedging instrument (e.g. a futures or options contract) has a different underlying to that of the hedged item or transaction. An example is a hedge of petrol prices using oil futures. A simple linear regression may establish a statistical relationship between the two variables, i.e. the price of oil and the price of petrol. The most common method to determine the regression line is called the least squares method. The method finds the best-fitting equation that minimises the sum of the (squared) distances between the data points and the regression line. Where there is a valid statistical relationship, the slope of the regression line can be used to establish the hedge ratio that will maximise expected effectiveness. [IAS 39.AG100]

More complex hedging strategies establish a relationship between one dependent and two or more independent variables by using multiple linear regression. However, as the objective of hedge effectiveness is to compare two variables, namely (i) the changes in fair value of the hedged risk of a hedged item with the change in fair value of a hedging instrument in a fair value hedge, or (ii) the cumulative change in fair value of the expected future cash flows on the hedged item from inception of the hedge with the cumulative gain or loss on the hedging instrument, a simple linear regression will normally be applied.

In order to conclude that the hedging relationship is highly effective using a regression analysis, R^2 should be equal to, or greater than 0.8, and the slope should be between a negative 0.8 and 1.25; and the F and *t* statistics should be evaluated at a 95 per cent confidence level. Only when all of these statistical objectives have been met can an entity claim a highly effective hedge relationship for the period.

The formula for a linear regression is as follows:

$$y = mx + b + x1.$$

where y — represents the dependent variable
m — represents the slope of the line
x — represents the independent variable
b — represents the y intercept
x1 — represents the error term

The table below provides information on how to evaluate the validity of a linear regression.

Factors that prove a regression analysis Is valid	Confidence level or numerical requirement	How to evaluate the confidence level or numerical requirement
R^2	> = 0.8	The R^2 output should be greater than or equal to 0.8. R^2 is the coefficient of determination which is the square of the coefficient of correlation or r. r indicates when two variables are linearly related.

Factors that prove a regression analysis Is valid	Confidence level or numerical require-ment	How to evaluate the confidence level or numerical requirement
		The value of r can range from –1 to +1. R^2 measures the proportion of variability in y that derives from x (i.e. how much of the change of y is explained by a change in x). The higher the value the higher the indication that y is related to x. R^2 is always positive as it is a squared number and cannot exceed 1 as x cannot explain more than 100 per cent in the change of y.
m — slope factor	Between –0.8 & –1.25	In the regression equation, the slope should be in the range provided. The slope of a line is the change in y over the change in x. An increasing or decreasing value indicates the positive or negative change in y for every change in x. For example, a slope of +1 would indicate that y is increasing at a positive rate with each change in x. In a hedging relationship, a hedge is used to achieve offsetting changes in the value of the hedged item, therefore, a regression equation for a hedging relationship should have a negative slope within the range previously specified as an entity will be long the exposure with the hedged item and short the exposure with the hedging instrument or vice versa. Additionally, 'm' represents the optimal hedge ratio for the hedge, indicating you need 'more' or 'less' of the hedging instrument to compensate for changes in the hedged item.
t — Statistic	95 Per cent Confidence Level	The t statistic for the x coefficient evaluates the probability that the slope is zero. A slope of zero indicates that there is no relationship between the x and y variables.

Factors that prove a regression analysis Is valid	Confidence level or numerical requirement	How to evaluate the confidence level or numerical requirement
		A high t statistic for the x coefficient, positive or negative, generally is a good indicator of correlation and thus a linear relationship. This statistic may be further evaluated by examining the p-value; a statistical output of the t statistic calculation. A low p-value associated with the t-statistic for the x variable, e.g. less than five per cent, indicates a low probability of the slope being zero and thus a high probability that the independent variable is useful in predicting the dependent variable.
F — Statistic	95 Per cent Confidence Level	The F statistic evaluates the probability that there is no linear relationship between the x and y variables. To achieve a 95 per cent confidence level, the significance of F should be less than five per cent. If the significance of F is less than five per cent then there is a less than five per cent probability that no linear relationship is present.

It has to be noted that all the factors have to be considered in determining whether a hedge relationship is highly effective. For example, if R^2 has a value near 1 then an m near the ranges of 80%-125% can be acceptable and vice versa.

If a hedge ratio other than one-for-one is applied (see **4.3.2** above), and historical regression analysis is used to determine this hedge ratio, when an entity actually assesses hedge effectiveness using regression values based on this hedge ratio, the entity would expect the 'perfect hedge' to have a gradient of 1 (not that of the hedge ratio). For example, if an entity has a hedge ratio of 0.7, i.e. 0.7 hedged items to 1 hedging instrument, for the purpose of assessing hedge effectiveness, the entity would still be expecting a gradient of the regression line of 0.8 to 1.25 in order to establish that the hedge was highly effective.

Users of regression must be aware of the concept of autocorrelation (i.e. serial correlation). This concept applies when the data points are correlated to each other over time, i.e. the data points are not random. One of the assumptions of a least squares regression is that the data points are uncorrelated to each other. If the data points are correlated to each other this will impact the output of the regression and will result in the R^2, m slope etc being misstated. When data points are taken over a period of time autocorrelation can occur if the different data points are sourced from the same period. For example, if one data point is the change in fair value of a derivative from 1 June to 30 August, and the second data point is the change in fair value from 1 August to 31 October, there is autocorrelation with respect to the month of August as it overlaps in both data points. Users of regression should ensure data is taken from discrete periods to avoid the data points being correlated with each other. Statistical techniques like the Durbin-Watson test can be applied to determine whether there is autocorrelation. Other statistical techniques, like the Prais-Winsten test can be used to restate the output from the model by removing the effects of autocorrelation. As IAS 39 provides no guidance on the use of statistical techniques, entities should use established statistical techniques that are known to provide a meaningful output that is consistent with the Standard's objective of assessing hedge effectiveness.

Further examples

An illustration of the accounting entries for a fair value hedge assessed for effectiveness using regression analysis is included in **5.1** in **chapter 10**.

4.6.1 Inputs in a regression analysis

Past data can be used to demonstrate that a hedge relationship is expected to be highly effective in a prospective hedge effectiveness test, and was highly effective in a retrospective hedge effectiveness test.

The data used in a regression is a series of matched-pair observations from a specified period of time. For example, an entity may wish to regress the change in fair value of an interest rate swap with the change in fair value of the interest rate portion of fixed rate debt on the first day of each month for a three year period. This will generate 36 matched-pair observations which will input into the regression model. An entity should apply a consistent number of data points as the regression is updated at a minimum at the end of each reporting period. If an entity is using a regression model for both prospective and retrospective hedge effectiveness tests it should also use the same number of data points in both tests, and should apply this consistently to other similar hedges.

It is typical to regress observations over the same period as the length of the hedge relationship. For example, if an entity is fair value hedging 5 year fixed rate debt from the date of issue for its full term, an entity would use observations from the last 5 years to demonstrate prospectively that a 5 year receive fixed pay floating interest rate swap is highly effective in fair value hedging the interest rate portion of the debt.

The more data points that are included in the data set will generally result in a more robust regression analysis. However, care must be taken not to include so many data points from such a long period that the data set is not representative of the hedge relationship. It is typical to use at least 30 observations, though in theory it is possible to have a highly effective hedge relationship with less than 30 observations when this is supported with an F-statistic and t-statistic that pass the required confidence levels if the underlying distribution can be assumed to be normal or approximately normal. However, as the number of observations must remain fixed throughout the hedge relationship, and therefore must be stated at inception in the hedge documentation, it is beneficial to use at least 30 observations in order to maximise the number of chances of passing the hedge effectiveness test in future reporting periods.

In both prospective and retrospective hedge effectiveness tests an entity will update the regression by adding new observations and excluding the same number of the oldest observations from the data set. This methodology ensures that the regression is consistently updated and interpreted throughout the hedge relationship.

If an entity wishes to designate a hedging relationship at initial recognition of the hedging instrument (in the case of a cash flow hedge) or at initial recognition of the hedging instrument and the hedged item (in the case of a fair value hedge) it will not necessarily have the data history for those particular instrument(s). This would be the case if the contract did not exist prior to the initial recognition date, or historical fair value data is not available for an instrument that did exist but was held by a different party. In this case the entity should consider using data from similar instruments or instead generate data points by calculating the hypothetical fair value of the instrument using historic market data assuming that instrument had existed prior to the initial recognition date.

4.6.2 *Differences in the results of regression and ratio analysis*

Ratio and regression analysis are clearly very different statistical techniques for assessing hedge effectiveness. Whichever technique is applied, whether for a prospective or/and retrospective assessment of hedge effectiveness, they are unlikely to achieve the same results for each period. The only exception to this perhaps is if the terms of the hedging instrument and hedged item are exactly the same and therefore for all periods the hedge effectiveness assessment would be highly effective. In such instances, entities may have a preference in applying ratio analysis instead of regression because it is simpler.

If an entity chooses to use regression analysis, and therefore must apply this technique consistently throughout the hedge relationship, the entity should be aware of other statistical techniques whose results could call into question the validity of the regression. An example would be a comparison of regression to ratio analysis. If an entity had chosen regression analysis and failed to be highly effective for a period using ratio analysis, it does not mean that the results of the regression are considered not highly effective for that period. Instead, the entity should be aware that if the entity would have failed using ratio analysis on multiple consecutive periods then this does call into question the validity and robustness of the regression analysis. In these instances, the entity should investigate the reasons for the divergence between ratio analysis and regression and if the reasons are not expected to recur in future periods the entity will pass the highly effective test in the current period, and can continue to apply regression analysis in future periods. For example, assume an entity was regressing Brent crude oil prices with aviation fuel prices over a 3 year period as it is hedging its forecast aviation fuel purchases in 3 years' time. After 4 quarters since the start of the hedge relationship, the retrospective hedge effectiveness assessment using regression passed every quarter, but ratio analysis failed every quarter. Upon further investigation of the difference, the entity noted there was a structural event in the market that will result in ratio analysis continuing to fail based on the current hedge designation. It is worth noting that the impact of this structural event will ultimately impact the regression analysis in future periods as new data is added each quarter and the oldest data is removed from the data set. Because the reasons for the divergence in regression and ratio analysis are expected to continue in future periods the entity would not achieve hedge accounting for the period, but the entity could re-designate the hedge relationship using a different hedge ratio and attempt to claim prospective hedge effectiveness based on the new designation.

In November 2006 the IFRIC issued a rejection notice that addressed testing of hedge effectiveness on a cumulative basis. One of the points made in the rejection notice was if the dollar-to-dollar comparison (i.e. ratio analysis) of the changes in the fair value or cash flows of the hedged items and the changes in the fair value or cash flows of the hedging instrument falls outside a range of 80–125 per cent this does not necessarily result in the entity failing to qualify for hedge accounting, provided that the dollar-to-dollar comparison is not the method documented at inception of the hedge for assessing hedge effectiveness. While this conclusion is certainly logical it is worth noting that the existence of a failing ratio analysis may provide evidence that the data being added to a regression analysis will result in a future failure of regression, which ultimately will impact an entity's ability to pass the prospective hedge effectiveness assessment. In short, entities should not be blinded by the output from statistical techniques nor should they look at the output in isolation as this will hinder their ability to assess the quality of the output and the soundness of statistical relationships.

5 Net investment hedge: advanced

Compared to other hedge accounting concepts net investment hedging is a relatively simple. The basic requirements of net investment hedges are described in 2.3 in *chapter 8*). Net investment hedging can become complicated when applied in large groups with multiple entities with different functional currencies. This section discusses some of these complexities and also demonstrates how cross currency swaps can be used in net investment hedges.

5.1 Hedging net investments with currency swaps

Net investment hedging with loans and forward contracts is discussed in **2.3** in **chapter 8**. Hedging net investments with foreign currency swaps is very similar to hedging with forwards. This is to be expected, as swaps with fixed cash flows are simply a series of forwards. As with forwards, it is important to be clear which risk is being hedged (i.e. the spot or forward rate).

Further examples

An illustration of the entries for a net investment hedge of a foreign operation using a cross currency interest rate swap that receives and pays:

- floating interest is shown at **4.3** in **chapter 10**.
- fixed interest is shown at **4.4** in **chapter 10**.

Whilst foreign currency swaps that swap from one currency to another can be used as hedging instruments of net investment hedges, it is difficult to get high effectiveness with cross currency fixed-for-floating interest rate swaps as the interest element of the swap does not reduce foreign exchange risk of the net investment in the foreign operation. This is the case when an entity is swapping currency as well as the basis of interest from floating to fixed rates and vice versa. Furthermore, since a derivative instrument must be designated in its entirety (except for the limited circumstances noted in **4.2** in **chapter 8**), the element that does not reduce foreign exchange risk cannot be excluded from the hedge designation.

Where the currency swap is fixed for fixed, or floating to floating, the derivative may qualify as a hedge of a net investment in a foreign operation. Hedging instruments such as floating to floating currency swaps respond closely to movements in spot rates. Thus, provided the notional of such an instrument does not exceed the net investment, it is likely to be an effective hedging instrument for a hedge of the spot risk associated with the net investment.

Fixed for fixed currency swaps may be used as hedging instruments in a hedge of either the forward or spot risk associated with the net investment. In either case there are potentially two ways of designating such an instrument. One would be to hedge an amount of net assets that is equal to the present value of the foreign currency interest and principal. This is in line with viewing the cross currency swap as comprising a combination of a loan payable in foreign currency and a loan receivable in the other currency. In this case an amount of net assets equal to the foreign currency principal of the swap should be designated as the hedged item. Alternatively, an amount of net assets equal to the sum of the undiscounted foreign currency principal and undiscounted foreign currency interest payments can be designated as the hedged item. This is in line with viewing the fixed for fixed swap as a combination of forwards with respect to interest payments and final principal exchange at maturity. Note that a greater amount of net assets would have to be available for the second method to be an effective hedge relationship. Whichever approach is applied, it should be applied consistently.

5.2 Hedging by multiple parent entities

IFRIC 16 clarified that within consolidated financial statements a parent that hedges a foreign operation can be an immediate parent, intermediate parent, or ultimate parent. The fact that the net investment is held through an intermediate parent does not affect the nature of the economic risk arising from the foreign currency exposure to the ultimate parent entity. [IFRIC 16.12] However, an exposure to foreign currency risk arising from a net investment in a foreign operation may qualify for hedge accounting only once in the consolidated financial statements. Therefore, if the same net assets of a foreign operation are hedged by more than one parent entity within the group (for example, both a direct and an indirect parent entity) for the same risk, only one hedging relationship will qualify for hedge accounting in the consolidated financial statements of the ultimate parent. [IFRIC 16.13]

If a hedging relationship is designated by one parent entity in its consolidated financial statements, it need not be maintained by another higher level parent entity. However, if it is not maintained by the higher level parent entity, the hedge accounting applied by the lower level parent must be reversed before the higher level parent's hedge accounting is recognised. [IFRIC 16.13] This is not unique to net investment hedging as hedge accounting by a subsidiary or by a sub-consolidated group need not be maintained in the consolidated financial statements that include the subsidiary or a sub-consolidated group. Conversely, hedge accounting could be designated in the consolidated financial statements but is not designated in the subsidiary only financial statements or the financial statements of a sub-consolidated group that forms part of the larger group. This flexibility is possible because hedge accounting is entirely voluntary.

Example 5.2

Hedge designations

The group structure of Group P is as follows:

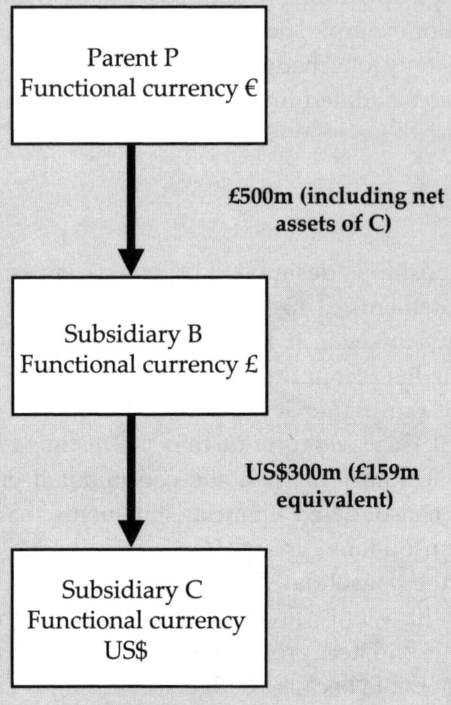

In the consolidated financial statements headed by Group P the maximum amount of net assets available to be hedged for the respective hedged risk in a qualifying hedge relationship is:

- $300m net assets for €/US$ risk between P and C; or
- £500m net assets for €/£ risk between P and B; or
- $300m net assets for £/US$ risk between B and C; or
- $300m net assets for £/US$ risk between B and C; and £500m net assets for €/£ risk between P and B; or
- $300m net assets for €/US$ risk between P and C; and £341m net assets for €/£ risk between P and B.

5.3 Location of hedging instrument within the group

IFRIC 16.14 states that the hedging instrument(s) may be held by any entity or entities within the group (except the foreign operation that itself is being hedged), as long as the designation, documentation and effectiveness requirements of IAS 39.88 for the net investment hedge are satisfied. IFRIC 16 notes that the hedge strategy must be clearly documented because of the possibility of different designations at different levels of the group.

Where the hedging instrument resides in an entity that has the same functional currency as the parent that has the investment in the foreign operation the hedge effectiveness calculations are easier to perform as hedge effectiveness is determined as if the parent that has the investment in the foreign operation also had the hedging instrument. Determining hedge effectiveness is more complex when the entity holding the hedging instrument has a different functional currency from that of the parent that has the exposure to the foreign operation. In such a case, IFRIC 16 requires hedge effectiveness to not only reflect the gain/loss residing in the entity holding the hedging instrument (which in the absence of hedge accounting would have been recognised in consolidated profit or loss), but also the effect of retranslating that hedging instrument as part of the translation of the net assets of the entity holding the hedging instrument into the parent's functional currency (which in the absence of hedge accounting would have been recognised in consolidated other comprehensive income). The IFRIC goes further to state that the assessment of effectiveness is not affected by whether the hedging instrument is a derivative or a non-derivative instrument or by the method of consolidation. [IFRIC 16.15]

Example 5.3

Assessing hedge effectiveness based on parent's functional currency

Parent P has a Euro functional currency and has two foreign operations, Subsidiary A which has a US dollar functional currency and Subsidiary B which has a New Zealand dollar functional currency. Subsidiary B holds a foreign currency forward contract to sell a fixed amount of US$ for a fixed amount of € at a specific date in the future. Parent P wishes to designate the foreign currency forward as a net investment hedge of its investment in Subsidiary A. The hedged risk is the €/US$ foreign currency exposure with respect to the translation of Subsidiary A's US$ net assets into €.

Parent P wishes to designate the spot foreign currency risk only (not the forward foreign currency risk). The opening net assets of Subsidiary A are $1,000 and the entire opening net assets are intended to be designated as being hedged by Parent P in its consolidated financial statements. For illustrative purposes the foreign currency forward's fair value is calculated using undiscounted spot rates and the foreign currency spot and forward rate are presumed to be the same (i.e. there is no gain/loss in respect of fair valuing the forward point differential).

	Opening spot rate	Closing spot rate	Average spot rate
€/US$	1.400	1.520	1.460
€/NZ$	2.200	1.850	2.025
US$/NZ$	1.571	1.217	1.394

Parent P's translation of Subsidiary A's designated net assets in the consolidated financial statements:

Opening designated net assets	US$1,000 @ 1.400 =	€714
Closing designated net assets	US$1,000 @ 1.520 =	€658
Loss on translation of Subsidiary A's net assets		€56

Gain/loss on the foreign currency forward with respect to spot rates in Subsidiary B's financial statements:

Receive €	(Buy €714 @ 1.850) =	NZ$1,321
Pay US$	(Sell US$1,000 @ 1.217) =	NZ$1,217
Gain/loss in the period		NZ$104

Impact of the derivative in consolidated profit or loss in the absence of hedge accounting with respect to the hedged risk:

Gain/loss NZ$104 @ 2.025 (average spot rate) = €51

If the translation of the hedging instrument from Subsidiary B's functional currency, NZ$, to the Parent P's functional currency, €, was ignored, the hedge relationship is partly ineffective. The hedge relationship would be 91% effective (€51/€56). As this remains within the 80% to 125% parameter it would have been deemed highly effective in the period.

IFRIC 16 requires the effectiveness to be determined by reference to the parent's functional currency. The effect of applying this approach is to include the difference between the average spot rate and the closing spot rate that is recognised in consolidated other comprehensive income with respect to the translation of the derivative in Subsidiary B, as part of the assessment of hedge effectiveness.

Gain/loss	NZ$104 @ 2.025 (average rates) =	€51
Gain/loss	NZ$104 @ 1.850 (closing rates) =	€56
Difference	=	€5

When the additional amount described above is included in the assessment of hedge effectiveness the hedge is 100% effective ((€51 + €5) / €56).

Had Parent P held the foreign currency forward, the gain/loss derived from the foreign currency forward would be driven solely by US$ as the € receive leg of the foreign currency forward does not generate foreign currency risk because Parent P has a € functional currency. The gain/loss on the hedging instrument would be an offset to the translation of Subsidiary A's US$ net assets to €. Considered differently, in the group accounts of Parent P the group has a long US$ position being the net assets of Subsidiary A, and a short US$ position being the US$ pay leg of the foreign currency forward contract and therefore the derivative would have been fully effective.

In February 2009 the IFRIC issued Exposure Draft ED/2009/1, *Post-implementation Revisions to IFRIC Interpretations – Proposed amendments to IFRIC 9 and IFRIC 16*, which proposed amending IFRIC 16.14 to allow the hedging instrument to be held by any entity within the group and thereby remove the restriction that the foreign operation that itself is being hedged cannot hold the hedging instrument. In the basis for conclusions of the exposure draft it states that the IFRIC believe that without hedge accounting part of the foreign exchange difference arising from the hedging instrument would be included in consolidated profit or loss and therefore the restriction that the foreign operation being hedged cannot hold the hedging instrument should be removed.

At the date of writing the proposed amendment to IFRIC 16 had not been finalised.

5.4 Hedging a portfolio of net investments with a single derivative

If a group has multiple foreign operations that have the same functional currency, the group can hedge the foreign operations either as a group, or individually. For example, Parent heads a group that includes two US$ subsidiaries, A and B, each with $500k of net assets, and $1m of third party borrowings. The Parent's interest in subsidiary A and B is held directly, i.e. Subsidiary B is not a subsidiary of Subsidiary A. The group may either designate the borrowings of $1m as a hedge of a group of foreign operations of $1m, or designate 50 per cent of the borrowings as hedging $500k of subsidiary A, and 50 per cent of the borrowings as hedging $500k of subsidiary B. When the designation is on a group basis the hedge documentation can be done on a group basis; however, hedge effectiveness must be assessed for each subsidiary individually.

Example 5.4

Hedging a portfolio of net investments with a single derivative

Entity P is a Sterling functional currency entity that has US$400m foreign currency denominated issued debt which it wishes to designate as a hedging instrument of the net investment in its US dollar foreign operations. The group structure is as follows:

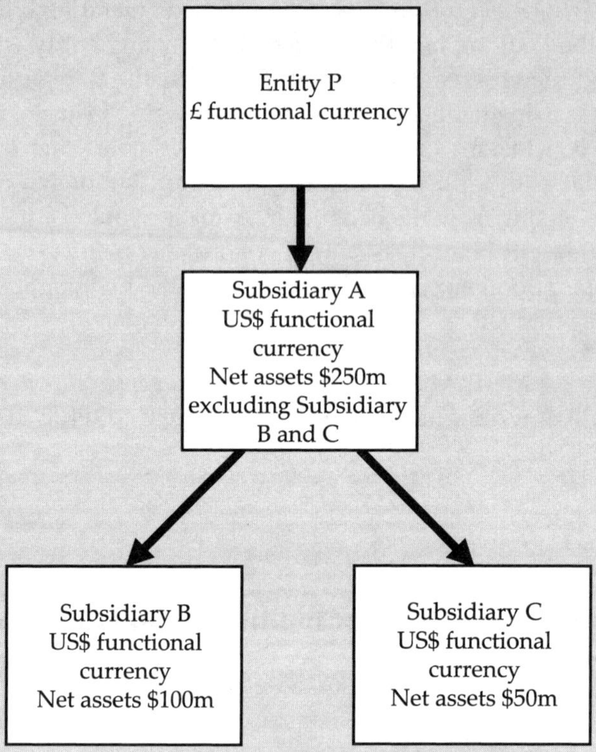

The following designations are permitted by IAS 39:

1. Entity P may designate US$400m debt as a hedging instrument of a net investment in the consolidated net assets of the sub-group headed by Subsidiary A;

2. Entity P may designate relevant proportions of the US$ debt as hedges of net investments in Subsidiary A, Subsidiary B, and Subsidiary C individually, i.e. 62.5 per cent of the US$ debt as a hedge of the net investment in subsidiary A, 25 per cent of the US$ debt as a hedge of the net investment in Subsidiary B, and 12.5 per cent of the US$ debt as the hedge of the net investment in Subsidiary C; or

3. Entity P may designate US$400m debt as a hedge of a portfolio of net investments in US$ subsidiaries.

IAS 21 *The Effects of Changes in Foreign Exchange Rates* views a net investment in a foreign operation as 'the amount of the reporting entity's interest in the net assets of that operation'. [IAS 21.8] The 'operation' is not defined and can be considered to be either the consolidated net assets of the sub-group headed by Entity A, or as a collection of net assets held by each of the three subsidiaries.

If Entity P chooses to designate a portfolio (designation 3 in the list above) it must have an expectation that each individual item in the portfolio will change in fair value approximately proportionally to the change in the fair value of the portfolio as a whole. Such an expectation would be appropriate if the net assets of the individual subsidiaries are expected to be stable or increasing, provided the designation is of 'the first US$ Xm of net assets of a subsidiary'. However, if the net assets of an individual subsidiary are expected to fall below the designated amount, Entity P could not expect that the items in the portfolio will move approximately proportionally to the movement in the portfolio as a whole.

If an entity can demonstrate a high expectation of effectiveness for the portfolio, the group must assess and measure hedge effectiveness based on the individual foreign operations within the portfolio. Therefore, to the extent that the net assets of one of the foreign operations fall below the designated net asset amount, or a subsidiary is sold, ineffectiveness will arise.

It should be noted that the amount of ineffectiveness that will be recognised if Entity P were to use the portfolio designation will be the same as that recognised if designation 2 was adopted. The only comparative advantage of the portfolio method is that the hedging documentation required is done for a portfolio as a whole (though it must include evidence supporting the expectation of approximately proportional movements in the fair value of individual investments in the portfolio to the fair value movements of the portfolio as a whole).

6 Cash flow hedge accounting – portfolio hedge of interest rate risk

An entity may wish to designate a derivative, or portfolio of derivatives, as a hedge of multiple variable interest rate payments or receipts. Instead of allocating each individual derivative to an individual cash inflow or outflow, the derivatives and the hedged cash flows are 'pooled' and hedged as a portfolio. IAS 39.IG.F.6.2 provides a series of questions and answers for an entity wishing to undertake such a hedge accounting strategy. IAS 39.IG.F.6.3 provides an illustrative example of the hedge strategy. The implementation guidance is very detailed and is complex. The objective of this section is to simplify the concepts and highlight some relevant conclusions that can be reached from this implementation guidance.

6.1 Hedged item

As stated in **2.2** in **chapter 8** a recognised floating rate debt instrument can either be hedged as a recognised financial instrument, or instead the floating interest inflows or outflows can be hedged as forecast transactions. If an entity regularly borrows or invests in floating rate debt instruments the entity has an exposure not only from the recognised debt instruments but also the debt instruments that it will invest or borrow in the future. An entity may, for example, borrow through short-term commercial paper, say up to a maturity of 90 days, that has an interest rate that resets monthly, but will rollover the recognised commercial paper into further commercial paper when the recognised commercial paper reaches its maturity. The entity has variability in cash flows with respect to its recognised commercial paper, but also the commercial paper it believes, with high probability, it borrow in the future.

IAS 39 provides flexibility in hedging forecast cash flows when an entity expects, with high probability, to reinvest cash flows from one instrument into another. When cash flow hedging interest rate risk, say LIBOR, an entity can have cash flow variability with respect to the following:

- the variability in LIBOR inflows or outflows on a recognised acquired or issued debt instrument when the basis of interest is determined by future LIBOR rates; or
- the variability in LIBOR inflows or outflows from a highly probable reinvestment or future borrowing of a new floating rate LIBOR debt instrument. As future interest inflows or outflows will be derived from future rates of LIBOR, the entity has an exposure to variability in LIBOR; or
- the effective interest rate that will be earned or paid if an entity has a highly probable forecast investment or issuance of fixed rate debt where the debt is priced off the LIBOR curve at the date the debt is issued; or
- the effective interest rate that will be earned or paid if an entity has a highly probable forecast investment or issuance of a fixed rate debt and the fixed interest rate is determined of the LIBOR curve prior to the debt being issued, and therefore the amount of proceeds received by the issuer, or paid by the acquirer has not yet been determined, i.e. it is variable. The resulting premium or discount to par at issue will impact profit or loss through the effective interest rate determined when the debt is issued.

The entity can aggregate its floating rate LIBOR exposures from the four examples above and plot them in time buckets so that the entity can determine when the LIBOR cash flows are set (i.e. when they fix), and therefore determine up to what period it has an exposure to LIBOR. For example, if an entity has issued 5-year floating rate 3-month LIBOR debt where the floating rate is set in advance, at the date of issue, the floating rate for the next 3 months will be determined based on the rate of LIBOR at the date the debt is issued. An entity cannot cash flow hedge the first payment of interest as that first payment is not actually variable as it has been fixed in advance. This payment will be excluded from the hedge designation. (If LIBOR was priced in arrears, or was priced in advance but some of the interest receipts or payments have not yet been set then this is the variability in LIBOR that could be designated.) However, all future interest payments that will be determined in 3 months' time and beyond, are today all variable, and until those floating rates are set, at the start of each respective quarter, the entity has exposure to LIBOR which it can hedge. As future LIBOR interest payments are set at the start of each quarter, the number of forecast transactions with respect to that debt instrument, falls, but is likely to be replaced by more forecast interest exposures in future periods if the entity expects to borrow more floating rate debt.

An entity does not need to state the maturity of the forecast floating or fixed debt it is expecting with high probability to invest in or borrow at. As long as the entity has a high probability of being exposed to LIBOR, as the entity is expected to invest in LIBOR debt instruments or borrow at LIBOR rates, the exact maturity of the instrument is not relevant. If an entity believes it will have an exposure to LIBOR for 3 years, it does not matter whether the entity expects to invest in a floating rate asset with a maturity of 6 months, that then rolls into another five 6-month term floating rate assets, or whether it expects to invest in a 12-month floating rate asset, and a subsequent investment in a further three 12-month floating rate assets. In both cases, and any other combination, the entity's *future* exposure to LIBOR is the same.

An entity also does not need to state whether it will invest or borrow in floating rate debt instruments, or fixed rate debt instruments, as long as any debt instrument it invests in or borrows is derived from the LIBOR curve. For example, if an entity expects to borrow in 6 months' time, up to the date it draws down the borrowing, it has an exposure to LIBOR. From today until 6-months' time, changes in LIBOR will impact the future interest payments on future floating rate debt, or will impact the fixed rate or amount of proceeds that will only be determined at the date the entity draws down the fixed rate borrowing. In both cases, the entity may designate its exposure to LIBOR for the next 6 months.

The portfolio approach to cash flow hedging interest rate risk is a dynamic approach in that an entity may choose to re-designate, almost on a continuous basis, though more likely every quarter if LIBOR resets quarterly. As the cash flows that are due to fix in the next period fall away from the designation, new forecast cash flows may be added to the designation.

As long as the entity can claim these new forecast transactions are highly probable and the entity has qualifying hedging instruments that are expected to be highly effective, the entity can pursue hedge accounting.

6.2 Hedging instrument

In the instance where the hedged risk is LIBOR the hedging instrument could be a LIBOR for fixed rate interest rate swap. Alternatively, it could be a LIBOR based purchased option. If the entity has an exposure to LIBOR inflows, and it chooses to hedge with a swap, it will have a pay LIBOR receive fixed rate interest rate swap; if the entity has an exposure to LIBOR outflows, and it chooses to hedge with a swap, it will have a receive LIBOR pay fixed rate interest swap. The entity must designate all, or a proportion, of the interest rate swap as a hedging instrument relating to the designated hedged item (forecast LIBOR interest inflows or outflows).

6.3 Hedge designation

In a hedge of forecast interest payments or receipts an entity will schedule the forecast transactions and will hedge these floating inflows or outflows up to the date they fix, i.e. when LIBOR is set. In more simple hedge designations, the timing of the fixing of the cash flows on the hedged items coincides with the timing of the refixing of the variable rate on the swap. This is considered a full term hedge, compared to a partial term hedge, as the full period up to the date when the forecast transaction is no longer subject to cash flow variability is hedged.

An entity will have exposure to LIBOR as long as the entity has a high probability of investing or borrowing in LIBOR-based debt instruments (whether floating or fixed of the future LIBOR curve). In order to designate all these exposures an entity can choose to partial term hedge these exposures until the next time LIBOR is set. As described in **6.1** above, if a LIBOR interest inflow or outflow is set, it no longer is variable and therefore cannot be hedged. An entity can use partial term hedging to hedge all variable LIBOR exposure for its forecast LIBOR-based transactions from today until the next time LIBOR resets. If LIBOR resets every quarter, the entity can partial term hedge all the future LIBOR exposures for just 3 months only. After 3 months, the entity will re-designate, for the next 3 months, and so on.

Example 6.3

Cash flow hedging the variability in reinvestment: designation

Entity A has a short-term recognised variable rate asset with 3 months remaining to maturity. At maturity of that asset Entity A will reinvest the proceeds from the asset into either fixed rate asset(s) or floating rate asset(s) of maturities that are not determined until those instruments are acquired. Entity A forecasts with high probability that it will reinvest for up to 4 years. As Entity A is exposed to interest rates from its reinvestment into new assets (irrespective of whether the asset is fixed or floating), it enters into a receive fixed pay floating 3m-LIBOR interest rate swap (IRS) that has a 2 year maturity (Entity A has a policy of hedging out only 2 years) to hedge the risk of variability in LIBOR. It is assumed that the floating rate on the recognised floating rate liability has already been set in advance and therefore there is no cash flow variability that can be hedged.

Entity A does not need to be specific as to the maturity of the future reinvested debt instruments. The instruments could have maturities of 3 months, 6 months, 9 months etc, and could also be fixed or floating. Up to the date the reinvestment occurs, Entity A has an exposure to LIBOR that it can cash flow hedge.

Entity A plots the notionals for the various time periods over the next 2 years which will determine the extent to which Entity A is exposed to LIBOR:

	t0	3m	6m	9m	12m	15m	18m	21m	24m
Specific 3m floating LIBOR asset (notional £m)	100								
Hedged item: Non specific assets that have LIBOR exposure (notional £m)		100	100	100	100	100	100	100	100
Hedging instrument: Receive fixed pay 3m-LIBOR (notional £m)	100	100	100	100	100	100	100	100	100

t0 = 1/1/X0

As the interest rate swap and the recognised floating rate asset have LIBOR set in advance, in this case on 1/1/X0, there is no cash flow variability on the LIBOR based asset with 3 months to maturity. All cash flows of that debt instrument are fixed, not variable, being the principal and one interest payment that have been determined at the date of designation. Therefore, the recognised floating rate LIBOR asset cannot be a hedged item in a cash flow hedge.

Entity A, therefore, can only designate the cash flow variability due to changes in LIBOR with respect to forecast transactions that occur after the first reset date of the swap (the first cash flows under the swap are already fixed at t0 as LIBOR is set in advance). The forecast transactions that Entity A chooses to hedge are the non-specific forecast exposure to LIBOR from reinvesting in LIBOR based assets from 1/4/X0 until 31/12/X1 (equal to the maturity of the IRS). At t0, Entity A designates the exposure of variability in LIBOR that occurs between 1/1/X0 and 31/3/X0 with respect to its forecast transaction (being the LIBOR variability on its forecast transactions occurring from 1/4/X0 to 31/12/X1). The exposure for the subsequent periods is specifically not hedged in this designation. Entity A has entered into a hedge of its exposure to LIBOR with respect to its reinvestment and rollover of LIBOR-based asset that are expected to occur in the 21 month period beginning 1/4/X0, due to changes in LIBOR that occur between 1/1/X0 and 31/3/X0.

Entity A is not specific as to the maturity of its reinvested assets that are acquired after 1/4/X0 as all assets will be subject to exposure to LIBOR until the date they are priced. As all non-specific forecast transaction are exposed to LIBOR and are deemed as highly probable Entity A is highly effective on a prospective basis.

6.4 Partial term cash flow hedging

Where there is a difference between the timing of the fixing of the LIBOR-based inflows or outflows of the hedged item and the timing of the fixing of LIBOR on the swap hedge ineffectiveness will generally arise as an entity hedges the full term of the forecast transaction, being the time period up to the date the interest receipt or payment is set to LIBOR.

Partial term cash flow hedging is an alternative technique which can be applied to hedged items that are financial instruments. Partial term cash flow hedging does not apply to non-financial items as explained in **2.2** above. In this instance where a forecast variable interest receipt or payment fixes at a date later than the respective fixing on the variable leg of the interest rate swap, an entity can purposely designate a partial term hedge of the period up to the date the variable leg on the interest rate swap refixes. For example, if the variable leg on the interest rate swap fixes for LIBOR on 1 October, yet the hedged item fixes for LIBOR on 1 November, the difference in timing of resetting cash flows is not part of the hedge designation. In this instance, variations in LIBOR between the designation date and 1 October are considered a partial term hedge of the variability in LIBOR that exists on the hedged item that will reset on 1 November. Partial term hedging 'carves' up the period to the next resetting on the hedged item and hedges only part of that period.

IAS 39.IG.F.6.3 endorses this type of designation as it states that 'when the interest rate swap is repriced in three months at the then current variable rate, the fixed rate and the variable rate on the interest rate swap become known and no longer provide hedge protection for the next three months. If the next forecast transaction does not occur until three months and ten days, the ten-day period that remains after the repricing of the interest rate swap is not hedged'. The term of the hedge designation is only for the next 3 months. The implementation guidance explains that the 'period of the exposure to interest rate changes on the portion of the cash flow exposures being hedged is:

- the period from the designation date to the repricing date of the interest rate swap that occurs within the quarterly period in which, but not before, the forecast transactions occur, and
- its effects for the period after the forecast transactions occur equal to the repricing interval of the interest rate swap.'

As the designation is the variability due to LIBOR prior to the debt instrument being acquired or issued, the fact that following the acquisition or recognition of the borrowing, LIBOR continues to change is irrelevant with respect to this specific partial term hedge designation, as the period following recognition of the asset or liability does not form part of this specific hedge.

6.5 Hedge effectiveness

Hedge ineffectiveness can be greatly reduced by using the above hedge accounting strategy for a number of reasons:

- The entity designates the LIBOR risk only, and excludes credit risk on the hedged items. Changes in the credit risk of the hedged item will not impact the effectiveness of the hedge as credit risk is not a designated hedged risk. The credit risk of the interest rate swap, however, must be monitored as this may be a source of ineffectiveness.
- Duration differences between the interest rate swap and the hedged forecast cash flow are not a source of ineffectiveness as the interest rate risk that is hedged is the risk relating to changes in the portion of the yield curve that corresponds with the period in which the variable rate leg of the interest rate swap is repriced.
- Timing differences between the date the swap resets to LIBOR and the date the hedged item resets to LIBOR are not a source of ineffectiveness when partial term hedging is applied.

Example 6.5

Cash flow hedging the variability in reinvestment: hedge effectiveness

Continuing with **example 6.3** above, assuming Entity A is subject to quarterly reporting where the period end coincides with the repricing on the swap, i.e. 31/3/X0, Entity A must perform a retrospective assessment of hedge effectiveness for the period gone, plus a prospective assessment if it wishes to continue to apply hedge accounting.

As part of the retrospective assessment of hedge effectiveness for the period it looks back at the transactions that occurred in the period to determine whether it has been highly effective. As at 1/1/X0 Entity A never claimed it was hedging cash flow variability for the first 3 months of 20X0 for its recognised asset as LIBOR had already been determined on that floating rate recognised asset and therefore it never formed part of the designation. However, Entity A must assess whether the forecast transactions that it had designated at 1/1/X0, being the full-term hedge of forecast reinvestments after 1/4/X0, is highly effective. Entity A did not need to apply partial term hedging as the date of the LIBOR reset on the interest rate swaps coincides with the date of the LIBOR reset of the forecast reinvestments. Where the forecast reinvestments remain highly probable the hedge will have been fully effective on a retrospective basis, assuming all other criteria are met. Entity A may therefore recognise the full amount of the fair value of the derivative in other comprehensive income at 31/3/X0 in accordance with IAS 39.96.

As part of the prospective assessment of hedge effectiveness at 1/4/X0 Entity A must reassess whether the future exposure to LIBOR is still highly probable. As the next reset date on the interest rate swap is 1/7/X0, Entity A is hedging those forecast transactions that are subject to LIBOR in the future that reset after 1/7/X0. Any LIBOR-based interest inflows that are fixed at 1/4/X0 are not designated as they are no longer variable, and any interest inflows that fix within the next 3 months are not part of the designation as they are not subject to variability in LIBOR for the next 3 months. Entity A can pass the prospective assessment of hedge effectiveness as long as all the forecast transactions are deemed to be highly probable.

7 Fair value hedge accounting – portfolio hedge of interest rate risk

The IASB published an amendment to IAS 39 in March 2004 that details how an entity can apply fair value hedge accounting to a portfolio of financial assets and/or financial liabilities for interest rate risk only. The main reasons for amending IAS 39 and a summary of the amendments are as described below.

7.1 Prepayable financial items

Fixed rate prepayable debt instruments may be prepaid prior to their contracted maturity. When interest rates move the change in the fair value of a prepayable item is caused by changes in the fair value of the contractual cash flows and changes in the fair value of the prepayment option. If the hedging instrument, e.g. an interest rate swap, is not prepayable, changes in the fair value of the hedged item are not expected to be offset by changes in fair value of the hedging instrument. This results in hedge ineffectiveness.

IAS 39 permits prepayable financial assets and liabilities to be hedged for changes in fair value attributable to changes in the hedged interest rate on the basis of expected rather than contractual repricing dates. [IAS 39.81A] This is achieved by analysing the portfolio of hedged items into time periods based on the expected repricing dates. The expected repricing date of an item is the earlier of the dates when the item is expected to mature or to reprice to market rates. [IAS 39.AG117] As a result, the computation of the effect of a change in interest rates on the fair value of the prepayment option embedded in a prepayable item is not required. Though, if the estimates of the time periods in which items are expected to repay change, ineffectiveness will arise.

7.2 Hedging a portfolio of items

IAS 39 allows similar assets or similar liabilities to be aggregated and hedged as a group only if the individual assets or individual liabilities in the group share the risk exposure that is designated as being hedged. Furthermore, the change in fair value attributable to the hedged risk for each individual item in the group must be expected to be approximately proportional to the overall change in fair value attributable to the hedged risk of the group of items. [IAS 39.83] As the individual hedged items are expected to behave differently in so far as they may prepay at different times, the change in the fair value of each hedged item cannot be expected to be proportional to the change in the fair value of the portfolio.

The general requirement is modified for a hedge of a portfolio for interest rate risk only. The items in the hedged portfolio must be items whose fair value changes in response to the hedged interest rate and must be items that could have qualified for fair value hedge accounting had they been designated individually. However, an entity is not required to demonstrate that the change in fair value of the individual hedged items is approximately proportional to the overall change in fair value of the portfolio due to interest rate risk. [IAS 39.AG118] For this type of hedge the designated hedged item is expressed as an 'amount of currency' (e.g. an amount of Sterling, US dollars, Euros etc) rather than as individual assets or liabilities. [IAS 39.81A]

7.3 Fair value hedge adjustments

IAS 39 requires that in an effective fair value hedge relationship the hedged item is adjusted by the change in its fair value due to the hedged risk. The adjustment to the hedged item may be amortised to profit or loss as soon as the adjustment exists, but shall begin no later than when the item ceases to be adjusted for the hedged risk. For a portfolio hedge this would require an adjustment to many items, as well as tracking the amortisation of the resultant adjustment to profit or loss. In most cases complex systems solutions would be required.

IAS 39 is modified to permit the adjustment to the hedged items for a portfolio hedge of interest rate risk to be recognised in two separate line items within assets or liabilities for those repricing time periods for which the hedged item is an asset or liability respectively. This adjustment shall be presented next to financial assets or financial liabilities. [IAS 39.89A] Furthermore, that adjustment may be amortised to profit or loss using a straight line method where amortising using a recalculated effective interest rate is not practicable. The adjustment should also be amortised to profit or loss by the expiry of the relevant repricing time period. [IAS 39.92]

7.4 Hedging a net position

Whilst IAS 39 prohibits the designation of an overall net position (e.g. the net of fixed rate assets and fixed rate liabilities), entities that hedge the net position in economic terms may designate a proportion of either the assets or liabilities as the hedged item. The net exposure will change each period due to the re-pricing of items, or through derecognition, impairment and origination of new instruments. It follows that the designated proportion of assets or liabilities will also need to be changed following such changes in the net exposure.

In the case of a portfolio hedge for interest rate risk only, the hedged item may be expressed as a *gross currency amount* of either assets or liabilities rather than as an individual asset (or liability). [IAS 39.81A] The benefit of this approach is that the effect of changes in interest rates on the amount of designated currency is determined in aggregate and not individually for each hedged item. [IAS 39.81A]

7.5 Demand deposits

IAS 39 states that the fair value of a financial liability with a demand feature is not less than the amount payable on demand, discounted from the first date that the amount could be required to be paid. [IAS 39.49] Many entities economically hedge their demand deposits on the basis that a certain core level of the demand deposits is not repaid on demand. For the core deposits the expected life extends well beyond the demand date and the balance of the portfolio is relatively stable because withdrawals on some accounts are offset by new deposits into others. The hedge relationships are entered into on the basis of the expected repayment dates of the total balance of the portfolio of deposits.

In a fair value hedge, accounting for demand deposits on the basis of their expected repayment dates is inconsistent with the measurement principle for a financial liability with a demand feature. Thus, for fair value hedges, demand deposits cannot be hedged beyond their demand date. Nevertheless, the deposits may be included in determining the entity's net exposure and the designated hedged item with one restriction: if the net exposure is a net liability and that liability is made up entirely or partly of demand deposits, the designated liability can only be up to an amount equal to the amount of non-demand deposit liabilities. The reason for this is that the fair value determined in accordance with IAS 39 of a demand deposit is not affected by changes in interest rates, i.e. there is no fair value exposure to hedge for accounting purposes.

7.6 Hedge ineffectiveness

In a fair value hedge of a portfolio hedge of interest rate risk, in addition to hedge ineffectiveness that arises on other fair value hedging relationships, additional hedge ineffectiveness may arise for the following reasons in a portfolio hedging relationship:

- actual repricing dates differ from those expected, or expected repricing dates are revised; and
- items in the hedged portfolio become impaired or are derecognised.

7.7 Application

IAS 39 sets out a number of steps that should be followed in achieving hedge accounting for a portfolio hedge of interest rate risk. These steps are summarised in the example below.

Example 7.7

Fair value hedging a portfolio of interest rate risk

Step 1: As part of its risk management process, Bank A identifies a portfolio of items whose interest rate risk it wishes to hedge. The portfolio may comprise only of financial assets, financial liabilities, or both. Since Bank A hedges its fixed rate originated mortgages, fixed rate liabilities and core deposits on a net basis, it identifies a portfolio containing these items as the portfolio it wishes to hedge. [IAS 39.AG114(a)]

Step 2: Bank A analyses the portfolio into repricing time periods based on expected, rather than contractual, repricing dates. The expected repricing dates are based on historical experience and other available information, including information and expectations regarding prepayment rates, interest rates and their interaction. Whilst the analysis into repricing time periods may be performed by scheduling cash flows into the periods in which they are expected to occur, the Bank schedules the notional principal amounts into all periods until repricing is expected to occur as follows: [IAS 39.AG114(b)]

	T1	T2	T3
Fixed rate assets	30	40	25
Fixed rate liabilities	(20)	(30)	(15)
Demand deposits	-	-	(35)
Net exposure	10	10	(25)

In addition to complying with all other hedge designation and documentation criteria, Bank A documents:

- which assets and liabilities are included in the portfolio hedge and the basis used for removing them from the portfolio; [IAS 39.AG119(a)]
- how Bank A estimates its repricing dates, including what interest rate assumptions underlie estimates of prepayments rates and the basis for changing those estimates; the same method is used for both the initial estimates made at the time an asset or liability is included in the hedged portfolio and for any later revisions to those estimates; [IAS 39.AG119(b)] and
- the number and duration of repricing time periods. [IAS 39.AG119(c)]

(for further documentation requirements see steps 3 and 5)

Step 3: Bank A determines the amount it wishes to hedge and designates as the hedged item in each repricing time period a gross currency amount of assets and/or liabilities from the identified portfolio equal to that amount.

	T1	T2	T3
Amount of assets (liabilities) designated as hedged item	10	10	(15)

This amount is converted into a percentage of assets or liabilities from the identified portfolio in each time period, which is used in testing hedge effectiveness. [IAS 39.AG114(c)]

	T1	T2	T3
Net exposure	10	10	(25)
Amount of assets (liabilities) designated as hedged item	10	10	(15) *
Hedge ratio (hedged item as a percentage of amount of qualifying assets (liabilities)	33.33% (10/30)	25% (10/40)	100% (15/15)

(* Note that the amount hedged may only be drawn from the fixed rate liabilities and not from the demand deposits as demand deposits cannot be a hedged item beyond their demand date.)

Bank A is therefore hedging 33.33 per cent of its assets in repricing time period T1, 25 per cent of its assets in repricing time period T2 and 100 per cent of its fixed rate liabilities in repricing time period T3.

In addition to complying with all other hedge accounting criteria, Bank A documents the methodology used to determine the amount of assets or liabilities that are designated as the hedged item, the hedge ratio and the percentage measure used when testing effectiveness. [IAS 39.AG119(e)]

Step 4: Bank A designates the interest rate risk hedged as a particular benchmark rate, e.g. LIBOR. [IAS 39.AG114(d)]

Step 5: Bank A designates one or more hedging instruments for each repricing time period. [IAS 39.AG114(e)] The derivatives designated for a repricing time period may comprise a number of derivatives with offsetting risk positions all of which contain exposure to LIBOR. None of the derivatives however may be a written option, or net written option as the Standard does not permit such options to be designated as hedging instruments except in certain limited circumstances (see **3.3** above for details). [IAS 39.AG120]

Bank A has the following interest rate swaps (by maturity):

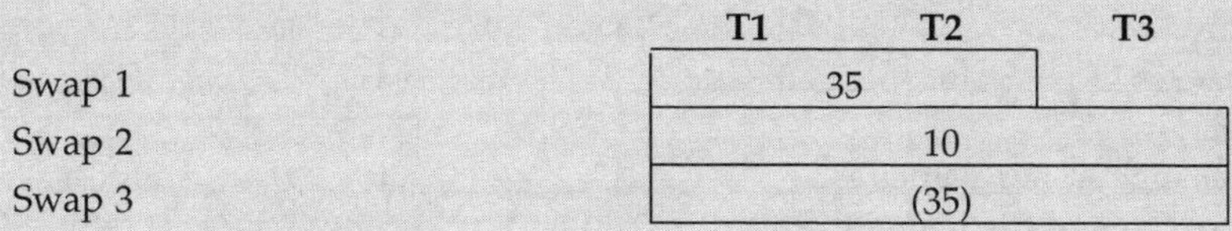

Bank A designates the following swaps or combination of swaps to hedge each of the time periods:

	T1	T2	T3
Swap 1	-	-	-
Swap 2	10	10	10
Swap 3	-	-	(25)
Total designated hedging instruments	10	10	(15)

In the above example swap 2 hedges more than one repricing time period and is thus allocated to all the time periods it hedges. [IAS 39.AG120]

Step 6: Using the designations made in steps 3–5 above, Bank A assesses at inception and in subsequent periods, whether the hedge is expected to be highly effective during the period for which the hedge is designated. [IAS 39.AG114(f)] It is not appropriate to assume that changes in the fair value of the hedged item equal changes in the value of the hedging instrument. [IAS 39.AG122] IAS 39 does allow the use of two techniques to measure the effectiveness of the hedging relationship: Bank A can calculate the effectiveness of the hedging relationship as the difference between the change in the fair value of the hedging instrument and the change in the fair value of the entire hedged item attributable to the hedged risk; [IAS 39.AG126(a)] or it can elect to use an approximation approach. [IAS 39.AG126(b)] Bank A applies this approximation method as is illustrated in steps A to E and step 7 below.

In addition to complying with all other hedge accounting criteria, Bank A documents:

- how often Bank A will test effectiveness (monthly in this case); [IAS 39.AG119(d)]
- which of the two effectiveness testing techniques Bank A is using; [IAS 39.AG119(d)] and
- when effectiveness is tested using the approximation approach, whether effectiveness will be assessed for each repricing time period individually, for all time periods in aggregate, or by using some combination of the two (in this case Bank A elects to assess effectiveness for all time periods in aggregate). [IAS 39.AG119(f)]

After one month, Bank A assesses the effectiveness of the hedging relationship using the approximation approach as follows:

Step A: Fair value changes of the hedged item (before determining the impact of changes in fair value due to revised repayment expectations and ignoring changes in fair value not attributable to interest rate movements) and of the hedging instruments are determined to be as follows:

	T1	**T2**	**T3**
Changes in fair value: hedged item	2	3	(1)
% change in fair value (as a percentage of the hedged assets (liabilities))	20% (2/10)	30% (3/10)	6.67% (1/15)
Changes in fair value: hedging instrument	(2)	(3)	1

Step B: A revised estimate of the amount of assets and liabilities in each repricing time period is determined in order to calculate the amount of the hedged item based on the revised estimates. Following a decrease in LIBOR, the assets and liabilities have repaid faster than initially expected. Bank A determines that its portfolio of assets and liabilities is now expected to reprice as follows:

	T1	**T2**	**T3**
Fixed rate assets	27	32	20
Fixed rate liabilities	(15)	(20)	(10)
Demand deposits	-	-	(20)
Net exposure *	12	12	(10)

(*Note that the above new net position is irrelevant for the purposes of determining the effectiveness of the hedging relationship for this period. It may however be relevant in the next period in determining the amount of hedged assets and liabilities.)

Step C: The percentage of the assets and liabilities hedged (as determined in step 3 above) is applied to the revised amount of assets and liabilities in each repricing period.
[IAS 39.AG126(b)(ii)]

	T1	**T2**	**T3**
Hedge ratio (from Step 3)	33.33%	25%	100%
Revised assets	27	32	-

Revised liabilities	-	-	(10)
Revised hedged assets	9 (33.33%*27)	8 (25%*32)	-
Revised hedged liabilities	-	-	(10) (100%*10)

Step D: The change in the fair value of the revised estimate of the hedged item that is attributable to the hedged risk is calculated by multiplying the change in fair value (as determined in Step A) by the new amount of assets (liabilities) in that repricing period (as determined in Step C) [IAS 39.AG126(b)(iii)]:

	T1	**T2**	**T3**
% change in fair value (Step A)	20%	30%	6.67%
Revised assets and liabilities (Step C)	9	8	(10)
Changes in fair value of the hedged item	1.8	2.4	(0.667)

Step E: The effectiveness of the hedging relationship is determined by comparing the change in the fair value of the hedging instrument to the change in the fair value of the hedged item:

	T1	**T2**	**T3**
Changes in fair value of the hedged item	1.8	2.4	(0.667)
Change in fair value of the hedging instrument(s)	(2)	(3)	1
Effectiveness (each time period)	90% (1.8/2)	80% (2.4/3)	66.7% (0.667/1)
Effectiveness (all time periods)		88.33% (1.8+2.4–0.667)/(-2–3+1)	

As the portfolio hedge is effective for all repricing time periods, in accordance with the documented method of testing hedge effectiveness (see step 6 above), Bank A concludes that the hedge is effective for the designated period.

In this example, for illustrative purposes only, all hedge ineffectiveness is due to changes in the amount of assets and liabilities at the start and the end of the reporting period due to changes in prepayment rates. In practice, ineffectiveness will also result due to impairment of assets, derecognition of assets and liabilities, and other valuation differences between the hedging instrument and hedged item like in any conventional fair value hedge.

Step 7: Bank A measures the change in the fair value of the hedged item attributable to the hedged risk on the basis of the expected repricing dates. Bank A recognises the change in fair value of the hedged item as a gain or loss in profit or loss and in one of two line items in the statement of financial position. Bank A recognises the following entry based on Step D above: [IAS 39.AG114(g)]

Dr	Separate statement of financial position line item (assets) [1.8+2.4]	4.2

Cr	Separate statement of financial position line item (liabilities)	0.667
Cr	Profit or loss	3.533

Step 8: Bank A measures the change in fair value of the hedging instrument(s) and recognises it as a gain or loss in profit or loss. The fair value of the hedging instrument(s) is recognised as an asset or liability in the statement of financial position. Bank A recognises the following journal entry based on Step A above:
[IAS 39.AG114(h)]

Dr	Profit or loss (fair value gains and losses on derivatives)	4
Dr	Derivative asset	1
Cr	Derivative liability	5

Step 9: Any ineffectiveness will be recognised in profit or loss as the difference arising from steps 7 and 8. The above hedging relationship resulted in an amount of 0.467 [4–3.533] being recognised in profit or loss as hedge ineffectiveness for the period. [IAS 39.AG114(i)]

Step 10: Bank A then establishes a new estimate of the total assets (liabilities) in each repricing time period, including new assets (liabilities) that have been originated since it last tested effectiveness, and designates a new amount as the hedged item and a new percentage as the hedged percentage. [IAS 39.AG127] The procedures set out above are then repeated at the next date the Bank tests effectiveness.

Step 11: The adjustment determined in Step 7 above should be amortised to profit or loss. Amortisation may begin as soon as an adjustment exists and shall begin no later than when the hedged item ceases to be adjusted for changes in its fair value attributable to the risk being hedged. Bank A concludes that amortising the adjustment using a recalculated effective interest rate is not practicable and instead will amortise the adjustment to profit or loss using a straight line approach. The adjustment will be amortised fully to profit or loss by the expiry of the relevant repricing time period. [IAS 39.92] Any amount relating to a particular time period that remains when the repricing time period expires should be recognised in profit or loss at that time. [IAS 39.AG129]

The example above does not account for the instances where, following the calculation of the hedge gain or loss, the hedged items are derecognised (e.g. through earlier than expected prepayment, impairment or sale). Should this occur, then the amount of change in fair value included in the statement of financial position (within a separate line item) that relates to the derecognised item shall be removed from the statement of financial position and be included in the gain or loss that arises on derecognition of the item. The knowledge of which repricing time period(s) the derecognised item was included in determines the repricing time periods from which to remove it, and therefore the amount to be removed from the separate line item. If it can be determined in which time period the derecognised item was included, it is removed from that time period. If not, it is removed from the earliest time period if the derecognition resulted from higher than expected prepayments or allocated to all time periods containing the derecognised item on a systematic and rational basis if the item was sold or became impaired. [IAS 39.AG128]

US GAAP comparison: The specific guidance in IFRS on fair value hedge accounting a portfolio of interest rate risk is in addition to more basic requirements on hedging a portfolio of items as described in **2.8** above. US guidance is limited to the basic requirements on hedging a portfolio of items which are largely similar to those described in IFRS. Fair value hedging of a portfolio of interest rate risk, as contemplated in the specific IFRS guidance referenced above is not permitted under US GAAP.

10 Hedge accounting – examples

1 Introduction

This chapter includes illustrative examples of hedge accounting. The chapter is divided into the three types of hedges.

Section 2	Fair value hedges
Section 3	Cash flow hedges
Section 4	Net investment hedges
Section 5	Hedge effectiveness assessment techniques

2 Fair value hedges

The following fair value hedges are illustrated in this section.

Section 2.1	Fair value hedging interest rate risk of fixed rate debt
Section 2.2	Fair value hedging a firm commitment with a non-derivative

2.1 Fair value hedging interest rate risk of fixed rate debt

The following example illustrates the entries for a fair value hedge of interest rate risk of fixed rate debt using an interest rate swap.

Fair value hedging fixed rate debt

On 1 January 20X0, Entity C issued £100 million of five-year 8 per cent fixed rate debt. Entity C has a BBB credit rating at the issuance date. The fixed interest rate on the debt is 150 basis points higher than the five-year swap rate. Interest on the debt is payable annually. Entity C's interest rate risk policy requires that all debt is at variable rates which is achieved either through issuing variable rate debt or by issuing fixed rate debt and swapping it into variable.

In order to maintain compliance with this policy Entity C entered into an interest rate swap on 1 January 20X0 to 'convert' the debt from fixed rate to variable and designated the swap (identifying and documenting all critical terms) as a fair value hedge of interest rate risk on the fixed rate debt (credit spreads are purposely not hedged). The swap is a five-year pay LIBOR, receive 6.50 per cent fixed interest rate swap.

Entity C satisfies the hedge accounting criteria.

- The fair value of Entity C's issued fixed rate debt will vary with changes in market interest rates. Such changes could have an impact in profit or loss if the debt is extinguished early. Hence, the debt qualifies for fair value hedge accounting (it is not a non-qualifying exposure).
- Entity C has formally documented the hedging relationship from inception, identifying all critical terms.
- The hedge is consistent with Entity C's risk management policy for that hedging relationship.
- Entity C expects its hedge to be highly effective and has documented this assessment –the primary potential source of ineffectiveness in a fair value hedge of fixed rate debt is credit risk. Entity C is using an interest rate swap to hedge interest rate risk only. Hence, changes in credit spreads between Entity C's BBB rate and swap rates will not generate hedge ineffectiveness.

Note that the principal terms of the hedged item and the hedging instrument match. IAS 39 recognises that if the principal terms of the hedging instrument and the hedged item are the same, then the changes in fair value attributable to the risk being hedged may be likely to offset each other fully, both at inception and afterwards. [IAS 39.AG108] Entity C is required, however to assess effectiveness on an ongoing basis. [IAS 39.IG.F.4.7]

The fair value of the swap and the carrying amount of the debt following the adjustment for changes in fair value attributable to the hedged risk are as follows.

	1/1/20X0	**30/6/20X0**	**31/12/20X0**
Issued debt	£(100m)	£(105m)	£(102m)
Swap	£nil	£5m	£2m

The required entries are as follows (£):

1 January 20X0

Dr	Cash	100,000,000
Cr	Debt	100,000,000

To record the issuance of debt.

No entries are required in respect of the swap as it was entered into at the money when the fair value was zero.

30 June 20X0

Dr	Profit or loss	5,000,000
Cr	Debt	5,000,000
Dr	Swap	5,000,000
Cr	Profit or loss	5,000,000

The net impact in profit or loss of £nil reflects that the changes in fair value of the swap offset fully the changes in the fair value of the debt for the designated risk.

31 December 20X0

Dr	Debt	3,000,000	
Cr	Profit or loss		3,000,000
Dr	Profit or loss		3,000,000
Cr	Swap		3,000,000

The net impact in profit or loss of £nil reflects that the changes in fair value of the swap offset fully the changes in the fair value of the debt for the designated risk.

Note that the carrying amount of the debt in the statement of financial position will not represent its full fair value but will be a hybrid of amortised cost and an element of its fair value which is due to movements in interest rates since the inception of the hedging relationship. As the entity's credit spread was purposely not hedged, the hedged item is not adjusted for movements in that risk.

2.2 Fair value hedging a firm commitment with a non-derivative

The following example illustrates the entries for a fair value hedge of foreign currency risk on a firm commitment using a foreign currency denominated deposit as a hedging instrument.

On 1 January 20X4, Entity B has a firm commitment to purchase equipment (a non-financial asset) from Entity M, a French entity. Entity B's functional currency is Sterling and Entity M's is Euro. The firm commitment requires B to pay €30 million for the equipment for delivery on 1 January 20X5. Entity B has a 31 March year-end.

Entity B currently has €30 million on deposit with a European bank maturing on 1 January 20X5 on which it currently recognises in profit or loss foreign exchange gains and losses at the end of each reporting period. Entity B would like to use its Euro deposit balance as a hedge of its commitment to purchase the equipment.

Entity B can designate the cash deposit as a hedging instrument in either a cash flow or a fair value hedge of the spot foreign currency risk of the firm commitment (see **2.1.2** above).

The spot foreign exchange rates are as follows.

Date	**Exchange rate**	**Sterling equivalent of €30m**	**Movement**
1 January 20X4	1.4321	20,948,257	
31 March 20X4	1.4282	21,005,461	57,204
1 January 20X5	1.4511	20,673,971	(331,490)

The entries below do not consider the accounting for the deposit before 1 January 20X4. Up to this date, the monetary asset will have been reported at the spot rate at the end of each reporting period, with exchange gains and losses reported in profit or loss.

Entity B designates the hedge as a *fair value hedge* of the spot foreign currency risk of the firm commitment.

1 January 20X4

There are no entries. The firm commitment has a fair value of zero.

31 March 20X4

Dr	Deposit	57,204
Cr	Profit or loss	57,204

To recognise the foreign exchange gain on remeasurement of the deposit.

Dr	Profit or loss	57,204
Cr	Firm commitment	57,204

To recognise the change in fair value of the firm commitment relating to the hedged risk (foreign currency spot movements).

1 January 20X5

Dr	Profit or loss	331,490
Cr	Deposit	331,490

To recognise the exchange loss on remeasurement of the deposit.

Dr	Firm commitment	331,490
Cr	Profit or loss	331,490

To recognise the change in fair value of the firm commitment relating to the hedged risk (foreign currency spot movements).

Dr	Property, plant, equipment	20,948,257
Cr	Firm commitment	274,286
Cr	Cash	20,673,971

To recognise the acquisition of the asset and derecognise the firm commitment that has now been extinguished. The carrying amount of the non-financial asset is the Sterling equivalent of €30 million, translated at the spot rate when the hedge was entered into.

Dr	Cash	20,673,971
Cr	Deposit	20,673,971

To account for the repayment of the deposit upon its maturity on 1 January 20X5.

Entity B designates the hedge as a *cash flow hedge* of the spot foreign currency risk of the firm commitment.

1 January 20X4

There are no entries.

31 March 20X4

Dr	Deposit	57,204
Cr	Cash flow hedge reserve	57,204

To recognise the foreign exchange gain on remeasurement of the deposit being fully effective in hedging the foreign currency risk of the forecast purchase.

1 January 20X5

Dr	Cash flow hedge reserve	331,490
Cr	Deposit	331,490

To recognise the exchange loss on remeasurement of the deposit being fully effective in hedging the foreign currency risk of the forecast purchase.

Dr	Property, plant, equipment	20,948,257
Cr	Cash flow hedge reserve	274,286
Cr	Cash	20,673,971

To recognise the cash paid on acquisition of the asset and perform a basis adjustment to remove the effective amount from equity and include it in the carrying amount of the asset. The carrying amount of the non-financial asset is the Sterling equivalent of €30 million, translated at the spot rate when the hedge was entered into.

Dr	Cash	20,673,971
Cr	Deposit	20,673,971

To account for the repayment of the deposit upon its maturity on 1 January 20X5.

If Entity B has an accounting policy not to apply basis adjustments to non-financial items in cash flow hedges, the amount recognised in other comprehensive income will be retained in equity at the acquisition date of the equipment and will be reclassified from equity to profit or loss in future periods when the depreciation of the equipment will impact profit or loss (see **2.2.3** in **chapter 8**). In this case, the carrying amount of the equipment would be €20,673,971.

3 Cash flow hedges

As cash flow hedging incorporates the hedging of financial and non-financial items, both recognised in the statement of financial position and forecast transactions that have yet to occur, there are many different examples. This section includes some of the more common examples in detail as well as some complex scenarios.

Section 3.1	Cash flow hedging a forecast sale of a non-financial item
Section 3.2	Cash flow hedging a forecast sale for foreign currency risk
Section 3.3	Basis adjusting the acquisition of a non-financial item
Section 3.4	Cash flow hedging a forecast sale and subsequent receivable
Section 3.5	Cash flow hedging variable rate interest with an interest rate swap
Section 3.6	Cash flow hedging variable rate debt with a purchased interest rate cap
Section 3.7	Cash flow hedging foreign currency risk of floating rate debt

3.1 Cash flow hedging a forecast sale of a non-financial item

The following example illustrates the entries for a cash flow hedge of market price risk on a forecast sale of a non-financial item using a forward contract.

Forecast sale of a non-financial item

On 4 January 20X0 Entity B has a forecast sale of 500 tonnes of wheat expected to occur on or about 31 December 20X0.

On 4 January 20X0 Entity B designates the cash flows of the forecasted sale as a hedged item and enters into a wheat futures contract to sell 500 tonnes at US$1.1 million on 31 December 20X0.

At inception of the hedge, the derivative is at-the-money (fair value is zero). The terms of the forecast sale and the derivative match. On 31 December 20X0, the wheat futures contract has a fair value of US$25,000 and is closed out. Entity B sells the inventory for US$1,075,000.

The required entries are as follows.

31 December 20X0

Dr	Wheat futures contract	US$25,000	
Cr	Other comprehensive income		US$25,000

To record the wheat futures contract at fair value (note that the changes in fair value of the derivative are recorded in other comprehensive income until the hedged forecast sale occurs).

31 December 20X0

Dr	Cash	US$25,000	
Cr	Wheat futures contract		US$25,000

To record the settlement of the wheat futures contract.

Dr	Cash	US$1,075,000
Dr	Cost of goods sold	US$1,000,000
Cr	Revenue	US$1,075,000
Cr	Inventory	US$1,000,000

To record the inventory sale

Dr	Other comprehensive income	US$25,000
Cr	Revenue	US$25,000

Revenue of US$1,100,000 is recognised. This represents US$1,075,000 from the sale of wheat at spot prices, plus the gain on the derivative. The sum of the two equals the sale of wheat at the hedged rate.

3.2 Cash flow hedging a forecast sale for foreign currency risk

The following example illustrates the entries for a cash flow hedge of foreign currency risk of a forecast sale using a forward exchange contract.

On 4 January 20X2 Entity D has a forecast sale of €4,000,000 of confectionery on or about 31 December 20X2 to a German retail outlet (Entity AG). Entity D has a Sterling functional currency, and Entity AG has a Euro functional currency. On 4 January 20X2, Entity D designates the cash flow of the forecast sale as a hedged item and enters into a currency forward to sell €4 million based on the forecast receipt. The forward contract locks in the value of the Euros to be received at a rate of €1.5:£. At inception of the hedge, the derivative is on-market (i.e. fair value is zero). The terms of the currency forward and the forecast sale match each other. The entity designates the forward foreign exchange risk as the hedged risk.

Potential sources of ineffectiveness include non-occurrence of the forecast transaction and changes in the date of sale. Any ineffectiveness will be recognised in profit or loss.

On 30 June 20X2, the fair value of the currency forward is negative £100,000 because the forward rate has changed, reflecting the fact that the Euro has strengthened against Sterling.

On 31 December 20X2 the transaction occurred as expected. The fair value of the forward is negative £111,111 as the Euro continued to strengthen against Sterling.

The required entries are as follows.

4 January 20X2
No entries are required since the forward was entered into 'on-market', and therefore had a fair value of zero at inception. Normally, there will be margin to be posted, associated with trading on a currency exchange, but this has been ignored for illustration purposes only. There may also be fees if the foreign exchange contract is an over-the-counter (OTC) transaction.

30 June 20X2

Dr	Other comprehensive income	£100,000
Cr	Forward	£100,000

To recognise the forward at fair value, reflecting that the forward contract is fully effective in hedging the forward rate of the forecast transaction.

31 December 20X2

Dr	Other comprehensive income	£11,111
Cr	Forward	£11,111

To record the change in fair value of the forward. The forward contract remains fully effective in hedging the forward rate of the forecast transaction.

Dr	Forward	£111,111
Cr	Cash	£111,111

To record the cash paid in settling the forward contract.

Dr	Cash	£2,777,778
Cr	Sales	£2,777,778

To record the receipt of €4m from the sale of confectionery translated at the spot rate of €1.44:£.

Dr	Sales	£111,111
Cr	Other comprehensive income	£111,111

To record the cumulative effective portion of the hedging instrument included in other comprehensive income that is reclassified from equity to profit or loss when the sale occurs.

The net effect of reclassifying the amount from equity to profit or loss when the sale occurred is equivalent to recognising in profit or loss the sale translated at the contracted rate inherent in the forward (i.e. €4,000,000 / €1.5:£).

Translation of sale at spot rate at 31 December 20X2	£2,777,778
Reclassified from equity to profit or loss at 31 December 20X2	(£111,111)
Sum	£2,666,667

Note: for the purposes of illustration only, the forward contract has not been discounted.

3.3 Basis adjusting the acquisition of a non-financial item

The following example illustrates the entries for a cash flow hedge of a non-financial item where a policy of basis adjustment is adopted.

On 4 January 20X2 Entity D has a forecast purchase of 100,000 kg of cocoa on or about 31 December 20X2 from a Brazilian supplier, Entity B. Entity D has a Sterling functional currency, and Entity B has a US$ functional currency. On 4 January 20X2, Entity D designates the cash flow of the forecast purchase as a hedged item and enters into a currency forward to buy US$180,000 based on the forecast payment (100,000 kg at US$1.8 per kg). The forward contract locks in the value of the US$ amount to be paid at a rate of US$1.8:£1. At inception of the hedge, the derivative is on-market (i.e. fair value is zero). The terms of the currency forward and the forecast purchase match each other, and the entity designates the forward foreign exchange risk as the hedged risk.

Potential sources of ineffectiveness include non-occurrence of the forecast transaction and changes in the date of purchase. Any ineffectiveness will be recognised in profit or loss.

On 30 June 20X2, the fair value of the currency forward is positive £10,000 because the forward rate has changed, reflecting the fact that the US$ has strengthened against Sterling.

On 31 December 20X2 the transaction occurred as expected. The fair value of the forward is positive £12,500 as the US$ continued to strengthen against Sterling.

The required entries are as follows.

4 January 20X2
No entries are required since the forward was entered into 'on-market', and therefore had a fair value of zero at inception. Normally, there will be margin to be posted associated with trading on a currency exchange, but this has been ignored for illustration purposes only. There may also be fees if the foreign exchange contract is an over-the-counter (OTC) transaction.

30 June 20X2

Dr	Forward	£10,000
Cr	Other comprehensive income	£10,000

To recognise the forward at fair value, reflecting that the forward contract is fully effective in hedging the forward rate of the forecast transaction.

31 December 20X2

Dr	Forward	£2,500
Cr	Other comprehensive income	£2,500

To record the change in fair value of the forward. The forward contract remains fully effective in hedging the forward rate of the forecast transaction.

Dr	Cash	£12,500
Cr	Forward	£12,500

To record the cash received in settling the forward contract.

Dr	Inventory	£112,500
Cr	Cash	£112,500

To record the payment of US$180,000 to purchase cocoa translated at the spot rate of $1.6:£1.

Dr	Other comprehensive income	£12,500
Cr	Inventory	£12,500

To record the cumulative effective portion of the hedging instrument included in other comprehensive income that is removed from equity and included as a basis adjustment in the initial carrying amount of the inventory.

The net effect of removing the amount from equity and including it in the carrying amount of the inventory is equivalent to recognising the inventory at the contracted rate inherent in the forward (i.e. US$180,000 / US$1.8:£1)

Translation of purchase at spot rate at 31 December 20X2	£112,500
Release from equity at 31 December 20X2	(£12,500)
Sum	£100,000

Note: for the purposes of illustration only, the forward contract has not been discounted.

3.4 Cash flow hedging a forecast sale and subsequent receivable

The following example illustrates the entries for a cash flow hedge of foreign currency risk of a forecast sale and the subsequent receivable using a forward exchange contract.

On 1 January 20X2, Entity A, a £ functional currency entity, has a highly probable forecast sale of US$100,000 in June 20X2. The receivable that is due with respect to the sale will be on 6 months credit terms. Entity A wishes to hedge the forecast sale and the receivable for foreign currency risk. Entity A will designate the forward US$:£ exchange rate, as opposed to the spot exchange rate. Entity A enters into a forward contract to sell US$100,000 and buy £50,481. As the currency, notional amount and maturity of the forward contract coincide with that of the highly probable forecast sale, Entity A expects the hedge relationship to be highly effective.

Date	Spot rate US$ / £	US$ interest rates	£ interest rates	Forward rate US$ / £	Fair value of forward contract (£)	Fair value movement of forward contract (£)
1/1/X2	2.000	4%	5%	1.981	0	0
31/3/X2	1.900	5%	6%	1.887	(2,418)	(2,418)
30/6/X2	1.850	4%	6%	1.832	(3,973)	(1,555)
30/9/X2	1.900	7%	8%	1.896	(2,230)	1,743
31/12/X2	2.100	8%	9%	2.100	2,862	5,092

The exchange of US$ at the spot rate at inception, being US$2.0:£, is equal to £50,000. The difference between this amount and the £50,481 contracted in the forward contract is £481 and represents the forward point differential in functional currency terms. This amount can be converted into a daily interest rate for use in allocating the systematic release of forward points to the periods pre and post the sale. The daily forward point differential is 0.0026%, calculated as (1+(481/50,000))$^{\wedge 1/365}$.

Period	£-equivalent US$	Forward point differential
1/1/X2	50,000	–
1/1/X2 to 30/6/X2	50,238	238
1/7/X2 to 30/9/X2	50,359	121
1/10/X2 to 31/12/X2	50,481	122

Entity A's documentation of the hedge is as follows.

Risk management objective and nature of risk being hedged	Cash flow hedge of the variability in functional currency equivalent cash flows associated with a forecast sale in 6 months and the cash to be paid on resulting receivable due in 12 months with respect to change in forward rates.
Date of designation	1 January 20X2
Hedging instrument	Forward contract entered into on 1 January 20X2 maturing on 31 December 20X2 to buy £50,481 and sell US$100,000.
Hedged item	Forecast US$100,000 denominated sale in June 20X2 with resulting receivable due December 20X2.
Assessment of hedge effectiveness	The critical terms of the derivative match that of the hedged item (in terms of maturity and notional), accordingly there is an expectation of high effectiveness. The entity will assess counterparty credit risk every period.
Measurement of hedge effectiveness	Hypothetical derivative method. The actual hedging instrument is the same as the hypothetical forward with exactly matching terms and therefore, no ineffectiveness is anticipated.

The following table illustrates the accounting entries for the transaction during its life in Sterling. Dr or (Cr) as indicated.

Date		Profit or loss	Receivable	Derivative	CFH reserve	Cash
31/3/X2	Fair value forward contract			(2,418)	2,418	
30/6/X2	Fair value of forward contract			(1,555)	1,555	
	Sale	(54,054)	54,054			
	Reclassification – spot	4,054			(4,054)	
	Reclassification – forward points	(238)			238	
30/9/X2	Fair value of forward contract			1,743	(1,743)	

Date		Profit or loss	Receivable	Derivative	CFH reserve	Cash
	Translation of receivable	1,422	(1,422)			
	Reclassification – spot	(1,422)			1,422	
	Reclassification – forward points	(121)			121	
31/12/X2	Fair value of forward contract			5,092	(5,092)	
	Translation of receivable	5,013	(5,013)			
	Reclassification – spot	(5,013)			5,013	
	Reclassification – forward points	(122)			122	
	Settle receivable		(47,619)			47,619
	Settle forward contract			(2,862)		2,862
		(50,481)	0	0	0	50,481
	Key	**A**			**B**	**C**

Key

A the amounts in profit or loss account can be considered as a sale at £50,000 (being a US$100,000 sale at the contracted forward rate of US$2.0:£), the retranslation loss on the receivable of £6,435 in accordance with IAS 21 with a corresponding fair value gain due to spot movements with respect to the forward contract of £6,435, plus the fair value gain of £481 arising from the forward point differential.

B nets to zero reflecting that all amounts in the cash flow hedge reserve in equity have been reclassified to profit or loss to offset the sale and the retranslation of the receivable to spot each period.

C reflects the £-equivalent cash from the receivable plus the receipt under the forward contract.

Entries in the financial statements for 20X2 are as follows.

1 January 20X2

No entry required as the forward contract has a fair value of nil at inception.

31 March 20X2

Dr	Other comprehensive income (cash flow hedge reserve)	2,418
Cr	Derivative	2,418

To recognise the fair value movements of the forward contract and the effective amount recognised in other comprehensive income (and taken to the cash flow hedge reserve in equity).

30 June 20X2

Dr	Other comprehensive income (cash flow hedge reserve)	1,555
Cr	Derivative	1,555

To recognise the fair value movements of the forward contract and the effective amount recognised in other comprehensive income (and taken to the cash flow hedge reserve in equity).

Dr	Receivable	54,054
Cr	Revenue	54,054

To recognise the sale at the spot rate.

Dr	Profit or loss	3,816
Cr	Other comprehensive income (cash flow hedge reserve)	3,816

To recognise the reclassification from equity (the cash flow hedge reserve) to profit or loss.

30 September 20X2

Dr	Derivative	1,743
Cr	Other comprehensive income (cash flow hedge reserve)	1,743

To recognise the fair value movements of the forward contract and the effective amount recognised in other comprehensive income (and taken to the cash flow hedge reserve in equity).

Dr	Profit or loss	1,422
Cr	Receivable	1,422

To recognise the retranslation of the receivable to spot rates in accordance with IAS 21.

Dr Other comprehensive income (cash flow hedge reserve) 1,543

Dr	Other comprehensive income (cash flow hedge reserve)	1,543
Cr	Profit or loss	1,543

To recognise the reclassification from equity (the cash flow hedge reserve) to profit or loss.

31 December 20X2

Dr	Derivative	5,092
Cr	Other comprehensive income (cash flow hedge reserve)	5,092

To recognise the fair value movements of the forward contract and the effective amount recognised in other comprehensive income (and taken to the cash flow hedge reserve in equity).

Dr	Profit or loss	5,013
Cr	Receivable	5,013

To recognise the retranslation of the receivable to spot rates in accordance with IAS 21.

Dr Other comprehensive income (cash flow hedge reserve)		5,135
Dr	Other comprehensive income (cash flow hedge reserve)	5,135
Cr	Profit or loss	5,135

To recognise the reclassification from equity (the cash flow hedge reserve) to profit or loss.

Dr	Cash	47,619
Cr	Receivable	47,619

To recognise the settlement of the receivable with the receipt of US$100,000 at the spot rate.

Dr	Cash	2,862
Cr	Derivative	2,862

To recognise the settlement of the derivative with receipt of £2,862 from the derivative counterparty.

3.5 Cash flow hedging variable rate interest with an interest rate swap

The following example illustrates the entries for a cash flow hedge of interest rate risk on variable rate debt using an interest rate swap.

Hedging variable rate interest on floating rate debt

Entity X issued US$100 million of five-year variable-rate debt on 1 January 20X0. The variable-rate on the debt is LIBOR plus a spread of 200 basis points. Initial LIBOR is 5 per cent. The debt pays interest on an annual basis and the swap resets on an annual basis on 31 December.

On 1 January 20X0, Entity X entered into a five-year pay fixed, receive LIBOR interest rate swap with a notional amount of US$100 million. The swap is designated as a cash flow hedge of the forecast interest payments on the LIBOR portion of the debt. Entity X does not intend to repurchase the debt prior to its maturity. The interest rate swap is on-market at inception and has a fair value of zero.

The terms of the interest rate swap are as follows.

Notional amount	US$100 million
Trade date	01/01/X0
Start date	01/01/X0
Maturity date	31/12/X4
Entity X pays	5.50 per cent
Entity X receives	LIBOR
Pay and receive dates	Annually on the debt-payment dates
Variable reset	Annually (on 31 December)

Initial LIBOR	5.00 per cent
First pay/receive date	31/12/X0
Last pay/receive date	31/12/X4

The interest rate swap is expected to be highly effective because the principal terms of the debt and the swap match. Hedge effectiveness will be assessed and measured, at a minimum, at the end of each reporting period. For illustration purposes only, this hedge relationship is deemed to be perfectly effective.

	LIBOR at inception and at each reset date	**Fair value of the interest rate swap**
1 January 20X0	5.00 per cent	US$0
31 December 20X0	6.57 per cent	US$4,068,000
31 December 20X1	7.70 per cent	US$5,793,000
31 December 20X2	6.79 per cent	US$2,303,000
31 December 20X3	5.76 per cent	US$241,000

Entity X accrues its interest expense at LIBOR plus 200 basis points on the debt and accrues the swap payments or receipts at the end of each reporting period as an adjustment to interest expense. The effect of the debt and swap accruals is a 7.50 per cent fixed rate. The fair value of the swap is recognised as an asset or liability with an offsetting amount in other comprehensive income to the extent the hedge relationship is effective. Any ineffectiveness is immediately recognised in net profit or loss.

1 January 20X0

Dr	Cash	US$100,000,000
Cr	Debt	US$100,000,000

To record the issuance of debt.

No entries are required in respect of the interest rate swap since it has a fair value of zero at inception.

Interest rates increased during the period ended 31 December 20X0 resulting in a fair value of the interest rate swap of US$4,068,000. Hedge ineffectiveness is assessed and measured at the end of the reporting period (determined to be zero), so the total change in fair value of the swap is recorded in other comprehensive income. Entity X paid US$500,000 in net cash settlements on the swap at 31 December 20X0. The LIBOR rate for the next period is 6.57 per cent.

31 December 20X0

Dr	Swap asset	US$4,068,000
Cr	Other comprehensive income	US$4,068,000

To record the fair value of derivative as a cash flow hedge.

Dr	Interest expense	US$7,000,000
Cr	Cash	US$7,000,000
Dr	Interest expense	US$500,000
Cr	Cash	US$500,000

To record payment of LIBOR plus 200 basis points (5.00 per cent + 2.00 per cent) on debt obligation and the net cash settlement payment on the swap as an adjustment to the yield on the debt. Effective yield is 7.50 per cent.

31 December 20X1

Interest rates increased further during the period ended 31 December 20X1 resulting in a fair value of the interest rate swap of $5,793,000. Hedge ineffectiveness is assessed and measured at the end of the reporting period (determined to be zero), so the total change in fair value of the swap is recorded in other comprehensive income. Entity X received US$1,070,000 in net cash settlements on the swap at 31 December 20X1. The LIBOR rate for the next period is 7.70 per cent.

Dr	Swap asset	US$1,725,000
Cr	Other comprehensive income	US$1,725,000

To record the change in fair value of derivative as a cash flow hedge.

Dr	Interest expense	US$8,570,000
Cr	Cash	US$8,570,000
Dr	Cash	US$1,070,000
Cr	Interest expense	US$1,070,000

To record payment of LIBOR plus 200 basis points (6.57 per cent + 2.00 per cent) on debt obligation and the net cash settlement receipt on the swap as an adjustment to the yield on the debt. Effective yield is 7.50 per cent.

Interest rates decreased during the period ended 31 December 20X2 resulting in a fair value of the interest rate swap of US$2,303,000. Hedge ineffectiveness is assessed and measured at the end of the reporting period (determined to be zero), so the total change in fair value of the swap is recorded in other comprehensive income. Entity X received US$2,200,000 in net cash settlements on the swap at 31 December 20X2. The LIBOR rate for the next period is 6.79 per cent.

31 December 20X2

Dr	Other comprehensive income	US$3,490,000
Cr	Swap asset	US$3,490,000

To record the fair value of derivative in other comprehensive income as a cash flow hedge.

Dr	Interest expense	US$9,700,000
Cr	Cash	US$9,700,000
Dr	Cash	US$2,200,000
Cr	Interest expense	US$2,200,000

To record payment of LIBOR plus 200 basis points (7.70 per cent + 2.00 per cent) on debt obligation and the net cash settlement receipt on the swap as an adjustment to the yield on the debt. Effective yield is 7.50 per cent.

Interest rates decreased during the period ended 31 December 20X3 resulting in a fair value of the interest rate swap of US$241,000. Hedge ineffectiveness is assessed and measured at the end of the reporting period (determined to be zero), so the total change in fair value of the swap is recorded in other comprehensive income. Entity X received US$1,290,000 in net cash settlements on the swap at 31 December 20X3. The LIBOR rate for the next period is 5.76 per cent.

31 December 20X3

Dr	Other comprehensive income	US$2,062,000
Cr	Swap asset	US$2,062,000

To record the change in fair value of derivative as a cash flow hedge.

Dr	Interest expense	US$8,790,000
Cr	Cash	US$8,790,000
Dr	Cash	US$1,290,000
Cr	Interest expense	US$1,290,000

To record payment of LIBOR plus 200 basis points (6.79 per cent + 2.00 per cent) on debt obligation and the net cash settlement receipt on the swap as an adjustment to the yield on the debt. Effective yield is 7.50 per cent.

The swap matured at 31 December 20X4. Entity X received US$260,000 in net cash settlements on the swap at 31 December 20X4.

31 December 20X4

Dr	Other comprehensive income	US$241,000
Cr	Swap asset	US$241,000

To record the change in fair value of derivative as a cash flow hedge.

Dr	Interest expense	US$7,760,000
Cr	Cash	US$7,760,000
Dr	Cash	US$260,000
Cr	Interest expense	US$260,000

To record payment of LIBOR plus 200 basis points (5.76 per cent +2.00 per cent) on debt obligation and the net cash settlement receipt on the swap as an adjustment to the yield on the debt. Effective yield is 7.50 per cent.

3.6 Hedging variable rate debt with a purchased interest rate cap

The following example illustrates the entries for a cash flow hedge of interest rate risk of variable rate debt using a purchased interest rate cap.

Example 4.7B

Hedging variable-rate debt with a purchased interest rate cap (1)

On 1 January 20X0, Entity X issued a 5-year CU100 million variable-rate bond. The bond pays interest based on CU LIBOR plus a spread of 200 basis points on an annual basis, reset in arrears on 31 December. Entity X wants to hedge against increases in interest rates by capping the maximum interest rate at 9 per cent (CU LIBOR of 7.00 per cent + 2.00 per cent spread). Entity X purchased an interest rate cap that is indexed to CU LIBOR with a CU100 million notional amount. The interest rate cap has no intrinsic value at inception. The counterparty to the cap pays Entity X the difference between 7 per cent and CU LIBOR if CU LIBOR rises above 7 per cent. The interest rate cap (intrinsic value only) is designated as a cash flow hedge of the variable-rate debt. The terms of the cap are as follows:

Notional amount	CU100 million
Trade date	01/01/X0
Start date	01/01/X0
Expiration date	31/12/X4
Strike price	7.00 per cent
Index	12 month CU LIBOR, set in arrears
Premium	CU1.44 million
Caplet expirations	31 December 20X0, 20X1, 20X2, 20X3 and 20X4

The payments on each caplet are made at expiration. For example, the caplet that expires on 31 December 20X0 will be paid, if applicable, on that date. The fair value of the cap throughout the term of the cap is summarised below:

Date	CU LIBOR	Cap rate	Fair value of cap $	Intrinsic value of cap (1) $	Time value of cap $	Cap cash receipts $
31 December 20X0	5.00	7.00	1,000,000	–	1,000,000	–
31 December 20X1	5.50	7.00	850,000	–	850,000	–
31December 20X2	7.50	7.00	1,500,000	895,000	605,000	500,000
31 December 20X3	8.00	7.00	1,000,000	600,000	400,000	1,000,000
31 December 20X4	7.00	7.00	–	–	–	–

(1) Intrinsic fair value is computed on a discounted basis.

The following entries are required:

1 January 20X0

Dr	Cash	CU100,000,000
Cr	Financial liability – debt	CU100,000,000

To record the issuance of debt.

Dr	Financial asset – option	CU1,440,000
Cr	Cash	CU1,440,000

To record the purchase of the interest rate cap.

31 December 20X0

Dr	Interest expense	CU7,000,000
Cr	Cash	CU7,000,000

To record the interest expense (CU LIBOR at reset plus 200 basis points (5.00 per cent + 2.00 per cent)) on the CU100 million principal amount.

Dr	Derivative loss	CU440,000
Cr	Financial asset – option	CU440,000

To record the cap option asset at fair value with changes in time value recognised in profit or loss (there was no intrinsic value to record).

31 December 20X1

Dr	Interest expense	CU7,500,000
Cr	Cash	CU7,500,000

To record the interest expense (CU LIBOR at reset plus 200 basis points (5.50 per cent + 2.00 per cent)) on the CU100 million principal amount.

Dr	Derivative loss	CU150,000
Cr	Financial asset – option	CU150,000

To record the cap option asset at fair value with changes in time value recognised in profit or loss (there was no intrinsic value to record).

31 December 20X2

Dr	Interest expense	CU9,500,000
Cr	Cash	CU9,500,000

To record the interest expense (CU LIBOR at reset plus 200 basis points (7.50 per cent + 2.00 per cent)) on the CU100 m principal amount.

Dr	Cash	CU500,000
Dr	Financial asset – option	CU650,000
Dr	Derivative loss	CU245,000
Cr	Other comprehensive income	CU1,395,000

To record the cash receipt and the cap option asset at fair value with changes in time value recognised in profit or loss and changes in intrinsic value recognised in other comprehensive income.

Dr	Other comprehensive income	CU500,000
Cr	Interest expense	CU500,000

To record the reclassification of amounts in equity to profit or loss. The reclassification of amounts from equity ((7.50 per cent CU LIBOR – 7.00 per cent cap rate) × CU100 million) results in an interest expense of 9.00 per cent.

31 December 20X3

Dr	Interest expense	CU10,000,000
Cr	Cash	CU10,000,000

To record the interest expense (CU LIBOR at reset plus 200 basis points (8.00 per cent + 2.00 per cent)) on the CU100 million principal amount.

Dr	Cash	CU1,000,000
Cr	Financial asset – asset	CU500,000
Dr	Derivative loss	CU205,000
Cr	Other comprehensive income	CU705,000

To record the cash receipt and the cap option asset at fair value with changes in time value recognised in profit or loss and changes in intrinsic value recognised in other comprehensive income.

Dr	Other comprehensive income	CU1,000,000
Cr	Interest expense	CU1,000,000

To record the reclassification of amounts in equity to profit or loss. The reclassification of amounts from equity ((8.00 per cent CU LIBOR – 7.00 per cent cap rate) × CU100 million) results in an interest expense of 9.00 per cent.

31 December 20X4

Dr	Interest expense	CU9,000,000
Cr	Cash	CU9,000,000

To record the interest expense (CU LIBOR at reset plus 200 basis points (7.00 per cent + 2.00 per cent)) on the CU100 million principal amount.

Dr	Derivative loss	CU400,000
Cr	Financial asset – option	CU1,000,000

Dr Other comprehensive income CU600,000

To record the cap option asset at fair value with changes in time value recognised in profit or loss and changes in intrinsic value recognised in other comprehensive income.

3.7 Cash flow hedging foreign currency risk of floating rate debt

The following example illustrates the entries for a cash flow hedge of foreign currency risk on variable rate debt using a cross currency interest rate swap.

On 1 January 20X2, Entity A, a Sterling functional currency entity, issues a US$ LIBOR +100 basis points (bp) floating rate debt instrument denominated in US dollars with a principal amount of US$100,000, that will mature on 31 December 20X6 at par. At 1 January 20X2, the spot rate on the US$ / £ is 1.75/1 so the principal of US$100,000 is equivalent to £57,143. On 1 January 20X2, Entity A also enters into a cross currency swap ('CCS') to exchange interest payments and principal at redemption on the same terms as the above debt and designates the CCS as a hedge of the variability of the £ functional currency equivalent cash flows on the debt. The terms are such that on each interest payment date (assume interest is paid annually on 31 December each year for both the debt and the cross currency swap), Entity A will receive US$ LIBOR + 100 basis points on a notional of US$100,000 and pay Sterling LIBOR + 106 bp based on a notional of £57,143. Because the currency, notional, coupons and interest payment dates match on both the CCS and the debt, Entity A expects the hedge relationship to be highly effective.

Date	**Spot rate US$ / £**	**Carrying amount of debt in US$**	**Carrying amount of debt in £**	**Cross currency swap fair value £**	**Net interest payment on the swap (£ LIBOR + 106 bp) – (US $ LIBOR + 100 bp)**
1/1/X2	1.75	100,000	57,143	0	0
31/12/X2	1.7	100,000	58,824	1,743	1,259
31/12/X3	1.6	100,000	62,500	5,520	1,476
31/12/X4	1.5	100,000	66,667	9,670	1,952
31/12/X5	1.8	100,000	55,556	(1,624)	1,042
31/12/X6	1.7	100,000	58,824	1,681	1,321

Entity A's documentation of the hedge is as follows.

Risk management objective and nature of risk being hedged	Cash flow hedge of the variability in functional currency equivalent cash flows associated with the foreign currency debt due to changes in spot rates.

Date of designation	1 January 20X2
Hedging instrument	Cross currency swap to exchange US$100,000 for £57,143 at maturity and receive US$ LIBOR + 100bp, pay £ LIBOR + 106bp interest annually over the term of the instrument.
Hedged item	The cross currency swap is designated as a hedge of the changes in the cash flows relating to the changes in foreign currency spot rates related to the debt and to the annual interest payments.
Assessment of hedge effectiveness	The critical terms of the derivative match (exchange of principal at maturity and annual interest payment), accordingly there is an expectation of high effectiveness. The entity will assess counterparty credit risk and probability of cash flows under the swap occurring every period.
Measurement of hedge effectiveness	Hypothetical derivative method. The actual hedging instrument is the same as the hypothetical cross currency swap with exactly matching terms and therefore, no ineffectiveness is anticipated.

The following table illustrates the accounting entries for the transaction during its life in Sterling. Dr or (Cr) as indicated.

31 Dec		Cash	CCS	Debt	CFH reserve	Interest expense	Translation loss (gain)
20X2	Issue debt	57,143		(57,143)			
	Pay interest on debt	(2,319)				2,319	
	Revalue debt to spot			(1,681)			1,681
	Net interest on CCS	(1,259)				1,259	
	Fair value of cross currency CCS		1,743		(62)		(1,681)
20X3	Pay interest on debt	(2,788)				2,788	
	Revalue debt to spot			(3,676)			3,676
	Net interest on CCS	(1,476)				1,476	

31 Dec		Cash	CCS	Debt	CFH reserve	Interest expense	Translation loss (gain)
	Fair value of cross currency CCS		3,777		(101)		(3,676)
20X4	Pay interest on debt	(2,469)				2,469	
	Revalue debt to spot			(4,167)			4,167
	Net interest on CCS	(1,952)				1,952	
	Fair value of cross currency CCS		4,150		17		(4,167)
20X5	Pay interest on debt	(2,879)				2,879	
	Revalue debt to spot			11,111			(11,111)
	Net interest on CCS	(1,042)				1,042	
	Fair value of cross currency CCS		(11,294)		183		11,111
20X6	Pay interest on debt	(3,171)				3,171	
	Revalue debt to spot			(3,268)			3,268
	Net interest on CCS	(1,321)				1,321	
	Fair value of cross currency CCS		3,305		(37)		(3,268)
	Settlement of swap	1,681	(1,681)				
	Repayment of debt	(58,824)		58,824			
		(20,676)	0	0	0	20,676	0
	Key				**A**	**B**	

* Numbers rounded.

Key

A Nets to zero reflecting that all amounts in the cash flow hedge reserve in equity have been reclassified to profit or loss to offset retranslation of the debt to spot each period and the recognition of interest.

B Reflects the total interest expense from US$ Debt and CCS. This amount equals the total interest expense that would have been incurred had Entity A actually issued £ debt at inception (£57,143 x (LIBOR + 106bp)) x 5 years = £20,675.

Entries in the consolidated financial statements for 20X2 for illustrative purposes

1 January 20X2

No entry required for CCS as fair value is nil at inception.

Dr	Cash	57,143
Cr	Debt	57,143

To record issue of 4% US$ bond in £ (retranslated at spot).

31 December 20X2

Dr	Interest expense	2,319
Cr	Cash	2,319

To record payment of the interest on US$ debt converted at average rates.

Dr	Retranslation loss (profit or loss)	1,681
Cr	Debt	1,681

To record loss on retranslation of the US$ debt at year end spot rates.

Dr	Interest expense	1,259
Cr	Cash	1,259

To record net interest paid on CCS.

Dr	CCS asset	1,743
Cr	Other comprehensive income (cash flow hedging reserve)	1,743

To record fair value movement in CCS in other comprehensive income (as 100 per cent effective).

Dr	Other comprehensive income (cash flow hedging reserve)	1,681
Cr	Retranslation gain (profit or loss)	1,681

To record reclassifying the effective portion of CCS from equity to profit or loss to offset the retranslation of the debt.

Similar entries would be recorded for the remaining term of the hedging relationship (20X3 -20X6).

Interest expense totalling £20,675 is recognised over the term of the hedging instrument and net profit or loss impact is as if Entity A had issued Sterling LIBOR + 106bp debt at inception. The CCS is fair valued at the end of each reporting period (after interest payments have been made as all interest payments are deemed to have taken place on last day of year which is also reset date for swap) with amounts recognised in other comprehensive income (and taken to the cash flow hedge reserve in equity). The amount of the CCS is reclassified from equity to profit or loss at the end of each reporting period to offset the amount recorded for retranslation of the US$ debt to Sterling spot rates and finally to offset the translation loss on repayment of principal at maturity of the debt.

It is worth noting that if there was no margin on the legs of the CCS, the CCS would reset at par each reset date (i.e. 31 December). In this case, the net figure in the statement of financial position (Debt and CCS) would be the same as if Entity A had issued Sterling debt at inception and therefore no amount would be taken to other comprehensive income at the end of each reporting period as the value of the CCS would be fully offset by the retranslation of the debt for spot rates. If there are margins on the legs of the swap, the changing yield curves result in fair value movements with respect to those margins, and therefore the CCS will not offset the retranslation of the debt notional for spot rates. Hence, where there is a margin, the fair value in respect of those amounts is initially recognised in other comprehensive income (and taken to the cash flow hedge reserve), to the extent it is effective, and reclassified from equity to profit or loss when interest on the debt is paid such that by the maturity of the debt and hedge relationship the amounts in the cash flow hedge reserve will be fully reclassified from equity to profit or loss.

3.8 Cash flow hedging foreign currency risk of fixed rate debt

The following example illustrates the entries for a cash flow hedge of foreign currency risk on fixed rate debt using a cross currency interest rate swap.

On 1 January 20X2, Entity A, a Sterling functional currency entity, issues a 4 per cent annual fixed coupon debt instrument denominated in US dollars (US$) with a notional amount of US$100,000, that will mature on 31 December 20X6 at par, and therefore the effective interest rate is 4 per cent. At 1 January 20X2, the spot rate on the US$ / £ is 1.75/1 so the notional of US$100,000 is equivalent to £57,143. On 1 January 20X2, Entity A also enters into a cross currency swap ('CCS') to exchange interest payments and principal at redemption on the same terms as the above debt and designates the CCS as a cash flow hedge of the variability of the £ functional currency equivalent cash flows on the debt. The terms are such that on each interest payment date (assume interest is paid annually on 31 December each year for both the debt and the cross currency swap), Entity A will receive 4 per cent on a notional of US$100,000 and pay 6 per cent based on a notional of £57,143. Because the currency, notional, coupons and interest payment dates match on both the cross currency swap and the debt, Entity A expects that the hedge relationship will be highly effective.

Date	Spot rate US$ / £	Carrying amount of debt in US$	Carrying amount of debt in £	Cross currency swap fair value £	Net interest payment on the swap £ (£ 6% – US$ 4%)
1/1/X2	1.75	100,000	57,143	0	0
31/12/X2	1.7	100,000	58,824	2,560	1,110
31/12/X3	1.6	100,000	62,500	7,723	1,004

Date	Spot rate US$ / £	Carrying amount of debt in US$	Carrying amount of debt in £	Cross currency swap fair value £	Net interest payment on the swap £ (£ 6% – US$ 4%)
31/12/X4	1.5	100,000	66,667	9,513	848
31/12/X5	1.8	100,000	55,556	(1,452)	1,004
31/12/X6	1.7	100,000	58,824	1,681	1,143

Entity A's documentation of the hedge is as follows.

Risk management objective and nature of risk being hedged	Cash flow hedge of the variability in functional currency equivalent cash flows associated with the foreign currency debt due to changes in forward rates.
Date of designation	1 January 20X2
Hedging instrument	Cross currency swap to receive US$ 4 per cent, pay £6 per cent interest annually based on notional of US$100,000 over the term of the instrument and exchange US$100,000 for £57,143 at maturity.
Hedged item	Changes in the £ functional currency equivalent cash flows relating to the changes in foreign currency spot rates related to the debt and to the annual interest payments.
Assessment of hedge effectiveness	The critical terms of the derivative match (exchange of principal at maturity and annual interest payments), accordingly there is an expectation of high effectiveness. The entity will assess counterparty credit risk and probability of cash flows under the swap occurring every period.
Measurement of hedge effectiveness	Hypothetical derivative method. The actual hedging instrument is the same as a hypothetical cross currency swap with exactly matching terms and therefore, no ineffectiveness is anticipated.

The following table illustrates the accounting entries for the transaction during its life in Sterling. Dr or (Cr) as indicated.

31 Dec		Cash	CCS statement of financial position	Debt	CFH reserve	Interest expense	Translation loss (gain)
20X2	Issue debt	57,143		(57,143)			
	Pay interest on debt	(2,319)				2,319	
	Revalue debt to spot			(1,681)			1,681
	Net interest on CCS	(1,110)				1,110	
	Fair value of cross currency CCS		2,560		(879)		(1,681)
20X3	Pay interest on debt	(2,424)				2,424	
	Revalue debt to spot			(3,676)			3,676
	Net interest on CCS	(1,004)				1,004	
	Fair value of cross currency CCS		5,163		(1,487)		(3,676)
20X4	Pay interest on debt	(2,581)				2,581	
	Revalue debt to spot			(4,167)			4,167
	Net interest on CCS	(848)				848	
	Fair value of cross currency CCS		1,790		2,377		(4,167)
20X5	Pay interest on debt	(2,424)				2,424	
	Revalue debt to spot			11,111			(11,111)

31 Dec		Cash	CCS statement of financial position	Debt	CFH reserve	Interest expense	Translation loss (gain)
	Net interest on CCS	(1,004)				1,004	
	Fair value of cross currency CCS		(10,965)		(146)		11,111
20X6	Pay interest on debt	(2,286)				2,286	
	Revalue debt to spot			(3,268)			3,268
	Net interest on CCS	(1,143)				1,143	
	Fair value of cross currency CCS		3,133		135		(3,268)
	Settlement of swap	1,681	(1,681)				
	Settlement of debt	(58,824)		58,824			
		(17,143)	0	0	0	17,143	0
	Key				**A**	**B**	

*Numbers rounded.

Key

A Nets to zero reflecting that all amounts in cash flow hedge reserve in equity have been reclassified to profit or loss.

B Reflects the total interest expense from US$ debt and CCS. Equals the total interest expense that would have been incurred had Entity A actually issued £ debt at inception (£57,143*6%) * 5 years = £17,143.

Entries in the consolidated financial statements for 20X2 for illustrative purposes

1 January 20X2

No entry required for CCS as fair value is nil at inception.

Dr	Cash	57,143
Cr	Debt	57,143

To record issue of 4 per cent US$ debt in £ (retranslated at spot).

31 December 20X2

Dr	Interest expense	2,319
Cr	Cash	2,319

To record payment of the interest on US$ debt converted at average rates.

Dr	Retranslation loss (profit or loss)	1,681
Cr	Debt	1,681

To record loss on retranslation of the US$ debt at year end spot rates.

Dr	Interest expense	1,110
Cr	Cash	1,110

To record net interest paid on CCS (£ 6% – US$ 4%).

Dr	CCS asset	2,560
Cr	Other comprehensive income (cash flow hedging reserve)	2,560

To record fair value movement in CCS in other comprehensive income (as 100% effective).

Dr	Other comprehensive income (cash flow hedging reserve)	1,681
Cr	Retranslation gain (profit or loss)	1,681

To record reclassifying the effective portion of CCS from equity to profit or loss to offset the retranslation of the debt.

Similar entries would be recorded for the remaining term of the hedging relationship (20X3 -20X6)

Interest expense totalling £17,143 is recognised over the term of the hedging instrument which is equivalent to Entity A having issued Sterling 6 per cent debt at inception. The CCS is fair valued at the end of each reporting period (after interest payments have been made as all interest payments for purposes of this illustration are deemed to have taken place on last day of year which is the reset date for the swap) with amounts recognised in other comprehensive income (and taken to the cash flow hedge reserve in equity). The amount of the CCS is reclassified from equity to profit or loss at the end of each reporting period to offset the amount recorded for retranslation of the US$ debt to Sterling spot rates.

3.9 Cash flow hedging foreign currency risk of zero coupon debt

The following example illustrates the entries for a cash flow hedge of foreign currency risk of zero coupon debt using a forward exchange contract.

On 1 January 20X2, Entity A, a £ functional currency entity, issues 5-year US$ denominated zero coupon debt with a notional amount of US$1,812,052 for US$1,419,791. The interest rate implicit in the debt is 5 per cent. The zero coupon debt will mature on 31 December 20X6. On the same date Entity A entered into a forward contract to buy US$1,812,052 for £1,000,000 at the forward rate of US$1.812:£ at 31 December 20X6. The £ interest rate implicit in the forward contract is 6 per cent. The carrying amount of the zero coupon debt at initial recognition in Entity A's functional currency, is £747,258 as spot rates at the date of issue are US$1.90:£.

The entity designates the forward exchange contract as a hedge of the variability of the £ functional currency equivalent cash flows on the zero coupon debt. As the currency, notional amount and maturity of the forward contract match that of the zero coupon debt Entity A expects the hedge relationship to be highly effective.

Date	**Spot rate US$ / £**	**Forward rate US$/£**	**US$ amortised cost (effective interest rate of 5%)**	**Synthetic £ zero coupon debt (effective interest rate of 6%)**	**Fair value of forward contract (£)**
1/1/X2	1.900	1.812	1,419,791	747,258	0
31/12/X2	1.800	1.733	1,490,780	792,094	36,117
31/12/X3	1.900	1.847	1,565,319	839,619	(15,767)
31/12/X4	1.900	1.900	1,643,585	889,996	(41,196)
31/12/X5	1.900	1.900	1,725,764	943,396	(43,668)
31/12/X6	1.900	1.900	1,812,052	1,000,000	(46,288)

The change in forward rates over the period reflects a combination of factors: (i) the pull of spot rates to forward rates over the period ending 31/12/X6; and (ii) an increase in US$ interest rates from 31/12/X4 to 31/12/X6 from 5% to 6%. Forward rates and spot rates coincide from 20X4 as there is no interest rate differential between US$ and £ as both are 6 per cent.

Entity A's documentation of the hedge is as follows.

Risk management objective and nature of risk being hedged	Cash flow hedge of the variability in functional currency equivalent cash flows associated with the foreign currency zero coupon debt due to changes in US$:£ forward rates.
Date of designation	1 January 20X2
Hedging instrument	Forward contract entered into on 1 January 20X2 maturing on 31 December 20X6 to buy US$1,812,052 and sell £1,000,000.
Hedged item	Zero coupon debt issued on 1 January 20X2 maturing on 31 December 20X6 with a notional amount of US$1,812,052 and issued for proceeds of US$1,419,791.

Assessment of hedge effectiveness	The critical terms of the derivative match those of the hedged item (in terms of currency, maturity and notional), accordingly there is an expectation of high effectiveness. The entity will assess counterparty credit risk every period.
Measurement of hedge effectiveness	Hypothetical derivative method. The actual hedging instrument is the same as the hypothetical forward with exactly matching terms and therefore, no ineffectiveness is anticipated.

The following table illustrates the accounting entries for the transaction during its life in Sterling. Dr or (Cr) as indicated.

Date		Cash	Forward	Debt	CFH reserve – equity	Interest expense	Foreign currency loss (gain)
1/1X2	Issue zero coupon debt	747,258		(747,258)			
31/12/X2	Accrue interest on debt			(39,439)		39,439	
	Revalue debt to spot			(41,514)			41,514
	Fair value forward contract		36,117			5,397	(41,514)
31/12/X3	Accrue interest on debt			(39,231)		39,231	
	Revalue debt to spot			43,590			(43,590)
	Fair value of forward contract		(51,885)			8,295	43,590
31/12/X4	Accrue interest on debt			(41,193)		41,193	
	Fair value of forward contract		(25,428)		16,245	9,183	
31/12/X5	Accrue interest on debt			(43,252)		43,252	
	Fair value of forward contract		(2,472)		(7,676)	10,148	
31/12/X6	Accrue interest on debt			(45,415)		45,415	

Date		Cash	Forward	Debt	CFH reserve – equity	Interest expense	Foreign currency loss (gain)
	Fair value of forward contract		(2,620)		(8,569)	11,189	
	Settlement of forward	(46,288)	46,288				
	Settlement of debt	(953,712)		953,712			
		(252,742)	0	0	0	252,742	0
	Key				**A**	**B**	

Key

A nets to zero reflecting that all amounts in the cash flow hedge reserve in equity have been reclassified to profit or loss to offset retranslation of the debt to spot each period and the recognition of total interest in £ at the £ rate implicit in the forward contract of 6 per cent.

B reflects the total interest expense from the US$ denominated zero coupon debt and the foreign currency forward contract. This is equal to a rate of 6 per cent as applied to the £747,258 (the £ equivalent of the proceeds at the spot rate when the zero coupon debt was issued). The interest amounts comprise two elements:

(i) the underlying 5 per cent interest on the US$ zero coupon debt retranslated into the functional currency; and

(ii) the systematic reclassification of the fair value movements of the forward contract from equity to profit or loss so as to increase the effective interest rate to 6 per cent.

Entries in the financial statements for 20X2 for illustrative purposes:

1 January 20X2

No entry required for forward contract as fair value is nil at inception.

Dr	Cash	747,258
Cr	Debt	747,258

To record the issue of the US$ denominated zero coupon debt in the £ functional currency (retranslated at spot).

31 December 20X2

Dr	Interest expense (profit or loss)	39,439
Cr	Debt	39,439

To record accrual of interest on zero coupon debt (5 per cent on US$1,419,791 translated at year end spot rate of US$1.8:£. Translation at year end spot rates is used for illustrative purposes only.

Dr	Retranslation loss (profit or loss)	41,514
Cr	Debt	41,514

To record loss on retranslation of US$ zero coupon debt at year end spot rate.

Dr	Forward contract	36,117
Dr	Interest expense (profit or loss)	5,397
Cr	Retranslation gain (profit or loss)	41,514

To record the fair value movement of the forward contract with the effective gain recognised in other comprehensive income (and taken to the cash flow hedge reserve) together with the appropriate reclassification from equity to profit or loss so as to offset the retranslation of the zero coupon debt to spot and to increase interest expense in profit or loss to total the rate that would have been accrued had the entity issued the zero coupon debt in Sterling.

In this period the effective gain recognised in other comprehensive income is reclassified from equity to profit or loss in the same period and therefore for illustrative purposes only the gross entries of recognising in other comprehensive income and reclassifying to profit or loss are not presented.

Similar entries would be recorded for the remaining term of the hedging relationship (20X3 -20X6).

Interest expense totalling £252,742 is recognised over the term of the hedging instrument and the net profit or loss is the same as if Entity A had issued £ denominated zero coupon debt for £747,258 on 1 January 20X2 which accrued interest at an effective rate of 6 per cent and matured with a payment of the notional of £1,000,000 at 31 December 20X6.

3.10 Cash flow hedging foreign currency risk of the principal only on interest-bearing debt

If the principal only cash flow of a debt instrument is cash flow hedged for foreign currency risk only part of a derivative's fair value will be reclassified to profit or loss over the period of the hedge relationship as only a part of the carrying value of the debt instrument that is retranslated into the functional currency represents the principal cash flow (as opposed to future interest flows) that impacts profit or loss. As the carrying amount of a loan is comprised of the discounted amount of both interest and principal discounted at the instrument's original effective interest rate, the amount that can be reclassified from equity to profit or loss in any given period will not equate to the whole fair value movement of the derivative. The amount to be reclassified will equal the portion of the change in fair value of the derivative equivalent to spot retranslation on the discounted principal at the period end plus the systematic release of forward points to the extent the entity is hedging the forward rate. Over the instrument's life, the proportion of the carrying value of the loan that equates to the discounted principal only will grow as the principal repayment date nears. It is not permitted to reclassify from equity to profit or loss the entirety of the derivative's fair value movement in the period as this would be overstating the foreign currency risk on the principal portion of the hedged loan. While the retranslation of the entire carrying amount of the loan will impact profit or loss under IAS 21, the principal only forms part of that carrying amount.

The following example illustrates the entries for a cash flow hedge of foreign currency risk of the principal payment only of interest-bearing debt using a forward exchange contract.

On 1 January 20X2, Entity A, a Euro functional currency entity, issues 3-year US$ denominated debt at par equal to US$100m for US$100m. The interest rate implicit in the debt is 5 per cent and is paid annually in arrears. The debt will mature on 31 December 20X4. On the issue date Entity A entered into a forward contract to buy US$100m for €78.69m at the forward rate of US$1.27:€ at 31 December 20X4 to hedge the principal payment only. The € interest rate implicit in the forward contract is 5.8 per cent. The carrying amount of the debt at initial recognition in Entity A's functional currency, is €76.92m as spot rates at the date of issue are US$1.30:€.

The entity designates the forward exchange contract as a hedge of the variability of the € functional currency equivalent cash flows on the principal payment only on the debt at maturity. As the currency, notional amount and maturity of the forward contract match the currency, notional amount and maturity of the debt, Entity A expects the hedge relationship to be highly effective.

Date	**Spot rate US$/ €**	**Forward rate US$/€**	**US$m amortised cost of the principal only (effective interest rate of 5%)**	**Synthetic €m amortised cost of the principal only (effective interest rate of 5.8%)**	**Fair value of forward contract (€m)**
1/1/X2	1.30	1.27	86.38	66.45	-
31/12/X2	1.25	1.21	90.70	70.30	3.22
31/12/X3	1.22	1.21	95.24	74.38	3.87
31/12/X4	1.38	1.38	100.00	78.69	(6.23)

Entity A's documentation of the hedge is as follows.

Risk management objective and nature of risk being hedged	Cash flow hedge of the variability in functional currency equivalent cash flows associated with the principal payment only of interest bearing debt due to changes in US$:€ forward rates.
Date of designation	1 January 20X2
Hedging instrument	Forward contract entered into on 1 January 20X2 maturing on 31 December 20X4 to buy US$100m and sell €78.69m.

Hedged item	Principal payment only on interest bearing US$ denominated debt issued at par of US$100m on 1 January 20X2 maturing on 31 December 20X4.
Assessment of hedge effectiveness	The critical terms of the derivative match those of the hedged item (in terms of currency, maturity and notional), accordingly there is an expectation of high effectiveness. The entity will assess counterparty credit risk every period.
Measurement of hedge effectiveness	Hypothetical derivative method. The actual hedging instrument is the same as the hypothetical forward with exactly matching terms and therefore, no ineffectiveness is anticipated.

The following table illustrates the accounting entries for the transaction during its life in Sterling. Dr or (Cr) as indicated.

Date		Cash	Forward	Debt	CFH reserve – equity	Profit or loss
1/1X2	Issue zero coupon debt	76.92		(76.92)		
31/12/X2	Accrue interest on debt at average rates			(3.92)		3.92
	Revalue debt to spot			(3.16)		3.16
	Pay interest at year end	(4.00)		4.00		
	Fair value forward contract		3.22		(3.22)	
	Reclassify amounts from equity to profit or loss				2.26	(2.26)
31/12/X3	Accrue interest on debt at average rates			(4.05)		4.05
	Revalue debt to spot			(2.02)		2.02
	Pay interest at year end	(4.10)		4.10		
	Fair value of forward contract		0.65		(0.65)	
	Reclassify amounts from equity to profit or loss				1.42	(1.42)

Date		Cash	Forward	Debt	CFH reserve – equity	Profit or loss
31/12/X4	Accrue interest on debt at average rates			(3.85)		3.85
	Revalue debt to spot			9.74		9.74
	Pay interest at year end	(3.62)		3.62		
	Fair value forward contract		(10.10)		10.10	
	Reclassify amounts from equity to profit or loss				(9.91)	9.91
	Settle forward contract	(6.23)	6.23			
	Settle principal on debt	(72.46)		72.46		
			0	0	0	32.97
	Key		**A**	**B**	**C**	**D**

Key

A nets to zero reflecting the forward is fully settled at maturity.

B net to zero reflecting the debt is fully settled at maturity.

C nets to zero reflecting that all amounts in the cash flow hedge reserve in equity have been reclassified to profit or loss to offset the retranslation of the principal only portion of the debt to spot each period and the systematic release of forward points relating to the principal only portion of the debt.

D the total impact in profit or loss reflects the US$ interest expense on the US$ denominated debt translated at average US$:€ rates, the translation on the US$ denominated debt to closing rates at each period end plus the impact of hedging the principal only from US$ to €.

The reclassified amounts from equity to profit or loss are equivalent to the amounts that would have been reclassified to profit or loss had the entity simply issued a US$100m denominated zero coupon bond for US$86.38m and immediately hedged it by exchanging US$100m at maturity for €78.69m. As Entity A only hedged the principal amount of the US$ denominated debt this is equivalent to hedging US$ zero coupon bond with the same maturity.

Entries in the financial statements for 20X2 for illustrative purposes:

1 January 20X2
No entry required for forward contract as fair value is nil at inception.

Dr	Cash	76.92
Cr	Debt	76.92

To record the issue of the US$ denominated debt in the € functional currency (retranslated at spot).

31 December 20X2

Dr	Interest expense (profit or loss)	3.92
Cr	Debt	3.92

To record the accrual of interest on the debt (5 per cent on US$100m translated at average rates of US$1.28:€).

Dr	Retranslation loss (profit or loss)	3.16
Cr	Debt	3.16

To record the loss on retranslation of US$ debt at year end spot rate. This amount consists of the translation of the opening carrying amount at closing rate compared to opening rate plus the interest accrual at closing rate compared to the average rate.

Dr	Debt	4.00
Cr	Cash	4.00

To record the payment of interest in cash at the year end at the actual rate.

Dr	Forward contract	3.22
Cr	Cash flow hedge reserve	3.22

To record the effective gain on the forward contract in other comprehensive income.

Dr	Cash flow hedge reserve	2.26
Cr	Profit or loss	2.26

To record the appropriate reclassification from equity to profit or loss so as to offset the retranslation of the principal portion of the debt to spot and to release the systematic release of forward points.

Similar entries would be recorded for the remaining term of the hedging relationship (20X3 and 20X4).

The amount of the debt that is hedged and the systematic release of forward points for the period ending 31 December 20X2 is described below.

At 1 January 20X2 the amount attributable to the interest and principal only components of the debt is determined in the foreign currency. This is calculated by discounting the principal cash flow due at maturity at the foreign currency original effective interest rate, US$100m / (1.05^3) = US$86.38m, with the balance being attributed to the interest only component (US$13.62m). At the next period end, 31 December 20X2, the amount attributable to the principal only component is US$90.70m (US$86.38m * 1.05), with the balance attributed to the interest only component (US$9.30m). The foreign currency risk that impacts profit or loss, that is being hedged, is the foreign currency translation of the principal only component.

Had Entity A issued the principal component in Euros, the entity's functional currency, as opposed to issuing in US$ (and then hedging the principal component into Euros), the principal component would have a value at issue of €66.45m (US$86.38 * US$:€1.30 [spot]) and would have an effective interest rate of 5.8%, being the Euro effective interest rate for a 3-year maturity. For the period ending 31 December 20X2 the impact in profit or loss for the principal component denominated in Euros would have been €3.85m, being €66.45m * 5.8%.

If the hedge is fully effective the profit or loss for the period will include the impact of the principal only component of the foreign currency debt as if it was issued in Euros. In other words, the effect of hedge accounting should be equivalent to Entity A issuing a Euro-denominated zero coupon bond with a yield of 5.8% for €66.45m and a 5% US$-denominated interest only strip with a notional of US$100m for US$13.62m, as opposed to issued a 5% US$-denominated debt at par of US$100m and hedging the principal only component to Euros. As Entity A is hedging the forward currency rate, not the spot rate, a systematic release of forward points included in the fair value of the forward contract recognised in equity will be reclassified to profit or loss to reflect that the principal only component is economically equivalent to it being denominated in Euros.

A reconciliation of the carrying value of the debt for 20X2 is illustrated below.

Carrying value of the debt	€m	Calculation
Net issue proceeds translated at the spot rate	76.92	US$100m @ US$1.30:€ [opening]
Interest at the effective interest of 5% translated at the average rate	3.92	US$100m * 5% @ US$1.28:€ [average]
Less interest at the effective interest of 5% paid in cash at the period end	(4.00)	US$100m * 5% @ US$1.25:€ [closing]
Foreign currency translation consisting of:		
- period end amortised cost balance in foreign currency translated at the closing rate compared to the opening rate	3.08	US$100m @ US$1.25:€ [closing] less US$100m @ US$1.30:€ [opening]
- the difference between the interest at the effective interest rate translated at the average and closing rate	0.08	US$100m * 5% @ US$1.25:€ [closing] less US$100m * 5% @ US$1.28:€ [average]
Carrying value at 31 December 20X2	80.00	

A reconciliation of the amounts recognised in profit or loss with respect to the principal only component that is cash flow hedged is illustrated below:

Profit or loss impact	€m	Calculation
Applying the US$ effective interest on the US$ principal only component	3.37	(US$86.38 * 5%) @ US$1.28: € [average]
Foreign currency translation consisting of:		

Profit or loss impact	€m	Calculation
- period end amortised cost balance in foreign currency translated at the closing rate compared to the opening rate	2.66	US$86.38m @ US$1.25:€ [closing] less US$86.38m @ US$1.30:€ [opening]
- the difference between the interest at the effective interest rate converted at the average and closing rate	0.08	US$86.38m * 5% @ US$1.25:€ [closing] less US$86.38m * 5% @ US$1.28:€ [average]
Less systematic release of forward points from equity to profit or loss	(2.26)	€66.45m * 5.8% less (3.39+2.66+0.07 above)
Net profit or loss impact had Entity A issued a Euro denominated zero coupon bond at 5.8% for €66.45m instead of issuing the principal only component of the US$ denominated debt at 5% for US$86.38	3.85	€66.45 * 5.8%

3.11 Designating a cash flow hedge in layers

The following example illustrates the entries for a cash flow hedge designated in layers for foreign currency risk of forecast revenue using forward exchange contracts.

Entity A, € functional currency, has a substantial export business to the United States where Entity A receives US$ receipts from the sales of goods. Entity A is exposed to variability of its future revenue from export sales due to fluctuations in currency rates between US$ and €.

Entity A reports under IFRS on a semi-annual basis and its period end is 31 December. On 1 January 20X0 Entity A establishes that it will have highly probable US$ sales amounting to US$10m on 30 June 20X1. In order to hedge its exposure to changes in the US$:€ forward exchange rate it enters into a forward contract to sell US$10m and buy € on 30 June 20X1. Entity A designates and documents the forward contract as a hedging instrument in a cash flow hedge of the US$:€ forward risk on a designated amount of highly probable US$ revenue.

The changes in the fair value of the derivative are shown in the table below:

Date	Fair value of forward (€ m)	Fair value change in period (€ m)
01.01.20X0	0	0
30.06.20X0	0.5	0.5
31.12.20X0	2.5	2.0
31.06.20X1	4.0	1.5

On 31 December 20X0 the entity revises its estimates of the US$ sales that will take place on 30 June 20X1 and determines that now only $7.5m of sales are highly probable. The entity is unable to identify a single event or change

in circumstances responsible for this revision in accordance with IAS 39.AG113. In addition to this, a further $0.5m of sales is expected to occur (but is not highly probable).

Whether Entity A designates and documents the forecast sales in multiple layers or a single layer does have an impact on the amount of the effective portion of the gain or loss on the derivative that is recognised in other comprehensive income in a cash flow hedge. The impact on profit or loss and other comprehensive income of the two designations is illustrated below.

The entries below are for the 6 months to 30 June 20X0 and 31 December 20X0 only.

Entity A specifies as part of its hedge documentation put in place on 1 January 20X0 that it has two designated hedge relationships, identified by two different layers:

- L1: a 75% proportion of the US$10m forward is designated as hedging the first $7.5m of US$ sales that are highly probable of occurring on 30 June 20X1; and
- L2: a 25% proportion of the US$10m forward is designated as hedging the next US$2.5m of highly probable US$ sales occurring on 30 June 20X1, i.e. sales US$ US$7.5m – US$10m.

6 months to 30 June 20X0

The full $10m forecast sales remain highly probable and therefore the total fair value movement of €0.5m will be recognised in other comprehensive income under L1 and L2 (both designations being perfectly effective hedging relationships).

Dr	Derivative asset	€0.5m
Cr	Other comprehensive income	€0.5m

To recognise the effective amount of the derivative gain in other comprehensive income

6 months to 31 December 20X0

(i) Entity A must assess whether any of the amounts recognised in other comprehensive income in equity at 30 June 20X0 should be reclassified from equity to profit or loss in the instance when some of the previously considered highly probable forecast transactions are no longer expected to occur. [IAS 39.101(c)] As US$8m of sales are still expected to occur (being US$7.5m that are highly probable and US$0.5m that are still expected to occur), compared to US$10m of sales at 30 June 20X0, 80 per cent of the €0.5m fair value movement previously recognised in other comprehensive income should remain in other comprehensive income with 20 per cent reclassified from equity to profit or loss. This in line with the principles outlined in **2.2.4** above.

Dr	Other comprehensive income	€0.1m
Cr	Profit or loss	€0.1m

To reclassify a fifth of the cash flow hedge gain from equity to profit or loss as a fifth of previously designated forecast transactions are no longer expected to occur

(ii) Entity A must assess whether the two hedging relationships (L1 and L2) have been highly effective for the 6 months to 31 December 20X0. Based on the revised estimates at 31 December 20X0 only US$7.5m of sales are highly probable. The L1 designation is considered to be highly effective as the total fair value movement in the designated proportion of the derivative is €1.5m (being 75 per cent of the total movement of €2.0m) and the change in fair value of the hedged cash flows, being US$7.5m, is €1.5m. L1 is therefore 100 per cent effective [€1.5m / €1.5m = 100 per cent].

All of the fair value movement of designation L2 (€0.5m, being 25 per cent of total movement of €2.0m) will be recognised in profit or loss as the hedge relationship is not highly effective due to the fall in the level of highly probable sales. As the amount of highly probable forecast sales between US$7.5m and US$10m is now nil, the hedge relationship is 0 per cent effective.

Dr	Derivative asset	€2.0m
Cr	Cash flow hedge reserve	€1.5m
Cr	Profit or loss	€0.5m

To recognise the effective amount of the derivative gain in other comprehensive income and remainder in profit or loss.

The amount of ineffectiveness recognised in profit or loss in the 6 months to 31 December 20X0 would be different were Entity A to designate the hedge of the forecast sales in a single layer.

As on 31 December 20X0, only US$7.5m of sales are considered to be highly probable, the hedging relationship is not highly effective: it is only 75 per cent effective as the total fair value movement in the derivative is €2.0m and the change in fair value of the hedged cash flows, being $7.5m, is €1.5m [€2.0m / €1.5m = 75 per cent]. Since hedge effectiveness is outside the range of 80 per cent – 125 per cent the entire fair value movement in the period of €2.0m will be recognised in profit or loss.

3.12 Cash flow hedging with an in-the-money option

The following example illustrates the entries for a cash flow hedge of interest rate risk on variable rate debt using a purchased in-the-money cap.

Entity B has a purchased European-style cap at 6% that matures in 6 months that has a notional of CU100m that corresponds with issued variable rate debt with the same notional that has a variable interest reset date also in 6 months time. Entity B wishes to designate the intrinsic value of the option as a hedge of future cash flow variability on its variable rate debt for the next 6 months with respect to changes in interest rates.

At the date of designation current interest rates are 8% and therefore the option is in-the-money. It is assumed for illustrative purposes the interest rate curve is flat and therefore both current and forward rates are 8%. The intrinsic value would be equal to (8%-6%) x CU100m discounted for 6 months. The fair value of the purchased cap with respect to intrinsic value will be included in the overall fair value of the derivative asset at the date of designation. At the date of designation the fair value of the intrinsic value is CU2m (for illustration purposes only discounting has been ignored throughout this example and fair value movements in time value are excluded as these gains/losses will always immediately be recognised in profit or loss as they are excluded from the hedge designation).

The date of designation is 1 October 20X9 and the reporting period end is 31 December 20X9. At the reporting period end four scenarios could arise.

Scenario 1 – interest rates rise (to 9%)

The option is further in-the-money.

Dr	Derivative asset	CU1m
Cr	Other comprehensive income – cash flow hedge reserve	CU1m

The option is fully effective at hedging increases in interest rates. In this case increases in interest rates of 1% would result in the at-the-money option being in-the-money by CU1m.

Scenario 2 – interest remain the same (at 8%)

The option remains in-the-money by the same degree as at the date of designation.

No entries are required as intrinsic value has remained the same as there has been no increase or decrease in interest rates. In this case as there is no change in interest rates an at-the-money option would continue to be at-the-money.

Scenario 3 – interest rates fall but remain above the cap (to 7%)

The option remains in-the-money but by a lesser amount.

Dr	Profit or loss	CU1m
Cr	Derivative asset	CU1m

The purchased cap is not effective at hedging changes in interest rates in the instance when interest rates fall below the level that existed when the option was designated. CU1m cannot be recognised in other comprehensive income as the option is not effective in the period in hedging future variability in interest rates. In this case a fall in interest rates for an at-the-money option would result in the option being out-of-the-money and therefore no intrinsic value could be recognised in other comprehensive income.

Scenario 4 – interest rates fall below the cap (to 5%)

The option is out-of-the-money.

Dr	Profit or loss	CU2m

Cr	Derivative asset	CU2m

The purchased cap is not effective at hedging changes in interest rates in the instance when interest rates fall below the level that existed when the option was designated. CU2m cannot be recognised in other comprehensive income as the option is not effective in the period in hedging future variability in interest rates. In this case a fall in interest rates for an at-the-money option would result in the option being out-of-the-money and therefore no intrinsic value could be recognised in other comprehensive income. In this instance the actual option is out-of-the-money so all intrinsic value that was recognised as an asset in the statement of financial position at the date of designation is recognised in profit or loss in the period.

If Scenario 1 occurred in the first quarter, but in the second quarter interest rates fell below the level of the cap then the amount recognised in the cash flow hedge reserve in the first quarter will be reversed through the cash flow hedge reserve until the cash flow hedge reserve is nil, and any excess is recognised in profit or loss.

If Scenario 4 occurred in the first quarter, but in the second quarter interest rates rose above the level of the cap then the amount recognised in profit or loss in the first quarter will be reversed in the second quarter in profit or loss. Any increase in intrinsic value above CU2m (being the intrinsic value at the date of designation) will be recognised in other comprehensive income.

3.13 Cash flow hedge ineffectiveness due to basis risk

The following example illustrates the entries for a cash flow hedge of interest rate risk on a forecast debt issuance using an interest rate swap with a different basis to the hedged item.

Entity X is expecting to issue €100 million of five-year fixed-rate bonds on 30 June 20X0. Entity X has a single A credit rating, it believes that interest rates may increase during the next six months and wants to hedge against such an increase by locking-in existing five-year fixed rates. Entity X enters into a forward starting five-year swap on 1 January 20X0 (the swap starts in six months) with a notional amount equal to the expected principal amount of the anticipated debt issuance. At the date of the hedge, swap rates were 5.50 per cent and five-year single A rates were 5.60 per cent.

Entity X assesses effectiveness based on the cumulative change in fair value of the derivative and the cumulative change in the discounted present value or fair value of expected future interest and principal payments on fixed-rate single A bonds. Changes in spreads during the hedge period will result in hedge ineffectiveness. At the inception of the hedge the spread between the swap rates and five-year single A corporate bonds was 10 basis points. Historically there is a high degree of correlation between swaps and single A corporate bonds.

The required entries are as follows.

1 January 20X0

No entry required as the derivative has a fair value of zero.

31 March 20X0

On 31 March 20X0 five-year swap rates are 5.10 per cent and five-year single A rates are 5.15 per cent. The derivative has a negative fair value of €1.744 million as a result of a decrease in five-year swap rates of 40 basis points subsequent to 1 January 20X0. The spread between five-year swap rates and five-year single A corporate bond rates decreased to 5 basis points. Because the hedge underperformed the changes in single A rates, the loss on the hedge is smaller than the present value decrease in expected future interest expense on the anticipated issuance of debt and, therefore, the hedge is fully effective. If the decrease in the expected future interest expense on the anticipated issuance of debt was lower than the loss on the hedge, a portion of the loss on the derivative would be recognised in profit or loss.

Dr	Other comprehensive income	€1,744,000	
Cr	Derivative liability		€1,744,000

To record the derivative at fair value with changes in fair value recorded in other comprehensive income.

30 June 20X0

On 30 June 20X0 five-year swap rates are 5.30 per cent and five-year single A rates are 5.40 per cent. The derivative has a negative fair value of €867,000 as a result of an increase in five-year swap rates of 20 basis points from 31 March 20X0; spreads at 31 March 20X0 returned to 10 basis points. The hedge is completely effective on a cumulative basis as the spreads returned to 10 basis points.

Dr	Derivative liability	€877,000	
Cr	Other comprehensive income		€877,000

To record the derivative at fair value with changes in fair value recorded in other comprehensive income.

On 30 June 20X0 Entity X issues €100 million of five-year bonds at a rate of 5.40 per cent. Entity X also closes out the derivative.

Dr	Cash	€100,000,000	
Cr	Debt obligation		€100,000,000
Dr	Derivative liability	€867,000	
Cr	Cash		€867,000

To record the debt issuance and close out of the derivative.

The €867,000 debit will be reclassified from equity to profit or loss when the interest on the debt is recognised in profit or loss. It will effectively result in a yield adjustment over the life of the bond (since the bond is issued at a greater discount) and an effective yield on the bond of approximately 5.60 per cent, which is the rate in effect at 1/1/X0, the date the hedge is initiated.

In the example basis risk exists between the risk exposure of the derivative, which is solely interest rates, and the risk exposure of the hedged item, which includes both interest rate risk and credit risk of the debt that has been issued. Even though there is basis risk, in this example, applying cash flow hedge accounting does not result in hedge ineffectiveness in profit or loss (as the hedge underperforms in the first period and is perfectly effective on a cumulative assessment basis for the second period).

3.14 Cash flow hedging share appreciation rights

The following example illustrates the entries for a cash flow hedge of equity price risk arising from an entity's IFRS 2 *Share-based Payment* charge using a purchased equity call option.

On 1 January 20X1, Entity A awarded its employees exclusively cash-settled share appreciation rights (SARs) that vest and can be exercised at 31 December 20X3 if the employees are still working for the entity on that date. Each of the 100 employees is granted one SAR with a strike price of CU10. Therefore, each right provides for a cash payment equal to the amount by which the share price of Entity A exceeds the strike price on the exercise date. No payment will be made if Entity A's share price is at or below CU10; Entity A's share price on 1 January 20X1 is CU10. Entity A estimates that 85 per cent of employees granted a SAR will be employed at 31 December 20X3 (it is estimated five employees leave the entity each year).

Entity A purchases a net cash-settled call option for CU70 with a strike price of CU10 that can only be settled at maturity on 31 December 20X3. The notional of the call option is over 70 shares, i.e. less than the 85 employees that are expected to be employed at the end of the scheme. Entity A hedges only 70 out of the 85 SARs that are expected to vest in order to reduce the risk over over-hedging should more employees leave than expected. Entity A excludes the time value of the option from the hedge designation to demonstrate prospectively that the relationship is expected to be highly effective. Entity A designates the intrinsic value of the derivative as hedging the cash flow variability of 70 employees' SARs and their profit or loss impact recognised in accordance with IFRS 2 *Share-based Payment*. At any given period, the IFRS 2 liability and corresponding cumulative profit or loss charge will be equal to the degree to which the hedging instrument is "in-the-money" apportioned for the period from the grant date to the vesting date.

The time value and intrinsic value of the hedging instrument are summarised below:

	1/1/X1	31/12/X1	31/12/X2	31/12/X3
Time value	70	40	20	–
Intrinsic value	–	210	280	140
Fair value	70	250	300	140

All amounts are expressed in CU (currency units).

1 January 20X1

Dr	Derivative asset	70
Cr	Cash	70

To recognise the fair value of the hedging instrument at initial recognition.

31 December 20X1

Entity A's share price is CU13, and three employees have left the entity in the period. Entity A changes its estimate of the number of employees expected to be employed at 31 December 20X3 to 91.

The share-based payment charge and liability is CU91 [((CU13 – CU10) × 91) × $^1/_3$ = CU91].

Dr	Employee expense	91
Cr	Share based payment liability	91

To recognise the share-based payment expense in the period.

The hedge was highly effective for the period since 70 employees are still expected to be employed at 31 December 20X3, and the hedging instrument provides a perfect offset to the cash flow variability of the liability for the payments to these employees.

Dr	Derivative asset	180 [250 – 70]
Dr	Profit or loss	30
Cr	Cash flow hedge reserve	210

To recognise the fair value movement of the derivative with the time value recognised in profit or loss and the effective portion recognised in other comprehensive income.

The period-end cash flow hedge reserve must be equal to the intrinsic value of 70 employee SARs that are still considered to be highly probable and that have not yet affected profit or loss through the IFRS 2 charge. Because the scheme is one-third through its life, the cash flow hedge reserve at the end of the period is CU140 [((CU13 – CU10) × 70) × $^2/_3$ = CU140].

Dr	Cash flow hedge reserve	70
Cr	Profit or loss	70

To recognise the reclassification from the cash flow hedge reserve in equity to profit or loss for the portion of intrinsic value of the derivative as a result of the SAR impacting profit or loss. The amount reclassified is determined as ((13–10) x 70) x $^1/_3$ = 70.

31 December 20X2

Entity A's share price is CU14, and four employees have left the entity in the period. The entity revises its estimates of the number of employees expected to be employed at 31 December 20X3 to 89.

The share-based payment liability is CU237 [((CU14 – CU10) × 89) × $^2/_3$ = CU237].

Dr	Employee expense	146
Cr	Share-based payment liability	146 [237 – 91]

To recognise the share-based payment expense in the period.

The hedge was highly effective for the period since 70 employees are still expected to be employed at 31 December 20X3, and the hedging instrument provides a perfect offset to the cash flow variability of the liability for the payments to these employees.

Dr	Derivative asset	50 [300 – 250]
Dr	Profit or loss	20
Cr	Cash flow hedge reserve	70

To recognise the fair value movement of the derivative with the time value recognised in profit or loss and the effective portion recognised in other comprehensive income.

The period-end cash flow hedge reserve must be equal to the intrinsic value of 70 employee SARs that are still considered to be highly probable and that have not yet affected profit or loss through the IFRS 2 charge. Because the scheme is two-thirds through its life, the cash flow hedge reserve at the end of the period is CU93 [((CU14 – CU10) × 70) × $^1/_3$ = CU93].

Dr	Cash flow hedge reserve	117
Cr	Profit or loss	117

To recognise the reclassification from the cash flow hedge reserve in equity to profit or loss for the portion of intrinsic value of the derivative as a result of the SAR impacting profit or loss. The amount reclassified is determined as [((14–10) x 70) x $^2/_3$] – 70 recognised in previous period = 117.

31 December 20X3

Entity A's share price is CU12, and five employees have left the entity in the period. In all, 12 employees have left over the three-year period [three in 20X1, four in 20X2, and five in 20X3].

The share-based payment liability is CU176 [((CU12 – CU10) × 88) × $^3/_3$ = CU176].

Dr	Share-based payment liability	61 [176 – 237]
Cr	Employee expense	61

To recognise the share-based payment expense in the period.

The hedge was highly effective for the period since 70 employees were employed at 31 December 20X3, and the hedging instrument provided a perfect offset to the cash flow variability of the liability for the payments to these employees.

Dr	Profit or loss	20
Dr	Cash flow hedge reserve	140
Cr	Derivative asset	160 [140 – 300]

To recognise the fair value movement of the derivative with the time value recognised in profit or loss and the effective portion recognised in other comprehensive income.

Since the 70 SARs vested at the period end, no amount should be left in the cash flow hedge reserve. Because the scheme is at the end of its life, the cash flow hedge reserve at the end of the period is CU0.

Dr	Cash flow hedge reserve	117
Cr	Profit or loss	117

To recognise the reclassification from the cash flow hedge reserve in equity to profit or loss for the portion of intrinsic value of the derivative as a result of the SAR impacting profit or loss. The amount reclassified is determined as [((12–10) x 70) x $^{3}/_{3}$] – (70 + 117) recognised in period periods = 47.

Dr	Share-based payment liability	176 [(12–10) x 88]
Cr	Cash	176

To recognise payment to employees on exercise of the SARs.

Dr	Cash	140
Cr	Derivative asset	140

To recognise cash received on settlement of the hedging instrument.

Summary of entries

Dr/(Cr)

Description	Derivative asset	Cash-settled share-based payment liability	Cash	Profit or loss	Cash flow hedge reserve
1/1/X1					
Hedging instrument	70		(70)		
31/12/X1					
Share-based payment		(91)		91	
Hedging instrument	180			(40)	(140)
31/12/X2					
Share-based payment		(146)		146	
Hedging instrument	50			(97)	47
31/12/X3					
Share-based payment		61		(61)	

Description	Derivative asset	Cash-settled share-based payment liability	Cash	Profit or loss	Cash flow hedge reserve
Hedging instrument	(160)			67	93
Share-based payment		176	(176)		
Hedging instrument	(140)		140		
Total	–	–	(106)	106	–

The net cash impact of hedging the cash-settled share-based payments is the total share-based payments of CU176, plus the up-front premium spent to acquire the hedging instrument of CU70, less the cash received on settlement of the hedging instrument of CU140. The profit or loss impact equates to the IFRS 2 charge of CU176 plus the net gain from the hedging instrument of CU70.

The net income in each period is not fully offset for the following reasons:

- Entity A did not hedge all its expected cash-settled share-based payment transactions. The entity hedged the first 70 share-based payment transactions, even though it expected at 1 January 20X1 that 85 of 100 employees would still be employed at 31 December 20X3.
- The time value of the SAR is not designated as part of the hedge relationship, which results in net income volatility in all periods.

In the above example the entity is negatively exposed to favourable movements in its own share price. The more the share increases in value, the greater the share-based payment liability that must be carried in the statement of financial position in accordance with IFRS 2, and the greater the ultimate cash payout will be at the maturity of the scheme. The cash-settled share-based payment presents an exposure to cash flows that affect profit or loss because the entity's liability under the scheme is remeasured with the movement in the share price. The transaction is deemed highly probable as a number of employees are expected to remain in employment for the period to enable them to exercise their SARs. It is possible to designate the cash flow variability arising from the SARs as the population of forecast transactions is homogenous, i.e. the SARs have the same maturity and the same strike price, and therefore result in the same cash payment at maturity.

To improve hedge effectiveness the time value of the hedging option will generally be excluded from the hedge designation. The effectiveness of the hedge will also be influenced by the number of SARs hedged compared to the number that is expected to, and ultimately does, vest. The effective portion of the gain and loss on the hedging instrument is recognised in other comprehensive income and is subsequently reclassified from equity to profit or loss in the same period during which the hedged item affects profit or loss. The ineffective portion of the gain or loss on the derivative must be recognised in profit or loss immediately.

3.15 Updating the hypothetical derivative

The following example illustrates the application of the hypothetical derivative method for a cash flow hedge of interest rate risk on a forecast issuance of debt where the timing of the forecast cash flows change.

On 1 July 20X1, Entity A considers with high probability that it will issue 5 year fixed rate debt with a notional of CU100m in six months' time. Interest will be payable semi-annually when the debt is issued. Entity A is concerned that interest rates will change during the next six months and therefore decides to hedge this exposure by entering into a forward starting interest rate swap to receive 6m-LIBOR pay fixed on a notional of CU100m for 5 years where the cash flows on the swap will be receivable and payable every six months starting in six months time. In six months time' when the fixed rate debt is issued Entity A will close out the forward starting interest rate swap and settle with the swap counterparty as Entity A will no longer be exposed to changes in interest rates because the fixed rate on the debt will have been determined. The forward starting interest rate swap has a fair value of zero at 1 July 20X1. The hypothetical derivative would have the same terms as the interest rate swap and is deemed to be perfectly effective at hedging changes in the six month forward 5-year LIBOR swap rate which will be an offset to the variability in the ten to-be-fixed interest payments on the debt that is forecast to be issued on 1 January 20X2.

The hedging instrument will be receive 6m-LIBOR (set in advance) pay 5% every six months starting 1 January 20X2 ending 31 December 20X6. Entity A has a calendar year reporting period and chooses to assess hedge effectiveness every quarter.

1 July 20X1

No entries are required as the fair value of the hedging instrument is zero at inception.

30 September 20X1

The derivative is remeasured to fair value and the effective portion of the gains/losses is recognised in other comprehensive income and taken to the cash flow hedge reserve in equity. As the timing of the forecast transaction and the credit quality of the counterparty remains unchanged the fair value of the derivative is deemed to be fully effective, i.e. the hypothetical derivative still equals the actual derivative. In the three month period since the derivative was entered into interest rates have fallen and therefore the derivative's fair value is negative, i.e. it is a financial liability. The valuation of the derivative is for illustrative purposes only.

Dr	Other comprehensive income (cash flow hedge reserve)	450,000
Cr	Derivative financial liability	450,000

To record the fair value movement of the derivative and the effective amount in other comprehensive income.

Reporting period	Fair value gain (loss) of derivative in the period	Cumulative fair value gain (loss) of derivative	Fair value gain (loss) of forecast transactions in the period	Cumulative fair value gain (loss) of forecast transactions	(Debit) credit in other comprehensive income (taken to cash flow hedge reserve in equity)	(Debit) credit to profit or loss	(Debit) credit to profit or loss
1 July to 30 September 20X1	(450,000)	(450,000)	450,000	450,000	(450,000)	–	100%

At 1 October 20X1 Entity A revises its estimates of forecast debt issuance due to changes in its funding needs and considers that the fixed rate debt is no longer expected to be issued at 1 January 20X2 and forecasts a30 day delay. In addition Entity A no longer believes it will issue CU100m of debt, rather it will issue CU95m. All other terms of the debt, e.g. frequency of interest payments, denomination, maturity remain the same as originally forecast. Two sources of hedge ineffectiveness have arisen: (i) change in timing of forecast transactions and (ii) reduction in amount of the forecast transaction. Entity A redefines the hypothetical derivative to reflect these changes in expectations. Entity A defines the hypothetical derivative that would have had a fair value of zero at 1 July 20X1 as the forward starting swap that will receive 6m-LIBOR (set in advance) pay fixed every six months starting 1 February 20X2 ending 31 January 20X7 with a notional of CU95m. The fixed rate that Entity A would have locked into for this revised hypothetical derivative would have been 5.2% (not the 5% fixed that the actual derivative and original hypothetical derivative achieved). The fair value of the revised hypothetical derivative at 1 October 20X1 is CU475,000.

Entity A decides to retain the actual derivative and continue to apply hedge accounting with the actual derivative to the extent that Entity A can be highly effective. The ten forecast interest payments are still expected to occur, though all ten forecast interest payments have shifted back 30 days and will be priced 30 days later because the issue date of the debt is delayed.

31 December 20X1

Interest rates continue to fall during the reporting period ended 31 December 20X2 and the fair value of the actual derivative liability is CU800,000. Entity A fair values the revised hypothetical derivative at 31 December 20X1 and the fair value is equal to (CU780,000). The difference in value between the revised hypothetical derivative and the actual derivative arises because the revised hypothetical derivative has a smaller notional but a higher fixed rate.

Period	Fair value gain (loss) of derivative in the period	Cumulative fair value gain (loss) of derivative	Fair value gain (loss) of forecast transactions in the period (revised cash flows)	Cumulative fair value gain (loss) of forecast transactions	(Debit) credit in other comprehensive income (taken to the cash flow hedge reserve in equity)	(Debit) credit to profit or loss	Hedge effectiveness
1 October to 31 December 20X1	(350,000)	(800,000)	305,000	780,000	(330,000)	(20,000)	97.5% (780,000 / 800,000)

Dr	Other comprehensive income (cash flow hedge reserve)	330,000
Dr	Profit or loss	20,000
Cr	Derivative financial liability	350,000

To record the fair value movement of the derivative in the period and the effective amount in other comprehensive income and ineffective amount in profit or loss.

The effect of the revision to the change in timing and amount of the forecast transaction is that for the quarter ending 31 December 20X1 not all the gains/losses of the actual derivative are recognised in other comprehensive income (and taken to the cash flow hedge reserve in equity) as the hedge is not fully effective. The hedge is only 97.5% effective and CU20,000 is recognised as ineffectiveness in the period as the cumulative gain/loss on the actual derivative from inception of the hedge is greater than the cumulative gain/loss on the revised hypothetical derivative from inception of the hedge.

At the start of each period for which hedge effectiveness is assessed Entity A would need to demonstrate that prospectively the hedge relationship will be highly effective. Even though the hedge was highly effective for the period ending 31 December 20X1 this of itself is not assurance that the hedge is expected to be highly effective for future periods. On 1 January 20X2 Entity A will perform the prospective hedge effectiveness test that will take into account the revised timing and amount of the forecast transactions.

Had the change in timing and amount of the forecast transaction been so significant that the entity failed hedge accounting in the period then Entity A would need to redesignate the hedge relationship in its entirety. A new hypothetical derivative would be determined for the new hedge relationship which as interest rate swap is a non-optional derivative, would have a fair value of zero at the new designation date.

4 Net investment hedges

The following net investment hedges are illustrated in this section.

Section 4.1 Net investment hedging the spot foreign currency rate

Section 4.2 Net investment hedging the forward foreign currency rate

Section 4.3	Net investment hedging with a floating to floating cross currency swap
Section 4.4	Net investment hedging with a fixed to fixed cross currency swap
Section 4.5	Net investment hedging on an after-tax basis

4.1 Net investment hedging the spot foreign currency rate

Below is an illustration of the accounting entries recorded in a net investment hedge of spot foreign currency risk using a forward contract.

On 1 November 20X1, Entity XYZ enters into a forward contract to sell US$1,000,000 and buy Sterling at a fixed rate of US$1.57:£1 on 30 January 20X2. Group XYZ has a 31 December year end and is headed by Entity XYZ, which has a Sterling functional currency. The forward contract is entered into to hedge the foreign exchange translation risk associated with movements in the spot rate relating to its investment in its US subsidiary with a US dollar functional currency, Entity ABC, which has net assets of US$1,000,000 in Group XYZ's consolidated group accounts.

The forward and spot US$/£ translation rates are as follows.

	1/11/X1	**31/12/X1**	**30/1/X2**
Spot	1.55	1.59	1.61
Forward (to 30/1/X2)	1.57	1.60	n/a

On 30 January 20X2, Entity XYZ closes out the forward contract, and also sells Entity ABC for US$1,200,000 which is equal to £745,342 translated at US$1.61:£1.

Translating US$1,000,000 at the above rates gives the following Sterling amounts:

	1/11/X1	**31/12/X1**	**30/1/X2**
Spot	1.55	1.59	1.61
Sterling amount	£645,161	£628,931	£621,118
Forward (to 30/1/X2)	1.57	1.60	n/a
Sterling amount	£636,943	£625,000	

Therefore, the value of the derivative is (for purposes of illustration, ignoring the time value of money):

Date	**Derivative value**	**How calculated**
31/12/X1	£11,943	£636,943 – £625,000
30/1/X2	£15,825	£636,943 – £621,118

Movements in the fair value of the premium (or discount) implicitly inherent in the fair value of the forward contract will not give rise to hedge ineffectiveness, as the designated hedged risk is movements in spot rate only and, therefore, those movements are excluded from the designated hedging relationship. However, movements in the fair value of these forward points will give rise to volatility in profit or loss.

The entries are as follows.

31 December 20X1

Dr	Other comprehensive income	£16,230	
Cr	Net assets	£16,230	

To recognise the foreign exchange difference on translation of the net assets at the spot rate (i.e. translating the investment at 1.59 rather than 1.55).

Dr	Derivative	£11,943	
Dr	Profit or loss	£4,287	(relates to forward points)
Cr	Other comprehensive income	£16,230	

To recognise the change in the fair value of the derivative, the effective portion in other comprehensive income and the undesignated portion in profit or loss.

30 January 20X2

Dr	Other comprehensive income	£7,813	
Cr	Net assets	£7,813	

To recognise the foreign exchange difference on translation of the net assets at the spot rate (i.e. translating the investment at 1.61 rather than 1.59).

Dr	Derivative	£3,882	
Dr	Profit or loss	£3,931	(relates to forward points)
Cr	Other comprehensive income	£7,813	

To recognise the change in the fair value of the derivative, the effective portion in other comprehensive income and the undesignated portion in profit or loss.

Dr	Cash	£15,825
Cr	Derivative	£15,825

To reflect cash settlement of the derivative at its maturity.

Dr	Cash	£745,342
Cr	Profit or loss	£100,181
Cr	Net assets	£621,118
Cr	Other comprehensive income	£24,043

To recognise the sale proceeds and profit on disposal.

Dr	Other comprehensive income	£24,043
Cr	Profit or loss	£24,043

To recognise the reclassification of the hedging gains and losses from equity to profit or loss.

The total, post hedge, profit on disposal is £124,224 (£100,181 + £24,043).

It is assumed for illustrative purposes only that the total net assets of the foreign operation are unaffected by the application of IFRS 5 *Non-current Assets Held for Sale and Discontinued Operations* to the disposal group, i.e. the carrying amount of the net assets is lower than the fair value less costs to sell.

4.2 Net investment hedging the forward foreign currency rate

Below is an illustration of the accounting entries recorded in a net investment hedge of spot foreign currency risk using a forward contract.

Movements in the fair value of the premium (or discount) implicit in the forward contract, the forward points, will now be recognised in other comprehensive income (rather than in profit or loss) and will therefore give rise to equity volatility. These amounts will be reclassified from equity to profit or loss when the subsidiary is sold.

The required entries are as follows.

31 December 20X1

Dr	Other comprehensive income	£16,230
Cr	Net assets	£16,230

To recognise the foreign exchange difference on translation of the net assets at the spot rate (i.e. translating the investment at 1.59):

Dr	Derivative	£11,943
Cr	Other comprehensive income	£11,943

To recognise the change in the fair value of the derivative that is fully effective.

30 January 20X2

Dr	Other comprehensive income	£7,813
Cr	Net assets	£7,813

To recognise the movements in the investment relating to the spot rate movement (i.e. translating the investment at 1.61):

Dr	Derivative	£3,882
Cr	Other comprehensive income	£3,882

To recognise the change in the fair value of the derivative that is fully effective.

Dr	Cash	£15,825
Cr	Derivative	£15,825

To reflect cash settlement of the derivative at its maturity.

Dr	Cash	£745,342
Cr	Profit or loss	£100,181
Cr	Net assets	£621,118
Cr	Other comprehensive income	£24,043

To recognise the sale proceeds and the profit on disposal.

Dr	Other comprehensive income	£15,825
Cr	Profit or loss	£15,825

To recognise the reclassification of the hedging gains and losses from equity to profit or loss

The total, post hedge, profit on disposal is £116,006 (£100,181 + £15,825).

Compared to **example 4.1** above, the profit on disposal is £8,218 lower as in the previous example the fair value of the forward points was recognised in profit or loss throughout the life of the hedge relationship.

It is assumed for illustrative purposes only that the total net assets of the foreign operation are unaffected by the application IFRS 5 *Non-current assets held for sale and discontinued operations* to the disposal group, i.e. the net assets are lower than the fair value less costs to sell.

4.3 Net investment hedging with a floating to floating cross currency swap

Below is an illustration of the accounting entries recorded for a net investment hedge of a foreign operation, using a cross currency interest rate swap that receives and pays floating interest.

On 1 January 20X2, Entity A, a Sterling functional currency entity, acquires a US subsidiary with a US dollar functional currency which has net assets of US$150,000. Entity A will be subject to foreign currency risk (between the US$ and £) on retranslation of the net investment in the consolidated financial statements and therefore wants to achieve hedge accounting for a specific level (US$100,000) of the net assets in the foreign operation. Entity A wishes to designate the first US$100,000 of net assets as the hedged item in a net investment in a foreign operation. At 1 January 20X2, the spot rate on the US$ / £ is 1.75/1 so the notional of US$100,000 is equivalent to £57,143. On the same date, Entity A enters into a cross currency swap ('CCS') to exchange interest payments and principal at redemption with a notional equal to the designated amount of net assets, and designates the cross currency swap as a hedge of the variability of the £ equivalent cash flows on the US$100,000 of the net assets of the foreign operation. The terms are such that on each interest payment date (assume interest is paid annually on 31 December each year for the cross currency swap), Entity A will pay US$ LIBOR + 100 basis points on a notional of US$100,000 and receive Sterling LIBOR + 106 basis points based on a notional of £57,143. Because the currency and notional on the swap match the net investment, and the swap is on-market at inception, Entity A expects that the hedging relationship will be highly effective.

Date	Spot rate US$ / £	Net assets of foreign operation in US$	Carrying amount of US$100,000 of net assets in £	Cross currency swap fair value £	Net interest receipt on the swap (£ LIBOR +106bp – US$ LIBOR +100bp)
31/12/X1	1.75	150,000	57,143	0	0
31/12/X2	1.7	160,000	58,824	(1,743)	1,259
31/12/X3	1.6	141,000	62,500	(5,520)	1,476
31/12/X4	1.5	121,000	66,667	(9,670)	1,952
31/12/X5	1.8	106,000	55,556	1,624	1,042
31/12/X6	1.7	115,000	58,824	(1,681)	1,321

Entity A's documentation of the hedge is as follows.

Risk management objective and nature of risk being hedged	Net investment hedge of the foreign currency exposure (due to US$/£ spot rate) to changes in the reporting entity's interest in the first US$100,000 of net assets in the foreign operation.
Date of designation	1 January 20X2
Hedging instrument	Cross currency swap to exchange US$100,000 at maturity and pay US$ LIBOR +100bp, receive £ LIBOR +106bp interest annually over the term of the instrument.
Hedged item	The first US$100,000 of net assets in the foreign operation.
Assessment of hedge effectiveness	The critical terms of the derivative (currency, notional) match that of the net investment. Although there are no interest payments from the net investment, the cross currency float to float swap responds closely to movements in undiscounted spot rates as the interest payments are made at the end of the reporting period. Accordingly there is an expectation of high effectiveness. The entity will assess counterparty credit risk and probability of cash flows under the swap occurring every period.
Measurement of hedge effectiveness	Comparison of the period-to-period retranslation on the first US$100,000 of net assets of the foreign operation using undiscounted spot rates compared to the fair value movement on the CCS.

Period-to-period assessment of hedge effectiveness using the dollar offset test:

Period	Fair value movement in spot rates in period for first US$100,000 of net assets £	Fair value movement in CCS in period £	% effective using period to period gains / losses	Hedge accounting permitted in period (80–125%)
20X2	1,681	1,743	96%	YES
20X3	3,676	3,777	97%	YES
20X4	4,167	4,150	100%	YES
20X5	(11,111)	(11,294)	98%	YES
20X6	3,268	3,305	99%	YES

The hedging relationship is deemed to be highly effective (80%-125%) throughout each period and therefore hedge accounting is permitted. Any ineffectiveness, being the difference between fair value movement of the CCS and the retranslation of the first US$100,000 of net assets using undiscounted spot rates, will be recognised in profit or loss in the period.

The following table illustrates the accounting entries for the transaction during its life in Sterling: Dr or (Cr) as indicated. For illustrative purposes only, the entries have recognised the translation on only US$100,000 of net assets and not actual net assets. IAS 21 would require translation of all net assets of the foreign operation to the cumulative translation reserve. As the total net assets never fall below US$100,000 at a period end, the illustrative journal for 'Consolidated net assets' is always the retranslation of US$100,000.

31 Dec		Cash	CCS	Consolidated net assets	Profit or loss (ineffective)	Interest income	Other comprehensive income (cumulative translation reserve)
20X2	Revalue US$100,000 net assets to spot			1,681			(1,681)
	Net interest on CCS	1,259				(1,259)	
	Fair value of CCS		(1,743)		62		1,681
20X3	Revalue US$100,000 net assets to spot			3,676			(3,676)
	Net interest on CCS	1,476				(1,476)	
	Fair value of CCS		(3,777)		101		3,676
20X4	Revalue US$100,000 net assets to spot			4,167			(4,167)
	Net interest on CCS	1,952				(1,952)	
	Fair value of CCS		(4,150)		(17)		4,167
20X5	Revalue US$100,000 net assets to spot			(11,111)			11,111
	Net interest on CCS	1,042				(1,042)	
	Fair value of CCS		11,294		(183)		(11,111)

31 Dec		Cash	CCS	Consolidated net assets	Profit or loss (ineffective)	Interest income	Other comprehensive income (cumulative translation reserve)
20X6	Revalue US$100,000 net assets to spot			3,268			(3,268)
	Net interest on CCS	1,321				(1,321)	
	Fair value of CCS		(3,305)		37		3,268
20X6		(7,050)	(1,681)	1,681	0	(7,050)	0
	Key		A	A	B		C

Key

A the remaining value on the CCS is the difference between the net assets retranslated at US$1.75/£ (original rate) and the US$1.70/£ (spot rate at date termination of swap). Hence total statement of financial position before final settlement of CCS is (net assets £58,824 – CCS £1,681) = £57,123 at 31/12/X6 which is equivalent to the original US$100,000 net assets at the original spot rate of US$1.75/£.

B Nets to zero as all amounts have been taken to profit or loss as ineffectiveness.

C As at least US$100,000 of net assets existed at each reporting period throughout the relationship, the hedge relationship was fully effective in hedging the first US$100,000 of net assets.

Entries in the consolidated financial statements for 20X2 for illustrative purposes.

1 January 20X2

No entry required by CCS as fair value is nil at inception.

31 December 20X2

Dr	Net assets	1,681
Cr	Other comprehensive income (cumulative translation reserve)	1,681

To record gain on retranslation of the US$100,000 of net assets at year-end spot rates.

Dr	Cash	1,259
Cr	Interest income	1,259

To record net interest income on the CCS

Dr	Other comprehensive income (cumulative translation reserve)	1,681
Dr	Profit or loss	62

Cr	Cross currency swap liability	1,743

To record fair value movement in CCS with corresponding entries to other comprehensive income (cumulative translation adjustment in equity to offset retranslation of net assets) and remainder recognised as ineffectiveness in profit or loss.

Similar entries would be recorded for the remaining term of the hedging relationship (20X3 -20X6). The amount in cumulative translation reserve will be reclassified from equity to profit or loss on disposal of the foreign operation.

Interest income totalling £7,050 is recognised over the term of the hedging instrument in profit or loss as the interest receipts represent the net financing on the swap. The reason the swap is not 100 per cent effective in hedging undiscounted spot is because the fair value of the swap is the present value of all future cash flows on the swap, which include some fixed cash flows. As both legs on the swap have fixed margins, the present value of these fixed margins will result in some hedge ineffectiveness. In the above example, the amount of ineffectiveness is not sufficient for the hedge relationship to fail hedge accounting.

4.4 Net investment hedging with fixed to fixed cross currency swap

Below is an illustration of the accounting entries recorded for a net investment hedge of a foreign operation, using a cross currency interest rate swap that receives and pays fixed interest.

On 1 January 20X2, Entity A, a Sterling functional currency entity, acquires a US subsidiary with a US dollar functional currency which has net assets of US$150,000. Entity A will be subject to foreign currency risk (between the US$ and £) on retranslation of the net investment in the consolidated financial statements and therefore wants to achieve hedge accounting for a specific level (US$100,000) of the net assets in the foreign operation. Entity A wishes to designate the first US$100,000 of net assets as the hedged item in a net investment hedge. At 1 January 20X2, the spot rate on the US$ / £ is 1.75/1 so the notional of US$100,000 is equivalent to £57,143. On the same date, Entity A enters into a cross currency swap ('CCS') to exchange interest payments and principal at redemption with a notional equal to the designated amount of net assets, and designates the cross currency swap as a hedge of the variability of the £ equivalent cash flows on the US$100,000 of the net assets of the foreign operation. The terms are such that on each interest payment date (assume interest is paid annually on 31 December each year for the cross currency swap), Entity A will pay US$ 4 per cent on a notional of US$100,000 and receive Sterling 6 per cent on a notional of £57,143. Because the currency and notional on the swap match the net investment, and the swap is on-market at inception, Entity A expects that the hedging relationship will be highly effective.

Date	Spot rate US$ / £	Net assets of foreign operation in US$	Carrying amount of US$100,000 of net assets in £	Cross currency swap fair value £ (liability)	Net interest receipts on the swap (US$ 4% – £ 6%)
31/12/X1	1.75	150,000	57,143	0	0
31/12/X2	1.7	160,000	58,824	(2,560)	1,110
31/12/X3	1.6	141,000	62,500	(7,723)	1,004
31/12/X4	1.5	121,000	66,667	(9,513)	848
31/12/X5	1.8	106,000	55,556	1,452	1,004
31/12/X6	1.7	115,000	58,824	(1,681)	1,143

Entity A's documentation of the hedge is as follows.

Risk management objective and nature of risk being hedged	Net investment hedge of the foreign currency exposure (due to US$/£ forward rates) to changes in the reporting entity's interest in the first US$100,000 of net assets in the foreign operation.
Date of designation	1 January 20X2
Hedging instrument	Cross currency swap to exchange US$100,000 at maturity and pay US$ 4%, receive £ 6% interest annually over the term of the instrument.
Hedged item	The first US$100,000 of net assets in the foreign operation.
Assessment of hedge effectiveness	The critical terms of the derivative (currency, notional) match those of the net investment. There is an expectation of high effectiveness. The entity will assess counterparty credit risk and probability of cash flows under the swap occurring every period.
Measurement of hedge effectiveness	Comparison of the fair value movement of the CCS and a hypothetical CCS with a notional amount equal to the hedged amount and terms that mirror those of the actual CCS.

The following table illustrates the accounting entries for the transaction during its life in Sterling: Dr or (Cr) as indicated. For illustrative purposes only, the entries have recognised the translation on only US$100,000 of net assets and not actual net assets. IAS 21 would require translation of all net assets of the foreign operation to the cumulative translation reserve. As the total net assets never fall below US$100,000 at a period end, the illustrative journal for 'Consolidated net assets' is always the retranslation of US$100,000.

For illustrative purposes the hedge relationship is deemed to be fully effective throughout its life.

31 Dec		Cash	CCS	Consolidated net assets	Profit or loss (ineffective)	Interest expense	Other comprehensive income (cumulative translation reserve)
20X2	Revalue US$100,000 net assets to spot			1,681			(1,681)
	Net interest on CCS	1,110				(1,110)	
	Fair value of CCS		(2,560)				2,560
20X3	Revalue US$100,000 net assets to spot			3,676			(3,676)
	Net interest on CCS	1,004				(1,004)	
	Fair value of CCS		(5,163)				5,163
20X4	Revalue US$100,000 net assets to spot			4,167			(4,167)
	Net interest on CCS	848				(848)	
	Fair value of CCS		(1,790)				1,790
20X5	Revalue US$100,000 net assets to spot			(11,111)			11,111
	Net interest on CCS	1,004				(1,004)	
	Fair value of CCS		10,965				(10,965)
20X6	Revalue US$100,000 net assets to spot			3,268			(3,268)

31 Dec		Cash	CCS	Consolidated net assets	Profit or loss (ineffective)	Interest expense	Other comprehensive income (cumulative translation reserve)
	Net interest on CCS	1,143				(1,143)	
	Fair value of CCS		(3,133)				3,133
20X6		5,109	(1,681)	1,681	0	(5,109)	0
	Key		**A**	**A**	**B**		**C**

Key

A the remaining value on the CCS is the difference between the net assets retranslated at US$1.75/£ (original rate) and the US$1.70/£ (spot rate at date termination of swap). Hence, total statement of financial position before final settlement of CCS is (net assets £58,824 – CCS £1,681) = £57,143 at 31/12/X6 which is equivalent to the original US$100,000 net assets at the original spot rate of US$1.75/£.

B Totals to zero as the hedge relationship was fully effective.

C As at least US$100,000 of net assets existed at each reporting period throughout the relationship, the hedge relationship was fully effective in hedging the first US$100,000 of net assets.

Entries in the consolidated financial statements for 20X2 for illustrative purposes

1 January 20X2

No entry required as fair value of CCS is nil at inception.

31 December 20X2

Dr	Net assets	1,681	
Cr	Other comprehensive income (cumulative translation reserve)		1,681

To record gain on retranslation of the US$100,000 of net assets at year-end spot rates.

Dr	Cash	1,110	
Cr	Interest expense		1,110

To record net interest receipt on the CCS

Dr	Other comprehensive income (cumulative translation reserve)	2,560	
Cr	CCS liability		2,560

To record fair value movement in CCS with corresponding entries to other comprehensive income (cumulative translation adjustment in equity).

Similar entries would be recorded for the remaining term of the hedging relationship (20X3 -20X6). The amount in cumulative translation reserve will be reclassified from equity to profit or loss on disposal of the foreign operation.

Interest income totalling £5,109 is recognised over the term of the hedging instrument in profit or loss as the interest receipts represent the net financing on the swap.

4.5 Net investment hedging on an after-tax basis

Below is an illustration of the entries for a net investment hedge of a foreign operation assessed for hedge effectiveness on an after tax basis.

Entity T, a Sterling functional currency, has an investment in a wholly owned subsidiary Entity U, a Euro functional currency. The consolidated financial statements headed by Entity T are presented in Sterling. Entity T's consolidated interest in its foreign operation, Entity U is equal to €840,000 of net assets as of 1/1/X1. Assume that the amount of net assets remains unchanged and that the foreign currency retranslation of the investment in the net assets of Entity U will not attract any taxation. On 1/1/X1 Entity T enters into a forward contract to sell €1,200,000 and buy Sterling at a rate of €1.5: £1 on 31/12/X2. The gain or loss arising on remeasurement of the forward contract at spot rates is subject to current tax at 30 per cent.

The forward and the spot EUR/£ translation rates are as follows.

	1/1/X1	**31/12/X1**	**31/12/X2**
Spot	1.4	1.6	1.7
Forward (to 31/12/X2)	1.5	1.66	–

Reporting €1,200,000 at the above rates gives the following Sterling amounts:

	1/1/X1	**31/12/X1**	**31/12/X2**
Spot	1.4	1.6	1.7
Sterling amount	£857,143	£750,000	£705,882
Forward (to 31/12/X2)	1.5	1.66	–
Sterling amount	£800,000	£722,892	

Therefore the fair value of the forward is:

Date	**Derivative value**	**Calculated as:**
31/12/X1	£77,108	£800,000 – £722,892
31/12/X2	£94,118	£800,000 – £705,882

(For illustration purposes only, the fair value of the forward ignores the time value of money.)

Reporting €840,000 at the above spot rates gives the following Sterling amounts:

	1/1/X1	31/12/X1	31/12/X2
Spot	1.4	1.6	1.7
Sterling amount	£600,000	£525,000	£494,118

The forward contract is designated as the hedging instrument in an after tax hedge of the spot retranslation risk on the first €840,000 net assets of the investment in the foreign operation in the consolidated financial statements. The notional of the forward contract is purposefully greater than the amount of net assets being designated as a hedged item to compensate for the fact that foreign currency movements on the hedged item (net assets) are not taxable while those on the hedging instrument (forward contract) are. The notional of the derivative of €1,200,000 equals the net assets grossed up for the tax rate (€840,000 / 1 – 0.30 tax rate).

Movements in the fair value due to the forward points will not give rise to hedge ineffectiveness, as the designated hedged risk is movements in spot rate only (on an after tax basis), i.e. these movements do not form part of the hedging relationship and will be recognised directly in profit or loss.

In accordance with the requirements of IAS 12 *Income Taxes* the current tax relating to the gain or loss remeasurement of the forward contract at spot rates will be recognised in other comprehensive income since the gain or loss itself is recognised in other comprehensive income.

The required entries are as follows.

31 December 20X1

Dr	Other comprehensive income	£75,000
Cr	Net assets	£75,000

To recognise the foreign exchange difference on translation of the net assets at the spot rate (i.e. translating the investment at 1.6 rather than 1.4).

Dr	Derivative	£77,108
Dr	Profit or loss	£30,035 (relates to forward points)
Cr	Other comprehensive income	£107,143

To recognise the change in the fair value of the derivative, the effective portion in other comprehensive income based on undiscounted spot rates, and the undesignated portion in profit or loss. It is presumed that the hedge relationship is fully effective, so the amount recognised in profit or loss is only the change in the fair value of forward points.

Dr	Other comprehensive income	£32,143 (30% of £107,143)
Cr	Tax liability	£32,143

To recognise the tax in respect of the gain on the derivative recognised in other comprehensive income.

On a post-tax hedge effectiveness assessment the hedge relationship has been fully effective. The post-tax foreign exchange loss on the net assets, £75,000, is equal to the post-tax foreign exchange gain on the derivative, £75,000 (£107,143 – £32,143).

31 December 20X2

Dr	Other comprehensive income	£30,882
Cr	Net assets	£30,882

To recognise the foreign exchange difference on translation of the net assets at the spot rate (i.e. translating the investment at 1.7 rather than 1.6).

Dr	Derivative	£17,010
Dr	Profit or loss	£27,108 (relates to forward points)
Cr	Other comprehensive income	£44,118

To recognise the change in the fair value of the derivative, the effective portion in other comprehensive income based on undiscounted spot rates, and the undesignated portion in profit or loss. It is presumed that the hedge relationship is fully effective, so the amount recognised in profit or loss is only the fair value of forward points.

Dr	Other comprehensive income	£13,236 (30% of £44,118)
Cr	Tax liability	£13,236

To recognise the tax in respect of the gain on the derivative recognised in other comprehensive income.

On a post-tax hedge effectiveness assessment the hedge relationship has been fully effective. The post-tax foreign exchange loss on the net assets, £30,882, is equal to the post-tax foreign exchange gain on the derivative, £30,882 (£44,118 – 13,236).

Dr	Cash	£94,118
Cr	Derivative	£94,118

To reflect cash settlement of the derivative at its maturity.

5 Hedge effectiveness assessment techniques

5.1 Regression analysis

Below is a detailed illustration of a fair value hedge where regression analysis is used to assess hedge effectiveness.

Bank A owns a €100 million portfolio of 10-year BBB corporate bonds. The bonds are eligible to be hedged as a portfolio because each item in the portfolio shares the same hedged risk (interest rate risk) and the change in fair value attributable for each individual item in the portfolio is expected to be approximately proportional to the overall change in the fair value attributable to the hedged risk of the group of items.

On 1 July 20X0, Bank A executes a fair value hedge of the interest rate risk on the bond portfolio using a Euro-bond indexed derivative. To establish a basis for hedge accounting at inception, Bank A computed a historical regression analysis on the monthly results for the previous six months and has assessed offset on a monthly and cumulative basis as summarised below. (For illustrative purposes only six data points have been regressed. As stated in **5.6.3** below more data points will generally be required.)

Month	Current period gain/(loss) on hedging instrument (€)	Current period gain/(loss) on hedged item (€)	(1) Current period R^2	(1) Current period slope	Current period ratio (per cent)
January	-700,000	300,000			-233.33
February	1,600,000	-1,500,000	0.970	1.11	-106.67
March	-2,050,000	2,200,000	0.980	0.99	-93.18
April	1,100,000	-1,020,000	0.988	1.00	-107.84
May	3,900,000	-3,980,000	0.995	0.99	-97.99
June	-12,350,000	11,900,000	1.000	1.03	-103.78

(1) Constant set to zero

	Cumulative gain/(loss) on hedging instrument (€)	Cumulative gain/(loss) on hedged item (€)	Cumulative ratio (per cent)
January	-700,000	300,000	-233.33
February	900,000	-1,200,000	-75.00
March	-1,150,000	1,000,000	-115.00
April	-50,000	-20,000	250.00
May	3,850,000	-4,000,000	-96.25
June	-8,500,000	7,900,000	-107.59

Based on the historical regression analysis, Bank A has a basis for concluding that the hedge is expected to be effective in offsetting changes in fair value. The ratio on a cumulative basis from January to June was within the acceptable 80 to 125 per cent range. Although there were two observations where the cumulative ratio was outside the acceptable 80 to 125 per cent range, based on the per-period ratio results and the strong statistical (regression) results, Bank A could conclude that the hedge was expected to be effective at providing offset. On a per-period basis, the ratio was within the acceptable 80 to 125 per cent range in all periods after the initial period. The regression statistics, with the constant set to zero, were well within the acceptable range of 0.80 to 1.25 for slope, while the range of 0.8 to 1.0 for R^2 indicates that a large element of changes in the fair value of the dependent variable are explained by fair value changes in the independent variable.

The **actual** cumulative and current period changes in fair value of the interest rate risk on the bond portfolio and the Euro-bond indexed derivative, from the date the hedge was initiated on 1 July, are summarised below. The R^2 and slope values were computed using the monthly observations from July to December.

Month	Current period gain/(loss) on hedging instrument (€)	Current period gain/(loss) on hedged item (€)	(1) current period R^2	(1) Current period slope	Current period ratio (per cent)	Current period ineffective portion of hedge
July	€8,575,000	€-7,885,000	1.000	1.05	-108.75	€690.000
August	425,000	-765,000	0.998	1.04	-55.56	-340,000
September	750,000	-350,000	0.998	1.05	-214.29	400,000
October	-1,000,000	800,000	0.998	1.05	-125.00	-200,000
November	2,500,000	-2,300,000	0.998	1.05	-108.70	200,000
December (2)	-2,775,000	2,775,000	0.998	1.05	-100.00	0

(1) Constant set to zero

(2) Note that only six observations were used for illustrative purposes to compute the regression statistics. Sufficient data points are required to render the results meaningful. However, there are also instances whereby data sourced over inappropriate lengths of time can obscure a change in the relationship between the hedged risk and the hedging instrument. Therefore, the context of how and why the data points have been sourced should be considered when judging which data should be applied to the assessment of effectiveness.

Month	Cumulative gain/(loss) on hedging instrument (€)	Cumulative gain/(loss) on hedged item (€)	Cumulative ratio (per cent)
July	75,000	15,000	500.00
August	500,000	-750,000	-66.67
September	1,250,000	-1,100,000	-113.64
October	250,000	-300,000	-83.33
November	2,750,000	-2,600,000	-105.77
December	-25,000	175,000	-14.29

Using a regression test measured on a period basis with the constant set to zero, the hedge was highly effective because the R^2 showed a strong level of explained changes in fair value, i.e. that was due to movements in interest rates, and the slope was within the range of negative 0.8–1.25. If the hedge was evaluated using period to period changes, the hedging relationship had periods of ineffectiveness in August and September using a ratio test and was always effective using a regression test. An entity's risk management policy should address when a failure to establish a hedging relationship, using either ratio or regression, would preclude hedge accounting.

Even though on a ratio basis the hedge failed the 80 to 125 per cent test in two months, the entity may conclude that hedge accounting was appropriate based on the strength of historical period to period offset provided that the entity had documented that it would assess hedge effectiveness on a cumulative basis. This assessment would only be appropriate if the entity's risk management policy specifically addresses hedge failures and indicates when such failures preclude hedge accounting.

It should be noted, however, that the measurement and recognition of the ineffective portion, which is computed on a monthly basis in the above example, is based on the degree of offset. Hence, for example, in July, €90,000 is recognised in profit or loss (€75,000 on the hedging instrument plus €15,000 on the hedged item). Although hedge accounting is permitted for the full period, the full extent of ineffectiveness is recognised in profit or loss for each month. For the months in which the effectiveness ratio fell outside the acceptable range, a relatively higher amount of hedge ineffectiveness is recognised in profit or loss.

Further, in this example it has been demonstrated that different methods of assessing hedge effectiveness can be applied, e.g. cumulative or period-to-period. An entity would need to document at the outset of the hedge relationship which method of assessment is going to be applied, and then use this method consistently. This method will also be documented in the entity's risk management strategy. It is not acceptable to switch methods part-way through a hedge relationship in order to 'cherry-pick' the method that produces the more acceptable results.

11 Disclosure

1 Introduction

In August 2005, the IASB issued IFRS 7 *Financial Instruments: Disclosures*. IFRS 7 is effective for annual periods beginning on or after 1 January 2007, and supersedes both IAS 30 *Disclosures in the Financial Statements of Banks and Similar Financial Institutions* and the disclosure requirements of IAS 32 *Financial Instruments: Disclosure and Presentation*. Following the introduction of IFRS 7, IAS 32 was renamed IAS 32 *Financial Instruments: Presentation* and continues to address the presentation requirements for financial instruments including classification of instruments as liabilities or equity, compound financial instruments, treasury shares, and the criteria for offsetting financial assets and financial liabilities.

Consequential amendments were made to a number of other Standards when IFRS 7 was issued. In particular, the disclosure requirements of IFRS 4 *Insurance Contracts* were realigned with those of IFRS 7. Also IAS 1 *Presentation of Financial Statements* was amended to include disclosures regarding an entity's capital.

In March 2009 the IASB issued an amendment to IFRS 7, *Improving Disclosures about Financial Instruments*. The amendments change the required disclosures for fair value measurement and liquidity risk and are effective for annual periods beginning on or after 1 January 2009 without the need for comparative information in the first year of application. If an entity chooses to apply the amendments prior to the effective date it should disclose this fact. The changes to IFRS 7 are reflected in this chapter. Entities preparing financial statements for annual periods beginning before 1 January 2009 not early adopting the amendments should refer to shaded boxes that begin, *For entities with annual reporting periods beginning before 1 January 2009*, which address the disclosures required in IFRS 7 prior to the amendment.

The Financial Stability Forum issued a report in April 2008, *Enhancing Market and Institutional Resilience*, which had two recommendations for the IASB. It suggests that the IASB should (i) enhance its guidance on valuing financial instruments when markets are no longer active, and (ii) strengthen its standards to achieve better disclosures about valuations, methodologies and the uncertainty associated with valuations. In response to the report the IASB's Expert Advisory Panel was set up and in October 2008 issued a report, *Measuring and disclosing the fair value of financial instruments in markets that are no longer active*. This report provides useful information and educational guidance for measuring and disclosing fair values. The report has not been approved by the IASB and does not establish new requirements. The report is intended to be used as application guidance in meeting the requirements of IFRSs. The disclosure aspects of this report are referred to in this chapter but as they do not represent official positions of the IASB are identified in a shaded box.

The objective of IFRS 7 is to require entities to provide disclosures in their financial statements that enable users to evaluate:
[IFRS 7.1]

(i) the significance of financial instruments for the entity's financial position and performance; and

(ii) the nature and extent of risks arising from financial instruments to which the entity is exposed during the period and at the end of the reporting period, and how the entity manages those risks.

These disclosures are designed to provide users of financial statements with additional information that would influence their assessment of the financial position, financial performance and of the amount, timing and uncertainty of future cash flows for that entity. Further disclosures are required to enable users to determine what accounting elections and judgements have been made when applying the requirements of IAS 32 and IAS 39, and their impact on the financial statements.

US GAAP comparison: Unlike IFRS 7 which is a single standard that provides disclosure requirements for *all* financial instruments and the risks arising from those instruments, the disclosure requirements for financial instruments under US GAAP are scattered across the various sources of guidance that deal with each financial instrument, risk, or activity.

This chapter discusses the requirements of IFRS 7 and IAS 32 in the following sections:

Section 2 Scope

Section 3 Classes of financial instruments

Section 4 Significance of financial instruments

Section 5 Nature and extent of risks arising from financial instruments

Section 6 Disclosure checklist

Section 7 Offsetting a financial asset and a financial liability

Whilst each disclosure requirement of IFRS 7 has been discussed separately, disclosures would, in practice, normally be presented as an integrated package with individual disclosures, in some instances, satisfying more than one requirement.

IFRS 7 contains mandatory application and non-mandatory Implementation Guidance, with the latter providing examples and guidance on how the requirements of IFRS 7 may be fulfilled. This chapter includes both. It also includes further examples, some extracted from financial statements of entities applying IFRS 7.

2 Scope

IFRS 7 is applicable to *all* entities and to *all* risks arising from *all* financial instruments, whether recognised or unrecognised, except where specifically mentioned below. Recognised financial instruments include financial assets and financial liabilities that are within the scope of IAS 39. Unrecognised financial instruments include some financial instruments that, although outside the scope of IAS 39, are within the scope of IFRS 7, such as certain loan commitments that are not designated or required to be carried at fair value through profit or loss. [IFRS 7.4]

> Whilst a loan commitment may eventually give rise to a recognised financial asset for the lender, to the extent that funds have not been drawn down by the counterparty, the commitment to lend meets the definition of a financial liability as the lender is *contractually obligated to deliver cash or another financial asset to another entity.* [IAS 32.11] Even though this commitment is not recognised and measured in accordance with IAS 39 it is considered to be an unrecognised financial liability to which IFRS 7 disclosure requirements apply. Similarly, the party with the right to draw down funds (the borrower) with respect to a loan commitment has an unrecognised financial asset to the extent that the funds have not yet been drawn down to which IFRS 7 disclosure requirements apply.

The table included in **section 2** of **chapter 1** summarises whether certain arrangements are in the scope of IFRS 7 or not.

> Regular way sales and purchases of financial assets accounted for using a settlement date accounting policy also give rise to unrecognised financial assets or liabilities that are within the scope of IFRS 7. See **2.2** in **chapter 7** for settlement date accounting.

IFRS 7 includes within its scope leases which meet the definition of a financial instrument. Finance leases are financial instruments whereas operating leases are not (except as regards individual payments currently due and payable). For further discussion see **3.4** in **chapter 1**.

IFRS 7 applies to the financial statements of subsidiaries. There is no exemption even if full disclosures are provided in the consolidated financial statements in which the subsidiary is included. The IASB has stated that where an entity prepares any financial statements in accordance with IFRSs, users of those financial statements should receive information of the same quality as users of general purpose financial statements prepared in accordance with IFRSs. [IFRS 7.BC11]

IFRS 7 applies to all contracts linked to interests in subsidiaries, associates or joint ventures that meet the definition of a derivative unless they meet the definition of an equity instrument. [IFRS 7.3(a)]

IFRS 7 scopes out derivatives over own equity that meet the definition of equity. This will include derivatives over shares in a subsidiary that meet the definition of equity in the consolidated financial statements. IFRS 7 does not appear to have a scope exception for non-derivative instruments classified as equity, such as ordinary shares and certain preference shares. This appears to be an oversight in the drafting of the Standard as IFRS 7.BC8 states that the scope exception of IFRS 7 is intended to be the same as IAS 32 (prior to IFRS 7 being issued) with one exception, namely 'derivatives based on interests in subsidiaries, associates or joint ventures if the derivatives meet the definition of an equity instrument in IAS 32'. The basis of conclusions justifies this position by stating that these instruments are not remeasured and hence "do not expose the issuer to balance sheet and income statement risk", and the disclosures about the significance of financial instruments for financial position and performance are not relevant to equity instruments. In addition, it states that these instruments are excluded from the scope of IFRS 7, but they are within the scope of IAS 32 for the purpose of determining whether they meet the definition of equity instruments. It seems reasonable that the scope exclusions for derivatives over own equity that meet the definition of equity would also apply to non-derivatives that meet the definition of equity as the justification in the basis of conclusions would be equally relevant.

IFRS 7 excludes from its scope those interests in subsidiaries, associates and joint ventures that are accounted for in accordance with IAS 27

Consolidated and Separate Financial Statements, IAS 28 *Investments in Associates* or IAS 31 *Interests in Joint Ventures*. [IFRS 7.3(a)] The only exception is where the entity applies IAS 39 for measuring its interests in a subsidiary, joint venture or associate as specifically permitted by IAS 27(2008).38 (previously IAS 27(2003).37), IAS 31.1 and IAS 28.1. IAS 27(2008).38 (previously IAS 27(2003).37) applies to the separate financial statements, IAS 31.1 and IAS 28.1 apply to investment in joint ventures and associates held by venture capital organisations, mutual funds, unit trusts and similar entities including investment-linked insurance funds.

Consolidated financial statements include all financial instruments of the subsidiary except those intragroup financial instruments that are fully eliminated on consolidation. Only if the financial instrument is fully eliminated on consolidation is it excluded from the scope of IFRS 7 in the consolidated financial statements.

IFRS 7 does not apply to an investment in an associate or joint venture accounted for under the equity method as the carrying amount represents the investor's initial cost adjusted for the post-acquisition changes in the investor's share of net assets of the investee.

It is less clear as to whether IFRS 7 applies to financial instruments of a proportionately consolidated joint venture. The application of proportionate consolidation means that the statement of financial position of the venturer includes its share of the assets that it controls jointly and its share of the liabilities for which it is jointly responsible. [IAS 31.33] As the assets and liabilities will include the venturer's share of financial instruments that are recognised and measured in accordance with IAS 39, it would seem reasonable that these financial instruments are subject to the disclosure requirements of IFRS 7.

IFRS 5 *Non-current Assets held for sale and Discontinued Operations* specifically states in paragraph 2 that the classification and presentation requirements of IFRS 5 apply to all non-current assets (or disposal groups) classified as held for sale and discontinued operations. A question arises as to whether IFRS 7 disclosures are also required for financial assets and financial liabilities classified as held for sale or that form part of disposal groups as there is no scope exemption in IFRS 7 in this respect. At the IFRIC's September 2007 meeting the IFRIC considered whether the disclosure requirements of other standards, in the absence of specific exclusion, would apply to non-current assets (or disposal groups) classified as held for sale or discontinued operations in accordance with IFRS 5. The IFRIC decided to refer the matter to the IASB for their consideration as part of the annual improvements process. The IASB issued an exposure draft of

Improvements to International Financial Reporting Standards in August 2008 that proposed clarifying that IFRS 5 and other IFRSs that specifically refer to non-current assets (or disposal groups) classified as held for sale or discontinued operations set out all the disclosures requirements in respect of those assets or operations. At the time of writing the amendment was not finalised.

Until finalisation of the proposed amendment to IFRS 5 there remains ambiguity about whether financial instruments included in non-current assets (or disposal groups) classified as held for sale or discontinued operations should be included within the scope of IFRS 7. The financial risk disclosures detailed in IFRS 7.31–42 and discussed in **section 5** below are likely to be useful for financial assets and liabilities classified as held for sale or that form part of a disposal group under IFRS 5 as those financial instruments do expose the entity to significant financial risks. If IFRS 7 is not applied in full to such assets and liabilities care should be taken in providing sufficient information that is consistent with the objectives of IFRS 7, namely providing information about the significance of financial instruments for the entity's financial position and performance, the nature and extent of risks arising from financial instruments and how those risks are managed.

It is important to remember that contracts to buy or sell non-financial items that may not be typically considered financial instruments, are within the scope of IFRS 7 if they are in the scope of IAS 39. Guidance on the recognition and measurement of contracts over non-financial items is detailed in **2.5** in **chapter 1**.

The extent to which an entity will provide financial instrument disclosures will depend on the entity's use of financial instruments and the associated risks. As many of the requirements of IFRS 7 are based on information provided internally to key management personnel, the depth of disclosure will reflect partly the information provided for use within the business. Entities with few financial instruments and associated risks will provide less disclosure than those entities that have significant financial instruments and related exposures to financial risk.

3 Classes of financial instruments

IFRS 7 specifies a number of disclosure requirements to be provided by 'class of financial instrument'. These include derecognition of financial assets (see **4.1.5** below); allowance account for credit losses if an entity chooses under IAS 39 to have a separate allowance account (see **4.1.7** below); impairment losses in the period (see **4.2.5** below); fair value of all financial instruments (see **4.3.3** below); 'day 1 profit or losses' (see **4.3.3** below); and, credit risk (see **5.2.1** below).

IFRS 7 requires the entity to group financial instruments into classes that are appropriate to the nature of the information disclosed and that take into account the characteristics of those financial instruments. The classes are to be reconciled to the line items presented in the statement of financial position. [IFRS 7.6] The classes are determined by the entity and are distinct from the categories of financial instruments specified by IAS 39. [IFRS 7.B1] At a minimum, the classes are required to distinguish between those financial instruments that are measured at amortised cost and those that are measured at fair value. The entity should treat as a separate class or classes those financial instruments that are outside the scope of IFRS 7 (where the entity wishes to provide additional disclosure over and above the requirements of IFRS 7). [IFRS 7.B2] In many instances, classes of financial instruments will be more granular than the categories of financial instruments. For example, loans and receivables is a financial instrument category that could comprise various classes like home loans, credit card loans, unsecured medium term loans etc.

The preparer of the financial statements must strike a balance between providing excessive detail and obscuring information as a result of too much aggregation. [IFRS 7.B3]

IFRS 7 is not clear whether the same classes of financial instruments are applied universally to all the disclosures that IFRS 7 requires by class. An advantage of applying the same classes of financial instruments across all the required disclosures is that it will enhance comparability and understanding between disclosures. However, such an approach may be in conflict with IFRS 7 in the following instances:

(i) disclosure by class is required for certain quantitative disclosures, yet, IFRS 7.34 requires this information to be consistent with that provided internally to key management personnel. If the information provided to key management for the quantitative disclosures required by the Standard is aggregated differently, depending on the applicable risk disclosure, this information must be disclosed. It would be inappropriate to aggregate classes differently to the aggregation provided to key management personnel.

(ii) IFRS 7.IG21 indicates that in determining classes for credit risk disclosures an entity should group financial instruments that share economic characteristics with respect to the risk being disclosed, for example, residential mortgages, unsecured consumer loans and commercial loans. This implies that classes vary depending on the type of information being disclosed. The classes applied to credit risk disclosure, therefore, may not be appropriate for the classes of financial instruments applied to fair value disclosure, for example the specific disclosures required for 'day 1 profit or loss' (see **4.3.3** below). If only a small number of items are included in the day 1 profit or loss disclosure, but the characteristics of the instruments or valuation techniques differ, an entity may consider it more appropriate to choose classes for this specific disclosure that differ to other required disclosures.

Care should be taken to ensure that the determination of classes is relevant to the disclosure requirement and provides the most meaningful information. If different classes of financial instruments are used for different disclosures then the entity should place greater emphasis on making clear how the classes are reconciled to the statement of financial position and between notes.

As IFRS does not prescribe captions for the statement of financial position, other than the minimum required by IAS 1 and other specific standards, an entity could choose to use its classes of financial instruments as a basis for its captions in the statement of financial position. Such an approach is likely to result in many more captions in the statement of financial position compared to the presentation where an entity uses the categories of financial assets in IAS 39 as the basis for captions in the statement of financial position.

Example 3

The extract below is an example of classes of financial instruments being used as captions in the statement of financial position

Extract from Nordea Annual Report 2008, p. 83:

		Group		Parent company	
EURm	Note	31 Dec 2008	31 Dec 2007	31 Dec 2008	31 Dec 2007
Assets					
Cash and balances with central banks		3,157	5,020	276	296
Treasury bills	15	6,545	5,193	2,098	567

EURm	Note	Group 31 Dec 2008	Group 31 Dec 2007	Parent company 31 Dec 2008	Parent company 31 Dec 2007
Loans and receivables to credit institutions	16	23,903	24,262	43,855	36,824
Loans and receivables to the public	16	265,100	244,682	29,240	26,640
Interest-bearing securities	17	44,830	38,782	10,080	5,216
Financial instruments pledged as collateral	18	7,937	4,790	3,097	2,806
Shares	19	10,669	17,644	1,107	2,034
Derivatives	20	86,838	31,498	3,562	1,281
Fair value changes of the hedged items in portfolio hedge of interest rate risk	21	413	(105)	27	(4)
Investments in group undertakings	22	–	–	15,866	15,488
Investments in associated undertakings	23	431	366	2	30
Intangible assets	24	2,535	2,725	757	819
Property and equipment	25,26	375	342	81	53
Investment property	27	3,334	3,492	–	–
Deferred tax assets	13	64	191	28	34
Current tax assets	13	344	142	76	52
Retirement benefit assets	37	168	123	–	–
Other assets	28	14,604	7,724	2,099	1,940
Prepaid expenses and accrued income	29	2,827	2,183	783	402
Total assets		474,074	389,054	113,034	94,478

Liabilities

EURm	Note	Group 31 Dec 2008	Group 31 Dec 2007	Parent company 31 Dec 2008	Parent company 31 Dec 2007
Liabilities					
Deposits by credit institutions	30	51,932	30,077	34,713	24,275
Deposits and borrowings from the public	31	148,591	142,329	33,457	32,296
Liabilities to policyholders	32	29,238	32,280	–	–
Debt securities in issue	33	108,989	99,792	17,949	13,839
Derivatives	20	85,538	33,023	2,756	1,581
Fair value changes of the hedged items in portfolio hedge of interest rate risk	21	532	–323	42	–69
Current tax liabilities	13	458	300	0	0
Other liabilities	34	17,970	22,860	4,229	4,014
Accrued expenses and prepaid income	35	3,278	2,762	465	341
Deferred tax liabilities	13	1,053	703	0	2
Provisions	36	143	73	3	2
Retirement benefit obligations	37	340	462	118	129
Subordinated liabilities	38	8,209	7,556	6,829	6,151
Total liabilities		456,271	371,894	100,561	82,561
Untaxed reserves	39	–	–	2	7
Equity	40				
Minority interests		78	78	–	–
Share capital		2,600	2,597	2,600	2,597
Other reserves		–888	–160	–5	5
Retained earnings		16,013	14,645	9,876	9,308
Total equity		17,803	17,160	12,471	11,910
Total liabilities and equity		474,074	389,054	113,034	94,478
Assets pledged as security for own liabilities	41	95,507	79,708	3,054	

EURm	Note	Group 31 Dec 2008	Group 31 Dec 2007	Parent company 31 Dec 2008	Parent company 31 Dec 2007
Other assets pledged	42	10,807	6,304	9,504	7,270
Contingent liabilities	43	26,287	24,254	21,947	14,066
Commitments excluding derivatives	44	88,434	87,006	24,139	29,474
Derivative commitments	20,44	3,802,101	3,405,332	104,378	299,852

4 Significance of financial instruments

One of the two key objectives of IFRS 7 is to require entities to provide disclosures in its financial statements that enable users to evaluate the significance of financial instruments for the entity's financial position and performance. To achieve this, disclosures must be provided for the statement of financial position, statement of comprehensive income and equity.

4.1 Statement of financial position disclosures

IFRS 7 requires specific disclosures about the statement of financial position. Some are very broad, for example, disclosing financial asset and financial liabilities by classification category, whereas some are very specific, for example, disclosures on collateral and derecognition.

4.1.1 Categories of financial assets and financial liabilities

An entity is required to disclose the carrying amount for each financial instrument category as defined by IAS 39 either in the statement of financial position or in the notes to the financial statements. Disclosure of carrying amount is required specifically of the following:
[IFRS 7.8]

(a) financial assets at fair value through profit or loss, showing separately (i) those designated as such upon initial recognition and (ii) those classified as held for trading;

(b) held-to-maturity investments;

(c) loans and receivables;

(d) available-for-sale financial assets;

(e) financial liabilities at fair value through profit or loss, showing separately (i) those designated as such upon initial recognition and (ii) those classified as held for trading; and

(f) financial liabilities measured at amortised cost.

These disclosures are intended to assist users in understanding the extent to which accounting policies affect the amounts at which financial assets and financial liabilities are recognised. [IFRS 7.BC14] Together with the disclosures of the gains and losses by category of financial instrument, the disclosure of the carrying amounts for each category of financial instrument allows users to appraise management on its decisions to buy, sell or hold financial assets and to incur, maintain or discharge financial liabilities.

Recognised derivative financial instruments other than those that are designated and effective hedging instruments are included within the fair value through profit or loss category. Derivatives that are designated as effective hedging instruments, however, are excluded from that category and IAS 39 does not include them in any other category or create a new category for them. It is reasonable, however, to include derivatives that are effective hedging instruments as a separate category in order to aid reconciliation between disclosures by category and the statement of financial position. Some entities choose to show derivatives in effective hedging relationship in a separate caption both in the statement of financial position and in the notes.

Example 4.1.1

The extract below is an example of the requirement in IFRS 7.8 to disclose the carrying amount of each classification category in IAS 39. The extract also includes non-financial items which is not a requirement of IFRS 7 as they are outside the scope of the Standard.

Extract from Nordea Annual Report 2008, p. 132:

Group 31 Dec 2008, EURm	Loans and receivables	Held to maturity	Financial assets at fair value through profit or loss: Held for trading	Financial assets at fair value through profit or loss: Designated at fair value through profit or loss	Derivatives used for hedging	Available for sale	Non-financial assets	Total
Assets								
Cash and balances with central banks	3,157							3,157
Treasury bills	9	183	6,353					6,545
Loans and receivables to credit institutions	18,731		5,172					23,903
Loans and receivables to the public	217,833		11,074	36,193				265,100
Interest-bearing securities		12,045	17,559	15,177		49		44,830
Financial instruments pledged as collateral			7,937					7,937
Shares			3,745	6,917		7		10,669
Derivatives			86,520		318			86,838
Fair value changes of the hedged items in portfolio hedge of interest rate risk	413							413
Investments in associated undertakings							431	431
Intangible assets							2,535	2,535
Property and equipment							375	375
Investment property							3,334	3,334
Deferred tax assets							64	64
Current tax assets							344	344
Retirement benefit assets							168	168
Other assets	5,738			8,829			37	14,604
Prepaid expenses and accrued income	2,090		312				425	2,827
Total	247,971	12,228	138,672	67,116	318	56	7,713	474,074

Liabilities

Group	Financial liabilities at fair value through profit or loss					
31 Dec 2008, EURm	Held for trading	Designated at fair value through profit or loss	Derivatives used for hedging	Other financial liabilities	Non-financial liabilities	Total
Liabilities						
Deposits by credit institutions	8,133	23,202		20,597		51,932
Deposits and borrowings from the public	2,999	4,914		140,678		148,591
Liabilities to policyholders	4,021				25,217	29,238
Debt securities in issue	5,242	27,153		76,594		108,989
Derivatives	83,277		2,261			85,538
Fair value changes of the hedged items in portfolio hedge of interest rate risk				532		532
Current tax liabilities					458	458
Other liabilities	4,056	2,641		10,780	493	17,970
Accrued expenses and prepaid income	614			1,763	901	3,278
Deferred tax liabilities					1,053	1,053
Provisions					143	143
Retirement benefit obligations					340	340
Subordinated liabilities	1			8,208		8,209
Total	108,343	57,910	2,261	259,152	28,605	456,271

4.1.2 Financial assets at fair value through profit or loss

IFRS 7.9 requires extensive disclosure where an entity has designated loans and receivables as at fair value through profit or loss (FVTPL), since applying the fair value option to these instruments may result in a significant impact on the financial statements caused by fair value movements, and in particular those movements caused by changes in credit risk.

IFRS 7 requires disclosure of:
[IFRS 7.9]

(a) the maximum exposure to *credit risk* of the loan or receivable designated as at fair value through profit or loss (or group of loans or receivables) at the end of the reporting period;

(b) the amount by which any related credit derivatives or similar instruments mitigate that maximum exposure to credit risk;

(c) the amount of change, during the period and cumulatively, in the fair value of the loan or receivable (or group of loans or receivables) that is attributable to changes in the credit risk of the financial asset determined either:

   (i) as the amount of change in its fair value that is not attributable to changes in market conditions that give rise to *market risk*; or

   (ii) using an alternative method the entity believes more faithfully represents the amount of change in its fair value that is attributable to changes in the credit risk of the asset.

   Changes in market conditions that give rise to market risk include changes in an observed (benchmark) interest rate, commodity price, foreign exchange rate or index of prices or rates; and

(d) the amount of the change in the fair value of any related credit derivatives or similar instruments that has occurred during the period and cumulatively since the loan or receivable was designated.

In addition, an entity shall disclose:
[IFRS 7.11]

(a) the methods used to comply with the requirements in (c) above;

(b) if the entity believes that the disclosure it has given to comply with the requirements in (c) above does not faithfully represent the change in the fair value of the financial asset attributable to changes in its credit risk, the reasons for reaching this conclusion and the factors it believes are relevant.

The maximum exposure to credit risk for a derivative is its carrying amount. [IFRS 7.BC50] The Standard is not clear whether the maximum exposure to credit risk for loans and receivables can also equal the carrying amount, which is fair value, when an entity designates those loans and receivables as at FVTPL.

The information to be disclosed regarding the maximum exposure to credit risk depends on whether exposure to credit loss is viewed as a 'cash loss' or a loss in the statement of comprehensive income. Credit risk is defined as *the risk that one party to a financial instrument will cause a financial loss for the other party by failing to discharge an obligation.* [IFRS 7(Appendix A)] Where the maximum exposure to credit risk is viewed as a cash loss, then the amount to be disclosed would be the amount owed, e.g. if the fair value of the debt is CU70 and the amount owed is CU100, then the maximum 'cash loss' is CU100. If, however, the maximum exposure to credit risk is viewed as a loss in the statement of comprehensive income, then the carrying amount, which is fair value of the loans and receivables in this instance, will be the amount that is required to be disclosed.

While either approach is supportable an entity must apply a consistent policy in disclosing the maximum exposure to credit risk for the loans and receivables that are designated as at FVTPL.

US GAAP comparison: FAS 159, *The Fair Value Option for Financial Assets and Financial Liabilities*, provides specific disclosure requirements for items elected to be measured at fair value under the fair value option, including loans and long-term receivables. Similar to IFRS, the disclosure requirements in FAS 159 focus on highlighting the credit quality of loans and long-term receivables elected to be measured at fair value. For example, for loans and long-term receivables elected to be measured at fair value under US GAAP, an entity is required to disclose: (1) the difference between the aggregate fair value and unpaid principal balance of the loan, (2) the aggregate fair value of loans that are 90 days or more past due, (3) the entity's policy for recognising interest income for loans elected to be carried at fair value, (4) the difference between the aggregate fair value and the aggregate unpaid principal balance for loans that are 90 days or more past due, in non-accrual status, or both, (5) the estimated amount of gain or loss included in earnings during the period attributable to changes in instrument-specific credit risk and (6) how the amount of gain and loss attributable to instrument-specific credit risks was determined.

Example 4.1.2A

Entity A acquired at the start of the prior period a portfolio of 9 per cent non-amortising unsecured long term loans with five years remaining to maturity and designated them as at FVTPL. The loans were acquired for CU905m when the effective interest rate was 10 per cent, consisting of 8 per cent interest rate and 2 per cent credit spread. The par amount of the loans is CU1bn. At the date of acquisition Entity A entered into a credit default swap with a financial institution to provide credit protection on the loans with a notional of CU500m. The credit default swap had an initial fair value of zero and remains outstanding at the year end.

The fair value of loans is CU896m at the year end (prior year: CU852m). At the year end interest rates for the remaining maturity are 8 per cent and credit spreads are 2.5 per cent (prior year: 9 per cent and 3 per cent respectively). The credit default swap has a fair value at the year end of CU35m (prior year: CU46m)

The items to be disclosed in accordance with IFRS 7.9 are as follows:

(*a*) *Maximum exposure to credit risk at the end of the reporting period*

If maximum exposure to credit risk is viewed as being loss in the statement of comprehensive income, then the amount to be disclosed would be CU896m (prior year: CU852m), being the fair value of the loans at the year end.

If the maximum exposure to credit risk is viewed as being equal to a cash loss, then the amount to be disclosed would be CU1bn (prior year: CU1bn), being the amount owed by the borrower at the year end.

Note: the entity cannot offset the loans and the credit default swaps as there is no right of set off and the financial instruments are with a different counterparty.

(*b*) *Amount by which any related credit derivatives or similar instruments mitigate that maximum exposure to credit risk*

The credit default swap provides credit protection on half of the loans. On a fair value basis, the maximum protection is equivalent to 56 per cent (prior year: 59 per cent) and on a cash loss basis is equivalent to 50 per cent (prior year: 50 per cent).

(*c*) *Amount of change, during the period and cumulative, in the fair value of loans that is attributable to changes in credit risk*

The cumulative change in fair value due to credit risk of the loans is a CU16m loss (prior year: CU27m loss). The change in fair value due to credit risk for the period was a CU11m gain.

(*d*) *Change in the fair value of any related credit derivatives*

The cumulative change in fair value of the credit default swap is a CU35m gain (prior year: CU46m gain). The change in fair value of the credit default swap for the period was a CU11m loss.

Example 4.1.2B

The extract below is an example of the requirement to disclose the maximum exposure to credit risk for loans and receivables designated as at FVTPL as well as changes in the fair value of the loans and receivables due to credit risk. [IFRS 7.9(a) & (c)].

Extract from Investec Annual Report 2008, p. 246

£'000	Carrying value	Fair value adjustment		Change in fair value attributable to credit risk		Maximum exposure to credit risk
		Year to date	Cumulative	Year to date	Cumulative	
14. Designated at fair value: loans and receivables and financial liabilities						
Loans and receivables						
2008						
Loans and advances to customers	1 104 940	47 962	132 766	76	(92)	1 104 940
2007						
Loans and advances to customers	1 055 702	(27 383)	(35 891)	168	(191)	1 055 702

Example 4.1.2C

The extract below is an example of the requirement to disclose the maximum exposure to credit risk for loans and receivables designated as at FVTPL, the amount by which related credit derivatives mitigate that exposure and the fair value movements on those credit derivatives, as well as changes in the fair value of the loans and receivables due to credit risk. [IFRS 7.9].

Extract from FirstRand Annual Report 2008, p. 292

41.1 Loans and receivables designated as at fair value through profit or loss

Certain instruments designated at fair value through profit or loss would meet the definition for classification as loans and receivables in terms of IAS 39 were it not for this designation. The table below contains details on the change in credit risk attributable to these instruments.

R MILLION			Change in fair value			
			Of mitigating instrument		Due to credit risk	
2008	Carrying value	Mitigated credit risk*	Current period	Cumulative	Current period	Cumulative
Included in advances	99 674	2 517	62	88	424	1 105
Included in investment securities	13 534	166	16	16	78	51
Included in non recourse investments	19 075	–	–	–	–	–
Total	132 283	2 683	78	104	502	1 156

* Amount by which any related credit derivatives or similar instruments mitigate the maximum exposure to credit risk.

Different methods are used to determine the current period and cumulative changes in fair value attributable to credit risk for investment securities and advances. This is due to the differing inherent credit risk of these instruments.

The methods used are described below:

Investment Securities

The change in fair value for investments designated at fair value through profit or loss is calculated by stripping out the movements which result from a change in market factors that give rise to market risk.

The change in fair value due to credit risk is then calculated as the balancing figure, after deducting the movement due to market risk from the total movement in fair value.

Advances

The current and cumulative change in fair value due to changes in credit risk for advances designated at fair value through profit or loss is calculated as the amount of change in fair value that is attributable to changes in credit risk.

The change in credit risk is the difference between fair value of the advances based on the original credit spreads and the fair value of the advances based on the most recent market observable credit spreads.

Example 4.1.2D

The extract below is an example of the requirement to disclose the maximum exposure to credit risk for loans and receivables designated as at FVTPL, the amount by which related credit derivatives mitigate that exposure and the fair value movements on those credit derivatives, as well as changes in the fair value of the loans and receivables due to credit risk. [IFRS 7.9].

Extract from Barclays Annual Report 2008, p. 215

13 Financial assets designated at fair value

Held on own account

	2008 £m	2007 £m
Loans and advances	30,187	23,491
Debt securities	8,628	24,217
Equity securities	6,496	5,376
Other financial assets	9,231	3,545
Financial assets designated at fair value – held on own account	54,542	56,629

The maximum exposure to credit risk on loans and advances designated at 31st December 2008 was £30,187m (2007: £23,491). The amounts by which related credit derivatives and similar instruments mitigate the exposure to credit risk at 31st December was £2,084m (2007: £2,605m).

The net loss attributable to changes in credit risk for loans and advances designated at fair value was £2,550m in 2008 (2007: £401m). The gains on related credit derivatives was £519m for the year (2007: £4m loss).

The cumulative net loss attributable to changes in credit risk for loans and advances designated at fair value since initial recognition is £2,149m at 31st December 2008 (2007: £401m). The cumulative change in fair value of related credit derivatives at 31st December 2008 is £523m (2007: £4m).

4.1.3 *Financial liabilities at fair value through profit or loss*

Where an entity has designated financial liabilities as at FVTPL, IFRS 7.10 requires extensive disclosure and in particular disclosure about creditworthiness. These disclosures have been included to help alleviate concerns that users may misinterpret the profit or loss effects of changes in issuer's credit risk. The perceived 'anomaly' of recording gains in profit or loss when the entity's credit rating deteriorates should be helped by disclosure of the changes in fair value attributable to credit risk.

IFRS 7 requires disclosure of:
[IFRS 7.10]

(a) the amount of change, during the period and cumulatively, in the fair value of the financial liability that is attributable to changes in the credit risk of that liability determined either:

  (i) as the amount of change in its fair value that is not attributable to changes in market conditions that give rise to market risk; or

  (ii) using an alternative method the entity believes more faithfully represents the amount of change in its fair value that is attributable to changes in the credit risk of the liability.

  Changes in market conditions that give rise to market risk include changes in a benchmark interest rate, the price of another entity's financial instrument, a commodity price, a foreign exchange rate or an index of prices or rates. For contracts that include a unit-linking feature, changes in market conditions include changes in the performance of the related internal or external investment fund.

(b) the difference between the financial liability's carrying amount and the amount the entity would be contractually required to pay at maturity to the holder of the obligation.

IFRS 7.BC22 states that the fair value may differ significantly from the settlement amount, i.e. amount contractually required to be paid at maturity, in particular for financial liabilities with a long duration when an entity has experienced a significant deterioration in creditworthiness since their issue. When complying with IFRS 7.10(b) as stated above the amount contractually required to be paid at maturity should be an undiscounted amount, not affected by the entity's own credit risk. To the extent the amount payable at maturity is subject to variability, for example because the principal is indexed-linked, an estimation of this amount should also be included, whether the index-linked feature is a separately accounted for embedded derivative or not. This is consistent with the principle applied for liquidity risk disclosures in IFRS 7.B16 as discussed in **5.2.2** below where the effects of any embedded derivatives are included on an undiscounted basis based on conditions existing at the end of the reporting period (incorporating forward rates as applicable).

The Standard also requires disclosure of:
[IFRS 7.11]

(a) the methods used to comply with the requirements in IFRS 7.10(a) above; and

(b) if the entity believes that the disclosure it has given to comply with the requirements in IFRS 7.10(a) above does not faithfully represent the change in the fair value of the financial liability attributable to changes in its credit risk, the reasons for reaching this conclusion and the factors it believes are relevant.

US GAAP Comparison: FAS 159, *The Fair Value Option for Financial Assets and Financial Liabilities*, provides specific disclosure requirements for financial liabilities designated as measured at fair value through profit or loss. Similar to IFRS, US GAAP requires the difference between the aggregate fair value and the aggregate unpaid principal balance of the financial liability and the estimated gains and losses for fair value changes included in earnings that are attributable to instrument-specific credit risk. Unlike IFRS, US GAAP also requires an entity to disclose qualitative information regarding what causes a change in instrument-specific credit risk and how that change was determined.

Example 4.1.3A

On the first day of its current financial period Entity B issued a 5-year bond in order to finance the expansion of its operations. The bond trades on a recognised bond exchange. Entity B's year-end is 31 December 20X1.

Maturity date:	31 December 20X5
Nominal value:	CU500million
Coupon:	9%, payable annually on 31 December in arrears
Issue price (1 January 20X1):	CU450million
Fair value (31 December 20X1):	CU400million
5-year LIBOR (1 January 20X1):	10.5%
4-year LIBOR (31 December 20X1):	12.75%

IFRS 7 requires disclosure of the amount of change in the fair value of the financial liability that is attributable to changes in the liability's credit risk. IFRS 7 permits an entity to determine this amount as the amount of change in the liability's fair value that is not attributable to changes in market conditions that give rise to market risk. If the only relevant changes in market conditions for a liability are changes in an observed (benchmark) interest rate, then this amount may be estimated as follows: [IFRS 7.B4]

(a) Determine the liability's internal rate of return at the start of the period using the observed market price of the liability and the liability's contractual cash flows at the start of the period.

Year 0	Year 1	Year 2	Year 3	Year 4	Year 5
-450,000,000[1]	45,000,000[2]	45,000,000[2]	45,000,000[2]	45,000,000[2]	545,000,000[3]

1 The bonds are recognised initially at fair value, being an amount of CU450million.

2 Yearly cash flows are determined as being 9% x CU500million.

3 The terminal cash flow is determined as the nominal value of the bonds plus the interest coupon.

The internal rate of return, equal to the effective interest rate, at issue is 11.76%.

(b) Deduct the observed (benchmark) interest rate at the start of the period from the internal rate of return to arrive at an instrument-specific component of the internal rate of return (i.e. the portion of the effective interest that relates to credit risk).

11.76% – 10.5% = 1.26% instrument specific component of the IRR

(c) Compute the present value of the cash flows of the liability using the liability's contractual cash flows at the end of the period and a discount rate equal to the sum of the observed benchmark interest rate at the end of the period and the instrument specific component of the internal rate of return determined above in (b).

Remaining cash flows to be discounted using an internal rate of return of 14.01% (12.75% + 1.26%)

Year 2	Year 3	Year 4	Year 5
45,000,000	45,000,000	45,000,000	545,000,000

Present value is equal to CU427,059,828 as at the end of the reporting period.

(d) Compute the change in the fair value of the liability that is not attributable to changes in the observed (benchmark) interest rate as being the difference between the observed market price of the liability and the amount determined above.

Change in fair value due to changes in credit risk is determined as CU27,059,828 (CU427,059,828 – CU400,000,000).

The disclosures may be provided as follows:

Financial liabilities

During the year, the group issued a commercial bond with a nominal value of CU500,000,000 with a maturity of five years that is designated as at fair value through profit or loss at initial recognition. The fair value and the change in that fair value that can be ascribed to changes in underlying credit risk are set out below:

	31 December 20X6	31 December 20X5
Fair value of commercial bond	CU400,000,000	–
Change in fair value of bonds not attributable to changes in market conditions	CU(27,059,828)	–
Difference between carrying amount and amount contractually required to be paid at maturity	CU100,000,000	–

The group estimates changes in fair value due to credit risk, by estimating the amount of change in the fair value that is not due to changes in market conditions that give rise to market risk.

The example above assumes that changes in the fair value arising from factors other than changes in the bond's credit risk or changes in interest rates are not significant. Had the bond above contained an embedded prepayment option, then the change in the fair value of the embedded derivative would need to be excluded in determining the amount to be disclosed. [IFRS 7.B4] Whether the embedded derivative is closely related or not, the effects of the embedded derivative need to be excluded.

The methodology illustrated above in **example 4.1.3A** is a reasonable approach in determining the fair value movements due to credit risk for plain vanilla debt instruments. Where there are other factors that affect the change in the instrument's fair value, such as embedded derivatives, then alternative methods may be used to calculate the amount of change in the fair value attributable to changes in credit risk of the liability. Such methods are required to be disclosed, as well as why those methods provide a more faithful representation than the method described in IFRS 7. [IFRS 7.BC21(a)] Liabilities, such as unit-linked insurance contracts, for which the amount of the liability reflects the performance of a defined pool of assets, present particular challenges.

Example 4.1.3B

The extract below is an example of the requirement to disclose the changes in fair value due to credit risk for financial liabilities designated as at fair value through profit or loss in accordance with IFRS 7.10(a) and the difference between the carrying amount and the amount contractually due at maturity in accordance with IFRS 7.10(b)

Extracts from HSBC Holdings plc Annual Report and Accounts 2008, p 419:

27. Financial liabilities designated at fair value (extract)

HSBC

	2008 US$m	2007 US$m
Deposits by banks and customer accounts	6,618	7,724
Liabilities to customers under investment contracts	9,283	16,053
Debt securities in issue (Note 28)	34,969	38,587

	2008 US$m	2007 US$m
Subordinated liabilities (Note 32)	20,316	22,831
Preference shares (Note 32)	3,401	4,744
	74,587	89,939

The carrying amount at 31 December 2008 of financial liabilities designated at fair value was US$1,851 million less than the contractual amount at maturity (2007: US$648 million less). At 31 December 2008, the cumulative amount of the change in fair value attributable to changes in credit risk was a gain of US$7,978 million (2007: gain of US$1,619 million).

4.1.4 Reclassification

Where an entity reclassifies financial assets in accordance with the requirements of IAS 39.51–54, from cost or amortised cost to fair value or vice versa, disclosure of the amount that has been reclassified into and out of each category is required, together with the reason for that reclassification. [IFRS 7.12] This disclosure will be relevant in the case where financial assets are reclassified from the held to maturity to available-for-sale category, and vice versa, or in the instance when an investment in, or derivative that results in the physical delivery of, an unlisted equity instrument becomes or ceases to become reliably measurable.

Some classification decisions depend on management's intent, for example, classification as held-to-maturity investments. Reclassifications from cost/amortised cost to fair value, and vice versa, may occur in limited circumstances and it is important to understand the reasons for such reclassifications since the understanding of the reasons may assist the users in judging how management follows through with its stated intentions. Such information is also useful to the user in understanding the performance of the entity since reclassifications of such instruments can have a significant effect on their measurement. [IFRS 7.BC23]

IFRS 7.12 requires disclosure of financial assets that are reclassified from cost or amortised cost to fair value, and vice versa. Whilst reclassification of financial liabilities is equally possible, the disclosure requirements in IFRS 7.12 do not refer to financial liabilities.

Although IFRS 7.12 appears not to require the same disclosure for financial liabilities, it is preferable to provide similar disclosures. For example, if an entity had written a call option over a non-listed third party equity security, where a fixed amount of the equity security would be delivered to the option holder upon exercise, the derivative instrument will be a financial liability. If the entity had previously held the derivative at cost as it could not measure the instrument reliably, and a reliable measure became available at a later date, the entity would be required to remeasure the derivative liability at fair value with changes in fair value recognised in profit or loss. [IAS 39.53] The amount and the reason for the reclassification would be equally relevant for a reclassification of the liability as it would be for a reclassification of an asset.

The amendment to IAS 39 issued in October 2008 relaxed the existing reclassification requirements for certain financial assets. Following the amendment, IAS 39 permits non-derivative financial assets to be reclassified out of the held-for-trading category and reclassification of available-for-sale debt instruments to loans and receivables subject to meeting specified criteria (see **section 4** in **chapter 2**). IFRS 7 was amended to introduce new disclosure requirements for such reclassifications: [IFRS 7.12A]

(a) the amount reclassified into and out of each category;

(b) for each reporting period until derecognition, the carrying amounts and fair values of all financial assets that have been reclassified in the current and previous reporting periods;

(c) if a financial asset was reclassified in accordance with paragraph 50B, the rare situation, and the facts and circumstances indicating that the situation was rare;

(d) for the reporting period when the financial asset was reclassified, the fair value gain or loss on the financial asset recognised in profit or loss or other comprehensive income in that reporting period and in the previous reporting period;

(e) for each reporting period following the reclassification (including the reporting period in which the financial asset was reclassified) until derecognition of the financial asset, the fair value gain or loss that would have been recognised in profit or loss or other comprehensive income if the financial asset had not been reclassified, and the gain, loss, income and expense recognised in profit or loss; and

(f) the effective interest rate and estimated amounts of cash flows the entity expects to recover, as at the date of reclassification of the financial asset.

The IASB introduced extensive disclosures for reclassifications out of fair value through profit or loss and out of available-for-sale to loans and receivables because of the significant effect these reclassifications can have on the financial statements. [IFRS 7.BC23A]

Example 4.1.4A

The extract below is an example of the disclosure requirements for assets reclassified out of fair value through profit or loss and out of available-for-sale to loans and receivables in accordance with IFRS 7.12A

Extracts from RBS Annual Report and Accounts 2008, p. 208:

Reclassification of financial instruments

As discussed in accounting policies on page 178, during 2008 the Group reclassified financial assets from the held-for-trading and available-for-sale categories into the loans and receivables category (as permitted by paragraph 50D of IAS 39 as amended) and from the held-for-trading category into the available-for-sale category (as permitted by paragraph 50B of IAS 39 as amended).

The turbulence in the financial markets during the second half of 2008 was regarded by management as rare circumstances in the context of paragraph 50B of IAS 39 as amended.

The balance sheet values of these assets, the effect of the reclassification on the income statement for the period from the date of reclassification to 31 December 2008 and the gains and losses relating to these assets recorded in the income statement for the years ended 31 December 2008, 2007 and 2006 were as follows:

						2008					2007	2008
	2008-on reclassification			31 December 2008			After reclassification					
	Carrying value	Effective interest rate	Expected cash flows	Carrying value	Fair value	Gains/losses up to the date of reclassification	Income	Impairment losses	Gains/(losses) in AFS reserves	Amount that would have been recognized	Gains-(losses) recognized in the income statement in prior periods	
	£m	%	£m	£m	£m	£m	£m	£m	£m	£m	£m	£m
Reclassified from HFT to LAR:												
Loans:												
Leveraged finance	3,602	10.15	6,083	4.304	2,523	(457)	454	–		(1,206)	(155)	–
Corporate loans	5,040	6.19	7,582	5,827	4,940	(76)	198	–		(681)	(50)	3
	8,642		13,665	10,131	7,463	(533)	652	–		(1,887)	(205)	3
Debt securities:												
CDO of RMBS	215	4.92	259	236	221	4	5	–		(11)	5	6
RMBS	1,765	6.05	2,136	2,011	1,536	(115)	157	–		(302)	(12)	–

						2008					2007	2008
	2008-on reclassification			31 December 2008			After reclassification					
	Carrying value	Effective interest rate	Expected cash flows	Carrying value	Fair value	Gains/losses up to the date of reclassification	Income	Impairment losses	Gains/(losses) in AFS reserves	Amount that would have been recognized	Gains-(losses) recognized in the income statement in prior periods	
	£m	%	£m	£m	£m	£m	£m	£m	£m	£m	£m	£m
CMBS	1	11.11	4	1	1	1	–	–		–	–	–
CLOs	835	6.34	1,141	952	717	(22)	104	–		(130)	(14)	(2)
Other ABS	2,203	5.07	3,202	2,514	2,028	(67)	129	–		(338)	3	(1)
Other	2,538	2.62	2,764	2,602	2,388	72	3	–		(166)	94	476
	7,557		9,506	8,316	6,891	(127)	398	–		(947)	76	479
Total	16,199		23,171	18,447	14,354	(660)	1,050	–		(2,834)	(129)	482
Reclassified from HFT to AFS:												
Debt securities:												
CDO of RMBS	6,228	8.14	8,822	5,695	5,695	(1,330)	1,147	(464)	(1,069)	(280)	(400)	–
RMBS	5,205	8.03	8,890	5,171	5,171	(530)	24	–	(162)	(122)	(4)	73
CMBS	32	6.81	85	31	31	(5)	5	–	(3)	2	(4)	–
CLOs	1,457	5.02	1,804	1,288	1,288	(168)	421		(383)	58	(36)	1
Other ABS	2,199	6.02	3,163	1,847	1,847	(366)	(10)	–	(354)	(311)	(42)	72
Other	614	12.55	1,311	698	698	–	130	–	(166)	(5)	(1)	–
	15,735		24,095	14,730	14,730	(2,389)	1,717	(464)	(2,137)	(658)	(487)	146
Reclassified from AFS to LAR:												
Debt securities	704	1.38	772	1,028	968	(12)(1)	6	–	–	(37)(1)	–	–
Total	32,638		48,038	34,205	30,052	(3,061)	2,773	(464)	(2,137)	(3,529)	(616)	628

Note:

(1) Gains (losses) recognized in the available-for-sale reserve.

4.1.5 *Derecognition*

Some transfers of financial assets do not qualify for derecognition. It is important for the users to be able to evaluate the significance of such transactions and the risks retained, the nature of the risks and rewards to which the entity continues to be exposed to, and the extent of its continuing involvement with, the asset. Disclosure is required of:
[IFRS 7.13]

(a) the nature of the assets involved;

(b) the nature of the risks and rewards of ownership to which the entity remains exposed;

(c) when the entity continues to recognise all of the assets, the carrying amounts of the assets and of the associated liabilities; and

(d) when the entity continues to recognise the assets to the extent of its continuing involvement, the total carrying amount of the original assets, the amount of the assets that the entity continues to recognise, and the carrying amount of the associated liabilities.

For example, a sale of a portfolio of receivables with a limited guarantee may result in the entity continuing to recognise the receivables and retaining some exposure to the receivables, but to a lesser extent than prior to the transfer.

IAS 1(2007).122 (previously IAS 1(2003).113 requires an entity to disclose in its accounting policies the judgements management makes in the process of applying its accounting policies. IAS 1(2007).123(b) (previously IAS 1(2003).114(b)) makes specific reference to disclosure of the judgement management makes in determining when substantially all the significant risks and rewards of ownership of financial assets and lease assets are transferred to other entities.

The disclosures for derecognition required by IFRS 7 are by class of financial asset and can be provided either by type of financial assets (i.e. differentiating by characteristics of the assets) or by type of risks or rewards of ownership to which the entity remains exposed.

US GAAP Comparison: FAS 140, *Accounting for Transfers and Servicing of Financial Assets and Extinguishments of Financial Liabilities,* provides disclosure requirements specific to the sale and securitisation of financial assets. Unlike IFRS 7, FAS 140 requires very specific disclosures of an entity's securitisation activities during a period. Specifically, FAS 140 requires an entity to disclose the following, if during any period presented in the financial statements the entity securitised financial assets: (1) the entity's accounting policy for initially measuring its interest that continue to be held after the transfer, (2) the methodology used to determine the fair value of items initially measured at fair value, (3) the characteristics of the securitisation transaction including the transferor's continuing involvement with the transferred assets, (4) the key assumptions used in measuring the fair value of interests that continue to be held at the time of securitisation including the discount rates, expected prepayments or expected weighted average life of the interest, and anticipated credit losses, and (5) the cash flows between the securitisation SPE and the transferor.

In addition to the disclosures specific to the securitisation activity, an entity that retains an interest in transferred financial assets must disclose the following regarding those retained interests: (1) its accounting policies for subsequently measuring those interests, including the methodology used in determining fair value, (2) the key assumptions used in subsequently measuring fair value of those interest, and (3) a sensitivity analysis or stress test showing the hypothetical effect on the fair value of those interest of two or more unfavourable variations from the expected levels of each key assumptions.

Example 4.1.5A

The extract below is an example of the application of the derecognition disclosure requirements in IFRS 7.13 where transferred assets continue to be fully recognised and fully derecognised

Extracts from ThyssenKrupp Annual Report 2007–2008 p.185

As of September 30, 2008, sales of receivables in the amount of €3 million (2007: €9 million) did not result in a derecognition from the balance sheet because the Group retained substantially all the risks and rewards of ownership. The corresponding liability is included in financial debt (see also Note 25). The sales resulted in net proceeds in the amount of €3 million (2006/2007: €9 million).

The amount of receivables sold and derecognized from the balance sheet as of September 30, 2008, was €972 million (2007: €929 million), resulting in net proceeds in the amount of €938 million (2006/2007: €899 million). In some cases, when the Group sells receivables it retains rights and immaterial obligations; these retained interests mainly consist of servicing as well as providing limited cash reserve accounts and dilution reserves. The recognized assets and provided guarantees which serve as a cash reserve account amounted to €72 million (2007: €70 million) as of September 30, 2008. Continuing involvement primarily resulting from the dilution reserve was €26 million (2007: €26 million) as of September 30, 2008.

Example 4.1.5B

The extract below is an example of application of the requirements in IFRS 7.13 for transferred assets that continue to be fully recognised

Extracts from RBS Annual Report and Accounts 2008, p 249:

Securitisations and other asset transfers

Continued recognition

The table below sets out the asset categories together with the carrying amounts of the assets and associated liabilities for those securitisations and other asset transfers where substantially all the risks and rewards of the asset have been retained by the Group.

	2008		2007	
Asset type	Assets £m	Liabilities £m	Assets £m	Liabilities £m
Residential mortgages	49,184	20,075	23,652	23,436
Credit card receivables	3,004	3,197	2,948	2,664
Other loans	1,679	1,071	1,703	1,149
Commercial paper conducts	36,395	35,835	32,613	31,193
Finance lease receivables	1,077	857	1,038	823
	91,339	61,035	61,964	59,265

4.1.6 Collateral

The entity is required to disclose the carrying amount of financial assets it has pledged as collateral (non-cash financial assets) for liabilities or contingent liabilities, including amounts the transferor has reclassified in accordance with IAS 39.37(a) where the transferee has the right to sell or pledge the collateral. The entity is also required to disclose the terms and conditions relating to its pledge. [IFRS 7.14] The terms and conditions may include:

- how much collateral needs to be maintained as security for the loans; and
- the type of collateral that needs to be provided as security for the loans.

Where an entity holds collateral (both financial and non-financial assets) as security for financial assets loaned to another entity and that it is permitted to sell or repledge in the absence of default by the owner of the collateral, the entity is required to disclose:

- the fair value of the collateral held;
- the fair value of any such collateral that has been sold or repledged, and whether the entity has an obligation to return it; and
- the terms and conditions associated with its use of the collateral. [IFRS 7.15]

The disclosure of the existence of such collateral is important since it provides information to the user of the financial statements of the amount of collateral used and available for use that may not be recognised in the statement of financial position of the entity.

Disclosure of collateral that the entity does not have the right to sell or pledge in the absence of default by the borrower is required in the credit risk disclosures note – see **6.2.1.2** below.

US GAAP Comparison: FAS 140, *Accounting for Transfers and Servicing of Financial Assets and Extinguishments of Financial Liabilities,* provides disclosure requirements specific to collateral arrangements.

Example 4.1.6A

The extract below is an example of application of the requirements in IFRS 7.14 for collateral pledged

Extract from Danske Bank Group Annual Report 2008, p. 122:

40 Assets deposited as collateral

At the end of 2008, the Group had deposited securities worth DKr278,324m as collateral with Danish and international clearing centres and other institutions (2007: DKr331,673m).

In connection with repo transactions, which involve selling securities to be repurchased at a later date, the securities remain on the balance sheet, and the amounts received are recognised as deposits. Repo transaction securities are treated as assets provided as collateral for liabilities. At the end of 2008, the carrying amount of such securities totalled DKr229,099m (2007: DKr277,379m). Counterparties are entitled to sell the securities or deposit them as collateral for other loans.

In connection with reverse transactions, which involve buying securities to be resold at a later date, the Group is entitled to sell the securities or deposit them as collateral for other loans. At the end of 2008, the fair value of reverse transaction securities was DKr369,999m (2007: DKr504,940m), of which securities sold totalled DKr41,769m (2007: DKr110,760m).

At the end of 2008, the Group had received cash and securities worth DKr26,186m as collateral for derivatives transactions (2007: DKr21,313m) and delivered cash and securities worth DKr66,440m (2007: DKr13,018m).

At the end of 2008, the Group had registered assets under insurance contracts worth DKr205,679m as collateral for the savings of policyholders (2007: DKr212,017m).

The Group had registered loans and advances at fair value worth DKr669,891m and other assets worth DKr0m as collateral for issued mortgage bonds, including mortgage-covered bonds, at the end at 2008 (2007: DKr627,809m and DKr3,035m, respectively).

At the end of 2008, the Group had registered loans and advances worth DKr78,842m and other assets worth DKr3,257m as collateral for covered bonds issued under Danish and Finnish law (2007: DKr23,886m and DKr0m, respectively).

Example 4.1.6B

The extract below is an example of application of the requirements in IFRS 7.15 for collateral held and in IFRS 7.38 for collateral obtained in the year.

Extracts from FirstRand Annual Report 2008, p. 291:

40.2 Collateral held

R MILLION	2008 Fair value	2008 Fair value of collateral sold or re-pledged	2007 Fair value	2007 Fair value of collateral sold or re-pledged
Collateral the Group holds which it has the ability to sell or repledge in the absence of default by the owner of the collateral				
Advances	29 609	14 519	19 914	6 285
Commodities	579	–	400	–
Total	30 188	14 519	20 314	6 285

When the Group takes possession of collateral which is not cash or not readily convertible into cash the Group determines a minimum sale amount ['pre-set sale amount'] and auctions the asset for the pre-set sale amount.

Where the Group is unable to obtain the pre-set sale amount in an auction the Group will continue to hold the asset while actively marketing it to ensure an appropriate value is obtained.

R MILLION	2008	2007
Collateral taken possession of and recognised on the balance sheet		
Vehicles	499	230
Total	499	230

4.1.7 Allowance account for credit losses

Where financial assets are impaired by credit losses, and the entity records the impairment in a separate allowance account rather than by directly reducing the carrying amount of an asset, the entity is required to disclose a reconciliation of changes in that account during the period. [IFRS 7.16] This disclosure is required by class of financial asset. The reconciliation is useful in assessing the adequacy of the allowance for impairment losses and enables comparison between entities.

IFRS 7 does not, however, specify components of the reconciliation. As the impairment for financial assets is determined differently from one entity to another, preparers are given flexibility in determining the most appropriate format for their needs. [IFRS 7.BC26]

For example, the reconciliation of the allowance account for credit losses may be presented with the following line items:

Opening balance	XX
Plus: impairment losses recognised	XX
Less: reversals of impairment losses	XX
Less: amounts written off during the year	XX
Plus/less: exchange gains and losses on foreign denominated items	XX
Less: unwind of discount	XX
Closing balance	XX

Entities may wish to expand on each of the above items. For instance:

- impairment losses recognised could be analysed between losses due to breach of contract, bankruptcy of the underlying debtor, adverse changes in payment status of borrowers and national or local economic conditions that correlate with defaults on the assets in the group and increases due to increases in effective interest rates (floating rate debt);
- reversals of impairment may similarly be analysed according to the underlying cause of the reversal; and
- amounts written off during the year may be analysed, for example, by type of exposure, type of client, geographical or industry segment.

The allowance account may be expanded to include any other items that the preparer of the financial statements considers to be material to the user's understanding of the financial statements.

US GAAP Comparison: FAS 114, *Accounting by Creditors for Impairment of a Loan,* provides disclosure requirements specific to impaired loans. While FAS 114 requires a similar reconciliation of impaired loans as depicted above, FAS 114 also requires the following to be disclosed regarding impaired loans: (1) the total recorded investment in impaired loans, (2) the amount of that recorded investment for which there is a related allowance for credit losses, (3) the amount of that recorded investment for which there is no related allowance for credit losses. In addition, FAS 114 requires a creditor to disclose its accounting policy for recognising interest income on impaired loans including how cash receipts are recorded. Finally, FAS 114 requires for each period presented, an entity to disclose the average recorded investment in impaired loans during the period, the related amount of interest income recognised on the impaired loan, and, unless not practicable, the amount of interest income recognised on an impaired loan using a cash-basis method of accounting.

Example 4.1.7

The extract below is an example of application of the requirements in IFRS 7.16 where an entity records impairment in a separate allowance account.

Extract from Deutsche Telekom Group Annual report 2008, p. 148:

18. Trade and other receivables (extract)

The following table shows the development of allowances on trade receivables:

millions of €	2008	2007
Allowances as of January 1	1,071	1,148
Currency translation adjustments	(7)	(8)
Additions (allowances recognized as expense)	547	662
Use	(437)	(510)
Reversal	(151)	(221)
Allowances as of December 31	1,023	1,071

The total additions of EUR 547 million (2007: EUR 662 million) relate to allowances for individual impairments of EUR 87 million (2007: EUR 144 million) and allowances for collective impairments of EUR 460 million (2007: EUR 518 million). Reversals were made of allowances for individual impairments of EUR 58 million (2007: EUR 85 million) and of allowances for collective impairments of EUR 84 million (2007: EUR 106 million).

4.1.8 Compound financial instruments with multiple embedded derivatives

IAS 32 prescribes how a compound financial instrument should be separated into its liability and equity components. For a compound financial instrument, the value of the debt or equity component may be affected by the other component. For instance, for convertible debt, the value of the debt component may depend in part on the relative attractiveness of early conversion. Hence, the aggregate fair value of the convertible bond could differ from the sum of the estimated fair values of the debt and equity components if these were valued independently of each other. IAS 32 assigns the full value of these interdependencies to the liability component and treats equity as the residual. This is arbitrary and can be argued to misstate the amount of the liability and thereby misstate the 'true' interest cost.

The interdependencies become even more significant when a compound instrument contains multiple embedded features whose values are also interdependent, e.g. the value of an embedded purchased call option and a written equity conversion option feature in a callable convertible debt instrument depend in part on each other as the equity conversion option is extinguished if the issuer exercises its purchased call option to redeem early, and vice versa, the value of the issuer purchased call option depends on the likelihood that the holder will exercise its right to convert early into shares. Because of the importance of these features, IFRS 7.17 requires an issuer of a compound instrument that has multiple embedded derivatives whose values are interdependent to disclose the existence of those features.

4.1.9 *Defaults and breaches*

For loans payable recognised at the end of the reporting period, disclosure is required of any defaults during the period of principal, interest, sinking fund, or redemption terms. In addition, the entity is required to disclose the carrying amount of any such loans that are in default at the end of the reporting period and whether the default was remedied, or the terms of the loans payable were renegotiated, before the financial statements were authorised for issue. [IFRS 7.18] Loans payable are defined as *'financial liabilities, other than short-term trade payables on normal credit terms'*. [IFRS 7(Appendix A)] It is important to note that disclosure of defaults is required of loans even where those defaults were rectified by the end of the reporting period.

If, during the period, there were breaches of loan agreement terms other than those described in the previous paragraph, the entity is required to disclose the same information as required above if those breaches permitted the lender to demand accelerated repayment (unless the breaches were remedied, or the terms of the loan were renegotiated, on or before the end of the reporting period). [IFRS 7.19] Examples of such defaults include breaches of collateral requirements or loan covenant features, or a failure to administer the loan in terms of the loan agreement.

Such disclosures are designed to provide the users with the relevant information about the entity's creditworthiness and its prospects of obtaining future loans. [IFRS 7.BC32]

The presentation of such loans as either current or non-current in accordance with the requirements of IAS 1 *Presentation of Financial Statements* may also be affected by such defaults.

4.2 Statement of comprehensive income disclosures

IFRS 7 requires disclosure of certain income, expense, gains or losses either in the statement of comprehensive income or in the notes to the financial statements.

4.2.1 *Net gains or net losses*

Disclosure of net gains or net losses is required for:
[IFRS 7.20(a)]

(i) financial assets or financial liabilities at fair value through profit or loss, showing separately those on financial assets or financial liabilities designated as such upon initial recognition, and those on financial assets or financial liabilities that are classified as held for trading in accordance with IAS 39;

(ii) available-for-sale financial assets, showing separately the amount of gain or loss recognised in other comprehensive income during the period and the amount reclassified from equity to profit or loss for the period;

(iii) held-to-maturity investments;

(iv) loans and receivables; and

(v) financial liabilities measured at amortised cost;

These disclosures are intended to assist users in understanding the extent to which accounting policies affect the performance of the entity and in understanding the nature of such gains and losses. [IFRS 7.BC33] The disclosures also provide useful financial information, together with the disclosures of the carrying amounts by category of financial instruments, which is designed to allow users to appraise management on the manner in which it has classified financial instruments and ultimately its decisions to buy, sell or hold financial assets and to incur, maintain or discharge financial liabilities.

IFRS 7.BC33 states that that the above disclosure of statement of comprehensive income "gains and losses by the measurement categories in IAS 39" complement the statement of financial position disclosures described in **4.1** above. Despite this claim it would appear that there is a difference between the requirements of the statement of financial position and statement of comprehensive income disclosures. As explained in **4.1** above IFRS 7.8 requires disclosure of the carrying amounts of: financial assets *and* financial liabilities designated at fair value through profit or loss upon initial recognition, as well as financial assets *and* financial liabilities classified as held for trading in accordance with IAS 39. The equivalent statement of comprehensive income disclosures refer to financial assets *or* financial liabilities. It is reasonable to presume this difference in wording was an oversight in the drafting and therefore an entity should disclose information on net gain or net losses in relation to *both* financial assets *and* financial liabilities.

Derivative financial instruments (or non-derivative financial instruments when hedging foreign currency risk) that have been designated as effective hedging instruments are not included in any of the financial instrument categories. Instead, the changes in fair values of those instruments will be reported in accordance with the hedge accounting disclosure requirements.

Example 4.2.1

The extract below is an example of application of the requirements in IFRS 7.20(a) requiring presentation of net gains and losses by category of financial instrument.

Extract from Deutsche Telekom Group Annual report 2008, p. 162:

27. Additional disclosures on financial instruments (extract)

Net gain/loss by measurement category

		From subsequent measurement				Net gain (loss)	
millions of €	From interest, dividends	At fair value	Currency translation	Impairment/ reversal of impairment	From derecognition	2008	2007
Loans and receivables (LaR)	162	n.a.	(956)	(782)	(1)	(1,577)	(2,083)
Held-to-maturity investments (HtM)	23	n.a.		(18)		5	9
Available-for-sale financial assets (AfS)	76			(11)	3	68	65
Financial instruments held for trading (FAHfT and FLHfT)	n.a.	383	n.a.	n.a.	383	(393)	
Financial liabilities measured at amortized cost (FLAC)	(2,757)	374	n.a.	(4)	(2,387)	(746)	
	(2,496)	383	(582)	(811)	(2)	(3,508)	(3,148)

Interest from financial instruments is recognized in finance costs, dividends in other financial income (please refer to Notes 7 and 9). Deutsche Telekom recognizes the other components of net gain/loss in other financial income/ expense, except for impairments/reversal of impairments of trade receivables (please refer to Note 18) that are classified as loans and receivables which are reported under selling expenses. The net gain from the subsequent measurement for financial instruments held for trading (EUR 383 million) also includes interest and currency translation effects. The net currency translation losses on financial assets classified as loans and receivables (EUR 956 million) are primarily attributable to the Group-internal transfer of foreign-currency loans taken out by Deutsche Telekom's financing company, Deutsche Telekom International Finance B.V., on the capital market. These were offset by corresponding currency translation gains on capital market liabilities of EUR 374 million. Finance costs from financial liabilities measured at amortized cost (EUR 2,757 million) primarily consist of interest expense on bonds and other (securitized) financial liabilities. The item also includes interest expenses from interest added back and interest income from interest discounted from trade payables. However, it does not include the interest expense and interest income from interest rate derivatives Deutsche Telekom used in the reporting period to hedge the fair value risk of financial liabilities (please refer to Note 7).

4.2.2 *Interest income and interest expense*

IFRS 7 requires disclosure of total interest income and total interest expense, determined using the effective interest method, for financial assets or financial liabilities that are not classified as at fair value through profit or loss. [IFRS 7.20(b)] Total interest expense is a component of the finance costs that are required to be disclosed as a line item in the statement of comprehensive income in accordance with IAS 1(2007).82(b) (previously IAS 1(2003).81(b)). Finance costs that are required to be disclosed in accordance with IAS 1 may also include amounts that arise on non-financial liabilities such as pension liabilities and income taxes. Separate disclosure of total interest expense allows the user to understand the extent to which financial instruments contribute to finance costs.

Example 4.2.2A

The extract below is an example of application of the requirements in IFRS 7.20(b) to present total interest income and total interest expense for financial instruments not at fair value through profit or loss.

Extract from Handelsbanken Annual Report 2008, p. 64:

G3 Net interest income

SEKm	2008	2007
Interest income		
Credit institutions and central banks	6,978	9,851
General public	75,272	56,636
Treasury bills and other eligible bills	3,948	2,301
Interest-bearing securities	7,024	9,195
Derivative instruments recognised as hedges	1,297	167
Other interest income	1,186	1,049
Total interest income	95,705	79,199
Of which interest expense reported in net gains/losses on financial items at fair value	12,350	13,975
Interest income according to income statement	83,355	65,224
Interest expense		
Credit institutions and central banks	-11,253	-15,172
General public	-16,809	-14,158
Issued securities	-32,374	-27,879
Derivative instruments recognised as hedges	-3,258	-239
Subordinated liabilities	-2,677	-2,748
Other interest expense	-8,557	-5,228
Total interest income, including trading-related	-74,928	-65,424
Of which interest expense reported in net gains/losses on financial items at fair value	-10,796	-15,808
Interest expense according to income statement	-64,132	-49,616
Net interest income	19,223	15,608

Includes interest income on bad debts SEK 113m (53).

- Total interest income on assets recognised at amortised cost and available-for-sale assets was SEK 77,029m (61,770).
- Total interest expense on liabilities recognised at amortised cost was SEK 46,214m (37,655).

Example 4.2.2B

The extract below is an example of application of the requirements in IFRS 7.20(b) to present total interest income and total interest expense for financial instruments not at fair value through profit or loss.

Extract from Nokia Annual Accounts 2008, p. 27:

10. Financial income and expenses

	2008 EURm	2007 EURm	2006 EURm
Dividend income on available-for-sale financial investments	1	–	–
Interest income on available-for-sale financial investments	353	338	225
Interest income on loans receivables carried at amortized cost	–	1	–
Interest expense on financial liabilities carried at amortized cost	(185)	(43)	(22)
Other financial income	17	43	55
Other financial expenses	(31)	(24)	(18)
Net foreign exchange gains (or losses)			
From foreign exchange derivatives designated at fair value through profit and loss account	432	37	75
From balance sheet items revaluation	(595)	(118)	(106)
Net gains (net losses) on other derivatives designated at fair value through profit and loss account	6	5	(2)
Total	(2)	239	207

During 2008, Nokia's interest expense increased significantly due to an increase in interest-bearing liabilities mainly related to financing of the NAVTEQ acquisition. Foreign exchange gains (or losses) increased due to a higher cost of hedging and increased volatility on the foreign exchange market.

4.2.3 *Fee income and expense*

IFRS 7 requires disclosure of fee income and expense, other than those amounts that are included in determining the effective interest rate, that arise from financial assets or financial liabilities that are not at fair value through profit or loss. Such items may include fee income earned as services are provided and fees that are earned on execution of a significant act. [IAS 18(Appendix Example 14(b) & (c)] In addition, disclosure is required of trust and other fiduciary activities that result in the holding or investing of assets on behalf of individuals, trusts, retirement benefit plans, and other institutions. [IFRS 7.20(c)] This information indicates the level of such activities and helps users to estimate possible future income of the entity. [IFRS 7.BC35]

The extent of disclosure will depend on the type of business. Lenders are likely to be subject to a significant level of disclosure. Examples of fees will include annual membership fee income for credit cards (payable irrespective of whether the card holder borrows using the card); interchange fees received each time a credit card is used; merchant service commission fees for processing debit and credit transactions; fees for withdrawing cash on a credit card; overdraft fee income received irrespective of whether the borrower utilises the overdraft facility, etc. Many fees with respect to specific borrowing and lending will meet the definition of a transaction cost and therefore will form part of the effective interest rate and thereby will not be subject to separate disclosure.

Example 4.2.3

The extract below is an example of application of the requirements in IFRS 7.20(c) to disclose fee income and expense

Extract from Close Brothers Annual Report 2008, p. 55:

3. Operating profit before tax (extract)

Fee income and expense (other than amounts calculated using the EIR method) on financial instruments that are not at fair value through profit and loss were £45.7 million (2007: £50.6 million) and £4.8 million (2007: £5.2 million). Fee income and expense arising from trust and other fiduciary activities amounted to £130.0 million (2007: £181.9 million) and £23.0 million (2007: £30.8 million).

4.2.4 *Interest on impaired financial assets*

Interest income on impaired financial assets is determined using the rate of interest used to discount the future cash flows for the purposes of measuring the impairment loss. [IFRS 7.20(d)]

The above requirement needs careful consideration in the case of financial assets impaired on a portfolio basis (see **6.2.4** in **chapter 6**).

If a loan within a portfolio is not individually assessed as being impaired, but is impaired on a collective basis prior to the loan being individually identified, and all cash flows with respect to the impaired loan are not recoverable, then no interest income will be disclosed in accordance with IFRS 7.20(d). In this case, following the impairment loss, there is no interest income on the loan that remains unidentified in the portfolio that is fully impaired (since no cash flows are expected).

In contrast, the entity may determine that an impairment loss is required in the instance where some, but not all, cash flows on unidentified loans are not recoverable. For disclosure of interest recognition post impairment the entity should use the effective interest rate that was applied in discounting the cash flows in determining the impairment loss. Even though the loans that are impaired are not identified yet, the entity is still required to disclose the amount of interest on the portfolio of loans that is impaired.

If an impairment loss is recognised in the period but is reversed prior to the period end an entity should still disclose the interest that arose during the part of the reporting period that the loan was impaired. As interest will be recognised throughout the instrument's life the entity will need to isolate the period immediately following the impairment event and prior to the impairment loss being reversed and determine the interest that was recognised during that period.

4.2.5 *Impairment losses*

IFRS requires disclosure of the amount of any impairment loss for each class of financial asset. [IFRS 7.20(e)] These amounts may be combined with the disclosures that are required for the allowance account mentioned above.

Example 4.2.5

The extract below is an example of application of the requirements in IFRS 7.20(e) to present impairment losses by class of financial asset

Extract from Barclays Bank Annual Accounts and Report 2008, p. 127:

48 Credit risk (extract)

The Group	At beginning of year £m	Acquisitions and disposals £m	Unwind of discount £m	Exchange and other adjustments £m	Amounts written off £m	Recoveries £m	Amounts charged to profit £m	Balance at 31st December £m
			2008					
Loans and advances to banks	3	–	–	1	–	7	40	51
Loans and advances to customers:								
Residential mortgage loans	132	–	(35)	19	(44)	3	232	307
Credit card receivables	8641	306	(68)	94	(845)	69	1,048	1,445
Other personal lending	1,373	1	(32)	134	(525)	42	890	1,883
Wholesale and corporate loans and advances	1,310	–	–	506	(1,428)	41	2,270	2,699
Finance lease receivables	113	–	–	37	(77)	12	104	189
Total loans and advances to customers	3,379	307	(135)	790	(2,919)	167	4.544	6,523
Total impairment allowance	3,772	307	(135)	791	(2,919)	174	4,584	6,574

4.3 Other disclosures

4.3.1 Accounting policies

IAS 1 requires disclosure of the measurement bases used in preparing the financial statements and the other accounting policies used that are relevant to an understanding of the financial statements. For financial instruments these would normally include:
[IFRS 7.B5]

(a) for financial assets or financial liabilities designated as at fair value through profit or loss:

  (i) the nature of the financial assets or financial liabilities that have been designated as at fair value through profit or loss;

  (ii) the criteria for so designating financial assets or financial liabilities on initial recognition; and

(iii) how the entity has satisfied the criteria in IAS 39 for such designation. That disclosure includes a narrative description of the circumstances underlying the measurement or recognition inconsistency that would otherwise arise and a narrative description of how designation at fair value through profit or loss is consistent with the entity's documented risk management or investment strategy where applicable.

US GAAP Comparison: Similar to IFRS, FAS 159, *The Fair Value Option for Financial Assets and Financial Liabilities*, provides specific disclosures regarding management's reasons for electing the fair value option for specific assets or liabilities. However, unlike IFRS, when the fair value option is elected under FAS 159 for some but not all eligible items within a group of similar eligible items, an entity must disclose (1) a description of items not elected at fair value, (2) why management did not elect to measure the entire group at fair value, and (3) the individual line items in the statement of financial position where the group of similar items is presented. Similarly, for each line item in the statement of financial position that includes an item or items that are measured at fair value under the fair value option, an entity is required to disclose the aggregate carrying amount of those items that are not carried at fair value.

Example 4.3.1A

The extract below is an example of application of the requirements in IFRS 7.B5(a) to disclose the nature of financial assets and liabilities designated as at fair value through profit or loss, as well as the criteria for designating such items

Extract from FirstRand Annual Report 2008 p.180

15.1.1 Financial instruments at fair value through profit or loss

This category has two sub categories: financial instruments held for trading, and those designated at fair value through profit or loss at inception.

A financial instrument is classified as a trading instrument if acquired principally for the purpose of selling in the short term or if it forms part of a portfolio of financial assets in which there is evidence of short term profit taking. Derivatives are also categorised as held for trading unless they are designated as effective hedges.

Financial assets and liabilities are designated on initial recognition as at fair value through profit and loss to the extent that it produces more relevant information because it either:

i. results in the reduction of measurement inconsistency [or accounting mismatch] that would arise as a result of measuring assets and liabilities and the gains and losses on them on a different basis; or

ii. is a group of financial assets and/or financial liabilities that is managed and its performance is evaluated on a fair value basis, in accordance with a documented risk management or investment strategy, and this is the basis on which information about the assets and/or liabilities is provided internally to the entity's key management personnel; or

iii. is a financial asset or liability containing significant embedded derivatives that clearly require bifurcation.

The main financial assets and liabilities designated at fair value through profit and loss under criteria [i] are:

- Various loans to customers, structured notes and other investments that form part of the Merchant Banking division. These financial instruments have been designated to eliminate the accounting mismatch between these assets and the underlying derivatives and funding instruments. If the assets were not designated at fair value, the mismatch would be as a result of the assets being recognised at amortised cost and the derivatives and funding instruments being recognised at fair value.
- Policyholder assets and liabilities under investment contracts. The liabilities under linked investment contracts have cash flows that are contractually determined with reference to the performance of the underlying assets. The changes in fair value of assets held in linked funds are recognised in the income statement. Liabilities to customers under other types of investment contracts are measured at amortised cost. If these assets were not designated on initial recognition, they would be classified as available-for-sale and the changes in their fair value would be recognised directly in equity. This would result in a significant accounting mismatch, as the movements in the fair value of the policyholder liability are recognised directly in the income statement.

Financial instruments designated under criteria [ii], include:

- certain private equity and other investment securities; and
- financial assets held to meet liabilities under insurance contracts.

The amount of change in the fair value, during the period and cumulatively, of designated loans and receivables and designated financial liabilities that is attributable to changes in credit risk, is determined as the amount of change in fair value that is not attributable to changes in market conditions that give rise to market risk, i e currency, interest rate and other price risk.

(b) the criteria for designating financial assets as available for sale;

Example 4.3.1B

The extract below is an example of disclosure of an accounting policy for designating financial instruments as available-for-sale assets

Extract from UBS Annual Report 2008, p.266

8) Financial investments available-for-sale (extract)

Financial investments available-for-sale are non-derivative financial assets that are not classified as held for trading, designated at fair value through profit or loss, or loans and receivables. They are recognized or a settlement date basis. Financial investments available-for-sale include strategic equity investments as well as instruments that, in management's opinion, may be sold in response to or in anticipation of needs for liquidity or changes in interest rates, foreign exchange rates or equity prices. Financial investments available-for-sale consist mainly of equity instruments, including certain

> private equity investments. In addition, certain debt instruments and non-performing loans acquired in the secondary market are classified as financial investments available-for-sale.

(c) whether regular way purchases and sales of financial assets are accounted for at trade date or at settlement date;

> **Example 4.3.1C**
>
> *The extract below is an example of application of the requirements in IFRS 7.B5(c) in disclosing the accounting policy for regular way transactions*
>
> *Extract from Anglo Irish Bank Annual Report and Accounts 2008 p. 41:*
>
> Purchases and sales of financial assets at fair value through profit or loss, held-to-maturity investments and available-for-sale financial assets are recognised on a trade date basis, being the date on which the Group commits to purchase or sell the asset. Loans and receivables are recognised when funds are advanced to the borrowers. Financial assets are initially recognised at fair value plus directly attributable transaction costs, with the exception of financial assets carried at fair value through profit or loss whose transaction costs are taken directly to the income statement. Financial assets are derecognised when the rights to receive cash flows from the financial assets have expired or where the Group has transferred substantially all the risks and rewards of ownership.

(d) when an allowance account is used to reduce the carrying amount of financial assets impaired by credit losses:

 (i) the criteria for determining when the carrying amount of impaired financial assets is reduced directly (or, in the case of a reversal of a write-down, increased directly) and when the allowance account is used; and

 (ii) the criteria for writing off amounts charged to the allowance account against the carrying amount of impaired financial assets;

(e) how net gains or net losses on each category of financial instrument are determined, for example, whether the net gains or net losses on items at fair value through profit or loss include interest or dividend income;

> It appears that the objective of the Standard in requiring an entity to disclose whether interest or dividends are shown separately from other fair value gains/losses was to make clear how interest and dividends were presented in income for non-derivative instruments that are carried at FVTPL. It is reasonable that if a derivative is not in a qualifying hedge relationship and is therefore is classified as a held for trading instrument, its fair value is a single number recognised in income and should not be split further across other profit or loss captions. This view is consistent with the SEC's view of US GAAP

that if a derivative does not qualify for hedge accounting, income, expenses, and fair value changes related to that derivative (whether realised or unrealised) must be recorded in one line item in the financial statements and this line item must not change.

For non-derivative financial instruments carried at FVTPL, some entities include interest income and expense and dividend income in gains and losses on financial assets and financial liabilities respectively and others include them in separate line items for interest and dividends. The disclosure of whether net gains and losses on financial assets or financial liabilities that are carried as at FVTPL include interest income and expense or dividend income is designed to aid comparability between entities.

It seems reasonable to have a separate policy for interest-bearing instruments, such as debt, and non-interest bearing instruments that earn a dividend, such as equity securities, but it is not acceptable to have a separate policy for interest bearing assets and a separate policy for interesting bearing liabilities as this would have the appearance of overstating or understating interest income and expense.

(f) the criteria the entity uses to determine that there is objective evidence that an impairment loss has occurred;

Example 4.3.1D

The extract below is an example of application of the requirements in IFRS 7.B5(f) in disclosing the criteria for determining objective evidence for impairment losses

Extract from RBS Annual Report and Accounts 2008, p. 183, 185–6:

16. Impairment of financial assets

The Group assesses at each balance sheet date whether there is any objective evidence that a financial asset or group of financial assets classified as held-to-maturity, available-for-sale or loans and receivables is impaired. A financial asset or portfolio of financial assets is impaired and an impairment loss incurred if there is objective evidence that an event or events since initial recognition of the asset have adversely affected the amount or timing of future cash flows from the asset.

Financial assets carried at amortised cost – if there is objective evidence that an impairment loss on a financial asset or group of financial assets classified as loans and receivables or as held-to-maturity investments has been incurred, the Group measures the amount of the loss as the difference between the carrying amount of the asset or group of assets and the present value of estimated future cash flows from the asset or group of assets discounted at the effective interest rate of the instrument at initial recognition.

Impairment losses are assessed individually for financial assets that are individually significant and individually or collectively for assets that are not individually significant. In making collective assessment of impairment, financial assets are grouped into portfolios on the basis of similar risk characteristics Future cash flows from these portfolios are estimated on the basis of the contractual cash flows and historical loss experience for assets with similar credit risk characteristics. Historical loss experience is adjusted, on the basis of current observable data, to reflect the effects of current conditions not affecting the period of historical experience.

Impairment losses are recognised in profit or loss and the carrying amount of the financial asset or group of financial assets reduced by establishing an allowance for impairment losses. If, in a subsequent period, the amount of the impairment loss reduces and the reduction can be ascribed to an event after the impairment was recognised, the previously recognised loss is reversed by adjusting the allowance. Once an impairment loss has been recognised on a financial asset or group of financial assets, interest income is recognised on the carrying amount using the rate of interest at which estimated future cash flows were discounted in measuring impairment.

Critical accounting policies and key sources of estimation uncertainty (extract)

Loan impairment provisions

The Group's loan impairment provisions are established to recognise incurred impairment losses in its portfolio of loans classified as loans and receivables and carried at amortised cost. A loan is impaired when there is objective evidence that events since the loan was granted have affected expected cash flows from the loan. The impairment loss is the difference between the carrying value of the loan and the present value of estimated future cash flows at the loan's original effective interest rate.

At 31 December 2008, gross loans and advances to customers totalled £885,611 million (2007 -£834,987 million) and customer loan impairment provisions amounted to £10,889 million (2007 – £6,449 million).

There are two components to the Group's loan impairment provisions: individual and collective.

Individual component – all impaired loans that exceed specific thresholds are individually assessed for impairment. Individually assessed loans principally comprise the Group's portfolio of commercial loans to medium and large businesses. Impairment losses are recognised as the difference between the carrying value of the loan and the discounted value of management's best estimate of future cash repayments and proceeds from any security held. These estimates take into account the customer's debt capacity and financial flexibility; the level and quality of its earnings; the amount and sources of cash flows; the industry in which the counterparty operates; and the realisable value of any security held. Estimating the quantum and timing of future recoveries involves significant judgement. The size of receipts will depend on the future performance of the borrower and the value of security both of which will be affected by future economic conditions; additionally, collateral may not be readily marketable. The actual amount of future cash flows and the date they are received may differ from these estimates and consequently actual losses incurred may differ from those recognised in these financial statements.

Collective component – this is made up of two elements: loan impairment provisions for impaired loans that are below individual assessment thresholds (collective impaired ban provisions) and for loan losses that have been incurred but have not been separately identified at the balance sheet date (latent loss provisions). These are established on a portfolio basis using a present value methodology taking into account the level of arrears, security, past loss experience, credit scores and defaults based on portfolio trends. The most significant factors in establishing these provisions are the expected loss rates and the related average life. These portfolios include credit card receivables and other personal advances including mortgages. The future credit quality of these portfolios is subject to uncertainties that could cause actual credit losses to differ materially from reported loan impairment provisions. These uncertainties include the economic environment, notably interest rates and their effect on customer spending, the unemployment level, payment behaviour and bankruptcy trends.

(g) when the terms of financial assets that would otherwise be past due or impaired have been renegotiated, the accounting policy for financial assets that are the subject of renegotiated terms.

The disclosure required is the entity's policy as to how it accounts for renegotiated debt assets, specifically how it determines whether the renegotiated debt is considered new debt and therefore old debt is derecognised, or whether it is considered the original debt with the original effective interest rate and the carrying amount adjusted according to IAS 39.AG8 at the date of renegotiation. This disclosure would be relevant since the only guidance in IFRSs on the accounting for debt modifications is with respect to financial liabilities in IAS 39.40 & AG62, whilst no guidance is provided for financial assets other than in the case of impairment. [IAS 39.IG.E.4.3]

Information that includes a description of the manner in which debt is renegotiated and the terms and conditions of the renegotiated debt may also provide valuable information.

4.3.2 *Hedge accounting*

Disclosures are required for entities that apply hedge accounting in accordance with IAS 39. [IFRS 7.22–24]

Hedging activities are integral to an entity's financial risk management and are often significant. Hedge accounting for such activities is a matter of choice under IAS 39 and this accounting choice can have a significant impact on the financial statements. In the absence of hedge accounting, changes in the fair value of all derivatives are reflected in profit or loss as they arise, often creating a mismatch with the timing of recognition of the gains and losses on the exposure that is being hedged. Hedge accounting corrects this measurement or recognition mismatch.

Hedge accounting disclosures are provided to allow the user to understand the nature of the entities' hedge relationships and the effect that those hedge relationships had on the performance of the entity both during the current period and what is expected in future periods.

For each type of hedge accounting that is applied (fair value hedge, cash flow hedge, or a hedge of net investment in a foreign operation), the entity must disclose the following:
[IFRS 7.22]

(a) a description of each type of hedge;

(b) a description of the financial instruments designated as hedging instruments and their fair values at the end of the reporting period; and

(c) the nature of the risks being hedged.

Additional disclosures are required for cash flow hedges as the entity has to make significant judgements about the expectation of future cash flows that are being hedged. Also, as cash flow hedging requires recognition of gains/losses in other comprehensive income and frequent reclassification from equity to profit or loss, the Standard requires these amounts to be transparent. An entity shall disclose:
[IFRS 7.23]

(a) the periods when the cash flows are expected to occur and when they are expected to affect profit or loss;

(b) a description of any forecast transaction for which hedge accounting had previously been used, but which is no longer expected to occur;

(c) the amount that was recognised in other comprehensive income during the period;

(d) the amount that was reclassified from equity to profit or loss for the period, showing the amount included in each line item in the statement of comprehensive income; and

(e) the amount that was removed from equity during the period and included in the initial cost or other carrying amount of a non-financial asset or a non-financial liability whose acquisition or incurrence was a hedged highly probable forecast transaction.

IFRS 7 requires an entity to disclose the extent to which hedge accounting has been effective in the period. For cash flow hedges and hedges of a net investment in a foreign operation, the amount of ineffectiveness may be disclosed either in the statement of comprehensive income (as all hedge ineffectiveness is recognised in profit or loss), or alternately in a note to the financial statements.

The disclosure requirements for fair value hedges are somewhat different, although the objective of disclosing hedge ineffectiveness is the same. In a fair value hedge, the gain or loss on the hedging instrument and the gain or loss on the hedged item are immediately recognised in profit or loss in all periods. The net of these amounts is equivalent to the hedge ineffectiveness that is recognised in profit or loss in the period. IFRS 7, therefore, requires an entity to disclose separately the gains or losses on the hedging instrument and on the hedged item that are attributable to the hedged risk. [IFRS 7.24] This may be disclosed either in the statement of comprehensive income or alternatively in a note to the financial statements.

If a fair value hedge is not highly effective, i.e. hedge effectiveness is outside the 80–125 per cent range, then hedge accounting cannot be applied for the period. The entity has not achieved hedge accounting and, therefore, is not required to disclose hedge ineffectiveness for that period with respect to that designated hedge.

For cash flow hedges and hedges of a net investment in a foreign operation if the hedge is not highly effective in the period, i.e. it is outside the 80–125 per cent range, hedge accounting is not applied in the period. The gains or losses on the hedging instrument will be recognised directly in profit or loss. The entity is not required to disclose hedge ineffectiveness. If previously designated forecast transactions are no longer expected to occur, this will generally result in reclassification from equity to profit or loss for some or all of the cumulative gains/losses brought forward from the prior period recognised in other comprehensive income (and accumulated in the cash flow hedging reserve in equity). This amount must be disclosed along with the other disclosures listed above.

US GAAP comparison: FAS 161, *Disclosures about Derivative Instruments and Hedging Activities* (*an amendment to FAS 133*), was issued in March 2008 and significantly amends the FAS 133 disclosure requirements specific to derivative instruments and hedging activities. FAS 161 is effective for fiscal years and interim periods beginning after November 15, 2008 and early application is encouraged. FAS 161 applies prospectively; however, comparative disclosure for earlier periods at initial adoption is also encouraged. The disclosure requirements in FAS 161 related to an entity's hedging activities are very similar to the disclosure requirements in IFRS 7. However, FAS 161 requires more extensive disclosures regarding general derivative activity relative to IFRS 7. For example, FAS 161 requires disclosure of an entity's derivative activity (whether part of a hedging relationship or not) be segregated by each instruments' primary underlying risk exposure (e.g. interest rate, credit, foreign exchange, interest and foreign exchange, or overall price risk). In addition, FAS 161 requires detailed tabular disclosures of the location and fair value amounts of derivatives instruments reported in the balance sheet and the change in value of those instruments included in the income statement. Further, under FAS 161, the effect of derivative instruments on the income statement is required to be segregated in tabular disclosure by (1) instruments that are designated in hedging relationships, and (2) instruments that are not designated in hedging relationships. For those instruments designated in hedging relationships, FAS 161 requires disclosure by (1) the type of hedging relationship (cash flows, fair value, net investment hedges), and (2) the type of derivative instrument (e.g., interest rate swap, forward, and option).

Example 4.3.2

The extract below is an example of application of the requirements in IFRS 7.22–24 to disclose information on hedge accounting

Extract from SEB Annual Report 2008, pp.72–3, 81–2

Hedge accounting

Hedge accounting is applied to derivatives used to reduce risks such as interest rate risks and currency risks in financial instruments and net investments in subsidiaries. The Group documents and designates at inception the relationship between hedged item and hedging instrument as well as the risk objective and hedge strategy. The Group also documents its assessment both at inception and on an ongoing basis whether prospectively the derivatives used are expected to be, and are highly effective when assessed retrospectively, in offsetting changes in fair values or cash flows of hedged item. The Group also assesses and documents that the likelihood of forecasted transactions to take place is highly probable.

The Group designates derivatives as either:

- hedges of the fair value of recognised assets or liabilities of firm commitments (fair value hedge)
- hedges of the fair value of the interest risk of a portfolio (macro hedging)
- hedges of highly probable future cash flows attributable to recognised assets or liabilities or a forecasted transaction (cash flow hedge)
- hedges of a net investment in a foreign operation (net investment hedge).

Fair value hedge

Fair value hedge is the hedging of exposure to changes in the fair value of an asset or a liability, or an identifiable component of such asset or liability, which is attributable to a certain risk that could affect the profit or loss. Changes in the fair value of derivatives that are designated and qualify as fair value hedges are recorded in the income statement together with changes in the fair value of the hedged item that are attributable to the hedged risk.

Where the Group hedges the fair value of interest rate exposure in a portfolio including financial assets or financial liabilities, so called portfolio hedging of interest rate risk, the gains or losses attributable to the hedged item are reported as a separate item under assets or as a separate item under liabilities in the balance sheet. The group applies the EU carve out version of IAS 39 for portfolio hedges of both assets and liabilities.

Fair value hedges are discontinued in the following situations:

- The hedging instrument expires or is sold, terminated or exercised
- The hedging relationship no longer meets the criteria for hedge accounting
- The hedging relationship is discontinued.

When hedge relationships are discontinued, any adjustment to the carrying amount of the hedged item is amortised to profit or loss over the period to maturity of the hedged item.

Cash flow hedge

Cash flow hedging is applied for the hedging of exposure to variations in future interest payments on assets or liabilities with variable interest rates. The portion of the gain or loss on the hedging instrument that is determined to be an effective hedge is recognised directly against equity. The ineffective portion of the gain or loss on the hedging instrument is recognised in profit or loss.

Gains or losses on hedging instruments reported directly against equity are recognised in profit or loss in the same period as interest income and interest expense from the hedged asset or liability.

Cash flow hedges are discontinued in the same situations as listed above regarding the termination of fair value hedges. When cash flow hedges are discontinued but future cash-flows still are expected to occur, accumulated gains or losses from the hedging instrument will remain as a separate item in equity. Accumulated gains or losses are subsequently reported in profit or loss in the same period in which the previously hedged interest flows are recognised in profit or loss.

Net investment hedge

The hedging of a net investment in a foreign operation refers to the hedge of equity in a foreign subsidiary against foreign exchange fluctuations. This type of hedge is accounted for similarly to cash flow hedges. Gains or losses on the hedging instrument attributable to the effective portion of the hedge are recognised in equity whilst the ineffective portion is recognised directly in profit or loss. Gains or losses accumulated in equity are included in profit or loss at the disposal of the foreign operation.

Fair value adjustment in hedge accounting

Fair value changes of the hedged items attributable to the hedged risk	–5,374	–1,363	–4,519	–854
Fair value changes of the hedging derivatives	4,831	907	4,417	842
Fair value hedges – ineffective portion	–543	–456	–102	–12
Fair value changes of the hedging derivatives	15	–14	15	–14
Cash-flow hedges – ineffective portion	15	–14	15	–14
Fair value changes of the hedged items	2,404	–691		
Fair value changes of the hedging derivatives	–1,922	1,029		
Fair value portfolio hedge of interest rate risk – ineffective portion	482	338		
Total	–46	–132	–87	–26

Fair value hedges and fair value portfolio hedges

The Group hedges a proportion of its existing interest rate risk, in financial assets payments and financial liabilities with fixed interest rates, against changes in fair value due to changes in the interest rates. For this purpose the Group uses interest rate swaps, cross-currency interest rate swaps and in some situations also options. The hedges are done either on an item by item or grouped by maturity basis.

Cash flow hedges

The Group uses interest rate swaps to hedge future cash flows from deposits and lending with floating interest rates. Interest flows from deposits and lending with floating interest rates are expected to be amortised in profit or loss during the period 2009 to 2037.

Net investment hedges

The Group hedges the currency translation risk of net investments in foreign operations through currency borrowings and currency forwards. Borrowing in foreign currency to an amount of SEK 55,899m (53,260) and currency forwards to an amount of SEK 4,486m (349) was designated as hedges of net investments in foreign operations. Ineffectiveness has been recognised with SEK -85m reported in Net financial income (note 5).

4.3.3 *Fair value*

Fair value information is required to be provided for all financial assets and liabilities (with limited exceptions) irrespective of whether they are carried at value or not. IFRS 7 requires an entity to group financial assets and financial liabilities into classes and provide fair value disclosures that permit comparability with the carrying amounts. An entity shall disclose how each class of financial asset and financial liabilities are fair valued, with particular emphasis on the use of valuation techniques. For financial instruments that are carried at fair value the disclosures are required to be provided by reference to the fair value hierarchy, with particular emphasis placed on instruments where fair value is not based on observable market data. Finally, an entity shall provide specific disclosures on 'day 1 profit or loss'.

4.3.3.1 *Fair value versus carrying value*

Fair value disclosures should be provided for each class of financial asset and financial liability, in a way that allows a comparison to be made to the corresponding carrying amounts in the statement of financial position. [IFRS 7.25] Financial assets and financial liabilities should be grouped into appropriate classes, but shall only be offset to the extent that their carrying amounts are offset in the statement of financial position. [IFRS 7.26]

Fair values reflect the financial markets' judgement about the present value of expected future cash flows from a financial instrument, and therefore provide a neutral basis of assessing management's decision to enter into financial instruments. Fair value information need not be disclosed for those financial instruments whose carrying amount reasonably approximates fair value, as is the case for most short-term trade receivables and payables. Additional exceptions exist for investments in unquoted equity instruments and derivatives linked to unquoted equity instruments when their fair value cannot be measured reliably, and contracts that contain a discretionary participation feature if their fair value cannot be measured reliably. [IFRS 7.29] However, where fair value cannot be measured reliably, additional disclosures are required to assist users of the financial statements in making their own judgements about the extent of possible differences between the carrying amount of those financial assets or financial liabilities and their fair value. These disclosures include a statement that fair value disclosure has not been provided as fair value cannot be measured reliably, a description of the instrument, its carrying amount, an explanation of why fair value cannot be measured reliably, information about the market for the instruments, and information about whether and how the entity intends to dispose of the financial instruments. Furthermore, if such instruments are subsequently derecognised, disclosures should be provided of the carrying amount at the date of disposal, the fact that fair value could not be reliably measured, and the gain or loss that results. [IFRS 7.30]

As noted above, IFRS 7 permits an entity to omit the fair value disclosure for derivatives that are *linked to equity instruments* that do not have a quoted market price in an active market and are measured at cost in accordance with IAS 39. It is worth noting that IAS 39.46 states that derivatives that are *linked to and must be settled by delivery of such unquoted equity instruments*, [emphasis added] shall be measured at cost. Thus, there is a difference in wording between the disclosure requirements of IFRS 7 and the measurement requirements of IAS 39. IAS 39 requires delivery of the unquoted equity instrument whereas IFRS 7 does not. However, while there is a difference in wording, the exception in IFRS 7 is not wider than in IAS 39 as a derivative that is linked to, but is not settled by the delivery of an unquoted equity is measured at fair value in accordance with IAS 39.

In the case of compound financial instruments (i.e. an instrument including a financial liability and equity component as described in **section 3** in **chapter 3**) the fair value disclosure will relate only to the financial liability component of the compound instrument as the equity component is scoped out of IFRS 7 (see **section 2** above). The fair value of the financial liability component will incorporate interest rate risk and the entity's own credit risk but will exclude any consideration of equity price risk.

Example 4.3.3.1A

Entity B (31 March 20X1)

	31 March 20X1		31 March 20X0	
Investments	**Carrying amount CUm**	**Fair value CUm**	**Carrying amount CUm**	**Fair value CUm**
Loans and receivables	3,428	3,543	5,200	5,602
Held-to-maturity investments	6,870	7,243	9,304	9,730

The assumptions used to estimate current fair values of investments are summarised below.

(i) For short-term loans and receivables (e.g. trade receivables) the carrying amount approximates to fair value because of their short maturities.

(ii) For long-term loans and receivables where the market rate of interest for that specific issuer is not readily determinable (e.g. non-quoted corporate debt issued by non-quoted companies), fair value has been calculated by discounting the future cash flows at the market rate of interest for a similar issuer with the same credit quality.

(iii) The fair values of held-to-maturity quoted corporate debt are derived from their external quoted prices.

	At 31 March 20X1		At 31 March 20X0	
Fair value of financial liabilities	**Carrying amount CUm**	**Fair value CUm**	**Carrying amount CUm**	**Fair value CUm**
Short-term creditors and borrowings	631	631	907	907
Current portion of long-term debt				
Bank Loans	50	52	32	31
Eurobonds	70	74	45	44
Sterling bond 20X1	82	84	52	50
Total current portion of long-term debt	202	210	129	125
Non-current portion of long-term debt				
Eurobonds	590	640	361	385
Sterling bond 20X1	674	732	413	441
European Investment Bank Loans	421	457	258	275
Total long-term debt	1,685	1,829	1,032	1,101

The assumptions used to estimate current fair values of debt and other financial instruments are summarised below:

(i) For short-term creditors and short-term borrowings (e.g. commercial paper and short-term borrowings under committed facilities) the carrying amount approximates to fair value because of their short maturities.

(ii) The fair values of the Sterling bond 20X1 and Bank loans have been calculated by discounting their future cash flows at the market rate that reflects current interest rates and current spreads for the entity.

(iii) The fair values of the Eurobonds have been derived from their external quoted prices.

Example 4.3.3.1B

The extract below is an example of the application of the requirements in IFRS 7.25 to disclose by class the fair value of financial instruments not measured at fair value

Extracts from UBS Annual Report 2008, pp. 324–5:

Financial instruments accounted for at amortized cost

The following table reflects the estimated fair values for the Group's instruments accounted for at amortized cost. Refer to Note 29 for an overview of financial assets classified as 'loans and receivables' and financial liabilities accounted for at amortized cost.

	31.12.08	
CHF billion	Carrying value	Fair value
Assets		
Loans to banks and customers	403.0	402.6
Cash collateral on securities borrowed and reverse repurchase agreements	347.5	347.7
Accrued income and prepaid expenses, other assets	9.4	9.4
Liabilities		
Due to banks and customers	600.4	600.4
Cash collateral on securities lent and repurchase agreements	116.6	116.6
Debt issued	201.2	199.7
Accrued expenses and deferred income, other liabilities	22.8	22.8

The fair values included in the table above were calculated for disclosure purposes only. The valuation techniques and assumptions described below provide a measurement of fair value of UBS's financial instruments accounted for at amortized cost. However, because other institutions may use different methods and assumptions for their fair value estimation, such fair value disclosures cannot necessarily be compared from one financial institution to another. UBS applies significant judgments and assumptions to arrive at these fair values, which are more holistic and less sophisticated than UBS's established fair value and model governance policies and processes applied for financial instruments accounted for at fair value, whose fair values impact UBS's balance sheet and net profit. Debt instruments reclassified in fourth quarter 2008 from 'held for trading' to 'loans and receivables' followed the same fair value measurement principles and governance policies as financial instruments accounted for at fair value. The following principles were applied when determining fair value estimates for financial instruments accounted for at amortized cost

- For short-term financial instruments with remaining maturities of one year or less, the carrying amount, which is net of credit loss allowances, is generally considered a reasonable estimate of fair value. The following financial instruments accounted for at amortized cost have remaining maturities of one year or less:

  100% of cash collateral on securities borrowed and reverse repurchase agreements; 97% of loans cue from banks; 61% of loans to customers; 98% or amounts due to banks and customers; 99% cash collateral on securities lent and repurchase agreements; 60% of debt issued. Refer to the chapter 'Liquidity and funding management' in the 'Risk and treasury management' section of this report.

- The fair value of variable-interest bearing financial instruments accounted for at amortized cost is assumed to be approximated by their carrying amounts, which are net of credit loss allowances, and does not reflect fair value changes in the credit quality of counterparties respectively UBS's own credit movements.

- For fixed-interest bearing financial instruments with remaining maturities above one year, fair value was estimated by discounting contractual cash flows using current rates at which similar cans would be transacted to borrowers with similar credit ratings and/or collateral and for the same remaining maturities. These estimates generally include adjustments for counterparty credit respectively UBS's own credit.

- The fair value estimates for repurchase and reverse repurchase agreements with variable and fixed interest rates, for all maturities, include the valuation of the interest rate component of these instrument. Credit and debit valuation adjustments nave not been included into the valuation due to the short-term nature of these instruments.
- For loans to customers from Global Wealth Management & Business Banking, many reflecting the impact of the Swiss Mortgage can portfolio with a fixed rate of interest, an excess of fair value over the carrying amount of CHF 3.0 billion was determined. This amount is largely attributable to the current CHF interest rate movements, which are significantly below the average levels over the last decade. The fair values of UBS's Investment Bank's loans to customers were CHF 3.4 billion below their carrying values, mainly reflecting credit valuation adjustments for debt instruments reclassified from 'held for trading' to 'loans and receivables' in fourth quarter 2008.
- For debt issued with remaining maturities greater than one year, the fair value was determined from quoted market prices, where available. Where quoted market prices were not available the fair value was derived by discounting contractual cash flows by using rates at which UBS could issue debt with similar remaining maturities. Adjustments for own credit movements have been included into fair value estimation.

The fair value of loans to banks and customers measured at amortized cost at 31 December 2007 was CHF 392.3 billion (carrying value: CHF 395.3 billion). The fair value of debt issued measured at amortized cost at 31 December 2007 was CHF 222.7 billion (carrying value: CHF 222.0 billion).

The fair values of UBS's fixed rate loans, long- and medium-term notes and bonds issued are predominantly hedged by derivative instruments. Refer to Note 23 and Note 1. The interest rate risk inherent in balance sheet positions with no specific maturity may also be hedged with derivative instruments based on management's view of their average cash flow and repricing behaviour.

4.3.3.2 *Fair value hierarchy*

Methods applied in fair valuing financial instruments are required to be disclosed by class of financial instruments. Where a valuation technique is used, disclosure of the assumptions used in determining fair value is required. This disclosure shall include information on, amongst others, prepayment rates, rates of estimated credit losses, and interest rates or discount rates. If there has been a change in valuation technique, the entity shall disclose that change and the reasons for making it. [IFRS 7(2009).27]

Disclosure of the method and significant assumptions used is very important as the use of valuation models inevitably involves a significant degree of judgement. Users of the financial statements should be in a position to understand the subjective and judgemental nature of the fair value numbers and to judge for themselves whether the assumptions made by management are reasonable.

The amendments to IFRS 7 issued in March 2009, *Improving Disclosures about Financial Instruments*, introduced a fair value hierarchy to be used in providing fair value disclosures for financial instruments carried at fair value in the statement of financial position. The hierarchy was noted as being useful by the IASB's Expert Advisory Panel in their report issued in October 2008, *Measuring and disclosing the fair value of financial instruments in markets that are no longer active*, as it was applied voluntarily by some financial institutions reporting under IFRS, and also applied by US GAAP entities following the requirements of FAS 157, *Fair value measurement*. For disclosure purposes the fair valuation hierarchy in IFRS 7(2009).27A has three levels:

Level	**Description**
Level 1	quoted prices (unadjusted) in active markets for identical assets or liabilities
Level 2	inputs other than quoted prices included within Level 1 that are observable for the asset or liability, either directly (i.e. as price) or indirectly (i.e. derived from prices)
Level 3	inputs for the asset or liability that are not based on observable market data (unobservable inputs)

The level in the fair value hierarchy within which the fair value of a financial instrument is categorised in its entirety shall be determined on the basis of the lowest level input that is significant to the fair value measurement in its entirety. For this purpose, the significance of an input is assessed against the fair value measurement in its entirety. If a fair value measurement uses observable inputs that require significant adjustment based on unobservable inputs, that measurement is a Level 3 measurement. Assessing the significance of a particular input to the fair value measurement as a whole requires judgement, considering factors specific to the asset or liability. [IFRS 7(2009).27A]

For financial instruments carried in the statement of financial position at fair value an entity is required to disclose for each class of financial instruments:
[IFRS 7(2009).27B]

(a) the level in the fair value hierarchy into which the fair value measurements are categorised in their entirety, using the levels described in the above table.

(b) any significant transfers between Level 1 and Level 2 of the fair value hierarchy and the reasons for those transfers. Transfers into each level shall be disclosed and discussed separately from transfers out of each level. For this purpose, significance shall be judged with respect to profit or loss, and total assets or total liabilities.

(c) for fair value measurements in Level 3 of the fair value hierarchy, a reconciliation from the beginning balances to the ending balances, disclosing separately changes during the period attributable to the following:

(i) total gains or losses for the period recognised in profit or loss, and a description of where they are presented in the statement of comprehensive income or the separate income statement (if presented);

(ii) total gains or losses recognised in other comprehensive income or the separate income statement (if presented);

(iii) purchases, sales, issues and settlements (each type of movement disclosed separately); and

(iv) transfers into or out of Level 3 (e.g. transfers attributable to changes in the observability of market data) and the reasons for those transfers. For significant transfers, transfers into Level 3 shall be disclosed and discussed separately from transfers out of Level 3.

(d) the amount of total gains or losses for the period in (c)(i) above included in profit or loss that are attributable to the change in gains or losses relating to those assets and liabilities held at the end of the reporting period and a description of where those gains or losses are presented in the statement of comprehensive income or the separate income statement (if presented).

(e) for fair value measurements in Level 3, if changing one or more of the inputs to reasonably possible alternative assumptions would change fair value significantly, the entity shall state that fact and disclose the effect of those changes. The entity shall disclose how the effect of a change to a reasonably possible alternative assumption was calculated. For this purpose, significance shall be judged with respect to profit or loss, and total assets or total liabilities, or, when changes in fair value are recognised in other comprehensive income, total equity.

An entity shall present the quantitative disclosures required by this paragraph in tabular format unless another format is more appropriate.

US GAAP comparison: The amendment made to IFRS 7 issued in March 2009 broadly aligns with the disclosure requirements in FAS 157, *Fair Value Measurement*, which require the use of tables illustrating fair value measurement by levels with a reconciliation of fair value for Level 3 fair values and extensive disclosure of the methods and assumptions that an entity uses to measure fair value. IFRS

7(2009).BC39B states the fair value hierarchy for disclosures is the same as that in FAS 157 but uses IFRS language pending completion of the IASB's fair value measurement project.

For entities with annual reporting periods beginning before 1 January 2009 and where the amendments to IFRS 7 issued in March 2009, *Improving Disclosures about Financial Instruments,* are not early adopted, the fair value disclosures are less extensive and prescriptive.

Specifically, disclosure of fair value measurement by levels and a reconciliation of the opening and closing balance of Level 3 fair value measurements are not required. Instead, IFRS 7(2006).27(b) requires entities to disclose whether fair value are determined using valuation techniques or published price quotations. This disclosure aims to show the extent to which fair value is observable and is non-observable and therefore serves the same objective to the more prescriptive disclosures showing fair value measurement by levels in the fair value hierarchy. IFRS 7(2006) does not require an entity to reconcile Level 3 fair value measurements. However, IFRS 7(2006).27(c & d) requires disclosure of whether fair value is determined in whole or in part using a valuation technique based on prices not supportable by observable current market transactions. For those financial instruments that fall into this category that are subsequently measured at fair value disclosure is required of the change in fair value recognised in profit or loss as well as the sensitivity of the fair value to a reasonable possible alternative assumptions. This latter requirement is similar to IFRS 7(2009)27(e) reproduced above.

Example 4.3.3.2A

Fair value disclosures

[IFRS 7.IG13A]

Assets measured at fair value

Description	31 Dec 20X2	Fair value measurement at end of the reporting period using: Level 1 CU million	Level 2 CU million	Level 3 CU million
Financial assets at fair value through profit or loss				
Trading securities	100	40	55	5
Trading derivatives	39	17	20	2
Available-for-sale financial assets				
Equity investments	75	30	40	5
Total	214	87	115	12

(Note: For liabilities, a similar table might be presented.)

Assets measured at fair value based on Level 3

	Fair value measurement at end of the reporting period using: Financial assets at fair value through profit or loss		Available-for-sale financial assets	Total
	Trading securities CU million	Trading derivatives CU million	Equity investments CU million	CU million
Opening balance	6	5	4	15
Total gains or losses				
- in profit or loss	(2)	(2)	–	(4)
- in other comprehensive income	–	–	(1)	(1)
- purchases	1	2	2	5
- issues	–	–	–	–
- settlements	–	(1)	–	(1)
- transfers out of Level 3	–	(2)	–	(2)
Closing balance	5	2	5	12
Total gains or losses for the period included in profit or loss for assets held at the end of the reporting period	(1)	(1)	–	(2)

(Note: For liabilities, a similar table might be presented.)

Gains or losses included in profit or loss for the period (above) are presented in trading income and in other income as follows:

	Trading income
Total gains or losses included in profit or loss for the period	(4)
Total gains or losses for the period included in profit or loss for assets held at the end of the reporting period	(2)

(Note: For liabilities, a similar table might be presented.)

Example 4.3.3.2B

The extract below is an example of the application of the requirements in IFRS 7(2009).27B(a) to disclose fair value measurements by a fair value hierarchy. Note: the extracts were included from financial statements prior to the introduction of this requirement in the amendment to IFRS 7, Improving Disclosures about Financial Instruments.

Extract from HSBC Annual Report 2008, p. 163 & 165

Determination of fair value

Fair values are determined according to the following hierarchy:

- *Quoted market price:* financial instruments with quoted prices for identical instruments in active markets.
- *Valuation technique using observable inputs:* financial instruments with quoted prices for similar instruments in active markets or quoted prices for identical or similar instruments in inactive markets and financial instruments valued using models where all significant inputs are observable.
- *Valuation technique with significant unobservable inputs:* financial instruments valued using valuation techniques where one or more significant inputs are unobservable.

Bases of valuing financial assets and liabilities measured at fair value

		Valuation technique		
	Quoted market price US$m	Using observ-able inputs US$m	With significant unobservable inputs US$m	Total US$m
At 31 December 2008				
Assets				
Trading assets	234,399	185,369	7,561	427,329
Financial assets designated at fair value	14,590	13,483	460	28,533
Derivatives	8,495	476,498	9,883	494,876
Financial investments: available for sale	103,949	173,157	9,116	286,222
Liabilities				
Trading liabilities	105,584	135,559	6,509	247,652
Financial liabilities designated at fair value	23,311	51,276	-	74,587
Derivatives	9,896	473,359	3,805	487,060

Example 4.3.3.2C

The extract below is an example of the application of the requirements in IFRS 7(2009).27B(c) to disclose a reconciliation of fair value measurements in Level 3. Note: the extract was taken a US GAAP reporting entity (not IFRS) as this requirement was introduced in March 2009 following the amendment to IFRS 7, Improving Disclosures about Financial Instruments. Also, note that US GAAP requires the separation of realised and unrealised gains and losses where as IFRS 7(2009).27B(c) does not.

Extract from Goldman Sachs Annual Report 2008, p. 96

The table below set forth a summary of changes in the fair value of the firm's level 3 financial assets and financial liabilities for the years ended November 2008 and November 2007. The tables reflect gains and losses, including gains and losses on financial assets and financial liabilities that were transferred to level 3 during the year, for all financial assets and financial liabilities categorized as level 3 as of November 2008 and November 2007, respectively. The tables do not include gains or losses that were reported in level 3 in prior periods for instruments that were sold or transferred out of level 3 prior to the end of the period presented.

Level 3 Financial Assets and Financial Liabilities
Year Ended November 2008

(in millions)	Cash Instruments: Assets	Cash Instruments: Liabilities	Derivative Contracts: Net	Unsecured Short Term Borrowings	Other Secured Financing	Unsecured Long-Term Borrowings
Balance, beginning of year	$54,451	$(554)	$2,056	$(4,271)	$ –	$ (767)
Realised gains/(losses)	1,930[(1)]	28[(3)]	267[(3)]	354[(3)]	87[(3)]	(20)[(3)]
Unrealised gains/(losses) relating to instruments still held at the reporting date	(11,485)[(1)]	(871)[(3)]	5,577[(3)(4)]	737[(3)]	838[(3)]	657[(3)]
Purchases, issuances and settlements	3,955	55	(1,813)	(1,353)	416	(1,314)
Transfers in and/or out of level 3	3,215[(2)]	(37)	(931)[(5)]	(626)	(5,161)[(6)]	(116)
Balance, end of year	$51,066	$(1,379)	$5,156	$(5,159)	$(3,820)	$(1,560)

(1) The aggregate amounts include approximately $(11.54) billion and $1.98 billion reported in "Trading and principal investments" and "interest income," respectfully, in the consolidated statements of earnings for the year ended November 2008. The aggregate amounts include approximately $(1.77) billion and $1.71 billion reported in "Trading and principal investments" and "interest income," respectively, in the consolidated statements of earnings for the year ended November 2007.

(2) Principally reflects transfers from level 2 within the fair value hierarchy of loans and securities backed by commercial real estate, reflecting reduced price transparency for these financial instruments.

(3) Substantially all is reported in "Trading and principal investments" in the consolidated statements of earnings.

(4) Principally resulted from changes in level 2 inputs.

(5) Principally reflects transfers to level 2 within the fair value hierarchy of mortgage-related derivative assets, as recent trading activity provided improved transparency of correlation inputs. This decrease was partially offset by transfers from level 2 within the fair value hierarchy of credit and equity-linked derivatives due to reduced price transparency.

(6) Consists of transfers from level 2 within the fair value hierarchy.

Example 4.3.3.2D

The extract below is an example of the application of the requirements in IFRS 7(2009).27B(e) to disclose sensitivity of fair value measurements for Level 3 fair value measurements.

Extract from HSBC Annual Report 2008, p. 167–168

Effect of changes in significant unobservable assumptions to reasonably possible alternatives

As discussed above, the fair value of financial instruments are, in certain circumstances, measured using valuation techniques that incorporate assumptions that are not evidenced by prices from observable current market transactions in the same instrument and are not based on observable market data. The following table shows the sensitivity of these fair values to reasonably possible alternative assumptions:

	Reflected in profit or loss		Reflected in equity	
	Favourable changes US$m	Unfavourable changes US$m	Favourable changes US$m	Unfavourable changes US$m
At 31 December 2008				
Derivatives, trading assets and trading liabilities[1]	1,266	(703)	–	–
Financial assets and liabilities designated at fair value	30	(30)	–	–

	Reflected in profit or loss		Reflected in equity	
	Favourable changes US$m	Unfavourable changes US$m	Favourable changes US$m	Unfavourable changes US$m
At 31 December 2008				
Financial investments: available for sale	–	–	984	(1,005)
At 31 December 2007				
Derivatives, trading assets and trading liabilities[1]	602	(415)	–	–
Financial assets and liabilities designated at fair value	30	(30)	–	–
Financial investments: available for sale	–	–	529	(591)

1 Derivatives, trading assets and trading liabilities are presented as one category to reflect the manner in which these financial instruments are risk-managed.

The increase in the effect of changes in significant unobservable inputs in relation to derivatives, trading assets and trading liabilities during the year primarily reflected increased sensitivity of instruments to unobservable parameters across asset and liability classes.

	Reflected in profit or loss		Reflected in equity	
	Favourable changes US$m	Unfavourable changes US$m	Favourable changes US$m	Unfavourable changes US$m
At 31 December 2008				
Private equity investments	28	(28)	234	(261)
Asset-backed securities	90	(91)	667	(660)
Leveraged finance	2	(2)	–	–
Loans held for securitisation	41	(41)	–	–
Structured notes	8	(8)	–	–
Derivatives with monolines	341	(250)	–	–
Other derivatives	652	(224)	–	–
Other portfolios	134	(89)	83	(84)

Favourable and unfavourable changes are determined on the basis of changes in the value of the instrument as a result of varying the levels of the unobservable parameter using statistical techniques. When parameters are not amenable to statistical analysis, quantification of uncertainty is judgemental.

When the fair value of a financial instrument is affected by more than one unobservable assumption, the above table reflects the most or most unfavourable change from varying the assumptions individually.

In respect of private equity investments, the valuations are assessed on an asset by asset basis using a valuation methodology appropriate to the specific investment, in line with industry guidelines. In many of the methodologies, the principal assumption is the valuation multiple to be applied to the main financial indicators, for example, multiples for comparable listed companies and discounts for marketability.

For ABSs whose prices are unobservable, models are used to generate the expected value of the asset, incorporating benchmark information on factors such as prepayment speeds, default rates, loss severities and the historical performance of the underlying assets. The models used are calibrated by using securities for which external market information is available.

For leveraged finance, loans held for securitisation and derivatives with monolines the principal assumptions concerns the appropriate value to be attributed to the counterparty credit risk. This requires exposure at default, probability of default and recovery in the event of default to be estimated. For loan transactions, assessment of exposure at default is straight-forward. For derivative transactions, a future exposure profile is generated based on current market data. Probabilities of default and recovery levels of estimated using market evidence, which may include financial information, historical experience, CDS spreads and consensus recovery levels.

In the absence of such evidence, management's best estimate is used.

For structured notes and other derivatives, principal assumptions concern the future volatility of asset values and future correlation between asset values. For such unobservable assumptions, estimates are based on available market data, which may include the use of a proxy method to derive a volatility or a correlation from comparable assets for which market data is more readily available, and/or an examination of historical levels.

Example 4.3.3.2E

The extract below is an example of the application of the requirements in IFRS 7(2009).27B(e) to disclose sensitivity of fair value measurements for Level 3 fair value measurements.

Extract from RBS Annual Report 2008, p. 202

Level 3 portfolios

Level 3 loans and advances decreased by £10 billion, primarily reflecting reclassification of certain loans (leveraged finance and other corporate loans) to loans and receivables (LAR) and fair value adjustments on the remaining portfolio at the end of the year.

Debt securities categorised as level 3 at the end of the year include £5.2 billion of asset-backed securities and £1.7 billion of corporate and other debt securities. The decrease during the year reflects termination of a deal in early 2008, reclassification of illiquid mortgage-backed securities (MBS) to loans and receivables, fair value changes, and the transfer of certain previous illiquid MBS, primarily sub-prime from level 3 to level 2.

Level 3 derivative assets at 31 December 2008 include credit derivative trades with credit derivative product companies (CDPCs) with a fair value of £3.5 billion after credit valuation adjustments of £1.3 billion. At 31 December 2007 these credit derivative trades with CDPCs had a fair value of £0.8 billion after a credit valuation of £44 million and were included within level 2 of the far value hierarchy. Other level 3 derivative assets at 31 December 2008 include illiquid credit default swaps (CDSs), other credit derivatives, commodity derivatives and illiquid interest rate derivatives.

Debt securities in issue, categorised as level 3, were structured medium term notes and the decrease in the year primarily reflects the termination of a deal in the first half of 2008.

The tables below presents the Level 3 financial instruments carried at fair value as at the balance sheet date, valuation basis, main assumptions used in the valuation of these instruments and reasonably possible increases or decreases in fair value based on reasonably possible alternative assumptions:

Assets	Valuation basis/ technique	Main assumptions	Carrying value £bn	Reasonably possible alternative assumptions: Increase in fair value £m	Decrease in fair value £m
Loans and advances	Proprietary model	Credit spreads, indices	3.1	70	50
Debt securities:					
– RMBS (1)	Industry standard model	Prepayment rates, probability of default, loss severity and yield	0.5	40	90
– CMBS (2)	Industry standard model	Prepayment rates, probability of default, loss severity and yield	0.6	30	30
– CDOs	Proprietary model	Implied collateral valuation, defaults rates housing prices, correlation	1.7	410	440
– CLOs (3)	Industry standard simulation model	Credit spreads, recovery rates, correlation	1.0	40	40
– Other	Proprietary model	Credit spreads	3.1	50	50
Derivatives					
– credit	Proprietary CVA model, industry option models, correlation model	Counterparty credit risk, correlation, volatility	8.0	1,030	1,200
– equity	Proprietary model	Volatility, correlation, dividends	0.1	–	10
– interest rate and commodity	Proprietary model	Volatility, correlation	2.2	130	130
Equity shares – private equity	Valuation statements	Fund valuations	1.1	80	160
31 December 2006			21.4	1,880	2,200
31 December 2007			32.7	610	700

4.3.3.3 *Day 1 profit or loss*

IAS 39 requires that no gain or loss should be recognised on initial recognition of a financial instrument where the valuation technique for that instrument does not solely use observable market data. A gain or loss shall be recognised subsequently only to the extent that it arises from a change in factor (including time) that market participants would consider in setting a price. As noted at **5.3.5** in **chapter 6** there is little clarity as to when day 1 profit or loss should be recognised since the standard does not specify how entities should account for those initial differences in subsequent periods. Disclosure is required, by class of financial instrument, of the accounting policy used to recognise that difference in profit or loss. In addition, the aggregate difference yet to be recognised in profit or loss at the beginning and end of the period should be disclosed together with a reconciliation of the changes in the balance during the period. [IFRS 7.28]

Example 4.3.3.3

The extract below is an example of an accounting policy for day 1 gain and losses and the application of IFRS 7.28 to disclose the amount of such gains or losses not yet recognised in profit or loss

Extract from Nordea Annual Report 2008 pp. 91,137:

10. Determination of fair value of financial instruments (extract)

For financial instruments, where fair value is estimated by a valuation technique, it is investigated whether the variables used in the valuation model are fully based on data from observable markets. By data from observable markets, Nordea considers data that can be collected from generally available external sources and where this data is judged to represent realistic market prices. If non-observable data is used, the instrument cannot be recognised initially at the fair value estimated by the valuation technique and any upfront gains are thereby deferred and amortised through the income statement over the contractual life of the contract

The valuation models applied by Nordea are consistent with accepted economic methodologies for pricing financial instruments, and incorporate the factors that market participants consider when setting a price.

New valuation models are subject to approval by Group Credit and Risk Control and all models are reviewed on a regular basis.

48. Deferred Day 1 profit or loss (extract)

In accordance with the Group's accounting policy as described in Note 1, if there are significant unobservable inputs used in the valuation technique, the financial instrument is recognised at the transaction price and any trade date profit is deferred. The table below shows the aggregate difference yet to be recognised in the income statement at the beginning and end of the period and a reconciliation of changes in the balance of this difference (movement of deferred Day 1 profit or loss).

	Group		Parent company	
EURm	31 Dec 2008	31 Dec 2007	31 Dec 2008	31 Dec 2007
Amount at beginning of year	105	58	17	0
Deferred profit/loss on new Transactions	62	82	1	18
Recognised in the income statement during the year	–63	–35	–9	–1
Amount at end of year	104	105	9	17

5 Nature and extent of risks arising from financial instruments

IFRS 7 has two key objectives: firstly to show the significance of financial instruments as discussed in **section 4** above; and, secondly, to require entities to disclose information that enables users of its financial statements to evaluate the nature and extent of risks arising from financial instruments to which the entity is exposed at the end of the reporting period as discussed below.

Both qualitative and quantitative disclosures are required about the risks that arise from financial instruments and how these risks have been managed. These risks typically include, but are not limited to, credit risk, liquidity risk and market risk. [IFRS 7.32] The disclosures provided should depend on the extent of an entity's use of financial instruments and the extent to which it assumes associated risks, though certain minimum disclosures are required for all entities. The guidance on how the disclosures should be provided has been developed so as to be consistent with the Basel Committee disclosure requirements for banks (so called 'Pillar 3' of Basel II) to allow banks to prepare a single set of co-ordinated disclosures about financial risk. [IFRS 7.BC41] It is of note that Pillar 3 disclosures are broader than those of IFRS 7 as they include operational risks.

The disclosures shall either be provided in the financial statements or incorporated by clear cross-reference from the financial statements to some other statement, such as a management commentary or risk report. Such a report must be available to users on the same terms as the financial statements and be available at the same time. Without such information the financial statements are incomplete. [IFRS 7.B6]

Where the disclosures are provided in a separate statement, the information should be clearly referenced as being part of the IFRS financial statements.

US GAAP Comparison: The disclosure requirements in IFRS 7 related to the nature and extent of the risks arising from financial instruments are more extensive than the equivalent disclosure requirements in US GAAP. Under US GAAP, FAS 107, *Disclosures about Fair Value of Financial Instruments* (as amended by FAS 133) requires an entity to disclose its concentrations of credit risk associated with all financial instruments including (1) the maximum potential amount of loss due to credit risk, (2) the entity's policy for requiring collateral or other security to support financial instruments subject to credit risk, and (3) an entity's policy of entering into master netting arrangements to mitigate credit risk of financial instruments. In addition to these required disclosure, FAS 107 encourages (but does not require) disclosures about market risk, such as (1) the hypothetical effects on comprehensive income (or net assets) or annual income of several possible changes in market prices, (2) a gap analysis of interest rate repricing or maturity dates, (3) the duration of financial instruments and (4) an entity's value at risk from derivatives and other position at the end of the reporting period and the average risk during the year. In addition to the disclosure requirements in FAS 107, AICPA SOP 94–6, *Disclosure of Certain Significant Risks and Uncertainties,* requires disclosures of the significant estimates used in the preparation of financial statements and of the vulnerabilities of an entity due to certain concentrations. FAS 161, *Disclosures about Derivative Instruments and Hedging Activities,* also requires detailed disclosures about how and why an entity uses derivatives, how they are accounted for, and how they affect financial position, financial performance, and cash flows. While many of the quantitative and qualitative disclosure in IFRS 7 regarding (1) market risk, (2) liquidity, or (3) credit risk are either optional or not required by US GAAP, SEC Regulation S-K, Item 305, *Quantitative and Qualitative Disclosures About Market Risk* requires SEC registrants to provide market risk disclosures somewhat similar to those in IFRS 7 as part of the registrant's Management Discussion & Analysis section of its quarterly and annual reports.

5.1 Qualitative disclosures

For each type of risk that an entity is exposed to, disclosure is required of the exposures to that risk, explanation of how the exposures arose, the entity's objective, policies and processes for managing the risk and the method used to measure it. Any changes from the previous period are also required to be disclosed. [IFRS 7.33]

As part of the IASB's annual improvements project for 2009 the IASB tentatively agreed at its Board meeting in December 2008 to state that the qualitative disclosures required by IFRS 7.33 should support and enhance the quantitative disclosures as required by IFRS 7.34–42 (see **5.2** below). The exposure draft of annual improvements is expected to be published in August 2009.

Disclosure may be provided on a gross basis or net of any risk transfer and other risk mitigating transactions. [IFRS 7.IG15(a)] Such information is useful since it highlights the relationship between financial instruments and provides the user of the financial statements with information to understand the effect that those relationships have on the nature, timing and uncertainty of future cash flows.

Disclosure of the entity's policies and processes for accepting, measuring, monitoring and controlling risk may include disclosure of the following: [IFRS 7.IG15(b) & (c)]

- the structure and organisation of the entity's risk management function;
- the scope and nature of risk reporting or measurement systems;
- policies for hedging or mitigating risk, including policies and procedures for taking collateral;
- the entity's processes for monitoring the continuing effectiveness of such hedges or mitigating devices; and
- disclosure of the policies and procedures that are undertaken to avoid excessive concentrations of risk.

An entity is required to disclose any changes in the qualitative information from the previous period. Such changes may result from changes in the risk exposure or from changes in the way in which the exposures are managed. [IFRS 7.IG17] This information is important since the user of the financial statements needs to understand the effect that such changes have on the nature, timing and uncertainty of future cash flows.

One of the objectives of the disclosure requirements is to enable users to evaluate an entity's ability to generate returns, and to appreciate the risks and uncertainties of those expected returns. This evaluation can only be meaningful if it is carried out in the context of the entity's risk management policies.

Example 5.1A

The extract below is an example of risk management disclosures as required by IFRS 7.33

Extracts from Diageo year ended 30 June 08 p.67

Risk management

The following section forms part of the audited financial statements.

The group's funding, liquidity and exposure to interest rate and foreign exchange rate risks are managed by the group's treasury department. The treasury department uses a combination of derivative and conventional financial instruments to manage these underlying risks.

Treasury operations are conducted within a framework of board-approved policies and guidelines, which are recommended and subsequently monitored by the finance committee. This committee is described in the corporate governance report. These policies and guidelines include benchmark exposure and/or hedge cover levels for key areas of treasury risk. The benchmarks, hedge cover and overall appropriateness of Diageo's risk management policies are reviewed by the board following, for example, significant business, strategic or accounting changes. The framework provides for limited defined levels of flexibility in execution to allow for the optimal application of the board-approved strategies. Transactions giving rise to exposures away from the defined benchmark levels arising on the application of this flexibility are separately monitored on a daily basis using value at risk analysis. These derivative financial instruments are carried at fair value and gains or losses are taken to the income statement as they arise. At 30 June 2008 gains and losses on these transactions were not material.

The finance committee receives monthly reports on the activities of the treasury department, including any exposures away from the defined benchmarks.

Currency risk The group publishes its consolidated financial statements in sterling and conducts business in many foreign currencies. As a result, it is subject to foreign currency exchange risk due to exchange rate movements, which will affect the group's transaction costs and the translation of the results and underlying net assets of its foreign operations.

Hedge of net investment in foreign operations. The group hedges a substantial portion of its exposure to fluctuations on the translation into sterling of its foreign operations by holding net borrowings in foreign currencies and by using foreign currency swaps and forwards. In February 2008, the board reviewed and approved the following revised foreign exchange risk management policy to effectively manage planning and rebalancing processes. Where a liquid foreign exchange market exists, the group's policy is to seek to hedge currency exposure on its net investment in foreign operations within the following percentage bands: 80% to 100% for US dollars, 80% to 100% for euros and 50% to 100% for other significant currencies. The group's previous policy was, where a liquid foreign exchange market exists, to seek to hedge currency exposure on its foreign equity investments before net borrowings at approximately the following percentages: 90% for US dollars, 90% for euros and 50% for other significant currencies. Exchange differences arising on the retranslation of foreign currency borrowings (including foreign currency swaps and forwards), to the extent that they are in an effective hedge relationship, are recognised in the statement of recognised income and expense to match exchange differences on foreign equity investments. Exchange differences on foreign currency borrowings not in a hedge relationship and any ineffectiveness are taken to the income statement.

Transaction exposure hedging. In February 2008, the board reviewed the group's foreign exchange risk management policy and approved the following revised policy. For currencies in which there is an active market, the group seeks to hedge between 60% and 100% of forecast transactional foreign exchange rate risk, for up to a maximum of 21 months forward, using forward foreign currency exchange contracts with coverage levels increasing nearer to the forecast transaction date. The group's previous policy for currencies in which there is an active market, was to seek to hedge between 80% and 100% of forecast transactional foreign exchange rate risk, for up to a maximum of 21 months forward, using forward foreign currency exchange contracts. The effective portion of the gain or loss on the hedge is recognised in the statement of recognised income and expense and recycled into the income statement at the same time as the underlying hedged transaction affects the income statement. Any ineffectiveness is taken to the income statement.

Hedge of foreign currency debt. The group uses cross currency interest rate swaps to hedge the forward foreign currency risk associated with certain foreign currency denominated bonds. The effective portion of the gain or loss on the hedge is recognised in the statement of recognised income and expense and recycled into the income statement at the same time as the underlying hedged transaction affects the income statement. Any ineffectiveness is taken to the income statement. Hedges are documented and tested for hedge effectiveness on an ongoing basis. Diageo expects hedges entered into to continue to be effective and therefore does not expect the impact of ineffectiveness on the income statement to be material.

Interest rate risk. The group has an exposure to interest rate risk, arising principally on changes in US dollar, euro and sterling interest rates. To manage interest rate risk, the group manages its proportion of fixed to floating rate borrowings within limits approved by the board, primarily through issuing fixed and floating rate term debt and commercial paper, and by utilising interest rate derivatives These practices serve to reduce the volatility of the group's reported financial performance. In June 2007, the board reviewed the group's interest rate risk management policy and approved the following revised policy, which allows for flexibility in executing the policy to facilitate operational efficiency and effective hedge accounting. The new policy was implemented during the year ended 30 June 2008. Fixed rate borrowings are maintained within a band of 40% to 60% of projected net borrowings for a time period approved by the board, and the overall net borrowings portfolio is managed according to a duration measure. The board approved template specifies different duration guidelines and fixed/floating amortisation periods (time taken for the fixed element of debt to reduce to zero) depending on different interest rate environments. During the year ended 30 June 2007, the profile of fixed rate to floating rate net borrowings was targeted according to a duration measure that was equivalent to an approximate 50% fixed and 50% floating amortising profile. The number of years within the amortising profile depended on the template approved by the board. The majority of Diageo's existing interest rate hedges are designated as hedges. Designated hedges are expected to be effective, and therefore the impact of ineffectiveness on the income statement is not expected to be material.

Liquidity risk The group's policy with regard to the expected maturity profile of group financing companies' borrowings is to limit the amount of such borrowings maturing within 12 months to 50% of gross borrowings less money market demand deposits and the level of commercial paper to 30% of gross borrowings less money market demand deposits. In addition, it is group policy to maintain backstop facility terms from relationship banks to support commercial paper obligations.

Credit risk Credit risk refers to the risk that a counterparty will default on its contractual obligations resulting in financial loss to the group. Credit risk arises from cash balances (including bank deposits and cash and cash equivalents), fixed income and money market investments and derivative financial instruments, as well as credit exposures to customers, including outstanding receivables, financial guarantees and committed transactions. Credit risk is managed on group basis separately for financial and business related credit exposures.

Financial credit risk. Diageo minimises its financial credit risk through the application of risk management policies approved and monitored by the board. While counterparties are limited to major banks and financial institutions, group policy ensures that individual counterparty limits are adhered to and that there are no significant concentrations of credit risk. Diageo monitors the credit ratings of its counterparties (where applicable) as part of its ongoing assessment of its credit exposure. Financial instruments are only transacted with major international financial institutions with a long term credit rating of A or better. The credit risk arising through the use of financial instruments for interest rate and foreign exchange management is estimated with reference to the fair value of contracts with a positive value, rather than the notional amount of the instruments themselves.

Business related credit risk. Trade and other receivables exposures are managed locally in the operating units where they arise and credit limits are set as deemed appropriate for the customer. There is no concentration of credit risk with respect to trade and other receivables as the group has a large number of customers which are internationally dispersed.

Commodity price risk. The group uses long term purchase and commodity futures contracts to hedge against price risk in certain commodities. Long term purchase contracts are used to secure prices with suppliers to protect against volatility in commodity prices. All commodity futures contracts hedge a projected future purchase of raw material. Commodity futures are then either closed out at the time the raw material is purchased or they are exchanged with the company manufacturing the raw material to determine the contract price. Commodity futures contracts are held in the balance sheet at fair value. To the extent that they are considered an effective hedge, the fair value movements are recognised in the statement of recognised income and expense and recycled into the income statement at the same time as the underlying hedged transaction affects the income statement.

Realised net gains recognised in the income statement in the year ended 30 June 2008 were £4 million (2007 – £2 million).There were no unrealised net gains on the balance sheet at 30 June 2008 (2007 – £1 million) as all commodity futures contracts had expired before that date.

Insurance. The group purchases insurance for commercial or, where required, for legal or contractual reasons. In addition, the group retains insurable risk where external insurance is not considered an economic means of mitigating these risks.

Example 5.1B

The extract below is an example of risk management disclosures as required by IFRS 7.33

Extracts from Barclays Bank Annual Report 2008 p. 103–4

46. Financial risk management (extract)

Barclays Bank PLC is a major global financial services provider engaged in retail and commercial banking, credit cards, investment banking, wealth management and investment management services. Financial instruments are fundamental to the Group's business and managing financial risks, especially credit risk, is a fundamental part of its business activity.

Barclays risk management policies and processes are designed to identify and analyse risk, to set appropriate risk appetite, limits, and controls, and to monitor the risks and adherence to limits by means of reliable and up-to-date data. Risk management policies, models and systems are regularly reviewed to reflect changes to markets, products and best market practice.

Risk responsibilities

The Board approves risk appetite and the Board Risk Committee monitors the Group's risk profile against this appetite:

– The Group Risk Director, under delegated authority from the Group Chief Executive and Group Finance Director, has responsibility for ensuring effective risk management and control;

– Business Heads are responsible for the identification and management of risk in their businesses;

– Business risk teams, each under the management of a Business Risk Director, are responsible for assisting Business Heads in the identification and management of their business risk profiles for implementing appropriate controls. These risk management teams also assist Group Risk in the formulation of Group Risk policy and the implementation of it across the businesses;

– Within Group risk, Risk-Type Heads and their teams are responsible for establishing a risk control framework and risk oversight; and

– Internal Audit is responsible for the independent review of risk management and the control environment.

Oversight of risk management is exercised by the Risk Oversight Committee which is chaired by the Group Risk Director under authority delegated by the Group Finance

Director. The Risk Oversight Committee oversees management of the Group's risk profile, exercised through the setting, review and challenge of the size and constitution of the profile when viewed against the Group risk appetite.

The Executive Committee monitors and manages risk-adjusted performance of businesses and receives a regular update on forward risk trends and the Group Risk Profile Report.

The Board Risk Committee (BRC) reviews the Group risk profile, approves the Group Control Framework and approves minimum control requirements for principal risks.

The Board Audit Committee (BAC) considers the adequacy and effectiveness of the Group Control Framework and receives quarterly reports on control issues of significance and half-yearly reports on impairment allowances and regulatory reports.

Both BRC and BAC also receive reports dealing in more depth with specific issues relevant at the time. The proceedings of both Committees are reported to the full Board. The Board approves the overall Group risk appetite.

The Risk Oversight Committee is chaired by the Group Risk Director and oversees the management of the Group's risk profile and all of its significant risks.

Oversight is exercised through the setting, review and challenge of the size and constitution of the profile when viewed against the Group's risk appetite.

It has delegated and apportioned responsibility for credit risk management to the Retail and Wholesale Credit Risk Management Committees.

The main financial risks affecting the Group are discussed in Notes 47 to 49.

47. Market Risk (extract)

Market risk management

Market risk is the risk that Barclays earnings or capital, or its ability to meet business objectives, will be adversely affected by changes in the level or volatility of market rates or prices such as interest rates, credit spreads, commodity prices, equity prices and foreign exchange rates. Market risk mainly arises from trading activities. Barclays is also exposed to market risk through interest rate risk on its non-trading activities and through the pension fund.

Organisation and structure

The Board approves market risk appetite for trading and non-trading activities. The Market Risk Director is responsible for the Market Risk Control Framework and, under delegated authority from the Group Risk Director, sets a limit framework within the context of the approved market risk appetite. A daily market risk report summarises Barclays market risk exposures against agreed limits. This daily report is sent to the Group Risk Director, the Market Risk Director, the Group Finance Director and the appropriate Business Risk Directors.

The head of each business, assisted by the business risk management team, is accountable for all market risks associated with its activities. Each business is responsible for the identification, measurement, management, control and reporting of market risk as outlined in Barclays Market Risk Control Framework. Oversight and support is provided to the business by the Market Risk Director, assisted by the central market risk team. The Market Risk Committee reviews, approves, and makes recommendations concerning the market risk profile across Barclays including risk appetite, limits and utilisation. The Committee meets monthly and is chaired by the Market Risk Director. Attendees include the Risk Director, respective business risk managers and senior managers from the central market risk team.

Traded market risk

Barclays policy is to concentrate trading activities in Barclays Capital. This includes transactions where Barclays Capital acts as principal with clients or with the market. For maximum efficiency, client and market activities are managed together.

Risk measurement and control

The measurement techniques used to measure and control traded market risk include Daily Value at Risk (DVaR), Expected Shortfall (ES), stress testing and scenario testing.

DVaR is an estimate of the potential loss arising from unfavourable market movements, if the current positions were to be held unchanged for one business day. Barclays Capital uses the historical simulation method with a two year unweighted historical period.

In 2008, the confidence level was changed to 95% from 98% as an increasing incidence of significant market movements made the existing measure more volatile and less effective for risk management purposes. Switching to 95% made DVaR more stable and consequently improved management, transparency and control of the market risk profile.

The historical simulation calculation can be split into three parts:

– Calculate hypothetical daily profit or loss for each position over the most recent two years, using observed daily market moves.

– Sum hypothetical profit or losses, for day 1giving one total profit or loss. This is repeated for all other days in the two year history.

– DVaR is the 95th percentile selected from the two years of daily hypothetical total profit or loss.

The DVaR model has been approved by the FSA to calculate regulatory capital for the trading book. The approval covers general market risk in interest rate, foreign exchange, commodities and equity products, and issuer specific risk for the majority of single name and portfolio traded credit products.

DVaR is an important market risk measurement and control tool, and consequently the model is regularly assessed. The main approach employed is the technique known as back-testing which counts the number of days when a loss, (as defined by the FSA in BIPRU 7.10), exceeds the corresponding DVaR estimate, measured at the 99% confidence level.

The FSA categorises a DVaR model as green (being best), amber or red. A green model is consistent with a good working DVaR model and is achieved for models that have four or less back testing exceptions in a 12- month period. For Barclays Capital's trading book, green model status was maintained for 2008 and 2007.

To further improve the control framework, formal daily monitoring of ES was started. This metric is the average of all the hypothetical losses beyond DVaR. Other controls include stress testing and scenario testing.

Stress testing provides an indication of the potential size of losses that could arise in extreme conditions. It helps to identify risk concentrations across business lines and assist senior management in capital planning decisions. A variety of different types of stress tests are performed in order to fulfil the objectives of stress testing. The global asset class stress tests have been designed to cover major asset classes including interest rate, credit spread, commodity, equity, foreign exchange rates and emerging markets.

Stress results are produced at least fortnightly. If a potential stress loss exceeds the corresponding trigger limit, the positions captured by the stress test are reviewed and discussed by Barclays Capital market risk management and the respective Barclays

Capital business heads. The minutes of the discussion, including the merits of the position and the appropriate course of action, are then sent to the Market Risk Director for review.

Scenario tests are hypothetical events which could lead to extreme yet plausible stress type moves under which profitability is seriously challenged. The scenarios are devised by senior risk managers and economists and are reviewed quarterly. Examples include 'Global Pandemic', 'Problems with GBP sovereign issuances' and 'Liquidity crisis'. The scenarios are calculated at least fortnightly and the results are included in the Traded Positions Risk Review meeting information pack.

5.2 Quantitative disclosures

For each type of risk that an entity is exposed to IFRS 7 requires an entity to provide quantitative information about exposure to that risk at the end of the reporting period, based on information reported internally to key management personnel. [IFRS 7.34(a)] Where more than one method is used to manage and report information about risk exposures, then disclosure of the method that provides the most relevant and reliable information shall be disclosed. [IFRS 7.B7] Disclosure based on management information provides a useful insight into how risk is viewed and managed by the entity, is based on information that has a more predictive value than information based on assumptions and methods that management does not use, provides disclosures which adapt to changes in the manner in which risk is measured and managed and allows users to use the same data that management uses to measure and manage risk. [IFRS 7.BC47]

Key management personnel are defined as *'those persons having authority and responsibility for planning, directing and controlling the activities of the entity, directly or indirectly, including any director (whether executive or otherwise) of that entity.'* [IAS 24.9]

Following the definition, any director, whether executive or non-executive, will be considered to be key management personnel. The definition of key management personnel is, however, wider than just directors of an entity. Key management personnel might, in some instances, include directors of subsidiaries who are not directors of the parent entity and senior managers who are not directors. Other managers may be included as key management personnel in some cases, and not in others. Consideration needs to be given to the relative autonomy of management and whether their decisions are subject to the approval of the Board of Directors. Take, for instance, a Treasury Manager in an organisation. Where that manager unilaterally reviews exposures and acts independently following only Board guidelines and objectives established by the Board , then that person may be considered to be included as part of the key management personnel of that entity. Where, however, that manager acts purely in accordance with the detailed treasury risk policy and framework as set out and approved by the board, then that person may in most instances be excluded from the definition of key management personnel. In all instances, a thorough understanding of a manager's role within the organisation and the realms within which they operate and report needs to be clearly understood in concluding whether that person is indeed included in the definition of key management personnel.

In addition to the above disclosures which are based on information provided to key management personnel, IFRS 7 requires, to the extent that these are not covered, disclosures of credit, liquidity and market risk, unless the risk is not material. [IFRS 7.34(b)]

As part of the IASB's annual improvements project for 2009 the IASB tentatively agreed at its Board meeting in December 2008 to remove the reference to materiality in IFRS 7.34(b). The IASB considered that the inclusion of the term could be read to imply that other disclosures in the standard are required even if not material. The exposure draft of annual improvements is expected to be published in August 2009.

Furthermore, disclosure of concentrations of risk shall be provided if not apparent from those disclosures. [IFRS 7.34(c)] Concentrations of risk arise from financial instruments that have similar characteristics and are affected similarly by changes in economic or other conditions. The identification of concentrations of risk requires judgement and must take into account the specific circumstances of the entity. Disclosures may include: [IFRS 7.B8]

- description of how concentrations are determined;
- description of the shared characteristic that identifies each concentration, e.g.: counterparty credit rating, geographical distribution, industry sector and other risks such as liquidity and market risks; and
- the amount of the risk exposure associated with all financial instruments that share that risk characteristic.

The quantitative information shall, in all instances, be provided for the risk exposures that exist at the end of the reporting period. Where such information is unrepresentative of the exposure to financial risk during the period, an entity should provide additional information, which may include, but not be limited to, disclosure of the highest, lowest and average amount of risk the entity was exposed to during the period. [IFRS 7.IG20]

US GAAP Comparison: While US GAAP does not require significant quantitative disclosure of the various risks an entity is exposed to in the footnotes to the financial statements, SEC Regulation S-K, Item 305, *Quantitative and Qualitative Disclosures About Market Risk* requires SEC registrants to provide disclosures regarding market risks including interest rate risk, foreign currency risk, and commodity risk as part of the registrant's Management Discussion & Analysis section of its quarterly and annual reports.

5.2.1 *Credit risk*

Credit risk is defined as 'the risk that one party to a financial instrument will cause a financial loss for the other party by failing to discharge an obligation'. [IFRS 7(Appendix A)] IFRS 7 disclosures about credit risk are substantial and are discussed in detail below. These disclosures are intended to provide the user with a sufficient understanding of the net risk position of financial assets at all stages and the extent of financial assets that are more likely to become impaired in the future. The disclosure requirements can be summarised in the following diagram.

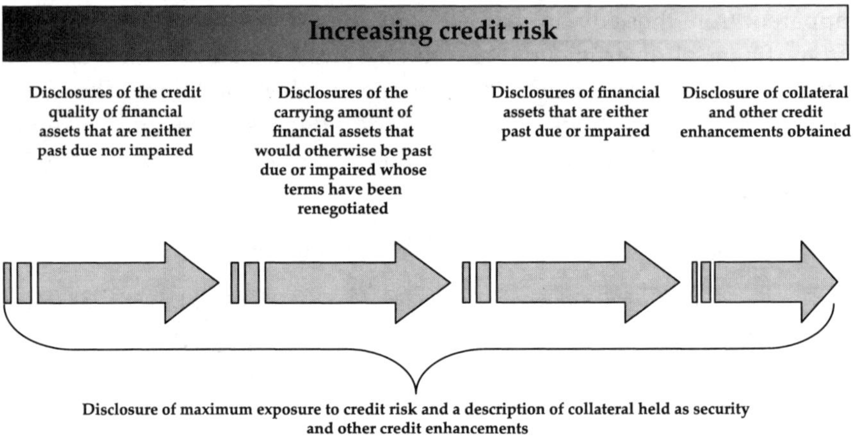

5.2.1.1 *Disclosure of the maximum exposure to credit risk*

For each class of financial asset disclosure is required of the amount that best represents its maximum credit risk exposure at the end of the reporting period, *excluding* any collateral and other amounts that do not qualify for offset in accordance with IAS 32. [IFRS 7.36(a)]

As part of the IASB's annual improvements project for 2009 the IASB tentatively agreed at its Board meeting in December 2008 to clarify that the disclosure requirements in IFRS 7.36(a) applies only to assets, and off balance sheet exposures, whose carrying amounts do not show the reporting entity's maximum exposure to credit loss. The exposure draft of annual improvements is expected to be published in August 2009.

These disclosures are designed to provide users of the financial statements with a consistent measure of the amounts exposed to credit risk and to allow for the possibility that the maximum exposure to loss may differ from the carrying amount of financial assets recognised at the end of the reporting period. [IFRS 7.BC49]

For financial assets exposed to credit risk, the maximum exposure to credit risk is typically the gross carrying amount, net of any amounts offset in accordance with IAS 32 and any impairment losses that are recognised in accordance with IAS 39. [IFRS 7.B9] In the case of derivatives that are measured at fair value, the maximum exposure to credit risk at the end of the reporting period will equal its carrying amount. [IFRS 7.B10(b)]

A derivative that will result in the delivery or receipt of an unquoted equity security where the underlying security cannot be fair valued with sufficient reliability will be recognised at cost in accordance with IAS 39.46(c) & 47(a). IFRS 7 does not state how to determine the maximum exposure to credit risk when the derivative is held at cost. For example, a gross physically settled purchased call over an unquoted equity security has a maximum exposure to credit risk equal to the value of the equity security that will be physically delivered to the entity less the exercise price to be paid. However, as the fair value of the instrument cannot be determined with sufficient reliability, and cost will generally be unrepresentative of the maximum exposure to credit risk, narrative disclosure of the terms of the instrument and the underlying would seem appropriate.

The maximum exposure to credit risk for financial guarantees that have been granted is equal to the maximum amount the entity would have to pay if the guarantee is called upon, irrespective of the likelihood of guarantee being exercised. This amount will generally be significantly greater than the amount recognised as a liability. [IFRS 7.B10(c)]

Whether the financial guarantees are accounted for within IFRS 4 or IAS 39 those contracts shall be disclosed in a similar manner. IFRS 4 requires disclosure of information about the credit risk of such contracts in the same manner as IFRS 7 requires credit risk disclosure for instruments that are measured in accordance with IAS 39. [IFRS 4.39(d)]

The maximum exposure to credit risk for a loan commitment that is irrevocable over the life of the facility, or is revocable only in response to a material adverse change, is the full amount of the commitment if the loan commitment cannot be settled net in cash or another financial asset. This is because it is uncertain whether the amount of any undrawn portion may be drawn upon in the future. Thus, the amount of the maximum exposure to credit risk for a loan commitment may be significantly greater than the amount recognised as a liability. [IFRS 7.B10(d)] Loan commitments that will be settled net in cash or other financial instruments are treated as derivative financial instruments and, thus, the maximum exposure to credit risk will, in that instance, be equal to their carrying value.

Whilst loan commitments that will not be settled net in cash or other financial instruments are outside the scope of IAS 39, they are within the scope of IFRS 7 as they are unrecognised financial assets or financial liabilities. [IFRS 7.4] If a loan commitment cannot be settled net, but is designated as at FVTPL and therefore is within the scope of IAS 39, the Standard is not clear whether it is possible to consider the maximum exposure to credit risk as being its fair value, as is the case for other derivative financial assets. As a loan commitment that cannot be settled net will always result in the origination of a loan if the commitment is exercised by the borrower, the most appropriate amount representing the maximum exposure to credit risk would seem to be the maximum that can be borrowed under the commitment. Disclosing this amount is consistent with the majority of gross settled loan commitments that are outside the scope of IAS 39.

The exposure under the loan to be originated under a loan commitment is the same as the exposure under a financial guarantee that can be claimed if the loan is in default. From the lender's perspective, both have credit risk.

IFRS 7.B10(c) states that the maximum exposure to credit risk for a written guarantee is the amount the entity could have to pay if the guarantee is called upon. It is reasonable to conclude that this amount should be based on the amount that could be required to be paid if the guarantee was called upon in its entirety, as opposed to the amount that could be claimed under the guarantee at the end of the reporting period based on the then level of lending that the lender has made to the borrower. This approach equally applies to loan commitments.

Example 5.2.1.1A

Maximum exposure to credit risk: loan commitment

Entity A issues a loan commitment to Entity B for US$100m. The maximum exposure to credit risk that will be disclosed in the bank's financial statements with respect to the loan commitment will be equal to the full amount of the loan that has been offered, US$100m. Assume Entity C issues a financial guarantee to Entity A with respect to their loan commitment to Entity B over US$100m. The guarantee will provide protection against Entity B defaulting on its loan to Bank A should Entity B draw down on the loan commitment. The maximum exposure to credit risk for Entity A will be US$100m, being the maximum potential loan under the loan irrespective of the guarantee it has acquired to reduce this potential loss. This amount will be disclosed at the end of the reporting period even if no draw down on the loan commitment is made by Entity B.

Entity C has credit risk on the financial guarantee written to Entity A. The maximum exposure to credit risk is also US$100m as this is the maximum amount Entity C could have to pay to Entity A if the guarantee is called upon.

Example 5.2.1.1B

Maximum exposure to credit risk: receivables

Group F is a listed retail group with a large customer base. Customers purchase goods under the group's standard credit terms. Group F also purchases goods from some of its major customers.

	30 June 20X2	**30 June 20X1**
	US$	**US$**
Gross trade receivables	365,500	323,700
Impairment loss	(14,620)	(12,948)
Net carrying amount	350,880	310,752
Amounts owed to customers	(75,500)	(62,250)

The group has an agreement with its customers to set off amounts owed by customers and amounts owed to customers, but only if the customer defaults. Group F does not meet the requirements to offset the asset and liability and there is not the intention and legal ability to set off the recognised amounts.

The maximum credit exposure to credit risk at the end of each reporting period is the gross amount less the allowance for impairment losses. The payables are excluded from the analysis as they are not offset in the statement of financial position.

Example 5.2.1.1C

Maximum exposure to credit risk: financial guarantee contracts

Entity B is a wholly owned operating subsidiary of Entity A, the ultimate parent of Group A. To finance its working capital requirements, Entity B has short-term banking facilities of €300million with various banks. Entity A has issued a variety of guarantees on behalf of its subsidiary and in favour of the banks which meet the definition of a financial guarantee contract. The schedule below details the drawn down banking facilities of Entity B and the amount guaranteed by Entity A at the period-end.

	30 June 20X2 €m	**30 June 20X1 €m**
Short-term banking facilities drawn down at year end	100	100
Guarantees issued by Entity A to lenders	250	250

The following amount will be disclosed as the maximum exposure to credit risk in Entity B, Entity A, and in the Group A financial statements.

- Entity B: € nil (20X1: €0) since Entity B is the borrower, it does not have an exposure to credit risk.
- Entity A: €250,000 (20X1: €250,000) – being the full amount of the guarantee that would be required to be paid if the guarantee is called upon. [IFRS 7.B10(c)]
- Group A: € nil (20X1: nil) since from a group perspective the group is the borrower and it does not have exposure to credit risk. The amount repayable is the same irrespective of whether Entity B repays the debt or Entity A repays the debt on Entity B's behalf.

Example 5.2.1.1D

The extract below is an example of application of the requirements in IFRS 7.36(a) to disclose maximum exposure to credit risk

Extract from Daimler Annual Report 2008 p. 199

Credit risk

Credit risk is the risk of economic loss arising from counterparty's failure to repay or service debt according to the contractual terms. Credit risk encompasses both the direct risk of default and the risk of a deterioration of credit worthiness as well as concentration risks.

The maximum risk positions of financial assets, which generally can be subject to credit risk, are equal to their carrying amounts and are shown in the following table:

in millions of €	See Note	Maximum risk position 2008	Maximum risk position 2007
Liquid assets		8,003	17,055
Receivables from financial services	13	42,387	39,213
Trade receivables	17	6,999	6,361
Derivatives (only assets)	14	4,072	3,389
Loan commitments	28	1,536	1,908
Other receivables and financial assets	14	2,089	3,581

Example 5.2.1.1E

The extract below is an example of application of the requirements in IFRS 7.36(a) to disclose maximum exposure to credit risk

Extract from Danske Bank Annual Report 2008 p. 135

Credit risk

The Group extends credit on the basis of the individual customer's financial position, which is reviewed regularly to assess whether the basis for granting credit has changed. Each facility must reasonably match the customer's credit quality and financial position. Furthermore, the customer must be able, in all probability, to demonstrate ability to repay the debt. If the term of a loan or credit facility exceeds five years, the customer is generally required to provide collateral. The Group is cautious about granting credit facilities to businesses and individuals if the Group will have obvious practical difficulties maintaining contact with the customer. The Group is particularly careful in granting credit to businesses in troubled or cyclical industries.

Credit exposure

The Group's credit exposure is calculated on the basis of selected items on and off the balance sheet

	2008	2007
Credit exposure relating to lending activities		
Balance sheet items:		
Demand deposits with central banks	9,968	6,813
Due from credit institutions and central banks	215,823	345,959
Loans and advances	1,352,113	1,360,413
Loans and advances at fair value	667,181	627,809
Off-balance-sheet items:		
Guarantees	107,648	109,242
Loan commitments < 1 year	51,874	97,598
Loan commitments > 1 year	115,263	131,940
Total credit exposure relating to lending activities	2,519,870	2,679,774
Credit exposure relating to trading and investment activities		
Balance sheet items:		
Trading portfolio assets	860,788	652,137
Investment securities	140,793	37,651

	2008	2007
Off-balance-sheet items:		
Other unutilised commitments	1,042	3,542
Total credit exposure relating to trading and investment activities	1,002,623	693,330
Total credit exposure	3,522,493	3,373,104

5.2.1.2 Disclosure of collateral held as security and other credit enhancements

IFRS 7 requires disclosure of the collateral held and other credit enhancements. [IFRS 7.36(b)] This requirement may be met by disclosing: [IFRS 7.IG23]

- the policies and processes for valuing and managing collateral and other credit enhancements obtained;
- a description of the main types of collateral and other credit enhancements (examples of the latter being guarantees, credit derivatives, and netting agreements that do not qualify for offset in accordance with IAS 32);
- the main types of counterparties to collateral and other credit enhancements and their creditworthiness; and
- information about risk concentrations within the collateral or other credit enhancements.

As part of the IASB's annual improvements project for 2009 the IASB tentatively agreed at its Board meeting in December 2008 to enhance the disclosure in IFRS 7.36(b) to include the financial effect of collateral held as security and other credit enhancements. The exposure draft of annual improvements is expected to be published in August 2009.

Example 5.2.1.2A

The extract below is an example of application of the requirements in IFRS 7.36(b) in describing collateral held as security and other credit enhancements.

Extract from Danske Annual Report 2008, p. 140

Collateral (extract)

The Group applies the various instruments available to reduce the risk on individual transactions, including collateral in the form of physical assets, netting agreements and guarantees.

Collateral is provided for a number of loan types to comply with statutory provisions or market practice, for example in the mortgage finance market. The most important instruments to reduce risk are charges, guarantees and netting agreements under derivatives master agreements. The types of collateral most frequently provided are real property, financial assets (shares and bonds) and motor vehicles.

The Group regularly assesses the value of collateral provided. It calculates the value as the price that would be obtained in a forced sale less deductions reflecting selling costs and the period over which the asset is up for sale. The Group has developed models to automatically estimate the value of the most frequently occurring types of collateral. For collateral for which no valuation model exists, the Group calculates the value manually. To allow for the uncertainty associated with calculating the value of collateral received, the Group reduces such value by haircuts. For real property, haircuts reflect the expected costs of a forced sale. For listed securities, haircuts are calculated on the basis of an internal price volatility model. For unlisted securities, the haircut is 100%.

2008	Retail personal customers	Retail, business customers	Corporate customers	Institutions	Governments	Securitisation	Total
Credit exposure	833,747	56,935	1,196,704	316,486	75,852	40,146	2,519,870
Collateral value	684,626	36,669	670,377	191,867	10,371	27,554	1,621,464
Total unsecured credit exposure	149,121	20,266	526,327	124,619	65,481	12,592	898,406
Unsecured portion of credit exposure (%)	17.9	35.6	44.0	39.4	86.3	31.4	35.7
2007							
Credit exposure	850,493	54,297	1,086,804	507,966	139,696	40,518	2,679,774
Collateral value	713,068	36,344	572,008	314,121	53,983	32,660	1,722,184
Total unsecured credit exposure	137,425	17,953	514,796	193,845	85,713	7,858	957,590
Unsecured portion of credit exposure (%)	16.2	33.1	47.4	38.2	61.4	19.4	35.7
2008							
Real property	663,239	26,363	352,314	1,864	1,007	23,701	1,068,488
Bank accounts	801	299	8,073	5	1	–	9,179
Custody accounts and securities	4,928	427	201,983	170,799	7,091	2,386	387,614
Vehicles	5,415	3,312	7,485	18	364	–	16,594
Equipment	92	1,526	13,987	52	50	–	15,707
Vessels and aircraft	113	129	28,928	–	1	–	29,171
Guarantees	8,809	4,271	20,720	14,302	1,002	–	49,104
Amounts due	66	150	3,888	10	60	1,147	5,321
Other assets	1,163	192	32,999	4,817	795	320	40,286
Total	684,626	36,669	670,377	191,867	10,371	27,554	1,621,464

5.2.1.3 *Disclosure of information of the credit quality of financial assets that are neither past due nor impaired*

Disclosures shall be provided of the credit quality of financial assets that are neither past due nor impaired. [IFRS 7.36(c)] A financial asset is not past due where the debtor has not missed a contractual payment (interest or capital) when contractually due [IFRS 7(Appendix A)], and a financial

asset is not impaired where there is no objective evidence of impairment. [IAS 39.59]] In providing these disclosures, the following information may be provided:
[IFRS 7.IG22]

(a) an analysis of credit exposures using an external or internal credit grading system;

(b) the nature of the counterparty;

(c) historical information about counterparty default rates; and

(d) any other information used to assess credit quality.

Such disclosures provide useful information and greater insight into the credit risk of assets and allow users to assess whether assets are more or less likely to become impaired in the future. Since all entities are different, each entity may determine its own way of providing the required information. [IFRS 7.BC54]

When an entity considers external ratings for managing and monitoring credit quality, the entity might disclose information about:
[IFRS 7.IG24]

(a) the amounts of credit exposures for each external credit grade;

(b) the rating agencies used;

(c) the amount of an entity's rated and unrated credit exposures; and

(d) the relationship between internal and external ratings.

When an entity considers internal credit ratings for managing and monitoring credit quality, the entity might disclose information about:
[IFRS 7.IG25]

(a) the internal credit ratings process;

(b) the amounts of credit exposures for each internal credit grade; and

(c) the relationship between internal and external ratings.

Disclosing information of exposures by credit grade reflects the strength of the debtors, especially where that debt is rated externally. The disclosure of one's internal credit rating process together with exposures by credit rating provides a useful insight into how the credit risk of financial assets is monitored internally and reflects how management measures and manages credit risk. Since comparative financial information will also be provided, the user will be able to understand how the credit risk of those financial assets that are neither past due nor impaired has changed over the financial period.

Example 5.2.1.3

The extract below is an example of application of the requirements in IFRS 7.36(c) to disclose credit quality of financial assets that are neither past due nor impaired.

Extract from Bank of Ireland, p. 118:

Financial assets neither past due nor impaired

The Group uses internal ratings as part of its credit risk management system. These have been mapped to the summary ratings below.

Mortgage, personal and commercial loans are assigned an internal credit grade based on an assessment of the credit quality of the borrower. A thirteen point grade scale is used for more complex, individually managed exposures, including wholesale, corporate and business lending. A seven point grade scale is used for standardised products (including mortgages, personal and small business loans). Other loans and financial instruments are assigned an internal rating supported by external ratings of the major rating agencies.

High quality ratings apply to highly rated financial obligors, strong corporate counterparties and personal borrowers (including residential mortgages) with whom the Group has an excellent repayment experience. High quality are derived from grades 1 to 4 on the thirteen point grade scale, grades 1 and 2 on the seven point grade scale and ratings equivalent to AAA, AA+, AA, AA-, A+, A, A-, BBB+ and BBB for the external major rating agencies.

Satisfactory quality ratings apply to financial assets that are performing as expected, including loans and advances to small and medium sized enterprises, leveraged entitles and more recently established businesses. Satisfactory quality also includes some element of the Group's retail portfolios. Satisfactory ratings are derived from grades 5 to 7 on the thirteen point grade scale, grade 3 on the seven point grade scale and external ratings equivalent to BBB- and BB+.

Acceptable quality ratings apply to customers with increased risk profiles that are subject to closer monitoring and scrutiny by lenders with the objective of managing risk and moving accounts to an improved rating category. Acceptable quality ratings are derived from grades 8 and 9 on the thirteen point grade scale, grade 4 outstandings that are neither past due nor impaired within the seven point scale and external ratings equivalent to BB- and B+.

The lower quality but not past due nor impaired rating applies to risks that are neither in arrears nor expected to result in loss but where the Group requires a work down or work out of the relationship unless an early reduction in risk is achievable. Lower quality ratings are derived from outstandings that are neither past due nor impaired within ratings grades 10 and 11 on the thirteen point grade scale and grade 5 on the seven point grade scale and external ratings equivalent to B or below.

All assets in grades 12 and 13 on the thirteen point grade scale and grades 6 and 7 on the seven point grade scale are impaired.

Group
31 March 2008

Risk profile of financial assets neither past due nor impaired	Mortgages €m	Personal €m	Commercial €m	Other financial instruments €m	Total €m
High quality	57.754	5,123	15,075	45,748	123,700
Satisfactory quality	545	1,394	45,152	8,977	56,068

Group
31 March 2008

Risk profile of financial assets neither past due nor impaired	Mortgages €m	Personal €m	Commercial €m	Other financial instruments €m	Total €m
Acceptable quality	21	170	6,336	65	6,592
Lower quality but not past due nor impaired	–	9	674	13	696
Total	58,320	6,696	67,237	54,803	187,056

5.2.1.4 *Disclosure of information of financial assets that would otherwise be past due or impaired whose terms have been renegotiated*

Disclosure shall be provided of the carrying amount of financial assets that would otherwise be past due or impaired whose terms have been renegotiated. [IFRS 7.36(d)]

An example where financial assets that would otherwise be past due whose terms have been renegotiated would be where the dates for repayment of a loan have been changed, e.g. previously a debtor was required to service a loan monthly but the loan has been renegotiated to require payments on a yearly basis. Were it not for the renegotiation of the terms, the loan would be past due as soon as a monthly repayment was missed.

If the terms of a financial asset are renegotiated or otherwise modified because of financial difficulties of the borrower or issuer, impairment may or may not have been recognised prior to the renegotiation as it will have depended on whether if an impairment trigger event had occurred. Where the lender, for economic or legal reasons relating to the borrower's financial difficulty, grants to the borrower a concession to the lender, this is evidence of impairment. [IAS 39.59(c) & IG.E.4.3] The renegotiation of the contractual cash flows of the debt may have avoided an impairment, and similarly, if there was an impairment prior to the renegotiation, the loan may no longer be impaired following the renegotiation because the contractual cash flows have changed.

An example where financial assets would otherwise be impaired whose terms have been renegotiated is where additional collateral or security has been provided on the loan as part of the terms of the debt renegotiation, e.g. previously the loan was unsecured and because of the debtor's worsening credit status, the debtor is required to provide collateral. If, by taking the collateral into account, the loan is no longer assessed to be impaired then such a loan would be classified as a loan that would otherwise be impaired whose terms have been renegotiated.

As part of the IASB's annual improvements project for 2009 the IASB tentatively agreed at its Board meeting in December 2008 to remove the disclosure requirement in IFRS 7.36(d) related to financial instruments renegotiated to avoid becoming past due or impaired. The IASB noted this disclosure requirement may have limited use as different approaches were being applied in meeting the requirement, financial assets are renegotiated for numerous reasons other than credit deterioration, and deleting the requirement would allow entities to redirect time and resources towards reporting and explaining information used internally to manage credit risk. The exposure draft of annual improvements is expected to be published in August 2009.

Example 5.2.1.4

The extract below is an example of application of the requirements in IFRS 7.36(d) for renegotiated loans

Extract from Anglo Irish Bank Annual Report and Accounts 2008, p. 112:

47. Banking credit risk (extract)

Renegotiated loans are those facilities that, during the financial year, have had their terms renegotiated resulting in an upgrade from impaired to performing status. This upgrade can be based, among other things, on subsequent good performance or an improvement in the credit profile of the borrower. Renegotiated loans and advances were €9m as at 30 September 2008 (2007: €42m).

5.2.1.5 Disclosure of financial assets that are either past due or impaired

Disclosure of financial information shall be provided by class of financial asset for financial assets that are either past due or impaired. [IFRS 7.37]

A financial asset is past due when the counterparty has failed to make a payment when contractually due. [IFRS 7(Appendix A)] Past due status can trigger various actions such as renegotiation, enforcement of covenants, or even legal proceedings. [IFRS 7.IG26] The new terms and conditions of debt that has been renegotiated apply in determining whether the financial asset is past due for the purposes of this disclosure item. [IFRS 7.IG27]

There is a subtle distinction between past due and impaired. Past due occurs when a payment that was contractually due is not made. This may not necessarily be equivalent to an impairment as the late payment may be added to the outstanding balance, with interest applied to the outstanding payment missed that is still deemed recoverable, so that from the lender's perspective the recoverable amount of the asset is the same, i.e. there is no impairment.

This disclosure shall include analysis of the age of financial assets that are past due but not impaired at the end of the reporting period. [IFRS 7.37(a)] An entity shall use its judgement to determine an appropriate number of time bands. [IFRS 7.IG28]

Since the quantitative disclosures of IFRS 7 should be based on the information that is provided internally to key management personnel of the entity, the disclosures for the ageing analysis based on internally reported time bands should be provided where available.

Providing an analysis of the age of financial assets that are past due, but not impaired, as at the end of the reporting period allows the user of the financial statements to understand the extent of financial assets that are more likely to become impaired because they are past due. This, in turn, assists users in estimating the level of future impairment losses. [IFRS 7.BC55(a)]

The disclosure of past due items may be particularly onerous for entities with accounts receivable. For example, if an entity has debtor repayment terms of 30 days from invoice date, yet it is customary for payment to be received after 60 days, then those receivables that remain outstanding at the end of the reporting period that are older than 30 days shall be disclosed as past due. This disclosure requirement is more onerous than that for breaches of loans payable, where short-term trade payables on normal credit terms are specifically excluded.

The disclosure shall include an analysis of financial assets that are individually determined to be impaired at the end of the reporting period and the factors that were considered in determining that those assets were impaired. [IFRS 7.37(b)] Such an analysis may include the carrying amount, before deducting any impairment losses, the amount of any related impairment losses, and the nature and fair value of collateral available and other credit enhancements obtained. [IFRS 7.IG29]

An analysis of impaired financial assets other than by age is useful because it helps users to understand why the impairment occurred. [IFRS 7.BC55(b)]

The disclosure shall also include disclosure of a description of collateral held by the entity as security and other credit enhancements and, unless impracticable, an estimate of their fair value. [IFRS 7.37(c)] Disclosure of the fair value of collateral for such debts provides useful information on the net risk position of those receivables.

As part of the IASB's annual improvements project for 2009 the IASB tentatively agreed at its Board meeting in December 2008 to remove the disclosure requirement in IFRS 7.37(c) related to collateral held as security or other credit enhancements. The exposure draft of annual improvements is expected to be published in August 2009.

Example 5.2.1.5A

The extract below is an example of application of the requirements in IFRS 7.37(a) to show an age analysis of financial assets past due but not impaired

Extract from RWE Annual Report 2008, p.201:

As of the cut-off date, there were unimpaired, past due receivables in the following amounts:

Receivables, past due and not impaired			Receivables not impaired, past due, by period				
€ million	Gross amount as of Dec 31, 2008	Receivables past due, impaired	less than 30 days	31 to 60 days	61 to 90 days	91 to 120 days	over 120 days
Financial receivables	5,911	41					
Trade accounts receivable	10,925	696					
Other receivables and other assets	14,775	4	1				1
	31,611	741	848	86	48	42	230

Example 5.2.1.5B

The extract below is an example of IFRS 7.37(a) to show an age analysis of financial assets past due but not impaired

Extract from SGS Annual Report 2008, p. 136:

Trade accounts and notes receivable

(CHF million)	2008	2007
Trade accounts and notes receivable	1 092	1 267
Allowance for doubtful accounts	(173)	(400)
Total	919	867

(CHF million)	2008	2007
Ageing of trade accounts and notes receivable not impaired:		
Not overdue	293	421
Past due not more than two months	376	307
Past due more than two months but not more than four months	100	68
Past due more than four months but not more than six months	40	37
Past due more than six months but not more than one year	35	34
Past due more than one year	75	–
Total	919	867

5.2.1.6 *Disclosure of collateral and other credit enhancements obtained*

Where an entity obtains financial or non-financial assets by taking possession of collateral or calling on other credit enhancements (e.g. financial guarantee contracts) at foreclosure, and such assets are required to be recognised in accordance with IAS 39 or another Standard, disclosure shall be provided of the nature and carrying amount of assets obtained. When those assets are not readily convertible into cash, then the entity's policies for disposing of those assets or using them in its operations shall also be disclosed. [IFRS 7.38] Disclosure of collateral in this instance is useful since it provides information about the frequency of such activities and the entity's ability to obtain and realise the value of the collateral.

As part of the IASB's annual improvements project for 2009 the IASB tentatively agreed at its Board meeting in December 2008 to clarify that the disclosure requirements in IFRS 7.38 applies only to foreclosed collateral held at the reporting date. The exposure draft of annual improvements is expected to be published in August 2009.

IFRSs do not define what readily convertible to cash means. As explained at **2.5.4** in **chapter 1**, the guidance in US GAAP may prove helpful in determining what is readily convertible into cash.

Consideration shall be given to the type of assets that are obtained as collateral and the ability to sell those assets. The mere fact that the collateral consists of listed securities does not indicate that it is readily convertible to cash as the liquidity of those assets and the size of holding should be considered.

Example 5.2.1.6A

Collateral and other credit enhancements obtained

Scenario 1

Bank A lends CU100,000 to a homeowner with property specified as collateral for the loan. During the period the homeowner defaults under loan and the property meets the criteria for recognition in the statement of financial position of Bank A before being disposed of. Bank A must comply with the disclosure requirements of IFRS 7.38 as noted above.

Scenario 2

Bank B lends CU1,000 to a retail customer. Concurrently it enters into a financial guarantee contract with Entity C under which if the retail customer fails to make payments under the loan agreement when due Entity C will reimburse Bank B the CU1,000 in cash. During the period the retail customer defaults under the loan and Bank B claims under the financial guarantee contract. The amount of CU1,000 is required to be disclosed following the requirements of IFRS 7.38.

Example 5.2.1.6B

The extract below is an example of application of the requirements in IFRS 7.38 to disclose information of collateral obtained

Extract from RBS Annual Report, p. 213:

The Group holds collateral in respect of certain loans and advances to banks and to customers that are past due or impaired. Such collateral includes mortgages over property (both personal and commercial); charges over business assets such as plant, inventories and trade debtors; and guarantees of lending from parties other than the borrower.

The following table shows financial and non-financial assets, recognised on the Group's balance sheet, obtained during the year by taking possession of collateral or calling on other credit enhancements.

Group	2008 £m	2007 £m
Residential property	41	32
Other property	6	8
Cash	59	18
Other assets	30	5
	136	63

In general, the Group seeks to dispose of property and other assets obtained by taking possession of collateral that are not readily convertible into cash as rapidly as the market for the individual asset permits.

Loans that have been renegotiated in the past 12 months that would otherwise have been past due or impaired amounted to £2,637 million as at 31 December 2008 (2007 – £930 million).

5.2.2 *Liquidity risk*

Liquidity risk is defined as the risk that an entity will encounter difficulty in meeting obligations associated with financial liabilities that are settled by delivering cash or another financial asset. [IFRS 7.(2009)(Appendix A)]

If a financial liability is exclusively settled in the issuer's own equity instruments, for example, a variable number of equity shares equal to a fixed monetary amount, then the financial liability will not be included in the liquidity risk disclosures. Equally, if the issuer has the right to deliver its own equity instruments instead of cash or another financial asset, the financial liability is deemed not to have liquidity risk as the issuer can avoid the delivery of cash or another financial asset by electing to deliver its own equity instruments. If the counterparty to the financial liability can demand cash or another financial asset, even if there is an equity settlement alternative, the financial liability must be included in the liquidity risk disclosures as the obligor cannot avoid settlement in cash or another financial asset if the counterparty chooses this settlement alternative.

If an entity has a contractual arrangement recognised as a financial liability where the entity is required to deliver a non-financial item only, for example gold, or the obligor has a choice of delivering a non-financial item instead of cash or another financial asset, then the financial liability is excluded from the liquidity risk disclosures, as the non-financial item is not cash or another financial asset (even if the non-financial item is regarded as readily convertible into cash). This will typically be the case for contracts for the delivery of non-financial assets that are included within the scope of IAS 39 as they are deemed net settled in accordance with IAS 39.5–7 (see **2.5** in **chapter 1**). Such instruments are generally classified as derivatives as at fair value through profit or loss and may be financial liabilities at the reporting period end.

Liquidity risk also arises because of the possibility (which may often be remote) that the entity could be required to pay its financial liabilities earlier than expected.

For entities with annual reporting periods beginning before 1 January 2009 and where the amendments to IFRS 7 issued in March 2009, *Improving Disclosures about Financial Instruments*, are not early adopted, the definition of liquidity risk differs. The definition of liquidity risk included no reference to the obligation being settled by the entity delivering cash or another financial asset. Consequently, the definition of liquidity risk contained in IFRS 7(2006) is broader than IFRS 7(2009) and, therefore, a greater number of financial liabilities are captured in the liquidity risk disclosures under the pre-amended definition. Specifically, if an entity has an obligation to deliver a non-financial item in exchange for a receipt of cash or another financial asset in the future, that is treated as a financial liability at the reporting period end within the scope of IAS 39, the non-financial item to be delivered will be included in the liquidity risk disclosures. Similarly, financial liabilities that will or may be settled by the issuer delivering its own equity instruments are included in the maturity analysis.

5.2.2.1 *Quantitative liquidity risk disclosures*

IFRS 7(2009) requires an entity to disclose summary quantitative information provided internally to key management personnel on its exposure to liquidity risk and how this data is determined. If the outflows of cash or another financial asset included in the data could occur significantly earlier or be for significantly different amounts than indicated in the data this fact should be disclosed and additional quantitative information should be disclosed to enable users of the financial statements to evaluate the risk. [IFRS 7(2009).B10A] The example provided in IFRS 7(2009) is where data on derivatives assumes net settlement but where the counterparty has the option to require gross settlement. However, additional quantitative information is not required if it is already included in the maturity analysis disclosure.

5.2.2.2 *Maturity analysis*

IFRS 7(2009).39 requires for financial liabilities disclosure of:

(a) a maturity analysis for non-derivative financial liabilities (including issued financial guarantee contracts) that shows the remaining contractual maturities.

(b) a maturity analysis for derivative financial liabilities. The maturity analysis shall include the remaining contractual maturities for those derivative financial liabilities for which contractual maturities are essential for an understanding of the timing of the cash flows (see Application Guidance paragraph AGB11B).

(c) a description of how it manages the liquidity risk inherent in (a) and (b)

IFRS 7(2009).B11B provides two examples where a quantitative maturity analysis for derivative financial liabilities showing remaining contractual maturities is deemed essential for an understanding of the timing of the cash flows. The first example is an interest rate swap with a remaining maturity of five years in a cash flow hedge of a variable rate financial asset or liability. The second example is all loan commitments.

A contractual maturity analysis of derivative liabilities is not required to be disclosed if the absence of information on contractual maturities is not essential for an understanding of the timing of cash flows. This may be the case where an entity frequently buys and sells derivatives, e.g. derivative liabilities included in a trading book in a financial institution. Showing the contractual maturities may not be essential for understanding of the timing of cash flows as the derivative liabilities will be settled through sale, as opposed to paying/receiving the contractual cash flows under the instrument until its contractual maturity. In such a case, the entity is still required to show a maturity analysis for derivative financial liabilities, but the analysis could be based on an alternative approach: for example, it could be based on expected maturities, or even on fair values at the reporting period end date where the entity's expectation is that the carrying amount, being its fair value, will be payable as a result of a disposal shortly after the reporting period end.

An entity shall exercise its judgement in determining the appropriate number of the time bands in the maturity analysis prescribed in (a) and (b) above.

Since quantitative information is required to be reported based on information reported to key management personnel, the time bands should, where applicable, be equivalent to those reported internally. Some entities may have many more time bands than others, such as banks that disclose liquidity for 1 day, 1–3 days, 3–7 days, 7–30 days etc. In any event, the entity should evaluate whether the liquidity analysis provides sufficient disclosure of the liquidity requirements by considering the relative timing of its liquidity needs. For example, an entity may have significant obligations due in a month's time, in which case aggregating all obligations of the first year into one band will not be appropriate.

For entities with annual reporting periods beginning before 1 January 2009 and where the amendments to IFRS 7 issued in March 2009, *Improving Disclosures about Financial Instruments,* are not early adopted, the maturity analysis for derivative instruments differed.

IFRS 7(2006) does not distinguish between derivative and non-derivative financial liabilities and requires a contractual maturity analysis for both. IFRS 7(2006).B15 states that it may be appropriate to disclose the maturity analysis of derivative financial instruments separately from non-derivative financial instruments, for example, in the case of gross settled derivative instruments, because the gross outflow may be accompanied by a related inflow.

5.2.2.3 *Contractual maturity analysis: determining which time band*

When a counterparty has a choice of when an amount is required to be paid, the liability is included on the basis of the earliest date on which the entity can be required to pay it, e.g. demand deposits shall be included in the earliest time band as the deposit holder can require repayment on demand. [IFRS 7.(2009)B11C(a)] Therefore, American-style written options that can be exercised by the holder at any time should be disclosed in the earliest time band in which the holder can exercise, whilst a European style option, which is only exercisable by the holder at maturity, should be included in the time period equivalent to its maturity date.

Where the counterparty has the choice of when an amount is to be paid, liquidity analysis is based on the 'worst case' scenario, i.e. the earliest period that the holder could be required to pay. [IFRS 7.BC 57] This also has implications for the treatment of financial liabilities that are callable by the issuer. IFRS 7.BC 57 would seem to imply that an issuer call is not taken into account for the purposes of the liquidity analysis. Therefore, for liquidity risk purposes, perpetual fixed rate debt that can be called by the issuer will be presented as if the call feature were absent and, therefore, the issuer has an obligation to pay cash flows into perpetuity. Similarly, if a financial liability has a maturity of 10 years but is callable by the issuer after 5 years, the cash flows included in the liquidity analysis would assume the instrument will remain outstanding until its contractual maturity. This approach applies even if it is highly likely that the call will be exercised by the issuer and also, if the effect of the call has been included in the determining the effective interest rate of the liability for the purpose of its measurement at amortised cost (see **section 4.1** in **chapter 6** for details).

When an entity is committed to make amounts available in instalments, each instalment is allocated to the earliest period in which the entity can be required to pay it, e.g. an undrawn loan commitment shall be included in the time band containing the earliest date that it can be drawn down. [IFRS

7(2009).B11C(b)] If loan commitments can be drawn by the holder at any time they should be included in the earliest time period.

While the loan commitment is undrawn, it is generally an unrecognised financial liability. However, IFRS 7.4 is clear that unrecognised financial liabilities are included within its scope. The requirement for the writer of the loan commitment, being the potential lender, to include in the contractual maturity analysis of liquidity risk its potential obligation to pay cash under undrawn loan commitments in the time band that reflects the earliest period the holder can draw down under the loan commitment is reasonable as it demonstrates the timing and amount of cash that the entity may be committed to pay to a borrower.

The approach applied to written loan commitments is equally applied to written financial guarantee contracts. The maximum amount that the writer could be required to pay to the holder of the guarantee shall be included in the time band that reflects the earliest period in which the guarantee could be called. [IFRS 7(2009).B11C]

If an entity has issued perpetual debt, the entity must consider how the cash flows which are due to perpetuity will be included in the maturity analysis. As the cash flows are perpetual it would be reasonable to determine the number of time bands based on all other financial liabilities that are not perpetual (i.e. that are term liabilities) and include undiscounted interest cash flows in relation to perpetual liabilities as appropriate in these time bands. In addition, it will be necessary to make clear through additional disclosure (in narrative form or a combination of an additional column with narrative disclosure) that the entity is subject to a stream of interest cash flows in relation to the perpetual instrument into infinity with disclosure of the key terms of the perpetual (such as rate of interest and notional).

5.2.2.4 Contractual maturity analysis: what amount to include in the time band

The amounts to be provided in the contractual maturity analysis are contractual, undiscounted cash flows. These amounts will differ from the amounts disclosed in the statement of financial position for financial liabilities since these are typically discounted amounts. [IFRS 7(2009).B11D]

Although not specifically mentioned in IFRS 7, the financial liabilities to be disclosed as part of the liquidity risk analysis should be after any amounts offset in accordance with IAS 32.

Examples of amounts included on an undiscounted basis include: [IFRS 7(2009).B11D]

- gross finance lease obligations, before deduction of finance charges;
- prices specified in forward agreements to purchase financial assets for cash;
- net amounts for pay (receive) floating/ receive (pay) fixed interest rate swaps for which net cash flows are exchanged;
- contractual amounts to be exchanged in a derivative financial instrument, such as a cross currency swap, for which gross cash flows are exchanged; and
- gross cash flows in respect of loan commitments.

For foreign denominated fixed or floating rate debt instruments the disclosure of principal and interest in the appropriate time bands is determined based on the interest rates curves in the foreign currency interest rate environment. These amounts may be disclosed in the foreign currency. Alternatively, they may be disclosed in the functional currency when preparing entity only financial statements, or alternatively disclosed in the group presentation currency when preparing consolidated financial statements.

Where the amount payable is not fixed, as is the case for issued debt that has a variable interest rate, the amount to be disclosed shall be determined by reference to the conditions existing at the end of the reporting period. If amount payable varies with changes in an index, the amount disclosed may be based on the level of the index at the end of the reporting period. [IFRS 7(2009).B11D]

What is not clear from IFRS 7(2009).B11D is whether 'conditions existing at the end of the reporting period' is referring solely to the absolute level of the index at the end of the reporting period, say the LIBOR rate at the end of the reporting period, or whether it is referring to conditions relating to future LIBOR that exist at the end of the reporting period. The former would result in say a five-year LIBOR based issued debt having five interest payments of the same amount, whereas the latter would have five interest payments based on the prevailing forward curve at the end of the reporting period, i.e. on what LIBOR is expected to be in the future. The most appropriate disclosure would seem to be the latter as it recognises the conditions at the period end relating to the entity's expected payments of cash or another financial asset.

A derivative may be an asset in one period and a liability in another period depending on its fair value at the end of the reporting period. In order to provide some comparability an entity may choose to project the undiscounted cash flows on the derivative (whether it is settled net or gross) and disclose these undiscounted cash flows in the appropriate time bands, irrespective of whether in a particular time band the entity is expecting a net cash inflow or a net cash outflow.

In the case of gross settled derivatives that are liabilities at the end of the reporting period the Standard only requires disclosure of the gross outflow leg. However, an entity may wish to disclose these derivatives separately from net settled derivatives so the user can distinguish the derivatives that will be accompanied by a gross inflow. An entity may also choose to provide the information in relation to the accompanying gross inflow to make clear the total cash flows on derivative instruments.

Disclosure of the gross outflow leg of gross settled derivative liabilities is required even if the outflow leg is not a cash leg, but the outflow is still the delivery of a financial instrument. For instance an entity may have entered into a forward contract to sell a particular corporate bond in exchange for £100m cash in 9 months' time with the contract being exclusively gross settled through delivery of the bond and receipt of the cash.

Consideration needs to be given how to present optional derivative financial liabilities that are not written loan commitments or financial guarantee contracts (whether standalone or embedded) in the maturity analysis. For instance, if a written credit default option that does not meet the definition of a financial guarantee contract because payout under the contract is driven not only by non-payment of a debtor but also by the credit rating of the borrower, it will be measured at fair value through profit or loss. The fair value of the written option will at each reporting period end comprise intrinsic value and time value. In determining the amount to be included in the liquidity analysis it would seem reasonable to draw on the principle in IFRS 7(2009).B11D and disclose an undiscounted amount that represents the expected payout under the option based on conditions at the end of the reporting period. Under this approach an amount of nil would be disclosed for options that are out-of-the-money (based on forward rates if applicable) at the end of the reporting period. For options that are in-the-money (based on forward rates if applicable) the amount of the expected payout would be included in the liquidity risk analysis. It should be noted that this amount will not take account of any of the option's time value as the time value is not payable by the writer to the counterparty, and will also differ from the intrinsic value of the option as this will include the effect of discounting.

If an entity is preparing a contractual maturity analysis and has a hybrid (combined) financial instrument, it shall not separate an embedded derivative for the purposes of including cash flows in the maturity analysis. [IFRS 7(2009).B11A] The entity will instead include the cash flows in the maturity analysis based on the terms of the whole arrangement, i.e. based on it being a non-derivative financial liability, whether embedded derivatives in the instrument are separately accounted for or not. If the hybrid (combined) financial instrument is a recognised financial asset an entity shall disclose cash flows in the maturity analysis based on the terms of the whole arrangement if that information is necessary to enable users of its financial statements to evaluate the nature and extent of liquidity risk (see **5.2.2.5** below). [IFRS 7.B11E]

The guidance in IFRS 7.B11A applies to hybrid (combined) financial instruments. An example would be an issued equity-linked bond or an issued debt instrument where the interest payments breach the 'double-double' test (see **7.3** in **chapter 5**).

IFRS 7 does not refer to the inclusion or exclusion of an embedded derivative that is a financial liability at the reporting period end that is embedded in a non-financial arrangement that is outside the scope of IFRS 7, for example a separately recognised embedded derivative in an unrecognised executory contract to receive a non-financial item. As the embedded derivative financial liability is fully within the scope of IFRS 7, on the face of it, it should be included within the maturity analysis if the embedded derivative results in the entity delivering cash or another financial asset. However, including the embedded derivative in the maturity analysis would appear to be in conflict with the principle in IFRS 7.B11A that requires an entity to consider the outflows of the whole contractual arrangement. As the whole contractual arrangement is not in the scope of IFRS 7, only the embedded derivative liability is, and the embedded derivative liability recognised may include imputed (not contractual) cash flows as a result of separating out part of the arrangement from the host contract, it is reasonable to exclude the embedded derivative from the maturity analysis.

For entities with annual reporting periods beginning before 1 January 2009 and where the amendments to IFRS 7 issued in March 2009, *Improving Disclosures about Financial Instruments*, are not early adopted, the guidance on liquidity risk disclosures is less extensive. IFRS 7(2006) makes no reference as to how to apply liquidity risk disclosures for hybrid (combined) contractual arrangements.

In the case of hybrid (combined) financial instruments an entity would apply one of the two policies and apply it consistently: (i) determine the contractual outflows based on the instrument as a whole (and therefore in the case of a host contract that is a financial asset there will be no outflows and no amounts are included in the maturity analysis), or (ii) include outflows only if the separately recognised embedded derivative is a financial liability at the reporting period end, as well as include outflows if the host contract is a financial liability.

In the case of hybrid (combined) arrangements where the host contract is outside the scope of IAS 39, and the embedded derivative is separately recognised as a financial liability at the period end, an entity should include the embedded derivative in the maturity analysis. However, it is acceptable to treat the embedded derivative as a net cash settled derivative since the cash flows on the embedded derivative are partly imputed as part of the exercise in separating the embedded derivative from its host contract. For example, a Sterling functional currency entity enters into an electricity sales contract to sell set quantities of electricity in the future in exchange for fixed amounts of Euro. The host contract to sell electricity in exchange for Sterling is considered to be an executory contract to sell a non-financial item that is outside the scope of IAS 39 and IFRS 7 (see **2.5** in **chapter 1**). However, on the basis of IAS 39.33(d), see **10.5** in **chapter 5**, the entity determines there is a non-closely related embedded derivative with respect to the foreign currency element. The embedded derivative is defined as a forward contract to sell Sterling and buy Euro that is within the scope of IAS 39 and IFRS 7(2006). If the embedded derivative is a financial liability at the period end, it is reasonable to regard the embedded derivative, as a net settled derivative given that the embedded derivative has been separated only for accounting purposes and there is no exchange of gross amounts of Sterling for gross amounts of Euro.

Example 5.2.2.4A

Liquidity risk disclosure: maturity analysis of financial liabilities

Bank M is a financial institution with a reporting period ending 31 December 20X1. Bank M accepts deposits from a wide range of investors with a variety of rates and maturities. The bank manages its exposure to liquidity risk through a separate and independent liquidity risk management board which reports monthly to the Board with a maturity analysis on the term structure of its deposit book. Bank M uses interest rate swaps to economically hedge its net interest margin. The interest rate swaps are not part of a trading book where there is frequent buying or selling. Bank M considers the inclusion of cash flows on its interest rate swaps in its liquidity risk maturity analysis is essential in order for users of the financial statements to understand the timing of cash flows.

The schedule below sets out the financial liabilities at the 31 December 20X2 (ignores comparative figures and assumes that all figures quoted in the table are the notional amounts only (where applicable).

Instrument type	CU'000
5.35% 15-day notice deposits	4,550
4.5% demand deposits	6,750
Fixed rate deposits	6,200
10% preference shares[4]	5,000
LIBOR-based financial liabilities[5]	10,000
Interest rate swaps[6]	1,200
Total	**33,700**

1 The notice deposits have a clause that allows for a depositor to elect to liquidate his/her deposit within 15 days. At the end of the reporting period, 40 per cent of the outstanding balance is in respect of depositors who have made this election.

2 The demand deposits are repayable within 30 days of notice being given. No persons had given notice at the end of the reporting period.

3 The fixed rate deposits vary between 60 days, 90 days and 120 days at varying rates. The year-end balance is made up as follows:

Maturity	Rate	Notional (CU'000)
60 days	4.90%	1,240
90 days	6.50%	1,860
120 days	7.36%	3,100

Interest is payable on maturity.

4 The preference shares are redeemable after 5 years. The interest on the preference shares is paid yearly on 31 December.

5 The LIBOR-based financial liabilities pay interest monthly with the interest rate re-setting to LIBOR in advance, with a bullet repayment of principal in 1 year's time. The forward curve at the end of the reporting period was as follows:

Month	Interest rate
January 20X2	5.53%
February 20X2	5.61%
March 20X2	6.12%
April 20X2	6.57%
May 20X2	6.59%
June 20X2	6.69%
July 20X2	6.71%
August 20X2	6.95%
September 20X2	7.06%
October 20X2	7.06%
November 20X2	7.30%
December 20X2	7.18%

6 The interest rate swaps net settle on a quarterly basis. The undiscounted future cash flows for all interest rate swap liabilities based on the forward curve at the end of the reporting period were as follows (negatives represent cash inflows):

Month	Net cash flow
March 20X3	600
June 20X3	500
September 20X3	400
December 20X3	350
March 20X4	300
June 20X4	200
September 20X4	100
December 20X4	50
March 20X5	-100
June 20X5	-150
September 20X5	-250
December 20X5	-300

Liquidity risk– maturity analysis
CU'000

	≤1 month	1-≤3 months	3-≤12 months	1-≤3 years	3-≤5 years
Notice deposits	4,560[1]				
Demand deposits	6,775[2]				
Fixed deposits		3,140[3]	3,175[3]		
Preference shares			500[4]	1,000[4]	6,000[4]
LIBOR-based financial liabilities		142[5]	10,520[5]		
Interest rate swaps		600[6]	1,250[6]	(150)[6]	
Total	11,335	3,882	15,445	850	6,000

Amounts determined as follows:

1 (4,550 x 5.35% x 40% x 15/365) + (4,550 x 5.35% x 60% x 16/365) + 4,550 = CU4,560

Whilst 40% of the depositors have indicated they will liquidate their deposit, on a worst case scenario basis, the remaining 60% will also all liquidate their deposits, by giving notice the very next day for their funds to be repaid within the next 15 days. Hence, the total liability will be settled within the next month, and the disclosure will need to include the principle plus interest due.

2 (6,750 x 4.5% x 30/365) + 6,750 = CU6,775
On a worst case basis, all of the demand deposits will be called within the following month. The amount to be disclosed will be the principal plus the interest for 30 days.

3 60 days: (1,240 x 4.90% x 60/365) + 1,240 = CU1,250
90 days: (1,860 x 6.50% x 90/365) + 1,860 = CU1,890
The fixed deposit is payable in tranches. The first two tranches fall due within the first 3 months. Total for 1–3 month time period = CU3,140
120 days: (3,100 x 7.36% x 120/365) + 3,100 = CU3,175
The fixed deposit is payable in tranches. The last tranche falls due in 120 days' time, i.e.: 3–12 month period.

4 1 year: (5,000 x 10%) = CU500
2, 3 years: (5,000 x 10% x 2) = CU1,000
4, 5 years: (5,000 x 10% x 2) +5,000 = CU6,000
The interest payment for the preference share falls due at the end of each year, with the capital being repaid at the end of 5 years.

5 Interest due is determined using the yield curve at the end of the reporting period, and is calculated as the product of the notional of the loan, the interest rate and the number of days.

Total for 1–3 months:

Month	Days	Time band	Rate	Cash flow
January 20X2	31	1–3 months	5.53%	47.00
February 20X2	28	1–3 months	5.61%	43.00
March 20X2	31	1–3 months	6.12%	52.00
Total				142.00

Total for 3–12 months:

Month	Days	Time band	Rate	Cash flow
April 20X2	30	3–12 months	5.53%	54.00
May 20X2	31	3–12 months	6.57%	56.00
June 20X2	30	3–12 months	6.59%	55.00
July 20X2	31	3–12 months	6.69%	57.00
August 20X2	31	3–12 months	6.71%	59.00
September 20X2	30	3–12 months	6.95%	58.00
October 20X2	31	3–12 months	7.06%	60.00
November 20X2	30	3–12 months	7.06%	60.00
December 20X2	31	3–12 months	7.30%	61.00
December 20X2	–	3–12 months	–	10,000
Total				**10,520**

6	The undiscounted forecasted cash flow for:	
	March 20X3 =	CU600
	June, September and December 20X3 =	CU1,250
	March 20X4 to December 20X7	(CU150)

Example 5.2.2.4B

The extract below is an example of application of the requirements of IFRS 7.39 to disclose liquidity risk management and a maturity analysis for financial liabilities

Extract from Anglo Irish Bank 2008 Annual Report and Accounts, p. 122:

Liquidity risk (extract)

The following tables present the cash flows payable by the Group under financial liabilities and off balance sheet contingent liabilities and commitments by remaining contractual maturities at the balance sheet date. The amounts disclosed in the tables for financial liabilities are contractual undiscounted cash flows and therefore differ from the carrying amounts of these liabilities in the consolidated balance sheet.

	30 September 2008							
The Group	Demand €m	Between one and eight days €m	Between nine days and one month €m	Between one and three months €m	Between three months and one year €m	Between one and five years €m	Over five years €m	Total €m
Deposits from banks	691	9.933	1.832	3,626	1,702	2,618	–	20,402
Customer accounts	3,015	21.312	9,844	8,629	8,432	828	112	52,172
Derivative financial instruments (1)	–	(53)	21	(80)	(317)	(141)	55	(515)
Debt securities in issue	–	1,374	1,321	3,030	4,606	7,864	98	18,293
Subordinated liabilities and other capital instruments	–	20	–	56	210	1,118	5,729	7,133
	3.706	32,586	13,018	15,261	14,633	12,287	5,994	97,485
Contingent liabilities (2)	14	16	15	142	226	267	56	736
Commitments to lend (2)	–	387	407	1,270	1,974	1,286	958	6,282
Total financial liabilities and off balance sheet items	3,720	32,989	13,440	16,673	16,833	13.840	7,008	104,503

Example 5.2.2.4C

The extract below is an example of application of the requirements in IFRS 7.39 to disclose liquidity risk management and a maturity analysis for financial liability

Extract from BASF Report 2008, p. 214–5:

Liquidity risks (extract)

We promptly recognize any risks from cash flow fluctuations as part of the liquidity planning. We have ready access to sufficient liquid funds from our ongoing commercial paper program and confirmed lines of credit from banks. Despite the current financial crisis, the commercial paper market for BASF continues to be liquid due to our good rating.

Maturities of contractual cash flows from financial liabilities

2008 (million €)

	Bonds and other liabilities to the capital markets	Liabilities to credit institutions	Liabilities resulting from derivative financial instruments	Miscellaneous liabilities
2009	5,691	943	1,497	1,012
2010	1,318	186	19	75
2011	1,501	201	2	31
2012	1,631	104	–	33
2013	1,531	619	–	31
2014 thereafter	2,580	77	–	313
	14,252	2,130	1,518	1,495

The interest and principal payments as well as other payments for derivative financial instruments are relevant for the presentation of the maturities of the contractual cash flows from financial liabilities. Future cash flows are not discounted here.

Derivatives are included using their net cash flows, provided they have a negative fair value and therefore represent a liability. Derivatives with positive fair values are assets and are not considered.

Trade accounts payable are generally interest free and fall due within one year. Therefore the carrying amount of trade accounts payable equals the sum of future cash flows.

Example 5.2.2.4D

The extract below is an example of application of the requirements in IFRS 7.39 to disclose a liquidity risk maturity analysis for financial liabilities for non-derivatives

Extract from Vodafone Annual Report 2008, p. 119:

Maturity of borrowings (extract)

The maturity profile of the anticipated future cash flows including interest in relation to the Group's non-derivative financial liabilities on an undiscounted basis, which, therefore, differs from both the carrying value and fair value is as follows:

	Bank loans £m	Redeem-able preference shares £m	Finance lease obliga-tions £m	Bonds £m	Other liabili-ties £m	Loans in fair value hedge relation-ships £m	Total £m
Within one year	838	43	12	1.368	1,788	1.443	5,492
In one to two years	369	104	12	464	110	4.168	5.227
In two to three years	1.490	77	12	214	2,732	398	4,923
In three to four years	346	43	12	1.671	–	1,016	3,088
In four to five years	142	43	11	139	223	1,082	1,640
In more than five years	423	1.132	26	2.990	137	9,459	14.167
	3,608	1,442	85	6,846	4,990	17,566	34,537
Effect of discount/financing rates	(133)	(457)	(16)	(1,282)	(258)	(5,197)	(7,343)
31 March 2008	3,475	985	69	5,564	4,732	12,369	27,194

5.2.2.5 Liquidity risk management

An entity is required to describe how it manages the liquidity risk inherent in the financial liabilities included in the maturity analysis (see **5.2.2.1** above). An entity shall disclose a maturity analysis of financial assets it holds for managing liquidity risk (for example financial assets that are readily saleable or expected to generate cash inflows to meet cash outflows on financial liabilities), if that information is necessary to enable users of its financial statements to evaluate the nature and extent of liquidity risk. [IFRS 7.B11E]

There is an apparent conflict between IFRS 7 which requires the disclosure of a liquidity analysis for all *financial liabilities* and IAS 1.65 which states that 'IFRS 7 requires disclosure of the maturity dates of *financial assets and financial liabilities*' [emphasis added]. An entity is not required to disclose a maturity analysis for financial assets in all cases. The minimum required disclosure is for a maturity analysis for financial liabilities only. However, a maturity analysis shall be disclosed for financial assets if it holds financial assets for managing liquidity risk and that information is necessary to enable users of its financial statements to evaluate the nature and extent of liquidity risk. [IFRS 7.B11E]

For entities with annual reporting periods beginning before 1 January 2009 and where the amendments to IFRS 7 issued in March 2009, *Improving Disclosures about Financial Instruments*, are not early adopted, there is no requirement to provide a maturity analysis for financial assets where providing such information is necessary to enable users of its financial statement to evaluate the nature and extent of liquidity risk. Instead, IFRS 7(2006).IG30 states that "If an entity manages liquidity risk on the basis of expected maturity dates, it might disclose a maturity analysis of the expected maturity dates of both financial liabilities and financial assets. If an entity discloses such an expected maturity analysis, it might clarify that expected dates are based on estimates made by management, and explain how the estimates are determined and the principal reasons for differences from the contractual maturity analysis . . .".

Other factors that an entity may wish to disclose in describing how it manages its liquidity risk include, but are not limited to, whether the entity:
[IFRS 7.B11F]

(a) has committed borrowing facilities (e.g. commercial paper facilities) or other lines of credit (e.g. stand-by credit facilities) that it can access to meet liquidity needs;

(b) holds deposits at central banks to meet liquidity needs;

(c) has very diverse funding sources;

(d) has significant concentrations of liquidity risk in either its assets or its funding sources;

(e) has internal control processes and contingency plans for managing liquidity risk;

(f) has instruments that include accelerated repayment terms (e.g. on the downgrade of the entity's credit rating);

(g) has instruments that could require the posting of collateral (e.g. margin calls for derivatives);

(h) has instruments that allows the entity to choose whether it settles its financial liabilities by delivering cash (or another financial asset) or by delivering its own shares; or

(i) has instruments that are subject to master netting agreements.

Example 5.2.2.5A

The extract below is an example of application of the requirements of IFRS 7.39(c) to disclose how the entity manages liquidity risk

Extract from Daimler Annual Report 2008, p. 201:

Liquidity risk

Liquidity risk comprises the risk that a company cannot meet its financial obligations in full.

Daimler manages its liquidity by holding adequate volumes of liquid assets and maintaining syndicated credit facilities in addition to the cash inflows generated by its operating business. In general, Daimler makes use of a broad spectrum of financial instruments to cover its funding requirements. Depending on funding requirements and market conditions, Daimler issues commercial paper, bonds and financial instruments secured by receivables in various currencies. Credit lines are also used to cover financing requirements. The funds raised are primarily used to finance the cash needs of the lease and financing business and the working capital and capital expenditure requirements. According to internal guidelines, the refunding of the lease and financing business is generally carried out with matching maturities of cash flows.

At year-end 2008, the Group had short-term and long-term credit lines totaling €22.7 billion, of which €8.5 billion was not utilized. These credit lines include a syndicated US $5 billion credit facility of Daimler AG. This facility will mature in December 2011. In order to bolster its group liquidity, Daimler signed a new €3 billion 364-day credit facility with a syndicate of international banks in October 2008. These facilities serve as a backup for commercial paper drawings and provide funds for general corporate purposes. At the end of 2008, neither of the facilities was utilized.

From an operating point of view, the management of the Group's liquidity exposures is centralized by a daily cash pooling process. This process enables Daimler to manage its liquidity surplus and liquidity requirements according to the actual needs of the Group and each subsidiary. The Group's short-term and midterm liquidity management takes into account the maturities of financial assets and financial liabilities and estimates of cash flows from the operating business.

Information on the Group's financing liabilities is also provided in Note 23 to the consolidated financial statements.

At present, refinancing in particular with regard to large amounts is only possible at significantly higher borrowing costs. In the case of a continued negative trend in the financial markets Daimler could be faced with ongoing high borrowing costs and lower financial flexibility. Higher borrowing costs would have an impact on the competitiveness and profitability of the Group's financial services business.

Example 5.2.2.5B

The extract below is an example of application of the requirements of IFRS 7.39(c) to disclose to disclose how the entity manages liquidity risk

Extract from Anglo Irish Bank 2008 Annual Report and Accounts, p. 122, 124, 125:

Liquidity risk

Liquidity risk is the risk that the Group does not have sufficient financial resources available at all times to meet its contractual and contingent cash flow obligations or can only secure these resources at excessive cost.

Liquidity risk is monitored centrally by ALCO, whose responsibilities in relation to liquidity include, but are not limited to:

- Setting liquidity risk strategy for the Group;
- Approving and maintaining Group funding and liquidity policy;
- Approving and maintaining the Group contingency funding plan;
- Maintaining internal and external liquidity risk limits;
- Liquidity stress testing and scenario analysis; and
- Providing the Board and relevant Board Committees with regular liquidity updates.

A dedicated ALCO Liquidity sub-committee, comprising key heads of funding and liquidity areas, provides an important forum for management and risk control matters relating to funding and liquidity. The subcommittee reports directly to ALCO and provides formal updates at each ALCO meeting. The Board and the Risk and Compliance Committee also receive formal liquidity reports and updates at each meeting.

Liquidity risk is measured using the cash flow mismatch approach where cash inflows and outflows are analysed to produce a net cash flow position over set time periods. Cash outflows are assumed to be paid at the earliest time period and cash inflows to be received at the latest potential time period. The Group mitigates liquidity risk through holding a stock of highly liquid assets which can be readily realised for cash and by actively managing the liquidity profile of its assets and liabilities.

Operational liquidity risk is short-term liquidity risk, ranging from intraday to one month. Execution of the Group's short term operational liquidity strategy and cash flow management on a daily and real time intraday basis is the responsibility of Group Treasury, operating within strict formal limits set by ALCO. Cash flow requirements are determined using contractual cash flows and conservative assumptions for non contractual cash flows which may fall due. Group Treasury provide formal updates to ALCO Liquidity subcommittee and ALCO on a regular basis.

Maintaining a portfolio of highly liquid assets eligible for repurchase agreements ('repo') to ensure the Group has a sufficient buffer to cope with unforeseen cash flow requirements is a core part of operational liquidity risk management.

Separate liquidity cash flow limits are in place for the management of liquidity in non-euro currencies ensuring foreign currency cash flow exposure is managed within approved risk tolerance limits.

The Group evaluates its longer term liquidity mismatch or structural liquidity risk on a regular basis. The management of structural liquidity risk is important in identifying future funding requirements.

ALCO is responsible for structural liquidity risk management and provides regular formal updates to the Risk and Compliance Committee and the Board.

Structural liquidity risk is managed under the guidelines set out in the Group funding policy. This policy seeks to build and maintain a funding book which is well diversified in terms of retail, corporate and wholesale markets on a customer, segmental, geographical and duration basis.

Liquid assets

An important part of the operational and structural liquidity risk strategy is maintaining a portfolio of highly liquid treasury assets which can be realised for cash at short notice through sale and repurchase agreements.

The Group maintains a portfolio of liquid assets comprising a sizeable holding of European government bonds and other high quality bank paper which is highly liquid in the bilateral or tri-party repo market.

Holding a portfolio of highly liquid assets has always formed part of the Group's liquidity management policy ensuring the Group has been able to receive and place cash in the repo market during periods of market volatility. During the year the Group pursued an active strategy of generating liquidity through securitisation and covered bonds issuance. As a result of these initiatives, the Group has increased its stock of repo eligible assets by €9.2bn since the start of the current market dislocation. This portfolio of liquid assets enhances the liquidity position of the Group even in times of severely dislocated markets.

Contingency planning

The Group maintains a comprehensive contingency funding plan to deal with periods of market liquidity stress. The plan includes detailed actions which would be required depending on the nature and severity of any potential liquidity stress. Early warning indicators are an important facet of the contingency funding plan. The plan is reviewed on a regular basis by ALCO and senior management.

Stress testing

An important element in the identification, management and control of liquidity risk is the use of stress tests and scenario analyses. The stress testing results enable ALCO to analyse the effects of low probability, yet high impact, events on the funding and liquidity position of the Group.

The Group has a comprehensive stress testing framework which is consistent with market best practice for liquidity risk stress and scenario testing. The suite of stress tests incorporates both market and Group specific stresses including moderate and severe events over different time horizons.

Some examples of the primary stress tests are the total closure of wholesale funding markets, one notch downgrade stress, two notch downgrade stress, Irish market specific stress and market risk stress. The Group has limits in place which set the maximum tolerance for the results of the various stress test scenarios, and also pre-defined courses of action to reduce the exposure to a particular stress if deemed appropriate.

Liquidity stress testing results are regularly reviewed by ALCO with updates provided to the Board and the Risk and Compliance Committee.

Regulatory liquidity requirements

The Irish Financial Regulator introduced new regulatory liquidity requirements in 2007, replacing the liquid stock approach with a more advanced cash flow mismatch approach. Minimum regulatory ratios are in place for the periods of 0 to 8 days and 9 to 30 days with strict conservative assumptions set for certain cash flow types. The Group is required to maintain a minimum of 100% coverage in the 0 to 8 day period and 90% coverage in the 9 to 30 day period. In addition the Irish Financial Regulator sets qualitative requirements regarded as best practice for liquidity risk management.

5.2.3 *Market risk*

Market risk is defined as 'the risk that the fair value or future cash flows of a financial instrument will fluctuate because of changes in market prices. Market risk comprises three types of risk: currency risk, interest rate risk and other price risk'. [IFRS 7(Appendix A)] Each of these risks is defined as follows:
[IFRS 7(Appendix A)]

(a) **Currency risk:** the risk that the fair value or future cash flows of a financial instrument will fluctuate because of changes in foreign exchange rates. Currency risk arises on financial instruments that are denominated in a different currency to the entity's functional currency.

(b) **Interest rate risk:** the risk that the fair value or future cash flows of a financial instrument will fluctuate because of changes in market interest rates. Interest rate risk arises on interest-bearing financial instruments that are recognised in the statement of financial position, e.g. loans and receivables and on some financial instruments that are not recognised in the statement of financial position, like some loan commitments.

(c) **Other price risk:** the risk that the fair value or future cash flows of a financial instrument will fluctuate because of changes in market prices (other than those arising from **interest rate risk** or **currency risk**), whether those changes are caused by factors specific to the individual financial instrument or its issuer, or factors affecting all similar financial instruments traded in the market'

Examples of other price risks include equity price risk, commodity price risk, prepayment risk and residual value risk.

For a financial asset or a liability that is classified as at fair value through profit or loss, whether a non-derivative or a derivative, credit risk will be a factor affecting its fair value and will impact profit or loss. For a debt security designated as available-for-sale, credit risk associated with the security will affect equity. However, it is questionable whether credit risk is a 'market price risk' in the same way that an equity price, foreign exchange rate or interest rate are. Also, as credit risk is specifically covered by a different set of detailed disclosures in IFRS 7, see **5.2.1** above, it is reasonable to assume credit risk was not intended to be included. While changes in the likelihood of the obligor defaulting under a financial instrument would not be treated as a type of *other price risk*, changes in fair value of an instrument due to, or cash flow payments contractually linked to, a variable such as a credit index which is not based on the ability of the obligor to meet its obligations under the financial instrument, which be viewed as a type of *other price risk*.

Market risk sensitivity analysis is required for each type of market risk to which the entity is exposed at the end of the reporting period showing how profit or loss and equity would have been affected by changes in the relevant risk variable that were reasonably possible at the end of the reporting period. In addition, disclosure should be provided of the methods and assumptions that were used in preparing the sensitivity analysis, any changes from the previous period in the methods and assumptions used, and the reasons for those changes. [IFRS 7.40]

An entity shall decide how it aggregates information to display the overall picture without combining information with different characteristics about exposures to risks from significantly different economic environments. For example:

(a) an entity that trades financial instruments might disclose this information separately for financial instruments held for trading and those not held for trading;

(b) an entity that has exposure to market risks from areas of hyperinflation and areas of very low inflation would disclose the information sensitivity for the two areas.

If an entity has exposure to only one type of market risk in only one economic environment, it would not show disaggregated information. [IFRS 7.B17]

The sensitivity analysis provides useful information since it is relatively easy to calculate and understand, is suitable for all entities and highlights the nature and extent of risks that arise from financial instruments. [IFRS 7.BC59]

It is not necessary to prepare an analysis that reflects inter-dependencies between risk variables, e.g. in preparing an interest rate sensitivity analysis an entity does not need to determine the impact of changes in interest rates would have on the relative strengthening and weakening of the currency with other currencies. Rather a simple sensitivity analysis that shows the change in only one variable is sufficient. [IFRS 7.BC60]

The preparation of a market risk sensitivity analysis requires the following steps:

(i) **Identify risk exposures**

All market risks to which the entity is exposed need to be identified.

(ii) **Identify the exposures at the end of the reporting period and how those exposures affect the sensitivity analysis**

All financial instruments at the end of the reporting period whose fair value and/ or cash flows are affected by changes in risk factors need to be identified.

Examples of financial instruments and their impact on *profit or loss* are included below.

- Floating rate debt instruments, whether an asset or liability, have a sensitivity to interest rates. The entity will flex interest rates for floating rate instruments that are outstanding at the period end showing how profit or loss would have varied in the period assuming the instruments at the period end were outstanding for the entire period.

- Foreign currency denominated debt instruments are sensitive to foreign currency rates as monetary items are retranslated into the functional currency of the entity at the period end. The sensitivity to foreign currency rates applies irrespective of whether the instrument is an asset or a liability, whether it is measured at fair value or amortised cost. This includes intercompany foreign currency denominated loans that are expected to be repaid in the foreseeable future where the foreign currency risk does not eliminate on consolidation.
- Any financial instrument at the period end that is designated as at fair value through profit or loss or is held for trading. The sensitivity will depend on the underlying risks of the instrument. A debt instrument may be sensitive to changes in interest rate, foreign currency risk, whereas an equity instrument may be sensitive to changes in equity prices and foreign currency risk.
- All derivatives in designated and qualifying fair value hedge accounting relationships.
- Fixed rate debt instruments that are hedged items in qualifying fair value hedges of interest rate risk are sensitive to changes in interest rates.

Examples of financial instruments and their impact in *equity* (*other comprehensive income*) are included below:

- foreign currency denominated debt instruments that are designated as a qualifying hedging instrument in a foreign currency cash flow or net investment hedge are sensitive to foreign currency rates;
- intragroup foreign currency denominated debt instruments to or from a foreign operation that are not expected to be repaid in the foreseeable future in accordance with IAS 21.15 are sensitive to foreign currency rates where the foreign currency risk does not eliminate on consolidation. Even though the debt instrument may form part of the foreign operation in accordance with IAS 39.102 it remains within the scope of IAS 39 and IFRS 7 and therefore should be included within sensitivity analysis;
- derivatives and embedded derivatives designated as effective hedging instruments in a cash flow hedge or a hedge of a net investment in a foreign operation;
- foreign currency denominated equity securities classified as available for sale are sensitive to foreign currency rates and equity prices;
- debt securities classified as available for sale are sensitive to interest rate risk and credit risk, and may also be sensitive to foreign currency risk.

Any recognised financial instrument at the end of the reporting period whose cash flows are contractually linked to a variable or whose fair value is dependent on a variable should be included in a sensitivity analysis to the extent changes in the variable will impact profit or loss or equity. For example, if an entity has issued debt that is contractually linked to inflation, where the inflation linkage is considered a closely related embedded derivative, the carrying value of the debt and its impact on profit or loss will depend on the level of inflation throughout the reporting period and at the period end. Alternatively, if the inflation linkage was not closely related, it would impact profit or loss through its re-measurement as a derivative at fair value through profit or loss.

An example of a financial instrument that has no impact on profit or loss or equity is a fixed rate debt instrument without any non-closely related embedded derivatives that is denominated in the entity's functional currency, whether an asset or a liability, provided that it is measured at amortised cost. Changes in interest rates or currency rates do not impact profit or loss or equity.

IFRS 7(Appendix A) defines currency risk as the *risk that the fair value or future cash flows of a financial instrument will fluctuate because of changes in foreign exchange rates*. IFRS 7.B23 states that *currency risk (or foreign exchange risk) arises on financial instruments that are denominated in a foreign currency, i.e. in a currency other than the functional currency in which they are measured*. The Standard is clear that any foreign currency monetary item at the period end will be included in the foreign currency risk sensitivity analysis. What is less clear is whether IFRS 7 requires an entity to also include in the foreign currency risk sensitivity analysis the extent to which the effective interest rate that is recognised in profit or loss in the period in respect of the period end monetary item would have differed had foreign currency rates differed. The foreign currency interest recognised in profit or loss is usually translated using the average monthly foreign currency rate and, therefore, profit or loss is sensitive to changes in foreign currency rates irrespective of whether the loan has fixed or floating foreign currency interest. As the monetary item impacts profit or loss through the recognition of interest, as well as the translation of the period end carrying amount, it would be meaningful to include both interest and principal of a monetary item within the foreign currency sensitivity analysis. This approach is consistent with the view that foreign currency interest is variable in the functional currency of the entity.

Financial instruments that are classified as equity in accordance with IAS 32 are not remeasured and therefore do not impact profit or loss or equity when sensitivity analysis is performed. [IFRS 7.B28]

It should be noted that if the entity is party to derivatives over own equity that are not classified as equity (e.g. if the entity has issued warrants with an exercise price in a currency other than the functional currency of the entity), then its own equity price risk will be a relevant example of an *other price risk*. As the instruments will be accounted for as derivatives at fair value through profit or loss with the underlying being the entity's own equity price they will need to be considered for the purposes of the sensitivity analysis.

(iii) Determine what is a reasonably possible change in the relevant risk variable that were reasonably possible at that date

An entity needs to determine what it considers to be a reasonably possible change in the relevant risk variable, and should consider both the economic environment in which it operates and the time frame over which it is making the assessment. A reasonably possible change in a relevant risk variable in one environment may not be the same in another environment, e.g. a reasonable possible change in interest rates may be 100bp for Sterling denominated debt, but the same could not be said for Yen denominated debt, for which a reasonably possible change may be substantially smaller. Entities are required to judge what those reasonably possible changes are and should not include remote or 'worse case scenarios' or 'stress tests'. A reasonably possible change in the relevant risk variable should be assessed over a time frame until the entity next presents these disclosures, which is usually the end of its next annual reporting period. [IFRS 7.B19]

While the range of reasonably possible changes may be wide, disclosure is not required for each change within that range. It is sufficient to disclose the effects of the changes at the limits of the reasonably possible range. [IFRS 7.B18(b)]

IFRS 7 requires comparative information to be presented. If the volatility of a given risk variable changes and, therefore, an entity alters its view of what is a reasonably possible change in that risk variable in relation to the prior year, this would not prompt restatement of the comparative risk disclosures. The entity should, however, carefully disclose the fact that there has been a change in what is considered a reasonably possible change in the risk variable.

(iv) Determine the appropriate level of aggregation that should be provided in the disclosures

An entity should aggregate the output from sensitivity analysis in order to provide a broad view of the entity's overall sensitivity to market risk but without combining information with different characteristics about exposures to risks from significantly different economic environments. Disclosure may, for instance, be provided separately for financial instruments that are held for trading from those that are not. Alternatively, disclosures may be disclosed for each risk. As a minimum, disclosure of sensitivity analyses for each currency to which an entity has a significant exposure shall be provided.
[IFRS 7.B24]

An entity shall provide sensitivity analyses for the whole of its business but may provide different types of sensitivity analyses for different classes of financial instruments. [IFRS 7.B21]

An entity could provide different types of sensitivity analysis for different parts of its business if this is consistent with how it manages risk internally. For example, a financial institution may comprise a retail banking division and an investment banking division. The entity could choose to provide a conventional sensitivity analysis, as described in the steps above, in relation to the retail banking division and a value-at-risk analysis in relation to the investment banking division, if the latter analysis is used for internal risk management purposes within the investment banking division. However, the entity in this case would need to consider carefully how to treat any transactions and exposures between the two divisions so that the disclosure is not misleading. See (vi) below for discussion of VaR as an alternative disclosure of market risk.

(v) Calculate and present the sensitivity analyses

Entities shall disclose the effect on profit or loss and equity for exposures at the end of the reporting period assuming that a reasonably possible change in the relevant risk variable had been applied to those exposures at the end of the reporting period. [IFRS 7.B18]

The sensitivity may be reported separately for different lines in profit or loss or for consolidated profit or loss and equity. An entity might disclose a sensitivity analysis for interest rate risk for each currency in which the entity has material exposures to interest rate risk. [IFRS 7.IG34]

The sensitivity of profit or loss and the sensitivity of equity shall be disclosed separately. [IFRS 7.B27]

The sensitivity analysis is prepared based on financial instruments that are recognised at the end of the reporting period. This is the case even where those exposures did not exist for the entire period or where the exposure changed materially during the period.

For example, an entity is building a road. To finance the construction of the road, it negotiates a floating rate debt facility. The entity starts to draw down on the facility half way through the year and at year end it has fully drawn down on the facility. A sensitivity analysis will be prepared for the loan showing profit or loss sensitivity assuming that the loan was in place for the entire period. A similar situation would arise in the case of an amortising loan where the exposure has reduced over the period due to part repayments of the principal. In that instance, the sensitivity analysis would be prepared on the basis of the exposure at the end of the reporting period, although it had significantly higher exposures during the period.

IFRS 7.35 does state that if the quantitative data disclosed as at the end of the reporting period is unrepresentative of an entity's exposure to risk during the period, an entity shall provide further information that is representative. For sensitivity analysis, an entity may provide supplementary disclosure illustrating the impact on profit or loss and equity based on the timing of recognition and derecognition of financial instruments in the period, in addition to the analysis based on financial instruments recognised at the period end.

Whilst IFRS 7 provides some guidance on the determination of reasonably possible changes in the relevant risk variable, no guidance is available on whether the degree of change at the end of the reporting period in the relevant risk variable should be extrapolated to the risk variables during the period, or whether the change should be determined as a fixed amount of change.

For example, an entity has a floating rate liability at year end. The current LIBOR rate is 5 per cent, and the entity estimates that a reasonably possible change in LIBOR is 100bp. During the year LIBOR was 2 per cent in the first half of the year, 3 per cent at half year and 4 per cent during the last 6 months. The volatility in cash flows during the year may either be expressed as:

(a) An *absolute change* of 100bp's to all rates. Thus, the sensitivity would be of 100bp increase and decrease to the loan's cash flows during the year; or

(b) A *percentage change*, where the change at the end of the reporting period is 20 per cent ($^1/_{5th}$) and, hence, all rates should change by 20 per cent during the period. Thus, the volatility in cash flows will be determined as the change of the above interest rate of 1.6 and 2.4 per cent, 2.4 and 3.6 per cent and 3.2 and 4.8 per cent (all increased and decreased by 20 per cent).

While either approach would be acceptable under IFRS 7, approach (a) provides information that seems more relevant and reliable than approach (b), since the sensitivity analysis will be more comparable with past periods. Whichever approach is used, disclosure of the method and assumptions should be provided.

IFRS 7 requires disclosure of a sensitivity analysis showing how profit or loss and equity would have been affected by changes in the relevant risk variable. The Standard is not clear whether sensitivity analysis should be provided on a pre or post tax basis. As equity is defined in IAS 32 as *the residual interest in the assets of the entity after deducting all of its liabilities*, and tax on gains or losses recognised in other comprehensive income (and taken to equity) will also be recognised in other comprehensive income (and taken to equity), it is reasonable to assume that for the purposes of the sensitivity analysis the analysis should be net of tax. Additionally, IFRS 7.IG36 provides an example of a sensitivity analysis which is determined on an after-tax basis.

Example 5.2.3A

Market risk disclosures: sensitivity analysis

Company D (ZAR functional currency) is a diversified oil and gas group. The earnings of the group are exposed to movements due to changes in market interest rates, equity prices, exchange rates and commodity prices. The entity expects the following to be reasonably possible changes in the relevant risk variable at the end of the reporting period:

ZAR market interest rates =	100 basis points
ZAR equity prices =	8%
ZAR/USD exchange rate =	15%
USD Brent crude price =	25%

Assume a tax rate of 30%. Profit after tax for the year ended 31 December 20X0 was:

ZAR 2,750million and equity was ZAR 1,000million. Company D has the following financial instruments that have an exposure to the relevant risk variable at the end of the reporting period.

1. USD denominated short term accounts receivable with a carrying value of ZAR 235million are held at amortised cost.

2. ZAR denominated listed equity investments that are classified as held for trading with a carrying value of ZAR 500million.

3. ZAR denominated listed equity investments that are classified as available-for-sale with a carrying value of ZAR 200million.

4. ZAR denominated fixed rate cash deposits with a carrying value ZAR 1,245million. The cash deposits are classified as loans and receivables and return a rate of 10 per cent per annum. The deposits were initially recognised at the beginning of the year.

5. ZAR denominated treasury bonds that have a fixed rate of interest of 12 per cent per annum with a carrying value of ZAR 765million. The bonds are designated as at fair value through profit or loss. A 100 basis point change in market interest rates is equivalent to a 4 per cent change in the fair value of the bond.

6. Purchased brent crude futures denominated in USD that are classified as held for trading and have a carrying value of ZAR 490million. A 100 basis point change in the ZAR market interest rate is equivalent to a 1 per cent change in the fair value of the futures and a 25 per cent change in the Brent crude oil price is equivalent to a 20 per cent change in the fair value of the futures.

7. USD denominated fixed rate borrowings initially recognised at the beginning of the year. The interest rate is 10 pr cent. The borrowings have been classified as a liability to be carried at amortised cost. The weighted average exchange rate during the reporting period was ZAR7:$1.These borrowings were designated as a hedge of a net investment of its foreign operation and had a carrying value at year end of ZAR 730million (USD100 million at a closing exchange rate of ZAR7.3:$1)

8. ZAR denominated floating rate borrowings of ZAR 350million that are classified as a financial liability held at amortised cost and were entered into at the beginning of the year for an amount of ZAR 350million. The floating interest resets on a quarterly basis in advance, with the quarterly rates during the past reporting period being as follows:

Month	**Rate**
1 January 20X0	14%
1 April 20X0	13%
1 July 20X0	12%
1 October 20X0	13%
1 January 20X1	14%

Company D wishes to present its sensitivity analysis by risk variable. Comparative financial data has been ignored for the purposes of this example.

The following represents the calculation of the market risk sensitivity analysis as required by IFRS 7.40.

Market interest rates

Items (1), (2), (3) and (4) do not affect profit or loss or equity if market interest rates change. In the case of item (4), the ZAR denominated fixed rate cash deposits that are classified as loans and receivables do not affect profit or loss or equity given a reasonably possible change in market interest rates since they are neither measured at fair value nor do they contain variable cash flows.

Item (5), the ZAR denominated fixed rate bonds that are designated at fair value through profit or loss will result in sensitivity in profit or loss of ZAR 765 million x 4% = **+/-ZAR 30.60million**.

Item (6), the Brent crude futures will result in sensitivity in profit or loss of +/-ZAR490 million x 1% = **+/-ZAR 4.90million**.

Item (7), the USD denominated fixed rate liability is designated as a hedging instrument for foreign currency risk only, with the carrying amount in foreign currency measured at amortised cost. This liability does not affect profit or loss or equity if market interest rates change since it is neither measured at fair value nor does it contain variable cash flows.

Item (8), the ZAR denominated floating rate borrowings are subject to floating interest rates. If market rates changed by 100 basis points during the period the sensitivity in interest cash flows would be 1.0% x ZAR 350million = **+/-ZAR 3.50million**

The treasury bond assets and the issued floating rate borrowings have the same directional sensitivity to interest rates with respect to their impact on profit or loss. As interest rates rise, the treasury bond assets fall in value, resulting in a loss in profit or loss, and the floating rate borrowing results in a higher interest expense in profit or loss. The vice versa is equally true when interest rates fall. Total profit or loss sensitivity as a result of changes in ZAR market interest rates is **+/-ZAR 39.00 million** after tax (30.60+4.90+3.50) * (1–30%).

ZAR Equity prices

Items (1), (4) – (8) do not affect profit or loss or equity is ZAR equity prices change.

Item (2), the ZAR listed investments that have been classified as held for trading will result in profit or loss sensitivity of ZAR 500million * 8% = +/-ZAR 40.00million.

Item (3), the ZAR listed investments that have been classified as available for sale will result in equity sensitivity of ZAR 200 million * 8% = +/-ZAR 16.00million.

Total profit or loss sensitivity as a result of changes in ZAR equity prices is **+/-ZAR 28.00million** after tax 40.00 * (1–30%).

Total equity sensitivity as a result of changes in ZAR equity prices is **+/-ZAR 11.20million** after tax 16.00 * (1–30%).

ZAR/USD exchange rate

Items (2), (3) (5) and (8) do not affect profit or loss or equity if ZAR/USD exchange rates change.

Item (1), the USD denominated accounts receivable will result in profit or loss sensitivity of ZAR 235million * 15% = +/-ZAR 35.25million.

Item (6), the USD denominated Brent crude derivatives will result in profit or loss sensitivity of ZAR 490million * 15% = +/-ZAR ZAR73.50million.

Item (7), the USD denominated borrowings will result in equity sensitivity of ZAR 730million * 15% = +/-ZAR 109.50million, being the re-translation of the borrowings at the end of the reporting period. Sensitivity of profit or loss due to recording interest cash flows during the year at a different exchange rate is determined as USD 100million * 10% interest rate * weighted average exchange rate during the year of ZAR7:$1 * sensitivity of 15% = ZAR 10.50 million

Total profit or loss sensitivity as a result of changes in the ZAR/USD exchange rate is
+/-ZAR 68.78million after tax (35.25+73.5–10.5) * (1–30%).

Total equity sensitivity as a result of changes in the ZAR/USD exchange rate is
+/-ZAR 76.65million after tax (109.5) * (1–30%).

USD Brent crude price

Items (1) – (5), (7) and (8) do not affect profit or loss or equity if USD Brent crude prices change.

Item (6), the USD denominated Brent crude futures will result in profit or loss sensitivity of ZAR 490million x 20% = +/- ZAR 98.00million.

Total profit or loss sensitivity as a result of changes in the Brent crude price is +/-ZAR 68.60million after tax 98.00 * (1–30%).

Disclosure

For financial instruments held, the company has used a sensitivity analysis technique that measures the change in the fair value and cash flows of the company's financial instruments for hypothetical changes in all relevant market risk variables.

The amounts generated from the sensitivity analysis are forward-looking estimates of market risk assuming certain market conditions. Actual results in the future may differ materially from those projected results due to the inherent uncertainty of global financial markets. The methods and assumptions used are the same as those applied in the previous reporting period.

The sensitivity of profit or loss and equity due to changes in the relevant risk variables as at 31 December 20X0 are set out in the table below. The methods and assumptions used in calculating are set out in note X1 to the financial statements.

The estimated change in fair values and cash flows for changes in market interest rates are based on an instantaneous increase or decrease of 100 basis points at the end of the reporting period, with all other variables remaining constant.

The estimated change in fair values for changes in ZAR equity prices are based on an instantaneous increase or decrease of 8 per cent for instruments at the end of the reporting period, with all other variables remaining constant.

The estimated change in fair values for changes in the ZAR/USD exchange rate are based on an instantaneous increase or decrease of 15 per cent for instruments at the end of the reporting period, with all other variables remaining constant.

The estimated change in fair values for changes in Brent crude prices are based on an instantaneous increase or decrease of 25 per cent for instruments at the end of the reporting period, with all other variables remaining constant.

The above-mentioned changes in the risk variables may result in non-proportional changes in fair values or cash flows due to the specific terms and nature of the relevant risk exposures.

The sensitivity analysis is for illustrative purposes only – in practice market rates rarely change in isolation and are likely to be interdependent.

The sensitivity of the relevant risk variables, on an after tax basis is as follows:

Market risk exposure	Profit or loss sensitivity ZAR million	Equity sensitivity ZAR million
Market interest rates	+/-39.00	–
ZAR equity prices	+/-28.00	+/-11.20
ZAR/USD exchange rates	+/-68.78	+/-76.65
USD Brent crude	+/-68.60	–

Example 5.2.3A above includes only non-optional derivatives, in this case Brent crude oil futures. Other non-optional derivatives include swaps and forward contracts. If these non-optional derivatives do not contain options

embedded within their contractual terms, like knock-out or knock-in options, early termination clauses that terminate at an amount other than at fair value, then the sensitivity to the underlying is likely to be the same irrespective of whether the price of the underlying moves up or down. This would not be the case for optional derivatives like options, or derivatives that are constructed using combinations of options, for example collars. As an option provides one-directional exposure, for example, protection against rising interest rates, then the fair value sensitivity of the option to increasing interest rates will be different from sensitivity to falling interest rates. The fair value sensitivity of optional derivatives will vary depending on the directional movement in the underlying market risk. The fair value sensitivity of an option to the underlying market risk will also depend on the price of the underlying at the end of the reporting period compared to the strike price of the option. If an option is nearly at-the-money it will have a greater sensitivity to changes in market risk when compared to an option that is deeply out-of-the-money.

Impairment of financial assets can also be affected by changes in an underlying market risk. However, it seems appropriate that for debt instruments only changes in existing impairment losses should be considered in the determination of the market risk sensitivity analysis. An entity should not project additional impairment losses that might occur given a movement in an underlying market risk. For example, if a loan is not impaired at the period end it will not be treated as impaired for the purposes of the sensitivity analysis.

If an available-for-sale debt instrument is impaired at the end of the reporting period and all the accumulated loss has been recognised in profit or loss in accordance with IAS 39.67–68, then the sensitivity of the fair value of the debt instrument for changes in interest rates will impact the extent of impairment recognised in profit or loss. Had interest rates been higher or lower, the amount of impairment recognised in profit or loss in the period would have differed as a different market interest rate would have resulted in a different fair value.

If an available-for-sale debt instrument is not impaired at the end of the reporting period, changes in the relevant risk variable should not result in an impairment charge. For example, the increased likelihood of a borrower defaulting in a higher interest rate environment should not result in the lender recognising an impairment charge in its interest rate sensitivity analysis. This view is consistent with the view that credit risk is not a market risk, as discussed at the start of this section.

If a floating rate financial asset is impaired at the end of the reporting period, the amount of interest income in the period will be sensitive to changes in the floating rates for the period. If the floating rate cash flows are themselves impaired, as opposed to the principal cash flow, then changes in the floating rate will impact the amount of impairment at the period end. This is not the case for a fixed rate asset as all cash flows are fixed and the effective interest rate is not sensitive to changes in interest rates.

In the case of sensitivity analysis of equity price risk of non-monetary available-for-sale financial assets, it is necessary to give careful consideration to whether a reasonably possible change in the relevant equity price would affect equity or profit or loss. Consider the case of an investment in an equity security that has already suffered impairment by the end of the reporting period. As reversals of impairment on equity securities classified as available-for-sale may not be recorded through profit or loss, in such a case a reasonably possible downward fall in the equity price will be shown as affecting profit or loss, but an equivalent upward shift would be shown as affecting equity. The fair value of an available-for-sale equity security that has not previously been impaired could become impaired depending on what is considered a reasonably possible downward shift in equity prices (based on a significant or prolonged decline in fair value of an investment in an equity security below cost in accordance with IAS 39.61). In such a case consideration must be given to whether a reasonably possible downward movement in the equity price would affect equity or profit or loss, taking into account an entity's impairment policy.

(vi) Provide additional disclosures

When the sensitivity analysis is unrepresentative of a risk inherent in a financial instrument, disclosure of that fact and the reason why the entity believes the sensitivity analysis is unrepresentative shall be provided. [IFRS 7.42] Examples where this may be the case include:
[IFRS 7.IG37]

(a) financial instruments contain terms and conditions whose effects are not apparent from the sensitivity analysis, e.g. options that are deep out of (or in) the money for the chosen change in risk variable;

(b) financial assets that are illiquid, such that the calculated changes in profit or loss are difficult to realise where there are low volumes of transactions or lack of counterparties to trade at those prices or rates;

(c) large holdings in financial assets that would be sold at a discount or premium to the quoted prices.

In these cases, additional disclosure may be provided of the terms and conditions of the financial instruments, the effect on profit or loss if the term or condition were met, description of how the risk is hedged and the reasons for illiquidity of the instruments concerned. [IFRS 7.IG38 and IG39]

IFRS 7.IG38(b) states that when financial instruments contain terms and conditions whose effects are not apparent from the sensitivity analysis, an entity may wish to state the effect on profit or loss if the term or condition were met. An entity may also wish to state the impact on equity, as this is consistent with the objective of sensitivity analysis of providing the user with the impact on profit or loss and equity. For example, an entity may have designated a purchased interest cap as a cash flow hedge of highly probable forecast floating interest payments where the option is so deeply out-of-the-money at the period end that no intrinsic value is recognised in other comprehensive income (and taken to equity). As the option is so deeply out-of-the-money, a moderate change in interest rates has little fair value sensitivity. If interest rates were to increase significantly, the option's fair value would be subject to fair value movements in profit or loss, and potentially would result in part of the fair value being recognised in other comprehensive income (and taken to equity) if interest rates are higher than the strike price of the cap. As the derivative is an effective hedging instrument in a cash flow hedge, illustrating the impact on equity is equally appropriate to illustrating the impact in profit or loss.

The sensitivity analysis may not give a true presentation of exposure to risk in the cases where the hedging instrument is in the scope of IFRS 7, but the hedged item is not. An example is a hedge of a net investment in a foreign operation. Changes in the sensitivity of the fair value of derivatives or foreign currency risk for non-derivative financial instruments will be reported in other comprehensive income if it is a qualifying hedging instrument in a net investment hedge. The changes in the hedged item, being the re-translation of the net assets in accordance with IAS 21 is not required to be reported in the sensitivity analysis since it is not a financial instrument within the scope of IFRS 7. An entity may choose to provide additional disclosure to explain that the retranslation of the net assets of the foreign operation would reduce the sensitivity of the hedging instrument in equity. For example, if the entity designates spot foreign currency risk as being hedged and the hedge is fully effective, the gains and losses on the hedging instrument recognised in other comprehensive income (and taken to equity) will be offset by the losses and gains on foreign currency translation on the net assets of the foreign operation, which are also recognised in other comprehensive income (and taken to equity). Similarly, additional disclosure may be appropriate for cash flow hedges or fair value hedges of non-financial items (including unrecognised 'off balance sheet' items). An entity may designate a foreign exchange forward contract in a highly effective hedge of a firm commitment to acquire plant and equipment, with the hedged risk being spot foreign currency risk. The forward contract will be included in the sensitivity analysis, while the fair value adjustment to the firm commitment to acquire a non-financial item will be outside the scope of IFRS 7. Additional disclosures may be useful to explain that the retranslation of the firm commitment at spot rates reduces the sensitivity of the hedging instrument in profit or loss.

Example 5.2.3B

Interest rate risk

[IFRS 7.IG36]

At 31 December 20X2, if interest rates at that date had been 10 basis points lower with all other variables held constant, post-tax profit for the year would have been CU1.7 million (20X1 – CU2.4 million) higher, arising mainly as a result of lower interest expense on variable borrowings, and other comprehensive income would have been CU2.8 million (20X1 – CU3.2 million) higher, arising mainly as a result of an increase in the fair value of fixed rate financial assets classified as available for sale. If interest rates had been 10 basis points higher, with all other variables held constant, post-tax profit would have been CU1.5 million (20X1 – CU2.1 million) lower, arising mainly as a result of higher interest expense on variable borrowings, and other comprehensive income would have been CU3.0 million (20X1 – CU3.4 million) lower, arising mainly as a result of a decrease in the fair value of fixed rate financial assets classified as available for sale. Profit is more sensitive to interest rate decreases than increases because of borrowings with capped interest rates. The sensitivity is lower in 20X2 than in 20X1 because of a reduction in outstanding borrowings that has occurred as the entity's debt has matured (see note X).

Foreign currency exchange rate risk

At 31 December 20X2, if the CU had weakened 10 per cent against the US dollar with all other variables held constant, post-tax profit for the year would have been CU2.8 million (20X1 – CU6.4 million) lower, and other comprehensive income would have been CU1.2 million (20X1 – CU1.1 million) higher. Conversely, if the CU had strengthened 10 per cent against the US dollar with all other variables held constant, post-tax profit would have been CU2.8 million (20X1 – CU6.4 million) higher, and other comprehensive income would have been CU1.2 million (20X1 – CU1.1 million) lower. The lower foreign currency exchange rate sensitivity in profit in 20X2 compared with 20X1 is attributable to a reduction in foreign currency denominated debt. Equity is more sensitive in 20X2 than in 20X1 because of the increased use of hedges of foreign currency purchases, offset by the reduction in foreign currency debt.

As an alternative to sensitivity analysis, disclosure may be provided of a ***value-at-risk analysis*** that reflects interdependencies between risk variables. An entity may only disclose value-at-risk analysis where the entity uses such a model to manage risk internally. Disclosure shall include an explanation of the method used in preparing such an analysis, how the model works (such as whether the model is based on a delta-normal variance-covariance approach, historical simulation or Monte Carlo simulation), the main parameters and assumptions underlying the data provided such as the holding period, confidence interval, historical observation period and weightings assigned to the observations, how options are dealt with and which volatilities and correlations are used. Disclosure of the objective of the method used and of the limitations that may result in the information not fully reflecting the fair value of the assets and liabilities involved shall also be provided [IFRS 7.41 & B20]

The value-at-risk analysis used internally may measure the potential for loss or gain including the effects of items that are outside the scope of IFRS 7 (e.g. contracts to buys or sell non-financial items outside the scope of IAS 39, hedged items that are outside the scope of IFRS 7 or risks such as credit risk which are not market risks). In contrast to conventional sensitivity analysis as discussed above, a value-at-risk analysis including such items would, if used as a model to manage risk internally, satisfy the requirements of the Standard. If such items are included, this fact should be clearly disclosed as part of the method used in preparing the analysis.

Example 5.2.3C

Market risk disclosures: value at risk

The Group manages the market risk in its trading and treasury portfolios through the use of value-at-risk (VaR) limits as well as stress testing, position and sensitivity limits. VaR is a technique that produces estimates of the potential negative change in the market value of a portfolio over a specified time horizon at a given confidence level. The table below sets out the trading and treasury VaR for the Group, which assumes a 95 per cent confidence level and a one-day time horizon. The VAR model uses largely historical data from the preceding three years to simulate scenarios of the future.

Year	Period end £m	Minimum £m	Maximum £m	Average £m
Trading VaR				
20X1	17.2	13.4	24.3	19.1
20X0	16.2	14.0	22.3	18.1
Treasury VaR				
20X1	8.1	6.6	12.1	9.5
20X0	8.0	6.9	13.1	8.5

The Group's VaR should be interpreted in light of the limitations of the methodologies used. These limitations include the following.

- Historical data may not provide the best estimate of the joint distribution of risk factor changes in the future and may fail to capture the risk of possible extreme adverse market movements which have not occurred in the historical window used in the calculations.
- VaR using a one-day time horizon does not fully capture the market risk of positions that cannot be liquidated or hedged within one day.
- The Group largely computes the VaR of the trading portfolios at the close of business and positions may change substantially during the course of the trading day. Controls are in place to limit the Group's intra-day exposure such as the calculation of VaR for selected portfolios.
- VaR using a 95 per cent confidence level does not reflect the extent of potential losses beyond that percentile.

These limitations and the nature of the VaR measure mean that the Group can neither guarantee that losses will not exceed the VaR amounts indicated nor that losses in excess of the VaR amounts will not occur more frequently than once in 20 business days.

Example 5.2.3D

The extract below is an example of application of the requirements in IFRS 7.42 to disclose sensitivity analysis of market risks

Extract from Novartis Annual Report 2008, p. 209–10:

Value at risk

The Group uses a value at risk (VAR) computation to estimate the potential ten-day loss in the fair value of its financial instruments.

A 10-day period is used because of an assumption that not all positions could be undone in one day given the size of the positions. The VAR computation includes the Group's financial debt, short-term and long-term investments, foreign currency forwards, swaps and options as well as anticipated transactions. Foreign currency trade payables and receivables as well as net investments in foreign subsidiaries are included in the computation.

The VAR estimates are made assuming normal market conditions, using a 95% confidence interval. The Group uses a 'Delta Normal' model to determine the observed inter-relationships between movements in interest rates, stock markets and various currencies. These inter-relationships are determined by observing interest rate, stock market movements and forward foreign currency rate movements over a 60 day period for the calculation of VAR amounts.

The estimated potential 10-day loss in pre-tax income from the Group's foreign currency instruments, the estimated potential 10-day loss of its equity holdings, and the estimated potential 10-day loss in fair value of its interest rate sensitive instruments (primarily financial debt and investments of liquid funds under normal market conditions) as calculated in the VAR model are the following:

	Dec 31, 2008 USD millions	Dec 31, 2007 USD millions
All financial Instruments	318	230
Analyzed by components:		
Instruments sensitive to foreign currency exchange rates	278	165
Instruments sensitive to equity market movements	181	110
Instruments sensitive to interest rates	21	12

The average, high, and low VAR amounts are as follows:

2008	Average USD millions	High USD millions	Low USD millions
All financial Instruments	196	318	135
Analyzed by components:			
Instruments sensitive to foreign currency exchange rates	158	278	74
Instruments sensitive to equity market movements	162	291	95
Instruments sensitive to Interest rates	73	233	10

2007	Average USD millions	High USD millions	Low USD millions
All financial instruments	108	230	52
Analyzed by components:			
Instruments sensitive to foreign currency exchange rates	56	165	30
Instruments sensitive to equity market movements	80	135	33
Instruments sensitive to Interest rates	25	40	8

The VAR computation is a risk analysis tool designed to statistically estimate the maximum potential ten day loss from adverse movements in foreign currency exchange rates, equity prices and interest rates under normal market conditions. The computation does not purport to represent actual losses in fair value on earnings to be incurred by the Group, nor does it consider the effect of favourable changes in market rates. The Group cannot predict actual future movements in such market rates and it does not claim that these VAR results are indicative of future movements in such market rates or to be representative of any actual impact that future changes in market rates may have on the Group's future results of operations or financial position.

In addition to these VAR analyses, the Group uses stress testing techniques that aim to reflect a worst case scenario on the financial assets monitored by Group Treasury. For these calculations, the Group uses the worst movements during a period of six months over the past 20 years in each category. For 2008 and 2007, the worst case loss scenario was configured as follows:

	Dec 31, 2008 USD millions	Dec 31, 2007 USD millions
All financial Instruments	300	474
Analyzed by components:		
Instruments sensitive to foreign currency exchange rates	144	60
Instruments sensitive to equity market movements	128	342
Instruments sensitive to Interest rates	28	72

In the Group's risk analysis, Novartis considered this worst case scenario acceptable as it could reduce income, but would not endanger the solvency or the investment grade credit standing of the Group. While it is highly unlikely that all worst case fluctuations would happen simultaneously, as shown in the model, the actual market can of course produce bigger movements in the future than it has historically. Additionally, in such a worst case environment, management actions could further mitigate the Group's exposure.

Example 5.2.3E

The extract below is an example of application of the requirements in IFRS 7.41–42 to disclose sensitivity analysis of market risks

Extract from BP Annual Report and Accounts 2008, p. 143–5

(a) Market risk

Market risk is the risk or uncertainty arising from possible market price movements and their impact on the future performance of a business. The market price movements that the group is exposed to include oil, natural gas and power prices (commodity price risk), foreign currency exchange rates, interest rates, equity prices and other indices that could adversely affect the value of the group's financial assets, liabilities or expected future cash flows. The group enters into derivatives in a well established entrepreneurial trading operation. In addition, the group has developed a control framework aimed at managing the volatility inherent in certain of its natural business exposures. In accordance with this control framework the group enters into various transactions using derivatives for risk management purposes.

During recent periods of increased volatility in financial markets the group's policies in relation to managing market risk continue to be appropriate and are outlined in further detail below. The group measures market risk exposure arising from its trading positions using value-at-risk techniques. These techniques are based on a variance/covariance model or a Monte Carlo simulation and make a statistical assessment of the market risk arising from possible future changes in market prices over a 24-hour period. The calculation of the range of potential changes in fair value takes into account a snapshot of the end-of-day exposures and the history of one-day price movements, together with the correlation of these price movements. The value-at-risk measure is supplemented by stress testing and tail risk analysis.

The trading value-at-risk model is used for derivative financial instrument types such as: interest rate forward and futures contracts, swap agreements, options and swaptions; foreign exchange forward and futures contracts, swap agreements and options; and oil, natural gas and power price forwards, futures, swap agreements and options. Additionally, where physical commodities or non-derivative forward contracts are held as part of a trading position, they are also reflected in the value-at-risk model. For options, a linear approximation is included in the value-at-risk models when full revaluation is not possible.

The value-at-risk table does not incorporate any of the group's natural business exposures or any derivatives entered into to risk manage those exposures. Market risk exposure in respect of embedded derivatives is also not included in the value-at-risk table. Instead separate sensitivity analyses are disclosed below.

Value-at-risk limits are in place for each trading activity and for the group's trading activity in total. The board has delegated an overall limit of $100 million value at risk in support of this trading activity. The high and low values at risk indicated in the table below for each type of activity are independent of each other. Through the portfolio effect the high value at risk for the group as a whole is lower than the sum of the highs for the constituent parts. The potential movement in fair values is expressed to a 95% confidence interval. This means that, in statistical terms, one would expect to see a decrease in fair values greater than the trading value at risk on one occasion per month if the portfolio were left unchanged.

Value at risk for 1 day at 95% confidence interval	$ million 2008				$ million 2007			
	High	Low	Average	Year end	High	Low	Average	Year end
Group trading	76	20	37	69	50	24	35	38
Oil price trading	69	12	25	63	46	16	26	34
Natural gas price trading	50	12	24	23	32	9	16	15
Power price trading	14	3	7	4	6	1	3	5
Currency trading	4	–	2	–	6	1	3	2
Interest rate trading	7	–	2	1	11	–	5	2
Other trading	5	1	2	2	7	–	2	1

(i) Commodity price risk

The group's integrated supply and trading function uses conventional financial and commodity instruments and physical cargoes available in the related commodity markets. Natural gas swaps, options and futures are used to mitigate price risk. Power trading is undertaken using a combination of over-the-counter forward contracts and other derivative contracts, including options and futures. This activity is on both a standalone basis and in conjunction with gas derivatives in relation to gas-generated power margin. In addition, NGLs are traded around certain US inventory locations using over-the-counter forward contracts in conjunction with over-the-counter swaps, options and physical inventories. Trading value-at-risk information in relation to these activities is shown in the table above.

As described above, the group also carries out risk management of certain short-term natural business exposures using over-the-counter swaps and exchange futures contracts with a duration of less than three years. In past periods commodity price risk relating to this activity has been managed using value-at-risk measures. For 2008 a separate control framework is now used as described under market risk above. For these derivative contracts the sensitivity of the net fair value to an immediate 10% increase or decrease in all reference prices would have been $90 million at 31 December 2008. This figure does not include any corresponding economic benefit or disbenefit that would arise from the natural business exposure which would be expected to largely offset the gain or loss on the derivatives.

In addition, the group has embedded derivatives relating to certain natural gas and crude oil contracts. The net fair value of these embedded derivatives was a liability of $1,867 million at 31 December 2008 (2007 liability of $2,085 million). Key information on the natural gas contracts is given below.

At 31 December	2008	2007
Remaining contract terms	1 year 9 months to 9 years 9 months	9 months to 11 years
Contractual/national amount	3,585 million therms	3,889 million therms
Discount rate- nominal risk free	2.5%	4.5%

For these embedded derivatives the sensitivity of the net fair value to an immediate 10% favourable or unfavourable change in the key assumptions is as follows.

	$ million 2008				$ million 2007			
At 31 December	Gas price	Oil price	Power price	Dis-count rate	Gas price	Oil price	Power price	Dis-count rate
Favourable 10% change	291	81	27	16	317	72	37	31
Unfavourable 10% change	(289)	(81)	(27)	(16)	(368)	(84)	(34)	(32)

The sensitivities for risk management activity and embedded derivatives are hypothetical and should not be considered to be predictive of future performance. In addition, for the purposes of this analysis, in the above table, the effect of a variation in a particular assumption on the fair value of the embedded derivatives is calculated independently of any change in another assumption. In reality, changes in one factor may contribute to changes in another, which may magnify or counteract the sensitivities. Furthermore, the estimated fair values as disclosed should not be considered indicative of future earnings on these contracts.

(ii) Foreign currency exchange risk

Where the group enters into foreign currency exchange contracts for entrepreneurial trading purposes the activity is controlled using trading value-at-risk techniques as explained above. This activity is described as currency trading in the value-at-risk table above.

Since BP has global operations, fluctuations in foreign currency exchange rates can have significant effects on the group's reported results. The effects of most exchange rate fluctuations are absorbed in business operating results through changing cost competitiveness, lags in market adjustment to movements in rates and conversion differences accounted for on specific transactions. For this reason, the total effect of exchange rate fluctuations is not identifiable separately in the group's reported results. The main underlying economic currency of the group's cash flows is the US dollar. This is because BP's major product, oil, is priced internationally in US dollars. BP's foreign currency exchange management policy is to minimize economic and material transactional exposures arising from currency movements against the US dollar. The group coordinates the handling of foreign currency exchange risks centrally, by netting off naturally-occurring opposite exposures wherever possible, and then dealing with any material residual foreign currency exchange risks.

The group manages these exposures by constantly reviewing the foreign currency economic value at risk and managing such risk to keep the 12-month foreign currency value at risk below $200 million. At 31 December 2008, the foreign currency value at risk was $70 million (2007 $60 million). At no point over the past three years did the value at risk exceed the maximum risk limit. The most significant exposures relate to capital expenditure commitments and other UK and European operational requirements, for which a hedging programme is in place and hedge accounting is claimed as outlined in Note 34.

For highly probable forecast capital expenditures the group locks in the US-dollar cost of non-US dollar supplies by using currency forwards and futures. The main exposures are sterling, euro, Norwegian krone, Australian dollar, Korean won and Canadian dollar, and at 31 December 2008 open contracts were in place for $949 million sterling, $553 million euro, $392 million Norwegian krone, $303 million Australian dollar, $187 million Korean won and $712 million Canadian dollar capital expenditures maturing within seven years, with over 65% of the deals maturing within two years (2007 $732 million sterling, $931 million euro, $479 million Norwegian krone, $38 million Australian dollar, $243 million Korean won and $7 million Ca nadian dollar capital expenditures maturing within eight years with over 80% of the deals maturing within two years).

For other UK, European, Canadian and Australian operational requirements the group uses cylinders and currency forwards to hedge the estimated exposures on a 12-month rolling basis. At 31 December 2008, the open positions relating to cylinders consisted of receive sterling, pay US dollar, purchased call and sold put options (cylinders) for $1,660 million (2007 $2,800 million); receive euro, pay US dollar cylinders for $1,612 million (2007 $1,400 million); receive Canadian dollar, pay US dollar cylinders for $250 million (2007 nil); and receive Australian dollar, pay US dollar cylinders for $455 million (2007 $382 million). At 31 December 2008, the open positions relating to currency forwards consisted of buy sterling, sell US dollar, currency forwards for $816 million (2007 nil); buy euro, sell US dollar currency forwards for $141 million (2007 nil); buy Canadian dollar, sell US dollar, currency forwards for $50 million (2007 nil); and buy Australian dollar, sell US dollar, currency forwards for $90 million (2007 nil).

In addition, most of the group's borrowings are in US dollars or are hedged with respect to the US dollar. At 31 December 2008, the total foreign currency net borrowings not swapped into US dollars amounted to $1,037 million (2007 $1,045 million). Of this total, $92 million was denominated in currencies other than the functional currency of the individual operating unit being entirely Canadian dollars (2007 $268 million, being $191 million in Canadian dollars and $77 million in Trinidad & Tobago dollars). It is estimated that a 10% change in the corresponding exchange rates would result in an exchange gain or loss in the income statement of $9 million (2007 $27 million).

(iii) Interest rate risk

Where the group enters into money market contracts for entrepreneurial trading purposes the activity is controlled using value-at-risk techniques as described above. This activity is described as interest rate trading in the value-at-risk table above.

BP is also exposed to interest rate risk from the possibility that changes in interest rates will affect future cash flows or the fair values of its financial instruments, principally finance debt.

While the group issues debt in a variety of currencies based on market opportunities, it uses derivatives to swap the debt to a US dollar floating rate exposure but in certain defined circumstances maintains a fixed rate exposure for a proportion of debt. The proportion of floating rate debt net of interest rate swaps at 31 December 2008 was 72% of total finance debt outstanding (2007 68%). The weighted average interest rate on finance debt at 31 December 2008 is 3% (2007 5%) and the weighted average maturity of fixed rate debt is three years (2007 two years).

The group's earnings are sensitive to changes in interest rates on the floating rate element of the group's finance debt. If the interest rates applicable to floating rate instruments were to have increased by 1% on 1 January 2009, it is estimated that the group's profit before taxation for 2009 would decrease by approximately $239 million (2007 $168 million decrease in 2008). This assumes that the amount and mix of fixed and floating rate debt, including finance leases, remains unchanged from that in place at 31 December 2008 and that the change in interest rates is effective from the beginning of the year. Where the interest rate applicable to an instrument is reset during a quarter it is assumed that this occurs at the beginning of the quarter and remains unchanged for the rest of the year. In reality, the fixed/floating rate mix will fluctuate over the year and interest rates will change continually. Furthermore, the effect on earnings shown by this analysis does not consider the effect of any other changes in general economic activity that may accompany such an increase in interest rates.

(iv) Equity price risk

The group holds equity investments, typically made for strategic purposes, that are classified as non-current available-for-sale financial assets and are measured initially at fair value with changes in fair value recognized directly in equity. Accumulated fair value changes are recycled to the income statement on disposal, or when the investment is impaired. Impairment losses of $546 million have been recognized in 2008 relating to listed non-current available-for-sale investments. For further information see Note 29.

At 31 December 2008, it is estimated that an increase of 10% in quoted equity prices would result in an immediate credit to equity of $59 million (2007 $162 million credit to equity), whilst a decrease of 10% in quoted equity prices would result in an immediate charge to profit or loss of $48 million and a charge to equity of $11 million (2007 $162 million charge to equity).

At 31 December 2008, 56% (2007 70%) of the carrying amount of non-current available-for-sale financial assets represented the group's stake in Rosneft, thus the group's exposure is concentrated on changes in the share price of this equity in particular.

6 Disclosure checklist

This checklist was up-to-dafte at the time of going to press. The checklist includes the amendments made to IFRS 7, *Improving disclosures about financial instruments*, issued in March 2009. The IASB continues to refine its standards via editorial corrections and annual improvements. Accordingly, reference should be made to the most recent versions of these standards when financial statements are being prepared.

IFRS 7 Reference	IFRS 7 Disclosure Checklist
7	An entity shall disclose information that enables users of its financial statements to evaluate the significance of financial instruments for its financial position and performance.
	Statement of financial position *Categories of financial assets and financial liabilities* The carrying amounts of each of the following categories, as defined in IAS 39, shall be disclosed either in the statement of financial position or in the notes:
8(a)	(a) financial assets at fair value through profit or loss, showing separately: i. those designated as such upon initial recognition; and ii. those classified as held for trading in accordance with IAS 39;
8(b)	(b) held-to-maturity investments;
8(c)	(c) loans and receivables;
8(d)	(d) available-for-sale financial assets;

8(e)	(e) financial liabilities at fair value through profit or loss, showing separately: i. those designated as such upon initial recognition; and ii. those classified as held for trading in accordance with IAS 39; and
8(f)	(f) financial liabilities measured at amortised cost.
	Financial assets or financial liabilities at fair value through profit or loss
	If the entity has designated a loan or receivable (or group of loans or receivables) as at fair value through profit or loss, it shall disclose:
9(a)	(a) the maximum exposure to credit risk of the loan or receivable (or group of loans or receivables) at the end of the reporting period;
36(a)	Note: The maximum exposure to credit risk reported should not take account of any collateral held or other credit enhancements (e.g. netting agreements that do not qualify for offset in accordance with IAS 32 (see also IFRS 7.B9 & B10).
9(b)	(b) the amount by which any related credit derivatives or similar instruments mitigate that maximum exposure to credit risk;
9(c)	(c) the amount of change, during the period and cumulatively, in the fair value of the loan or receivable (or group of loans or receivables) that is attributable to changes in the credit risk of the financial asset determined either: i. as the amount of change in its fair value that is not attributable to changes in market conditions that give rise to market risk; or ii. using an alternative method the entity believes more faithfully represents the amount of change in its fair value that is attributable to changes in the credit risk of the asset;
9(c)	Note: Changes in market conditions that give rise to market risk include changes in an observed (benchmark) interest rate, commodity price, foreign exchange rate or index of prices or rates.
9(d)	(d) the amount of the change in the fair value of any related credit derivatives or similar instruments that has occurred during the period and cumulatively since the loan or receivable was designated.

	If the entity has designated a financial liability as at fair value through profit or loss in accordance with paragraph 9 of IAS 39, it shall disclose:
10(a)	(a) the amount of change, during the period and cumulatively, in the fair value of the financial liability that is attributable to changes in the credit risk of that liability determined either: i. as the amount of change in its fair value that is not attributable to changes in market conditions that give rise to market risk (see also IFRS 7.B4); or ii. using an alternative method the entity believes more faithfully represents the amount of change in its fair value that is attributable to changes in the credit risk of the liability;
10(a)	Note: Changes in market conditions that give rise to market risk include changes in a benchmark interest rate, the price of another entity's financial instrument, a commodity price, a foreign exchange rate or an index of prices or rates. For contracts that include a unit-linking feature, changes in market conditions include changes in the performance of the related internal or external investment fund.
10(b)	(b) the difference between the financial liability's carrying amount and the amount the entity would be contractually required to pay at maturity to the holder of the obligation.
	The entity shall disclose:
11(a)	(a) the methods used to determine the amount of change that is attributable to changes in the credit risk in compliance with the requirements in paragraphs 9(c) and 10(a) of IFRS 7 (see above).
11(b)	(b) if the entity believes that the disclosure it has given to comply with the requirements in paragraph 9(c) or 10(a) of IFRS 7 does not faithfully represent the change in the fair value of the financial asset or financial liability attributable to changes in its credit risk, the reasons for reaching this conclusion and the factors it believes are relevant.
	Reclassification
12	If the entity has reclassified a financial asset (in accordance with paragraphs 51–54 of IAS 39) as one measured: (a) at cost or amortised cost, rather than at fair value; or (b) at fair value, rather than at cost or amortised cost,

	it shall disclose the amount reclassified into and out of each category and the reason for that reclassification.
12A	If the entity has reclassified a financial asset out of the fair value through profit or loss category in accordance with paragraph 50B or 50D of IAS 39 or out of the available-for-sale category in accordance with paragraph 50E of IAS 39, it shall disclose:
	(a) the amount reclassified into and out of each category;
	(b) for each reporting period until derecognition, the carrying amounts and fair values of all financial assets that have been reclassified in the current and previous reporting periods;
	(c) if a financial asset was reclassified in accordance with paragraph 50B, the rare situation, and the facts and circumstances indicating that the situation was rare;
	(d) for the reporting period when the financial asset was reclassified, the fair value gain or loss on the financial asset recognised in profit or loss or other comprehensive income in that reporting period and in the previous reporting period;
	(e) for each reporting period following the reclassification (including the reporting period in which the financial asset was reclassified) until derecognition of the financial asset, the fair value gain or loss that would have been recognised in profit or loss or other comprehensive income if the financial asset had not been reclassified, and the gain, loss, income and expense recognised in profit or loss; and
	(f) the effective interest rate and estimated amounts of cash flows the entity expects to recover, as at the date of reclassification of the financial asset.
	Derecognition
	An entity may have transferred financial assets in such a way that part or all of the financial assets do not qualify for derecognition. The entity shall disclose for each class of such financial assets:
13(a)	(a) the nature of the assets;
13(b)	(b) the nature of the risks and rewards of ownership to which the entity remains exposed;
13(c)	(c) when the entity continues to recognise all of the assets, the carrying amounts of the assets and of the associated liabilities; and

13(d)	(d) when the entity continues to recognise the assets to the extent of its continuing involvement, the total carrying amount of the original assets, the amount of the assets that the entity continues to recognise, and the carrying amount of the associated liabilities.
	Collateral
	An entity shall disclose:
14(a)	(a) the carrying amount of financial assets it has pledged as collateral for liabilities or contingent liabilities, including amounts that have been reclassified in the statement of financial position separately from other assets as the transferee has the right to sell or repledge the collateral.
14(b)	(b) the terms and conditions relating to its pledge.
	When an entity holds collateral (of financial or non-financial assets) and is permitted to sell or repledge the collateral in the absence of default by the owner of the collateral, it shall disclose:
15(a)	(a) the fair value of the collateral held;
15(b)	(b) the fair value of any such collateral sold or repledged, and whether the entity has an obligation to return it; and
15(c)	(c) the terms and conditions associated with its use of the collateral.
	Allowance account for credit losses
16	When financial assets are impaired by credit losses and the entity records the impairment in a separate account (e.g. an allowance account used to record individual impairments or a similar account used to record a collective impairment of assets) rather than directly reducing the carrying amount of the asset, it shall disclose a reconciliation of changes in that account during the period for each class of financial assets.
	Compound financial instruments with multiple embedded derivatives
17	If an entity has issued an instrument that contains both a liability and an equity component and the instrument has multiple embedded derivatives whose values are interdependent (such as a callable convertible debt instrument), it shall disclose the existence of those features.
	Defaults and breaches
	For loans payable recognised at the end of the reporting period, an entity shall disclose:

18(a)	(a) details of any defaults during the period of principal, interest, sinking fund, or redemption terms of those loans payable;
18(b)	(b) the carrying amount of the loans payable in default at the end of the reporting period; and
18(c)	(c) whether the default was remedied, or the terms of the loans payable were renegotiated, before the financial statements were authorised for issue.
19	If, during the period, there were breaches of loan agreement terms other than those described in paragraph 18 of IFRS 7 (see above), an entity shall disclose the same information as required by paragraph 18 if those breaches permitted the lender to demand accelerated repayment (unless the breaches were remedied, or the terms of the loan were renegotiated, on or before the end of the reporting period).
	Statement of comprehensive income *Items of income, expense, gains or losses* An entity shall disclose the following items of income, expense, gains or losses either in the statement of comprehensive income or in the notes:
20(a)	(a) net gains or net losses on: i. financial assets or financial liabilities at fair value through profit or loss, showing separately those on financial assets or financial liabilities designated as such upon initial recognition, and those on financial assets or financial liabilities that are classified as held for trading; ii. available-for-sale financial assets, showing separately the amount of gain or loss recognised in other comprehensive income during the period and the amount reclassified from equity to profit or loss for the period; iii. held-to-maturity investments; iv. loans and receivables; and v. financial liabilities measured at amortised cost;
20(b)	(b) total interest income and total interest expense (calculated using the effective interest method) for financial assets or financial liabilities that are not at fair value through profit or loss;
20(c)	(c) fee income and expense (other than amounts included in determining the effective interest rate) arising from: i. financial assets or financial liabilities that are not at fair value through profit or loss; and

	ii. trust and other fiduciary activities that result in the holding or investing of assets on behalf of individuals, trusts, retirement benefit plans, and other institutions;
20(d)	(d) accrued interest income on impaired financial assets; and
20(e)	(e) the amount of any impairment loss for each class of financial asset.
	Other disclosures
	Accounting policies
21	In accordance with paragraph 117 of IAS 1 Presentation of Financial Statements (as revised in 2007), an entity discloses, in the summary of significant accounting policies, the measurement basis (or bases) used in preparing the financial statements and the other accounting policies used that are relevant to an understanding of the financial statements, including:
B5(a)	for financial assets or financial liabilities designated as at fair value through profit or loss: (i) the nature of the financial assets or financial liabilities the entity has designated as at fair value through profit or loss; (ii) the criteria for so designating such financial assets or financial liabilities on initial recognition; and (iii) how the entity has satisfied the conditions for such designation including where appropriate a narrative description of the circumstances underlying the measurement or recognition inconsistency that would otherwise arise, or how designation at fair value through profit or loss is consistent with the entity's documented risk management or investment strategy.
B5(b)	the criteria for designating financial assets as available for sale.
B5(c)	whether regular way purchases and sales of financial assets are accounted for at trade date or at settlement date.
B5(d)	when an allowance account is used to reduce the carrying amount of financial assets impaired by credit losses:

	(i) the criteria for determining when the carrying amount of impaired financial assets is reduced directly (or, in the case of a reversal of a write-down, increased directly) and when the allowance account is used; and (ii) the criteria for writing off amounts charged to the allowance account against the carrying amount of impaired financial assets.
B5(e)	how net gains or net losses on each category of financial instrument are determined, for example, whether the net gains or net losses on items at fair value through profit or loss include interest or dividend income.
B5(f)	the criteria the entity uses to determine that there is objective evidence that an impairment loss has occurred.
B5(g)	when the terms of financial assets that would otherwise be past due or impaired have been renegotiated, the accounting policy for financial assets that are the subject of renegotiated terms.
B5	Note. Paragraph 122 of IAS 1 (as revised in 2007) also requires entities to disclose, in the summary of significant accounting policies or other notes, the judgements, apart from those involving estimations, that management has made in the process of applying the entity's accounting policies and that have the most significant effect on the amounts recognised in the financial statements.
	Hedge accounting
	An entity shall disclose the following separately for each type of hedge (i.e. fair value hedges, cash flow hedges, and hedges of net investments in foreign operations):
22(a)	(a) a description of each type of hedge;
22(b)	(b) a description of the financial instruments designated as hedging instruments and their fair values at the end of the reporting period; and
22(c)	(c) the nature of the risks being hedged.
	For cash flow hedges, an entity shall disclose:
23(a)	(a) the periods when the cash flows are expected to occur and when they are expected to affect profit or loss;
23(b)	(b) a description of any forecast transaction for which hedge accounting had previously been used, but which is no longer expected to occur;
23(c)	(c) the amount that was recognised in other comprehensive income during the period;

23(d)	(d) the amount that was reclassified from equity to profit or loss for the period, showing the amount included in each line item in the statement of comprehensive income; and
23(e)	(e) the amount that was removed from equity during the period and included in the initial cost or other carrying amount of a non-financial asset or non-financial liability whose acquisition or incurrence was a hedged highly probable forecast transaction.
	An entity shall disclose separately:
24(a)	(a) in fair value hedges, gains or losses: i. on the hedging instrument; and ii. on the hedged item attributable to the hedged risk;
24(b)	(b) the ineffectiveness recognised in profit or loss that arises from cash flow hedges; and
24(c)	(c) the ineffectiveness recognised in profit or loss that arises from hedges of net investments in foreign operations.
	Fair value
25	Except as set out in paragraph 29 of IFRS 7 (see below), for each class of financial assets and financial liabilities, an entity shall disclose the fair value of that class of assets and liabilities in a way that permits it to be compared with its carrying amount.
26	Note: In disclosing fair values, an entity shall group financial assets and financial liabilities into classes, but shall offset them only to the extent that their carrying amounts are offset in the statement of financial position.
	An entity shall disclose:
27	the methods and, when a valuation technique is used, the assumptions applied in determining fair values of each class of financial assets or financial liabilities. If there has been a change in valuation technique, the entity shall disclose that change and the reasons for making it. Note: For example, if applicable, an entity discloses information about the assumptions relating to prepayment rates, rates of estimated credit losses, and interest rates or discount rates.
27A	To make the disclosures required by IFRS 7.27B (see below) an entity shall classify fair value measurements using a fair value hierarchy that reflects the significance of the inputs used in making the measurements. The fair value hierarchy shall have the following levels:

	(a) quoted prices (unadjusted) in active markets for identical assets or liabilities (Level 1); (b) inputs other than quoted prices included within Level 1 that are observable for the asset or liability, either directly (i.e. as prices) or indirectly (i.e. derived from prices) (Level 2); and (c) inputs for the asset or liability that are not based on observable market data (unobservable inputs) (Level 3). The level in the fair value hierarchy within which the fair value measurement is categorised in its entirety shall be determined on the basis of the lowest level input that is significant to the fair value measurement in its entirety. For this purpose, the significance of an input is assessed against the fair value measurement in its entirety. If a fair value measurement uses observable inputs that require significant adjustment based on unobservable inputs, that measurement is a Level 3 measurement. Assessing the significance of a particular input to the fair value measurement in its entirety requires judgement, considering factors specific to the asset or liability.
27B	For fair value measurements recognised in the statement of financial position an entity shall disclose for each class of financial instruments: (a) the level in the fair value hierarchy into which the fair value measurements are categorised in their entirety, segregating fair value measurements in accordance with the levels defined in paragraph 27A. (b) any significant transfers between Level 1 and Level 2 of the fair value hierarchy and the reasons for those transfers. Transfers into each level shall be disclosed and discussed separately from transfers out of each level. For this purpose, significance shall be judged with respect to profit or loss, and total assets or total liabilities. (c) for fair value measurements in Level 3 of the fair value hierarchy, a reconciliation from the beginning balances to the ending balances, disclosing separately changes during the period attributable to the following: total gains or losses for the period recognised in profit or loss, and a description of where they are presented in the statement of comprehensive income or the separate income statement (if presented);

	total gains or losses recognised in other comprehensive income; purchases, sales, issues and settlements (each type of movement disclosed separately); and transfers into or out of Level 3 (e.g. transfers attributable to changes in the observability of market data) and the reasons for those transfers. For significant transfers, transfers into Level 3 shall be disclosed and discussed separately from transfers out of Level 3. (d) the amount of total gains or losses for the period in (c)(i) above included in profit or loss that are attributable to gains or losses relating to those assets and liabilities held at the end of the reporting period and a description of where those gains or losses are presented in the statement of comprehensive income or the separate income statement (if presented). (e) for fair value measurements in Level 3, if changing one or more of the inputs to reasonably possible alternative assumptions would change fair value significantly, the entity shall state that fact and disclose the effect of those changes. The entity shall disclose how the effect of a change to a reasonably possible alternative assumption was calculated. For this purpose, significance shall be judged with respect to profit or loss, and total assets or total liabilities, or, when changes in fair value are recognised in other comprehensive income, total equity. Note: An entity shall present the quantitative disclosures required by this paragraph in tabular format unless another format is more appropriate.
28	Note: If the market for a financial instrument is not active, an entity establishes its fair value using a valuation technique. Nevertheless, the best evidence of fair value at initial recognition is the transaction price, unless the fair value of the instrument concerned is evidenced by comparison with other observable current market transactions in the same instrument or based on a valuation technique whose variables include only data from observable markets. It follows that there could be a difference between the fair value at initial recognition and the amount that would be determined at that date using the valuation technique. Disclosures of fair value are not required:

29(a)	(a) when the carrying amount is a reasonable approximation of fair value, for example, for financial instruments such as short-term trade receivables and payables;
29(b)	(b) for an investment in equity instruments that do not have a quoted market price in an active market, or derivatives linked to such equity instruments, that is measured at cost because its fair value cannot be measured reliably; or
29(c)	(c) for a contract containing a discretionary participation feature (as described in IFRS 4 *Insurance Contracts*) if the fair value of that feature cannot be measured reliably.
	In the cases described in paragraphs 29(b) and (c) of IFRS 7 (see above), an entity shall disclose information to help users of the financial statements make their own judgements about the extent of possible differences between the carrying amount of those financial assets or financial liabilities and their fair value, including:
30(a)	(a) the fact that fair value information has not been disclosed for these instruments because their fair value cannot be measured reliably;
30(b)	(b) a description of the financial instruments, their carrying amount, and an explanation of why fair value cannot be measured reliably;
30(c)	(c) information about the market for the instruments;
30(d)	(d) information about whether and how the entity intends to dispose of the financial instruments; and
30(e)	(e) if financial instruments whose fair value previously could not be reliably measured are derecognised, that fact, their carrying amount at the time of derecognition, and the amount of gain or loss recognised.
	Nature and extent of risks arising from financial instruments
31	An entity shall disclose information that enables users of its financial statements to evaluate the nature and extent of risks arising from financial instruments to which the entity is exposed at the end of the reporting period.
	Notes:

32	1. The disclosures required by paragraphs 33 to 42 of IFRS 7 (see below) focus on the risks that arise from financial instruments and how they have been managed. These risks typically include, but are not limited to, credit risk, liquidity risk and market risk.
B6	2. The disclosures required by paragraphs 31–42 shall be either given in the financial statements or incorporated by cross-reference from the financial statements to some other statement, such as a management commentary or risk report, that is available to users of the financial statements on the same terms as the financial statements and at the same time. Without the information incorporated by cross-reference, the financial statements are incomplete.
	Qualitative disclosures
	For each type of risk arising from financial instruments, an entity shall disclose:
33(a)	(a) the exposures to risk and how they arise;
33(b)	(b) its objectives, policies and processes for managing the risk and the methods used to measure the risk; and
33(c)	(c) any changes in 33(a) or (b) (see above) from the previous period.
	Quantitative disclosures
	For each type of risk arising from financial instruments, an entity shall disclose:
34(a)	(a) summary quantitative data about its exposure to that risk at the end of the reporting period. This disclosure shall be based on the information provided internally to key management personnel of the entity (as defined in IAS 24 Related Party Disclosures), for example the entity's board of directors or chief executive officer.
B7	Note: When an entity uses several methods to manage a risk exposure, the entity shall disclose information using the method or methods that provide the most relevant and reliable information.
34(b)	(b) the disclosures required by paragraphs 36 to 42 of IFRS 7 (see below), to the extent not provided in paragraph 34(a) (see above), unless the risk is not material.
34(b)	Note: See paragraphs 29 to 31 of IAS 1 *Presentation of Financial Statements* for a discussion of materiality.
34(c) B8	(c) concentrations of risk if not apparent from 34(a) and (b) (see above), including:

	1. a description of how management determines concentrations; 2. a description of the shared characteristic that identifies each concentration (e.g. counterparty, geographical area, currency or market); and 3. the amount of the risk exposure associated with all financial instruments sharing that characteristic.
B8	Note: Concentrations of risk arise from financial instruments that have similar characteristics and are affected similarly by changes in economic or other conditions. The identification of concentrations of risk requires judgement taking into account the circumstances of the entity.
35	If the quantitative data disclosed as at the end of the reporting period are unrepresentative of an entity's exposure to risk during the period, an entity shall provide further information that is representative.
	Credit risk
	An entity shall disclose by class of financial instrument:
36(a)	(a) the amount that best represents its maximum exposure to credit risk at the end of the reporting period without taking account of any collateral held or other credit enhancements (e.g. netting agreements that do not qualify for offset in accordance with IAS 32 Financial Instruments: Presentation) (see also IFRS 7.B9 & B10);
B9, B10	Notes: 1. For a financial asset the entity's maximum exposure to credit risk is typically the gross carrying amount net of any amounts offset in accordance with IAS 32 and any impairment losses. 2. Activities that give rise to credit risk include granting loans, receivables, financial guarantees, making irrevocable loan commitments and entering into derivative contracts. Further guidance is included in IFRS 7.B10.
36(b)	(b) in respect of the amount disclosed in 36(a) (see above), a description of collateral held as security and other credit enhancements;
36(c)	(c) information about the credit quality of financial assets that are neither past due nor impaired; and
36(d)	(d) the carrying amount of financial assets that would otherwise be past due or impaired whose terms have been renegotiated.

	Financial assets that are either past due or impaired
	An entity shall disclose by class of financial asset:
37(a)	(a) an analysis of the age of financial assets that are past due as at the end of the reporting period but not impaired;
37(b)	(b) an analysis of financial assets that are individually determined to be impaired as at the end of the reporting period, including the factors the entity considered in determining that they are impaired; and
37(c)	(c) for the amounts disclosed in 37(a) and (b) (see above), a description of collateral held by the entity as security and other credit enhancements and, unless impracticable, an estimate of their fair value.
	Collateral and other credit enhancements obtained
	When an entity obtains financial or non-financial assets during the period by taking possession of collateral it holds as security or calling on other credit enhancements (e.g. guarantees), and such assets meet the recognition criteria in other Standards, an entity shall disclose:
38(a)	(a) the nature and carrying amount of the assets obtained; and
38(b)	(b) when the assets are not readily convertible into cash, its policies for disposing of such assets or for using them in its operations.
	Liquidity risk
39(a)	An entity shall disclose a maturity analysis for non-derivative financial liabilities (including issued financial guarantee contracts) that shows the remaining contractual maturities.
39(b)	An entity shall disclose a maturity analysis for derivative financial liabilities. The maturity analysis shall include the remaining contractual maturities for those derivative financial liabilities for which contractual maturities are essential for an understanding of the timing of the cash flows.

B10A	An entity must disclose summary quantitative data about its exposure to liquidity risk on the basis of information provided internally to key management personnel. If the outflows of cash (or another financial asset) included in that data could either occur significantly earlier or be for significantly different amounts than indicated in the data the entity shall state that fact and provide quantitative information that enables users of its financial statements to evaluate the extent of this risk unless that information is included in the contractual maturity analysis required by IFRS 7.39(a) and (b) above.
B11 to B16	Notes: 1. An entity must use its judgement to determine an appropriate number of time bands; 2. an entity shall not separate an embedded derivative from a hybrid (combined) financial instrument. For such an instrument, an entity shall apply IFRS 7.39(a) 3. an entity must discloses a quantitative maturity analysis for derivative financial liabilities that shows remaining contractual maturities if the contractual maturities are essential for an understanding of the timing of the cash flows. For example, this would be the case for an interest rate swap with a remaining maturity of five years in a cash flow hedge of a variable rate financial asset or liability and all loan commitments. *Contractual maturity analysis* 4. when a counterparty has a choice of when an amount is paid, the liability is allocated to the earliest period in which the entity can be required to pay. For example, financial liabilities that an entity can be required to repay on demand (e.g. demand deposits) are included in the earliest time band. 5. when an entity is committed to make amounts available in instalments, each instalment is allocated to the earliest period in which the entity can be required to pay. For example, an undrawn loan commitment is included in the time band containing the earliest date it can be drawn down. 6. for issued financial guarantee contracts the maximum amount of the guarantee is allocated to the earliest period in which the guarantee could be called.

	7. the amounts disclosed in the maturity analysis are the contractual undiscounted cash flows. Such undiscounted cash flows differ from the amount included in the statement of financial position because the amount in the statement of financial position is based on discounted cash flows. See IFRS 7.B11D for more detail. 8. when the amount payable is not fixed, the amount disclosed is determined by reference to the conditions existing at the end of the reporting period.
39(c)	An entity shall disclose a description of how it manages the liquidity risk inherent in 39(a) and (b) (see above).
B11E to B11F	Notes 1. An entity shall disclose a maturity analysis of financial assets it holds for managing liquidity risk (e.g. financial assets that are readily saleable or expected to generate cash inflows to meet cash outflows on financial liabilities), if that information is necessary to enable users of its financial statements to evaluate the nature and extent of liquidity risk. 2. Factors an entity might include might consider disclosing to meet the requirement of IFRS 7.36(c) are whether the entity: (a) has committed borrowing facilities (e.g. commercial paper facilities) or other lines of credit (e.g. stand-by credit facilities) that it can access to meet liquidity needs; (b) holds deposits at central banks to meet liquidity needs; (c) has very diverse funding sources; (d) has significant concentrations of liquidity risk in either its assets or its funding sources; (e) has internal control processes and contingency plans for managing liquidity risk; (f) has instruments that include accelerated repayment terms (e.g. on the downgrade of the entity's credit rating); (g) has instruments that could require the posting of collateral (e.g. margin calls for derivatives); (h) has instruments that allows the entity to choose whether it settles its financial liabilities by delivering cash (or another financial asset) or by delivering its own shares; or

	(i) has instruments that are subject to master netting agreements.
	Market risk
B17 to B28	*Sensitivity analysis*
	Unless an entity complies with paragraph 41 of IFRS 7 (see below), it shall disclose:
40(a)	(a) a sensitivity analysis for each type of market risk to which the entity is exposed at the end of the reporting period, showing how profit or loss and equity would have been affected by changes in the relevant risk variable that were reasonably possible at that date;
B17 to B28	Notes:
	1. An entity decides how it aggregates information to display the overall picture without combining information with different characteristics about exposures to risks from significantly different economic environments. If an entity has exposure to only one type of market risk in only one economic environment, it would not show disaggregated information;
	2. an entity discloses the effect on profit or loss and equity at the end of the reporting period assuming that a reasonably possible change in the relevant risk variable had occurred at the end of the reporting period and had been applied to the risk exposures in existence at that date;
	3. an entity is not required to disclose the effect on profit or loss and equity for each change within a range of reasonably possible changes of the relevant risk variable. Disclosure of the effects of the changes at the limits of the reasonably possible range would be sufficient; and
	4. an entity shall provide sensitivity analyses for the whole of its business, but may provide different types of sensitivity analysis for different classes of financial instruments.
	Further guidance is included in IFRS 7.B17 – B28.
40(b)	(b) the methods and assumptions used in preparing the sensitivity analysis; and
40(c)	(c) changes from the previous period in the methods and assumptions used, and the reasons for such changes.

41	If an entity prepares a sensitivity analysis, such as value-at-risk, that reflects interdependencies between risk variables (e.g. interest rates and exchange rates) and uses it to manage financial risks, it may use that sensitivity analysis in place of the analysis specified in paragraph 40 of IFRS 7 (see above).
B20	Notes: 1. This applies even if such a methodology measures only the potential for loss and does not measure the potential for gain. 2. An entity may also disclose the historical observation period and weightings applied to observations within that period, an explanation of how options are dealt with in the calculations, and which volatilities and correlations (or, alternatively, Monte Carlo probability distribution simulations) are used.
	The entity shall also disclose:
41(a)	(a) an explanation of the method used in preparing such a sensitivity analysis, and of the main parameters and assumptions underlying the data provided; and
41(b)	(b) an explanation of the objective of the method used and of limitations that may result in the information not fully reflecting the fair value of the assets and liabilities involved.
	Other market risk disclosures
42	When the sensitivity analyses disclosed in accordance with paragraph 40 or 41 of IFRS 7 (see above) are unrepresentative of a risk inherent in a financial instrument (for example because the year-end exposure does not reflect the exposure during the year), the entity shall disclose that fact and the reason it believes the sensitivity analyses are unrepresentative.
	Adoption of Standard before effective date
43	If an entity applies IFRS 7 for a period beginning before 1 January 2007, it shall disclose that fact.
	Exemption in the first period of adoption before 1 January 2006 from presenting certain comparative information
44	If an entity applies IFRS 7 for annual periods beginning before 1 January 2006, it need not present comparative information for the disclosures required by paragraphs 31 to 42 of the Standard about the nature and extent of risks arising from financial instruments (see above).

7 Offsetting a financial asset and a financial liability

7.1 General principle

IAS 32 requires that a financial asset and a financial liability shall be offset as a net amount in the statement of financial position when, and only when, both of the following conditions are satisfied:

- the entity currently has a legally enforceable right to set off the recognised amounts of the asset and liability; and
- the entity intends to settle on a net basis, or to realise the asset and settle the liability simultaneously.

In the case of a transfer of a financial asset that does not qualify for derecognition under IAS 39, the entity shall not offset the transferred asset and the associated liability (for further details on derecognition refer to **3.3** in **chapter 7**). [IAS 32.42]

When offset is applied, the entity will have the right to pay or receive a single net amount in relation to the two instruments, and intends to do so, and therefore in effect, the entity only has a single financial asset or financial liability. If the conditions of offset are not met then the two financial instruments are presented separately. Whether or not a financial asset and a financial liability is offset, they shall be measured in accordance with the normal measurement guidance with respect to financial assets and financial liabilities.

It should be noted that offsetting a financial asset and a financial liability (and the consequent net presentation in the statement of financial position) is different from derecognition of those financial instruments. In contrast to offsetting, derecognition of a financial asset or a financial liability not only removes the financial instrument in question from the statement of financial position, but also may give rise to a gain or loss on derecognition. [IAS 32.44] Offset does not result in the asset or liability being removed from the statement of financial position, but in net presentation of the asset and liability as either a net asset or a net liability. A gain or loss does not arise because of the offsetting requirements, although it may arise because of the measurement requirements applicable to the asset or liability, respectively.

US GAAP comparison: US GAAP has the same general principle that assets and liabilities should not be offset except where a right of set-off exists. In order to achieve offset, the following criteria must all be satisfied:

- each of the parties owe determinable amounts (not necessarily in the same currency) but where maturities differ, only the party with the nearer maturity can set-off;

- there is a right to set-off the amount owed with the amount owed from the other party;

- there is an intention to set-off (met where there is an acknowledgement of the intent by the reporting party); and

- the right of set-off is enforceable at law.

The above criteria are similar to the criteria in IAS 32 described above. However, under US GAAP, FIN 39: *Offsetting of Amounts Related to Certain Contracts* and FIN 41: *Offsetting of Amounts Related to Certain Repurchase and Reverse Repurchase Agreements*, offsetting is elective and not mandatory, that is, an entity may, but is not required to offset amounts if the above criteria are met. Under IFRS, there is no option: if the criteria are met, the entity must offset the relevant amounts. There is also a US GAAP and IFRS difference in respect of master netting arrangements. FIN 39, as amended by FSP FIN 39–1, allows the fair value amounts recognised for derivative instruments executed with the same counterparty under a master netting arrangement to be offset. The reporting entity's choice to offset must be applied consistently. As described in **7.5** below, IFRS does not permit offset for master netting agreements where these do not give rise to a currently enforceable right of offset (as opposed to the right conditional on default, for instance) and where there is no intention to settle on a net basis.

7.2 Legal right of offset

IAS 32 defines the right of offset as a debtor's legal right, by contract or otherwise, to settle or otherwise eliminate all or a portion of an amount due to a creditor by applying against that amount an amount due from the creditor. As the right is specifically a legal right, the circumstances that give rise to such a right will vary from one legal jurisdiction to another. Thus, for each relationship between the two parties (of debtor and creditor) it will be necessary to consider the particular laws applicable to it. [IAS 32.45]

In certain circumstances the debtor may have a legal right to apply an amount due from a third party against the amount due to a creditor provided that there is an agreement between the three parties that clearly establishes the debtor's right to offset. [IAS 32.45]

Legal rights do not need to be established in a single document between the three parties. For example, a debtor might obtain set-off rights separately from the third party and from the creditor. In establishing the validity of the legal right to set-off, it is necessary to understand the terms of the particular contracts, as well as the context within which set-off is to be applied. The legal right to set-off could, inter alia, be evidenced with reference to a legal opinion, or be established by statutory or regulatory provisions which have been clearly demonstrated as applicable to and governing the particular transaction.

For a discussion of considerations surrounding master netting agreements refer to **7.6** below.

US GAAP comparison: According to FIN 39.6 offsetting amounts due from and owed to different counterparties is not permitted.

7.3 Intention to settle on a net basis, or to realise the asset and settle the liability simultaneously

The existence of the legal right of offset (while it affects the entity's rights and obligations and may affect its credit exposure) is not sufficient in itself for offsetting. Where there is a legal right, and an entity intends to exercise the right of offset, or to settle simultaneously, the entity is, in effect, exposed to a net amount, which reflects the timing of the expected cash flows and the risks to which those cash flows are exposed, and therefore presentation of the financial instruments on a net basis is appropriate. [IAS 32.46]

The intention by one or both parties to settle on a net basis without the legal right to do so is not sufficient to justify offsetting a financial asset and a financial liability. This is due to the fact that the legal rights and obligations pertaining to the individual financial assets and financial liabilities are not altered. [IAS 32.45]

Intention may be demonstrated through management representations that are not contradicted by past experience or other relevant circumstances (e.g. normal business practices, requirements of financial markets, circumstances that limit the ability to settle net) and, also, may take into account reference to the entity's risk management policies, if appropriate. There is no requirement for an assessment of the counterparty's intent.

The operation of a clearing house in an organised financial market, or a face to face exchange may facilitate the simultaneous settlement of two financial instruments. In such circumstances the cash flows are, in effect, equivalent to a single net amount and the exposure to credit or liquidity risk does not pertain to the gross amounts. This is different from a situation where the entity will settle two instruments separately by receiving and paying the gross amounts, even if the period between settlement of the two instruments is short. In the latter case the entity is exposed to credit risk on the asset and liquidity risk on the liability, both of which may be significant. In such circumstances net presentation is not appropriate. Realisation of a financial asset and settlement of a financial liability are treated as simultaneous only when the transactions occur at the same moment. [IAS 32.48]

Example 7.3

Offset: unmatched payments and receipts

Assume that the legal right of offset exists in the following scenario. Company X owes Company Y four payments of CU10 million each at the end of each calendar quarter (31 March, 30 June, 30 September, 31 December), totalling CU40 million. As part of another contract, Company Y owes Company X two payments of CU15 million at 30 June and 31 December, totalling CU30 million.

The intention to settle simultaneously can only be demonstrated in respect of the 30 June and 31 December cash flows. At the beginning of the year, Company X will, therefore, reflect a financial liability of CU20 million (being the 31 March and 30 September payments) and a separate financial asset of CU10 million (representing the difference between the CU10 million payable and CU15 million receivable from Company Y on 30 June and 31 December). Although Company X's net position over the whole year is a financial liability of CU10 million, since it cannot demonstrate the intention to settle net or simultaneously for all payments, the criteria for offset are not satisfied in respect of those unmatched payments and separate presentation is required. Company Y correspondingly has an asset of CU20 million and a liability of CU10 million.

It is common for entities to have amounts on deposit with a financial institution and simultaneously have a drawn down borrowing facility, sometimes referred to as an 'overdraft', with the same financial institution. The entity has a separate financial asset and a financial liability with the same counterparty. It is usually not possible to achieve offset for the asset and the liability as in most cases the entity cannot assert that the asset will be used to settle the liability. The asset will rise and fall as the entity deposits further cash on deposit or withdraws cash to settle other obligations. Although the asset at the reporting period end could be used to settle the overdraft, the entity cannot claim offset as the entity does not have the intention at the reporting period end to settle the overdraft liability with the deposit asset. Rather the entity's intention is to use the deposit asset at the reporting period end, and potentially draw down more borrowings if needed, to meet its working capital needs.

7.4 Circumstances in which offsetting is usually not appropriate

Due to the principles outlined in **7.1** above not being met, offsetting is specifically identified in IAS 32 as not being appropriate where:

(a) several different financial instruments are used to emulate the features of a single financial instrument (known as a 'synthetic instrument').

Example 7.4

Offset: synthetic instrument accounting

Assume an entity issues long term floating rate debt in the market and concurrently enters into an interest rate swap with the bank that involves receiving floating rate payments and making fixed rate payments with a maturity equal to that of the debt. The combination of the issued debt and the interest rate swap could be seen as synthetically amounting to fixed rate long term debt.

Each of the two instruments (floating rate liability and receive floating rate pay fixed rate interest rate swap) represent contractually separate arrangements with their own terms and conditions and each may be transferred or settled separately. Moreover, each of the two instruments will be exposed to risks that differ from those to which the other instrument is exposed. The offset conditions are not met since there is no legal right of set-off, and while the cash flows under the two instruments may occur within a short space of time from each other, they are not simultaneous. Hence, the debt and swap are not presented on a net basis in the entity's statement of financial position.

(b) financial assets and financial liabilities arise from financial instruments with the same primary risk exposure (for example, assets and liabilities within a portfolio of forward contracts or other derivative instruments) but with different counterparties;

(c) financial or other assets are pledged as collateral for non-recourse financial liabilities;

(d) financial assets are set aside in trust by a debtor for the purpose of discharging an obligation without those assets having been accepted by the creditor in settlement of the obligation (for example, a sinking fund arrangement); or

(e) obligations incurred as a result of events giving rise to losses are expected to be recovered from a third party by virtue of a claim made under an insurance policy. [IAS 32.49]

7.5 Circumstances in which offset conditions are met only in relation to some cash flows

There may be circumstances where the offset requirements are met only in relation to some of the cash flows of a contractually single financial asset and a contractually single financial liability. In such circumstances the offset requirements are applied to the extent that the conditions are met. This is illustrated in the following example:

Example 7.5

Offset: partial offset of cash flows

Company A and Company B are independent entities. On 1 January 20X1 Company A borrows CU100 from Company B ('instrument 1'). The terms of instrument 1 require repayment after 6 years (at 31 December 20X6) of CU100 and annual interest of 6 per cent on the notional of CU100. One year later, on 1 January 20X2 Company A lends CU50 to Company B ('instrument 2') on terms that require repayment of CU50 after 5 years (at 31 December 20X6) and annual interest of 6 per cent on the notional of CU50.

The terms of the instruments give both parties the legally enforceable right to settle the principal amounts repayable on a net basis on maturity of the instruments (i.e. through Company A paying a net amount of CU50 to Company B on 31 December 20X6). Both parties intend to settle the principal amounts on this basis. In respect of the 6 per cent interest payments/receipts over the life of the two instruments there is no ability to settle on a net basis.

Company A measures both the financial liability (instrument 1) and the financial asset (instrument 2) at amortised cost, using the effective interest rate method.

Company A should offset the financial asset and liability to the extent that the financial asset and financial liability meet the condition for offset. The offset conditions are met in respect of a proportion of the principal payments on the two instruments at 1 January 20X2 onwards. Therefore, offsetting is appropriate in respect of these amounts. However, offsetting is not appropriate in respect of the interest amounts.

Assume the amortised cost carrying value of instrument 1 (before considering offset) at 1 January 20X2 is CU100 which comprises an amount of CU75 being the present value of the principal payment and an amount of CU25 being the present value of the interest payments. Similarly the amortised cost carrying value of instrument 2 (before considering offset) comprises an amount of CU37.5 representing the present value of the principal payment and an amount of CU12.5 representing the present value of the interest payments.

Applying offset to the proportion of principal payments but not to the interest components of the financial asset and financial liability will result in a liability of CU62.5 and asset of CU12.5 being shown in the statement of financial position of Company A. This balance is summarised below:

	CU	CU
Asset		
Present value of interest flows on instrument 2		12.5
Liability		
Present value of interest flows on instrument 1		25
Present value of principal flow on instrument 1	75	
Less offset of principal flow on instrument 2	(37.5)	
Net principal flow		37.5
		62.5

The offset that is achieved by Company A can equally apply to Company B; Company B will present a liability of CU12.5 to Company A, and a loan and receivable of CU62.5 from Company A.

7.6 Master netting agreements

An entity that undertakes a number of financial instrument transactions with a single counterparty may enter into a 'master netting agreement' covering all of its transactions with that counterparty. Such an agreement creates a legally enforceable right of offset that comes into effect and affects the realisation of individual financial assets and settlement of individual financial liabilities only on the occurrence of a specified event of default, or other events not expected to happen in the normal course of business. Such agreements are typically used by financial institutions to provide a degree of protection in the event of bankruptcy or other circumstances that render a counterparty unable to meet its obligations. Once the triggering event takes place, the contract will typically provide for a single net settlement of all financial instruments covered by the agreement.

The existence of a master netting agreement does not in itself provide a basis for offsetting assets and liabilities covered by the agreement: firstly, the master netting agreement creates only a conditional right to set off recognised amounts, which falls short of the IAS 32 requirement that the entity must have the *currently enforceable* legal right to set off recognised amounts; and secondly, the entity may not have the intention or ability to either settle on a net basis or realise the asset and settle the liability simultaneously. [IAS 32.50]

Example 7.6A

Offset: master netting agreement

Bank X, an investment bank, enters into several swap transactions with different reset dates to manage the interest rate risk arising from its corporate loans portfolio. Although these transactions are with a range of other banks as counterparties, Bank X's systems aggregate all exposures on a daily basis to enable them to recognise the net profit or loss due to the change in fair value of all open (i.e. unexpired) contracts. Certain contracts have a positive fair value while others are in a loss position. ISDA (International Swaps and Derivatives Association) Master Netting Agreements are in place with some, but not all of these counterparties. Bank X does not net the settlements across swap positions with counterparties on reset dates.

Bank X does not meet the criteria for offsetting financial assets and liabilities related to its swap positions. It does not settle on a net basis and, due to the mismatch in reset dates across its swaps book, cannot demonstrate the simultaneous settlement of swap cash flows. Additionally, the ISDA Master Netting Agreements are not, in themselves sufficient to provide the Bank with the legal right to set off its settlement cash flows across contracts except in the conditional event of default or termination by one of the parties.

Example 7.6B

Offset: options

Company X, a gold producer in South Africa, manages its exposure to changes in the gold price and locks in the cost of funding future capital expenditure by entering into option strategies with several investment banks. These strategies require Company X to both purchase call options and to write put options at various strike prices and with various maturity dates. The transactions are expected to be settled in cash and hence meet the definition of a derivative in IAS 39.

The investment banks require Company X to enter into ISDA Master Netting agreements which give either party the legal right of offset on termination of the contract, or on default of the other party. These agreements do not provide for the offset of settlements in the ordinary course of business.

Company X may not offset the financial assets and financial liabilities arising from the premiums paid and received and subsequent measurement of these options to fair value. The master netting agreement establishes a legally enforceable right of offset only in the event of a contingent event (i.e. default or on termination by one of the parties) and not in respect of ongoing settlements. Additionally, by virtue of the different maturity dates, the company does not demonstrate the intention to settle on a net basis or to realise the asset and settle the liability simultaneously. Therefore, the requirements in IAS 32 are not satisfied. Even in the case where the premiums are settled on the same date, the continuing exposure to credit risk on the party writing the option precludes set-off.

US GAAP comparison: Under US GAAP, a reporting entity may offset fair value amounts recognised for derivative instruments and fair value amounts recognised for the right to reclaim cash collateral (or the obligation to return cash collateral) subject to master netting agreements in accordance with FIN 39. Similarly, repurchase and reverse repurchase agreements subject to master netting agreements that meet certain conditions can be offset for presentation purposes in accordance with FIN 41.

12 First-time adoption of IFRSs

1 Introduction

1.1 First-time adoption

A first-time adopter of IFRSs is an entity that prepares its first IFRS annual financial statements containing an explicit and unreserved statement of compliance with IFRSs. [IFRS 1.3] The date of transition to IFRSs for a first-time adopter is the beginning of the earliest period for which an entity presents full comparative information under IFRSs in its first IFRS financial statements. [IFRS 1(Appendix A)]

In general, IFRS 1 *First-time Adoption of International Financial Reporting Standards*, which applies to first-time adopters, requires an entity to comply retrospectively with each IFRS effective at the end of the reporting period for its first IFRS financial statements. [IFRS 1.7] IFRS 1 grants limited exemptions from these requirements in specified areas, including financial instruments (e.g. see **3.7** below) and prohibits retrospective application in others, also including financial instruments (see **section 4** below).

This chapter explores some of the aspects of first-time adoption of IFRSs on an entity's accounting for financial instruments that are within the scope of IAS 32 and IAS 39:

- the requirement to identify, classify and measure as appropriate all financial instruments in the scope of IAS 32 and IAS 39 (see **sections 3** to **3.6** below);
- IFRS 1's elective exemption from retrospective application of IAS 32 to compound instruments where the liability component is no longer outstanding (see **3.7** below); and
- IFRS 1's mandatory prohibitions from retrospective application of IAS 39 in respect of derecognition, hedge accounting, and estimates (see **4.1**, **4.3** and **3.5** below).

This chapter is set out differently from preceding chapters, as a series of questions and answers, and constitutes an amalgamation of questions frequently asked by first-time adopters. It includes the following sections:

Section 2	Reconciliations for first-time adopters
Section 3	Transition to IFRSs with respect to financial instruments
Section 4	Prohibition on retrospective application of IAS 32 and IAS 39

2 Reconciliations for first-time adopters

Example 2

Reconciliations for first-time adopters

Question

Which reconciliations must a first-time adopter, Entity Y, with a 31 December 2009 year end, provide in the 2009 financial statements?

Answer

- On transition, a first-time adopter is required to explain how the transition from previous GAAP to IFRSs affected its reported financial position, financial performance, and cash flows. [IFRS 1.23] In order to explain how the transition from previous GAAP to IFRSs has affected its financial position and financial performance, IFRS 1.24 requires the following reconciliations to be included in the entity's first IFRS financial statements:

(a) reconciliations of equity reported under previous GAAP to equity under IFRSs (with sufficient detail to enable users to understand the material adjustments to the statement of financial position) for the following dates:

    (i) the date of transition to IFRSs; and

    (ii) the end of latest period presented in the entity's most recent annual financial statements under previous GAAP; and

(b) a reconciliation of total comprehensive income reported under previous GAAP for the latest period in the entity's most recent annual financial statements to its profit or loss under IFRSs (with sufficient detail to enable users to understand the material adjustments to the statement of comprehensive income).

Entity Y is required therefore to provide the following reconciliations in accordance with IFRS 1.24 in its first IFRS financial statements:

- a reconciliation of equity under previous GAAP to equity under IFRSs (including IAS 32 and IAS 39) as at 1 January 2008 (this being Entity Y's date of transition to IFRS);
- a reconciliation of equity under previous GAAP to equity under IFRS (including IAS 32 and IAS 39) as at 31 December 2008 (this being the end of latest period presented in the Entity Y's most recent annual financial statements under previous GAAP); and

- a reconciliation of total comprehensive income under previous GAAP to total comprehensive income under IFRSs (including IAS 32 and IAS 39) for the year ended 31 December 2007 (this being the latest period in the Entity Y's most recent annual financial statements).

3 Transition to IFRSs with respect to financial instruments

IFRS 1 contains specific transitional provisions in respect of financial instruments. These are discussed in this section and **section 4** below. A first-time adopter is required to identify, recognise, classify and measure as appropriate all financial assets and financial liabilities at the date of transition that qualify for recognition in accordance with IAS 32 and IAS 39, and treat any adjustment to the carrying amount of a financial asset or financial liability as a result of the adoption of the two Standards as a transition adjustment to be recognised in the opening balance of retained earnings at the date of transition to IFRSs. [IFRS 1.IG58A]

IAS 8 applies to adjustments resulting from changes in estimates. Where it not possible to determine whether a particular portion of the adjustment is a transition adjustment or a change in estimate, it should be treated as a change in accounting estimate under IAS 8, with appropriate disclosures. [IFRS 1.IG58B]

At the date of transition a first-time adopter is required to derecognise assets and liabilities that do not qualify for recognition in accordance with IAS 32 and IAS 39, for example, gains and losses deferred as assets and/or liabilities in the statement of financial position in respect of hedge relationships under previous GAAP that do not qualify for recognition as assets and liabilities under IFRSs (see **4.3** below).

3.1 The key steps to conversion to IFRSs for financial instruments

Example 3.1

Key steps for first-time adoption

Question

What are the key steps an entity should consider for conversion to IFRSs in respect of financial instruments?

Answer

The key steps to ensure that an entity complies with IAS 32 and IAS 39 can be summarised as follows:

(a) identify all financial instruments and other contracts that fall within the scope of IAS 32 and IAS 39 including embedded derivatives and other contracts scoped into those two standards, not accounted for as financial instruments under previous GAAP (see **chapter 1**);

(b) recognise and classify all financial instruments in accordance with the financial asset and financial liability classifications of IAS 39 and the rules on equity or liability classification in IAS 32 (see **chapters 2** and **3**);

(c) derecognise items if IAS 32 and IAS 39 do not permit their recognition, for example, gains and losses deferred as assets and/or liabilities in the statement of financial position in respect of hedge relationships under previous GAAP that do not qualify for recognition as assets and liabilities under IFRSs (see **4.1** below);

(d) designate and document qualifying hedge relationships before the date of transition to IAS 39 to ensure these comply with IAS 39's hedge accounting criteria should an entity wish to apply hedge accounting prospectively from the date of transition to IAS 39 (see **4.3** below and **chapters 8 and 9**);

(e) apply IAS 32 and IAS 39 in measuring all financial assets and financial liabilities in accordance with their classification (see **3.4** below and **chapters 2**, **3** and **6**); and

(f) design and implement controls and procedures for continued compliance with (a) to (e) above.

3.2 Identification of all financial assets and financial liabilities on first-time adoption

Example 3.2

Unrecognised financial instruments under previous GAAP

Question

For a first-time adopter of IFRSs in 2009, which previously unrecognised items under previous GAAP will require first-time recognition as financial assets and financial liabilities?

Answer

It depends. Typically a number of items would **not** have been recognised under previous GAAP compared to IFRSs. These include:

(a) all derivatives, including:

(i) contracts to buy or sell a non-financial item, scoped into IAS 39 if they can be settled net in cash or another financial instrument, or by exchanging financial instruments, and are not entered into or held in accordance with the entity's expected purchase, sale or usage requirements (see **2.5** in **chapter 1**);

(ii) issued guarantees falling within the scope of IAS 39 that do not meet the definition of a financial guarantee contract (see **2.3.2** in **chapter 1**);

(iii) derivatives on an interest in a subsidiary, associate or joint venture unless they meet the definition of an equity instrument of the entity in accordance with IAS 32 or because they will result in a business combination at a future date (see **2.1** and **3.2** in **chapter 1**);

(iv) derivatives based on climatic, geological or other physical variables unless they meet the definition of an insurance contract and are within the scope of IFRS 4 (see **2.3.3** in **chapter 1**); and

(v) loan commitments that can be settled net in cash or another financial instrument, loan commitments that the issuer designates as financial assets or liabilities at fair value through profit or loss or loan commitments to provide a loan at a below-market interest rate (see **3.5** in **chapter 1**);

(b) all embedded derivatives that are required to be separately accounted for, i.e. the entire contract is not one measured at fair value through profit or loss and the embedded derivative is not closely related to the non-derivative financial host contract (see **chapter 5**);

(c) other interests, such as servicing rights or servicing liabilities, retained after a derecognition transaction and still existing at the date of transition to IFRSs (see **chapter 7**); and

(d) financial instruments that are held in special purpose entities (SPEs) that were not consolidated under the previous GAAP, but are consolidated under IFRS because the entity controls the SPE at the date of transition to IFRSs (see **3.1.1** in **chapter 7**).

3.2.1 *Embedded derivatives*

Example 3.2.1

Embedded derivative

Question

IAS 39 requires separate accounting treatment for embedded derivatives not closely related to the host contract, where the entire contract is not one measured at fair value through profit or loss. On transition to IFRSs, does an entity assess whether an embedded derivative is closely related to the host contract or not, at the date of transition, or at the date when that contract would have been initially recognised if IAS 39 had always been applied?

Answer

Full retrospective application of IAS 39 is required in this area. IFRIC 9 *Reassessment of Embedded Derivatives* clarifies that a first-time adopter should make its assessment of whether an embedded derivative is to be separated on the later of when becoming party to the contract or when the contract is substantially modified (for a discussion of the 'substantially modified' criterion see **section 3** in **chapter 5**). Assuming in the above scenario there was no substantial modification of the arrangement the assessment of whether the embedded derivative is closely related is made at the date when the entity first became party to the contract and not on the date of transition to IFRSs. The initial carrying amounts of the embedded derivative and the host contract reflect circumstances at the date the whole instrument satisfied the recognition criteria of IAS 39. [IFRS 1.IG55] Once the carrying amount at initial recognition of an embedded derivative that is not closely related to the host contract is separately determined (see **chapter 5**), it is then possible to determine the appropriate carrying values at the date of transition. These adjustments are recognised in the opening balance of retained earnings at the date of transition to IFRSs.

If the entity cannot determine the initial carrying amounts of the embedded derivative and host contract reliably, it treats the entire combined contract as a financial instrument held for trading (see **section 12** in **chapter 5**) measured at fair value through profit or loss. [IFRS 1.IG55]

3.3 Recognition of all financial instruments on first-time adoption

Subject to the exception discussed in **4.1** below on the retrospective application of IAS 39's derecognition rules, at the date of transition to IFRSs an entity recognises all financial assets and financial liabilities that qualify for recognition under IAS 39, for example, all derivative instruments that have not qualified for derecognition under IAS 39. [IFRS 1.IG53]

3.4 Classification and measurement of financial assets and financial liabilities on transition

A first-time adopter applies IAS 39's classification and measurement criteria to its financial assets and financial liabilities at the date of transition to IFRSs.

For those financial assets and financial liabilities classified at the date of transition in an amortised cost category, an entity determines their amortised cost on the basis of circumstances existing when the assets and liabilities first satisfied the recognition criteria in IAS 39. However, if the entity acquired those financial assets and financial liabilities in a past business combination, their carrying amount under previous GAAP immediately following the business combination is their deemed cost under IFRSs at that date. [IFRS 1.IG57]

Example 3.4A

Determining classification and measurement at date of transition to IFRSs

Question

Entity ABC is a Norwegian listed entity with a 31 December year end and a first-time adopter in 2008. Its date of transition to IFRSs is 1 January 2008. How does Entity ABC apply the requirements of IAS 39 in respect of the classification and measurement of its financial assets and financial liabilities?

Answer

At 1 January 2008, Entity ABC applies IAS 39's classification and measurement criteria to its financial assets and financial liabilities as if it had initially recognised those financial assets and financial liabilities in accordance with the Standard as illustrated.

- Entity ABC can classify those financial assets meeting the criteria for classification as held-to-maturity (HTM) investments (see **3.2** in **chapter 2**) in that category; its intent and ability to hold such assets to their maturity is made at the date of transition. [IFRS 1.IG56(a)] Entity ABC recognises any adjustment to financial assets classified in the HTM category to measure them at the appropriate amortised cost balance, as if that measurement basis had been applied since the date they first qualified for recognition in accordance with IAS 39, directly in retained earnings. It follows that sales or transfers of held-to-maturity investments before the date of transition to IFRSs do not trigger the 'tainting' rules (see **3.3** in **chapter 2**).

- It can classify those financial assets that satisfied the loans and receivables definition (see **3.4** in **chapter 2**) when the financial assets first satisfied the recognition criteria in IAS 39 for that category. [IFRS 1.IG56(b)] Entity ABC recognises any adjustment to financial assets classified in the loans and receivables category to measure them at the appropriate amortised cost amount, as if that measurement basis had been applied since the date they first qualified for recognition as loans and receivables in accordance with IAS 39, directly in retained earnings.

- Entity ABC can designate any non-derivative financial asset that is not held for trading and required to be measured at fair value through profit or loss, as available-for-sale (see **3.5** in **chapter 2**). [IFRS 1.29] Like the designation of available-for-sale assets at initial recognition, the designation in this category on transition to IFRSs is irrevocable. The fair value gain or loss on transition for assets designated as available-for-sale financial assets on the date of transition and hence measured at fair value is taken to a separate component of equity as if those assets had been accounted for since initial recognition as available-for-sale financial assets, except for impairment losses, foreign exchange gains or losses on monetary assets and interest income calculated using the effective interest method on those assets. [IFRS 1.IG59]

- Entity ABC recognises any derivative financial assets and derivative financial liabilities that are in the scope of IAS 39 at fair value (see **3.1.2** in **chapter 2** and **7.1.1** in **chapter 3**) with fair value gains or losses on transition accounted for as an adjustment to retained earnings, except for derivatives that were part of a net investment hedge or cash flow hedge under previous GAAP.

- Entity ABC classifies non-derivative financial assets or non-derivative financial liabilities in its opening IFRS statement of financial position as held for trading (hence measured at fair value through profit or loss) if, the assets or liabilities were: (i) acquired or incurred principally for the purpose of selling or repurchasing in the near term; or (ii) at the date of transition to IFRSs, part of a portfolio of identified financial instruments that were managed together and for which there was evidence of a recent actual pattern of short-term profit-taking. [IFRS 1.IG56(d)] The fair value gain or loss on transition is accounted for as an adjustment to retained earnings.

- At the date of transition to IAS 39, Entity ABC is also permitted to designate any financial asset or financial liability as one to be measured at fair value through profit or loss if specified criteria are met, i.e. the 'fair value option' (see **3.1.1** in **chapter 2** and **7.1.2** in **chapter 3**) is available as a one-off choice on transition. [IFRS 1.D19(b)] The fair value gain or loss on transition for financial assets or financial liabilities designated as at fair value through profit or loss at the date of transition, is accounted for as an adjustment through retained earnings, i.e. the assets or liabilities are accounted for as if designated at fair value through profit or loss from the date of initial recognition. Entity ABC must disclose the fair value of any financial assets or financial liabilities designated into the 'financial assets at fair value through profit or loss' and 'financial liabilities at fair value through profit or loss' categories and their classification and carrying amount in its previous financial statements. [IFRS 1.29]

- Entity ABC classifies financial liabilities that are not measured at fair value through profit or loss, either because the 'fair value option' has not been applied or because the items are not held for trading, as other financial liabilities measured at amortised cost (see **7.2** in **chapter 3**). It recognises any adjustment to measure them at the appropriate amortised cost amount as if that measurement basis had been applied since the date they first qualified for recognition in accordance with IAS 39, in retained earnings.

Example 3.4B

Derivative not fair valued under previous GAAP

Question

Entity P is a first-time adopter of IFRSs and has a financial year end of 31 March. Entity P prepares its first annual IFRS financial statements for the year ended 31 March 2009.

Entity P has some derivative financial instruments. Under previous GAAP these instruments were not recognised at fair value in the statement of financial position as they were considered to be hedging instruments. The derivatives were instead held on an accruals basis and were included in the carrying amount of the item being hedged. At the date of transition the instruments have a fair value of CU(2) million and do not qualify as hedging instruments in accordance with IAS 39 as they are net written options. How does Entity P account for these derivative instruments on first-time adoption of IFRSs?

Answer

On Entity P's date of transition to IFRSs, i.e. 1 April 2008, it recognises the derivative liability in its statement of financial position with the corresponding entry recognised in retained earnings. The entity cannot include the loss in a cash flow hedge accounting reserve as the derivative is not a qualifying hedge accounting instrument under IAS 39.

Under previous GAAP the derivatives had been netted against the item being hedged. Not only is the measurement basis not compliant with IFRSs, but also the financial instruments could not be offset unless the criteria for offset in IAS 32 were met (see **section 7** in **chapter 11**).

An adjustment will be required to the hedged items to recognise them at the appropriate carrying amounts (see **4.3** below).

Example 3.4C

Determining amortised cost

Question

Entity MNO's year end is 31 December 2009. Entity MNO's date of transition to IFRSs is 1 January 2008. Entity MNO has the following two zero coupon bond assets, which are not quoted in an active market.

- Bond 1 was purchased at original issuance on 1 January 2005 for €1,000. It is redeemable in 5 years' time at €1,250. The effective interest rate on this instrument is 4.56 per cent.
- Bond 2 has the same terms as Bond 1, but the bond was acquired in a business combination on 1 January 2006. The fair value of the bond on the date of the business combination was €1,100. The bond has risen in

value since it was issued because of the accretion of the zero coupon and because interest rates have fallen since the bond had been issued. The effective interest rate calculated at the time of the business combination is 3.25 per cent.

How does Entity MNO recognise its investments in Bonds 1 and 2 on the date of transition to IFRSs?

Answer

The bonds are not quoted in an active market and the entity chooses not to designate the bonds as available-for-sale financial assets. Hence, at the date of its transition to IFRS, 1 January 2008, Entity MNO classifies both bonds as loans and receivables (see **3.4** in **chapter 2**) measured at amortised cost. Entity MNO determines the carrying amount of Bond 1 as if it had been accounted for at amortised cost since acquisition using the bond's effective interest rate of 4.56 per cent. The amortised cost on 1 January 2008 is €1,092, representing two years of amortisation at 4.56 per cent.

Entity MNO determines the carrying amount of Bond 2 as if it had been accounted for at amortised cost since acquired in the business combination using the bond's effective interest rate of 3.25 per cent. The amortised cost on 1 January 2008 is €1,136, representing 1 year of amortisation at 3.25 per cent.

Alternatively, the fair value option could have been applied to the bonds on transition to IFRSs if the specified criteria were met.

3.5 Impairment and other estimates

IFRS 1 prohibits retrospective application of IFRSs in respect of estimates, unless there is objective evidence that previous estimates were in error. [IFRS 1.14]

The principal area where estimates are involved in the measurement of financial instruments is in assessments of impairment. IFRS 1.IG58 confirms that an entity's estimates of loan impairments at the date of transition to IFRS are consistent with estimates made for the same date under previous GAAP (after adjustments to reflect any difference in accounting policies), unless there is objective evidence that those assumptions were in error. [IFRS 1.14] It is important to distinguish between a change in estimate and a change in accounting policy for the purpose of recognition of impairment on transition. For example, a change in accounting policy would be moving from an undiscounted basis of measuring impairment under previous GAAP to a discounted basis under IFRSs. The effect of such a change in accounting policy would be reflected in the adjustment to the opening balance of retained earnings on transition. Generally, reconsidering the extent of cash flows that are then subject to discounting under IFRSs is reassessment of an estimate. Such a change in estimate would not be reflected in the adjustment to the opening balance of retained earnings on transition. An exception may arise in the case of purchased guarantees. In this case, the accounting treatment of the guarantee may differ between previous GAAP and IFRSs, thus resulting in an adjustment to the carrying value of loans and potentially retained earnings on transition. This is because IFRSs include the potential recovery under the guarantee as part of the impairment analysis whereas previous GAAP may not. Impairment is described in greater detail in **chapter 6**.

3.5.1 *Change in impairment policy*

Example 3.5.1

Change in impairment policy

Question

Under previous GAAP, Entity A measured impairment of financial assets carried at cost on an undiscounted basis. Entity A is a first-time adopter of IFRSs.

IAS 39 requires impairment losses to be measured using discounted cash flows. [IAS 39.63] Therefore, at the date of transition to IFRS, Entity A makes an adjustment to the carrying amount of those financial assets that are measured at amortised cost under IAS 39 to reflect the effect of discounting expected future cash flows.

Is this adjustment recognised as an adjustment to the opening balance of retained earnings at the date of transition in accordance with IFRS 1?

Answer

Yes. In accordance with IFRS 1.11, 14 & IG58, Entity A should recognise this measurement adjustment as a consequence of change in accounting policy in respect of the impairment of financial assets (e.g. loans and receivables) in the opening balance of retained earnings at the date of transition to IFRSs.

3.6 Classification as a financial liability or equity

In its opening IFRS statement of financial position, an entity applies the criteria in IAS 32 to classify financial instruments issued (or components of compound instruments issued) as either financial liabilities or equity instruments in accordance with the substance of the contractual arrangement when the instrument first satisfied the recognition criteria in IAS 32.15, without considering events after that date, other than changes to the terms of the instruments. [IFRS 1.IG35]

Example 3.6

Assessing terms at date of transition to IFRSs

Question

Entity P issued a capital instrument two years before its date of transition to IFRSs, 1 January 2006. Entity P's date of transition to IFRS is 1 January 2008. If IAS 32 was applied at the date of issue of the instrument, the instrument would have been classified as a liability as the instrument's contingent settlement provision (requiring redemption in cash) would have been judged to be genuine, i.e. the circumstances in which redemption is triggered would not have been considered to be extremely rare. At transition date these circumstances (not the terms of the instrument) have changed such that redemption is now extremely rare.

Answer

In its opening IFRS statement of financial position an entity classifies financial instruments issued or their component parts as either financial liabilities or equity instruments based on the substance of the contractual arrangements and the definitions of a financial liability and equity at the time when the instrument first satisfied the recognition requirements of IAS 32 (see **section 2** in **chapter 3**). Subsequent events or changes in market conditions are not taken into account, except for changes in the terms of the instrument. [IFRS 1.IG35]

Entity P therefore classifies its instrument as a financial liability on transition notwithstanding the fact that if it issued an instrument with the same terms at 1 January 2008 it would recognise an equity instrument.

3.7 Compound instruments

To the extent that the liability component is no longer outstanding at the date of transition to IFRSs, full retrospective application of IAS 32 with regard to such compound financial instruments is not required. Full retrospective application would involve separating two components of equity: one portion representing the cumulative interest accrued on the liability component during its life using the effective interest rate method, which would normally reside in retained earnings; and the second portion representing the original equity component that would have been separated on initial recognition of the instrument. [IFRS 1.D18]

Example 3.7A

Convertible debt: outstanding at date of transition to IFRSs

Question

Entity H is a first-time adopter in 2009. Entity H issued 2,000 convertible bonds on 1 January 2006. The bonds have a four-year term, and were issued at par with a face value of CU1,000 per bond, giving total proceeds of CU2 million. Interest is payable annually in arrears at an annual interest rate of 6 per cent. Each bond is convertible, at the holder's discretion, at any time up to maturity into 250 ordinary shares. When the bonds were issued, the market interest rate for similar debt without the conversion option was 9 per cent.

How does Entity H account for its convertible debt on first-time adoption of IFRSs?

Answer

An entity that has an issued compound instrument outstanding at the date of transition to IFRSs determines the initial carrying amounts of the liability and equity components based on circumstances existing when the instrument was issued. [IFRS 1.IG36]

IAS 32 requires that the liability component is valued first. The liability component is calculated as the present value of the contractual cash flows using the discount rate of 9 per cent, which was the market interest rate for similar bonds with the same credit standing having no conversion rights when the bonds were issued. The difference between the proceeds of the bond issue and the fair value of the liability at the time of original issuance is assigned to the equity component. The equity component is not remeasured. An adjustment in the opening balance of retained earnings is required to measure the liability component at its appropriate amortised cost at the date of transition.

Example 3.7B

Convertible debt: not outstanding at date of transition to IFRSs

Question

Entity Q, on the other hand, also a first-time adopter in 2009 (with a December year end), issued convertible bonds on 1 January 2003. The bonds had a three-year term, were convertible at any time up to maturity into 250 ordinary shares of the entity, and were redeemed at maturity.

How does Entity Q account for its convertible debt on first-time adoption of IFRSs?

Answer

The liability component of Entity Q's convertible instruments is no longer outstanding at its date of transition to IFRSs, 1 January 2008. Entity Q is not required to do a full retrospective application of IAS 32 with regard to its convertible. IFRS 1 permits a first-time adopter not to separate the two components of equity which would have resulted if full retrospective application had been applied: one component representing the cumulative interest accrued on the liability component during its life using the effective interest rate method, which would normally reside in retained earnings; and the second portion representing the original equity component that would have been separated on initial recognition of the instrument.

Example 3.7C

Convertible debt: redeemed after date of transition to IFRSs

Question

Using the facts as in **example 3.7B** above, if Entity Q's convertible had a maturity of 1 January 2009, i.e. it had a six-year term, and was expected to be redeemed on its maturity on 1 January 2009, would Entity Q be exempted from full retrospective application of IAS 32 for its convertible?

Answer

No. Entity Q's date of transition to IFRS is the beginning of its first IFRS reporting period, 1 January 2008. The liability component of its convertible instrument, in this instance, is still outstanding at the date of transition. Hence, Entity Q would be required to apply IAS 32 retrospectively to its convertible debt and separate out the equity component that would have been separated on initial recognition of the instrument in accordance with IAS 32.

3.8 Designation of previously recognised financial instruments

Any entity is permitted to designate any financial asset, other than an asset that meets the definition of held for trading, as an available-for-sale financial asset at the date of transition to IFRSs. [IFRS 1.29]

A first-time adopter of IFRSs must de-designate financial assets and financial liabilities that under previous GAAP were designated as at fair value through profit or loss (FVTPL), but they do not qualify for such designation under IAS 39.

Example 3.8

Date of designation

Entity B prepares its first set of IFRS financial statements for the year ended 31 December 2009. In February 2008, Entity B issued fixed rate debentures that are measured at amortised cost on initial recognition. At the same time, Entity B uses the proceeds of the debt to acquire a portfolio of fixed rate assets which it designates as available-for-sale with changes in fair value recognised in other comprehensive income. The fair value changes on the assets tend to offset the fair value movements on the debenture liabilities.

> During 2008, Entity B realises the measurement and recognition inconsistency in measuring the fixed rate debt liability at amortised cost whilst measuring the fixed rate assets at fair value with gains and losses recognised in other comprehensive income.
>
> Entity B cannot re-designate the fixed rate debt instruments after initial recognition. At initial recognition, in February 2008, Entity B chose to designate the fixed rate debentures at amortised cost and not at fair value through profit or loss. A designation as at fair value through profit or loss must be made at the later of initial recognition or date of transition to IFRSs.
>
> If the fixed rate debentures were acquired prior to the date of transition to IFRSs, i.e. prior to 1 January 2008, Entity B could have designated those fixed rate debentures as at fair value through profit or loss as at the date of transition to IFRSs if the specified criteria were met.

Entities are required to disclose the fair value of the financial assets or financial liabilities designated into each category (available-for-sale or at fair value through profit or loss) at the date of designation and their classification and carrying amount in the previous financial statements. [IFRS 1.29]

3.9 Fair value measurement of financial assets or financial liabilities

As all financial assets and liabilities are required to be initially recognised at fair value an entity must consider the specific guidance in IAS 39 on fair value when determining the carrying amount of financial assets and liabilities at the date of transition to IFRSs. This applies even if the financial asset or financial liability is not subsequently measured at fair value, as fair value at initial recognition will be the opening carrying amount at the date of transition to IFRSs.

IAS 39 has very specific guidance on determining fair value at initial recognition for financial assets and liabilities that are not traded in an active market. The Standard limits upfront gain/loss recognition unless the fair value of the instrument is evidenced by comparison with other observable current market transactions in the same instrument (i.e. without modification or repackaging) or based on a valuation technique whose variables include only data from observable markets. This is often referred to as "day 1 P&L" and is discussed in more depth at **5.3.5** in **chapter 6**. IFRS 1.D20 has specific transition requirements when applying the day 1 P&L guidance. IFRS 1 permits an entity to apply the day 1 P&L guidance (with specific reference from IFRS 1 to the last sentence of IAS 39.AG76 and to IAS 39.AG76A in any one of the following ways:

- retrospectively;

- prospectively to transactions entered into after 25 October 2002; or
- prospectively to transactions entered into after 1 January 2004.

The unique transition requirements listed above were introduced when the day 1 P&L guidance was originally included in IAS 39. Full retrospective application was not required as constituents raised concerns that retrospective application would diverge from the requirements of US GAAP, would be difficult and expensive to implement, and might require subjective assumptions about what was observable and what was not.

4 Prohibition on retrospective application of IAS 32 and IAS 39

IFRS 1.B1 prohibits retrospective application of IFRSs relating to:

(a) derecognition of financial assets and financial liabilities except as specified in **4.2** below;

(b) hedge accounting; and

4.1 Transitional requirements on derecognition for first-time adopters

A first-time adopter is required by IFRS 1.B2 to apply the derecognition rules in IAS 39 prospectively from the effective date of IAS 39, 1 January 2004 (the effective date of the original version of the Standard published in December 2003) unless it chooses to apply the derecognition rules of IAS 39 retrospectively from a date of its choosing in accordance with IFRS 1.B3 (see **4.2** below). Hence, if a first-time adopter derecognised financial assets under its previous GAAP in a securitisation, transfer or other derecognition transaction that occurred before 1 January 2004, it does not recognise those assets and liabilities at the date of transition (even if these would not have qualified for derecognition under IAS 39), unless they qualify for recognition as a result of a later transaction or event.

Example 4.1A

Transfers after 1 January 2004

Question

If a securitisation, transfer, or other derecognition transaction was entered into before 1 January 2004, and derecognition treatment was permitted under previous GAAP, are further transfers of financial assets as part of the same scheme after this date (for example, to maintain a specified balance of mortgage or credit card receivables) subject to the derecognition criteria of IAS 39?

Answer

Yes. Any further transfers of financial assets as part of the same scheme after 1 January 2004 (effective date of application of the recognition requirements in IAS 39) would have to satisfy the derecognition criteria of IAS 39 in order to qualify for derecognition treatment. [IFRS 1.B2 & B3]

A first-time adopter must recognise, however, any financial interest retained as a result of a derecognition transaction prior to 1 January 2004 that still exists at the date of transition to IFRSs, for example, any derivatives and other interests, such as servicing rights or servicing liabilities.

Furthermore, the exemption from applying the derecognition requirements prior to 1 January 2004 is not extended to consolidation. A first-time adopter must consolidate all special purpose entities (SPEs) that it controls at the date of transition to IFRSs, even if the SPEs existed before the date of transition to IFRS or hold financial assets or financial liabilities that were derecognised under previous GAAP. [IFRS 1.IG26] Hence, although a group may have derecognised financial assets under its previous GAAP as a result of a transfer of assets to an SPE occurring before 1 January 2004, those assets may be consolidated back into the group's statement of financial position if the SPE to which the financial assets were transferred is deemed to be controlled by the group in accordance with SIC-12 *Consolidation – Special Purpose Entities*, and the SPE did not derecognise the assets under the previous GAAP. If this is the case, the IAS 39 derecognition decision tree will be applied to the new group as defined by IFRSs.

Example 4.1B

Transfers to a consolidated entity

Entity X is part of Group Y. The date of transition to IFRSs is 1 January 2008 for Entity X and for the group. The entity and group do not apply the election available under IFRS 1.B3 (see **4.2** below) to apply the derecognition rules to transactions derecognised prior to 1 January 2004.

Entity X derecognised financial assets under its previous GAAP on 30 September 2003. These assets were transferred to Entity Z. Entity Z is not a member of Group Y under previous GAAP. Entity Z is a special purpose entity that issues beneficial interests in the underlying financial assets transferred to it by Entity X to unrelated third party investors, and provides servicing of those financial assets.

On the date of transition to IFRSs, in accordance with SIC-12, Entity Z is now considered to be part of Group Y and must be consolidated by Group Y.

Individual financial statements of Entity X under IFRSs

As Entity X derecognised the financial assets under its previous GAAP in a transaction occurring prior to 1 January 2004, the transferred assets continue to be derecognised under IFRSs.

Group Y's financial statements under IFRSs

As Group Y now includes Entity Z, the derecognition requirements must be applied to the enlarged group. If Entity Z could not derecognise the financial assets under its previous GAAP, and the assets continue to be recognised under IFRSs, then the Group continues to recognise those assets. If Entity Z did derecognise the financial assets under its previous GAAP, the assets will remain derecognised ('off balance sheet') under IFRSs because they were derecognised under previous GAAP in a transaction occurring prior to 1 January 2004.

Where the entity and group had made the election available under IFRS 1.B3 to apply the derecognition requirements of IAS 39 to derecognition transactions occurring before 1 January 2004 (see **4.2** below), the derecognition requirements of IAS 39 would be applied to the transaction on 30 September 2003. If the transfer of financial assets qualified for derecognition by both Entity X and Group Y (including Entity Z) under IAS 39, the assets would remain derecognised ('off-balance sheet') on the adoption of IFRSs by Group Y on 1 January 2008.

4.2 Option to apply derecognition rules retrospectively from a chosen date

Notwithstanding the requirement to apply IAS 39's rules on derecognition prospectively from 1 January 2004, an entity may choose to apply them retrospectively from a date of the entity's choosing, provided that the information needed to apply IAS 39 to financial assets and financial liabilities derecognised as a result of past transactions was obtained at the time of initially accounting for those transactions. [IFRS 1.B3] (See **example 4.1B** above.)

4.3 Hedge accounting

IFRS 1 prohibits retrospective application of IAS 39 in respect of hedge accounting. [IFRS 1.B4-B6] This is consistent with the general hedging requirements of IAS 39 under which hedge accounting is only ever available prospectively if the hedge relationship is appropriately designated, documented, is expected to be highly effective and satisfies all other hedge accounting criteria (see **chapters 8 – 10**).

At the date of transition to IFRS, an entity must measure all derivatives at fair value and eliminate all deferred gains and losses arising on derivatives that were reported under previous GAAP as assets or liabilities in the statement of financial position in respect of hedge relationships under previous GAAP since these do not qualify for recognition as assets and liabilities under IFRSs. [IFRS 1.B4]

If, before the date of transition to IFRSs, a transaction had been designated as a hedge but the hedge does not meet the conditions for hedge accounting in IAS 39, the requirements of IAS 39.91 and IAS 39.101 should be applied to discontinue hedge accounting. [IFRS 1.B6]

The designation and documentation of a hedge relationship must be completed on or before the date of transition to IFRSs if the hedge relationship is to qualify for hedge accounting from that date. Hedge accounting can be applied prospectively only from the date that the hedge relationship is fully designated and documented. [IFRS 1.IG60]

4.3.1 Re-designation or discontinuation of hedge relationships of a type that do not comply with IAS 39

Where a first-time adopter has a hedge relationship of a type that does not qualify for hedge accounting under IAS 39, for example, where the hedging instrument is a cash instrument or written option or where the hedged item is a net position, or the designated risk is interest rate risk in a held-to-maturity investment (see **sections 3** and **4** in **chapter 8** on qualifying hedged items and qualifying hedging instruments respectively), the entity shall not reflect that hedge relationship in its opening IFRS statement of financial position. However, if an entity designated a net position as a hedged item under previous GAAP, it may designate an individual item within that net position as a hedged item under IFRSs, provided that it does so no later than the date of transition to IFRSs and provided all other hedge accounting criteria are met. [IFRS 1.B5]

4.3.1.1 Fair value hedge under previous GAAP that of a type does not qualify as a fair value hedge under IFRSs

Example 4.3.1.1A

Non-qualifying hedge (1)

Question

Entity H is fair value hedging a fixed rate debt instrument for interest rate risk under previous GAAP. Entity H intends to classify the instrument as held-to-maturity under IFRSs. Held-to-maturity investments cannot be hedged items with respect to interest rate risk under IFRSs because designation of an investment as held-to-maturity requires an intention to hold the investment till maturity without regard to the changes in fair value attributable to changes in interest rates. Hence, the hedge relationship does not qualify for hedge accounting under IAS 39, and the entity is not permitted to reflect the hedge relationship in its opening IFRS statement of financial position. [IFRS 1.B5] Under IFRSs, the held-to-maturity debt security will be accounted for at amortised cost. How should the previous fair value adjustments to the carrying amount of the hedged item be accounted for on the first-time adoption of IFRSs, and thereby, the initial application of IAS 39?

Answer

As the held-to-maturity investments are not qualifying hedged items under IFRSs in respect of interest rate risk, the carrying amount on the date of transition to IFRSs should reflect the balance that would have existed had the entity always applied IFRSs, i.e. the balance that would have existed had the entity never applied hedge accounting. The held-to-maturity investment will be measured at amortised cost and thus any previous adjustments recognised under previous GAAP should be reversed to the extent that they have resulted in a carrying amount that differs from the amortised cost balance that would have been reported had the entity applied IFRSs and measured the item at amortised cost throughout its life.

The derivative will be recognised in the statement of financial position at its fair value with an adjustment to retained earnings on the date of transition.

Example 4.3.1.1B

Non-qualifying hedge (2)

Question

Entity J is fair value hedging a fixed rate, non pre-payable debt instrument for interest rate risk under previous GAAP with an interest rate swap whereby Entity J receives a fixed rate of interest and pays LIBOR. The interest rate swap contains an option for the Bank to cancel the swap at any time at a settlement amount of zero (the bank will cancel the swap where it is out of the money to them). Under IFRSs, the debt instrument will be carried at amortised cost. How should this relationship be accounted for on the first time adoption of IFRSs, and thereby, the initial application of IAS 39?

Answer

Entity J has written an option embedded in the swap. A written option or net written option does not qualify as a hedging instrument unless it is designated as an offset to a purchased option, including one that is embedded in another financial instrument. [IAS 39.77 and IAS 39.AG94] As the debt is non pre-payable, and therefore does not have an equal and opposite embedded purchased option, the hedging instrument is not a qualifying instrument. [IAS 39.AG94] The difference between the fair value of the interest rate swap and its previously reported carrying amount, together with the difference between the debt's amortised cost and its previously reported carrying amount should be recognised directly in opening retained earnings. No fair value hedging adjustment to the hedged debt is allowed.

4.3.1.2 *Cash flow hedge under previous GAAP that does not qualify as a cash flow hedge under IFRS*

Example 4.3.1.2

Non-qualifying hedge (3)

Question

If a forecasted transaction is not expected to occur at the date of transition to IFRSs how should any net cumulative gains or losses arising on measurement at fair value of the hedging instrument be accounted for at the date of transition?

Answer

If, at the date of transition to IFRSs, the forecasted transaction is not expected to occur the hedge does not qualify as a cash flow hedge. A first-time adopter reclassifies any net cumulative gain or loss reported in other comprehensive income under previous GAAP to retained earnings at the date of transition in accordance with IFRS 1.11.

If the derivative instrument was carried at cost, and no changes in value of the derivative were recognised in other comprehensive income, the full amount of the adjustment to the derivative asset or liability necessary to recognise the derivative at fair value should be recorded in retained earnings where hedge accounting is not permitted. If the derivative instrument was carried at an amount other than fair value with a deferred debit or credit in the statement of financial position recorded as an offset, that deferred debit or credit should be reversed through retained earnings if it does not meet the appropriate recognition criteria under IFRSs, and the value of the derivative brought up to its fair value at the date of transition.

4.3.2 *Hedge relationships of a type that continue to qualify under IAS 39*

For a hedge relationship to continue to qualify as a hedge relationship at the date of transition to IFRSs, it must meet all the hedge accounting criteria (see **chapters 8** and **9**). In particular, the designation and documentation of a hedge relationship must be completed on or before the date of transition to IFRSs if the hedge relationship is to qualify for hedge accounting from that date. Hedge accounting can be applied prospectively only from the date that the hedge relationship is fully designated and documented.

For a first-time adopter of IFRSs this may be a significant change to previous GAAP which may not have required such rigorous hedge designation and documentation. Hedge accounting under IAS 39, and hence on first-time adoption of IFRSs, can only be applied prospectively from the date that the hedge relationship is fully designated and documented subject to all other hedge accounting requirements of IAS 39 being met.

4.3.2.1 *Qualifying fair value hedges*

Under its previous GAAP, an entity may have deferred or not recognised gains and losses on a fair value hedge of a hedged item that is not measured at fair value. In these circumstances IFRS 1 requires an adjustment (in the opening balance of retained earnings) to the carrying amount of the hedged item at the date of transition provided the hedge is of a type that would be a qualifying hedge relationship under IAS 39. This adjustment is the lower of:

(a) that portion of the cumulative change in the fair value of the hedged item that reflects the designated hedged risk and was not recognised under previous GAAP; and

(b) that portion of the cumulative change in the fair value of the hedging instrument that reflects the designated hedged risk and, under previous GAAP, was either (i) not recognised or (ii) deferred in the statement of financial position as an asset or liability. [IFRS 1.IG60A]

These requirements result in the hedged item being adjusted by the cumulative change in the fair value of the hedged item due to the designated risk where the fair value of the hedging instrument is more than the exposure on the hedged item. This entry is equivalent to the entry that would have been recognised had the entity always applied IFRSs.

If the derivative is less than exposure of the hedged item, the hedged item is adjusted to the value of the derivative which would have been different had the entity always applied IFRSs.

Example 4.3.2.1

Qualifying fair value hedges

Assume for both of the following scenarios that the hedge relationship is one that is a qualifying hedge relationship under IAS 39 and hence, qualifies for hedge accounting at the date of transition to IFRSs.

Scenario A

Entity D has an issued fixed rate bond (CU100 million) and a receive fixed rate CU pay floating 3 month CU LIBOR interest rate swap that it has designated in a fair value hedge of the fixed rate bond (with the designated risk being fair value interest rate exposure due to changes in 3 month CU LIBOR. Under Entity D's previous GAAP changes in the fair value of the swap were not recognised in the financial statements and the carrying value of the debt was not adjusted for changes in fair value attributable to the designated risk (3 month CU LIBOR).

At the date of transition to IFRSs the fair value of the bond is CU70 million. Of the CU30 million cumulative changes in the value of the bond since its issue (when its fair value was equal to CU100 million) CU20 million is determined to be due to changes in the 3 month CU LIBOR interest rate while CU10 million relates to changes in Entity D's credit risk. At the date of transition the cumulative changes in fair value of the swap (not reflected in the financial statements under previous GAAP) amount to CU21 million of which CU19.5 million is attributable to the hedged risk (changes in the 3 month CU LIBOR rate).

In accordance with IFRS 1.IG60A, on transition to IFRSs, the hedged item (the fixed rate bond) is adjusted by CU19.5 million such that its carrying amount in the opening statement of financial position is CU80.5 million (CU100 million less the adjustment of CU19.5 million). The CU19.5 million adjustment is the lower of the portion of the cumulative change in the fair value of the hedged item due to the designated hedged risk and the portion of the cumulative change in the fair value of the hedging instrument due to the designated hedged risk (CU20 million and CU19.5 million respectively).

At the date of transition Entity D makes the following entries:

Dr Fixed rate bond	CU19.5 million
Cr Retained earnings	CU19.5 million
To adjust the hedged item for the designated risk	
Dr Retained earnings	CU21.0 million
Cr Derivative liability	CU21.0 million
To recognise the swap at fair value	

Scenario B

Entity F has a fixed rate investment that is not classified as held-to-maturity that it originally acquired for CU100 million some years ago. On acquisition of the investment Entity F also entered into a receive floating 1 month CU LIBOR pay fixed CU interest rate swap that it designated under previous GAAP as a hedging instrument in a fair value hedge of the fixed rate investment (with the hedged risk being fair value interest rate risk due to changes in the one-month CU LIBOR rate).

At the date of transition to IFRSs, the fair value of the fixed rate investment is CU115 million. Changes in fair value of the investment have not been recognised under previous GAAP. Of the CU15 million cumulative change in the value of the fixed rate investment since it was acquired (when its fair value was equal to CU100 million), CU13 million is determined to be due to fair value changes due to changes in the one-month CU LIBOR rate while CU2 million relates to changes in the issuer's credit risk. At the date of transition the cumulative change in the fair value of the swap (not reflected in the financial statements under previous GAAP) amounts to CU12 million, all of which is determined to relate to the hedged risk (changes in the one-month CU LIBOR rate).

At the date of transition, the fixed rate investment is adjusted by CU12 million such that its carrying amount in the opening statement of financial position is CU112 million (CU100 million plus the adjustment of CU12 million). This adjustment is the lower of the portion of the cumulative change in the fair value of the hedged item due to the designated hedged risk and the portion of the cumulative change in the fair value of the hedging instrument due to the designated hedged risk (CU13 million and CU12 million respectively).

On transition Entity D makes the following entries:

Dr Fixed rate investment	CU12 million
Cr Retained earnings	CU12 million
To adjust the hedged item	
Dr Retained earnings	CU12 million
Cr Derivative liability	CU12 million
To recognise the swap at fair value	

4.3.2.2 *Qualifying cash flow hedges*

An entity may have deferred gains and losses on a cash flow hedge of a forecast transaction. If, at the date of transition to IFRSs, the hedge relationship is of a type that would be a qualifying hedge relationship under IAS 39, i.e. the forecast transaction is highly probable, or if it is not highly probable, it is still expected to occur, the entire deferred gain or loss on the hedging instrument is recognised in equity. [IFRS 1.IG60B] Note that this initial entry in or reclassification into equity (depending on whether the gains and losses were either previously not recognised or deferred in the statement of financial position outside of equity) comprises the entire cumulative gain or loss on the hedging instrument as at the date of transition regardless of its effectiveness up to that date.

Any net cumulative gain or loss that is reclassified to equity on initial application of IAS 39 remains in equity until:

(a) the forecast transaction subsequently results in the recognition of a non-financial asset or non-financial liability and the amount deferred in equity, depending on the accounting policy choice of the entity, is either included in the initial carrying value of the non-financial asset or non-financial liability, i.e. it is accounted for as a basis adjustment to the item, or remains in equity and is reclassified from equity to profit or loss when the item affects profit or loss (see **2.2.3** in **chapter 8**);

(b) the forecast transaction affects profit or loss and the amount deferred in equity is reclassified from equity to profit or loss, for example, when a hedged highly probable forecast sale actually occurs; or

(c) the forecast transaction is no longer expected to occur, in which case any related net cumulative gain or loss is reclassified from equity to profit or loss.

Example 4.3.2.2

Qualifying cash flow hedges

Prior to the date of transition, a Sterling functional currency entity expects, with a high degree of probability, to sell goods to one of its customers for €1 million on a date after the date of transition to IFRSs. The entity enters into a forward contract to sell €1 million and buy £ at a forward rate of £0.7:€1 on the expected date of sale of the goods. Under previous GAAP the entity did not recognise the fair value of the forward contract in its statement of financial position.

Assume that on date of transition:

- the fair value of the forward contract is £(200,000), i.e. it is a liability; and
- the sale of goods for €1 million at the date originally forecast is still a highly probable forecast transaction.

At the date of transition, the entire cumulative loss on the forward contract to date is recorded in equity as follows:

Dr Equity	£200,000
Cr Forward contract	£200,000

After the date of transition the accounting treatment depends on the likelihood of the forecast transaction occurring.

(a) If the forecast transaction is no longer expected to occur, the entire cumulative gain/loss on the forward contract deferred in equity until that date (including that portion deferred on transition) is immediately reclassified from equity to profit or loss.

(b) If after the date of transition the forecast transaction becomes no longer highly probable but is still expected to occur, the hedged transaction no longer qualifies for hedge accounting (since it is no longer highly probable). Hence, subsequent gains and losses on the forward contract are recognised in profit or loss. However, the cumulative gain/loss on the forward contract deferred in equity (including that portion deferred on transition) up until the forecast transaction is no longer highly probable, remains in equity until either the transaction takes place (see (c) below) or it is no longer expected to occur (see (a) above).

(c) The highly probable forecast transaction takes place as expected. The cumulative gains/losses on the hedging instrument (including that portion deferred on transition) will be released to profit or loss at the same time as the highly probable forecast transaction (in the form of € denominated revenues) affects profit or loss, i.e. when the Euro denominated sale occurs.

4.3.2.3 Qualifying net investment hedges

IAS 39 and IFRS 1 do not contain any explicit guidance as to the transitional requirements in respect of hedges of a net investment in a foreign operation.

In accordance with IAS 39.102 hedges of a net investment in a foreign operation are accounted for similarly to cash flow hedges. It may therefore be argued that similar transitional provisions to those for cash flow hedging should be applied in the case of hedges of a net investment in a foreign operation. This would imply that, provided that the hedge relationship qualifies for hedge accounting under IAS 39 the cumulative gain/loss on the hedging instrument at the date of transition (that under previous GAAP may or may not have been recorded in the statement of financial position) is recognised in equity. Hence, for a derivative hedging instrument (e.g. cross currency swap or foreign currency forward contract) not previously reflected in the statement of financial position under previous GAAP, the following journal entry is required:

Dr/Cr Fair value of derivative (statement of financial position)	X	
Cr/Dr Equity		X

This amount classified in equity is released to profit or loss upon disposal of the foreign operation in accordance with the requirements of IAS 39.102 (see **2.3** in **chapter 8** for more details on hedging a net investment in a foreign operation). The reclassification of the deferred fair value gains/losses on the hedging instrument from equity to profit or loss will offset either fully or partially the foreign exchange gains/losses recognised in other comprehensive income arising on the retranslation of the net assets of the foreign operation in accordance with IAS 21 *The Effects of Changes in Foreign Exchange Rates*.

Pre-transition gains and losses recognised in equity will not be reclassified from equity to profit or loss in accordance with IAS 39.102 when an entity has elected to reset the cumulative translation reserve in equity to zero in accordance with IFRS 1.D13. Applying the exemption in IFRS 1.D13, the cumulative translation differences for all foreign operations are deemed to be zero at the date of transition and therefore only subsequent translation differences that arise after the date of the transition will be reclassified from equity to profit or loss on disposal of the foreign operation. If an entity has applied net investment hedge accounting in the consolidated financial statements under previous GAAP and the related hedging reserve is set to zero at the date of transition to IFRSs, the gains and losses on the hedging instrument prior to the date of transition, shall be recognised in the opening balance of retained earnings.

Appendix – Illustrative IFRS 7 disclosures

1 Introduction

The following illustrative IFRS 7 disclosures are included by way of example only and do not necessarily represent the only disclosures which may be appropriate for particular financial instruments and do not cover all financial instruments that may be used in practice. Material on a grey shaded background does not form part of the illustrative disclosures but is included to provide commentary and draw attention to disclosure requirements that have not been illustrated.

The illustrative disclosures reflect the disclosures required by the amendments to IFRS 7, *Improving Disclosures about Financial Instruments,* issued in March 2009. The amendments are effective for annual reporting periods beginning on or after 1 January 2009 without the need for comparative information for the first period of application.

Due to the pervasive nature of financial instruments, the application of IFRS 7 will impact a number of the disclosures throughout a set of financial statements. The amount of disclosure will depend on the underlying business, the extent of financial instruments, the complexity of those instruments and how the risks of the financial instruments are managed.

2 Illustrative disclosures

Source reference

3. Significant accounting policies

[extract only]

Example accounting policies

The following illustrations are quoted by way of example only, and do not necessarily represent the only treatment which may be appropriate for the item concerned and do not cover all items that should be considered for inclusion in the summary of accounting policies.

For example:

- an entity may elect to or not to adjust the initial measurement of the cost of a non-financial asset or a non-financial liability arising from a hedged forecast transaction by the amount deferred in equity
- an entity may elect to recognise and derecognise financial assets on settlement date or trade date basis
- a parent entity may elect to measure investments in subsidiaries, jointly controlled entities and associates, that are not classified as held for sale, either at cost or in accordance with IAS 39 'Financial Instruments: Recognition and Measurement'
- an entity may elect to amortise the fair value hedge adjustment to the hedged item for which the effective interest method is used into profit or loss from the date the adjustment is made or only begin the amortisation when the hedge accounting is discontinued.

(f) Derivative financial instruments

IFRS 7.21

The Group enters into a variety of derivative financial instruments to manage its exposure to interest rate and foreign exchange rate risk, including forward foreign exchange contracts, interest rate swaps and cross currency swaps. Further details of derivative financial instruments are disclosed in note 46 to the financial statements.

Derivatives are initially recognised at fair value on the date a derivative contract is entered into and are subsequently remeasured to their fair value at each reporting date. The resulting gain or loss is recognised in profit or loss immediately unless the derivative is designated and effective as a hedging instrument, in which event, the timing of the recognition in profit or loss depends on the nature of the hedge relationship. The Group designates certain derivatives as either hedges of the fair value of recognised assets or liabilities or firm commitments (fair value hedges), hedges of highly probable forecast transactions or hedges of foreign currency risk of firm commitments (cash flow hedges), or hedges of net investments in foreign operations.

The fair value of derivatives is classified as a non-current asset or a non-current liability if the remaining maturity of the instrument is more than 12 months and it is not expected to be realised or settled within 12 months.

<u>Embedded derivatives</u>

Derivatives embedded in other financial instruments or other host contracts are treated as separate derivatives when their risks and characteristics are not closely related to those of host contracts and the host contracts are not measured at fair value with changes in fair value recognised in profit or loss.

<u>Hedge accounting</u>

The Group designates certain hedging instruments, which include derivatives, embedded derivatives and non-derivatives in respect of foreign currency risk, as either fair value hedges, cash flow hedges, or hedges of net investments in foreign operations. Hedges of foreign exchange risk on firm commitments are accounted for as cash flow hedges.

Source reference

3. **Significant accounting policies (cont'd)**

At the inception of the hedge relationship the entity documents the relationship between the hedging instrument and hedged item, along with its risk management objectives and its strategy for undertaking various hedge transactions. Furthermore, at the inception of the hedge and on an ongoing basis, the Group documents whether the hedging instrument is highly effective in offsetting changes in fair values or cash flows of the hedged item.

Note 46 contains details of the fair values of the derivative instruments used for hedging purposes. Movements on the hedging reserve in equity are also detailed in note 32.

Where a statement of changes in equity is presented showing all changes in equity, the above sentence would refer to that statement rather than note 32.

Fair value hedge

Changes in the fair value of derivatives that are designated and qualify as fair value hedges are recorded in profit or loss immediately, together with any changes in the fair value of the hedged asset or liability that is attributable to the hedged risk. The change in the fair value of the hedging instrument and the change in the hedged item attributable to the hedged risk are recognised in the line of the income statement relating to the hedged item.

Hedge accounting is discontinued when the Group revokes the hedging relationship, the hedge instrument expires or is sold, terminated, exercised, or no longer qualifies for hedge accounting. The adjustment to the carrying amount of the hedged item arising from the hedged risk is amortised to profit or loss from that date.

Cash flow hedge

The effective portion of changes in the fair value of derivatives that are designated and qualify as cash flow hedges are recognised initially in other comprehensive income. The gain or loss relating to the ineffective portion is recognised immediately in profit or loss, and is included in the "other gains and losses" line of the income statement.

Amounts deferred in equity are recycled in profit or loss in the periods when the hedged item is recognised in profit or loss, in the same line of the income statement as the recognised hedged item. However, when the forecast transaction that is hedged results in the recognition of a non-financial asset or a non-financial liability, the gains and losses previously deferred in equity are transferred from equity and included in the initial measurement of the cost of the asset or liability.

Hedge accounting is discontinued when the Group revokes the hedging relationship, the hedging instrument expires or is sold, terminated, or exercised, or no longer qualifies for hedge accounting. At that time, any cumulative gain or loss deferred in equity at that time remains in equity and is recognised when the forecast transaction is ultimately recognised in profit or loss. When a forecast transaction is no longer expected to occur, the cumulative gain or loss that was deferred in equity is recognised immediately in profit or loss.

Hedges of net investments in foreign operations

Hedges of net investments in foreign operations are accounted for similarly to cash flow hedges. Any gain or loss on the hedging instrument relating to the effective portion of the hedge is initially recognised in other comprehensive income in the foreign currency translation reserve. The gain or loss relating to the ineffective portion is recognised immediately in profit or loss and is included in the 'other gains and losses' line of the income statement.

The effective gains and losses of the hedging instrument are deferred in the foreign currency translation reserve in equity and are recycled from that reserve to profit or loss when the foreign operation is disposed of.

Source reference

3. Significant accounting policies (cont'd)

(h) Financial assets

IFRS 7.21

Investments are recognised and derecognised on trade date where the purchase or sale of an investment is under a contract whose terms require delivery of the investment within the timeframe established by the market concerned, and are initially measured at fair value, plus transaction costs except for those financial assets classified as at fair value through profit or loss, which are initially measured at fair value.

Subsequent to initial recognition, investments in subsidiaries are measured at cost. Subsequent to initial recognition, investments in associates are accounted for under the equity method in the consolidated financial statements and the cost method in the company financial statements.

Other financial assets are classified into the following specified categories: financial assets as 'at fair value through profit or loss', 'held-to-maturity investments', 'available-for-sale' financial assets and 'loans and receivables'. The classification depends on the nature and purpose of the financial assets and is determined at the time of initial recognition.

Financial assets at fair value through profit or loss

Financial assets are classified as financial assets at fair value through profit or loss (FVTPL) where the financial asset is either held for trading or is designated as at FVTPL. A financial asset is held for trading if the Group acquires it principally for the purpose of selling in the near term, the financial asset is a part of an identified portfolio of financial instruments that the Group manages together and has a recent actual pattern of short term profit taking or it is a derivative that is not designated and effective as a hedging instrument..

IFRS 7.21, app.B5(a)

Where an entity designates financial assets into the financial assets at fair value through profit or loss category it discloses:

(i) the nature of the financial assets;

(ii) the criteria for so designating such financial assets on initial recognition; and

(iii) how the entity has satisfied the requirements in IAS 39 for such designation, including a narrative description of the circumstances underlying the measurement or recognition inconsistency that would otherwise arise or of how designation at fair value through profit or loss is consistent with the entity's documented risk management or investment strategy, as appropriate.

A financial asset other than a financial asset held for trading may be designated as at FVTPL upon initial recognition if:

- such designation eliminates or significantly reduces a measurement or recognition inconsistency that would otherwise arise; or
- the financial asset forms part of a group of financial assets or financial liabilities or both, which is managed and its performance is evaluated on a fair value basis, in accordance with the Group's documented risk management or investment strategy, and information about the grouping is provided internally on that basis; or
- it forms part of a contract containing one or more embedded derivatives, and IAS 39 Financial Instruments: Recognition and Measurement permits the entire combined contract (asset or liability) to be designated as at FVTPL.

Financial assets at fair value through profit or loss are stated at fair value, with any resultant gain or loss recognised in profit or loss. The net gain or loss recognised in profit or loss incorporates any dividend or interest earned on the financial asset. Fair value is determined in the manner described in note 46.

Source reference

3. Significant accounting policies (cont'd)

Effective interest method

The effective interest method is a method of calculating the amortised cost of a financial asset and of allocating interest income over the relevant period. The effective interest rate is the rate that exactly discounts estimated future cash receipts (including all fees on points paid or received that form an integral part of the effective interest rate, transaction costs and other premiums or discounts) through the expected life of the financial asset, or, where appropriate, a shorter period.

Debt instruments that are held-to-maturity, are available-for-sale, or are loans and receivables recognise income on an effective interest rate basis.

Held-to-maturity investments

Bills of exchange and debentures with fixed or determinable payments and fixed maturity where the Group has the positive intent and ability to hold to maturity are classified as held-to-maturity investments. Held-to-maturity investments are recorded at amortised cost using the effective interest method less impairment, with revenue recognised on an effective yield basis.

IFRS 7.appB5(b)

Where an entity designates a financial asset into the available-for-sale category it should disclose the criteria used in making the designation.

Available-for-sale financial assets

Unlisted shares and listed redeemable notes held by the Group are classified as being available-for-sale and are stated at fair value. Fair value is determined in the manner described in note 46. Gains and losses arising from changes in fair value are recognised directly in equity in the investments revaluation reserve with the exception of impairment losses, interest calculated using the effective interest method and foreign exchange gains and losses on monetary assets which are recognised directly in profit or loss. Where the investment is disposed of or is determined to be impaired, the cumulative gain or loss previously recognised in the investments revaluation reserve is included in profit or loss for the period.

Dividends on available-for-sale equity instruments are recognised in profit and loss when the Group's right to receive payments is established.

The fair value of available-for-sale monetary assets denominated in a foreign currency is determined in that foreign currency and translated at the spot rate at the reporting date. The change in fair value attributable to translation differences that result from a change in amortised cost of the asset is recognised in profit or loss, and other changes are recognised in equity.

Loans and receivables

Trade receivables, loans and other receivables that have fixed or determinable payments that are not quoted in an active market are classified as 'loans and receivables'. Loans and receivables are measured at amortised cost using the effective interest method less any impairment.

Interest income is recognised by applying the effective interest rate, except for short-term receivables when the recognition of interest would be immaterial.

Source reference

3. Significant accounting policies (cont'd)

Impairment of financial assets

Financial assets, other than those at FVTPL, are assessed for indicators of impairment at each reporting period end date. Financial assets are impaired where there is objective evidence that as a result of one or more events that occurred after the initial recognition of the financial asset the estimated future cash flows of the investment have been impacted.

IFRS 7.B5(f)
IFRS 7.37(b)

For unlisted shares classified as AFS, a significant or prolonged decline in the fair value of the security below its cost is considered to be objective evidence of impairment.

For all other financial assets, including redeemable notes classified as AFS and finance lease receivables, objective evidence of impairment could include:

- significant financial difficulty of the issuer or counterparty; or
- default or delinquency in interest or principal payments; or
- it becoming probable that the borrower will enter bankruptcy or financial re-organisation.

For certain categories of financial asset, such as trade receivables, assets that are assessed not to be impaired individually are subsequently assessed for impairment on a collective basis. Objective evidence of impairment for a portfolio of receivables could include the Group's past experience of collecting payments, an increase in the number of delayed payments in the portfolio past the average credit period of 60 days, as well as observable changes in national or local economic conditions that correlate with default on receivables.

For financial assets carried at amortised cost, the amount of the impairment is the difference between the asset's carrying amount and the present value of estimated future cash flows, discounted at the financial asset's original effective interest rate.

The carrying amount of the financial asset is reduced by the impairment loss directly for all financial assets with the exception of trade receivables where the carrying amount is reduced through the use of an allowance account. When a trade receivable is uncollectible, it is written off against the allowance account. Subsequent recoveries of amounts previously written off are credited against the allowance account. Changes in the carrying amount of the allowance account are recognised in profit or loss.

With the exception of available-for-sale equity instruments, if, in a subsequent period, the amount of the impairment loss decreases and the decrease can be related objectively to an event occurring after the impairment was recognised, the previously recognised impairment loss is reversed through profit or loss to the extent the carrying amount of the investment at the date the impairment is reversed does not exceed what the amortised cost would have been had the impairment not been recognised.

In respect of available-for-sale equity securities, impairment losses previously recognised through profit or loss are not reversed through profit or loss. Any subsequent increase in fair value after an impairment loss is recognised directly in equity.

IFRS 7.appB5(g)

When the terms of financial assets that would otherwise be past due or impaired have been renegotiated the entity should disclose the accounting policy for financial assets that are the subject of renegotiated terms.

Source reference

3. Significant accounting policies (cont'd)

Reclassification of financial assets

IFRS 7.21

The Group may reclassify certain non-derivative financial assets out of held for trading, part of the fair value through profit or loss category, to available-for-sale financial assets or held-to-maturity investments. Reclassification is only permitted in rare circumstances and where the asset is no longer held for the purpose of selling in the near term. In addition, it may also reclassify certain non-derivative financial assets out of held for trading to loans and receivables where the asset is no longer held for the purpose of selling in the near term and where the Group has the intention and ability to hold the financial asset for the foreseeable future or until maturity. The Group may also reclassify non-derivative financial assets from available-for-sale to loans and receivables where the Group has the intention and ability to hold the financial asset for the foreseeable future or until maturity. In all cases reclassification of financial assets is limited to debt instruments and is reclassified at the fair value of the financial asset at the date of reclassification. Where the Group reclassifies non-derivative financial assets to loans and receivables it assesses compliance with the definition of loans and receivables at the date of reclassification.

Derecognition of financial assets

The Group derecognises a financial asset only when the contractual rights to the cash flows from the asset expire; or it transfers the financial asset and substantially all the risks and rewards of ownership of the asset to another entity. If the Group neither transfers nor retains substantially all the risks and rewards of ownership and continues to control the transferred asset, the Group recognises its retained interest in the asset and an associated liability for amounts it may have to pay. If the Group retains substantially all the risks and rewards of ownership of a transferred financial asset, the Group continues to recognise the financial asset and also recognises a collateralised borrowing for the proceeds received.

(i) Financial instruments issued by the Group

IFRS 7.21

Debt and equity instruments

Debt and equity instruments are classified as either financial liabilities or as equity in accordance with the substance of the contractual arrangement.

Equity instruments

An equity instrument is any contract that evidences a residual interest in the assets of an entity after deducting all of its liabilities. Equity instruments issued by the Group are recorded at the proceeds received, net of direct issue costs.

Compound instruments

The component parts of compound instruments issued by the Group are classified separately as financial liabilities and equity in accordance with the substance of the contractual arrangement. At the date of issue, the fair value of the liability component is estimated using the prevailing market interest rate for a similar non-convertible instrument. This amount is recorded as a liability on an amortised cost basis using the effective interest method until extinguished on conversion or upon the instrument reaching maturity. The equity component is determined by deducting the amount of the liability component from the fair value of the compound instrument as a whole. This is recognised and included in equity, net of income tax effects and is not subsequently remeasured.

Financial guarantee contract liabilities

Financial guarantee contract liabilities are measured initially at their fair values and subsequently at the higher of:

Source reference

3. Significant accounting policies (cont'd)

- the amount of the obligation under the contract, as determined in accordance with IAS 37 Provisions, Contingent Liabilities and Contingent Assets; and
- the amount initially recognised less, where appropriate, cumulative amortisation recognised in accordance with the revenue recognition policies described in note x

Financial liabilities

Financial liabilities are classified as either financial liabilities 'at fair value through profit or loss' or 'other financial liabilities'.

Financial liabilities at fair value through profit or loss

Financial liabilities are classified as at FVTPL where the financial liability is either held for trading or it is designated as at FVTPL.

A financial liability is classified as held for trading if:

- it has been incurred principally for the purpose of repurchasing in the near future; or
- it is a part of an identified portfolio of financial instruments that the Group manages together and has a recent actual pattern of short-term profit-taking; or
- it is a derivative that is not designated and effective as a hedging instrument.

IFRS 7.21

Where an entity designates financial liabilities into the financial liability at fair value through profit or loss category it is required to disclose:

(i) the nature of the financial liabilities;

(ii) the criteria for so designating such financial liabilities on initial recognition; and

(iii) how the entity has satisfied the requirements in IAS 39 for such designation, including a narrative description of the circumstances underlying the measurement or recognition inconsistency that would otherwise arise or of how designation at fair value through profit or loss is consistent with the entity's documented risk management or investment strategy, as appropriate.

A financial liability other than a financial liability held for trading may be designated as at FVTPL upon initial recognition if:

- such designation eliminates or significantly reduces a measurement or recognition inconsistency that would otherwise arise; or
- the financial liability forms part of a group of financial assets or financial liabilities or both, which is managed and its performance is evaluated on a fair value basis, in accordance with the Group's documented risk management or investment strategy, and information about the grouping is provided internally on that basis; or
- it forms part of a contract containing one or more embedded derivatives, and IAS 39 Financial Instruments: Recognition and Measurement permits the entire combined contract (asset or liability) to be designated as at FVTPL.

Financial liabilities at fair value through profit or loss are initially measured at fair value and subsequently stated at fair value, with any resultant gain or loss recognised in profit or loss. The net gain or loss recognised in profit or loss incorporates any interest paid on the financial liability. Fair value is determined in the manner described in note 46.

Source reference

3. Significant accounting policies (cont'd)

Other financial liabilities

Other financial liabilities are initially measured at fair value, net of transaction costs.

Other financial liabilities are subsequently measured at amortised cost using the effective interest method, with interest expense recognised on an effective yield basis.

The effective interest method is a method of calculating the amortised cost of a financial liability and of allocating interest expense over the relevant period. The effective interest rate is the rate that exactly discounts estimated future cash payments through the expected life of the financial liability, or, where appropriate, a shorter period.

Derecognition of financial liabilities

The Group derecognises financial liabilities when, and only when, the Group's obligations are discharged, cancelled or they expire.

Classes of financial instruments

The Group considers the following to be its classes of financial assets: cash and bank deposits; trade receivables; finance lease receivables; loans; derivatives; financial assets designated at FVTPL; bills of exchange and debentures; shares; and redeemable notes.

The following financial liabilities are presented as separate classes of financial liabilities: bank overdrafts; bank loans; other loans; financial liabilities designated as at FVTPL; derivatives; redeemable cumulative preference shares; convertible notes; perpetual notes; transferred receivables; finance lease liabilities; and financial guarantee contracts.

IFRS 7.6

When disclosure by class of financial instrument is required by IFRS 7, an entity should group financial instruments into classes that are appropriate to the nature of the information disclosed and that take into account the characteristics of those financial instruments. An entity should provide sufficient information to permit reconciliation to the line items presented in the statement of financial position.

7. Revenue

[extract only]

Source reference		Consolidated		Company	
		2009 £'000	2008 £'000	2009 £'000	2008 £'000
	Interest revenue:				
	Bank deposits				
	Loans				
	Debentures				
	Redeemable notes				
IFRS 7.20(d)	Impaired financial assets				
	Unwinding of discount on bills of exchange				
	Other				
IFRS 7.20(b)					

Source reference

8. Other gains and losses

[extract only]

Source reference		Consolidated		Company	
		2009	2008	2009	2008
		£'000	£'000	£'000	£'000
	Continuing operations				
IFRS 7.20(a)(i)	Change in fair value of financial assets designated as at FVTPL				
IFRS 7.20(a)(i)	Change in fair value of financial assets classified as held for trading				
IFRS 7.20(a)(i)	Change in fair value of financial liabilities designated as at FVTPL				
IFRS 7.20(a)(i)	Change in fair value of financial liabilities classified as held for trading				
IFRS 7.20(a)(ii)	Recycling of gain/(loss) from equity on disposal of investments classified as available-for-sale				
IFRS 7.24(b)	Hedge ineffectiveness on cash flow hedges				
IFRS 7.24(c)	Hedge ineffectiveness on net investment hedges				

IFRS 7.20(a)(i)

If the redeemable cumulative preference shares are designated as financial liabilities at FVTPL, the following items would also be included in this note:

	Consolidated		Company	
	2009	2008	2009	2008
	£'000	£'000	£'000	£'000
Continuing operations				
Change in fair value of financial liabilities designated as at FVTPL (i)				
Change in fair value of financial assets classified as held for trading (ii)				

(i) The net loss on redeemable cumulative preference shares designated as at FVTPL includes dividends of £____ paid during the year.

(ii) Interest rate swap that economically hedges the fair value of cumulative preference shares, but for which hedge accounting was not applied. The net loss on the interest rate swap includes net interest of £____ paid during the year.

Source reference

9. Finance costs
[extract only]

Source reference		Consolidated		Company	
		2009 £'000	2008 £'000	2009 £'000	2008 £'000
	Interest on bank overdrafts and loans				
	Interest on obligations under finance leases				
	Dividends on instruments classified as financial liabilities				
	Interest on convertible notes				
	Interest on perpetual notes				
	Other interest expense				
IFRS 7.20(b)	Total interest expense				
	Less: amounts included in the cost of qualifying assets				
IFRS 7.24(a)(i)	Loss/(gains) arising on derivatives in a designated fair value hedge accounting relationship				
IFRS 7.24(a)(ii)	(Gains)/loss arising on adjustment to hedged item in a designated fair value hedge accounting relationship				
IFRS 7.23(d)	Fair value gains transferred from equity on interest rate swaps designated as cash flow hedges of floating rate debt				
	Unwinding of discounts on provisions				
	Unwinding of discount on costs to sell non-current assets classified as held for sale				
	Other finance costs				
	Attributable to:				
	Continuing operations				
	Discontinued operations				

The weighted average capitalisation rate on funds borrowed generally is 8.0 per cent p.a. (2008: 7.8 per cent p.a.).

Preparers of financial reports should apply judgment in deciding whether hedging gains and losses form part of finance costs or another part of expenses. In so doing, they should consider among other factors, their accounting policies, the nature of the instrument and objectives in entering into the hedging instruments.
If cumulative preference shares are designated as financial liabilities at FVTPL, the dividend on the redeemable cumulative preference shares would not be shown as part of finance costs above. Instead, it would be included in note 8 in accordance with the Group's accounting policy to include any interest paid on a financial liability at FVTPL in the net gain or loss.

Source reference

10. Profit for the year

[extract only]

Profit/(loss) before tax has been arrived at after crediting/(charging) the following gains and losses:

Source reference		Consolidated 2009 £'000	Consolidated 2008 £'000	Company 2009 £'000	Company 2008 £'000
	Net foreign exchange gains/(losses)				
	Other				
IFRS 7.20(e)	Impairment of cash and bank deposits				
IFRS 7.20(e)	Impairment of trade receivables				
IFRS 7.20(e)	Impairment of loans				
IFRS 7.20(e)	Impairment of bills of exchange and debentures				
IFRS 7.20(e)	Impairment of shares				
IFRS 7.20(e)	Impairment of redeemable notes				
	Gains attributable to:				
	Continuing operations				
	Discontinued operations				
	Losses attributable to:				
	Continuing operations				
	Discontinued operations				

IFRS 7.20(c)

An entity should disclose, either on the face of the financial report or in the notes, fee income and expense (other than amounts included in determining the effective interest rate) arising from:

(i) financial assets or financial liabilities that are not at fair value through profit or loss; and

(ii) trust and other fiduciary activities that result in the holding or investing of assets on behalf of individuals, trusts, retirement benefit plans, and other institutions.

Source reference

11. Net gain and losses on financial instruments

Consolidated

Source reference		Available-for-sale £'000	Held-to-maturity £'000	Loans and receivables £'000	Designated at FVTPL £'000	Held for trading £'000	Other liabilities £'000
	2009						
	Impairment loss reclassified from equity on available-for-sale financial instruments						
	Reclassification of gain/(loss) on disposal of available-for-sale financial instruments						
IFRS 7.20(a)(ii)	Total reclassified from equity and recognised in profit or loss						
	Interest revenue						
	Dividends						
	Net foreign exchange gain/loss on financial instruments not designated at FVTPL and not held for trading						
	Fair value gain/(loss) recognised on subsequent measurement or disposal						
	Total recognised in profit or loss						
IFRS 7.20(a)(ii)	Fair value gain/ Reclassified from equity to profit and loss for available-for-sale financial instruments						
IFRS 7.20(a)	Total net gain/(loss)						

Source reference

11. Net gain and losses on financial instruments (cont'd)

Source reference		Available-for-sale £'000	Held-to-maturity £'000	Loans and receivables £'000	Designated at FVTPL £'000	Held for trading £'000	Other liabilities £'000
	2008						
	Impairment loss reclassified from equity on available-for-sale financial instruments						
	Reclassification of gain/(loss) on disposal of available-for-sale financial instruments						
IFRS 7.20(a)(ii)	Total reclassified from equity and recognised in profit or loss						
	Interest revenue						
	Dividends						
	Net foreign exchange gain/loss on financial instruments not designated at FVTPL and not held for trading						
	Fair value gain/(loss) recognised on subsequent measurement or disposal						
	Total recognised in profit or loss						
IFRS 7.20(a)(ii)	Fair value gain/(loss) recognised directly in other comprehensive income						
	Reclassified from equity to profit and loss for available-for-sale financial instruments						
IFRS 7.20(a)	Total net gain/(loss)						

Source reference

11. Net gain and losses on financial instruments (cont'd)

Company

Source reference		Available-for-sale £'000	Held-to-maturity £'000	Loans and receivables £'000	Designated at FVTPL £'000	Held for trading £'000	Other liabilities £'000
	2009						
	Impairment loss reclassified from equity on available-for-sale financial instruments						
	Reclassification of gain/(loss) on disposal of available-for-sale financial instruments						
IFRS 7.20(a)(ii)	Total reclassified from equity and recognised in profit or loss						
	Interest revenue						
	Dividends						
	Net foreign exchange gain/loss on financial instruments not designated at FVTPL and not held for trading						
	Fair value gain/(loss) recognised on subsequent measurement or disposal						
	Total recognised in profit or loss						
IFRS 7.20(a)(ii)	Fair value gain/(loss) recognised directly in other comprehensive income						
	Reclassified from equity to profit and loss for available-for-sale financial instruments						
IFRS 7.20(a)	Total net gain/(loss)						

Source reference

11. Net gain and losses on financial instruments (cont'd)

Company (con'd)

Source reference		Available-for-sale £'000	Held-to-maturity £'000	Loans and receivables £'000	Designated at FVTPL £'000	Held for trading £'000	Other liabilities £'000
	2008						
	Impairment loss reclassified from equity on available-for-sale financial instruments						
	Reclassification of gain/(loss) on disposal of available-for-sale financial instruments						
IFRS 7.20(a)(ii)	Total reclassified from equity and recognised in profit or loss						
	Interest revenue						
	Dividends						
	Net foreign exchange gain/loss on financial instruments not designated at FVTPL and not held for trading						
	Fair value gain/(loss) recognised on subsequent measurement or disposal						
	Total recognised in profit or loss						
IFRS 7.20(a)(ii)	Fair value gain/(loss) recognised directly in other comprehensive income						
	Reclassified from equity to profit and loss for available-for-sale financial instruments						
IFRS 7.20(a)	Total net gain/(loss)						

Source reference

12. Trade and other receivables

Source reference		Consolidated 2009 £'000	Consolidated 2008 £'000	Company 2009 £'000	Company 2008 £'000
	Trade receivables (i)				
IAS 39.63	Allowance for doubtful debts (ii)				
	Finance lease receivable (note x)				
	Allowance for uncollectible minimum lease payments (iii)				
	Deferred sales proceeds (note x)				
	Operating lease receivable				
	Amounts due from customers under construction contracts (note x)				
	Goods and services tax recoverable				
	Other [describe]				

IFRS 7.36(c),37

(i) The average credit period on sales of goods is 60 days. No interest is charged on the trade receivables for the first 60 days from the date of the invoice. Thereafter, interest is charged at two per cent per annum on the outstanding balance. The Group has provided fully for all receivables over 120 days. Trade receivables between 60 and 120 days are provided for based on estimated irrecoverable amounts from the sale of goods, determined by reference to past default experience.

IFRS 7.36(c), 34(c)

Before accepting any new customer, the Group uses an external credit scoring system to assess the potential customer's credit quality and defines credit limits by customer. Limits and scoring attributed to customers are reviewed twice a year. 80% of the trade receivables that are neither past due nor impaired have the best credit scoring attributable under the external credit scoring system used by the Group. Of the trade receivables balance at the end of the year, £ (2008: £) is due from Company E, the Group's largest customer (see notes X and X).There are no other customers who represent more than 5% of the total balance of trade receivables.

The company uses the same method of assessing credit quality as the Group. 85% of the trade receivables that are neither past due nor impaired have the best credit scoring attributable under the external credit scoring system used by the Group. There are no customers who represent more than 5% of the total balance of trade receivables.

IFRS 7.37(a), (c)

Included in the Group's trade receivable balance are debtors with a carrying amount of £___ (2008: £___) which are past due at the reporting date for which the Group has not provided as there has not been a significant change in credit quality and the Group believes that the amounts are still considered fully recoverable. The Group does not hold any collateral over these balances. The average age of these receivables is 84 days (2008: 85 days).

Source reference

12. Trade and other receivables (cont'd)

Included in the company's trade receivable balance are debtors with a carrying amount of £___ (2008: £___) which are past due at the reporting date for which the company has not provided as there has not been a significant change in credit quality and the Group believes that the amounts are still considered fully recoverable. The company does not hold any collateral over these balances. The average age of these receivables is 75 days (2008: 79 days).

IFRS 7.37(a) Ageing of past due but not impaired

60-90 days		
90-120 days		
Total		

IFRS 7.16 (ii) Movement in the allowance for doubtful debts

	Balance at beginning of the year		
IFRS 7.20(e)	Impairment losses recognised on receivables		
	Amounts written off during the year		
	Amounts recovered during the year		
	Impairment losses reversed		
	Balance at end of the year		

In determining the recoverability of the trade receivable, the Group considers any change in the credit quality of the trade receivable from the date credit was initially granted up to the reporting date. The concentration of credit risk is limited due to the customer base being large and unrelated. Accordingly, the directors believe that there is no further credit provision required in excess of the allowance for doubtful debts.

IFRS 7.37(b) Included in the allowance for doubtful debts are specific trade receivables with a balance of £___ (2008: £___) for the Group and nil (2008: nil) for the company which have been placed under liquidation. The impairment represents the difference between the carrying amount of the specific trade receivable and present value of the expected liquidation proceeds. The Group and the company do not hold any collateral over these balances.

IFRS 7 .37(b) Ageing of impaired trade receivables

	Consolidated		Company	
	2009	2008	2009	2008
	£'000	£'000	£'000	£'000
60-90 days				
90-120 days				
120+ days				
Total				

Source reference	
	12. Trade and other receivables (cont'd)
IFRS 7.16	(iii) Movement in the allowance for uncollectible minimum lease payments

Balance at beginning of the year		
Impairment losses recognised on receivables		
Amounts written off during the year		
Amounts recovered during the year		
Impairment losses reversed		
Balance at end of the year		

IFRS 7 .37(b)

Ageing of impaired finance lease receivables		
60-90 days		
90-120 days		
120+ days		
Total		

IFRS 7.37(a)

There are no past finance lease receivable balances that are past due but not impaired.

IFRS 7. 37(b)-(c)

Included in the allowance for doubtful debts are specific finance lease receivables with a balance of £____ (2008: £____) for the Group and nil (2008: nil) for the company which are considered to be impaired. The terms of these leases are currently in the process of renegotiation with the lessees who are experiencing some financial difficulties. The impairment represents the difference between the carrying amount of the specific finance lease receivables and the present value of the expected future renegotiated lease receipts discounted using the original effective interest rate. The balances are secured over the leased equipment and the fair value of the collateral held by the Group is £ (2008: £___) and nil (2008: nil) for the company.

IFRS 7.36(b)-(c), 34(c)

Before entering into a finance lease arrangement, the Group and company use an external credit scoring system to assess the potential lessee's credit quality and define credit limits by customer. Limits and scoring attributed to lessees are reviewed twice a year. 90% of the Group and company finance lease receivables that are neither past due nor impaired have the second best credit scoring attributable under the external credit scoring system used by the Group and company. The balances are secured over the leased equipment and the fair value of the collateral held by the Group is £___ (2008: £___) and £___ (2008: £___) for the company. There are no customers who represent more than 5% of the total balance of finance lease receivables.

Source reference	
	12. Trade and other receivables (cont'd)
IFRS 7.37	**An entity should disclose by class of financial asset:** (a) an analysis of the age of financial assets that are past due as at the reporting date but not impaired; (b) an analysis of financial assets that are individually determined to be impaired as at the reporting date, including the factors the entity considered in determining that they are impaired; and (c) for the amounts disclosed in (a) and (b), a description of collateral held by the entity as security and other credit enhancements and, unless impracticable, an estimate of their fair value.
IFRS 7.36(d)	An entity should disclose by class of financial instrument the carrying amount of financial assets that would otherwise be past due or impaired whose terms have been renegotiated. For each asset line item that combines amounts expected to be recovered or settled (a) no more than twelve months after the reporting date, and (b) more than twelve months after the reporting date, an entity should disclose the amount expected to be recovered or settled after more than twelve months.
IFRS 7.13, 14	During the period the Group transferred £___ (2008: Nil) of trade receivables to an unrelated party. As a part of the transfer, the Group provided the transferee a credit guarantee over the expected losses of those receivables. The Group continues to recognise the full carrying amount of the receivables and has recognised the cash received on the transfer as a secured borrowing (refer to note 25). At the reporting date the carrying amount of the transferred short term receivables which have been pledged as security for the borrowing, is £___ and the associated liability is £___. The transferee is entitled to sell the trade receivables or deposit them as security for other loans.
IFRS 7.13	**Derecognition of financial assets** An entity may have transferred financial assets in such a way that part or all of the financial assets do not qualify for derecognition. The entity should disclose for each class of such financial assets: (a) the nature of the assets; (b) the nature of the risks and rewards of ownership to which the entity remains exposed; (c) when the entity continues to recognise all of the assets, the carrying amounts of the assets and of the associated liabilities; and (d) when the entity continues to recognise the assets to the extent of its continuing involvement, the total carrying amount of the original assets, the amount of the assets that the entity continues to recognise and the carrying amount of the associated liabilities.

Source reference

13. Other financial assets

	Consolidated		Company	
	2009	2008	2009	2008
	£'000	£'000	£'000	£'000
Investments carried at cost:				
Non-current				
Investments in subsidiaries				
Investments in associates				
Investments in jointly controlled entities				
Derivatives that are designated and effective as hedging instruments carried at fair value:				
Current				
Foreign currency forward contracts				
Interest rate swaps				
Non-current				
Interest rate swaps				
Financial assets carried at value through profit or loss:				
Current				
[describe]				
Non-current				
[describe]				
Held-to-maturity investments carried at amortised cost:				
Current				
Bills of exchange (v)				
Debentures (v)				
Non-current				
Bills of exchange (v)				
Available-for-sale investments carried at fair value:				
Current				
Shares				
Non-current				
Redeemable notes (i)				
Shares (ii)				
Asset-backed securities (vii)				
Loans carried at amortised cost:				
Current				
Bank deposits (vi)				
Loans to subsidiaries (iii)				
Loans to other related parties (iv)				
Non-current				
[describe]				
Disclosed in the financial statements as:				
Current other financial assets				
Non-current other financial assets				

Source reference	
	13. Other financial assets (cont'd)
IFRS 7.7, 34(c), 36(b)-(c).	(i) The Group holds listed redeemable notes returning 7 per cent p.a. The notes are redeemed at par value in 2010. The notes are held with a single counterparty with an AA credit rating. The Group doe not hold collateral over this balance.
	(ii) The Group holds 20 per cent (2008: 20 per cent) of the ordinary share capital of Rocket Corp Limited, a company involved in the refining and distribution of fuel products. The directors of the Group do not believe that the Group is able to exert significant influence over Rocket Corp Limited as the other 80 per cent is controlled by one shareholder, who also manages the day-to-day operations of the company.
IFRS 7.7, 34(c), . 36(b)-(c)	(iii) Receivables from entities within the wholly-owned Group are unsecured and include amounts arising under the Group's tax funding arrangement.
IFRS 7.7, 34(c), 36(b)-(c).	(iv) The Group has provided a joint venture with a short term loan at rate comparable to the average commercial rate of interest. The loan is secured over the property, plant and equipment of the joint venture. The fair value of the collateral exceeds the carrying amount of the loan. The group is not able to resell or repledge collateral in the absence of the default by the joint venture.
IFRS 7.7, 34(c), . 36(b)-(c)	(v) The Group holds bills of exchange and debentures with the counterparties with a minimum A credit rating for bills of exchange and a minimum of B credit rating for debentures. All of the assets are not past due and not impaired, and 70% of the assets have AA credit rating. Refer note 46 for significant concentrations of credit risk.
IFRS 7.7, 34(c), 36(b)-(c).	(vi) The Group and company hold bank deposits with financial institutions with a minimum of an A credit rating. All of the assets are not past due and not impaired, and 90% of the assets have AA credit rating. Refer note 46 for significant concentrations of credit risk.
IFRS 7.7, 34(c), 36(b)-(c).	(vii) The Group and company holds investments in asset-backed securities which have an underlying exposures to a pool of fixed rate corporate bonds. The reference portfolios of fixed fate corporate bonds are managed by a third party fund manager under a predetermined investment mandate. The investment mandate permits the fund manager to buy and sell the specific named corporate bonds subject to meeting specified credit ratings of AA or above. The asset-backed securities have been reclassified from held for trading to available-for-sale in the period. See note 24 on reclassification of financial assets. The contractual cash flows on the asset-backed securities have not been past due and the have not been subject to impairment since the date of reclassification.
	Financial assets carried at fair value through profit or loss
IFRS 7.8(a)	Where an entity carries financial assets at fair value through profit or loss, the entity should disclose separately the carrying amount of: (i) financial assets that, upon initial recognition, were designated by the entity as financial assets at fair value through profit or loss; and (ii) financial assets that are classified as held for trading.
	Financial assets that are either past due or impaired
IFRS 7.37(c)	In respect of financial assets that are past due as at the reporting date but not impaired and financial assets that are individually determined to be impaired as at the reporting date, an entity should provide a description of collateral held by the entity as security and other credit enhancements and, unless impracticable, an estimate of their fair value.
IFRS 7.36(d)	An entity should disclose by class of financial instrument the carrying amount of financial assets that would otherwise be past due or impaired whose terms have been renegotiated.

Source reference

21. Assets received as collateral

IFRS 7.15

As disclosed in note 12, finance lease receivable balances are secured over the storage equipment leased. The Group is not permitted to sell or repledge the collateral in the absence of default by the lessee.

IFRS 7.15

When an entity holds collateral (of financial and non-financial assets) and is permitted to sell or repledge the collateral in the absence of default by the owner of the collateral, it should disclose:

(a) the fair value of the collateral held (financial and non-financial assets);

(b) the fair value of any such collateral sold or repledged and whether the entity has an obligation to return it; and

(c) any material terms and conditions associated with its use of this collateral.

IFRS 7.38

When an entity obtains financial or non-financial assets during the period by taking possession of collateral it holds as security or calling on other credit enhancements (e.g. guarantees), and such assets meet the recognition criteria in other International Accounting Standards, an entity should disclose:

(a) the nature and carrying amount of the assets obtained; and

(b) when the assets are not readily convertible into cash, its policies for disposing of such assets or for using them in its operations.

22. Assets pledged as security

IFRS 7.14

Trade receivables transferred pledged as a security for the associated borrowing are disclosed in note 12.

In accordance with the security arrangements of liabilities, as disclosed in note 25 to the financial statements, all non-current assets of the Group, except goodwill and deferred tax assets, have been pledged as security. The holder of the security does not have the right to sell or re-pledge the assets.

The Group does not hold title to the equipment under finance lease pledged as security.

The financial report should disclose the following:

(a) the carrying amount of inventories pledged as security for liabilities

(b) the existence and carrying amounts of intangible assets whose title is restricted and the carrying amounts of intangible assets pledged as security for liabilities

(c) the carrying amount of the property, plant and equipment pledged and the related existence and amounts of restrictions on title

(d) the existence and amounts of restrictions on the realisability of investment property or the remittance of income and proceeds of disposal

IFRS 7.14

(e) the carrying amount of financial assets it has pledged as collateral for liabilities, or contingent liabilities, including amounts that have been reclassified as a result of a transfer of a financial asset in accordance with paragraph 37(a) of IAS 39, and the terms and conditions relating to its pledge.

Source reference

23. Trade and other payables

	Consolidated		Company	
	2009	2008	2009	2008
	£'000	£'000	£'000	£'000
Trade payables (i)				
Cash-settled share-based payments (note x) (ii)				
Amounts due to customers under construction contracts (note x)				
Goods and services tax payable				
Other [describe]				

IFRS 7.7

(i) The average credit period on purchases of certain goods from the United States is 4 months. No interest is charged on the trade payables for the first 60 days from the date of the invoice. Thereafter, interest is charged at two per cent per annum on the outstanding balance. The Group has financial risk management policies in place to ensure that all payables are paid within the credit timeframe.

(ii) At the reporting date, the intrinsic value of vested cash-settled share-based payments for the company and the Group is £nil (2008: £nil).

For each liability line item that combines amounts expected to be recovered or settled (a) no more than twelve months after the reporting date, and (b) more than twelve months after the reporting date, an entity should disclose the amount expected to be recovered or settled after more than twelve months.

	Consolidated		Company	
Disclosed in the financial statements as:				
Current				
Non-current				

Source reference	
	24. Reclassification of financial assets
	Reclassification of financial assets
IFRS 7.12	In the circumstances that a financial asset is reclassified as one measured at cost or amortised cost rather than at fair value, or at fair value, rather than at cost or amortised cost, an entity should disclose the amount and the reason for the reclassification. This disclosure is limited to those assets reclassified under IAS 39.51-54, i.e. those not reclassified out of held for trading (part of fair value through profit or loss) and out of available-for-sale to loans and receivables as permitted by IAS 39.50.

Source reference		Period end carrying amount		Period end fair value	
		2009 £'000	2008 £'000	2009 £'000	2008 £'000
IFRS 7.12A(b)	**Financial assets reclassified on 1 July 2009**				
	Consolidated				
	Reclassified from HFT to L&R				
	Reclassified from AFS to L&R				
	Total				
	Company				
	Reclassified from HFT to L&R				
	Reclassified from AFS to L&R				
	Total				

Source reference		Consolidated		Company	
		2009 £'000	2008 £'000	2009 £'000	2008 £'000
IFRS 7.12A(a)	**Fair value at the date of reclassification**				
	Reclassified from HFT to L&R				
	Reclassified from AFS to L&R				
	Total				

IFRS 7.12A(c)

The reclassifications of assets from HFT to AFS is limited to certain asset-backed securities where the Group's original intention at initial recognition was to sell the financial assets in the short-term. The severe reduction in the liquidity of those assets in the mar kets in which they would trade accompanied by a deterioration of price transparency and reduction in investor appetite to acquire the assets led to the Group concluding that for those reclassified assets at 1 July 2009 the circumstances were rare and that the Group no longer has the intention to sell the assets in the short-term.

Source reference

24. Reclassification of financial assets (cont'd)

Source reference		Consolidated		Company	
		2009	2008	2009	2008
		£'000	£'000	£'000	£'000
IFRS 7.12A(d)	**Fair value gain/loss recognised in the period**				
	Reclassified from HFT to L&R – income statement				
	Reclassified from AFS to L&R – other comprehensive income				
	Total				
IFRS 7.12A(e)	**Gain, loss, income and expense that would have been recognised had the financial assets not been reclassified**				
	Reclassified from HFT to L&R – fair value gains/losses in the income statement				
	Reclassified from AFS to L&R – interest income recognised using the effective interest rate in the income statement				
	Reclassified from AFS to L&R – impairment losses in the income statement				
	Reclassified from AFS to L&R – foreign currency gains/losses in the income statement				
	Total – income statement				
	Reclassified from AFS to L&R – fair value gains/losses in other comprehensive income				

As a result of the reclassifications undertaken at 1 July 2009, the profit or loss is £___ higher, and other comprehensive income £___ higher, for the period ending 31 December 2009, than would have been the case had the financial assets not been reclassified.

Source reference		Reclassified from HFT to L&R		Reclassified from AFS to L&R	
		Consolidated	Company	Consolidated	Company
		2009	2008	2009	2008
		£'000	£'000	£'000	£'000
IFRS 7.12A(f)	**Effective interest at the date of reclassification from financial assets:**				
	Effective interest rate (range)				
	Effective interest rate (weighted average)				
IFRS 7.12A(f)	**Expected recoverable cash flows at the date of reclassification:**				
	< 1year				
	≥ 1 year ≤ 3 years				
	≥ 3 years < 5 years				
	≥ 5 years				
	Total				

Source reference

25. Borrowings

	Consolidated		Company	
	2009 £'000	2008 £'000	2009 £'000	2008 £'000
Unsecured – at amortised cost				
Current				
Bank overdrafts				
Other loans				
Bills of exchange (v)				
Loans from:				
Subsidiaries (i)				
Other related parties (ii)				
Other entities				
Other [describe]				
Non-current				
Bills of exchange (v)				
Loans from:				
Subsidiaries (i)				
Other related parties (ii)				
Other entities				
Redeemable cumulative preference shares (iii)				
Convertible notes (note 27)				
Perpetual notes (iv)				
Other [describe]				
Secured – at amortised cost				
Current				
Bank overdrafts				
Bank loans (vi), (vii)				
Transferred receivables (ix)				
Finance lease liabilities (viii) (note x)				
Other [describe]				
Non-current				
Bank loans (vii)				
Other loans (vii)				
Finance lease liabilities (viii) (note x)				
Other [describe]				
Disclosed in the financial statements as:				
Current borrowings				
Non-current borrowings				

IFRS 7.7

(i) Payables to entities within the wholly-owned Group include amounts arising under the entity's tax funding arrangement (refer to note x for details).

(ii) Amounts repayable to related parties of the Group. Interest of 8.0% - 8.2% per annum is charged on the outstanding loan balances (2008: 8.0% - 8.2% per annum). The Group hedges a portion of the loans via an interest rate swap exchanging fixed rate interest for variable rate interest. The outstanding balance is adjusted for fair value movements in the hedged risk, being movements in the US dollar inter-bank rate.

Source reference

25. Borrowings (cont'd)

IFRS 7.7

(iii) 3 million 7 per cent redeemable cumulative preference shares were issued on 1 June 2009 at an issue price of £_ per share. The shares are redeemable on 31 May 2010 at £_ per share.

IFRS 7.7

(iv) 2,500 6 per cent perpetual notes were issued on 27 August 2009 at £__ principal value. Issue costs of £__ were incurred.

(v) Bills of exchange with a variable interest rate were issued in 2000. The current weighted average effective interest rate on the bills is 6.8% per annum (2008: 6.8% per annum).

(vi) Relates to the current portion of long-term borrowings.

(vii) Secured by a mortgage over the Group's freehold land and buildings. The current weighted average effective interest rate on the bank loans is 8.30% per annum (2008: 8.32% per annum).

(viii) Secured by the assets leased. The borrowings are mix of a variable and fixed interest rate debt with repayment terms not exceeding 5 years.

(ix) Secured by a charge over certain of the Group's trade receivables (refer to note 12 for details).

Defaults and breaches

IFRS 7.18

For loans payable recognised at the reporting date, an entity should disclose:

(a) details of any defaults during the period of principal, interest, sinking fund, or redemption terms of those loans payable;

(b) the carrying amount of the loans payable in default at the reporting date; and

(c) whether the default was remedied, or the terms of the loans payable were renegotiated, before the financial statements were authorised for issue.

IFRS 7.19

If, during the period, there were breaches of loan agreement terms other than those described above, an entity shall disclose the same information as required above if those breaches permitted the lender to demand accelerated repayment (unless the breaches were remedied, or the terms of the loan were renegotiated, on or before the reporting date).

IFRS 7.18

During 2009, the Group was late in paying interest for the first quarter on one of its loans with a carrying amount of CU5 million. The delay arose because of a temporary lack of funds on the date interest was payable due to a technical problem on settlement. The interest payment outstanding of CU107,500 was repaid in full on the following day, including the additional interest and penalty. The lender did not request accelerated repayment of the loan and the terms of the loan were not changed. Management has reviewed the Group's settlement procedures to ensure that such circumstances do not recur.

If the redeemable cumulative preference shares are designated as financial liabilities at FVTPL, redeemable cumulative preference shares would be shown as liabilities as at FVTPL in note 26.

Source reference

26. Other financial liabilities

	Consolidated		Company	
	2009	2008	2009	2008
	£'000	£'000	£'000	£'000
Financial guarantee contracts				
Current				
Non-current				
Derivatives				
Derivatives that are designated and effective as hedging instruments carried at fair value:				
Current				
Foreign currency forward contracts				
Interest rate swaps				
Currency swaps				
Other [describe]				
Non-current				
Other [describe]				
Derivatives that are classified as held for trading:				
Current				
Other [describe]				
Non-current				
Other [describe]				
Disclosed in the financial statements as:				
Current other financial liabilities				
Non-current other financial liabilities				

Financial liabilities carried at fair value through profit or loss

IFRS 7.8(e) An entity should disclose the carrying amount of:

(i) financial liabilities that are classified as held for trading; and

(ii) financial liabilities that, upon initial recognition, were designated by the entity as financial liabilities at fair value through profit or loss.

If the redeemable cumulative preference shares are designated as financial liabilities at FVTPL, the following additional amounts would be included in note 26 below

Source reference

26. Other financial liabilities (cont'd)

(extract)

	Consolidated		Company	
	2009 £'000	2008 £'000	2009 £'000	2008 £'000
Financial liabilities carried at fair value through profit or loss (FVTPL)				
Non-derivative financial liabilities designated as at FVTPL				
Current				
Cumulative preference shares (i)				
Non-current				
Cumulative preference shares (i)				
Held for trading non-derivative financial liabilities				
Current				
Other [describe]				
Non-current				
Other [describe]				
Derivatives				
Held for trading derivatives that are not designated in hedge accounting relationships				
Current				
Interest rate swap (ii)				
Non-current				
Interest rate swap (ii)				

(i) 3,000,000 7% redeemable cumulative preference shares were issued on 1 June 2009 at an issue price of CU5 per share. The shares are redeemable on 31 May 2010 at CU5 per share. The shares are unsecured borrowings of the Group and are designated as at FVTPL.

(ii) A pay-floating receive-fixed interest rate swap economically hedges fair value interest rate risk of redeemable cumulative preference shares. The swap matures on 31 May 2010.

The Group has designated its redeemable cumulative preference shares as financial liabilities at fair value through profit or loss (FVTPL) as permitted by IAS 39 *Financial Instruments: Recognition and Measurement*. The preference shares have fixed interest payments and mature on 31 May 2010. To reduce the fair value risk of changing interest rates, the Group has entered into a pay-floating receive-fixed interest rate swap. The swap's notional principal is CU15 million and matches the principal of the cumulative redeemable preference shares. The swap matures on 31 May 2010. The designation of preference shares as at FVTPL eliminates the accounting mismatch arising on measuring the liability at amortised cost and measuring the derivative at FVTPL.

Source reference

27. Convertible notes

4.5 million £ denominated 5.5 per cent convertible notes were issued on 1 September 2009 at an issue price of £_ per note. The conversion price is at a 30% premium to the share price of the ordinary shares at the date the convertible notes were issued. Each note entitles the holder to convert to one ordinary share at a cost of £__ per ordinary share. Conversion may occur any time between 1 July 2012 and 31 August 2012. Unconverted notes mature at £__ on 1 September 2012. Interest of 5.5% will be paid quarterly up until that settlement date.

IAS 32.28 — The net proceeds received from the issue of the convertible notes have been split between the liability element and an equity component, representing the residual attributable to the option to convert the liability into equity of the Group, as follows:

	Consolidated and Company	
	2009	2008
	£'000	£'000
Proceeds of issue (net of apportioned transaction costs)		
Liability component at date of issue		
Equity component		

The equity component of £__has been credited to equity (option premium on convertible notes – see note x).

The interest charged for the year is calculated by applying an effective interest rate of 8%. The liability component is measured at amortised cost. The difference between the carrying amount of the liability component at the date of issue (£) and the amount reported in the statement of financial position at 31 December 2009 (£) represents the effective interest rate less interest paid to that date.

32. Reserves

[extract only]

Source reference		Consolidated		Company	
		2009	2008	2009	2008
		£'000	£'000	£'000	£'000
	Investments revaluation reserve				
	Balance at beginning of financial year				
	Effect of change in ability to designate investment in shares as 'at fair value through profit or loss'				
	Restated opening balance				
IFRS 7.20(a)(ii)	Increase arising on revaluation of available-for-sale financial assets Cumulative (gain)/loss reclassified to the income statement on sale of available-for-sale financial assets				
IFRS 7.20(a)(ii)	Cumulative (gain)/loss reclassified to the income statement on impairment of available-for-sale financial assets				
	Related income tax				
	Balance at end of financial year				

Source reference

32. Reserves (cont'd)

The investments revaluation reserve arises on the revaluation of available-for-sale financial assets. Where a revalued financial asset is sold that portion of the reserve which relates to that financial asset is recognised in profit or loss. Where a revalued financial asset is impaired that portion of the reserve which relates to that financial asset is recognised in profit or loss.

Hedging reserve

Source reference			
	Balance at beginning of financial year		
IFRS 7.23(c)	Gain/(loss) recognised on cash flow hedges:		
	Forward exchange contracts		
	Interest rate swaps		
	Currency swaps		
	Income tax related to gains/ losses recognised in equity		
IFRS 7.23(d)	Reclassified to profit or loss (i):		
	Forward exchange contracts		
	Interest rate swaps		
	Currency swaps		
	Income tax related to amounts transferred to profit or loss		
IFRS 7.23(e)	Reclassified to initial carrying amount of hedged item:		
	Forward exchange contracts		
	Income tax related to amounts transferred to initial carrying amount of hedged item		
	Other [describe]		
	Balance at end of financial year		

The hedging reserve represents hedging gains and losses recognised on the effective portion of cash flow hedges. The cumulative deferred gain or loss on the hedge is recognised in profit or loss when the hedged transaction impacts the profit or loss, or is included as a basis adjustment to the non-financial hedged item, consistent with the applicable accounting policy.

IFRS 7.23(d)

(i) Gains and losses reclassified from equity into profit or loss during the period are included in the following line items on the face of the income statement:

Revenue		
Other income		
Finance costs		
Other expenses		
Income tax expense		
Other [describe]		

Source reference

46. Financial instruments

IAS 1.134, 135

(a) Capital risk management

The Group manages its capital to ensure that entities in the Group and company will be able to continue as a going concern while maximising the return to stakeholders through the optimisation of the debt and equity balance. The Group and company's overall strategy remains unchanged from 2008.

The capital structure of the Group consists of debt, which includes the borrowings disclosed in note 25, cash and cash equivalents and equity attributable to equity holders of the parent, comprising issued capital, reserves and retained earnings as disclosed in notes x, 32 and x respectively.

The Group's risk management committee reviews the capital structure of the company and Group on a semi-annual basis. As a part of this review the committee considers the cost of capital and the risks associated with each class of capital. The Group has a target gearing ratio of 20-25% determined as the proportion of net debt to equity. Based on the committee's recommendations, the Group expects to increase its gearing ratio closer to 25% through the issue of new debt and the payment of dividends.

The company has a target gearing ratio of 50% determined in the same way as for the Group. Based on the current committee's recommendations, the company expects to maintain its current gearing ratio unchanged.

Gearing ratio

	Consolidated		Company	
	2009	2008	2009	2008
	£'000	£'000	£'000	£'000
Debt				
Cash and cash equivalents				
Net debt				
Net debt to equity ratio				

(i) Debt is defined as long- and short-term borrowings, as detailed in note 32.

(ii) Equity includes all capital and reserves of the Group.

Externally imposed capital requirements

IAS 1.135(d)

When an entity is subject to externally imposed capital requirements, it should disclose the nature of those requirements and how those requirements are incorporated into the management of capital.

IAS 1.135(e)

When the entity has not complied with such externally imposed capital requirements, it should disclose the consequences of such non-compliance.

IFRS 7.21

(b) Significant accounting policies

Details of the significant accounting policies and methods adopted, including the criteria for recognition, the basis of measurement and the basis on which income and expenses are recognised, in respect of each class of financial asset, financial liability and equity instrument are disclosed in note 3 to the financial statements.

Source reference

46. Financial instruments

(c) Categories of financial instruments

Source reference		Consolidated 2009 £'000	Consolidated 2008 £'000	Company 2009 £'000	Company 2008 £'000
	Financial assets				
	Cash				
	Fair value through profit or loss				
IFRS 7.8(a)	Held for trading				
IFRS 7.8(a)	Designated (i)				
	Derivative instruments in designated hedge accounting relationships				
IFRS 7.8(b)	Held-to-maturity investments				
IFRS 7.8(c)	Loans and receivables				
IFRS 7.8(d)	Available-for-sale financial assets				
	Financial liabilities				
	Fair value through profit or loss				
IFRS 7.8(e)	Held for trading				
IFRS 7.8(e)	Designated (ii)				
	Derivative instruments in designated hedge accounting relationships				
IFRS 7.8(f)	Amortised cost				
	Financial guarantee contracts				

(i) Loans and receivables designated as at 'fair value through profit or loss'

Source reference		Consolidated 2009 £'000	Consolidated 2008 £'000	Company 2009 £'000	Company 2008 £'000
	Carrying amount of loans and receivables designated as at 'fair value through profit or loss'				
IFRS 7.9(c)	Cumulative changes in fair value attributable to changes in credit risk				
IFRS 7.9(c)	Changes in fair value attributable to changes in credit risk recognised during the period				

IFRS 7.9(a) At the reporting date there are no significant concentrations of credit risk for loans and receivables designated as at fair value through profit or loss. The carrying amount reflected above represents the company's and the Group's maximum exposure to credit risk for such loans and receivables.

IFRS 7.9(b) If the entity has designated a loan or receivable (or group of loans or receivables) as at fair value through profit or loss, it should disclose the amount by which any related credit derivatives or similar instruments mitigate that maximum exposure to credit risk.

IFRS 7.11(a) An entity should disclose the methods used to comply with the requirements in IFRS 7 to disclose the amount of change, during the period and cumulatively, in the fair value of the loan or receivable (or group of loans or receivables) that is attributable to changes in the credit risk of the financial asset.

Source reference	
	46. Financial instruments (cont'd)
IFRS 7.11(b)	If the entity believes that the disclosure it has given to comply with the requirements in IFRS 7 to disclose the amount of change, during the period and cumulatively, in the fair value of the loan or receivable (or group of loans or receivables) that is attributable to changes in the credit risk of the financial asset does not faithfully represent the change in the fair value of the financial asset attributable to changes in its credit risk, it should disclose the reasons for reaching this conclusion and the factors it believes are relevant.
IFRS 7.9(d)	Credit derivatives over loans and receivables at fair value

	Consolidated		Company	
	2009 £'000	2008 £'000	2009 £'000	2008 £'000
Opening fair value				
Change in fair value				
Closing fair value				

(ii) Financial liabilities designated as at 'fair value through profit or loss'

Source reference		Consolidated		Company	
		2009 £'000	2008 £'000	2009 £'000	2008 £'000
IFRS 7.10(a)	Cumulative changes in fair value attributable to changes in credit risk (ii)				
IFRS 7.10(a)	Changes in fair value attributable to changes in credit risk recognised during the period (i)				

IFRS 7.10(b) Difference between carrying amount and maturity amount

	Consolidated		Company	
	2009 £'000	2008 £'000	2009 £'000	2008 £'000
Financial liabilities at fair value (i)				
Amount payable at maturity (i)				

If the redeemable cumulative preference shares are designated as financial liabilities at FVTPL:

(i) Financial liabilities at fair value reflect the fair value of cumulative redeemable preference shares and the amount payable at maturity would be the redemption amount on 31 May 2010 as per note 26.

The following additional information would be required:

IFRS 7.11(a) (ii) The change in fair value attributable to change in credit risk is calculated as the difference between total change in fair value of cumulative preference shares of (£___) and the change in fair value of preference shares due to change in market risk factors alone (£___). The change in fair value due to market risk factors was calculated using benchmark interest yield curves as at the reporting period end date holding credit risk margin constant. The fair value of cumulative redeemable preference shares was estimated by discounting future cash flows using quoted benchmark interest yield curves as at the reporting period end date and by obtaining lender quotes for borrowing of similar maturity to estimate credit risk margin.

Source reference	
	46. Financial instruments (cont'd)
IFRS 7.11(a)	An entity should disclose the methods used to comply with the requirements in IFRS 7 to disclose the amount of change, during the period and cumulatively, in the fair value of the financial liability that is attributable to changes in the credit risk of the financial liability.
IFRS 7.11(b)	If the entity believes that the disclosure it has given to comply with the requirements in IFRS 7 to disclose the amount of change, during the period and cumulatively, in the fair value of the financial liability that is attributable to changes in the credit risk of the financial liability does not faithfully represent the change in the fair value of the financial liability attributable to changes in its credit risk, it should disclose the reasons for reaching this conclusion and the factors it believes are relevant.
	Financial risk management
IFRS 7.31	An entity should disclose information that enables users of its financial statements to evaluate the nature and extent of risks arising from financial instruments to which the entity is exposed at the reporting date.
IFRS 7.32	IFRS 7 requires certain disclosures be made about the nature and extent of risks arising from financial instruments. These disclosures focus on the risks that arise from financial instruments and how they have been managed. These risks typically include, but are not limited to, credit risk, liquidity risk and market risk.
IFRS 7.33	For each type of risk arising from financial instruments, an entity should disclose: (a) the exposures to risk and how they arise; (b) its objectives, policies and processes for managing the risk and the methods used to measure the risk; and (c) any changes in (a) or (b) from the previous period.
IFRS 7.34	For each type of risk arising from financial instruments, an entity should disclose: (a) summary quantitative data about its exposure to that risk at the reporting date. This disclosure should be based on the information provided internally to key management personnel of the entity, for example the entity's board of directors or chief executive officer; (b) the disclosures about credit risk, liquidity risk and market risk required by the standard (refer IFRS 7 paragraphs 36 to 42), to the extent not provided in (a), unless the risk is not material; and (c) concentrations of risk if not apparent from (a) and (b).
IFRS 7.34, appB8	Disclosure of concentrations of risk should include: (a) a description of how management determines concentrations; (b) a description of the shared characteristic that identifies each concentration (e.g. counterparty, geographical area, currency or market); and (c) the amount of the risk exposure associated with all financial instruments sharing that characteristic.
IFRS 7.31	**(d) Financial risk management objectives** The Group's Corporate Treasury function provides services to the business, coordinates access to domestic and international financial markets, monitors and manages the financial risks relating to the operations of the Group through internal risk reports which analyse exposures by degree and magnitude of risks. These risks include market risk (including currency risk, fair value interest rate risk and price risk), credit risk, liquidity risk and cash flow interest rate risk. The Group seeks to minimise the effects of these risks, by using derivative financial instruments to hedge these risk exposures. The use of financial derivatives is governed by the Group's policies approved by the board of directors, which provide written principles on foreign exchange risk, interest rate risk, credit risk, the use of financial derivatives and non-derivative financial instruments, and the investment of excess liquidity. Compliance with policies and exposure limits is reviewed by the internal auditors on a continuous basis. The Group does not enter into or trade financial instruments, including derivative financial instruments, for speculative purposes.

Source reference	
	46. Financial instruments (cont'd)
	The Corporate Treasury function reports quarterly to the Group's risk management committee, an independent body that monitors risks and policies implemented to mitigate risk exposures.
IFRS 7.33	**(e) Market risk** The Group's activities expose it primarily to the financial risks of changes in foreign currency exchange rates (refer to section g) and interest rates (refer to section h). The Group enters into a variety of derivative financial instruments to manage its exposure to interest rate and foreign currency risk, including: • forward foreign exchange contracts to hedge the exchange rate risk arising on the export of widgets to the United States and Japan; • interest rate swaps to mitigate the risk of rising interest rates. • forward foreign exchange contracts to hedge the risk arising on translation of the Group's investment in foreign operation Subfour Limited which has a US dollar functional currency. At a Group level market risk exposures are measured using value-at-risk (VaR) and are supplemented by sensitivity analysis. At a company level market risks are managed through sensitivity analyses.
IFRS 7.33(c)	There has been no change to the Group and company's exposure to market risks or the manner in which these risks are managed and measured.
	Market risk – sensitivity analysis
IFRS 7.40	An entity should disclose: (a) a sensitivity analysis for each type of market risk to which the entity is exposed at the reporting date, showing how profit or loss and equity would have been affected by changes in the relevant risk variable that were reasonably possible at that date;
IFRS 7.appB19	In determining what a reasonably possible change in the relevant risk variable is, an entity should consider: i. the economic environments in which it operates. A reasonably possible change should not include remote or 'worst case' scenarios or 'stress tests'. Moreover, if the rate of change in the underlying risk variable is stable, the entity need not alter the chosen reasonably possible change in the risk variable; and ii. the time frame over which it is making the assessment. The sensitivity analysis should show the effects of changes that are considered to be reasonably possible over the period until the entity will next present these disclosures, which is usually its next annual reporting period. (b) the methods and assumptions used in preparing the sensitivity analysis; and (c) changes from the previous period in the methods and assumptions used, and the reasons for such changes.
IFRS 7.41	If an entity prepares a sensitivity analysis, such as value-at-risk, that reflects interdependencies between risk variables (e.g. interest rates and exchange rates) and uses it to manage financial risks, it may use that sensitivity analysis in place of the analysis specified above. The entity should also disclose: (a) an explanation of the method used in preparing such a sensitivity analysis, and of the main parameters and assumptions underlying the data provided; and (b) an explanation of the objective of the method used and of limitations that may result in the information not fully reflecting the fair value of the assets and liabilities involved.
IFRS 7.42	When the sensitivity analyses disclosed are unrepresentative of a risk inherent in a financial instrument (e.g. because the year-end exposure does not reflect the exposure during the year), the entity should disclose that fact and the reason it believes the sensitivity analyses are unrepresentative.

Source reference

46. Financial instruments (cont'd)

(f) VaR Analysis

The VaR risk measure estimates the potential loss in pre-taxation profit over a given holding period for a specified confidence level. The VaR methodology is a statistically defined, probability-based approach that takes into account market volatilities as well as risk diversification by recognising offsetting positions and correlations between products and markets. Risks can be measured consistently across all markets and products, and risk measures can be aggregated to arrive at a single risk number. The one-day 99 per cent VaR number used by the Group reflects the 99 per cent probability that the daily loss will not exceed the reported VaR.

The VaR methodologies employed to calculate daily risk numbers include the historical and variance–covariance approaches. In addition to these two methodologies, Monte Carlo simulations are applied to the various portfolios on a monthly basis to determine potential future exposure.

While VaR captures the Group's daily exposure to currency and interest rate risk, sensitivity analysis evaluates the impact of a reasonably possible change in interest or foreign currency rates over a year. The longer time frame of sensitivity analysis complements VaR and helps the Group to assess its market risk exposures. Details of sensitivity analysis for foreign currency risk are set out below.

Historical VaR	**Average**		**Minimum**		**Maximum**		**Year-end**	
(99%, one-day)	**2009**	**2008**	**2009**	**2008**	**2009**	**2008**	**2009**	**2008**
by risk type	**£'000**	**£'000**	**£'000**	**£'000**	**£'000**	**£'000**	**£'000**	**£'000**
Foreign exchange								
Interest rate								
Diversification								
Total VaR exposure								

(g) Foreign currency risk management

IFRS 7.33, 34

The Group undertakes certain transactions denominated in foreign currencies, hence exposures to exchange rate fluctuations arise. Exchange rate exposures are managed within approved policy parameters utilising forward foreign exchange contracts.

The carrying amounts of the Group's foreign currency denominated monetary assets and monetary liabilities at the reporting date are as follows:

	Liabilities		**Assets**	
	2009	**2008**	**2009**	**2008**
	£'000	**£'000**	**£'000**	**£'000**
USD				
Japanese Yen				
Other				

The company does not have any exposures to foreign currencies at the reporting date (2008: nil).

Foreign currency sensitivity

The Group is mainly exposed to US dollars and Japanese Yen.

IFRS 7.40(b)

The following table details the Group's sensitivity to a 10 per cent increase in pounds sterling against the respective foreign currencies. The 10 per cent is the rate used when reporting foreign currency risk internally to key management personnel and represents management's assessment of the reasonably possible change in foreign exchange rates. The sensitivity analysis includes only outstanding foreign currency denominated monetary items and adjusts their translation at the period end for a 10 per cent change in foreign currency rates. The sensitivity analysis includes external loans as well as loans to foreign operations within the Group where the denomination of the loan is in a currency other than the currency of the lender or the borrower. A positive number below indicates an increase in profit and other equity where the pound sterling strengthens 10 per cent against the relevant currency. For a 10 per cent weakening of the pound sterling against the relevant currency, there would be an equal and opposite impact on the profit and other equity, and the balances below would be negative.

Source reference

46. Financial instruments (cont'd)

	USD Impact				Japanese Yen Impact			
	Consolidated		Company		Consolidated		Company	
	2009 £'000	2008 £'000	2009 £'000	2008 £'000	2009 £'000	2008 £'000	2009 £'000	2008 £'000
IFRS 7.40(a) Profit or loss				(i)				(iii)
IFRS 7.40(a) Other equity				(ii)				(iv)

(i) This is mainly attributable to the exposure outstanding USD receivables and payables at year end in the Group.

(ii) This is mainly as a result of the changes in fair value of derivative instruments designated as cash flow hedges and hedges of a net investment in a foreign operation.

(iii) This is mainly attributable to the exposure to outstanding Japanese Yen payables at the year end.

(iv) This is mainly as a result of the changes in fair value of derivative instruments designated as cash flow hedges.

IFRS 7.33(c)

The Group's sensitivity to foreign currency has decreased during the current period mainly due to the disposal of certain USD investments and the reduction in USD sales in the last quarter of the financial year which has resulted in lower USD denominated trade receivables.

IFRS 7.42

In management's opinion, the sensitivity analysis is unrepresentative of the inherent foreign exchange risk as the year end exposure does not reflect the exposure during the year. USD denominated sales are seasonal with lower sales volumes in the last quarter of the financial year, which results in a reduction in USD receivables at year end. Additionally, the change in equity due to a 10 per cent change in pounds sterling against all exchange rates for the translation of net investment hedging instruments would be a decrease/ increase of £____ (2008: £____). However, there would be no net impact on equity as there would be an offset in the currency translation of the foreign operation.

Forward foreign exchange contracts

IFRS 7.22, 33, 34

It is the policy of the Group to enter into forward foreign exchange contracts to cover specific foreign currency payments and receipts within 70 to 80 per cent of the exposure generated. The Group also enters into forward foreign exchange contracts to manage the risk associated with anticipated sales and purchase transactions out to 6 months within 40 to 50 per cent of the exposure generated. Basis adjustments are made to the carrying amounts of non-financial hedged items when the anticipated sale or purchase transaction takes place. As mentioned above, the company does not have any exposures to foreign currencies at the reporting date (2008: nil) and consequently does not hold any foreign currency derivatives.

In the current year, the Group has designated certain forward contracts as a hedge of its net investment in Subfour Limited, which has US dollar functional currency. The Group's policy has been reviewed and, due to the increased volatility in US dollar, it was decided to hedge up to 50% of the net assets of the Subfour Limited for forward foreign currency risk arising on translation of the foreign operation. The Group utlilises a rollover hedging strategy, using contract with terms of up to 6 months. Upon the maturity of a forward contract, the Group enters into a new contract designated as a separate hedging relationship.

The following table details the forward foreign currency contracts outstanding as at reporting date:

Source reference

46. Financial instruments (cont'd)

Outstanding contracts	Average exchange rate		Foreign currency		Contract value		Fair value	
			FC'000	FC'000	£'000	£'000	£'000	£'000
	2009	2008	2009	2008	2009	2008	2009	2008
Consolidated								
Cash flow hedges								
Buy US Dollars								
Less than 3 months								
3 to 6 months								
Sell US Dollars								
Less than 3 months								
Buy Japanese Yen								
Less than 3 months								
Net investment hedge								
Sell US dollars								
3 to 6 months								

IFRS 7.34(a)

The table above provides an example of summary quantitative data about exposure to foreign exchange risks at the reporting date that an entity may provide internally to key management personnel of the entity.

If there were foreign currency derivatives held by the company, and if similar information was provided internally to key management personnel for the company as for the Group, the following table would be disclosed for the company.

Outstanding contracts	Average exchange rate		Foreign currency		Contract value		Fair value	
			FC'000	FC'000	£'000	£'000	£'000	£'000
	2009	2008	2009	2008	2009	2008	2009	2008
Company								

[describe]

The Group has entered into contracts to supply widgets to customers in the United States. The Group has entered into forward foreign exchange contracts (for terms not exceeding 3 months) to hedge the exchange rate risk arising from these anticipated future transactions, which are designated as cash flow hedges.

IFRS 7.23(a)

As at the reporting date the aggregate amount of losses under forward foreign exchange contracts deferred in the hedging reserve relating to the exposure on these anticipated future transactions is £___ (2008: gains of £___). It is anticipated that the sales will take place during the first 3 months of the next financial year at which stage the amount deferred in equity will be released into profit or loss.

The Group has entered into contracts to purchase raw materials from suppliers in the United States and Japan. The Group has entered into forward foreign exchange contracts (for terms not exceeding 6 months) to hedge the exchange rate risk arising from these anticipated future purchases, which are designated into cash flow hedges.

IFRS 7.23(a)

As at the reporting date the aggregate amount of gains under forward foreign exchange contracts deferred in the hedging reserve relating to these anticipated future transactions is £___ (2008: gains of £___). It is anticipated that the purchases will take place during the first 6 months of the next financial year at which stage the amount deferred in equity will be included in the carrying values of the raw materials. It is anticipated that the raw materials will be converted into inventory and sold within 12 months after purchase at which stage the amount deferred in equity will impact profit or loss.

Source reference	
	46. Financial instruments (cont'd)
IFRS 7.23(b)	The Group has reduced its forecasts on sales of widgets to the United States due to an increased local competition and higher shipping costs. The Group had previously hedged US$___ of future sales of which US$___ are no longer expected to occur, and US$___ remain highly probable. The revision to forecasts was determined at the start of the third quarter. Accordingly, the Group, has recycled £___ of losses on foreign currency forward contracts relating to forecast transactions that are no longer expected to occur into profit or loss.
IFRS 7.24(c)	As at 31 December 2009 there has been no ineffectiveness recognised in profit or loss arising from hedging the net investment in Subfour Limited.
IFRS 7.33, 34	**(h) Interest rate risk management**
	The Group and the company are exposed to interest rate risk as entities in the Group borrow funds at both fixed and floating interest rates. The risk is managed by the Group by maintaining an appropriate mix between fixed and floating rate borrowings, by the use of interest rate swap contracts and forward interest rate contracts. Hedging activities are evaluated regularly to align with interest rate views and defined risk appetite; ensuring optimal hedging strategies are applied, by either positioning the statement of financial position or protecting interest expense through different interest rate cycles.
	The Group and the company's exposures to interest rates on financial assets and financial liabilities are detailed in the liquidity risk management section of this note.
	Interest rate sensitivity
IFRS 7.40(b), 34(a)	The sensitivity analyses below have been determined based on the exposure to interest rates for both derivatives and non-derivative instruments at the reporting date. For floating rate liabilities, the analysis is prepared assuming the amount of liability outstanding at the reporting period end date was outstanding for the whole year. A 50 basis point increase or decrease is used when reporting interest rate risk internally to key management personnel and represents management's assessment of the reasonably possible change in interest rates.
IFRS 7.40(a)	At reporting date, if interest rates had been 50 basis points higher/lower and all other variables were held constant, the Group's: • net profit would decrease/increase by £___ (2008: decrease/increase by £___). This is mainly attributable to the Group's exposure to interest rates on its variable rate borrowings; • other equity reserves would decrease/increase by £___ (2008: decrease/increase by £___) mainly as a result of the changes in the fair value of available-for-sale fixed rate debt instruments.
IFRS 7.33(c)	The Group's sensitivity to interest rates has decreased during the current period mainly due to the reduction in variable rate debt instruments and the increase in interest rate swaps to swap floating rate debt to fixed.
IFRS 7.40(a)	At the reporting date, if interest rates had been 50 basis points higher/lower and all other variables were held constant, the company's: • net profit would decrease/increase by £___ (2008: decrease/increase by £___). This is mainly attributable to the company's exposure to interest rates on its variable rate borrowings and cash deposits; • other equity reserves would decrease/increase by £___ (2008: decrease/increase by £___) mainly as a result of the changes in fair value of available-for-sale fixed rate instruments.
	The company's sensitivity to interest rates has decreased during the current period mainly due to the reduction in variable rate debt instruments.

Source reference

46. Financial instruments (cont'd)

Interest rate swap contracts

IFRS 7.22, 33, 34

Under interest rate swap contracts, the Group and company agree to exchange the difference between fixed and floating rate interest amounts calculated on agreed notional principal amounts. Such contracts enable the Group and company to mitigate the risk of changing interest rates on the fair value of issued fixed rate debt held and the cash flow exposures on the issued variable rate debt. The fair value of interest rate swaps at the year end are determined by discounting the future cash flows using the year end curves and the credit risk inherent in the contract, and are disclosed below. The average interest rate is based on the outstanding balances at the end of the financial year.

The following tables detail the notional principal amounts and remaining terms of interest rate swap contracts outstanding as at reporting date:

Cash flow hedges	Average contracted fixed interest rate		Notional principal amount		Fair value	
Outstanding receive floating pay fixed contracts	2009	2008	2009	2008	2009	2008
Consolidated						
Less than 1 year						
1 to 2 years						
2 to 5 years						
5 years +						
Company						
Less than 1 year						
[describe]						

IFRS 7.34(a)

The table above provides an example of summary quantitative data about exposure interest rate risks at the reporting date that an entity may provide internally to key management personnel.

The interest rate swaps settle on a quarterly basis. The basis of floating rates is 3-month LIBOR which at the reporting period end was ___ (2008 :___) The Group and company will settle the difference between the fixed and floating interest rate on a net basis.

IFRS 7.22, 23(a)

All interest rate swap contracts exchanging floating rate interest amounts for fixed rate interest amounts are designated as cash flow hedges in order to reduce the Group and company's cash flow exposure resulting from variable interest rates on borrowings. The interest rate swaps and the interest payments on the loan occur simultaneously and the amount deferred in equity is recognised in profit or loss over the period that the floating rate interest payments on debt impact profit or loss.

Fair value hedges	Average contracted fixed interest rate		Notional principal amount		Fair value	
Outstanding receive fixed pay floating contracts	2009	2008	2009	2008	2009	2008
Consolidated						
Less than 1 year						
[describe]						
Company						
Less than 1 year						
[describe]						

IFRS 7.34(a)

The table above provides an example of summary quantitative data about exposure to interest rate risks at the reporting date that an entity may provide internally to key management personnel.

Source reference

46. Financial instruments (cont'd)

If cumulative preference shares are designated as at FVTPL, the following additional information would be required:

Fair value hedges	**Average contracted fixed interest rate**		**Notional principal amount**		**Fair value**	
	2009	**2008**	**2009**	**2008**	**2009**	**2008**
Outstanding receive fixed pay floating contracts						
Held for trading interest rate swap 1 to 2 years						

The interest rate swaps settle on a quarterly basis. The basis of floating rates is 3-month LIBOR which at the reporting period end was ____ (2008:___). The Group and company will settle the difference between the fixed and floating interest rate on a net basis.

IFRS 7.24(a) Interest rate swap contracts exchanging fixed rate interest for floating rate interest are designated and effective as fair value hedges in respect of interest rates. During the period the Group and company's hedge was 100 per cent effective in hedging the fair value exposure to interest rate movements and as a result the carrying amount of the loan in the Group and company was adjusted by £___ which was included in profit or loss at the same time that the fair value of the interest rate swap was included in profit or loss.

(i) Other price risks

The Group and company are exposed to equity price risks arising from equity investments. Equity investments are held for strategic rather than trading purposes. The Group and company do not actively trade in these investments.

Equity price sensitivity

IFRS 7.40(b) The sensitivity analyses below have been determined based on the exposure to equity price risks at the reporting date.

IFRS 7.40(a) If equity prices had been 5 per cent higher/lower

- net profit would have been unaffected as the equity investments are classified as available-for-sale and no investments were disposed of or impaired;
- other equity reserves would increase/decrease by £___ (2008: increase/decrease by £___) for the Group and £___ (2008: £___) for the company as a result of the changes in fair value of available-for-sale shares.

IFRS 7.40(c) The Group and company's sensitivity to equity prices has not changed significantly from the prior year.

IFRS 7.36, appB8 **(j) Credit risk management**

Credit risk refers to the risk that a counterparty will default on its contractual obligations resulting in financial loss to the Group. The Group has adopted a policy of only dealing with creditworthy counterparties and obtaining sufficient collateral where appropriate, as a means of mitigating the risk of financial loss from defaults. The Group and company only transact with entities that are rated the equivalent of investment grade and above. This information is supplied by independent rating agencies where available and, if not available, the Group and company use other publicly available financial information and its own trading records to rate the major customers. The Group and company's exposure and the credit ratings of its counterparties are continuously monitored and the aggregate value of transactions concluded is spread amongst approved counterparties. Credit exposure is controlled by counterparty limits that are reviewed and approved by the risk management committee annually.

Source reference

46. Financial instruments (cont'd)

Trade receivables consist of a large number of customers, spread across diverse industries and geographical areas. Ongoing credit evaluation is performed on the financial condition of accounts receivable and, where appropriate, credit guarantee insurance cover is purchased.

The Group does not have any significant credit risk exposure to any single counterparty or any Group of counterparties having similar characteristics. The Group defines counterparties as having similar characteristics if they are related entities. Concentration of credit risk did not exceed 5% of gross monetary assets at any time during the year. The credit risk on liquid funds and derivative financial instruments is limited because the counterparties are banks with high credit-ratings assigned by international credit-rating agencies.

Except as detailed in the following table, the carrying amount of financial assets recorded in the financial statements, which is net of impairment losses, represents the Group's maximum exposure to credit risk without taking account of the value of any collateral obtained:

	Maximum credit risk	
	2009	2008
	£'000	£'000
Financial assets and other credit exposures		
Consolidated		
Guarantee provided by a subsidiary to secure financing for a sister company controlled by the Group's overseas parent		
Guarantee provided to lender on a jointly controlled entity's loan		
Other [describe]		
Company		
Guarantee provided to lender on subsidiary's borrowing		
Guarantee provided under the deed of cross guarantee		
Other [describe]		

IFRS 7.36(b) An entity should disclose a description of collateral held as security and other credit enhancements in respect of the amounts disclosed above.

IFRS 7.34(c) The table below shows the credit limit and balance of 3 major counterparties for the Group and company at the reporting period end date using the Standard and Poor's credit rating symbols.

Counterparty	Location	Rating	2009 Credit limit	2009 Carrying amount	2008 Credit limit	2008 Carrying amount
			£'000	£'000	£'000	£'000
Consolidated						
Company A	United Kingdom	AA				
Company B	Japan	B				
Company C	United States	BB				
Company						
Company A	United Kingdom	AA				
Company D	United Kingdom	B				
Company E	United Kingdom	B				

Source reference

46. Financial instruments (cont'd)

IFRS 7.appB10

Activities that give rise to credit risk and the associated maximum exposure to credit risk include, but are not limited to:

- granting loans and receivables to customers and placing deposits with other entities. In these cases, the maximum exposure to credit risk is the carrying amount of the related financial assets;
- entering into derivative contracts, for example, foreign exchange contracts and interest rate swaps. When the resulting asset is measured at fair value, the maximum exposure to credit risk at the reporting date will equal the carrying amount;
- entering into credit derivatives. When the resulting asset is measured at fair value, the maximum exposure to credit risk at the reporting date will equal the carrying amount. When the resulting liability is measured at fair value, the maximum exposure to credit risk at the reporting date is the maximum amount the entity could have to pay, which may be significantly greater than the amount recognised as a liability;
- granting financial guarantees. In this case, the maximum exposure to credit risk is the maximum amount the entity could have to pay if the guarantee is called on, which may be significantly greater than the amount recognised as a liability; and
- making a loan commitment that is irrevocable over the life of the facility or is revocable only in response to a material adverse change. If the issuer cannot settle the loan commitment net in cash or another financial instrument, the maximum credit exposure is the full amount of the commitment. This is because it is uncertain whether the amount of any undrawn portion may be drawn upon in the future. This may be significantly greater than the amount recognised as a liability.

(k) Liquidity risk management

IFRS 7.33, 39(c)

Ultimate responsibility for liquidity risk management rests with the board of directors, which has built an appropriate liquidity risk management framework for the management of the Group and company's short, medium and long-term funding and liquidity management requirements. The Group and company manage liquidity risk by maintaining adequate reserves, banking facilities and reserve borrowing facilities by continuously monitoring forecast and actual cash flows and matching the maturity profiles of financial assets and liabilities. Included in note x is a listing of additional undrawn facilities that the Group/company has at its disposal to further reduce liquidity risk.

Liquidity and interest risk tables

IFRS 7.34, 35, 39(a)(b)

The following tables detail the company's and the Group's remaining contractual maturity for its *non-derivative* financial liabilities (including issued financial guarantee contracts). The tables below have been drawn up based on the undiscounted contractual cash flows of the financial liabilities including both interest and principal cash flows. To the extent interest flows are floating rate the undiscounted amount is derived from interest rate curves at the reporting period end. The contractual maturity is based on the earliest date on which company and the Group may be required to pay.

IFRS 7.34(a)

The tables below includes the weighted average effective interest rate as an example of summary quantitative data about exposure to interest rates at the reporting date that an entity may provide internally to key management personnel.

Source reference

46. Financial instruments (cont'd)

Consolidated

	Weighted average effective interest rate %	Less than 1 month £'000	1–3 months £'000	3 months to 1 year £'000	1–5 years £'000	5+ years £'000	Total £'000
2009							
Non-interest bearing:							
Financial guarantee contracts							
Interest bearing:							
Finance lease liability							
Variable interest rate instruments							
Fixed interest rate instruments							
2008							
Non-interest bearing:							
Financial guarantee contracts							
Interest bearing:							
Finance lease liability							
Variable interest rate instruments							
Fixed interest rate instruments							

Company

	Weighted average effective interest rate %	Less than 1 month £'000	1–3 months £'000	3 months to 1 year £'000	1–5 years £'000	5+ years £'000	Total £'000
2009							
Non-interest bearing:							
Financial guarantee contracts							
Interest bearing:							
Variable interest rate instruments							
Fixed interest rate instruments							
2008							
Non-interest bearing:							
Financial guarantee contracts							
Interest bearing:							
Variable interest rate instruments							
Fixed interest rate instruments							

IFRS 7.B10A(a)

The Group/company has the ability to early redeem its variable interest rate instruments at the end of year 2 and therefore the principal amounts included in the maturity analysis could be settled at that date as opposed to year 6 as described above. In such cases the interest payments included in years 3-6 will not be payable however the Group/company may incur interest payments to the extent the early redemption of variable interest rate instruments is funded by new borrowings.

Source reference

46. Financial instruments (cont'd)

IFRS 7.B10(b)

The amounts included above for financial guarantee contracts are the maximum amount the Group/company could be forced to settle under the arrangement for the full guaranteed amount if that amount is claimed by the counterparty to the guarantee. Based on expectations at the reporting period end the Group/company considers it is more likely than not that nil amount will be payable under the arrangement. However, this amount is subject change depending on the probability of the counterparty claiming under the guarantee which is a function of the likelihood that the financial receivables held by the counterparty which are guaranteed suffer credit losses.

IFRS 7.34, 35

The following tables detail the company's and the Group's expected maturity for its *non-derivative financial assets*. The tables below have been drawn up based on the undiscounted cash flows of the financial assets including interest that will be earned on those assets. The inclusion of information on non-derivative financial assets is necessary in order to understand the Group's liquidity risk management as the liquidity is managed on a net asset and liability basis.

Consolidated

	Weighted average effective interest rate %	Less than 1 month £'000	1–3 months £'000	3 months to 1 year £'000	1–5 years £'000	5+ years £'000	Total £'000
2009							
Non-interest bearing							
Interest bearing:							
Finance lease receivable							
Variable interest rate instruments							
Fixed interest rate instruments							
2008							
Non-interest bearing							
Interest bearing:							
Finance lease receivable							
Variable interest rate instruments							
Fixed interest rate instruments							

IFRS 7.B10A(b)

The amounts included above for variable interest rate instruments for both non-derivative financial assets and liabilities is subject to change should changes in variable interest rates differ to those estimates of interest rates determined at the reporting period end.

IFRS 7.39(c)

The Group has access to financing facilities, the total unused amount which is £___ (2008: £___) at the reporting period end date. The Group expects to meet its other obligations from operating cash flows and proceeds of maturing financial assets. The Group expects to maintain its existing current debt to equity ratio, within a 20-25% range. This will be achieved through the issue of new debt and the increased use of secured bank loan facilities.

Source reference

46. Financial instruments (cont'd)

Company

	Weighted average effective interest rate %	Less than 1 month £'000	1–3 months £'000	3 months to 1 year £'000	1–5 years £'000	5+ years £'000	Total £'000
2009							
Non-interest bearing							
Interest bearing:							
Variable interest rate instruments							
Fixed interest rate instruments							
2008							
Non-interest bearing							
Interest bearing:							
Variable interest rate instruments							
Fixed interest rate instruments							

IFRS 7.39(c) The Company has access to financing facilities, the total unused amount which is £___ (2008: £___) at the reporting period end date. The company expects to meet its other obligations from operating cash flows and proceeds of maturing financial assets.

IFRS 7.34, 35 The following table details the Group's contractual maturity for its *derivative financial assets and liabilities*. Derivatives are designated in highly effective hedge relationships and are anticipated to be retained until their contractual maturity in order to act as an offset to the gains or losses on the hedged item. The table has been drawn up based on the undiscounted net cash inflows/(outflows) on the derivative instruments that settle on a net basis and the undiscounted gross inflows and (outflows) on those derivatives that require gross settlement. When the amount payable or receivable is not fixed, the amount disclosed has been determined by reference to the projected interest rates as illustrated by the yield curves existing at the reporting date.

The company does not hold any derivative financial instruments (2008: nil).

	Less than 1 month £'000	1–3 months £'000	3 months to 1 year £'000	1–5 years £'000	5+ years £'000
2009					
Net settled:					
Interest rate swaps					
Foreign exchange forward contracts					
Gross settled:					
Foreign exchange forward contracts					
2008					
Net settled:					
Interest rate swaps					
Forward exchange contracts					
Gross settled:					
Foreign exchange forward contracts					

Source reference

46. Financial instruments (cont'd)

IFRS 7.B11D

The amounts disclosed in the maturity analysis are the contractual undiscounted cash flows, for example:

(a) gross finance lease obligations (before deducting finance charges);

(b) prices specified in forward agreements to purchase financial assets for cash;

(c) net amounts for pay-floating/receive-fixed interest rate swaps for which net cash flows are exchanged;

(d) contractual amounts to be exchanged in a derivative financial instrument (e.g. a currency swap) for which gross cash flows are exchanged; and

(e) gross loan commitments.

(l) Fair value of financial instruments

IFRS 7.27

The fair values of financial assets and financial liabilities are determined as follows:

- the fair value of financial assets and financial liabilities with standard terms and conditions and traded on active liquid markets are determined with reference to quoted market prices
- the fair value of other financial assets and financial liabilities (excluding derivative instruments) are determined in accordance with generally accepted pricing models based on discounted cash flow analysis using prices from observable current market transactions and dealer quotes or similar instruments
- the fair value of derivative instruments, are calculated using quoted prices. Where such prices are not available, use is made of discounted cash flow analysis using the applicable yield curve for the duration of the instruments for non-optional derivatives, and option pricing models for optional derivatives
- the fair value of financial guarantee contracts is determined using option pricing models where the main assumptions are the probability of default by the specified counterparty extrapolated from market-based credit information and the amount of loss, given the default.

Quoted prices

Financial assets in this category include listed redeemable notes, bills of exchange and debentures. Financial liabilities include bills of exchange and perpetual notes.

Derivatives

Foreign currency forward contracts are measured using quoted forward exchange rates and yield curves derived from quoted interest rates matching maturities of the contracts.

Interest rate swaps are measured at the present value of future cash flows estimated and discounted based on the applicable yield curves derived from quoted interest rates.

Credit risk adjustments for counterparty or own credit risk are applied to derivative fair valuations reflecting an collateral posted or received as well any master netting agreements that will apply in the case of default to the extent the Group/company has multiple derivatives with the same counterparty.

IFRS 7.25, 29(a)

Except as detailed in the following table, the directors consider that the carrying amount of financial assets and financial liabilities recorded in the financial statements approximates their fair values.

Source reference

46. Financial instruments (cont'd)

	Carrying amount £'000	Fair value £'000
2009		
Consolidated		
Financial assets:		
Loans and receivables:		
Bank deposits		
Loans to related parties		
Held-to-maturity:		
Bills of exchange		
Debentures		
Finance lease receivables		
Financial liabilities		
Amortised cost:		
Bills of exchange		
Redeemable cumulative preference shares		
Convertible notes		
Perpetual notes		
Bank loans at fixed interest rate		
Loans from related parties at fixed interest rate		
Loans from other entities at fixed interest rate		
Financial guarantees issued		
Finance lease payables		

(I) Fair value of financial instruments

IFRS 7.27

The fair values of financial assets and financial liabilities are determined as follows:

- s and conditions and traded on active liquid markets are determined with reference to quoted market prices
- the fair value of other financial assets and financial liabilities (excluding derivative instruments) are determined in accordance with generally accepted pricing models based on discounted cash flow analysis using prices from observable current market transactions and dealer quotes or similar instruments
- the fair value of derivative instruments, are calculated using quoted prices. Where such prices are not available, use is made of discounted cash flow analysis using the applicable yield curve for the duration of the instruments for non-optional derivatives, and option pricing models for optional derivatives
- the fair value of financial guarantee contracts is determined using option pricing models where the main assumptions are the probability of default by the specified counterparty extrapolated from market-based credit information and the amount of loss, given the default.

Quoted prices

Financial assets in this category include listed redeemable notes, bills of exchange and debentures. Financial liabilities include bills of exchange and perpetual notes.

Source reference

46. Financial instruments (cont'd)

Derivatives

Foreign currency forward contracts are measured using quoted forward exchange rates and yield curves derived from quoted interest rates matching maturities of the contracts.

- Interest rate swaps are measured at the present value of future cash flows estimated and discounted based on the applicable yield curves derived from quoted interest rates.

IFRS 7.25, 29(a)

Except as detailed in the following table, the Group consider that the carrying amount of financial assets and financial liabilities recognised in the statement of financial position approximates their fair values.

	Carrying amount £'000	Fair value £'000
Consolidated		
Financial assets:		
Loans and receivables:		
Bank deposits		
Loans to related parties		
Held-to-maturity:		
Bills of exchange		
Debentures		
Finance lease receivables		
Financial liabilities		
Amortised cost:		
Bills of exchange		
Redeemable cumulative preference shares		
Convertible notes		
Perpetual notes		
Bank loans at fixed interest rate		
Loans from related parties at fixed interest rate		
Loans from other entities at fixed interest rate		
Financial guarantees issued		
Finance lease payables		

	Carrying amount £'000	Fair value £'000
2009		
Company		
Financial assets at amortised cost		
Loans and receivables:		
Bank deposits		
Loans to subsidiaries		
Finance lease receivables		

Source reference

46. Financial instruments (cont'd)

	Carrying amount £'000	Fair value £'000
Financial liabilities		
Amortised cost:		
Bills of exchange		
Redeemable cumulative preference shares		
Convertible notes		
Perpetual notes		
Bank loans at fixed interest rate		
Loans from other entities at fixed interest rate		
Financial guarantees issued		
Finance lease payables		

	Carrying amount £'000	Fair value £'000
2008		
Consolidated		
Financial assets		
Loans and receivables:		
Bank deposits		
Loans to related parties		
Held-to-maturity:		
Bills of exchange		
Debentures		
Finance lease receivables		
Financial liabilities		
Amortised cost:		
Bills of exchange		
Bank loans at fixed interest rate		
Loans from related parties at fixed interest rate		
Loans from other entities at fixed interest rate		
Financial guarantees issued		
Finance lease payables		
Company		
Financial assets		
Loans and receivables:		
Bank deposits		
Loans to subsidiaries		
Finance lease receivables		
Financial liabilities		
Amortised cost:		
Bills of exchange		
Bank loans at fixed interest rate		
Loans from other entities at fixed interest rate		
Financial guarantees issued		
Finance lease payables		

Source reference

46. Financial instruments (cont'd)

IFRS 7.27

The financial statements include holdings in unlisted shares which are measured at fair value (note x). Fair value is estimated using a discounted cash flow model, which includes some assumptions that are not supportable by observable market prices or rates.

IFRS 7.27A

For financial instruments that subsequently measured at fair value the fair value measurements are grouped into Level 1 to 3 based on the degree to which the fair value is observable. Level 1 fair value measurements are those derived from quoted prices (unadjusted) in active markets for identical assets or liabilities; Level 2 fair value measurements are those derived from inputs other than quoted prices included within Level 1 that are observable for the asset or liability, either directly (i.e. as price) or indirectly (i.e. derived from prices), and Level 3 fair value measurements are those derived from valuation techniques that include inputs for the asset or liability that are not based on observable market data (unobservable inputs).

Group and Company	**Level 1**		**Level 2**		**Level 3**		**Total**	
Fair value at the reporting period end	**2009**	**2008**	**2009**	**2008**	**2009**	**2008**	**2009**	**2008**
date	**£'000**	**£'000**	**£'000**	**£'000**	**£'000**	**£'000**	**£'000**	**£'000**
Fair value through profit or loss:								
Asset-backed securities								
Derivatives								
Loans								
Available for sale:								
Corporate bonds								
Government bonds								
Equity securities								
Total								

IFRS 7.27B(b)

There were no transfers between Level 1 and 2 in the period.

The table above only includes financial assets as there are no financial liabilities subsequently measured at fair value.

IFRS 7.27B(c)

Group and Company	**Fair value through profit or loss**				**Available-for-sale**		**Total**	
	Asset-backed securities		**Derivatives**		**Corporate bonds**			
	2009	**2008**	**2009**	**2008**	**2009**	**2008**	**2009**	**2008**
	£'000	**£'000**	**£'000**	**£'000**	**£'000**	**£'000**	**£'000**	**£'000**
Opening balance								
Total gains or losses								
- in profit or loss								
- in other comprehensive income								
- purchases								
- issues								
- settlements								
- transfers out of Level 3								
Closing balance								

IFRS 7.27B(d)

Of the total gains or losses for the period included in profit or loss £ (2008: £) and £ (2008: £) relates to asset-backed securities and derivatives respectively held at the end of the reporting period. Fair value gains or losses on asset-backed securities are included in trading income and fair value gains or losses on derivatives are included in revenue or in the foreign exchange translation reserve as they are designated in highly effective hedge accounting relationships of revenue transactions and net investments in foreign operations. Any hedge ineffectiveness is recognised in 'other gains or losses' but hedge ineffectiveness is nil in the current and prior period.

Source reference

46. Financial instruments (cont'd)

Valuation methods and assumptions applied in valuations techniques

IFRS 7.27 — An entity shall disclose for each class of financial instruments: the methods and, when a valuation technique is used, the assumptions applied in determining fair values of each class of financial assets or financial liabilities. For example, if applicable, an entity discloses information about the assumptions relating to prepayment rates, rates of estimated credit losses, and interest rates or discount rates. If there has been a change in valuation technique, the entity shall disclose that change and the reasons for making it.

Level 3 fair value measurements

IFRS 7.27B(e) — For Level 3 financial assets subsequently measured at fair value, if changing one or more of the inputs to reasonably possible alternative assumptions would change fair value significantly, the entity shall state that fact and disclose the effect of those changes. The entity shall disclose how the effect of a change to a reasonably possible alternative assumption was calculated. For this purpose, significance shall be judged with respect to profit or loss, and total assets or total liabilities, or, when changes in fair value are recognised in other comprehensive income, total equity.

IFRS 7.27(d) — The entity should disclose the total amount of the change in fair value estimated using a valuation technique that was recognised in profit or loss during the period.

Fair value not reliably determinable

IFRS 7.29(b), (c), 30 — Disclosures of fair value is not required for an investment in equity instruments that does not have a quoted market price in an active market, or a derivative linked to such an equity instrument, that is measured at cost in accordance with IAS 39 because its fair value cannot be measured reliably; or for a contract containing a discretionary participation feature (as described in IFRS 4) if the fair value of that feature cannot be measured reliably.

In the cases described above an entity should disclose information to help users of the financial report make their own judgments about the extent of possible differences between the carrying amount of those financial assets or financial liabilities and their fair value, including:

(a) the fact that fair value information has not been disclosed for these instruments because their fair value cannot be measured reliably;
(b) a description of the financial instruments, their carrying amount, and an explanation of why fair value cannot be measured reliably;
(c) information about the market for the instruments;
(d) information about whether and how the entity intends to dispose of the financial instruments; and
(e) if financial instruments whose fair value previously could not be reliably measured are derecognised, that fact, their carrying amount at the time of derecognition, and the amount of gain or loss recognised.

Accounting for deferred 'day 1' gains

IFRS 7.28 — Where an entity is precluded from recognising a 'day 1' gain or loss on a financial instrument the entity should disclose, by class of financial instrument:

(a) its accounting policy for recognising that difference in profit or loss to reflect a change in factors (including time) that market participants would consider in setting a price; and
(b) the aggregate difference yet to be recognised in profit or loss at the beginning and end of the period and a reconciliation of changes in the balance of this difference.

Compound financial instruments with multiple embedded derivatives

IFRS 7.17 — If an entity has issued an instrument that contains both a liability and an equity component and the instrument has multiple embedded derivatives whose values are interdependent (such as a callable convertible debt instrument), it should disclose the existence of those features.

Index